The Meat Buyer's Guide®

Guía para Compradores de Carne®

1910 Association Drive • Reston, VA 20191 USA
+1 703.758.1900 • Fax: +1 703.758.8001 • www.namp.com

$79.00
ISBN 978-1-935593-38-6
57900>
9 781935 593386

NAMP
North American Meat Processors Association
Association Amérique du Nord des Transformateurs de Viande
Asociación Norteamericana de Procesadores de Carne

contents

Note: Table of contents for Spanish content is located on page xxix.

Importante: el índice del contenido en español se encuentra en la página xxix.

North American Meat Processors Association

The North American Meat Processors Association is a non-profit trade association comprised of meat processing companies and associates that share a continuing commitment to provide their foodservice customers with reliable and consistent meat, poultry, seafood, game, and other food products. The association, which was founded in 1942, has member companies both large and small throughout the United States, Canada, Mexico, and other parts of the world. The organization is best known by its acronym, NAMP, and is universally recognized for its world-renowned publication, *The Meat Buyer's Guide®*.

NAMP is a member-driven organization that provides both services and educational opportunities for the benefit of its membership, the meat & poultry industry, and culinary professionals. These programs are designed to provide individual growth and help members achieve business success. Each year, NAMP presents its prestigious and coveted Harry L. Rudnick Educator's Award to a distinguished educator to recognize outstanding contributions in the field of meat education. NAMP also presents special awards for accomplishment and service to its individual members. In addition, the association and its members encourage students, culinary and hospitality institutions, and industry-wide scientific and educational endeavors. NAMP provides leadership on issues that affect both the industry and the public, and strives to address them for the benefit of all parties.

It is in this spirit that the North American Meat Processors Association has undertaken the publication of

The Meat Buyer's Guide®

Learn more about NAMP at www.namp.com. Consider becoming a member to take full advantage of all NAMP's benefits.

our mission

To provide our members a forum for success with exceptional education, advocacy, and access to resources while fostering life-long relationships and long-term prosperity.

North American Meat Processors Association (NAMP)

1910 Association Drive Reston, VA 20191 USA

+1 703.758.1900 Fax: +1 703.758.8001

www.namp.com

preface

The North American Meat Processors Association (NAMP) is proud to present this revised and expanded version of *The Meat Buyer's Guide®* to purchasers of meat and poultry products worldwide. This book is our newest and most authoritative version of our widely regarded and renowned publication.

From its inception in 1961, *The Meat Buyer's Guide* has been the premier resource publication for foodservice purchasers, educators, students, meat processing companies, culinary professionals, and the many others who deal with the public and our industry. *The Guide* has been revised a number of times since its origin, most recently in 2010.

This edition of *The Meat Buyer's Guide* includes new information and a new look. Spanish translations have been included, making the book even more useful to a wider audience. In addition, information on grading, labeling, and nomenclature specific to Canada is available throughout the book, making it fully applicable to the Canadian meat trade. Information on the meat industry in Mexico also has been added, as well as the names of the most popular beef and pork cuts in Latin American countries. These additions make the book more North American in scope.

Many changes have occurred in the meat and poultry industries. Research conducted at meat science universities has led to the identification of new uses for previously undervalued muscles in meat carcasses. New trim levels and shifts in consumer usage to more convenience-oriented products have also created a desire for a host of new items. Expanded international trade and increasing ethnic diversity in eating habits have resulted in increased product diversification as well.

NAMP, in its effort to address the many changes in the industry and to meet the demands of the twenty-first century, took this opportunity to meet these challenges through the publication of an entirely new version of *The Meat Buyer's Guide*. Accordingly, users of *The Guide* will find new photographs and descriptions depicting products, trim and processing options, along with information on packaging, food safety, nutrition, cooking, and an enhanced glossary.

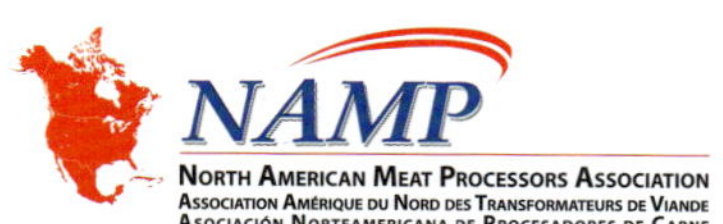

acknowledgements

This publication would not have been possible without the dedicated assistance of NAMP's *Meat Buyer's Guide* Revision Committee and its Species Committees, the complete support of our membership, various meat groups, and many individuals from industry and government who have given so generously of their time, energy and expertise. The current version of *The Meat Buyer's Guide* is based upon the latest in the series of Institutional Meat Purchasing Specifications (IMPS) of the United States Department of Agriculture's (USDA), Agricultural Marketing Service's (AMS), Livestock and Seed Program's Standardization Branch and the Poultry Program's applicable U.S. Trade Descriptions for Poultry. NAMP is very appreciative of the Department's valuable assistance in all facets of *The Guide*.

This edition of *The Guide* also incorporates information from the Canadian Food Inspection Agency (CFIA) Meat Cuts Manual regarding Canadian government specifications. Assistance was provided by the Beef Information Centre (Canada).

The U.S. Meat Export Federation (USMEF) also contributed to the preparation of this English/Spanish version of *The Guide*. NAMP appreciates the expertise of the USMEF and BIC staffs and the partnership with each organization for the betterment of the entire North American meat industry.

We sincerely thank all of those who assisted us in this endeavor. Each and every one played an important role in furthering the value of *The Meat Buyer's Guide* both as an educational resource and as a purchasing tool for the foodservice and retail industries and the public at large. We are sure that users of *The Guide* will be pleased with the results as well.

Since 1961, foodservice organizations have recognized The Meat Buyer's Guide as the premier publication for education and information on the subject of meat and poultry cuts. Governments, culinary schools, foodservice establishments and their employees, industry food organizations, and others wishing to gain knowledge about meat rely daily on this publication.

These organizations endorsed the 6th edition of the *Meat Buyer's Guide,* which is in English with Spanish translations of the meat cut names. This 7th edition adds a complete Spanish translation of the 6th edition, plus the endorsements of the two Mexican trade associations.

American Association of Meat Processors

American Lamb Board

American Meat Institute

American Meat Science Association

Asociación Nacional de Establecimientos TIF, A.C. (ANETIF)

Beef Information Centre (Canada)

Chicago Midwest Meat Association

Consejo Mexicano de la Carne

Culinary Institute of America

Meat & Livestock Australia

National Cattlemen's Beef Association

National Chicken Council

This latest edition of The Guide offers additional valuable information on food safety, nutrition, and new products. The North American Meat Processors Association has responded to the needs of our industry and this new publication has received the support of the organizations listed.

National Meat Association

National Pork Board

National Poultry & Food Distributors Association

National Restaurant Association

National Turkey Federation

Research Chefs Association

Southeastern Meat Association

Southwest Meat Association

USA Poultry & Egg Export Council

U.S. Meat Export Federation

USDA

United States Department of Agriculture

Office of the Secretary
Washington, D.C. 20250

JUL 1 0 2009

The Board of Directors
North American Meat Processors Association
1910 Association Drive
Reston, Virginia 20191

Dear Board of Directors:

Congratulations on completing the 2010 revision of the *Meat Buyers Guide (MBG)*. I am confident that the *MBG* will continue to be the foremost resource publication for the foodservice community and serve as a valuable aid to the marketing of meat and poultry products.

Many in the meat industry have come to rely on the *MBG* as a resource which provides excellent color pictorials for the Department of Agriculture's (USDA) Institutional Meat Purchase Specifications. Additionally, the revised *MBG* reflects the increase in product diversification and the ongoing industry trend towards the marketing of value-added meat cuts. This resource publication is a great example of the successful partnership and cooperation between the meat industry and Government.

USDA has appreciated the opportunity to work with the North American Meat Processors Association over the years and looks forward to maintaining this cooperative spirit to meet the needs of an ever-expanding marketplace.

Sincerely,

Thomas J. Vilsack
Secretary

NAMP
NORTH AMERICAN MEAT PROCESSORS ASSOCIATION
ASSOCIATION AMÉRIQUE DU NORD DES TRANSFORMATEURS DE VIANDE
ASOCIACIÓN NORTEAMERICANA DE PROCESADORES DE CARNE

The NAMPOMETER, Bacterial Guidelines

Meat products are extremely perishable and the temperature of meat storage and cookery has an especially critical role in the microbiological safety of meat products. The "NAMPOMETER" on this page illustrates the important relationship between temperature and meat product bacterial growth. Maximum bacterial growth for most spoilage and pathogenic organisms associated with meat products is between 4°C or 40°F and 60°C or 140°F. The thermal destruction of microorganisms is based on both time and temperature. The temperatures shown on this chart do not reflect the time and temperature relationships. Therefore, individual processes may differ with respect to the minimum temperature required to destroy specific microorganisms based on time of application. U.S. foodservice facilities may be required to operate under the U.S. Food and Drug Administration's Food Code, as may be adopted by individual states. The NAMPOMETERs represent guidelines for meat processors and may not reflect the specific temperatures required by state, provincial, or federal regulation for restaurant operations.

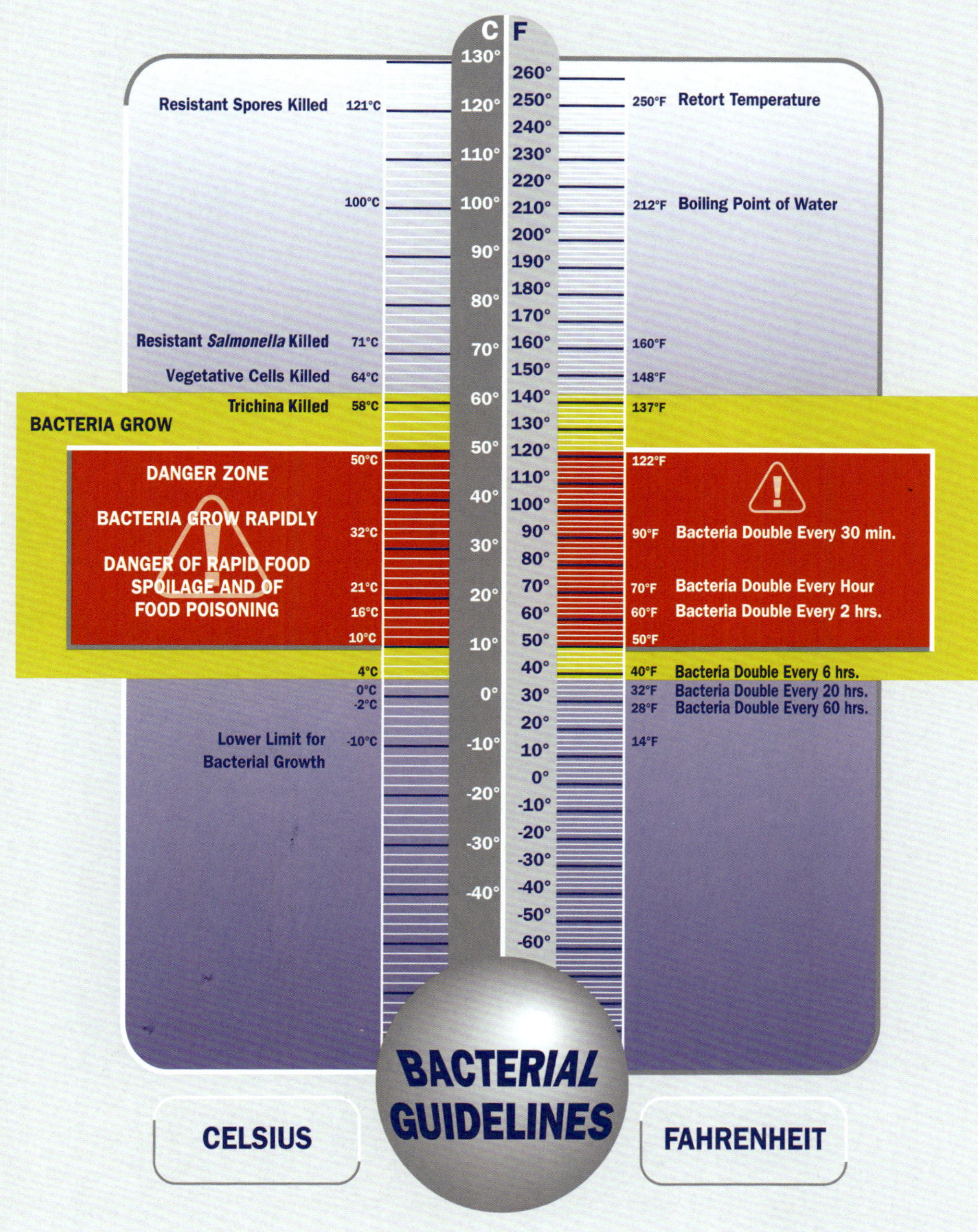

The NAMPOMETER, Meat Guidelines

Temperature plays an important role in the relationship of meat storage and cookery to meat product palatability. The "NAMPOMETER" shown on this page displays the desired storage temperatures to retain maximum freshness for both fresh and frozen meat products. In addition, the internal meat temperatures necessary to achieve specific levels of doneness are shown. The degree of doneness (and hence internal temperature) of a meat product will have a major influence on the eating qualities of that product. U.S. foodservice facilities may be required to operate under the U.S. Food and Drug Administration's Food Code, as may be adopted by individual states. The NAMPOMETERs represent guidelines for meat processors and may not reflect the specific temperatures required by state, provincial, or federal regulation for restaurant operations.

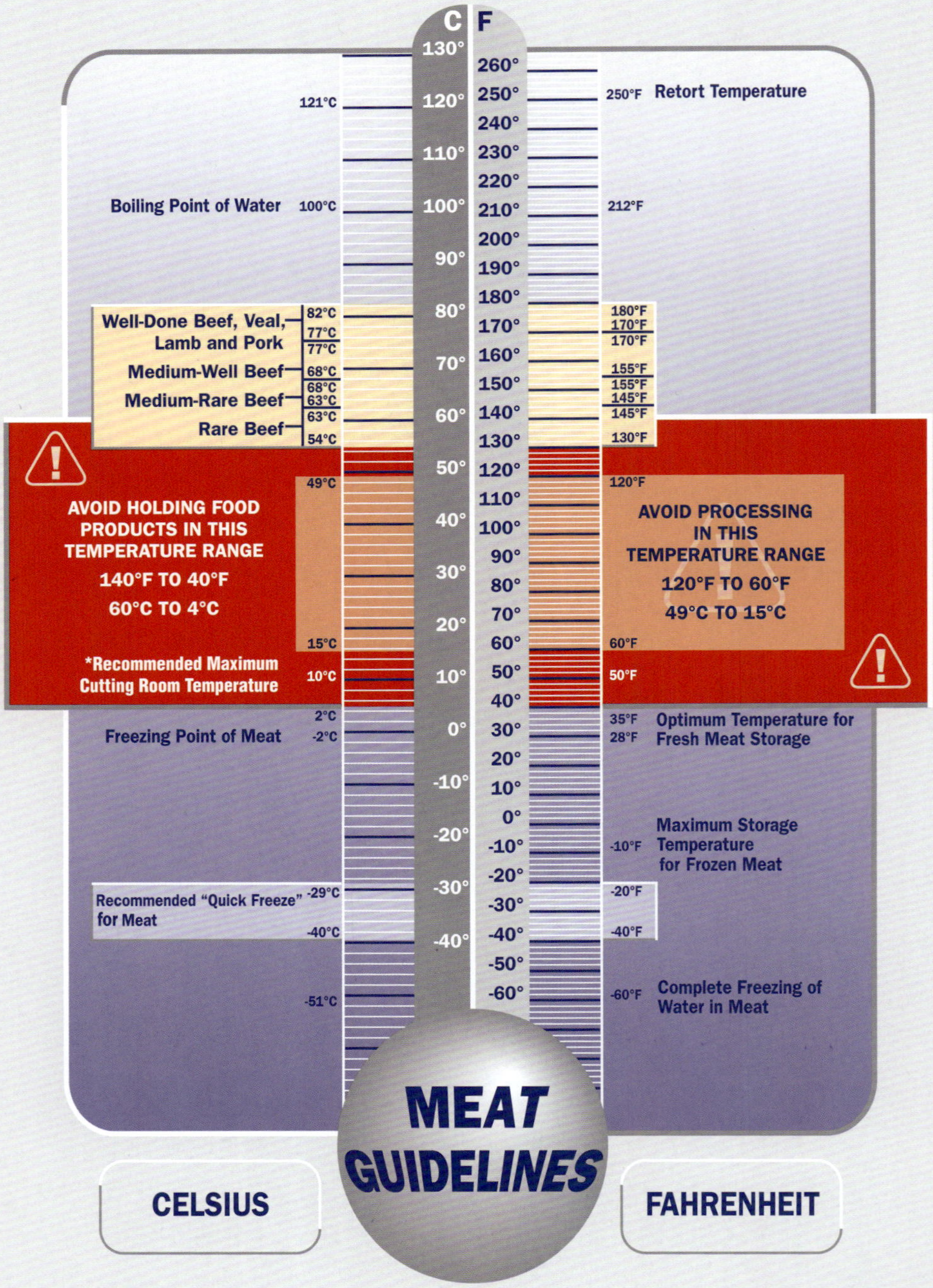

*Product temperature should be maintained below 45°F.

The NAMPOMETER for Poultry

Poultry products are extremely perishable and the temperature of poultry storage and cookery has an especially critical role in the microbiological safety of poultry products. Temperature also plays an important role in the relationship of poultry storage and cookery to poultry product palatability. The poultry thermometer on this page illustrates the important relationship between temperature and poultry product bacterial growth and the desired storage temperatures to retain maximum freshness for both fresh and frozen poultry products. The internal temperatures necessary to achieve specific levels of doneness are also shown. U.S. foodservice facilities may be required to operate under the U.S. Food and Drug Administration's Food Code, as may be adopted by individual states. The NAMPOMETERs represent guidelines for meat processors and may not reflect the specific temperatures required by state, provincial, or federal regulation for restaurant operations.

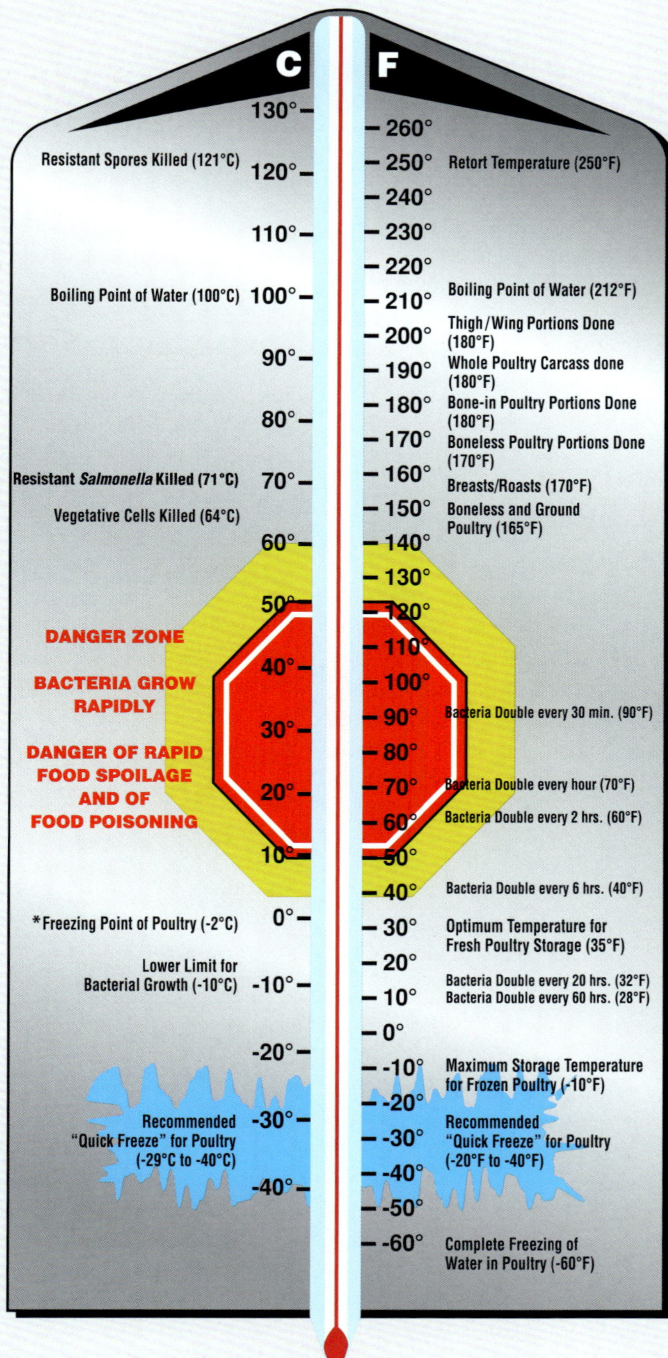

*For additional information see pg. xix.

Food Safety

In the United States, the U.S. Department of Agriculture's Food Safety and Inspection Service (FSIS) is the federal health agency responsible for ensuring that the U.S. commercial supply of meat and poultry products is safe, wholesome, and correctly labeled and packaged. In addition to daily plant inspection and oversight, FSIS analyzes products for microbiological and chemical adulterants, and animal diseases. It also educates consumers about foodborne illness.

In Canada, Health Canada is the federal department responsible for helping Canadians maintain and improve their health. The Canadian Food Inspection Agency (CFIA) provides all federal inspection services related to food and enforces the food safety and nutritional quality standards established by Health Canada.

In Mexico, the Secretariat of Health (Sec-Salud) is the federal department responsible for the administration of the National Health Program and national food safety. The meat inspection program at municipal slaughterhouses is overseen by the Sec-Salud Commission for Prevention of Sanitary Risks (COFEPRIS). SENASICA (which stands for the Health, Agri-Food Safety and Quality Services) is a separate agency of the Secretariat of Livestock Agriculture, Rural Development, Fisheries and Food (SAGARPA) that complements Sec Salud functions in terms of meat and poultry safety by certifying and providing meat inspection services related to the so called Federally Inspected Type (TIF) domestic establishments. SENASICA also is responsible for the re-inspection of imported meats and the authorization of foreign plants exporting meats and poultry to Mexico.

HACCP: Hazard Analysis Critical Control Point System

In the U.S., the USDA's Food Safety and Inspection Service (FSIS) established a food safety and pathogen reduction program called the Hazard Analysis Critical Control Point (HACCP) System. It is applied to both domestic and imported meat and poultry production. The system relies on science-based techniques to meet present-day food safety needs. It replaces reliance on decades-old organoleptic inspection methods and command and control regulations. The HACCP system instead substitutes process controls and incorporates scientific data to address food safety needs.

In Canada, meat processing facilities also operate under a HACCP system. To be most effective, the HACCP system requires that all in the food chain, from farm to table, accept their share of responsibility to ensure that meat and poultry, as well as seafood and other foods, are produced and cared for under the most rigorous food safety disciplines.

In Mexico, HACCP is not mandatory. HACCP prerequisites are generally applied in slaughterhouses and meat processing facilities. However, all Mexican establishments eligible to export meat and poultry to the U.S. operate under a HACCP system.

NAMP members assure you of their dedication to this effort.

Safe Handling of Meat and Poultry Products

All uncooked and precooked meat products must be properly stored, handled, and cooked to ensure public safety. However, safe food handling does not end with the meat processor.

Refrigerated meat should be stored at temperatures less than 4°C or 40°F and frozen meat should be stored at less than -18°C or 0°F. In order to prevent foodborne illness, foods must be cooked properly to their individual minimum internal temperatures, promptly chilled for storage if not consumed immediately, and kept at proper storage temperatures.

For more information on critical temperatures for meat and poultry storage, handling, and cooking, please refer to the NAMPOMETERs in this section.

Food handlers must take care not to cross-contaminate food. Do not use the same cutting boards or utensils for both raw and cooked products without proper cleaning of the items between usage. Store raw food products away from other cooked or raw food items. Food handlers must wash their hands with hot soapy water before and after handling raw or cooked meat products.

U.S. Food Safety and Inspection Service

For questions or problems with meat or poultry products outside Washington, D.C., call toll free, +1 800.535.4555; within the Washington, D.C., metropolitan area, call +1 202.720.3333.

You may also visit the FSIS website at www.fsis.usda.gov.

Canadian Food Inspection Agency

For questions or problems with meat and poultry products in Canada, call toll free +1 800.442.2342 or +1 613.225.2342 or visit www.inspection.gc.ca

Health, Agri-Food Safety and Quality Services of Mexico (SENASICA)

For questions or problems with meat and poultry products in Mexico, you may call 011-52-55-5905-1000, ext. 50911, or visit www.senasica.gob.mx

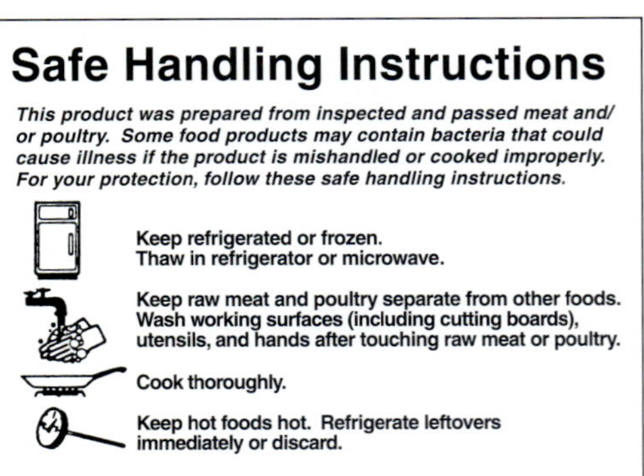

Material Requirements
for Beef, Veal, Lamb, Pork, and Poultry

All product offered shall comply with the following material requirements and the requirements of the specific item description. These requirements are based upon the Institutional Meat Purchase Specifications (IMPS) General Requirements and Quality Assurance Provisions.

Quality

Product Condition

All product offered for sale must be in excellent condition. The exposed lean and fat surfaces shall be of a color and bloom normally associated with the class, grade, and cut of meat specified. All meat shall be practically free of bruises, blood clots, bloody tissue, blood discoloration, spinal cord portions, exposed blood vessels, cod and/or udder fat, gambrel cord or any other conditions that would negatively affect the use of the product. Except in ground and flaked items, dark cutting and/or calloused beef is not acceptable. The meat must be maintained in excellent condition through processing, storage, and transit. Cut surfaces and naturally exposed lean surfaces, as well as fat, shall show no more than slight darkening or discoloration due to dehydration, aging, and/or microbial activity or oxidation unless the product was specified to be dry aged. No other odors foreign to fresh meat shall be present. Changes in color and odors characteristically associated with vacuum-packaged meat in excellent condition, however, shall be acceptable. Product shall show no evidence of any mishandling. Neither should the product show evidence of freezing or defrosting unless either was requested by the purchaser.

Portion-cut and ground items to be delivered frozen may be produced from frozen meat cuts, provided such cuts show no evidence of deterioration. Unless otherwise specified, portion-cut items shall maintain their approximate original shape. Products thus produced shall be packaged, packed, and returned promptly to the freezer.

Cutting, Trimming, and Boning

The cutting, trimming, and boning of the items shall be accomplished with sufficient care so that each cut retains its identity and is devoid of objectionable scores in the lean. Ragged edges shall be removed close to the lean surfaces. Except for cuts that are separated through natural seams, all cut surfaces shall be made at approximate right angles with the skin surface. No more than a slight amount of lean, fat, or bone, provided the item is being prepared bone in, shall be included from an adjacent cut. No bone shall be present in a boneless item.

When portioning steaks, except those that are cubed and/or knitted or otherwise described differently, the steaks shall be cut in full slices in a straight line, reasonably perpendicular to the outer surface and at an approximate right angle to the length of the cut being sliced or portioned. Individual steaks shall remain intact when suspended 0.5 inch (13 mm) from the outer edge. Portion-cut items shall be practically free of fractures, tag ends, and knife scores.

Conversion Chart

Fractional equivalents to decimal and metric measurements used throughout this guide are as follows:

Inches	Decimal	Metric
1/8	0.125	3 mm
1/4	0.25	6 mm
3/8	0.375	9 mm
1/2	0.50	13 mm
5/8	0.625	16 mm
3/4	0.75	19 mm
7/8	0.875	22 mm
1	1.0	2.5 cm

Peeled/Denuded

The term "peeled" implies surface fat and muscle separation through natural seams so that the resulting cut's seamed surface ("silver" or "blue" tissue) is exposed with remaining "flake" fat not to exceed 1.0 inch (2.5 cm) in the longest dimension and/or 0.125 inch (3 mm) in depth at any point. The term "denuded" implies all surface fat is removed so that the resulting cut's seamed surface ("silver" or "blue" tissue") is exposed with remaining "flake" fat not to exceed 1.0 inch (2.5 cm) in any dimension and/or 0.125 inch (3 mm) in depth at any point.

Peeled/Denuded, Surface Membrane Removed

When the surface membrane ("silver" or "blue" tissue) is required to be removed (skinned), the resulting cut surface shall expose at least 90 percent lean with remaining "flake" fat not to exceed 0.125 inch (3 mm) in depth.

Due to the concerns regarding bovine spongiform encephalopathy (BSE), the Food Safety and Inspection Service (FSIS) in 2004 amended its inspection regulations to prohibit specific parts of cattle and beef carcasses from use as human food. In cattle over 30 months of age, items that were designated as specified risk materials (SRMs) included the brain, skull, eyes, trigeminal ganglia, spinal cord, vertebral column (excluding the vertebrae of the tail, the transverse processes of the thoracic and lumbar vertebrae, and the wings of the sacrum), and the dorsal root ganglia contained in the vertebral column. In addition, in cattle of all ages, FSIS designated that tonsils and the *distal ileum* of the small intestine be classified as SRMs.

FSIS required as an additional food safety measure that all non-ambulatory disabled cattle presented for slaughter must be condemned and not enter the food chain. BSE has never been found in the muscle tissue of beef carcasses. Primarily, all foodservice beef items come from younger cattle much less than 30 months of age, and generally approximately 20 months old. See the FSIS website at www.fsis.usda.gov for more information.

Similar regulations and requirements are in place in Canada and Mexico. For more information, go to www.inspection.gc.ca or www.senasica.gob.mx/?id=816.

Fat Trim

Trimming of external fat shall be accomplished by smoothly removing the fat following the contour of the underlying muscle surface. Merely beveling the edges of a cut or portion, so as to appear to achieve a desired fat trim, is not acceptable. Two terms used for describing fat limitations are: (1) maximum fat thickness at any one point and (2) average fat thickness. These fat thickness requirements may be applicable both to the external surface and/or seam fat within an item. Instead of selecting a specific measurement to determine the maximum and average fat thicknesses, a purchaser may specify either one of the two fat trim requirements at the left as an alternative.

Method for Determining Fat Thickness in Cuts and Roast Items

The maximum fat thickness at any one point is determined by visually examining the area of a cut that has the most fat thickness and measuring the fat thickness or depth at this point.

The average fat thickness is determined by visually selecting the different areas where surface fat appears on the cut or roast and then taking measurements of the fat thickness or depth only in these areas. The average fat thickness is then determined by adding the fat thickness measurements together and dividing the total by the number of measurements. For example, in the case of three measurements of surface area of 0.2 inch (5 mm) in depth, 0.3 inch (8 mm) in depth, and 0.4 inch (10 mm) in depth, the average fat thickness or depth would be 0.3 inch (8 mm).

The above measurements of fat are made on the edges of the cut or roast by probing or scoring the overlying surface fat as necessary, in a manner that determines the actual fat thickness and reveals any natural depression or seam that could affect the measurement.

Bridging Method of Fat Measurement

When a natural depression occurs in a muscle, only the fat above the portion of the depression that is more than 0.75 inch (19mm) in width is considered in making the fat thickness determination. See Figure 1.

Planing Method of Fat Measurement

When seam of fat occurs between adjacent muscles only the fat above the level of the involved muscles is measured. See Figure 1.

Method for Determining Fat Trim in Diced and Steak Portion-Cut Items

The maximum fat thickness at any one point is determined by visually selecting the areas on the edges of either side of the diced or portion-cut item that has the thickest amount of fat, and measuring the thickness or depth of surface fat at this point.

The average fat thickness is determined by visually selecting the different areas where surface fat appears on the diced or portion-cut item and then taking measurements and computing the average fat thickness as in the preceding Cuts and Roasts explanation.

The actual measurements of surface fat are made on the edges of the cut and by probing or scoring the fat surface as necessary in a manner that reveals the actual fat thickness. For steak items, the bridging and/or the planing methods shall be applied to take into account any natural depression occurring in a muscle and/or when a seam of fat occurs between adjacent muscles.

In the event a purchaser specifies a maximum seam fat limitation width at any one point, then that limit shall be visually determined and measured at the points between the layers of lean muscles on the side of the cut that has the thickest or widest deposits of fat. The average thickness shall be determined by computing the average fat thickness as in the preceding Cuts and Roasts explanation.

For steak items, the bridging and/or planing methods shall be applied to take into account the irregular widths of the seam fat within a muscle depression or between adjacent muscles in order to reveal the actual fat thickness (width) of fat within a seam. Seam fat shall be evaluated no closer than 0.75 inch (19 mm) from the contour (projected perimeter when symmetrically formed or unformed) of the outer edge of the steak.

Whenever a fat limitation of either Peeled/Denuded or Peeled/Denuded, Surface Membrane Removed is specified, only the Bridging Method shall be used in evaluating the fat above a natural depression in a muscle or the fat occurring in the seam between adjacent muscles.

> **Whenever a fat limitation of either Peeled/Denuded or Peeled/Denuded, Surface Membrane Removed is specified, only the Bridging Method shall be used in evaluating the fat above a natural depression in a muscle or the fat occurring in the seam between adjacent muscles.**

FIGURE 1 - Bridging and Planing

Bridging

When a natural depression occurs in a muscle, only the fat above the portion of the depression which is more than 0.75 inch (19 mm) in width is considered.

Planing

When a seam of fat occurs between adjacent muscles only the fat above the level of the involved muscles is measured.

NAMP
NORTH AMERICAN MEAT PROCESSORS ASSOCIATION
ASSOCIATION AMÉRIQUE DU NORD DES TRANSFORMATEURS DE VIANDE
ASOCIACIÓN NORTEAMERICANA DE PROCESADORES DE CARNE

Netting or Tying

When netting or tying is specified by the purchaser or required by the item description, stretchable netting or any other equivalent FSIS or CFIA approved material shall be used to make roasts firm and compact. Unless otherwise specified, roasts shall be netted so that all portions are held intact without any portions protruding through the ends of the netting. Alternatively, roasts may be string-tied by loops of twine uniformly spaced at no more than approximately 2.0 inch (5.0 cm) intervals girthwise or perpendicular to item length. When girthwise tying does not make roasts firm and compact, lengthwise tying shall also be used. All netting and tying materials shall be included with other packaging materials in determining the tare weight.

Chop, Block-Ready, or Steak-Ready

The use of the terms Chop, Block-Ready, or Steak-Ready indicate that the cuts are ready to be further processed into chops or steaks simply by using a knife or saw. When the terms chop or block-ready are used in conjunction with Veal Rack items they specifically mean that the items are split, the chine and feather bones, blade bone, related cartilage, back strap, and the lifter muscles associated with the blade bone have been excluded. When the terms are used with Veal Loin items they specifically mean that they are split, the chine and rib bones excluded, the cavity is clean, and the flank has been excluded by a straight cut that is no more than 1.0 inch (2.5 cm) below the *longissimus dorsi* muscle on the rib or sirloin ends. Some Lamb items are identified as block or roast-ready with further explanation of the meaning in the item description. Pork loins may also at times be identified as chop or block-ready. The term steak-ready usually applies to beef rib or loin items.

Notch Cut

Generally, notch cutting is made on rack, loin, and sirloin portions of lamb, veal, and pork. Starting on the split surface of the chine bone, saw cuts shall be made between vertebrae junctures to a point into the lean so that the rack, loin or sirloin items are left intact and the user may slice items into portions with a knife before or after roasting. Lamb shoulder and breast ribs may be notched by cutting across the ribs into the overlying muscles, leaving the overlying muscles intact.

Individual Muscle (IM)

When "IM" appears with the name of an item, it designates that the roast or steak is composed of one muscle. Variation of quality will be eliminated since IM cuts will yield highly uniform slices as compared to multiple muscle cuts. When portioning IM cuts, they should be sliced at an approximate right angle to the grain (direction of muscle fibers).

Order of Tenderness

Research has shown that the most tender major muscles of beef include:

Psoas major
Infraspinatus
Spinalis dorsi
Serratus ventralis
Teres major
Tensor facia latae
Rectus femoris
Longissimus dorsi

The tenderness of muscles in the beef carcass may be measured in several ways and can be affected by a variety of factors. For more specific and complete information on beef muscle tenderness, go to www.beefresearch.org.

The purpose of the following requirements is to provide a purchaser with a variety of meat handling and packaging options that conform to good manufacturing practices.

Purchasers may request any other specific requirements they wish. Some additional requirements may be imposed when product is ordered under certification procedures. The following explanations may not be inclusive.

State of Refrigeration

Each of the species and product sections in this guide provide information as to whether the item may be ordered fresh, frozen, or in a further processed condition. The applicable temperature requirements are also described. Purchasers may, if they desire, request that products be stored and/ or shipped subject to specific temperature requirements.

For poultry, effective December 17, 1997, the term "fresh" may be used only on raw poultry products whose internal temperature has never fallen below -3°C or 26°F. Poultry product held at a temperature of -18°C or 0°F or below must be labeled "frozen," or, if thawed, "previously frozen." There is neither label designation nor terminology for raw poultry between -18°C and -3°C or 0°F and 26°F.

Packaging and Packing

There are different requirements for packaging depending on the type and size of the cut and the purchaser's specifications. Carcasses, sides, quarters, and primal cuts need not be wrapped or boxed unless so specified by the purchaser. Bone-in or boneless subprimal cuts, cured, smoked, cooked, dried, and variety meats, if not individually packaged, shall be packed into boxes lined with plastic bags. Portion-cut items shall be packaged or layer packed in small cartons with spacers between the layers. Packaging may consist of a vacuum-packaging-type barrier film with or without a modified atmosphere application, or with any other approved wrapping material, or as the purchaser may specify.

Frozen bulk items, such as trimmings, shall be packed into wax-coated or impregnated cartons without liners. Ground and diced meat items shall be packaged in plastic bags or casings and may be packed in cartons. Patties may be packed in wax-coated or impregnated cartons with or without plastic bags or in non-coated cartons lined with plastic bags. Patties shall be separated from each other in a manner that prevents them from sticking together. In addition, purchasers may specify that metal-detection equipment be used on all types of ground products. Products such as fresh, smoked, and cooked links may be packed in any appropriate small carton with or without separators between the layers. Bacon layers shall be separated or individually packaged.

All packaging material shall comply with FSIS or CFIA regulations, and packages must be labeled in accordance with FSIS or CFIA regulations. Packaging requirements in Mexico are controlled by COFEPRIS and are based on regulations homologated with those of FSIS. Small cartons may be master packed. Master or shipping cartons shall be of a size and bursting strength suitable for the purpose. All packaging shall be done in a manner that will safeguard the product. Products may be palletized when appropriate.

Grading
Quality and Yield Grade Descriptions and Marks of Identification

In the introductory section of each species section in *The Guide* you will find a reference to grading. In the U.S. beef, lamb, veal, pork, and poultry products may be quality graded, whereas only beef, lamb, and pork may be yield graded. Beef and lamb use names to designate quality and numerals to identify yield. Veal quality grades are also identified by name. Quality and yield grades are combined into a single numerical designation for pork. Poultry grades are identified by letters. In the U.S., the grade names and procedures for their use are supervised by the United States Department of Agriculture (USDA), Agricultural Marketing Service (AMS), Livestock & Seed Program (LSP), Meat Grading and Certification Branch (MGC) (+1 202.720.1113) and the USDA, AMS, Poultry Programs (+1 202.720.4476), Washington, DC, www.ams.usda.gov. While the use of meat grading services is voluntary, only the Meat Grading and Certification Branch or the Poultry Programs may apply official grade marks. When requested, this service shall be paid for either on an hourly or long-term contract basis by those using the service. In addition, the user shall also comply with the Food Safety and Inspection Service (FSIS) grade labeling procedures. The official USDA grade designation may appear in any one or any combination of the following ways: (1) container markings, (2) on individual bags, (3) legible roller brand appearing on the meat, or (4) by a USDA shield stamp that incorporates the quality and/or yield grade. For more information, write or telephone the MGC Branch or Poultry Programs. The MGC Branch and Poultry Programs staff, through its field offices and field personnel, is responsible for implementing the grading service's day-to-day activities.

In addition, we have provided information on the Canadian Grading Systems is provided on the following pages. For complete information on Canadian Grading Systems, go to: http://laws.justice.gc.ca/en/C-0.4/SOR-92-541

Three voluntary regulations have been issued in Mexico as guidelines for grading carcasses of beef (NMX-FF-078-SCFI-2002), pork (NMX-FF-081-SCFI-2003), and lamb (NMX-FF-106-SCFI-2006). Some northern states of Mexico have developed and implemented beef grading standards to be used locally. However, none of the above has been adopted as a federal standard by the national meat industry.

Beef Grading: http://portal.veracruz.gob.mx/pls/portal/docs/PAGE/COVECAINICIO/IMAGENES/ARCHIVOSPDF/TAB3885839/NMX-FF-078-SCFI-2002.PDF

Pork Grading: http://www.colpos.mx/bancodenormas/nmexicanas/NMX-FF-081-2003.PDF

An explanation of the applicable quality and yield grades for each species follows.

Beef Grading

Beef Grading in the U.S.

Beef carcasses may be graded, for quality alone, yield alone, a combination of quality and yield, or left ungraded as established by the regulations and as suits the needs of slaughterers and their customers. The use of the system is entirely voluntary and on a fee-for-service basis.

U.S. Quality Grades

Quality grades serve to identify the eating characteristics of the product. They are a guide to identify the tenderness and palatability of the meat. In the U.S., there are eight beef quality grades. The grades, in order from the highest to lowest quality, are as follows: U.S. Prime, U.S. Choice, U.S. Select, U.S. Standard, U.S. Commercial, U.S. Utility, U.S. Cutter, and U.S. Canner. Beef steers and heifers are eligible for all the above grade designations. Cows are eligible for all but Prime grade. Bullocks may only be graded Prime, Choice, Select, Standard, and Utility. Bulls may not be quality graded. Each grade level is identified by its own grade stamp. See examples on page xx. The grade designation assigned to a carcass is determined by an evaluation of its sex characteristics, maturity, the quality of the lean muscle, and the degree of marbling present. See examples and explanations of marbling scores on page 3. The goal for the use of these criteria is to provide purchasers with a system that measures and predicts quality by methods that maximize consistency and reliability. Upon request, the grading service may establish specific grade specification programs for purchasers or suppliers using the above criteria. A number of these purchase specification programs are presently in existence.

U.S. Yield Grades

Yield Grades 1, 2, 3, 4, and 5, are applicable to beef carcasses. Yield Grade (YG) 1 means that the animal will have the most useable lean or produce the greatest cutability from the carcasses, whereas YG 5 will produce the least. In other words, YG 1 is the leanest, whereas YG 5 is the fattest. The assessment is made by an equation that includes the measurement of the ribeye, the presence of heart and pelvic fat, if applicable by the species requirements, and fat cover thickness. Generally speaking, the higher the quality grade, the higher the yield grade. Consequently,

U.S. Beef Grading

Quality Grades	Classification			
	Steers/ Heifers	Cows	Bullocks	Bulls
U.S. Prime	•		•	
U.S. Choice	•	•	•	
U.S. Select	•	•	•	
U.S. Standard	•	•	•	
U.S. Commercial	•	•		
U.S. Utility	•	•	•	
U.S. Cutter	•	•		
U.S. Canner	•	•		

most restaurant-quality Prime and Choice quality animals will fall in YG 3 and occasionally higher. In beef animals, the adoption of cross-breeding techniques, improved diet, and genetic changes have gone a long way toward eliminating excess fat so that the quantity of YGs 1 and 2 are increasing and those of YGs 4 and 5 are decreasing. In most instances, due to further trimming by suppliers, the YG will not appear on the product.

Yield Grade		
		Yield Grade
Leanest		1
		2
		3
		4
Fattest		5

Beef Grading in Canada

The Canadian Beef Grading Agency (CBGA) is accredited by the Canadian Food Inspection Agency (CFIA) to assess beef carcass grades in accordance with Canada's national standards. Carcasses can be both quality and yield graded. Quality grades include for youthful cattle include: Canada Prime, Canada AAA, Canada AA, and Canada A.

The Canadian marbling standards mirror the copyrighted marbling standards of the U.S. and are used to determine quality grades (see page 3 for more information). In addition to marbling, quality grades in Canada are based upon the following factors to be considered for Canada's top four grades:

- Maturity: only carcasses assessed as youthful
- Meat Color: only beef that is a bright red color
- Fat Color: only carcasses with no yellow fat
- Meat Texture: only firm muscle texture
- Muscling: only good muscling or better

In addition to the grades for youthful cattle, Canada also has quality grades for mature animals. Bulls are assigned an E grade and cows are placed into one of four D grades.

Canadian Yield Grades

In Canada, three measurements are used to determine yield:

a. Rib-eye length
b. Rib-eye width
c. Fat depth on the rib-eye

These values are then inserted into a lean yield prediction equation. Yield grades 1, 2, or 3 are assigned in accordance with the lean yield percentages calculated.

Beef Grading in Mexico

Voluntary regulations have been issued in Mexico as guidelines for grading carcasses of beef (see page xx).

Ovine (Lamb and Mutton) Grading

Ovine Grading in the U.S.

Ovine carcasses, if offered for grading, must be simultaneously graded with both a quality grade and a yield grade. The regulations require that the kidney fat be removed prior to grading. As with beef, official U.S. grading of lamb, yearling mutton and mutton carcasses is a voluntary service, available only from the MGC Branch on a fee-for-service basis.

U.S. Quality Grades

As with the other species, quality grades serve to identify the eating characteristics of the product. They are a guide to identify the tenderness and palatability of the meat. There are four quality grades for lamb and yearling mutton. The grades, in order from the highest to lowest quality, are as follows: U.S. Prime, U.S. Choice, U.S. Good, and U.S. Utility. Mutton may only be graded U.S. Choice, U.S. Good, U.S. Utility, or U.S. Cull. The distinction between lamb, yearling mutton, and mutton is based primarily on the absence or presence of a spool or break joint on the foreleg trotter. Lamb, the youngest Ovine class designation, will not display a spool joint. Although it is not part of the official U.S. grading standards, the term "Spring Lamb" has been used by the industry to designate young lamb carcasses. In determining the quality grade, consideration is given to the animal's maturity based on its lean and skeletal development along with the degree of fat streaking on the flank.

U.S. Yield Grades

Yield grades (YG) of lamb, yearling mutton, and mutton carcasses are calculated based on the external fat covering of the carcass. Yield grades are identified by the numbers 1, 2, 3, 4, and 5, with YG 1 having the least external fat and YG 5 having the most external fat. Generally speaking, only Prime and Choice quality grade lamb is offered for grading. Since quality and yield grading are coupled, all graded carcasses will bear both the quality and yield grade marks. Consequently there are more YG 2s in the Choice category.

U.S. Ovine Grading			
	Classification		
Quality Grades	**Lamb**	**Yearling Mutton**	**Mutton**
U.S. Prime	•	•	
U.S. Choice	•	•	•
U.S. Good	•	•	•
U.S. Utility	•	•	•
U.S. Cull			•

Ovine Grading in Canada

In Canada, there are five grades for ovine carcasses: Canada AAA, Canada C1, Canada C2, Canada D1, and Canada D4. Quality grades are based upon maturity, muscle score, flank muscle color and streaking, and fat cover.

A yield class is assigned to carcasses that grade Canada AAA by taking a fat measurement. Classes are Canada 1 through Canada 4, with Canada 1 having the least fat.

Lamb carcasses have fewer than two permanent incisors, two break joints (or in the case of one break joint and one spool joint, the break joint must have four intact and well-defined ridges with at least a slightly red and damp surface), and ribs that are no more than slightly wide. Lamb carcasses are eligible to grade Canada AAA, C1, or C2.

Mutton carcasses have two or more permanent incisors, two spool joints (or in the case of one break joint and one spool joint, the break joint has a dry, white surface), and ribs that are wide, flat, and white. Mutton carcasses are only eligible to grade Canada D1 or D4.

Ovine Grading in Mexico

Voluntary regulations have been issued in Mexico as guidelines for grading carcasses of ovine (see page xx).

Veal and Calf Grading

Veal and Calf Grading in the U.S.

U.S. Veal & Calf Grading	
Quality Grades	Classification
	Veal & Calf
U.S. Prime	•
U.S. Choice	•
U.S. Good	•
U.S. Standard	•
U.S. Utility	•

Veal and calf carcasses may only be quality graded. Yield grades do not apply. Relatively small numbers of veal and calf carcasses are graded. As in beef and lamb, the use of the system is entirely voluntary and on a fee-for-service basis.

U.S. Quality Grades

As with the other species quality grades serve to identify the eating characteristics of the product. They are a guide to identify the tenderness and palatability of the meat. There are five quality grades for veal and calf. The grades, in order from the highest to lowest quality, are as follows: U.S. Prime, U.S. Choice, U.S. Good, U.S. Standard, and U.S. Utility. Most of the small number of carcasses graded are Choice grade with some Prime. The reason that few veal and calf carcasses are graded is accounted for by the fact that higher-quality product is identified and sold as product produced by special management techniques.

U.S. Yield Grades

Because there is relatively little fat cover on veal and calf carcasses there has been no demonstrated need for the use of yield grades.

Veal and Calf Grading in Canada

To be classified as veal in Canada, carcasses must weigh between 80 kg (176 lbs.) and 180 kg (397 lbs.). There are 10 grades of veal carcasses: Canada A1, A2, A3, A4, B1, B2, B3, B4, C1, and C2. Grades are assigned based on muscle condition, muscle color, fat color and coverage, and carcass maturity.

Veal and Calf Grading in Mexico

There is no system for grading veal in Mexico.

Pork Grading

Pork Grading in the U.S.

Pork grading is not a major factor in determining quality at the foodservice level. Quality grade and yield are combined in the pork grading system and expressed primarily in numerical terms. In the U.S., the identifiers are U.S. No. 1, U.S. No. 2, U.S. No. 3, U.S. No. 4, and U.S. Utility for barrows and gilts. Sows are graded U.S. No. 1, 2, 3, U.S. Medium, and U.S. Cull. Boars and Stags are not graded. See the Pork Section of this guide, page 151, for additional information about grade.

Pork Grading in Canada

There is no federal system for grading pork in Canada.

Pork Grading in Mexico

Voluntary regulations have been issued in Mexico as guidelines for grading carcasses of pork (see page xx).

Poultry

Poultry Grading in the U.S.

In the U.S., a number of factors are used to determine the quality grade designation of ready-to-cook poultry carcasses, parts, or products.

Specifically, for ready-to-cook poultry carcasses and parts, the quality factors considered in assessing the grade are:

1. Conformation
2. Fleshing
3. Fat Covering
4. Defeathering
5. Exposed Flesh
6. Discolorations
7. Disjointed and Broken Bones
8. Missing Parts
9. Freezing Defects

In determining the quality grade of other poultry products, the following factors are considered:

1. Presence of Bone, Tendons, and Cartilage
2. Bruising and Blood Clots
3. Other Product-Specific Factors

Poultry Grading in Canada

There are three grades of poultry carcasses in Canada: Canada A, Canada Utility, and Canada C. Factors that determine the quality grade include carcass composition, fat cover, discolorations, skin condition, bone condition, weight, and maturity.

Poultry Grading in Mexico

There is no federal system for grading poultry in Mexico.

The items pictured and described in the *Meat Buyer's Guide* have been selected from the U.S. Institutional Meat Purchase Specifications (IMPS). IMPS are a series of meat product specifications maintained by USDA/AMS. They are developed as voluntary consensus specifications. Large volume purchasers such as federal, state and local government agencies, schools, restaurants, hotels, and other food service users reference the IMPS for procuring meat products. The products in this guide represent the items most commonly used by foodservice establishments and institutional purchasers. The descriptions use terminology that will best identify the product in terms that will assure purchasers that they will receive merchandise meeting their expectations. Purchasers should be able to identify their purchase requirements by the item number and product name listed in *The Guide*. Purchasers, however, may want additional products or ones with different specifications. Your NAMP suppliers will be pleased to assist you in meeting your requirements.

A number of products included in *The Meat Buyer's Guide* allow for Purchaser Specified Options (PSO). Some item descriptions list trim level requirements, or provide a number of choices, or contain other specific requirements. The material requirements for beef, lamb, veal, pork, and poultry and the General Product Requirements in this section also describe a number of general conditions affecting purchases. In addition, each species and product introductory section appearing later in *The Guide* also contains some general product guidelines. Purchasers should take the opportunity to acquaint themselves with all the conditions and product choices that may affect the items they wish to buy.

Universal Product Code (UPC)

Universal Product Codes or UPC numbers are used in retail to identify products by electronic devices for both inventory control and pricing. For more information on UPC codes, visit www.meattrack.com.

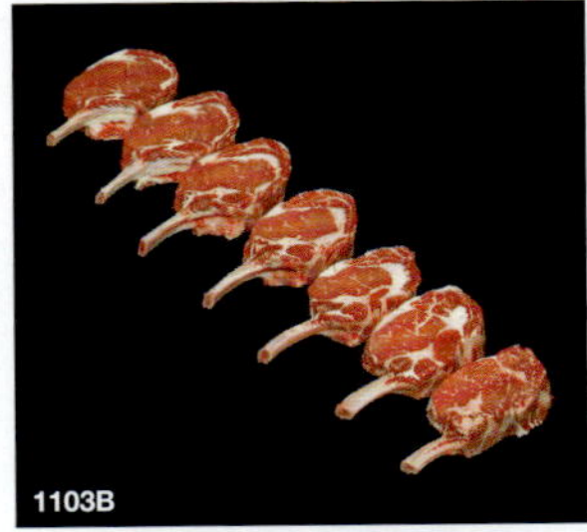

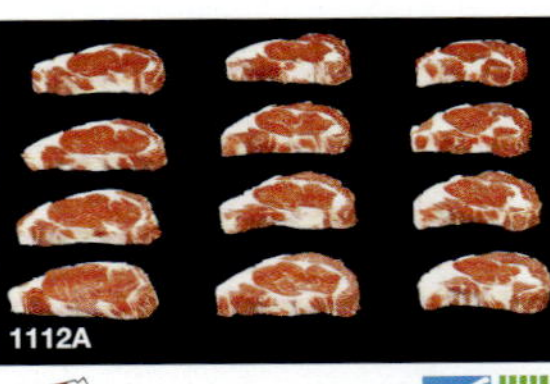

portion cuts / cortes porcionados

1103B — Beef Rib, Rib Steak, Bone In, Frenched

This item is prepared as described in Item No. 1103 except that each steak must be cut between the rib bones. The rib bone shall be completely trimmed of the intercostal meat, lean, and fat so that the bone is exposed from the ventral edge of the *longissimus dorsi* to the end of the rib bone. This item is also referred to as a "Cowboy Steak."

Alternative Purchaser Specified Options (PSO):

PSO: 1 – Purchaser may request that the rib be prepared as a roast to the same specifications as Item No. 1103B but instead of being cut into steaks, it be left intact.

2 – Purchaser may request that the rib be prepared as a roast as in PSO 1 and then partially cut into steaks and the balance left as a roast.

3 – Purchaser may request that the rib steaks in Item No. 1103B or PSO 2 be split into two steaks by a saw cut through the center of the rib bone.

1103B — Chuletón (Espaldar), Bistec del Chuletón, Con Hueso, Estilo Francés

Esta pieza se prepara según descripción de la pieza número 1103, salvo que cada bistec debe ser cortado entre los huesos de las costillas. El hueso de la costilla deberá ser recortado completamente de carne intercostal, carne magra y grasa, de forma que el hueso quede expuesto desde el borde ventral del *longissimus dorsi* hasta el extremo de la costilla. Esta pieza es llamada a veces "Bistec del Cowboy".

Opciones alternativas especificadas por el comprador:

PSO: 1 – El comprador puede solicitar que el chuletón, en vez de hacerlo bistecs, se prepare como un trozo rosbif, según las mismas especificaciones de la pieza número 1103B, pero que en vez de ser cortado en bistecs, quede intacto.

2 – El comprador puede solicitar que el chuletón se prepare como un trozo rosbif, como figura en la opción 1 especificada por el comprador, y luego se corte parcialmente en bistecs, dejando lo remanente como rosbif.

3 – El comprador puede solicitar que los bistecs de chuletón detallados en la pieza número 1103B o en la opción 2 especificada por el comprador, se separen en dos bistecs mediante un corte de sierra a través del centro del hueso de las costillas.

1112A — Beef Rib, Ribeye Steak, Lip-On, Boneless

Boneless ribeye steaks, lip-on shall be prepared from a rib item meeting the end requirements of Item No. 112A. The lip shall be cut on the short rib side with a straight cut that is ventral to, but no more than 2.0 inches (5.0 cm) from, the *longissimus dorsi*, leaving the lip firmly attached.

🍁 In Canada, steaks containing muscles other than the *longissimus dorsi* and *spinalis dorsi* must be called "Boneless Rib Steaks".

1112A — Chuletón (Espaldar), Bistec de Ribeye, Con Cordón, Deshuesado

Los bistecs de ribeye deshuesado, por su cola, llamada "cordón" o "gota", se conocen también como "ribeye gota", y deberán prepararse a partir de una pieza de chuletón que reúna los requisitos finales de la pieza número 112A. Se deberá cortar el cordón del lado del lomo corto con un corte recto ventral al *longissimus dorsi*, sin que supere los 5.0 cm (2.0 pulgadas) dejando el cordón firmemente unido.

🍁 En Canadá, los bistecs que contienen músculos que no sean el *longissimus dorsi* y el *spinalis dorsi* deben llamarse "Bistecs del Chuletón Deshuesados" (en inglés, "Boneless Rib Steaks").

Additional information about the IMPS or the specifications may be obtained from:

United States Department of Agriculture Agricultural Marketing Service

Livestock and Seed Program Standardization Branch
1400 Independence Ave. SW, STOP 0254
Washington, DC 20250
+1 202.720.4486

Poultry Programs Standardization Branch
1400 Independence Ave. SW, STOP 0259
Washington, DC 20250
+1 202.720.3506

www.ams.usda.gov

Any member of the North American Meat Processors Association (NAMP) will be happy to assist you in your product selection and will also be pleased to help you determine the trim and quality most appropriate for your business needs. NAMP members are located in many communities across the U.S., Canada, Mexico, and Australia.

A list of NAMP members in your area may also be obtained by calling the NAMP office at +1 703.758.1900.

Trim Levels

The following graph represents the most common fat trim level specifications currently used in the industry. Purchasers have the option of specifying the trim level best suited to their need unless, however, a trim level is specifically required by the product item description. In keeping with the current health and nutrition recommendations of the U.S. Department of Agriculture, NAMP has chosen to illustrate either 0.25 inch (6 mm) or 0.125 inch (3 mm) fat trim dimensions in the photographs. Actual fat thickness trim on any product, unless otherwise restricted, is to be agreed upon by the Buyer and Seller.

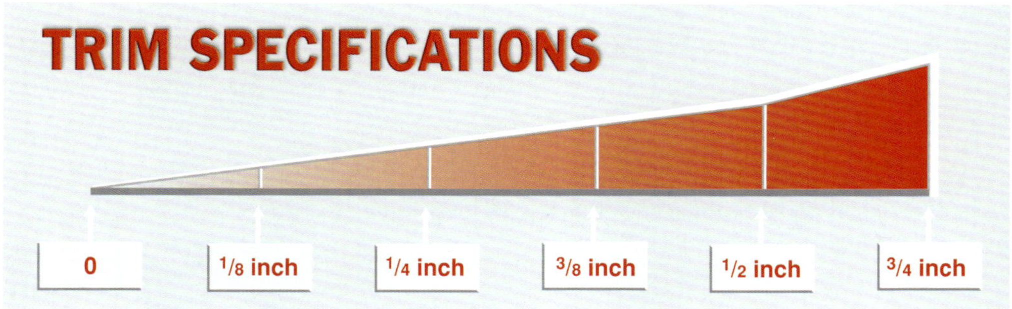

Meat Product Nomenclature in Canada

In Canada, the Meat Inspection Act and Regulations, the Food and Drugs Act and Regulations, and the Consumer Packaging and Labelling Act and Regulations, which are administered and enforced by the Canadian Food Inspection Agency (CFIA), require meat cuts, organs and other carcass parts to be labeled with common names at all levels of trade. Common names to be used are provided in the CFIA Meat Cuts Manual.

Significant deviations between common names prescribed by the CFIA Meat Cuts Manual and the NAMP nomenclature used in this guide are noted next to the individual items within *The Guide*. Please look for ❁ symbol indicating such a deviation.

Processors and restaurant purchasers and operators are encouraged to consult the CFIA Meat Cuts Manual to ensure common names used on product labels and restaurant menus are compliant with CFIA requirements.

Links

CFIA Meat Cuts Manual:
http://www.inspection.gc.ca/english/fssa/labeti/mcmancv/mcmancve.shtml

CFIA Food Labelling Information Service:
http://www.inspection.gc.ca/english/fssa/labeti/guide/ch1e.shtml#offbur

Acts and Regulations administered and enforced by the CFIA:
http://www.inspection.gc.ca/english/reg/rege.shtml

Meat Product Nomenclature in Mexico

Except for the existing guidelines on pork fabrication (NMX-FF-081-SCFI-2003), there is no official nomenclature for meat products in Mexico.

The pork guidelines can be found at
http://www.colpos.mx/bancodenormas/nmexicanas/NMX-FF-081-2003.PDF

Icons

In order to help you make use of *The Meat Buyer's Guide*, some items and descriptions in *The Guide* are annotated with icons. The symbols are used to aid in the identification of Educational, Measurement, Portion, and Canadian requirements.

A mortarboard indicates cuts that are no longer commonly used and may not be readily available in the marketplace. They have been included in *The Guide* as an educational reference.

Educational

A ruler indicates cuts that have a specific measurement, such as length or thickness.

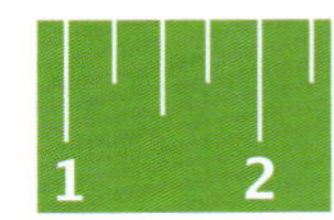

Measurement

A knife represents portion-cutting and/or those cuts for which trimming is designated.

Cutting And Trimming

A maple leaf indicates a deviation between the CFIA Meat Cuts Manual and the NAMP/IMPS item name or description.

Canadian

For poultry icons, see page 240.

Putting U.S. Meat on the World's Table

The United States red meat industry is a global leader in providing safe, high quality, nutritious products. The demand for red meat is growing along with global populations and economies, and the United States is helping meet this demand.

The U.S. red meat industry makes a commitment to its global customers to ensure the safety of the red meat products it produces. A unique interaction between industry, academia and government provides the United States with a structure to identify and implement technologies and interventions to continually make advances in the safety of red meat products. The mission of the U.S. Department of Agriculture (USDA) is to protect and promote food, agriculture and natural resources.

The USDA's Food Safety and Inspection Service (FSIS) is responsible for ensuring that the nation's commercial meat supply is safe, wholesome, and correctly labeled and packaged. Its federal, HACCP-based system of inspection and oversight of animal welfare and meat production is respected around the world.

The Animal and Plant Health Inspection Service (APHIS) protects and promotes U.S. agricultural health, regulating genetically engineered organisms, administering the Animal Welfare Act and carrying out wildlife damage management activities.

The Agricultural Marketing Service (AMS) is responsible for developing the quality grade standards that are recognized throughout the world.

The United States is committed to scientific principles and the ideal that strong risk assessment, risk management and risk communication, followed by evaluation and validation of mitigation procedures, provide for the strongest food safety system infrastructure. The natural resources found in the United States allow it to be an extremely competitive producer of red meat products. U.S. producers and the U.S. industry are committed to sustainability and responsible environmental stewardship. U.S. cattle raisers don't overgraze the land and they protect the nation's waterways. The U.S. hog industry treats its effluent and recycles it into agriculture in such a way as to help modern farming methods such as minimum tilling.

A commitment to quality is the hallmark of the United States red meat industry. It begins with production systems that utilize technologies and scientific advances in breeding, genetics and nutrition. Through the use of product evaluation technologies and palatability enhancing techniques, the U.S. red meat industry focuses on creating — with domestic grains and soybeans — a year-round supply of products that are world renowned for a consistent high quality — ensuring that consumers enjoy a good eating experience time and again.

www.USMEF.org

Bobby Hatoff
President
Allen Brothers, Inc.

Jeff Saval
Vice President
Deli Brands of America

Mike Satzow
Treasuer
North Country Smokehouse

Tony Gahn, Jr.
Assistant Treasurer
Gahn Meat Co., Inc.

Gary Malenke
Chairman
Sioux-Preme Pork Products

Philip Kimball, CAE
Director Ejecutivo
NAMP

Board of Directors:
Chris Appert
Andy Becker
Guenter Becker
Michael Bernstein
John Bloch
Peter Bozzo
Doug Bush
David Carriere
John Chlopek
Darren Dies
Steve Falcigno
John Fell
Lee Friedheim
Mike Gangel
Kirk Halpern
Mick Hamilton
Beau Heeps
Ron Hemauer
Deanna Hofing
Joseph F. Kinnealey
Jose Ramon Lozano
Joe Maas
Don Macgregor
Chris Mason
Mark Mitchell
Ray Parsons
Noel Reyes
Scott Rich
Kent Seelig
Ross Shuket
Thomas M. Stachecki
Andrew Sussman
Kevin Tulley
John Vatri
Tim Vlcek

February 2011

Dear *Meat Buyer's Guide®* User:

Congratulations for using the NAMP *Meat Buyer's Guide®*, the definitive reference and standards resource for the meat and poultry industry. First published in 1961, this publication represents the 7th edition of the book and is the direct result of the hard work and dedication of hundreds of meat industry professionals in industry, government and academia.

As you can see, the *Meat Buyer's Guide®* is divided into sections - each representing major meat protein groups – beef, pork, veal, lamb and poultry – and the content is designed to help you with manufacturing, purchasing and sales specifications. Additionally, reference material provides important information designed to help you in your business or profession.

The North American Meat Processors Association (NAMP), author and publisher of the *Meat Buyer's Guide®*, represents meat and poultry processors and suppliers throughout North America. We offer services and educational programs for the betterment of our members and the industry at large, and our members are dedicated to the highest standards of professionalism. We are proud to work alongside others in our food industry, sharing the goal to help provide the safest and most wholesome food products for our customers.

We are confident that you will find the *Meat Buyer's Guide®* a daily tool which will help you in your business, and we invite you to give us your feedback on how we can make the *Meat Buyer's Guide®* even more useful.

Sincerely,

Philip H. Kimball

Philip H. Kimball, CAE
Executive Director
North American Meat Processors Association

North American Headquarters
Washington, DC
1910 Association Drive, Reston, Virginia 20191 E.U.A.

Canada Office
203-2525 St. Laurent Blvd.
Ottawa, Ontario K1H 8P5, CANADÁ

www.namp.com info@namp.com
+1 703.758.1900 (main)
+1 703.758.8001 (fax)
+1 800.368.3043 (member services)

rdevalk@namp.com
+1 613.739.8500 (main)
+1 613.733.9501 (fax)

contenido

NAMP
NORTH AMERICAN MEAT PROCESSORS ASSOCIATION
Association Amérique du Nord des Transformateurs de Viande
Asociación Norteamericana de Procesadores de Carne

Asociación Norteamericana de Procesadores de Carne

Comité de revisión de la Guía para compradores de carne® (2010)

Presidente	John DeBenedetti, Del Monte Meat Co., Sacramento, CA
General	Ken Johnson, H. K. Johnson Associates, Inc., Winfield, IL Michael Strauss, Colorado Boxed Beef Co., Inverness, IL
Carne de res	John Stowell, Dole & Bailey, Woburn, MA
Carne de cordero	Mark DeNittis, Johnson & Wales University, y DeNCo Enterprise, LLC & Il Mondo Vechhio Salumi, Denver, CO
Carne de ternera	Bryan Scott, Dutch Valley Foods – Brown Packing Co., South Holland, IL
Carne de cerdo	Peter Bozzo, Chicago Meat Authority, Chicago, IL Gary Malenke, Sioux-Preme Pork Products, Sioux City, IA
Carne de aves	Lee Freidheim, Cougle Commission Co., Chicago, IL
Departamento de Agricultura de E.U.A.	Steve Olson, Servicio de Mercadeo Agrícola del Departamento de Agricultura de E.U.A., Washington, DC Darin Doerscher, Servicio de Mercadeo Agrícola del Departamento de Agricultura de E.U.A., Washington, DC
Personal	Ann Wells, Directora de Asuntos Científicos y Normativos, NAMP, Reston, VA Phil Kimball, CAE, Director Ejecutivo, NAMP, Reston, VA
USMEF	Nelson Huerta Leidenz, Ph. D., Director de Servicios Técnicos, U.S. Meat Export Federation, México D.F., México
BIC	John Baker, Director Ejecutivo de Mercadeo Comercial, Beef Information Centre (Canada), Calgary, AB

Los miembros de NAMP y otras organizaciones de todo Estados Unidos y Canadá que participaron en los comités de especies individuales han realizado contribuciones adicionales.

La Asociación Norteamericana de Procesadores de Carne es una asociación sin fines de lucro formada por empresas de procesamiento de carne y asociados que comparten un compromiso continuo por ofrecer carne, aves, mariscos, caza mayor y menor y otros alimentos a los clientes de la industria de servicios de alimentación. La asociación, que se fundó en 1942, tiene grandes y pequeñas empresas afiliadas en todo el territorio de Estados Unidos, Canadá, México y otras partes del mundo. La organización es más conocida por su acrónimo, NAMP, y universalmente reconocida por su famosa publicación a nivel mundial, *la Guía para compradores de carne®*.

NAMP es una organización orientada a los miembros que proporciona servicios y oportunidades educativas para el beneficio de sus miembros, la industria de la carne y las aves, y los profesionales de la gastronomía. Estos programas están diseñados para ofrecer crecimiento individual y ayudar a los miembros a lograr éxitos empresariales. Cada año, NAMP presenta su prestigioso y codiciado Premio del Educador Harry L. Rudnick a un educador distinguido en reconocimiento por sus aportes destacados en el campo de la educación sobre la carne. NAMP también presenta premios especiales por logros y servicios a sus miembros individuales. Además, la asociación y sus miembros alientan a los estudiantes e instituciones culinarias y de hospitalidad, y fomentan las iniciativas científicas y educativas de toda la industria. NAMP ofrece liderazgo en los temas que afectan a la industria y al público, y se esfuerza por atenderlos en beneficio de todas las partes.

nuestra misión

Proporcionar a nuestros miembros un foro a fin de que tengan éxito con una educación excepcional, la defensa y el acceso a los recursos mientras fomentan relaciones duraderas y prósperas a largo plazo.

Con este espíritu, la Asociación Norteamericana de Procesadores de Carne ha asumido la tarea de la publicación de la

Guía para compradores de carne®

Obtenga más información acerca de NAMP en www.namp.com. Piense en convertirse en miembro para aprovechar al máximo todos los beneficios de NAMP.

Asociación Norteamericana de Procesadores de Carne (NAMP)

**1910 Association Drive
Reston, VA 20191 USA**

**+1 703.758.1900
Fax: +1 703.758.8001**

www.namp.com

prefacio

La Asociación Norteamericana de Procesadores de Carne (NAMP) tiene el orgullo de presentar esta versión revisada y ampliada de *la Guía para compradores de carne®* a los compradores de productos cárnicos y avícolas de todo el mundo. Este libro es nuestra versión más reciente y autorizada de nuestra ampliamente respetada y reconocida publicación.

Desde sus comienzos en 1961, *la Guía para compradores de carne* ha sido la publicación y recurso principal para compradores de la industria de servicios de alimentación, docentes, estudiantes, empresas de procesamiento de carne, profesionales de la gastronomía y muchos otros que atienden al público en nuestra industria. *La Guía* se ha revisado en varias ocasiones desde su origen y más recientemente en 2010.

Esta edición de *la Guía para compradores de carne* incluye nueva información y una nueva presentación. Se incluye la traducción al español, haciendo que el libro resulte aún más útil para un público más amplio. Además, en todo el libro se ofrece información acerca de la clasificación por grados, etiquetado y nomenclatura específica para Canadá, para que sea completamente aplicable al comercio de carne canadiense. También se ha agregado información sobre la industria cárnica en México, así como los nombres de los cortes más populares de res y cerdo en los países de América Latina. Estos agregados hacen que el libro tenga una mayor cobertura de América del Norte.

Se han producido muchos cambios en las industrias de la carne y las aves. Las investigaciones en ciencia de la carne realizadas en las universidades han permitido la identificación de nuevos usos de músculos anteriormente subvalorados en las canales de carne. Los nuevos niveles de recorte grasa y limpieza y los cambios en los hábitos de los consumidores hacia productos más convenientes también han favorecido un deseo por una mayor cantidad de nuevas piezas. El comercio internacional ampliado y la creciente diversidad étnica en los hábitos alimenticios también han provocado una mayor diversificación de los productos.

La Asociación Norteamericana de Procesadores de Carne (NAMP), en su esfuerzo por atender los diversos cambios en la industria y satisfacer las demandas del siglo XXI, aprovechó esta oportunidad para cumplir con estos desafíos a través de la publicación de una versión completamente nueva de *la Guía para compradores de carne*. En consecuencia, los usuarios de *la Guía* encontrarán nuevas fotografías y descripciones que representan los productos, los recortes de grasa y limpieza y las opciones de procesamiento, junto con información acerca del embalaje, inocuidad alimentaria, nutrición, cocción y un glosario mejorado.

agradecimientos

Esta publicación no hubiese sido posible sin la ayuda dedicada del Comité de Revisión de la *Guía para compradores de carne* de la Asociación Norteamericana de Procesadores de Carne o NAMP y sus Comités de Especies, y sin el apoyo completo de nuestros miembros, diversos grupos relacionados con la carne y muchas personas de la industria y el gobierno que han aportado tan generosamente su tiempo, energía y experiencia. La versión actual de *la Guía para compradores de carne* está basada en la última serie de Especificaciones Institucionales de Compra de Carne (IMPS) del Departamento de Agricultura de E.U.A. (USDA), el Servicio de Mercadeo Agrícola (AMS), la División de Estandarización del Programa de Ganado y Granos y las Descripciones de Comercio de E.U.A. aplicables del Programa de Carne de Aves para Productos Avícolas. La Asociación Norteamericana de Procesadores de Carne aprecia mucho la valiosa ayuda del Departamento en todas las facetas de *la Guía*.

Esta edición de *la Guía* también incorpora información del Manual de Cortes de Carne de la Agencia Canadiense de Inspección de Alimentos (CFIA) en lo que respecta a especificaciones del gobierno canadiense. El Centro de Información de Carne de Res (Canadá) aportó su colaboración.

La Federación de Exportadores de Carnes de los E.U.A. (USMEF, por sus siglas en inglés) también contribuyó con la preparación de esta versión en inglés/español de *la Guía*. NAMP agradece la experiencia del personal de USMEF y de BIC, y la alianza con cada una de las organizaciones para la mejora de toda la industria de la carne en América del Norte.

Sinceramente agradecemos a todos los que nos ayudaron en este emprendimiento. Cada uno desempeñó un papel importante en aumentar el valor de *la Guía para compradores de carne* tanto como un recurso educativo como una herramienta de compra para la industria de servicios de alimentación y las industrias de venta al detalle, así como para el público en general. Estamos seguros de que los usuarios de *la Guía* también estarán satisfechos con los resultados.

Desde 1961, las organizaciones de la industria de servicios de alimentación han reconocido a la Guía para compradores de carne como la principal publicación para la educación e información acerca del tema de cortes de carne y aves. Los gobiernos, escuelas gastronómicas, establecimientos de la industria de servicios de alimentación y sus empleados, organizaciones de la industria de la alimentación y otros que deseen obtener conocimientos acerca de la carne confían diariamente en esta publicación.

Estas organizaciones han aprobado la 6ª edición de la *Guía para Compradores de Carne*, que se presenta en inglés, con las traducciones al español de los nombres de los cortes de carne. Esta 7ª edición incluye una traducción completa al español de la 6ª edición, y cuenta además con la aprobación de las dos asociaciones mexicanas de la industria.

American Association of Meat Processors (Asociación Norteamericana de Procesadores de Carne)

American Lamb Board (Junta Americana del Cordero)

American Meat Institute (Instituto Americano de la Carne)

American Meat Science Association (Asociación Americana de Ciencia de la Carne)

Asociación Nacional de Establecimientos TIF, A.C. (ANETIF)

Beef Information Centre (Canadá) [Centro de Información sobre Carne de Res (Canadá)]

Chicago Midwest Meat Association (Asociación de Carne de Chicago Medio-Oeste)

Consejo Mexicano de la Carne

Culinary Institute of America (Instituto Culinario de América)

Meat & Livestock Australia (Carne y Ganado de Australia)

National Cattlemen's Beef Association (Asociación Nacional de Criadores de Ganado de Carne)

National Chicken Council (Consejo Nacional del Pollo)

Esta última edición de la Guía ofrece información adicional valiosa acerca de la seguridad alimentaria, la nutrición y los nuevos productos. La Asociación Norteamericana de Procesadores de Carne ha dado respuesta a las necesidades de nuestra industria y esta nueva publicación ha recibido el apoyo de las organizaciones enumeradas.

National Meat Association (Asociación Nacional de la Carne)

National Pork Board (Junta Nacional del Cerdo)

National Poultry & Food Distributors Association (Asociación Nacional de Distribuidores de Aves y Alimentos Avícolas)

National Restaurant Association (Asociación Nacional de Restaurantes)

National Turkey Federation (Federación Nacional del Pavo)

Research Chefs Association (Asociación de Chefs de Investigación)

Southeastern Meat Association (Asociación de Carne del Sudeste)

Southwest Meat Association (Asociación de Carne del Sudoeste)

USA Poultry & Egg Export Council (Consejo de Exportación de Aves y Huevos de E.U.A.)

U.S. Meat Export Federation (Federación de Exportadores de Carnes de los E.U.A.)

United States Department of Agriculture

Office of the Secretary
Washington, D.C. 20250

Consejo de Administración
Asociación Norteamericana de Procesadores de Carne
1910 Association Drive
Reston, Virginia 20191

Estimado Consejo de Administración:

Felicitaciones por finalizar la revisión 2010 de la Guía para Compradores de Carne. Tengo la certeza de que la Guía continuará siendo la publicación y el recurso principal para la comunidad de la industria de servicios de alimentación y servirá como valiosa ayuda para la comercialización de productos cárnicos y avícolas.

Para muchas personas en la industria de la carne, la Guía se ha convertido en un recurso que brinda excelentes ilustraciones a color para las Especificaciones Institucionales de Compra de Carne del Departamento de Agricultura (USDA). Además, la Guía revisada refleja el aumento de la diversificación de los productos y la tendencia continua de la industria hacia la comercialización de cortes de carne con valor agregado. Esta publicación es un gran ejemplo de la exitosa alianza y cooperación entre la industria de la carne y el Gobierno.

USDA ha valorado la oportunidad de trabajar con la Asociación Norteamericana de Procesadores de Carne a través de los años y espera mantener este espíritu de cooperación para satisfacer las necesidades de un mercado en continua expansión.

Atentamente,

Thomas J. Vilsack
Secretario

NAMPÓMETRO: guías bacterianas

Los productos cárnicos son extremadamente perecederos y la temperatura de almacenamiento y cocción de la carne cumple un papel especialmente preponderante en la seguridad microbiológica de los productos cárnicos. El "NAMPÓMETRO" de esta página ilustra la relación entre la temperatura y el crecimiento bacteriano de los productos cárnicos. El máximo crecimiento bacteriano para la mayoría de los organismos patógenos y de descomposición asociados con los productos cárnicos se produce entre 4 °C o 40 °F y 60 °C o 140 °F. La destrucción térmica de los microorganismos se basa en el tiempo y la temperatura. Las temperaturas indicadas en este diagrama no reflejan las relaciones de tiempo y temperatura. Por lo tanto, los procesos individuales pueden variar con respecto a la temperatura mínima necesaria para destruir un microorganismo específico según el tiempo de aplicación. Es posible que las instalaciones de la industria de servicios de alimentación en E.U.A. tengan que operar según el Código de Alimentos de la Administración de Alimentos y Medicamentos de E.U.A., en caso de que el estado lo adopte. Los NAMPÓMETROS representan guías para los procesadores de carne y es posible que no reflejen las temperaturas específicas exigidas por los reglamentos estatales, provinciales o federales para la operación de restaurantes.

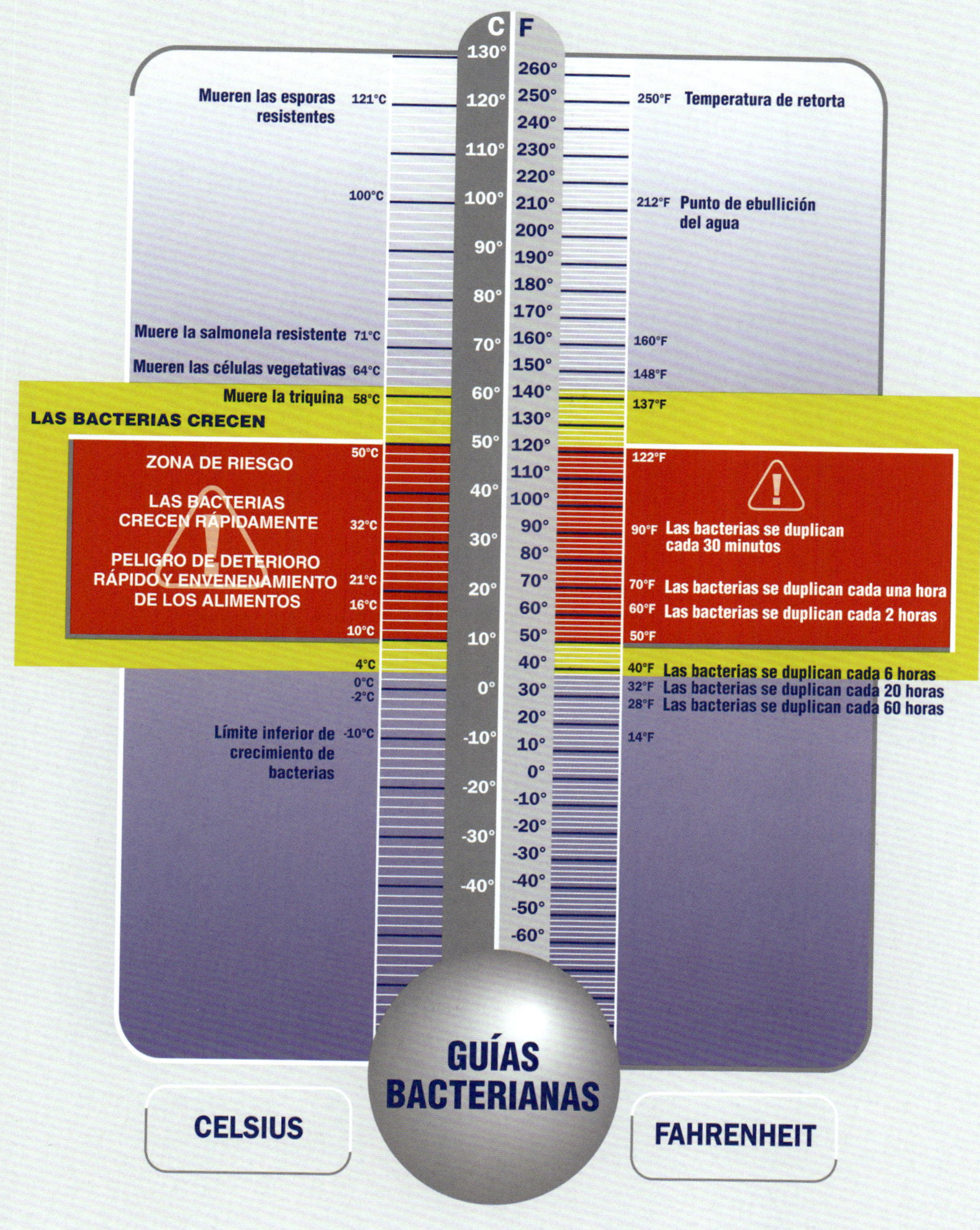

NAMPÓMETRO para carne

La temperatura tiene un papel importante en la relación del almacenamiento y cocción de la carne con la palatabilidad de los productos cárnicos. El "NAMPÓMETRO" que se muestra en esta página indica las temperaturas óptimas de almacenamiento para conservar la máxima frescura de los productos cárnicos frescos y congelados. Además, se indican las temperaturas internas de la carne necesarias para alcanzar los niveles específicos de cocción. El grado de cocción (y por lo tanto la temperatura interna) de un producto cárnico tendrá una influencia muy importante en las características de ese producto. Es posible que las instalaciones de la industria de servicios de alimentación en E.U.A. tengan que operar según el Código de Alimentos de la Administración de Alimentos y Medicamentos de E.U.A., en caso de que el estado lo adopte. Los NAMPÓMETRO representan guías para los procesadores de carne y es posible que no reflejen las temperaturas específicas exigidas por los reglamentos estatales, provinciales o federales para la operación de restaurantes.

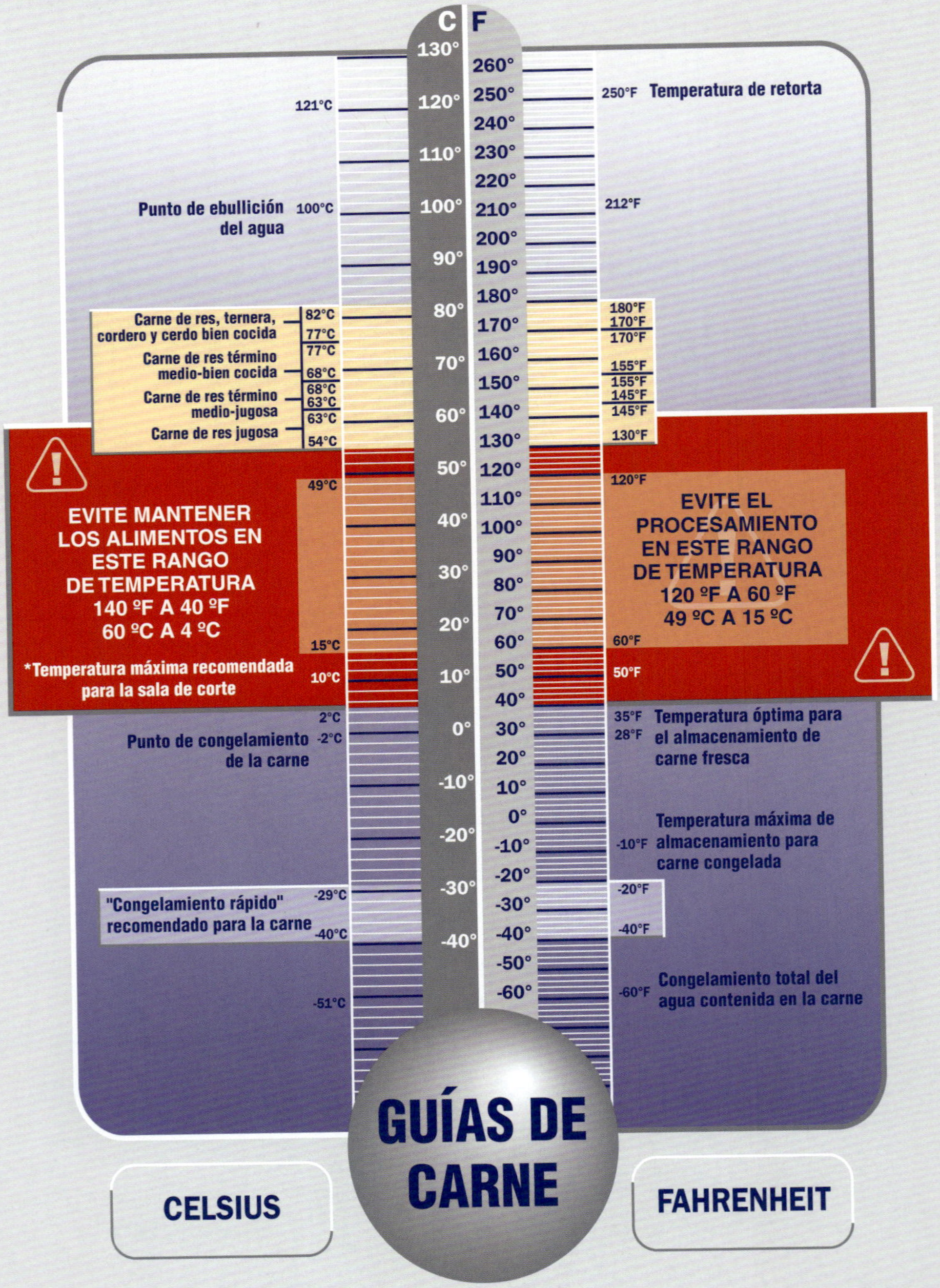

*La temperatura del producto debe mantenerse por debajo de los 7 °C (45 °F).

NAMPÓMETRO para aves

Los productos avícolas son extremadamente perecederos y la temperatura de almacenamiento y cocción de la carne de aves cumple un papel especialmente preponderante en la seguridad microbiológica de los productos avícolas. La temperatura también desempeña un papel importante en la relación del almacenamiento y cocción de la carne de aves con lo paladeable del producto avícola. El termómetro para la carne de aves de esta página ilustra la relación entre la temperatura y el crecimiento bacteriano en los productos avícolas y las temperaturas deseadas para conservar la máxima frescura para los productos avícolas frescos y congelados. También se muestran las temperaturas internas necesarias para lograr niveles específicos de cocción. Se puede exigir que los centros de la industria de servicios de alimentación en E.U.A. operen de acuerdo con el Código de Alimentos de la Administración de Alimentos y Medicamentos de E.U.A., según lo adopten cada uno de los estados de la nación. El NAMPÓMETRO representa sólo una guía a seguir por los procesadores de carne y puede no reflejar las temperaturas específicas que requieren los reglamentos estatales, provinciales o federales para los sistemas operativos de los restaurantes.

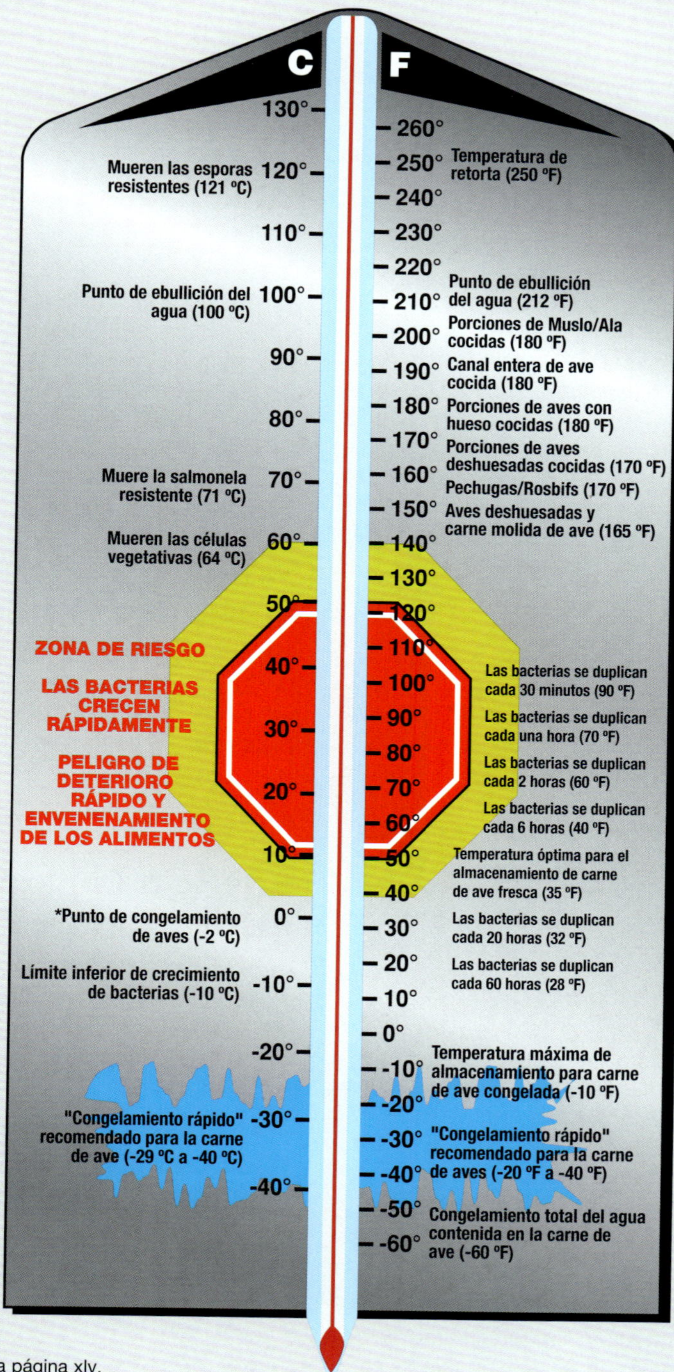

Para obtener más información, consulte la página xlv.

Inocuidad alimentaria

En Estados Unidos, el Servicio de Inspección e Inocuidad Alimentaria del Departamento de Agricultura de E.U.A. es la agencia de sanidad federal responsable de garantizar que el suministro comercial estadounidense de productos cárnicos y avícolas sea seguro y salubre, y que estos se encuentren correctamente etiquetados y embalados. Además de la inspección y supervisión diaria de la planta, el Servicio de Inspección e Inocuidad Alimentaria realiza un análisis de adulterantes microbiológicos y químicos, y de enfermedades animales en los productos. También informa a los consumidores acerca de las enfermedades de origen alimentario.

En Canadá, Health Canada es el departamento federal que se encarga de ayudar a los canadienses a mantener y mejorar su estado de salud. La Agencia Canadiense de Inspección de Alimentos proporciona todos los servicios de inspección federal relacionados con los alimentos e impone los estándares de inocuidad alimentaria y calidad nutricional que establece Health Canada.

En México, la Secretaría de Salud (Sec-Salud) es el departamento federal responsable de la administración del Programa Nacional de Salud e inocuidad alimentaria en el país. El programa de inspección de carnes en los rastros municipales se encuentra supervisado por la Comisión para la Protección contra Riesgos Sanitarios (COFEPRIS) de la Secretaría de Salud. SENASICA (Servicio Nacional de Sanidad, Inocuidad y Calidad Agroalimentaria) es un organismo separado de la Secretaría de Agricultura, Ganadería, Desarrollo Rural, Pesca y Alimentación (SAGARPA) que complementa las funciones de la Secretaría de Salud en términos de inocuidad cárnica y avícola mediante la certificación y la realización de servicios de inspección de carnes relacionados con los denominados establecimientos domésticos TIF (Tipo de Inspección Federal). SENASICA también es responsable de la reinspección de las carnes importadas y de la autorización de las plantas extranjeras que exportan carnes y aves a México.

Análisis de riesgos y puntos críticos de control (HACCP)

El Servicio de Inspección e Inocuidad Alimentaria del Departamento de Agricultura de E.U.A. estableció un programa de inocuidad alimentaria y de disminución de patógenos llamado sistema de análisis de riesgos y puntos críticos de control (HACCP). Este se aplica tanto en la producción dentro de E.U.A. como en los productos importados de carne de res y aves. El sistema se basa en técnicas con bases científicas para satisfacer las necesidades actuales de inocuidad alimentaria. Este sistema sustituye la dependencia de métodos de inspección que solo utilizan los órganos de los sentidos (inspección organoléptica) y las reglamentaciones de ordenanzas y control que tienen décadas de antigüedad. El HACCP, en cambio, sustituye los controles del proceso e incorpora datos científicos para atender las necesidades en materia de inocuidad alimentaria.

En Canadá, las plantas de procesamiento de carne también funcionan de acuerdo con dicho sistema. Para que resulte más efectivo, el sistema HACCP exige que todos los que participan en la cadena alimentaria, desde la granja hasta la mesa, acepten su cuota de responsabilidad para garantizar que la carne y productos avícolas, así como los mariscos y otros alimentos, se produzcan y se resguarden bajo las más rigurosas disciplinas de inocuidad alimentaria.

En México, HACCP no es obligatorio. Los requisitos previos de HACCP generalmente se aplican en los rastros y en los establecimientos de procesamiento de carne. Sin embargo, todos los establecimientos mexicanos que cumplen con los requisitos para exportar carne y aves a E.U.A. operan según el sistema HACCP.

Los miembros de la Asociación Norteamericana de Procesadores de Carne o NAMP le garantizan su dedicación a este esfuerzo.

Manejo seguro de productos cárnicos y avícolas

Todos los productos cárnicos sin cocer y precocidos se deben almacenar, manejar y cocer de forma apropiada para garantizar la seguridad del público. Sin embargo, el manejo seguro de los alimentos no termina con el procesador de carne.

La carne refrigerada se debe almacenar a temperaturas inferiores a 4 °C o 40 °F, y la carne congelada se debe almacenar a menos de -18 °C o 0 °F. Para evitar las enfermedades de origen alimentario, los alimentos se deben cocer adecuadamente a sus temperaturas internas mínimas correspondientes, refrigerar rápidamente para su almacenamiento si no se consumen de inmediato y conservarlos a temperaturas de almacenamiento adecuadas.

Para obtener más información acerca de las temperaturas críticas para el almacenamiento, manejo y cocción de carne y productos avícolas, consulte las pautas de NAMPÓMETRO.

Las personas que manipulan alimentos deben tener cuidado de no exponerlos a la contaminación cruzada. No utilice las mismas tablas para picar ni los mismos utensilios para los productos crudos y cocidos sin una limpieza adecuada de los elementos entre un uso y otro. Almacene los productos y alimentos crudos separados de otros alimentos cocidos o crudos. Las personas que manipulan alimentos se deben lavar las manos con agua tibia y jabón antes y después de tocar productos cárnicos crudos o cocidos.

Servicio de Inspección e Inocuidad Alimentaria de E.U.A.

Para enviar preguntas o consultas acerca de problemas con productos cárnicos o avícolas fuera de Washington, D.C., llame a la línea sin cargo, +1 800.535.4555; dentro del área metropolitana de Washington, D.C., llame al +1 202.720.3333.

También puede visitar el sitio web del Servicio de Inspección e Inocuidad Alimentaria, www.fsis.usda.gov.

Agencia Canadiense de Inspección de Alimentos

Para enviar preguntas o consultas acerca de problemas con productos cárnicos o avícolas en Canadá, llame a la línea sin cargo al +1 800.442.2342, o llame al +1 613.225.2342 o visite www.inspection.gc.ca

Servicio Nacional de Sanidad, Inocuidad y Calidad Agroalimentaria de México (SENASICA)

Para consultas o problemas con productos cárnicos y avícolas en México puede llamar al 011-52-55-5905-1000, ext. 50911, o visitar www.senasica.gob.mx.

Requisitos materiales
para carne de res, ternera, cordero, cerdo y aves

Todos los productos ofrecidos deben cumplir con los siguientes requisitos materiales y los requisitos de la descripción para la pieza específica. Estos requisitos se basan en los requisitos generales y las disposiciones de control de calidad de las Especificaciones Institucionales de Compra de Carne (IMPS).

Calidad

Condición del producto

Todos los productos ofrecidos para la venta deben estar en excelente estado. Las superficies expuestas de carne magra y grasa deben tener un color que se asocie normalmente con la clase, grado y corte de carne especificado. Toda la carne debe estar prácticamente libre de hematomas, coágulos de sangre, tejido sanguíneo, decoloración sanguínea, porciones de médula espinal, vasos sanguíneos expuestos, grasa del escroto o la ubre, tendón de Aquiles o cualquier otra condición que pudiese afectar negativamente el uso del producto. Excepto en las piezas molidas y rebanadas en hojuelas, no se acepta la carne de res de corte oscuro o callosa. La carne se debe mantener en un excelente estado durante el procesamiento, almacenamiento y transporte. Las superficies de corte y las superficies de carne magra expuestas naturalmente, al igual que la grasa, no deben mostrar más que un leve oscurecimiento o decoloración debido a la deshidratación, maduración o actividad microbiana u oxidación, a menos que se haya especificado que el producto se haya madurado en seco. No se deben percibir olores extraños en la carne fresca. Sin embargo, se aceptarán los cambios de coloración y los olores característicamente asociados con la carne envasada al vacío en excelente estado. El producto no debe mostrar evidencia alguna de manejo indebido. El producto tampoco debe mostrar evidencias de congelación o descongelación, a menos que el comprador lo haya solicitado.

Las piezas en cortes porcionados o molidas que se entreguen congeladas se pueden producir de cortes de carne congelados, siempre y cuando dichos cortes no muestren evidencia alguna de deterioro. A menos que se especifique lo contrario, las piezas en cortes porcionados deben mantener aproximadamente su forma original. Los productos que se creen de ese modo se deben envasar, empaquetar y regresar al refrigerador.

Corte, Recorte de Grasa y Limpieza, y Deshuesado

El corte, recorte de grasa y limpieza y el deshuesado de las piezas se debe lograr con el suficiente cuidado como para que cada pieza conserve su identidad y carezca de incisiones profundas objetables en la carne magra. Se deberán quitar los bordes irregulares cerca de las superficies de carne magra. Excepto para aquellos cortes que están divididos por vetas naturales, todas las superficies de corte se deben realizar en ángulos aproximadamente rectos con respecto a la lámina conectiva superficial que los recubre ("la piel"). No se debe incluir más que una pequeña cantidad de carne magra, grasa o hueso, siempre y cuando la pieza se prepare con hueso, derivados de un corte adyacente. Ningún hueso puede estar presente en una pieza deshuesada.

Cuando se corten bistecs porcionados, excepto los que hayan sido suavizados o entretejidos o bien descritos de forma diferente, los bistecs se deben cortar en rebanadas completas en una línea recta, razonablemente perpendicular a la superficie exterior en un ángulo aproximadamente recto con respecto al largo del corte que se está rebanando o porcionando. Los bistecs individuales deben permanecer intactos cuando se suspenden 13 mm (0.5 pulgadas) desde el borde exterior. Las piezas en cortes porcionados deben estar prácticamente libres de fracturas, extremos marcados e incisiones profundas de las cuchillas.

Tabla de conversión

A continuación se indican fracciones equivalentes a medidas decimales y métricas utilizadas en esta guía:

Pulgadas	Decimal	Métrico
1/8	0.125	3 mm
1/4	0.25	6 mm
3/8	0.375	9 mm
1/2	0.50	13 mm
5/8	0.625	16 mm
3/4	0.75	19 mm
7/8	0.875	22 mm
1	1.0	2.5 cm

Desprovisto de grasa/ Prácticamente desnudo de grasa

La expresión "Desprovisto de grasa" implica retiro de la cubierta de grasa y la separación del músculo por disección a través de las vetas naturales para que la superficie descubierta del corte que resulta de la disección (membrana "plateada" o "azulada", llamada "espejo") quede expuesta con una "escama" de grasa restante que no debe superar los 2.5 cm (1.0 pulgada) en la dimensión más larga o 3 mm (0.125 pulgadas) de profundidad en ningún punto. La expresión "Prácticamente desnudo de grasa" implica la eliminación de toda la cubierta de grasa para que la superficie muscular descubierta del corte que resulta de su disección (membrana "plateada" o "azulada", llamada "espejo") quede expuesta con una "escama" de grasa restante que no debe superar los 2.5 cm (1.0 pulgada) en ninguna dimensión o 3 mm (0.125 pulgadas) de profundidad en ningún punto.

Desprovisto de grasa/ Prácticamente desnudo de grasa, Membrana superficial retirada

Cuando se requiere el retiro (despellejado) de la membrana superficial ("plateada" o "azulada" llamada "espejo"), la superficie de corte resultante deberá exponer como mínimo el 90% de carne magra con una "escama" de grasa restante que no debe superar los 3 mm (0.125 pulgadas) de profundidad.

Debido a la preocupación acerca de la encefalopatía espongiforme bovina (EEB, por sus siglas en inglés), el Servicio de Inspección e Inocuidad Alimentaria (FSIS) enmendó en 2004 sus reglamentos de inspección para prohibir que algunas partes específicas de ganado y canales de res se utilicen como alimento para seres humanos. En el caso del ganado bovino mayor de 30 meses de edad, las partes que se designaron como materiales de riesgo especificado (SRM, por sus siglas en inglés) incluían los sesos, cráneo, ojos, ganglios trigéminos, médula espinal, columna vertebral (excluidas las vértebras de la cola, las apófisis transversas de las vértebras toráxicas y lumbares y las alas del sacro) y los ganglios de raíz dorsal contenidos en la columna vertebral. Además, en el caso del ganado bovino de todas las edades, el Servicio de Inspección e Inocuidad Alimentaria indicó que las amígdalas y el *íleon distal* del intestino delgado se deben clasificar como materiales de riesgo especificado.

El Servicio de Inspección e Inocuidad Alimentaria requería como una medida de inocuidad adicional que se condenara el sacrificio de todo el ganado discapacitado no ambulatorio y que no se introdujera en la cadena alimentaria. La encefalopatía espongiforme bovina (EEB) nunca se ha encontrado en el tejido muscular de las canales de carne de res. En primer lugar, todas las piezas y productos de carne de res de la industria de servicios de alimentación provienen de ganado joven mucho menor de 30 meses de edad, generalmente de aproximadamente 20 meses de edad. Consulte el sitio web del Servicio de Inspección e Inocuidad Alimentaria en http://www.fsis.usda.gov para obtener más información.

Existen reglamentos y requisitos similares en Canadá y México. Para obtener más información, visite www.inspection.gc.ca o www.senasica.gob.mx/?id=816.

Recortes para limpieza de grasa

El recorte de grasa externa se logrará al retirar suavemente la grasa siguiendo el contorno de la superficie muscular subyacente. No es aceptable que simplemente se haga un biselado de los bordes de un corte o porción, para que parezca que se logró el recorte de grasa deseado. Dos términos que se utilizan para describir las limitaciones de grasa son: (1) grosor máximo de grasa en cualquier punto y (2) grosor promedio de grasa. Estos requisitos de grosor de grasa se pueden aplicar a la superficie externa o a las vetas de grasa intermuscular en una pieza. En lugar de seleccionar una medida específica para determinar los grosores máximo y promedio, el comprador puede especificar uno de los dos requisitos de recorte de grasa a la izquierda como una alternativa.

Método para determinar el grosor de la grasa en cortes y rosbifs

El grosor máximo de grasa en cualquier punto se determina mediante un examen visual del área que exhiba el mayor grosor de grasa en un corte y proceder a medir el grosor o la profundidad de grasa en ese punto.

El grosor máximo de grasa en cualquier punto se determina mediante un examen visual del área que exhiba el mayor grosor de grasa en un corte y proceder a medir el grosor o la profundidad de grasa en ese punto. El grosor promedio de grasa se determina después sumando todas las medidas del grosor de grasa y dividiendo el total entre la cantidad de medidas tomadas. Por ejemplo, en el caso de tres medidas de un área de superficie de 5 mm (0.2 pulgadas) de profundidad, 8 mm (0.3 pulgadas) de profundidad y 10 mm (0.4 pulgadas) de profundidad, el grosor o profundidad promedio de la grasa sería de 8 mm (0.3 pulgadas).

Las medidas de grasa antes mencionadas se toman en los bordes del corte o rosbif, según sea necesario, con un calado o incisión profunda de la cubierta de grasa que recubre la pieza, de modo que determine el grosor real de la grasa y revele cualquier depresión natural o veta que pueda afectar la medición.

Método de transición (Bridging Method) de medición de grasa

Cuando un músculo presente una depresión natural, únicamente se considerará la grasa que recubra esa parte de la depresión cuando tenga un ancho superior a 19 mm (0.75 pulgadas) para determinar así el grosor de la grasa. Ver imagen 1.

Método planimétrico de la medición de grasa

Cuando se presenta una veta de grasa entre músculos adyacentes, únicamente se medirá la grasa que queda por encima del nivel de los músculos que intervienen. Ver imagen 1.

Método para determinar el recorte de grasa en piezas troceadas en cubos y de bistecs derivados de cortes porcionados

El grosor máximo de grasa en cualquier punto se determina mediante una selección visual de las áreas en los bordes de cualquiera de los lados de la pieza troceada o de los cortes porcionados que tengan la cantidad más gruesa de grasa y midiendo el grosor o profundidad de la cubierta de grasa en ese punto.

El grosor promedio de grasa se determina mediante una selección visual de distintas áreas en las que aparezca cubierta de grasa en la pieza troceada en cubos o en los cortes porcionados y luego se toman las medidas correspondientes para calcular el grosor promedio de grasa, como se explicó anteriormente para cortes y rosbifs.

Las mediciones reales de la cubierta de grasa se toman en los bordes del corte y mediante un calado o incisión profunda de la cubierta de grasa, según sea necesario, de modo que se pueda revelar el grosor real de la grasa. Para las piezas hechas bistecs, los métodos de transición o el planimétrico se deben aplicar para tener en cuenta cualquier depresión natural que presente un músculo o cuando se interpone una veta de grasa entre músculos adyacentes.

En el caso de que un comprador especifique un límite máximo del ancho de las vetas de grasa intermuscular en cualquier punto, dicho límite se debe determinar visualmente y medir en los puntos entre las capas de músculos magros del lado del corte que tenga los depósitos de grasa más gruesos o más anchos. El grosor promedio se debe determinar mediante el cálculo del grosor promedio de grasa como se explicó anteriormente para cortes y rosbifs.

Para las piezas hechas bistecs, los métodos de transición o planimétricos se deben aplicar para tener en cuenta los anchos irregulares de las vetas de grasa intermuscular en una depresión muscular o entre músculos adyacentes para revelar el grosor de grasa real (ancho) de la grasa que se encuentra intercalada en una veta. Las vetas de grasa intermuscular se deben evaluar en un punto que no se acerque en más de 19 mm (0.75 pulgadas) al contorno (perímetro proyectado cuando se moldea de forma simétrica o aún sin moldear) del borde exterior del bistec.

Siempre que se especifique una limitación de grasa "Desprovisto de grasa/Prácticamente Desnudo de grasa, Membrana superficial retirada", solo se podrá utilizar el método de transición para evaluar la grasa que cubre una depresión natural en un músculo o la grasa presente en las vetas entre músculos adyacentes.

IMAGEN 1: Transición y Planificación

Transición

Cuando un músculo presenta una depresión natural, únicamente se considera la grasa por encima de esa porción de depresión que tenga un ancho superior a 19 mm (0.75 pulgadas).

Planificación

Cuando se presenta una veta de grasa entre músculos adyacentes, únicamente se mide la grasa por encima del nivel de los músculos involucrados.

requisitos materiales

Colocación en una malla o amarrado

Cuando el comprador lo especifica o la descripción de la pieza requiere que se amarre o se coloque en una malla, se debe utilizar una malla elástica o cualquier otro material equivalente aprobado por el Servicio de Inspección e Inocuidad Alimentaria o la Agencia Canadiense de Inspección de Alimentos para que los rosbifs queden firmes y compactos. A menos que se especifique de otro modo, los rosbifs deben colocarse en mallas para que todas las porciones se mantengan intactas y que ninguna porción sobresalga por los extremos de dicha malla. De forma alternativa, los rosbifs se pueden amarrar con cuerdas por medio de lazos trenzados uniformemente a intervalos espaciados de no más de 5.0 cm (2.0 pulgadas) aproximadamente de forma circunferencial o perpendicular al largo de la pieza. Si se amarra de forma circunferencial y los rosbifs no quedan firmes y compactos, también se debe amarrar de forma longitudinal. Todos los materiales de las mallas y amarres se deben incluir con otros materiales de embalaje para determinar el peso de la tara.

Listo para Chuletas, Listo para Tablajear o Listo para Filetear

El uso de los términos Listo para Chuletas, Listo para Tablajear o Listo para Filetear indica que los cortes están listos para procesarse en chuletas o bistecs, utilizando simplemente una cuchilla o sierra. Cuando se utilizan los términos Listo para Chuletas o Listo para Tablajear junto con piezas de costillar de ternera, significan específicamente que las piezas están divididas y que se han quitado las puntas del espinazo, el hueso de la paleta, los cartílagos relacionados, la banda ligamentosa nucal y los músculos elevadores asociados con el hueso de la paleta. Cuando se utilizan los términos con piezas del lomo de ternera, significan específicamente que se han dividido, que se le han quitado las puntas del espinazo y los huesos de las costillas, que la cavidad está limpia y se ha quitado la falda con un corte recto que se encuentra a no más de 2.5 cm (1.0 pulgada) por debajo del músculo *longissimus dorsi* en los extremos adyacentes al espaldar o sirloin. Algunas piezas de carne de cordero se identifican como Listas para Tablajear o Listas para Rosbifs con una explicación adicional del significado en la descripción de la pieza. Los lomos de cerdo a veces también se pueden identificar como Listos para Chuletas o Listos para Tablajear. El término Listos para Bistecs generalmente corresponde a piezas de chuletón o lomo de res.

Corte de muesca

Generalmente, el corte de muesca se realiza en las porciones de costillar, lomo y sirloin de cordero, ternera y cerdo. Comenzando desde la superficie dividida de las vértebras torácicas del espinazo, se harán cortes a sierra entre vértebras hasta profundizar en un punto tal de la carne magra que las piezas derivadas del costillar, el lomo y el sirloin queden intactas y el usuario pueda cortar fácilmente las piezas en porciones con una cuchilla, antes o después de asarlas. Se pueden realizar cortes de muesca en las costillas de la espaldilla y el pecho de cordero cortando a través de las costillas en los músculos que las recubren, dejando dichos músculos intactos.

Músculo individual (MI)

Cuando aparece "MI" con el nombre de una pieza, significa que el rosbif o bistec se compone de un sólo músculo. Así se eliminará la variación en calidad, ya que los cortes MI rendirán rebanadas sumamente uniformes en comparación con los cortes de múltiples músculos. Al hacer porciones de cortes MI, se deben rebanar aproximadamente en ángulo recto al grano (a través de las fibras del músculo).

Orden de suavidad

La investigación científica ha demostrado que entre los principales músculos de mayor terneza o suavidad para la carne de res se encuentran:

Psoas mayor
Infraspinatus
Spinalis dorsi
Serratus ventralis
Teres mayor
Tensor de la fascia lata
Rectus femoris
Longissimus dorsi

La suavidad de los músculos en la canal de res se puede medir de varias formas y puede verse afectada por diversos factores. Para obtener información más completa y específica acerca de la suavidad de los músculos en la carne de res, visite www.beefresearch.org.

La finalidad de los siguientes requisitos es proporcionarle al comprador una variedad de opciones de manejo y embalaje de la carne que cumplan con las buenas prácticas de fabricación.

Los compradores pueden solicitar cualquier otro requisito específico que deseen. Es posible que se impongan algunos requisitos adicionales cuando se realice el pedido del producto de acuerdo con ciertos procedimientos de certificación. Las siguientes explicaciones pueden no ser incluyentes.

Estado de refrigeración

Cada una de las secciones en esta guía dedicadas a especies y productos proporcionan información acerca de la posibilidad de realizar los pedidos de las piezas en estado fresco, congelado o como productos ya procesados. También se describen las exigencias de temperatura correspondientes. Los compradores pueden solicitar, si lo desean, que los productos se almacenen o se envíen sujetos a exigencias específicas de temperatura.

Para la carne de aves, a partir del 17 de diciembre de 1997, el término "fresh" (fresco) se puede emplear únicamente en productos crudos de carne de ave cuya temperatura interna no haya estado nunca por debajo de los -3 °C o 26 °F. Los productos de carne de aves que se conserven a una temperatura de -18 °C o 0 °F o inferior se deben etiquetar como "frozen" (congelado) o, en caso de estar descongelados, "previously frozen" (previamente congelado). No existe designación de etiqueta ni terminología para la carne cruda de aves entre -18 °C y -3 °C o 0 °F y 26 °F.

Embalaje y empaque

Existen diferentes requisitos para el embalaje, en función del tipo y tamaño del corte y de las especificaciones del cliente. Las canales, los lados, cuartos y cortes primarios no necesitan envasarse ni colocarse en cajas a menos que el comprador así lo especifique. Los cortes subprimarios con hueso o deshuesados, curados, ahumados, cocidos, secos y variedades cárnicas (coproductos comestibles), se deben colocar en cajas revestidas con bolsas plásticas. Las piezas en cortes porcionados se deben empaquetar o embalar en capas en cajas pequeñas con espaciadores entre las capas. El embalaje puede consistir en una película de barrera tipo envasado al vacío con o sin una aplicación de atmósfera modificada, o con cualquier otro material de embalaje aprobado o lo que el comprador especifique.

Las piezas a granel congeladas, como los recortes, se pueden empaquetar en cajas recubiertas o impregnadas de cera sin forros. Las piezas de carne molida o troceada en cubos se deben embalar en bolsas o envoltorios plásticos y se pueden empaquetar en cajas. Las hamburguesas o tortitas de carne se pueden empaquetar en cajas recubiertas o impregnadas con cera con o sin bolsas plásticas, o en cajas sin recubrimiento forradas con bolsas plásticas. Las hamburguesas o tortitas de carne se deben separar unas de otras para evitar que se adhieran entre sí. Además, los compradores pueden especificar que se utilicen equipos detectores de metales en todos los tipos de productos molidos. Los productos en ristras frescas, ahumadas y cocidas se pueden empaquetar en cualquier tipo de caja pequeña apropiada, con o sin separadores entre las capas. Las capas de tocino se deben separar o empaquetar individualmente.

Todos los materiales de embalaje deberán cumplir con las reglamentaciones del Servicio de Inspección e Inocuidad Alimentaria o de la Agencia Canadiense de Inspección de Alimentos, y los paquetes se deben etiquetar de acuerdo con dichas reglamentaciones. Los requisitos de embalaje en México son controlados por COFEPRIS y se basan en reglamentos homologados con los de FSIS. Algunas cajas pequeñas se podrán colocar en empaques maestros. Las cajas maestras o de embarque deberán tener un tamaño y una resistencia a las roturas que sean acordes a su propósito. Todo el embalaje se debe realizar de una forma que proteja el producto. Los productos se pueden colocar en tarimas cuando corresponda.

Clasificación por grados
Descripciones de grado de calidad y rendimiento y marcas de identificación

En la sección introductoria de las secciones de cada especie en *la Guía* encontrará una referencia para la clasificación por grados. En Estados Unidos, los productos de carne de res, cordero, ternera, cerdo y aves se pueden clasificar por grados en cuanto a la calidad, aunque sólo se pueden clasificar por grado de rendimiento los de carne de res, cordero y cerdo. La carne de res y de cordero utilizan nombres para denotar la calidad y números para identificar el rendimiento. Los grados de calidad de la carne de ternera también se identifican por nombres. Los grados de calidad y rendimiento se combinan en una única designación numérica para la carne de cerdo. Los grados para las aves se identifican con letras. En E.U.A., los nombres de grados y los procedimientos para su utilización los supervisa el Departamento de Agricultura de Estados Unidos o USDA, el Servicio Mercadeo Agrícola o AMS, el Programa de Ganado y Granos o LSP, la División de Certificación y Clasificación de Carne o MGC (+1 202.720.1113) y los Programas de carne de aves de USDA y AMS (+1 202.720.4476), Washington, DC, www.ams.usda.gov. Si bien la utilización de los servicios de clasificación por grados de la carne es voluntaria, únicamente la División de Certificación y Clasificación de Carne o los Programas de carne de aves pueden aplicar las calificaciones oficiales de grado. Cuando se solicite, los usuarios pagarán este servicio por hora o en base a un contrato a largo plazo. Además, el usuario también debe cumplir con los procedimientos de etiquetado del Servicio de Inspección e Inocuidad Alimentaria (FSIS). La designación oficial de grados del Departamento de Agricultura de E.U.A. puede aparecer de alguna de las siguientes formas o combinación de ellas: (1) marcas en los envases, (2) en bolsas individuales, (3) impresiones legibles de marca comercial sobre la carne, o (4) sello del escudo del Departamento de Agricultura de E.U.A. que incorpora el grado de calidad o rendimiento. Para más información, escribir o llamar por teléfono a la División de Certificación y Clasificación de Carne o a los Programas de Carne de Aves. El personal de la División de Certificación y Clasificación de Carne y los Programas de Carne de Aves, a través del personal y sus oficinas regionales, es responsable por la implementación de las actividades cotidianas del servicio de clasificación por grados.

Se ofrece información acerca de los sistemas de clasificación por grados canadienses en las siguientes páginas. Para obtener información completa acerca de los sistemas de clasificación por grados canadienses, visite: http://laws.justice.gc.ca/en/C-0.4/SOR-92-541

En México se han emitido tres reglamentos voluntarios como pautas para la clasificación por grados de las canales de res (NMX-FF-078-SCFI-2002), cerdo (NMX-FF-081-SCFI-2003) y cordero (NMX-FF-106-SCFI-2006). Algunos estados del norte de México han desarrollado e implementado estándares de clasificación de carne de res para uso local. Sin embargo, la industria cárnica nacional no ha adoptado ninguno de ellos como estándar federal.

Clasificación de carne de res: http://portal.veracruz.gob.mx/pls/portal/docs/PAGE/COVECAINICIO/IMAGENES/ARCHIVOSPDF/TAB3885839/NMX-FF-078-SCFI-2002.PDF

Clasificación de cerdo: http://www.colpos.mx/bancodenormas/nmexicanas/NMX-FF-081-2003.PDF

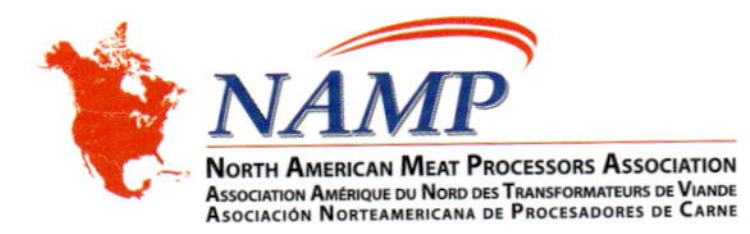

A continuación se incluye una explicación de la calidad correspondiente y los grados de rendimiento de cada especie.

Clasificación por grados de las canales de carne de res

Clasificación por grados en E.U.A.

Las canales de carne de res se pueden clasificar por grados de calidad únicamente, por grado de rendimiento únicamente, o combinando simultáneamente grados de calidad y rendimiento, o bien, se pueden dejar sin clasificar por grados según lo que establezcan los reglamentos y atendiendo las necesidades de los industriales y sus clientes. La utilización del sistema es completamente voluntaria y con pago de una tarifa por los servicios prestados.

Grados de calidad de E.U.A.

Los grados de calidad sirven para identificar las cualidades comestibles del producto. Son una guía para identificar la suavidad (terneza) y lo paladeable de la carne. En E.U.A., existen ocho grados de calidad para la carne de res. Los grados, en el orden de mayor a menor calidad, son los siguientes: Prime de E.U.A., Choice de E.U.A., Select de E.U.A., Standard de E.U.A., Commercial de E.U.A., Utility de E.U.A., Cutter de E.U.A. y Canner de E.U.A. La carne de res de novillos y vaquillas puede recibir todas las designaciones de grados mencionadas. Las vacas pueden recibir todos, menos el grado Prime. Los toretes se pueden clasificar únicamente para Prime, Choice, Select, Standard y Utility. Los toros no se pueden clasificar por calidad. Cada grado se identifica con su propio sello. Consulte los ejemplos en la página xx. La designación del grado en el cual califica una canal se determina mediante una evaluación de sus características sexuales, madurez, calidad del músculo magro y grado de marmoleado presente. Consulte los ejemplos y explicaciones de cortes profundos de marmoleado en la página 3. El objetivo del uso de estos criterios es proporcionar a los compradores un sistema que pueda medir y predecir la calidad mediante métodos que maximicen la coherencia y la confiabilidad. Cuando se solicite, el servicio de clasificación por grados puede, utilizando los criterios mencionados anteriormente, establecer programas de especificaciones de grados específicos para los compradores y proveedores. Actualmente, existe una serie de estos programas de especificaciones de compra.

Grados de rendimiento de E.U.A.

Los grados de rendimiento 1, 2, 3, 4 y 5 corresponden a las canales de carne de res. El grado de rendimiento (YG, por su sigla en inglés) 1 significa que la res tendrá la mayor proporción de carne magra utilizable o producirá el rendimiento más alto de cortes de sus canales, mientras que el grado de rendimiento 5 producirá lo mínimo. En otras palabras, el grado de rendimiento 1 representa a las canales más magras, mientras que el grado de rendimiento 5 representa a las canales con más grasa. La evaluación se realiza con una ecuación que incluye la medida del ribeye, la presencia de grasa alrededor del corazón y en la cavidad pélvica si corresponde, según los requisitos de la especie, y el grosor de la cubierta de grasa. En términos generales, cuanto mayor sea el grado de calidad, mayor será el valor numérico del rendimiento. Por consiguiente, la mayoría de los animales de calidad de restaurante Prime y Choice corresponderán al grado de rendimiento 3 y ocasionalmente de un número superior. En ganado de carne, la adopción de técnicas de inseminación cruzada, dieta mejorada y cambios genéticos han permitido avanzar mucho hacia la eliminación del exceso de grasa, de modo que el número de reses que clasifica en los grados de rendimiento 1 y 2 está aumentando mientras que la de los grados de rendimiento 4 y 5 está disminuyendo. En la mayoría de los casos, debido al recorte de grasa posterior que realizan los proveedores, el grado de rendimiento ya no es necesario indicarlo y no aparecerá en el producto.

Las fotografías de carne de res que aparecen en esta guía se tomaron utilizando canales de madurez "A" identificadas como la media del grado Choice de E.U.A. Los productos grado Choice o Prime son aquellos que generalmente se sirven en hoteles, clubes y restaurantes. Los establecimientos de la industria de servicios de alimentación normalmente indican que sus compras deben ser de una calidad específica.

Clasificación y designación de grados para las canales de res de E.U.A.

Grados de calidad	Clasificación			
	Novillos/Vaquillas	Vacas	Toretes	Toros
Prime de E.U.A.	•		•	
Choice de E.U.A.	•	•	•	
Select de E.U.A.	•	•	•	
Standard de E.U.A.	•	•	•	
Commercial de E.U.A.	•	•		
Utility de E.U.A.	•	•	•	
Cutter de E.U.A.	•	•		
Canner de E.U.A.	•	•		

Clasificación por grados de las canales de carne de res en Canadá

La Agencia Canadiense de Clasificación de Carne de Res (CBGA, por sus siglas en inglés) está acreditada por la Agencia Canadiense de Inspección de Alimentos (CFIA, por sus siglas en inglés) para evaluar los grados de la canal de res de acuerdo con los estándares nacionales de Canadá. Las canales se pueden clasificar por ambos grados, de calidad y de rendimiento. Los grados de calidad para el ganado joven incluyen: Prime de Canadá, AAA de Canadá, AA de Canadá y A de Canadá.

Los estándares canadienses de marmoleado reflejan los mismos estándares de marmoleado de E.U.A., que son marca registrada y se utilizan para determinar los grados de calidad (consulte la página 3 para obtener más información). Además del marmoleado, los grados de calidad en Canadá se basan en los siguientes factores que se deben tener en cuenta para los cuatro grados más altos de Canadá:

- Madurez: únicamente canales que califiquen como jóvenes
- Color de la carne: únicamente carne de res que tenga un color rojo brillante
- Color de la grasa: únicamente canales sin grasa amarilla
- Textura de la carne: únicamente textura firme del músculo
- Musculatura: únicamente con buena o mejor musculatura

Además de los grados para el ganado joven, Canadá también tiene grados de calidad para reses adultas. A los toros se les asigna el grado E y las vacas se clasifican en uno de los cuatro grados D.

Grado de rendimiento en Canadá

En Canadá, se utilizan tres medidas para determinar el rendimiento:

a. Largo del rib-eye
b. Ancho del rib-eye
c. Profundidad de grasa del rib-eye

Estos valores se insertan después en una ecuación de predicción del rendimiento en carne magra. Los grados de rendimiento 1, 2 o 3 se asignan de acuerdo con los porcentajes calculados de rendimiento en carne magra.

Grado de rendimiento en México

En México, se han emitido reglamentaciones voluntarias como lineamientos para la clasificación de canales de res (ver página xx).

Clasificación por grados de las canales ovinas (cordero y carnero)

Clasificación por grados de las canales ovinas (cordero y carnero) en E.U.A.

Las canales ovinas, si se ofrecen para la clasificación por grados, deberán recibir simultáneamente un grado de calidad y un grado de rendimiento. Las reglamentaciones exigen que se elimine la grasa de riñonada antes de la clasificación. Como en el caso de la canal de carne de res, la clasificación por grados de la canal de cordero, carnero añojo y carnero es un servicio voluntario, disponible únicamente en la División de Certificación y Clasificación de Carnes con una tarifa de pago por servicios prestados.

Grado de rendimiento	
La de mayor magrez	Grado de rendimiento
	1
	2
	3
	4
La más grasosa	5

Grados de calidad de E.U.A.

Como sucede en las otras especies, los grados de calidad sirven para identificar las cualidades comestibles del producto. Son una guía para identificar la suavidad (terneza) y lo paladeable de la carne. Existen cuatro grados de calidad para la carne de cordero y carnero añojo. Los grados, en orden de mayor a menor calidad, son los siguientes: Prime de E.U.A., Choice de E.U.A., Good de E.U.A. y Utility de E.U.A. La carne de carnero únicamente se puede clasificar por los grados Choice de E.U.A., Good de E.U.A., Utility de E.U.A. o Cull de E.U.A. La distinción entre cordero, carnero añojo y carnero se basa principalmente en la ausencia o presencia de una articulación fácil de quebrar ("coyuntura de quiebre") o de una canilla osificada que ya no se puede quebrar (coyuntura de "carrete") en el jarrete de la pata delantera. El cordero, la clase más joven designada para la canal ovina, no presentará una coyuntura de carrete. Aunque no forma parte de los estándares de clasificación oficial por grados de E.U.A., el término "Spring Lamb" (cordero de primavera) se ha utilizado en la industria estadounidense para designar las canales de cordero joven. Para determinar el grado de calidad, se considera la madurez del animal en base a su desarrollo muscular y óseo junto con el grado de veteado de grasa en el flanco (faldas).

Grados de rendimiento de E.U.A.

Los grados de rendimiento (YG, por sus siglas en inglés) de las canales de cordero, carnero añojo y carnero se calculan en base a la cubierta de grasa externa de la canal. Los grados de rendimiento se identifican con los números 1, 2, 3, 4 y 5, el grado de rendimiento 1 es el que tiene menos grasa externa y el grado de rendimiento 5 es el que tiene más grasa externa. En términos generales, únicamente se ofrecen para la clasificación por grados los corderos de grado de calidad Prime y Choice. Como la clasificación por grados de calidad y de rendimiento están acopladas, todas las canales clasificadas lucirán tanto sus clasificaciones por grado de calidad como de rendimiento. Por consiguiente, existen más grados de rendimiento 2 en la categoría Choice.

Clasificación por grados de las canales ovinas en Canadá

En Canadá, existen cinco grados para las canales ovinas: AAA de Canadá, C1 de Canadá, C2 de Canadá, D1 de Canadá y D4 de Canadá. Los grados de calidad se basan en la madurez, la calificación del músculo, el color y veteado de grasa del músculo del flanco (falda) y la cubierta de grasa.

Se asigna una clase de rendimiento a las canales que obtienen un grado AAA de Canadá tomando una medida de la grasa. Las clases van de Canadá 1 a Canadá 4 y la clase Canadá 1 es la que tiene menos grasa.

Las canales de cordero tienen menos de dos incisivos permanentes, dos coyunturas de quiebre (o en el caso de una coyuntura de quiebre y una coyuntura de carrete, la coyuntura de quiebre debe tener cuatro surcos intactos y bien definidos con al menos una superficie ligeramente roja y

Grados de calidad	Clasificación		
	Cordero	Carnero añojo	Carnero
Prime de E.U.A.	•	•	
Choice de E.U.A.	•	•	•
Good de E.U.A.	•	•	•
Utility de E.U.A.	•	•	•
Cull de E.U.A.			•

Clasificación y designación de grados para las canales ovinas de E.U.A.

húmeda) y costillas que no pasan de ser ligeramente anchas. Las canales de cordero pueden clasificarse con grado AAA, C1 o C2 de Canadá.

Las canales de carnero tienen dos o más incisivos permanentes, dos coyunturas de quiebre (o en el caso de una coyuntura de quiebre y una coyuntura de carrete, la coyuntura de quiebre debe tener una superficie seca y blanca) y costillas que son anchas, planas y blancas. Las canales de carnero se pueden clasificar únicamente con grado D1 o D4 de Canadá.

Clasificación por grados de las canales ovinas en México

En México, se han emitido reglamentaciones voluntarias como lineamientos para la clasificación de canales ovinas (ver página xx).

Clasificación por grados de las canales de ternera y becerro

Clasificación por grados de las canales de ternera y becerro en E.U.A.

Clasificación y designación de grados para las canales de ternera y becerro de E.U.A.	Clasificación
Grados de calidad	Ternera y Becerro
Prime de E.U.A.	•
Choice de E.U.A.	•
Good de E.U.A.	•
Standard de E.U.A.	•
Utility de E.U.A.	•

Las canales de ternera y becerro se pueden clasificar únicamente en cuanto a la calidad. No corresponden los grados de rendimiento. Se clasifica un número relativamente pequeño de canales de ternera y becerro. Como en el caso de la carne de res y de cordero, la utilización del sistema es completamente voluntaria y con una tarifa de pago por servicios prestados.

Grados de calidad de E.U.A.

Como en el caso de las otras especies, los grados de calidad sirven para identificar las cualidades comestibles del producto. Son una guía para identificar la suavidad (terneza) y lo paladeable de la carne. Existen cinco grados de rendimiento para la carne de ternera y becerro. Los grados, en el orden de mayor a menor calidad, son los siguientes: Prime de E.U.A., Choice de E.U.A., Good de E.U.A., Standard de E.U.A. y Utility de E.U.A. La mayoría de las pocas canales que llegan a clasificarse son de grado Choice y algunas son Prime. El motivo por el que se clasifican pocas canales de ternera y becerro se debe al hecho de que el producto de mayor calidad se identifica y vende como un producto logrado con técnicas de manejo especiales.

Grados de rendimiento de E.U.A.

Debido a que las canales de ternera y becerro tienen una cubierta de grasa relativamente pequeña, no se ha justificado la necesidad de utilizar los grados de rendimiento.

Clasificación por grados de las canales de ternera y becerro en Canadá

Para que se clasifiquen como ternera en Canadá, las canales deben pesar entre 80 kg (176 lbs.) y 180 kg (397 lbs.). Existen 10 grados de canales de ternera: A1, A2, A3, A4, B1, B2, B3, B4, C1 y C2 de Canadá. Los grados se asignan en base a la condición muscular, el color del músculo, el color y la cubierta de la grasa y la madurez de la canal.

Clasificación por grados de las canales de ternera y becerro en México

No existe un sistema para clasificar por grados a las canales de ternera en México.

Clasificación por grados de la canal porcina

Clasificación por grados de la canal porcina en E.U.A.

La clasificación por grados de la carne de cerdo no es un factor relevante para determinar la calidad a nivel de la industria de servicios de alimentación. El grado de calidad se combina con el de rendimiento en el sistema de clasificación por grados de la carne de cerdo, y esto se expresa principalmente en términos numéricos. En E.U.A. los identificadores son Nº 1 de E.U.A., Nº 2 de E.U.A., Nº 3 de E.U.A., Nº 4 de E.U.A. y Utility de E.U.A. para cerdos jóvenes castrados o hembras primerizas. La carne de cerdas hembras se clasifica con Nº 1, 2, 3 de E.U.A., Medium de E.U.A. y Cull de E.U.A. La carne de padrotes y verracos no se clasifica por grados. Consulte la sección de carne de cerdo de esta guía, página 151, para obtener más información acerca de los grados.

Clasificación por grados de la carne de cerdo en Canadá

No existe un sistema federal para clasificar por grados a los cerdos en Canadá.

Clasificación por grados de la carne de cerdo en México

En México, se han emitido reglamentaciones voluntarias como lineamientos para la clasificación de canales de cerdo (ver página xx).

Carne de aves

En E.U.A., se utiliza una serie de factores para determinar la designación del grado de calidad de las canales, piezas o productos de aves listos para cocinar.

Específicamente para las canales y piezas de aves listas para cocinar, los factores de calidad que se consideran en la evaluación del grado son:

1. Conformación
2. Descarnado
3. Cubierta de grasa
4. Desplumado
5. Carne expuesta
6. Decoloraciones
7. Huesos dislocados o quebrados
8. Partes faltantes
9. Defectos de congelación

Para determinar el grado de calidad de otros productos avícolas, se consideran los siguientes factores:

1. Presencia de huesos, tendones y cartílagos
2. Hematomas y coágulos de sangre
3. Otros factores específicos del producto

Clasificación por grados de la carne de aves en Canadá

Existen tres grados de canales de aves en Canadá: A de Canadá, Utility de Canadá y C de Canadá. Los factores que determinan el grado de calidad incluyen composición de la canal, cubierta de grasa, condición de la piel, condición ósea, peso y madurez.

Clasificación por grados de la carne de aves en México

En México, se han emitido reglamentaciones voluntarias como lineamientos para la clasificación de carne de aves.

cómo utilizar su Guía para compradores de carne

Las piezas que se ilustran y describen en la *Guía para Compradores de Carne* han sido seleccionadas de las Especificaciones Institucionales de Compra de Carne (IMPS, por sus siglas en inglés) de E.U.A. Las IMPS son una serie de especificaciones de productos cárnicos que mantienen el Departamento de Agricultura de E.U.A. y el Servicio de Comercialización Agrícola. Se desarrollan como especificaciones voluntarias por consenso. Los compradores de grandes volúmenes como los organismos federales, estatales y locales, las escuelas, los restaurantes, los hoteles y otros usuarios del servicio de alimentos hacen referencia a las IMPS para obtener productos cárnicos. Los productos de esta guía representan las piezas más utilizadas por los establecimientos de la industria de servicios alimenticios y los compradores institucionales. Las descripciones emplean una terminología que identificará al producto del mejor modo con términos que garantizarán a los compradores que recibirán una mercadería que cumple con sus expectativas. Los compradores deberán poder identificar los requisitos de su compra con el número de pieza y el nombre del producto que se indican en *la Guía*. No obstante, los compradores pueden querer otros productos o productos con especificaciones diferentes. Sus proveedores de NAMP estarán encantados de ayudarlo para cumplir con sus requisitos.

Una serie de productos incluidos en *la Guía para compradores de carne* admiten opciones especificadas por el comprador (PSO, por su sigla en inglés). Algunas descripciones de piezas indican requisitos de nivel de recorte de grasa, u ofrecen una serie de opciones, o incluyen otros requisitos específicos. Los requisitos materiales para la carne de res, cordero, ternera, cerdo y aves y los requisitos de productos generales de esta sección también describen una serie de condiciones generales que inciden en las compras. Además, cada una de las secciones introductorias de especies y productos que aparecen posteriormente en *la Guía* también contienen algunas pautas generales acerca de los productos. Los compradores deben aprovechar la oportunidad de familiarizarse con todas las condiciones y opciones de productos que pueden afectar las piezas que desean comprar.

Código Universal de Productos (UPC, por sus siglas en inglés)

Los códigos universales de productos o números UPC se utilizan en los comercios de venta al detalle para identificar los productos mediante equipos electrónicos, a fin de controlar el inventario y el marcado de precios. Para obtener más información acerca de los códigos UPC, visite www.meattrack.com.

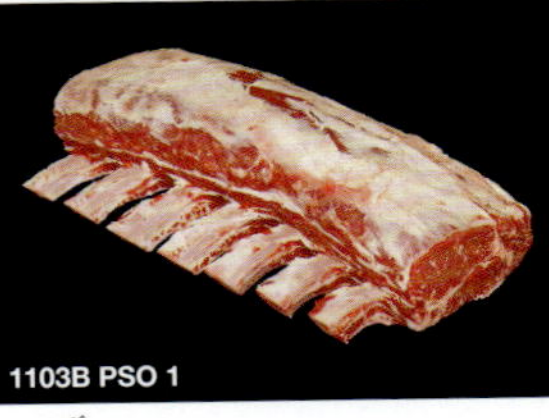

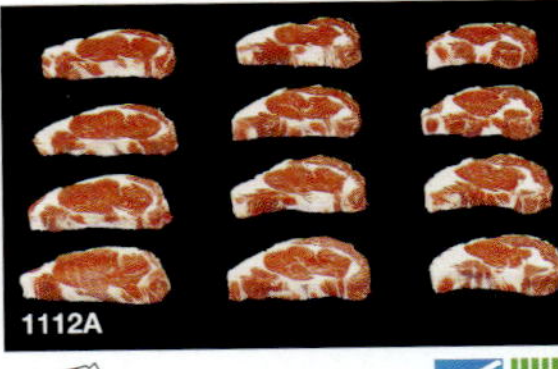

portion cuts / cortes porcionados

1103B Beef Rib, Rib Steak, Bone In, Frenched

This item is prepared as described in Item No. 1103 except that each steak must be cut between the rib bones. The rib bone shall be completely trimmed of the intercostal meat, lean, and fat so that the bone is exposed from the ventral edge of the *longissimus dorsi* to the end of the rib bone. This item is also referred to as a "Cowboy Steak."

Alternative Purchaser Specified Options (PSO):

PSO: 1 – Purchaser may request that the rib be prepared as a roast to the same specifications as Item No. 1103B but instead of being cut into steaks, it be left intact.

2 – Purchaser may request that the rib be prepared as a roast as in PSO 1 and then partially cut into steaks and the balance left as a roast.

3 – Purchaser may request that the rib steaks in Item No. 1103B or PSO 2 be split into two steaks by a saw cut through the center of the rib bone.

1103B Chuletón (Espaldar), Bistec del Chuletón, Con Hueso, Estilo Francés

Esta pieza se prepara según descripción de la pieza número 1103, salvo que cada bistec debe ser cortado entre los huesos de las costillas. El hueso de la costilla deberá ser recortado completamente de carne intercostal, carne magra y grasa, de forma que el hueso quede expuesto desde el borde ventral del *longissimus dorsi* hasta el extremo de la costilla. Esta pieza es llamada a veces "Bistec del Cowboy".

Opciones alternativas especificadas por el comprador:

PSO: 1 – El comprador puede solicitar que el chuletón, en vez de hacerlo bistecs, se prepare como un trozo rosbif, según las mismas especificaciones de la pieza número 1103B, pero que en vez de ser cortado en bistecs, quede intacto.

2 – El comprador puede solicitar que el chuletón se prepare como un trozo rosbif, como figura en la opción 1 especificada por el comprador, y luego se corte parcialmente en bistecs, dejando lo remanente como rosbif.

3 – El comprador puede solicitar que los bistecs de chuletón detallados en la pieza número 1103B o en la opción 2 especificada por el comprador, se separen en dos bistecs mediante un corte de sierra a través del centro del hueso de las costillas.

1103B

1103B PSO 1

1112A Beef Rib, Ribeye Steak, Lip-On, Boneless

Boneless ribeye steaks, lip-on shall be prepared from a rib item meeting the end requirements of Item No. 112A. The lip shall be cut on the short rib side with a straight cut that is ventral to, but no more than 2.0 inches (5.0 cm) from, the *longissimus dorsi*, leaving the lip firmly attached.

🍁 In Canada, steaks containing muscles other than the *longissimus dorsi* and *spinalis dorsi* must be called "Boneless Rib Steaks".

1112A Chuletón (Espaldar), Bistec de Ribeye, Con Cordón, Deshuesado

Los bistecs de ribeye deshuesado, por su cola, llamada "cordón" o "gota", se conocen también como "ribeye gota", y deberán prepararse a partir de una pieza de chuletón que reúna los requisitos finales de la pieza número 112A. Se deberá cortar el cordón del lado del lomo corto con un corte recto ventral al *longissimus dorsi*, sin que supere los 5.0 cm (2.0 pulgadas) dejando el cordón firmemente unido.

🍁 En Canadá, los bistecs que contienen músculos que no sean el *longissimus dorsi* y el *spinalis dorsi* deben llamarse "Bistecs del Chuletón Deshuesados" (en inglés, "Boneless Rib Steaks").

1112A

NAMP
North American Meat Processors Association
Association Américaine du Nord des Transformateurs de Viande
Asociación Norteamericana de Procesadores de Carne

The Meat Buyer's Guide • 71

Se puede obtener información adicional acerca de las **Especificaciones Institucionales de Compra de Carne o IMPS, por sus siglas en inglés, del:**

Departamento de Agricultura de Estados Unidos
Servicio de Mercadeo Agrícola

Programa de Ganado y Granos
División de Estandarización
1400 Independence Ave. SW, STOP 0254
Washington, DC 20250
202.720.4486

Programas Avícolas
División de Estandarización
1400 Independence Ave. SW, STOP 0259
Washington, DC 20250
202.720.3506

www.ams.usda.gov

Cualquier miembro de la Asociación Norteamericana de Procesadores de Carne (NAMP) tendrá el gusto de ayudarle en la selección de productos, y también estará encantado de ayudarle a determinar la limpieza y la calidad que más se ajusten a las necesidades de su empresa. Los miembros de NAMP están ubicados en muchas comunidades de Estados Unidos, Canadá, México y Australia.

También se puede obtener una lista de los miembros de NAMP llamando a la oficina de NAMP al 001-703.758.1900.

Niveles de recorte de grasa

El siguiente gráfico representa las especificaciones más comunes de niveles para recorte de grasa actualmente utilizadas en la industria. Los compradores tienen la opción de especificar el nivel de recorte de grasa que mejor se ajuste a sus necesidades, a menos que la descripción de la pieza requiera específicamente un nivel de recorte de grasa. Para cumplir con las actuales recomendaciones de salud y nutrición del Departamento de Agricultura de Estados Unidos, NAMP ha optado por ilustrar en las fotografías las dimensiones de recorte de grasa de 6 mm (0.25 pulgadas) o 3 mm (0.125 pulgadas). El comprador y el vendedor deberán acordar el grosor del recorte de grasa real en cualquier producto, a menos que se establezca otra limitación.

Nomenclatura de productos cárnicos en Canadá

En Canadá, la Ley de Inspección de Carnes y sus reglamentos, la Ley de Alimentos y Medicamentos y sus reglamentos así como la Ley de Embalaje y Etiquetado para el Consumidor y sus reglamentos, que administra e impone la Agencia Canadiense de Inspección de Alimentos, exigen que los cortes de carne, órganos y otras piezas de canal se etiqueten con nombres comunes en todos los niveles del comercio. El Manual de Cortes de Carne de la Agencia Canadiense de Inspección de Alimentos proporciona los nombres comunes que se deben utilizar.

Las variaciones significativas entre los nombres comunes que prescribe el Manual de Cortes de Carne de la Agencia Canadiense de Inspección de Alimentos y la nomenclatura utilizada en esta guía se indican junto a las piezas individuales en *la Guía*. Busque el símbolo 🍁 que indica dicha variación.

Se recomienda a los procesadores, compradores de carne y operadores restaurantes que consulten el Manual de Cortes de Carne de la Agencia Canadiense de Inspección de Alimentos para asegurarse de que los nombres comunes que se utilizan en las etiquetas de los productos y los menús de los restaurantes cumplan con los requisitos de la Agencia Canadiense de Inspección de Alimentos.

Vínculos

Manual de Cortes de Carne de la Agencia Canadiense de Inspección de Alimentos:
http://www.inspection.gc.ca/english/fssa/labeti/mcmancv/mcmancve.shtml

Servicio de Información de Etiquetado de Alimentos de la Agencia Canadiense de Inspección de Alimentos:
http://www.inspection.gc.ca/english/fssa/labeti/guide/ch1e.shtml#offbur

Leyes y reglamentaciones administradas e impuestas por la Agencia Canadiense de Inspección de Alimentos:
http://www.inspection.gc.ca/english/reg/rege.shtml

Nomenclatura de productos cárnicos en México

Excepto por las pautas de fabricación de cerdo (NMX-FF-081-SCFI-2003), no existe una nomenclatura oficial para los productos cárnicos en México.

Los lineamientos sobre carne de cerdo se pueden consultar en http://www.colpos.mx/bancodenormas/nmexicanas/NMX-FF-081-2003.PDF

Íconos

Para ayudarle a utilizar *la Guía para compradores de carne*,
algunas piezas y descripciones en *la Guía* aparecen acompañadas
de iconos. Los símbolos se utilizan como ayuda en la identificación
de requisitos educativos, de medidas, para porcionar y las
exigencias.

El birrete indica aquellos cortes que ya no se utilizan comúnmente
y es posible que no estén disponibles en el mercado. Se han incluido en *la Guía* como referencia educativa.

Educativo

Una regla indica los cortes que tienen una medida específica, como
el largo o el grosor.

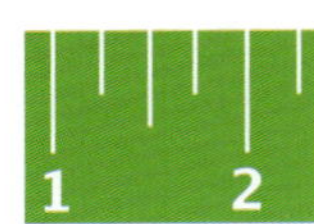

Medición

Un cuchillo representa los cortes porcionados o aquellos cortes
para los que se indica recorte de grasa y limpieza.

Corte y recorte de grasa, y limpieza

Una hoja de arce indica una variación entre el Manual de Cortes
de Carne de la Agencia Canadiense de Inspección de Alimentos y
el nombre o descripción de pieza de NAMP/IMPS.

Canadiense

Para obtener información acerca de los íconos de carne de aves, consulte la
página 240.

Carne de res y cerdo de E.U.A.: calidad de la granja al tenedor

La industria de carnes rojas de Estados Unidos es líder mundial en la oferta de productos seguros, de alta calidad y nutritivos. La demanda de carne roja aumenta junto con las poblaciones y economías del mundo, y Estados Unidos está ayudando a satisfacer esta demanda.

La industria de carnes rojas de E.U.A. se compromete con sus clientes de todo el mundo para garantizar la inocuidad de los productos de carne roja que produce. Una interacción única entre la industria, la comunidad académica y el gobierno proporciona a Estados Unidos una estructura para identificar e implementar tecnologías e intervenciones a fin de avanzar continuamente en la seguridad de los productos de carne roja. La misión del Departamento de Agricultura de E.U.A. (USDA) es proteger y promover los alimentos, la agricultura y los recursos naturales.

El Servicio de Inspección e Inocuidad Alimentaria (FSIS) del Departamento de Agricultura de E.U.A. es responsable de garantizar que la oferta comercial de carne del país sea inocua, salubre y esté correctamente etiquetada y envasada. Su sistema federal de inspección y supervisión del bienestar animal y la producción de carne basado en HACCP (Análisis de riesgos y puntos críticos de control, por sus siglas en inglés) es respetado en todo el mundo.

El Servicio de Inspección Sanitaria de Animales y Plantas (APHIS, por sus siglas en inglés) protege y promueve la salud agrícola en E.U.A., al regular los organismos diseñados genéticamente, administrar la Ley de bienestar animal (Animal Welfare Act) y desarrollar actividades de manejo de daños a la vida silvestre.

El Servicio de Mercadeo Agrícola (AMS, por sus siglas en inglés) es responsable de desarrollar las normas de grado de calidad reconocidas en todo el mundo.

Estados Unidos está comprometido con los principios científicos y el ideal de que una sólida evaluación, manejo y comunicación de riesgos, seguidos por la evaluación y comprobación de los procedimientos de mitigación, resultan en la más sólida infraestructura de un sistema de inocuidad alimentaria. Los recursos naturales que se encuentran en Estados Unidos permiten que sea un productor extremadamente competitivo de productos de carne roja. Tanto los productores como la industria de E.U.A. están comprometidos con la sustentabilidad y un manejo responsable del medio ambiente. Los criadores de ganado de E.U.A. no hacen un pastoreo excesivo de la tierra y protegen las vías fluviales del país. La industria de carne de cerdo de E.U.A. trata las aguas residuales y las recicla para la agricultura a fin de contribuir con los métodos de cultivo modernos como la labranza mínima.

El compromiso con la calidad es el sello distintivo de la industria de la carne roja de Estados Unidos. Comienza con sistemas de producción que utilizan tecnologías y avances científicos para cría, genética y nutrición. Mediante el uso de tecnologías para la evaluación de productos y técnicas de mejora del gusto, la industria de la carne roja de E.U.A. se concentra en la creación, utilizando granos y soya nacionales, de un suministro para todo el año de productos reconocidos en todo el mundo por una alta calidad en forma constante, asegurando que los consumidores disfruten de una buena experiencia alimentaria una y otra vez.

www.USMEF.org

Bobby Hatoff
Presidente
Allen Brothers, Inc.

Jeff Saval
Vicepresidente
Deli Brands of America

Mike Satzow
Tesorero
North Country Smokehouse

Tony Gahn, Jr.
Tesorero adjunto
Gahn Meat Co., Inc.

Gary Malenke
Presidente del Directorio
Sioux-Preme Pork Products

Philip Kimball, CAE
Director Ejecutivo
NAMP

Consejo de Directores:
Chris Appert
Andy Becker
Guenter Becker
Michael Bernstein
John Bloch
Peter Bozzo
Doug Bush
David Carriere
John Chlopek
Darren Dies
Steve Falcigno
John Fell
Lee Friedheim
Mike Gangel
Kirk Halpern
Mick Hamilton
Beau Heeps
Ron Hemauer
Deanna Hofing
Joseph F. Kinnealey
Jose Ramon Lozano
Joe Maas
Don Macgregor
Chris Mason
Mark Mitchell
Ray Parsons
Noel Reyes
Scott Rich
Kent Seelig
Ross Shuket
Thomas M. Stachecki
Andrew Sussman
Kevin Tulley
John Vatri
Tim Vlcek

Febrero de 2011

Estimado usuario de la *La Guía para Compradores de Carne®*:

Felicitaciones por usar *La Guía para Compradores de Carne®* de NAMP, la referencia obligatoria y el recurso normativo para la industria de la carne roja y de aves. La guía, publicada por primera vez en 1961, representa la 7ª edición del libro y es el resultado directo del gran esfuerzo y dedicación de cientos de profesionales del sector de la carne en la industria, el gobierno y el ámbito académico.

Como puede ver, *La Guía para Compradores de Carne®* se divide en secciones, cada una de las cuales representa uno de los grandes grupos de proteínas: carne de res, cerdo, ternera, cordero y aves, y el contenido está diseñado para ayudarle con las especificaciones de fabricación, compra y venta. El material de referencia también proporciona información importante diseñada para ayudarle en su negocio o profesión.

La Asociación Norteamericana de Procesadores de Carne (NAMP), autora y editora de *La Guía para Compradores de Carne®*, representa a procesadores y proveedores de carne roja y aves de toda Norteamérica. Ofrecemos servicios y programas educativos para la mejora de nuestros miembros y la industria en general, y nuestros miembros están comprometidos con las más altas normas de profesionalismo. Estamos orgullosos de trabajar junto con otros en nuestra industria de la alimentación, compartiendo la meta de ayudar a proporcionar los productos alimenticios más seguros y saludables para nuestros clientes.

Confiamos en que *La Guía para Compradores de Carne®* le resultará una herramienta diaria que le ayudará en su negocio, y lo invitamos a decirnos cómo podemos hacer que *La Guía para Compradores de Carne®* sea aún más útil.

Atentamente,

Philip H. Kimball

Philip H. Kimball, CAE
Director Ejecutivo
Asociación Norteamericana de Procesadores de Carne

Oficina central de Norteamérica
Washington, DC
1910 Association Drive, Reston, Virginia 20191 E.U.A.

Oficina en Canadá
*203-2525 St. Laurent Blvd.
Ottawa, Ontario K1H 8P5, CANADÁ*

*www.namp.com info@namp.com
+1 703.758.1900 (principal)
+1 703.758.8001 (fax)
+1 800.368.3043 (servicios para miembros)*

*rdevalk@namp.com
+1 613.739.8500 (principal)
+1 613.733.9501 (fax)*

Nomenclature of the most common beef and pork cuts in selected Central American and Caribbean countries
Nomenclatura de cortes de carne de res y de cerdo en países seleccionados de Centroamérica y el Caribe

Beef / Carne de res

USA / E.U.A.	COSTA RICA	EL SALVADOR	GUATEMALA	HONDURAS	NICARAGUA	PANAMÁ	REP. DOMINICANA
Chuck Roll	Lomo de Aguja-Quititeña	Solomo-Posta de Gallina	Marranito-Tasbal	Quititeña	Posta de Gallina	Costillón	Costillón
Chuck Tender	Cacho de Paleta	Cachito	Cachito	Cachito	Paleta Pequeña	Lomo de Paleta	Lomo de Paleta
Shoulder Clod	Corazón de Paleta	Posta de Paleta	Posta Paleta	Paleta-Chuleta 7	Posta de Paleta	Lomo Chato- Pulpa Blanca	Paleta
Short plate	Costilla	Costilla Alta	Costilla	Costilla	Costilla	Costilla	Costilla
Brisket	Pecho	Pecho	Pecho	Pecho	Pecho	Pecho	Pecho
Fore Shank	Ratón	Gato	Camote	Gato	Caracú-Ratón	Jarrete	Jarrete
Flank*	Cecina-Alipego	Aleta	Cecina	Falda	Trasera de Cecina	Falda	Falda
Ribeye Roll	Lomo Entero-Delmónico	Lomo Rollizo	Lomo Grande	Lomo Grande	Lomo Grande	Lomo de Costillón	Lomo de Costillón
Loin	Lomo Ancho	Lomo Pacho	Viuda	Lomo Chato	Trasera de Lomo	Lomo de Cinta	Lomo de Cinta
Top Sirloin	Vuelta de Lomo, Posta de cuarto	Angelina	Rochoy	Cabeza de Lomo	Cabeza de Lomo	Bola de Rincón	Rincón
Tri-tip	Gallinilla-Cacho de Vuelta de Lomo	Punta-Manita-Posta de Cinta	Manita de Rochoy			Punta de Rincón	Punta de Rincón
Tenderloin	Lomito	Filete de Lomito-de Aguja	Lomito	Filete	Filete	Filete	Filete
Rump (Top Sirloin cap)**	Punta de Solomo	Puyaso	Puyaso	Punta de Pierna-Puyaso	Puyaso	Punta de Palomilla	Punta de Palomilla
Outside Round	Solomo	Posta Pacha	Caña	Tajo Largo	Salón Blanco	Palomilla	Pulpa Blanca-Palomilla
Inside Round	Posta de Cuarto	Posta Negra	Pieza	Tajo Negro	Posta de Pierna	Pulpa Negra	Pulpa Negra
Eye of Round	Mano de Piedra	Salón	Bolovique	Mano de Piedra	Mano de Piedra	Lomo Mulato/ Redondo	Lomo Mulato-Redondo
Knuckle	Bolita	Choquezuela	Badilla	Cusuco	Posta de Corona	Babilla	Babilla

* Refered to the cut composed by the abdominal muscles (mainly the transversus and obliccus abdominis)
** In most Latin American Countries NAMP 171 G (rump) and NAMP 184D (Top Sirloin Cap) are referred as the same cut.
* Con referencia al corte compuesto por los músculos abdominales (principalmente los músculos transversus y obliccus abdominis)
** En la mayoría de los países de América Latina los cortes NAMP 171 G (Tajo Anterior de Pulpa Blanca) y NAMP 184D (Tapa del Aguayón) son considerados como el mismo corte.

Pork / Carne de cerdo

USA / E.U.A.	COSTA RICA	EL SALVADOR	GUATEMALA	HONDURAS	NICARAGUA	PANAMÁ	REP. DOMINICANA
Jowl	Papada	Quijada	Buche-Cachete	Cachete	Cachete	Papada	Papada
Picnic Shoulder	Paleta	Posta de Brazuelo	Brazuelo	Tajo de Paleta	Paleta	Picnic	Paleta
Boston Butt	Cabeza de Lomo	Posta de Nuca	Nuca	Tajo de Paleta	Cabeza de Lomo	Cogote	Cuello
Loin	Chuleta de Riñonada	Lomo	Chuletero-Lomo de Cinta	Lomo	Chuleta	Chuleta	Lomo
Back Fat	Tocino-Lonja	Grasa de Espalda	Lonja-Grasa de Espalda	Lonja-Grasa Dorsal	Cuero con Grasa (de espalda)	Grasa de Espalda	Grasa de Lomo
Belly	Tocineta	Tocineta	Tocineta-Panza	Tocineta	Tocino	Tocino	Tocineta
Spare Ribs	Costilla de Segunda	Costilla de Costillón	Costilla	Costillas	Costillas	Costilla Americana	Costillar
Leg (Ham)	Pierna	Posta de Pierna	Pierna	Pierna	Posta de Pierna	Pierna	Pierna

Membership Information
Información sobre la membresía

Want your personal network to include the real decision-makers at the most successful meat & poultry processors and suppliers in North America?

THEN JOIN NAMP!

Founded in 1942, the North American Meat Processors Association (NAMP) is an international member-driven association of **progressive meat processors, distributors, center-of-the-plate specialists,** and suppliers selling primarily to the foodservice industry. NAMP provides exceptional value through high-caliber support programs and governmental representation to help ensure our members' success in the industry.

The Meat Buyer's Guide® is a NAMP publication. NAMP members can participate in the review/update process of each edition.

BENEFITS OF MEMBERSHIP

- 35% discount on *The Meat Buyers Guide®*
- A relaxed networking and learning environment at two major industry-wide meetings a year
- Learning opportunities at NAMP's 16+ food safety conferences and workshops: pay lower member fees
- NAMP's weekly report, *NewsLine,* which contains industry information and updates and NAMP's weekly Market Report, with complete up-to-date pricing information
- Unlimited free access to NAMP's College of Experts, our team of 34 Ph.D.-level consultants on 19 subjects important to your business
- A voice in government rulemaking: NAMP is a North American organization that effectively represents your interests to USDA-FSIS, USDA-AMS, and CFIA
- A cross-referenced *Member Resource Directory* for networking and enriching your business prospects
- Fast, on-line help from other members through NAMP's Listserve called "Bull Session"
- Exclusive technical/educational info on the Members Only section at www.namp.com

Members also enjoy toll-free access to NAMP's experienced staff and off-site consultants who are ready to help you with just about any problem, question or concern you may have. *It's like having your own team of experts without the added expense - an incredible value for your dues dollar!*

Membership in NAMP offers an unparalleled and unique opportunity to learn and network with your peers. Join today and you'll enrich your business prospects and benefit from other members' experiences. *It's what our long-time members call "The Magic of NAMP".*

WE INVITE YOU TO JOIN TODAY

To apply, go to www.namp.com or call +1 703.758.1900.

¿Quiere que su red personal incluya a quienes en verdad toman las decisiones y a los más exitosos procesadores y proveedores de carne roja y aves de América del Norte?

¡ENTONCES ÚNASE A NAMP!

La Asociación Norteamericana de Procesadores de Carne (NAMP), fundada en 1942, es una asociación internacional dedicada a sus integrantes, que incluyen **procesadores, distribuidores, especialistas en ingredientes principales del plato** y proveedores progresistas que venden principalmente a la industria de servicios de alimentación. NAMP ofrece un valor excepcional a través de programas de apoyo de gran nivel y representación en el gobierno para ayudar a garantizar el éxito de nuestros miembros en la industria.

La Guía para Compradores de Carne® es una publicación de NAMP. Los miembros de NAMP pueden participar en el proceso de revisión y actualización de cada edición.

BENEFICIOS DE LA MEMBRESÍA

- 35% de descuento en *La Guía para Compradores de Carne®*
- Un ambiente relajado para establecer contactos y aprender en dos grandes reuniones de toda la industria por año
- Oportunidades de aprendizaje en las conferencias y los talleres de inocuidad alimentaria de NAMP: pague tarifas más bajas para miembros
- Informe semanal de NAMP, *NewsLine,* que contiene información y actualizaciones de la industria, y el Informe de Mercado semanal de NAMP, con la información de precios completa y al día
- Acceso gratis ilimitado al colegio de expertos de NAMP, nuestro equipo de 34 con nivel de doctorado en 19 áreas importantes para su negocio
- Una voz en las normativas del gobierno: NAMP es una organización norteamericana que representa sus intereses de manera eficaz ante FSIS (Servicio de Inspección e Inocuidad Alimentaria) de USDA (Departamento de Agricultura de E.U.A.), AMS (Servicio de Mercadeo Agrícola) de USDA y la Agencia Canadiense de Inspección de Alimentos
- Un *Directorio de recursos de miembros* con referencia cruzada para establecer contactos y enriquecer las posibilidades de su negocio
- Ayuda rápida en Internet de otros miembros a través del Listserve de NAMP llamado "Bull Session"
- Información técnica y educativa exclusiva en la sección Members Only (sólo para miembros) de www.namp.com

Los miembros también disponen de acceso a través de un número telefónico sin cargo al experimentado personal de NAMP y a consultores descentralizados que están listos para ayudarle con prácticamente cualquier problema, consulta o inquietud que pueda tener. *Es como tener su propio equipo de expertos sin el gasto adicional ¡un increíble rendimiento por el valor de su suscripción!*

La membresía de NAMP ofrece una oportunidad única e incomparable de aprender y establecer contactos con sus colegas. Suscríbase hoy para enriquecer las posibilidades de su negocio y beneficiarse de la experiencia de otros miembros. *Es lo que nuestros miembros de muchos años llaman "La magia de NAMP".*

LO INVITAMOS A UNIRSE HOY

Para solicitar su inscripción, visite www.namp.com o llame al +1 703.758.1900.

beef / carne de res

114D PSO 1 Beef Chuck, Shoulder (Clod), Top Blade / Paleta (Espaldilla), Planchuela

116A Beef Chuck, Chuck Roll
Paleta (Espaldilla), Rollo de Diezmillo

120 Beef Brisket, Deckle-Off, Boneless / Pecho, Sin Grasa Endurecida ní Carne Intercostal, Deshuesado

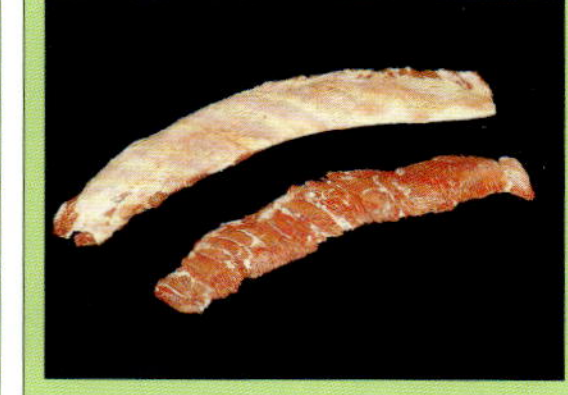

121C Beef Plate, Outside Skirt (IM)
Costillar, Arrachera Delgada Regular (M. Diafragma)

109 Beef Rib, Roast-Ready
Chuletón (Espaldar), Listo para Rostizar

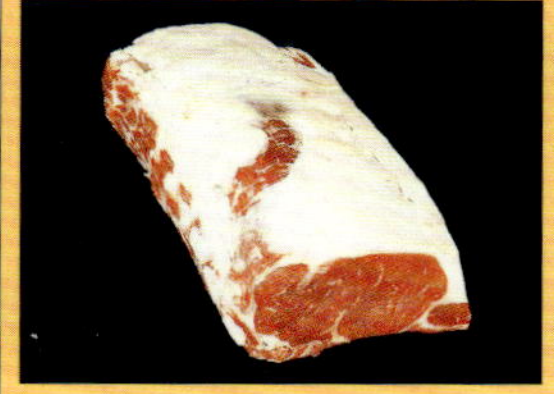

109D Beef Rib, Roast-Ready, Cover Off, Short Cut (Export Style) / Chuletón (Espaldar), Listo para Rostizar, Sin Tapa, Pieza Corta (de Exportación)

193 Beef Flank, Flank Steak
Falda (Ijar), Concha de Falda

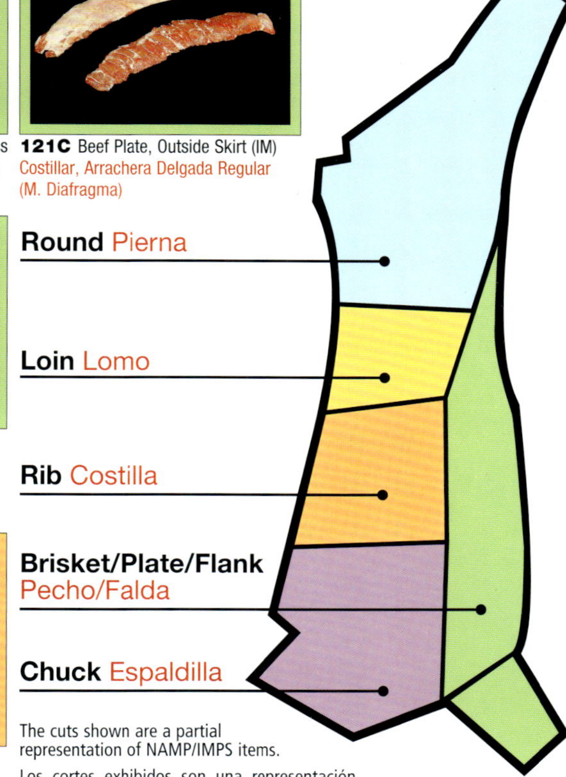

Round Pierna

Loin Lomo

Rib Costilla

Brisket/Plate/Flank
Pecho/Falda

Chuck Espaldilla

The cuts shown are a partial representation of NAMP/IMPS items.

Los cortes exhibidos son una representación parcial de las piezas de NAMP/IMPS.

1103B Beef Rib, Rib Steak, Bone In, Frenched / Chuletón (Espaldar), Bistec del Chuletón, Con Hueso, Estilo Francés

112A Beef Rib, Ribeye, Lip-On
Chuletón (Espaldar), Rollo Ribeye, con Cordón

1112 Beef Rib, Ribeye Roll Steak, Boneless / Chuletón (Espaldar), Bistec de Rollo Ribeye, Deshuesado

180 Beef Loin, Strip Loin, Boneless
Lomo, Strip Loin (New York), Deshuesado

1180 Beef Loin, Strip Loin Steak, Boneless / Bistec de Lomo de Res, Deshuesado

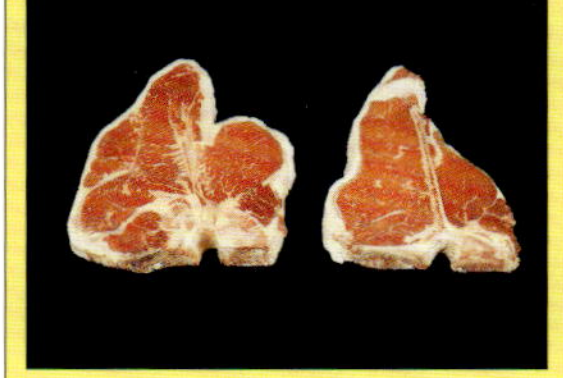

1173 Beef Loin, Porterhouse Steak
Lomo, Bistec "Porterhouse"

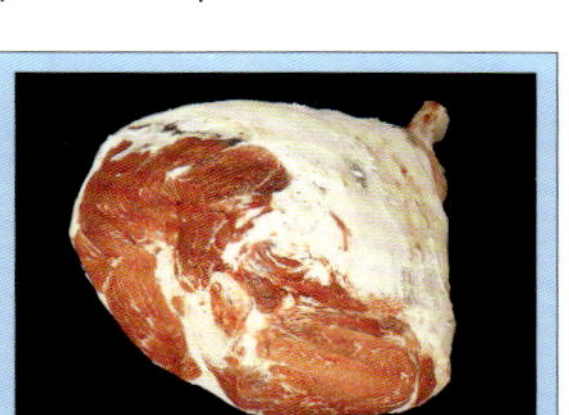

166B Beef Round, Rump and Shank Partially Off, Handle On
Pierna (Piña), Corta, Sin Tajo Anterior de Pulpa Blanca ni Chamberete, con Mango

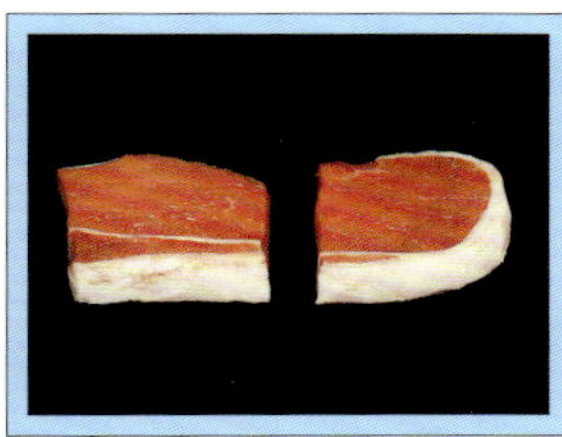

1169 Beef Round, Top (Inside) Round Steak / Pierna (Piña), Bistec de Pulpa Negra (Cara/Centro)

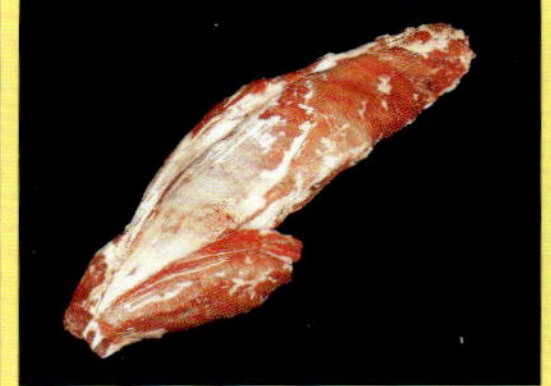

189A Beef Loin, Tenderloin, Full, Side Muscle On, Defatted / Lomo, Filete, Completo, con Cuerda (Psoas Menor) Pegado, Limpio de Grasa

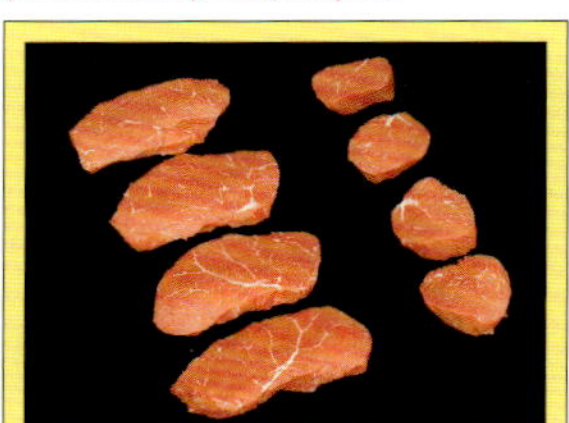

1190A Beef Loin, Tenderloin Steak, Side Muscle Off, Skinned
Lomo, Medallón de Filete, sin Cuerda (Psoas Menor), Despellejado

184B PSO 1 Beef Loin, Top Sirloin Butt, Center-Cut, Boneless, Cap Off (IM)
Lomo, Top Sirloin, Aguayón sin Tapa, Corte del Centro, Deshuesado

169A Beef Round, Top (Inside), Cap Off / Pierna (Piña), Pulpa Negra (Cara/Centro) sin Tapa

171B Beef Round, Outside Round (Flat) / Pierna (Piña), Contracara, Pulpa Blanca

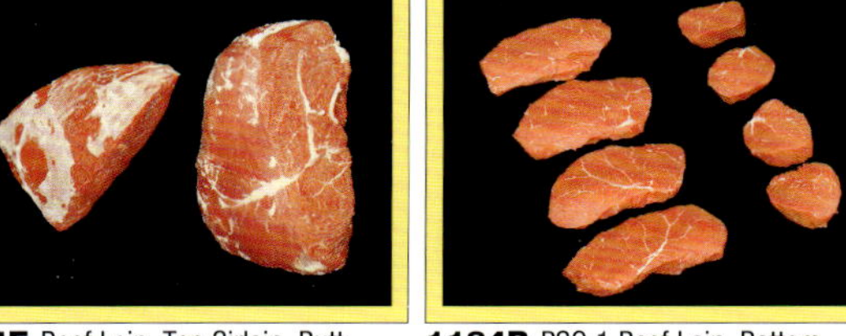

184E Beef Loin, Top Sirloin, Butt, Boneless, 2-Piece / Lomo, Pulpa del Aguayón Superior/Top Sirloin (Aguayón y Tapa), Deshuesados y Recortados de grasa, en 2 piezas

1184B PSO 1 Beef Loin, Bottom Sirloin Butt Steak, Center-Cut, Boneless (IM) / Lomo, Bistec de Pulpa del Aguayón Superior/Top Sirloin, Bistec de Aguayón sin Tapa, Corte del Centro, Deshuesado (M. Glúteo Medio)

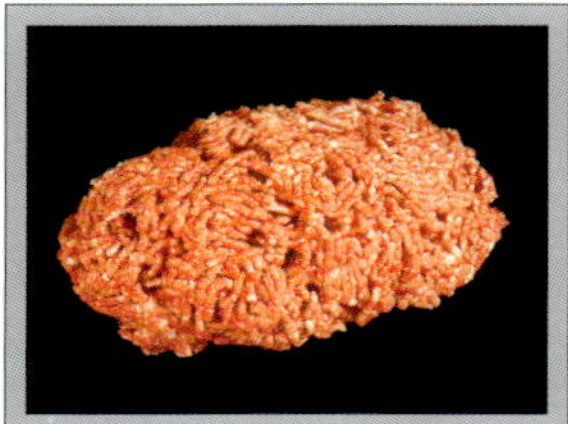

135A Beef for Stewing
Trozos de Res en Cubos para Cocido/Guisado

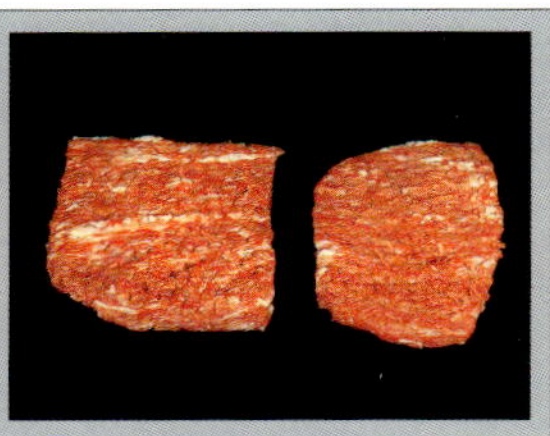

136 Ground Beef
Carne Molida de Res

1100 Beef Cubed Steak
Bistec Suavizado

1

carne de res australiana

Australia es uno de los más grandes productores y exportadores de carne de res en el mundo. El compromiso de nuestra industria sobre inocuidad alimentaria e integridad y rastreabilidad de los productos, significa que podemos entregar de forma constante los productos de carne de res, con los estándares más altos, a nuestros clientes en todo el mundo.

La industria de la carne de res australiana produce una de las carnes de mayor calidad del mundo. A pesar de que nuestra industria se ha orientado tradicionalmente a la producción de carne de res de alta calidad y alimentada con pasto, ahora tenemos a su disposición productos naturales y orgánicos de reses alimentadas con granos y que son específicos para cada raza, como Wagyu y Angus. La industria de la carne de res australiana también satisface las necesidades de diferentes culturas, y muchos empacadores australianos producen carne halal de acuerdo a las leyes islámicas.

No importa lo que usted necesite para sus clientes más exigentes—desde carne sin grasa elaborada para hamburguesas, de reses alimentadas con granos o productos orgánicos, hasta reses alimentadas de modo natural y con pasto—cuando compra carne de res australiana, usted sabe que está adquiriendo un producto que cumple con las normas mundiales más estrictas en cuanto a calidad, rastreabilidad e inocuidad.

Libre de enfermedades

Australia está reconocida como un país libre de todas las principales enfermedades epidémicas del ganado, incluyendo la fiebre aftosa (FA). Hemos sido líderes mundiales en promulgar leyes que impiden la alimentación con carne y huesos a los rumiantes, y también hemos implementado programas de vigilancia de las enfermedades de acuerdo a las normas internacionales para hacer cumplir esta prohibición. Como resultado de estos programas y de nuestras regulaciones estrictas sobre cuarentena, nuestra industria es una de las pocas en el mundo que ha sido declarada perteneciente a un país de "Riesgo insignificante" de encefalopatía espongiforme bovina (EEB) por la Organización Mundial de Sanidad Animal.

Integridad de los productos y sistemas de rastreabilidad

La industria de la carne de res australiana ha sido líder mundial en la implementación de sistemas de integridad y rastreabilidad en todos sus campos, para garantizar la calidad de nuestros productos. A continuación se incluye un resumen de estos sistemas. Se puede encontrar más información en la pestaña Programas de la Industria en www.mla.com.au.

La Garantía de Producción del Ganado (LPA, por sus siglas en inglés) es un programa de inocuidad alimentaria en los ranchos que ayuda a los ganaderos a registrar y declarar la situación de inocuidad alimentaria de sus reses. Bajo la LPA los rancheros deben hacer un resumen de la situación de seguridad alimenticia del ganado consignado para venta o sacrificio en un formulario denominado Declaración de Vendedor Nacional (NVD), el cual está relacionado con la propiedad del vendedor por medio de un único código de identificación de propiedad (PIC) de ocho dígitos. El sistema es auditado al azar y los vendedores que proporcionan información falsa se enfrentan a penas severas.

El Sistema Nacional de Identificación del Ganado (NLIS) consiste de etiquetas electrónicas en las orejas y una base de datos gestionada centralmente que ofrece identificación y rastreabilidad individual para el ganado hasta la propiedad de nacimiento.

Australia es líder mundial en identificación animal al haber hecho obligatorio el programa en 2005. El ganado está vinculado a una propiedad por un PIC emitido por los gobiernos estatales e impresos en las etiquetas NLIS y en los formularios NVD de cada ranchero.

Siempre que un animal es trasladado de la propiedad, la base de datos se actualiza para proporcionar una rastreabilidad completa que, cuando se combina con los registros de tratamiento y manejo mantenidos bajo la LPA y el Plan de Acreditación de Corrales de Engorde Nacionales (NFAS), permite que el historial de salud y alimentación de los animales pueda rastrearse hasta la propiedad de nacimiento.

La norma australiana y el Servicio Australiano de Inspección y Cuarentena (AQIS)

Todos los empacadores de carne con licencia de exportación operan bajo la Norma Australiana para una producción higiénica y transporte de carne y productos cárnicos para consumo humano (AS4696:2007), la cual se basa en algunas de las mejores prácticas del mundo y concuerda con la norma ISO 9001:2000. La garantía de calidad basada en HACCP es obligatoria para todos los empacadores australianos de exportación.

El Servicio Australiano de Inspección y Cuarentena (AQIS) es la autoridad gubernamental que audita las normas y la carne no puede ser exportada hasta que no tenga un certificado de salud emitido por AQIS.

Para hacer cumplir la Norma, AQIS también monitorea la E. coli y la Salmonella, mientras que otro programa gubernamental, denominado Inspección Nacional de Residuos (NRS), monitorea los residuos contaminantes agrícolas, veterinarios, ambientales e industriales. Todo producto exportado a Estados Unidos debe cumplir con los requisitos estrictos de este país y está sujeto a la inspección del gobierno estadounidense en el puerto de entrada.

Para obtener más información sobre la forma de disfrutar de los beneficios de la saludable carne de res australiana, visite la sección de comercio de nuestro galardonado sitio web en www.australian-meat.com

Empaquetado y tiempo de conservación

El sector australiano de procesamiento emplea las últimas tecnologías de empaquetado para garantizar que nuestra carne sea entregada en los mercados de exportación en las mismas condiciones de alta calidad en las cuales salió de la empacadora. Los cortes primarios de carne australiana enfriada son empaquetados al vacío para mantener la frescura y la calidad y para garantizar un tiempo extenso de conservación. Se mantiene un control estricto de la temperatura a través de todo el proceso de entrega, inhibiendo el crecimiento bacterial y dándole a la carne de res australiana enfriada un tiempo de conservación de hasta 120 días (la cadena de frío intacta a 32°F) y a la carne de res australiana congelada, un tiempo de conservación de hasta 12 meses (la cadena de frío intacta a 5°F).

Australian Beef User Guide

Australia is one of the largest producers and exporters of beef in the world. Our industry's commitment to food safety, product integrity and traceability means we can consistently deliver beef products of the highest standard to our customers worldwide.

The Australian beef industry produces some of the finest beef in the world. While our industry is traditionally geared toward producing high quality, grass fed beef; Natural, Organic, grain fed beef and breed specific products such as Wagyu and Angus are now available. The Australian beef industry also caters to the needs of different cultures, and many Australian packers produce Halal beef in accordance with Islamic laws.

No matter what you require for your most discerning customers – from lean manufacturing beef for hamburgers, grainfed beef to organic, natural and grassfed beef – when you buy Australian beef you know you are purchasing a product that meets the strictest quality, traceability and safety standards in the world.

Free from Disease

Australia is recognized as being free of all major epidemic diseases of cattle including Foot and Mouth Disease (FMD). We have been world leaders by enacting legislation to prevent the feeding of meat and bone meal to ruminants and have also implemented disease surveillance programs in line with international standards to verify this ban. As a result of these programs and our strict quarantine regulations, our industry is one of only a few in the world to be declared a "Negligible Risk" country of Bovine Spongiform Encephalopathy (BSE) by the World Organization for Animal Health.

Product Integrity and Traceability Systems

The Australian beef industry has been a world leader in implementing industry wide integrity and traceability systems to safeguard the quality of our products. A summary of these systems is provided below. More information can be found under the Industry Programs tab at www.mla.com.au

Packaging and Shelf Life

The Australian processing sector employs the latest packaging technologies to ensure that our beef is delivered to export markets in the same high quality condition in which it left the packinghouse. Australian chilled beef primal cuts are vacuum packaged to maintain freshness and quality and to ensure extended shelf life. Strict temperature control is maintained throughout the delivery process inhibiting bacterial growth and giving Australian chilled beef a shelf life of up to 120 days (cold chain intact at 32°F) and Australian frozen beef a shelf life up to 12 months (cold chain intact at 5°F).

Livestock Production Assurance (LPA) is an on-farm food safety program that assists ranchers to record and declare the food safety status of their livestock. Under LPA ranchers summarize the food safety status of livestock consigned for sale or slaughter on a National Vendor Declaration (NVD) form which is linked to the vendor's property by a unique eight-digit property identification code (PIC). The system is audited at random and vendors providing false information face severe penalties.

The National Livestock Identification System (NLIS) consists of electronic ear tags and a centrally managed database providing individual identification and traceability for cattle back to their property of birth.

Australia is a world leader in animal identification mandating the program in 2005. Cattle are linked to a property by a PIC which is issued by State Governments and printed on each rancher's NLIS tags and NVD form.

Whenever an animal is moved from the property the database is updated to provide complete traceability which, when combined with the treatment and handling records kept under LPA and the National Feedlot Accreditation Scheme (NFAS), allows the health and feeding history of animals to be traced back to their property of birth.

The Australian Standard and Australian Quarantine Inspection Service (AQIS)

All export licensed beef packers operate under the Australian Standard for hygienic production and transportation of meat and meat products for human consumption (AS4696:2007) which is based on some of the world's best practices and is consistent with the ISO 9001:2000 standard. HACCP-based quality assurance is mandatory for all Australian export packers.

The Australian Quarantine Inspection Service (AQIS) is the government authority that audits against the standard and beef cannot be released for export until it has an accompanying health certificate issued by AQIS.

To comply with the Standard, AQIS also monitors for *E. coli* and *Salmonella* while another government program, called the National Reside Survey (NRS), monitors for residues of agricultural, veterinary, environmental and industrial contaminants. All product exported to the United States must meet strict U.S. requirements and is subject to U.S. government inspection at the port of import.

For more information on how you can enjoy the benefits of wholesome Australian beef, visit the trade section of our award-winning website at www.australian-meat.com

MEAT & LIVESTOCK AUSTRALIA, NORTH AMERICAN OFFICE
1401 K Street, NW Suite 602, Washington, DC 20005

202.521.2551 main
202.521.2699 fax

www.australian-meat.com
info@mlana.com

Popular Australian Cuts (Cortes australianos populares)

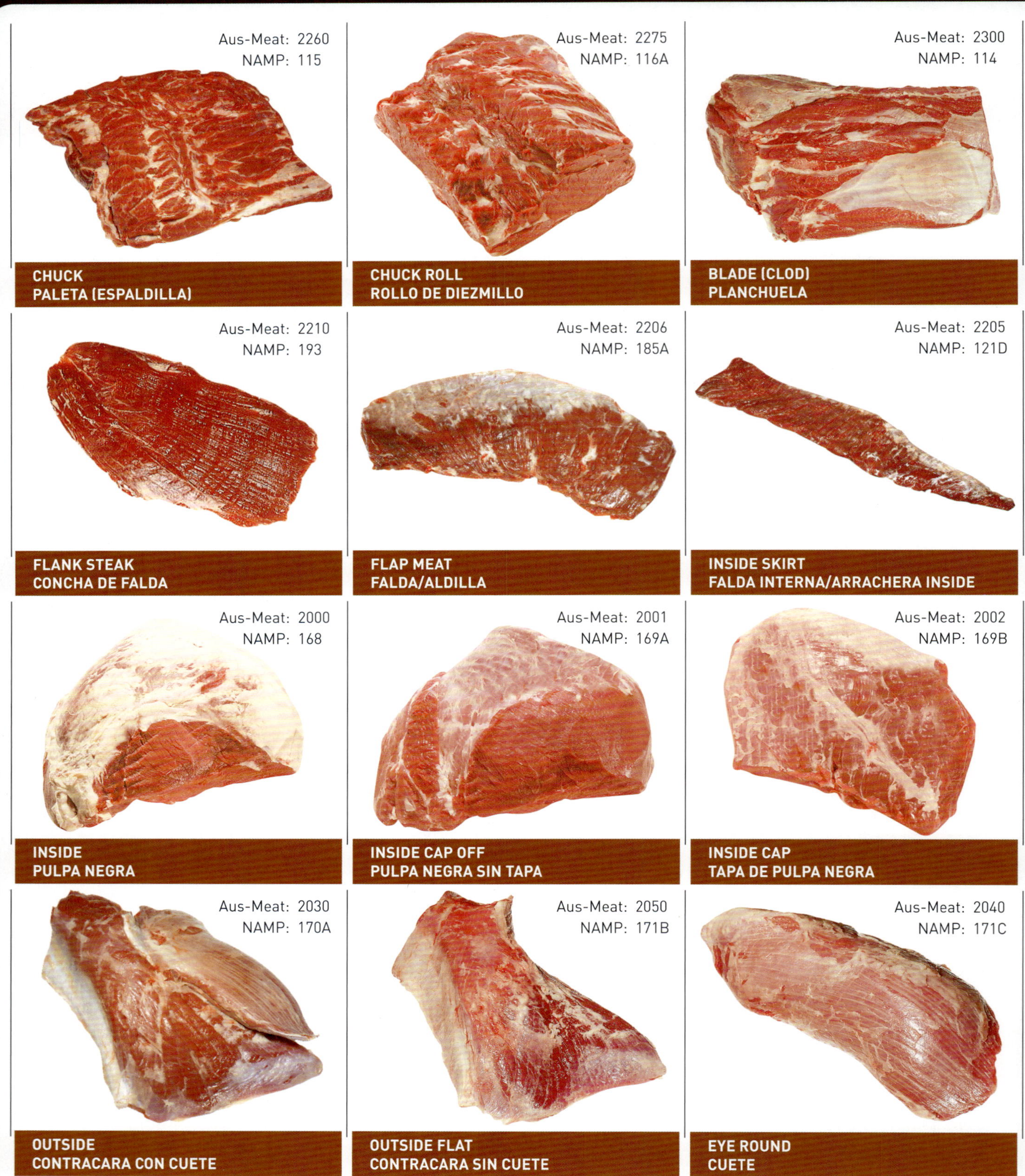

All of the cuts listed are the major cuts that are exported to the U.S.
For points of specification regarding these and the full range of cuts and information
on the Australian beef industry, go to www.australian-beef.com

Todos los cortes de la lista son los cortes principales que se exportan a E.U.A. Para conocer los puntos de especificaciones relacionados con estos cortes y con la variedad completa de cortes, y para obtener información sobre la industria de la carne de res australiana, visite www.australian-meat.com/carne-australia

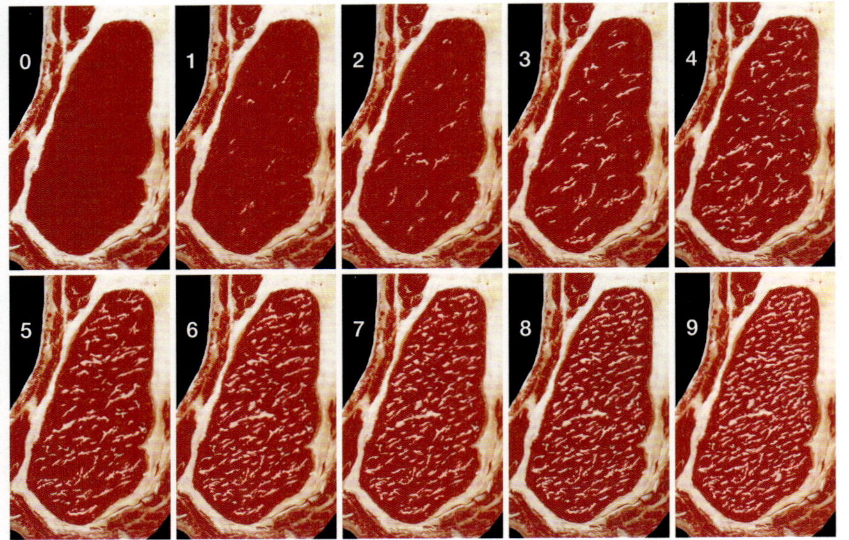

Marmoleado

El sistema de marmoleado de AUS-MEAT proporciona una indicación de la cantidad de marmoleado en la carne de res. El marmoleado es la grasa que se deposita entre las fibras musculares del músculo *M. longissumus dorsi*. El marmoleado es evaluado y calificado de acuerdo a las normas de referencia de marmoleado de AUS-MEAT.

Información sobre Etiquetado para la Carne de Res Australiana

Todas las cajas de cartón de la carne de res y de cordero australianos están identificadas con etiquetas que contienen la información sobre el producto. Las etiquetas de las cajas poseen información obligatoria exigida por las regulaciones del gobierno de Australia, y concuerda con los requisitos de etiquetado para los productos cárnicos importados que exigen el Departamento de Agricultura de E.U.A. (USDA), la Agencia Canadiense de Inspección de Alimentos (CFIA) y la Secretaría de Agricultura, Ganadería, Desarrollo Rural, Pesca y Alimentación (SAGARPA). Además de la información obligatoria, y por motivos comerciales, las empacadoras australianas pueden incluir en la etiqueta otra información opcional que permita una mayor descripción del producto.

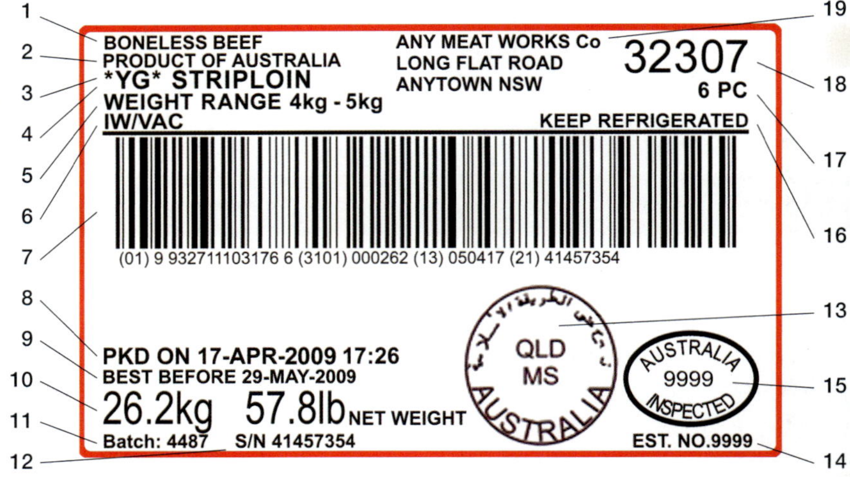

Como ejemplo, los siguientes elementos pueden ser incluidos en las etiquetas de todas las cajas de cartón de carne roja australiana:

1. Información genérica: Carne con hueso o deshuesada, e identificación de la especie

2. País de origen

3. Identificación de la canal: Código de categoría que identifica la edad y el sexo de la canal

4. Identificación del producto: Descripción del corte primario tal como se muestra en el Manual de Carnes Australianas

5. Límites de peso del corte primario: Indica que cada corte primario de la caja se encuentra dentro de los límites mínimo y máximo que se indican en la etiqueta

6. Tipo de empaquetado: Corresponde al código de empaquetado de AUS-MEAT

7. Código de barras: Desarrollado de conformidad con las normas GS1 (EAN. UCC) para las industrias internacionales de la carne

8. Fecha de empacado: Día, mes, año y hora en que el producto fue empacado en la caja

9. Fecha hasta la cual se recomienda el mejor consumo ("best before"): Fin del período para la carne almacenada de conformidad con cualquier condición estipulada. La carne marcada con esta fecha recomendada puede seguirse vendiendo después de dicha fecha siempre y cuando no esté dañada, deteriorada o estropeada. La carne marcada con fecha de caducidad ("use by") no puede ser vendida después de esa fecha

10. Peso neto: El contenido de carne en la caja, menos todos los materiales de empaquetado, que se muestra con hasta dos cifras decimales en kilogramos y libras

11. Número de lote: Número de identificación interno de la compañía, para hacer el seguimiento del producto si fuese necesario

12. Número de serie de la caja: Número de identificación individual para la caja

13. Aprobación Halal: Producto que ha sido sacrificado ritualmente y certificado por una organización islámica aprobada

14. Número de establecimiento: Número de identificación de una planta registrada

15. Sello de AI: Inspeccionada por el gobierno de Australia

16. Declaración de refrigeración: "Mantener frío / refrigerado" indica que el producto en la caja ha sido mantenido en condiciones controladas de enfriamiento desde el momento del empaquetado

17. Número de piezas: Número de cortes primarios que van en la caja

18. Código de compañía: Identificación interna del producto contenido en la caja

19. Nombre comercial de la compañía: Nombre de la empacadora del producto

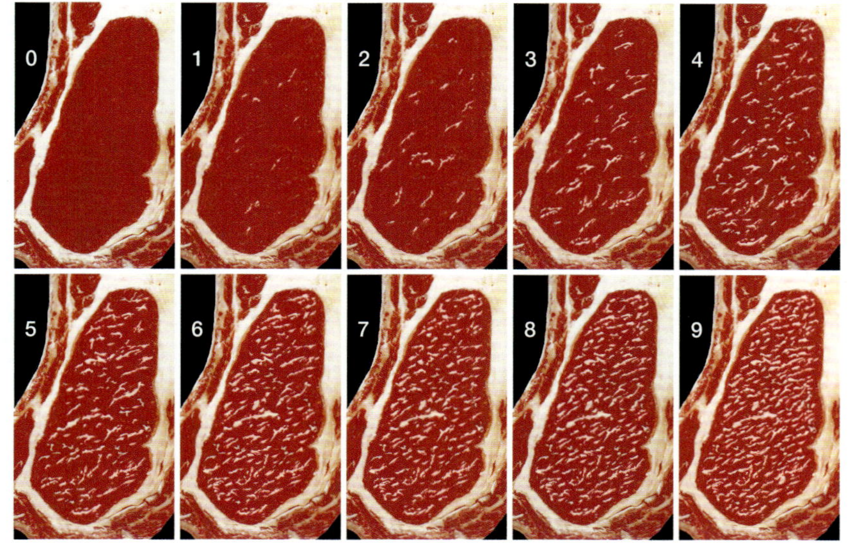

Marbling

The AUS-MEAT marbling system provides an indication of the amount of marbling in beef. Marbling is the fat that is deposited between muscle fibers of the M. *longissumus dorsi* muscle. Marbling is assessed and scored against the AUS-MEAT marbling reference standards.

Labeling Information

All cartons of Australian red meat are identified with labels with information about the product. Carton labels consist of mandatory information that is required under Australian government regulation and is consistent with the U.S. Department of Agriculture (USDA), the Canadian Food Inspection Agency (CFIA) and Secretaria de Agricultura, Ganaderia, Desarrollo Rural, Pesca y Alimentacion (SAGARPA) requirements for labeling of imported meat products. In addition to mandatory information, Australian packers may include optional information on the label, allowing for further description for trade purposes.

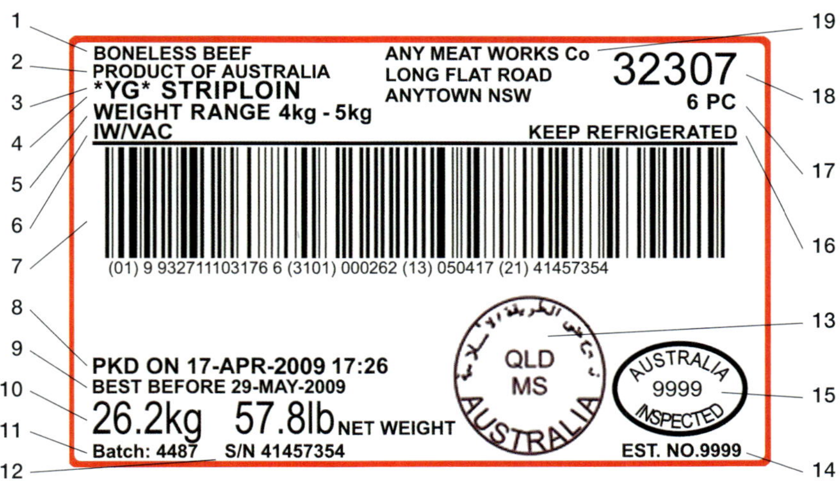

As an example, the following elements may be and can be included on labels for all Australian red meat cartons:

1. Generic statement: Bone-in or boneless and identification of species

2. Country of Origin

3. Carcass Identification: Category code which identifies the carcass age and sex

4. Product Identification: Primal cut description as shown in the Handbook of Australian Meat

5. Primal Weight Range: indicates that each primal cut in the carton is the minimum / maximum weight range as shown on the label

6. Packaging Type: AUS-MEAT packaging code

7. Bar code: Most developed and compliant with the GS1 (EAN.UCC) international meat industry guidelines

8. Packed on date: Day, month, year and time that the product was packed into the carton

9. Best Before date: End of the period for meat stored in accordance with any stated storage condition. Meat marked with best before date can continue to be sold after that date provided that the meat is not damaged, deteriorated or perished. Meat marked with use by date cannot be sold after that date.

10. Net Weight: Meat content, less all the packing material, shown to two decimal places in kilograms and pounds

11. Batch Number: In-house company identification number for product tracing when required

12. Carton Serial Number: Individual identification number for carton

13. Halal Approved: Product has been ritually slaughtered and certified by an approved Islamic organization

14. Establishment Number: Plant-registered identification number

15. AI Stamp: Australia-government Inspected

16. Refrigeration Statement: "keep chilled / refrigerated" indicates that the product in the carton has been held in a controlled chilled condition from the time of packing

17. Number of Pieces: Number of primal cuts in the carton

18. Company Code: In-house identification code for product in the carton

19. Company Trading Name: Name of the packer of the product

Sistema canadiense de clasificación de carne de res

La Agencia Canadiense de Clasificación de Carne de Res (CBGA, por sus siglas en inglés) fue creada en 1996. Está acreditada por la Agencia Canadiense de Inspección de Alimentos (CFIA, por sus siglas en inglés) para evaluar los grados de acuerdo con las normas nacionales de Canadá. El objetivo del sistema de clasificación es facilitar las decisiones de mercadeo y producción y lograr una mayor uniformidad y previsibilidad en la calidad de los alimentos. Además de la clasificación, CBGA participa en la certificación de marcas, como las marcas de carne de res producida a partir de una raza de ganado específica. Esta verificación independiente garantiza a los compradores el pleno cumplimiento con las normas de los programas de carne de res de marca de Canadá.

En Canadá se permite que únicamente los examinadores calificados asignen un grado a una canal de carne de res. Cada examinador debe completar satisfactoriamente un programa de capacitación integral aprobado por CBGA y luego aprobar un examen escrito y práctico. Una vez que obtienen la certificación, los examinadores son auditados regularmente por funcionarios de CBGA y a través del Programa Nacional de Monitoreo de Grados administrado por la Agencia Canadiense de Inspección de Alimentos. Estas auditorías continuas garantizan que la clasificación se realice de manera uniforme y que refleje fielmente los requisitos nacionales de Canadá para la carne de res de alta calidad.

Proceso de clasificación para la carne de res canadiense de alta calidad

Únicamente se podrá clasificar una canal después de que haya sido inspeccionada y de que se le haya colocado el sello de inspección de carne que indica que la carne de res cumple con todos los requisitos de inocuidad alimentaria. Se deben cumplir todos los requisitos de atributos de calidad para recibir los grados A, AA, AAA y Prime de Canadá, y no se podrá compensar un defecto con otra característica. Únicamente un examinador que cuente con la certificación de la Agencia Canadiense de Clasificación de Carne de Res puede asignar grados de calidad y rendimiento a las canales.

La Agencia Canadiense de Clasificación de Carne de Res está acreditada por la Agencia Canadiense de Inspección de Alimentos para asignar grados de carne de res canadiense de acuerdo con las normas nacionales definidas por las leyes federales.

Grados de calidad de Canadá

Los grados de calidad de Canadá para la carne de res proveniente de canales jóvenes son A de Canadá, AA de Canadá, AAA de Canadá y Prime de Canadá. Para asignar estos grados, un examinador certificado realiza una evaluación detallada de la canal después de que haya sido refrigerada por un mínimo de 12 horas. Los atributos evaluados incluyen madurez, color de la carne, color de la grasa, musculatura de la canal, cobertura y textura de la grasa, textura de la carne y nivel de marmoleado.

Grados de rendimiento de Canadá

El grado de rendimiento es una medida relacionada con la cantidad de carne magra o músculo en la canal. Los grados de rendimiento 1 de Canadá, 2 de Canadá y 3 de Canadá se evalúan según el porcentaje de rendimiento de carne magra, que se calcula utilizando medidas obtenidas con una regla especialmente diseñada. Estas medidas permiten la determinación de la clase de grasa y también la clasificación de músculo, que se utilizan para determinar el grado de rendimiento.

Se deben cumplir todos los requisitos de atributos de calidad para recibir los grados A, AA, AAA y Prime de Canadá y no se podrá compensar un defecto con otra característica.

Normas de grado de calidad para ganado joven

Grado	Marmoleado*	Madurez**	Color de la carne	Color de la grasa	Musculatura	Textura de la carne*
CANADÁ						
Prime	Ligeramente abundante	Joven	Sólo rojo intenso	No se permite grasa amarilla	Buena musculatura o mejor	Sólo firme
AAA	Pequeño	Joven	Sólo rojo intenso	No se permite grasa amarilla	Buena musculatura o mejor	Sólo firme
AA	Ligero	Joven	Sólo rojo intenso	No se permite grasa amarilla	Buena musculatura o mejor	Sólo firme
A	Rastros	Joven	Sólo rojo intenso	No se permite grasa amarilla	Buena musculatura o mejor	Sólo firme

*Marmoleado mínimo y textura de la carne permitidos para la clasificación de grado de calidad.   **Las categorías de madurez reflejan los requisitos nacionales.

Normas de marmoleado para ganado joven

En 1996 se modificaron las normas canadienses de marmoleado para reflejar las normas de marmoleado protegidas por derechos de autor de Estados Unidos. Las normas de marmoleado mínimas que se utilizan para el Departamento de Agricultura de E.U.A. Prime (ligeramente abundante), Choice (pequeño) y Select (ligero) son las mismas normas mínimas que se usan en Canadá.

CANADIAN BEEF
Quality that inspires confidence.™

Beef Information Centre

The Canadian Beef Grading System

The Canadian Beef Grading Agency (CBGA) was created in 1996. It is accredited by the Canadian Food Inspection Agency (CFIA) to assess grades in accordance with Canada's national standards. The grading system functions to facilitate marketing and production decisions and to achieve greater consistency and predictability in eating quality. In addition to grading, the CBGA is involved in certification of brands, such as those for beef produced only from a specific breed of cattle. This independent verification assures buyers that the standards for Canadian branded beef programs are being fully satisfied.

Only qualified graders are permitted to grade a beef carcass in Canada. Each grader must successfully complete a comprehensive training program approved by the CBGA, followed by a written and a practical examination. Once certified, graders are regularly audited by CBGA officials and through the National Grade Monitoring Program administered by the CFIA. These ongoing audits ensure that grading is performed in a manner which is consistent and accurately reflects Canada's national requirements for high quality beef.

The Grading Process for High Quality Canadian Beef

A carcass may be graded only after it has been inspected and received the meat inspection stamp, indicating that the beef satisfies all food safety requirements. Each requirement for quality attributes must be met to qualify for the Canada A, AA, AAA and Prime grades and any deficiency cannot be offset by other traits. Quality and yield grades can only be assigned to carcasses by a certified Canadian Beef Grading Agency grader.

The Canadian Beef Grading Agency is accredited by the Canadian Food Inspection Agency to assign Canadian beef grades in accordance with national standards defined by federal law.

Canada's Quality Grades

Canada's quality grades for beef from youthful carcasses are Canada A, Canada AA, Canada AAA and Canada Prime. To assign these grades, a detailed assessment of the carcass is made by a certified grader following chilling for a minimum of 12 hours. Attributes evaluated include maturity, meat color, fat color, carcass muscling, fat coverage and texture, meat texture and marbling level.

Canada's Yield Grades

The yield grade is a measure related to the amount of lean or muscle in the carcass. The Canada 1, Canada 2, and Canada 3 yield grades are assessed on the basis of lean yield percentage, calculated using measurements obtained with a specially designed ruler. These measurements allow the determination of both fat class and muscle score, which is used to determine the yield grade.

Each requirement for quality attributes must be satisfied to qualify for the Canada A, AA, AAA and Prime grades and any deficiency cannot be offset by other traits.

Quality Grade Standards for Youthful Cattle

Grade	Marbling*	Maturity**	Meat Color	Fat Color	Muscling	Meat Texture*
CANADA						
Prime	Slightly abundant	Youthful	Bright red only	No yellow fat permitted	Good muscling or better	Firm only
AAA	Small	Youthful	Bright red only	No yellow fat permitted	Good muscling or better	Firm only
AA	Slight	Youthful	Bright red only	No yellow fat permitted	Good muscling or better	Firm only
A	Trace	Youthful	Bright red only	No yellow fat permitted	Good muscling or better	Firm only

*Minimum marbling and meat texture permitted for quality grade class.   **Maturity categories reflect domestic requirements.

Marbling Standards for Youthful Cattle

The Canadian marbling standards were changed in 1996 to mirror the copyrighted marbling standards of the United States. The minimum marbling standards used for USDA Prime (slightly abundant), Choice (small) and Select (slight) are the same minimum standards used in Canada.

CANADIAN BEEF
Quality that inspires confidence.™

Beef Information Centre

Ganaderos y rancheros: Ecologistas de la vida diaria

La preservación, conservación y restauración de los recursos naturales de este país como los espacios abiertos, las praderas, los pantanos, el aire puro y el hábitat de la fauna silvestre son tan importantes para las familias rancheras como lo son para las familias de todo el país. Su objetivo es dejarle un medio ambiente mejor a la próxima generación. Para los ganaderos y rancheros estadounidenses, la tierra no sólo es donde crían ganado, también es donde crían a sus familias.

La conservación es una parte importante de la vida en la granja

Para las familias de agricultores y rancheros, la sustentabilidad significa asegurarse de que la tierra pueda abastecer a la próxima generación.

Los ranchos ganaderos mantienen mucho más que sólo ganado. La misma tierra que proporciona alimentos y espacios abiertos para la cría de ganado también ofrece un hogar para diversos tipos de vida silvestre, incluyendo especies de peces, mamíferos, pájaros y plantas amenazados o en peligro de extinción. Los agricultores y los rancheros ayudan a la vida silvestre al proporcionar alimentos, retrasar la cosecha de heno hasta después de la época de desovado y mantener o restaurar las plantas y pasturas.

El agua es una fuente de vida para todos los habitantes de la granja, incluyendo el ganado, la vida silvestre y las familias que los crían y protegen. Los esfuerzos diarios para la conservación del agua incluyen la realización de análisis de calidad del agua, el cercado de arroyos para proteger a los peces y las vías fluviales y la creación de estanques artificiales para irrigación.

Las familias ganaderas de todo el país administran cuidadosamente la tierra que tienen a su cuidado, protegiendo los espacios abiertos de Estados Unidos. El pastoreo del ganado estabiliza el suelo y estimula el crecimiento de las pasturas beneficiosas mientras que protege contra la erosión y los incendios forestales. Las prácticas de control de la erosión, incluyendo el pastoreo rotacional, el control de las malezas y la labranza mínima protegen este frágil ecosistema.

Beneficios diarios de las granjas de ganado y la carne de res nutritiva

En la actualidad, los agricultores y rancheros usan menos recursos naturales para producir una oferta más rica y accesible de carne de res con un buen sabor y rica en nutrientes. Los animales que pastan en tierras que no son adecuadas para el cultivo aumentan a más del doble el área que se puede utilizar para producir alimentos.

El ganado desempeña un papel valioso en el ecosistema al convertir plantas que los humanos no pueden consumir en un alimento con alto contenido de nutrientes. La deficiencia de hierro es la deficiencia nutricional más común en todo el mundo. La carne de res ofrece la fuente de hierro más abundante y fácil de absorber. De hecho, una porción de apenas 3 onzas de carne de res proporciona el 51% del valor diario (VD) de proteínas, el 38% del VD de zinc y el 14% del VD de hierro.

Visite www.ExploreBeef.org y www.beeffoodservice.com para obtener más información, o comuníquese con National Cattlemen's Beef Association: 303-694-0605

Cattle Farmers and Ranchers: Everyday Environmentalists

Preserving, conserving and restoring this country's natural resources such as open space, grasslands, wetlands, clean air and wildlife habitat are as important to ranching families as they are to families across the country. Their goal is to leave the environment in better shape for the next generation. For America's cattle farmers and ranchers, the land is not just where they raise cattle; it's also where they raise their families.

Conservation is an Important Part of Farm Life

Sustainability to farming and ranching families means ensuring that the land will provide for the next generation.

Cattle ranches support a lot more than just cattle. The same land that provides food and open space for raising cattle also offers a home for many types of wildlife, including threatened and endangered species of fish, mammals, birds and plants. Farmers and ranchers help wildlife by providing feed, delaying hay harvest until after nesting season and maintaining or restoring native plants and grasses.

Water is a source of life for everyone on the farm, including the cattle, the wildlife and the families who raise and protect them. Everyday water conservation efforts include conducting water quality tests, fencing off streams to protect the fish and waterways and creating man-made irrigation ponds.

Farm families across the country carefully manage the land in their care, protecting America's open spaces. Cattle grazing stabilizes the soil and promotes growth of beneficial grasses while protecting against erosion and forest fires. Erosion control practices, including rotational grazing, brush control management and no-till farming, protect this fragile ecosystem.

The Everyday Benefits of Cattle Farms and Nutritious Beef

Today's farmers and ranchers are using fewer natural resources to produce a more abundant and affordable supply of great-tasting, nutrient rich beef. Grazing animals on land not suitable for producing crops more than doubles the land area that can be used to produce food.

Cattle serve a valuable role in the ecosystem by converting plants humans cannot consume into a nutrient-dense food. Iron deficiency is the most common nutritional deficiency worldwide. Beef provides the most readily available and easily absorbed source of iron. In fact, just one 3-ounce serving of beef supplies 51 percent of the Daily Value (DV) for protein, 38 percent of the DV for zinc and 14 percent of the DV for iron.

Visit www.ExploreBeef.org and www.beeffoodservice.com for more information,
or contact National Cattlemen's Beef Association: 303-694-0605

Guía de colores del bistec de res

Grados de cocción

ROJO/INGLÉS
Aprox. 55 °C, 130 °F

JUGOSO
Aprox. 60 °C, 140 °F

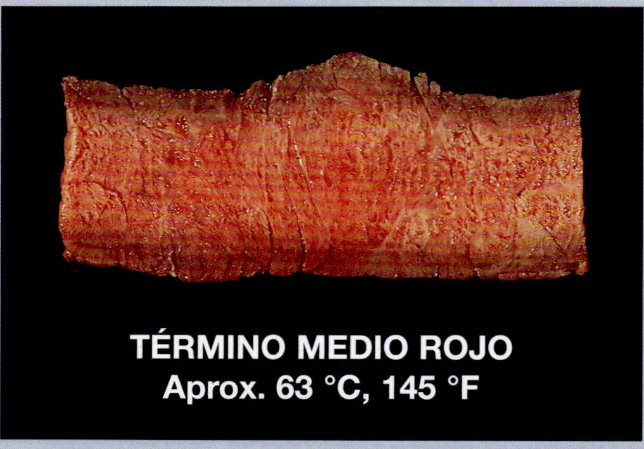

TÉRMINO MEDIO ROJO
Aprox. 63 °C, 145 °F

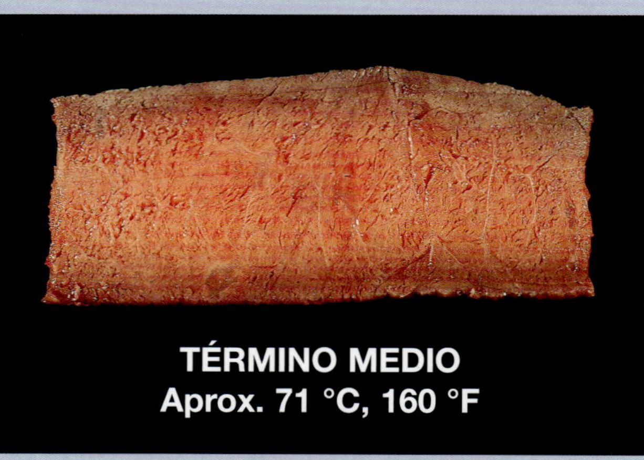

TÉRMINO MEDIO
Aprox. 71 °C, 160 °F

BIEN COCIDO/TRES CUARTOS
Aprox. 77 °C, 170 °F

MUY COCIDO
Aprox. 82 °C, 180 °F

Esta guía de colores es una publicación producto de la colaboración entre National Cattlemen's Beef Association, American Meat Science Association y el Departamento de Agricultura/ARS de E.U.A.

Beef Steak Color Guide

Degrees of Doneness

VERY RARE
Approx. 130°F, 55°C

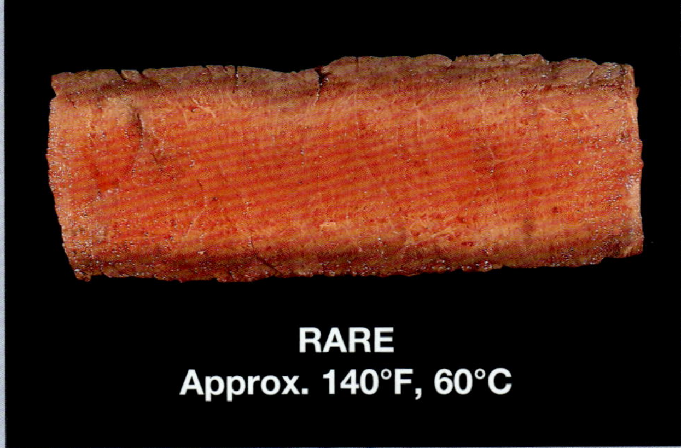

RARE
Approx. 140°F, 60°C

MEDIUM RARE
Approx. 145°F, 63°C

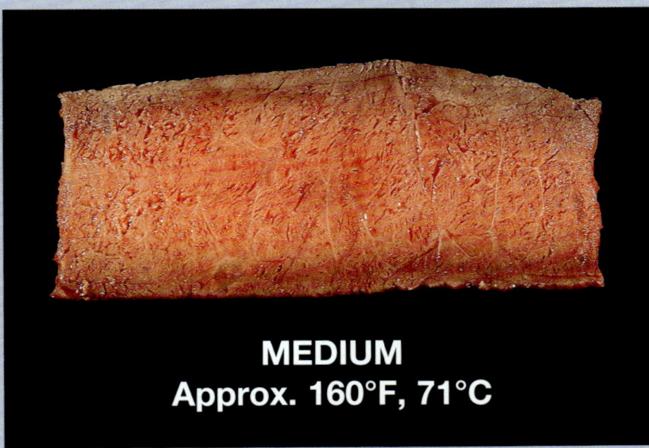

MEDIUM
Approx. 160°F, 71°C

WELL DONE
Approx. 170°F, 77°C

VERY WELL DONE
Approx. 180°F, 82°C

This color guide is presented as a cooperative publication by the National Cattlemen's Beef Association, the American Meat Science Association and the U.S. Department of Agriculture/ARS.

©2010 National Cattlemen's Beef Association

MARMOLEADO
Descripciones e ilustraciones

Descripción de los grados de calidad

A la derecha aparecen los seis grados de marmoleado que se encuentran más comúnmente a disposición de los compradores de la industria de servicios de alimentación.

Las descripciones se aplican a canales de reses de 9 a 30 meses de edad aproximadamente. El Departamento de Agricultura de E.U.A. categoriza a los animales de esta edad como de madurez "A" dentro de sus estándares de clasificación oficiales.

El 95% o más de las reses sometidas a clasificación oficial a disposición de los compradores de la industria de servicios de alimentación son de madurez "A".

Descripciones de grados de marmoleado

- El grado de marmoleado ilustra la cantidad mínima necesaria para cumplir con los siguientes grados de calidad canadienses y de E.U.A.

- Si bien no se pueden considerar como oficiales, salvo para Prime (E.U.A.) o Choice (E.U.A.), las fotografías de grados de marmoleado sí identifican los puntos de marmoleado requeridos dentro de cada nivel de grado.

- La Agencia Canadiense de Clasificación de Carne de Res, que está acreditada ante la Agencia Canadiense de Inspección de Alimentos, usa los mismos estándares de marmoleado utilizados por el Departamento de Agricultura de E.U.A.

Para obtener información adicional sobre clasificación de canal de carne de res tanto en E.U.A. como en Canadá, consulte la sección de Clasificación por grados de esta Guía, que comienza en la página xlvi.

Debido a que el marmoleado es un factor tan importante en la clasificación por grados de calidad de los productos de carne de res, las siguientes ilustraciones reflejan los límites más bajos de seis grados de marmoleado: Moderadamente Abundante, Levemente Abundante, Moderado, Modesto, Pequeño y Leve.

Debe observarse que existen diez grados de marmoleado a los que se hace referencia en los Estándares Oficiales de E.U.A. para Grados de Canales Bovinas. Estas fotografías a color se han elaborado para ayudar al gobierno, a la industria y al campo académico a aplicar correctamente los estándares oficiales en materia de clasificación por grados.

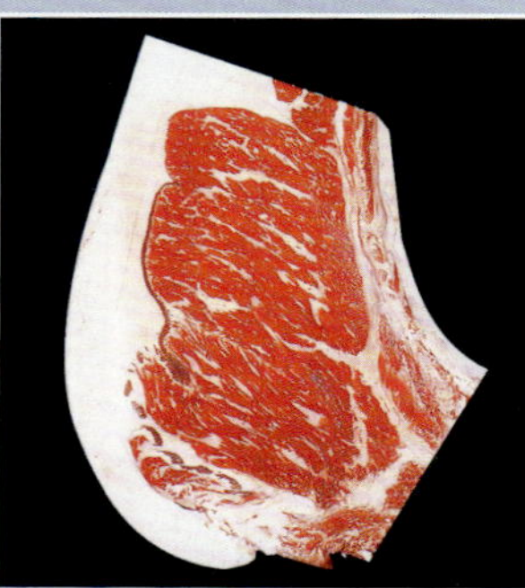

Moderadamente Abundante

- Grado mínimo de marmoleado necesario para promediar el grado de calidad Prime de E.U.A.

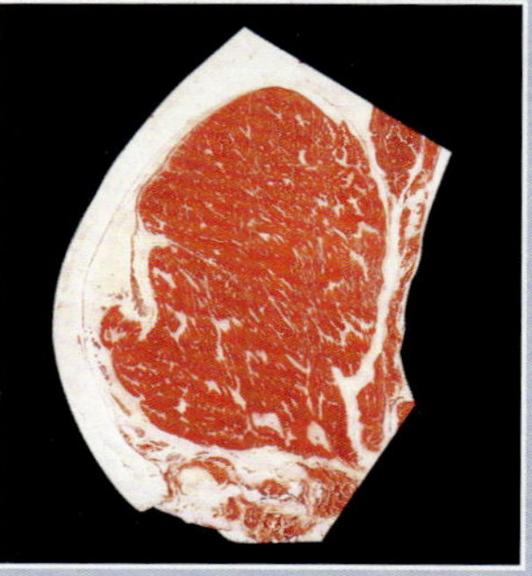

Levemente Abundante

- El grado de calidad Prime de E.U.A., como nivel mínimo, debe ser representativo de Levemente Abundante.

- Marmoleado mínimo necesario para cumplir con los requisitos del grado Prime de E.U.A.

- Marmoleado mínimo necesario para cumplir con los requisitos del grado de calidad Prime de Canadá.

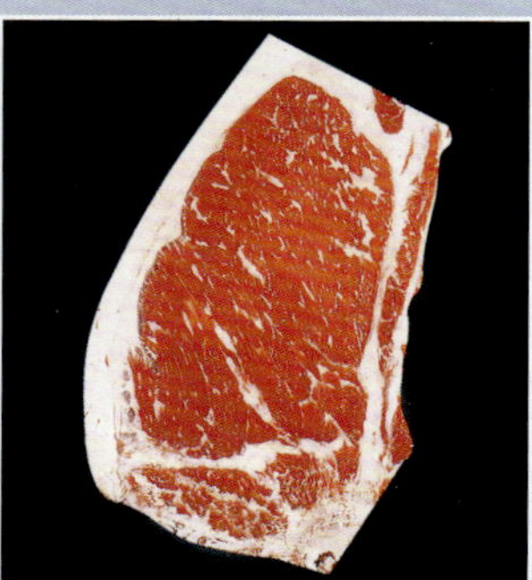

Moderado

- Grado mínimo de marmoleado necesario para cumplir con los requisitos del grado de calidad Choice alto de E.U.A.

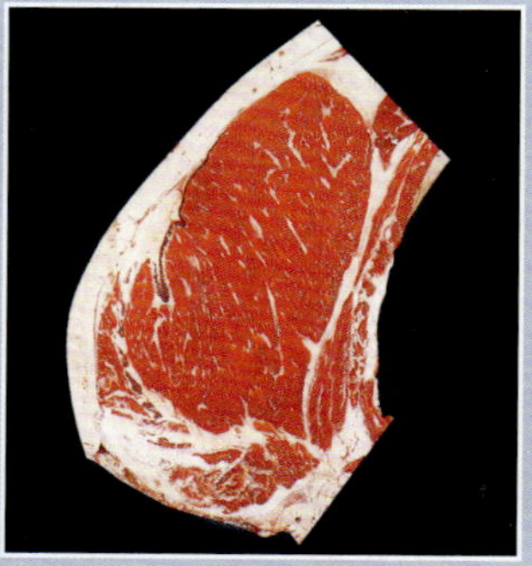

Modesto

- Grado mínimo de marmoleado necesario para promediar el grado de calidad Choice de E.U.A.

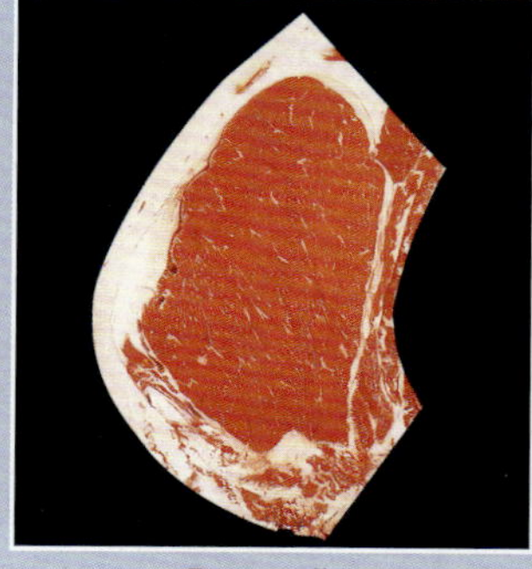

Pequeño

- El grado de calidad Choice de E.U.A., como nivel mínimo, debe ser representativo de Pequeño.

- Marmoleado mínimo necesario para cumplir con los requisitos del grado de calidad Choice de E.U.A.

- Marmoleado mínimo necesario para cumplir con los requisitos del grado AAA de Canadá.

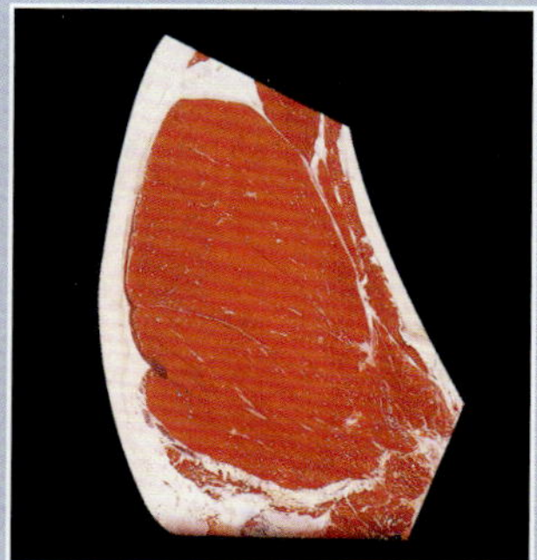

Leve

- El grado de calidad Select de E.U.A., como nivel mínimo, debe ser representativo de Leve.

- Marmoleado mínimo necesario para cumplir con los requisitos del grado AA de Canadá.

Las ilustraciones anteriores son reproducciones reducidas de fotografías de marmoleado oficiales del Departamento de Agricultura de E.U.A., preparadas y suministradas por la Asociación Nacional de Criadores de Ganado de Carne para dicho Departamento de Agricultura.

MARBLING
Descriptions & Illustrations

Quality Grade Description

At right appear the six most commonly found marbling degrees available to foodservice purchasers.

The descriptions apply to beef carcasses from animals of approximately nine to 30 months of age. The U.S. Department of Agriculture designates this age animal to be "A" maturity in its official grading standards.

95 percent or more of the officially graded beef that is made available to foodservice purchasers is of "A" maturity.

Marbling Descriptions

- The degree of marbling illustrates the minimum amount of marbling necessary to qualify for the following U.S. and Canadian quality grades.

- Though not officially graded except as U.S. Prime or U.S. Choice, the degree-of-marbling photographs do identify the points within each grade level.

- The Canadian Beef Grading Agency, which is accredited by the Canadian Food Inspection Agency, uses the same marbling standards as the USDA.

For further information on beef carcass grading in both the United States and Canada, please refer to the Grading section of the Guide, which begins on page xx.

Since marbling is such an important factor in grading beef quality, the following pictures illustrate the lower limits of six marbling degrees: Moderately Abundant, Slightly Abundant, Moderate, Modest, Small, and Slight.

It should be noted that there are 10 degrees of marbling referred to in the Official United States Standards for Grades of Carcass Beef. These color photographs have been developed to assist government, industry, and academia in the proper application of official grade standards.

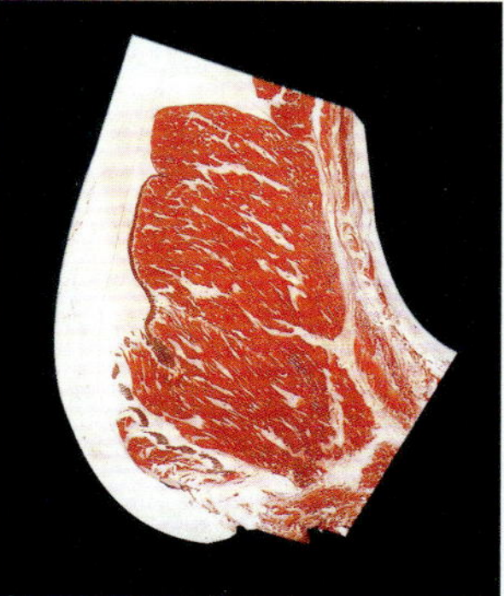

Moderately Abundant

- The minimum marbling degree necessary for average U.S. Prime.

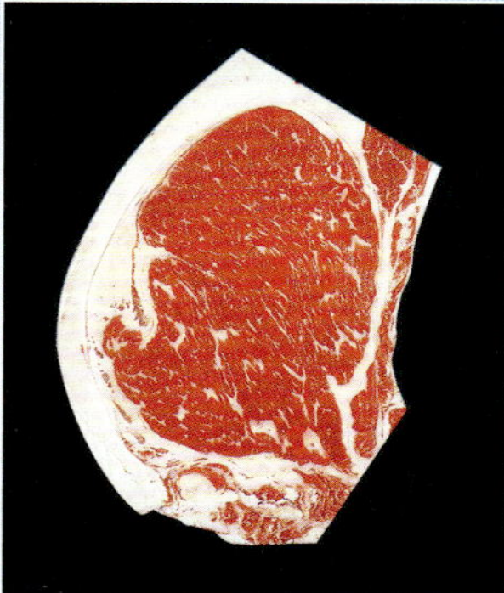

Slightly Abundant

- U.S. Prime must, at the minimum level, be representative of Slightly Abundant.
- The minimum marbling necessary to qualify for U.S. Prime grade.
- The minimum marbling necessary to qualify for Canada Prime.

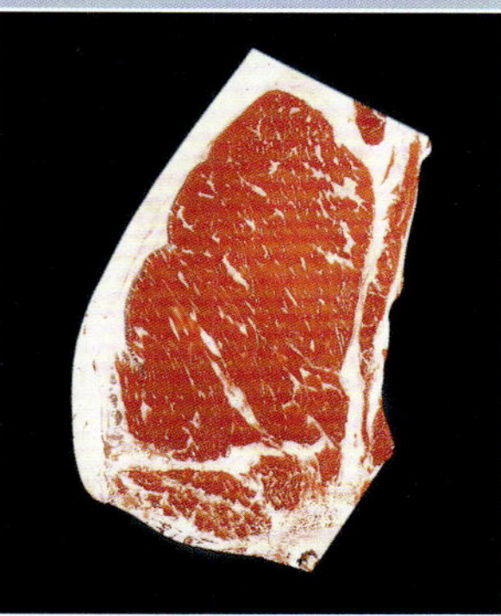

Moderate

- The minimum marbling degree necessary for high U.S. Choice.

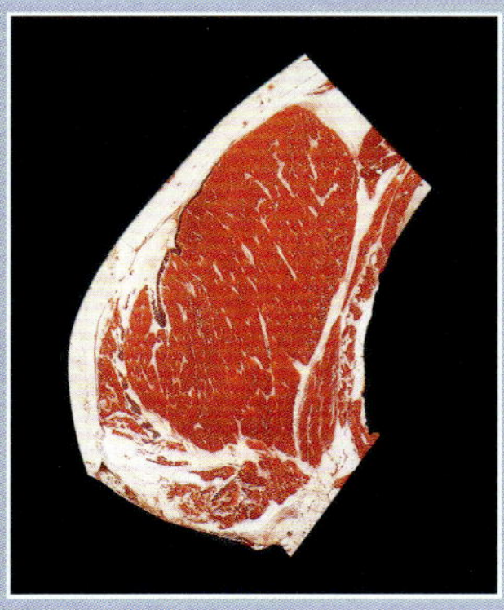

Modest

- The minimum marbling degree necessary for average U.S. Choice.

Small

- U.S. Choice must, at the minimum level, be representative of Small.
- The minimum marbling necessary to qualify for U.S. Choice grade.
- The minimum marbling necessary to qualify for Canada AAA.

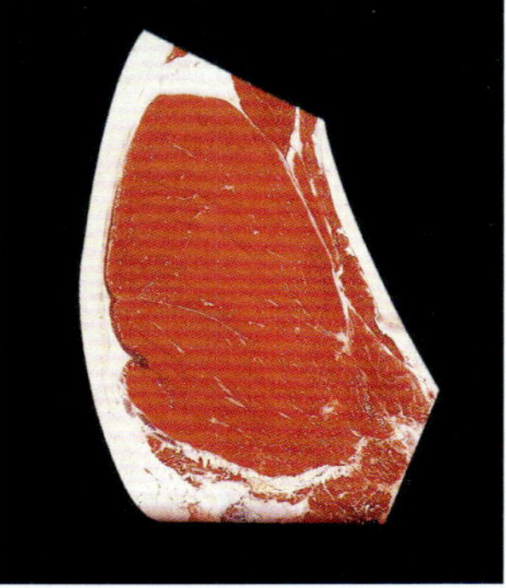

Slight

- U.S. Select must, at the minimum level, be representative of Slight.
- The minimum marbling necessary to qualify for Canada AA.

The above illustrations are reduced reproductions of the Official USDA Marbling Photographs prepared for the U.S. Department of Agriculture by and available from the National Cattlemen's Beef Association.

Beef Skeletal Chart / Diagrama de estructura esquelética de res

Location, Structure, and Names of Bones
Ubicación, estructura y nombres de los huesos

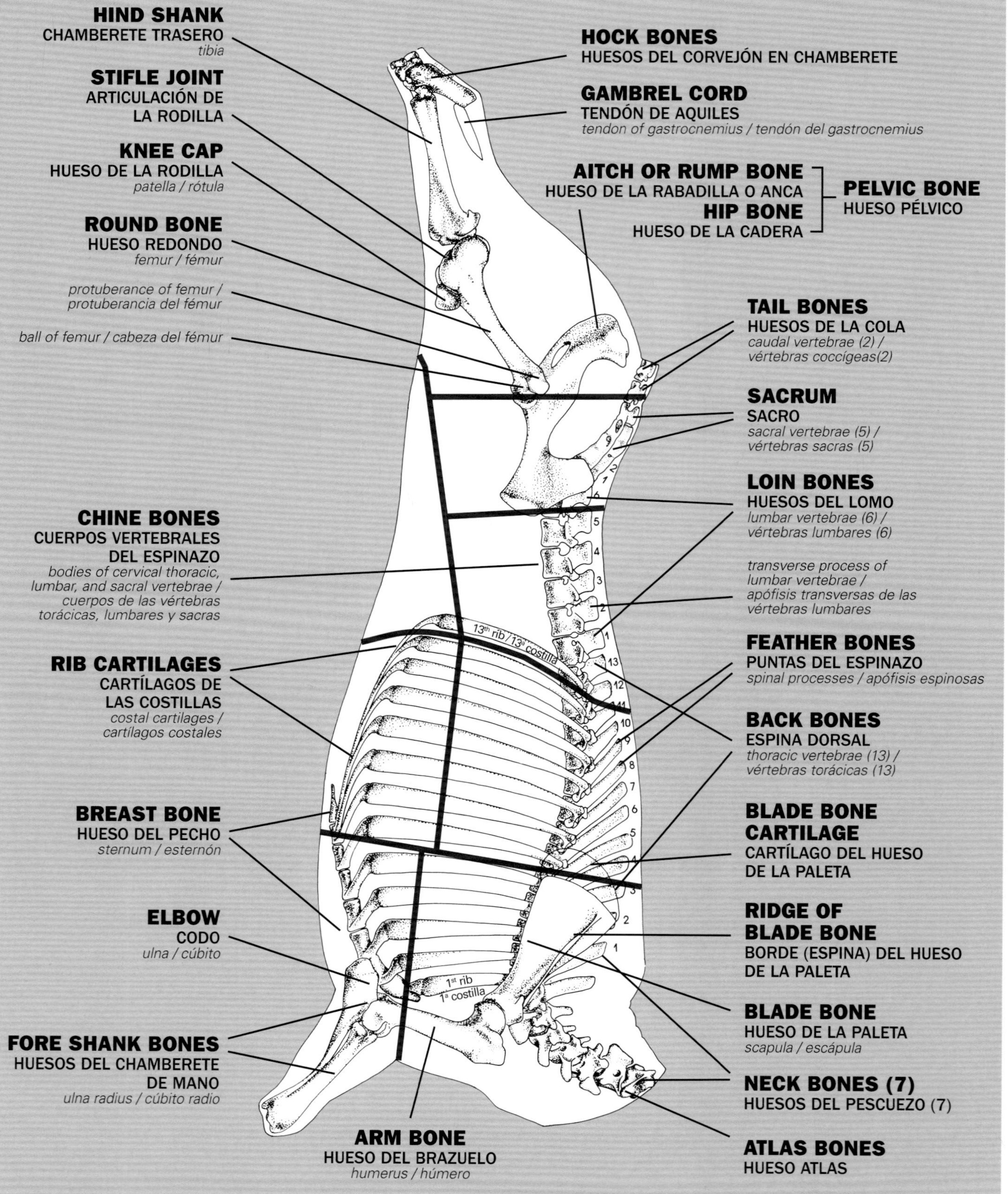

HIND SHANK
CHAMBERETE TRASERO
tibia

STIFLE JOINT
ARTICULACIÓN DE
LA RODILLA

KNEE CAP
HUESO DE LA RODILLA
patella / rótula

ROUND BONE
HUESO REDONDO
femur / fémur

protuberance of femur / protuberancia del fémur

ball of femur / cabeza del fémur

CHINE BONES
CUERPOS VERTEBRALES
DEL ESPINAZO
bodies of cervical thoracic, lumbar, and sacral vertebrae / cuerpos de las vértebras torácicas, lumbares y sacras

RIB CARTILAGES
CARTÍLAGOS DE
LAS COSTILLAS
costal cartilages / cartílagos costales

BREAST BONE
HUESO DEL PECHO
sternum / esternón

ELBOW
CODO
ulna / cúbito

FORE SHANK BONES
HUESOS DEL CHAMBERETE
DE MANO
ulna radius / cúbito radio

HOCK BONES
HUESOS DEL CORVEJÓN EN CHAMBERETE

GAMBREL CORD
TENDÓN DE AQUILES
tendon of gastrocnemius / tendón del gastrocnemius

AITCH OR RUMP BONE
HUESO DE LA RABADILLA O ANCA
HIP BONE
HUESO DE LA CADERA

PELVIC BONE
HUESO PÉLVICO

TAIL BONES
HUESOS DE LA COLA
caudal vertebrae (2) / vértebras coccígeas(2)

SACRUM
SACRO
sacral vertebrae (5) / vértebras sacras (5)

LOIN BONES
HUESOS DEL LOMO
lumbar vertebrae (6) / vértebras lumbares (6)

transverse process of lumbar vertebrae / apófisis transversas de las vértebras lumbares

FEATHER BONES
PUNTAS DEL ESPINAZO
spinal processes / apófisis espinosas

BACK BONES
ESPINA DORSAL
thoracic vertebrae (13) / vértebras torácicas (13)

BLADE BONE CARTILAGE
CARTÍLAGO DEL HUESO
DE LA PALETA

RIDGE OF BLADE BONE
BORDE (ESPINA) DEL HUESO
DE LA PALETA

BLADE BONE
HUESO DE LA PALETA
scapula / escápula

NECK BONES (7)
HUESOS DEL PESCUEZO (7)

ATLAS BONES
HUESO ATLAS

ARM BONE
HUESO DEL BRAZUELO
humerus / húmero

13th rib / 13ª costilla

1st rib / 1ª costilla

Courtesy of the American Meat Science Association. / Cortesía de la Asociación Americana de Ciencia de la Carne.

Beef Primal Cuts / Cortes de res primarios

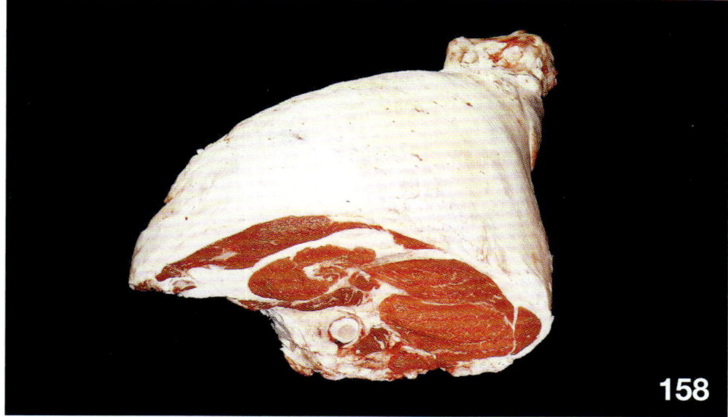

Beef Round
Pierna (Piña), Pieza Primaria

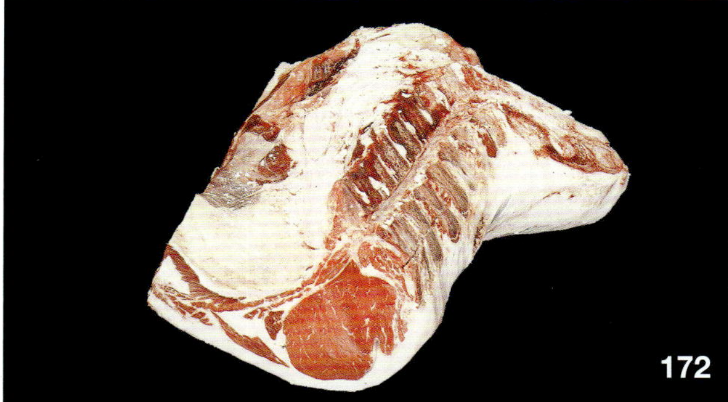

Beef Loin, Trimmed
Lomo, Lomo Completo (Full Loin), Recortado de Grasa y Limpio

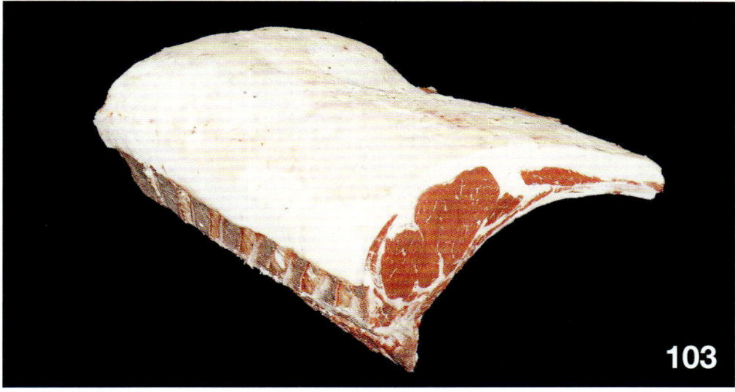

Beef Rib
Chuletón (Espaldar), Pieza Primaria

Beef Chuck, Square-Cut
Paleta (Espaldilla), Corte Cuadrado

Loin-Round Separation
Separación Lomo-Pierna

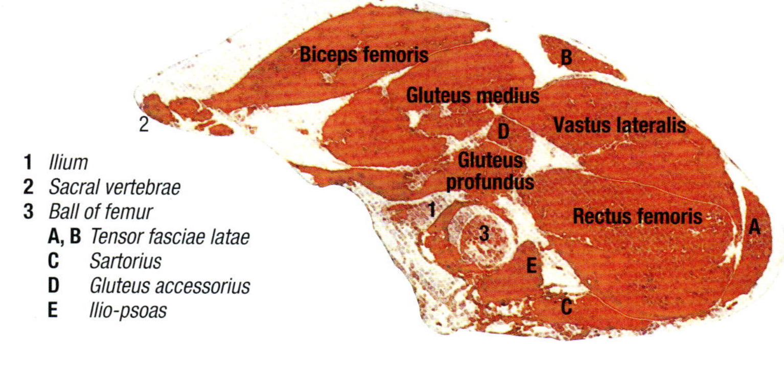

1 Ilium
2 Sacral vertebrae
3 Ball of femur
A, B Tensor fasciae latae
C Sartorius
D Gluteus accessorius
E Ilio-psoas

Rib-Loin Separation
Separación Chuletón (Espaldar)-Lomo

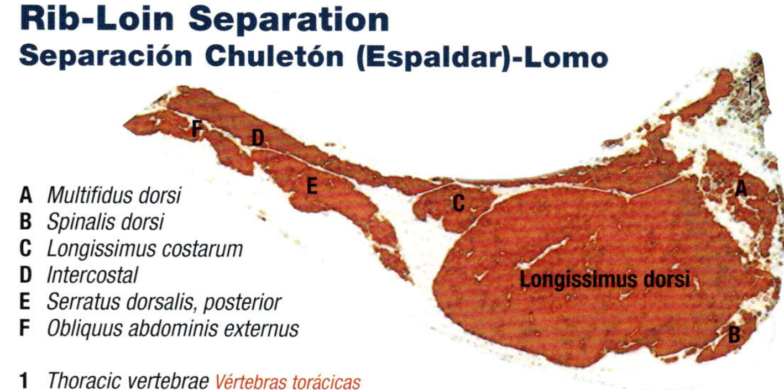

A Multifidus dorsi
B Spinalis dorsi
C Longissimus costarum
D Intercostal
E Serratus dorsalis, posterior
F Obliquus abdominis externus

1 Thoracic vertebrae *Vértebras torácicas*

Rib-Chuck Separation
Separación Chuletón (Espaldar)-Paleta

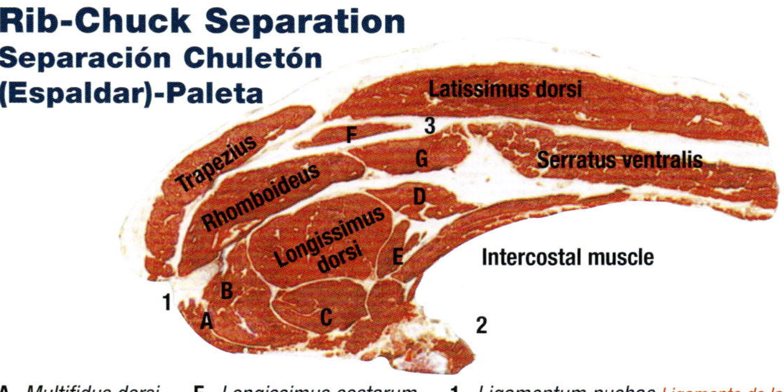

A Multifidus dorsi	E Longissimus costarum	1 Ligamentum nuchae *Ligamento de la nuca o banda ligamentosa nucal*
B Spinalis dorsi	F Infraspinatus	2 Thoracic vertebrae *Vértebras torácicas*
C Complexus	G Subscapularis	3 Scapula *Escápula*
D Serratus dorsalis		

Chuck-Brisket Separation
Separación Paleta-Pecho

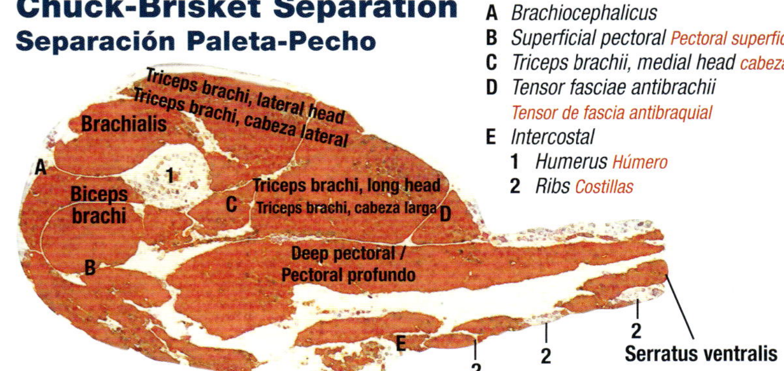

A Brachiocephalicus
B Superficial pectoral *Pectoral superficial*
C Triceps brachii, medial head *cabeza media*
D Tensor fasciae antibrachii *Tensor de fascia antibraquial*
E Intercostal
1 Humerus *Húmero*
2 Ribs *Costillas*

Index / Índice

Beef Products and Weight Ranges
Productos de res y escalas de peso

ITEM PIEZA	PRODUCT NAME / NOMBRE DE PRODUCTO	PG. PÁG.	Weight Ranges (pounds) / Escalas de peso (libras/kg) A	B	C	D
100	**Carcass** / Canal	15	500-600 (226.8-272.2)	600-700 (272.2-317.5)	700-800 (317.5-362.9)	800-up (Más de 362.9)
101	**Side** / Media Canal	15	250-300 (113.4-136.1)	300-350 (136.1-158.8)	350-400 (158.8-181.4)	400-up (Más de 181.4)
102	**Forequarter** / Cuarto Delantero	15	131-157 (59.4-71.2)	157-183 (71.2-83)	183-400 (83-181.4)	400-up (Más de 181.4)
103	**Rib, Primal** / Chuletón (Espaldar), Corte Primario	16	24–28 (10.9-12.7)	28–33 (12.7-15)	33–38 (15-17.2)	38-up (Más de 17.2)
107	**Rib, Oven-Prepared** / Chuletón (Espaldar), Preparado para Hornear	16	17–19 (7.7-8.6)	19–23 (8.6-10.4)	23–26 (10.4-11.8)	26-up (Más de 11.8)
109	**Rib, Roast-Ready** / Chuletón (Espaldar), Listo para Rostizar	17	14–16 (6.4-7.3)	16–19 (7.3-8.6)	19–22 (8.6-10)	22-up (Más de 10)
109A	**Rib, Roast-Ready, Special** / Chuletón (Espaldar), Listo para Rostizar, Especial	18	14–16 (6.4-7.3)	16–19 (7.3-8.6)	19–22 (8.6-10)	22-up (Más de 10)
109B	**Rib, Blade Meat** / Chuletón (Espaldar), Carne de Paleta (Tapas Interior y Exterior)	18	3-up (Más de 1.4)			
109D	**Rib, Roast-Ready, Cover Off, Short-Cut (Export Style)** / Chuletón (Espaldar), Listo para Rostizar, Sin Tapa, Pieza Corta (de Exportación)	18	12-14 (5.4-6.4)	14 – 17 (6.4-7.7)	17–20 (7.7-9.1)	20-up (Más de 9.1)
109E	**Rib, Ribeye Roll, Lip-On, Bone In (Export Style)** / Chuletón (Espaldar), Rollo de Ribeye, Con Cordón, Con Hueso (de Exportación)	19	11–13 (5-5.9)	13–16 (5.9-7.3)	16–19 (7.3-8.6)	20-up (Más de 9.1)
110	**Rib, Roast-Ready, Boneless** / Chuletón (Espaldar), Listo para Rostizar, Deshuesado	19	11–13 (5-5.9)	13–16 (5.9-7.3)	16–19 (7.3-8.6)	19-up (Más de 8.6)
112	**Rib, Ribeye Roll** / Chuletón (Espaldar), Rollo Ribeye	20	5–6 (2.3-2.7)	6–8 (2.7-3.6)	8-10 (3.6-4.5)	10-up (Más de 4.5)
112A	**Rib, Ribeye Roll, Lip-On** / Chuletón (Espaldar), Rollo Ribeye, con Cordón	19	6–7 (2.7-3.2)	7–9 (3.2-4.1)	9–11 (4.1-5)	11-up (Más de 5)
112C	**Rib, Ribeye (IM)** / Chuletón (Espaldar), Ribeye (Ojo del Chuletón), (MI)	20	4–6 (1.8-2.7)	6–8 (2.7-3.6)	8-10 (3.6-4.5)	10-up (Más de 4.5)
112D	**Rib, Ribeye Cap (IM)** / Chuletón (Espaldar), Tapa del Ribeye (MI)	20	Under 2 (Menos de 0.90)	2–4 (0.9-1.8)	4-up (Más de 1.8)	
113	**Chuck, Square-Cut** / Paleta (Espaldilla), Corte Cuadrado	21	66–79 (29.9-35.8)	79–93 (35.8-42.2)	93–106 (42.2-48.1)	106-up (Más de 48.1)
114	**Chuck, Shoulder (Clod)** / Paleta (Espaldilla), Planchuela	22	13–15 (5.9-6.8)	15–18 (6.8-8.2)	18–21 (8.2-9.5)	21-up (Más de 9.5)
114C	**Chuck, Shoulder (Clod), Trimmed** / Paleta (Espaldilla), Planchuela, Recortada de grasa	22	Under 12 (Menos de 5.4)	12-14 (5.4-6.4)	14 – 18 (6.4-8.2)	18-up (Más de 8.2)
114D	**Chuck, Shoulder (Clod), Top Blade** / Paleta (Espaldilla), Planchuela, Paletilla California (M. Infraespinoso)	23	Under 8 (Menos de 3.6)	8–10	10-12 (4.5–5.4)	12-up (Más de 5.4)
114E	**Chuck, Shoulder (Clod), Arm Roast** / Paleta (Espaldilla), Planchuela, Trozo Rosbif de Brazuelo	23	Under 8 (Menos de 3.6)	8-10 (3.6–4.5)	10-12 (4.5–5.4)	12-up (Más de 5.4)
114F	**Chuck, Shoulder Tender (IM)** / Paleta, Espaldilla, Teres Filé (MI)	24	Under 0.5 (Menos de 0.2)	0.5-up (Más de 0.2)		
115	**Chuck, Square-Cut, Boneless** / Paleta (Espaldilla), Corte Cuadrado, Deshuesada	24	54–65 (24.5-29.5)	65–77 (29.5-34.9)	77–88 (34.9-39.9)	88-up (Más de 39.9)
115D	**Chuck, Square-Cut, Pectoral Meat (IM)** / Paleta (Espaldilla), Corte Cuadrado, Carne del Pectoral (MI)	25	Under 5 (Menos de 2.3)	5-up (Más de 2.3)		
116A	**Chuck, Chuck Roll** / Paleta (Espaldilla), Rollo de Diezmillo, Deshuesado	25	13–15 (5.9-6.8)	15–18 (6.8-8.2)	18–21 (8.2-9.5)	21-up (Más de 9.5)
116B	**Chuck, Chuck Tender (IM)** / Paleta (Espaldilla), Juil (MI)	26	Under 1 (Menos de 0.45)	1–3 (0.45-1.4)	3-up (Más de 1.4)	
116D	**Chuck, Chuck Eye Roll** / Paleta (Espaldilla), Centro del Rollo de Diezmillo	26	Under 8 (Menos de 3.6)	8-10 (3.6–4.5)	10 – 14 (4.5-6.4)	14-up (Más de 6.4)
116E	**Chuck, Under Blade Roast** / Paleta (Espaldilla), Trozo Rosbif de la Tapa Interior de la Planchuela (Debajo de la Paleta)	26	Under 8 (Menos de 3.6)	8-10 (3.6–4.5)	10 – 14 (4.5-6.4)	14-up (Más de 6.4)
116G	**Chuck, Under Blade, Center-Cut (IM)** / Paleta (Espaldilla), Tapa Interior de la Planchuela, Corte del Centro (Rosbif Denver) (MI)	27	Under 7 (Menos de 3.2)	7-up (Más de 3.2)		
116H	**Chuck, Chuck Eye (IM)** / Paleta (Espaldilla), Corazón del Diezmillo (MI)	27	Under 4 (Menos de 1.8)	4-up (Más de 1.8)		
116I	**Chuck, Neck Roast** / Paleta (Espaldilla), Trozo Rosbif de Pescuezo	27	Under 5 (Menos de 2.3)	5-up (Más de 2.3)		
116K	**Chuck Roll, 3-Way** / Rollo de Diezmillo, en 3 piezas	27	10-12 (4.5–5.4)	12–16 (5.4-7.3)	16–19 (7.3-8.6)	19-up (Más de 8.6)
117	**Foreshank** / Chamberete de Mano	28	7–8 (3.2-3.6)	8-10 (3.6–4.5)	10-12 (4.5–5.4)	12-up (Más de 5.4)
120	**Brisket, Deckle-Off, Boneless** / Pecho, Sin Grasa Endurecida ni Carne Intercostal, Deshuesado	28	6–8 (2.7-3.6)	8-10 (3.6–4.5)	10-12 (4.5–5.4)	12-up (Más de 5.4)

ITEM PIEZA	PRODUCT NAME / NOMBRE DE PRODUCTO	PG. PÁG.	Weight Ranges (pounds) / Escalas de peso (libras/kg)			
			A	B	C	D
120A	**Brisket, Flat Cut, Boneless (IM)** Pecho, Falda de Pecho, Deshuesada (MI)	28	4–6 (1.8-2.7)	6–8 (2.7-3.6)	8-10 (3.6–4.5)	10-up (Más de 4.5)
120B	**Brisket, Point Cut, Boneless (IM)** Pecho, Punta de Pecho, Deshuesada (MI)	28	Under 3 (Menos de 1.4)	3–4 (1.4-1.8)	4–6 (1.8-2.7)	6-up (Más de 2.7)
120C	**Brisket, 2-Piece, Boneless** Pecho, en 2 piezas (Falda y Punta), Deshuesado	29	6–8 (2.7-3.6)	8-10 (3.6–4.5)	10-12 (4.5–5.4)	12-up (Más de 5.4)
121	**Plate, Short Plate** Costillar (Aguja), Costillar Corto (Costilla Cargada Completa)	29	20–27 (9.1-12.2)	27–31 (12.2-14.1)	31–35 (14.1-15.9)	35-up (Más de 15.9)
121C	**Plate, Outside Skirt (IM)** Costillar, Arrachera Delgada Regular (MI)	29	1–2 (0.45-0.90)	2–3 (0.90-1.4)	3-up (Más de 1.4)	
121D	**Plate, Inside Skirt (IM)** Costillar, Falda Interna/Arrachera Inside (MI)	29	1–3 (0.45-1.4)	3–4 (1.4-1.8)	4-up (Más de 1.8)	
123	**Short Ribs** Costillar, Costillas (Agujas) Cortas, 2 o 5 Costillas (6ª-10ª) (M. Serrato Ventral)	30	2–3 (0.90-1.4)	3–4 (1.4-1.8)	4–5 (1.8-2.3)	5-up (Más de 2.3)
123A	**Short Plate, Short Ribs, Trimmed** Costillar, Costilla Cargada, Costillas (Agujas) Cortas (6ª-8ª), Recortadas de Grasa y Limpias	30	Amount as Specified / Cantidad según lo especificado			
123B	**Rib, Short Ribs, Trimmed** Chuletón (Espaldar), Costillas (Agujas) Cortas (6ª-8ª), Limpias	31	Amount as Specified / Cantidad según lo especificado			
123C	**Rib, Short Ribs** Chuletón (Espaldar), Costillas (Agujas) Cortas (6ª-8ª)	31	Amount as Specified / Cantidad según lo especificado			
123D	**Short Ribs, Boneless (IM)** Costilla Cargada, Costillas (Agujas) Cortas (6ª-8ª), (MI)	31	1–2 (0.45-0.90)	2–3 (0.90-1.4)	3–4 (1.4-1.8)	4-up (Más de 1.8)
124	**Rib, Back Ribs** Chuletón (Espaldar), Costillas del Chuletón/Ribeye	31	Amount as Specified / Cantidad según lo especificado			
124A	**Rib, Back Rib, Rib Fingers** Chuletón (Espaldar), Costillas del Chuletón, Tiras de Entrecostilla (M. Intercostales)	32	Amount as Specified / Cantidad según lo especificado			
130	**Chuck, Short Ribs** Paleta (Espaldilla), Costillas Cortas de Espaldilla (2ª-5ª)	32	2–3 (0.90-1.4)	3–4 (1.4-1.8)	4–5 (1.8-2.3)	5-up (Más de 2.3)
130A	**Chuck, Short Ribs, Boneless** Paleta (Espaldilla), Costillas Cortas de Espaldilla (2ª-5ª), Deshuesadas (M. Serrato Ventral)	32	.5–1.5 (0.22-0.68)	1.5–2.5 (0.68-1.1)	2.5–3.5 (1.1-1.6)	3.5-up (Más de 1.6)
134	**Beef Bones** Huesos de la Res	33	Amount as Specified / Cantidad según lo especificado			
135	**Diced Beef** Trozos de Res en Cubos	33	Amount as Specified / Cantidad según lo especificado			
135A	**Beef for Stewing** Trozos de Res en Cubos para Cocido/Guisado	33	Amount as Specified / Cantidad según lo especificado			
135B	**Beef for Kabobs** Trozos de Res para Brochetas	34	Amount as Specified / Cantidad según lo especificado			
136	**Ground Beef** Carne Molida de Res	34	Amount as Specified / Cantidad según lo especificado			
136A	**Beef and Soy Protein Product Patty Mix** Carne Molida de Res con Producto Proteico Vegetal (PPV) Añadido Según La Normativa	36	Amount as Specified / Cantidad según lo especificado			
136C	**Beef Patty Mix, Not to Exceed (NTE) 10% Fat** Mezcla para Hamburguesa de Res (con PPV Sin Exceder 10%), Magra (sin Exceder 10% Grasa)	37	Amount as Specified / Cantidad según lo especificado			
136D	**Pure Beef** Pura Carne de Res	37	Amount as Specified / Cantidad según lo especificado			
137	**Ground Beef, Special** Carne Molida de Res, Especial	38	Amount as Specified / Cantidad según lo especificado			
138	**Beef Trimmings** Carne de Res, Recortes	39	Amount as Specified / Cantidad según lo especificado			
139	**Beef Special Trim, Boneless** Carne de Res, Recortes Especiales, Deshuesados	39	Amount as Specified / Cantidad según lo especificado			
140	**Hanging Tender (IM)** Arrachera Gallo (MI)	39	Under 3 (Menos de 1.4)	3-up (Más de 1.4)		
155	**Hindquarter** Cuarto Trasero	15	119–143 (54-64.9)	143–167 (64.9-75.8)	167–190 (75.8-86.2)	190-up (Más de 86.2)
158	**Round, Primal** Pierna (Piña), Pieza Primaria Hip / Cadera	40	59–71 (26.8-32.2)	71–83 (32.2-37.6)	83–95 (37.6-43.1)	95-up (Más de 43.1)
158A	**Round, Diamond-Cut** Pierna (Piña), Forma Diamante	40	63–76 (28.6-34.5)	76–89 (34.5-40.4)	89–102 (40.4-46.3)	102-up (Más de 46.3)
159	**Round, Primal, Boneless** Pierna (Piña), Pieza Primaria, Deshuesada	41	44–53 (20-24)	53–62 (24-28.1)	62–71 (28.1-32.2)	71-up (Más de 32.2)
160	**Round, Shank Off, Partially Boneless** Pierna (Piña), sin Chamberete, Parcialmente Deshuesada	41	47–57 (21.3-25.9)	57–67 (25.9-30.4)	67–76 (30.4-34.5)	76-up (Más de 34.5)

Index / Índice

Beef Products and Weight Ranges
Productos de res y escalas de peso

ITEM PIEZA	PRODUCT NAME / NOMBRE DE PRODUCTO	PG. PÁG.	Weight Ranges (pounds) / Escalas de peso (libras/kg)			
			A	B	C	D
160B	Round, Heel and Shank Off, Semi-Boneless Pierna (Piña), sin Talón/Copete ni Chamberete, Parcialmente Deshuesada	42	38–46 (17.2-20.9)	46–54 (20.9-24.5)	54–60 (24.5-27.2)	60-up (Más de 27.2)
161	Round, Shank Off, Boneless Pierna (Piña), sin Chamberete, Deshuesada	42	42–51 (19.1-23.1)	51–62 (23.1-28.1)	62–71 (28.1-32.2)	71-up (Más de 32.2)
161B	Round, Heel & Shank Off, Without Sirloin Tip (Knuckle), Boneless Pierna (Piña), sin Talón/Copete, Sin Chamberete ni Pulpa Bola, Deshuesada	42	30–37 (13.6-16.8)	37–44 (16.8-19.9)	44–51 (19.9-23.1)	51-up (Más de 23.1)
163	Round, Shank Off, 3-Way, Boneless Pierna (Piña), sin Chamberete, 3 Piezas, Deshuesada	42	41–50 (18.6-22.7)	50–58 (22.7-26.3)	58–66 (26.3-29.9)	66-up (Más de 29.9)
166A	Round, Rump Partially Removed, Shank Off Pierna (Piña) Corta, Tajo Anterior de Pulpa Blanca Parcialmente Retirado, Sin Chamberete, Deshuesada, Atada en Malla	43	44–52 (20-23.6)	52–61 (23.6-27.7)	61–70 (27.7-31.8)	70-up (Más de 31.8)
166B	Round, Rump and Shank Partially Off, Handle On Pierna (Piña) Corta, Sin Tajo Anterior de Pulpa Blanca ni Chamberete, Con Mango	43	44–52 (20-23.6)	52–61 (23.6-27.7)	61–70 (27.7-31.8)	70-up (Más de 31.8)
167	Round, Sirloin Tip (Knuckle) Pierna (Piña), Punta de Sirloin (Pulpa Bola)	44	8–9 (3.6-4.1)	9–11 (4.1-5)	11–13 (5-5.9)	13-up (Más de 5.9)
167A	Round, Sirloin Tip (Knuckle), Peeled Pierna (Piña), Punta de Sirloin (Pulpa Bola), Desprovisto de Grasa	44	7–8 (3.2-3.6)	8-10 (3.6–4.5)	10-12 (4.5-5.4)	12-up (Más de 5.4)
167D	Round, Sirloin Tip (Knuckle), Peeled, 2-Piece Pierna (Piña), Punta de Sirloin (Pulpa Bola), Desprovistas de Grasa, 2 piezas	45	5 – 7 (2.3-3.2)	7–9 (3.2-4.1)	9–12 (4.1-5.4)	12-up (Más de 5.4)
167E	Round, Sirloin Tip (Knuckle), Center Roast (IM) Pierna (Piña), Punta de Sirloin (Pulpa Bola), Trozo Rosbif del Centro (MI)	45	2–3 (0.90-1.4)	3 – 5 (1.4-2.3)	5-up (Más de 2.3)	
167F	Round, Sirloin Tip (Knuckle), Side Roast (IM) Pierna (Piña), Punta de Sirloin (Pulpa Bola), Trozo Rosbif Lateral (MI)	45	2–3 (0.90-1.4)	3–4 (1.4-1.8)	4-up (Más de 1.8)	
168	Round, Top (Inside), Untrimmed Pierna (Piña), Pulpa Negra (Cara/Centro), sin Recortado de Grasa y sin Limpiar	45	14 – 17 (6.4-7.7)	17–20 (7.7-9.1)	20–23 (9.1-10.4)	23-up (Más de 10.4)
169	Round, Top (Inside) Pierna (Piña), Pulpa Negra (Cara/Centro), Semi-Recortada de Grasa	46	14 – 17 (6.4-7.7)	17–20 (7.7-9.1)	20–23 (9.1-10.4)	23-up (Más de 10.4)
169A	Round, Top (Inside), Cap Off Pierna (Piña), Pulpa Negra (Cara/Centro), sin Tapa	46	12–15 (5.4-6.8)	15–18 (6.8-8.2)	18–20 (8.2-9.1)	20-up (Más de 9.1)
169B	Round, Top (Inside), Cap (IM) Pierna (Piña), Pulpa Negra (Cara/Centro), Tapa (MI)	46	1–2 (0.45-0.90)	2–3 (0.90-1.4)	3-up (Más de 1.4)	
169C	Round, Top (Inside), Front Side Muscle (IM) Pierna (Piña), Pulpa Negra (Cara/Centro), Músculo del Lado Frontal (MI)	47	Under 1 (Menos de 0.45)	1-up (Más de 0.45)		
170	Round, Bottom (Gooseneck) Pierna (Piña), Contracara con Cuete	47	18–23 (8.2-10.4)	23–27 (10.4-12.2)	27–31 (12.2-14.1)	31-up (Más de 14.1)
170A	Round, Bottom (Gooseneck), Heel Out Pierna (Piña), Contracara con Cuete, sin Talón/Copete	47	17–20 (7.7-9.1)	20–24 (9.1-10.9)	24–28 (10.9-12.7)	28-up (Más de 12.7)
171B	Round, Outside Round (Flat) Pierna (Piña), Contracara, Pulpa Blanca	48	8-10 (3.6-4.5)	10–13 (4.5-5.9)	13–16 (5.9-7.3)	16-up (Más de 7.3)
171C	Round, Eye of Round (IM) Pierna (Piña), Contracara, Cuete (MI)	48	Under 3 (Menos de 1.4)	3 – 5 (1.4-2.3)	5-up (Más de 2.3)	
171D	Round, Outside Round, Side Muscle Removed (IM) Pierna (Piña), Contracara, Pulpa Blanca, Retirando Músculo de al lado (MI)	48	4–6 (1.8-2.7)	6–8 (2.7-3.6)	8–12 (3.6-5.4)	12-up (Más de 5.4)
171E	Round, Outside Round, Side Roast (IM) Pierna (Piña), Contracara (Pulpa Blanca), Trozo Rosbif de Músculo Pegado al Lado (MI)	49	2–3 (0.90-1.4)	3 – 5 (1.4-2.3)	5-up (Más de 2.3)	
171F	Round, Outside Round, Heel Pierna (Piña), Contracara, Talón (Copete)	49	3 – 5 (1.4-2.3)	5 – 7 (2.3-3.2)	7-up (Más de 3.2)	
171G	Round, Outside Round, Rump (IM) Pierna (Piña), Contracara, Tajo Anterior de Pulpa Blanca (MI)	49	2–3 (0.90-1.4)	3 – 5 (1.4-2.3)	5-up (Más de 2.3)	
172	Loin, Full Loin, Trimmed Lomo, Lomo Completo (Full Loin), Recortado de Grasa y Limpio	50	30–37 (13.6-16.8)	37–45 (16.8-20.4)	45–52 (20.4-23.6)	52-up (Más de 23.6)
172A	Loin, Full Loin, Diamond-Cut, Trimmed Lomo, Lomo Completo (Full Loin), Forma Diamante, Recortado de Grasa y Limpio	50	35–42 (15.9-19.1)	42–50 (19.1-22.7)	50–57 (22.7-25.9)	57-up (Más de 25.9)
174	Loin, Short Loin, Short-Cut Lomo, Lomo Corto (Short Loin), Acortado	51	14–20 (6.4-9.1)	20–25 (9.1-11.3)	25–30 (11.3-13.6)	30-up (Más de 13.6)
175	Loin, Strip Loin, Bone In Lomo, Strip Loin (New York), Con Hueso	52	11–14 (5-6.4)	14 – 18 (6.4-8.2)	18 – 22 (8.2-10)	22-up (Más de 10)
176	Loin, Steak Tail Lomo, Bistec de Cola de Falda	53	0.6–0.75 (0.27-0.34)	0.75–0.9 (0.34-0.41)	0.9–1.00 (0.41-0.45)	1-up (Más de 0.45)
180	Loin, Strip Loin, Boneless Lomo, Strip Loin (New York), Deshuesado	53	8-10 (3.6-4.5)	10-12 (4.5-5.4)	12-14 (5.4-6.4)	14-up (Más de 6.4)
180B	Loin, Strip Loin, Split, Boneless Lomo, Strip Loin (New York), Dividido, Deshuesado	54	8-10 (3.6-4.5)	10-12 (4.5-5.4)	12-14 (5.4-6.4)	14-up (Más de 6.4)

ITEM PIEZA	PRODUCT NAME NOMBRE DE PRODUCTO	PG. PÁG.	Weight Ranges (pounds) / Escalas de peso (libras/kg)			
			A	B	C	D
181	**Loin, Sirloin** Lomo, Sirloin (Aguayón) con Hueso	54	16–19 (7.3-8.6)	19–24 (8.6-10.9)	24–28 (10.9-12.7)	28-up (Más de 12.7)
181A	**Loin, Top Sirloin, Bone In** Lomo, Top Sirloin (Aguayón Superior y Algo de Empuje), Con Hueso	54	11–14 (5-6.4)	14 – 17 (6.4-7.7)	17–20 (7.7-9.1)	20-up (Más de 9.1)
184	**Loin, Top Sirloin Butt, Boneless** Lomo, Pulpa del Aguayón Superior/Top Sirloin, Aguayón con Tapa, Deshuesado	55	8-10 (3.6–4.5)	10-12 (4.5-5.4)	12-14 (5.4–6.4)	14-up (Más de 6.4)
184A	**Loin, Top Sirloin Butt, Semi Center-Cut, Boneless** Lomo, Pulpa del Aguayón Superior/Top Sirloin, Aguayón sin Tapa, Corte Casi del Centro, Deshuesado	55	7–9 (3.2-4.1)	9–11 (4.1-5)	11–13 (5-5.9)	13-up (Más de 5.9)
184B	**Loin, Top Sirloin Butt, Center-Cut, Boneless, Cap Off (IM)** Lomo, Pulpa del Aguayón Superior/Top Sirloin (Aguayón sin Tapa), Corte del Centro, Deshuesado (MI)	56	5 – 7 (2.3-3.2)	7–9 (3.2-4.1)	9–11 (4.1-5)	11-up (Más de 5)
184D	**Loin, Top Sirloin, Cap (IM)** Lomo, Aguayón Superior/Top Sirloin, Tapa del Aguayón (MI)	56	1–2 (0.45-0.90)	2–3 (0.90-1.4)	3–4 (1.4-1.8)	4-up (Más de 1.8)
184E	**Loin, Top Sirloin Butt, Boneless, 2-Piece** Lomo, Pulpa del Aguayón Superior/Top Sirloin (Aguayón y Tapa), Deshuesados y Recortados de grasa, en 2 piezas	56	8–9 (3.6-4.1)	9–11 (4.1-5)	11–13 (5-5.9)	13-up (Más de 5.9)
184F	**Loin, Top Sirloin Butt, Center-Cut, Boneless, Seamed, Dorsal Side (IM)** Lomo, Pulpa del Aguayón Superior/Top Sirloin, Aguayón, Corte del Centro, Deshuesado, Diseccionado por las Vetas Naturales, Lado Dorsal (MI)	57	Under 3 (Menos de 1.4)	3-up (Más de 1.4)		
185	**Loin, Bottom Sirloin Butt, Boneless** Lomo, Pulpa del Aguayón Inferior/Bottom Sirloin (Empuje, Punta de Pulpa Bola y Falda), Deshuesado	57	5–6 (2.3-2.7)	6–7 (2.7-3.2)	7–8 (3.2-3.6)	8-up (Más de 3.6)
185A	**Loin, Bottom Sirloin Butt, Flap, Boneless (IM)** Lomo, Pulpa del Aguayón Inferior/Bottom Sirloin, Falda/Aldilla, Deshuesada (MI)	57	1–3 (0.45-1.4)	3-up (Más de 1.4)		
185B	**Loin, Bottom Sirloin Butt, Ball Tip, Boneless** Lomo, Pulpa del Aguayón Inferior/Bottom Sirloin, Punta de Pulpa Bola, Deshuesada	58	1.5–3 (0.68-1.4)	3-up (Más de 1.4)		
185C	**Loin, Bottom Sirloin Butt, Tri-Tip, Boneless (IM)** Lomo, Pulpa del Aguayón Inferior/Bottom Sirloin, Empuje (Punta Triangular), Deshuesado (MI)	58	1.5–3 (0.68-1.4)	3-up (Más de 1.4)		
185D	**Loin, Bottom Sirloin Butt, Tri-Tip, Boneless, Defatted (IM)** Lomo, Pulpa del Aguayón Inferior/Bottom Sirloin, Empuje (Punta Triangular), Deshuesado, Limpio de Grasa (MI)	58	1.5–3 (0.68-1.4)	3-up (Más de 1.4)		
188	**Loin, Tenderloin, Bone In** Lomo, Filete Cabrería Corto, con Hueso	58	5–6 (2.3-2.7)	6–7 (2.7-3.2)	7–8 (3.2-3.6)	8-up (Más de 3.6)
189	**Loin, Tenderloin, Full** Lomo, Filete, Completo, sin Hueso	59	4–5 (1.8-2.3)	5–6 (2.3-2.7)	6–7 (2.7-3.2)	7-up (Más de 3.2)
189A	**Loin, Tenderloin, Full, Side Muscle On, Defatted** Lomo, Filete, Completo, con Cuerda (Psoas Menor) Pegado, Limpio de Grasa	59	3–4 (1.4-1.8)	4–5 (1.8-2.3)	5–6 (2.3-2.7)	6-up (Más de 2.7)
190	**Loin, Tenderloin, Full, Side Muscle Off, Defatted** Lomo, Filete, Completo, sin Cuerda (Psoas Menor), Limpio de Grasa	60	2–3 (0.90-1.4)	3–4 (1.4-1.8)	4-up (Más de 1.8)	
190A	**Loin, Tenderloin, Full, Side Muscle Off, Skinned** Lomo, Filete, Completo, sin Cuerda (Psoas Menor), Despellejado	60	2–3 (0.90-1.4)	3–4 (1.4-1.8)	4-up (Más de 1.8)	
190B	**Loin, Tenderloin, Full, Side Muscle Off, Center-Cut, Skinned (IM)** Lomo, Filete, Completo, sin Cuerda (Psoas Menor), Corte del Medio (Sin Cabeza ni Cola), Despellejado (MI)	60	1.5-2.5 (0.68-1.1)	2.5-3.5 (1.1-1.6)	3.5-up (Más de 1.6)	
191	**Loin, Tenderloin, Butt** Lomo, Filete, Cabeza (Porción en el Aguayón)	61	1–2 (0.45-0.90)	2–3 (0.90-1.4)	3–4 (1.4-1.8)	4-up (Más de 1.8)
191A	**Loin, Tenderloin, Butt, Defatted** Lomo, Filete, Cabeza, Limpia de Grasa	61	1–2 (0.45-0.90)	2–3 (0.90-1.4)	3–4 (1.4-1.8)	4-up (Más de 1.8)
191B	**Loin, Tenderloin, Butt, Skinned** Lomo, Filete, Cabeza, Despellejada	61	Under 2 (Menos de 0.90)	2–3 (0.90-1.4)	3-up (Más de 1.4)	
192	**Loin, Tenderloin, Short** Lomo, Filete, Corto	62	2–3 (0.90-1.4)	3–4 (1.4-1.8)	4-up (Más de 1.8)	
192A	**Loin, Tenderloin Tails** Lomo, Filete, Colas (Puntas)	62	Amount as Specified Cantidad según lo especificado			
193	**Flank, Flank Steak (IM)** Falda (Ijar), Concha de Falda (MI)	62	Under 1 (Menos de 0.45)	1–2 (0.45-0.90)	2-up (Más de 0.90)	

Información para hacer los pedidos

Opciones especificadas por el comprador

Los compradores pueden especificar varias opciones diferentes en los productos que desean comprar. Estas opciones incluyen, entre otras, el grado de calidad, el grado oficial de rendimiento, el estado de refrigeración, las medidas de limitación de grasa y las instrucciones de procesamiento. Los aspectos detallados en el texto pueden incluir también requisitos específicos de la descripción de la pieza del producto, u ofrecer una variedad de opciones de especificaciones del comprador. Algunas de estas opciones se explican más detalladamente en la sección introductoria al comienzo de la *Guía para Compradores de Carne*, o más adelante en esta sección, o en la descripción de la pieza correspondiente. Los compradores que tengan necesidades o especificaciones especiales deben comunicarse con sus proveedores.

Estado de refrigeración

A **FRESCO**	−2.2 °C (28 °F) o mayor
B **CONGELADO**	−2.2 °C (28 °F) o menor
C **OPCIÓN ESPECIFICADA POR EL COMPRADOR**	−17.8 °C (0 °F) o menor

El producto se puede pedir fresco o congelado. El término *refrigerado en estado fresco* es utilizado por el Servicio de Mercadeo Agrícola del Departamento de Agricultura de E.U.A. para describir los productos que no han sido congelados anteriormente.

Grado

Los compradores pueden solicitar una clasificación por grado de calidad o de rendimiento específicos, o una combinación de grado de calidad y grado de rendimiento. También pueden realizar su compra de carne de res sin estipular ningún tipo de grado. La sección al frente de esta guía contiene descripciones de clasificación por grados de calidad y de rendimiento de carne de res, ilustraciones de marmoleado de carne de res, una explicación de las opciones de clasificación disponibles, y los requisitos de etiquetado que se aplican para identificar el producto, paquete o recipiente. La División de Certificación y Clasificación de Carne del Servicio de Mercadeo Agrícola del Departamento de Agricultura de E.U.A. o, en Canadá, la Agencia Canadiense de Clasificación de Carne de Res determinan oficialmente los grados de calidad de la carne de res.

Opciones para limitar la grasa

Canales y Cuartos

El comprador deberá especificar el grado de rendimiento y/o el grosor promedio máximo de cubierta de grasa.

Cortes y Rosbifs

El comprador especificará uno de los siguientes grosores promedio máximos de cubierta de grasa, a menos que se indiquen limitaciones precisas de grasa en la descripción detallada de la pieza.

Cortes y Rosbifs		
N° de opción	**Grosor promedio máximo**	**Máximo en un punto cualquiera**
1	19 mm (0.75 pulgadas) con recorte de grasa y limpieza tipo commodity	2.5 cm (1.0 pulgada)
2	6 mm (0.25 pulgadas)	13 mm (0.50 pulgadas)
3	3 mm (0.125 pulgadas)	6 mm (0.25 pulgadas)
4	Prácticamente libre de grasa (el 75% de la superficie es carne magra/superficie muscular descubierta por la disección)	3 mm (0.125 pulgadas)
5	Desprovisto de grasa/Prácticamente desnudo de grasa* [la grasa que queda no debe exceder los 2.5 cm (1.0 pulgada) en la dimensión más larga y/o 3 mm (0.125 pulgadas) de grosor]	3 mm (0.125 pulgadas)
6	Desprovisto de grasa/Prácticamente desnudo de grasa, Membrana superficial retirada** (el 90% de la superficie expuesta es magra)	3 mm (0.125 pulgadas)

*/** − consulte la definición en la página xlii

*** Importante: cuando se especifiquen los grosores promedio de grasa en la descripción de la pieza, se aplicará la limitación "Máximo en un punto cualquiera" correspondiente.**

Es posible encontrar información sobre nomenclatura acerca de musculatura bovina en el sitio web de la Universidad de Nebraska, en: http://bovine.unl.edu

Ordering Data

Purchaser Specified Options (PSO)

Purchasers may specify a number of different options on the products they wish to purchase. These options (PSO) include, among others, quality grade, yield grade, state of refrigeration, fat limitation measurements, and processing instructions. Items listed in the text may also include specific requirements in the Item Description of the product, and/or offer a range of PSO choices. Some of these options are explained in more detail in the Introductory Section at the front of *The Meat Buyer's Guide*, or later in this section, or in the appropriate Item Description. Purchasers who have special needs or specifications should contact their suppliers.

State of Refrigeration

A **FRESH**	28°F (−2.2°C) or higher
B **FROZEN**	28°F (−2.2°C) or lower
C **PSO**	0°F (−17.8°C) or lower

Product may be ordered fresh or frozen. The term *fresh chilled* is used by the USDA Agricultural Marketing Service to describe product that has not been previously frozen.

Grade

Purchasers may request a specific quality or yield grade, or a combination of quality and yield grade, or make their beef purchase without stipulating any grade whatsoever. Descriptions of beef quality and yield grades, beef marbling pictures, an explanation of the available grading options, and the labeling requirements that apply to identify the product, package, or container appear in the front section of this guide. Beef quality grades are officially determined by the Meat Grading and Certification Branch of the USDA Agricultural Marketing Service or in Canada by the Canadian Beef Grading Agency.

Fat Limitation Options (FLO)

Carcasses and Quarters

The purchaser shall specify yield grade and/or maximum average thickness of surface fat.

Cuts and Roasts

The purchaser shall specify one of the following maximum average thicknesses of surface fat unless definite fat limitations are indicated in the detailed Item Descriptions.

Cuts and Roasts

Option No.	Maximum Average Thickness	Maximum at Any One Point
1	0.75 inch (19 mm) "Commodity trim"	1.0 inch (2.5 cm)
2	0.25 inch (6 mm)	0.50 inch (13 mm)
3	0.125 inch (3 mm)	0.25 inch (6 mm)
4	Practically Free (75 percent lean/seam surface exposed)	0.125 inch (3 mm)
5	Peeled/Denuded* (remaining fat shall not exceed 1.0 inch (2.5 cm) in the longest dimension and/or 0.125 inch (3 mm) in thickness)	0.125 inch (3 mm)
6	Peeled/Denuded, Surface Membrane Removed** (90 percent lean exposed)	0.125 inch (3 mm)

*/** – see page xvi for definition

*** Note: When average fat thicknesses are specified in Item Descriptions, the appropriate "Maximum at Any One Point" limitation shall apply.**

Information on Beef muscle nomenclature may be found on the University of Nebraska website at: http://bovine.unl.edu

Center of the Plate Training®

from the producers of *The Meat Buyer's Guide®*

Capacitación en ingredientes principales del plato

de los realizadores de la Guía para Compradores de Carne®

Course Specifics

Center of the Plate Training® offered by the North American Meat Processors Association (NAMP) is a first-hand look at how carcasses are converted into portioned items commonly traded in the foodservice and retail meat business. The course covers all the major center of the plate protein items: beef, veal, lamb, pork, and poultry (in some locations).

This course is held two to three times annually across North America. It spans two to three days of classroom learning, with presentations by industry experts. You also will receive a copy of the NAMP *Meat Buyer's Guide®*, which is used extensively in the course.

What You Will Learn From This Course

- The IMPS/NAMP numbering system, purchase specified options, and standards common to the industry.

- A knowledge of meat items as described by IMPS and by NAMP's *Meat Buyer's Guide®*.

- Where meat products originate and how this affects their final use.

- The importance of standards and how they keep products consistent, wholesome, and fair throughout the market.

- Common defects or inconsistencies in meat products that you should look for to prevent dissatisfied customers or unpleasant dining experiences.

- Current trends in the foodservice industry, new menu ideas and options.

- How value is determined for different meat products and how this is affected by quality parameters.

If you're involved in the buying and selling of meat products - from restaurants and supermarkets to foodservice distributors and meat companies - gain a competitive edge by applying the valuable information you'll learn from this course.

Visit www.namp.com for more information on specific courses, locations, and dates.

Visite www.namp.com para obtener información adicional sobre cursos específicos, sitios y fechas.

Detalles del curso

La Capacitación en ingredientes principales del plato que ofrece la Asociación Norteamericana de Procesadores de Carne (NAMP) es una mirada de primera mano a la forma en que las canales se convierten en piezas porcionadas comúnmente comercializadas en la industria de servicios de alimentación y los negocios minoristas de carne. El curso comprende las principales piezas proteicas que constituyen los ingredientes principales del plato: carne de res, ternera, cordero, cerdo y aves (en algunos lugares).

Este curso se dicta dos o tres veces al año en toda Norteamérica. Abarca de dos a tres días de aprendizaje en un salón de clase, con presentaciones a cargo de expertos de la industria. También recibirá una copia de *La Guía para Compradores de Carne®* de NAMP (Asociación Norteamericana de Procesadores de Carne, por sus siglas en inglés) que se utilizará exhaustivamente en el curso.

Qué aprenderá en este curso

- El sistema de numeración IMPS/NAMP, las opciones especificadas de compra y las normas comunes de la industria.

- Un conocimiento de las piezas de carne como se describen en las IMPS (Especificaciones Institucionales de Compra de Carne, por sus siglas en inglés) y en *La Guía para Compradores de Carne®* de NAMP.

- Dónde se originan los productos de carne y cómo afecta esto su uso final.

- La importancia de las normas y cómo logran que los productos sean uniformes, saludables y buenos en todo el mercado.

- Defectos o anomalías en los productos de carne que debería buscar para evitar clientes insatisfechos o que tengan experiencias desagradables en la mesa.

- Las tendencias actuales de la industria de servicios de alimentación, nuevas ideas y opciones para su menú.

- Cómo se determina el valor de diferentes productos de carne y cómo éste se ve afectado por los parámetros de calidad.

Si participa en la compra y venta de productos de carne, ya sea en restaurantes y supermercados o distribuidores de la industria de servicios de alimentación y empresas de carne, obtenga una ventaja competitiva aplicando la valiosa información que aprenderá en este curso.

100 — Beef Carcass

The carcass shall consist of two matched sides, each consisting of a forequarter and a hindquarter. The sides shall be produced by splitting the carcass down the back exposing the spinal groove at least 75 percent of the length of either side. No more than a minor amount of major muscles shall be removed from either side. The forequarters and hindquarters are produced by completely or partially separating the quarters from the carcass by a cut following the natural curvature between the 12th and 13th ribs. The diaphragm may be excluded; however, if present, it shall be firmly attached and the membranous portion shall be trimmed close to the lean. The thymus gland and heart fat shall be closely trimmed and excluded. Purchasers for export may request that carcasses be separated differently.

100 — Canal

La canal consistirá en dos medias canales o lados equivalentes, cada uno consistente en un cuarto delantero y un cuarto trasero. Las medias canales deberán obtenerse mediante la separación de la canal a lo largo de la columna vertebral, exponiendo el canal raquídeo al menos en el 75% de la longitud de cada lado. No se retirará más de una pequeña cantidad de los músculos principales de cada lado. Los cuartos delanteros y los cuartos traseros se obtienen separando completa o parcialmente los cuartos de la canal mediante un corte que siga la curvatura natural entre la 12ª y la 13ª costilla. Puede excluirse el diafragma; pero si está presente, deberá estar firmemente unido y la porción membranosa deberá ser despellejada de grasa casi hasta la parte magra. Se deberá limpiar y extraer cuidadosamente el timo y la grasa del corazón. Para exportación, los compradores pueden solicitar que las canales se separen en forma diferente.

101 — Beef Side

This item is as described in Item No. 100, except the side is one matched forequarter and hindquarter. The side shall be trimmed as described in Item No. 100.

101 — Media Canal

Esta pieza aparece descrita en la pieza número 100, excepto que el cuarto delantero y el cuarto trasero pertenecen al mismo lado. La media canal deberá ser recortada de grasa según se describe en la pieza número 100.

102 — Beef Forequarter

The beef forequarter is the anterior portion of the side after severance from the hindquarter as described in Item No. 100. The forequarter shall be trimmed as described in Item No. 100.

102 — Cuarto Delantero

El cuarto delantero es la pieza anterior de la media canal después de su separación del cuarto trasero como se describe en la pieza número 100. El cuarto delantero deberá ser recortado de grasa según la descripción contenida en la pieza número 100.

155 — Beef Hindquarter

The hindquarter is the posterior portion of the side after severance from the forequarter as described in Item No. 100.

155 — Cuarto Trasero

El cuarto trasero es la pieza posterior de la media canal después de su separación del cuarto delantero según se describe en la pieza número 100.

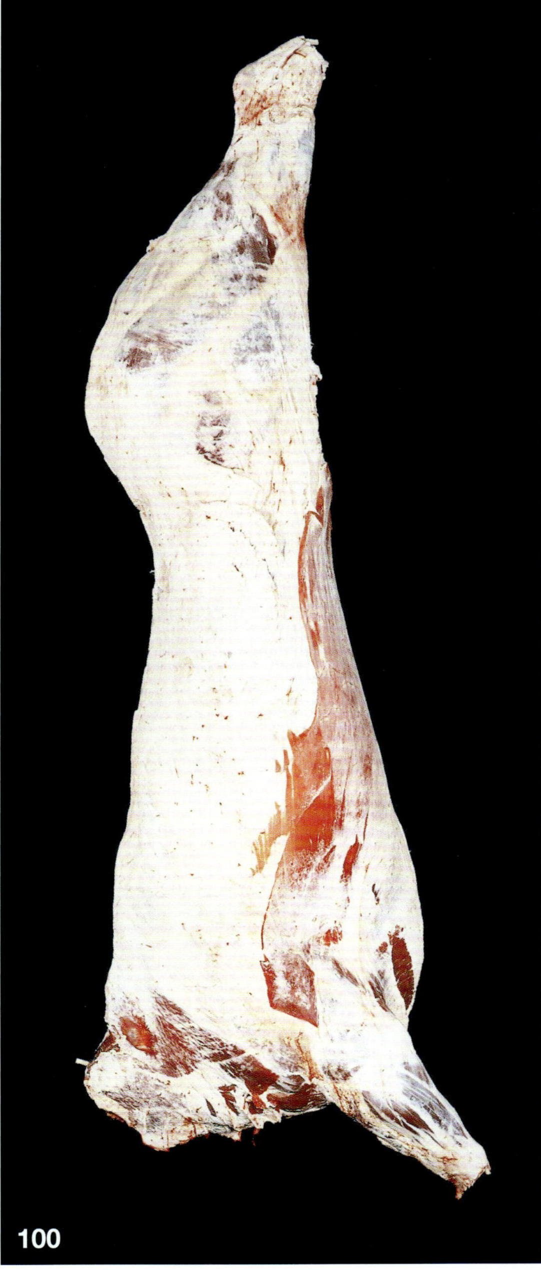

100

100
101
102
155

NAMP
NORTH AMERICAN MEAT PROCESSORS ASSOCIATION
ASSOCIATION AMÉRIQUE DU NORD DES TRANSFORMATEURS DE VIANDE
ASOCIACIÓN NORTEAMERICANA DE PROCESADORES DE CARNE

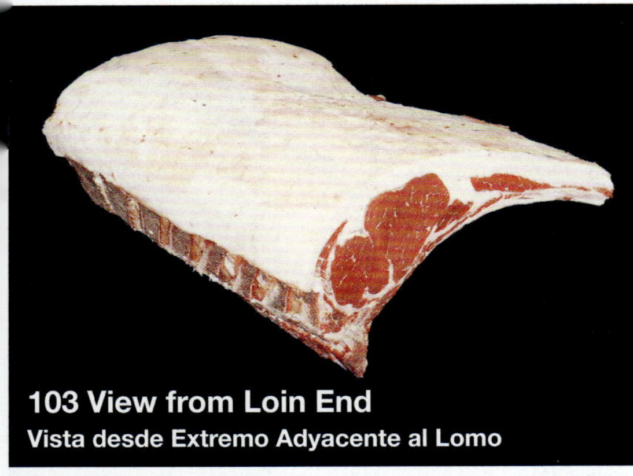

103 View from Loin End
Vista desde Extremo Adyacente al Lomo

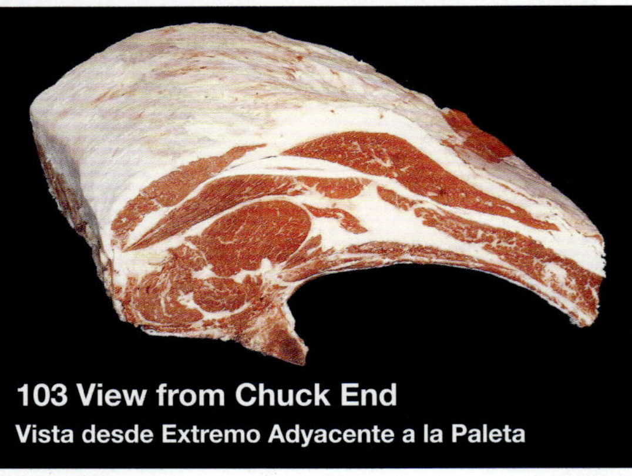

103 View from Chuck End
Vista desde Extremo Adyacente a la Paleta

103 Beef Rib, Primal

The primal rib is that portion of the forequarter remaining after excluding the cross-cut chuck and short plate and shall contain seven ribs (6th to 12th inclusive). The posterior tip of the blade bone (scapula), and the thoracic vertebrae remain attached to the ribs. The loin end shall follow the natural curvature of the 12th rib. The chuck is excluded by a straight cut between the 5th and 6th ribs. The short plate is excluded by a straight cut that is ventral to, but not more than 6.0 inches (15.0 cm) from, the *longissimus dorsi* at the loin end, to a point on the chuck end ventral to, but not more than 10.0 inches (25.4 cm) from, the *longissimus dorsi*. The diaphragm and fat on the ventral surface of the vertebrae shall be excluded.

103 Chuletón (Espaldar), Pieza Primaria

El chuletón primario, también conocido como "Costillar primario", es la porción del cuarto delantero que queda después de excluir la paleta de corte cruzado y el costillar corto, y deberá contener siete costillas (de la 6ª a la 12ª inclusive). La punta posterior del hueso de la paleta (escápula) y las vértebras torácicas permanecen unidas a las costillas. El extremo adyacente al lomo deberá seguir la curvatura natural de la 12ª costilla. La paleta primaria se excluye mediante un corte recto entre la 5ª y 6ª costilla. Se excluirá el costillar corto mediante un corte recto ventral al *longissimus dorsi*, pero a no más de 15.0 cm (6.0 pulgadas) del mismo en el extremo adyacente al lomo, hasta un punto en el extremo adyacente a la paleta, ventral al *longissimus dorsi,* pero a no más de 25.4 cm (10.0 pulgadas) del mismo. Se deberá excluir el diafragma y la grasa sobre la superficie ventral de las vértebras.

107 View from Loin End
Vista desde Extremo Adyacente al Lomo

107 View from Chuck End
Vista desde Extremo Adyacente a la Paleta

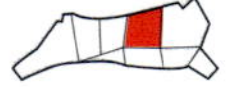

107 Beef Rib, Oven-Prepared

This item is prepared as described in Item No. 103, except the short plate shall be excluded by a straight cut that is ventral to, but not more than 3.0 inches (7.5 cm) from, the *longissimus dorsi* at the loin end, to a point on the chuck end ventral to, but not more than 4.0 inches (10.0 cm) from, the *longissimus dorsi*. The chine bone shall be excluded so that the lean is exposed between the ribs and the feather bone and vertebrae junctures, leaving the feather bones attached. The blade bone and related cartilage shall be excluded.

107 Chuletón (Espaldar), Preparado para Hornear

Esta pieza se prepara según la descripción de la pieza número 103, salvo que se excluirá el costillar corto mediante un corte recto ventral al *longissimus dorsi* pero a no más de 7.5 cm (3.0 pulgadas) del mismo, en el extremo adyacente al lomo, hasta un punto en el extremo adyacente a la paleta, ventral al *longissimus dorsi*, pero a no más de 10.0 cm (4.0 pulgadas) del mismo. Se deberá excluir los cuerpos vertebrales del espinazo a fin de exponer la carne magra que queda entre las costillas y las puntas del espinazo y las articulaciones vertebrales, dejando adheridas las puntas del espinazo. Se deberá excluir el hueso de la paleta y el cartílago conexo.

109 — Beef Rib, Roast-Ready

This item is prepared from a rib item meeting the end requirements of Item No. 107. In addition, the backstrap, *latissimus dorsi*, *infraspinatus*, *subscapularis*, *rhomboideus*, and *trapezius* shall be excluded. The exterior fat cover that had been over the *latissimus dorsi* and *trapezius* may be separated from the rib to accommodate removal of the backstrap and then returned to its original position. The fat cover shall be trimmed even with the short plate side and shall not have holes larger than 2.0 square inches (12.9 sq cm) or exceed 1.0 inch (2.5 cm) in depth at any point. The rib shall be netted or tied.

109 — Chuletón (Espaldar), Listo para Rostizar

Esta pieza se prepara a partir de una pieza de chuletón que cumpla con los requisitos de la pieza número 107. Además, se excluirá la banda ligamentosa (a veces referida por los carniceros como "mecapal") y los músculos *latissimus dorsi*, *infraspinatus*, *subscapularis*, *rhomboideus* y *trapezius*. La cubierta de grasa exterior que había estado superpuesta a los músculos *latissimus dorsi* y el *trapezius* puede apartarse del costillar para facilitar la extracción de la banda ligamentosa nucal y luego volverla a poner en su lugar original. La cubierta de grasa se recortará emparejándola con el lado del costillar corto y no podrá tener orificios superiores a 12.9 cm cuadrados (2.0 pulgadas cuadradas) ni exceder 2.5 cm (1.0 pulgada) de profundidad en ningún punto. El chuletón deberá colocarse en una red o amarrarse.

109 View from Loin End
Vista desde Extremo Adyacente al Lomo

109 View from Chuck End
Vista desde Extremo Adyacente a la Paleta

109 Processing View, Roast-Ready
Vista del Despiece, Listo para Rostizar

109A

109A Beef Rib, Roast-Ready, Special

This item is as described in Item No. 109, except feather bones are also excluded. In addition, the exterior fat cover that had covered the *latissimus dorsi, trapezius, longissimus dorsi,* and *spinalis dorsi* shall be separated to facilitate trimming of the underlying fat to a uniform thickness over the entire seamed surface. The exterior fat covering shall be replaced in its original position so that it extends from the feather bone edge of the rib bones toward the edges of the rib bones at the short plate side. Any fat cover extending beyond the short plate edges of the ribs shall be excluded.

109A Chuletón (Espaldar), Listo para Rostizar, Especial

Esta pieza aparece descrita en la pieza número 109, salvo que también se excluyen las puntas del espinazo en su sección torácica. Además, la cubierta de grasa exterior superpuesta a los músculos *latissimus dorsi, trapezius, longissimus dorsi* y *spinalis dorsi* deberá ser apartada para facilitar el recortado de la grasa subyacente hasta lograr un grosor uniforme sobre toda la superficie muscular descubierta con la disección. La cubierta de grasa exterior se volverá a colocar en su posición original de modo que se extienda desde el borde de las puntas del espinazo hacia los bordes de los huesos de las costillas en el lado del costillar corto. Cualquier cubierta de grasa que se extienda por fuera de los bordes del costillar corto deberá eliminarse.

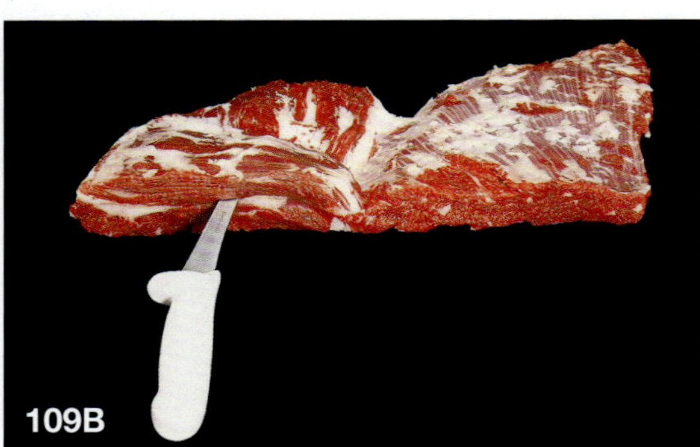

109B

109B Beef Rib, Blade Meat

This item consists of portions of those muscles that are immediately below (*subscapularis* and *rhomboideus*) and above (*latissimus dorsi, infraspinatus,* and *trapezius*) the blade bone and related cartilage of the primal rib. The lean surfaces shall be trimmed practically free of fat. All bones and cartilages shall be excluded.

109B Chuletón (Espaldar), Carne de Paleta (Tapas Interior y Exterior)

Esta pieza, también conocida a veces como "Sobrepaleta" consiste en porciones de aquellos músculos que se ubican inmediatamente por debajo (*subscapularis* y *rhomboideus*) y por encima (*latissimus dorsi, infraspinatus* y *trapezius*) del hueso de la paleta y cartílago relacionado a la pieza primaria del chuletón. Las superficies magras deberán ser recortadas hasta que estén prácticamente libres de grasa. Se excluirán todos los huesos y cartílagos.

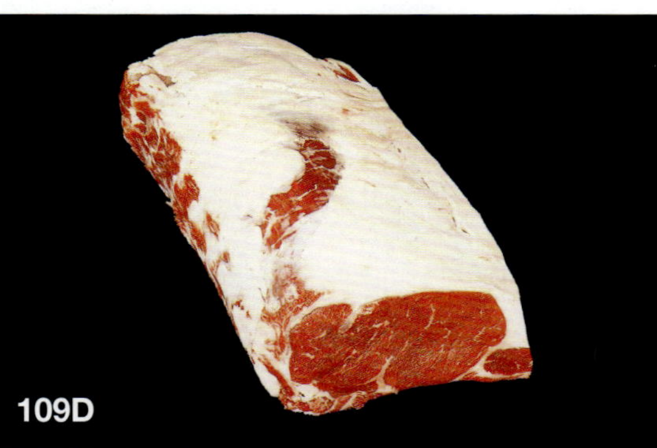

109B

109D Beef Rib, Roast-Ready, Cover Off, Short-Cut (Export Style)

This item is prepared from a rib as described in Item No. 109A, except the fat cover shall be excluded. In addition, the short plate shall be further excluded by a straight cut that is ventral to, but not more than 2.0 inches (5.0 cm) from, the *longissimus dorsi* at the loin end to a point on the chuck end ventral to, but not more than 3.0 inches (7.5 cm) from, the *longissimus dorsi.*

109D Chuletón (Espaldar), Listo para Rostizar, Sin Tapa, Pieza Corta (de Exportación)

Esta pieza se prepara de un chuletón según la descripción de la pieza número 109A, salvo que la cubierta de grasa deberá excluirse. Además, también se excluirá el costillar corto mediante un corte recto ventral al músculo *longissimus dorsi* en el extremo adyacente al lomo, pero a no más de 5.0 cm (2.0 pulgadas) hasta un punto en el extremo adyacente a la paleta ventral al *longissimus dorsi,* pero no más de 7.5 cm (3.0 pulgadas).

109D

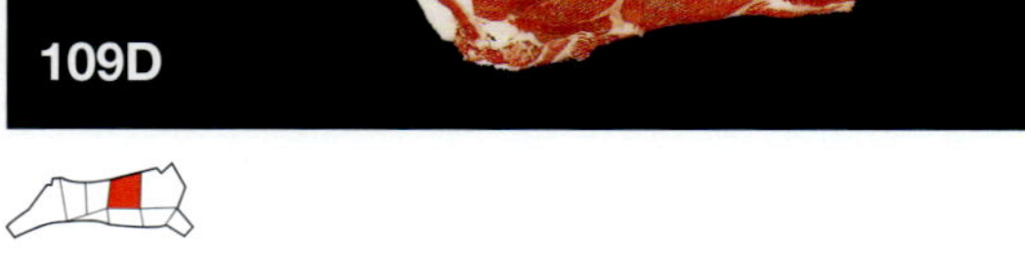

109E — Beef Rib, Ribeye Roll, Lip-On, Bone In (Export Style)

This item is as described in Item 109D, except the short plate shall be removed by a straight cut that is ventral to, but not more than 2.0 inches (5.0 cm) from, the *longissimus dorsi* at either end of the rib. The purchaser has the option in addition to specify one of the following PSO's for short plate removal.

PSO: 1 – 1.0 inch (2.5 cm) x 1.0 inch (2.5 cm)

    2 – 0 inch x 0 inch (product name shall omit reference to "lip-on")

    3 – Other

109E — Chuletón (Espaldar), Rollo Ribeye, Con Cordón, Con Hueso (de Exportación)

Esta pieza aparece descrita en la pieza número 109D, salvo que el costillar corto se extraerá mediante un corte recto ventral al músculo *longissimus dorsi*, pero a no más de 5.0 cm (2.0 pulgadas) del mismo, a ambos extremos del costillar. El comprador también tiene la opción de especificar una de las siguientes opciones para la extracción del costillar corto.

PSO: 1 – 2.5 cm (1.0 pulgada) x 2.5 cm (1.0 pulgada)

    2 – 0 cm x 0 cm (el nombre del producto omitirá la referencia a "con cordón")

    3 – Otros

110 — Beef Rib, Roast-Ready, Boneless

This item is prepared the same as Item No. 109, except in addition, all bones and intercostal meat shall be excluded. The exterior fat cover shall not extend beyond the short plate edge. The boneless roast shall be netted or tied.

110 — Chuletón (Espaldar), Listo para Rostizar, Deshuesado

Esta pieza se prepara igual que la pieza número 109, salvo que además, todos los huesos y la carne intercostal deberán excluirse. La cubierta de grasa exterior no deberá extenderse más allá del borde del costillar corto. El rosbif deshuesado deberá colocarse en una red o amarrarse.

110

112A — Beef Rib, Ribeye, Lip-On

The boneless ribeye, lip-on may be prepared from any rib item meeting the end requirements of Item No. 109. The item contains the *longissimus dorsi*, *spinalis dorsi*, *complexus*, and *multifidus dorsi* muscles and a lip consisting of the *serratus dorsalis* and *longissimus costarum* muscles and related intermuscular fat on the short plate side. The lip length shall be prepared with a straight cut that is ventral to, but not more than 2.0 inches (5.0 cm) from, the *longissimus dorsi.* The item shall be practically free of surface fat and intercostal meat. All other muscles, bones, cartilages, backstrap, and the exterior fat cover shall be excluded.

112A — Chuletón (Espaldar), Rollo Ribeye, con Cordón

El ribeye deshuesado, con el cordón (también conocido como "gota" o "cola" en sus bistecs), también se le refiere como "lomo delantero" y puede prepararse a partir de cualquier pieza de chuletón que cumpla con los requisitos de la pieza número 109. La pieza contiene los músculos *longissimus dorsi*, *spinalis dorsi*, *complexus* y *multifidus dorsi* así como un cordón que consiste en los músculos *serratus dorsalis* y *longissimus costarum*, y la grasa intermuscular relacionada con estos músculos en el lado del costillar corto. La longitud del cordón se preparará con un corte recto ventral al músculo *longissimus dorsi*, sin sobrepasar los 5.0 cm (2.0 pulgadas). La pieza deberá estar prácticamente libre de cubierta de grasa y de carne intercostal. Todos los demás músculos, huesos, cartílagos, banda ligamentosa y cubierta de grasa exterior deberán retirarse.

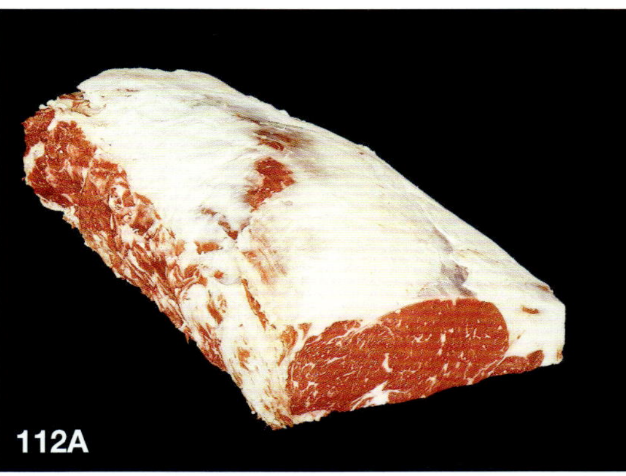

112A

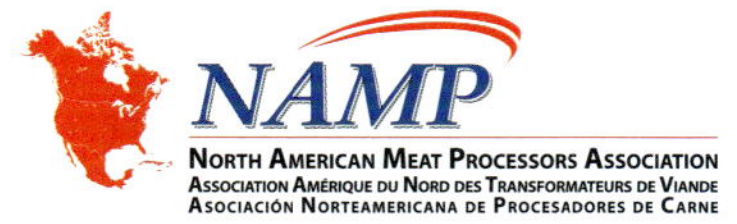

112

112 — Beef Rib, Ribeye Roll

This boneless item is the same as Item No. 112A, except the lip portion shall be excluded at the natural seam immediately ventral to the *longissimus dorsi*.

112 — Chuletón (Espaldar), Rollo Ribeye

Esta pieza deshuesada, a menudo referida como Entrecot, es la misma que la pieza número 112A, salvo que la porción de cordón deberá quitarse por la veta natural inmediatamente ventral al músculo *longissimus dorsi*.

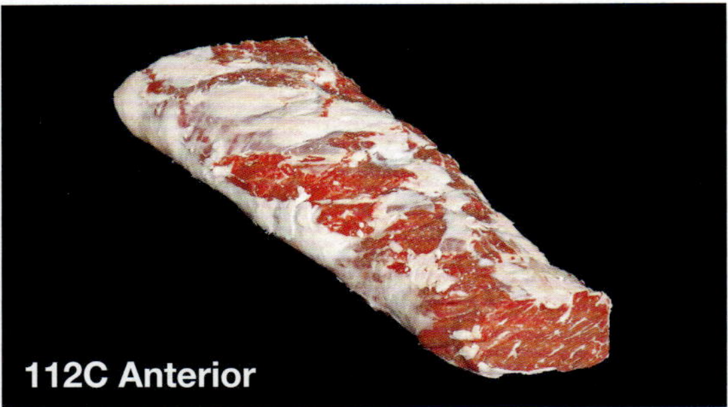

112C Anterior

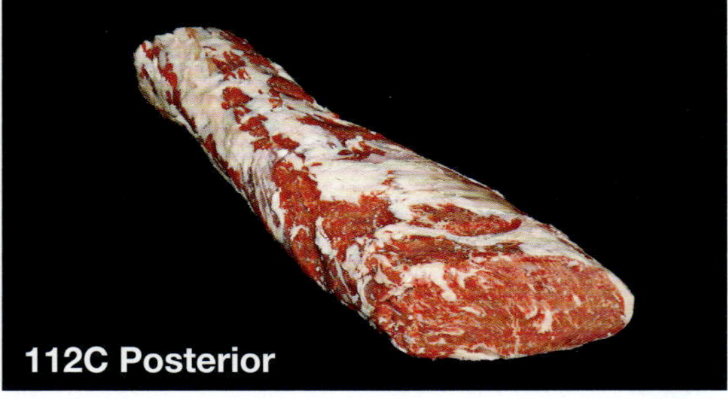

112C Posterior

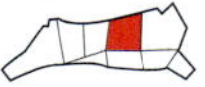

112C — Beef Rib, Ribeye (IM)

This item shall consist of the *longissimus* muscle only from the ribeye roll. The *complexus* and *spinalis* muscles have been removed by cutting through the natural seams.

112C — Chuletón (Espaldar), Ribeye (Ojo del Chuletón), (MI)

Esta pieza deberá consistir en el músculo *longissimus* únicamente proveniente del rollo de ribeye. Los músculos *complexus* y *spinalis* se han extraído cortando a lo largo de las vetas naturales.

112D

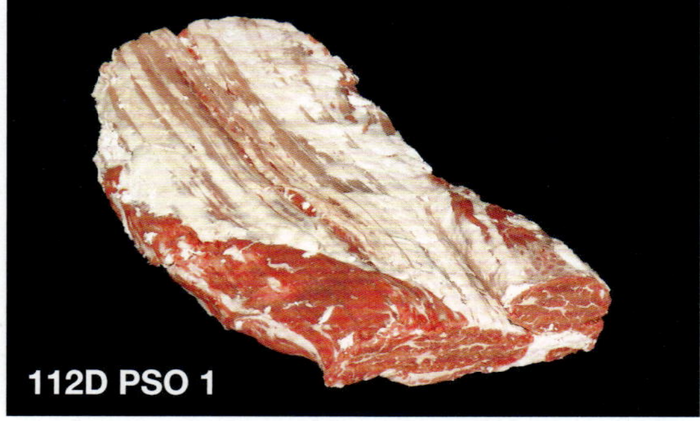

112D PSO 1

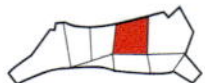

112D — Beef Rib, Ribeye Cap (IM)

This item will consist of the *spinalis dorsi/multifidus dorsi* muscle from the ribeye roll. The *longissimus* and *complexus* muscles have been removed by cutting through the natural seams.

PSO: 1 – *Complexus* muscle included.

112D — Chuletón (Espaldar), Tapa del Ribeye (MI)

Esta pieza consistirá en el músculo *spinalis dorsi/multifidus dorsi* del rollo del ribeye. Los músculos *longissimus* y *complexus* se han extraído cortando a lo largo de las vetas naturales.

PSO: 1 – *Músculo Complexus* incluido.

113 Beef Chuck, Square-Cut

This item is the portion of the forequarter after removal of the rib, short plate, foreshank, and brisket. The rib end of the chuck shall be prepared by a straight cut between the 5th and 6th ribs. The brisket and foreshank shall be removed by a straight cut that is at an approximate right angle to the rib end. Evidence of the cartilaginous juncture of the 1st rib and the sternum shall be present on the brisket side. The thymus gland and heart fat shall be closely removed and excluded.

Purchasers may specify that Item No. 113 be separated into a blade and arm portion. If so, request Item No. 113A. The separation is made at a point no more than 5.0 inches (12.5 cm) or less than 3.0 inches (7.5 cm) from the *longissimus dorsi*. Purchasers who in addition desire that the neck portion of the blade separation be excluded should request Item No. 113B. Item No. 113C consists of the blade portion of Item No. 113B and the arm roast described in Item No. 114E, which are each individually packaged and placed in the same container.

113 Paleta (Espaldilla), Corte Cuadrado

Esta pieza es la porción del cuarto delantero una vez extraída la costilla, el costillar corto, el chamberete de mano (antebrazo) y el pecho. El extremo de la paleta adyacente al chuletón deberá prepararse mediante un corte recto entre la 5ª y la 6ª costilla. El pecho y el chamberete de mano deberán extraerse mediante un corte derecho en un ángulo recto aproximado respecto al extremo del costillar. En el lado del pecho deberán quedar rastros de la articulación cartilaginosa de la 1ª costilla con el esternón. El timo y la grasa del corazón se deberán extraer cuidadosamente de forma total.

Los compradores pueden especificar que la pieza número 113 sea separada en una porción de paleta y una porción de brazuelo. [Nota: de la porción de la paleta con hueso se podrán cortar las llamadas chuletas "del 7" (llamadas así por la forma del corte del hueso de la paleta); del brazuelo con hueso se podrán cortar las chuletas "del Cero" (llamadas así por la forma redonda del corte transversal del hueso del brazo)]. En dicho caso, solicite la pieza número 113A. La separación se realiza en un punto no mayor a 12.5 cm (5.0 pulgadas) o menor de 7.5 cm (3.0 pulgadas) del músculo *longissimus dorsi*. Los compradores que además desean que se excluya la porción del pescuezo al separar la paleta, deberán solicitar la pieza número 113B. La pieza número 113C consiste en la porción de la pieza número 113B y el rosbif de brazuelo descrito en la pieza número 114E, que se empacan individualmente y se colocan en el mismo envase.

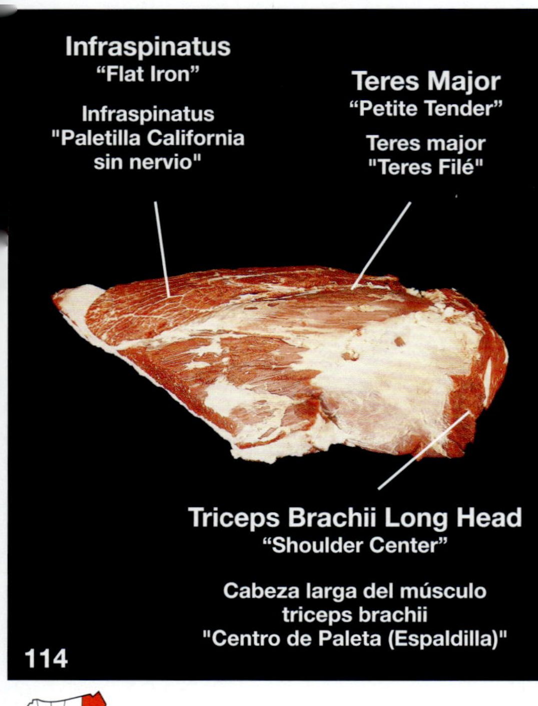

114 — Beef Chuck, Shoulder (Clod)

The shoulder, or "clod," the term by which this item is usually identified, is the large muscle system that lies above and to the rear of the elbow joint and below and to the rear of the ridge of the scapula and the 6th rib bone. The *cutaneous* muscle or "shoulder rose" shall be removed when the underlying fat exceeds the surface fat thickness specified by the purchaser. The presence of the *trapezius, cutaneous trunci, teres major*, and the minor muscles over the humerus are optional. The tendons on the elbow shall be trimmed to even with the lean. All bones and cartilages shall be removed.

If roasts are desired to be prepared from the clod, the purchaser should specify Item No. 114A. No roast shall be less than 1 inch (2.5 cm) thick, except within 0.75 inch (19 mm) of the juncture of the *trapezius* and *latissimus dorsi* muscles so as to comply with the surface fat requirements. The roasts are to be prepared horizontally and may be further divided in approximate sizes or weights specified by the purchaser. Cuts should be made at a right angle to the length and in approximate equal portions. All roasts shall be netted or tied.

114 — Paleta (Espaldilla), Planchuela

La paleta deshuesada, es a veces referida como "asado de paleta". "Planchuela" es el término que por lo general identifica a esta pieza y consiste en el gran sistema muscular que yace por encima y en la parte posterior de la articulación del codo y por debajo y en la parte posterior al borde (espina) del hueso de la paleta (escápula) y de la 6ª costilla. El músculo *cutáneo* o "suadero" deberá extraerse cuando la grasa subyacente exceda el grosor de la cubierta de grasa especificada por el comprador. La presencia de los músculos *trapezius, cutaneous trunci, teres major* y los músculos menores rodeando al húmero son opcionales. Los tendones del codo deberán ser recortados para emparejar con la carne magra. Todos los huesos y cartílagos deberán extraerse.

Si se desea que los rosbifs se preparen a partir de la planchuela, el comprador debe especificar la pieza número 114A. Los rosbifs no deben tener un grosor inferior a 2.5 cm (1 pulgada), excepto dentro de 19 mm (0.75 pulgadas) de la articulación de los músculos *trapezius* y *latissimus dorsi* a fin de cumplir con los requisitos de cubierta de grasa. Los rosbifs deben prepararse horizontalmente, y pueden dividirse en tamaños o pesos aproximados especificados por el comprador. Los cortes deben realizarse en un ángulo recto respecto al largo y en porciones aproximadamente iguales. Todos los rosbifs deben ser colocados en una red o amarrados.

114C — Beef Chuck, Shoulder (Clod), Trimmed

This item is as described in Item No. 114, except the *cutaneous trunci* (shoulder rose), *latissimus dorsi*, the optional minor muscles (*trapezius, teres major*), and muscles over the humerus shall be removed. To facilitate packaging, the *infraspinatus* may be separated and included.

114C — Paleta (Espaldilla), Planchuela, Recortada de grasa

Esta pieza aparece descrita en la pieza número 114, con excepción de que los músculos *cutaneous trunci* (suadero), *latissimus dorsi*, los músculos menores opcionales *trapecio, teres major*, y los músculos rodeando al húmero deberán ser extraídos. Para facilitar el empaque, el *infraspinatus* puede ser separado e incluido.

114D — Beef Chuck, Shoulder (Clod), Top Blade

This item is derived from Item No. 114 and shall consist of the *infraspinatus* muscle, untrimmed.

PSO: 1 – Purchaser may request that this item be further trimmed to remove the internal connective tissue or shoulder tendon. To remove the tissue or tendon it must be completely exposed by a butterfly cut prior to its removal. Purchaser may also request that this item then be separated into two pieces after completely removing the shoulder tendon. After the removal of the tendon the item is sometimes referred to as a "Flat Iron."

114D — Paleta (Espaldilla), Planchuela, Paletilla California (M. Infraespinoso)

Esta pieza, a veces referida como "bistec de planchuela" o "bistec de espaldilla" proviene de la pieza número 114 y consistirá en el músculo *infraspinatus*, sin recortado de grasa.

PSO: 1 – El comprador puede solicitar que a esta pieza se le aplique mayor recortado de grasa y limpieza a fin de extraer el tejido conjuntivo o tendón ("nervio" de la paletilla) que lo atraviesa. Para exponer y extraer el tejido conjuntivo o tendón, antes la paletilla debe abrirse completamente mediante un corte mariposa. El comprador puede también solicitar que esta pieza posteriormente se separe en dos, una vez que se haya extraído completamente el tendón de la paletilla. Después de la extracción del tendón, la pieza es llamada "Paletilla California sin Nervio".

114D

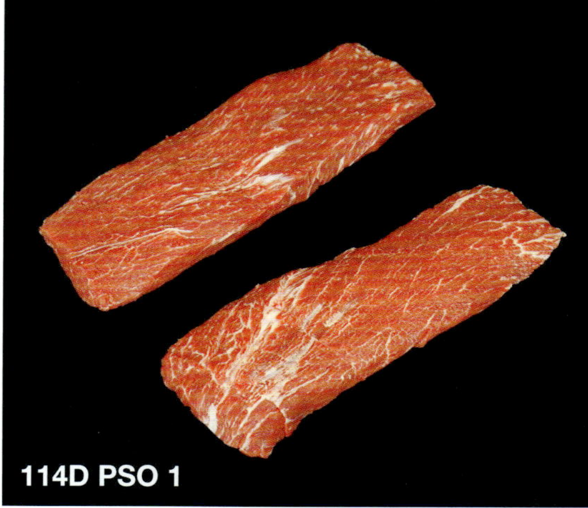
114D PSO 1

114E — Beef Chuck, Shoulder (Clod), Arm Roast

This item is derived from Item No. 114 and shall consist of the large muscle system of the thick end of the clod (*triceps brachii long head*, *triceps brachii lateral head*, and may consist of the *triceps brachii medial head* and *tensor fascia antibrachii*).

PSO: 1 – Purchaser may request that only the *triceps brachii long head* and a small portion of the *triceps brachii lateral head* muscles at the thick end of the Clod shall remain after being separated from the other muscles identified in Item No. 114E. The heavy part of the elbow tendon should be removed. The muscle is to be completely trimmed of all fat and connective tissue. The item is usually referred to as the "Clod Heart" or "Shoulder Center." Photograph is from the shank or ventral side.

114E — Paleta, (Espaldilla), Planchuela, Trozo Rosbif de Brazuelo

Esta pieza proviene de la pieza número 114 y deberá consistir en el gran sistema muscular del extremo grueso de la planchuela (*cabeza larga del músculo triceps brachii, cabeza lateral del músculo triceps brachii*, y puede consistir en *la cabeza medial del músculo triceps brachii* y el músculo *tensor fascia antibraquial*).

PSO: 1 – Es posible que el comprador solicite que queden únicamente la *cabeza larga del músculo triceps brachii* y una pequeña porción de la *cabeza lateral de los músculos triceps brachii* en el extremo grueso de la Planchuela, luego de separarlos de los otros músculos identificados en la pieza 114E. La parte gruesa del tendón del codo debe ser extraída. El músculo debe quedar completamente recortado de grasa y tejido conjuntivo. La pieza generalmente se llama "Corazón de Planchuela" o "Centro de Paleta" (Espaldilla). También se le ha referido como "Pulpa de Paleta". La fotografía corresponde al chamberete o al lado ventral.

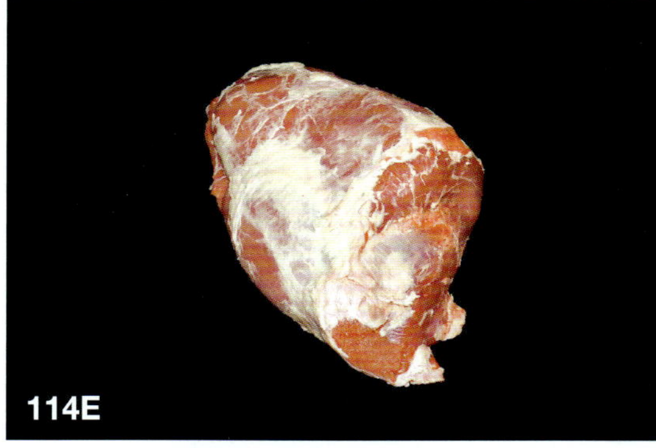
114E

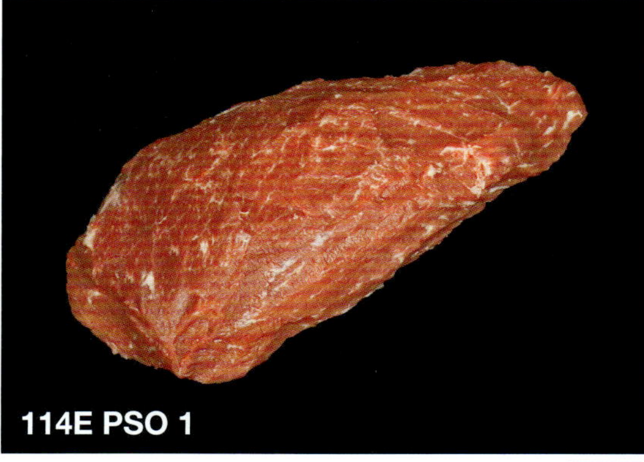
114E PSO 1

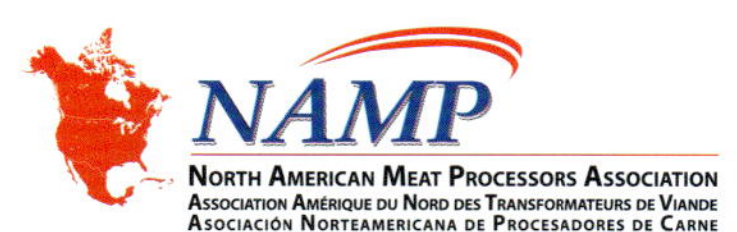

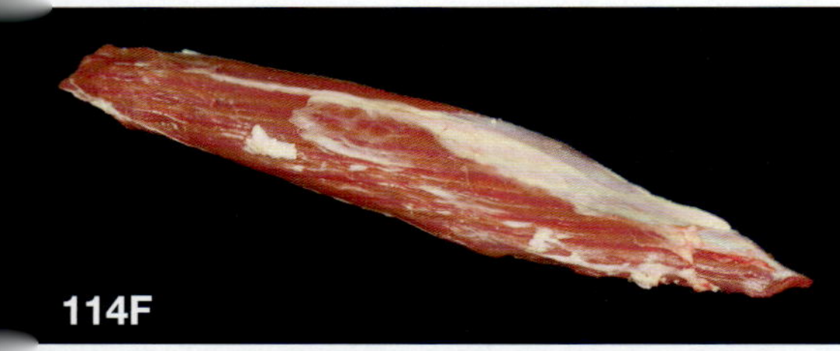
114F

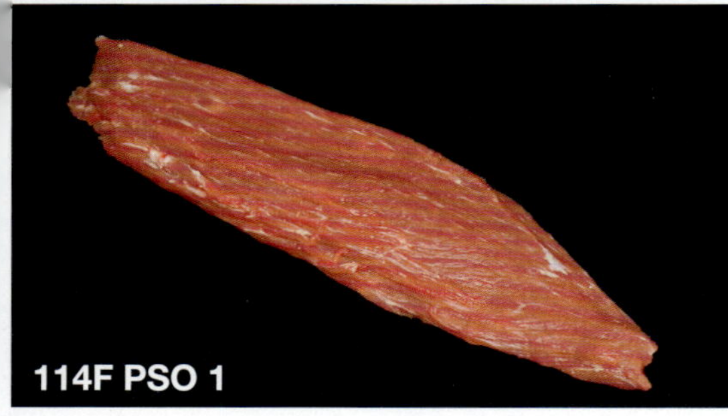
114F PSO 1

114F Beef Chuck, Shoulder Tender (IM)

This Item shall be prepared from Item No. 114 and shall consist of the *teres major* muscle, which is derived from the clod by cutting through the natural seam. This individual muscle (IM) is sometimes referred to as the "Petite Tender."

PSO: 1 – Purchaser may specify that this item shall be trimmed to FLO 6, Peeled/Denuded, Surface Membrane Removed (see page 13).

114F Paleta (Espaldilla), Teres Filé (MI)

Esta pieza debe prepararse a partir de la pieza 114 y deberá consistir en el músculo *teres major*, que se extrae de la planchuela cortando a través de la veta natural. Este músculo individual (MI) anatómicamente también se le conoce como Redondo Mayor y en el argot del mercado recientemente se le ha dado en llamar "Teres Filé" o "Petite Tender".

PSO: 1 – El comprador puede especificar que esta pieza debe quedar recortada según la opción 6 para limitar la grasa, "Desprovisto de grasa/ Prácticamente desnudo de grasa, Membrana superficial retirada" (ver página 12).

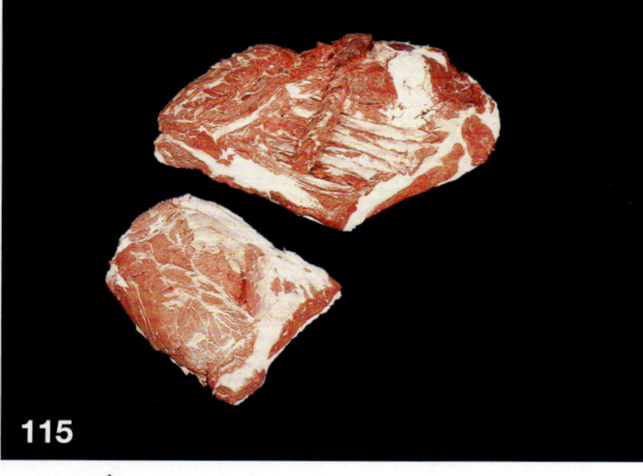
115

115 Beef Chuck, Square-Cut, Boneless

This boneless item is prepared from any chuck item with the brisket and foreshank removed. The full clod shall be separated (but included) as described in Item No. 114 and may be separated prior to cutting the brisket side. On the rib end, the *longissimus dorsi* shall be twice as large as the *complexus*. No fewer than 5 rib marks shall be present. The brisket side and rib end shall be straight cuts forming an approximate right angle. On the brisket side, the deep pectoral shall extend to the 3rd rib mark but not past the 5th rib mark. Though this item is normally available in the two pieces as pictured and described above, the item also may be purchased separated into three pieces as hereafter described. After separating the clod, the blade portion shall then be separated from the arm portion by a straight cut, approximately perpendicular with the rib end, which is ventral to, but not more than 5.0 inches (12.5 cm) or less than 3.0 inches (7.5 cm) from, the *longissimus dorsi* at the rib end. All bones, cartilages, backstrap, prescapular lymph gland, heart fat, and thymus gland shall be excluded.

When Item No. 115 has been prepared in three pieces, Item No. 115A describes the specifications for the Beef Chuck, Blade Portion, Boneless, and Item No. 115B describes the specifications for the Beef Chuck, Arm-Out, Boneless. These items may be purchased individually.

115 Paleta (Espaldilla), Corte Cuadrado, Deshuesada

Esta pieza deshuesada se prepara a partir de cualquier paleta, quitándosele el pecho y el chamberete de mano. Se separará la planchuela entera (que se encuentra presente en esta pieza) según se describe en la pieza número 114, y la misma podrá separarse antes de cortar el lado del pecho. En el extremo adyacente al chuletón, el músculo *longissimus dorsi* duplicará el tamaño del *complexus*. No habrá menos de 5 marcas de costillas. El lado del pecho y el extremo adyacente al chuletón se constituirán por cortes derechos que formen aproximadamente un ángulo recto. Del lado del pecho, el pectoral profundo se extenderá hasta la marca de la tercera costilla, sin pasar la marca de la quinta. Si bien este corte generalmente se consigue en dos piezas, como se muestra y se describe anteriormente, también puede comprarse en tres piezas separadas, como se describe a continuación. Una vez separada la planchuela, la porción de la paleta se separará de la porción del brazuelo mediante un corte recto, aproximadamente perpendicular al extremo adyacente al chuletón, que es ventral al músculo *longissimus dorsi*, pero de no más de 12.5 cm (5.0 pulgadas) o menos de 7.5 cm (3.0 pulgadas) en el extremo adyacente al chuletón. Se extraerán todos los huesos, banda ligamentosa nucal, ganglios linfáticos prescapulares, grasa del corazón, así como el timo.

Cuando se ha preparado la pieza número 115 en tres piezas, la pieza número 115A describe las especificaciones para la Paleta, Porción de la Paleta, Deshuesada, y la pieza número 115B describe las especificaciones de la Paleta, sin Brazuelo, Deshuesada. Es posible comprar estas piezas en forma individual.

115D — Beef Chuck, Square-Cut, Pectoral Meat (IM)

This item consists of the *deep pectoral* muscle that remains in the square cut chuck after the brisket is removed. It is removed from the chuck by cutting through the natural seams.

115D — Paleta (Espaldilla), Corte Cuadrado, Carne del Pectoral (MI)

Esta pieza consiste en el músculo *pectoral profundo* que permanece en el corte cuadrado de la paleta una vez extraído el pecho. Se extrae de la paleta cortando por las vetas naturales.

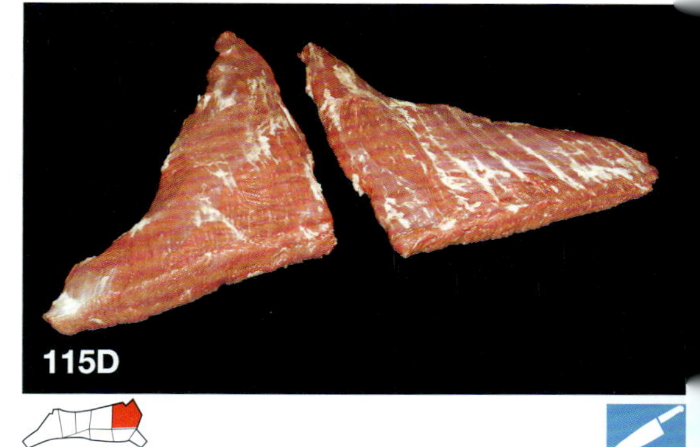

116A — Beef Chuck, Chuck Roll

This boneless item is prepared from a neck off boneless square-cut chuck and consists only of the large muscle system that lies under the blade bone that contains the *longissimus dorsi, rhomboideus, spinalis dorsi, complexus, multifidus dorsi, serratus ventralis, subscapularis,* and *splenius*. The rib end shall be made by a straight cut exposing the *longissimus dorsi* to be at least twice as large as the *complexus* and forms an approximate right angle with the length of the chuck roll. The neck shall be removed by a straight cut which is approximately parallel with the rib end and is anterior to, but not more than .50 inch (13 mm) from, the *serratus ventralis*. The arm portion shall be excluded by a straight cut that is not more than 3.0 inches (7.5 cm) ventral from the *longissimus dorsi* at the rib end and not more than 4.0 inches (10.0 cm) from the *complexus* at the neck end. Any cartilages, backstrap, *trapezius, supraspinatus,* intercostal meat (rib fingers), and prescapular lymph gland shall also be excluded. When smaller roasts are specified, the boneless chuck roll shall be divided into approximately equal portions by cutting through the meat perpendicular to the length of the chuck roll. This item shall be netted or tied when specified.

The purchaser may specify a different length arm portion exclusion (PSO) as follows:

PSO: 1 – Arm excluded 1.0 inch (2.5 cm) x 1.0 inch (2.5 cm) from the rib (*longissimus dorsi*) and neck (*complexus*) ends.

2 – Arm excluded by straight cut immediately ventral to the *longissimus dorsi* and *complexus*.

3 – The *subscapularis* shall be excluded.

4 – The "hump meat" (dorsal portion of the *rhomboideus*) shall be removed so that the dorsal edge is a straight cut parallel to the arm (ventral) edge.

116A — Paleta (Espaldilla), Rollo de Diezmillo, Deshuesado

Esta pieza deshuesada, también denominada "rollo de espaldilla", se prepara a partir de una paleta de corte cuadrado deshuesada sin pescuezo y consiste solamente en el gran sistema muscular que yace debajo del hueso de la paleta y que contiene los músculos *longissimus dorsi, rhomboideus, spinalis dorsi, complexus, multifidus dorsi, serratus ventralis, subscapularis* y *splenius*. El extremo adyacente al Chuletón (Espaldar) se elaborará aplicando un corte recto que exponga el músculo *longissimus dorsi* de modo que sea al menos dos veces más grande que el músculo *complexus*, formando un ángulo aproximadamente recto con el largo del rollo de diezmillo. Se extraerá el pescuezo mediante un corte recto aproximadamente paralelo al extremo adyacente al chuletón y anterior al músculo *serratus ventralis*, pero sin superar los 13 mm (0.50 pulgadas). Se extraerá la porción de brazuelo mediante un corte recto de no más de 7.5 cm (3.0 pulgadas) ventrales respecto al músculo *longissimus dorsi* en el extremo del chuletón y a no más de 10.0 cm (4.0 pulgadas) del músculo *complexus* en el extremo del pescuezo. También se extraerá cualquier cartílago, banda ligamentosa nucal, *trapezius, supraspinatus,* carne intercostal (tiras de entrecostilla) y ganglios linfáticos prescapulares. Cuando se especifiquen rosbifs más pequeños, el rollo de diezmillo deshuesado deberá dividirse en porciones iguales, aproximadamente, cortando la carne en forma perpendicular a lo largo del rollo de diezmillo. Esta pieza deberá ser colocada en una red o amarrada cuando así se especifique.

El comprador puede especificar una diferente exclusión con respecto al largo del brazuelo (PSO), según las siguientes opciones:

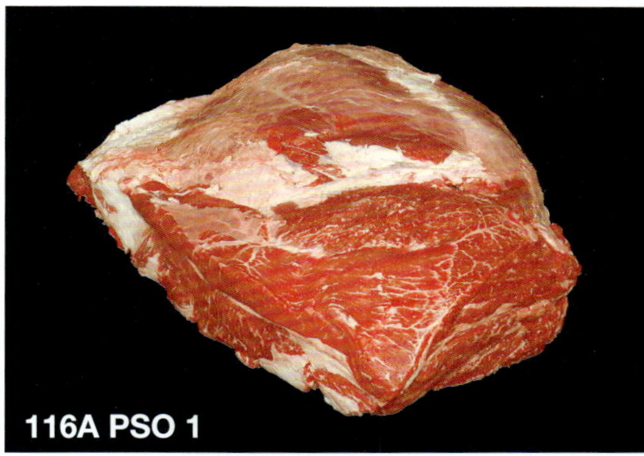

PSO: 1 – Brazuelo excluido 2.5 cm (1.0 pulgada) x 2.5 cm (1.0 pulgada) de los extremos adyacentes al *longissimus dorsi* del chuletón y *complexus* del cuello.

2 – Brazuelo excluido mediante corte recto inmediatamente ventral a los músculos *longissimus dorsi* y *complexus*.

3 – El músculo *subscapularis* deberá ser excluido.

4 – La "carne de la giba" (porción dorsal del músculo *rhomboideus* deberá extraerse de manera que el borde dorsal sea un corte recto paralelo al borde (ventral) del brazuelo.

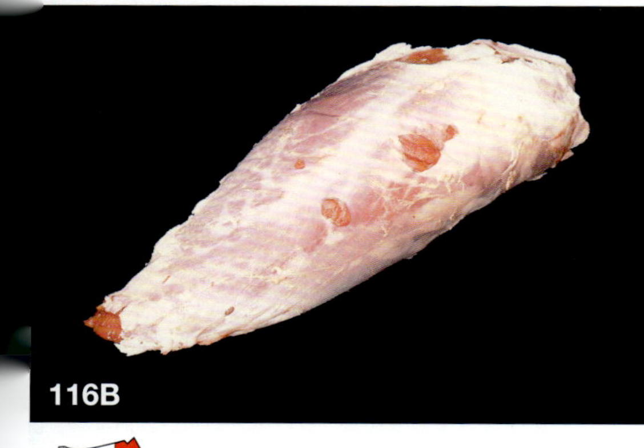

116B

116B Beef Chuck, Chuck Tender (IM)

This item consists of the *supraspinatus* muscle that lies dorsal to the medial ridge of the blade bone. The chuck tender shall be separated from the other muscles through the natural seams.

PSO: 1 – The heavy connective tissue on the thick end of the chuck tender shall be exposed and removed by a butterfly cut leaving a score that is no more than 2.0 inches (5 cm) into the lean.

116B Paleta (Espaldilla), Juil (MI)

Esta pieza consiste en el músculo *supraspinatus* que yace en la fosa superior respecto al borde óseo (espina) del hueso de la paleta. El juil se separará de los otros músculos a través de las vetas naturales.

PSO: 1 – El tejido conectivo grueso del extremo grueso del juil se verá expuesto y se extraerá mediante un corte mariposa, dejando una marca de no más de 5 cm (2.0 pulgadas) en la carne magra.

116D

116D Beef Chuck, Chuck Eye Roll

This item is the muscle group from Item No. 116A that consists of the *longissimus dorsi, spinalis dorsi, complexus,* and *multifidus dorsi.* The chuck eye roll shall be separated from the chuck roll by cutting through the natural seams and shall be practically free of surface fat.

116D Paleta (Espaldilla), Centro del Rollo de Diezmillo

Esta pieza es el grupo muscular de la pieza número 116A que consiste de los músculos *longissimus dorsi, spinalis dorsi, complexus* y *multifidus dorsi.* El centro del rollo del diezmillo se separará del rollo del diezmillo mediante un corte a lo largo de las vetas naturales y deberán estar prácticamente libres de cubierta de grasa.

116E

116E Beef Chuck, Under Blade Roast

This item is derived from Item No. 116A, after the exclusion of Item No. 116D Beef Chuck, Chuck Eye Roll and shall consist of the *serratus ventralis, rhomboideus,* and *splenius* muscles. The dorsal and ventral edges shall be straight cuts that are approximately parallel with each other.

116E Paleta (Espaldilla), Trozo Rosbif de la Tapa Interior de la Planchuela (Debajo de la Paleta)

Esta pieza proviene de la pieza número 116A, después de la exclusión de la pieza número 116D, Paleta (Espaldilla), Centro del Rollo de Diezmillo, y deberá consistir en los músculos *serratus ventralis, rhomboideus* y *splenius.* Los bordes dorsal y ventral deberán conformar cortes rectos aproximadamente paralelos entre sí.

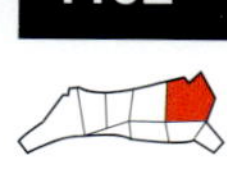

116G — Beef Chuck, Under Blade, Center-Cut (IM)

This item will consist of the *serratus ventralis* muscle in its entirety from the Chuck Roll (Item No. 116A) or Under Blade (Item No. 116E). This item is sometimes referred to as "Denver Cut".

PSO: 1 – The item may consist of any portion of the item 116G. When made from the portion of the *serratus ventralis* that is removed from the ventral edge of the Chuck Roll to comply with PSO 1 of Item No. 116A, the item is commonly referred to as the "Edge Roast" or "Chuck Flap".

116G — Paleta (Espaldilla), Tapa Interior de la Planchuela, Corte del Centro (Rosbif Denver) (MI)

Esta pieza consistirá en el músculo *serratus ventralis* en su totalidad, proveniente del Rollo de Diezmillo (pieza número 116A) o de la Tapa Interior de la Planchuela (pieza número 116E). En ocasiones, a esta pieza también se le llama "Corte Denver".

PSO: 1 – La pieza puede consistir en cualquier porción de la pieza número 116G. Cuando se la elabora a partir de la porción de *serratus ventralis* que se extrae del borde ventral del Rollo del Diezmillo para cumplir con las exigencias de la PSO 1 de la pieza número 116A, la pieza habitualmente se denomina "Trozo Rosbif del Borde" o "Tapa de Paleta".

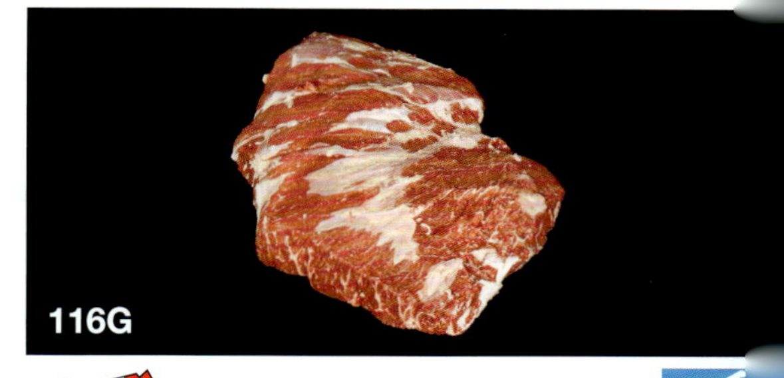

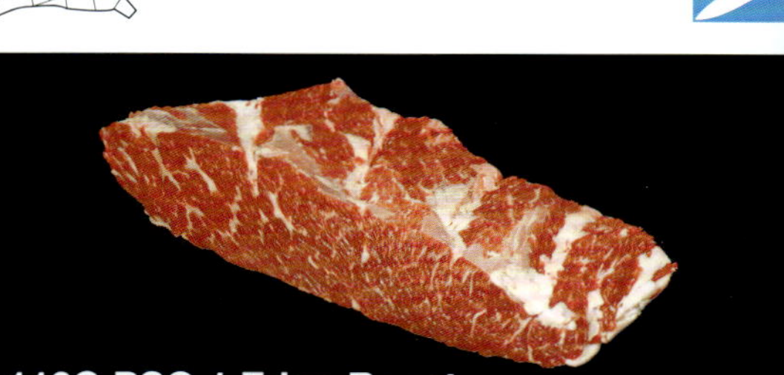

116H — Beef Chuck, Chuck Eye (IM)

This item shall consist of the *complexus* muscle that is derived from the Chuck Eye Roll.

116H — Paleta (Espaldilla), Corazón del Diezmillo (MI)

Esta pieza deberá consistir en el músculo *complexus* que proviene del Centro del Rollo de Diezmillo.

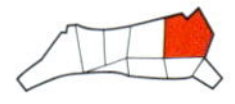

116I — Beef Chuck, Neck Roast

This item is derived from the anterior end of the untrimmed chuck roll. It is removed from the chuck roll as described in Item No. 116A.

116I — Paleta (Espaldilla), Trozo Rosbif de Pescuezo

Esta pieza proviene del extremo anterior del rollo de diezmillo sin recortado de grasa y limpieza. Se extrae del rollo de diezmillo según se describe en la pieza número 116A.

116K — Beef Chuck Roll, 3-Way

This item shall consist of the Chuck Eye Roll (Item No. 116D), and *serratus ventralis* and *splenius* muscles from the Under Blade (Item No. 116E). The *serratus ventralis* (Item No. 116G) and *splenius* muscles shall be separated from each other and the *rhomboideus* by cutting through the natural seams. The 3 pieces shall be individually packaged and placed into the same container.

116K — Rollo de Diezmillo, en 3 piezas

Esta pieza deberá consistir en el Centro del Rollo de Diezmillo (pieza número 116D) y los músculos *serratus ventralis* y *splenius*, de la Tapa Interior de la Planchuela (pieza número 116E). Los músculos *serratus ventralis* (pieza número 116G) y *splenius* deberán separarse entre sí y del *rhomboideus* mediante cortes por las vetas naturales. Las 3 piezas deberán ser empaquetadas individualmente y colocadas en el mismo recipiente.

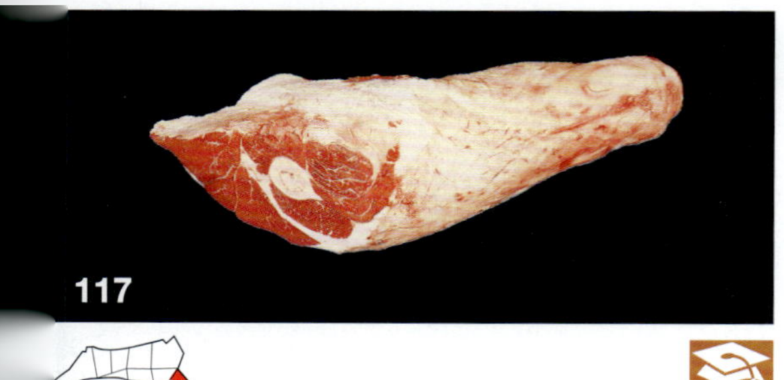

117

117 Beef Foreshank

A bone in foreshank is the item produced from an Item No. 102, after its separation from a square-cut chuck and brisket. The foreshank is made by a straight cut exposing a cross section of the humerus bone. The brisket is excluded by a cut through the natural seam.

117 Chamberete de Mano

El chamberete de mano con hueso es la pieza que se obtiene a partir de la pieza número 102, después de su separación de la paleta de corte cuadrado y el pecho. El chamberete de mano se logra mediante un corte recto que expone la superficie del corte transversal del hueso húmero. Se excluye el pecho mediante un corte a través de la veta natural.

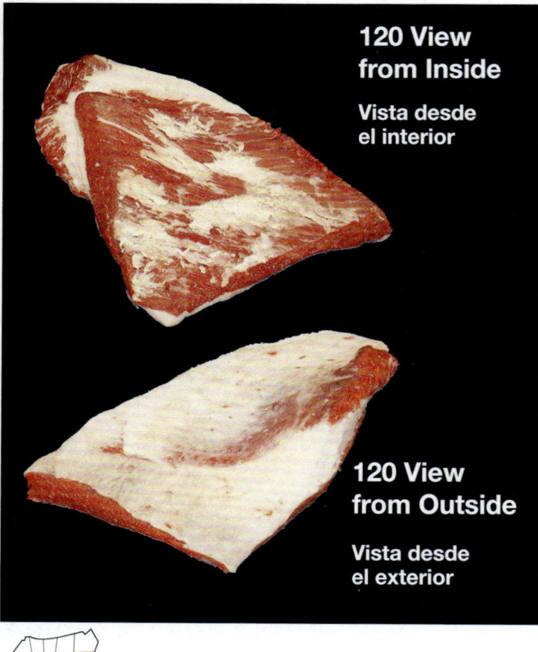

120 Beef Brisket, Deckle-Off, Boneless

This boneless and cartilage-free item is prepared from a bone in brisket produced as described in Item No. 117. The deckle, which is the hard fat and intercostal meat on the inside surface, shall be excluded at the natural seam exposing the lean surface of the *deep pectoral* muscle, which terminates just prior to the short plate separation. The hard fat along the sternum edge shall be trimmed level with the boned surface. The inside lean surface shall be trimmed practically free of fat. Purchasers may request the exterior fat cover be further trimmed.

120 Pecho, Sin Grasa Endurecida ni Carne Intercostal, Deshuesado

Esta pieza deshuesada y sin cartílagos se prepara a partir de un pecho con hueso que se obtiene según la descripción de la pieza número 117. La grasa endurecida, conocida en inglés como "deckle", y la carne intercostal de la superficie interna, deberá excluirse siguiendo la veta natural y exponiendo la superficie magra del músculo pectoral profundo, que termina justo antes de la separación del costillar corto. La grasa dura a lo largo del borde del esternón deberá recortarse a nivel de la superficie con hueso. La superficie magra interna deberá ser recortada hasta que esté prácticamente libre de grasa. Los compradores pueden solicitar que se recorte más profundamente el recubrimiento de grasa exterior.

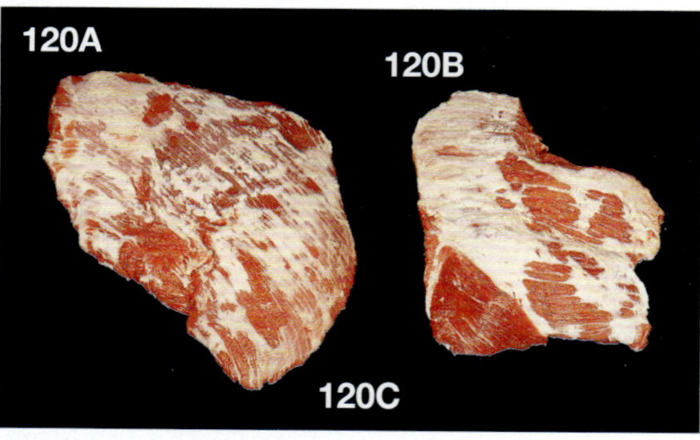

120A Beef Brisket, Flat Cut, Boneless (IM)

This item is the *deep pectoral* muscle from a boneless brisket. All surfaces shall be trimmed practically free of fat and the item itself shall be no less than 0.5 inch (13 mm) thick at any point.

120A Pecho, Falda de Pecho, Deshuesada (MI)

Esta pieza es el músculo *pectoral profundo* que proviene de un pecho deshuesado. Todas las superficies deberán recortarse hasta que estén prácticamente libres de grasa y la pieza misma no deberá tener un grosor inferior a 13 mm (0.5 pulgadas) en ningún punto.

120B Beef Brisket, Point Cut, Boneless (IM)

This item is the *superficial pectoral* muscle from a boneless brisket. All surfaces shall be trimmed practically free of fat and the item itself shall be no less than 0.5 inch (13 mm) thick at any point.

120B Pecho, Punta de Pecho, Deshuesada (MI)

Esta pieza es el músculo *pectoral superficial* que proviene de un pecho deshuesado. Todas las superficies deberán recortarse hasta que estén prácticamente libres de grasa y la pieza misma no deberá tener un grosor inferior a 13 mm (0.5 pulgadas) en ningún punto.

120C — Beef Brisket, 2-Piece, Boneless

This item shall consist of Item No. 120A and Item No. 120B packaged together.

120C — Pecho, en 2 piezas (Falda y Punta), Deshuesado

Esta pieza deberá consistir en la pieza número 120A y la pieza número 120B empacadas conjuntamente.

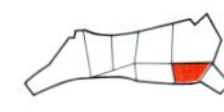

121 — Beef Plate, Short Plate

This item is that portion of the forequarter immediately ventral to Item No. 103. The flank end shall follow the natural curvature of the 12th rib. The *deep pectoral* muscle shall not completely extend to the dorsal edge of the brisket side. Seven ribs shall be present. The rib side shall be a straight cut that exposes the *serratus ventralis* to be continuous for at least 2 ribs. The diaphragm may be excluded, but if present shall be firmly attached and the membranous portion shall be trimmed close to the lean.

121 — Costillar (Aguja), Costillar Corto (Costilla Cargada Completa)

Esta pieza es la porción del cuarto delantero inmediatamente ventral a la pieza número 103. El extremo adyacente a la falda deberá seguir la curvatura natural de la 12ª costilla. El músculo *pectoral profundo* no deberá extenderse completamente al extremo dorsal del lado del pecho. Deberá haber siete costillas. Del lado de las costillas se verá un corte recto que exponga el *serratus ventralis* en forma continua por al menos 2 costillas. Puede excluirse el diafragma; pero si está presente, deberá estar firmemente unido y la porción membranosa deberá ser despellejada de grasa casi hasta la parte magra.

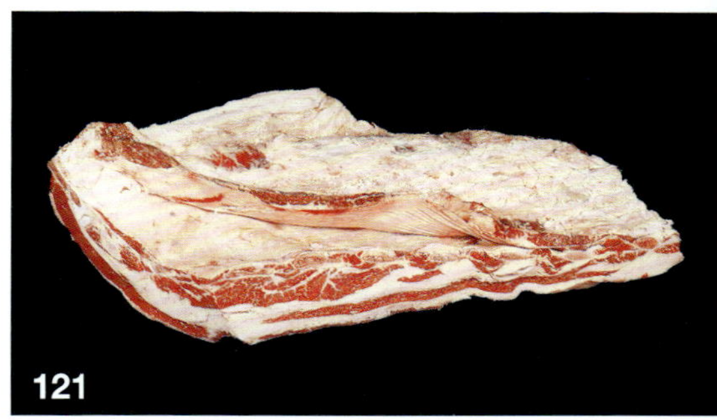
121

121C — Beef Plate, Outside Skirt (IM)

This item is removed from the short plate. The outside skirt shall consist of the diaphragm, which may have the *serous membrane (peritoneum)* attached. The membrane portion must be trimmed close to the lean.

Purchasers who desire this item to have the *serous membrane* or *peritoneum* excluded from both sides of the outside skirt or diaphragm should request Item No. 121E. The ends shall also be squared.

121C — Costillar, Arrachera Delgada Regular (MI)

Esta pieza, a veces referida como "entraña" o "fajita original", se retira del costillar corto. La arrachera regular deberá consistir en el diafragma, que puede tener unida la *membrana serosa (peritoneo)*. La porción de la membrana debe limpiarse casi hasta la carne magra.

Los compradores que desean que se excluya de esta pieza la *membrana serosa* o el *peritoneo*, de ambos lados de la arrachera regular o diafragma, deben solicitar la pieza número 121E. También se recortarán los extremos.

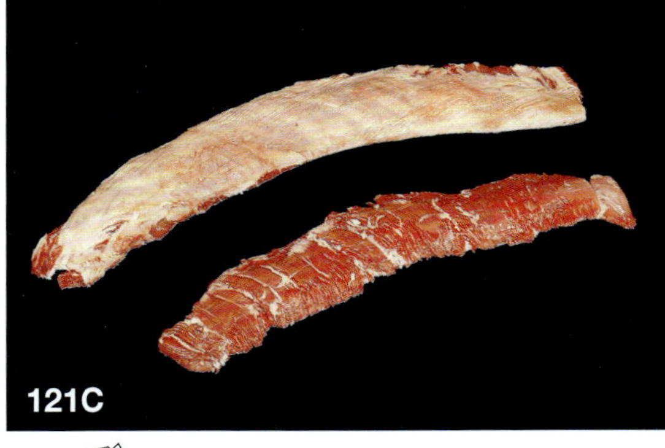
121C

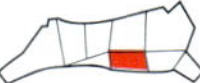

121D — Beef Plate, Inside Skirt (IM)

This item shall consist of the *transversus abdominis* muscle only. The *serous membrane (peritoneum)* shall be excluded. The lean surface shall be trimmed practically free of fat.

121D — Costillar, Falda Interna/ Arrachera Inside (MI)

Esta pieza, perteneciente al grupo de faldas o aldillas, deberá consistir solamente en el músculo *transversus abdominis*. Se excluirá la *membrana serosa (peritoneo)*. La superficie magra deberá ser recortada hasta que esté prácticamente libre de grasa.

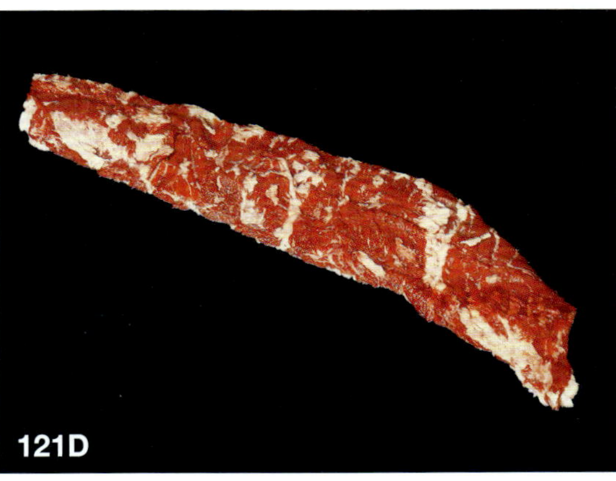
121D

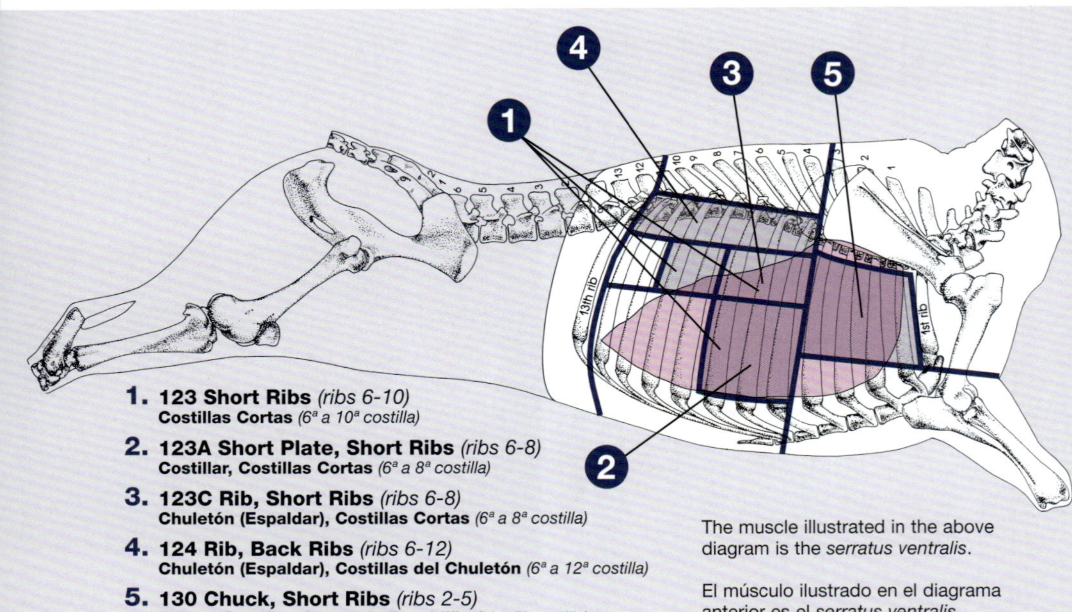

Beef Bone Structure Chart & Rib Guide

Tabla de estructura esquelética de res y guía de costillas

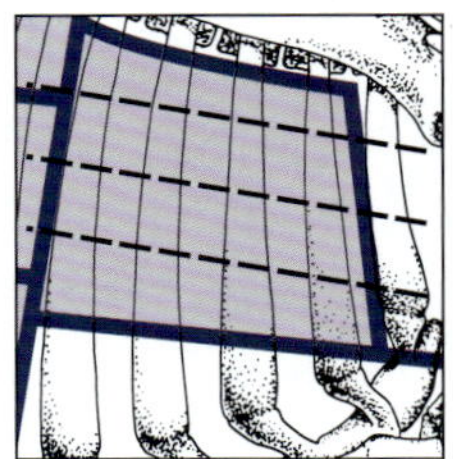

1. 123 Short Ribs *(ribs 6-10)*
Costillas Cortas *(6ª a 10ª costilla)*

2. 123A Short Plate, Short Ribs *(ribs 6-8)*
Costillar, Costillas Cortas *(6ª a 8ª costilla)*

3. 123C Rib, Short Ribs *(ribs 6-8)*
Chuletón (Espaldar), Costillas Cortas *(6ª a 8ª costilla)*

4. 124 Rib, Back Ribs *(ribs 6-12)*
Chuletón (Espaldar), Costillas del Chuletón *(6ª a 12ª costilla)*

5. 130 Chuck, Short Ribs *(ribs 2-5)*
Paleta, Costillas Cortas de Espaldilla *(2ª a 5ª costilla)*

The muscle illustrated in the above diagram is the *serratus ventralis.*

El músculo ilustrado en el diagrama anterior es el *serratus ventralis.*

Flanken Style Ribs (see Item No. 1123) are produced from any chuck, rib, or plate short rib item by cutting at a right angle to the rib bones.

Las Costillas Estilo Flanken (ver pieza número 1123) se obtienen de cualquier pieza de paleta, chuletón o costillas cortas, cortando en ángulo recto hasta los huesos de las costillas.

123 Beef Short Ribs

This item consists of the rib section from any rib and/or plate item and shall contain at least 2 but no more than 5 ribs (ribs 6 through 10). The dorsal side shall be at an approximate right angle to the rib bones and the *latissimus dorsi* shall be continuous across the cut surface. The ventral side shall be a straight cut that is approximately parallel to the dorsal side and does not contain any costal cartilages. The *cutaneous trunci, diaphragm,* and *serous membrane (peritoneum)* shall be excluded. The surface fat shall be trimmed to not exceed 0.25 inch (6 mm) at any point. The purchaser shall specify the number of ribs and the width (distance between the dorsal and ventral sides) of the rib sections.

123 Costillar, Costillas (Agujas) Cortas, 2 o 5 Costillas (6ª-10ª) M. Serrato Ventral

Esta pieza consiste en la sección de costillas proveniente de cualquier pieza de chuletón o costillar y deberá contener por lo menos 2 pero no más de 5 costillas (de la 6ª a la 10ª costilla). El lado dorsal deberá estar aproximadamente en ángulo recto a los huesos de las costillas y el *latissimus dorsi* deberá desplegarse a través de la superficie del corte. El lado ventral deberá resultar en un corte recto que sea aproximadamente paralelo al lado dorsal y que no contenga ningún cartílago costal. Se retirará el *cutaneous trunci (suadero),* el *diafragma* y la *membrana serosa (peritoneo).* Se deberá recortar la cubierta de grasa de forma que no exceda los 6 mm (0.25 pulgadas) en ningún punto. El comprador deberá especificar el número de costillas y el grosor (distancia entre los lados dorsal y ventral) de las piezas de costillas.

123A Beef Short Plate, Short Ribs, Trimmed

This item is as described in Item No. 123, except it shall be derived from the 6th, 7th, and 8th ribs of the short plate. The *serratus ventralis* shall be continuous across the cut surface for at least 2 ribs on both the dorsal and ventral sides, and the exterior fat cover and the *latissimus dorsi* shall be excluded.

123A Costillar, Costilla Cargada, Costillas (Agujas) Cortas (6ª-8ª), Recortadas de Grasa y Limpias

Esta pieza aparece descrita en la pieza número 123, salvo que provendrá de la 6ª, 7ª y 8ª costillas del costillar corto. El *serratus ventralis* deberá desplazarse en forma continua por la superficie del corte por al menos 2 costillas tanto en el lado dorsal como ventral, y se deberá excluir la cubierta de grasa exterior y el *latissimus dorsi.*

NAMP
North American Meat Processors Association
Association Amérique du Nord des Transformateurs de Viande
Asociación Norteamericana de Procesadores de Carne

123B — Beef Rib, Short Ribs, Trimmed

This item is as described in Item No. 123, except it shall be derived from the 6th, 7th, and 8th ribs of the primal rib. The *serratus ventralis* shall be exposed and continuous for at least 2 ribs on one side only, and the exterior fat cover and the *latissimus dorsi* shall be excluded. This item shall be trimmed practically free of surface fat.

123B — Chuletón (Espaldar), Costillas (Agujas) Cortas (6ª-8ª), Limpias

Esta pieza aparece descrita en la pieza número 123, salvo que provendrá de la 6ª, 7ª y 8ª costillas del chuletón primario. El *serratus ventralis* deberá estar expuesto y desplazarse en forma continua por al menos 2 costillas de un solo lado, y deberán excluirse la cubierta de grasa exterior, así como el *latissimus dorsi*. Esta pieza deberá ser recortada hasta quedar prácticamente libre de cubierta de grasa.

123C — Beef Rib, Short Ribs

This item is as described in Item No. 123, except it shall be derived from the 6th, 7th, and 8th ribs of the primal rib. The *serratus ventralis* shall be exposed and continuous for at least 2 ribs on one side only.

123C — Chuletón (Espaldar), Costillas (Agujas) Cortas (6ª-8ª)

Esta pieza aparece descrita en la pieza número 123, salvo que provendrá de la 6ª, 7ª y 8ª costillas del chuletón primario. El *serratus ventralis* deberá exponerse y continuar por al menos 2 costillas de un lado solamente.

123D — Beef Short Ribs, Boneless (IM)

This item shall consist of the *serratus ventralis* muscle from any short rib item. The rib bones and intercostal meat shall be excluded.

123D — Costilla Cargada, Costillas (Agujas) Cortas (6ª-8ª), Deshuesadas (MI)

Esta pieza deberá consistir en el músculo *serratus ventralis* proveniente de cualquier pieza de costillas cortas. Se deberán excluir los huesos de las costillas y la carne intercostal.

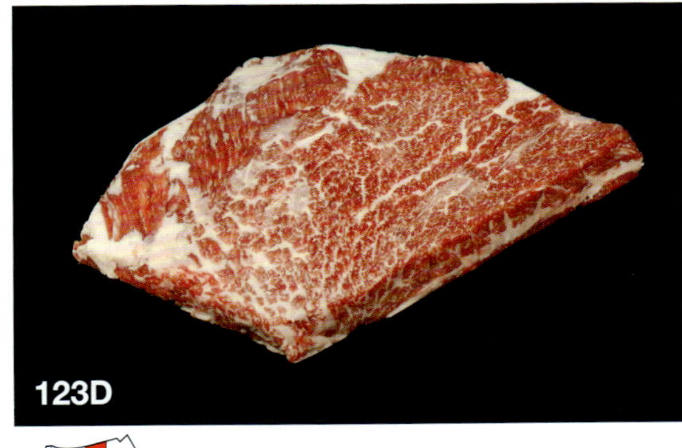

124 — Beef Rib, Back Ribs

This item is the intact portion of the seven ribs and intercostal meat from Item Nos. 109 or 109A. The chine bone and thoracic vertebrae shall be removed exposing the sawed ends of the rib bones. Unless otherwise specified, back ribs shall be no less than 6.0 inches (15.0 cm) or more than 8.0 inches (20.0 cm) wide at any point measured across the sawed ends of the rib bones.

124 — Costilla Cargada, Costillas (Agujas) Cortas (6ª-8ª), Deshuesadas

Esta pieza es la porción intacta de las siete costillas y la carne intercostal de las piezas número 109 o 109A. El cuerpo de las vértebras torácicas y sus puntas (llamadas también "espinas" o "puntas del espinazo") divididas a sierra de las vértebras torácicas deberán extraerse exponiéndose los extremos de las costillas cortados a sierra. A menos que se especifique lo contrario, las costillas del espaldar deberán tener por lo menos 15.0 cm (6.0 pulgadas) o más de 20.0 cm (8.0 pulgadas) de ancho en cualquier punto a lo largo de los extremos de las costillas cortados a sierra.

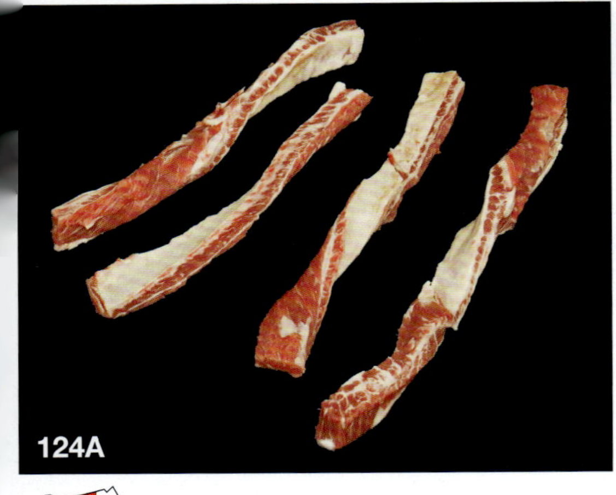

124A

124A Beef Rib,
Back Rib, Rib Fingers

This item will consist of the intercostal muscles that are removed from between the back ribs. Purchaser may specify that the costal cartilage be removed as is pictured.

124A Chuletón (Espaldar),
Costillas del Chuletón,
Tiras de Entrecostilla
(M. Intercostales)

Esta pieza consistirá en los músculos *intercostales* que se extraen entre las costillas del espaldar. El comprador puede especificar que se retire el cartílago costal como se muestra en la ilustración.

130

130 Beef Chuck,
Short Ribs

This item may be prepared from the arm portion of any chuck item and shall consist of the ribs numbers 2 through 5, the intercostal meat, and *serratus ventralis* muscle. This item shall be trimmed practically free of surface fat. The dorsal edge shall have no evidence of the cartilaginous junctures of the ribs and thoracic vertebrae.

130 Paleta (Espaldilla),
Costillas Cortas de
Espaldilla (2ª-5ª)

Esta pieza puede prepararse a partir de la porción del brazuelo de cualquier pieza de paleta y consistirá en las costillas número 2 a 5, la carne intercostal y el músculo *serratus ventralis*. Esta pieza deberá ser recortada hasta quedar prácticamente libre de grasa de cubierta. En el borde dorsal no deben quedar rastros de las coyunturas cartilaginosas de las costillas ni de las vértebras torácicas.

130A

130A Beef Chuck,
Short Ribs,
Boneless

This item is prepared from Item No. 130 and shall consist of the *serratus ventralis* muscle from the arm portion of the chuck. The ribs and intercostal muscles shall be removed. This item shall have at least four rib marks extending to the dorsal and ventral edge of the *serratus ventralis* muscle. This item shall be trimmed practically free of fat and shall be no less than .5 in (13 mm) thick at any point.

130A Paleta (Espaldilla),
Costillas Cortas de
Espaldilla (2ª-5ª),
Deshuesadas (M.
Serrato Ventral)

Esta pieza se prepara a partir de la pieza número 130 y deberá consistir en el músculo *serratus ventralis* de la porción del brazuelo de la paleta. Deberán retirarse las costillas y los músculos intercostales. Esta pieza deberá tener un mínimo de cuatro costillas marcadas, extendiéndose al borde dorsal y ventral del músculo *serratus ventralis*. Esta pieza deberá limpiarse para que quede prácticamente libre de grasa, y no podrá tener un grosor superior a 13 mm (0.5 pulgadas) en ningún punto.

134   Beef Bones

This item consists of any one or combination of shank, femur, or humerus bones sawed into sections of lengths as specified by the purchaser. Marrow shall be exposed on at least one end of each sawed section.

134   Huesos de la Res

Esta pieza consiste en cualquiera o una combinación de los huesos de chamberete, fémur o húmero cortados a sierra en secciones de longitudes especificadas por el comprador. La médula ósea deberá estar expuesta en al menos en un extremo de cada sección aserrada.

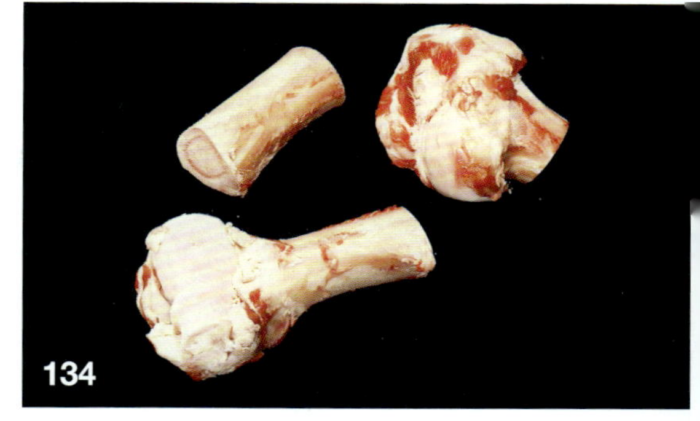

134

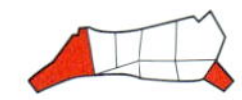

135   Diced Beef

Diced beef shall be prepared from any portion of the carcass exclusive of the shank, detached *cutaneous* muscles, and heel meat unless otherwise specified. When heel meat is allowed by the purchaser, the *superficial digital flexor* shall be separated and excluded from the *gastrocnemius* through the natural seams. The meat shall be either hand-diced or mechanically diced. Grinding is not permitted. To facilitate dicing, meat may be frozen and/or tempered, one time only. Dices shall be free of bones, cartilages, heavy connective tissue, and lymph glands. Unless otherwise specified, at least 75 percent by weight of the resulting dices shall be of a size equivalent of not less than a 0.75 inch (19 mm) cube nor not more than a 1.5 inch (3.8 cm) cube and no individual surface shall be more than 2.5 inches (6.3 cm) in length. The surface and/or seam fat shall not exceed 0.5 inch (13 mm) thickness at any point.

135   Trozos de Res en Cubos

Los trozos de res en cubos deberán prepararse a partir de la canal excluyendo el chamberete, los músculos *cutáneos* sueltos y la carne del talón, a menos que se especifique lo contrario. Cuando el comprador permite la carne del talón, se deberá retirar el *flexor digital superficial* del *gastrocnemius* siguiendo las vetas naturales. La carne deberá trocearse ya sea a mano o mecánicamente. La molienda no está permitida. Para facilitar el troceado, la carne puede estar congelada o atemperada, una sola vez. Los cubos deberán estar libres de huesos, cartílagos, tejido conectivo grueso y ganglios linfáticos. A menos que se especifique lo contrario, al menos el 75% por peso de los cubos resultantes deberán ser de un tamaño equivalente a por lo menos 19 mm (0.75 pulgadas) sin superar los 3.8 cm (1.5 pulgadas), y ninguna superficie individual podrá tener más de 6.3 cm (2.5 pulgadas) de longitud. La cubierta de grasa o entre los músculos no deberá exceder un grosor de 13 mm (0.5 pulgadas) en ningún punto.

135

135A   Beef for Stewing

This item is as described in Item No. 135, except unless otherwise specified at least 85 percent by weight of the resulting dices shall meet the Item No. 135 dice size requirements. In addition, the fat thickness of the surface and/or seam fat shall not exceed 0.25 inch (6 mm) at any point.

135A   Trozos de Res en Cubos para Cocido/Guisado

Este producto es como aparece descrito en el número 135; salvo que se especifique lo contrario, al menos el 85% por peso de los trozos resultantes deberá cumplir con los requisitos de tamaño correspondientes del producto número 135. Además, el grosor de la cubierta de grasa o entre los músculos no deberá exceder 6 mm (0.25 pulgadas) en ningún punto.

135A

135B

135B Beef for Kabobs

The raw material requirements of this item are as described in Item No. 135. The kabobs shall be prepared so that unless otherwise specified at least 90 percent by weight of the resulting dices shall be of a size equivalent not less than a 1.0 inch (2.5 cm) or more than a 1.5 inch (3.8 cm) cube and no individual surface shall be more than 2.5 inches (6.3 cm) in length. The fat thickness of the surface and/or seam fat shall not exceed 0.125 inch (3 mm) at any point.

135B Trozos de Res para Brochetas

Los requisitos sobre la materia prima de este producto son los descritos en el producto número 135. Las brochetas deberán ser preparadas de manera que, a menos que se especifique lo contrario, al menos el 90% por peso de los trozos resultantes sean de un tamaño equivalente a cubos no menores a 2.5 cm (1.0 pulgadas) ni más de 3.8 cm (1.5 pulgadas), y ninguna superficie individual deberá tener más de 6.3 cm (2.5 pulgadas) de longitud. El grosor de la cubierta de grasa o entre los músculos no deberá exceder 3 mm (0.125 pulgadas) en ningún punto.

136 Ground Beef

Material - Ground beef shall be prepared from any portion of a boneless graded or ungraded carcass. The meat shall be free of bones; cartilages; prefemoral, popliteal, and prescapular, and other exposed lymph glands; heavy connective tissue; and the tendinous ends of shanks, shoulder clods, and tips (knuckles) to a point that exposes at least 75 percent lean on a cross-sectional cut. Unless otherwise specified, ground beef may be derived from frozen and stockpiled boneless meat. The purchaser may specify the maximum amount of frozen boneless meat that can be mixed with fresh-chilled meat prior to final grinding.

When specified by the purchaser, "finely textured beef", low temperature rendered beef that is processed from boneless beef trimmings, is allowed to be combined with boneless beef meeting the above material requirements provided it does not exceed 20 percent by weight of the combined finished product. When finely textured beef is used, the following criteria must be met:

- Red Color - The producer of finely textured beef shall assure that the product has a discernible redness in color. The finely textured beef shall maintain the same redness in color until the time of blending and grinding to minimize the effect of the color to the finished ground beef.

- Fat Content - Does not exceed 10 percent fat.

Processing – Grinding equipment shall have sharp knives and plates and be equipped with a bone/collector system. The boneless meat shall be ground at least once through a plate having holes not larger than 1.0 inch (2.5 cm) in diameter unless specified otherwise. Alternatively, boneless beef may be chopped or machine-cut by any method provided the texture and appearance of the product after final grinding is typical of ground beef prepared by grinding only. Unless otherwise specified, final grinding shall be through a plate having holes 0.125 inch (3 mm) in diameter. Beef shall be thoroughly blended at least once prior to final grinding. The ground beef shall not be mixed again after final grinding. Initial reduction in size, blending, and final grinding shall be a continuous sequence.

The purchaser may specify the use of a bone collector/ extruder system to help exclude objectionable materials such as bone, cartilage, connective tissue, etc. when using a 0.1875 inch (5 mm) or smaller plate on the final grind. This material may not be reintroduced into the finished product. For certification purposes, the purchaser may waive an examination for trimming defects provided the use of a bone collector/extruder system is specified.

When coarse ground beef is specified the boneless meat shall be ground once through a plate having holes no larger than 1.0 inch (2.5 cm) or smaller than 0.625 inch (16 mm) in diameter. Alternatively, the boneless meat may be ground twice, with the smallest plate having holes no larger than 1.0 inch (2.5 cm) or smaller than 0.75 inch (19 mm) in diameter. Coarse ground meat may be blended after grinding or between grinds in order to assure uniformity of the fat content throughout the product. The term "coarse ground" shall appear on the product label in accord with FSIS regulations.

Fat Content – Unless otherwise specified, the fat content shall be 20 percent fat. The purchaser may specify a different fat content provided it does not exceed 30 percent.

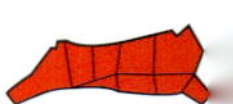

136   Carne Molida de Res

Material - La carne molida de res deberá prepararse a partir de cualquier porción de una canal deshuesada clasificada por grados o sin clasificar. La carne deberá estar libre de huesos, cartílagos, ganglios prefemorales, poplíteos y prescapulares, y otros ganglios linfáticos expuestos; tejido conectivo grueso y los extremos tendinosos de los chamberetes; planchuelas y pulpas bola, hasta un punto en que se exponga por lo menos el 75% de carne magra en un corte transversal. A menos que se especifique lo contrario, la carne molida de res puede provenir de carne deshuesada congelada y almacenada. El comprador puede especificar la cantidad máxima de carne congelada y deshuesada que se puede mezclar con carne refrigerada en estado fresco previamente a la molienda final.

Cuando el comprador lo especifica, "carne de res finamente texturizada", la carne de res a baja temperatura que se procesa a partir de recortes de carne de res deshuesada, puede ser combinada con carne de res deshuesada, cumpliendo los requisitos de los materiales antes detallados, siempre que no exceda el 20% por peso del producto combinado terminado. Cuando se usa carne de res finamente texturizada, se debe cumplir con las siguientes pautas:

- Color Rojo - El productor de carne de res finamente texturizada deberá garantizar que el producto tenga un color rojo discernible. La carne de res finamente texturizada deberá mantener el mismo color rojo hasta el momento de mezclarse y molerse para reducir el efecto del color en la carne molida terminada.

- Contenido de grasa - No excede el 10% de grasa.

Procesamiento - El equipo de molienda deberá tener cuchillas y hojas afiladas y contar con un sistema de recolección de huesos. La carne deshuesada deberá molerse al menos una vez a través de placas con orificios que no superen los 2.5 cm (1.0 pulgada) de diámetro, a menos que se especifique lo contrario. Por otra parte, la carne de res deshuesada puede ser picada o cortada a máquina por cualquier método, siempre que la textura y la apariencia del producto después del molido final sea la típica de la carne molida de res tal como se prepara únicamente mediante la molienda. A menos que se especifique lo contrario, la molienda final deberá realizarse con una placa con orificios de 3 mm (0.125 pulgadas) de diámetro. La carne de res debe mezclarse muy bien, al menos una vez antes de la molienda final. La carne molida de res no podrá mezclarse nuevamente después de la molienda final. La reducción inicial en tamaño, mezcla y molienda final deberá constituir una secuencia continua.

El comprador puede especificar el uso de un sistema expulsor y colector de huesos para ayudar a expeler materiales cuestionables como hueso, cartílago, tejido conectivo, etc. cuando en la molienda final se use una placa de 5 mm (0.1875 pulgadas) o menos. Este material no puede volver a ser introducido en el producto terminado. A efectos de certificaciones, el comprador puede renunciar a la realización de un examen para constatar defectos de recorte si se especifica el uso de un sistema expulsor y colector de huesos.

Cuando se especifique que la carne de res sea molida gruesa, la carne deshuesada deberá molerse una vez a través de una placa con orificios que no superen 2.5 cm (1.0 pulgada) ni sean inferiores a 16 mm (0.625 pulgadas) de diámetro. De lo contrario, la carne deshuesada puede molerse dos veces, con la placa más pequeña de orificios que no superen 2.5 cm (1.0 pulgada) ni sean inferiores a 19 mm (0.75 pulgadas) de diámetro. La carne molida gruesa puede mezclarse después de molerse o entre moliendas a fin de asegurar la uniformidad del contenido de grasa en todo el producto. El término "coarse ground" (molido grueso) deberá aparecer en la etiqueta del producto, de acuerdo con los reglamentos del Servicio de Inspección e Inocuidad Alimentaria.

Contenido de grasa – A menos que se especifique lo contrario, el contenido de grasa deberá ser del 20%. El comprador puede especificar un contenido de grasa diferente, siempre que no exceda el 30%.

136A — Beef and Soy Protein Product Patty Mix

This item is as described in Item No. 136 except that soy protein product (SPP) shall be added. Source (e.g., soy), Type[1] (flour, concentrate, or isolate), and Texture (granular or textured) of SPP shall be specified by the purchaser. The SPP may be used dry, partially hydrated, or fully hydrated. If not specified, the dry SPP shall be fully hydrated to yield a minimum of 18 percent protein. To determine the maximum amount of water to be mixed with the dry SPP to yield 18 percent protein in the mixture, the following equation shall be used:

$$\frac{[\text{Percent protein on ``as is'' basis}]}{[\quad 18 \quad]} - 1 = x$$

x = maximum pounds of water to be added to each pound of dry SPP.

The SPP shall be hydrated for the length of time listed on the product label. If this information is not available, the product shall be hydrated until all water is absorbed. The purchaser shall specify any level of substitution of hydrated SPP in the combined finished product up to 30 percent. If not specified, the maximum percent of hydrated protein product in the combined finished product shall not exceed 20 percent. The hydrated SPP shall be used in the same working day in which it was hydrated. The hydrated SPP shall be blended with the raw meat (in the specified ratio) following the initial reduction in size.

SPP hydrated and frozen by the SPP manufacturer may be used provided that: (1) the protein content of the hydrated product (as specifically stated on the manufacturer's label) is not less than 18 percent: (2) the product may be tempered, but not thawed, prior to use; and (3) no additional water may be added.

[1] Any one or combination of the following types of SPP may be used. When a combination of these are produced by the SPP manufacturer, the amount of each type and minimum protein content (as is basis) of the mixture shall be declared on the manufacturer's label.

Type	Protein (%) as is basis
Flour	50.0
Concentrate	65.0
Isolate	85.0

136A — Carne Molida de Res con Producto Proteico Vegetal (PPV) Añadido Según La Normativa

Esta pieza aparece descrita en la pieza número 136, salvo que se agregará el producto proteico vegetal (PPV). La fuente (por ej., soya), el tipo [1] (harina, concentrado o aislado), y la textura (granulada o texturizada) del PPV serán especificados por el comprador. El PPV puede utilizarse en seco, parcial o completamente hidratado. Si no se especifica, el PPV seco deberá hidratarse por completo para rendir un mínimo del 18% de proteína. A fin de determinar la cantidad máxima de agua a mezclarse con el PPV seco, para que rinda 18% de proteína en la mezcla, se deberá utilizar la siguiente ecuación:

$$\frac{[\text{Porcentaje de proteína en las condiciones en que se encuentra}]}{[\quad 18 \quad]} - 1 = x$$

x = máximo de libras de agua a agregarse por cada libra de PPV seco.

El PPV deberá ser hidratado por el período de tiempo detallado en la etiqueta del producto. Si no se dispone de esta información, el producto deberá hidratarse hasta que se absorba toda el agua. El comprador deberá especificar cualquier nivel de sustitución de PPV hidratado en el producto terminado combinado en hasta 30%. Si no se especifica, el porcentaje máximo de producto proteico hidratado en el producto terminado combinado no deberá exceder el 20%. El PPV deberá utilizarse el mismo día de la semana en que se hidrató. El PPV hidratado deberá mezclarse con la carne cruda (en el porcentaje indicado), siguiendo la reducción inicial en tamaño.

El fabricante del PPV podrá usar el PPV hidratado y congelado siempre que: (1) el contenido proteico del producto hidratado (como se indica específicamente en la etiqueta del fabricante) no sea menor al 18%; (2) el producto podrá atemperarse, pero no descongelarse, antes de su uso; y (3) no se le podrá agregar más agua.

[1] Es posible usar cualquiera de los siguientes tipos de PPV o una combinación de los mismos. Cuando el fabricante de PPV produce una combinación de éstos, la cantidad de cada tipo y el contenido proteico mínimo (tal como se encuentra) de la mezcla deberán aparecer declarados en la etiqueta.

Tipo	Proteína (%) tal como se encuentra
Harina	50.0
Concentrado	65.0
Aislado	85.0

136C — Beef Patty Mix, Not to Exceed (NTE) 10% Fat

This item is as described in Item No. 136 except that the fat content shall not exceed 10 percent. Additional ingredients may be added to enhance product acceptability. Such ingredients shall not exceed 10 percent of the combined finished product. The purchaser may specify the ingredients that will be allowed.

136C — Mezcla para Hamburguesa de Res, (con PPV Sin Exceder 10%), Magra (sin Exceder 10% Grasa)

Esta pieza aparece descrita en la pieza número 136, salvo que el contenido de grasa no deberá exceder el 10%. Es posible agregar ingredientes adicionales para mejorar la aceptación del producto. Esos ingredientes no podrán exceder el 10% del producto combinado terminado. El comprador puede especificar los ingredientes que serán permitidos.

136D — Pure Beef

This item is as described in Item No. 136 except that the finely textured beef that is labeled as partially defatted chopped beef or that does not comply with the criteria listed in Item No. 136 may be used to not exceed 20 percent by weight of the combined finished product.

136D — Pura Carne de Res

Este producto aparece descrito en el producto número 136, salvo que la carne de res de textura fina que está etiquetada como carne de res parcialmente limpia de grasa y picada o la que no cumple con los criterios detallados en el producto número 136, puede ser usada para no exceder el 20% por peso del producto combinado terminado.

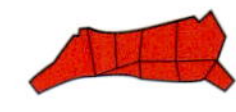

137 Ground Beef, Special

This item is as described in Item No. 136, except not less than 50 percent by weight of the product shall be from any combination of boneless primal or subprimal portions of rounds, loins, ribs, or square-cut chucks. The remaining portion, not to exceed 50 percent by weight, may be composed of trimmings or cuts from any allowable portion of the carcass. The purchaser may specify a quality grade requirement for the primal or subprimal portion and/or the remaining portion. Formulation requirements shall be determined on a boneless basis. Primal or subprimal cuts that have more than a minor amount of lean removed are not eligible for the primal portion.

The purchaser has an option to select a ground beef style derived from one of the specific primal portions described below. If no such selection is made, Style 1 will apply. Product produced in accordance with the following styles shall be labeled accordingly.

Style 1 Ground Beef, Special

As described above.

Style 2 Ground Beef, Chuck

Ground beef chuck may be derived from any portion of a boneless chuck item including the foreshank provided that the shank meat in the mixture not exceed its natural 6 percent proportions. If, however, the purchaser specifies the product's fat content to be 20 percent or less, or when the producer's label declares that the fat content of packaged ground beef chuck product is 20 percent or less, then, unless otherwise specified, the producer will be allowed to use foreshanks up to 50 percent of the formulation as a source for lean, provided the shanks have been mechanically desinewed.

Style 3 Ground Beef, Round

Ground beef round may be derived from any portion of a boneless round item including the hindshank, provided that the shank meat in the mixture not exceed its 6.0 percent natural proportions. If, however, the purchaser specifies the product's fat content to be 15 percent or less, or when the producer's label declares that the fat content of packaged ground beef round product is 15 percent or less, then the producer, unless otherwise specified, will be allowed to use hindshanks up to 50 percent of the formulation as a source for lean, provided the shanks have been mechanically desinewed.

Style 4 Ground Beef, Sirloin

Ground beef sirloin may be derived from any portion of a boneless sirloin item. When the purchaser specifies the product's fat content to be 15 percent or less, or when the producer's label declares that the fat content of packaged ground beef sirloin product is 15 percent or less, then the producer, unless otherwise specified, will be allowed to use any portion of a boneless sirloin tip (knuckle) item up to 50 percent of the formulation as a lean source.

If purchasers desire any of the above formulations prepared with SPP, they may specify Item No. 137A, Beef and Soy Protein Product Mix, Special. The SPP shall be added as described in Item No. 136A.

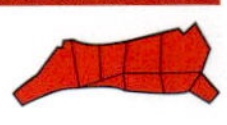

137 Carne Molida de Res, Especial

Este producto aparece descrito en el producto número 136, salvo que al menos un 50% por peso del producto deberá provenir de una combinación de porciones primarias o subprimarias deshuesadas de piernas, lomos, costillas o paletas de corte cuadrado. La porción restante, que no deberá superar el 50% por peso, puede estar compuesta de recortes o cortes de cualquier porción permitida de la canal. El cliente puede especificar un requisito de grado de calidad para la porción primaria o subprimaria o para la porción restante. Los requisitos de la fórmula deben determinarse en función del producto deshuesado. Los cortes primarios o subprimarios a los que se les ha quitado más de una pequeña cantidad de carne magra no cumplen con los requisitos para constituir una porción primaria.

El comprador tiene la opción de seleccionar un estilo de carne molida derivado de las porciones primarias específicas descritas más abajo. Si no se hace dicha selección, se aplicará el Estilo 1. El producto elaborado según los siguientes estilos deberá ser etiquetado según corresponda.

Carne Molida de Res, Especial, Estilo 1

Según la descripción anterior.

Carne Molida de Res, Paleta, Estilo 2

La carne molida de paleta de res puede provenir de cualquier porción de una pieza de paleta deshuesada, inclusive el chamberete de mano, siempre que la carne del chamberete que forme parte de la mezcla no exceda la proporción natural del 6%. No obstante, si el comprador especifica que el contenido de grasa del producto debe ser del 20% o menos, o cuando la etiqueta del productor declara que el contenido de grasa del producto empaquetado de carne molida de paleta de res es del 20% o menos, entonces, a menos que se especifique lo contrario, el productor podrá usar hasta el 50% de la formulación en chamberetes como fuente de carne magra, siempre que se hayan eliminado mecánicamente los pellejos y demás tejidos conectivos de los chamberetes.

Carne Molida de Res, Pierna, Estilo 3

La carne molida de res puede provenir de cualquier porción de la pierna deshuesada, inclusive del chamberete trasero, siempre que la carne del chamberete que forme parte de la mezcla no exceda la proporción natural del 6.0%. Si, no obstante, el comprador especifica que el contenido de grasa del producto debe ser del 15% o menos, o cuando la etiqueta del productor declara que el contenido de grasa del producto empaquetado de carne molida de res es del 15% o menos, entonces el productor, a menos que se especifique lo contrario, podrá usar los chamberetes traseros en una cantidad de hasta el 50% de la fórmula como fuente de carne magra, siempre que se hayan eliminado mecánicamente los pellejos y demás tejidos conectivos de los chamberetes.

Carne Molida de Res, Aguayón, Estilo 4

La carne molida de aguayón de res puede provenir de cualquier porción del aguayón deshuesado. Cuando el comprador especifica que el contenido de grasa del producto debe ser del 15% o menos, o cuando la etiqueta del productor declara que el contenido de grasa del producto empaquetado de aguayón de carne molida de res es del 15% o menos, entonces el productor, a menos que se especifique lo contrario, podrá usar cualquier porción de la pulpa bola en un porcentaje de hasta el 50% de la fórmula, como fuente de carne magra.

Si los compradores desean que cualquiera de las fórmulas detalladas anteriormente se preparen con PPV, pueden especificar la pieza número 137A, Mezcla de Producto de Proteína de Soya y Carne de Res, Especial. El PPV deberá agregarse según se describe en la pieza número 136A.

138   Beef Trimmings

Beef trimmings may be prepared from any portion of the carcass which yields product that meets end item requirements. All objectionable materials shall be removed. Ground product is not permitted. Unless otherwise specified by the purchaser, trimmings derived from automatic deboning machines and advance lean retrieval systems shall be excluded.

138   Carne de Res, Recortes

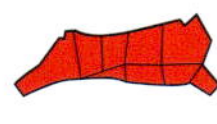

Los recortes de carne de res pueden prepararse a partir de cualquier porción de canal que dé como resultado un producto que cumpla con los requisitos de la pieza final. Todos los materiales objetables deberán retirarse. No se permite un producto molido. A menos que el comprador especifique lo contrario, se deberán excluir los recortes provenientes de máquinas deshuesadoras automáticas y sistemas avanzados para recuperar la carne.

139   Beef, Special Trim, Boneless

Beef special trim may be prepared from any portion of the carcass which yields product that meets the end item requirements. Unless otherwise specified, shank and heel meat shall be excluded. When heel meat is allowed by the purchaser, the *superficial digital flexor* shall be removed from the *gastrocnemius* through the natural seams. Unless otherwise specified, trimmings shall consist of pieces which have a surface area on one side which is no less than 8.0 square inches (51.6 sq. cm) and are no less than .50 inch (13 mm) thick at any point. All bones, cartilages, heavy connective tissue, detached cutaneous muscles, and lymph glands shall be removed. Trimmings shall be practically free of surface and seam fat.

139   Carne de Res, Recortes Especiales, Deshuesados

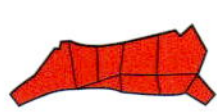

Los recortes especiales de carne de res pueden prepararse a partir de cualquier porción de la canal que dé como resultado un producto que cumpla con los requisitos de la pieza final. A menos que se especifique lo contrario, se excluirá la carne del chamberete y el talón. Cuando el comprador permite la carne de talón, el *flexor digital superficial* deberá retirarse del *gastrocnemius* siguiendo las vetas naturales. A menos que se especifique lo contrario, los recortes consistirán en piezas cuyos lados tengan un área superficial que no sea inferior a 51.6 cm cuadrados (8.0 pulgadas cuadradas) y cuyo grosor no sea inferior a 13 mm (0.50 pulgadas) en ningún punto. Se deben quitar todos los huesos, cartílagos, tejido conectivo grueso, músculos cutáneos sueltos y ganglios linfáticos. Los recortes quedarán prácticamente libres de cubierta de grasa y vetas de grasa intermuscular.

140   Beef, Hanging Tender (IM)

The hanging tender is a soft, grainy-textured, elliptical-shaped muscle that is attached to the diaphragm and the juncture of the lumbar/thoracic vertebrae. There is only one hanging tender per carcass.

PSO: 1 – The heavy connective tissue within the center shall be exposed and removed by a butterfly cut. The resulting product is sometimes referred to as "Pillars".

140   Arrachera Gallo (MI)

La arrachera gallo es un músculo suave, de textura granulada y forma elíptica que está unido al diafragma y a la articulación de las vértebras lumbares y torácicas. Hay solamente una arrachera gallo por canal.

PSO: 1 – El tejido conectivo grueso dentro del centro deberá exponerse y extraerse mediante un corte mariposa. A veces al producto resultante se le llama "Pilares" por tratarse de los pilares del diafragma.

140

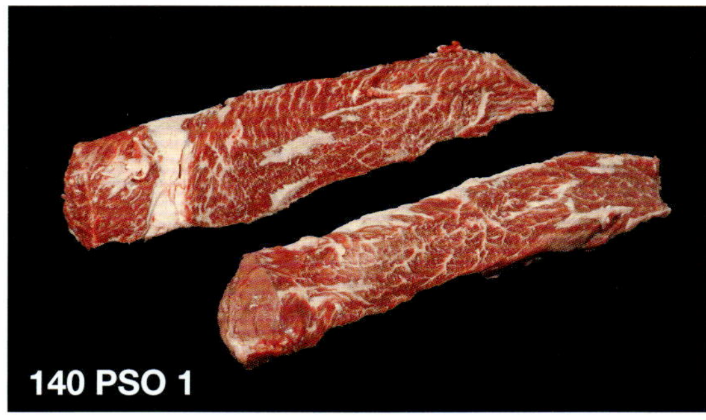

140 PSO 1

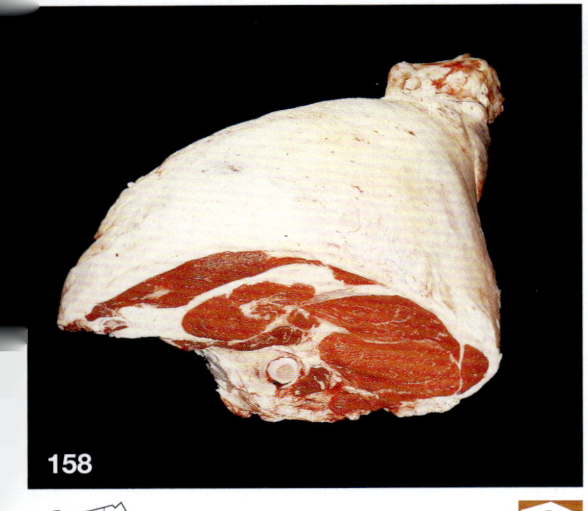

158

158 Beef Round, Primal

This bone in item consists of the top, bottom, sirloin tip (knuckle) portion (Item No. 167), rump, heel, and shank. It remains after Item No. 172 is separated from the hindquarter Item No. 155. The loin end shall be exposed by a straight cut beginning at the juncture of the last sacral and the first caudal vertebrae, exposing the ball of the femur without severing the protuberance. No more than two vertebra shall remain on the round. The *tensor fasciae latae* shall not extend completely around the outside of the knuckle. The *obliquus abdominis internus* or flank muscle shall be excluded.

❧ In Canada, this item is referred to as the Hip. The Round refers to the Top Round (Item No. 169D) and Bottom Round (Item No. 170) collectively.

Beef Round, Components

A 171F Heel
B 169D Top (Inside)
C *Pectineus*
D *Sartorius*
E 167A Sirloin Tip (Knuckle), Peeled
F 171B Outside (Flat)
G 171C Eye of Round

158 Pierna (Piña), Pieza Primaria

Esta pieza con hueso consiste en la porción de pulpa negra (cara/centro), pulpa blanca (contracara), pulpa bola (pieza número 167), tajo anterior de pulpa blanca, talón y chamberete. Se obtiene después de que se separa la pieza número 172 de la pieza número 155 del cuarto trasero. El extremo posterior deberá exponerse mediante un corte recto que comience en la articulación de la última vértebra sacra con la primera vértebra coccígea, exponiéndose la cabeza del fémur sin cortar la protuberancia. No quedarán más de dos vértebras en la pierna. El *tensor de la fascia lata* no deberá extenderse completamente alrededor del exterior de la pulpa bola. El músculo *obliquus abdominis internus* o músculo de la falda deberá ser excluido.

❧ En Canadá, esta pieza se le conoce como la Cadera. La Pierna se refiere al conjunto de la Pulpa Negra (Cara) [pieza número 169D] y Pulpa Blanca (Contracara) [pieza número 170].

Componentes de la Pierna de Res

A 171F Talón
B 169D Pulpa Negra (Cara/Centro)
C *Pectineus*
D *Sartorius*
E 167A Punta de Sirloin (Pulpa Bola), Desprovisto de Grasa
F 171B Contracara (Contracuete)
G 171C Cuete

158A Beef Round, Diamond-Cut

This bone in item consists of the top, bottom, full sirloin tip (knuckle) (Item No. 167B), rump, heel and shank. It remains after Item No. 172A is separated from the hindquarter Item No. 155. The loin end shall be exposed by two straight cuts which exposes the ball of the femur without severing the protuberance and leaves the full sirloin tip (knuckle) attached. The first cut shall start at a point passing through the 4th sacral vertebra and extend to the ball of the femur. The second cut shall extend from the ball of the femur to a point on the ventral edge exposing the *tensor fasciae latae* extending completely around the outside of the sirloin tip (knuckle). The *obliquus abdominis internus*, or flap muscle, shall be excluded. The full sirloin tip (knuckle) may be separated from the round. If separated, it shall be separated as described in Item No. 167. The full sirloin tip (knuckle) shall be individually packaged and packed in the same container.

158A Pierna (Piña), Forma Diamante

Esta pieza con hueso consiste en la porción de pulpa negra (cara/centro), pulpa blanca (contracara), pulpa bola completa (pieza número 167B), aguayón, talón y chamberete. Se obtiene después de que se separa la pieza número 172A de la pieza número 155, cuarto trasero. El extremo posterior deberá estar expuesto por dos cortes rectos que exponen la cabeza del fémur sin cortar la protuberancia, dejando toda la pulpa bola unida. El primer corte deberá comenzar en un punto que pase por la 4ª vértebra sacra y se extienda hacia la cabeza del fémur. El segundo corte deberá extenderse desde la cabeza del fémur hasta un punto en el borde ventral que exponga el músculo *tensor de la fascia lata*, extendiéndose completamente alrededor de la parte externa de la pulpa bola. Se deberá excluir el músculo *obliquus abdominis internus* o músculo de la falda. La pulpa bola completa puede ser separada de la pierna. Si se separa, deberá procederse según se describe en la pieza número 167, y la pulpa bola se deberá empaquetar individualmente y empacar en el mismo recipiente.

159 — Beef Round, Primal, Boneless

This boneless item is prepared from Item No. 158. The top (inside) round shall be separated from the sirloin tip (knuckle) through the natural seam. The *tensor fasciae latae* shall not extend completely around the outside of the sirloin tip (knuckle). All bones, cartilages, *obliquus abdominis internus,* the *sacrosciatic* ligament, the lean and fat that overlaid the *sacrosciatic* ligament, the lean and fat (oyster) that overlaid the aitch bone, the thick opaque portion of the *gracilis* membrane, and *popliteal* and *prefemoral* lymph glands shall be excluded. The tendinous ends of the shank and sirloin tip (knuckle) shall be cut to evidence no less than 75 percent lean. The sirloin tip (knuckle) may be separated from the boneless round. If separated, it shall be separated as described in Item No. 167 and individually packaged and packed into the same container.

159 — Pierna (Piña), Pieza Primaria, Deshuesada

Esta pieza deshuesada se prepara a partir de la pieza número 158. La porción de pulpa negra (cara/centro) deberá ser separada de la pulpa bola siguiendo las vetas naturales. El *tensor de la fascia lata* no deberá extenderse completamente alrededor del exterior de la pulpa bola. Se excluirán todos los huesos, cartílagos, *obliquus abdominis internus*, el ligamento *sacrociático*, la carne magra y la grasa que recubren el ligamento *sacrociático*, la carne magra y la grasa ("ostra" de la cadera) que recubre el hueso de la cadera, la porción gruesa opaca de la membrana del músculo *gracilis* y los ganglios linfáticos *poplíteos* y *prefemorales*. Los extremos tendinosos de chamberete y la pulpa bola deberán cortarse de forma que se muestre por lo menos el 75% de la carne magra. La pulpa bola puede ser separada de la pierna deshuesada. Si se separa, deberá procederse según se describe en la pieza número 167 y se deberá empaquetar individualmente y empacar en el mismo recipiente.

160 — Beef Round, Shank Off, Partially Boneless

This partially boneless item is prepared as described in Item No. 158, except the aitch bone and the fat and lean overlying it (oyster), tail bones (sacral vertebrae), *sacrosciatic* ligament and the fat and lean overlying the ligament, the thick opaque portion of the *gracilis* membrane, exposed lymph glands, and the hindshank shall be excluded. The hindshank is excluded by a cut through the stifle joint along the natural seam between the heel and hindshank. The sirloin tip (knuckle) may be separated from the partially boneless round. If separated, it shall be separated as described in Item No. 167 and individually packaged and packed into the same container.

160 — Pierna (Piña), sin Chamberete, Parcialmente Deshuesada

Esta pieza parcialmente deshuesada se prepara según se describe en la pieza número 158, salvo que deberán excluirse el hueso de la cadera y la carne magra que lo recubre ("ostra" de la cadera), los huesos de la cola (vértebras sacras), el ligamento *sacrociático* y la grasa y la carne magra que recubre el ligamento, la porción gruesa opaca de la membrana del músculo *gracilis*, los ganglios linfáticos expuestos y el chamberete trasero. El chamberete trasero se excluye mediante un corte a través de la articulación de la rodilla, siguiendo la veta natural entre el talón y el chamberete trasero. La pulpa bola puede ser separada de la pierna parcialmente deshuesada. Si se separa, deberá procederse según se describe en la pieza número 167 y se deberá empaquetar individualmente y empacar en el mismo recipiente.

160 View from Loin End
Vista desde el Extremo Adyacente al Lomo

160 View from Shank End
Vista desde el Extremo Adyacente al Chamberete

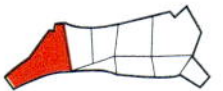

160B Beef Round, Heel and Shank Off, Semi-Boneless

This item is described in Item No. 160, except, in addition, the heel is excluded by cutting through the natural seams.

160B Pierna (Piña), sin Talón/Copete ni Chamberete, Parcialmente Deshuesada

Esta pieza está descrita en la pieza número 160, salvo que, además, se retira el talón cortándolo por las vetas naturales.

161 Beef Round, Shank Off, Boneless

This boneless item is as prepared in Item No. 159, except, in addition, the hindshank is excluded as described in Item No. 160. Unless otherwise specified, the *popliteal* lymph gland shall also be excluded.

161 Pierna (Piña), sin Chamberete, Deshuesada

Esta pieza deshuesada se prepara como la pieza número 159, salvo que, además, se retira el chamberete trasero como se describe en la pieza número 160. A menos que se especifique lo contrario, el ganglio linfático *poplíteo* también deberá retirarse.

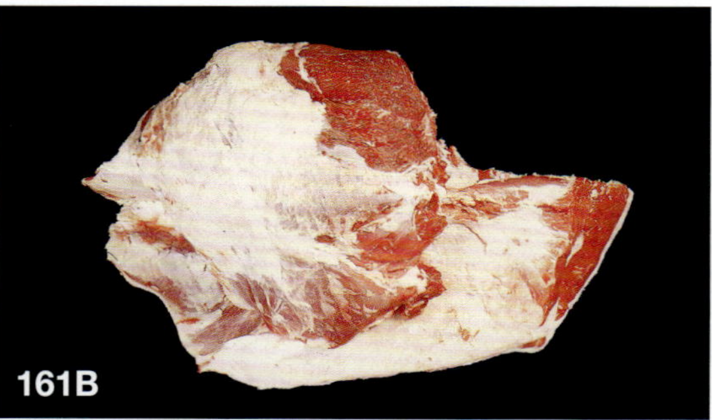

161B

161B Beef Round, Heel and Shank Off, Without Sirloin Tip (Knuckle), Boneless

This item is as described in Item No. 161, except, in addition, the heel and sirloin tip (knuckle) shall be excluded by cutting through natural seams.

161B Pierna (Piña), sin Talón/Copete, sin Chamberete ni Pulpa Bola, Deshuesada

Esta pieza aparece descrita en la pieza número 161, excepto que, además, el talón y la pulpa bola deberán excluirse cortando por las vetas naturales.

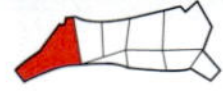

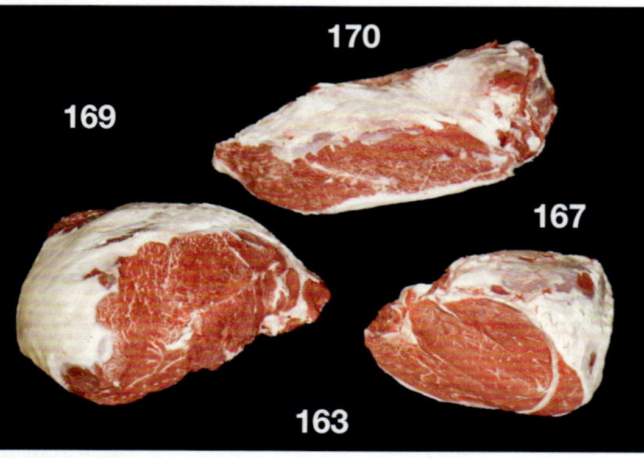

163 Beef Round, Shank Off, 3-Way, Boneless

This item shall consist of the following items that are individually packaged and packed into the same container:

Item No. 167 - Beef Round, Sirloin Tip (Knuckle)

Item No. 169 - Beef Round, Top (Inside)

Item No. 170 - Beef Round, Bottom (Gooseneck)

163 Pierna (Piña), sin Chamberete, 3 Piezas, Deshuesada

Esta pieza deberá consistir en las siguientes piezas empaquetadas individualmente y empacadas en el mismo recipiente:

Pieza número 167 - Pierna (Piña), Punta de Sirloin (Pulpa Bola)

Pieza número 169 - Pierna (Piña), Pulpa Negra (Cara/Centro), Semi-Recortada de Grasa

Pieza número 170 - Pierna (Piña), Contracara con Cuete

166A — Beef Round, Rump Partially Removed, Shank Off

This item is as described in Item No. 160, except, in addition, the rump shall be partially excluded. The rump portion shall be removed anterior to the top or inside round exposing the *semitendinosus*, the ball, and the protuberance of the femur. Neither the ball nor the medial portion of the *rectus femoris* may be severed. The *vastus lateralis* and/or the main portion of the *rectus femoris*, however, may be severed. As in Item No. 160, the aitch bone and overlying fat and lean (oyster), tail bones, *sacrosciatic* ligament and overlying lean and fat, exposed lymph glands, and the thick opaque portion of the *gracilis* membrane are excluded along with the rump.

166A — Pierna (Piña) Corta, Tajo Anterior de Pulpa Blanca Parcialmente Retirado, Sin Chamberete, Deshuesada, Atada en Malla

Esta pieza aparece descrita en la pieza número 160, salvo que, además, el aguayón se deberá retirar parcialmente. La porción del Tajo Anterior de Pulpa Blanca deberá ser retirada en su parte anterior a la pulpa negra (cara/centro), exponiendo el músculo *semitendinosus*, la bola y la protuberancia del fémur. No se puede separar ni la bola ni la porción media del *rectus femoris*. No obstante, se puede separar el músculo *vastus lateralis* o la porción principal del *rectus femoris*. Como en la pieza número 160, se excluyen, conjuntamente con el tajo anterior de pulpa blanca, el hueso de la cadera, la grasa que recubre y la carne magra ("ostra" de la cadera), los huesos de la cola, el ligamento *sacrociático* y la carne magra y grasa que lo recubre, los ganglios linfáticos expuestos así como la porción gruesa opaca de la membrana del músculo *gracilis*.

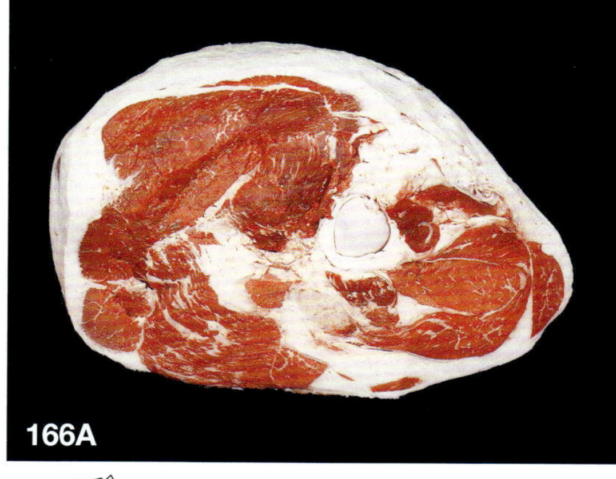

166A

166B — Beef Round, Rump and Shank Partially Off, Handle On

In preparing this item the rump is excluded together with the aitch bone and other portions described in Item No. 166A by a straight cut that exposes the *semitendinosus*, and a cross section of the ball of the femur. This cut must not sever the medial portion of the *rectus femoris* but may sever the *vastus lateralis* and/or main portion of the *rectus femoris*. Further, the hindshank and heel meat shall be excluded from the tibia or shank bone by a straight cut perpendicular to the ventral edge of the round that is posterior to, but no more than 2.0 inches (5.0 cm) from, the stifle joint, leaving no more than 4.0 inches (10.0 cm) of the shank bone exposed and firmly intact. The exposed shank bone shall be trimmed practically free of lean. A commonly used name to describe this item is "Baron of Beef."

166B — Pierna (Piña) Corta, Sin Tajo Anterior de Pulpa Blanca ni Chamberete, Con Mango

Al preparar esta pieza, se excluye el aguayón conjuntamente con el hueso de la cadera y otras porciones descritas en la pieza número 166A mediante un corte recto que expone el músculo *semitendinosus*, y un corte transversal de la cabeza del fémur. Este corte no debe separar la porción media del músculo *rectus femoris*, pero puede separar el *vastus lateralis* o la porción principal del *rectus femoris*. Además, la carne del chamberete trasero y del talón deberá ser excluida del hueso de la tibia o el chamberete mediante un corte recto perpendicular al borde ventral de la pierna posterior a la articulación de la rodilla pero sin superar los 5.0 cm (2.0 pulgadas) de la misma, dejando no más de 10.0 cm (4.0 pulgadas) del hueso del chamberete expuesto y firmemente intacto. El hueso del chamberete expuesto deberá ser recortado de grasa hasta quedar prácticamente libre de grasa. Un nombre comúnmente usado para describir esta pieza es Barón de la Carne ("Baron of Beef").

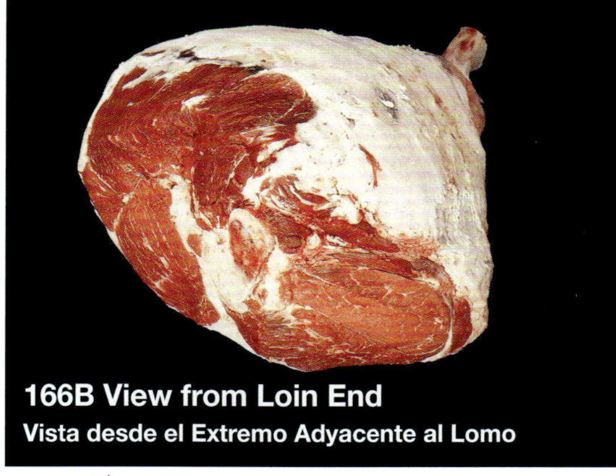

166B View from Loin End
Vista desde el Extremo Adyacente al Lomo

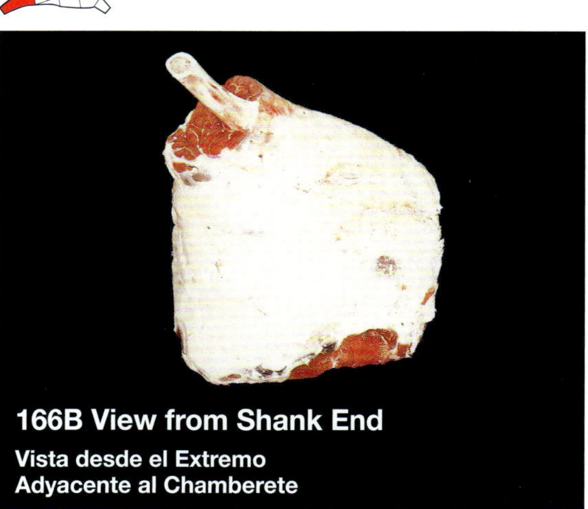

166B View from Shank End
Vista desde el Extremo Adyacente al Chamberete

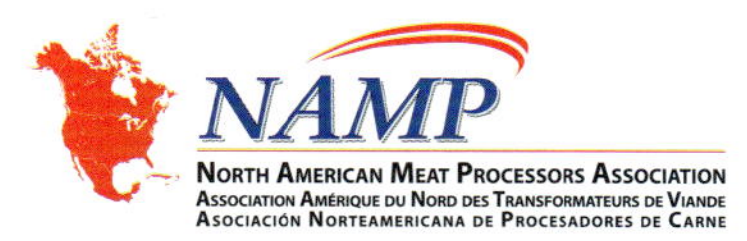

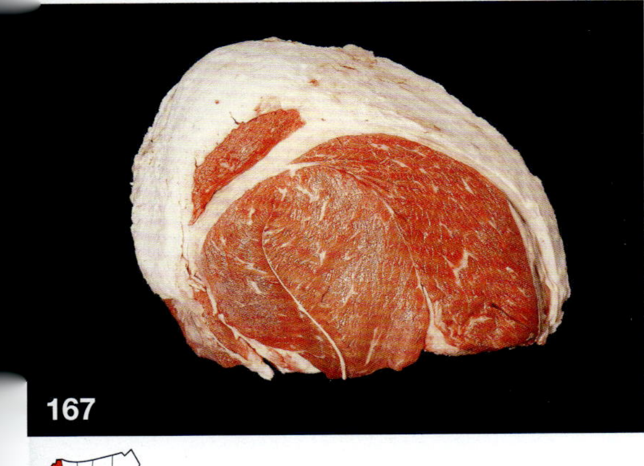

167

167 — Beef Round, Sirloin Tip (Knuckle)

This boneless item is prepared from Item No. 158 and consists of the posterior portion of the full sirloin tip (knuckle) comprised of the *vastus intermedius*, *vastus lateralis*, *vastus medialis*, and *rectus femoris*. A portion of the *sartorius* may remain, if firmly attached. In addition the *tensor fasciae latae*, though not completely extending around the outside of the sirloin tip (knuckle), shall be exposed on the loin end. The sirloin tip (knuckle) is separated from the top (inside) round and bottom (gooseneck) round between the natural seams. All bones and cartilages shall be excluded. The tendinous end shall also be excluded exposing no less than 75 percent lean. When specified, the sirloin tip (knuckle) shall be split lengthwise into approximate equal portions.

*When the full sirloin tip (IMPS Item No. 167B) is removed by cutting through the natural seams and left attached to the bottom sirloin prior to separation of the round from the sirloin, then the full sirloin tip may be referred to as Beef Loin, Bottom Sirloin, Full Sirloin Tip.

167 — Pierna (Piña), Punta de Sirloin (Pulpa Bola)

Esta pieza deshuesada se prepara a partir de la pieza número 158 y consiste en la porción posterior de la pulpa bola completa, conformada por los músculos *vastus intermedius*, *vastus lateralis*, *vastus medialis* y *rectus femoris*. Puede quedar una porción del músculo *sartorius*, si permanece firmemente unido. Además, el *tensor de la fascia lata*, aunque sin extenderse por completo alrededor del exterior de la pulpa bola, deberá exponerse en el extremo adyacente al lomo. La pulpa bola se separa de la pulpa negra (cara/centro) y de la pulpa blanca con cuete (contracara) abriendo entre las vetas naturales. Se excluirán todos los huesos y cartílagos. El extremo tendinoso deberá también excluirse, y se expondrá por lo menos el 75% de la carne magra. Cuando se especifique así, la pulpa bola deberá separarse longitudinalmente en porciones aproximadamente iguales.

*Cuando se retira la pulpa bola completa (pieza número 167B de las especificaciones IMPS), cortando por las vetas naturales, y se deja unida al bottom sirloin (aguayón inferior), antes de separar la pierna del aguayón, la pulpa bola completa puede llamarse "Lomo de Res, Sirloin Inferior o Pulpa Bola Completa".

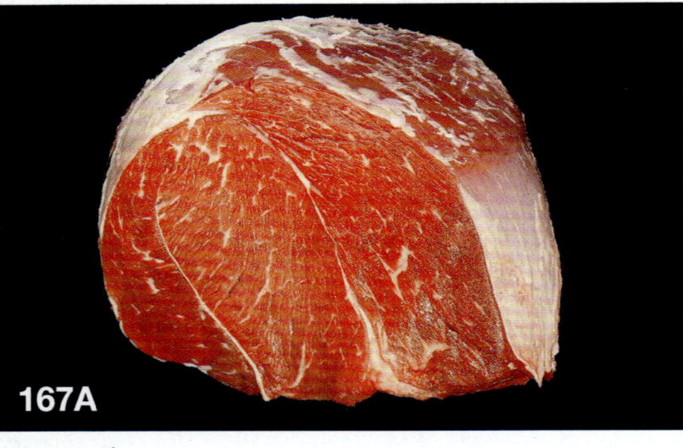

167A

167A — Beef Round, Sirloin Tip (Knuckle), Peeled

This boneless item is as prepared in Item No. 167, except, in addition, the *tensor fasciae latae*, fat, and skin tissue are excluded. When smaller roasts are specified, the sirloin tip (knuckle) shall be split lengthwise into approximate equal portions.

PSO: 1 – The *vastus intermedius* and *vastus medialis* muscles shall be removed.

167A — Pierna (Piña), Punta de Sirloin (Pulpa Bola), Desprovisto de Grasa

Esta pieza deshuesada está preparada según las indicaciones de la pieza número 167, salvo que, además, se excluyen el empuje (*tensor de la fascia lata*), la grasa y el tejido cutáneo. Cuando se especifiquen rosbifs más pequeños, la pulpa bola deberá separarse longitudinalmente en porciones aproximadamente iguales.

PSO: 1 – Se deberán retirar los músculos *vastus intermedius* y *vastus medialis*.

167D — Beef Round, Sirloin Tip (Knuckle), Peeled, 2-Piece

This item is as described in Item No. 167A, except, in addition, the *vastus lateralis* and the *rectus femoris* are separated by cutting through the seam. The *sartorius*, *vastus medialis*, and *vastus intermedialis* shall be removed by cutting through the natural seams.

167D — Pierna (Piña), Punta de Sirloin (Pulpa Bola), Desprovistas de Grasa, 2 piezas

Esta pieza aparece descrita en la pieza número 167A, salvo que, además, el *vastus lateralis* y el *rectus femoris* están separados por un corte que sigue la veta. Se retirarán los músculos *sartorius*, *vastus medialis* y *vastus intermedialis* mediante un corte por las vetas naturales.

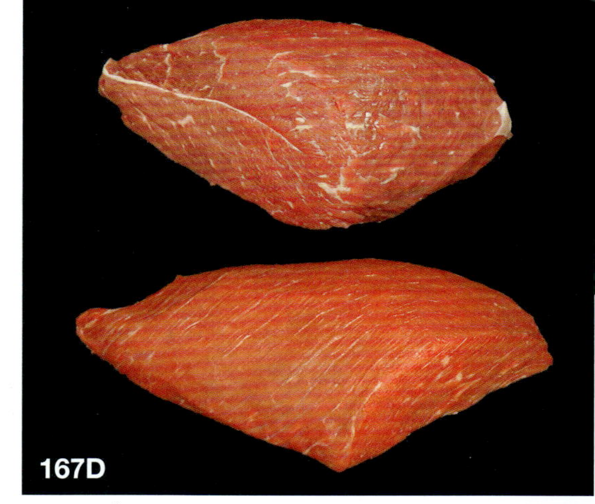
167D

167E — Beef Round, Sirloin Tip (Knuckle), Center Roast (IM)

This item consists of the *rectus femoris* muscle only from any Round Sirloin Tip (Knuckle) item. It is separated from the other muscles as described in Item No. 167D.

167E — Pierna (Piña), Punta de Sirloin (Pulpa Bola), Trozo Rosbif del Centro (MI)

Esta pieza consiste en el músculo *rectus femoris* que provenga solamente de una pieza de la punta de la pulpa bola. Está separada de los otros músculos como se describe en la pieza número 167D.

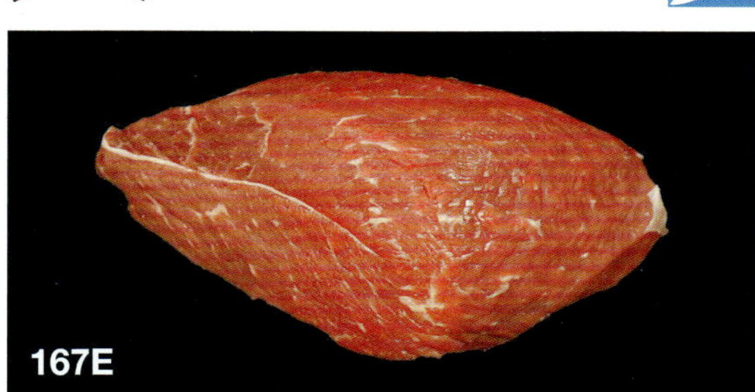
167E

167F — Beef Round, Sirloin Tip (Knuckle), Side Roast (IM)

This item consists of the *vastus lateralis* muscle only from any Round Sirloin Tip (Knuckle) item. It is separated from the other muscles as described in Item No. 167D.

167F — Pierna (Piña), Punta de Sirloin (Pulpa Bola), Trozo Rosbif Lateral (MI)

Esta pieza consiste en el músculo *vastus lateralis* que provenga solamente de una pieza de la punta de pulpa bola. Está separada de los otros músculos como se describe en la pieza número 167D.

167F

168 — Beef Round, Top (Inside), Untrimmed

This boneless item consists of the *semimembranosus*, *sartorius*, *adductor*, *gracilis*, and *pectineus* and is separated from the bottom round and sirloin tip (knuckle) through the natural seams. The *iliopsoas* may remain if firmly attached. All bones, cartilages, and exposed lymph glands shall be removed. Purchasers may request that this item be further trimmed. Purchasers may also request that the item be split into smaller pieces as well as netted or tied if so desired.

168 — Pierna (Piña), Pulpa Negra (Cara/Centro), sin Recortado de Grasa y sin Limpiar

Esta pieza deshuesada consiste en el *semimembranosus*, *sartorius*, *adductor*, *gracilis* y *pectineus*, y se separa de la pulpa blanca y de la pulpa bola siguiendo las vetas naturales. Es posible que el *iliopsoas* se mantenga si permanece firmemente unido. Se deberán extraer todos los huesos, cartílagos y ganglios linfáticos expuestos. Es posible que los compradores soliciten que el recorte de grasa y limpieza a esta pieza sea más minucioso. También, quizás los compradores soliciten que la pieza sea dividida en trozos más pequeños, así como colocados en redes o amarrados si lo desean.

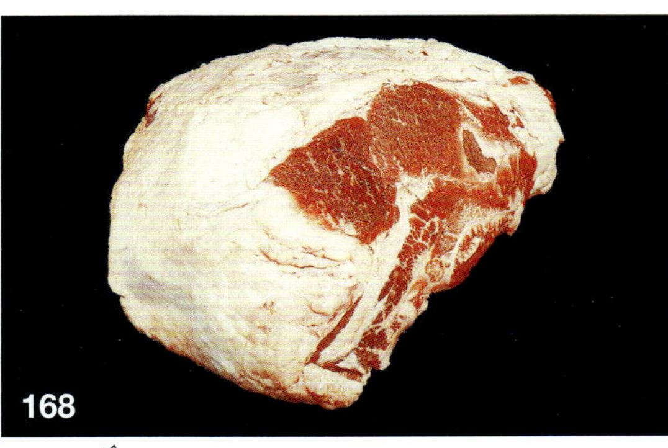
168

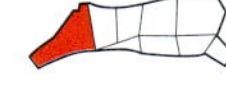

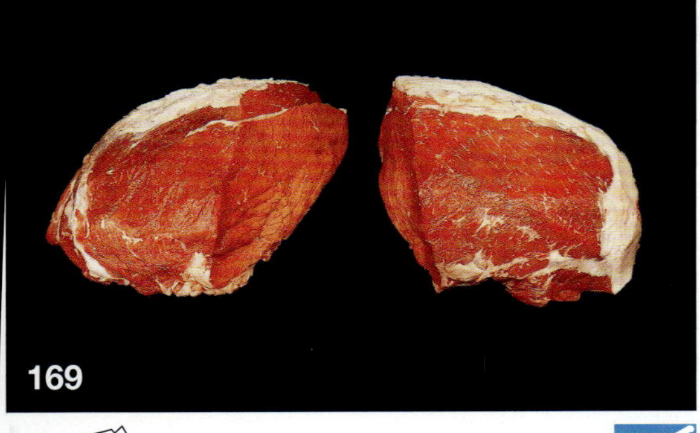

169

169 Beef Round, Top (Inside)

This boneless item is as described in Item No. 168, except the thick opaque portion of the *gracilis* membrane shall be removed. When smaller roasts are specified, the top round shall be split by no more than two lengthwise cuts, and subsequent cuts, if necessary, shall be made girthwise separating the item into approximate equal portions. Purchasers may also request further trimming and netting or tying of the product.

169 Pierna (Piña), Pulpa Negra (Cara/Centro), Semi-Recortada de Grasa

Esta pieza deshuesada aparece descrita en la pieza número 168, salvo que se deberá eliminar la porción opaca y gruesa de la membrana del músculo *gracilis*. Cuando se especifican rosbifs más pequeños, la cara/centro de la pierna deberá dividirse mediante no más de dos cortes longitudinales y los cortes subsiguientes, en caso de tener lugar, deberán hacerse a lo largo del contorno, separando la pieza en porciones aproximadamente iguales. También es posible que los compradores soliciten una limpieza más minuciosa, además de poner el producto en redes o amarrarlo.

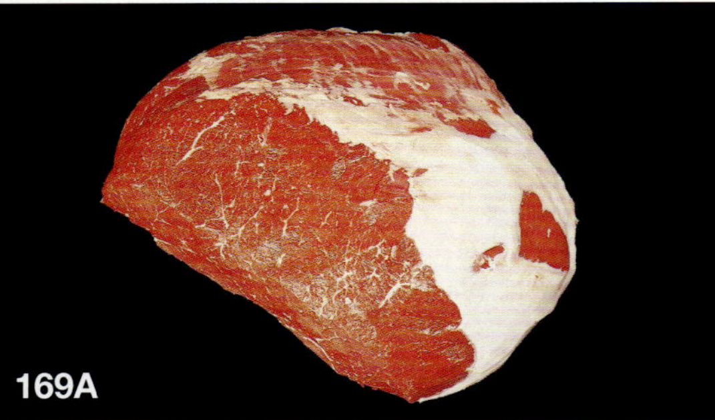

169A

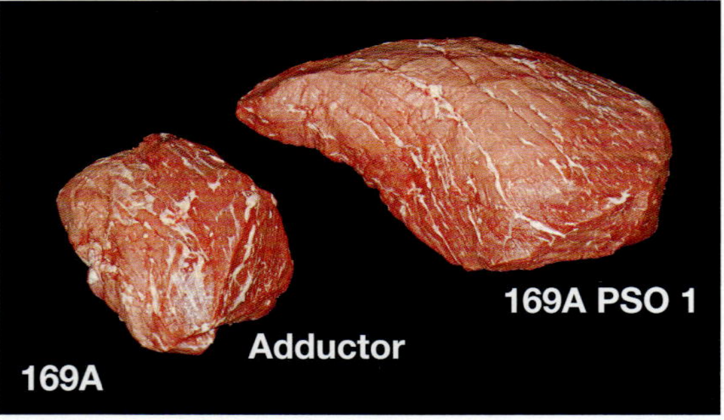

169A PSO 1

Adductor

169A

169A Beef Round, Top (Inside), Cap Off

This item is as described in Item No. 169, except, in addition, the *gracilis* muscle and the soft side *pectineus* and *sartorius* muscles shall be excluded by cutting through the natural seams.

PSO: 1 – The *adductor* muscle shall be removed and excluded by cutting through the natural seams.

169A Pierna (Piña), Pulpa Negra (Cara/Centro), sin Tapa

Esta pieza, también conocida como "Centro de Cara", aparece descrita en la pieza número 169, salvo que, además, el músculo *gracilis* y el lado blando de los músculos *pectineus* y *sartorius* deberán excluirse siguiendo el curso de las vetas naturales.

PSO: 1 – Se deberá retirar y excluir el músculo *adductor* cortando por las vetas naturales.

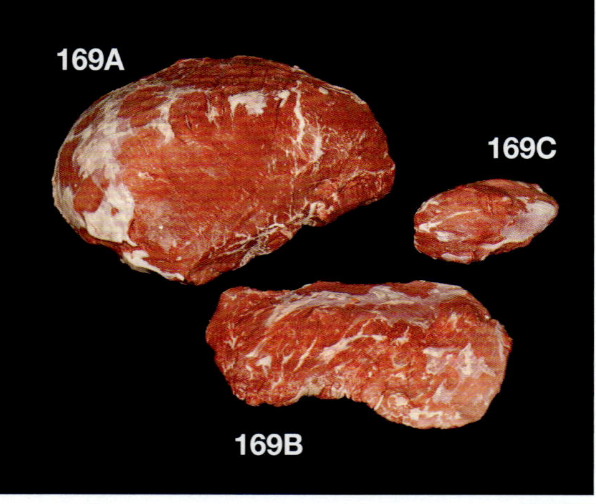

169A

169C

169B

169B Beef Round, Top (Inside), Cap (IM)

This item shall consist of the *gracilis* muscle that was separated from the top round as described in Item No. 169A.

169B Pierna (Piña), Pulpa Negra (Cara/Centro), Tapa (MI)

Esta pieza consistirá en el músculo *gracilis* que fue separado de la cara/centro de la pierna según la descripción de la pieza número 169A.

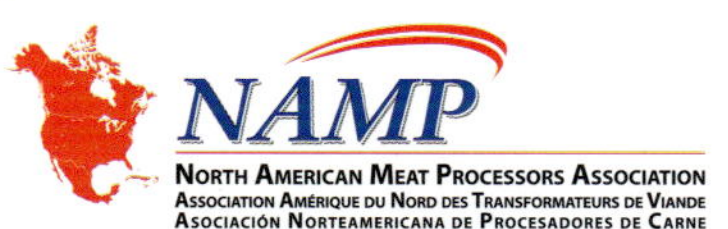

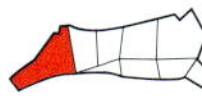

169C — Beef Round, Top (Inside), Front Side Muscle (IM)

This item shall consist of the *pectinius* muscle only. This item is removed from the ventral (soft) side of the top round by cutting through the natural seam.

169C — Pierna (Piña), Pulpa Negra (Cara/Centro), Músculo del Lado Frontal (MI)

Esta pieza consistirá únicamente en el músculo *pectinius*. Esta pieza se extrae desde el lado ventral (blando) de la cara/centro de la pierna, cortando por la veta natural.

170 — Beef Round, Bottom (Gooseneck)

The bottom or gooseneck round is produced by separating the boneless item from the top round, sirloin tip (knuckle), and shank between the natural seams. The item consists of the *semitendinosus*, *biceps femoris*, and heel and, in addition, may contain the *gluteus medius*, *gluteus accessorius*, and *gluteus profundus*. The *semitendinosus* muscle shall not be exposed on the loin end. All bones, cartilages, *sacrosciatic* ligament, the lean and fat that overlaid the *sacrosciatic* ligament, *popliteal* lymph gland, and the heavy opaque connective tissue separating the bottom round from the sirloin tip (knuckle) shall be excluded.

170 — Pierna (Piña), Contracara con Cuete

La contracara con cuete se elabora separando la pieza deshuesada de la cara/centro de la pierna, pulpa bola y chamberete a lo largo de las vetas naturales. La pieza consiste en los músculos *semitendinosus*, *biceps femoris* y talón, y además, puede contener los músculos *gluteus medius*, *gluteus accessorius* y *gluteus profundus*. El músculo *semitendinosus* no deberá exponerse en el extremo posterior. Se deberán excluir todos los huesos, cartílagos, ligamento *sacrociático*, la grasa y la carne magra que recubre el ligamento *sacrociático*, el ganglio linfático *poplíteo* y el tejido conectivo opaco grueso que separa la pulpa blanca de la pulpa bola.

170 View from Rump End
Vista desde el Extremo Adyacente al Aguayón

170 View from Shank End
Vista desde el Extremo Adyacente al Chamberete

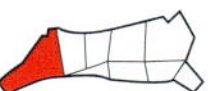

170A — Beef Round, Bottom (Gooseneck), Heel Out

This item is as described in Item No. 170, except, in addition, the heel is excluded. The heel is removed by separating it along the natural seam adjacent to the *semitendinosus* and *biceps femoris*. When specified, the bottom round shall be split into approximate equal portions by cutting at an approximate right angle to the length of the item.

170A — Pierna (Piña), Contracara con Cuete, sin Talón/Copete

Esta pieza aparece descrita en la pieza número 170, salvo que, además, se excluye el talón. El talón se retira separándolo por las vetas naturales adyacentes a los músculos *semitendinosus* y *biceps femoris*. Cuando se especifique, la pulpa blanca se dividirá en porciones de tamaño aproximado, cortando en un ángulo recto aproximado a la longitud de la pieza.

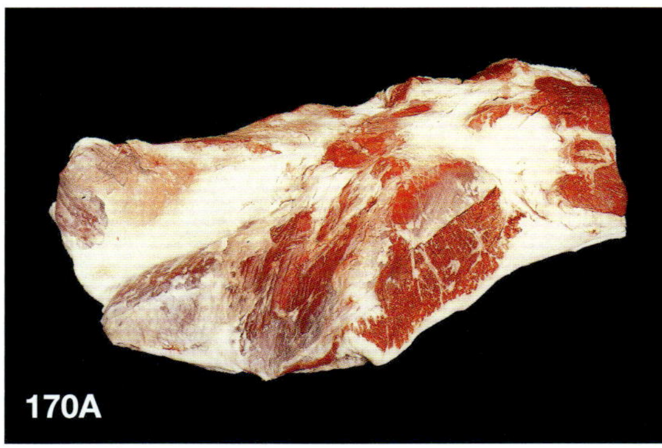

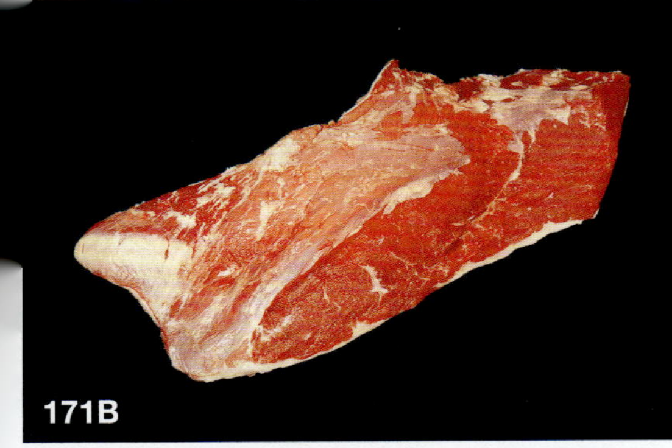

171B

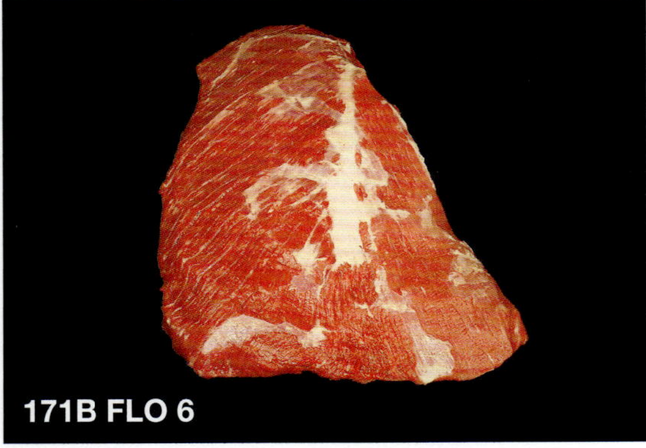

171B FLO 6

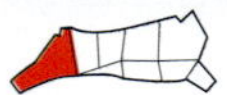

171B — Beef Round, Outside Round (Flat)

The outside round or flat is produced by separating the boneless item from the top round, sirloin tip (knuckle), heel, and *semitendinosus* or eye of round between the natural seams. The item consists of the biceps femoris and may contain the *gluteus medius, gluteus profundus,* and *gluteus accessorius*. The loin end shall expose the *biceps femoris* equal to or larger than the *gluteus medius* if it is present. All bones, cartilages, *sacrosciatic* ligament, and the lean and fat that overlaid the ligament, the opaque heavy connective tissue or silver skin along the ventral side, and the *popliteal* lymph gland shall be excluded.

PSO: 1 – After being trimmed to meet FLO 6 Peeled/ Denuded, Surface Membrane Removed requirements as shown (see page 13), item may be split into 2 parts as in Item Nos. 171D and 171E.

171B — Pierna (Piña), Contracara, Pulpa Blanca

La contracara, también conocida como contracuete o pulpa larga, se obtiene separando la pieza deshuesada de la cara/centro de la pierna, la pulpa bola, el talón y el *semitendinosus* o cuete de res, por las vetas naturales. La pieza consiste en el biceps femoris y puede contener los músculos *gluteus medius, gluteus profundus* y *gluteus accessorius*. El extremo posterior deberá exponer el *biceps femoris* igual o más largo que el *gluteus medius* si está presente. Se deberán excluir todos los huesos, los cartílagos, el ligamento *sacrociático* y la grasa y carne magra que recubren el ligamento, el tejido conectivo opaco grueso o membrana plateada (llamada "espejo") a lo largo del lado ventral, y el ganglio linfático *poplíteo*.

PSO: 1 – Una vez que la pieza sea recortada a fin de cumplir con los requisitos de la opción 6 para limitar la grasa, "Desprovisto de grasa/ Prácticamente desnudo de grasa, Membrana superficial retirada", según se exponen a la vista (ver página 12), la pieza se puede dividir en dos partes como en las piezas números 171D y 171E.

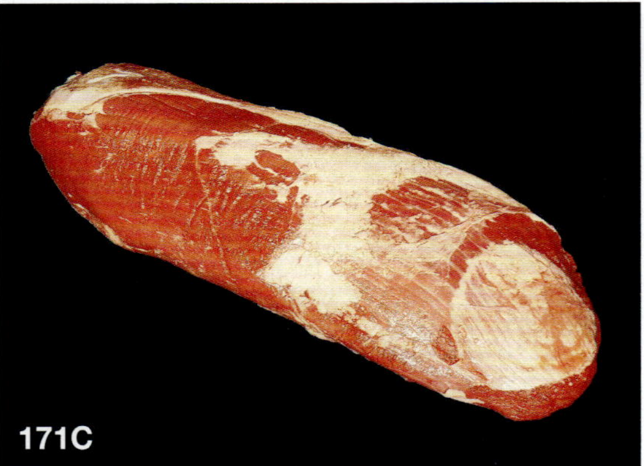

171C

171C — Beef Round, Eye of Round (IM)

This boneless item consists of the *semitendinosus* muscle and is produced by separating the eye of round from the top and outside rounds and heel between the natural seams. It shall not be severed on either end.

171C — Pierna (Piña), Contracara, Cuete (MI)

Esta pieza deshuesada consiste en el músculo *semitendinosus* y se obtiene al separar el cuete del talón así como de la cara y contracara de la pierna, siguiendo las vetas naturales. No deberá cortarse en ninguno de los dos extremos.

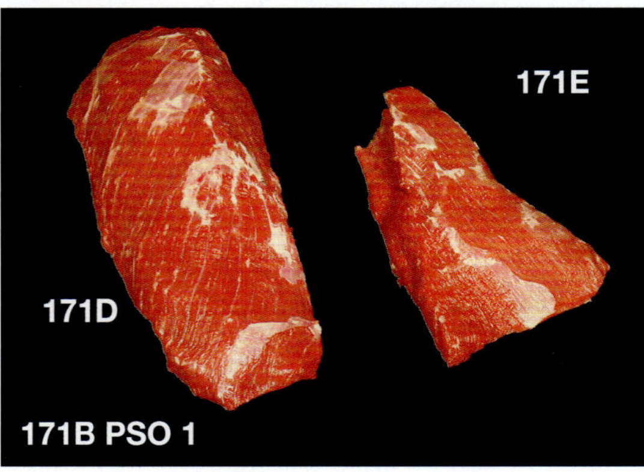

171E

171D

171B PSO 1

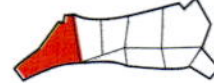

171D — Beef Round, Outside Round, Side Muscle Removed (IM)

This item is as described in Item No. 171B except that the side muscle (*biceps femoris ishiatic* head) is removed by cutting through the natural seam.

171D — Pierna (Piña), Contracara, Pulpa Blanca, Retirando Músculo de al lado (MI)

Esta pieza aparece descrita en la pieza número 171B, salvo que el músculo lateral (cabeza isquiática del *biceps femoris*) se retira mediante un corte que sigue la veta natural.

NAMP
NORTH AMERICAN MEAT PROCESSORS ASSOCIATION
ASSOCIATION AMÉRIQUE DU NORD DES TRANSFORMATEURS DE VIANDE
ASOCIACIÓN NORTEAMERICANA DE PROCESADORES DE CARNE

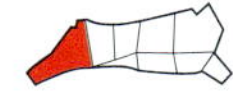

171E — Beef Round, Outside Round, Side Roast (IM)

This item consists of the *biceps femoris ishiatic* head from the outside round. It is separated from the main portion of the *biceps femoris* by cutting through the natural seam.

171E — Pierna (Piña), Contracara (Pulpa Blanca), Trozo Rosbif de Músculo Pegado al Lado (MI)

Esta pieza consiste en la cabeza isquiática del *biceps femoris* de la contracara. Se separa de la porción principal del *biceps femoris* mediante un corte que sigue la veta natural.

171F — Beef Round, Outside Round, Heel

This will consist of the heel portion of the bottom (gooseneck) round. It is separated as described in Item No. 170A.

PSO 1 – *Superficial digital flexor* muscle shall be removed.

171F — Pierna (Piña), Contracara, Talón (Copete)

Esto consistirá en la porción del talón de la contracara con cuete. Se separa según descripción de la pieza número 170A.

PSO 1 – *El músculo flexor digital superficial* deberá retirarse.

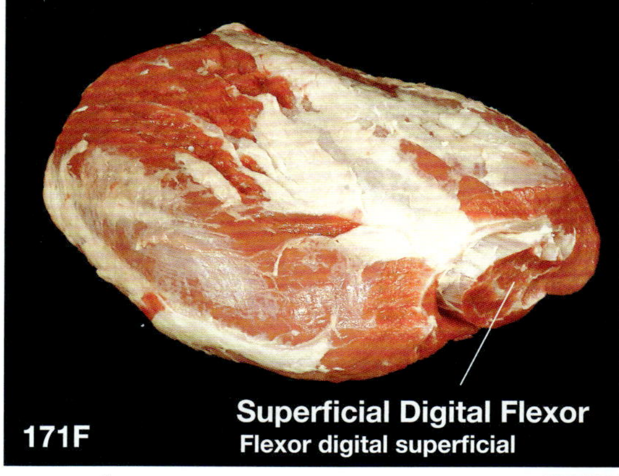

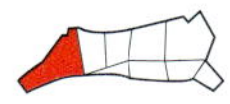

171G — Beef Round, Outside Round, Rump (IM)

This item shall consist of the anterior portion of the *biceps femoris* muscle of Item No. 171B. The *gluteus medius, gluteus profundus,* and *gluteus accessorius* shall be excluded. The rump shall be removed from the outside round by a cut that is at or immediately anterior to the *biceps femoris ishiatic* head.

171G — Pierna (Piña), Contracara, Tajo Anterior de Pulpa Blanca (MI)

Esta pieza deberá consistir en la porción anterior del músculo *biceps femoris* de la pieza número 171B. Deberán excluirse el *gluteus medius, gluteus profundus* y *gluteus accessorius*. El tajo anterior de pulpa blanca deberá separarse de la contracara de la pierna mediante un corte en la cabeza isquiática del *biceps femoris* o inmediatamente anterior a la misma.

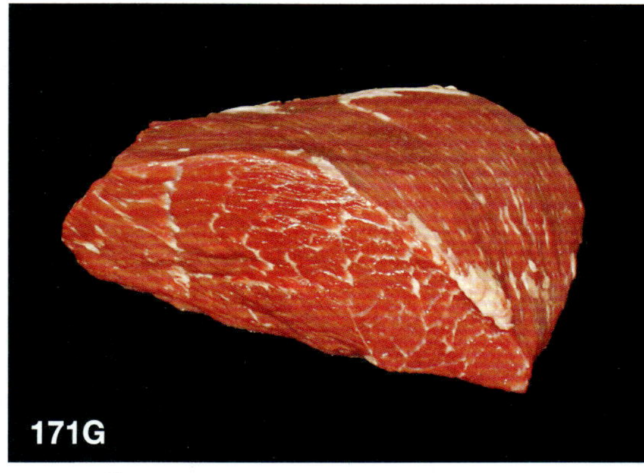

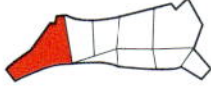

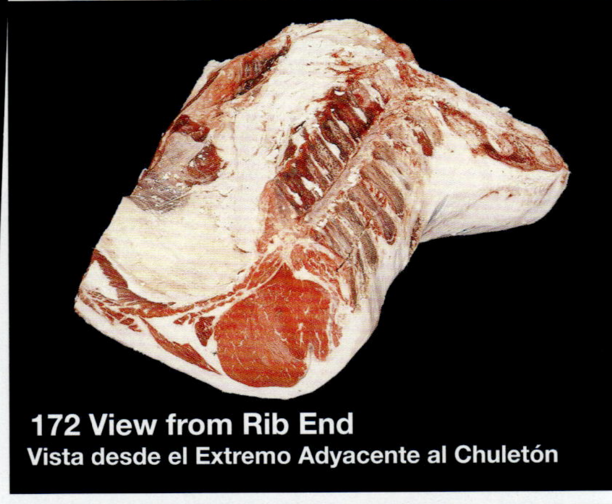

172 View from Rib End
Vista desde el Extremo Adyacente al Chuletón

172 View from Sirloin End
Vista desde el Extremo
Adyacente al Aguayón

172 — Beef Loin, Full Loin, Trimmed

This item is that portion of the hindquarter remaining after the removal of Item No. 158 and the flank. The trimmed loin shall consist of the short loin, sirloin, and the 13th rib. The hanging tender, kidney, and kidney knob and excess internal fat including that over the 13th rib bone shall be excluded. The flank shall be excluded by a straight cut ventral to, but not more than 6.0 inches (15.0 cm) from, the *longissimus dorsi* at the rib end to a point on the round end that is ventral to, but not more than 1.0 inch (2.5 cm) from, the *tensor fasciae latae*. The fat covering the lumbar, sacral, and tenderloin regions shall be trimmed to not exceed 1.0 inch (2.5 cm) in depth at any point.

172 — Lomo, Lomo Completo (Full Loin), Recortado de Grasa y Limpio

Esta pieza es la porción del cuarto trasero que se obtiene después de la extracción de la pieza número 158 y la falda. El lomo recortado de grasa deberá consistir en el lomo corto, el aguayón y la 13ª costilla. Deberá excluirse la arrachera gallo (arrachera colgante), los riñones, la grasa pélvico renal y la grasa interna en exceso, inclusive la que cubre la 13ª costilla. La falda se excluirá mediante un corte recto ventral al *longissimus dorsi* en el extremo adyacente al chuletón, pero sin superar los 15.0 cm (6.0 pulgadas), hasta un punto en el extremo adyacente a la pierna, ventral al empuje (*tensor de la fascia lata*), pero sin superar los 2.0 cm (1.5 pulgadas). Se deberá recortar la grasa que cubre las regiones lumbar, sacra y del filete, de forma que no exceda los 2.5 cm (1.0 pulgada) de profundidad en ningún punto.

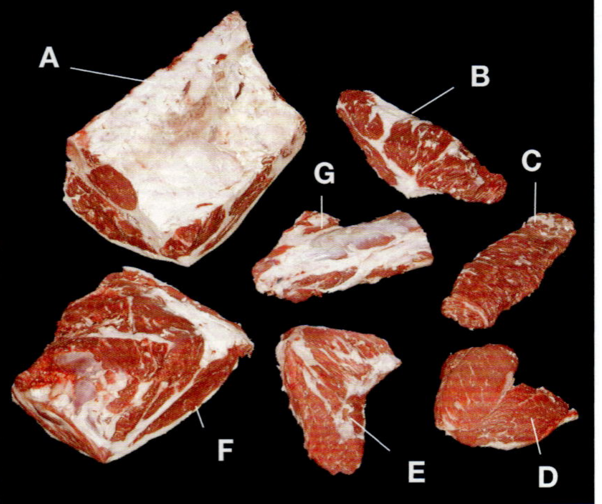

Beef Loin, Components

A	174	Short Loin
B	185A	Flap
C	176	Steak Tails
D	185B	Ball Tip
E	185C	Tri-Tip
F	184	Top Sirloin Butt
G	191	Butt Tender

Lomo de res, componentes

A	174	Lomo corto
B	185A	Tapa
C	176	Steak Tails (Bistecs de cola)
D	185B	Punta de la pulpa bola
E	185C	Empuje
F	184	Pulpa del Aguayón Superior/Top Sirloin, Aguayón con Tapa
G	191	Cabeza de Filete

172A — Beef Loin, Full Loin, Diamond-Cut, Trimmed

This item is that portion of the hindquarter remaining after the removal of Item No. 158A and the flank. The flank removal measurements, fat covering thickness, and trim specifications for this item are the same as those for Item No. 172.

172A — Lomo, Lomo Completo (Full Loin), Forma Diamante, Recortado de Grasa y Limpio

Esta pieza es la porción del cuarto trasero que se obtiene después de la extracción de la pieza número 158A y la falda. Las medidas de extracción de la falda, el grosor del recubrimiento de grasa y las especificaciones de limpieza para esta pieza son iguales que para la pieza número 172.

174 Beef Loin, Short Loin, Short-Cut

This item is prepared from the short loin portion of Item Nos. 172 or 172A. The short loin includes the 13th rib and is separated from the sirloin by a straight cut at a right angle to its length anterior to the hip cartilage that exposes the *gluteus medius*. The flank shall be excluded by a straight cut ventral to, but not more than 3.0 inches (7.5 cm) from, the *longissimus dorsi* at the rib end to a point on the sirloin end ventral to, but not more than 2.0 inches (5.0 cm) from, the *longissimus dorsi.*

The purchaser specified options (PSO) for flank removal by a straight cut ventral to the *longissimus dorsi* are as follows: (Rib end x Sirloin end)

PSO: 1 – 1.0 inch (2.5 cm) x 1.0 inch (2.5 cm)

2 – 1.0 inch (2.5 cm) x 0 inch (immediately ventral)

3 – Other as specified

174 Lomo, Lomo Corto (Short Loin), Acortado

Esta pieza se prepara a partir de la porción de lomo corto de las piezas número 172 o 172A. El lomo corto incluye la costilla 13ª y se separa del aguayón mediante un corte derecho en ángulo recto a su longitud anterior al cartílago de la cadera, que expone el *gluteus medius*. La falda se excluirá mediante un corte recto ventral al *longissimus dorsi* en el extremo del costillar, pero sin superar los 7.5 cm (3.0 pulgadas), hasta un punto en el extremo adyacente al aguayón ventral al *longissimus dorsi*, pero sin superar los 5.0 cm (2.0 pulgadas).

Las opciones de especificación del comprador para la extracción de falda mediante corte recto ventral al *longissimus dorsi* son las siguientes: (Extremo Adyacente al Chuletón x Extremo Adyacente al Aguayón)

PSO: 1 – 2.5 cm (1.0 pulgada) x 2.5 cm (1.0 pulgada)

2 – 2.5 cm x (1.0 pulgada) x 0 cm (inmediatamente ventral)

3 – Otras, según especificación

174 View from Rib End
Vista desde el Extremo Adyacente al Chuletón

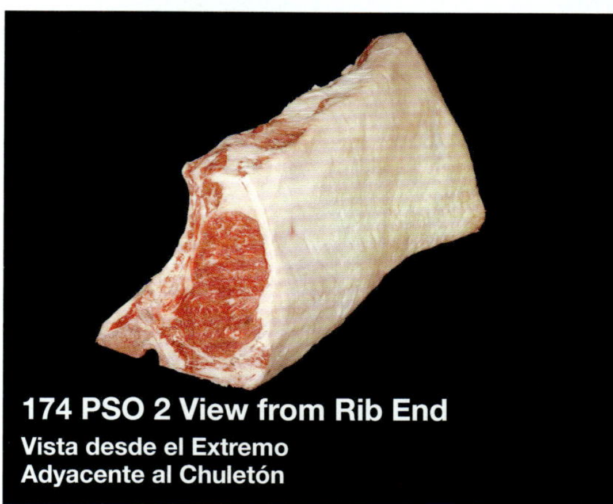

174 PSO 2 View from Rib End
Vista desde el Extremo
Adyacente al Chuletón

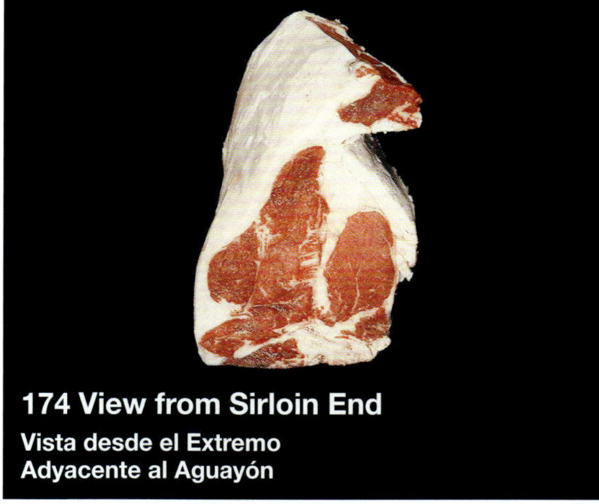

174 View from Sirloin End
Vista desde el Extremo
Adyacente al Aguayón

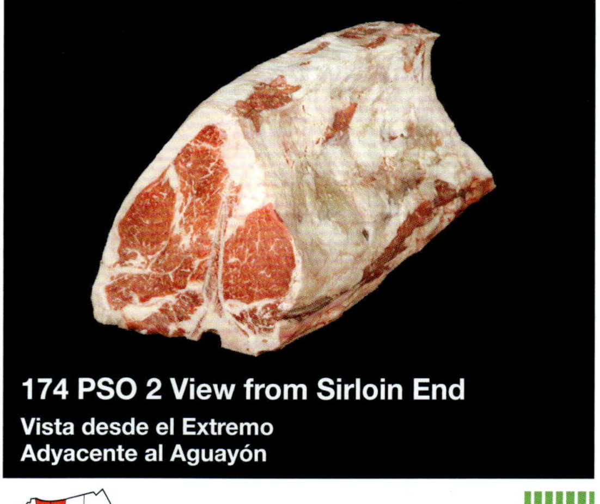

174 PSO 2 View from Sirloin End
Vista desde el Extremo
Adyacente al Aguayón

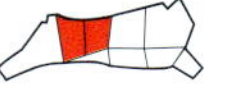

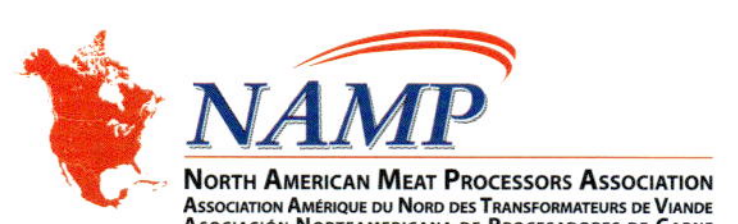

175 View from Rib End
Vista desde el Extremo
Adyacente al Chuletón

175 View from Sirloin End
Vista desde el Extremo Adyacente al Aguayón

175 PSO 4 View from Rib End
Vista desde el Extremo Adyacente al Chuletón

175 PSO 4 View from Sirloin End
Vista desde el Extremo Adyacente al Aguayón

175 — Beef Loin, Strip Loin, Bone In

This item is prepared from the short loin portion of Item Nos. 172 or 172A as described in Item No. 174, except the flank shall be excluded by a straight cut ventral to, but not more than 6.0 inches (15.0 cm) from, the *longissimus dorsi* at the rib end to a point on the sirloin end ventral to, but not more than 4.0 inches (10.0 cm) from, the *longissimus dorsi*. In addition the tenderloin and the protruding edge of the chine bone are excluded. The chine bone shall be removed along the dorsal edge of the spinal groove without scoring the *longissimus dorsi* in the event that it is exposed.

The purchaser specified options (PSO) for flank removal by a straight cut ventral to the *longissimus dorsi* are as follows: (Rib end x Sirloin end)

PSO: 1 – 4.0 inches (10.0 cm) x
        3.0 inches (7.5 cm)

2 – 3.0 inches (7.5 cm) x
     2.0 inches (5.0 cm)

3 – 1.0 inch (2.5 cm) x 1.0 inch (2.5 cm)

4 – 1.0 inch (2.5 cm) x 0 inch

5 – 0 inch x 0 inch

6 – Other as specified

175 — Lomo, Strip Loin (New York), Con Hueso

Esta pieza, también conocida como "Lomo Plano", "Lomo Trasero" o "Lomo Corto", se prepara a partir de la porción de Short Loin de las piezas número 172 o 172A según la descripción en la pieza número 174, salvo que la falda deberá excluirse mediante un corte recto, ventral al *longissimus dorsi* en el extremo adyacente al chuletón, sin superar los 15.0 cm (6.0 pulgadas), hasta un punto ventral al *longissimus dorsi* en el extremo adyacente al aguayón, sin superar los 10.0 cm (4.0 pulgadas). Además, se excluyen el filete y el borde protuberante del espinazo. Se eliminarán los cuerpos vertebrales del espinazo conjuntamente con el canal raquídeo, sin cortar el *longissimus dorsi* en caso de que esté expuesto.

Las opciones de especificación del comprador para la extracción de falda mediante corte recto ventral al *longissimus dorsi* son las siguientes: (Extremo Adyacente al Chuletón x Extremo Adyacente al Aguayón)

PSO: 1 – 10.0 cm (4.0 pulgadas) x
        7.5 cm (3.0 pulgadas)

2 – 7.5 cm (3.0 pulgadas) x
     5.0 cm (2.0 pulgadas)

3 – 2.5 cm (1.0 pulgada) x
     2.5 cm (1.0 pulgada)

4 – 2.5 cm (1.0 pulgada) x 0 cm

5 – 0 cm x 0 cm

6 – Otras, según especificación

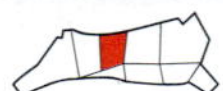

176 — Beef Loin, Steak Tail

This item, which may include both the *obliquus adominis internus* and *obliquus adominis externus* muscles, may be prepared from the flank portion of any beef hindquarter, ventral to the short loin, or part thereof of any full loin, short loin, or bone in or boneless strip loin item from which it is possible to produce the item. Unless otherwise specified by the purchaser the Fat Limitations Option (FLO) 4, Practically Free of Fat (75 percent lean/seam surface exposed), shall apply. The size of the individual pieces shall measure 8 square inches (20 square cm) or more. See page 13 for other FLO options.

176 — Lomo, Bistec de Cola de Falda

Esta pieza, que puede incluir los músculos *obliquus adominis internus* y *obliquuus adominis externus*, puede ser preparada a partir de la porción de falda de cualquier cuarto trasero, ventral al lomo corto o parte del mismo, de cualquier lomo entero, lomo corto, o de una pieza de Short Loin deshuesada o no, lomo corto o cualquier lomo entero, de donde sea posible elaborar la pieza. A menos que el comprador especifique lo contrario, se aplicará la opción 4 para limitar la grasa, Prácticamente libre de grasa (exposición del 75% de superficie magra/superficie muscular descubierta por la disección). El tamaño de las piezas individuales deberá ser de 20 cm cuadrados (8 pulgadas cuadradas) o más. Consulte la página 12 para ver otras opciones para limitar la grasa.

176

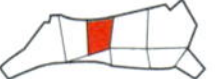

180 View from Rib End
Vista desde el Extremo Adyacente al Chuletón

180 View from Sirloin End
Vista desde el Extremo Adyacente al Aguayón

180 PSO 2 View from Rib End
Vista desde el Extremo Adyacente al Chuletón

180 PSO 2 View from Sirloin End
Vista desde el Extremo Adyacente al Aguayón

180 — Beef Loin, Strip Loin, Boneless

This boneless item is prepared from any loin item that meets the end item requirements. The item on the rib end displays the 13th rib mark and shall follow the natural curvature of the 13th rib. The sirloin end shall be anterior to the hip cartilage, forming an approximate right angle with the length of the loin, and exposing the *gluteus medius*. The flank side shall be ventral to, but not more than 3.0 inches (7.5 cm) from, the *longissimus dorsi* at the rib end to a point on the sirloin end ventral to, but not more than 2.0 inches (5.0 cm) from, the *longissimus dorsi*.

The purchaser specified options (PSO) for flank removal by a straight cut ventral to the longissimus dorsi are as follows: (Rib end x Sirloin end)

PSO: 1 – 2.0 inches (5.0 cm) x 1.0 inch (2.5 cm)

2 – 1.0 inch (2.5 cm) x 0 inch

3 – 1.0 inch (2.5 cm) x 1.0 inch (2.5 cm)

4 – 0.0 inch x 0 inch

5 – Other as specified

180 — Lomo, Strip Loin (New York), Deshuesado

Esta pieza deshuesada se prepara a partir de cualquier pieza de lomo que cumpla los requisitos finales de la misma. La pieza en el extremo adyacente al chuletón despliega la marca de la 13ª costilla y seguirá la curvatura natural de dicha costilla. El extremo adyacente al aguayón será anterior al cartílago de la cadera, formando un ángulo recto aproximado con la longitud del lomo, y exponiendo el *gluteus medius*. El lado que da a la falda deberá ubicarse en forma ventral al *longissimus dorsi* en el extremo adyacente al chuletón, pero sin superar los 7.5 cm (3.0 pulgadas), hasta un punto en el extremo adyacente al aguayón, ventral al *longissimus dorsi*, pero sin superar los 5.0 cm (2.0 pulgadas).

Las opciones de especificación del comprador para la extracción de la falda mediante un corte ventral al longissimus dorsi son las siguientes: (Extremo Adyacente al Chuletón x Extremo Adyacente al Aguayón)

PSO: 1 – 5.0 cm (2.0 pulgadas) x 2.5 cm (1.0 pulgadas)

2 – 2.5 cm (1.0 pulgada) x 0 cm

3 – 2.5 cm (1.0 pulgada) x 2.5 cm (1.0 pulgada)

4 – 0.0 cm x 0 cm

5 – Otras, según especificación

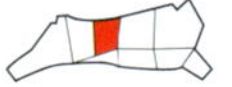

180B

180B Beef Loin, Strip Loin, Split, Boneless

This item is as described in Item No. 180 PSO 3 except that the heavy connective tissue overlying the *longissimus* muscle shall be removed. The item shall split by a lengthwise cut into two approximate equal in size sections.

PSO: 1 – The *multifidus dorsi* shall be removed.

2 – The posterior end of the strip loin shall be removed so that the *gluteus medius* is not present.

180B Lomo, Strip Loin (New York), Despellejado, Dividido, Deshuesado

Esta pieza aparece descrita en la pieza número 180, opción 3 de especificación del comprador, salvo que se deberá eliminar el tejido conectivo grueso que recubre el músculo *longissimus*. Esta pieza deberá ser dividida en dos por un corte, lo que proporcionará dos secciones aproximadamente iguales en tamaño.

PSO: 1 – Se deberá extraer el *multifidus dorsi*.

2 – El extremo posterior del Strip Loin deberá extraerse a fin de que no quede presente el *gluteus medius.*

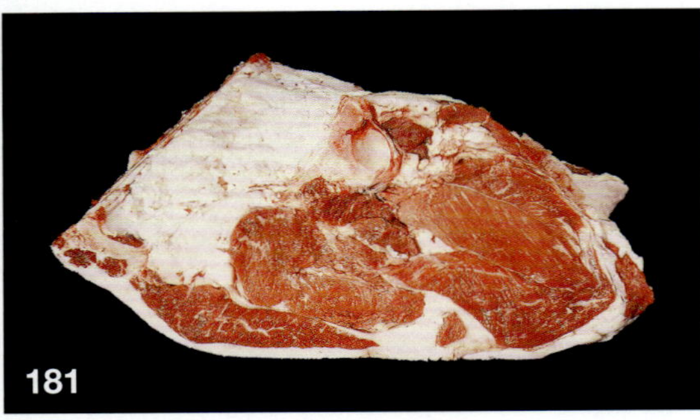

181

181 Beef Loin, Sirloin

The bone in sirloin is the posterior section of a full loin remaining after its separation from the short loin. See Item Nos. 172 and 174 for detailed specifications. The fat covering the lumbar, sacral, and tenderloin regions shall be trimmed not to exceed 1.0 inch (2.5 cm) in depth at any point.

181 Lomo, Sirloin (Aguayón) con Hueso

El Aguayón o Sirloin Completo con hueso corresponde a la sección posterior de un lomo completo obtenido luego de su separación del lomo corto. Vea las piezas número 172 y 174 para obtener especificaciones detalladas. Se deberá recortar la grasa que cubre las regiones lumbar, sacra y del filete, de forma que no exceda los 2.5 cm (1.0 pulgada) de profundidad en ningún punto.

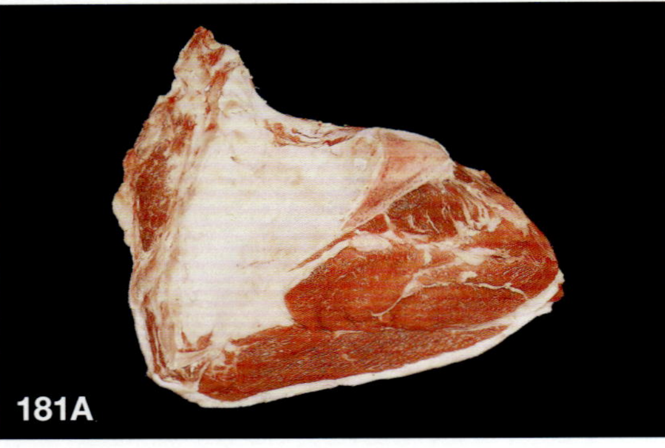

181A

181A Beef Loin, Top Sirloin, Bone In

This bone in item is prepared from Item No. 181 and is what remains after both the butt tenderloin and the bottom sirloin butt are separated from the bone in sirloin. The bottom sirloin butt is excluded by a straight cut along the natural seam between the *gluteus medius* and the sirloin tip (knuckle). The separation continues to the outside surface of the sirloin leaving a portion of the *tensor fasciae latae* attached to the top sirloin. The butt tender is excluded by separating it from the hip bone. The protruding points of the hip bone socket and the first sacral vertebrae shall also be excluded to facilitate handling and packaging.

181A Lomo, Top Sirloin (Aguayón Superior y Algo de Empuje), Con Hueso

Esta pieza con hueso se prepara a partir de la pieza número 181 y es lo que permanece después de que tanto la cabeza del filete como la pulpa del aguayón inferior se separan del lomo con hueso. Se excluye la pulpa del aguayón inferior mediante un corte recto por la veta natural entre el *gluteus medius* y la pulpa bola. La separación continúa hacia la superficie exterior del aguayón, dejando una porción del *tensor de la fascia lata* (empuje) unida al aguayón superior. La cabeza del filete se excluye separándola del hueso de la cadera. También se extraerán los puntos protuberantes de la cuenca del hueso de la cadera y las primeras vértebras sacras, para facilitar el manejo y el embalaje.

184 — Beef Loin, Top Sirloin Butt, Boneless

This boneless item is prepared from Item Nos. 181 or 181A and contains the *gluteus medius, gluteus accessorius, gluteus profundus,* and the *biceps femoris.* The short loin end of the top butt shall be approximately parallel to the round end exposing the *gluteus medius.* On the round end, the *biceps femoris* shall be approximately equal to or larger than the *gluteus medius.* All bones, cartilages, tenderloin, and the *sacrosciatic* ligament and the lean and fat that overlaid the ligament shall be removed.

184 — Lomo, Pulpa del Aguayón Superior/Top Sirloin (Aguayón con Tapa), Deshuesado

Esta pieza deshuesada se prepara a partir de las piezas número 181 o 181A y contiene el *gluteus medius, gluteus accessorius, gluteus profundus* y el *biceps femoris.* El extremo adyacente al lomo corto deberá estar aproximadamente paralelo a la pierna y exponiendo el *gluteus medius.* En el extremo de la pierna, el *biceps femoris* deberá ser aproximadamente igual o más grande que el *gluteus medius.* Se deberán quitar todos los huesos, cartílagos, filetes y el ligamento *sacrociático,* así como la grasa y la carne que recubren el ligamento.

184 View from Strip Loin End
Vista desde el Extremo Adyacente al Strip Loin

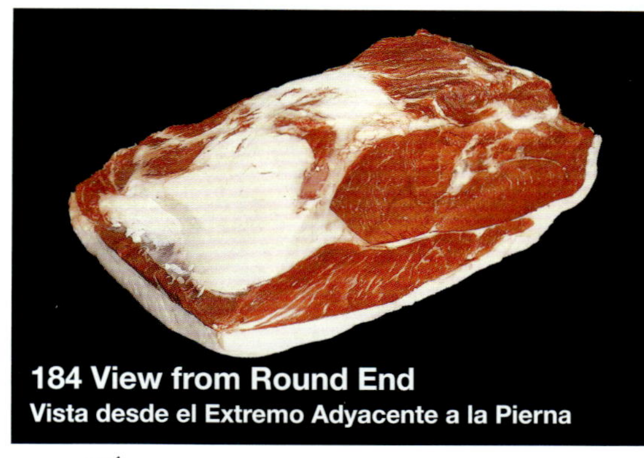

184 View from Round End
Vista desde el Extremo Adyacente a la Pierna

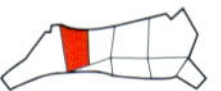

184A — Beef Loin, Top Sirloin Butt, Semi Center-Cut, Boneless

This boneless item is as described in Item No. 184, except the *biceps femoris* (cap) shall be excluded. When smaller sized roasts are specified, this item shall be split lengthwise into approximate equal portions.

184A — Lomo, Pulpa del Aguayón Superior/Top Sirloin (Aguayón sin Tapa), Corte Casi del Centro, Deshuesado

Esta pieza deshuesada aparece descrita en la pieza número 184, salvo que se deberá excluir el *biceps femoris* (tapa). Cuando se especifiquen rosbifs de tamaño más pequeño, esta pieza deberá ser dividida longitudinalmente en porciones aproximadamente iguales.

184A

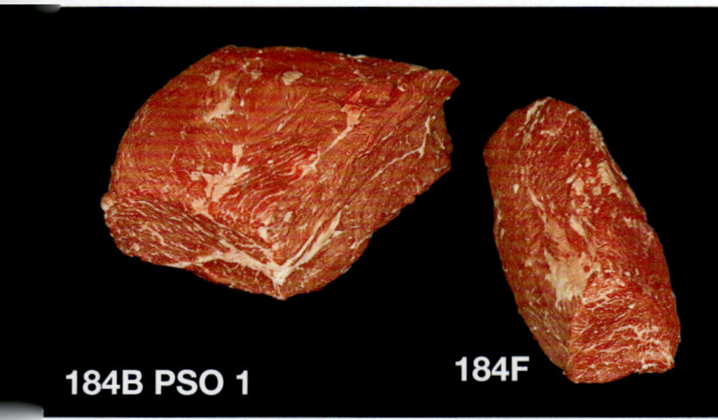

184B — Beef Loin, Top Sirloin Butt, Center-Cut, Boneless, Cap Off (IM)

This boneless item is as described in Item No. 184, except all muscles other than the *gluteus medius* shall be excluded. The flakes of surface fat remaining over the *gluteus medius* shall not exceed 1.0 inch (2.5 cm) in their dimension nor 0.125 inch in depth at any one point. When smaller-sized roasts are specified, this item shall be split lengthwise into approximate equal portions.

PSO: 1 – The dorsal portion of the *gluteus medius* shall be detached from the main portion by cutting through the seam. The two pieces shall be packaged together and placed within the same shipping container.

184B — Lomo, Pulpa del Aguayón Superior/Top Sirloin (Aguayón sin Tapa), Corte del Centro, Deshuesado (MI)

Esta pieza deshuesada, también conocida como "Palomilla" aparece descrita en la pieza número 184, salvo que deberán excluirse todos los músculos con excepción del *gluteus medius*. Las pequeñas capas de grasa que permanezcan sobre la superficie del *gluteus medius* no deberán exceder los 2.5 cm (1.0 pulgada) de dimensión ni tampoco 0.31 cm (0.125 pulgadas) de profundidad en ningún punto. Cuando se especifiquen rosbifs de tamaño más pequeño, esta pieza deberá ser dividida longitudinalmente en porciones aproximadamente iguales.

PSO: 1 – La porción dorsal del *gluteus medius* deberá separarse de la porción principal mediante el corte correspondiente siguiendo la veta. La dos piezas deben empaquetarse juntas y colocarse en el mismo recipiente.

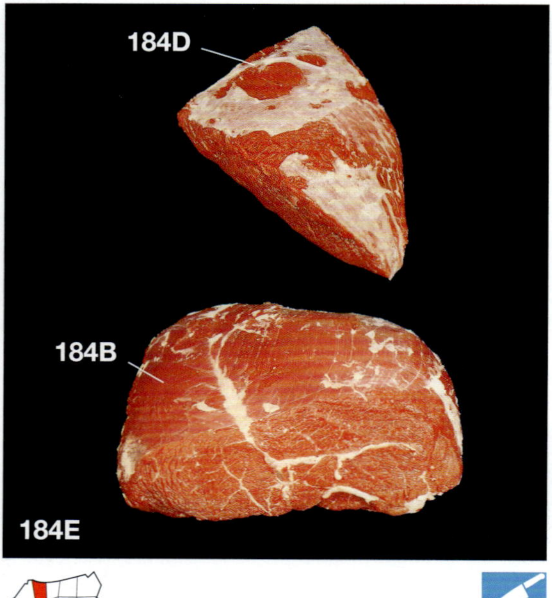

184D — Beef Loin, Top Sirloin, Cap (IM)

This item shall consist of the *biceps femoris* muscle. It is obtained when preparing Item No. 184B by a separation through the natural seam. Purchasers may specify the exterior fat cover trim desired. This item is often referred to as the "Coulotte".

184D — Lomo, Aguayón Superior/Top Sirloin, Tapa del Aguayón (MI)

Esta pieza deberá consistir en el músculo *biceps femoris*. Se obtiene al preparar la pieza número 184B mediante una separación a través de la veta natural. Los compradores pueden especificar la limpieza deseada de cubierta de grasa exterior. Esta pieza con frecuencia se llama "Coulotte".

184E — Beef Loin, Top Sirloin Butt, Boneless, 2-Piece

This item is as described in Item No. 184, except the cap muscle shall be separated from the top sirloin. The two pieces, Item Nos. 184B and 184D, shall be trimmed to comply with specified fat thickness requirements and packaged together.

184E — Lomo, Pulpa del Aguayón Superior/Top Sirloin (Aguayón y Tapa), Deshuesados y Recortados de Grasa, en 2 piezas

Esta pieza aparece descrita en la pieza número 184, salvo que la tapa del músculo deberá separarse del aguayón superior. Las dos piezas, números 184B y 184D, deberán recortarse a fin de cumplir con los requisitos especificados sobre el grosor de la grasa, y deberán empacarse juntas.

184F — Beef Loin, Top Sirloin Butt, Center-Cut, Boneless, Seamed, Dorsal Side (IM)

This item is prepared from Item No. 184B and shall consist of the dorsal portion of the *gluteus medius*, which is removed from the main portion by cutting through the natural seam. This item is commonly referred to as the "baseball cut". *(Pictured with Item No. 184B.)*

184F — Lomo, Pulpa del Aguayón Superior/Top Sirloin, Aguayón, Corte del Centro, Deshuesado, Diseccionado por las Vetas Naturales, Lado Dorsal (MI)

Esta pieza se prepara a partir de la pieza número 184B, y deberá consistir en la porción dorsal del *gluteus medius*, que se extrae de la porción principal cortando por la veta natural. Esta pieza se llama habitualmente "corte pelota de béisbol". *(Se incluye ilustración con la pieza número 184B.)*

185 — Beef Loin, Bottom Sirloin Butt, Boneless

This item is prepared from Item No. 181. The separation of the bottom sirloin butt is described in Item No. 181A. The boneless bottom sirloin butt consists of 3 parts. They are the *tensor fasciae latae*, or tri-tip; the *vastus medialis, vastus lateralis,* and *rectus femoris*, or ball tip; and the *obliquus abdominis intermus*, or flap. All bones and cartilages shall be excluded.

185 — Lomo, Pulpa del Aguayón Inferior/ Bottom Sirloin (Empuje, Punta de Pulpa Bola y Falda), Deshuesado

Esta pieza se prepara a partir de la pieza número 181. La separación de aguayón con tapa se describe en la pieza número 181A. El aguayón inferior con tapa deshuesado consiste en tres partes. Son el *tensor de la fascia lata*, o empuje; el *vastus medialis, el vastus lateralis* y el *rectus femoris*, o punta de la pulpa bola; y el *obiquus abdominis intermus*, o tapa. Se excluirán todos los huesos y cartílagos.

185 View from Strip Loin End
Vista desde el Extremo Adyacente al Strip Loin

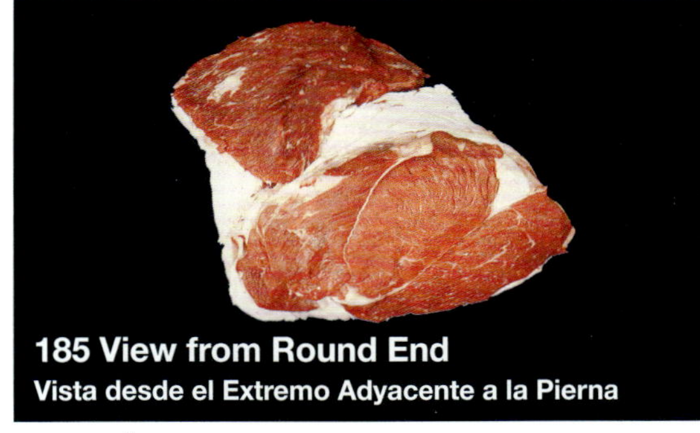

185 View from Round End
Vista desde el Extremo Adyacente a la Pierna

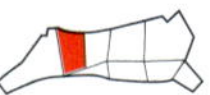

185A — Beef Loin, Bottom Sirloin Butt, Flap, Boneless (IM)

This item consists of the *obliquus abdominis internus* muscle from the bottom sirloin butt. The boneless flap is separated from the ball tip and the tri-tip through the natural seam. The heavy connective tissue and any cartilage shall be excluded.

The accompanying picture represents Fat Limitation Option (FLO) 6 but is available untrimmed by specifying FLO Option 1. See page 13 for more information.

185A — Lomo, Pulpa del Aguayón Inferior/Bottom Sirloin, Falda/Aldilla, Deshuesada (MI)

Esta pieza consiste en el músculo *obliquus abdominis internus* del aguayón inferior. La tapa deshuesada se separa de la punta de la pulpa bola y del tensor de la fascia lata (empuje) a través de la veta natural. El tejido conectivo grueso y cualquier cartílago presente debe excluirse.

La ilustración que acompaña esta descripción representa la opción 6 para limitar la grasa, pero está disponible sin recortar la grasa si se especifica la opción 1. Consulte la página 12 para obtener información adicional.

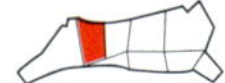

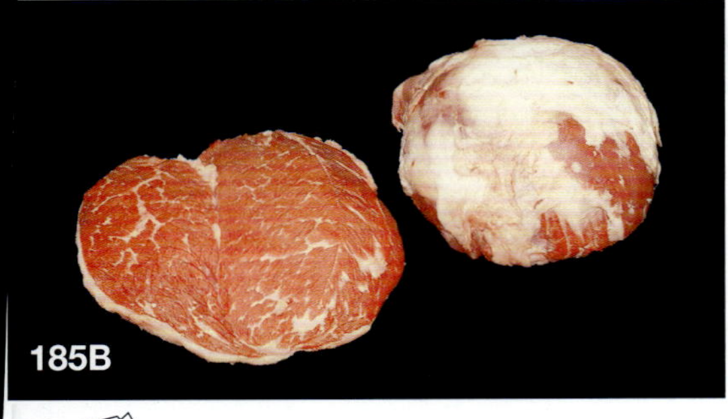

185B

Beef Loin, Bottom Sirloin Butt, Ball Tip, Boneless

This item consists of the *vastus medialis, vastus lateralis,* and *rectus femoris* muscles from the bottom sirloin butt. The boneless ball tip is separated from the tri-tip and the flap through the natural seam. All bones, cartilages, and the outside skin tissue shall be excluded.

185B

Lomo, Pulpa del Aguayón Inferior/Bottom Sirloin, Punta de Pulpa Bola, Deshuesada

Esta pieza consiste en los músculos *vastus medialis, vastus lateralis* y *rectus femoris* del aguayón inferior. La punta de la pulpa bola deshuesada se separa del empuje y la tapa siguiendo la veta natural. Se deberán excluir todos los huesos, los cartílagos y el tejido exterior cutáneo.

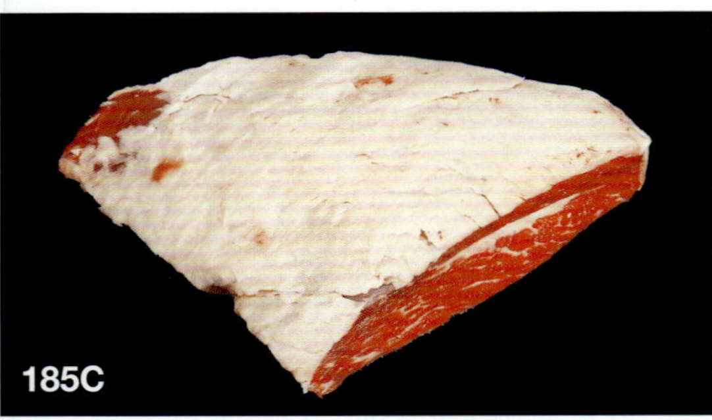

185C

Beef Loin, Bottom Sirloin Butt, Tri-Tip, Boneless (IM)

This item consists of the *tensor fasciae latae* muscle from the bottom sirloin butt. The boneless tri-tip is separated from the ball tip and the flap through the natural seam. Any cartilage or connective tissue shall be excluded.

185C

Lomo, Pulpa del Aguayón Inferior/Bottom Sirloin, Empuje (Punta Triangular), Deshuesado (MI)

Esta pieza o músculo triangular, referida también como "Punta de Palomilla" o "Punta de Cuarto", consiste en el músculo de forma triangular *tensor de la fascia lata* de la pulpa del aguayón inferior. El empuje deshuesado se separa de la punta de la pulpa bola y de la tapa siguiendo la veta natural. Se excluirá cualquier cartílago o tejido conectivo presente.

185D

Beef Loin, Bottom Sirloin Butt, Tri-Tip, Boneless, Defatted (IM)

This item is as described in Item No. 185C, except it shall be trimmed practically free of fat.

185D

Lomo, Pulpa del Aguayón Inferior/Bottom Sirloin, Empuje (Punta Triangular), Deshuesado, Limpio de Grasa (MI)

Esta pieza aparece descrita en la pieza número 185C, salvo que deberá ser recortada de grasa hasta que esté prácticamente libre de la misma.

188

Beef Loin, Tenderloin, Bone In

This item is derived from a short loin and consists of *psoas major* and *psoas minor,* attached to the transverse process of the *lumbar vertebrae.* The anterior end shall be removed so that the *psoas major* is no less than 2.5 inches (6.25 cm) in the longest dimension.

188

Lomo, Filete Cabrería Corto, con Hueso

Esta pieza proviene de un lomo y consiste en el *psoas mayor* y el *psoas menor,* unidos a las apofisis transversales de las *vértebras lumbares.* El extremo anterior deberá extraerse de manera que el *psoas mayor* no mida más de 6.25 cm (2.5 pulgadas) en la dimensión más extensa.

189 — Beef Loin, Tenderloin, Full

This item is derived from a full loin as described in either Item Nos. 172 or 172A. The boneless item shall consist of the *psoas major, psoas minor, iliacus,* and may show the presence of the *sartorius.* The *obliquus abdominis internus* muscle, or flap, if present, shall be trimmed level with the fat surface. The sirloin butt end of the tenderloin shall expose the *psoas major, iliacus,* and if present, the *sartorius.* The surface fat shall be trimmed so as not to exceed 0.75 inch (19 mm) in depth at any point measured along the tenderloin from the head or butt end to the exposed lymph gland. The surface fat from the lymph gland toward the tail shall be tapered down to the lean at a point not beyond three-quarters the length of the entire tenderloin. The tenderloin shall also be trimmed free of ragged edges. A score into the tenderloin exceeding 0.5 inch (13 mm) in depth is not acceptable.

189 — Lomo, Filete, Completo, sin Hueso

Esta pieza proviene de un lomo completo, como se describe en las piezas 172 o 172A. La pieza deshuesada deberá consistir en los músculos *psoas mayor, psoas menor e iliacus,* y puede mostrar la presencia del *sartorius.* El músculo *obliquus abdominis internus,* o tapa, si está presente, deberá recortarse al mismo nivel de la cubierta de grasa. El aguayón sin tapa del filete deberá exponer los músculos *psoas mayor e iliacus* y, si está presente, el *sartorius.* La cubierta de grasa deberá ser recortada de manera que no exceda los 19 mm (0.75 pulgadas) de profundidad en ningún punto medido a lo largo del filete, desde el extremo de la cabeza o aguayón hasta el ganglio linfático expuesto. La cubierta de grasa desde el ganglio linfático a la cola deberá rebajarse hasta la superficie magra no más allá de las tres cuartas partes del largo total del filete. Asimismo, el filete deberá ser recortado de grasa y limpio para emparejar los bordes irregulares. Un corte profundo del filete que exceda los 13 mm (0.5 pulgadas) de grosor no es aceptable.

189 View from Fat Side
Vista desde el lado de la grasa

189 View from Bone Side
Vista desde el lado del hueso

189A — Beef Loin, Tenderloin, Full, Side Muscle On, Defatted

This item is as described in Item No. 189, except the entire tenderloin shall be practically free of surface and wing fat. Wing fat is the fat lying between the main body of the tenderloin and the *iliacus* muscle, or wing, as it is often called.

189A — Lomo, Filete, Completo, con Cuerda (Psoas Menor) Pegado, Limpio de Grasa

Esta pieza aparece descrita en la pieza número 189, salvo que el filete completo deberá presentarse prácticamente libre de cubierta de grasa y de la grasa que se intercala entre los músculos ("grasa del ala"). La grasa del "ala" del filete es la grasa intermuscular que yace entre el cuerpo principal del lomo y el músculo *iliacus,* o "ala del filete", como se le llama habitualmente a este músculo.

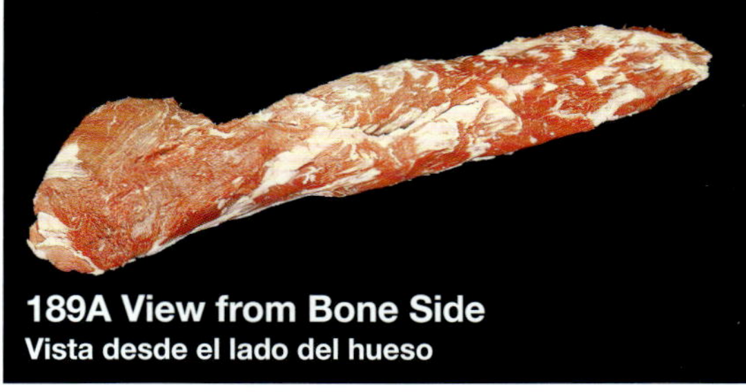

189A View from Bone Side
Vista desde el lado del hueso

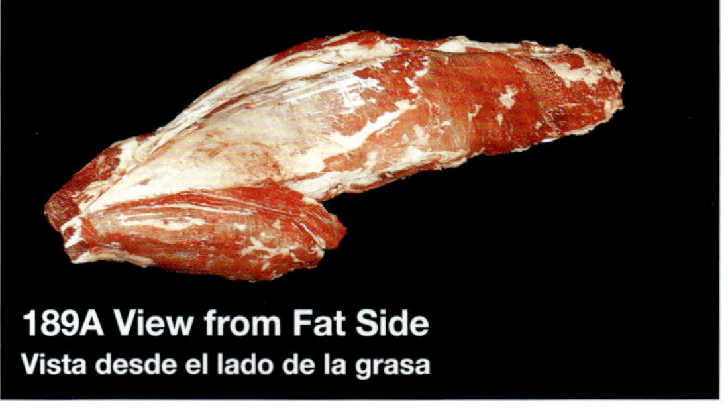

189A View from Fat Side
Vista desde el lado de la grasa

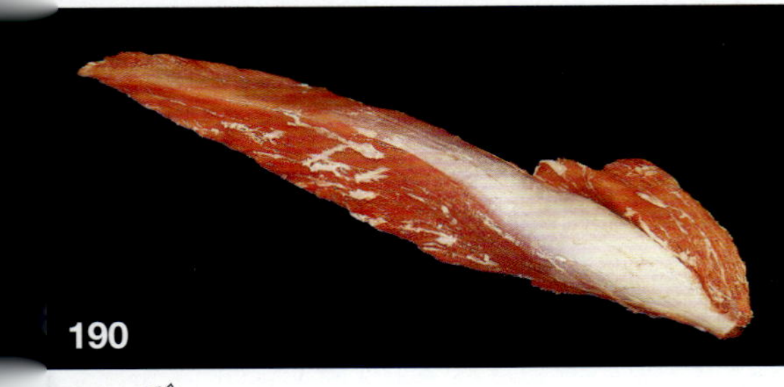

190 — Beef Loin, Tenderloin, Full, Side Muscle Off, Defatted

This item is as described in Item No. 189A, except the side muscle, or *psoas minor*, shall be excluded. The principal membranous tissue over the main body of the tenderloin, or *psoas major*, shall remain intact.

190 — Lomo, Filete, Completo, sin Cuerda (Psoas Menor), Limpio de Grasa

Esta pieza, también conocida como "Filete Entero con Cordón" o "Caña de Filete" aparece descrita en la pieza número 189A, salvo que se deberá excluir el músculo del lado o *psoas menor*. El tejido membranoso principal ('espejo') sobre el cuerpo principal del filete, o *psoas mayor*, deberá permanecer intacto.

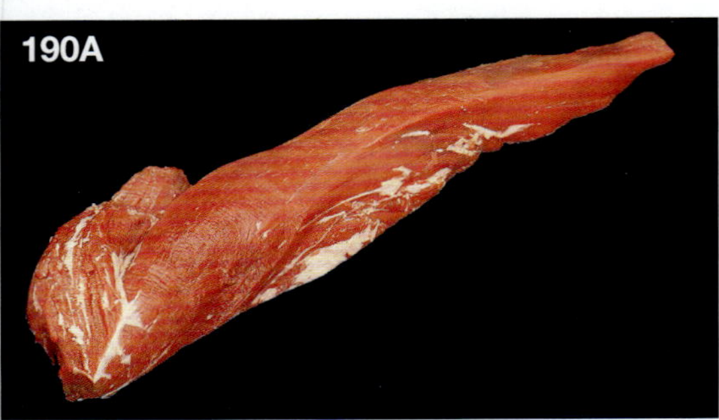

190A — Beef Loin, Tenderloin, Full, Side Muscle Off, Skinned

This item is as described in Item No. 190, except the principal membranous tissue covering the *psoas major* shall be excluded.

190A — Lomo, Filete, Completo, sin Cuerda (Psoas Menor), Despellejado

Esta pieza limpia, también llamada "caña de filete sin cordón", aparece descrita en la pieza número 190, salvo que el tejido membranoso principal ("espejo") que recubre el *psoas mayor* deberá excluirse.

190B — Beef Loin, Tenderloin, Full, Side Muscle Off, Center-Cut, Skinned (IM)

This item is as described in Item No. 190A except that the tenderloin tail (Item No. 192A) and butt tenderloin (Item No. 191A) shall be removed. This item is sometime referred to as a "barrel" cut.

190B — Lomo, Filete, Completo, sin Cuerda (Psoas Menor), Corte del Medio (Sin Cabeza ni Cola), Despellejado (MI)

Esta pieza aparece descrita en la pieza número 190A, salvo que se deberá retirar la cola del filete (pieza número 192A) y la cabeza del filete (pieza número 191A). Esta pieza algunas veces se llama corte "barril".

191 — Beef Loin, Tenderloin, Butt

This item shall consist of the sirloin butt portion of the tenderloin. The sirloin, or butt end, shall expose the *psoas major, psoas minor, iliacus,* and if present, the *sartorius*. Further, the *obliquus abdominis internus,* or flap, if also present, shall be trimmed level with the fat surface. The anterior, or short loin, end shall be exposed by a straight cut that displays the *psoas major* and the *psoas minor* muscles no further along the length of the tenderloin than 0.5 inch (13 mm) inch beyond the *iliacus*. The surface fat shall be trimmed so as not to exceed 0.75 inch (19 mm) in depth at any point. The large lymph gland shall be exposed. A score into the butt tenderloin exceeding 0.5 inch (13 mm) is not acceptable.

191 — Lomo, Filete, Cabeza (Porción en el Aguayón)

Esta pieza deberá consistir en la porción de aguayón sin tapa del filete. El sirloin, o aguayón sin tapa, deberá exponer los músculos *psoas mayor, psoas menor, iliacus* y, si está presente, el *sartorius*. Además, el *obliquus abdominis internus*, o tapa, si también se encuentra presente, deberá recortarse a nivel de la superficie de grasa. El extremo anterior, o adyacente al lomo, deberá exponerse mediante un corte recto que exhiba los músculos *psoas mayor* y *psoas menor*, sin sobrepasar la longitud del filete en 13 mm (0.5 pulgadas) más allá del *iliacus*. La cubierta de grasa deberá recortarse de manera que no exceda los 19 mm (0.75 pulgadas) de profundidad en ningún punto. El ganglio linfático grande deberá exponerse. Un corte profundo de la cabeza del filete que exceda los 13 mm (0.5 pulgadas) no es aceptable.

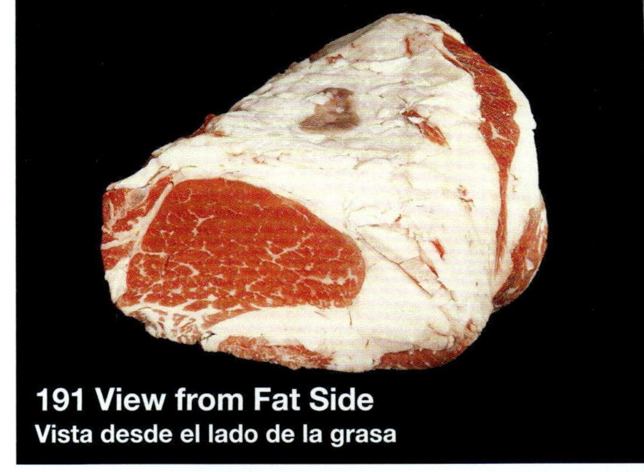

191 View from Fat Side
Vista desde el lado de la grasa

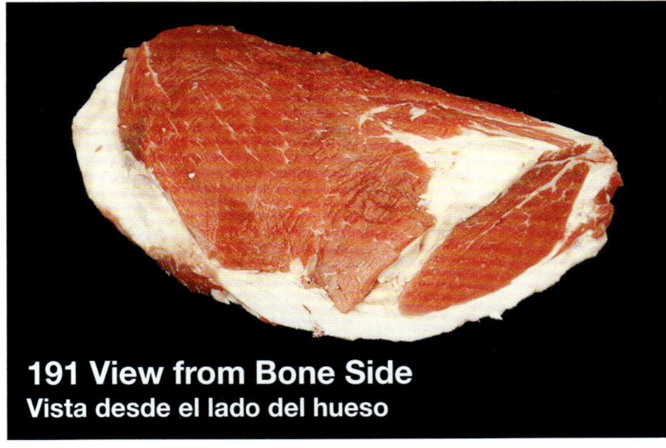

191 View from Bone Side
Vista desde el lado del hueso

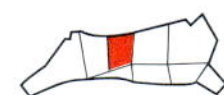

191A — Beef Loin, Tenderloin, Butt, Defatted

This item is as described in Item No. 191, except the surface and wing fat, as explained in Item No. 189A, shall be trimmed practically free.

191A — Lomo, Filete, Cabeza, Limpia de Grasa

Esta pieza aparece descrita en la pieza número 191, salvo que la cubierta de grasa y la grasa entre los músculos del filete, como se explica en la pieza número 189A, deberán recortarse hasta que ésta quede prácticamente libre de grasa.

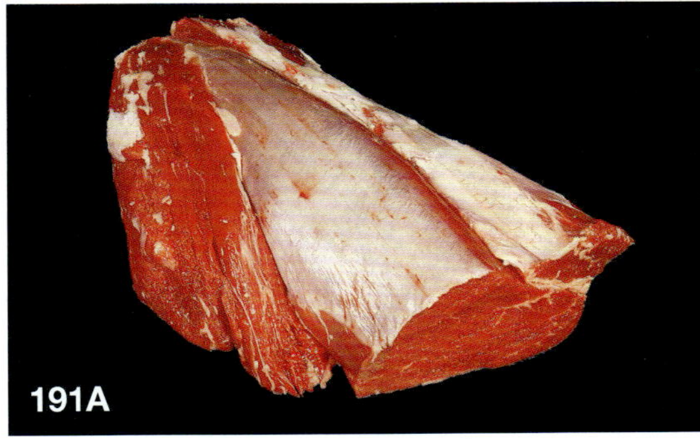

191A

191B — Beef Loin, Tenderloin, Butt, Skinned

This item is as described in Item No. 191A, except the principal membranous tissue covering the *psoas major* muscle shall be excluded.

191B — Lomo, Filete, Cabeza, Despellejada

Esta pieza aparece descrita en la pieza número 191A, salvo que el tejido membranoso principal que recubre el músculo *psoas mayor* deberá excluirse.

191B

192 — Beef Loin, Tenderloin, Short

This item shall consist of the short loin portion of the tenderloin and consists only of the *psoas major* and *psoas minor* muscles. The fat shall be trimmed to not exceed 0.5 inch (13 mm) in depth at any point over the *psoas major* at the sirloin butt end and shall be tapered down to the lean of the *psoas major* prior to the thin or tail end. A score into the short tenderloin exceeding 0.5 inch (13 mm) is not acceptable.

192 — Lomo, Filete, Corto

Esta pieza deberá consistir en la porción del filete en el lomo corto y proviene únicamente de los músculos *psoas mayor* y *psoas menor*. La grasa deberá recortarse de forma que no exceda los 13 mm (0.5 pulgadas) de grosor en ningún lugar sobre el *psoas mayor* en el extremo adyacente al aguayón sin tapa y deberá darle forma de huso a la parte magra del *psoas mayor* antes del extremo delgado o cola. Un corte profundo del filete corto que exceda los 13 mm (0.5 pulgadas) no es aceptable.

192A — Beef Loin, Tenderloin Tails

This item shall consist of the thin or tail portion of the *psoas major*. The *psoas minor*, however, may remain firmly attached.

192A — Lomo, Filete, Colas (Puntas)

Esta pieza deberá consistir en el extremo delgado o la cola del *psoas mayor*. El *psoas menor*, no obstante, puede permanecer firmemente unido.

193 — Beef Flank, Flank Steak (IM)

This boneless item consists of the *rectus abdominis* muscle from the flank region of the carcass. The flank steak is located at the cod or udder end. It is separated from the *transversus abdominis*, *obliquus abdominis internus*, and *obliquus abdominis externus* muscles through the natural seams. The item shall be prepared practically free of fat and the membranous tissue.

193 — Falda (Ijar), Concha de Falda (MI)

Esta pieza deshuesada consiste en el músculo *rectus abdominis* de la región de la falda de la canal. El bistec de concha de falda se ubica en el extremo del canal inguinal o de la ubre. Se separa de los músculos *transversus abdominis*, *obliquus abdominis internus* y *obliquus abdominis externus* a través de las vetas naturales. La pieza deberá prepararse de manera que quede prácticamente libre de grasa y del tejido membranoso.

NAMP
NORTH AMERICAN MEAT PROCESSORS ASSOCIATION
Association Amérique du Nord des Transformateurs de Viande
Asociación Norteamericana de Procesadores de Carne

Photo courtesy of The Beef Checkoff.
Fotografía cortesía del programa The Beef Checkoff.

Index / Índice

Beef Portion Cuts and Weight Ranges
Cortes porcionados de carne de res y escalas de peso

ITEM PIEZA	PRODUCT NAME NOMBRE DE PRODUCTO	PG. PÁG.	Suggested Portion Weight Range Porción Sugerida Escala de Peso
1100	Cubed Steak Bistec Suavizado	69	3 – 8 oz. (85-226.8 gr)
1101	Cubed Steak, Special Bistec Suavizado, Especial	69	3 – 8 oz. (85-226.8 gr)
1102	Braising Steak, Swiss Bistec para Brasear, Estilo Suizo	70	4 – 8 oz. (113.4-226.8 gr)
1103	Rib, Rib Steak, Bone In Chuletón (Espaldar), Bistec del Chuletón, Con Hueso	70	8 – 18 oz. (226.8-510.3 gr)
1103B	Rib, Rib Steak, Bone In, Frenched Chuletón (Espaldar), Bistec del Chuletón, Con Hueso, Estilo Francés	71	12 – 20 oz. (340.2-567 gr)
1112	Rib, Ribeye Roll Steak, Boneless Chuletón (Espaldar), Bistec de Rollo Ribeye, Deshuesado	72	4 – 12 oz. (113.4-340.2 gr)
1112A	Rib, Ribeye Steak, Lip-On, Boneless Chuletón (Espaldar), Bistec de Ribeye, Con Cordón, Deshuesado ♣ Bistecs del Chuletón Deshuesado	71	8 – 14 oz. (226.8-396.9 gr)
1112B	Rib, Ribeye Steak, Lip-On, Short-Cut, Boneless Chuletón (Espaldar), Bistec de Ribeye, Con Cordón, Corte Corto, Deshuesado ♣ Bistecs del Chuletón Deshuesado	72	4 – 12 oz. (113.4-340.2 gr)
1112C	Rib, Ribeye Cap Steak (IM) Chuletón (Espaldar), Bistec de Ribeye/Entrecot (M. Longissimus dorsi)	72	4 – 12 oz. (113.4-340.2 gr)
1112D	Rib, Ribeye Cap Steak (IM) Chuletón (Espaldar), Tapa del Ribeye (M. Spinalis dorsi/Multifidus dorsi)	72	4 – 8 oz. (113.4-226.8 gr)
1114D	Shoulder, Top Blade Steak (IM) Paleta (Espaldilla), Bistec de "Paletilla California" (M. Infraespinoso)	73	4 – 8 oz. (113.4-226.8 gr)
1114E	Shoulder, Arm Steak Paleta (Espaldilla), Bistec de Brazuelo	73	4 – 8 oz. (113.4-226.8 gr)
1114F	Shoulder Tender, Portioned Teres Filé, Porcionado (M. Teres/Redondo Mayor)	73	2 – 14 oz. (56.7-396.9 gr)
1116D	Chuck, Chuck Eye Roll Steak, Boneless Paleta (Espaldilla), Bistec del Centro de Rollo de Diezmillo, Deshuesado	74	4 – 12 oz. (113.4-340.2 gr)
1116G	Chuck, Under Blade, Center-Cut Steak Paleta (Espaldilla), Tapa Interior de la Planchuela, Bistec del Centro	74	4 – 12 oz. (113.4-340.2 gr)
1121D	Plate, Inside Skirt Steak, Boneless (IM) Costillar, Falda Interna/Arrachera Inside, Deshuesada (M. Transverso del Abdomen)	75	4 – 8 oz. (113.4-226.8 gr)
1121E	Plate, Outside Skirt Steak, Skinned (IM) Costillar, Arrachera Delgada Regular, Despellejada (M. Diafragma)	75	4 – 8 oz. (113.4-226.8 gr)
1123	Short Rib, Bone In Costilla Corta (Costilla Cargada), Con Hueso	75	3 – 10 oz. (85-283.5 gr)
1136	Ground Beef Patties Hamburguesas de Carne Molida de Res	76	Desired ounces or number per pound Onzas o cantidad por libras deseadas
1136A	Beef and Soy Protein Product Patties Hamburguesas de Res con Producto Proteico Vegetal (PPV) Añadido según la Normativa	76	Desired ounces or number per pound Onzas o cantidad por libras deseadas
1137	Ground Beef Patties, Special Hamburguesa de Carne Molida de Res, Especial	76	Desired ounces or number per pound Onzas o cantidad por libras deseadas
1140	Hanging Tender Steak Bistec de Arrachera Gallo (Pilares o Arrachera Colgante del Lomo)	77	3 – 10 oz. (85-283.5 gr)
1167	Round, Sirloin Tip (Knuckle) Steak Pierna (Piña), Bistec de Punta de Sirloin (Pulpa Bola)	77	3 – 10 oz. (85-283.5 gr)
1167A	Round, Sirloin Tip (Knuckle) Steak Pierna (Piña), Bistec de Punta de Sirloin (Pulpa Bola), Desprovisto de Grasa	77	3 – 10 oz. (85-283.5 gr)
1167D	Round, Sirloin Tip (Knuckle) Steak Pierna (Piña), Bistec de Punta Sirloin (Pulpa Bola), Desprovisto de Grasa, Especial	78	4 – 8 oz. (113.4-226.8 gr)
1167E	Round, Sirloin Tip (Knuckle), Side Steak (IM) Pierna (Piña), Punta de Sirloin (Pulpa Bola), Bistec del Centro (M. Recto Femoral)	78	4 – 8 oz. (113.4-226.8 gr)
1167F	Round, Sirloin Tip (Knuckle), Side Steak (IM) Pierna (Piña), Punta de Sirloin (Pulpa Bola), Bistec del Músculo Lateral (M. Vasto Lateral)	78	4 – 8 oz. (113.4-226.8 gr)
1169	Round, Top (Inside) Round Steak Pierna (Piña), Bistec de Pulpa Negra (Cara/Centro)	79	3 – 12 oz. (85-340.2 gr)

portion cuts / cortes porcionados

ITEM PIEZA	PRODUCT NAME / NOMBRE DE PRODUCTO	PG. PÁG.	Suggested Portion Weight Range / Porción Sugerida Escala de Peso
1169C	Top (Inside) Round, Front Side Steak Pierna (Piña), Pulpa Nuez (M. Pectíneo) de la Pulpa Negra, Porcionado	79	3 – 12 oz. (85-340.2 gr)
1170A	Round, Bottom (Gooseneck) Round Steak Pierna (Piña), Bistec de Contracara con Cuete	79	3 – 24 oz. (85-680.4 gr)
1171D	Round, Outside Round Steak (IM) Pierna (Piña), Bistec de Pulpa Blanca (MI)	79	3 – 24 oz. (85-680.4 gr)
1173	Loin, Porterhouse Steak Lomo, Bistec Porterhouse	80	12 – 24 oz. (340.2-680.4 gr)
1174	Loin, T-Bone Steak Lomo, Bistec T-Bone	80	10 – 22 oz. (283.5-623.7 gr)
1179	Loin, Strip Loin Steak, Bone In Lomo, Bistec Strip Loin (New York), con Hueso	81	8 – 24 oz. (226.8-680.4 gr)
1179A	Loin, Strip Loin Steak, Bone In, Center-Cut Lomo, Bistec Strip Loin (New York), con Hueso, del Centro	81	8 – 24 oz. (226.8-680.4 gr)
1180	Loin, Strip Loin Steak, Boneless Lomo, Bistec Strip Loin (New York), Deshuesado, del Centro	82	6 – 20 oz. (170.1-567 gr)
1180A	Loin, Strip Loin Steak, Boneless, Center-Cut Lomo, Bistec Strip Loin (New York), Deshuesado, del Centro	82	6 – 20 oz. (170.1-567 gr)
1180B	Loin, Strip Loin Steak, Split, Boneless Lomo, Bistec Strip Loin (Club Steak), Dividido, Deshuesado	83	4 – 12 oz. (113.4-340.2 gr)
1184	Loin, Top Sirloin Butt Steak, Boneless Lomo, Bistec de Pulpa del Aguayón Superior/Top Sirloin, Deshuesado	83	4 – 24 oz. (113.4-680.4 gr)
1184A	Loin, Top Sirloin Butt Steak, Semi Center-Cut, Boneless Lomo, Bistec de Pulpa del Aguayón Superior/Top Sirloin, Sin Tapa, Corte Casi del Centro, Deshuesado	83	4 – 16 oz. (113.4-453.6 gr)
1184B	Loin, Top Sirloin Butt Steak, Center-Cut, Boneless (IM) Lomo, Bistec de Pulpa del Aguayón Superior/Top Sirloin, Sin Tapa, Corte del Centro, Deshuesado (MI)	84	4 – 16 oz. (113.4-453.6 gr)
1184D	Loin, Top Sirloin Cap Steak, Boneless (IM) Lomo, Bistec de Tapa del Aguayón, Deshuesado (MI)	84	4 – 8 oz. (113.4-226.8 gr)
1184F	Loin, Top Sirloin Butt Steak, Center-Cut, Boneless, Seamed, Dorsal Side (IM) Lomo, Bistec de Pulpa del Aguayón Superior/Top Sirloin, Sin Tapa, Corte del Centro, Deshuesado, Diseccionado por las Vetas Naturales, Lado Dorsal (MI)	85	3 – 8 oz. (85-226.8 gr)
1185A	Loin, Bottom Sirloin Butt, Flap Steak (IM) Lomo, Pulpa del Aguayón Inferior/Bottom Sirloin, Bistec de Falda (MI)	85	3 – 8 oz. (85-226.8 gr)
1185B	Loin, Bottom Sirloin Butt, Ball Tip Steak Lomo, Pulpa del Aguayón Inferior/Bottom Sirloin, Bistec de Punta de Pulpa Bola, Deshuesada (M. Recto Femoral y Vasto Lateral)	85	3 – 10 oz. (85-283.5 gr)
1185C	Loin, Bottom Sirloin Butt, Tri-Tip Steak (IM) Lomo, Pulpa del Aguayón Inferior/Bottom Sirloin, Bistec de Empuje (Punta Triangular) (MI)	86	3 – 8 oz. (85-226.8 gr)
1185D	Loin, Bottom Sirloin Butt, Tri-Tip Steak, Defatted (IM) Lomo, Pulpa del Aguayón Inferior/Bottom Sirloin, Bistec de Empuje (Punta Triangular), Limpio de Grasa (MI)	86	3 – 8 oz. (85-226.8 gr)
1188	Loin, Tenderloin Steak, Bone In Lomo, Tablita de Filete (Bistec Cabrería), Con Hueso	86	8 – 20 oz. (226.8-557 gr)
1189	Loin, Tenderloin Steak Lomo, Medallón de Filete	87	4 – 14 oz. (113.4-396.9 gr)
1189A	Loin, Tenderloin Steak, Side Muscle On, Defatted Lomo, Medallón de Filete, Con Cuerda (Psoas Menor), Limpio de Grasa	87	3 – 14 oz. (85-396.9 gr)
1190	Loin, Tenderloin Steak, Side Muscle Off, Defatted Lomo, Medallón de Filete, sin Cuerda (Psoas Menor), Limpio de Grasa	87	3 – 14 oz. (85-396.9 gr)
1190A	Loin, Tenderloin Steak, Side Muscle Off, Skinned Lomo, Medallón de Filete, sin Cuerda (Psoas Menor), Despellejado	88	3 – 14 oz. (85-396.9 gr)
1190B	Loin, Tenderloin Steak, Full, Side Muscle Off, Skinned, Center-Cut (IM) Lomo, Medallón de Filete, sin Cuerda (Psoas Menor), Corte del Medio (Sin Cabeza ni Cola), Despellejado (MI)	88	3 – 14 oz. (85-396.9 gr)
1190C	Loin, Tenderloin Tips Lomo, Colas (Puntas) de Filete	88	Amount as Specified Cantidad según lo especificado

Información para hacer los pedidos

Tolerancias de peso y grosor de la porción*

El comprador especificará el peso y/o el grosor que desea. Para obtener ayuda en la especificación del peso, consulte las tablas de escalas de peso. A menos que el comprador especifique otras tolerancias de peso y/o grosor, se deberán utilizar las tablas que aparecen a continuación. Cuando se especifique tanto el peso como el grosor, se recomienda que esos requisitos se limiten a piezas prensadas y/o rebanadas de forma mecánica.

Opciones para limitar la grasa

Cortes de porciones

El comprador especificará uno de los siguientes grosores máximos de cubierta de grasa (en un punto cualquiera) en los bordes del bistec, a menos que se indiquen limitaciones precisas de grasa en la descripción detallada de la pieza. En caso de que no se especifique, el grosor de la grasa no excederá los 6 mm (0.25 pulgadas) en ningún punto.

Cortes de porciones

Número de opción	Grosor máximo de grasa en un punto cualquiera del corte en porciones
1	6 mm (0.25 pulgadas)
2	3 mm (0.125 pulgadas)
3	Prácticamente libre de grasa [75% de superficie magra/superficie muscular descubierta por la disección, y con grasa remanente que no debe exceder los 3 mm (0.125 pulgadas)]
4	Desprovisto de grasa/Prácticamente desnudo de grasa* [la grasa restante no debe exceder los 2.5 cm (1.0 pulgada) en la dimensión más larga y/o 3 mm (0.125 pulgadas) de grosor]
5	Desprovisto de grasa/Prácticamente desnudo de grasa, Membrana superficial retirada** (el 90% de la superficie magra es expuesta) y la grasa que queda no debe exceder los 3 mm (0.125 pulgadas)

*/** - Consulte la página xlii para leer la definición

Tolerancias de grosor de la porción

Grosor especificado	Tolerancia de grosor	Uniformidad de grosor
2.5 cm o menos (1.0 pulgada)	± 5 mm (0.1875 pulgadas)	5 mm (0.1875 pulgadas)
Más de 2.5 cm (1.0 pulgada)	± 6 mm (0.25 pulgadas)	6 mm (0.25 pulgadas)

Tolerancia de peso de la porción

Peso especificado	Tolerancia de peso	Uniformidad de grosor
Menor que 170 g (6.0 oz.)	± 7 g (0.25 oz.)	5 mm (0.1875 pulgadas)
170 g (6.0 oz.) a 340 g (12.0 oz.)	± 14 g (0.50 oz.)	6 mm (0.25 pulgadas)
341 g (12.01 oz.) a 680 g (24.0 oz.)	± 21 g (0.75 oz.)	9 mm (0.375 pulgadas)
681 g (24.01 oz.) o más	± 28 g (1.0 oz.)	13 mm (0.50 pulgadas)

Los compradores que tengan necesidades o especificaciones especiales deben comunicarse con sus proveedores.

* Las medidas de grosor no se aplican a una distancia de 6 mm (0.25 pulgadas) del borde. Además, el valor que se indica en la uniformidad de grosor es la máxima diferencia admitida entre la medida más fina y la más gruesa de una chuleta o un bistec individual.

Ordering Data

Portion-Cut Weight and Thickness Tolerances*

The purchaser shall specify the portion weight and/or thickness desired. For assistance in specifying weight, see weight range tables. Unless other portion weight and/or thickness tolerances are specified by the purchaser, the following tables shall be used. When both weight and thickness are specified, it is recommended that those requirements be limited to items that are mechanically pressed and/or sliced.

Fat Limitation Options (FLO)

Portion Cuts

The purchaser shall specify one of the following maximum (at any one point) thicknesses of surface fat on the edges of the steak unless definite fat limitations are indicated in the detailed Item Descriptions. If not specified, fat thickness shall not exceed 0.25 inch (6 mm) at any one point.

Portion Cuts

Option No.	Maximum Fat Thickness at Any One Point for Portion Cuts
1	0.25 inch (6 mm)
2	0.125 inch (3 mm)
3	Practically free (75 percent lean/seam surface exposed and remaining fat shall not exceed 0.125 inch (3 mm)
4	Peeled/Denuded* (remaining fat shall not exceed 1.0 inch (2.5 cm) in the longest dimension and/or 0.125 inch (3 mm) in thickness)
5	Peeled/Denuded, Surface Membrane Removed** (90 percent lean exposed) and remaining fat shall not exceed 0.125 inch (3 mm)

*/** – see page xvi for definition

Portion Thickness Tolerances

Specified Thickness	Thickness Tolerance	Thickness Uniformity
1.0 inch (2.5 cm or less)	± 0.1875 inch (5 mm)	0.1875 inch (5 mm)
More than 1.0 inch (2.5 cm)	± 0.25 inch (6 mm)	0.25 inch (6 mm)

Portion Weight Tolerance

Specified Weight	Weight Tolerance	Thickness Uniformity
Less than 6.0 oz. (170 g)	± 0.25 oz. (7 g)	0.1875 inch (5 mm)
6.0 oz. (170 g) to 12.0 oz. (340 g)	± 0.50 oz. (14 g)	0.25 inch (6 mm)
12.01 oz. (341 g) to 24.0 oz. (680 g)	± 0.75 oz. (21 g)	0.375 inch (9 mm)
24.01 oz. (681 g) or more	± 1.0 oz. (28 g)	0.50 inch (13 mm)

Purchasers with special needs or specifications should contact their suppliers.

* Thickness measurements not applicable with 0.25 inch (6 mm) of edge. Also, value listed under thickness uniformity is the maximum allowable difference between the thinnest and thickest measurement of an individual chop or steak.

Membership Information
Información sobre la membresía

Want your personal network to include the real decision-makers at the most successful meat & poultry processors and suppliers in North America?

THEN JOIN NAMP!

Founded in 1942, the North American Meat Processors Association (NAMP) is an international member-driven association of *progressive meat processors, distributors, center-of-the-plate specialists,* and suppliers selling primarily to the foodservice industry. NAMP provides exceptional value through high-caliber support programs and governmental representation to help ensure our members' success in the industry.

The Meat Buyer's Guide® is a NAMP publication. NAMP members can participate in the review/update process of each edition.

BENEFITS OF MEMBERSHIP

- 35% discount on *The Meat Buyers Guide®*
- A relaxed networking and learning environment at two major industry-wide meetings a year
- Learning opportunities at NAMP's 16+ food safety conferences and workshops: pay lower member fees
- NAMP's weekly report, *NewsLine,* which contains industry information and updates and NAMP's weekly Market Report, with complete up-to-date pricing information
- Unlimited free access to NAMP's College of Experts, our team of 34 Ph.D.-level consultants on 19 subjects important to your business
- A voice in government rulemaking: NAMP is a North American organization that effectively represents your interests to USDA-FSIS, USDA-AMS, and CFIA
- A cross-referenced *Member Resource Directory* for networking and enriching your business prospects
- Fast, on-line help from other members through NAMP's Listserve called "Bull Session"
- Exclusive technical/educational info on the Members Only section at www.namp.com

Members also enjoy toll-free access to NAMP's experienced staff and off-site consultants who are ready to help you with just about any problem, question or concern you may have. *It's like having your own team of experts without the added expense - an incredible value for your dues dollar!*

Membership in NAMP offers an unparalleled and unique opportunity to learn and network with your peers. Join today and you'll enrich your business prospects and benefit from other members' experiences. *It's what our long-time members call "The Magic of NAMP".*

WE INVITE YOU TO JOIN TODAY

To apply, go to www.namp.com or call +1 703.758.1900.

¿Quiere que su red personal incluya a quienes en verdad toman las decisiones y a los más exitosos procesadores y proveedores de carne roja y aves de América del Norte?

¡ENTONCES ÚNASE A NAMP!

La Asociación Norteamericana de Procesadores de Carne (NAMP), fundada en 1942, es una asociación internacional dedicada a sus integrantes, que incluyen *procesadores, distribuidores, especialistas en ingredientes principales del plato* y proveedores progresistas que venden principalmente a la industria de servicios de alimentación. NAMP ofrece un valor excepcional a través de programas de apoyo de gran nivel y representación en el gobierno para ayudar a garantizar el éxito de nuestros miembros en la industria.

La Guía para Compradores de Carne® es una publicación de NAMP. Los miembros de NAMP pueden participar en el proceso de revisión y actualización de cada edición.

BENEFICIOS DE LA MEMBRESÍA

- 35% de descuento en *La Guía para Compradores de Carne®*
- Un ambiente relajado para establecer contactos y aprender en dos grandes reuniones de toda la industria por año
- Oportunidades de aprendizaje en las conferencias y los talleres de inocuidad alimentaria de NAMP: pague tarifas más bajas para miembros
- Informe semanal de NAMP, *NewsLine,* que contiene información y actualizaciones de la industria, y el Informe de Mercado semanal de NAMP, con la información de precios completa y al día
- Acceso gratis ilimitado al colegio de expertos de NAMP, nuestro equipo de 34 con nivel de doctorado en 19 áreas importantes para su negocio
- Una voz en las normativas del gobierno: NAMP es una organización norteamericana que representa sus intereses de manera eficaz ante FSIS (Servicio de Inspección e Inocuidad Alimentaria) de USDA (Departamento de Agricultura de E.U.A.), AMS (Servicio de Mercadeo Agrícola) de USDA y la Agencia Canadiense de Inspección de Alimentos
- Un *Directorio de recursos de miembros* con referencia cruzada para establecer contactos y enriquecer las posibilidades de su negocio
- Ayuda rápida en Internet de otros miembros a través del Listserve de NAMP llamado "Bull Session"
- Información técnica y educativa exclusiva en la sección Members Only (sólo para miembros) de www.namp.com

Los miembros también disponen de acceso a través de un número telefónico sin cargo al experimentado personal de NAMP y a consultores descentralizados que están listos para ayudarle con prácticamente cualquier problema, consulta o inquietud que pueda tener. *Es como tener su propio equipo de expertos sin el gasto adicional ¡un increíble rendimiento por el valor de su suscripción!*

La membresía de NAMP ofrece una oportunidad única e incomparable de aprender y establecer contactos con sus colegas. Suscríbase hoy para enriquecer las posibilidades de su negocio y beneficiarse de la experiencia de otros miembros. *Es lo que nuestros miembros de muchos años llaman "La magia de NAMP".*

LO INVITAMOS A UNIRSE HOY

Para solicitar su inscripción, visite www.namp.com o llame al +1 703.758.1900.

1100 — Beef Cubed Steak

Cube steaks shall be prepared from any portion of the carcass excluding the shank and heel meat that yields product that meets the end-item requirements. Unless otherwise specified, the steaks shall be cubed twice at approximate right angles. Knitting of two or more pieces and folding the meat when cubing is permissible. After cubing, surface and seam fat shall not exceed 15 percent of the total area on either side of the steak. Individual steaks shall remain intact when suspended 0.5 inch (13 mm) from the outer edge. The steaks shall be free of heavy connective tissue, bones, cartilages, and lymph glands.

❖ In Canada, the name of this product must include the cut the steak was prepared from, and must use the qualifier "minute" instead of "cubed".

1100 — Bistec Suavizado de Carne de Res

Los bistecs suavizados mecánicamente deberán prepararse a partir de cualquier porción de la canal, salvo la carne del chamberete y del talón, dando como resultado un producto que cumpla con los requisitos de la pieza final. A menos que se especifique lo contrario, los bistecs deberán suavizarse dos veces en ángulos rectos aproximados. Se permite unir dos o más piezas y plegar la carne al suavizarla. Después de suavizarla, la cubierta de grasa y las vetas de grasa intermuscular no deberán exceder el 15% del área total en ningún lado del bistec. Los bistecs individuales deben permanecer intactos cuando se suspenden 13 mm (0.5 pulgadas) del borde exterior. Los bistecs deberán estar libres de tejido conectivo grueso, huesos, cartílagos y ganglios linfáticos.

❖ En Canadá, el nombre de este producto debe incluir el corte del cual proviene el bistec, y se debe utilizar el calificativo "cortado en diminuto" ("minute") en vez de "suavizado" ("cubed").

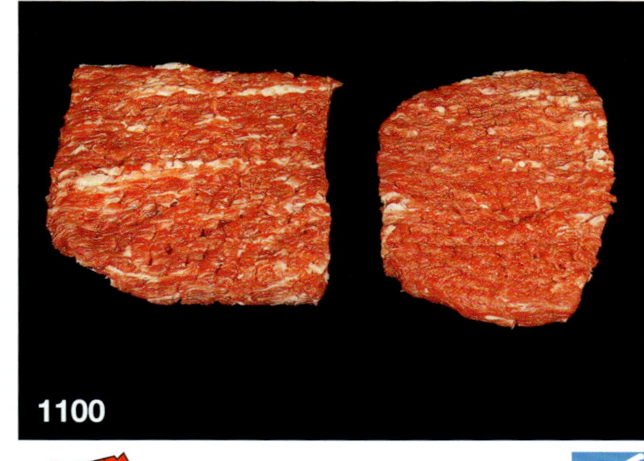

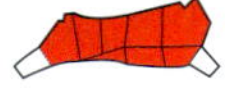

1101 — Beef Cubed Steak, Special

This item is as described in Item No. 1100, except the steaks shall be prepared from any combination of lean from the round, loin, rib, or chuck sections of the carcass excluding the shank and heel meat. Knitting of two or more pieces and folding the meat when cubing is not permissible.

1101 — Bistec Suavizado, Especial

Esta pieza está descrita en la pieza número 1100, salvo que los bistecs deberán prepararse de cualquier combinación de carne magra de las secciones de pierna, lomo, chuletón o paleta de la canal, excluyendo la carne del chamberete y el talón. No está permitido unir dos o más piezas ni plegar la carne al suavizarla.

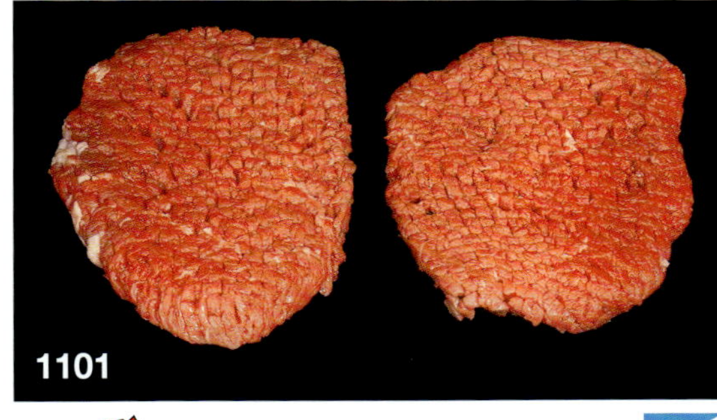

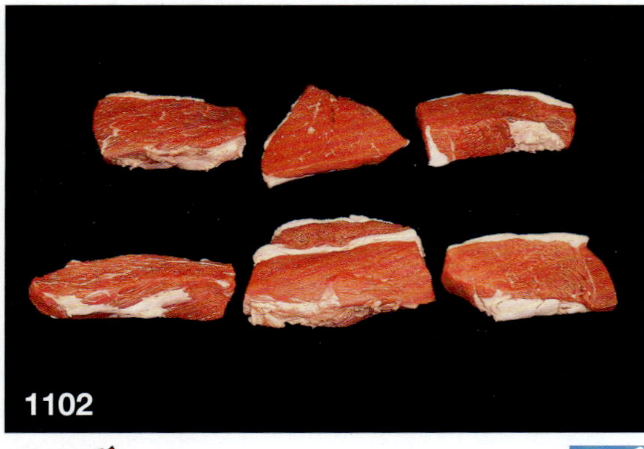

1102

1102 — Beef Braising Steak, Swiss

Braising steaks shall be prepared from any combination of lean from the round, loin, rib, or chuck sections of the carcass excluding the shank and heel meat that yields product that meets the end-item requirements. The steaks shall be free of heavy connective tissue, bones, cartilages, and lymph glands. When specified, the raw materials or the steaks shall be mechanically tenderized by using the multiple probe or pinning method not more than one time. Pressing, knitting, or folding two pieces of meat together is not permissible. Surface and seam fat shall not exceed an average of 0.25 inch (6 mm) in thickness and the thickness at any one point shall not exceed 0.5 inch (13 mm). Surface fat, measuring 0.1 inch (2 mm) or more in thickness, shall not exceed 50 percent of the circumference of the steak. Individual steaks shall remain intact when suspended 0.5 inch (13 mm) from the outer edge. Alternatively, the purchaser may specify surface and seam fat limitations in terms of maximum surface area percentage. Both surface and seam fat of the total cut surface on either side of the steak shall not exceed the percentage specified by the purchaser.

1102 — Bistec para Brasear, Estilo Suizo

Los bistecs para brasear deberán prepararse a partir de cualquier combinación de carne magra de las secciones de la pierna, lomo, chuletón o paleta de la canal, salvo la carne del chamberete y el talón para que rinda un producto que cumple con los requerimientos de la pieza final. Los bistecs deberán estar libres de tejido conectivo grueso, huesos, cartílagos y ganglios linfáticos. Cuando se especifique, las materias primas o los bistecs se ablandarán mecánicamente mediante el uso del método de múltiples vástagos, lancetas o puntas, no más de una vez. No está permitido prensar, unir ni plegar dos piezas de carne. La cubierta de grasa y las vetas de grasa intermuscular no deberán exceder los 6 mm (0.25 pulgadas) de espesor como promedio, y el grosor en ningún punto deberá exceder los 13 mm (0.5 pulgadas). La cubierta de grasa, de un espesor de 2 mm (0.1 pulgadas) o más, no deberá exceder el 50% de la circunferencia del bistec. Los bistecs individuales deben permanecer intactos cuando se suspenden a 13 mm (0.5 pulgadas) del borde exterior. Asimismo, el comprador puede especificar limitaciones de cubierta de grasa y vetas de grasa intermuscular en términos de porcentajes máximos del área total de la superficie del corte. Ni la cubierta de grasa ni la veta de grasa intermuscular sobre la superficie total del corte en cada lado del bistec deberán exceder el porcentaje especificado por el comprador.

1103

1103 — Beef Rib, Rib Steak, Bone In

Bone-in rib steaks may be prepared from any bone in rib item. The *latissimus dorsi, infraspinatus,* and *trapezius* muscles above the blade bone and the *subscapularis* and *rhomboideus* muscles below it including the blade bone, related cartilage, feather bones, chine bones, and backstrap shall be excluded. The short ribs shall be excluded at a point that is no more than 3.0 inches (7.5 cm) from the ventral edge of the *longissimus dorsi* muscle.

1103 — Chuletón (Espaldar), Bistec del Chuletón, Con Hueso

Los bistecs con hueso pueden prepararse a partir de cualquier pieza del chuletón con hueso. Se deberán extraer los músculos *latissimus dorsi, infraspinatus* y *trapezius* por encima del hueso de la paleta y los músculos *subscapularis* y *rhomboideus* por debajo de la misma, así como el hueso y cartílago de la paleta, las puntas del espinazo y la banda ligamentosa nucal. Se deberán extraer las costillas cortas en un punto que no esté a más de 7.5 cm (3.0 pulgadas) del borde ventral del músculo *longissimus dorsi*.

1103B — Beef Rib, Rib Steak, Bone In, Frenched

This item is prepared as described in Item No. 1103 except that each steak must be cut between the rib bones. The rib bone shall be completely trimmed of the intercostal meat, lean, and fat so that the bone is exposed from the ventral edge of the *longissimus dorsi* to the end of the rib bone. This item is also referred to as a "Cowboy Steak."

Alternative Purchaser Specified Options (PSO):

PSO: 1 – Purchaser may request that the rib be prepared as a roast to the same specifications as Item No. 1103B but instead of being cut into steaks, it be left intact.

2 – Purchaser may request that the rib be prepared as a roast as in PSO 1 and then partially cut into steaks and the balance left as a roast.

3 – Purchaser may request that the rib steaks in Item No. 1103B or PSO 2 be split into two steaks by a saw cut through the center of the rib bone.

1103B — Chuletón (Espaldar), Bistec del Chuletón, Con Hueso, Estilo Francés

Esta pieza se prepara según descripción de la pieza número 1103, salvo que cada bistec debe ser cortado entre los huesos de las costillas. El hueso de la costilla deberá ser recortado completamente de carne intercostal, carne magra y grasa, de forma que el hueso quede expuesto desde el borde ventral del *longissimus dorsi* hasta el extremo de la costilla. Esta pieza es llamada a veces "Bistec del Cowboy".

Opciones alternativas especificadas por el comprador:

PSO: 1 – El comprador puede solicitar que el chuletón, en vez de hacerlo bistecs, se prepare como un trozo rosbif, según las mismas especificaciones de la pieza número 1103B, pero que en vez de ser cortado en bistecs, quede intacto.

2 – El comprador puede solicitar que el chuletón se prepare como un trozo rosbif, como figura en la opción 1 especificada por el comprador, y luego se corte parcialmente en bistecs, dejando lo remanente como rosbif.

3 – El comprador puede solicitar que los bistecs de chuletón detallados en la pieza número 1103B o en la opción 2 especificada por el comprador, se separen en dos bistecs mediante un corte de sierra a través del centro del hueso de las costillas.

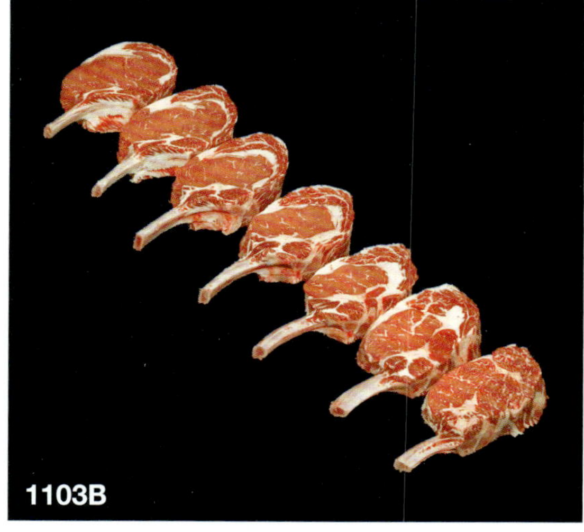

1103B

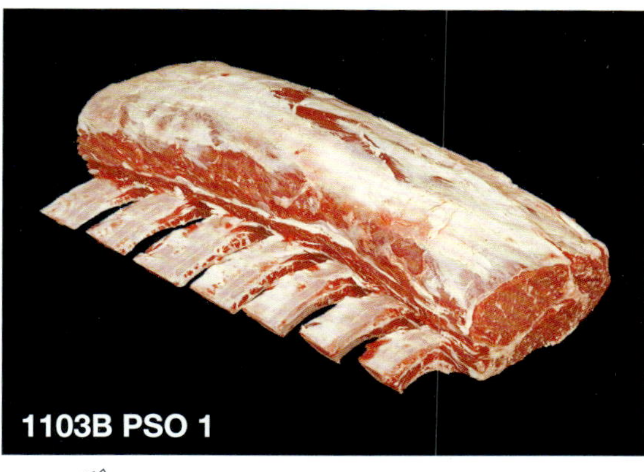

1103B PSO 1

1112A — Beef Rib, Ribeye Steak, Lip-On, Boneless

Boneless ribeye steaks, lip-on shall be prepared from a rib item meeting the end requirements of Item No. 112A. The lip shall be cut on the short rib side with a straight cut that is ventral to, but no more than 2.0 inches (5.0 cm) from, the *longissimus dorsi,* leaving the lip firmly attached.

 In Canada, steaks containing muscles other than the *longissimus dorsi* and *spinalis dorsi* must be called "Boneless Rib Steaks".

1112A — Chuletón (Espaldar), Bistec de Ribeye, Con Cordón, Deshuesado

Los bistecs de ribeye deshuesado, por su cola, llamada "cordón" o "gota", se conocen también como "ribeye gota", y deberán prepararse a partir de una pieza de chuletón que reúna los requisitos finales de la pieza número 112A. Se deberá cortar el cordón del lado del lomo corto con un corte recto ventral al *longissimus dorsi*, sin que supere los 5.0 cm (2.0 pulgadas) dejando el cordón firmemente unido.

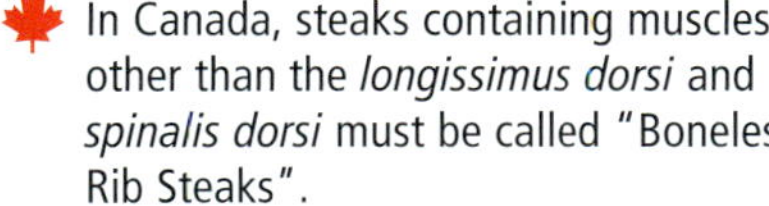 En Canadá, los bistecs que contienen músculos que no sean el *longissimus dorsi* y el *spinalis dorsi* deben llamarse "Bistecs del Chuletón Deshuesados" (en inglés, "Boneless Rib Steaks").

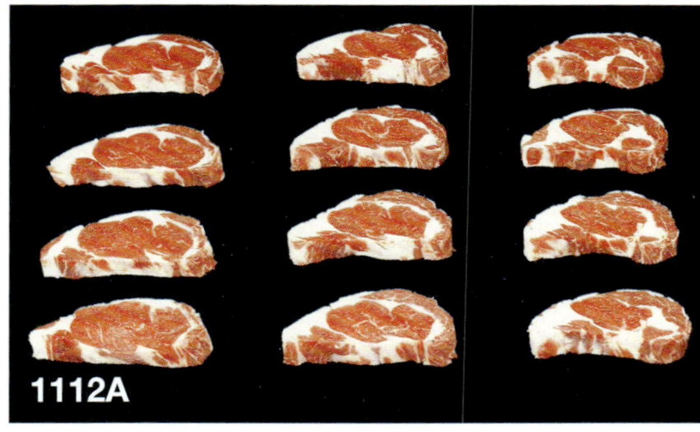

1112A

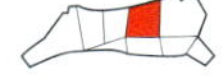

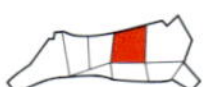

1112B — Beef Rib, Ribeye Steak, Lip-On, Short-Cut, Boneless

This item is as described in Item No. 1112A, except in this item the lip shall be cut on the short rib side ventral to, but no more than 1.0 inch (2.5 cm) from, the *longissimus dorsi.*

🍁 In Canada, steaks containing muscles other than the *longissimus dorsi* and *spinalis dorsi* must be called "Boneless Rib Steaks".

1112B — Chuletón (Espaldar), Bistec de Ribeye, Con Cordón, Corte Corto, Deshuesado

Esta pieza está descrita en la pieza número 1112A, salvo que en ésta, el cordón deberá cortarse del lado de la costilla corta, en forma ventral al *longissimus dorsi,* pero sin superar los 2.5 cm (1.0 pulgada).

🍁 En Canadá, los bistecs que contienen músculos que no sean el *longissimus dorsi* y el *spinalis dorsi* deben llamarse "Bistecs del Chuletón Deshuesados" (en inglés, "Boneless Rib Steaks").

1112

1112 — Beef Rib, Ribeye Roll Steak, Boneless

Boneless ribeye roll steaks shall be prepared from any boneless ribeye roll item. Any lip, if present on the product being used to prepare this item, shall be excluded so as to expose the natural seam immediately ventral to the *longissimus dorsi* muscle.

1112 — Chuletón (Espaldar), Bistec de Rollo Ribeye, Deshuesado

Los bistecs de rollo ribeye deshuesados deberán prepararse a partir de cualquier pieza de rollo ribeye deshuesado. Cualquier cordón que estuviera presente en la pieza se deberá excluir, a fin de exponer la veta natural inmediatamente ventral al músculo *longissimus dorsi.*

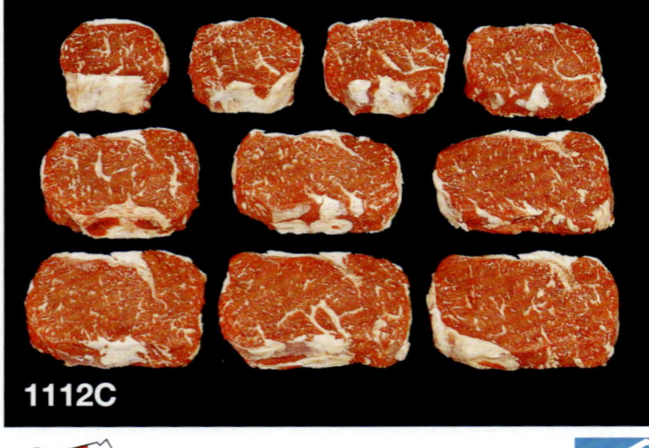
1112C

1112C — Beef Rib, Ribeye Steak (IM)

Boneless ribeye steaks shall be prepared from the *longissimus* muscle of any ribeye roll item.

1112C — Chuletón (Espaldar), Bistec de Ribeye/ Entrecot (MI)

Los bistecs de ribeye deshuesado deberán prepararse a partir del músculo *longissimus* proveniente de cualquier pieza de rollo de ribeye.

1112D — Beef Rib, Ribeye Cap Steak (IM)

Boneless ribeye cap steaks shall be prepared from the *spinalis dorsi/multifidus dorsi* muscle from any ribeye roll item. For portioning, slice the ribeye cap at a right angle to the grain or direction of muscle fibers.

1112D — Chuletón (Espaldar), Tapa del Ribeye (MI)

Los bistecs deshuesados de tapa del ribeye deberán prepararse a partir del músculo *spinalis dorsi/multifidus dorsi* proveniente de cualquier pieza de rollo de ribeye. Para realizar las porciones, rebane la tapa del ribeye en ángulo recto al grano o en la dirección de las fibras musculares.

1114D — Beef Shoulder, Top Blade Steak (IM)

This item is prepared from Item No. 114D. However, this item is generally prepared as PSO 1, see below.

PSO: 1 – This steak is prepared from Item No. 114D, PSO 1, which specifies that the shoulder tissue or tendon be removed and is commonly called a "Flat Iron Steak."

1114D — Paleta (Espaldilla), Bistec de "Paletilla California" (MI)

Esta pieza se prepara con la pieza número 114D. Sin embargo, esta pieza generalmente se prepara según la opción 1 especificada por el comprador; consulte a continuación.

PSO: 1 – Este bistec se prepara a partir de la pieza número 114D, opción 1, especificada por el comprador. Dicha opción especifica que el "nervio" o tendón de la paletilla debe extraerse; habitualmente se llama Paletilla California sin "Nervio".

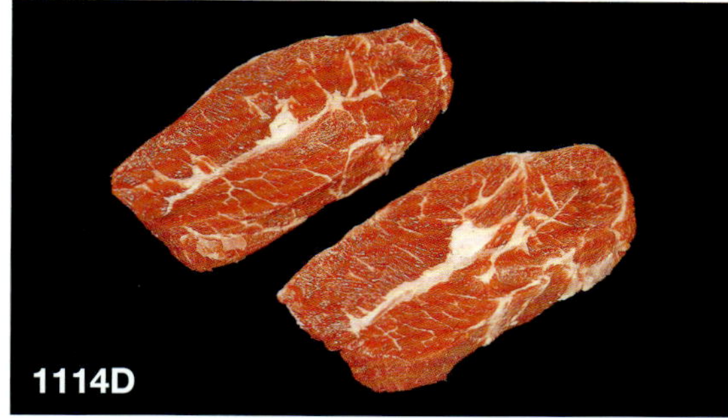

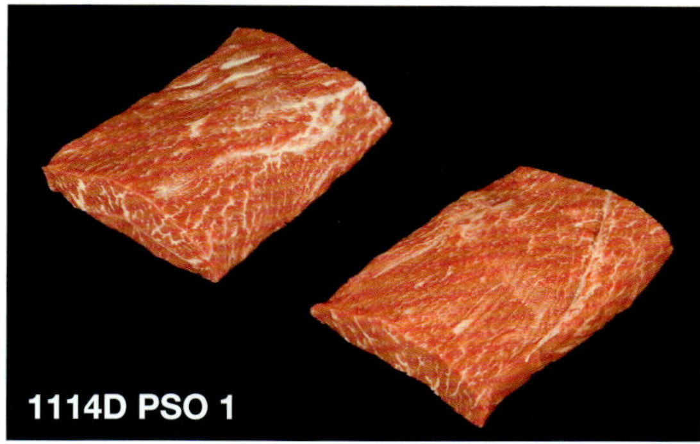

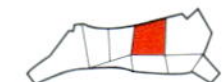

1114E — Beef Shoulder, Arm Steak

The boneless arm steaks shall be prepared from Item No. 114E after the *triceps brachii medial head* has been removed. The steaks will be sliced across the grain of the *triceps brachii long head*.

PSO: 1 – Purchaser may specify that this item be prepared from Item No. 114E, PSO 1. The steaks are commonly referred to as "Ranch Steaks." The steaks are completely trimmed of all fat and connective tissue.

1114E — Paleta (Espaldilla), Bistec de Brazuelo

Los bistecs de brazuelo deshuesado deberán prepararse a partir de la pieza número 114E una vez extraída la cabeza medial del músculo *triceps brachii*. Los bistecs deberán ser rebanados a través del grano de la cabeza larga del músculo *triceps brachii*.

PSO: 1 – El comprador puede especificar que esta pieza sea preparada a partir de la pieza número 114E, opción 1, especificada por el comprador. Los bistecs se llaman comúnmente "bistecs rancheros". Los bistecs se recortan completamente de toda la grasa y tejido conectivo.

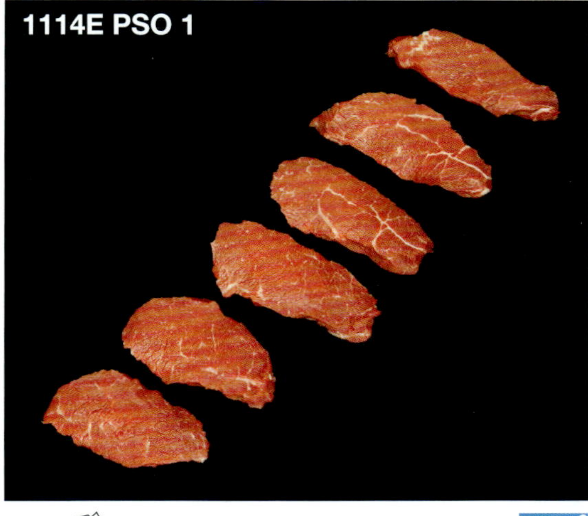

1114F — Beef Shoulder Tender, Portioned

1114F — Teres Filé, Porcionado (M. Teres/Redondo Mayor)

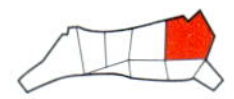

This item shall be prepared from Item No. 114F Beef Chuck, Shoulder Tender (IM), PSO 1. The individual steaks, sometimes referred to as "Petite Tender Medallions," shall be prepared by a straight cut across the grain in accordance with the purchaser's specification with respect to thickness or weight.

Esta pieza se prepara con la pieza número 114F: "Paleta (Espaldilla), Teres Filé (M. Teres Mayor)", opción 1 especificada por el comprador. Los bistecs individuales, algunas veces llamados "Medallones de Teres Filé", deberán prepararse mediante un corte recto a través del grano según la especificación del comprador con respecto al grosor o peso.

NAMP
NORTH AMERICAN MEAT PROCESSORS ASSOCIATION
ASSOCIATION AMÉRIQUE DU NORD DES TRANSFORMATEURS DE VIANDE
ASOCIACIÓN NORTEAMERICANA DE PROCESADORES DE CARNE

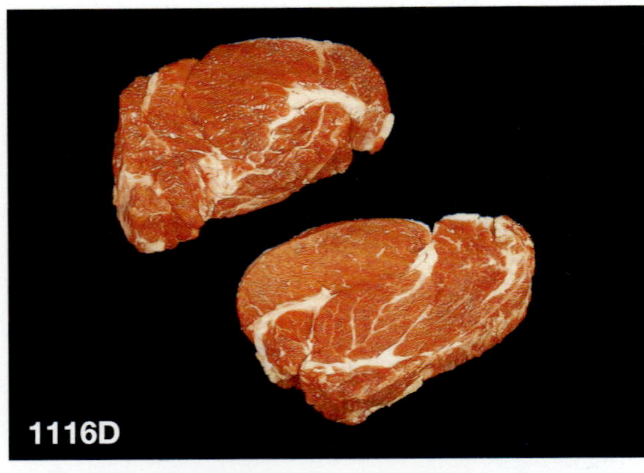

1116D

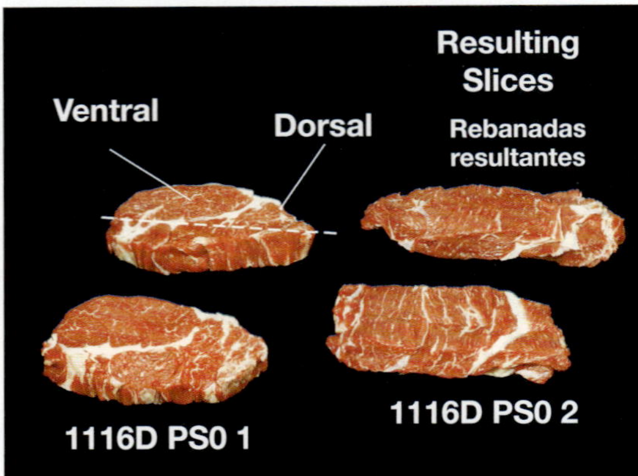

Resulting Slices

Rebanadas resultantes

Ventral   Dorsal

1116D PSO 1

1116D PSO 2

1116D — Beef Chuck, Chuck Eye Roll Steak, Boneless

Boneless chuck eye roll steaks shall be prepared from product meeting the end requirements of Item No. 116D.

PSO: 1 – The purchaser may specify steaks to be derived from the portion of the chuck eye roll that has the *longissimus* present. The *longissimus* must be present on at least one side of the steak. This item is sometimes referred to as "Beef Chuck, Delmonico Steak".

2 – The purchaser may specify steaks made from any portion of the chuck eye roll that are cut into two pieces by slicing the individual steaks with a cut that starts at the ventral side and ends at a point on dorsal side (where the feather bones were). (See illustration) Alternatively, the chuck eye roll in its entirety may be cut into two approximate equal sized portions by making a lengthwise cut which starts at the ventral side to a point on the dorsal edge (where the feather bones were), and then sliced into portions according to the purchaser's specification for size or thickness. This item is sometimes referred to as a "Boneless Country-Style Ribs'.

1116D — Paleta (Espaldilla), Bistec del Centro de Rollo de Diezmillo, Deshuesado

Los bistecs de centro del rollo de diezmillo deshuesados deberán prepararse a partir de un producto que cumpla con los requisitos finales de la pieza número 116D.

PSO: 1 - El comprador puede especificar que los bistecs provenientes de la porción de la paleta contengan el *longissimus*. El *longissimus* debe estar presente en al menos un lado del bistec. A esta pieza se le llama, algunas veces, "Paleta de Res, Bistec Delmonico ".

2 – El comprador puede especificar que los bistecs provenientes de cualquier porción del centro del rollo de diezmillo deben cortarse en dos piezas al rebanar los bistecs individuales con un corte que comience del lado ventral y termine en un punto del lado dorsal (donde estaban las puntas del espinazo). (Consulte la ilustración.) En forma alternativa, es posible cortar el centro del rollo de diezmillo entero en dos porciones de tamaño aproximado, aplicando un corte longitudinal que comience del lado ventral hasta un punto en el borde dorsal (donde estaban las puntas del espinazo), y luego rebanarse en porciones según las especificaciones del comprador en cuanto a tamaño o espesor. Esta pieza algunas veces se llama "Costillas Deshuesadas Estilo Campestre".

1116G

1116G — Beef Chuck, Under Blade, Center Cut Steak

This item shall be prepared from any portion of the *serratus ventralis* muscle as described within Item No. 116G and made into steaks by slicing across the grain. This item is sometimes referred to as "Denver Cut".

1116G — Paleta (Espaldilla), Tapa Interior de la Planchuela, Bistec del Centro

Esta pieza deberá prepararse a partir de cualquier porción del músculo *serratus ventralis*, según la descripción contenida en la pieza número 116G, y procesarse en forma de bistecs al rebanar a través del grano. En ocasiones, a esta pieza también se le llama "Corte Denver".

1121D — Beef Plate, Inside Skirt Steak, Boneless (IM)

The boneless steaks shall be prepared from product meeting the end requirements of Item No. 121D.

1121D — Costillar, Falda Interna/Arrachera Inside, Deshuesada (MI)

Los bistecs deshuesados deberán prepararse a partir de un producto que cumpla con los requisitos finales de la pieza número 121D.

1121E — Beef Plate, Outside Skirt Steak, Skinned (IM)

The steaks shall be prepared from an outside skirt or diaphragm muscle meeting the end requirements of Item No. 121E.

1121E — Costillar, Arrachera Delgada Regular, Despellejada (MI)

Los bistecs deberán prepararse a partir de una arrachera regular o de un músculo del diafragma a fin de cumplir con los requisitos finales de la pieza número 121E.

1123 — Beef Short Rib, Bone In

This item may be prepared from any beef chuck, rib, or plate short rib item as described in Item No. 123. The bone in short rib shall consist of the ribs, intercostal meat, and the intact *serratus ventralis* muscle. The *serratus ventralis* muscle shall be continuous across both the dorsal and ventral side of the specified portion. The ribs shall be cut flanken style by cutting them at a right angle to the rib bones. Purchaser shall specify both the width of the cut and the number of ribs in each portion.

Purchasers also have the option to request that the bone in short ribs be prepared from product described in Item Nos. 123A, 123B, or 123C.

Purchasers who desire a boneless short rib should specify that the item be prepared from Item No. 123D.

1123 — Costilla Corta (Costilla Cargada), Con Hueso

Esta pieza puede prepararse de cualquier pieza de paleta de res, chuletón o agujas cortas del costillar según la descripción de la pieza número 123. La costilla cargada con hueso consistirá en las costillas, la carne intercostal y el músculo *serratus ventralis* intacto. El músculo *serratus ventralis* debe permanecer continuo a través del lado dorsal, así como del lado ventral de la porción especificada. Las costillas deben cortarse al estilo alemán ("flanken") mediante un corte en ángulo recto a las costillas. El comprador deberá especificar el grosor del corte y la cantidad de costillas en cada porción.

Los compradores también tienen la opción de solicitar que las costillas cortas (costilla cargada) con hueso se preparen a partir del producto descrito en las piezas 123A, 123B o 123C.

Los compradores que desean el costillar corto deshuesado (Carne de costillas) deberán especificar que la pieza debe ser preparada según la pieza número 123D.

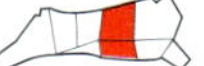

1136 — Ground Beef Patties

The patties shall be prepared from product described in Item No. 136. The ground meat shall be mechanically formed into patties of the shape and size specified by the purchaser. Patties shall be separated from each other by a means that will prevent them from sticking together when packaged. Patties shall be frozen unless specified fresh.

1136 — Hamburguesas de Carne Molida de Res

Las hamburguesas deberán prepararse a partir del producto descrito en la pieza 136. La carne molida será procesada mecánicamente para elaborar hamburguesas de la forma y tamaño especificados por el comprador. Las hamburguesas se deberán separar entre sí de forma que no se peguen unas con otras al empaquetarse. Las hamburguesas deberán congelarse a menos que la solicitud las especifique frescas.

1136A — Beef and Soy Protein Product Patties

The patties shall be prepared from Item No. 136A. The patties shall be formed and packaged as described in Item No. 1136. Patties shall be frozen.

1136A — Hamburguesas de Res con Producto Proteico Vegetal (PPV) Añadido según la Normativa

Las hamburguesas se prepararán con la pieza número 136A. Las hamburguesas se elaborarán y empaquetarán según descripción de la pieza número 1136. Las hamburguesas deberán congelarse.

1137 — Ground Beef Patties, Special

The patties shall be prepared from Item No. 137. The purchaser has an option to select a ground beef style derived from one of the specific primal portions described. If no such selection is made, Style 1 will apply. Product shall be labeled accordingly. Patties shall be formed and packaged as described in Item No. 1136. Patties shall be frozen unless specified fresh.

If purchasers desire frozen patties from any of the above formulations prepared with SPP, they should specify Item No. 1137A, which is prepared from product described in Item No. 137A.

1137 — Hamburguesas de Carne Molida de Res, Especial

Las hamburguesas se prepararán con la pieza número 137. El comprador tiene la opción de seleccionar un estilo de carne molida derivado de las porciones primarias específicas descritas. Si no se hace dicha selección, se aplicará el Estilo 1. El producto deberá etiquetarse de manera correspondiente. Las hamburguesas deberán formarse y empaquetarse según la descripción de la pieza número 1136. Las hamburguesas deberán congelarse a menos que se especifiquen refrigeradas en fresco.

Si los compradores desean hamburguesas congeladas de cualquiera de las fórmulas anteriores preparadas con PPV, deberán especificar la pieza número 1137A, que se prepara a partir del producto descrito en la pieza número 137A.

1140 — Hanging Tender Steak

This steak is prepared from Item No. 140 by straight cuts across the grain along the length of hanging tender to the specifications of the purchaser for size. The steaks shall be trimmed along the edges and top and bottom sides so that the steaks are free of any heavy connective tissue or loose fat. The steak is sometimes referred to as a "Hanger Steak", "Onglet Steak" or "Pillar".

1140 — Bistec de Arrachera Gallo (Pilares o Arrachera Colgante del Lomo)

Esta pieza se prepara con la pieza número 140 mediante cortes rectos a través del grano, a lo largo de la arrachera gallo, según las especificaciones de tamaño del comprador. Los bistecs deberán ser recortados de grasa en los bordes y en los lados superior e inferior de manera que se eliminen los restos de tejido conectivo grueso o grasa suelta. Al bistec se le llama, algunas veces, "Hanger Steak", "Onglet steak" o "Pillar".

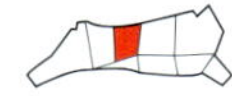

1167 — Beef Round, Sirloin Tip (Knuckle) Steak

The steaks shall be prepared from any beef sirloin tip (knuckle) item. The sirloin tip (knuckle) may be separated lengthwise into sections to accommodate the cutting of specified portion-size steaks.

1167 — Pierna (Piña), Bistec de Punta de Sirloin (Pulpa Bola)

Los bistecs deberán prepararse a partir de cualquier pieza de pulpa bola. La pulpa bola puede separarse longitudinalmente en secciones para facilitar los cortes de bistecs con tamaños de porción especificados.

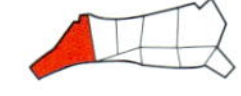

1167A — Beef Round, Sirloin Tip (Knuckle) Steak, Peeled

The steaks may be prepared from any beef sirloin tip (knuckle) item, provided the product used meets the end-item requirements described in Item No. 167A or 167C, which excludes the *tensor fasciae latae* muscle, fat, and "skin" tissue. The sirloin tip (knuckle) may be separated lengthwise into sections to accommodate the cutting of specified portion-size steaks.

PSO: 1 – The *vastus intermedius* and *vastus medialis* muscles shall be removed prior to portioning.

1167A — Pierna (Piña), Bistec de Punta de Sirloin (Pulpa Bola), Desprovisto de Grasa

Los bistecs pueden ser preparados a partir de cualquier pieza de pulpa bola, siempre que el producto utilizado reúna los requisitos finales de la pieza descritos en la pieza número 167A o 167C, que excluyen el músculo *tensor de la fascia lata* (empuje), la grasa y el tejido de la llamada "piel". La pulpa bola puede separarse longitudinalmente en secciones para facilitar los cortes de bistecs con tamaños de porción especificados.

PSO: 1 – Los músculos *vastus intermedius* y *vastus medialis* deberán extraerse antes de realizar las porciones.

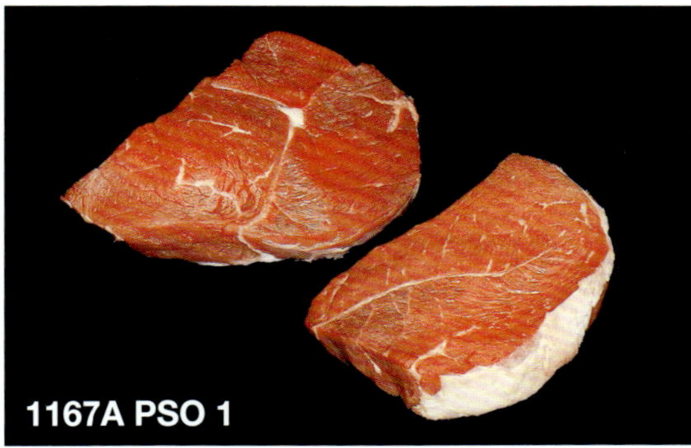

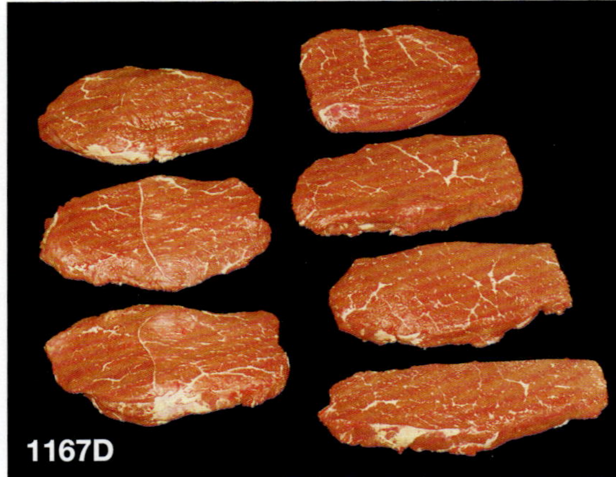

1167D

1167D — Beef Round, Sirloin Tip (Knuckle) Steak, Peeled, Special

This item shall be prepared from only the *vastus lateralis and rectus femoris* muscles of the beef sirloin tip (knuckle) that have been separated from each other by cutting through the natural seam. These muscles may be derived from any beef sirloin tip (knuckle) item that meets the end requirements described in Item No. 167D. In preparing the steaks any remaining fat, skin tissue, and heavy opaque connective tissue shall be excluded. The steaks shall be made into specified portion size or thickness by slicing the pieces at a right angle to the grain or direction of the muscle fibers.

1167D — Pierna (Piña), Bistec de Punta de Sirloin (Pulpa Bola), Desprovisto de Grasa, Especial

Esta pieza deberá prepararse únicamente de los músculos *vastus lateralis y rectus femoris* de la pulpa bola que se han separado entre sí cortando por la veta natural. Estos músculos pueden provenir de cualquier pieza de pulpa bola que cumpla con los requisitos finales descritos en la pieza número 167D. Al preparar los bistecs, se deberá retirar toda la grasa, tejido cutáneo y tejido conectivo opaco grueso remanentes. Los bistecs se harán coincidir con el tamaño o espesor de porción especificados al rebanar las piezas en ángulo recto con respecto al grano o en la dirección de las fibras de los músculos.

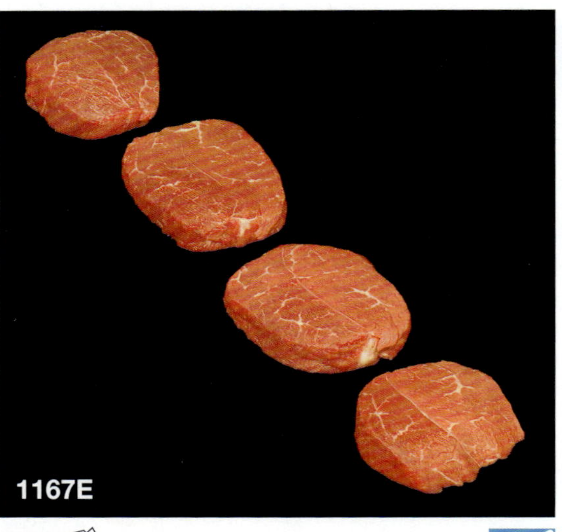

1167E

1167E — Beef Round, Sirloin Tip (Knuckle), Center Steak (IM)

This steak is prepared from Item No. 167E Beef Round, Sirloin Tip (Knuckle), Center Roast (IM) by cuts across the grain or at right angles to it, if necessary, to fulfill the purchaser's specification as to portion size or thickness.

1167E — Pierna (Piña), Punta de Sirloin (Pulpa Bola), Bistec del Centro (MI)

Esta pieza se prepara con la pieza número 167E: "Pierna (Piña), Punta de Sirloin (Pulpa Bola), Trozo Rosbif del Centro (MI)", mediante cortes a través del grano o en ángulos rectos del mismo, si fuese necesario, para cumplir con la especificación del comprador en cuanto a tamaño o grosor de las porciones.

1167F

1167F — Beef Round, Sirloin Tip (Knuckle), Side Steak (IM)

This steak is prepared from Item No. 167F Beef Round, Sirloin Tip (Knuckle), Side Roast (IM) by cuts across the grain or at right angles to it, if necessary, to fulfill the purchaser's specification as to portion size or thickness.

1167F — Pierna (Piña), Punta de Sirloin (Pulpa Bola), Bistec del Músculo Lateral (MI)

Esta pieza se prepara con la pieza número 167F: "Pierna (Piña), Punta de Sirloin (Pulpa Bola), Trozo Rosbif Lateral (MI)", mediante cortes a través del grano o a ángulos rectos del mismo, si fuese necesario, para cumplir la especificación del comprador en cuanto a tamaño o grosor de las porciones.

1169 — Beef Round, Top (Inside) Round Steak

The steaks may be prepared from any top (inside) round item. The thick opaque portion of the *gracilis* membrane shall be removed as described in Item No. 169. The top round may be separated lengthwise into sections to accommodate the cutting of specified portion-size steaks.

1169 — Pierna (Piña), Bistec de Pulpa Negra (Cara/Centro)

Los bistecs pueden prepararse de cualquier pieza de pulpa negra (cara/centro de pierna). Se deberá eliminar la porción gruesa opaca de la membrana del *gracilis,* según la descripción en la pieza número 169. La cara/centro de la pieza puede separarse longitudinalmente en secciones para permitir los cortes de bistecs con un tamaño de porción especificado.

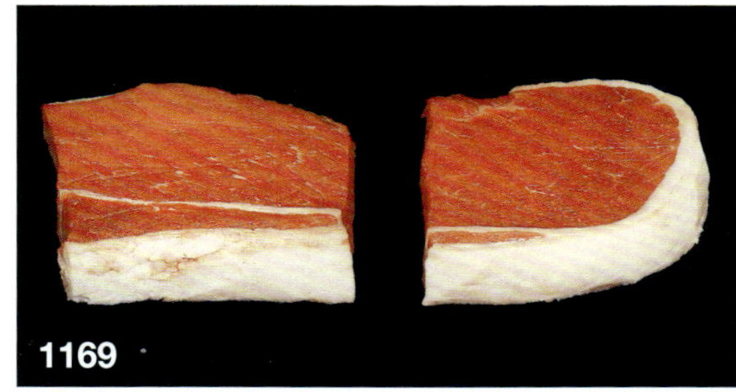
1169

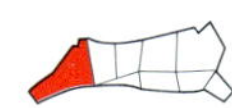

1169C — Beef Top (Inside) Round, Front Side Steak

This item shall be prepared from Item No. 169C Beef Round, Top (Inside), Front Side Muscle (IM), which consists of the *pectineus* muscle. The individual steak shall be prepared by a straight cut across the grain in accordance with the purchaser's specification with respect to thickness and weight.

1169C — Pierna (Piña), Pulpa Nuez (M. Pectíneo) de la Pulpa Negra, Porcionado

Esta pieza se prepara con la pieza número 169C: "Pierna (Piña), Pulpa Negra (Cara/Centro), Músculo del Lado Frontal (M. Sartorio)", que consiste en el músculo *pectíneo*. El bistec individual deberá prepararse mediante un corte recto a través del grano según la especificación del comprador sobre grosor y peso.

1170A — Beef Round, Bottom (Gooseneck) Round Steak

The steaks may be prepared from any beef bottom round item meeting the end item requirements of Item No. 170A. The bottom round may be separated lengthwise into sections to accommodate the cutting of specified portion-size steaks.

1170A — Pierna (Piña), Bistec de Contracara con Cuete

Los bistecs pueden prepararse a partir de cualquier pieza de contracara de pierna de res que cumpla con los requisitos finales de la pieza número 170A. La contracara puede separarse longitudinalmente para permitir el corte de bistecs con tamaños de porción especificados.

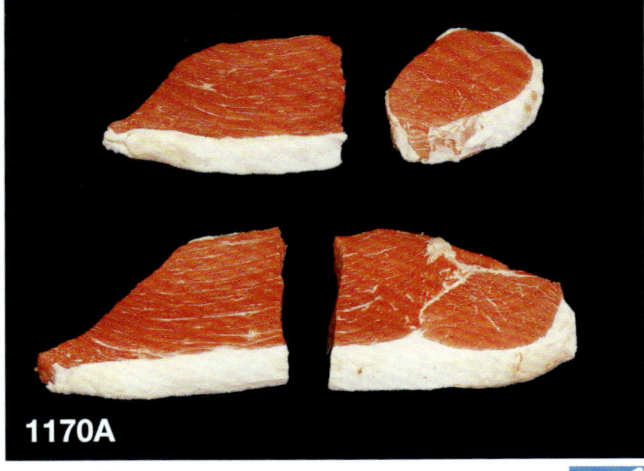
1170A

1171D — Beef Round, Outside Round Steak (IM)

This item is derived from the *biceps femoris* muscle (with the side muscle (*biceps femoris ishiatic* head) removed) as described in Item No. 171D. The steaks shall be made by slicing perpendicular to the grain of the muscles. This item is sometimes referred to as a "Western Griller".

1171D — Pierna (Piña), Bistec de Pulpa Blanca (MI)

Esta pieza proviene del músculo *biceps femoris* (después de retirar la cabeza isquiática del *biceps femoris* del músculo lateral), según la descripción de la pieza número 171D. Los bistecs deberán prepararse rebanando en forma perpendicular al grano de los músculos. Esta pieza algunas veces se llama "Western Griller".

1171D

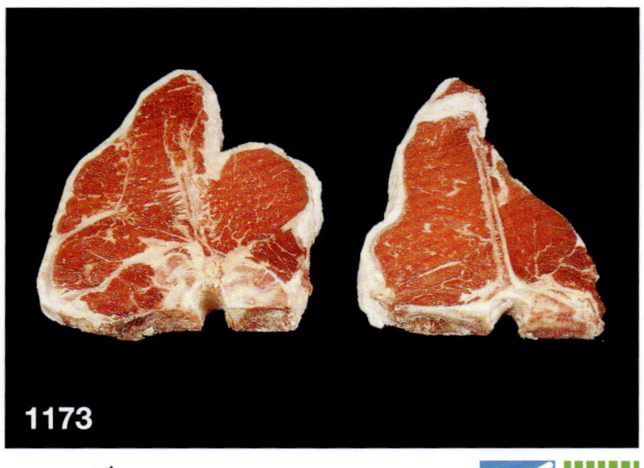

1173 — Beef Loin, Porterhouse Steak

The steaks shall be prepared from any beef short loin item. The minimum width of the tenderloin shall be at least 1.25 inches (3.2 cm) when measured parallel to the length of the back bone.

The purchaser may specify the following tail length options for Item No. 1173 above, and Item Nos. 1174, 1179, 1179A, 1180, and 1180A, which follow. If not specified, the tail length will not exceed 1.0 inch (2.5 cm) from the *longissimus dorsi*.

PSO: 1 – 4.0 inches (10.0 cm)
     2 – 3.0 inches (7.5 cm)
     3 – 2.0 inches (5.0 cm)
     4 – 1.0 inch (2.5 cm)
     5 – No tail except that of the specified fat trim dimension
     6 – Other as specified

In Canada, no minimum tenderloin size is associated with this item. Porterhouse Steaks must be cut from the portion of the short loin anterior to the *gluteus medius*.

1173 — Lomo, Bistec Porterhouse

Los bistecs deberán prepararse a partir de cualquier pieza de lomo corto de carne de res. El ancho mínimo del filete deberá ser de 3.2 cm (1.25 pulgadas) al medirlo paralelo a la longitud de la columna vertebral.

El comprador puede especificar las siguientes opciones de longitud de la cola para la pieza 1173 antes descrita, y las piezas números 1174, 1179, 1179A, 1180 y 1180A, a continuación. En caso de que no se especifique, la longitud de la cola no excederá los 2.5 cm (1.0 pulgada) desde el *longissimus dorsi*.

PSO: 1 – 10.0 cm (4.0 pulgadas)
     2 – 7.5 cm (3.0 pulgadas)
     3 – 5.0 cm (2.0 pulgadas)
     4 – 2.5 cm (1.0 pulgada)
     5 – Sin cola, salvo lo especificado sobre dimensión de recortado de grasa
     6 – Otros, según especificación

En Canadá no existe un tamaño mínimo de filete que se asocie con esta pieza. Los bistecs Porterhouse deben cortarse de la porción del lomo corto anterior al *gluteus medius*.

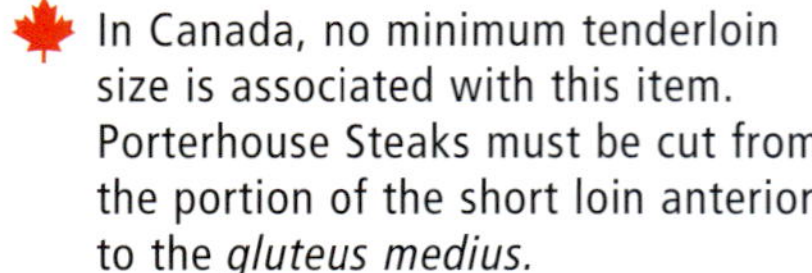

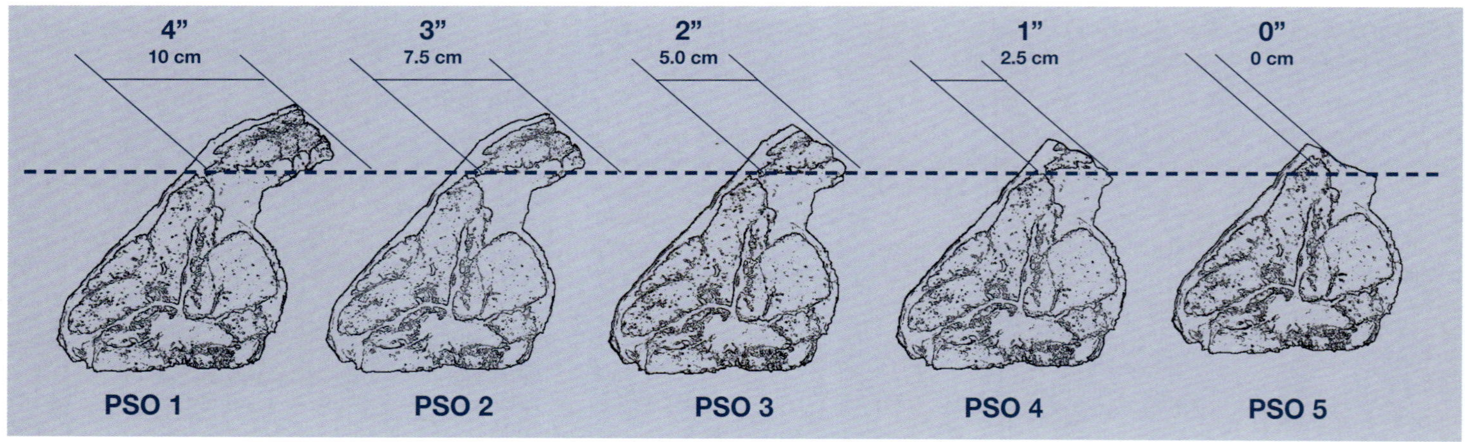

Graphic illustration of the length of tail difference on porterhouse and T-bone steaks.
Ilustración gráfica sobre la diferencia de longitud de la cola en bistecs porterhouse y T-bone.

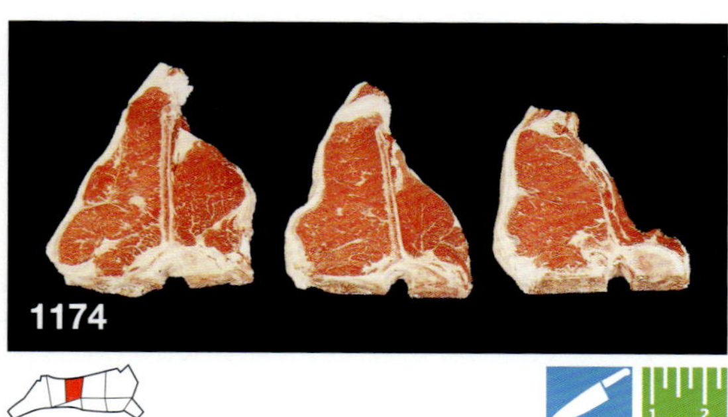

1174 — Beef Loin, T-Bone Steak

The steaks shall be prepared from any beef short loin item. The minimum width of the tenderloin shall be at least 0.5 inch (13 mm) when measured parallel to the length of the back bone. *See Item No. 1173 for purchaser tail length options.*

In Canada, no minimum tenderloin size is associated with this item.

1174 — Lomo, Bistec T-Bone

Los bistecs, al igual que a los de Porterhouse, a veces se les refiere como "Chuleta de Doble Lomo". Deberán prepararse a partir de cualquier pieza de lomo corto de carne de res. El ancho mínimo del filete deberá ser de 13 cm (0.5 pulgadas) al medirlo paralelo a la longitud de la columna vertebral. *Consulte la pieza número 1173 para informarse sobre las opciones del comprador sobre el largo de la cola.*

En Canadá no existe un tamaño mínimo de filete que se asocie con esta pieza.

1179 — Beef Loin, Strip Loin Steak, Bone In

The steaks shall be prepared from any beef short loin or bone in strip loin item provided the item meets the end requirements described in Item No. 175. In further preparing the steaks, the protruding edge of the chine bone shall be excluded so that no portion of the spinal groove is present. *See Item No. 1173 for purchaser tail length options.*

1179 — Lomo, Bistec Strip Loin (New York), con Hueso

Los bistecs deberán prepararse de cualquier pieza de lomo corto o strip loin con hueso, de carne de res, siempre que la pieza cumpla con los requisitos finales descritos en la pieza número 175. En la consiguiente preparación de los bistecs, el borde protuberante de las puntas del espinazo deberá excluirse a fin de eliminar toda presencia del canal raquídeo. *Consulte la pieza número 1173 para informarse sobre las opciones del comprador sobre el largo de la cola.*

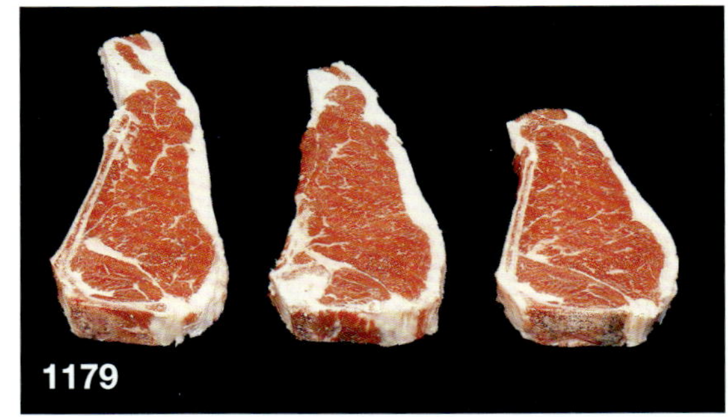

1179A — Beef Loin, Strip Loin Steak, Bone In, Center-Cut

This item, in addition to meeting the requirements of Item No. 1179, shall be further prepared by excluding the posterior or sirloin butt end of the bone in strip loin at or anterior to the *gluteus medius. The gluteus medius*, if present, may appear only on one side of the steak. *See Item No. 1173 for purchaser tail length options.*

* In Canada, "center-cut" is not an approved modifier. See page xxv for more information.

1179A — Lomo, Bistec Strip Loin (New York), con Hueso, del Centro

Esta pieza, además de cumplir con los requisitos de la pieza número 1179, deberá ser posteriormente preparada excluyendo del strip loin con hueso la parte posterior o extremo adyacente al aguayón justo en el *gluteus medius,* o antes de éste. *El gluteus medius,* si está presente, solamente puede aparecer de un solo lado del bistec. *Consulte la pieza número 1173 para informarse sobre las opciones del comprador sobre el largo de la cola.*

* En Canadá, "corte del centro" no está aprobado como un modificador. Consulte la pág. li para obtener información adicional.

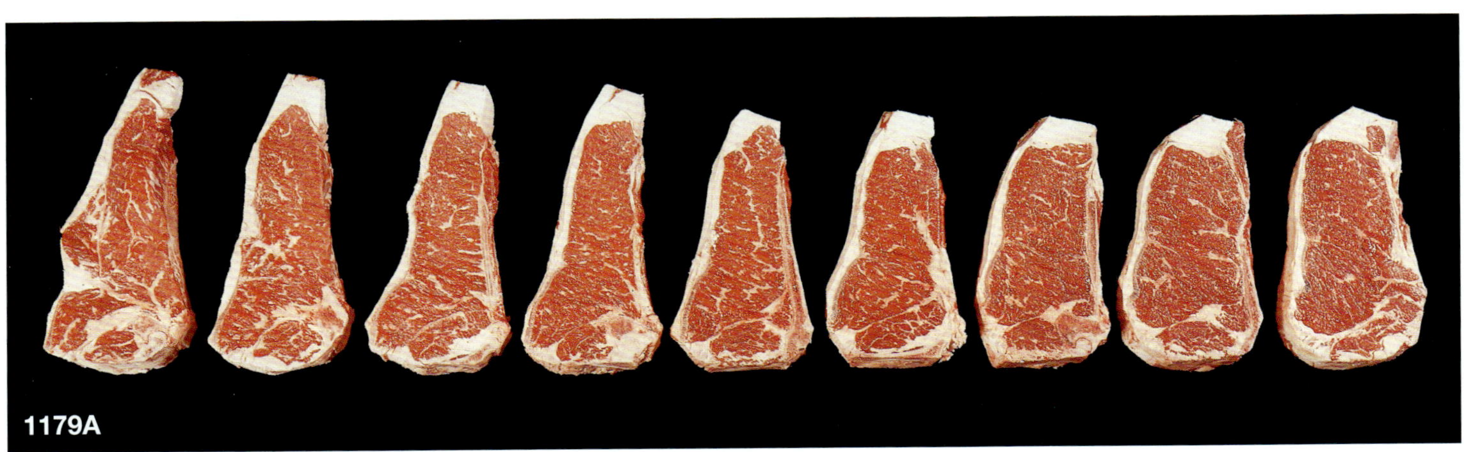

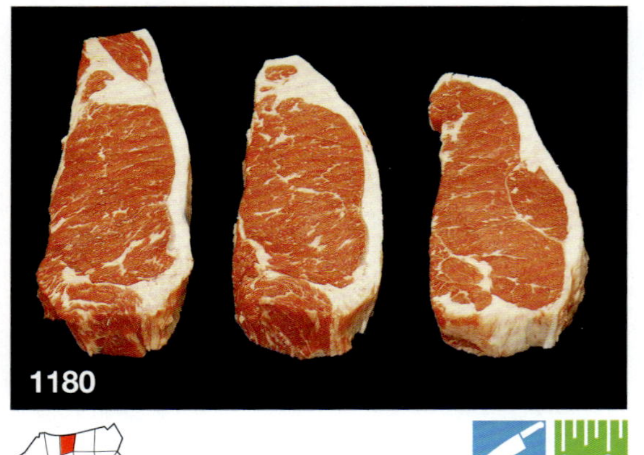

1180 — Beef Loin, Strip Loin Steak, Boneless

The boneless steaks shall be prepared from any beef short loin, bone in strip loin, or boneless strip loin item, provided the item meets the end requirements of Item No. 180. All bones and cartilages shall be excluded. *See Item No. 1173 for purchaser tail length options.*

1180 — Lomo, Bistec Strip Loin (New York), Deshuesado, del Centro

Los bistecs deshuesados deberán prepararse a partir de cualquier pieza de lomo corto de carne de res, strip loin con hueso, o de una pieza de strip loin deshuesada, siempre que la pieza cumpla con los requisitos finales de la pieza número 180. Se deberán excluir todos los huesos y cartílagos. *Consulte la pieza número 1173 para informarse sobre las opciones del comprador sobre el largo de la cola.*

1180A — Beef Loin, Strip Loin Steak, Boneless, Center-Cut

This item, in addition to meeting the requirements of Item No. 1180, shall be further prepared by excluding the posterior or sirloin butt end of the boneless strip loin at or anterior to the *gluteus medius*. The *gluteus medius*, if present, may appear only on one side of the steak.

🍁 In Canada, "center-cut" is not an approved modifier. See page xxv for more information.

1180A — Lomo, Bistec Strip Loin (New York), Deshuesado, del Centro

Esta pieza, además de cumplir con los requisitos de la pieza número 1180, deberá ser posteriormente preparada excluyendo la parte posterior o extremo adyacente al aguayón del strip loin deshuesado justo en el *gluteus medius* o antes de éste. El *gluteus medius*, si está presente, puede aparecer solamente de un solo lado del bistec.

🍁 En Canadá, "corte del centro" no está aprobado como un modificador. Consulte la página li para obtener información adicional.

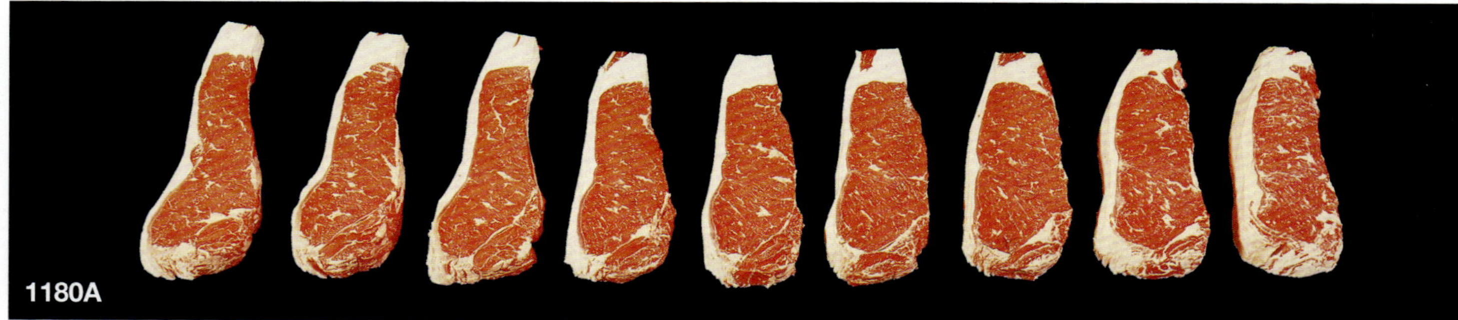

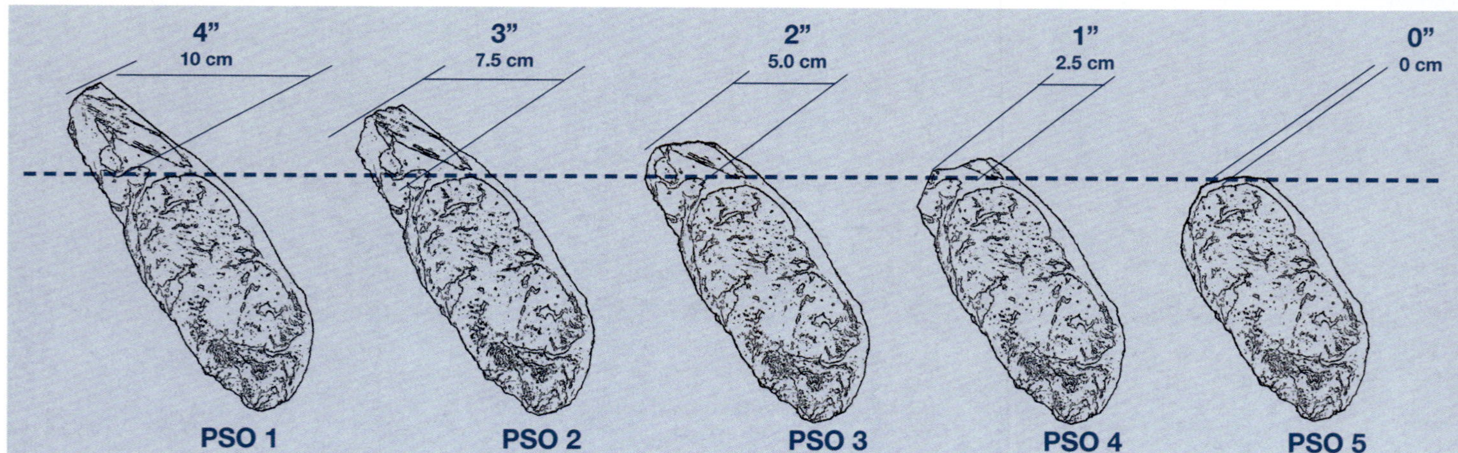

Graphic illustration of the length of tail difference on strip loin steaks, (bone in and boneless).
Ilustración gráfica sobre la diferencia de longitud de la cola en bistecs strip loin (con hueso y deshuesados).

1180B — Beef Loin, Strip Loin Steak, Split, Boneless

This item is prepared from any boneless strip loin item that is processed as described in Item No. 180B. This item is sometimes referred to as "strip steak filet" or "club cut".

PSO: 1 – The *multifidus dorsi* shall be removed.

2 – The posterior end of the strip loin shall be removed so that the *gluteus medius* is not present.

1180B — Lomo, Bistec Strip Loin (Club Steak), Dividido, Deshuesado

Esta pieza se prepara a partir de cualquier pieza de strip loin deshuesado, procesada según la descripción de la pieza número 180B. Esta pieza algunas veces es llamada "strip steak filet" o "club cut".

PSO: 1 – Se deberá extraer el *multifidus dorsi*.

2 – El extremo posterior del strip loin deberá extraerse a fin de que el *gluteus medius* no esté presente.

1180B

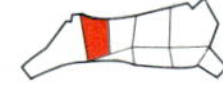

1184 — Beef Loin, Top Sirloin Butt Steak, Boneless

The boneless steaks may be prepared from any top sirloin butt, provided the item meets the end requirements of Item No. 184. Prior to cutting the top sirloin butt into steaks, it shall be faced by a straight cut to exclude the heavy connective tissue closely associated with the protuberance of the femur so that the appearance of the *gluteus medius* is oval in shape. The boneless top sirloin butt may be separated into sections reasonably parallel to the backbone line to accommodate the cutting of specified portion-size steaks. The sections shall be cut into steaks reasonably parallel to the cut surface of the round end.

1184 — Lomo, Bistec de Pulpa del Aguayón Superior/Top Sirloin, Deshuesado

Los bistecs deshuesados pueden prepararse con cualquier pieza de aguayón superior, siempre que cumpla con los requisitos de la pieza número 184. Antes de cortar la pulpa del aguayón superior en bistecs, se aplicará un corte recto para excluir el tejido conectivo grueso muy relacionado con la protuberancia del fémur, a fin de que el *gluteus medius* tome un aspecto ovalado. El aguayón deshuesado puede separarse en secciones razonablemente paralelas a la línea del espinazo a fin de facilitar el tamaño de los cortes de las porciones especificadas de los bistecs. Las secciones deberán ser cortadas en bistecs razonablemente paralelos a la superficie de corte del extremo adyacente a la pierna.

1184

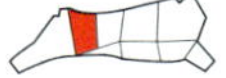

1184A — Beef Loin, Top Sirloin Butt Steak, Semi Center-Cut, Boneless

These steaks shall be as described in Item No. 1184 except that the *biceps femoris* shall be removed. The *longissimus dorsi* may or may not be present.

� In Canada, "semi center-cut" is not an approved modifier. *See page xxv for more information.*

1184A — Lomo, Bistec de Pulpa del Aguayón Superior/Top Sirloin, Sin Tapa, Corte Casi del Centro, Deshuesado

Estos bistecs deberán cumplir con las especificaciones de la pieza número 1184, salvo que deberá extraerse el *biceps femoris*. El *longissimus dorsi* podrá, o no, estar presente.

� En Canadá, "corte casi del centro" no está aprobado como un modificador. *Consulte la pág. li para obtener información adicional.*

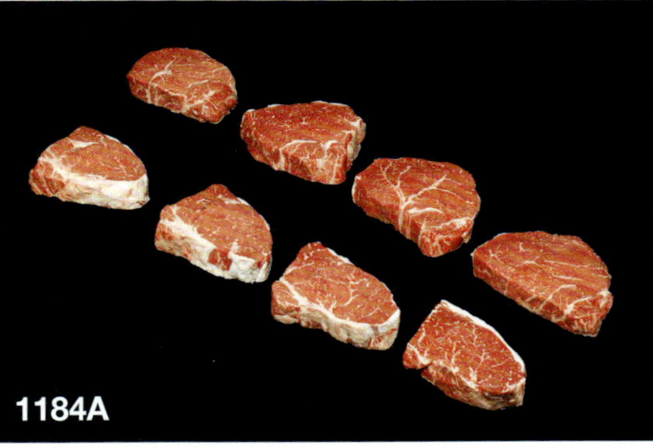

1184A

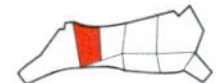

1184B

1184B Beef Loin, Top Sirloin Butt Steak, Center-Cut, Boneless (IM)

In addition to the preparation requirements described in Item No. 1184, these boneless top sirloin steaks shall be prepared only from the *gluteus medius* muscle.

PSO: 1 – Purchaser may specify that steaks are prepared after the separation of the dorsal portion of the *gluteus medius* from the main portion as described in Item No. 184B PSO 1.

🍁 In Canada, "center-cut" is not an approved modifier. See page xxv for more information.

1184B Lomo, Bistec de Pulpa del Aguayón Superior/Top Sirloin, Sin Tapa, Corte del Centro, Deshuesado (MI)

Además de los requisitos de preparación descritos en la pieza número 1184, estos bistecs de aguayón deshuesado sin tapa deberán prepararse únicamente del músculo *gluteus medius*.

PSO: 1 – El comprador puede especificar que los bistecs sean preparados después de realizada la separación entre la porción dorsal del *gluteus medius* y la porción principal, según descripción de la pieza número 184B, opción 1, especificada por el comprador.

🍁 En Canadá, "corte del centro" no está aprobado como un modificador. Consulte la pág. li para obtener información adicional.

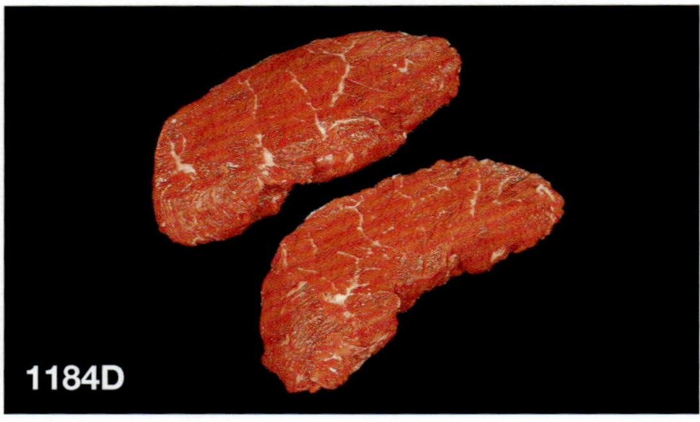

1184D

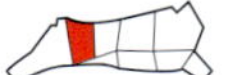

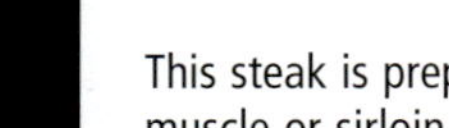

1184D Beef Loin, Top Sirloin Cap Steak, Boneless (IM)

This steak is prepared from the *biceps femoris* muscle or sirloin cap from any beef top sirloin item, provided the sirloin cap meets the end requirements of Item No. 184D. The boneless steaks shall be made into specified portion size or thickness by slicing the sirloin cap at an approximate right angle to the grain or direction of the muscle fibers. This item is sometimes referred to as a "Coulotte Steak."

1184D Lomo, Bistec de Tapa del Aguayón, Deshuesado (MI)

Este bistec se prepara a partir del músculo *biceps femoris* o tapa de aguayón de cualquier pieza de aguayón de res, siempre que la tapa de aguayón cumpla con los requisitos finales de la pieza número 184D. Los bistecs deshuesados se harán coincidir con el tamaño o grosor de porción especificados al rebanar la tapa del aguayón aproximadamente en ángulo recto al grano o en la dirección de las fibras de los músculos. A esta pieza a veces se la llama "Bistec Coulotte".

1184F — Beef Loin, Top Sirloin Butt Steak, Center-Cut, Boneless, Seamed, Dorsal Side (IM)

These steaks are prepared from the dorsal portion of the gluteus medius as described in Item No. 184F. The steaks are commonly referred to as "Baseball Cut".

* In Canada, "center-cut" is not an approved modifier. See page xxv for more information.

Photo shown is Fat Limitation Option (FLO) 5 - Peeled, Denuded, Surface Membrane Removed. *For more information, see pg. 67.*

1184F — Lomo, Bistec de Pulpa del Aguayón Superior/Top Sirloin, Sin Tapa, Corte del Centro, Deshuesado, Diseccionado por las Vetas Naturales, Lado Dorsal (MI)

Estos bistecs se preparan a partir de la porción dorsal del *gluteus medius,* según la descripción de la pieza número 184F. Los bistecs se llaman comúnmente "Corte Pelota de Béisbol".

* En Canadá, "corte del centro" no está aprobado como un modificador. Consulte la pág. xxv para obtener información adicional.

La foto muestra la opción 5 para limitar la grasa: "Desprovisto de grasa/Prácticamente desnudo de grasa, Membrana superficial retirada". *Para obtener más información, consulte la página 66.*

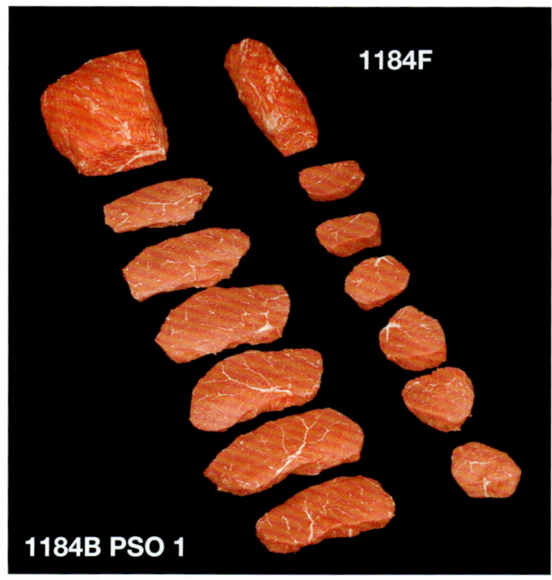

1185A — Beef Loin, Bottom Sirloin Butt, Flap Steak (IM)

The steaks shall be prepared from the *obliquus abdominis internus* muscle or flap portion of the bottom sirloin butt as described in Item No. 185A. The boneless steaks shall be made into specified portion size or thickness by slicing the flap at an approximate right angle to the grain or direction of the muscle fibers.

1185A — Lomo, Pulpa del Aguayón Inferior/Bottom Sirloin, Bistec de Falda (MI)

Los bistecs deberán prepararse a partir del músculo *obliquus abdominis internus* o de la porción de la tapa del aguayón, según descripción de la pieza número 185A. Los bistecs deshuesados se harán coincidir con el tamaño o grosor de porción especificados al rebanar la tapa en ángulo recto aproximado al grano o en la dirección de las fibras de los músculos.

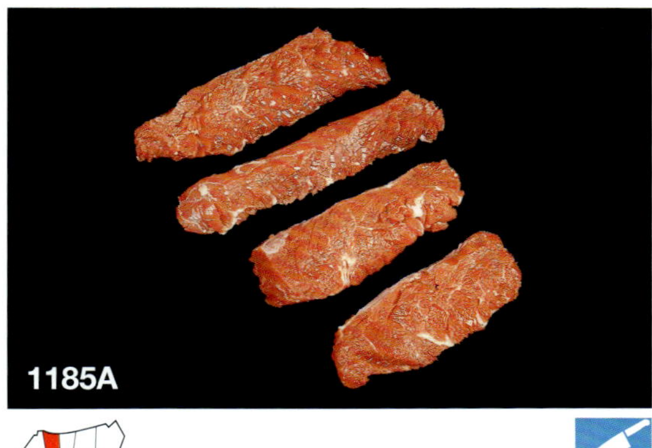

1185B — Beef Loin, Bottom Sirloin Butt, Ball Tip Steak

The steaks shall be prepared from the *rectus femoris* and *vastus lateralis* muscles or sirloin tip (knuckle) portion of the bottom sirloin butt as described in Item No. 185B. The boneless steaks shall be made into specified portion size or thickness by slicing the ball tip at an approximate right angle to the grain or direction of the muscle fibers.

1185B — Lomo, Pulpa del Aguayón Inferior/Bottom Sirloin, Bistec de Punta de Pulpa Bola, Deshuesada (M. Recto Femoral y Vasto Lateral)

Los bistecs deberán prepararse a partir de los músculos *rectus femoris* y *vastus lateralis* o la porción de pulpa bola del aguayón según la descripción de la pieza número 185B. Los bistecs deshuesados deberán cumplir con el tamaño o grosor de porción especificados al rebanar la punta de la pulpa bola en ángulo recto aproximado al grano o en la dirección de las fibras de los músculos.

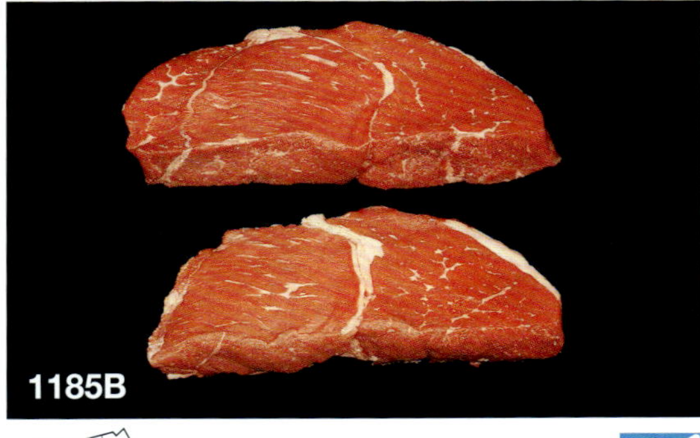

1185C

1185C Beef Loin, Bottom Sirloin Butt, Tri-Tip Steak (IM)

The steaks shall be prepared from the *tensor fasciae latae* muscle or triangle portion of the bottom sirloin butt as described in Item No. 185C. The boneless steaks shall be made into specified portion size or thickness by slicing the tri-tip at an approximate right angle to the grain or direction of the muscle fibers.

1185C Lomo, Pulpa del Aguayón Inferior/ Bottom Sirloin, Bistec de Empuje (Punta Triangular) (MI)

Los bistecs deberán prepararse a partir del músculo *tensor de la fascia lata* o porción triangular (empuje) del aguayón inferior según descripción de la pieza número 185C. Los bistecs deshuesados deberán cumplir con el tamaño o grosor de porción especificados al rebanar la punta triangular (empuje) en ángulo recto aproximado al grano o en la dirección de las fibras de los músculos.

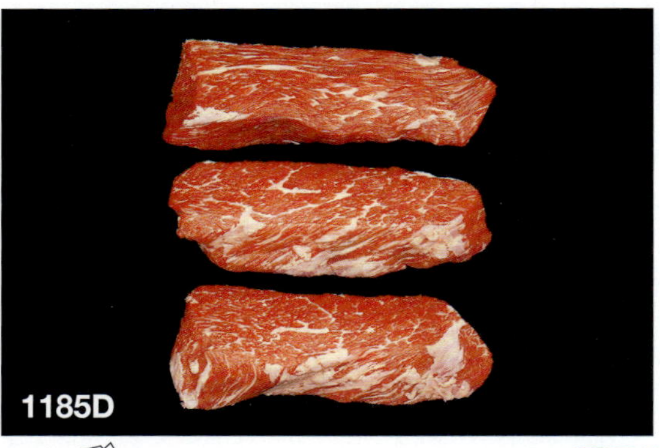

1185D

1185D Beef Loin, Bottom Sirloin Butt, Tri-Tip Steak, Defatted (IM)

This item is as described in Item No. 1185C, except steaks shall be trimmed practically free of fat.

1185D Lomo, Pulpa del Aguayón Inferior/ Bottom Sirloin, Bistec de Empuje (Punta Triangular), Limpio de Grasa (MI)

Esta pieza aparece descrita en la pieza número 1185C, salvo que los bistecs deberán ser recortados hasta quedar prácticamente libres de grasa.

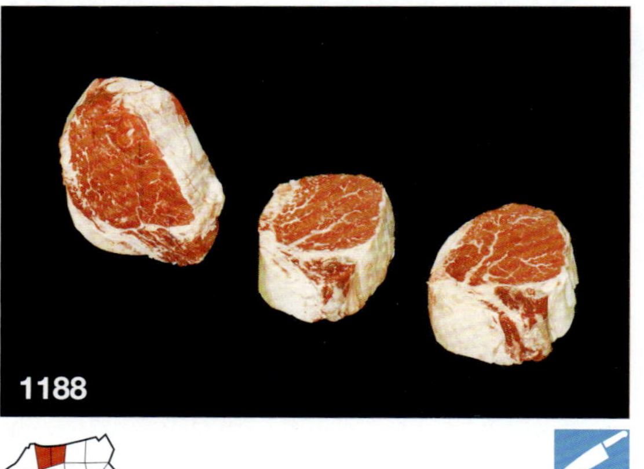

1188

1188 Beef Loin, Tenderloin Steak, Bone In

This item is derived from a short loin or Item No. 188, Beef Loin, Tenderloin, Bone In, and consists of the consists of *psoas major* and *psoas minor*, attached to the transverse process of the lumbar vertebrae. No steaks shall have a diameter of the *psoas major* less than 1.5 inches (3.75 cm) in the longest dimension.

1188 Lomo, Tablita de Filete (Bistec Cabrería), Con Hueso

Esta pieza proviene de un lomo corto o pieza número 188 "Lomo, Filete Cabrería Corto, con Hueso", y consiste en el *psoas mayor* y el *psoas menor*, unidos a las apófisis transversas de las vértebras lumbares. El *psoas mayor* de ningún bistec deberá tener un diámetro inferior a 3.75 cm (1.5 pulgadas) en su dimensión más larga.

NAMP
North American Meat Processors Association
Association Amérique du Nord des Transformateurs de Viande
Asociación Norteamericana de Procesadores de Carne

1189 — Beef Loin, Tenderloin Steak

The steaks shall be prepared from any beef tenderloin item meeting the end requirements of Item No. 189. The narrowest diameter of the cut surface of the *psoas major* or main tenderloin muscle, exclusive of its fat cover, must be a minimum of 1.0 inch (2.5 cm). Any fat or lean not firmly attached to the *psoas major* shall be excluded. Maximum surface fat thickness where present shall be 0.125 inch (3 mm) unless otherwise specified by the purchaser.

1189 — Lomo, Medallón de Filete

Los medallones deberán prepararse a partir de cualquier pieza de filete de carne de res, según los requisitos finales de la pieza número 189. El diámetro más angosto de la superficie del corte del *psoas mayor* o músculo principal del filete, sin tomar en cuenta su cubierta de grasa, debe ser de un mínimo de 2.5 cm (1.0 pulgada). Se deberá excluir la grasa o la carne magra presentes que no estén firmemente unidas al *psoas mayor*. El espesor máximo de la cubierta de grasa, cuando esté presente, deberá ser de 3 mm (0.125 pulgadas) a menos que el comprador haya especificado lo contrario.

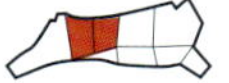

1189A — Beef Loin, Tenderloin Steak, Side Muscle On, Defatted

The defatted steaks shall be prepared from any beef tenderloin item meeting the end requirements described in Item No. 189A. The narrowest diameter of the cut surface of the *psoas major* or main tenderloin muscle, exclusive of any remaining surface fat cover, must be a minimum of 1.0 inch (2.5 cm).

1189A — Lomo, Medallón de Filete, Con Cuerda (Psoas Menor), Limpio de Grasa

Los medallones limpios de grasa deberán prepararse a partir de cualquier pieza de filete de carne de res que cumpla con los requisitos finales descritos en la pieza número 189A. El diámetro más angosto de la superficie de corte del *psoas mayor* o músculo principal del filete, sin tener en cuenta cualquier resto de cubierta de grasa, debe ser de un mínimo de 2.5 cm (1.0 pulgada).

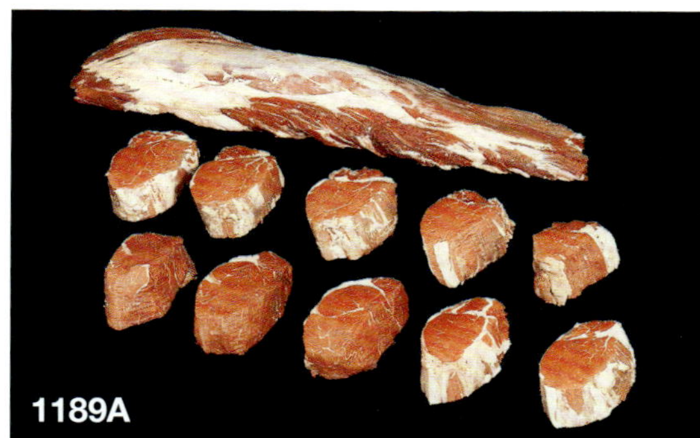

1190 — Beef Loin, Tenderloin Steak, Side Muscle Off, Defatted

The side muscle or chain off steaks shall be prepared from any beef tenderloin item meeting the end requirements described in Item No. 190. The narrowest diameter of the cut surface of the *psoas major* or main tenderloin muscle, exclusive of any remaining traces of surface fat cover, must be a minimum of 1.0 inch (2.5 cm).

1190 — Lomo, Medallón de Filete, sin Cuerda (Psoas Menor), Limpio de Grasa

Los bistecs sin el músculo lateral o cadena deberán prepararse a partir de cualquier pieza de filete de res que cumpla con los requisitos finales descritos en la pieza número 190. El diámetro más angosto de la superficie de corte del *psoas mayor* o músculo principal del filete, sin tener en cuenta cualquier resto de cubierta de grasa, debe ser de un mínimo de 2.5 cm (1.0 pulgada).

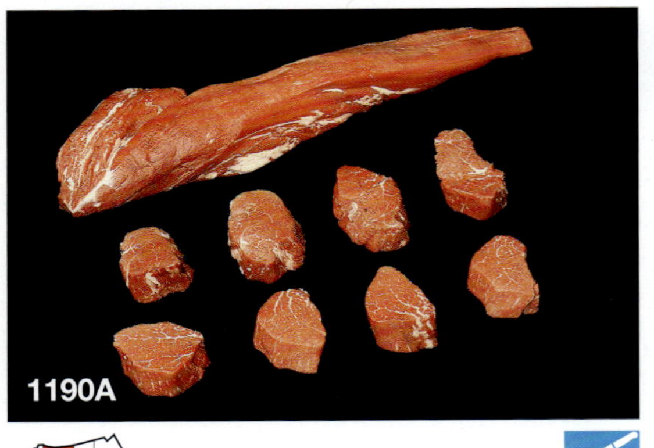

1190A — Beef Loin, Tenderloin Steak, Side Muscle Off, Skinned

The side muscle or chain off steaks shall be prepared from any beef tenderloin item meeting the end requirements described in Item No. 190A. The narrowest diameter of the cut surface of the *psoas major* or main tenderloin muscle, exclusive of any traces of remaining surface fat cover, must be a minimum of 1.0 inch (2.5 cm).

1190A — Lomo, Medallón de Filete, sin Cuerda (Psoas Menor), Despellejado

Los bistecs sin el músculo lateral o cadena deberán prepararse a partir de cualquier pieza de filete de res que cumpla con los requisitos finales descritos en la pieza número 190A. El diámetro más angosto de la superficie de corte del *psoas mayor* o músculo principal del filete, sin tener en cuenta cualquier cubierta de grasa, debe ser de un mínimo de 2.5 cm (1.0 pulgada).

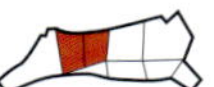

1190B — Beef Loin, Tenderloin Steak, Full, Side Muscle Off, Center-Cut, Skinned (IM)

This item is from Item No. 190B and shall consist of the psoas major only. It is commonly referred to as a "barrel cut".

🍁 In Canada, "center-cut" is not an approved modifier. See page xxv for more information.

1190B — Lomo, Medallón de Filete, sin Cuerda (Psoas Menor), Corte del Medio (Sin Cabeza ni Cola), Despellejado (MI)

Esta pieza se prepara de la pieza número 190B y consistirá únicamente en el psoas mayor. Habitualmente, se la llama "corte barril".

🍁 En Canadá, "corte del centro" no está aprobado como un modificador. Consulte la pág. li para obtener información adicional.

1190C — Beef Loin, Tenderloin Tips

Tenderloin tips shall be prepared from any beef tenderloin item that meets these requirements. Tips may consist of any portion of the thin end of the *psoas major*, *psoas minor*, or *iliacus* muscles and shall consist of pieces that are no less than 1.5 square inches (3.8 sq cm) and are no less than 0.5 inch (13 mm) thick at any point.

1190C — Lomo, Colas (Puntas) de Filete

Las colas (puntas) de filete deberán prepararse a partir de cualquier pieza de filete de res que cumpla con estos requisitos. Las colas (puntas) pueden consistir en cualquier porción del extremo angosto de los músculos *psoas mayor*, *psoas menor* o *iliacus*, conformadas por piezas de un tamaño de por lo menos 3.8 cm cuadrados (1.5 pulgadas cuadradas) y un grosor de por lo menos 13 mm (0.5 pulgadas) en cualquier punto.

lamb / cordero

208 Lamb Shoulder, Square-Cut, Boneless / Paleta (Espaldilla), Corte Cuadrado, Deshuesada

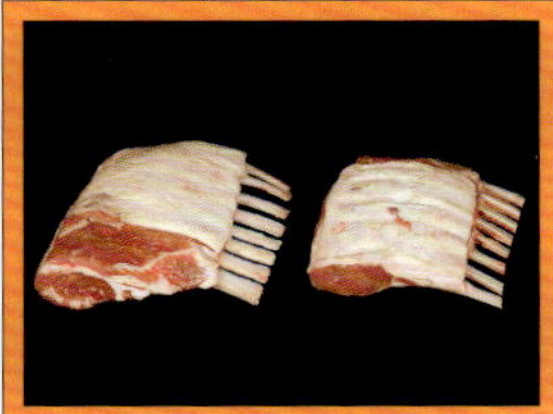

204C Lamb Rack, Roast-Ready, Frenched / Costillar, Listo para Rostizar, Estilo Francés

204D Lamb Rack, Roast-Ready, Frenched, Special (Cap Off) Costillar, Listo para Rostizar, Estilo Francés, Especial, Sin Tapa

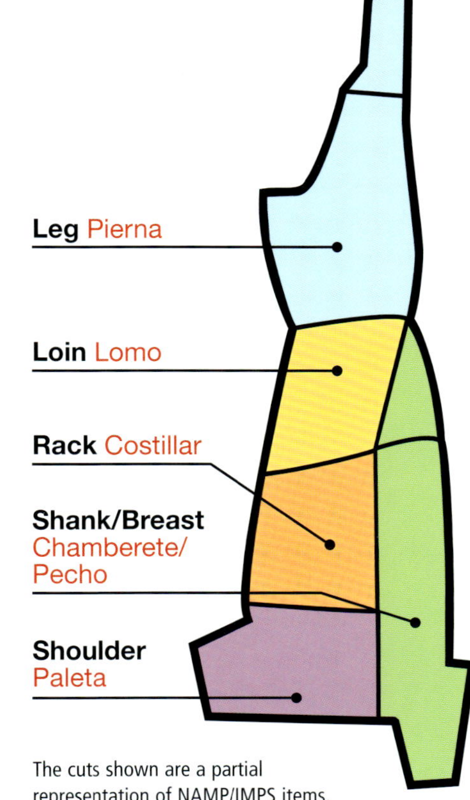

Leg Pierna

Loin Lomo

Rack Costillar

Shank/Breast Chamberete/ Pecho

Shoulder Paleta

The cuts shown are a partial representation of NAMP/IMPS items.

Los cortes exhibidos son una representación parcial de las piezas de NAMP/IMPS.

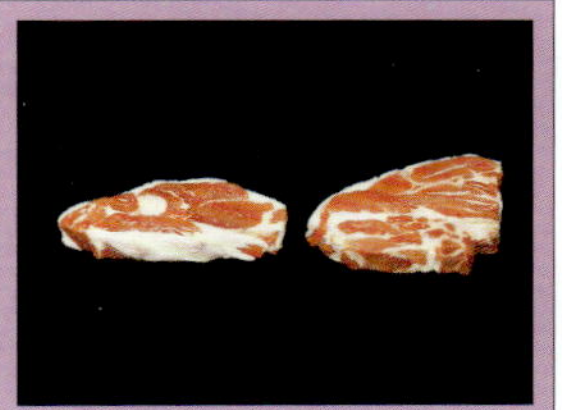

1207 Lamb Shoulder Chops Chuletas de Brazuelo y Paleta/Chuletas del 7

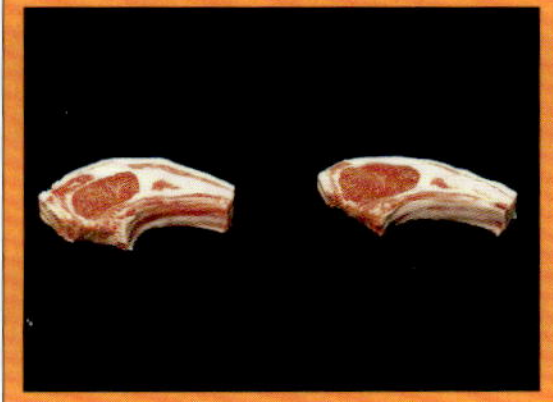

1204B Lamb Rib Chops Chuletas del Espaldar

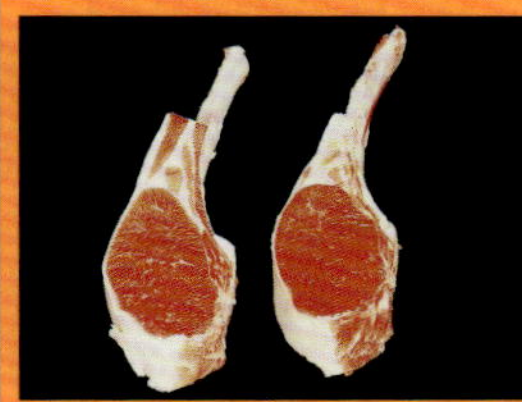

1204D Lamb Rib Chops, Frenched, Special / Chuletas del Espaldar, Estilo Francés, Especiales

209B Lamb Shoulder Ribs Paleta (Espaldilla), Costillas

1204F Lamb Rib Chops, Frenched, Fancy / Chuletas del Espaldar, Estilo Francés, De Gala

232A Lamb Loin, Block-Ready, Trimmed / Lomo, Listo para Tablajear, Recortado de Grasa y Limpio

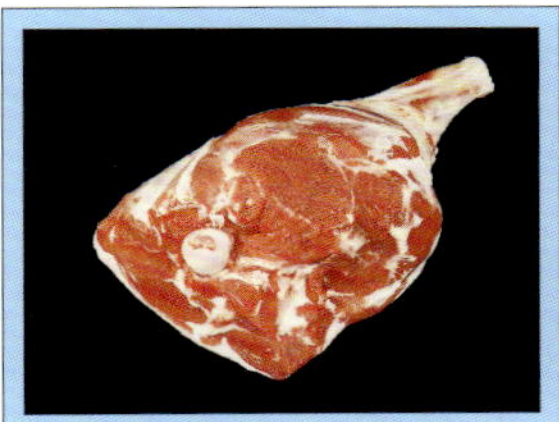

233E Lamb Leg, Steamship, 3/4, Aitch Bone Removed / Pierna, sin Caña/ Jarrete (3/4), Sin Hueso de Cadera

234 Lamb Leg, Boneless Pierna, Deshuesada

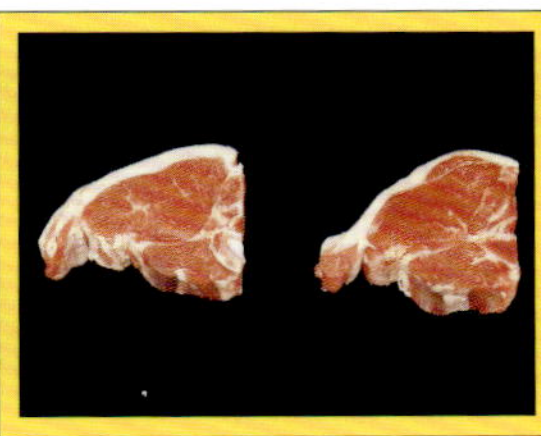

1232A Lamb Loin Chops Chuletas de Lomo

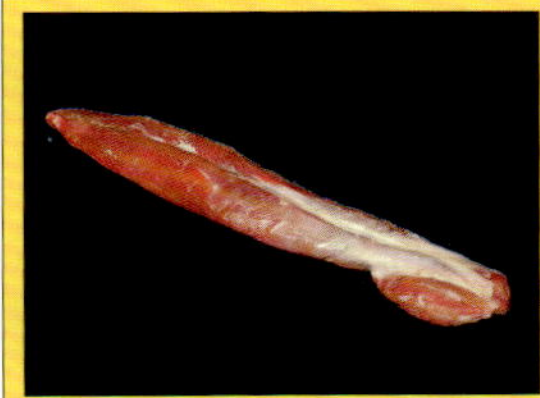

246 Lamb Tenderloin Filete de Cordero

232C Lamb Loin, Single, Boneless Lomo, Individual, Deshuesado

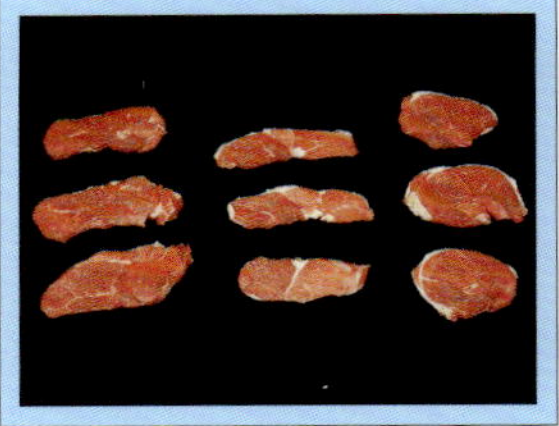

1234A Lamb Leg, Cutlet, Boneless / Pierna, Escalopas, Deshuesadas

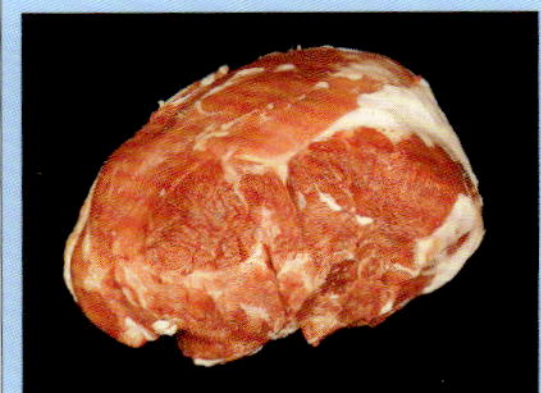

234E Lamb Leg, Inside, Boneless Pierna, Pulpa Negra (Cara/Centro), Deshuensada

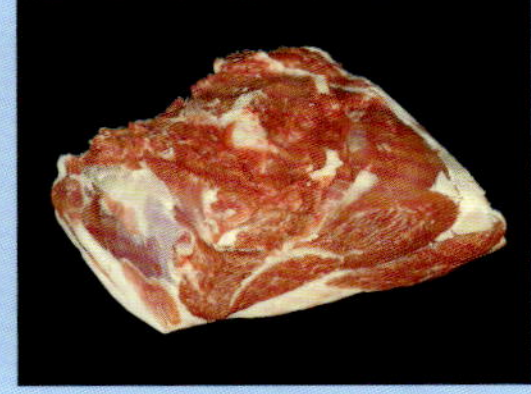

234G PSO 2 Lamb Top Sirloin, Boneless / Aguayón Superior (Top Sirloin), Deshuesado

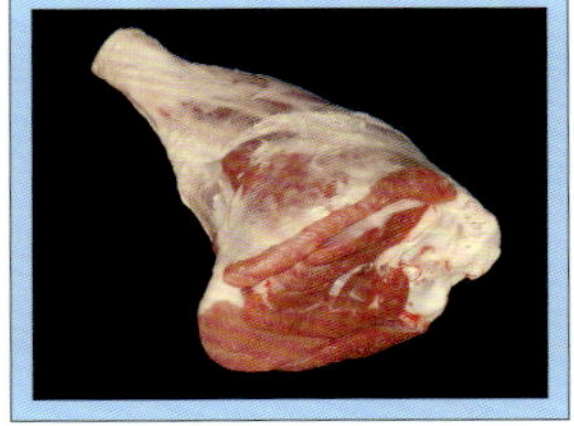

233G Lamb Leg, Hindshank, Heel On Pierna, Chamberete Trasero, con Talón

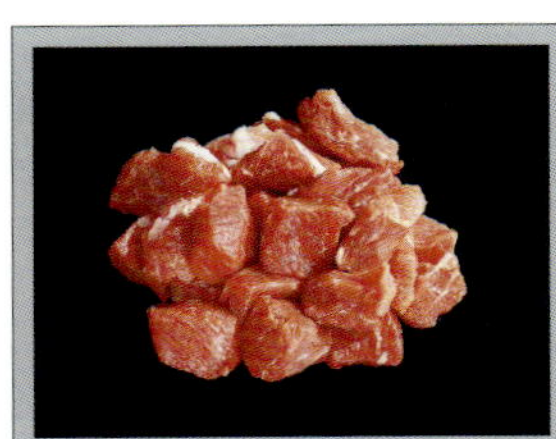

295 Lamb for Stewing / Trozos de Cordero para Cocido/Guisado

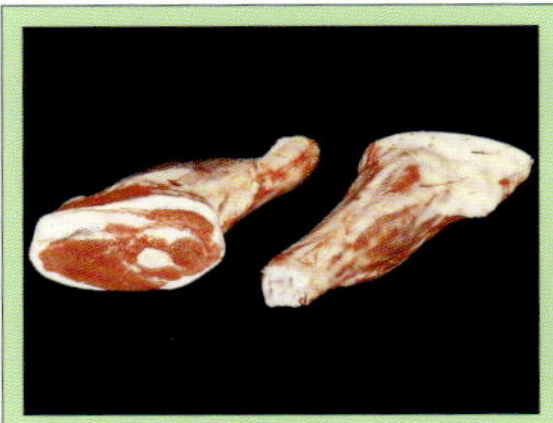

210 Lamb Foreshank Chamberete de Mano

209A Lamb Ribs, Breast Bones Off / Costillas, Sin Hueso del Pecho

Center of the Plate Training®
from the producers of *The Meat Buyer's Guide®*

Capacitación en ingredientes principales del plato
de los realizadores de la Guía para Compradores de Carne®

Course Specifics

Center of the Plate Training® offered by the North American Meat Processors Association (NAMP) is a first-hand look at how carcasses are converted into portioned items commonly traded in the foodservice and retail meat business. The course covers all the major center of the plate protein items: beef, veal, lamb, pork, and poultry (in some locations).

This course is held two to three times annually across North America. It spans two to three days of classroom learning, with presentations by industry experts. You also will receive a copy of the NAMP *Meat Buyer's Guide®*, which is used extensively in the course.

What You Will Learn From This Course

- The IMPS/NAMP numbering system, purchase specified options, and standards common to the industry.

- A knowledge of meat items as described by IMPS and by NAMP's *Meat Buyer's Guide®*.

- Where meat products originate and how this affects their final use.

- The importance of standards and how they keep products consistent, wholesome, and fair throughout the market.

- Common defects or inconsistencies in meat products that you should look for to prevent dissatisfied customers or unpleasant dining experiences.

- Current trends in the foodservice industry, new menu ideas and options.

- How value is determined for different meat products and how this is affected by quality parameters.

If you're involved in the buying and selling of meat products - from restaurants and supermarkets to foodservice distributors and meat companies - gain a competitive edge by applying the valuable information you'll learn from this course.

Visit www.namp.com for more information on specific courses, locations, and dates.

Visite www.namp.com para obtener información adicional sobre cursos específicos, sitios y fechas.

Detalles del curso

La Capacitación en ingredientes principales del plato que ofrece la Asociación Norteamericana de Procesadores de Carne (NAMP) es una mirada de primera mano a la forma en que las canales se convierten en piezas porcionadas comúnmente comercializadas en la industria de servicios de alimentación y los negocios minoristas de carne. El curso comprende las principales piezas proteicas que constituyen los ingredientes principales del plato: carne de res, ternera, cordero, cerdo y aves (en algunos lugares).

Este curso se dicta dos o tres veces al año en toda Norteamérica. Abarca de dos a tres días de aprendizaje en un salón de clase, con presentaciones a cargo de expertos de la industria. También recibirá una copia de *La Guía para Compradores de Carne®* de NAMP (Asociación Norteamericana de Procesadores de Carne, por sus siglas en inglés) que se utilizará exhaustivamente en el curso.

Qué aprenderá en este curso

- El sistema de numeración IMPS/NAMP, las opciones especificadas de compra y las normas comunes de la industria.

- Un conocimiento de las piezas de carne como se describen en las IMPS (Especificaciones Institucionales de Compra de Carne, por sus siglas en inglés) y en *La Guía para Compradores de Carne®* de NAMP.

- Dónde se originan los productos de carne y cómo afecta esto su uso final.

- La importancia de las normas y cómo logran que los productos sean uniformes, saludables y buenos en todo el mercado.

- Defectos o anomalías en los productos de carne que debería buscar para evitar clientes insatisfechos o que tengan experiencias desagradables en la mesa.

- Las tendencias actuales de la industria de servicios de alimentación, nuevas ideas y opciones para su menú.

- Cómo se determina el valor de diferentes productos de carne y cómo éste se ve afectado por los parámetros de calidad.

Si participa en la compra y venta de productos de carne, ya sea en restaurantes y supermercados o distribuidores de la industria de servicios de alimentación y empresas de carne, obtenga una ventaja competitiva aplicando la valiosa información que aprenderá en este curso.

Cooking lamb is similar to cooking other meats. Just follow these simple steps:

1. Do not overcook lamb. A meat thermometer is the best tool to determine the doneness of lamb. Insert the thermometer into the center of the meat, being careful not to touch any fat, bone or the bottom of the pan.

   145°F for medium-rare   160°F for medium   170°F for well

   *Ground meat should be cooked to an internal temperature of 160°F

2. Let your lamb rest for 5 to 10 minutes before serving – the rest allows the meat's juices to settle. Keep in mind that the meat will continue to cook slightly upon standing so remove the lamb from oven at a slightly lower degree of doneness than you prefer.

3. Find information on cuts and nutrition as well as recipes at **www.americanlamb.com**

Cocinar cordero es similar a cocinar otras carnes. Simplemente siga estos sencillos pasos:

1. No cocine el cordero en forma excesiva. Un termómetro de carne es la mejor herramienta para determinar el grado de cocción del cordero. Inserte el termómetro en el centro de la carne, con cuidado de no tocar la grasa, el hueso ni el fondo de la cacerola.

   145 °F para término medio jugoso   160 °F para término medio   170 °F para bien cocido

   *La carne molida se debe cocinar hasta que alcance una temperatura interna de 160 °F

2. Deje reposar el cordero durante 5 a 10 minutos antes de servirlo para permitir que los jugos de la carne se asienten. Recuerde que la carne seguirá cociéndose ligeramente mientras la deje reposar, así que debe retirar el cordero del horno a un grado de cocción ligeramente menor al que prefiere.

3. Obtenga información sobre cortes, nutrición y recetas en **www.americanlamb.com**

Lamb Skeletal Chart / Diagrama de estructura esquelética del cordero

Location, Structure, and Names of Bones
Ubicación, estructura y nombres de los huesos

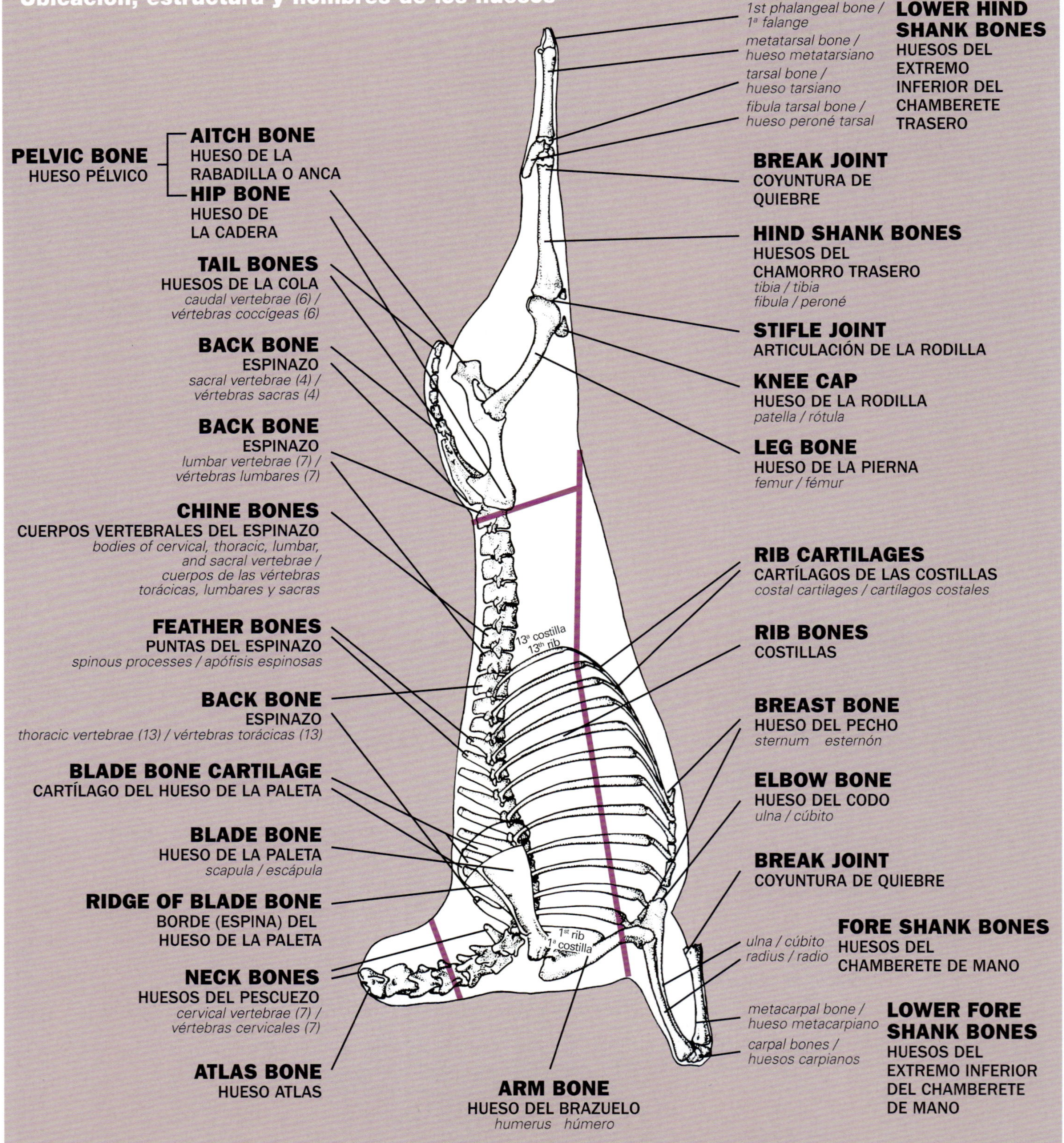

NAMP
NORTH AMERICAN MEAT PROCESSORS ASSOCIATION
Association Amérique du Nord des Transformateurs de Viande
Asociación Norteamericana de Procesadores de Carne

Lamb Primal Cuts / Cortes Primarios del Cordero

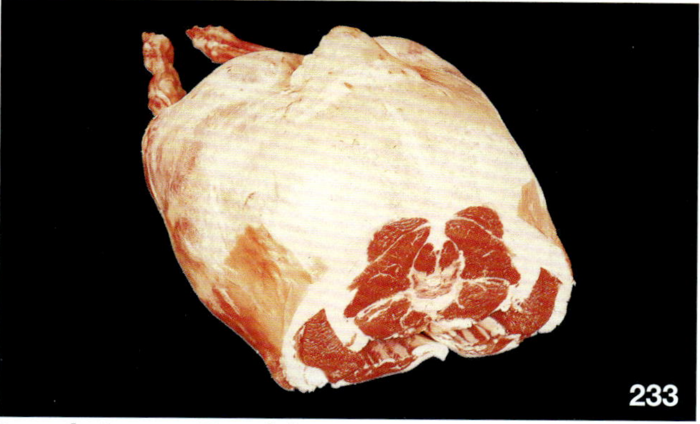

Lamb Legs, Double
Piernas de Cordero, En Pareja

233

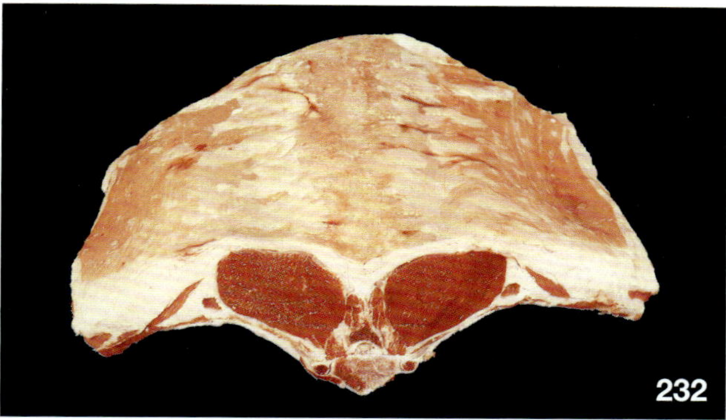

Lamb Loin, Double
Lomos de Cordero, En Pareja

232

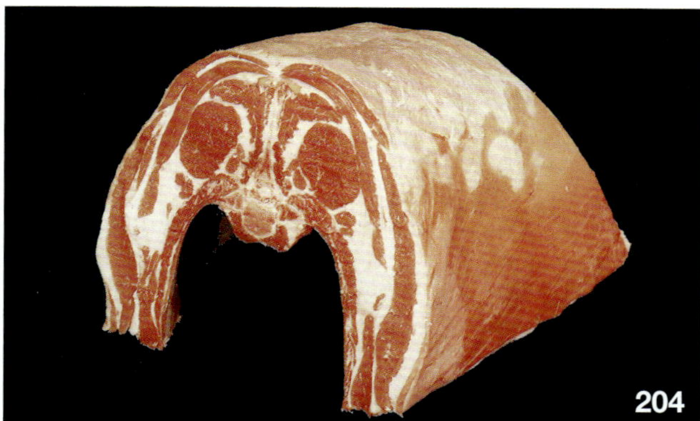

Lamb Hotel Rack
Costillar de Cordero Clase Hotelera

204

Lamb Shoulder, Square-Cut
Espaldilla de Cordero, Corte Cuadrado

207

Loin-Leg Separation
Separación Lomo-Pierna

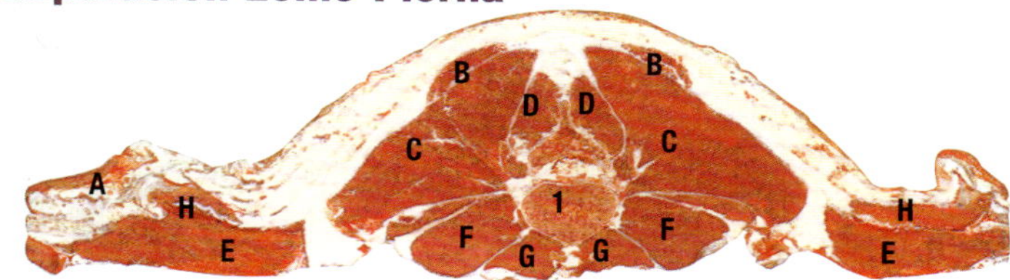

A Cutaneus trunci	**E** Obliquus internus abdominis	**H** Obliquus externus abdominis
B Gluteus medius	**F** Psoas major / mayor	**1** Vertebrae (Backbone)
C Longissimus dorsi	**G** Psoas minor / menor	Vértebras (Espinazo)
D Multifidus dorsi		

Loin-Rack Separation
Separación Lomo-Costillar

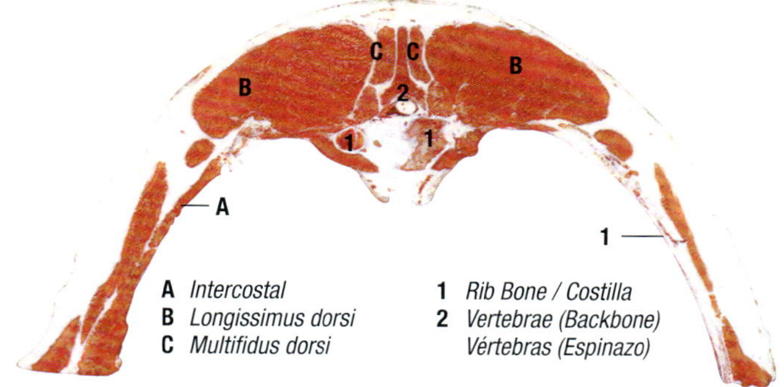

A Intercostal	**1** Rib Bone / Costilla
B Longissimus dorsi	**2** Vertebrae (Backbone)
C Multifidus dorsi	Vértebras (Espinazo)

Rack-Shoulder Separation
Separación Costillar-Espaldilla

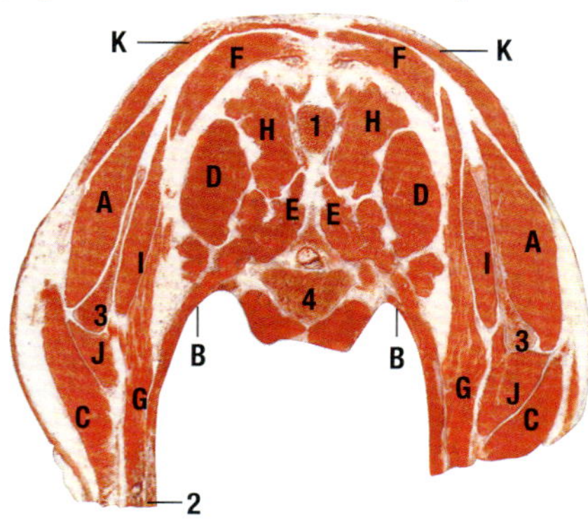

A Infraspinatus
B Intercostal
C Latissimus dorsi
D Longissimus dorsi
E Multifidus dorsi
F Rhomboideus
G Serratus ventralis
H Spinalis dorsi
I Subcapularis
J Teres major / mayor
K Trapezius
1 Feather Bones
Puntas del espinazo
2 Rib Bone / Costilla
3 Scapula (Blade Bone)
Escápula (hueso de la paleta)
4 Vertebrae (Backbone)
Vértebras (Espinazo)

Shoulder-Brisket Separation
Separación Espaldilla-Pecho

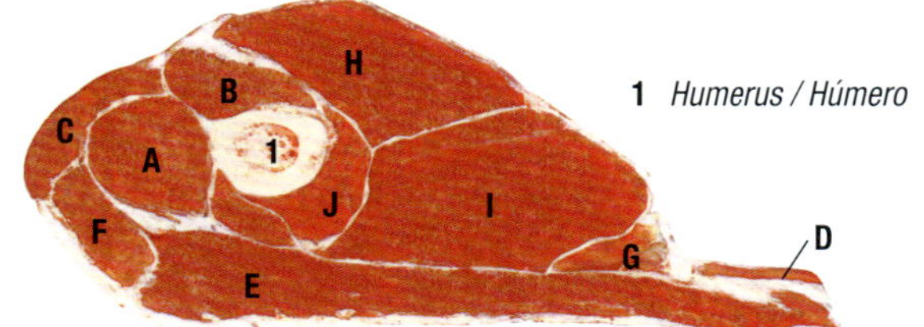

1 Humerus / Húmero

A Biceps brachii	**F** Pectoralis superficialis	**I** Triceps brachii, long head / cabeza larga
B Brachialis	**G** Tensor fasciae antebrachii	**J** Triceps brachii, medial head / cabeza media
C Brachiocephalicus	**H** Triceps brachii, lateral head / cabeza lateral	
D Cutaneus trunci		
E Pectoralis profundus		

Index / Índice

Lamb Products and Weight Ranges
Productos de cordero y escalas de peso

ITEM PIEZA	PRODUCT NAME / NOMBRE DE PRODUCTO	PG. PÁG.	Weight Ranges (pounds) / Escalas de peso (libras/kg)			
			A	B	C	D
200	Carcass / Canal	99	41–55 (18.6-24.9)	55–65 (24.9-29.5)	65–75 (29.5-34)	75-up (Más de 34)
200A	Carcass, 3-Way / Canal, en 3 piezas	99	41–55 (18.6-24.9)	55–65 (24.9-29.5)	65–75 (29.5-34)	75-up (Más de 34)
200B	Carcass, Block-Ready / Canal, Listo para Tablajear	99	41–55 (18.6-24.9)	55–65 (24.9-29.5)	65–75 (29.5-34)	75-up (Más de 34)
204	Rack / Costillar	100	4–5 (1.8-2.3)	5–7 (2.3-3.2)	7–9 (3.2-4.1)	9-up (Más de 4.1)
204A	Rack, Chined / Costillar, con Espinazo Rebajado	100	2-down (Menos de 0.90)	2–3 (0.90-1.4)	3–4 (1.4-1.8)	4-up (Más de 1.8)
204B	Rack, Roast-Ready / Costillar, Listo para Rostizar	101	2-down (Menos de 0.90)	2–3 (0.90-1.4)	3–4 (1.4-1.8)	4-up (Más de 1.8)
204C	Rack, Roast-Ready, Frenched / Costillar, Listo para Rostizar, Estilo Francés	101	2-down (Menos de 0.90)	2–3 (0.90-1.4)	3–4 (1.4-1.8)	4-up (Más de 1.8)
204D	Rack, Roast-Ready, Frenched, Special, Cap Off / Costillar, Listo para Rostizar, Estilo Francés, Especial, Sin Tapa	102	1.5-down (Menos de 0.68)	1.5–2.5 (0.68-1.1)	2.5–3.5 (1.1-1.6)	3.5-up (Más de 1.6)
206	Shoulder / Paleta (Espaldilla)	102	14–19 (6.4-8.6)	19–23 (8.6-10.4)	23–27 (10.4-12.2)	27-up (Más de 12.2)
207	Shoulder, Square-Cut / Paleta (Espaldilla), Corte Cuadrado	102	5–6 (2.3-2.7)	6–8 (2.7-3.6)	8-10 (3.6-4.5)	10-up (Más de 4.5)
208	Shoulder, Square-Cut, Boneless / Paleta (Espaldilla), Corte Cuadrado, Deshuesada	103	4–5 (1.8-2.3)	5–7 (2.3-3.2)	7–9 (3.2-4.1)	9-up (Más de 4.1)
208D	Shoulder, Pectoral Meat / Paleta (Espaldilla), Carne del Pectoral	103	2 – 3 oz. (57-85 gr)	3 – 5 oz. (85-142 gr)	5 – 7 oz. (142-198 gr)	8 oz.-up (227 gr)
209	Breast / Pecho	103	2-down (Menos de 0.90)	2–3 (0.90-1.4)	3–4 (1.4-1.8)	4-up (Más de 1.8)
209A	Ribs, Breast Bones Off / Costillas, Sin Hueso del Pecho	104	2-down (Menos de 0.90)	2–3 (0.90-1.4)	3–4 (1.4-1.8)	4-up (Más de 1.8)
209B	Shoulder, Ribs / Paleta (Espaldilla), Costillas	105	1-down (Menos de 0.45)	1–2 (0.45-0.90)	3–4 (1.4-1.8)	4-up (Más de 1.8)
210	Foreshank / Chamberete de Mano	105	0.5–1 (0.23-0.45)	1 – 1.5 (0.45-0.68)	1.5–2 (0.68-0.90)	2-up (Más de 0.90)
229A	Hindsaddle, Long-Cut, Trimmed / Cuarto Trasero en Silla de Montar, Trasero Largo (8-9 costillas), Recortado de Grasa y Limpio	106	23–29 (10.4-13.2)	29–36 (13.2-16.3)	36–41 (16.3-18.6)	41-up (Más de 18.6)
230	Hindsaddle / Cuarto Trasero en Silla de Montar	106	20–25 (9.1-11.3)	25–30 (11.3-13.6)	30–35 (13.6-15.9)	35-up (Más de 15.9)
231	Loins, Saddle / Lomos	106	6–8 (2.7-3.6)	8–11 (3.6-5)	11–13 (5-5.9)	13-up (Más de 5.9)
232	Loins, Saddle, Trimmed / Lomos, Recortados de Grasa y Limpios	107	4–5 (1.8-2.3)	5 – 7 (2.3-3.2)	7–9 (3.2-4.1)	9-up (Más de 4.1)
232A	Loin, Block-Ready, Trimmed / Lomo, Listo para Tablajear, Recortado de Grasa y Limpio	107	1–2 (0.45-0.90)	2–3 (0.90-1.4)	3–4 (1.4-1.8)	4-up (Más de 1.8)
232B	Loins, Double, Boneless / Lomos, En Pareja, Deshuesados	108	2-down (Menos de 0.90)	2–3 (0.90-1.4)	3 – 5 (1.4-2.3)	5-up (Más de 2.3)
232C	Loin, Single, Boneless / Lomo, Individual, Deshuesado	108	1-down (Menos de 0.45)	1 – 1.5 (0.45-0.68)	1.5–2.5 (0.68-1.1)	2.5-up (Más de 1.1)
232D	Loin, Short Tenderloin / Lomo, Filete Corto	108	0.5-down (Menos de 0.23)	0.5–1 (0.23-0.45)	1–2 (0.45-0.90)	2-up (Más de 0.90)
232E	Flank, Untrimmed / Falda/Aldilla, sin Recortado de Grasa y sin Limpiar	108	.5-down (Menos de 0.23)	0.5 – 1 (0.23-0.45)	1-up (Más de 0.45)	
233	Legs / Piernas	109	6–9 (2.7-4.1)	9–13 (4.1-5.9)	13–17 (5.9-7.7)	17-up (Más de 7.7)
233A	Leg, Trotter Off / Pierna, sin Caña/Jarrete	109	5–9 (2.3-4.1)	9–13 (4.1-5.9)	13–17 (5.9-7.7)	17-up (Más de 7.7)
233C	Leg, Trotter Off, Semi-Boneless / Pierna, sin Caña/Jarrete, Parcialmente Deshuesada	109	4 – 8 (1.8-3.6)	8–12 (3.6-5.4)	12–16 (5.4-7.3)	16-up (Más de 7.3)
233D	Leg, Shank Off, Semi-Boneless / Pierna, sin Chamberete, Parcialmente Deshuesada	110	3 – 5 (1.4-2.3)	5 – 7 (2.3-3.2)	7 – 10 (3.2-4.5)	10-up (Más de 4.5)
233E	Leg, Steamship, 3/4, Aitch Bone Removed / Pierna, sin Caña/Jarrete (3/4), Sin Hueso de Cadera	110	5 – 7 (2.3-3.2)	7–9 (3.2-4.1)	9–11 (4.1-5)	11-up (Más de 5)

NAMP
North American Meat Processors Association
Association Amérique du Nord des Transformateurs de Viande
Asociación Norteamericana de Procesadores de Carne

ITEM PIEZA	PRODUCT NAME NOMBRE DE PRODUCTO	PG. PÁG.	Weight Ranges (pounds) / Escalas de peso (libras/kg)			
			A	B	C	D
233F	**Leg, Hindshank** Pierna, Chamberete Trasero	110	1-down (Menos de 0.45)	1–2 (0.45-0.90)	2-up (Más de 0.90)	
233G	**Leg, Hindshank, Heel On** Pierna, Chamberete Trasero, con Talón	111	1-down (Menos de 0.45)	1-up (Más de 0.45)		
234	**Leg, Boneless** Pierna, Deshuesada	111	5–8 (2.3-3.6)	8–11 (3.6-5)	11–13 (5-5.9)	13-up (Más de 5.9)
234A	**Leg, Shank Off, Boneless** Pierna, sin Chamberete, Deshuesada	111	6–8 (2.7-3.6)	8–9 (3.6-4.1)	9–11 (4.1-5)	11-up (Más de 5)
234C	**Leg, Bottom, Boneless** Pierna, Pulpa Blanca-Aguayón-Pulpa Bola, Deshuesada	112	1–3 (0.45-1.4)	2–4 (0.9-1.8)	4–6 (1.8-2.7)	6-up (Más de 2.7)
234D	**Leg, Outside, Boneless** Pierna, Contracara-Aguayón sin Talón (Copete), Deshuesada	112	1-down (Menos de 0.45)	1 – 1.5 (0.45-0.68)	1.5–3 (0.68-1.4)	3-up (Más de 1.4)
234E	**Leg, Inside, Boneless** Pierna, Pulpa Negra (Cara/Centro), Deshuesada	113	1-down (Menos de 0.45)	1 – 1.5 (0.45-0.68)	1.5–2 (0.68-0.90)	2-up (Más de 0.90)
234F	**Leg, Sirloin Tip, Boneless** Pierna, Punta de Sirloin, Deshuesada	113	0.5-down (Menos de 0.23)	0.5–1.5 (0.23-0.68)	1.5–2.5 (0.68-1.1)	2.5-up (Más de 1.1)
234G	**Top Sirloin, Boneless** Aguayón Superior (Top Sirloin), Deshuesado	114	2-down (Menos de 0.90)	2–3 (0.90-1.4)	3–4 (1.4-1.8)	4-up (Más de 1.8)
235	**Back** Espaldar	114	11–12 (5-5.4)	12-14 (5.4-6.4)	14–16 (6.4-7.3)	16–18 (7.3-8.2)
236	**Back, Trimmed** Espaldar, Recortado de Grasa y Limpio	115	8–11 (3.6-5)	11–13 (5-5.9)	13–15 (5.9-6.8)	15-up (Más de 6.8)
238	**Trimmings** Recortes	115	Amount as Specified Cantidad según lo especificado			
239	**Special Trimmings** Recortes Especiales	116	Amount as Specified Cantidad según lo especificado			
245	**Leg, Sirloin, Bone In** Pierna, Aguayón (Sirloin), Con Hueso	116	2-down (Menos de 0.90)	2–3 (0.90-1.4)	3–4 (1.4-1.8)	4-up (Más de 1.8)
246	**Tenderloin** Filete de Cordero	116	0.5-down (Menos de 0.23)	0.5–1.5 (0.23-0.68)	1.5–2.5 (0.68-1.1)	2.5-up (Más de 1.1)
295	**Lamb for Stewing** Trozos de Cordero para Cocido/Guisado	117	Amount as Specified Cantidad según lo especificado			
295A	**Lamb for Kabobs** Trozos de Cordero para Brochetas	117	Amount as Specified Cantidad según lo especificado			
296	**Ground Lamb** Carne Molida de Cordero	118	Amount as Specified Cantidad según lo especificado			

Información para hacer los pedidos

Opciones especificadas por el comprador

Los compradores pueden especificar varias opciones diferentes en los productos que desean comprar. Estas opciones incluyen, entre otras, una combinación del grado de calidad y el grado de rendimiento, el estado de refrigeración, las medidas de limitación de grasa y las instrucciones de procesamiento. Algunas de estas opciones se explican más detalladamente en la sección introductoria al comienzo de la *Guía para Compradores de Carne*, más adelante en esta sección, o en la descripción de la pieza correspondiente. Los compradores que tengan necesidades o especificaciones especiales deben comunicarse con sus proveedores.

Estado de refrigeración

A **FRESCO**	–2.2 °C (28 °F) o mayor
B **CONGELADO**	–2.2 °C (28 °F) o menor
C **OPCIÓN ESPECIFICADA POR EL COMPRADOR**	–17.8 °C (0 °F) o menor

El producto se puede pedir fresco o congelado. El término *refrigerado en estado fresco* es utilizado por el Servicio de Mercadeo Agrícola del Departamento de Agricultura de E.U.A. para describir los productos que no han sido congelados anteriormente.

Grado

El sistema de clasificación del cordero y el carnero en E.U.A. y Canadá se explica en detalle en la sección introductoria al comienzo de la *Guía para Compradores de Carne*. Dentro de las especies ovinas, las canales se clasifican como de cordero, carnero añojo, o carnero, dependiendo de la madurez evidente según lo indique el desarrollo de los sistemas muscular y esquelético. Las canales más jóvenes reciben el nombre de cordero, y este es el producto que se utiliza con mayor frecuencia en la industria de servicios de alimentación. Todos los productos que se presentan en la *Guía para Compradores de Carne* son de cordero.

El comprador puede especificar el grado de calidad y el grado de rendimiento para cualquier pieza. En la mayoría de los casos, debido a la limpieza posterior de los cortes que realizan los proveedores, el grado de rendimiento no aparecerá en el producto. La designación oficial del grado aparecerá de alguna de las siguientes formas o combinación de ellas: (1) etiquetas en el envase, (2) en bolsas individuales o material autoadhesivo para envolver, o (3) impresiones legibles de marca comercial sobre la carne. El procesador cumplirá con los procedimientos de etiquetado de grado de FSIS (Servicio de Inspección e Inocuidad Alimentaria, por sus siglas en inglés) o CFIA (Agencia Canadiense de Inspección de Alimentos, por sus siglas en inglés).

Opciones para limitar la grasa

Canales y Cuartos

El comprador puede especificar el grado de rendimiento y/o el grosor promedio máximo de cubierta de grasa.

Cortes y Trozos Rosbifs

Excepto en las piezas de chamberetes, el comprador especificará uno de los siguientes grosores promedio máximos de cubierta de grasa, a menos que se indiquen limitaciones precisas de grasa en la descripción detallada de la pieza.

Número de opción	Grosor promedio máximo	Máximo en un punto cualquiera
1	19 mm (0.75 pulgadas) con recorte de grasa tipo commodity	2.5 cm (1.0 pulgada)
2	6 mm (0.25 pulgadas)	13 mm (0.50 pulgadas)
3	3 mm (0.125 pulgadas)	6 mm (0.25 pulgadas)
4	Prácticamente libre de grasa (el 75% de la superficie expuesta es carne magra/vetas de grasa intermuscular)	3 mm (0.125 pulgadas)
5	Desprovisto de grasa/Prácticamente desnudo de grasa* [la grasa que queda no debe exceder los 2.5 cm (1.0 pulgada) en la dimensión más larga y/o 3 mm (0.125 pulgadas) de grosor]	3 mm (0.125 pulgadas)
6	Desprovisto de grasa/Prácticamente desnudo de grasa, Membrana superficial retirada** (el 90% de la superficie expuesta es magra)	3 mm (0.125 pulgadas)

*/** – consulte la definición en la página xlv

*** NOTA: cuando se especifiquen los grosores promedio de grasa en la descripción de la pieza, aplicará la limitación "Máximo en un punto cualquiera" correspondiente.**

Chuletas

El comprador especificará uno de las siguientes grosores máximos de cubierta de grasa (en un punto cualquiera) sobre los bordes de la chuleta a menos que se indiquen limitaciones precisas de grasa en la descripción detallada de la pieza. En caso de que no se especifique, el grosor de grasa no excederá los 6 mm (0.25 pulgadas) en ningún punto.

Grosor máximo de grasa en un punto cualquiera del corte de la porción[†]
6 mm (0.25 pulgadas)
3 mm (0.125 pulgadas)
Prácticamente libre de grasa [el 75% de la superficie es carne magra/superficie muscular descubierta por la disección y la grasa que queda no debe exceder los 3 mm (0.125 pulgadas)]
Desprovisto de grasa/Prácticamente desnudo de grasa [la grasa que queda no debe exceder los 2.5 cm (1.0 pulgada) en ninguna dimensión y/o 3 mm (0.125 pulgadas) de grosor]
Desprovisto de grasa/Prácticamente desnudo de grasa, Membrana superficial retirada [el 90% de la superficie expuesta es magra y la grasa que queda no debe exceder los 3 mm (0.125 pulgadas)]

[†] Cuando el comprador especifica los requisitos de recorte de grasa o éstos se especifican en la descripción de la pieza, se deberá quitar toda la membrana dérmica laxa.

Ordering Data

Purchaser Specified Options (PSO)

Purchasers may specify a number of different options on the products they wish to purchase. These options (PSO) include, among others, a combination of quality grade and yield grade, state of refrigeration, fat limitation measurements, and processing instructions. Some of these options are explained in more detail in the Introductory Section at the front of *The Meat Buyer's Guide*, or later in this section, or in the appropriate Item Description. Purchasers who have special needs or specifications should contact their suppliers.

State of Refrigeration

A **FRESH**	28°F (−2.2°C) or higher
B **FROZEN**	28°F (−2.2°C) or lower
C **PSO**	0°F (−17.8°C) or lower

Product may be ordered fresh or frozen. The term *fresh chilled* is used by the USDA Agricultural Marketing Service to describe product that has not been previously frozen.

Grade

The system of lamb and mutton grading in both the U.S. and Canada is explained in detail in the Introductory Section at the front of *The Meat Buyer's Guide*. Carcasses within the ovine species are classified as lamb, yearling mutton, or mutton depending upon their evidences of maturity as indicated by the development of muscular and skeletal systems. The youngest carcasses are called Lamb, and this is the product primarily used in foodservice establishments. All product featured in *The Meat Buyer's Guide* is lamb.

The purchaser may specify the quality and yield grade desired for any item. In most instances, due to further trimming by suppliers, the yield grade will not appear on the product. The official grade designation will appear in any one or any combination of the following ways: (1) container markings, (2) on individual bags or wrapping material, or (3) legible roller brand appearing on the meat. The processor shall comply with FSIS or CFIA grade labeling procedures.

Fat Limitation Options (FLO)

Carcasses and Quarters

The purchaser may specify yield grade and/or maximum average thickness of surface fat.

Cuts and Roasts

Except for shank items, the purchaser shall specify one of the following maximum average thicknesses of surface fat unless definite fat limitations are indicated in the detailed Item Descriptions.

Option No.	Maximum Average Thickness	Maximum at Any One Point
1	0.75 inch (19 mm) "Commodity trim"	1.0 inch (2.5 cm)
2	0.25 inch (6 mm)	0.50 inch (13 mm)
3	0.125 inch (3 mm)	0.25 inch (6 mm)
4	Practically Free (75 percent lean/seam surface exposed)	0.125 inch (3 mm)
5	Peeled/Denuded* (remaining fat shall not exceed 1.0 inch (2.5 cm) in the longest dimension and/or 0.125 inch (3 mm) in thickness)	0.125 inch (3 mm)
6	Peeled/Denuded, Surface Membrane Removed** (90 percent lean exposed)	0.125 inch (3 mm)

*/** − see page xvi for definition

*** NOTE: When average fat thicknesses are specified in Item Descriptions, the appropriate "Maximum at Any One Point" limitation shall apply.**

Chops

The purchaser shall specify one of the following maximum (at any one point) thicknesses of surface fat on the edges of the chop unless definite fat limitations are indicated in the detailed Item Descriptions. If not specified, fat thickness shall not exceed 0.25 inch (6 mm) at any one point.

Maximum Fat Thickness at Any One Point for Portion Cuts†

0.25 inch (6 mm)
0.125 inch (3 mm)
Practically Free (75 percent lean/seam surface exposed and remaining fat shall not exceed 0.125 inch (3 mm))
Peeled/Denuded (remaining fat shall not exceed 1.0 inch (2.5 cm) in any dimension and/or 0.125 inch (3 mm) in thickness)
Peeled/Denuded, Surface Membrane Removed (90 percent lean exposed and remaining fat shall not exceed 0.125 inch (3 mm))

† When fat trim requirements are specified by the purchaser or within the individual Item Description, all fell shall be removed

Cutting Instructions / Instrucciones de corte — Style A / Estilo A

Separation A — Style A / Separación A — Estilo A
Shoulder-Bracelet Separation / Separación Espaldilla-Brazalete

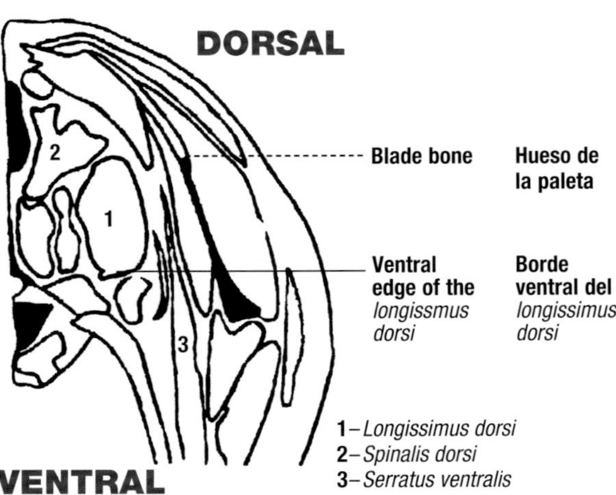

The shoulder is separated from the bracelet by a straight cut between the 4th and 5th ribs, leaving 4 ribs on the shoulder. The cut surface (see figure) shall expose the *spinalis dorsi* to be dorsal in relationship to the *longissimus dorsi*.

La espaldilla se separa del brazalete mediante un corte recto entre la 4ª y la 5ª costilla, dejando 4 costillas en la espaldilla. La superficie de corte (ver figura) debe exponer el *spinalis dorsi* dorsal en relación con el *longissimus dorsi*.

Separation B — Style A / Separación B — Estilo A
Bracelet-Loin Separation / Separación Brazalete-Lomo

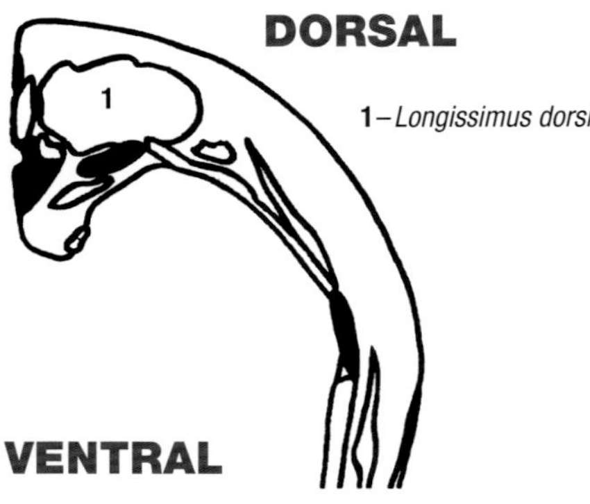

The bracelet is separated from the loin by a cut that follows the natural curvature between the 12th and 13th ribs. Leaving 8 ribs (ribs 5–12) with the bracelet and no more than 1 rib remaining with the loin.

El brazalete se separa del lomo mediante un corte que siga la curvatura natural del costillar entre la 12ª y 13ª costilla. Se dejan 8 costillas (costillas 5-12) con el brazalete y no más de una costilla con el lomo.

Separation C — Style A / Separación C — Estilo A
Loin-Leg Separation / Separación Lomo-Pierna

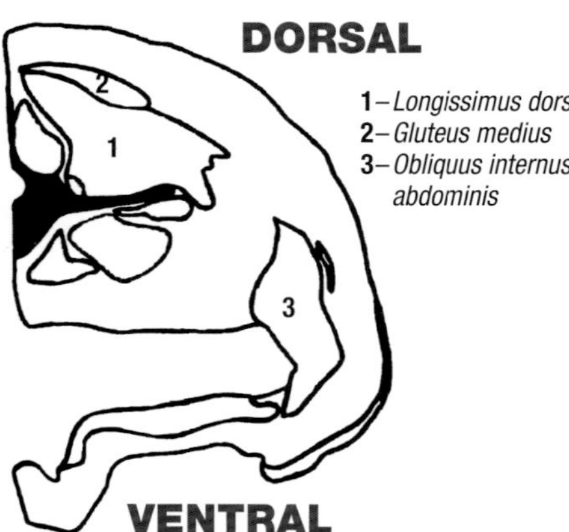

The leg is separated from the loin by a straight cut, approximately perpendicular to the length of the leg, passing anterior to the hip bone and hip bone cartilage. The cut surface, which is approximately perpendicular to the length of the leg, exposes the *gluteus medius* and does not expose the *tensor fasciae latae* (see figure).

La pierna se separa del lomo mediante un corte recto, aproximadamente perpendicular al largo de la pierna, pasando delante del hueso y cartílago de la cadera. La superficie del corte, que es aproximadamente perpendicular al largo de la pierna, expone el *gluteus medius* y no expone el tensor de la fascia lata (ver figura).

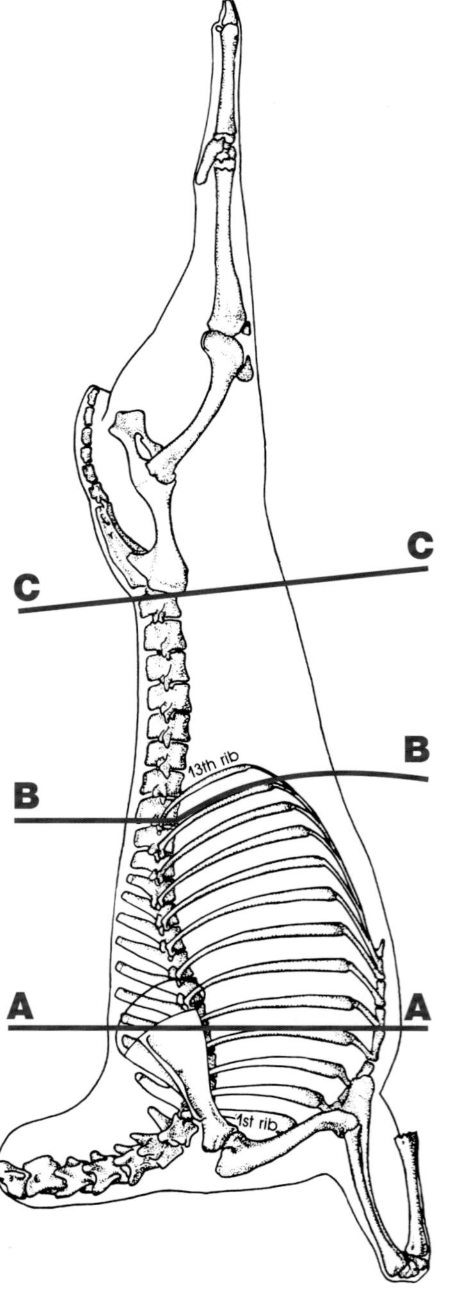

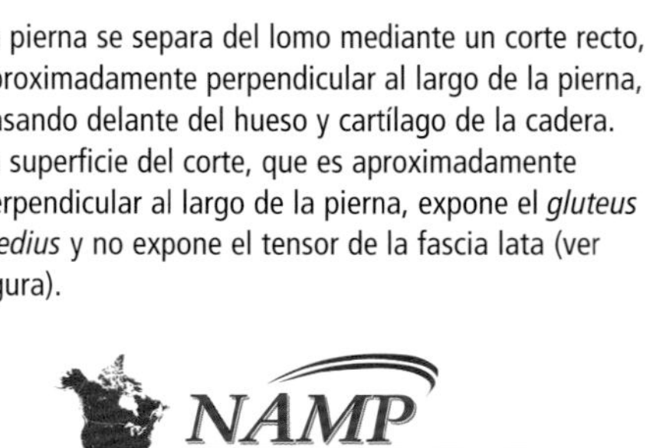

Cutting Instructions — Style B
Instrucciones de corte — Estilo B

Separation A — Style B / Separación A — Estilo B
Shoulder-Bracelet Separation / Separación Espaldilla-Brazalete

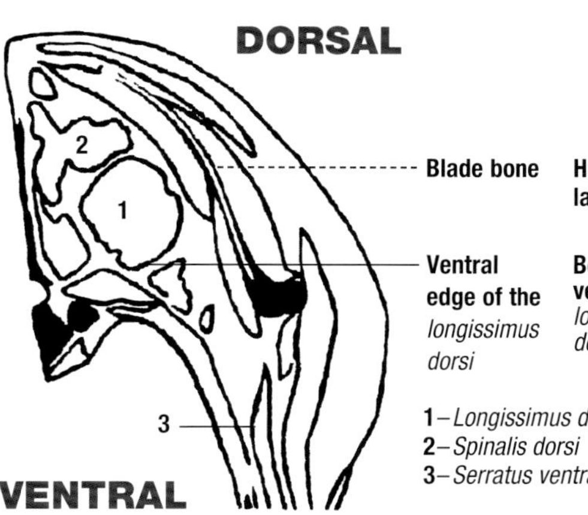

The shoulder is separated from the bracelet by a straight cut between the 5th and 6th ribs, leaving 5 ribs on the shoulder. The cut surface (see figure) shall expose the *spinalis dorsi* to be dorsal in relationship to the *longissimus dorsi*, and the *serratus ventralis* shall not extend past (dorsal to) the ventral edge of the *longissimus dorsi*.

La espaldilla se separa del "brazalete" constituido por espaldar-costilla mediante un corte recto entre la 5ª y la 6ª costilla, y se dejan 5 costillas en la espaldilla. La superficie del corte (ver figura) debe exponer al *spinalis dorsi* dorsal en relación con el *longissimus dorsi*, y el *serratus ventralis* no debe extenderse más allá del (dorsal al) borde ventral del *longissimus dorsi*.

Separation B — Style B / Separación B — Estilo B
Bracelet-Loin Separation / Separación Brazalete-Lomo

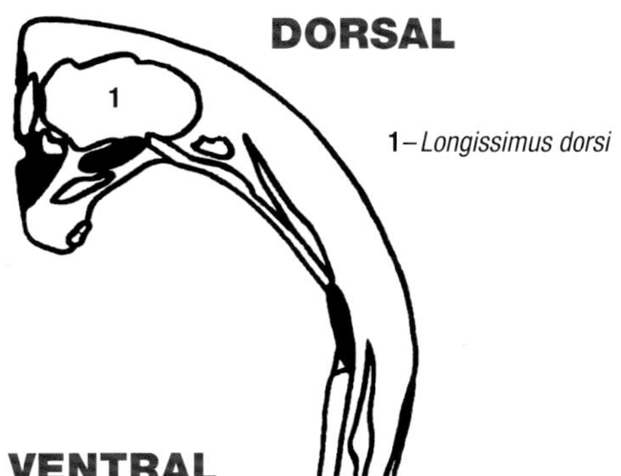

The bracelet is separated from the loin by a cut that follows the natural curvature posterior to the 13th rib. Leaving 8 ribs (ribs 6–13) with the bracelet and no rib remaining with the loin.

El brazalete espaldar-costillar se separa del lomo mediante un corte que siga la curvatura natural posterior a la 13ª costilla. Se dejan 8 costillas (costillas 6-13) con el brazalete y ninguna costilla se deja con el lomo.

Separation C — Style B / Separación C — Estilo B
Loin-Leg Separation / Separación Lomo-Pierna

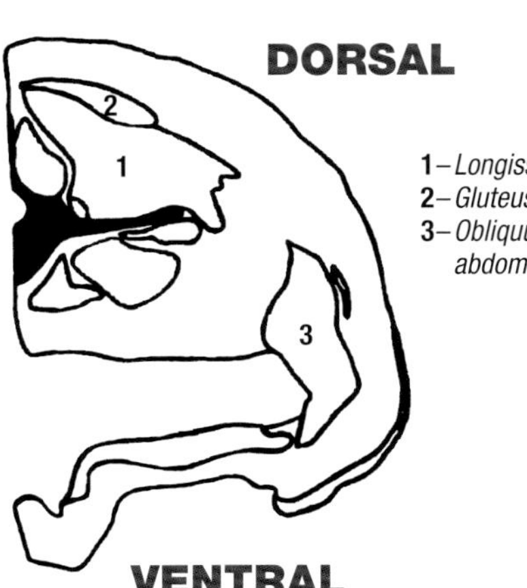

The leg is separated from the loin by a straight cut, approximately perpendicular to the length of the leg, passing anterior to the hip bone and hip bone cartilage. The cut surface, which is approximately perpendicular to the length of the leg, exposes the *gluteus medius* and does not expose the *tensor fasciae latae* (see figure).

La pierna se separa del lomo mediante un corte recto, aproximadamente perpendicular a lo largo de la pierna, pasando al frente del hueso y cartílago de la cadera. La superficie del corte, que es aproximadamente perpendicular al largo de la pierna, expone el *gluteus medius* y no expone el tensor de la fascia lata (ver figura).

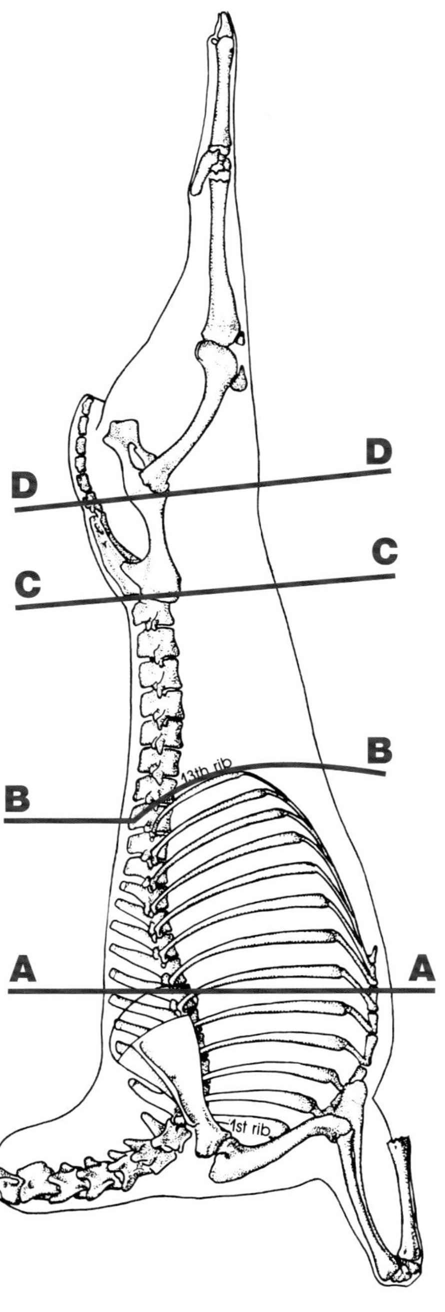

Cutting Instructions — Style B
Instrucciones de corte — Estilo B

Separation D — Style B / Separación D — Estilo B
Sirloin-Leg Separation / Separación Sirloin-Pierna

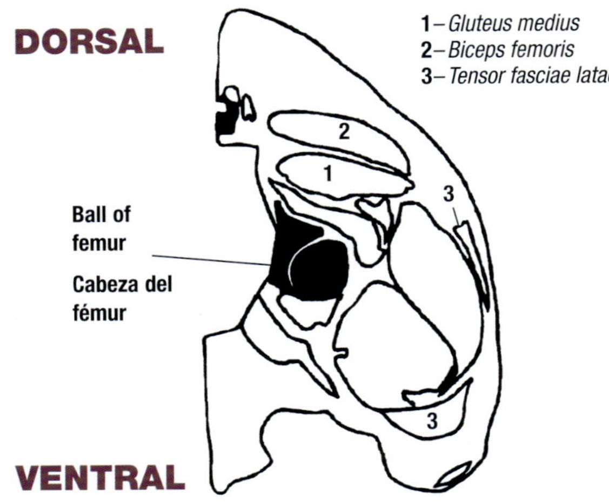

The leg is separated from the sirloin by a straight cut: (1) approximately perpendicular to the length of the leg; (2) starting at the juncture of the last sacral and first caudal vertebra and (3) passing anterior to the protuberance of the femur (while exposing the ball of the femur). The cut surface (see figure) shall expose: (1) the *gluteus medius* to be approximately equal in size to the *biceps femoris* and (2) the *tensor fasciae latae* shall be exposed and shall not extend around the knuckle.

Cutting styles for lamb vary slightly in Canada from the styles described here.

In accordance with the CFIA Meat Cuts Manual, the forequarter (front half) is separated from the hindquarter (hind half) between the 11th and 12th ribs.

In addition, the shoulder (front) is separated from the bracelet (whole loin and flank) between the 6th and 7th ribs.

La pierna se separa del sirloin mediante un corte recto: (1) aproximadamente perpendicular al largo de la pierna; (2) comenzando en la unión de la última vértebra sacra con la primera vértebra caudal y (3) pasando por delante de la protuberancia del fémur (exponiendo la cabeza del fémur). La superficie de corte (ver figura) debe exponer: (1) el *gluteus medius* aproximadamente del mismo tamaño que el *biceps femoris* y (2) el tensor de la fascia lata debe quedar expuesto y no prolongarse en la pulpa bola.

Los estilos de corte del cordero en Canadá tienen pequeñas variaciones con respecto a los estilos que se describen aquí.

De acuerdo al Manual de Cortes de Carne de la Agencia Canadiense de Inspección de Alimentos el cuarto delantero (mitad delantera) se separa del cuarto trasero (mitad trasera) entre la 11ª y la 12ª costilla.

Además, la espaldilla (delantera) se separa del brazalete (lomo y falda enteros) entre la 6ª y la 7ª costilla.

200 — Lamb Carcass

A lamb, yearling mutton, or mutton carcass is the entire unsplit carcass. Bloody tissue, frayed ends at the neck, and practically all heart fat shall be removed. The diaphragm and the hanging tender may be removed. However, if present, the membranous portion shall be trimmed close to the lean.

200 — Cordero, Canal

La canal de cordero, carnero añojo o carnero quedará entera sin dividir. Se deberán eliminar los tejidos sanguíneos, los extremos desflecados en el pescuezo y prácticamente toda la grasa del corazón. También se puede quitar el diafragma y la arrachera gallo (pilares o arrachera colgante). Sin embargo, si se conserva, la porción membranosa deberá despellejarse hasta descubrir la carne magra.

200A — Lamb Carcass, 3-Way

This item is as described in Item No. 200, except the carcass is separated into 3 portions. The portions are a double shoulder, back, and leg. All 3 double portions are packaged together. The carcass separation is made according to Style A, unless Style B is specified.

200A — Cordero, Canal, en 3 Piezas

Esta pieza es igual a la pieza número 200, excepto que la canal se separa en 3 porciones. Las porciones son espaldilla, espaldar y pierna, todas dobles. Las 3 porciones dobles se empacan juntas. La separación de la canal se realiza de acuerdo con el Estilo A, a menos que se especifique que se realice según el Estilo B.

200B — Lamb Carcass, Block-Ready

This item is as described in Item No. 200, except, unless otherwise specified, the carcass is separated into single portions. The portions are square-cut shoulders, racks, loins, foreshanks, breasts, and legs. The individual single portions are packaged together. The foreshank separation from the brisket end of the breast is made through the natural seam by a cut that passes through the web *(pectorales superficialis)*. The trotter or lower foreshank shall be removed at the knee joint. The hanging tender and kidneys are to be excluded. The carcass separation is made according to Style A, unless Style B is specified.

200B — Cordero, Canal, Listo para Tablajear

Esta pieza es igual a la pieza número 200, excepto que, a menos que se especifique lo contrario, la canal se divide en porciones individuales. Las porciones son espaldillas de corte cuadrado, costillares, lomos, chamberetes de mano, pechos y piernas. Las porciones individuales se empacan juntas. La separación del chamberete de mano del extremo del pecho se realiza a través de la veta natural mediante un corte que pasa a través del tejido muscular *(pectorales superficialis)*. El jarrete o extremo inferior del chamberete delantero deberá quitarse en la articulación del codillo. También se deben quitar los riñones y la arrachera gallo (pilares o arrachera colgante). La separación de la canal se realiza de acuerdo con el Estilo A, a menos que se especifique que se realice según el Estilo B.

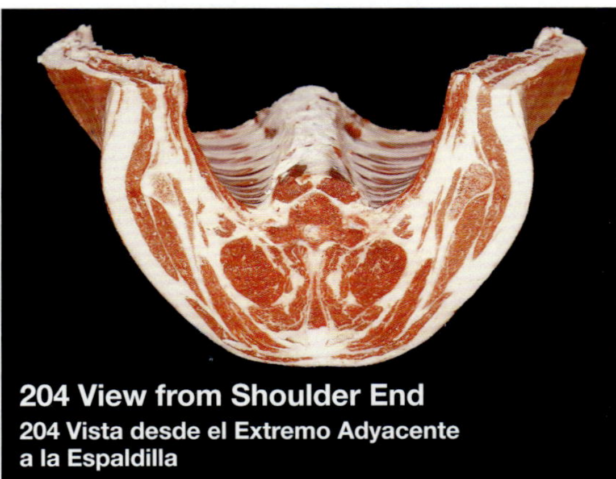

204 View from Shoulder End
204 Vista desde el Extremo Adyacente a la Espaldilla

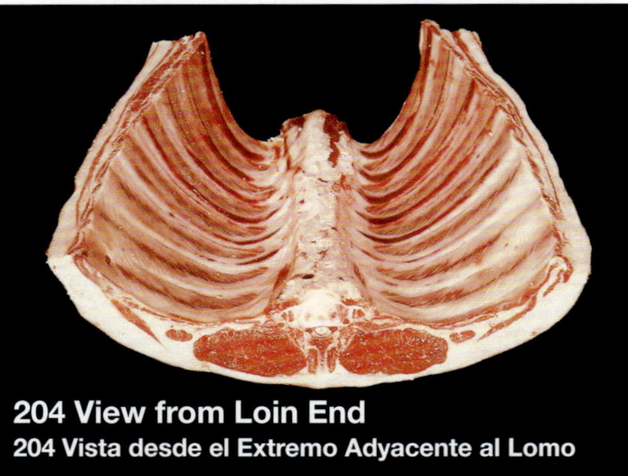

204 View from Loin End
204 Vista desde el Extremo Adyacente al Lomo

204 Lamb Rack, Single
204 Costillar de Cordero, Individual

204 — Lamb Rack

The rib rack is the portion remaining after the removal of the shoulder, breast, and loin portions of the carcass, and contains 8 ribs. The loin is removed as in Style A unless Style B is specified. The breast is removed by a straight cut no more than 4 inches (10.0 cm) from the ventral edge of the *longissimus dorsi* (ribeye) muscle. The diaphragm and fat along the ventral side of the vertebrae shall be removed. Unless otherwise specified, the rack is often packaged split.

204 — Cordero, Costillar

El costillar es la porción que queda luego de que se quitan de la canal las porciones de espaldilla, pecho y lomo, y contiene 8 costillas. El lomo se quita según el Estilo A, a menos que se especifique que se debe realizar según el Estilo B. El pecho se quita mediante un corte recto a no más de 10.0 cm (4 pulgadas) del borde ventral del músculo *longissimus dorsi* (ribeye). También se debe quitar el diafragma y la grasa a lo largo del lado ventral de las vértebras. A menos que se especifique lo contrario, el costillar generalmente se empaca dividido.

204A

204A — Lamb Rack, Chined

This item is prepared from a split rack as described in Item No. 204. The chine bone or protruding edge of the vertebrae shall be removed such that the lean is exposed between the ribs and the feather bones, leaving the feather bones attached. The blade bone and associated cartilage and fell membrane shall also be excluded.

PSO: 1 – Purchaser may specify a ½ rack (4 rib rack) for this item.

204A — Costillar de Cordero, con Espinazo Rebajado

Esta pieza se prepara con un costillar dividido tal como se describe en la pieza número 204. Las puntas del espinazo o los bordes sobresalientes de los cuerpos vertebrales deberán quitarse de forma que la carne magra quede expuesta entre las costillas y las puntas del espinazo, dejando las puntas del espinazo anexas. También se deberá quitar el hueso de la paleta y el cartílago asociado así como la membrana dérmica laxa.

PSO: 1 – El comprador puede especificar un ½ costillar (costillar de 4 costillas) para esta pieza.

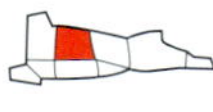 

204B — Lamb Rack, Roast-Ready

The term *Block-Ready* is used interchangeably with *Roast-Ready* in describing this item.

This item, as described in Item No. 204A, is further prepared by removing the feather bones, exterior fat cover, back strap, blade bone and overlying muscles (*trapezius*, *infraspinatus*, and *latissumis dorsi*), making the item partially cap off. The measurement from the ventral edge of the *longissimus dorsi* to the point at which the breast is removed shall be no more than 4 inches (10.0 cm). The purchaser may specify a different tail length option, or PSO, as described below:

PSO: 1 – 3.0 inches (7.5 cm)

2 – 2.0 inches (5 cm)

3 – 1.0 inch (2.5 cm)

4 – 0.0 inch

5 – Purchaser may specify a ½ rack (4 rib rack) for this item.

6 – In addition, the *rhomboideus* and *subscapularis* muscles below the blade bone shall be removed, making the item cap off.

204B — Costillar de Cordero, Listo para Rostizar

El término *Listo para Tablajear* se utiliza de forma indistinta con el término *Listo para Rostizar* en la descripción de esta pieza.

Esta pieza es igual a la pieza número 204A, pero se prepara posteriormente quitando las puntas del espinazo, la cubierta de grasa exterior, la banda ligamentosa nucal, el hueso de la paleta y los músculos que lo recubren (*trapezius*, *infraspinatus* y *latissumis dorsi*), haciendo que la pieza quede parcialmente sin tapa. La medida desde el borde ventral del *longissimus dorsi* hasta el punto en que se quita el pecho no debe exceder los 10 cm (4 pulgadas). El comprador puede especificar una medida diferente para la longitud de la cola, o PSO, tal como se describe a continuación:

PSO: 1 – 7.5 cm (3.0 pulgadas)

2 – 5 cm (2.0 pulgadas)

3 – 2.5 cm (1.0 pulgada)

4 – 0.0 cm

5 – El comprador puede especificar un ½ costillar (costillar de 4 costillas) para esta pieza.

6 – Además, se deberán quitar los músculos *rhomboideus* y *subscapularis* que se encuentran debajo del hueso de la paleta, haciendo que la pieza quede sin tapa.

204C — Lamb Rack, Roast-Ready, Frenched

The term *Block-Ready* is used interchangeably with *Roast-Ready* in describing this item.

This item as described in Item No. 204B is further prepared by removing the intercostal meat and lean and fat over the rib bones. Neither the exposed rib bone (Frenched) nor remaining intercostal meat, lean, and fat over the rib bones shall exceed 2 inches (5.0 cm) in length.

PSO: 1 – The length from the ventral edge of the *longissimus dorsi* to the point at which the breast is removed shall be no more than 3 inches (7.5 cm), and neither the exposed rib bone nor remaining intercostal meat, lean, and fat over the rib bones shall exceed 1.5 inches (3.8 cm) in length.

2 – Purchaser may specify a ½ rack (4 rib rack) for this item.

3 – The intercostal meat and lean and fat over the rib bones shall be removed (Frenched) to the base of the loin eye.

204C — Costillar de Cordero, Listo para Rostizar, Estilo Francés

El término *Listo para Tablajear* se utiliza de forma indistinta con el término *Listo para Rostizar* en la descripción de esta pieza.

Como se describe en el número 204B, esta pieza se prepara quitando la carne intercostal, así como la grasa y la carne magra que se encuentra sobre las costillas. Ni la costilla expuesta (al estilo francés) ni la carne intercostal, grasa o carne magra sobre las costillas debe exceder los 5.0 cm (2 pulgadas) de longitud.

PSO: 1 – La distancia desde el borde ventral del *longissimus dorsi* hasta el punto en donde se quita el pecho no debe exceder los 7.5 cm (3 pulgadas), y ninguna de las costillas expuestas ni la carne intercostal, grasa o carne magra sobre las costillas deben exceder los 3.8 cm (1.5 pulgadas) de longitud.

2 – El comprador puede especificar un ½ costillar (costillar de 4 costillas) para esta pieza.

3 – Se deberá quitar la carne intercostal, así como la grasa y la carne magra sobre las costillas (estilo francés) hasta la base del ojo del lomo.

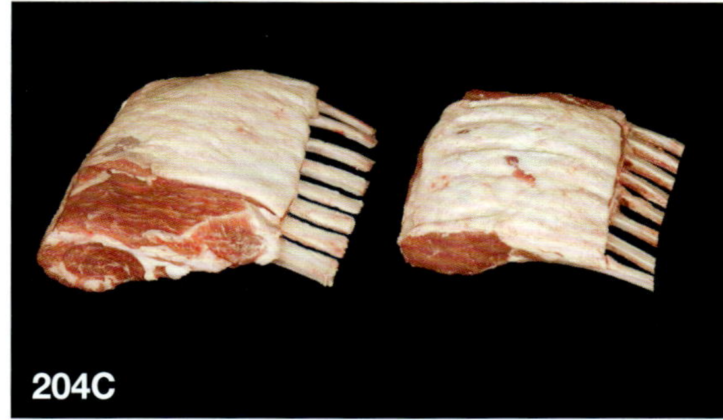

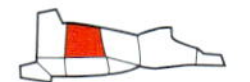 

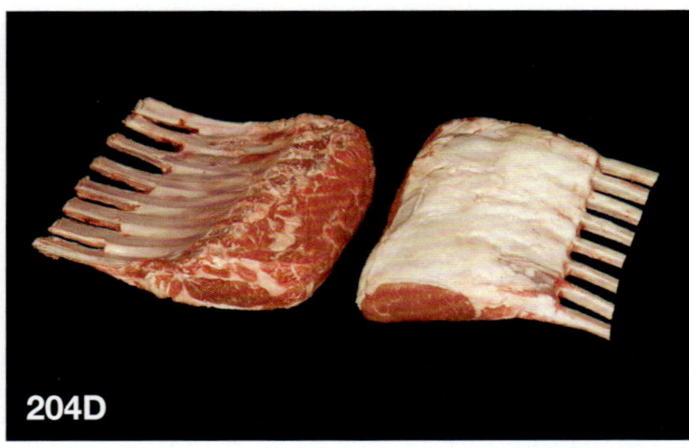

204D

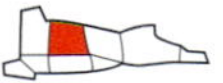

204D — Lamb Rack, Roast-Ready, Frenched, Special (Cap Off)

The term *Block-Ready* is used interchangeably with *Roast-Ready* in describing this item.

This item is as described in Item 204C except in addition, the firmly attached *rhomboideus* and *subscapularis* muscles below where the blade bone had been removed shall also be excluded.

PSO: 1 – The length from the ventral edge of the *longissimus dorsi* to the point at which the breast is removed shall be no more than 3 inches (7.5 cm), and neither the exposed rib bone nor remaining intercostal meat, lean, and fat over the rib bones shall exceed 1.5 inches (3.8 cm) in length.

2 – Purchaser may specify a ½ rack (4 rib rack) for this item.

3 – The intercostal meat and lean and fat over the rib bones shall be removed (Frenched) to the base of the loin eye.

204D — Costillar de Cordero, Listo para Rostizar, Estilo Francés, Especial (sin Tapa)

El término *Listo para Tablajear* se utiliza de forma indistinta con el término *Listo para Rostizar* en la descripción de esta pieza.

Esta pieza es igual a la pieza 204C excepto que además se deberán retirar también los músculos *rhomboideus* y *subscapularis* que se encuentran firmemente adheridos debajo del lugar donde se quitó el hueso de la paleta.

PSO: 1 – La distancia desde el borde ventral del *longissimus dorsi* hasta el punto en donde se quita el pecho no debe exceder los 7.5 cm (3 pulgadas), y ninguna de las costillas expuestas ni la carne intercostal, grasa o carne magra sobre las costillas deben exceder los 3.8 cm (1.5 pulgadas) de longitud.

2 – El comprador puede especificar un ½ costillar (costillar de 4 costillas) para esta pieza.

3 – Se deberá quitar la carne intercostal, y la grasa y la carne magra sobre las costillas (estilo francés) hasta la base del ojo del lomo.

206 — Lamb Shoulder

All shoulders are available either as Style A: 4 Ribs (ribs 1 to 4) or Style B: 5 Ribs (ribs 1 to 5). Unless otherwise specified, the carcass separation is made according to Style A.

The thymus gland (sweetbread) and heart fat shall be closely removed. Purchaser may specify either a single or double shoulder.

206 — Paleta (Espaldilla) de Cordero

Todas las espaldillas están disponibles en Estilo A: 4 costillas (costillas 1 a la 4) o Estilo B: 5 costillas (costillas 1 a la 5). A menos que se especifique lo contrario, la separación de la canal se realizará de acuerdo al Estilo A.

La glándula del timo (molleja) y la grasa del corazón deberán quitarse cuidadosamente. El comprador puede especificar si desea una espaldilla individual o doble.

207

207 — Lamb Shoulder, Square-Cut

In addition to the requirements of Item No. 206, the foreshank and brisket portion of the breast, as well as the neck, shall be removed by a straight cut approximately perpendicular to the rack side. The cut through the foreshank and brisket shall pass through the cartilaginous juncture of the first rib, and the cut removing the neck shall not leave more than 1.0 inch (2.5 cm) of neck on the shoulder. Purchaser may specify either a single or double shoulder.

207 — Paleta (Espaldilla) de Cordero, Corte Cuadrado

Además de los requisitos de la pieza número 206, el chamberete de mano y la porción de pecho, así como el pescuezo, deben quitarse mediante un corte recto, aproximadamente perpendicular al lado del costillar. El corte a través del chamberete de mano y del pecho debe pasar a través de la coyuntura cartilaginosa de la primera costilla, y el corte para quitar el pescuezo no debe dejar más de 2.5 cm (1.0 pulgada) del pescuezo sobre la espaldilla. El comprador puede especificar si desea una espaldilla individual o doble.

208 — Lamb Shoulder, Square-Cut, Boneless

This item is further prepared from a single Item No. 207 Shoulder by excluding all bones, cartilages, backstrap, fell, prescapular lymph gland, and heart fat. The brisket side shall expose the *pectoralis profundus* extending posterior to the 3rd rib mark and form an approximate right angle with the rib end. The shoulder shall be rolled with the ribeye lengthwise to the roll and netted or tied.

208 — Paleta (Espaldilla) de Cordero, Corte Cuadrado, Deshuesada

Esta pieza se prepara a partir de una pieza única, la número 207, Espaldilla, quitando todos los huesos, cartílagos, banda ligamentosa nucal, membrana dérmica laxa, ganglios linfáticos prescapulares y grasa del corazón. El lado adyacente al pecho debe mostrar el músculo *pectoralis profundus* que se extiende por detrás de la marca de la 3ª costilla y forman un ángulo aproximadamente recto con el extremo adyacente al espaldar. La espaldilla debe enrollarse con el ribeye a lo largo del rollo y atarse o amarrarse con una red.

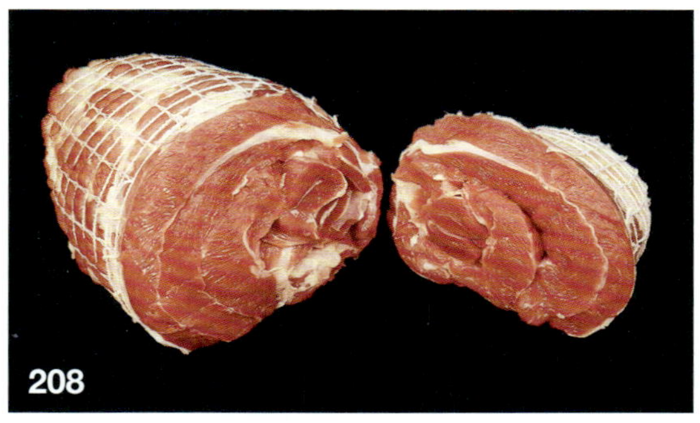

208D — Lamb Shoulder, Pectoral Meat

This item will consist of the *pectoralis profundis* muscle that is removed from any boneless shoulder item.

208D — Paleta (Espaldilla) de Cordero, Carne del Pectoral

Esta pieza consistirá en el músculo *pectoralis profundis* que se retira de cualquier pieza de la espaldilla sin hueso.

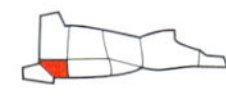

209 — Lamb Breast

This item is that portion of the carcass ventral to the separation of the Item No. 204 Rack and posterior to the separation of the Item No. 206 Shoulder. The diaphragm may be removed. However, if present, the membranous portion of the diaphragm shall be trimmed close to the lean. The heart fat shall be closely removed.

209 — Cordero, Pecho

Esta pieza es la porción de la canal ventral a la separación de la pieza número 204, Costillar, y posterior a la separación de la pieza número 206, Espaldilla. También puede quitarse el diafragma. Sin embargo, si se conserva, la porción membranosa del diafragma deberá despellejarse hasta descubrir la carne magra. La grasa del corazón deberá quitarse cuidadosamente.

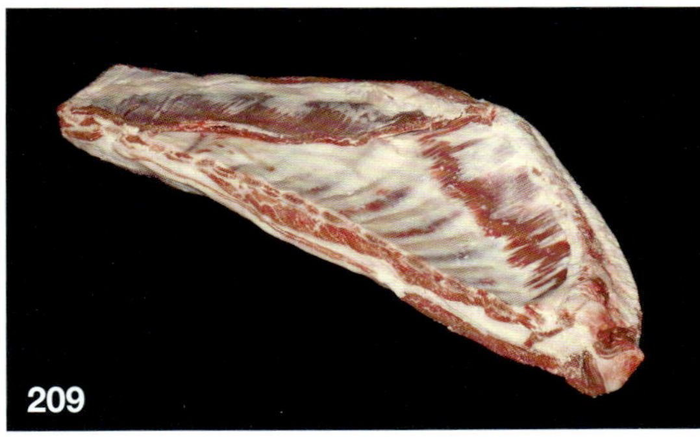

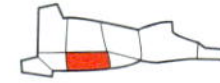

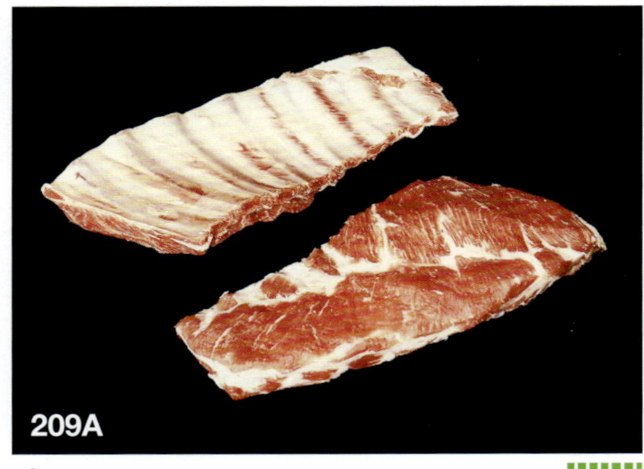

209A

Lamb Ribs, Breast Bones Off

This item is prepared from Item No. 209 and shall consist of at least 7 ribs, and the intercostal muscles, *serratus ventralis,* and associated muscles immediately overlying the ribs. The cut shall be not less than 3.0 inches (7.5 cm) in width. The sternum and ventral edges of the costal cartilages shall be removed. The fell, *cutaneous trunci,* exterior fat cover, *latissimus dorsi,* and diaphragm shall be removed. This item shall be trimmed practically free of surface fat. This item is sometimes referred to as "Denver Style Ribs."

PSO: 1 – Notched/Split: When specified, notching of lamb ribs shall be accomplished by making saw cuts across the ribs at 1.0 inch (2.5 cm) intervals. The saw cuts shall pass through the rib bones and intercostal meat while leaving the lean (*serratus ventralis*) intact.

2 – Special/Frenched: When specified, the ribs shall be frenched. Prior to frenching the costal cartilages shall be removed by a straight cut parallel with the dorsal edge. The ribs will then be frenched by detaching the *serratus ventralis* and removing the intercostal meat from the rib bones for a distance of 2 inches (5 cm) from the ventral (sternum/costal cartilage) side. The *serratus ventralis* shall be rolled and tied to the dorsal edge.

209A

Costillas de Cordero, Sin Hueso del Pecho

Esta pieza se prepara con la pieza número 209 y consistirá en al menos 7 costillas y los músculos intercostales, el *serratus ventralis,* y otros músculos asociados que recubren inmediatamente las costillas. El corte deberá tener al menos 7.5 cm (3.0 pulgadas) de grosor. Se deberá quitar el esternón y los bordes ventrales de los cartílagos costales. Se deberá quitar la piel, el *cutaneous trunci* (suadero), la cobertura de grasa exterior, el *latissimus dorsi,* y el diafragma. La pieza debe recortarse y limpiarse para que quede prácticamente libre de cobertura de grasa. En ocasiones a esta pieza también se le llama "Costillas Denver".

PSO: 1 – Corte de muesca/División: cuando se especifique, el corte de muesca de las costillas de cordero debe realizarse con cortes de sierra a través de las costillas, a intervalos de 2.5 cm (1.0 pulgadas). Los cortes de sierra deberán pasar a través de los huesos de las costillas y la carne intercostal, dejando la carne magra (*serratus ventralis*) intacta.

2 – Especial/Estilo Francés: cuando así se especifique, las costillas deben prepararse al estilo francés. Antes de preparar las costillas al estilo francés, se deberán retirar los cartílagos costales mediante un corte recto y paralelo al borde dorsal. Luego se prepararán las costillas al estilo francés separando el *serratus ventralis* y quitando la carne intercostal de las costillas a una distancia de 5 cm (2 pulgadas) del lado ventral (esternón/cartílago costal). El *serratus ventralis* deberá enrollarse y amarrarse al borde dorsal.

209B — Lamb Shoulder, Ribs

This item may be derived from any bone in, square-cut shoulder item and shall include at least 4 ribs and the *intercostal* and *serratus ventralis* muscles. The item shall be trimmed practically free of surface fat. The dorsal edge shall have no evidence of the cartilaginous junctures of the ribs and thoracic vertebrae.

PSO: 1 – Notched/Split: When specified, notching of lamb ribs shall be accomplished by making saw cuts across the ribs at 1.0 inch (2.5 cm) intervals. The saw cuts shall pass through the rib bones and intercostal meat while leaving the lean (*serratus ventralis*) intact.

2 – Special/Frenched: When specified, the ribs shall be frenched. Prior to frenching the costal cartilages shall be removed by a straight cut parallel with the dorsal edge. The ribs will then be frenched by detaching the *serratus ventralis* and removing the intercostal meat from the rib bones for a distance of 2 inches (5 cm) from the ventral (sternum/costal cartilage) side. The *serratus ventralis* shall be rolled and tied to the dorsal edge.

209B — Paleta (Espaldilla) de Cordero, Costillas

Esta pieza puede prepararse con cualquier pieza de espaldilla de corte cuadrado con hueso y debe incluir 4 costillas y los músculos *intercostal* y *serratus ventralis*. La pieza debe recortarse y limpiarse para que quede prácticamente libre de cobertura de grasa. En el borde dorsal no deben quedar rastros de las coyunturas cartilaginosas de las costillas ni de las vértebras torácicas.

PSO: 1 – Corte de muesca/División: cuando se especifique, el corte de muesca de las costillas de cordero debe realizarse con cortes de sierra a través de las costillas, en intervalos de 2.5 cm (1.0 pulgadas). Los cortes de sierra deberán pasar a través de los huesos de las costillas y la carne intercostal, dejando la carne magra (*serratus ventralis*) intacta.

2 – Especial/Estilo Francés: cuando así se especifique, las costillas deben prepararse al estilo francés. Antes de preparar las costillas al estilo francés, se deberán retirar los cartílagos costales mediante un corte recto y paralelo al borde dorsal. Luego se prepararán las costillas al estilo francés separando el *serratus ventralis* y quitando la carne intercostal de los huesos de las costillas a una distancia de 5 cm (2 pulgadas) del lado ventral (esternón/cartílago costal). El *serratus ventralis* deberá enrollarse y amarrarse al borde dorsal.

209B

210 — Lamb Foreshank

The foreshank shall be removed from the shoulder by a straight cut exposing the humerus and removed from the brisket by a cut through the natural seam and may contain a portion of the web muscle (*pectoralis superficialis*). The trotter or lower foreshank shall be removed at or above the knee joint.

210 — Cordero, Chamberete de Mano

El chamberete de mano debe separarse de la espaldilla mediante un corte recto que deje el húmero expuesto, y separarse del pecho mediante un corte a través de la veta natural, y puede contener una porción de tejido muscular (*pectoralis superficialis*). El jarrete o extremo inferior del chamberete delantero deberá quitarse en la articulación del codillo o por encima de ella.

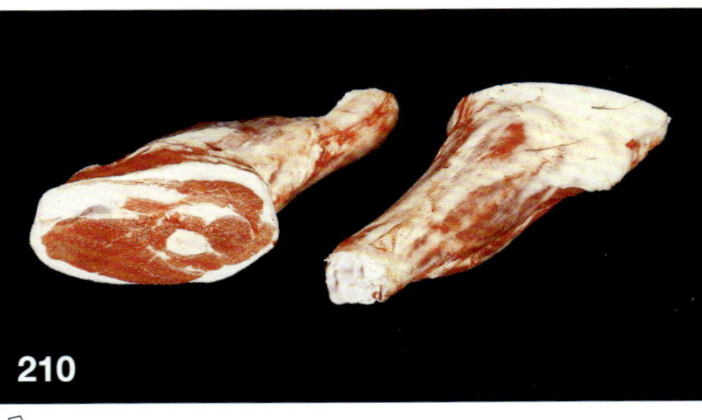

210

229A — Lamb Hindsaddle, Long-Cut, Trimmed

This item is prepared from Item No. 200, and the carcass separation is made according to Style A, containing 9 ribs, unless Style B, containing 8 ribs is specified. The breasts and the flanks are removed by straight cuts ventral to, but no more than 4.0 inches (10.0 cm) from, the *longissimus dorsi* at the shoulder end, to a point that is immediately ventral to the *tensor fasciae latae* on the leg.

229A — Cordero, Cuarto Trasero en Silla de Montar, Trasero Largo (8-9 costillas), Recortado de Grasa y Limpio

Esta pieza se prepara con la pieza número 200 y la separación de la canal se realiza según el Estilo A, incluyendo 9 costillas, a menos que se especifique que se realice según el Estilo B, incluyendo 8 costillas. Los pechos y las faldas se retiran mediante cortes rectos ventrales al *longissimus dorsi*, pero a no más de 10.0 cm (4.0 pulgadas) del mismo en el extremo adyacente a la espaldilla, hasta un punto que se encuentre inmediatamente ventral al tensor de la fascia lata en la pierna.

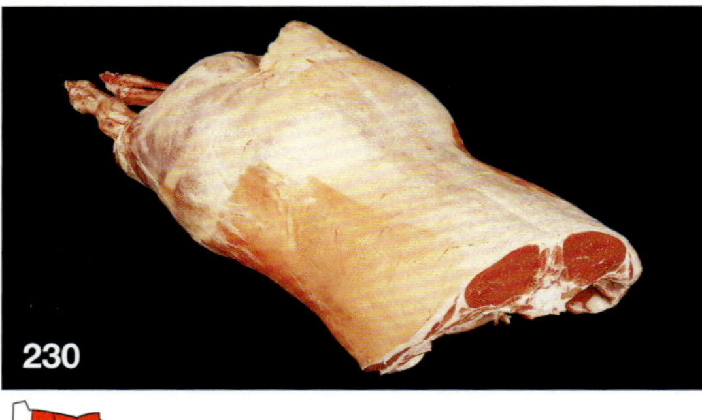

230

230 — Lamb Hindsaddle

This item is prepared from Item No. 200, and the carcass separation is made according to Style A, containing 1 rib, unless Style B, without a rib is specified. The separation follows the natural curvature of the 13th rib bone either posterior or anterior to it depending on the style. The item shall be practically free of all kidney and pelvic fat. The diaphragm and the hanging tender may be excluded. If present, however, the membranous portion of the diaphragm shall be trimmed close to the lean.

230 — Cordero, Cuarto Trasero en Silla de Montar

Esta pieza se prepara con la pieza número 200, y la separación de la canal se realiza según el Estilo A, con una costilla, a menos que se especifique que se realice según el Estilo B, sin costilla. La separación sigue la curvatura natural de la 13ª costilla, ya sea anterior o posterior a ella, dependiendo del estilo. La pieza debe encontrarse prácticamente libre de grasa pélvica y de riñonada. El diafragma y la arrachera gallo (pilares o arrachera colgante del lomo) pueden quitarse. Sin embargo, si se conserva, la porción membranosa del diafragma deberá despellejarse hasta descubrir la carne magra.

231 View from Rack End
231 Vista desde el Extremo del Costillar

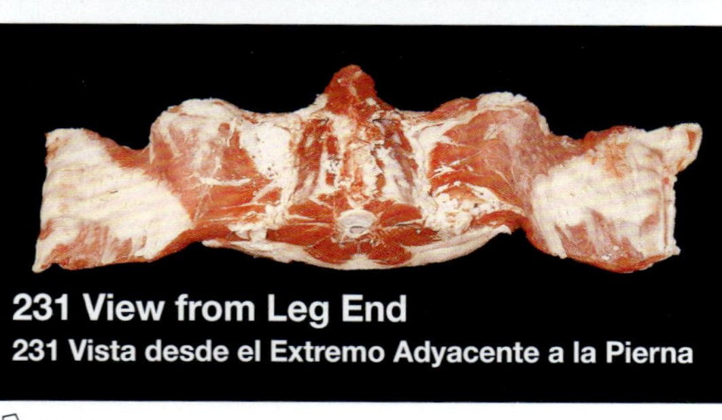

231 View from Leg End
231 Vista desde el Extremo Adyacente a la Pierna

231 — Lamb Loins, Saddle

This item is prepared from Item No. 230. The legs shall be removed at separation point "C" depicted on the Cutting Instruction Charts for Styles A and B. This item shall be practically free of all kidney and lumbar fat.

231 — Lomos de Cordero

Esta pieza se prepara con la pieza número 230. Las piernas deben retirarse en el punto "C" representado en las gráficas de instrucciones de corte para los Estilos A y B. Esta pieza debe encontrarse prácticamente libre de grasa pélvica y de riñonada.

232 — Lamb Loins, Saddle, Trimmed

This item is prepared from Item No. 231. The flank is removed by a straight cut that is not more than 4.0 inches (10.0 cm) from the *longissimus dorsi,* both at the rack end and at a point on the leg side that also is not more than 4.0 inches (10.0 cm) ventral from it. The diaphragm, hanging tender, and kidneys shall be excluded.

232 — Lomos de Cordero, Recortados de Grasa y Limpios

Esta pieza se prepara con la pieza número 231. La falda se quita mediante un corte recto que no supera 10.0 cm (4.0 pulgadas) desde el músculo *longissimus dorsi,* tanto en el extremo adyacente al espaldar como en un punto del lado adyacente a la pierna que tampoco sobrepasa los 10.0 cm (4.0 pulgadas) debajo de este músculo. El diafragma, la arrachera gallo (pilares o arrachera colgante del lomo) y los riñones deben quitarse.

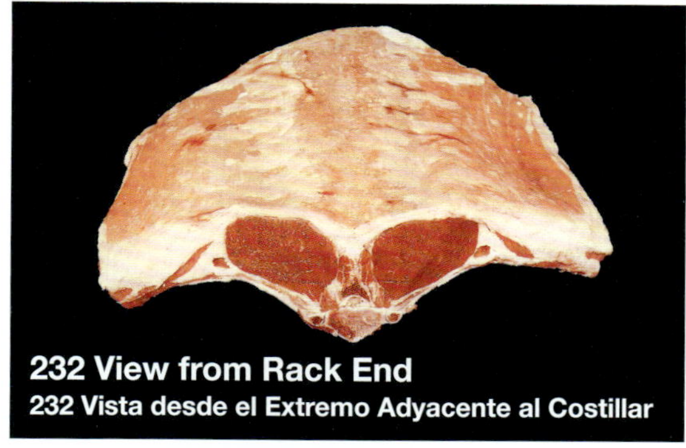

232 View from Rack End
232 Vista desde el Extremo Adyacente al Costillar

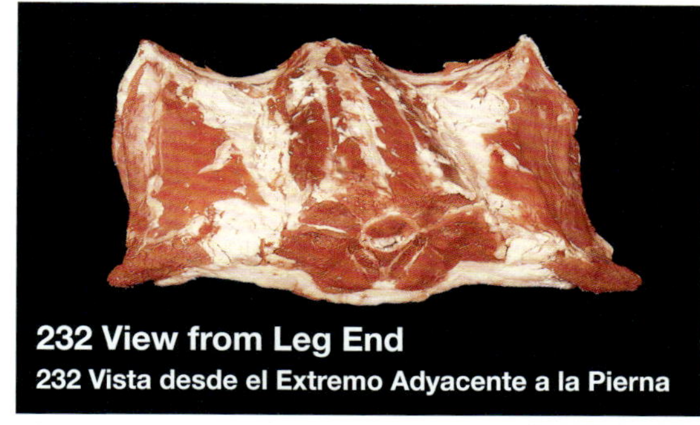

232 View from Leg End
232 Vista desde el Extremo Adyacente a la Pierna

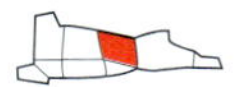

232A — Lamb Loin, Block-Ready, Trimmed

This item may be derived from Item No. 232 or any other loin item that yields product that meets the end-item requirements. It is a single loin with the flank removed so that the tail length measurement, ventral from the edge of the *longissimus dorsi* at both the rack and leg ends, is not more than 4.0 inches (10 cm). If desired, purchasers may specify a different tail length option. The options are:

PSO: 1 – 3.0 inches (7.5 cm)

2 – 2.0 inches (5 cm)

3 – 1.0 inch (2.5 cm)

4 – 0.0 inch

5 – Purchaser may request the Item is notched. See pg. xviii for more information

232A — Lomo de Cordero, Listo para Tablajear, Recortado de Grasa y Limpio

Esta pieza puede prepararse con la pieza número 232 o con cualquier pieza de lomo que dé como resultado un producto que cumpla con los requisitos de la pieza final. Es un lomo individual al que se le quitó la falda de modo que la longitud de la cola, ventral al borde del *longissimus dorsi* en el extremo del costillar y de las piernas no sea mayor a 10 cm (4.0 pulgadas). Si así lo desea, el comprador puede especificar una medida diferente de la longitud de la cola. Las opciones son:

PSO: 1 – 7.5 cm (3.0 pulgadas)

2 – 5 cm (2.0 pulgadas)

3 – 2.5 cm (1.0 pulgada)

4 – 0.0 cm

5 – El comprador puede solicitar la pieza con corte de muesca. Consulte la pág. xviii para obtener información adicional

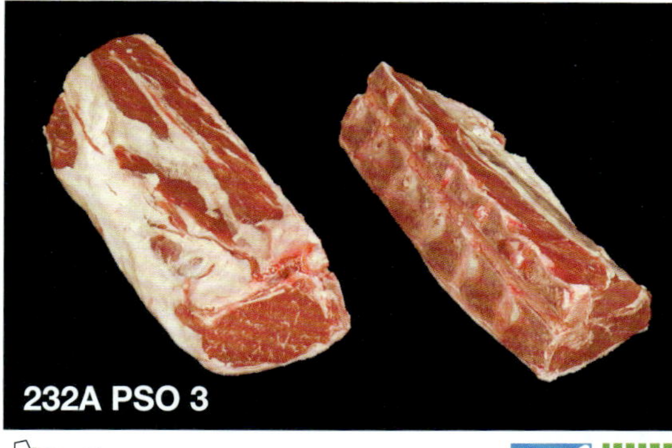

232A PSO 3

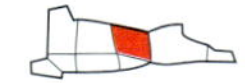

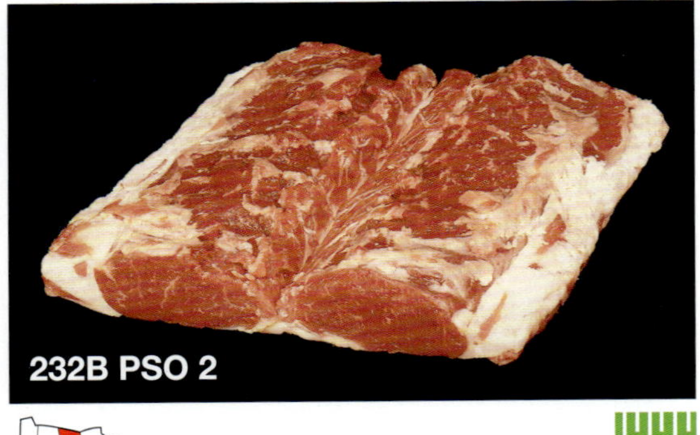

232B PSO 2

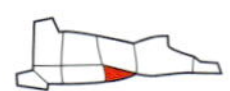

232B Lamb Loins, Double, Boneless

This item may be derived from any unsplit loin. The tail length shall be not more than 3.0 inches (7.5 cm) unless another tail length option is specified as listed in Item No. 232A. All bones, cartilages, hanging tender, kidneys, and tenderloins shall be excluded while leaving the double boneless loins attached. This item may be netted or tied.

232B Lomos de Cordero, En Pareja, Deshuesados

Esta pieza puede prepararse con cualquier lomo sin dividir. El largo de la cola no será mayor a 7.5 cm (3.0 pulgadas) a menos que se especifique otra opción de longitud de la cola tal como se enumera en la pieza número 232A. Se deberán quitar todos los huesos, los cartílagos, la arrachera gallo (arrachera colgante), los riñones y los filetes, y se dejarán unidos los lomos en pareja y deshuesados. Esta pieza puede atarse o amarrarse con una red.

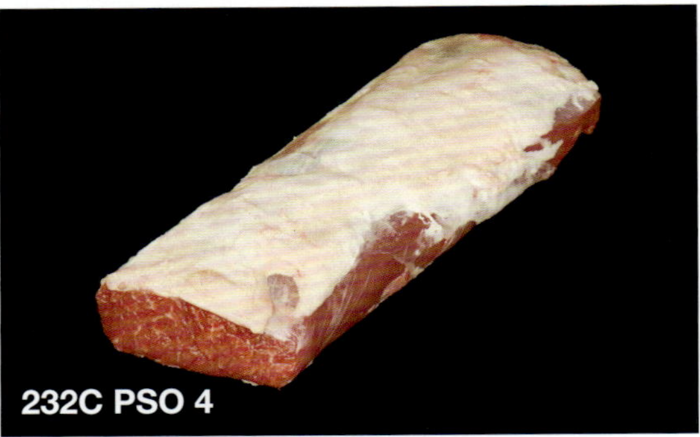

232C PSO 4

232C Lamb Loin, Single, Boneless

This item shall be prepared in the same manner as Item No. 232B except that it shall be a single loin. The item tail length options described in Item No. 232A shall also apply. The item maybe requested FLO 5, Peeled/Denuded (remaining fat shall not exceed 1.0 inch (2.5 cm) in any dimension).

232C Lomo de Cordero, Individual, Deshuesado

Esta pieza se preparará de la misma forma que la pieza número 232B, excepto que debe ser un lomo individual. También se aplicarán las opciones de la longitud de la cola descritas en la pieza número 232A. Para esta pieza se puede solicitar la opción 5 "Desprovisto de grasa/Prácticamente desnudo de grasa" para limitar la grasa [la grasa que queda no debe exceder los 2.5 cm (1.0 pulgadas) en ninguna dimensión].

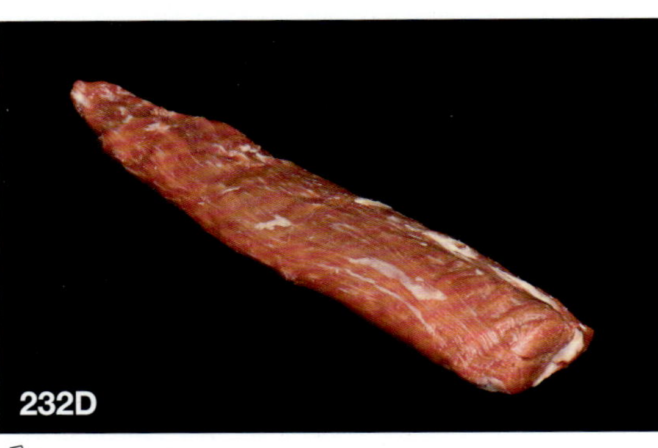

232D

232D Lamb Loin, Short Tenderloin

This item consists of the tenderloin portion of any loin item. It is similar to a short loin tender and shall consist of the *psoas major* and *psoas minor* muscles only. It shall be practically free of fat, and any bone, cartilage, or ragged edges shall be removed. A score into the tenderloin exceeding 0.50 inch (13 mm) in depth is not acceptable.

See Item No. 246 for whole tenderloin.

232D Lomo de Cordero, Filete Corto

Esta pieza consiste en la porción de filete de cualquier pieza del lomo. Es similar al filete del lomo corto y consiste en los músculos *psoas mayor* y *psoas menor* únicamente. Deberá estar prácticamente libre de grasa, y se deberán quitar todos los huesos, cartílagos o bordes irregulares. No se aceptará ningún corte en el filete que exceda los 13 mm (0.50 pulgadas) de profundidad.

Consulte la pieza número 246 para ver el filete entero.

232E Flank, Untrimmed

This item shall contain the abdominal muscles ventral to the loin. Costal cartilages and rib bones shall be removed.

232E Falda/Aldilla, sin Recortado de Grasa y sin Limpiar

Esta pieza contendrá los músculos abdominales ventrales al lomo. Se deberán quitar los cartílagos costales y los huesos de las costillas.

233 — Lamb Legs

This double item may be derived from the posterior portion of the carcass or hindsaddle. The legs are removed by a straight cut anterior to the hip bone cartilage that forms an approximate right angle to the length of the legs, depicted as separation point "C" on the Cutting Instruction Charts for Styles A and B.

233 — Cordero, Piernas

Esta pieza doble puede derivarse de una porción posterior de la canal o cuarto trasero. Las piernas se retiran mediante un corte recto anterior al cartílago del hueso de la cadera formando un ángulo aproximadamente recto con respecto al largo de las piernas, representado como el punto de separación "C" en las gráficas de instrucciones de corte para los Estilos A y B.

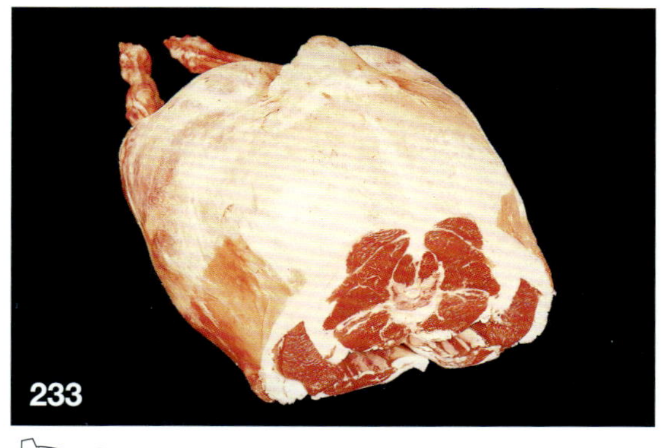

233

233A — Lamb Leg, Trotter-Off

This single bone in leg has the trotter (lower hindshank) removed at the break joint. The gambrel cord (Achilles tendon) is also removed.

This, as well as the following 233 items, unless described differently in the item description, are derived from a leg made at separation point "C" of Style A or B unless the purchaser specifies it be prepared from a leg made at separation point "D" of Style B. These separation points are depicted on the Cutting Instruction Charts for each style.

233A — Pierna de Cordero, sin Caña/Jarrete

A este hueso de la pierna se le retira el jarrete (extremo inferior del chamberete trasero) por la coyuntura de quiebre. El tendón de Aquiles también se quita.

Esta pieza, así como las siguientes piezas que se incluyen en el número 233, a menos que se detalle de otra forma en la descripción de la pieza, se derivan de una pierna cortada en el punto de separación "C" del Estilo A o B, a menos que el comprador especifique que se prepare con una pierna cortada en el punto "D" del Estilo B. Estos puntos de separación se encuentran representados en las gráficas de instrucciones de corte para cada estilo.

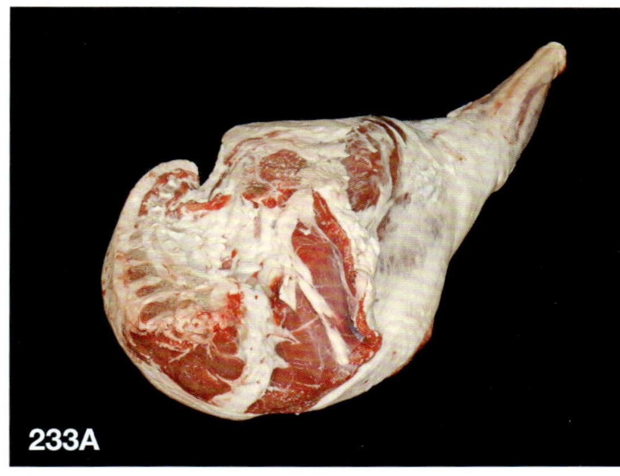

233A

233C — Lamb Leg, Trotter-Off, Semi-Boneless

This item is as described in Item No. 233A, except the pelvic, vertebrae, tail bones, lean and fat overlying the pelvic bone, flank, and practically all cod and udder fat shall be removed.

PSO: 1 – The femur shall be removed

    2 – Frenched - the lean and fat shall be removed from the (lower hindshank) trotter end so the shank bone is exposed for a distance of 2.0 inches (5 cm).

Purchaser may specify both PSO 1 and 2.

233C — Pierna de Cordero, sin Caña/Jarrete, Parcialmente Deshuesada

Esta pieza es igual a la pieza número 233A, excepto que el hueso pélvico, las vértebras y los huesos de la cola, la carne magra y la grasa que recubren el hueso pélvico, la falda y prácticamente toda la grasa del canal inguinal o de la ubre deberán quitarse.

PSO: 1 – Se deberá quitar el fémur.

    2 – Estilo francés: se deberá quitar la carne magra y la grasa del extremo del jarrete (extremo inferior del chamberete trasero) de forma que el hueso del chamberete quede expuesto por una longitud de 5 cm (2.0 pulgadas).

El comprador puede especificar ambas opciones 1 y 2.

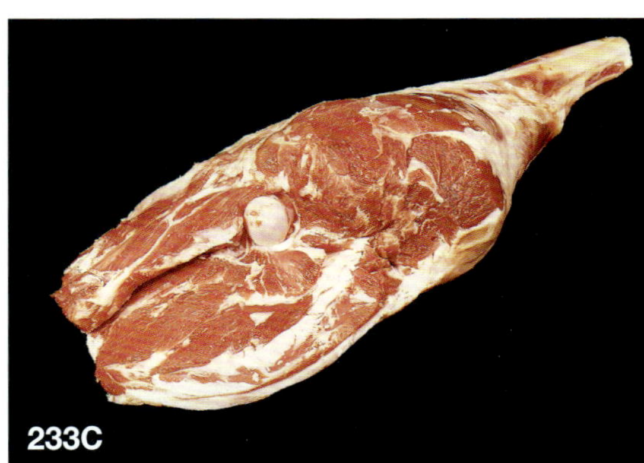

233C

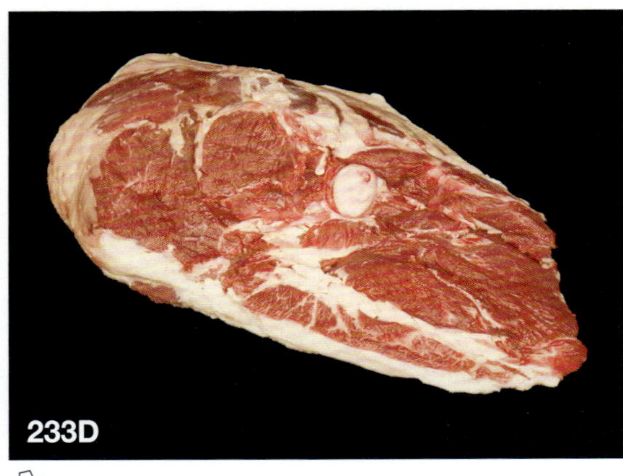

233D

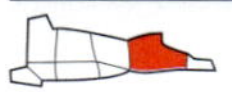

233D — Lamb Leg, Shank Off, Semi-Boneless

This item is as described in Item No. 233C, except the hindshank is removed by a straight cut through the stifle joint and then follows the natural seam between the shank and the heel.

PSO: 1 – Heel Off - The heel is removed along with the shank through the natural seams between the *biceps femoris* (outside leg) and heel.

233D — Pierna de Cordero, sin Chamberete, Parcialmente Deshuesada

Esta pieza es igual a la pieza número 233C, excepto que se quita el chamberete trasero mediante un corte recto a través de la articulación de la rodilla y luego se continúa a lo largo de la veta natural entre el chamberete y el talón.

PSO: 1 – Sin Talón: se quita el talón junto con el chamberete a través de las vetas naturales entre el *biceps femoris* (contracara de la pierna) y el talón.

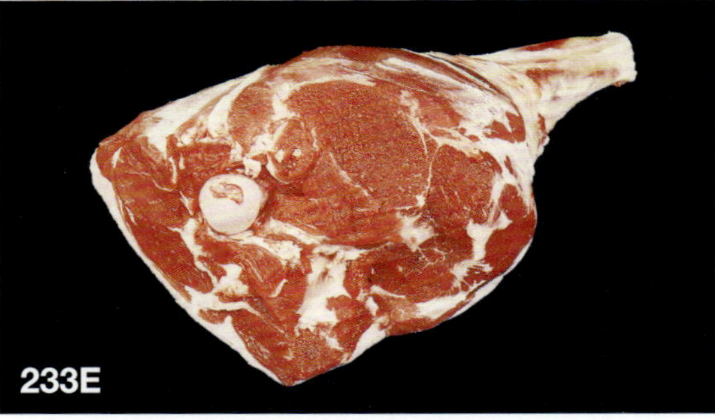

233E

233E PSO 2

233E Opción 2 especificada por el comprador

233E — Lamb Leg, Steamship, 3/4, Aitch Bone Removed

This item is as described in Item No. 233C, except the sirloin is removed from the leg by a straight cut at separation point "D" of Style B.

PSO: 1 – The femur shall be removed

2 – Frenched - the lean and fat shall be removed from the (lower hindshank) trotter end so the shank bone is exposed for a distance of 2.0 inches (5 cm).

233E — Pierna de Cordero, sin Caña/Jarrete, 3/4, Sin Hueso de Cadera

Esta pieza es igual a la pieza número 233C, excepto que el sirloin se separa de la pierna mediante un corte recto en el punto de separación "D" del Estilo B.

PSO: 1 – Se deberá quitar el fémur.

2 – Estilo francés: se deberá quitar la carne magra y la grasa del extremo del jarrete (extremo inferior del chamberete trasero) de forma que el hueso del chamberete quede expuesto por una longitud de 5 cm (2.0 pulgadas).

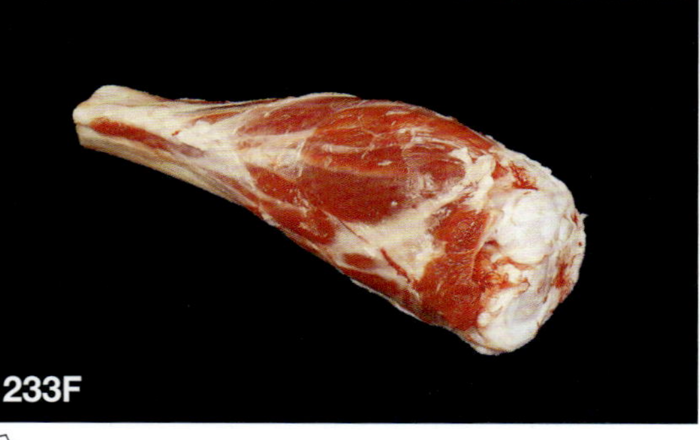

233F

233F — Lamb Leg, Hindshank

This item is prepared by a cut through the stifle joint that follows on through the natural seam between the shank and the heel. Both the trotter (lower hindshank) and the gambrel cord (Achilles tendon) are excluded.

PSO: 1 – Frenched - the lean and fat shall be removed from the (lower hindshank) trotter end so the shank bone is exposed for a distance of 2.0 inches (5 cm).

233F — Pierna de Cordero, Chamberete Trasero

Esta pieza se prepara mediante un corte a través de la articulación de la rodilla que sigue a lo largo de la veta natural entre el chamberete y el talón. Tanto el jarrete (extremo inferior del chamberete trasero) como el tendón de Aquiles deben ser retirados.

PSO: 1 – Estilo francés: se deberá retirar la carne magra y la grasa del extremo del jarrete (extremo inferior del chamberete trasero) de forma que el hueso del chamberete quede expuesto en una longitud de 5 cm (2.0 pulgadas).

233G — Lamb Leg, Hindshank, Heel On

This item is removed from any shank-on leg by a straight cut through to the stifle joint at an approximate right angle to the shank bone leaving the heel or any portion of the heel attached to the shank. The trotter (lower hindshank) is removed at the break joint and the gambrel cord is removed.

PSO: 1 – Frenched - the lean and fat shall be removed from the (lower hindshank) trotter end so the shank bone is exposed for a distance of 2.0 inches (5 cm).

233G — Pierna de Cordero, Chamberete Trasero, con Talón

Esta pieza se prepara con cualquier pierna con chamberete mediante un corte recto a través de la articulación de la rodilla aproximadamente en ángulo recto al hueso del chamberete, dejando el talón o cualquier porción del talón unido al chamberete. El jarrete (extremo inferior del chamberete trasero) se quita en la coyuntura de quiebre y se quita el tendón de Aquiles.

PSO: 1 – Estilo francés: se deberá retirar la carne magra y la grasa del extremo del jarrete (extremo inferior del chamberete trasero) de forma que el hueso del chamberete quede expuesto en una longitud de 5 cm (2.0 pulgadas).

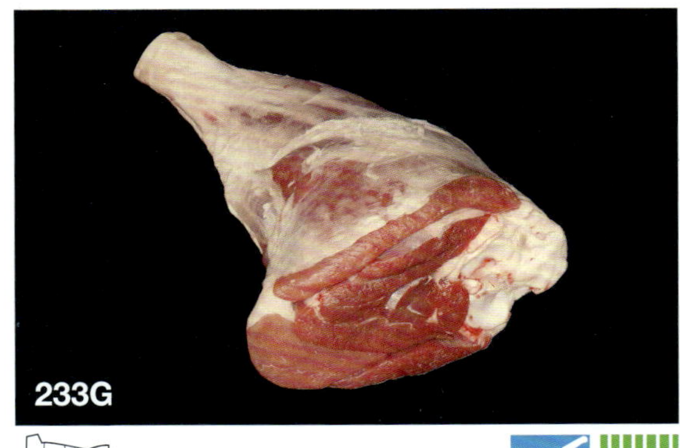

234 — Lamb Leg, Boneless

This item is prepared from a leg meeting the Item No. 233A Leg requirements. The leg is separated at point "C" of Styles A and B unless purchaser specifies point "D" of Style B. The femur bone is removed by a cut through the natural seam between the knuckle and the inside portions. All bones, cartilages, *sacrosciatic* ligament including the lean and fat overlying it, *popliteal* and exposed lymph glands, gambrel cord (Achilles tendon) if present, flank, and tendinous ends of the shank and knuckle, which expose less than 75 percent lean on the cross-sectional cut, shall be excluded. The shank meat from the leg may be folded or placed into the femur cavity. This item shall be netted or tied.

234 — Cordero, Pierna, Deshuesada

Esta pieza se prepara con una pierna que cumpla con los requisitos de la pieza número 233A, Pierna. La pierna se separa en el punto "C" de los Estilos A y B a menos que el comprador especifique el punto "D" del Estilo B. El hueso del fémur se retira mediante un corte a través de la veta natural entre la pulpa bola y las porciones de pulpa negra (cara/centro). Se deberán quitar todos los huesos, cartílagos, el ligamento *sacrociático* incluyendo la carne magra y la grasa que lo recubren, los ganglios linfáticos *poplíteos* y expuestos, el tendón de Aquiles si estuviera presente, la falda, y los extremos tendinosos del chamberete y la pulpa bola que presenten menos de 75% de carne magra en un corte transversal. La carne del chamberete de la pierna puede plegarse o colocarse dentro de la cuenca dejada por el fémur. Esta pieza se deberá atar o amarrar con una red.

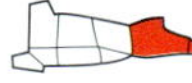

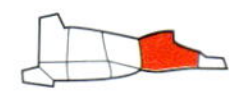

234A — Lamb Leg, Shank Off, Boneless

This item is as described in Item No. 234 except the shank meat shall be excluded. The boneless leg shall be netted or tied.

234A — Pierna de Cordero, sin Chamberete, Deshuesada

Esta pieza es igual a la pieza número 234, excepto que se quita la carne del chamberete. La pierna deshuesada se atará o amarrará con una red.

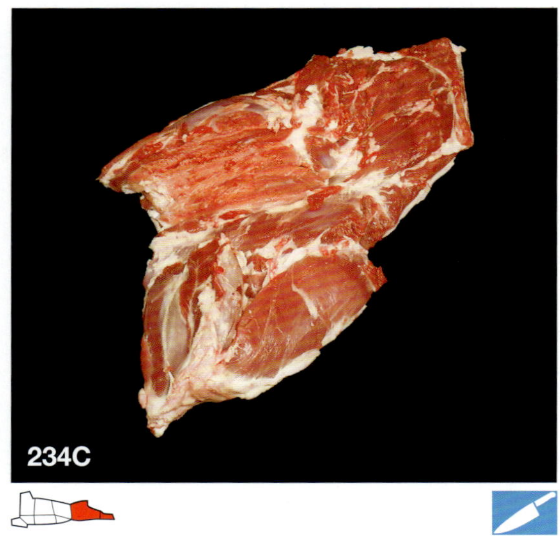

234C

Lamb Leg, Bottom, Boneless

This boneless item may be prepared from any boneless leg and consists of the outside (*biceps femoris* and *semitendinosus* muscles) attached to the sirloin tip (*quadriceps femoris* group and *tensor fasciae latae* muscles) portions. Presence of the top sirloin portion (*gluteus medius* muscle) and heel (*gastrocnemius* and *superficial digital flexor* muscles) are optional.

PSO: 1 – The top sirloin (*gluteus medius* muscle) shall remain.

2 – The heel and *popliteal* lymph gland shall be removed by cutting through the natural seam.

3 – Butterfly: Purchaser may specifiy that the cut be butterflied by cutting the sirloin tip (*quadriceps femoris* group and *tensor fasciae latae* muscles) lengthwise toward the void in the shank area. Fold the butterflied sirloin tip into the void of the shank area to create a uniformly shaped cut.

234C

Pierna de Cordero, Pulpa Blanca-Aguayón-Pulpa Bola, Deshuesada

Esta pieza deshuesada puede prepararse con cualquier pierna deshuesada y consiste en la contracara (músculos *biceps femoris* y *semitendinosus*) unida a las porciones de punta de sirloin (grupo de cuádriceps femoral y tensor de la fascia lata). La presencia de la porción de aguayón (músculo *gluteus medius*) y el talón (músculos *gastrocnemius* y *flexor digital superficial*) es opcional.

PSO: 1 – El aguayón (músculo *gluteus medius*) deberá conservarse.

2 – El talón y los ganglios linfáticos *poplíteos* deberán quitarse mediante un corte a través de las vetas naturales.

3 – Mariposa: el comprador puede especificar que la pieza se abra por la mitad realizando un corte a lo largo de la punta de sirloin (grupo *cuádriceps femoral* y *tensor de la fascia lata*) hacia el espacio vacío que queda en la zona del chamberete. Doble la punta de sirloin abierta a la mitad al estilo mariposa hacia el espacio vacío que queda en la zona del chamberete para crear un corte de forma uniforme.

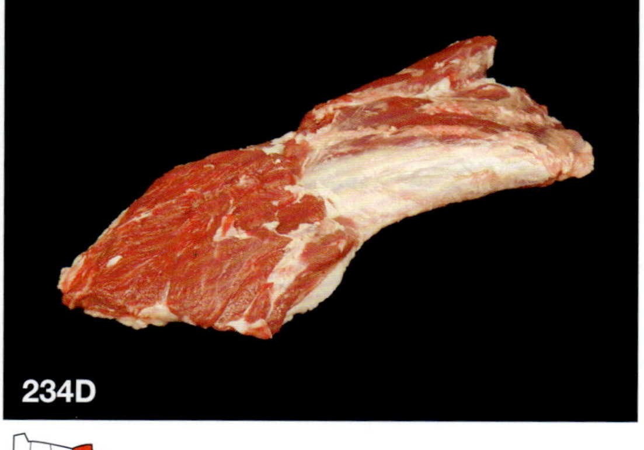

234D

Lamb Leg, Outside, Boneless

This item may be prepared from the outside portion (*biceps femoris* and *semitendinosus*) of any boneless leg item. The *gluteus medius* shall also be included unless purchaser specifies that it not be. The heel (*gastrocnemius* and *superficial digital flexor* muscles) and *popliteal* lymph gland shall be excluded by cutting through the natural seam. When specified by the purchaser, two outside portions shall be reversed and netted or tied together to form a uniformly thick roast.

234D

Pierna de Cordero, Contracara-Aguayón sin Talón (Copete), Deshuesada

Esta pieza puede prepararse con la porción de contracara (*biceps femoris* y *semitendinosus*) de cualquier pieza de pierna deshuesada. El *gluteus medius* también debe incluirse a menos que el comprador especifique lo contrario. El talón (músculos *gastrocnemius* y *flexor digital superficial*) y los ganglios linfáticos *poplíteos* deberán quitarse realizando un corte a través de la veta natural. Cuando el comprador así lo solicite, se deben invertir y atar o amarrar con una red dos porciones de contracara a manera de formar un trozo rosbif grueso y uniforme.

234E — Lamb Leg, Inside, Boneless

This item may be prepared from the inside portion (*semimembranosus*, *adductor*, and firmly attached muscles) of any boneless leg. The inside is to be separated from the bottom and knuckle portions along the natural seams. When specified by the purchaser, two inside portions shall be reversed and netted or tied together to form a uniformly thick roast.

PSO: 1 – The *gracilis* muscle (cap) shall be removed by cutting through the natural seams.

234E — Pierna de Cordero, Pulpa Negra (Cara/Centro), Deshuesada

Esta pieza puede prepararse con la porción de pulpa negra (cara/centro) (músculos *semimembranosus*, *adductor*, y músculos firmemente unidos) de cualquier pierna deshuesada. La pulpa negra (cara/centro) debe separarse de las porciones de contracara y pulpa bola a lo largo de las vetas naturales. Cuando el comprador así lo solicite, se deben invertir y atar o amarrar con una red dos porciones de pulpa negra (cara/centro) a manera de formar un trozo rosbif y uniforme.

PSO: 1 – El músculo *gracilis* (tapa) debe ser retirado mediante un corte a través de las vetas naturales.

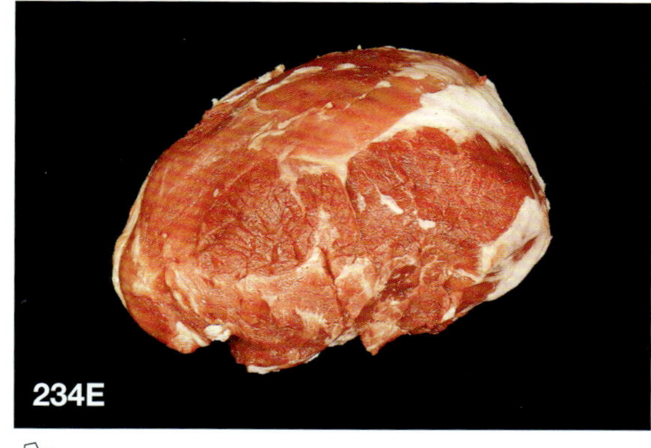
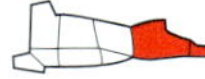

234F — Lamb Leg, Sirloin Tip, Boneless

This item may be prepared from the knuckle portion (*quadriceps femoris* group) and *tensor fasciae latae* of any boneless leg item. The sirloin tip is separated from the inside and outside portions along the natural seams. Any cartilage and tendinous ends exposing less than 75 percent lean on a cross-sectional cut shall be excluded.

234F — Pierna de Cordero, Punta de Sirloin, Deshuesada

Esta pieza puede prepararse con la porción de pulpa bola (grupo de cuádriceps femoral) y el tensor de la fascia lata (empuje) de cualquier pieza de pierna deshuesada. La punta de sirloin se separa de la porción de pulpa negra (cara/centro) y la contracara a lo largo de las vetas naturales. Todos los extremos cartilaginosos y tendinosos en los que se observe menos de 75% de carne magra se deberán quitar por un corte transversal.

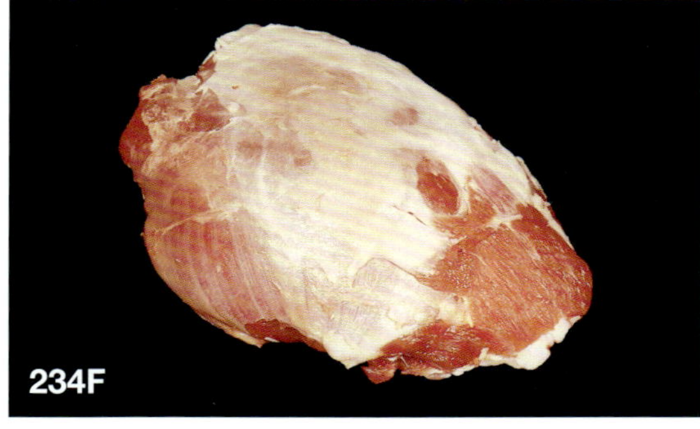

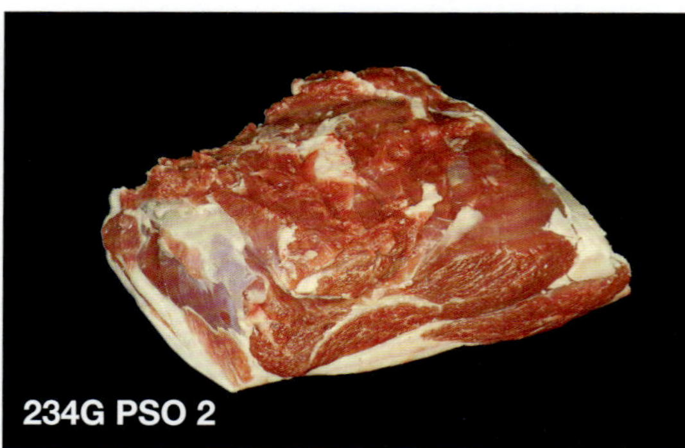

234G PSO 2

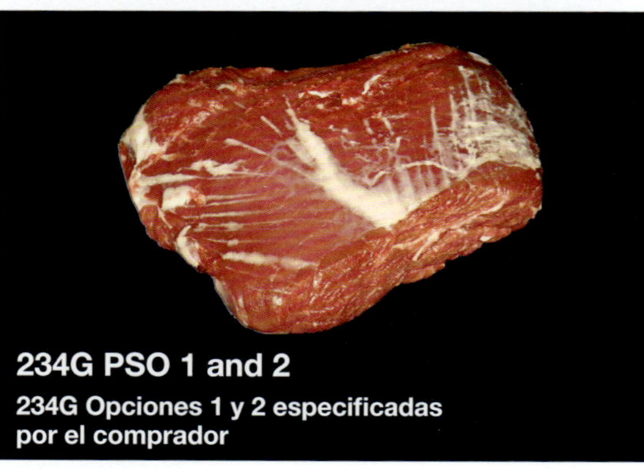

234G PSO 1 and 2
234G Opciones 1 y 2 especificadas por el comprador

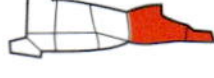

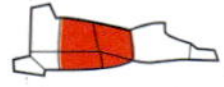

234G Lamb Top Sirloin, Boneless

This boneless item is prepared from the muscles (*biceps femoris*, *gluteus medius*, *gluteus accessorius*, and *gluteus profundus*) lying between the "C" and "D" separation points of Style B depicted on the Cutting Instruction Chart. The bottom sirloin shall be removed by cutting along the natural seam (between the *gluteus medius* and *rectus femoris*) continuing to the outside surface leaving a portion of the *tensor fasciae latae* attached to the boneless top sirloin. All bones, cartilages, tenderloin, and the sacrosciatic ligament and the lean and fat which overlaid the ligament shall be removed.

This item is most commonly sold with the tenderloin attached.

PSO: 1 – The *biceps femoris* (cap) shall be removed by cutting through the natural seams

2 – The tenderloin shall be removed.

3 – The *tensor fascia latae* shall remain attached to the sirloin.

234G Aguayón Superior (Top Sirloin) de Cordero, Deshuesado

Esta pieza deshuesada se prepara con los músculos (*biceps femoris*, *gluteus medius*, *gluteus accessorius*, y *gluteus profundus* que se encuentran entre los puntos de separación "C" y "D" del Estilo B, representado en la gráfica de instrucciones de corte. Se deberá quitar el bottom sirloin (aguayón inferior) mediante un corte a lo largo de la veta natural (entre el *gluteus medius* y el *rectus femoris*), continuando hacia la superficie exterior y dejando una porción del tensor de la fascia lata (empuje) unido al aguayón deshuesado. Se deberán quitar todos los huesos, cartílagos, filetes, y el ligamento sacrociático, así como la grasa y la carne que recubren el ligamento.

Por lo general, esta pieza se vende con el filete unido.

PSO: 1 – El músculo *biceps femoris* (tapa) debe ser retirado mediante un corte a través de las vetas naturales.

2 – Se deberá quitar el filete.

3 – El tensor de la fascia lata deberá permanecer unido al sirloin (aguayón).

235 Lamb Back

This item consists of the unsplit rack and loin with flank and breast portions attached. The separation at the shoulder and leg is made according to Style A, unless a Style B separation at the shoulder is specified. The diaphragm may be removed. If present, however, the membranous portion of the diaphragm shall be trimmed close to the lean. The back shall be practically free of all internal fat.

235 Cordero, Espaldar

Esta pieza consiste en el espaldar con costillar y el lomo sin dividirlos con las porciones de falda y pecho unidas. Las separaciones de la espaldilla y la pierna se realizan de acuerdo con el Estilo A, a menos que se especifique una separación Estilo B de la espaldilla. También puede quitarse el diafragma. Sin embargo, la cubierta membranosa del mismo deberá despellejarse hasta descubrir la carne magra. El espaldar debe estar prácticamente libre de grasa interna.

236 — Lamb Back, Trimmed

This item is the same as described in Item No. 235, except the flank and breast portions are removed by a straight cut that is ventral to, but no more than 4.0 inches (10.0 cm) from, the *longissimus dorsi* on both shoulder and leg ends. The kidneys and hanging tender shall also be excluded.

236 — Cordero, Espaldar, Recortado de Grasa y Limpio

Esta pieza es igual a la pieza número 235, excepto que las porciones de falda y pecho se quitan mediante un corte recto y ventral al *longissimus dorsi*, a no más de 10.0 cm (4.0 pulgadas) de él, tanto en el extremo adyacente a la espaldilla como el de la pierna. Los riñones y la arrachera gallo (pilares o arrachera colgante) también deben quitarse.

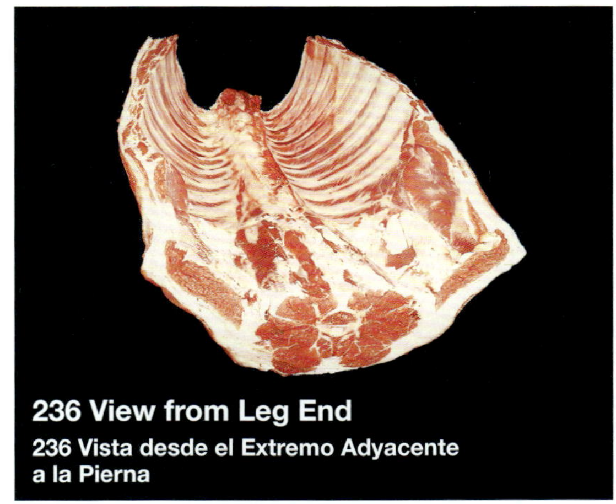

236 View from Leg End
236 Vista desde el Extremo Adyacente a la Pierna

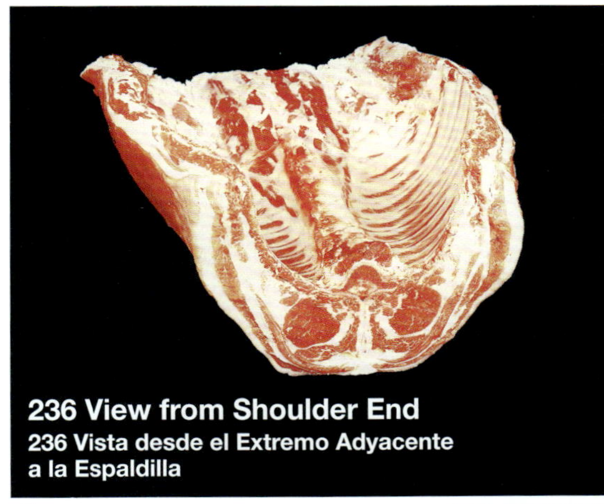

236 View from Shoulder End
236 Vista desde el Extremo Adyacente a la Espaldilla

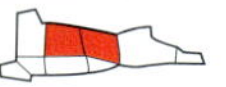

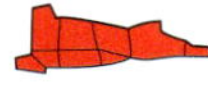

238 — Lamb Trimmings

Trimmings may be prepared from any portion of the carcass which yields product that meets the end item requirements. All fell, bones, cartilages, backstrap, heavy connective tissue, and lymph glands shall be removed. The fat content shall be specified by the purchaser.

238 — Cordero, Recortes

Los recortes pueden prepararse con cualquier porción de la canal que dé como resultado un producto que cumpla con los requisitos de la pieza final. Se debe quitar toda la piel, huesos, cartílagos, banda ligamentosa, tejido conectivo grueso y ganglios linfáticos. El comprador especificará el contenido de grasa.

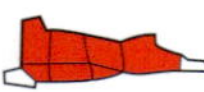

239 — Lamb Special Trimmings

Trimmings may be prepared from any portion of the carcass which yields product that meets the end item requirements. Unless otherwise specified, shank and heel meat shall be excluded. Unless otherwise specified, trimmings shall consist of pieces which have a surface area on one side which is no less than 6.0 square inches (15.0 square cm) and are no less than 0.3 inch (8 mm) thick at any point. All fell, bones,cartilages, backstrap, heavy connective tissue, detached cutaneous muscles, and lymph glands shall be removed. Trimmings shall be practically free of surface and seam fat.

239 — Cordero, Recortes Especiales

Los recortes pueden prepararse con cualquier porción de la canal que dé como resultado un producto que cumpla con los requisitos exigidos al producto final. A menos que se especifique lo contrario, se excluirá la carne del chamberete y el talón. A menos que se especifique lo contrario, los recortes consistirán en piezas que en uno de sus lados tengan una superficie no menor a 15.0 cm cuadrados (6.0 pulgadas cuadradas) y cuyo grosor no sea inferior a 8 mm (0.3 pulgadas) en ningún punto. Se debe quitar toda la piel, huesos, cartílagos, banda ligamentosa, tejido conectivo grueso, músculos cutáneos sueltos y ganglios linfáticos. Los recortes deben estar prácticamente libres de cubierta de grasa y vetas de grasa intermuscular.

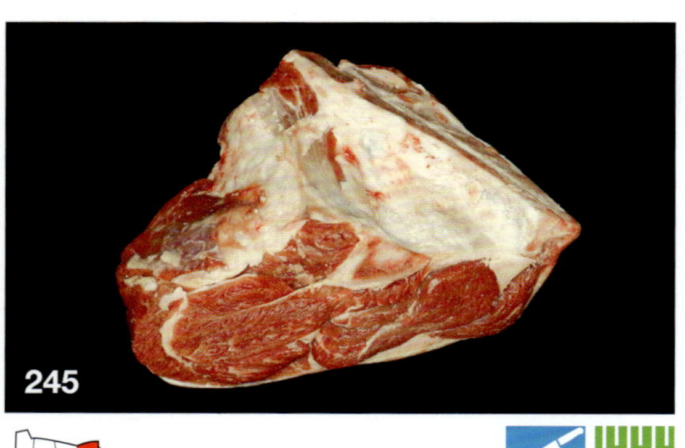

245 — Lamb Leg, Sirloin, Bone In

This item is separated from the carcass as described for separations "C" and "D" within Style B. The flank is removed by a straight cut from a point which is not more than 4.0 inches (10.0 cm) from the *gluteus medius* to a point which is not more than 0.25 inch (6 mm) from the *tensor fasciae latae*.

PSO: 1 – Purchaser may request the Item is notched. See pg. xviii for more information.

245 — Pierna de Cordero, Aguayón (Sirloin), con Hueso

Esta pieza se separa de la canal tal como se describe en las separaciones "C" y "D" dentro del Estilo B. La falda se separa mediante un corte recto desde un punto que no se encuentre a más de 10.0 cm (4.0 pulgadas) del *gluteus medius* hasta un punto que no se encuentre a más de 6 mm (0.25 pulgadas) del tensor de la fascia lata (empuje).

PSO: 1 – El comprador puede solicitar la pieza con corte de muesca. Consulte la pág. xviii para obtener información adicional.

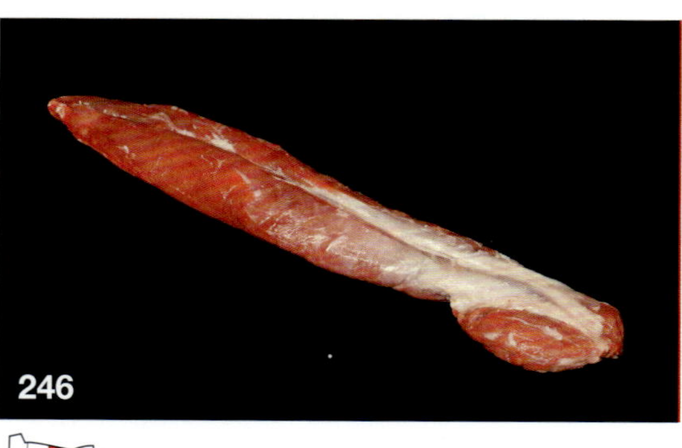

246 — Lamb Tenderloin

This item is derived from any loin item that has a bone in sirloin attached to it that was removed from the leg at point of separation "D" in Style B. The full tender consists of the *psoas major*, *psoas minor*, and *iliacus* (wing). Any portion of *psoas minor* that is not firmly attached shall be excluded along with any bone or cartilage. The tenderloin shall be trimmed practically free of kidney fat.

246 — Filete de Cordero

Esta pieza es un derivado de cualquier pieza de lomo que tenga un hueso unido al sirloin que haya sido separado de la pierna en el punto de separación "D" del Estilo B. El filete completo consiste en el *psoas mayor*, *psoas menor*, e *iliacus* (ala). Cualquier porción del *psoas menor* que no esté firmemente adherida debe ser retirada junto con cualquier hueso o cartílago. El filete debe recortarse y limpiarse para que quede prácticamente libre de grasa de riñonada.

295 — Lamb for Stewing

Unless otherwise specified this item shall be prepared from any portion of the carcass that yields product that meets the end-item requirements. However, meat from the heel and shank must be excluded. All bones, cartilage, backstrap, heavy connective tissue, exposed large blood vessels, and exposed lymph glands shall also be excluded. The boneless meat shall be hand-diced or processed through a dicing machine (grinding is not permitted). Hand-dicing must be specifically requested. Not less than 85 percent by weight of the resulting pieces shall be of a size that is equivalent to not less than a 0.5 inch (13 mm) cube or more than a 1.25 inch (3.1 cm) cube and no individual surface on these pieces shall exceed 2.5 inch (6.2 cm) in length. If requested by the purchaser, this item may also be prepared from yearling mutton or mutton as specified and labeled accordingly. Further, this item, if requested by the purchaser, may be specified to be prepared from an individual cut or cuts, such as the leg, sirloin, loin, rack, or square-cut shoulder, and labeled accordingly.

295 — Trozos de Cordero para Cocido/Guisado

A menos que se especifique lo contrario, esta pieza se preparará con cualquier porción de la canal que dé como resultado un producto que cumpla con los requisitos exigidos por la pieza final. Sin embargo, se debe excluir la carne del talón y el chamberete. También se deben retirar todos los huesos, cartílagos, banda ligamentosa nucal, tejido conectivo grueso, grandes vasos sanguíneos expuestos y ganglios linfáticos expuestos. La carne deshuesada debe trocearse en cubos a mano o procesarse a través de una máquina de cubicado (la molienda no está permitida). El troceado en cubos a mano debe solicitarse de forma específica. Al menos el 85% del peso de las piezas resultantes debe tener un tamaño equivalente a un cubo de no menos de 13 mm (0.5 pulgadas) ni más de 3.1 cm (1.25 pulgadas) y ninguna superficie individual de estas piezas excederá los 6.2 cm (2.5 pulgadas) de longitud. En caso de que el comprador lo solicite, estas piezas también pueden prepararse con carnero añojo o carnero, según corresponda en la especificación y etiquetado. Además, si así lo solicita el comprador, se puede especificar que esta pieza se prepare de un corte o cortes individuales, como pierna, sirloin (aguayón), lomo, costillar, o espaldilla de corte cuadrado, y que se etiquete según corresponda.

295

295A — Lamb for Kabobs

This item is as described in Item No. 295, except that at least 90 percent by weight of the resulting dices, unless otherwise specified, shall be of a size equivalent to not less than a 0.75 inch (19 mm) cube or more than a 1.25 inch (3.1 cm) cube, and no individual surface shall be more than 2.5 inches (6.2 cm) in length.

295A — Trozos de Cordero para Brochetas

Esta pieza es igual a la pieza número 295, excepto que al menos un 90% del peso de los cubos resultantes, siempre que no se especifique de otro modo, debe tener un tamaño equivalente a un cubo de no menos de 19 mm (0.75 pulgadas) y no más de 3.1 cm (1.25 pulgadas), y ninguna superficie individual debe ser mayor a 6.2 cm (2.5 pulgadas) de longitud.

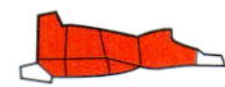

296 Ground Lamb

This item shall be prepared from any portion of a lamb carcass. If requested by the purchaser this item may also be prepared from yearling mutton or mutton as specified and labeled accordingly. Unless otherwise specified, the fat content shall not exceed 20 percent. Purchasers, however, may specify a different fat content provided it does not exceed 30 percent. The meat used shall be free of fell, bones, cartilage, backstrap, exposed lymph glands, heavy connective tissue, exposed large blood vessels, and the tendinous ends of shanks and knuckles to a point that exposes at least 75 percent lean on a cross-sectional cut. Unless otherwise specified, frozen product may be incorporated into the mixture.

The meat shall be ground at least once through a plate having holes not larger than 1.0 inch (2.5 cm) in diameter. Alternatively, the meat may be chopped or machine-cut by any method provided that the texture and appearance of the product after final grinding is typical of ground lamb prepared by grinding only. Unless otherwise specified, the final grinding shall be through a plate having holes 0.125 inch (3 mm) in diameter. The lamb shall be thoroughly blended at least once prior to final grinding. The meat shall not be mixed after the final grind. The grinding process and product labeling shall be done in conformity with FSIS requirements.

296 Carne Molida de Cordero

Esta pieza se preparará a partir de cualquier porción de la canal del cordero. En caso de que el comprador así lo solicite, esta pieza también puede prepararse con carnero añojo o carnero, según se especifica y cataloga consecuentemente. A menos que se especifique lo contrario, el contenido de grasa no debe superar el 20%. Los compradores, sin embargo, pueden especificar un contenido de grasa distinto siempre que no exceda el 30%. La carne utilizada deberá estar libre de piel, huesos, cartílagos, banda ligamentosa, ganglios linfáticos expuestos, tejido conectivo grueso, grandes vasos sanguíneos expuestos, y extremos tendinosos de chamberetes y pulpa bola, de forma que se pueda ver la carne magra al menos en un 75% de la superficie al corte transversal. A menos que se especifique lo contrario, se puede incorporar producto congelado a la mezcla.

La carne debe molerse al menos una vez a través de una placa con orificios no mayores a 2.5 cm (1.0 pulgada) de diámetro. De forma alternativa, la carne puede picarse o cortarse·a máquina mediante cualquier método, siempre y cuando la textura y la apariencia del producto después de la molienda final sean las típicas de la carne molida de cordero preparada únicamente mediante molienda. A menos que se especifique de otro modo, la molienda final deberá realizarse con una placa con orificios de 3 mm (0.125 pulgadas) de diámetro. El cordero debe mezclarse al máximo, al menos una vez antes de la molienda final. La carne no debe mezclarse después de la molienda final. El proceso de molienda y etiquetado del producto debe realizarse de acuerdo con los requisitos del Servicio de Inspección e Inocuidad Alimentaria.

North American Meat Processors Association
Association Amérique du Nord des Transformateurs de Viande
Asociación Norteamericana de Procesadores de Carne

Membership Information
Información sobre la membresía

Want your personal network to include the real decision-makers at the most successful meat & poultry processors and suppliers in North America?

THEN JOIN NAMP!

Founded in 1942, the North American Meat Processors Association (NAMP) is an international member-driven association of *progressive meat processors, distributors, center-of-the-plate specialists,* and suppliers selling primarily to the foodservice industry. NAMP provides exceptional value through high-caliber support programs and governmental representation to help ensure our members' success in the industry.

The Meat Buyer's Guide® is a NAMP publication. NAMP members can participate in the review/update process of each edition.

BENEFITS OF MEMBERSHIP

- 35% discount on *The Meat Buyers Guide®*
- A relaxed networking and learning environment at two major industry-wide meetings a year
- Learning opportunities at NAMP's 16+ food safety conferences and workshops: pay lower member fees
- NAMP's weekly report, *NewsLine,* which contains industry information and updates and NAMP's weekly Market Report, with complete up-to-date pricing information
- Unlimited free access to NAMP's College of Experts, our team of 34 Ph.D.-level consultants on 19 subjects important to your business
- A voice in government rulemaking: NAMP is a North American organization that effectively represents your interests to USDA-FSIS, USDA-AMS, and CFIA
- A cross-referenced *Member Resource Directory* for networking and enriching your business prospects
- Fast, on-line help from other members through NAMP's Listserve called "Bull Session"
- Exclusive technical/educational info on the Members Only section at www.namp.com

Members also enjoy toll-free access to NAMP's experienced staff and off-site consultants who are ready to help you with just about any problem, question or concern you may have. *It's like having your own team of experts without the added expense - an incredible value for your dues dollar!*

Membership in NAMP offers an unparalleled and unique opportunity to learn and network with your peers. Join today and you'll enrich your business prospects and benefit from other members' experiences. *It's what our long-time members call "The Magic of NAMP".*

WE INVITE YOU TO JOIN TODAY

To apply, go to www.namp.com or call +1 703.758.1900.

¿Quiere que su red personal incluya a quienes en verdad toman las decisiones y a los más exitosos procesadores y proveedores de carne roja y aves de América del Norte?

¡ENTONCES ÚNASE A NAMP!

La Asociación Norteamericana de Procesadores de Carne (NAMP), fundada en 1942, es una asociación internacional dedicada a sus integrantes, que incluyen *procesadores, distribuidores, especialistas en ingredientes principales del plato* y proveedores progresistas que venden principalmente a la industria de servicios de alimentación. NAMP ofrece un valor excepcional a través de programas de apoyo de gran nivel y representación en el gobierno para ayudar a garantizar el éxito de nuestros miembros en la industria.

La Guía para Compradores de Carne® es una publicación de NAMP. Los miembros de NAMP pueden participar en el proceso de revisión y actualización de cada edición.

BENEFICIOS DE LA MEMBRESÍA

- 35% de descuento en *La Guía para Compradores de Carne®*
- Un ambiente relajado para establecer contactos y aprender en dos grandes reuniones de toda la industria por año
- Oportunidades de aprendizaje en las conferencias y los talleres de inocuidad alimentaria de NAMP: pague tarifas más bajas para miembros
- Informe semanal de NAMP, *NewsLine*, que contiene información y actualizaciones de la industria, y el Informe de Mercado semanal de NAMP, con la información de precios completa y al día
- Acceso gratis ilimitado al colegio de expertos de NAMP, nuestro equipo de 34 con nivel de doctorado en 19 áreas importantes para su negocio
- Una voz en las normativas del gobierno: NAMP es una organización norteamericana que representa sus intereses de manera eficaz ante FSIS (Servicio de Inspección e Inocuidad Alimentaria) de USDA (Departamento de Agricultura de E.U.A.), AMS (Servicio de Mercadeo Agrícola) de USDA y la Agencia Canadiense de Inspección de Alimentos
- Un *Directorio de recursos de miembros* con referencia cruzada para establecer contactos y enriquecer las posibilidades de su negocio
- Ayuda rápida en Internet de otros miembros a través del Listserve de NAMP llamado "Bull Session"
- Información técnica y educativa exclusiva en la sección Members Only (sólo para miembros) de www.namp.com

Los miembros también disponen de acceso a través de un número telefónico sin cargo al experimentado personal de NAMP y a consultores descentralizados que están listos para ayudarle con prácticamente cualquier problema, consulta o inquietud que pueda tener. *Es como tener su propio equipo de expertos sin el gasto adicional ¡un increíble rendimiento por el valor de su suscripción!*

La membresía de NAMP ofrece una oportunidad única e incomparable de aprender y establecer contactos con sus colegas. Suscríbase hoy para enriquecer las posibilidades de su negocio y beneficiarse de la experiencia de otros miembros. *Es lo que nuestros miembros de muchos años llaman "La magia de NAMP".*

LO INVITAMOS A UNIRSE HOY

Para solicitar su inscripción, visite www.namp.com o llame al +1 703.758.1900.

Index / Índice

Lamb Products and Weight Ranges
Productos de cordero y escalas de peso

Información para hacer los pedidos

Tal como se ejemplifica en las instrucciones de corte en las páginas 83-85, el comprador puede especificar una separación o elaboración de la canal al Estilo A o B, siempre que en la descripción de la pieza individual se permita realizar esta elección. Cuando no se permita realizar esta elección o el comprador no realice especificaciones, la separación o elaboración de la canal se llevará a cabo según las instrucciones de corte para el Estilo A. El Estilo B se utiliza comúnmente para el comercio internacional.

Opciones para limitar la grasa

Cortes de porciones

El comprador puede especificar uno de los siguientes grosores promedio máximos (en un punto cualquiera) de cubierta de grasa cuando las limitaciones de grasa que se indican en la descripción detallada de la pieza no son las deseadas.

Cortes de porciones

Nº de opción	Grosor máximo de grasa en un punto cualquiera del corte en porciones
1	6 mm (0.25 pulgadas)
2	3 mm (0.125 pulgadas)
3	Prácticamente libre de grasa [el 75% de la superficie expuesta es magra/desgrasada y la grasa que queda no debe exceder los 3 mm (0.125 pulgadas)]
4	Desprovisto(a) de grasa/Prácticamente Desnudo(a) de grasa* [la grasa que queda no debe exceder los 2.5 cm (1.0 pulgada)en la dimensión más larga y/o 3 mm (0.125 pulgadas) de grosor]
5	Desprovisto(a) de grasa/Prácticamente desnudo(a) de grasa, Membrana superficial retirada** [el 90% de la superficie expuesta es magra y la grasa que queda no debe exceder los 3 mm (0.125 pulgadas)]

*/** – consulte la definición en la página xlv

Tolerancias de peso y grosor de la porción[†]

El comprador especificará el peso y/o el grosor que desea. A menos que el comprador especifique otras tolerancias de peso y/o grosor, se deberán utilizar las tablas que aparecen a continuación. Cuando se especifique tanto el peso como el grosor, se recomienda que esos requisitos se limiten a piezas prensadas y/o rebanadas de forma mecánica.

Tolerancias de grosor de la porción

Grosor especificado	Tolerancia de grosor	Uniformidad de grosor
2.5 cm (1.0 pulgada) o menos	± 5 mm (0.1875 pulgadas)	5 mm (0.1875 pulgadas)
Más de 2.5 cm (1.0 pulgadas)	± 6 mm (0.25 pulgadas)	6 mm (0.25 pulgadas)

Tolerancia de peso de la porción

Peso especificado	Tolerancia de peso	Uniformidad de grosor
Menos de 170 g (6.0 onzas)	± 7 g (0.25 onzas)	5 mm (0.1875 pulgadas)
170 g (6.0 onzas) a 340 g (12.0 onzas)	± 14 g (0.50 onzas)	6 mm (0.25 pulgadas)

[†] Las medidas de grosor no se aplican a menos de una distancia de 6 mm (0.25 pulgadas) desde el borde. Además, el valor que se indica en la uniformidad de grosor es la máxima diferencia admitida entre la medida más fina y la más gruesa de una chuleta o tajada individual.

Los compradores que tengan necesidades o especificaciones especiales deben comunicarse con sus proveedores.

Ordering Data

As illustrated in the Cutting Instructions on pages 83-85, the purchaser may specify either Style A or B carcass separation or fabrication, provided an option is allowed by the language of the individual Item Description. When an option is not provided for or not specified by the purchaser, the style of carcass separation or fabrication shall be in accordance with the Cutting Instructions for Style A. Style B is most commonly used for international trading.

Purchasers with special needs or specifications should contact their suppliers.

Fat Limitation Options (FLO)

Portion Cuts

The purchaser may specify one of the following maximum (at any point) thicknesses of surface fat when the fat limitations indicated in the detailed Item Descriptions are not desired.

Portion Cuts

Option No.	Maximum Fat Thickness at Any One Point for Portion Cuts
1	0.25 inch (6 mm)
2	0.125 inch (3 mm)
3	Practically free (75 percent lean/seam surface exposed and remaining fat shall not exceed 0.125 inch (3 mm))
4	Peeled/Denuded* (remaining fat shall not exceed 1.0 inch (2.5 cm) in the longest dimension and/or 0.125 inch (3 mm) in thickness)
5	Peeled/Denuded, Surface Membrane Removed** (90 percent lean exposed and remaining fat shall not exceed 0.125 inch (3 mm))

*/** – see page xvi for definition

Portion-Cut Weight and Thickness Tolerances[†]

The purchaser shall specify the portion weight and/or thickness desired. Unless other portion weight and/or thickness tolerances are specified by the purchaser, the following tables shall be used. When both weight and thickness are specified, it is recommended that those requirements be limited to items that are mechanically pressed and/or sliced.

Portion Thickness Tolerances

Specified Thickness	Thickness Tolerance	Thickness Uniformity
1.0 inch (2.5 cm) or less	± 0.1875 inch (5 mm)	0.1875 inch (5 mm)
More than 1.0 inch (2.5 cm)	± 0.25 inch (6 mm)	0.25 inch (6 mm)

Portion Weight Tolerance

Specified Weight	Weight Tolerance	Thickness Uniformity
Less than 6.0 oz. (170 g)	± 0.25 oz. (7 g)	0.1875 inch (5 mm)
6.0 oz. (170 g) to 12.0 oz. (340 g)	± 0.50 oz. (14 g)	0.25 inch (6 mm)

[†] Thickness measurements not applicable within 0.25 inch (6 mm) of the edge. Also, value listed under thickness uniformity is the maximum allowable difference between the thinnest and thickest measurement of an individual chop or steak.

1200 — Lamb Cubed Steaks

Cubed steaks shall be prepared from any portion of the carcass that yields product that meets the end-item requirements. Shank and heel meat shall be excluded, and the steaks shall also be free of heavy connective tissue, bones, cartilages, and lymph glands. Unless otherwise specified, the steaks shall be cubed twice at approximate right angles while in the fresh state. Knitting 2 or more pieces together and folding the meat while cubing is permissible. After cubing, the surface and seam fat shall not exceed 15 percent of the total area on either side of the steak. Individual steaks shall remain intact when suspended 0.50 inch (13 mm) from the outer edge.

1200 — Cordero, Tajadas Suavizadas (Ablandadas por Machacado, Rayado)

Las tajadas suavizadas se prepararán con cualquier porción de la canal que dé como resultado un producto que cumpla con los requisitos de la pieza final. Se retirará la carne del chamberete y del talón, y además las escalopas deberán estar libres de tejido conectivo grueso, huesos, cartílagos y ganglios linfáticos. A menos que se especifique de otro modo, las tajadas se suavizarán mecánicamente dos veces en ángulos aproximadamente rectos mientras se encuentren en estado fresco. Se permite unir dos o más piezas y plegar la carne al suavizarla mecánicamente. Después de suavizarla, la cubierta de grasa y las vetas de grasa intermuscular no deberán exceder el 15% del área total en ningún lado de la tajada. Las tajadas individuales deben permanecer intactas cuando se suspenden a 13 mm (0.50 pulgadas) desde el borde exterior.

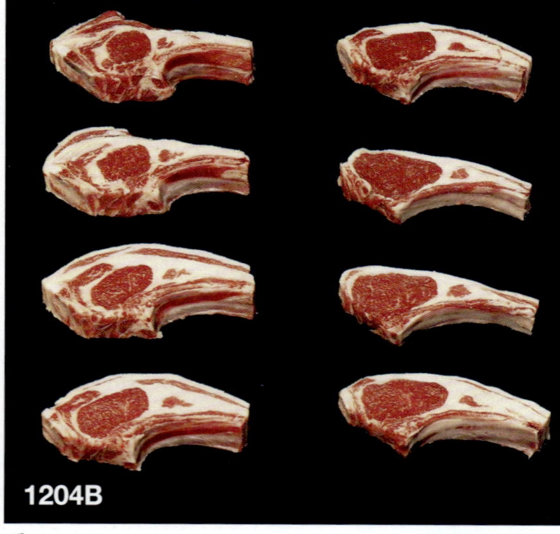

1204B — Lamb Rib Chops

This item shall be prepared from any Style A bone in rack that yields product that meets the end-item requirement unless the purchaser specifies that Style B be used. The feather bones, exterior fat cover, fell, backstrap, blade bone, and the *trapezius, infraspinatus,* and *latissimus dorsi* muscles shall also be excluded. The tail length of the chop shall be not more than 4.0 inches (10 cm) from the ventral edge of the *longissimus dorsi* muscle unless purchaser specifies another option as described below.

PSO: 1 – 3.0 inches (7.5 cm)
     2 – 2.0 inches (5 cm)
     3 – 1.0 inch (2.5 cm)
     4 – 0.0 inch

1204B — Cordero, Chuletas del Espaldar

Esta pieza se preparará con cualquier costillar con hueso Estilo A que dé como resultado un producto que cumpla con los requisitos de la pieza final, a menos que el comprador especifique que se debe utilizar el Estilo B. También se deberán quitar las puntas del espinazo, la cobertura de grasa exterior, la piel, la banda ligamentosa nucal, el hueso de la paleta y los músculos *trapezius, infraspinatus* y *latissimus dorsi*. La longitud de la cola de la chuleta no deberá exceder los 10 cm (4.0 pulgadas) desde el borde ventral al músculo *longissimus dorsi* a menos que el comprador especifique otra opción tal como se describe a continuación.

PSO: 1 – 7.5 cm (3.0 pulgadas)
     2 – 5 cm (2.0 pulgadas)
     3 – 2.5 cm (1.0 pulgada)
     4 – 0.0 cm

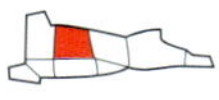

1204C — Lamb Rib Chops, Frenched

This item is as described in Item No. 1204B, except the breast side of the ribs shall be Frenched by the removal of the intercostal meat and the lean and fat over a portion of the rib bones. Exposed portions of the rib bones shall not exceed 2 inches (5 cm) in length, and the remaining intercostal meat and lean and fat over the ribs bones shall not exceed 2 inches (5 cm) from the ventral edge of the *longissimus dorsi* muscle. Chops having more than one rib bone shall have the rib bone nearest the center of the chop Frenched and the other rib bone(s) removed for the distance that the Frenched rib bone is exposed. The weight of each chop will determine the number of bones per chop unless purchaser specifies that each chop have a specific number of bones regardless of weight.

1204C — Chuletas del Espaldar de Cordero, Estilo Francés

Esta pieza es igual a la pieza número 1204B, excepto que las costillas deben prepararse al Estilo Francés quitando la carne intercostal, la grasa y la carne magra sobre una porción de las costillas hacia el lado del pecho. Las porciones de las costillas que quedan expuestas no deben exceder los 5 cm (2 pulgadas) de longitud, y la carne intercostal, la grasa y la carne magra sobre las costillas no deben exceder los 5 cm (2 pulgadas) desde el borde ventral del músculo *longissimus dorsi*. En las chuletas que contengan más de una costilla, la costilla que se encuentre más al centro debe estar preparada al Estilo Francés y la(s) otra(s) costilla(s) se deberán quitar a la altura en que queda expuesta la costilla preparada al Estilo Francés. El peso de cada chuleta determinará la cantidad de costillas por chuleta, a menos que el comprador especifique que, independientemente de su peso, cada chuleta incluya una cantidad determinada de costillas.

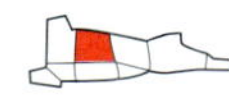

1204D — Lamb Rib Chops, Frenched, Special

This item is as described in Item No. 1204C, except in addition, the firmly attached *rhomboideus* and *subscapularis* muscles below where the blade bone has been removed shall also be excluded.

1204D — Cordero, Chuletas del Espaldar, Estilo Francés, Especiales

Esta pieza es igual a la pieza número 1204C excepto que además se deberán retirar los músculos *rhomboideus* y *subscapularis* que se encuentran firmemente adheridos debajo del lugar donde se quitó el hueso de la paleta.

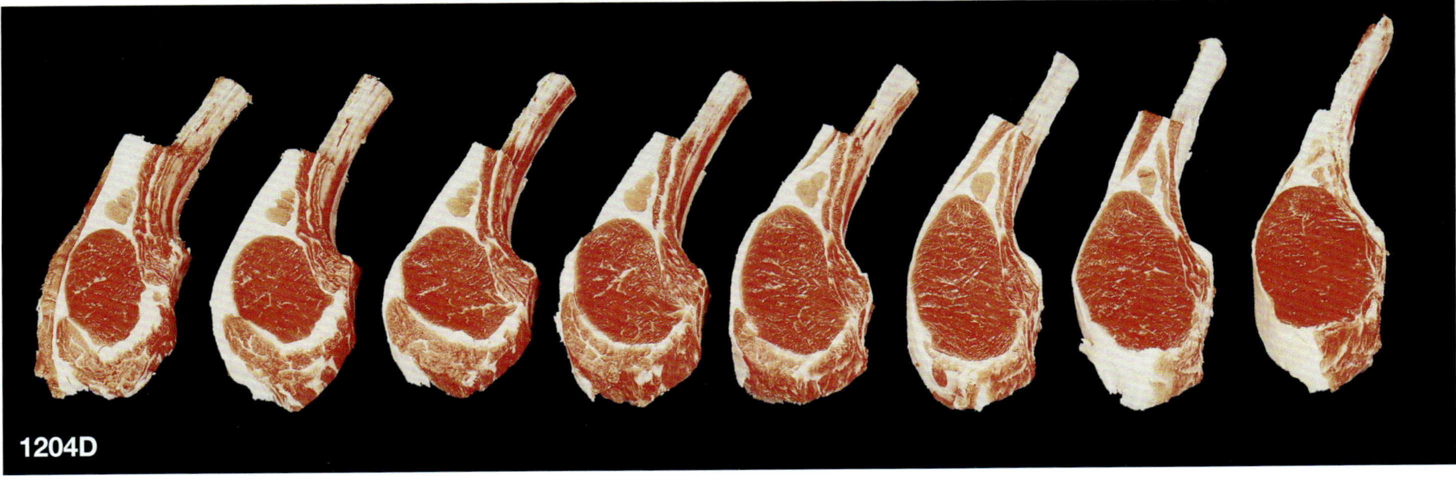

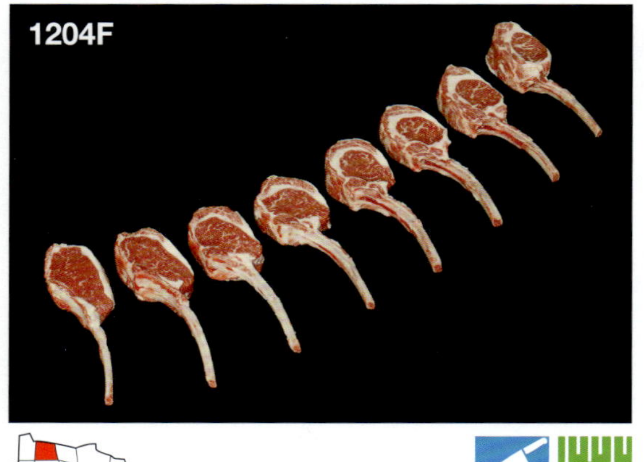

1204F — Lamb Rib Chops, Frenched, Fancy

This item is as described in Item No. 1204D, except all of the intercostal meat and lean and fat over the visible rib bone shall have been Frenched from a point immediately ventral to the *longissimus dorsi* muscle. Any other rib bone(s) shall also be removed at this same point. The maximum tail length of the bone shall be no more than 4.0 inches (10 cm) unless specified by a PSO length described in Item No. 1204B.

1204F — Cordero, Chuletas del Espaldar, Estilo Francés, De Gala

Esta pieza es igual a la pieza número 1204D, excepto que toda la carne intercostal, la grasa y la carne magra sobre la costilla visible deberán ser retiradas al estilo francés desde un punto inmediatamente ventral al músculo *longissimus dorsi*. Cualquier otra costilla también se deberá quitar en el mismo punto. La longitud máxima de la cola del hueso no deberá ser mayor a 10 cm (4 pulgadas), a menos que así lo especifique una longitud PSO descrita en la pieza número 1204B.

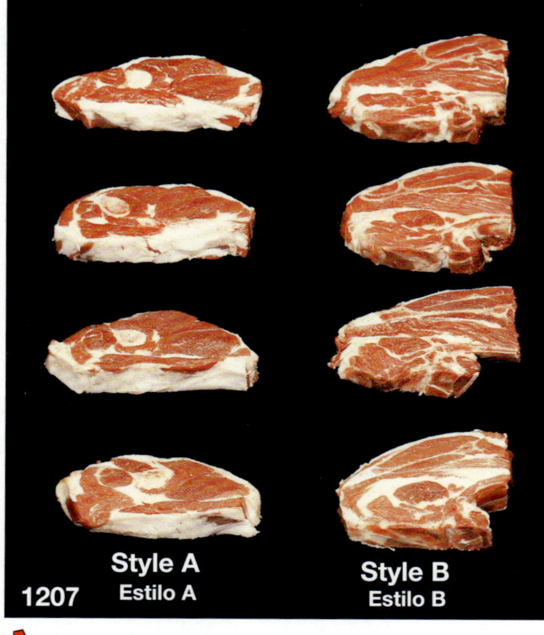

1207 — Lamb Shoulder Chops

Shoulder chops shall be prepared in proportional quantities from both the arm and blade bone portions of a single square-cut shoulder as described in Item No. 207. Chops shall be cut parallel to the line of the shoulder separations and meet the individual trim requirements for each style of chop. Purchaser, however, has an option to specify a single chop style as described below.

Style: A – Arm chops - These are derived from the arm portion of Item No. 207 Shoulder and shall contain a cross section of the humerus bone. Any rib bone and intercostal meat shall be excluded.

PSO: 1 – Rib bones are left attached if seam fat is less than .25 inch (6 mm) between the *pectoral* muscle and rib bones.

Style: B – Blade chops - These are derived from the blade or dorsal portion of Item No. 207 Shoulder. These chops shall contain a portion of the blade bone.

PSO: 1 – Chops may be prepared as "Country-style" by cutting the chops between the blade bone and rib bone to a point ending near the feather bone.

1207 — Cordero, Chuletas de Brazuelo y Paleta/ Chuletas del 7

Las chuletas de espaldilla se prepararán en cantidades proporcionales de porciones del hueso del brazuelo y de la paleta de una espaldilla de corte cuadrado, tal como se describe en la pieza número 207. Las chuletas deberán cortarse paralelas a la veta de separación de la espaldilla y cumplir con los requisitos de recorte individual para cada estilo de chuleta. El comprador, sin embargo, tiene la opción de especificar un único estilo de chuleta, tal como se especifica a continuación.

Estilo: A – Chuletas de brazuelo: estas chuletas se preparan con la porción de brazuelo de la pieza número 207, Espaldilla, e incluirá un corte transversal del húmero. Se deberán excluir las costillas y la carne intercostal.

PSO: 1 – Las costillas se dejarán unidas si las vetas de grasa intermuscular son menores de 6 mm (0.25 pulgadas) entre el músculo *pectoral* y las costillas.

Estilo: B – Chuletas de paleta: estas chuletas se preparan con la paleta o la porción dorsal de la pieza número 207; Espaldilla. Estas chuletas deben contener una porción del hueso de la paleta.

PSO: 1 – Las chuletas pueden prepararse al "estilo campestre", cortando las chuletas entre el hueso de la paleta y la costilla hasta un punto cercano a la punta del espinazo.

1209 — Lamb Short Rib, Bone In

This item may be prepared from any lamb shoulder or breast item as described in Item Nos. 206 or 209. The bone in short rib shall consist of the ribs, intercostal meat, and the intact *serratus ventralis* muscle. The *serratus ventralis* muscle shall be continuous across both the dorsal and ventral side of the specified portion. The ribs shall be cut flaken style by cutting them at a right angle to the rib bones. Purchaser may specify both the width of the cut and the number of ribs in each portion.

PSO: 1 – The ribs shall come from the shoulder portion only.

1209 — Cordero, Costilla Corta (Costilla Cargada), Con Hueso

Esta pieza puede prepararse con cualquier pieza de espaldilla o pecho de cordero tal como se describe en las piezas número 206 o 209. La costilla corta con hueso consistirá en las costillas, la carne intercostal y el músculo *serratus ventralis* intacto. El músculo *serratus ventralis* debe ser continuo a lo largo de los lados dorsal y ventral de la porción especificada. Las costillas deben cortarse al estilo alemán (flanken) mediante un corte en ángulo recto a las costillas. El comprador puede especificar el grosor del corte y la cantidad de costillas en cada porción.

PSO: 1 – Las costillas deben proceder únicamente de la porción de espaldilla.

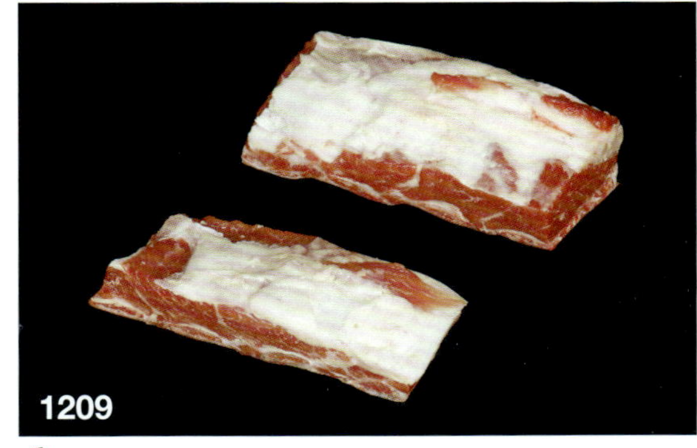
1209

1232A — Lamb Loin Chops

These chops shall be prepared from any bone in loin item that yields product that meets the end-item requirements. No chop shall contain any portion of the hipbone. The tail length shall be no longer than 4.0 inches (10 cm) from the ventral edge of the *longissimus dorsi* unless an optional tail length, as described below, is specified.

PSO: 1 – 3.0 inches (7.5 cm)

2 – 2.0 inch (5 cm)

3 – 1.0 inch (2.5 cm)

4 – 0.0 inch

1232A — Cordero, Chuletas de Lomo

Esta pieza se prepara con cualquier pieza de lomo con hueso que dé como resultado un producto que cumpla con los requisitos de la pieza final. Las costillas no incluirán ninguna porción de hueso de la cadera. La longitud de la cola no superará los 10 cm (4.0 pulgadas) desde el borde ventral del *longissimus dorsi*, a menos que se especifique una longitud opcional para la cola, tal como se describe a continuación.

PSO: 1 – 7.5 cm (3.0 pulgadas)

2 – 5 cm (2.0 pulgadas)

3 – 2.5 cm (1.0 pulgada)

4 – 0.0 cm

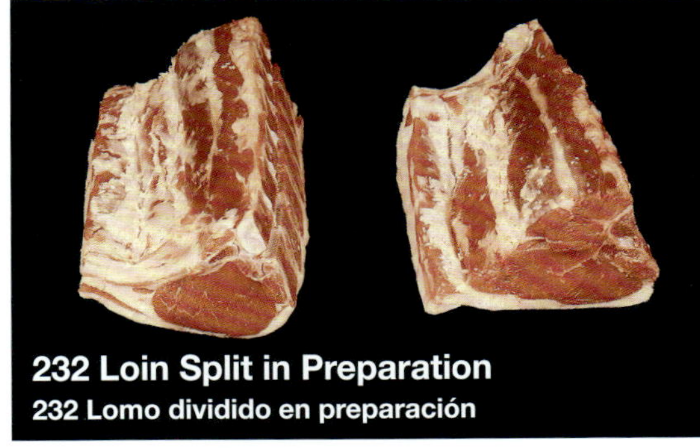
232 Loin Split in Preparation
232 Lomo dividido en preparación

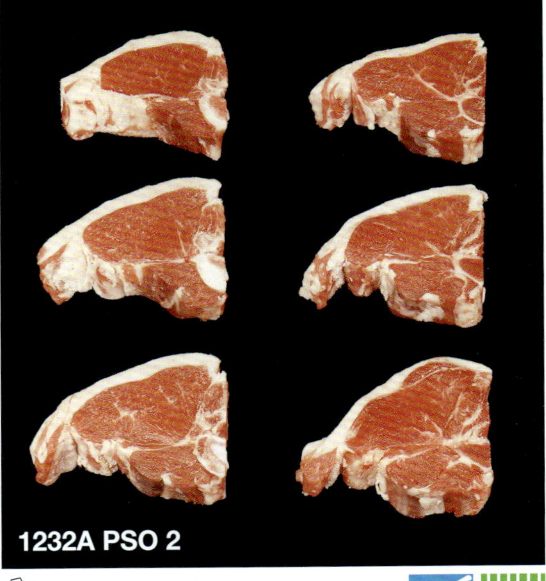
1232A PSO 2

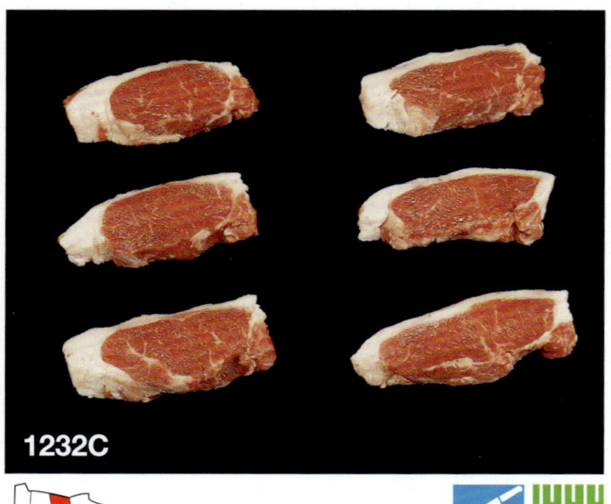

1232C — Lamb Loin Chops, Single, Boneless

These chops shall be prepared from any boneless loin item that yields product that meets the end-item requirements. The tail length shall be no longer than 4.0 inches (10 cm) from the ventral edge of the *longissimus dorsi* unless an optional tail length, as described in Item No. 1232A, is specified.

1232C — Cordero, Chuletas de Lomo, Individuales, Deshuesadas

Esta pieza se prepara con cualquier pieza de lomo sin hueso que dé como resultado un producto que cumpla con los requisitos de la pieza final. La longitud de la cola no superará los 10 cm (4.0 pulgadas) desde el borde ventral del *longissimus dorsi*, a menos que se especifique una longitud opcional para la cola, tal como se describe en la pieza número 1232A.

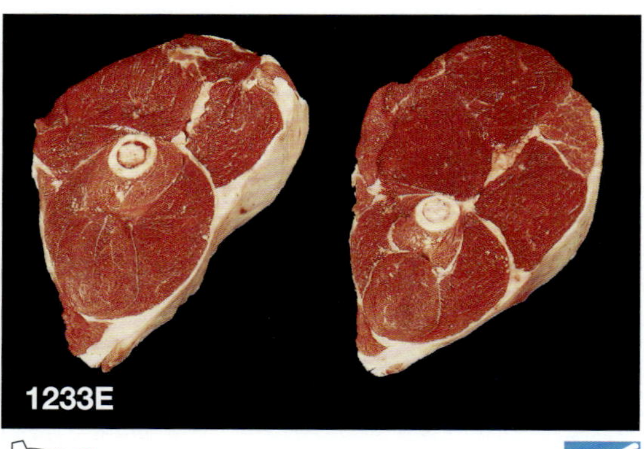

1233E — Lamb Leg, Center-Cut Chops

This item may be prepared from any bone in leg item that yields product that meets the end-item requirements. Each chop shall display a cross section of the femur bone on both sides of the chop. No other bone or cartilage shall be present.

- In Canada, "center-cut" is not an approved modifier. See page xxv for more information.

1233E — Pierna de Cordero, Chuletas del Centro

Esta pieza puede prepararse con cualquier pieza de pierna con hueso que dé como resultado un producto que cumpla con los requisitos de la pieza final. Cada chuleta debe presentar un corte transversal del fémur en sus dos lados. No deben existir otros huesos ni cartílagos.

- En Canadá, "corte central" no es un modificador aprobado. Consulte la pág. xxv para obtener información adicional.

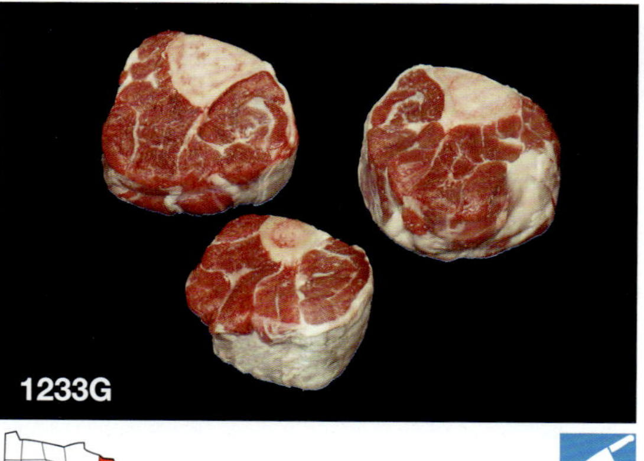

1233G — Lamb Osso Bucco, Hindshank

This item shall be prepared from Item No. 233G. The hindshank portions shall be cut to a thickness as specified by the purchaser. The slices shall be cut approximately perpendicular to the bone length so as to display a cross-section surface at least 75 percent lean on each side.

1233G — Osobuco de Cordero, Chamberete Trasero

Esta pieza se prepara con la pieza número 233G. Las porciones de chamberete trasero se cortarán del grosor que el comprador especifique. Las rebanadas deberán cortarse en forma aproximadamente perpendicular a la longitud del hueso de forma tal que la superficie del corte transversal presente un 75% de carne magra en cada lado.

NAMP
NORTH AMERICAN MEAT PROCESSORS ASSOCIATION
ASSOCIATION AMÉRIQUE DU NORD DES TRANSFORMATEURS DE VIANDE
ASOCIACIÓN NORTEAMERICANA DE PROCESADORES DE CARNE

1234A — Lamb Leg, Cutlet, Boneless

1234A — Pierna de Cordero, Escalopas, Deshuesadas

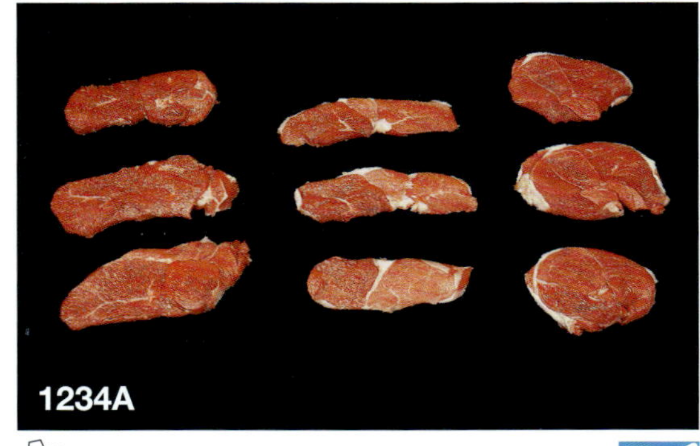

This item shall be prepared from any combination of boneless portions of inside, outside, sirloin tip, and sirloin muscles that yields a product that meets the end-item requirements. All shank and heel meat shall be excluded, and the cutlets shall be free of heavy connective tissue, cartilages, and lymph glands and trimmed of fat to meet purchaser specifications.

If cubing is specified, the cutlets shall be cubed the specified number of times at approximate right angles while in a fresh state. Knitting two or more pieces together and folding the meat while cubing is not permissible.

Esta pieza se preparará con cualquier combinación de porciones deshuesadas de músculos de pulpa negra (cara/centro), contracara, punta de sirloin y sirloin que den como resultado un producto que cumpla con los requisitos de la pieza final. Se excluirá toda la carne del chamberete y del talón, y las escalopas deben estar libres de tejido conectivo grueso, cartílagos, ganglios linfáticos y un recortado de grasa que cumpla con las especificaciones del comprador.

Si se especifica que las escalopas deben pasarse por máquina para suavizarlas, se deberá hacerlo la cantidad de veces que se especifique, en ángulos aproximadamente rectos, mientras se encuentren en estado fresco. No está permitido unir dos o más piezas ni plegar la carne al suavizarla.

1296 — Ground Lamb Patties

1296 — Hamburguesas de Carne Molida de Cordero

The patties shall be prepared from Item No. 296.

Las hamburguesas se prepararán con la pieza número 296.

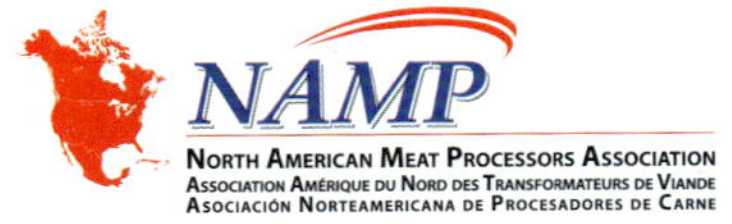

Center of the Plate Training®

from the producers of
The Meat Buyer's Guide®

Capacitación en ingredientes principales del plato

de los realizadores de la Guía
para Compradores de Carne®

Course Specifics

Center of the Plate Training® offered by the North American Meat Processors Association (NAMP) is a first-hand look at how carcasses are converted into portioned items commonly traded in the foodservice and retail meat business. The course covers all the major center of the plate protein items: beef, veal, lamb, pork, and poultry (in some locations).

This course is held two to three times annually across North America. It spans two to three days of classroom learning, with presentations by industry experts. You also will receive a copy of the NAMP *Meat Buyer's Guide®*, which is used extensively in the course.

What You Will Learn From This Course

- The IMPS/NAMP numbering system, purchase specified options, and standards common to the industry.

- A knowledge of meat items as described by IMPS and by NAMP's *Meat Buyer's Guide®*.

- Where meat products originate and how this affects their final use.

- The importance of standards and how they keep products consistent, wholesome, and fair throughout the market.

- Common defects or inconsistencies in meat products that you should look for to prevent dissatisfied customers or unpleasant dining experiences.

- Current trends in the foodservice industry, new menu ideas and options.

- How value is determined for different meat products and how this is affected by quality parameters.

If you're involved in the buying and selling of meat products - from restaurants and supermarkets to foodservice distributors and meat companies - gain a competitive edge by applying the valuable information you'll learn from this course.

Visit www.namp.com for more information on specific courses, locations, and dates.

Visite www.namp.com para obtener información adicional sobre cursos específicos, sitios y fechas.

Detalles del curso

La Capacitación en ingredientes principales del plato que ofrece la Asociación Norteamericana de Procesadores de Carne (NAMP) es una mirada de primera mano a la forma en que las canales se convierten en piezas porcionadas comúnmente comercializadas en la industria de servicios de alimentación y los negocios minoristas de carne. El curso comprende las principales piezas proteicas que constituyen los ingredientes principales del plato: carne de res, ternera, cordero, cerdo y aves (en algunos lugares).

Este curso se dicta dos o tres veces al año en toda Norteamérica. Abarca de dos a tres días de aprendizaje en un salón de clase, con presentaciones a cargo de expertos de la industria. También recibirá una copia de *La Guía para Compradores de Carne®* de NAMP (Asociación Norteamericana de Procesadores de Carne, por sus siglas en inglés) que se utilizará exhaustivamente en el curso.

Qué aprenderá en este curso

- El sistema de numeración IMPS/NAMP, las opciones especificadas de compra y las normas comunes de la industria.

- Un conocimiento de las piezas de carne como se describen en las IMPS (Especificaciones Institucionales de Compra de Carne, por sus siglas en inglés) y en *La Guía para Compradores de Carne®* de NAMP.

- Dónde se originan los productos de carne y cómo afecta esto su uso final.

- La importancia de las normas y cómo logran que los productos sean uniformes, saludables y buenos en todo el mercado.

- Defectos o anomalías en los productos de carne que debería buscar para evitar clientes insatisfechos o que tengan experiencias desagradables en la mesa.

- Las tendencias actuales de la industria de servicios de alimentación, nuevas ideas y opciones para su menú.

- Cómo se determina el valor de diferentes productos de carne y cómo éste se ve afectado por los parámetros de calidad.

Si participa en la compra y venta de productos de carne, ya sea en restaurantes y supermercados o distribuidores de la industria de servicios de alimentación y empresas de carne, obtenga una ventaja competitiva aplicando la valiosa información que aprenderá en este curso.

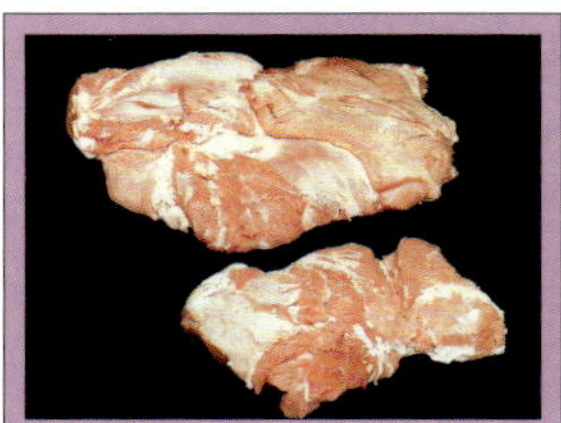

309B Veal Chuck, Square-Cut, 4 Ribs, Boneless / Paleta (Espaldilla sin Pecho ni Chamberetes), Corte Cuadrado, 4 Costillas, Deshuesada

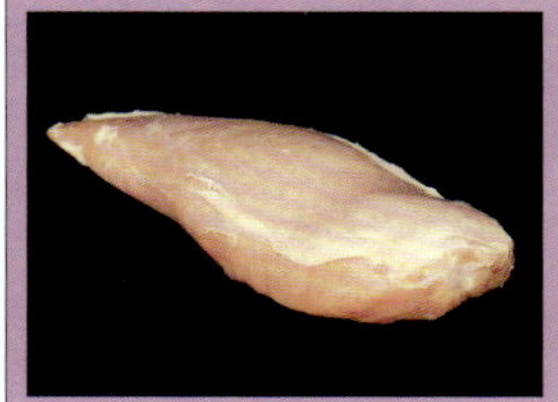

310C Veal Chuck Tender
Juil de Ternera

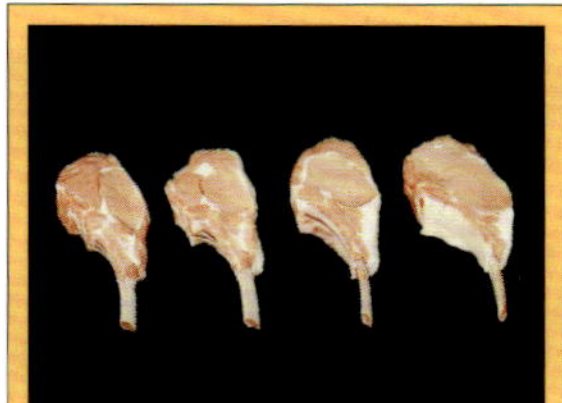

1306E Veal Rack, Rib Chops, Frenched, 6 Rib / Costillar, Chuletas, Estilo Francés, de 6 Costillas

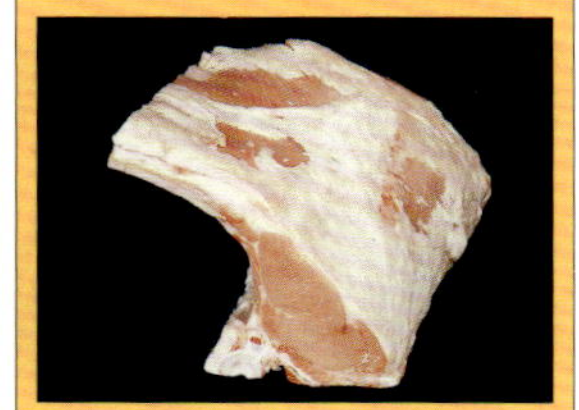

306 Veal Hotel Rack, 7 Rib
Costillar Clase Hotelera, 7 Costillas

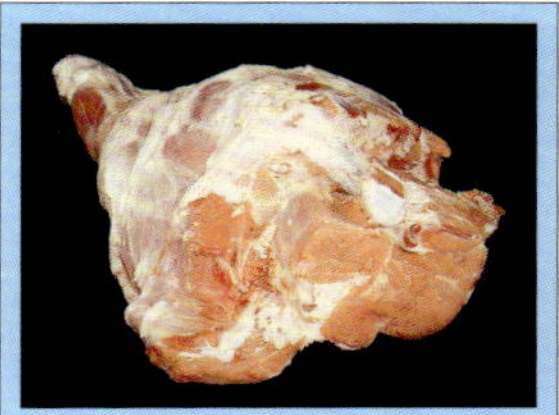

334 Veal Legs
Piernas

306C Veal Hotel Rack, Chop-Ready, 6 Ribs / Costillar Clase Hotelera, Listo Para Chuletas, 6 Costillas

307 Veal Rack, Ribeye, Boneless, 7 Ribs
Costillar, Ribeye, 7 Costillas

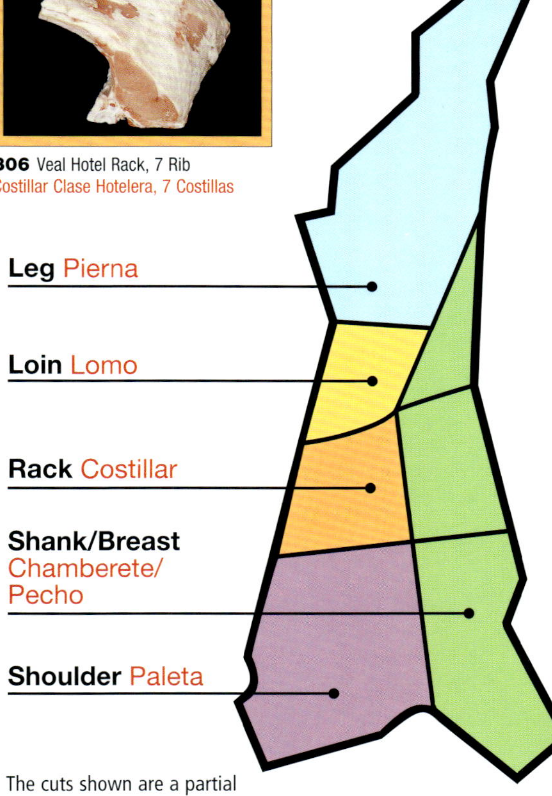

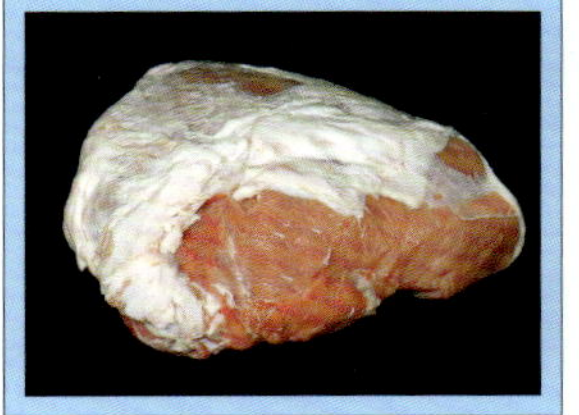

349 Veal Leg, Top Round (Inside), Cap On / Pierna, Pulpa Negra (Cara/Centro de Pierna), con Tapa

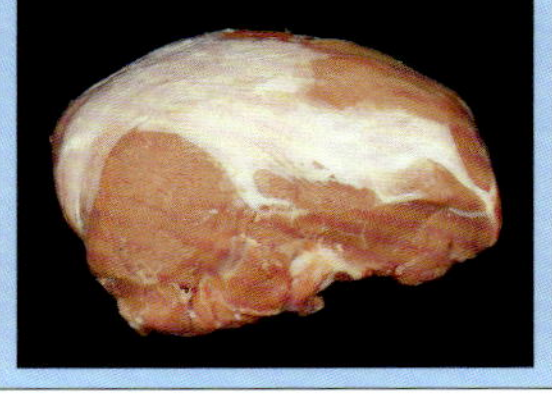

349A Veal Leg, Top Round, Cap Off / Pierna, Pulpa Negra (Cara/Centro de Pierna), sin Tapa

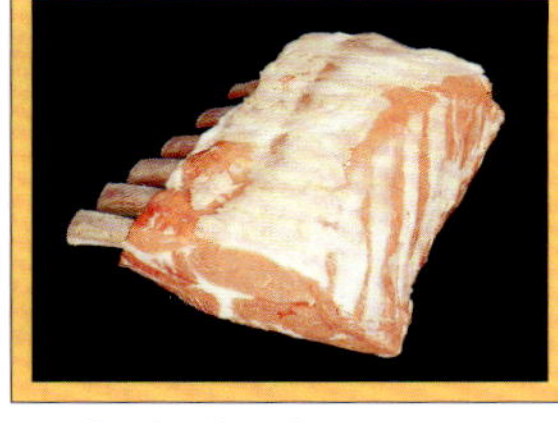

306E Veal Hotel Rack, Chop-Ready, 6 Ribs, Frenched Costillar Clase Hotelera, Listo Para Chuletas, 6 Costillas, Estilo Francés

The cuts shown are a partial representation of NAMP/IMPS items.

Los cortes exhibidos son una representación parcial de las piezas de NAMP/IMPS.

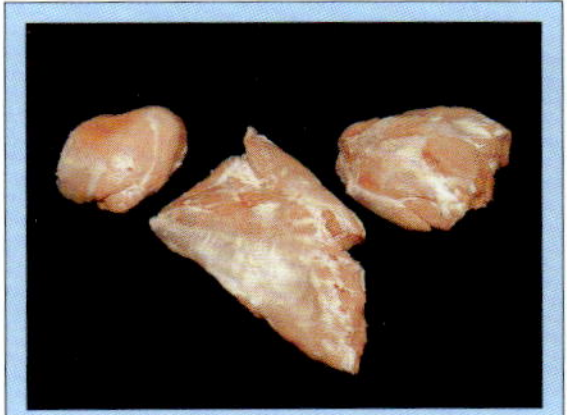

363A Veal Leg, TBS, 3 Parts
Pierna, Deshuesada, 3 piezas

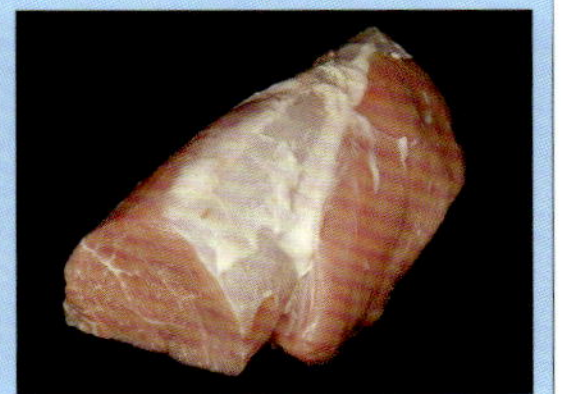

346 Veal Leg, Butt Tenderloin, Trimmed / Pierna, Cabeza de Filete, recortado de grasa y limpio

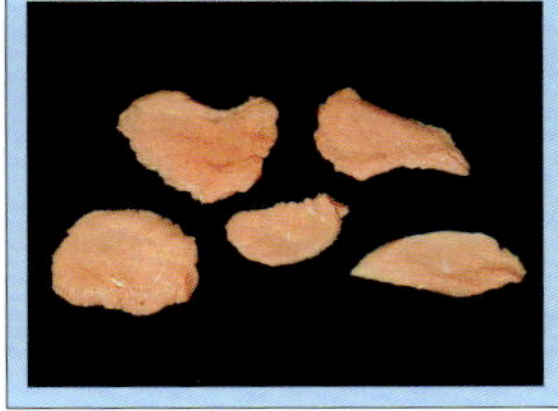

1336 Veal Cutlets, Boneless
Escalopas de Ternera, Deshuesadas

312A Veal Foreshank, Center-Cut
Chamberete de Mano, Corte del Centro

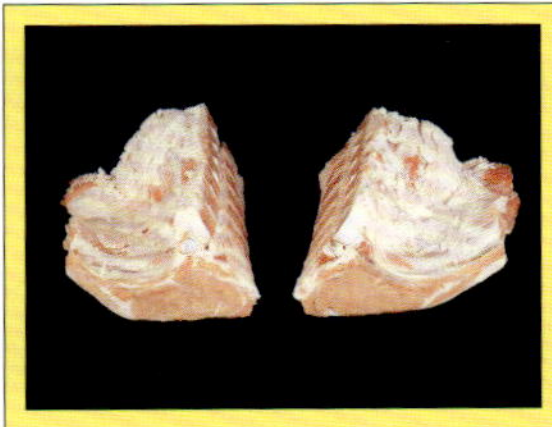

332 Veal Loins, Trimmed
Lomos, Recortados de Grasa y Limpios

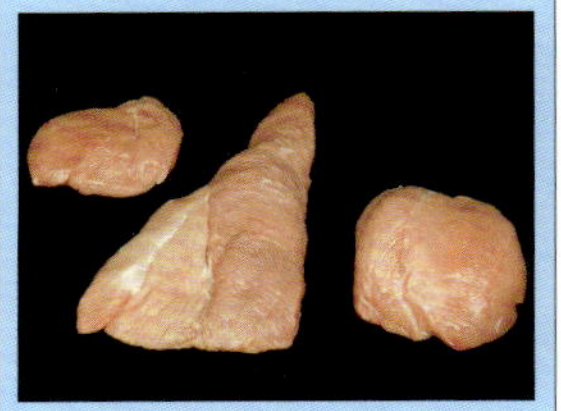

363B Veal Leg, BHS, 3 Parts
Pierna, Deshuesada, 3 piezas

1337 Veal Osso Buco, Hindshank
Osobuco de Ternera, Chamberete Trasero

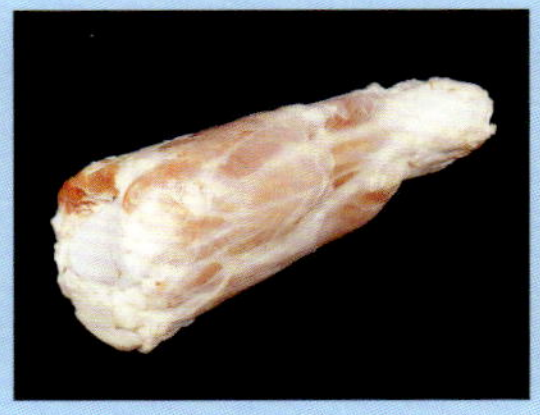

337 Veal Hindshank
Chamberete Trasero

344 Veal Loin, Strip Loin, Boneless
Lomo, Strip Loin, Deshuesado

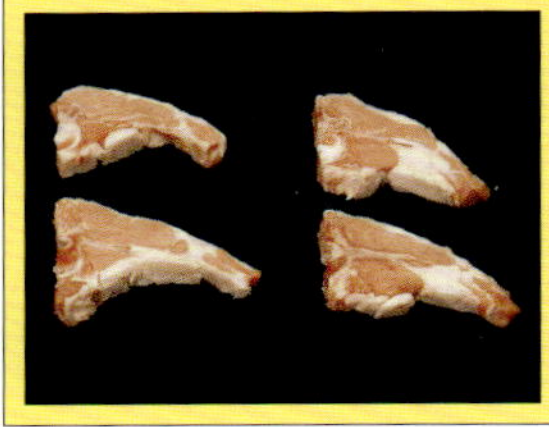

1332 Veal Loin Chops
Chuletas del Lomo

1300 Veal Cubed Steak, Boneless
Bistec Suavizado (Ablandado por Machacado, Rayado), Deshuesado

395A Veal (or Calf) for Kabobs
Trozos de Ternera para Brochetas

NAMP/IMPS Number (North American Meat Processors Association/Institutional Meat Purchase Specifications)
©2011 North American Meat Processors Association
www.namp.com

Número de NAMP/IMPS (Asociación Norteamericana de Procesadores de Carne/Especificaciones Institucionales de Compra de Carne)
©2011 Asociación Norteamericana de Procesadores de Carne
www.namp.com

Para obtener más información, comuníquese con National Cattlemen's Beef Association.

Producción de ternera

Desarrollo de la industria de ternera con alimentación especial

La producción de ternera en Estados Unidos está relacionada con la industria lechera. Por lo tanto, los becerros se crían principalmente en estados con una importante producción lechera. Para mantener una producción de leche eficiente, las vacas lecheras deben tener crías una vez al año. Se cría a las terneras hembras, o vaquillas, para la producción de leche. Las terneras macho, o toros, se comercializan a criadores de terneras para la producción de carne de ternera.

La ternera como la conocemos hoy tiene su origen en Europa. En la década de 1950, los productores lecheros de E.U.A. producían grandes excedentes de leche desnatada, un coproducto del procesamiento de mantequilla y queso, que se vendía a un bajo costo a los productores de ternera en los Países Bajos. Al igual que para todos los animales jóvenes, la leche es un componente básico de la dieta de las terneras. Los productores de ternera de los Países Bajos descubrieron que al alimentar a sus becerros con una dieta de leche desnatada, suero de leche y grasa obtenían una ternera de mayor peso y mejor calidad.

Al mejorar la calidad de la ternera, la demanda de ternera alimentada con leche aumentó en Europa y se expandió a E.U.A. Con el tiempo mejoraron los procesos empleados para la producción de raciones, junto con las prácticas de crianza de terneras. Actualmente se conoce a los becerros criados con ración producida a partir de suero reconstituido o líquido como terneras "con alimentación especial". El producto final tiene características únicas que incluyen un color rosa claro y un sabor suave. La ternera con alimentación especial es el tipo de ternera más usado en la industria de servicios de alimentación de primer nivel.

Producción de ternera: compasiva y saludable

En los últimos años se ha demostrado preocupación sobre la producción de ternera. Las críticas se han centrado en los establecimientos y la dieta de los animales. Para ayudar a los chefs y a los comensales a entender estos temas, ofrecemos una descripción general de la producción de ternera y la realidad de la industria de ternera en la actualidad.

De acuerdo con la American Veal Association (Asociación de Ternera de E.U.A), una organización de productores de ternera dedicados a establecer y mantener las normas de la industria, no había realmente un enfoque moderno y científico para la producción de ternera. Antes de la demanda de ternera al estilo europeo: "Se comercializaba a los becerros dentro de los tres o cuatro días después de su nacimiento. Todavía no había interés en crear el tipo de producto que se encontraba en Europa. Sin embargo, una vez que las prácticas de alimentación especial comenzaron a tener éxito en Estados Unidos, las prácticas de cuidado y alimentación de los animales mejoraron rápidamente". Los sistemas actuales de producción de ternera garantizan la salud del animal y la integridad del producto de ternera. Hoy en día, los productores de ternera invierten en la construcción de establos para terneras bien iluminados, climatizados y ventilados. Se aloja a los becerros en establos individuales construidos especialmente. Estos establos individuales reducen el contacto entre becerros, que es la mejor manera de evitar la propagación de enfermedades. Los establos individuales también maximizan la calidad del cuidado que los productores y veterinarios pueden dar a los becerros. Por ejemplo, se garantiza que cada becerro reciba cantidades adecuadas de alimento, en lugar de tener que competir con otros becerros en un lugar grupal. Además, las canaletas en el piso de los establos permiten retirar los desechos de manera eficiente. Por último, los establos tienen un tamaño adecuado que permite que los becerros se paren, estiren, echen y limpien solos.

La dieta con alimentación especial de los becerros se formula en etapas para producir animales sanos. Los productores de ternera y sus proveedores de alimentos supervisan cada becerro y extraen muestras de sangre regularmente para asegurar que todos los becerros reciban suficientes nutrientes.

De hecho, los productores de ternera tienen un interés personal en asegurar que sus becerros se críen en un entrono saludable. Con los años, los productores de ternera han demostrado ser innovadores en el cuidado y manejo de animales, lo que ha resultado en un producto de calidad.

Clases de ternera actuales. Estados Unidos produce entre 300 y 400 millones de libras de ternera al año. Existen básicamente tres tipos de ternera que se determinan según la manera en que se cría y alimenta a los becerros y se clasifican según el color y la textura de la carne.

A los becerros de ternera con alimentación especial se les alimenta con un suplemento lácteo nutricionalmente completo hasta que alcanzan las 18 a 20 semanas de edad y generalmente pesan entre 400 y 450 libras. La carne es de color marfil o rosa cremoso, y tiene una textura firme, fina y aterciopelada. Aproximadamente el 85% de la ternera que se consume en E.U.A. es ternera con alimentación especial. Este es el producto de calidad superior de la industria de ternera.

A las terneras lechales se les alimenta con leche. Por lo general pesan menos de 150 libras y tienen aproximadamente tres semanas cuando se comercializan. La carne tiene un color rosa claro y una textura suave.

A los becerros alimentados con granos se les alimenta inicialmente con leche y luego reciben una dieta de granos, heno y fórmulas de nutrición. La carne tiende a tener un color más oscuro y tiene un marmoleado adicional, y a su vez suele tener grasa visible. Los becerros alimentados con granos generalmente se comercializan de 5 a 6 meses de edad y pesan entre 450 y 600 libras.

Inspección y clasificación de la ternera

Al igual que todos los animales utilizados para la producción de carne, el Departamento de Agricultura de E.U.A. inspecciona dos veces a los becerros, una vez antes del procesamiento para verificar el estado de salud general y el bienestar del animal y otra vez después del procesamiento para verificar su sanidad.

Para garantizar la sanidad de la ternera, el Servicio de Inspección e Inocuidad Alimentaria del Departamento de Agricultura de E.U.A. también toma muestras de canales de ternera al azar para detectar la presencia de residuos antes de la venta. Sólo se han encontrado infracciones de residuos en un pequeño porcentaje de la muestra. Para combatir mejor cualquier problema con la inocuidad de los alimentos, la American Veal Association ha establecido un programa de control de calidad para la ternera con alimentación especial que requiere un estricto cumplimiento de las buenas prácticas de cría de animales. Desde el establecimiento del programa, el porcentaje de becerros en los que se detectaron infracciones de residuos cayó de 0.86% a 0.07%.

Además de las inspecciones antes del procesamiento y las muestras para la detección de residuos, se puede clasificar a las canales de ternera según su calidad. Los examinadores evalúan la conformidad de las canales (forma), su color y otros factores. Los examinadores de calidad identifican las características alimentarias del producto. Estas características son una guía sobre la ternura y el gusto de la carne.

Hay cinco grados de calidad para la ternera. Los grados, en orden de mayor a menor calidad, son los siguientes: U.S. Prime, U.S. Choice, U.S. Good, U.S. Standard y U.S. Utility. Más del 93% de la ternera evaluada es de calidad Prime o Choice. Los operadores de la industria de servicios de alimentación que compran ternera con alimentación especial están seguros de que reciben ternera Prime o Choice, debido a la uniformidad del producto que resulta de las prácticas modernas de producción de ternera.

Veal Production

Development of the Special-Fed Veal Industry

Veal production in the United States is tied to the dairy industry. Consequently, veal calves are primarily raised in major dairy production states. To remain efficient milk producers, dairy cows must give birth once a year. Female calves, or heifers, are raised to give milk. The male calves, or bulls, are marketed to veal farmers for veal production.

Veal as we know it today has its origins in Europe. In the 1950s, U.S. dairy farmers produced large surpluses of skim milk, a by-product of butter and cheese processing, which was sold inexpensively to veal producers in the Netherlands. Like all young animals, milk is a staple of a veal calf's diet. Dutch veal producers found that feeding their veal calves a diet of skim milk, whey and fat led to increased weights and an improved quality of veal.

As veal quality improved, demand for milk-fed veal increased in Europe and spread to the U.S. Over time, the processes used for manufacturing feed advanced, along with veal raising practices. Now, veal calves raised on feed made of reconstituted or liquid whey are known as "special-fed" veal. The final product has unique qualities that include a light-pink color and subtle flavor. Special-fed veal is the most popular type of veal used in up scale foodservice operations.

Veal Production: Humane and Healthy

In recent years, concerns have been raised over the production of veal. Criticism has focused on animal housing and diet. To help chefs and diners understand these issues, we offer an overview of veal production and the facts regarding the veal industry today.

According to the American Veal Association, an organization of veal producers dedicated to setting and maintaining industry standards, there really wasn't a modern and scientific approach to veal production. Prior to the demand for Europen-style veal. "Veal calves were marketed within three to four days of birth. There wasn't an interest yet in creating the type of product found in Europe. However, once the special-fed practices took off in the United States, improved animal care and feeding practices quickly evolved." Current veal production systems ensure the health of the animal and the integrity of the veal product. Today, veal producers invest in building well-lit, climate-controlled and ventilated veal barns. Veal calves are housed in specially constructed, individual stalls. These individual stalls reduce calf-to-calf contact, which is the best way to prevent the spread of disease. Individual stalls also maximize the quality of care producers and veterinarians can give the calves. For example, each calf is assured of receiving adequate amounts of food rather than having to compete with other calves in a group setting. In addition, the stalls' slotted floors allow for efficient removal of waste. Finally, the stalls are of adequate size to allow the calves to stand, stretch, lie down and groom themselves.

The special-fed calves' diet is formulated in stages to produce healthy animals. Veal producers and their feed suppliers monitor each calf and regularly draw blood samples to ensure all calves receive enough nutrients.

The fact is, veal producers have a vested interest in ensuring that their veal calves are raised in a healthy environment. Over the years, veal producers have proven themselves innovators in animal care and management, which has resulted in a quality product.

Classes of Veal Today The United States produces between 300 to 400 million pounds of veal annually. There are essentially three veal types; each is determined by the way calves are raised and fed, and are categorized by the color and texture of the meat.

Special-Fed Veal calves are fed a nutritionally complete milk supplement until they reach 18 to 20 weeks of age and typically weigh from 400 to 450 pounds. The meat is ivory or creamy pink, with a firm, fine and velvety texture. Approximately 85% of the veal consumed in the U.S. is special-fed veal. This is the veal industry's premium product.

Bob Veal calves are fed milk. They usually weigh less than 150 pounds and are approximately three weeks old when marketed. The meat has a light-pink color and a soft texture.

Grain-Fed Veal calves are initially fed milk, and then receive a diet of grain, hay and nutrition formulas. The meat tends to be darker in color and has additional marbling and often visible fat. Grain-fed veal calves are usually marketed at 5 to 6 months of age and weigh from 450 to 600 pounds.

Veal Inspection and Grading

Like all animals used in meat production, veal calves are inspected twice by the USDA - once before processing for the general health and well-being of the animal, and once after processing for wholesomeness.

To further ensure the wholesomeness of veal, the Food Safety and Inspection Service of the USDA surveys random samples of veal carcasses for the presence of residues prior to sale. Residue violations have shown up in only a very small percentage of the sample. To further combat any concerns about food safety, the American Veal Association has established a Quality Assurance Program for special- fed veal that requires strict compliance with good husbandry practices. Since the establishment of the program, the percentage of calves found to have residue violations has dropped from 0.86% to 0.07%.

In addition to inspection before processing and sampling for violative residues, veal carcasses can be graded for quality. Veal graders evaluate a carcass on conformity (shape), color and other factors. Quality grades identify the eating characteristics of the product. They are a guide to the tenderness and palatability of the meat.

There are five quality grades for veal. The grades in order from the highest to lowest quality are as follows: U.S. Prime, U.S. Choice, U.S. Good, U.S. Standard and U.S. Utility. More than 93% of graded veal is of Prime or Choice quality. Foodservice operators who purchase special-fed veal are assured of getting Prime or Choice veal, due to the product consistency that results from modern veal production practices.

Veal Skeletal Chart / Diagrama de estructura esquelética de la ternera

Location, Structure, and Names of Bones
Ubicación, estructura y nombres de los huesos

Courtesy of the American Meat Science Association. / Cortesía de la Asociación Americana de Ciencia de la Carne.

Veal Primal Cuts / Piezas Primarias de la Ternera

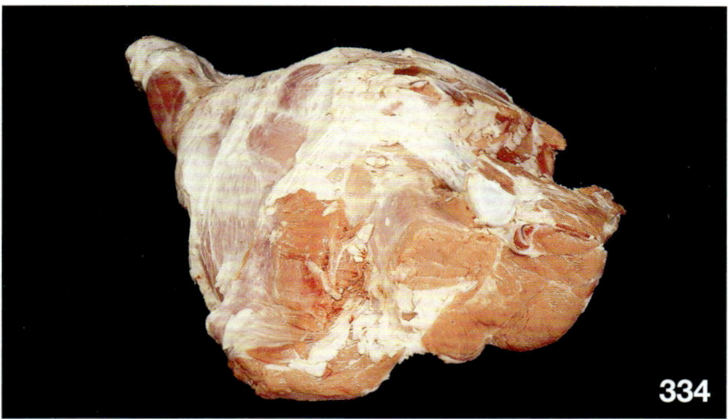

Veal Legs

Piernas de Ternera

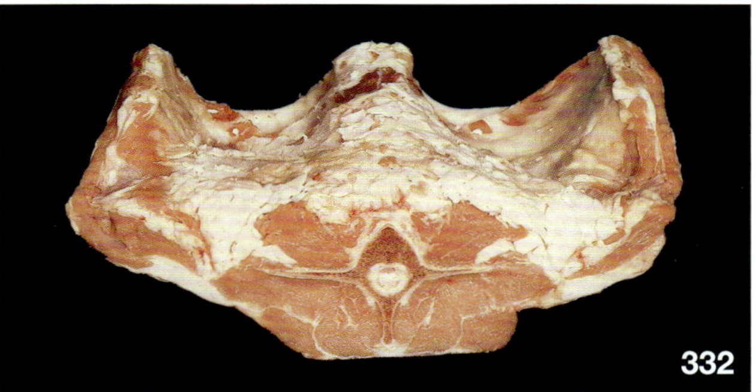

Veal Loins, Trimmed

Lomos de Ternera, Recortados de Grasa y Limpios

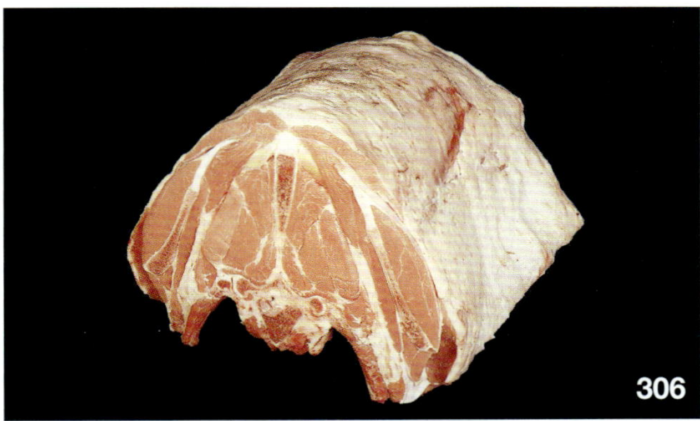

Veal Hotel Rack, 7 Ribs

Costillar Clase Hotelera, 7 Costillas

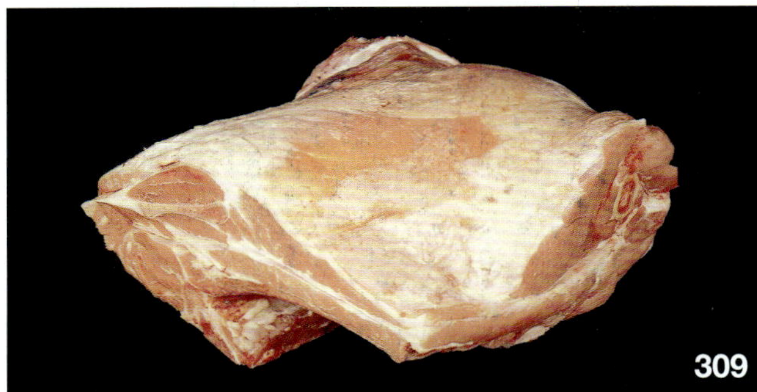

Veal Chuck, Square-Cut, 4 Ribs

Paleta de Ternera (Espaldilla sin Pecho ni Chamberetes),
Corte Cuadrado, 4 costillas

Loin-Leg Separation / Separación Lomo-Pierna

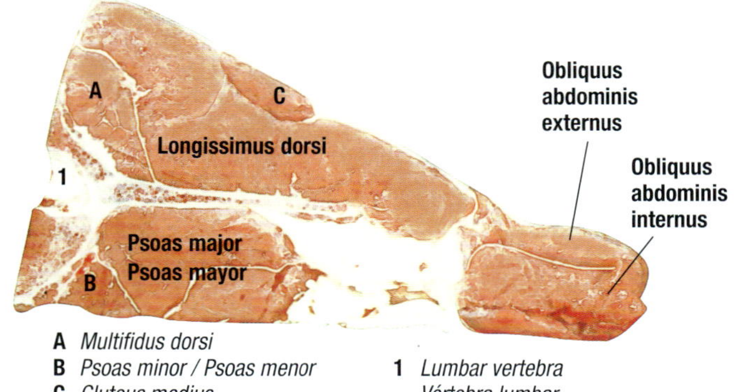

A Multifidus dorsi
B Psoas minor / Psoas menor
C Gluteus medius
1 Lumbar vertebra
Vértebra lumbar

Loin-Rack Separation / Separación Lomo-Costillar

A Multifidus dorsi
B Spinalis dorsi
C Longissimus costarum
D Intercostal
E Obliquus abdominis externus

1 Thoracic vertebra
Vértebra torácica

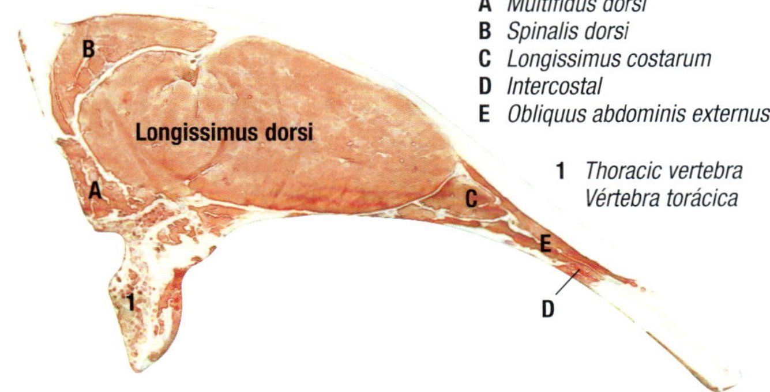

Rack-Chuck Separation
Separación Costillar-Paleta

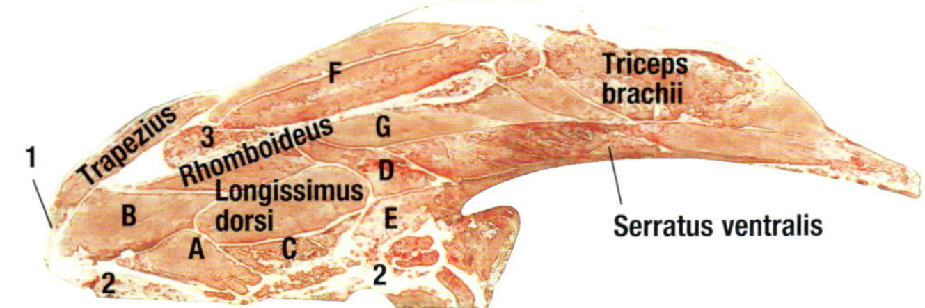

A Multifidus dorsi
B Spinalis dorsi
C Complexus
D Serratus dorsalis

E Longissimus costarum
F Infraspinatus
G Subcapularis

1 Ligamentum nuchae
2 Thoracic vertebra
Vértebra torácica
3 Scapula / Escápula

Chuck-Breast Separation
Separación Paleta-Pecho

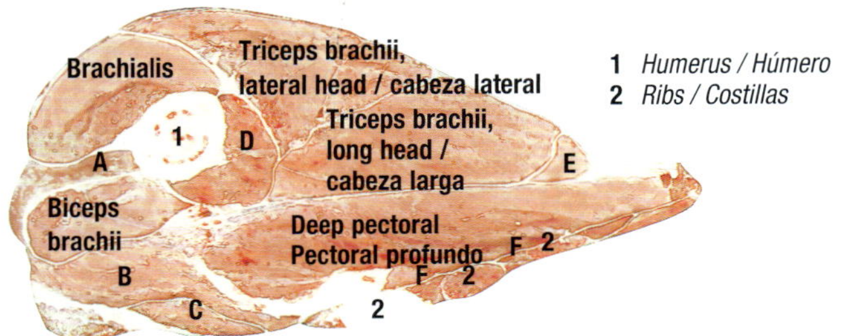

1 Humerus / Húmero
2 Ribs / Costillas

A Brachiocephalicus
B Superficial pectoral
Pectoral superficial

C Sterno-cleido mastoid
Esterno cleido mastoideo
D Triceps brachii, medial
head / cabeza media

E Tensor fascia antibrachii
F Intercostal muscles
Músculos intercostales

Index/Índice

Veal & Calf Products and Weight Ranges
Productos de Ternera y Becerro y Escalas de Peso

ITEM PIEZA	PRODUCT NAME / NOMBRE DE PRODUCTO	PG. PÁG.	Weight Ranges (pounds) / Escalas de peso (libras/kg) A	B	C	D	E
300	**Carcass** — Canal	140	50–70 (22.7-31.8)	70–175 (31.8-79.4)	175–245 (79.4-111.1)	245–300 (111.1-136.1)	300-up (Más de 136.1)
303	**Side** — Media Canal	140	25–35 (11.3-15.9)	35–87 (15.9-39.5)	87–122 (39.5-55.3)	122–150 (55.3-68)	150-up (Más de 68)
304	**Foresaddle, 11 Ribs Front Half** — Cuarto Delantero, 11 Costillas - Mitad Delantera ❋ Front Half	140	25–34 (11.3-15.4)	34–86 (15.4-39)	86–120 (39-54.4)	120–147 (54.4-66.7)	147-up (Más de 66.7)
304A	**Forequarter, 11 Ribs** — Cuarto Delantero, 11 Costillas	140	12–17 (5.4-7.7)	17–43 (7.7-19.5)	43–60 (19.5-27.2)	60–74 (27.2-33.6)	74-up (Más de 33.6)
306	**Hotel Rack, 7 Ribs** — Costillar Clase Hotelera, 7 Costillas	141	4–6 (1.8-2.7)	6–14 (2.7-6.4)	14–20 (6.4-9.1)	20–25 (9.1-11.3)	25-up (Más de 11.3)
306A	**Hotel Rack, 6 Ribs** — Costillar Clase Hotelera, 6 Costillas	142	3–5 (1.4-2.3)	5–13 (2.3-5.9)	13–19 (5.9-8.6)	19–24 (8.6-10.9)	24-up (Más de 10.9)
306B	**Hotel Rack, Chop-Ready, 7 Ribs** — Costillar Clase Hotelera, Listo Para Chuletas, 7 Costillas	142	1–2 (0.45-0.90)	2–5 (0.90-2.3)	5–7 (2.3-3.2)	7–9 (3.2-4.1)	9-up (Más de 4.1)
306C	**Hotel Rack, Chop-Ready, 6 Ribs** — Costillar Clase Hotelera, Listo Para Chuletas, 6 Costillas	142	1–2 (0.45-0.90)	2–4 (0.9-1.8)	4–6 (1.8-2.7)	6–8 (2.7-3.6)	8-up (Más de 3.6)
306D	**Hotel Rack, Chop-Ready, 7 Ribs, Frenched** — Costillar Clase Hotelera, Listo Para Chuletas, 7 Costillas, Estilo Francés	142	1–2 (0.45-0.90)	2–5 (0.90-2.3)	5–7 (2.3-3.2)	7–9 (3.2-4.1)	9-up (Más de 4.1)
306E	**Hotel Rack, Chop-Ready, 6 Ribs, Frenched** — Costillar Clase Hotelera, Listo Para Chuletas, 6 Costillas, Estilo Francés	143	1–2 (0.45-0.90)	2–4 (0.9-1.8)	4–6 (1.8-2.7)	6–8 (2.7-3.6)	8-up (Más de 3.6)
307	**Rack, Ribeye, Boneless, 7 Ribs** — Costillar, Ribeye, Deshuesado, 7 Costillas	143	0.5–2 (0.23-0.90)	2–4 (0.9-1.8)	4–6 (1.8-2.7)	6–9 (2.7-4.1)	9-up (Más de 4.1)
308	**Chucks, 4 Ribs** — Paleta (Espaldilla con Pecho y Chamberetes), 4 costillas	143	14–20 (6.4-9.1)	20–49 (9.1-22.2)	49–69 (22.2-31.3)	69–85 (31.3-38.6)	85-up (Más de 38.6)
308B	**Chucks, Arm Chucks, 4 Ribs** — Paletas (Espaldilla sin Pecho, con Chamberetes) de Ternera, 4 costillas	144	14–20 (6.4-9.1)	20–49 (9.1-22.2)	49–69 (22.2-31.3)	69–85 (31.3-38.6)	85-up (Más de 38.6)
309	**Chucks, Square-Cut, 4 Ribs** — Paleta (Espaldilla sin Pecho ni Chamberetes), Corte Cuadrado, 4 Costillas	144	11–16 (5-7.3)	16–39 (7.3-17.7)	39–55 (17.7-24.9)	55–68 (24.9-30.8)	68-up (Más de 30.8)
309B	**Chucks, Square-Cut, 4 Ribs, Boneless** — Paleta (Espaldilla sin Pecho ni Chamberetes), Corte Cuadrado, 4 Costillas, Deshuesada	144	10–19 (4.5-8.6)	19–26 (8.6-11.8)	26–33 (11.8-15)	33–40 (15-18.1)	40-up (Más de 18.1)
309G	**Chuck, Square-Cut, Clod Out, Boneless** — Paleta (Espaldilla sin Pecho ni Chamberetes), Corte Cuadrado, Sin Planchuela, Rollo Atado	145	9–15 (4.1-6.8)	15–20 (6.8-9.1)	20–30 (9.1-13.6)	30–38 (13.6-17.2)	38-up (Más de 17.2)
310	**Chuck, Outside Shoulder, Boneless** — Paleta (Espaldilla), Contracara de Planchuela, Deshuesada	145	2–4 (0.9-1.8)	4–5 (1.8-2.3)	5–7 (2.3-3.2)	7–9 (3.2-4.1)	9-up (Más de 4.1)
310C	**Chuck Tender (IM)** — Juil de Ternera (MI)	146	0.5–1 (0.23-0.45)	1–2 (0.45-0.90)	2-up (Más de 0.90)		
310D	**Chuck, Outside Shoulder** — Paleta (Espaldilla), Contracara de Planchuela con Brazuelo y Chamberete	146	2-5 (0.90-2.3)	5-8 (2.3-3.6)	8-10 (3.6-4.5)	10-13 (4.5-5.9)	13-up (Más de 5.9)
311	**Chuck, Blade Portion, Neck Off, Boneless** — Paleta (Espaldilla), Porción de la Paleta, Sin Pescuezo ni Juil, Deshuesada	147	7–13 (3.2-5.9)	13–21 (5.9-9.5)	21–28 (9.5-12.7)	28–38 (12.7-17.2)	38-up (Más de 17.2)
311A	**Chuck, Inside Roll, Boneless** — Paleta (Espaldilla), Rollo de Adentro de la Planchuela, Deshuesado	147	4–9 (1.8-4.1)	9–13 (4.1-5.9)	13–16 (5.9-7.3)	16–19 (7.3-8.6)	19-up (Más de 8.6)
311B	**Chuck, Chuck Eye Roll, Boneless** — Paleta (Espaldilla), Rollo de Corazón de Diezmillo, Deshuesado	148	2–3 (0.90-1.4)	3–5 (1.4-2.3)	5–7 (2.3-3.2)	7–10 (3.2-4.5)	10-up (Más de 4.5)
311C	**Chuck, Under Blade Roast, Boneless** — Paleta (Espaldilla), Tapa Interior de la Planchuela, Deshuesada	148	2–6	6–9 (2.7-4.1)	9–12 (4.1-5.4)	12–15 (5.4-6.8)	15-up (Más de 6.8)
312	**Foreshank** — Chamberete de Mano	148	1–2 (0.45-0.90)	2–3 (0.90-1.4)	3–4 (1.4-1.8)	4–5 (1.8-2.3)	5-up (Más de 2.3)
312A	**Foreshank, Center-Cut** — Chamberete de Mano, Corte del Centro	149	Under 1 (Menos de 0.45)	1–2 (0.45-0.90)	2–3 (0.90-1.4)	3–4 (1.4-1.8)	4-up (Más de 1.8)
313	**Breast** — Pecho	149	3–4 (1.4-1.8)	4–10 (1.8-4.5)	10–15 (4.5-6.8)	15–18 (6.8-8.2)	18-up (Más de 8.2)
314	**Breast with Pocket** — Pecho con Bolsillo	149	3–4 (1.4-1.8)	4–10 (1.8-4.5)	10–15 (4.5-6.8)	15–18 (6.8-8.2)	18-up (Más de 8.2)
323	**Short Ribs** — Costillas Cortas (Costilla Cargada)	150	Amount as Specified / Cantidad según lo especificado				
330	**Hindsaddle, 2 Ribs** — Cuarto Trasero, 2 Costillas - Mitad Trasera ❋ Hindhalf	141	25–36 (11.3-16.3)	36–89 (16.3-40.4)	89–125 (40.4-56.7)	125–153 (56.7-69.4)	153-up (Más de 69.4)
330A	**Hindquarter, 2 Ribs** — Cuarto Trasero, 2 Costillas	141	12–18 (5.4-8.2)	18–45 (8.2-20.4)	45–63 (20.4-28.6)	63–76 (28.6-34.5)	76-up (Más de 34.5)

ITEM / PIEZA	PRODUCT NAME / NOMBRE DE PRODUCTO	PG. / PÁG.	Weight Ranges (pounds) / Escalas de peso (libras/kg)				
			A	B	C	D	E
331	**Loins** Lomos	150	6–12 (2.7-5.4)	12–18 (5.4-8.2)	18–30 (8.2-13.6)	30–36 (13.6-16.3)	36-up (Más de 16.3)
332	**Loins, Trimmed** Lomos, Recortados de Grasa y Limpios	150	3–7 (1.4-3.2)	7–18 (3.2-8.2)	18–26 (8.2-11.8)	26–30 (11.8-13.6)	30-up (Más de 13.6)
332A	**Loins, Block-Ready, Trimmed** Lomos, Listos Para Tablajear, Recortados de Grasa y Limpios	151	Under 3 (Menos de 3)	3 – 5 (1.4-2.3)	5 – 7 (2.3-3.2)	7–8 (3.2-3.6)	8-up (Más de 3.6)
334	**Legs** Piernas	151	19–27 (8.6-12.2)	27–68 (12.2-30.8)	68–95 (30.8-43.1)	95–117 (43.1-53.1)	117-up (Más de 80.3)
335	**Leg, Boneless** Pierna, Deshuesada	151	8–11 (3.6-5)	11–26 (5-11.8)	26–36 (11.8-16.3)	36–45 (16.3-20.4)	45-up (Más de 20.4)
336	**Leg, Shank Off, Boneless** Pierna, sin Chamberete, Deshuesada	152	7 – 10 (3.2-4.5)	10–24 (4.5-10.9)	24–34 (10.9-15.4)	34–42 (15.4-19.1)	42-up (Más de 19.1)
337	**Hindshank** Chamberete Trasero	152	1–2 (0.45-0.90)	2–5 (0.90-2.3)	5–6 (2.3-2.7)	6–8 (2.7-3.6)	8-up (Más de 3.6)
337A	**Hindshank, Center-Cut** Chamberete Trasero de Ternera, Corte del Centro	152	1–2 (0.45-0.90)	2–3 (0.90-1.4)	3–4 (1.4-1.8)	4–5 (1.8-2.3)	5–6 (2.3-2.7)
341	**Back, Trimmed** Espaldar, Recortado de Grasa y Limpio	153	8–13 (3.6-5.9)	13–32 (5.9-14.5)	32–46 (14.5-20.9)	46–58 (20.9-26.3)	58-up (Más de 26.3)
344	**Loin, Strip Loin, Boneless** Lomo, Strip Loin, Deshuesado	153	2–3 (0.90-1.4)	3 – 5 (1.4-2.3)	5 – 7 (2.3-3.2)	7–8 (3.2-3.6)	8-up (Más de 3.6)
344A	**Loin, Strip Loin, Boneless, Skinned, 0x0** Lomo, Strip Loin, Deshuesado, Despellajado, 0x0	154	2–3 (0.90-1.4)	3 – 5 (1.4-2.3)	5-up (Más de 2.3)		
346	**Leg, Butt Tenderloin, Trimmed** Pierna, Cabeza de Filete, Recortado de Grasa y Limpio	154	1 – 1.5 (0.45-0.68)	1.5-up (0.68 y más)			
346A	**Leg, Butt Tenderloin, Skinned** Pierna, Cabeza de Filete, Despellejado	154	0.5–1 (0.23-0.45)	1-up (Más de 0.45)			
347	**Loin, Short Tenderloin** Lomo, Filete Corto	154	0.5–1 (0.23-0.45)	1-up (Más de 0.45)			
348	**Tenderloin** Filete de Ternera	155	Under 1 (Menos de 0.45)	1.5-2 (0.68-0.9)	2-2.5 (0.9-1.1)	2.5-3 (1.1-1.4)	3-up (Más de 1.4)
349	**Leg, Top Round (Inside), Cap On** Pierna, Pulpa Negra (Cara/Centro de Pierna), con Tapa	155	3–8 (1.4-3.6)	8–12 (3.6-5.4)	12-14 (5.4–6.4)	14–16 (6.4-7.3)	16-up (Más de 7.3)
349A	**Leg, Top Round, Cap Off** Pierna, Pulpa Negra (Cara/Centro de Pierna), sin Tapa	156	3–8 (1.4-3.6)	8–10 (3.6–4.5)	10–13 (4.5-5.9)	13–15 (5.9-6.8)	15-up (Más de 6.8)
350	**Leg, Bottom (Gooseneck), Heel Out** Pierna, Pulpa Blanca y Cuete, sin Chamberete, Deshuesada	156	Under 2 (Menos de 0.9)	2–3.5 (0.9-1.6)	3.5–5 (1.6-2.3)	5 – 7 (2.3-3.2)	7-up (Más de 3.2)
351A	**Leg, Sirloin Tip (Knuckle), Cap Off, Trimmed** Pierna, Pulpa Bola, sin Tapa, Recortada de Grasa y Limpia	157	Under 1 (Menos de 0.45)	1–2 (0.45-0.90)	2–3 (0.90-1.4)	3–4 (1.4-1.8)	4-up (Más de 1.8)
352A	**Leg, Hip, Cap Off, Boneless** Pierna, Cadera, sin Tapa, Deshuesada	157	Under 1 (Menos de 0.45)	1 – 1.5 (0.45-0.68)	1.5–2 (0.68-0.90)	2–2.5 (0.90-1.1)	2.5-up (Más de 1.1)
353	**Leg, Eye of Round (Leg)** Pierna, Cuete	158	Under 0.25 (Menos de 0.11)	0.25–0.5 (0.11-0.23)	0.5–1 (0.23-0.45)	1 – 1.5 (0.45-0.68)	1.5-up (0.68 y más)
363	**Leg, TBS, 4 Parts** Pierna, Deshuesada, 4 piezas	158	8–11 (3.6-5)	11–27 (5-12.2)	27–38 (12.2-17.2)	38–47 (17.2-21.3)	47-up (Más de 21.3)
363A	**Leg, TBS, 3 Parts** Pierna, Deshuesada, 3 piezas	158	6–9 (2.7-4.1)	9–24 (4.1-10.9)	24–32 (10.9-14.5)	32–39 (14.5-17.7)	39-up (Más de 17.7)
363B	**Leg, BHS, 3 Parts** Pierna, Deshuesada, 3 piezas	159	6–12 (2.7-5.4)	12–27 (5.4-12.2)	27–35 (12.2-15.9)	35–42 (15.9-19.1)	42-up (Más de 19.1)
388	**Bones, Mixed** Huesos, Variados	159	Amount as Specified Cantidad según lo especificado				
389	**Bones, Marrow** Huesos, Tuétano	159	Amount as Specified Cantidad según lo especificado				
393	**Flank, Flank Steak** Falda de Ternera, Concha (Bistec de Falda) (M. Rectus Abdominis)	159	Under 0.25 (Menos de 0.11)	0.25–0.3 (0.11-0.13)	0.3–0.5 (0.13-0.23)	0.5–0.75 (0.23-0.34)	0.75-up (Más de 0.34)
395	**Veal (or Calf) for Stewing** Trozos de Ternera para Cocer/Guisar	160	Amount as Specified Cantidad según lo especificado				
395A	**Veal (or Calf) for Kabobs** Trozos de Ternera para Brochetas	160	Amount as Specified Cantidad según lo especificado				
396	**Ground Veal** Carne Molida de Ternera	161	Amount as Specified Cantidad según lo especificado				

Información para hacer los pedidos

Grado

El sistema de clasificación por grados de la canal de ternera y becerro en E.U.A. y Canadá se explica en detalle en la sección introductoria al comienzo de la *Guía para Compradores de Carne*. El comprador puede especificar el grado y/o la clase de canales de donde se desea extraer las piezas. La División de Certificación y Clasificación del Servicio de Mercadeo Agrícola del Departamento de Agricultura de E.U.A. determina oficialmente los grados de calidad de la ternera y el becerro mediante la evaluación de la madurez de la canal, la calidad de la carne magra y la conformación. No existen grados de rendimiento para la ternera y el becerro. Del total, muy pocas canales de terneras o becerros se someten a gradación. Las fotografías que aparecen en esta guía se tomaron utilizando canales provenientes de las opciones C o D de la descripción a la derecha en el cuadro titulado Clases de terneras.

Estado de refrigeración

A **FRESCO**	−2.2 °C (28 °F) o mayor
B **CONGELADO**	−2.2 °C (28 °F) o menor
C **OPCIÓN ESPECIFICADA POR EL COMPRADOR**	−17.8 °C (0 °F) o menor

El producto se puede pedir fresco o congelado. El término *refrigerado en estado fresco* es utilizado por el Servicio de Mercadeo Agrícola del Departamento de Agricultura de E.U.A. para describir los productos que no han sido congelados anteriormente.

Opciones especificadas por el comprador

Los compradores pueden especificar una cantidad de opciones diferentes sobre los productos que desean comprar. Estas opciones incluyen, entre otras, grado de calidad, estado de refrigeración, mediciones sobre límites de la grasa e instrucciones de procesamiento. Los aspectos detallados en el texto pueden incluir también requisitos específicos de la descripción de la pieza del producto, u ofrecer una variedad de opciones de especificaciones del comprador. Algunas de estas opciones se explican más detalladamente en la sección introductoria al comienzo de la *Guía para Compradores de Carne*, más adelante en esta sección, o en la descripción de la pieza correspondiente. Los compradores que tengan necesidades o especificaciones especiales deben comunicarse con sus proveedores.

Clase

La diferenciación entre las clases "ternera" y "becerro" en E.U.A. se basa primordialmente en el color de la carne magra. Las canales de ternera típicas tienen un color rosa grisáceo de carne magra con una textura muy lisa y aterciopelada. En contraste, la carne magra de las canales de becerro típicas son de un color rojo grisáceo. Cuanto más evidencia de color rojo en la carne magra, más correlación habrá con una madurez avanzada y con la dieta. La siguiente tabla proporciona información para el comprador y opciones sobre los diversos tipos de ternera y becerro a su disposición.

Clases de ternera

Opción	Tipo	Lb	Kg	Color	Edad	Dieta
A	Ternera lechal	50–70	22–31	Rosa grisácea clara	<21 días	Leche/fórmula
B	Ternera intermedia	70–175	70–175	Rosa grisácea	3–14 sem.	Leche/fórmula
C	Ternera alimentada con fórmula/leche	175–225	79–102	Rosa grisácea	14-18 sem.	Leche/fórmula
D	Ternera con alimentación especial	225–300	102–136	Rosa grisácea	18-20 sem.	Leche/fórmula
E	Becerro	+ 300	+ 136	Rojo grisáceo	+ 18 sem.	Grano/forraje

El procesador deberá cumplir con todos los procedimientos de etiquetado sobre grados y productos del Servicio de Inspección e Inocuidad Alimentaria (FSIS, por sus siglas en inglés). Para fines de etiquetado, cuando se especifica la Opción A, B, C o D, el producto deberá llevar la etiqueta con la palabra "Veal" [ternera] (si se desea, la opción A puede etiquetarse como "Bob Veal" [ternera lechal]). Cuando se especifica la opción E dentro de una variedad de opciones (por ej., de A a E), el producto deberá llevar la etiqueta con la palabra "Veal or Calf" (Ternera o Becerro). Cuando solamente se especifica la opción E, el producto debe etiquetarse como "Calf" (Becerro).

Los tipos individuales de A a D descritos anteriormente no pueden ser verificados mediante una evaluación de las canales o los cortes. El comprador puede solicitar un documento del vendedor que declare que las canales o los cortes proporcionados provienen del o los tipos especificados requeridos.

 En Canadá, las canales de menos de 180 kg (397 libras) pueden etiquetarse como ternera. Canadá tiene dos clases de ternera: ternera lechal, alimentada con leche, que proviene de becerros que alcanzan un peso de mercado de 204 a 227 kg (450 a 500 libras), y ternera alimentada con granos, que proviene de becerros que alcanzan un peso de mercado de 295 a 318 kg (650 a 700 libras).

Información para hacer los pedidos

Opciones para limitar la grasa

Cortes y Trozos Rosbifs

A menos que se especifique lo contrario en la descripción de la pieza, el comprador puede especificar uno de los siguientes niveles de recorte para eliminación de la cubierta de grasa y/o membrana superficial ("membrana conectiva azul" o "plateada" llamada "Espejo") de las superficies de los cortes y los trozos rosbifs.

Cortes y Trozos Rosbifs

N° de opción	Máximo de Grosor Promedio	Máximo en un Punto Cualquiera
1	19 mm (0.75 pulgadas) con recorte de grasa tipo commodity	2.5 cm (1.0 pulgadas)
2	6 mm (0.25 pulgadas)	13 mm (0.50 pulgadas)
3	3 mm (0.125 pulgadas)	6 mm (0.25 pulgadas)
4	Prácticamente Libre (75% de superficie magra/superficie muscular descubierta por la disección)	3 mm (0.125 pulgadas)
5	Desprovisto de grasa/Prácticamente desnudo de grasa* [la grasa que queda no debe exceder los 2.5 cm (1.0 pulgadas) en la dimensión más larga y/o 3 mm (0.125 pulgadas) de grosor]	3 mm (0.125 pulgadas)
6	Desprovisto de grasa/Prácticamente desnudo de grasa, Membrana superficial retirada** (el 90% de la superficie expuesta es magra)	3 mm (0.125 pulgadas)

*/** – consulte la definición en la página xlv

* NOTA: cuando se especifiquen los grosores promedio de grasa en la descripción de la pieza, se aplicará la limitación "Máximo en un punto cualquiera" correspondiente.

Ordering Data

Grade

The system of veal and calf carcass grading in both the U.S. and Canada is explained in detail in the Introductory Section at the front of *The Meat Buyer's Guide*. The purchaser may specify the grade and/or class of carcasses from which the items they want are to be derived. In the U.S., veal and calf quality grades are officially determined by evaluation of carcass maturity, quality of lean, and conformation by the Meat Grading and Certification Branch of the USDA Agricultural Marketing Service. There are no yield grades for veal and calf. In total, very few veal or calf carcasses are graded. The photographs that appear in this guide were taken using carcasses from Options C or D described at the right in the Classes of Veal table.

State of Refrigeration

A FRESH	28°F (–2.2°C) or higher
B FROZEN	28°F (–2.2°C) or lower
C PSO	0°F (–17.8°C) or lower

Product may be ordered fresh or frozen. The term *fresh chilled* is used by the USDA Agricultural Marketing Service to describe product that has not been previously frozen.

Purchaser Specified Options (PSO)

Purchasers may specify a number of different options on the products they wish to purchase. These options (PSO) include among others, quality grade, state of refrigeration, fat limitation measurements, and processing instructions. Items listed in the text may also include specific requirements in the Item Description of the product, and/or offer a range of PSO choices. Some of these options are explained in more detail in the Introductory Section at the front of *The Meat Buyer's Guide,* or later in this section, or in the appropriate Item Description. Purchasers who have special needs or specifications should contact their suppliers.

Class

Differentiation between the classes "veal" and "calf" in the U.S. is made primarily on the basis of the color of lean. Typical veal carcasses have a grayish pink color of lean that is very smooth and velvety in texture. By contrast, typical calf carcasses have a grayish red color of lean. The more evidence of red color of lean correlates with advanced maturity and diet. The following table provides purchaser information and options for the various types of veal and calf available.

Classes of Veal

Option	Type	Lbs	Kg	Color	Age	Diet
A	Bob Veal	50–70	22–31	Light grayish-pink	<21 days	Milk/ formula
B	Intermediate Veal	70–175	70–175	Grayish-pink	3–14 wk	Milk/ formula
C	Milk/Formula-Fed Veal	175–225	79–102	Grayish-pink	14–18 wk	Milk/ formula
D	Special-Fed Veal	225–300	102–136	Grayish-pink	18–20 wk	Milk/ formula
E	Calf	300+	136+	Grayish-red	18 wk+	Grain/ roughage

The processor shall comply with all FSIS grade labeling and product labeling procedures. For labeling purposes, when Option A, B, C, or D is specified, the product shall be labeled "Veal" (if desired Option A may be labeled "Bob Veal"). When Option E is specified within a range of options (i.e., A–E), product shall be labeled "Veal or Calf." When only E is specified, product shall be labeled "Calf."

The individual types, A–D described above, cannot be verified by evaluation of carcasses or cuts. The purchaser may request documentation from the vendor, stating that carcasses or cuts supplied are derived from the specified type(s) requested.

 In Canada, carcasses under 180 kg (397 lbs.) may be labeled as veal. Canada has two classes of veal: milk fed veal, which is from calves who reach a market weight of 450-500 pounds, and grain fed veal, which is from calves that reach a market weight of 650-700 pounds.

Ordering Data

Fat Limitation Options (FLO)

Cuts and Roasts

Unless stated differently within the Item Description, the purchaser may specify one of the following trim levels for removal of surface fat and/or surface membrane ("silver" or "blue tissue") from the surfaces of cuts and roasts.

Cuts and Roasts

Option No.	Maximum Average Thickness	Maximum at Any One Point
1	0.75 inch (19 mm) "Commodity trim"	1.0 inch (2.5 cm)
2	0.25 inch (6 mm)	0.50 inch (13 mm)
3	0.125 inch (3 mm)	0.25 inch (6 mm)
4	Practically Free (75 percent lean/seam surface exposed)	0.125 inch (3 mm)
5	Peeled/Denuded* (remaining fat shall not exceed 1.0 inch (2.5 cm) in the longest dimension and/or 0.125 inch (3 mm) in thickness)	0.125 inch (3 mm)
6	Peeled/Denuded, Surface Membrane Removed** (90 percent lean exposed)	0.125 inch (3 mm)

*/** – see page xvi for definition

*** NOTE: When average fat thicknesses are specified in Item Descriptions, the appropriate "Maximum at Any One Point" limitation shall apply.**

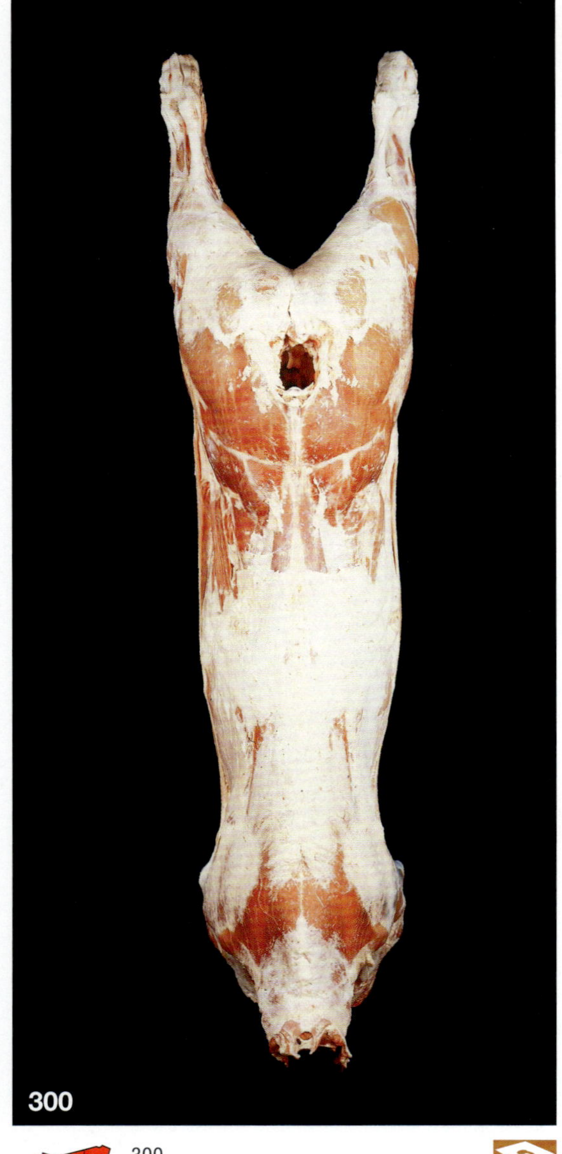

300

300 Veal Carcass

This item is the unsplit carcass with not more than two tail vertebrae remaining attached. The hanging tender and diaphragm may be removed, but if not removed, the membranous portion of the diaphragm shall be trimmed close to the lean.

300 Canal de Ternera

Esta pieza es la canal sin dividir con un máximo de dos vértebras de la cola aún unidas. Es posible extraer la falda colgante del lomo (arrachera gallo) y el diafragma, pero si no se eliminan, la porción membranosa del diafragma deberá ser despellejada llegando a descubrir la carne magra.

303 Veal Side

A side consists of one half of the carcass. It is produced by splitting the carcass through the vertebral column (backbone) exposing the spinal cord groove at least 75 percent of the length of the side. The hanging tender and the diaphragm may be removed, but if not removed, the diaphragm shall be trimmed as described in Item No. 300.

303 Media Canal de Ternera

La media canal consiste en una mitad de la canal. Se obtiene dividiendo la canal a lo largo de la columna vertebral (espinazo), exponiendo el canal raquídeo al menos en un 75% de la longitud de la media canal. Es posible extraer la falda colgante del lomo (arrachera gallo) y el diafragma, pero si no se eliminan, se deberá recortar de grasa y limpiar el diafragma según la descripción de la pieza número 300.

304 Veal Foresaddle, 11 Ribs

The foresaddle is the anterior portion of the carcass that includes the 1st through 11th ribs. It remains after removal of the Item No. 330 Hindsaddle, 2 Ribs from the carcass, by a cut following the natural curvature between the 11th and 12th ribs. The diaphragm may or may not be removed as described in Item No. 300.

In Canada, this item is referred to as the Front Half.

304 Cuarto Delantero, 11 Costillas - Mitad Delantera

El cuarto delantero es la porción anterior de la canal que incluye las costillas 1ª a la 11ª. Se obtiene después de retirar la pieza número 330: "Cuarto trasero, 2 Costillas - Mitad Trasera", mediante un corte que siga la curvatura natural entre las costillas 11ª y 12ª. El diafragma puede o no extraerse, según la descripción de la pieza número 300.

En Canadá, esta pieza se la conoce como la "Front Half" (Mitad Delantera).

304A Veal Forequarter, 11 Ribs

This item is the split half of Item No. 304. It is also produced after Item No. 330A Hindquarter, 2 Ribs is separated from Item No. 303.

304A Cuarto Delantero, 11 Costillas

Esta pieza es la mitad dividida de la pieza número 304. También se obtiene después de que la pieza número 330A: "Cuarto trasero, 2 Costillas", se separa de la pieza número 303.

300

303

304

304A

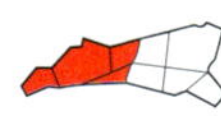

330 — Veal Hindsaddle, 2 Ribs

The hindsaddle is the posterior portion of the carcass remaining after the removal of Item No. 304. It includes the 12th and 13th ribs. The hanging tender and diaphragm may or may not be removed as described in Item No. 300.

 In Canada, this item is referred to as the Hind Half.

330 — Cuarto Trasero de Ternera, 2 Costillas - Mitad Trasera

El cuarto trasero es la porción posterior de la canal que permanece después de extraer la pieza número 304. Incluye las costillas 12ª y 13ª. La arrachera gallo (falda colgante del lomo) y el diafragma pueden, o no, extraerse según la descripción de la pieza número 300.

En Canadá, esta pieza se conoce como la "Hind Half" (mitad trasera).

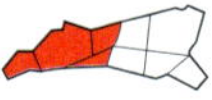

330A — Veal Hindquarter, 2 Ribs

The item in the split half of Item N. 330. It is also produced after Item No. 304A Forequarter, 11 Ribs is separated from Item No. 303.

330A — Cuarto Trasero, 2 Costillas

Es la pieza dividida por la mitad de la pieza número 330. También se obtiene después de que la pieza número 304A: "Cuarto delantero, 11 Costillas", se separa de la pieza número 303.

306 — Veal Hotel Rack, 7 Ribs

This 7 rib item is prepared from Item No. 304 by a straight cut between the 4th and 5th ribs and includes ribs 5 through 11. The plate portion of the breast is separated by a straight cut across the ribs that is no more than 4.0 inches (10.0 cm) from the outer tip of the ribeye muscle (*longissimus dorsi*). The ribeye muscle shall be approximately equal to or larger than the *complexus* muscle on the cut surface of the chuck end. Purchaser may request this item be split.

306 — Costillar Clase Hotelera, 7 Costillas

Esta pieza de 7 costillas se prepara con la pieza número 304 mediante un corte recto entre la costilla 4ª y la 5ª, e incluye las costillas 5ª a la 11ª. La porción del costillar del pecho se separa mediante un corte recto a través de las costillas, de no más de 10.0 cm (4.0 pulgadas) desde la punta externa del músculo del ribeye (*longissimus dorsi*). El músculo del ribeye deberá ser aproximadamente igual o mayor en tamaño que el músculo *complexus* sobre la superficie de corte del extremo adyacente a la paleta. El comprador puede solicitar que esta pieza esté separada.

306 View from Chuck End, Split
Vista desde el Extremo Adyacente a la Paleta, Dividida

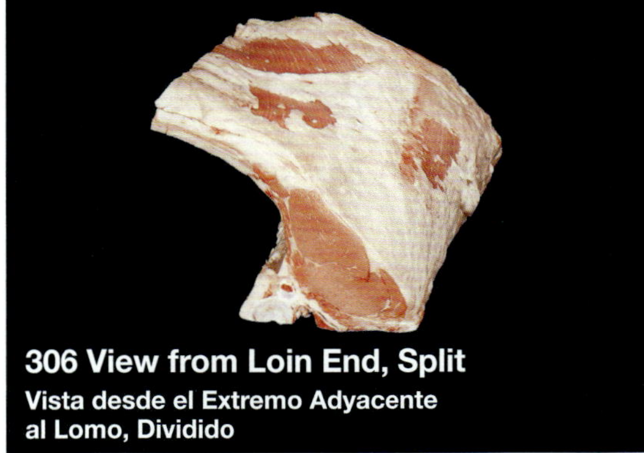
306 View from Loin End, Split
Vista desde el Extremo Adyacente al Lomo, Dividido

306 View from Chuck End, Unsplit
Vista desde el Extremo Adyacente a la Paleta, Sin Dividir

306A — Veal Hotel Rack, 6 Ribs

This is a 6 rib item prepared from Item No. 304 by a straight cut between the 5th and 6th ribs to include ribs 6 through 11. All the other specifications and options applicable to Item No. 306 also apply to this item.

306A — Costillar Clase Hotelera, 6 Costillas

Esta pieza de 6 costillas se prepara a partir de la pieza número 304 mediante un corte recto entre la 5ª y la 6ª costilla, para incluir las costillas 6ª a 11ª. Todas las demás especificaciones y opciones aplicables a la pieza número 306 también se aplican a esta pieza.

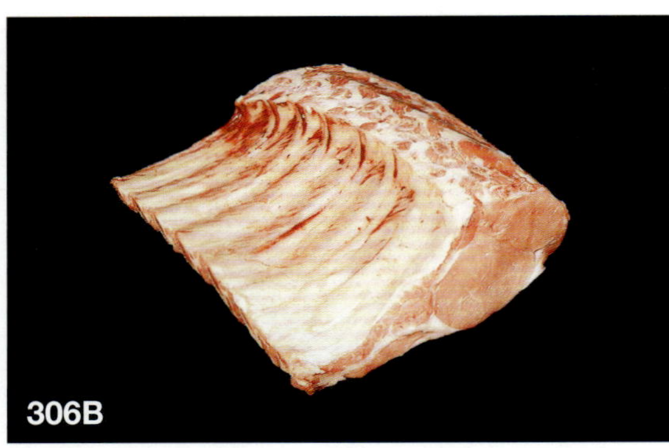

306B

306B — Veal Hotel Rack, Chop-Ready, 7 Ribs

This item is a single rack prepared as described in Item No. 306. In addition the chine (vertebrae), feather bones, blade bone, related cartilage, and backstrap as well as the lifter muscles (*trapezius, infraspinatus, latissimus dorsi, rhomboideus, subscapularis*) shall be excluded.

306B — Costillar Clase Hotelera, Listo Para Chuletas, 7 Costillas

Esta pieza es un costillar individual preparado según la descripción de la pieza número 306. Además, deberán excluirse el espinazo (cuerpos vertebrales), las puntas del espinazo, el hueso de la paleta, el cartílago correspondiente y la banda ligamentosa nucal, así como los músculos de elevación (*trapezius, infraspinatus, latissimus dorsi, rhomboideus, subscapularis*).

306C

306C — Veal Hotel Rack, Chop-Ready, 6 Ribs

This 6 rib item from a single rack, as described in Item No. 306A, is further prepared as explained in Item No. 306B.

306C — Costillar Clase Hotelera, Listo Para Chuletas, 6 Costillas

La preparación de esta pieza de 6 costillas proveniente de un solo costillar, según la descripción de la pieza número 306A, continúa según se explica en la pieza número 306B.

306D — Veal Hotel Rack, Chop-Ready, 7 Ribs, Frenched

This item is as described in Item No. 306B, except the breast side of the ribs shall be Frenched by the exclusion of the intercostal meat and lean and fat between and over the ribs. The exposed portions of the rib bones shall not exceed 1.5 inches (3.8 cm), and the remaining intercostal meat and lean and fat over the rib bones shall not exceed 2.5 inches (6.3 cm) from the outer edge of the *longissimus dorsi* muscle as described in Item No. 306.

306D — Costillar Clase Hotelera, Listo Para Chuletas, 7 Costillas, Estilo Francés

Esta pieza está descrita en la pieza número 306B, salvo que el lado del pecho de las costillas debe ser preparado al Estilo francés, quitando la carne intercostal, y la grasa y carne magra que queda entre las costillas y por encima de ellas. Las porciones expuestas de las costillas no deben exceder los 3.8 cm (1.5 pulgadas), y la carne intercostal restante, así como la grasa y carne magra sobre las costillas, no deberán exceder los 6.3 cm (2.5 pulgadas) desde el borde externo del músculo *longissimus dorsi*, según la descripción de la pieza número 306.

306E — Veal Hotel Rack, Chop-Ready, 6 Ribs, Frenched

This 6 rib bone item is as described in Item No. 306C and is further prepared to the same specifications as described in Item No. 306D.

306E — Costillar Clase Hotelera, Listo Para Chuletas, 6 Costillas, Estilo Francés

Esta pieza de 6 costillas está descrita en la pieza número 306C, y su preparación continúa con las mismas especificaciones de la pieza número 306D.

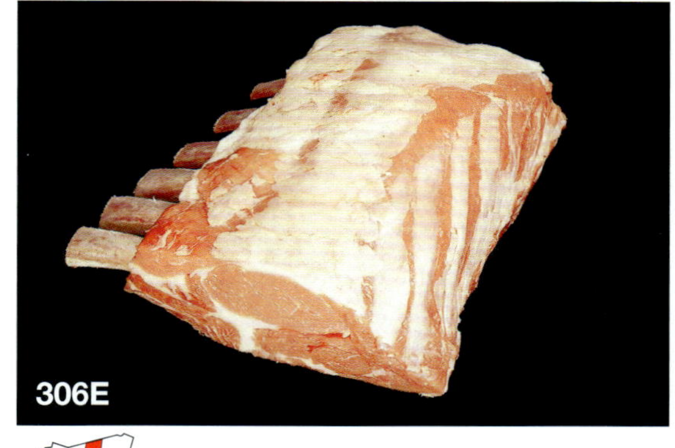

307 — Veal Rack, Ribeye, Boneless, 7 Ribs

This item consists only of the *longissimus dorsi, spinalis dorsi, complexus,* and *multifidus dorsi* muscles of a single 7 rib rack meeting the requirements of Item No. 306. In addition all bones, cartilages, backstrap, and exterior fat covering shall be excluded. The seam surface overlying the *spinalis* and *longissimus dorsi* shall be trimmed practically free of fat. If the purchaser desires a ribeye produced from a 6 rib rack, specify Item No. 307A.

307 — Costillar de Ternera, Ribeye, Deshuesado, 7 Costillas

Esta pieza consiste solamente en los músculos *longissimus dorsi, spinalis dorsi, complexus* y *multifidus dorsi* de un costillar de 7 costillas que cumple con los requisitos de la pieza número 306. Además, se deberán excluir todos los huesos, cartílagos, banda ligamentosa nucal y la cubierta de grasa externa. La superficie magra que recubre el *spinalis* y el *longissimus dorsi* deberá recortarse hasta quedar prácticamente libre de grasa. Si el comprador desea un ribeye producido de un costillar de 6 costillas, se deberá especificar la pieza número 307A.

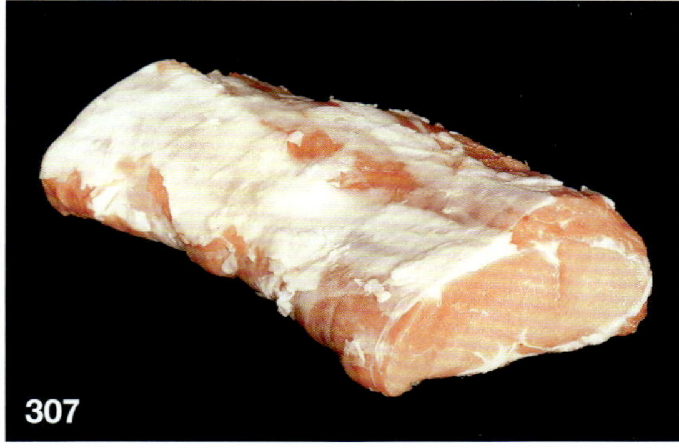

308 — Veal Chucks, 4 Ribs

The chucks are that portion of foresaddle remaining after excluding the hotel rack and plate portions of the breast as described in Item No. 306. The veal foreshanks (Item No. 312) and brisket may either be attached or separated and packaged with the chucks. Purchaser may request this item be split. If the purchaser desires 5 rib chucks, specify Item No. 308A.

308 — Paleta de Ternera (Espaldilla con Pecho y Chamberetes), 4 costillas

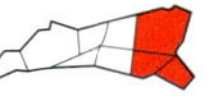

Las paletas son la porción del cuarto delantero que queda después de extraer las porciones de costillar clase hotelera y costillar de la paleta del pecho, según la descripción de la pieza número 306. Los chamberetes de mano (pieza número 312) y pecho de ternera pueden estar unidos o separados y empacados con las paletas. El comprador puede solicitar que esta pieza esté separada. Si el comprador desea paletas de 5 costillas, se debe especificar la pieza número 308A.

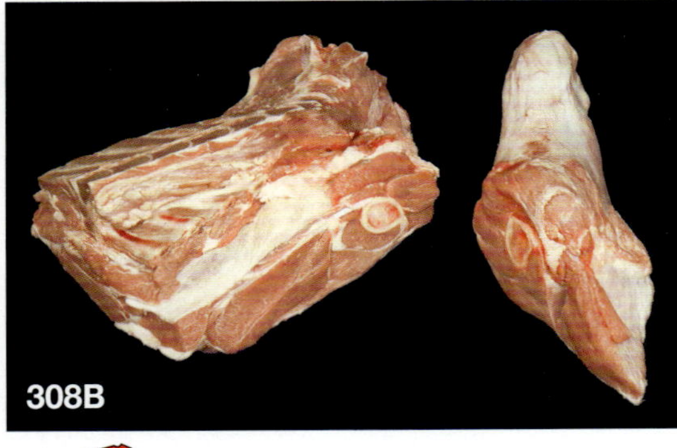

308B

308B Veal Chucks, Arm Chucks, 4 Ribs

This item is described within Item No. 308 except that the brisket is removed by a straight cut at right angles to the rack side, passing through the cartilaginous juncture of the first rib and sternum. The foreshank may either be attached or separated and packaged with the chucks. If desired, the purchaser may request 5 rib Arm Chucks.

308B Paleta (Espaldilla sin Pecho, con Chamberetes) de Ternera, 4 costillas

Esta pieza se describe como parte de la pieza número 308, salvo que el pecho se extrae mediante un corte recto, en ángulos rectos con respecto al lado del costillar, pasando a través de la unión cartilaginosa de la primera costilla y el esternón. El chamberete de mano puede estar unido o separado y ser empacado con las paletas. Si lo desea, el comprador puede solicitar paletas con chamberetes, de 5 costillas.

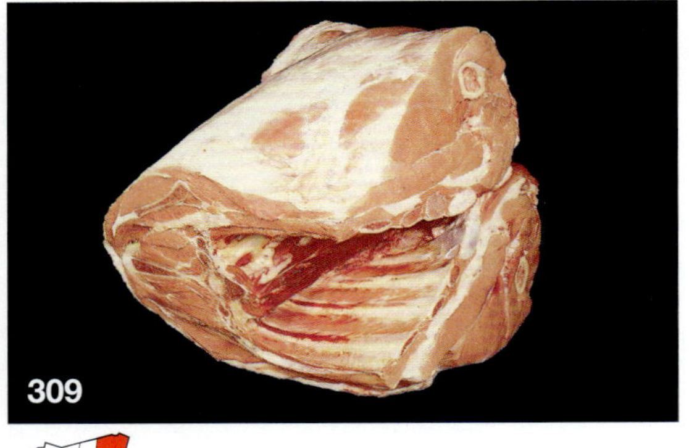

309

309 Veal Chucks, Square-Cut, 4 Ribs

This item is as described in Item No. 308, except the foreshanks and brisket portions of the breast are removed by a straight cut perpendicular to the rack side that passes through the cartilaginous juncture of the first rib and the sternum. Purchaser may request this item be split. If the purchaser desires 5 rib chucks, specify Item No. 309A.

309 Paleta de Ternera (Espaldilla sin Pecho ni Chamberetes), Corte Cuadrado, 4 costillas

Esta pieza se describe en la pieza número 308, salvo que los chamberetes de mano y las porciones de pecho se extraen mediante un corte recto perpendicular al lado del costillar, que pasa a través de la unión cartilaginosa de la primera costilla y el esternón. El comprador puede solicitar que esta pieza esté separada. Si el comprador desea paletas de 5 costillas, se debe especificar la pieza número 309A.

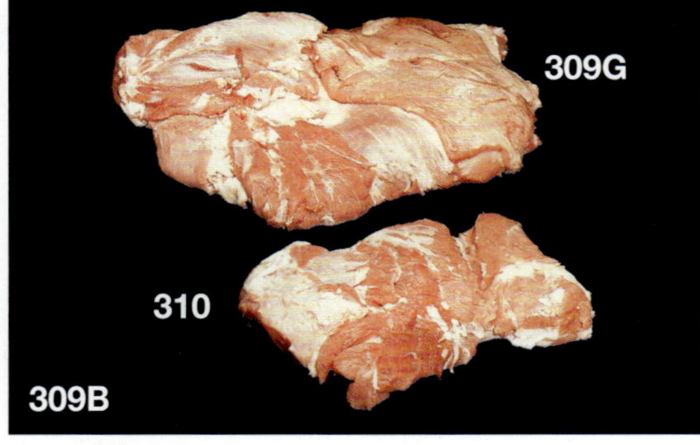

309G

310

309B

309B Veal Chucks, Square-Cut, 4 Ribs, Boneless

This boneless item is produced from a single split chuck described in Item No. 309. All bones, cartilages, backstrap, and the *prescapular* lymph gland and surrounding fat in excess of 0.5 inch (13 mm) shall be excluded. The outside shoulder or clod, with or without the Chuck Tender (*supraspinatus* muscle) attached, shall be separated from, but packaged together with, the balance of the boneless chuck. If the purchaser desires this item from a 5 rib chuck, specify Item No. 309C.

309B Paleta de Ternera (Espaldilla sin Pecho ni Chamberetes), Corte Cuadrado, 4 Costillas, Deshuesada

Esta pieza deshuesada se produce a partir de una sola paleta dividida, descrita en la pieza número 309. Deberán excluirse todos los huesos, los cartílagos, la banda ligamentosa nucal y el ganglio linfático *prescapular*, así como la grasa circundante que sobrepase los 13 mm (0.5 pulgadas). La contracara de la planchuela con brazuelo y chamberete, o planchuela, con o sin el juil de ternera (músculo *supraspinatus*), deberá separarse de lo que queda de la paleta deshuesada, pero se empacará con la misma. Si el comprador desea esta pieza proveniente de una paleta de 5 costillas, se deberá especificar la pieza número 309C.

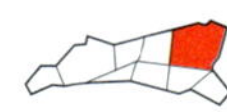

309G — Veal Chuck, Square-Cut, Clod Out, Boneless

This item is the same as Item Nos. 309B or 309C depending or whether a 4 rib or 5 rib chuck is specified, except the outside shoulder or clod with or without the Chuck Tender (*supraspinatus* muscle) shall be excluded. The boneless chuck shall be netted or tied as described in Item No. 309D.

See photo with Item No. 309B.

309G — Paleta de Ternera (Espaldilla sin Pecho ni Chamberetes), Corte Cuadrado, Sin Planchuela, Rollo Atado

Esta pieza es la misma que las piezas número 309B o 309C, según se especifique una paleta de 4 o 5 costillas, salvo que se deberá excluir la contracara de la planchuela con o sin el juil de ternera (músculo *supraspinatus*). La paleta deshuesada deberá colocarse en una malla o amarrarse según la descripción de la pieza número 309D.

Observe la foto con la pieza número 309B.

310 — Veal Chuck, Outside Shoulder, Boneless

This item may be prepared from any veal chuck by cutting through the web muscle (*superficial pectoral*) and following the natural seam to a point immediately medial to the blade cartilage. The thick (arm) end includes the *latissimus dorsi, triceps brachii* group, and other minor muscles. The thin (blade) end includes the *supraspinatus, infraspinatus,* and *latissimus dorsi* muscles. The shoulder rose or *cutaneous* muscle shall be removed when the underlying fat exceeds the surface fat thickness specified by the purchaser. All bones and cartilaginous material shall be excluded and the tendons on the elbow end trimmed even with the lean. If specified by the purchaser, this item may be netted or tied. This item is commonly referred to as a shoulder clod.

PSO 1 — All sides of the clod shall be trimmed so the minimum thickness is not less than 0.5 inch (13 mm) at any one point. If specified by the purchaser, the clod shall be split lengthwise, the ends reversed, and the boned surfaces placed together and either netted or tied. If purchaser specifies larger roasts, they may be produced by reversing the ends of two clods and holding the boned surfaces together by netting or tying.

310 — Paleta de Ternera (Espaldilla), Contracara de Planchuela, Deshuesada

Esta pieza puede prepararse a partir de cualquier paleta de ternera, cortando a través del músculo telaraña *superficial pectoral*, y siguiendo la veta natural hasta un punto inmediatamente medial al cartílago del hueso de la paleta. El extremo grueso (brazuelo) incluye el grupo de *latissimus dorsi, triceps brachii* y otros músculos menores. El extremo delgado (adyacente a la paleta) incluye los músculos *supraspinatus, infraspinatus* y *latissimus dorsi*. El suadero o músculo *cutáneo* deberá extraerse cuando la grasa subyacente exceda el grosor de la cubierta de grasa especificada por el comprador. Se deberán retirar todos los huesos y material cartilaginoso, y recortar la grasa de los tendones del extremo del codo, hasta emparejar con la carne magra. Si el comprador lo especifica, esta pieza puede colocarse en una malla o amarrarse. Esta pieza con frecuencia se llama "planchuela".

PSO 1 — Todos los lados de la planchuela deberán recortarse de grasa, de forma que el grosor mínimo no sea menor que 13 mm (0.5 pulgadas) en ningún punto. Si el comprador lo especifica, la planchuela deberá separarse longitudinalmente, los extremos deberán darse vuelta y las superficies con huesos deberán colocarse juntas en una malla o amarrarse. Si el comprador especifica trozos rosbifs más grandes, pueden ser producidos dando vuelta a los extremos de dos planchuelas y manteniendo unidas las superficies deshuesadas mediante una malla o amarrándolas.

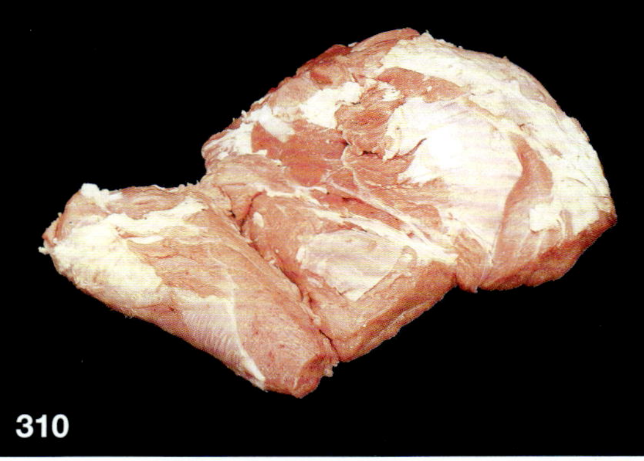

310

310 Netted
En Malla

310C — Veal Chuck Tender (IM)

This item consists of the *supraspinatus* muscle. It lies along the dorsal side of the medial ridge of the blade bone. It shall be separated from adjacent muscles through the natural seams. The Chuck Tender is sometimes referred to as the "Mock" or "Scotch" Tender.

310C — Juil de Ternera (MI)

Esta pieza consiste en el músculo *supraspinatus*. Yace a lo largo de la fosa superior respecto al borde óseo (espina) del hueso de la paleta. Se deberá separar de músculos adyacentes siguiendo las vetas naturales. El Juil de Ternera algunas veces es llamado "Mock" o "Scotch Tender".

310D — Veal Chuck, Outside Shoulder

This item shall consist of the shank, humerus, and blade bone and associated muscles of the chuck. It may be prepared from the chuck prior to removal of the rack and breast. This item is prepared by cutting through the natural seam between the triceps *brachii* and deep *pectoral/serratus ventralis* muscles. The cut follows the natural seam to a point immediately to the dorsal edge of the blade cartilage. The thick end (arm end) shall include the shank and humerus bones and overlying lean (*latissimus dorsi, triceps brachii* group, and minor muscles associated with the humerus). The thin end (blade end) shall consist of the blade bone and muscles overlying the blade bone (*supraspinatus, infraspinatus,* and *latissimus dorsi* and immediately below the blade bone (*subscapularis* and *teres major*). The *cutaneous* muscle (shoulder rose) shall be removed when the underlying fat exceeds the surface fat thickness specified. All sides shall be trimmed following the natural curvature of the major muscles and the scapula. This item is commonly referred to as a "paddle".

310D — Paleta (Espaldilla) de Ternera, Contracara de Planchuela con Brazuelo y Chamberete

Esta pieza consistirá en el chamberete, húmero y hueso de la paleta, así como los músculos asociados a ésta. Puede prepararse a partir de la paleta antes de la extracción del costillar y el pecho. Esta pieza se prepara cortando por la veta natural entre los músculos *triceps brachii* y los músculos profundos *pectoral/serratus ventralis*. El corte sigue la veta natural hasta un punto inmediatamente anterior al borde dorsal del cartílago de la paleta. El extremo grueso (extremo adyacente al brazuelo) deberá incluir los huesos del chamberete y el húmero y el recubrimiento de carne magra (grupo *latissimus dorsi, triceps brachii* y los músculos menores relacionados con el húmero). El extremo delgado (extremo adyacente a la paleta) deberá incluir el hueso de la paleta y los músculos que lo cubren (*supraspinatus, infraspinatus* y *latissimus dorsi*) e inmediatamente por debajo del hueso de la paleta (*subscapularis* y *teres mayor*). El músculo *cutáneo* (suadero) deberá extraerse cuando la grasa subyacente exceda el grosor de la cubierta de grasa especificada por el comprador. Se deberá recortar la grasa de todos los lados, siguiendo la curvatura natural de los principales músculos y del hueso de la paleta (la escápula). Esta pieza con frecuencia se llama "paddle".

311 — Veal Chuck, Blade Portion, Neck Off, Boneless

This item is what remains after the clod has been removed from a boneless 4 or 5 rib neck off chuck. The item shall be netted or tied and may be made into smaller roasts if specified by the purchaser. The *supraspinatus* muscle need not be present.

311 — Paleta (Espaldilla) de Ternera, Porción de la Paleta, Sin Pescuezo ni Juil, Deshuesada

Esta pieza es lo que permanece después de extraerse la planchuela de una paleta sin pescuezo, deshuesado, de 4 o de 5 costillas. La pieza deberá colocarse en una malla o amarrarse, y es posible procesarla en trozos rosbifs más pequeños si el comprador lo especifica. No es necesario que el músculo *supraspinatus* esté presente.

311A — Veal Chuck, Inside Roll, Boneless

This is as described in Item No. 311 except that the *supraspinatus* and the *trapezius* (chuck cover) shall be removed. This item consists of the large muscle system of the blade portion of the chuck that lies beneath (medial) the blade bone and *trapezius*. Unless otherwise specified below, the arm portion shall be removed by a straight cut that is at an approximate right angle to the rib end and is not more than 3.0 inches (7.5 cm), ventral from the *longissimus dorsi* at the rack end and not more than 4.0 inches (10 cm) from the *complexus* at the neck end. When smaller roasts are specified, a straight cut, perpendicular to its length, shall divide the chuck roll into approximately equal portions. If specified by the purchaser, this item may be netted and tied.

The purchaser may specify alternative arm removal options:

Maximum distance from *Longissimus* on the rack end x Maximum distance from the *complexus* on the neck end.

PSO: 1 – 2.0 inches (5 cm) x 3.0 inches (7.5 cm)

2 – 1.0 inch (2.5 cm) x 2.0 inches (5 cm)

3 – 0.0 inch x 1.0 inch (2.5 cm)

4 – The neck shall be removed by a straight cut approximately parallel to the rack end and is anterior to, but not more than 0.5 inch (13 mm) from, the *serratus ventralis* muscle.

311A — Paleta (Espaldilla) de Ternera, Rollo de Adentro de la Planchuela, Deshuesado

311A

Este procedimiento es igual al descrito en la pieza 311, salvo que se deberán extraer el *supraspinatus* y el *trapezius* (tapa de la paleta). Esta pieza consiste en el gran sistema muscular que rodea a la paleta y que se encuentra por debajo (medial) del hueso de la paleta y del *trapezius*. A menos que se especifique lo contrario a continuación, la porción del brazuelo deberá extraerse mediante un corte recto en ángulo recto aproximado respecto al extremo del costillar, de no más de 7.5 cm (3.0 pulgadas), ventral desde el *longissimus dorsi* en el extremo del costillar y a no más de 10 cm (4.0 pulgadas) desde el *complexus* en el extremo adyacente al pescuezo. Cuando se especifiquen trozos rosbifs más pequeños, un corte recto, perpendicular a su longitud, dividirá el rollo de diezmillo en porciones aproximadamente iguales. Si el comprador lo especifica, esta pieza puede ser colocada en una malla y amarrada.

El comprador puede especificar opciones alternativas para la extracción del brazuelo:

Distancia máxima desde el *Longissimus* en el extremo del costillar x distancia máxima desde el *complexus* en el extremo del pescuezo.

PSO: 1 – 5 cm (2.0 pulgadas) x 7.5 cm (3.0 pulgadas)

2 – 2.5 cm (1.0 pulgada) x 5 cm (2.0 pulgadas)

3 – 0.0 pulgadas x 2.5 cm (1.0 pulgada)

4 – Se extraerá el pescuezo mediante un corte recto aproximadamente paralelo al extremo adyacente al costillar y que es anterior al músculo *serratus ventralis*, pero sin superar los 13 mm (0.5 pulgadas).

311B Veal Chuck, Chuck Eye Roll, Boneless

This item is derived from Item No. 311A with the neck removed as described within PSO 4. The chuck eye roll is the large muscle system consisting of the *longissimus dorsi, spinalis dorsi, multifidus dorsi, complexus,* and minor muscles immediately ventral to the *longissimus dorsi*. It is separated from the inside roll by cutting through the natural seams. This item shall be practically free of surface fat. All bones, cartilage, backstrap, *rhomboideus, serratus ventralis,* and *intercostal* meat shall be removed. If specified by the purchaser, this item may be netted and tied.

311B Paleta (Espaldilla) de Ternera, Rollo de Corazón de Diezmillo, Deshuesado

Esta pieza se prepara con la pieza número 311A, extrayéndose el pescuezo como se describe en la PSO 4. El rollo de corazón de diezmillo es el gran sistema muscular conformado por el *longissimus dorsi, spinalis dorsi, multifidus dorsi, complexus* y músculos menores inmediatamente ventrales al *longissimus dorsi*. Se separa del rollo de adentro de la planchuela cortando por las vetas naturales. Esta pieza deberá quedar prácticamente libre de cubierta de grasa. Se deberán eliminar todos los huesos, los cartílagos, la banda ligamentosa nucal, *el rhomboideus, el serratus ventralis* y la carne *intercostal*. Si el comprador lo especifica, esta pieza puede ser colocada en una malla y amarrada.

311C Veal Chuck, Under Blade Roast, Boneless

The item is the remaining portion of the inside roll after removal of the chuck eye roll. It shall consist of the *serratus ventralis, rhomboideus* and *splenius* muscles. This item shall be practically free of surface fat. All bones, cartilage, backstrap, neck meat and intercostal meat shall be removed. If specified by the purchaser, this item may be netted and tied.

311C Paleta de Ternera (Espaldilla), Tapa Interior de la Planchuela, Deshuesada

Esta pieza es la porción restante del rollo de adentro de la planchuela, después de la extracción del rollo de corazón de diezmillo. Consistirá en los músculos *serratus ventralis, rhomboideus* y *splenius*. Esta pieza deberá quedar prácticamente libre de cubierta de grasa. Deberán extraerse todos los huesos, cartílagos, banda ligamentosa nucal, carne del pescuezo y carne intercostal. Si el comprador lo especifica, esta pieza puede ser colocada en una malla y amarrada.

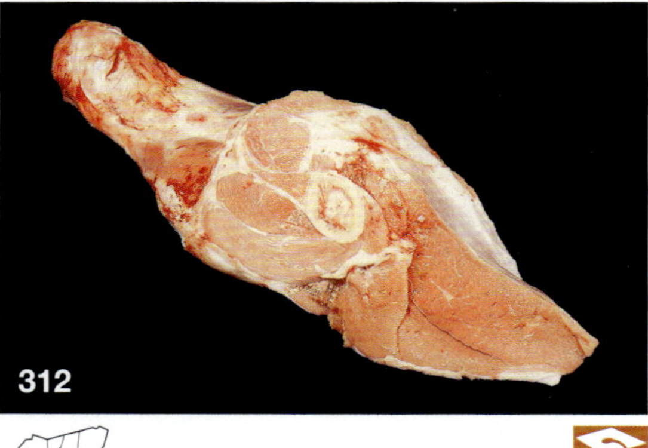

312 Veal Foreshank

This item is the foreleg portion from the chuck. A cross section of the arm bone (*humerus*) shall be exposed. The foreshank is separated from the brisket by cutting through the natural seam. A small portion of the web muscle (*pectoralis superficialis*) may remain attached to the foreshank.

312 Chamberete de Mano de Ternera

Esta pieza es la porción de la pata delantera de la paleta. Se expondrá una sección transversal del hueso del brazuelo (*húmero*). El chamberete de mano se separa del pecho aplicando un corte por la veta natural. Es posible que una porción pequeña del músculo telaraña (*pectoralis superficialis*) permanezca unida al chamberete de mano.

NAMP
NORTH AMERICAN MEAT PROCESSORS ASSOCIATION
Association Amérique du Nord des Transformateurs de Viande
Asociación Norteamericana de Procesadores de Carne

312A Veal Foreshank, Center-Cut

This item is prepared from Item No. 312 by straight cuts so that cross sections of the ulna and the radius are evident at both ends of the foreshank.

🍁 In Canada, center-cut is not an approved modifier. See page xxv for more information.

312A Chamberete de Mano de Ternera, Corte del Centro

Esta pieza se prepara con la pieza número 312 mediante cortes rectos, a fin de que las secciones transversales del cúbito y del radio se vean en ambos extremos del chamberete de mano.

🍁 En Canadá, "corte central" no es un modificador aprobado. Consulte la página xxv para obtener información adicional.

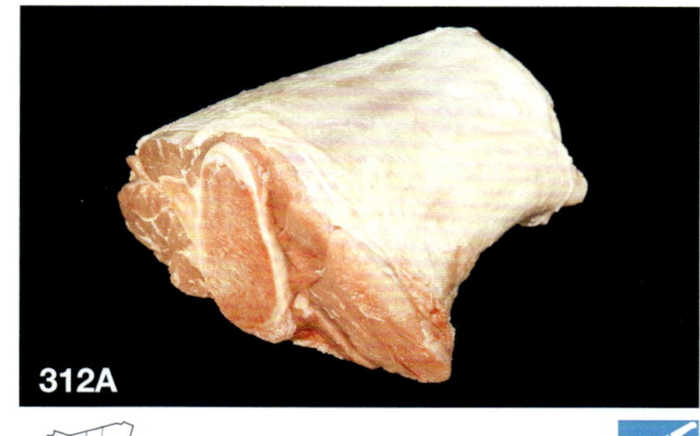

313 Veal Breast

The breast shall contain 11 ribs and consists of the intact plate and brisket portion of the forequarter. The diaphragm may be removed, but if present, the membranous portion shall be trimmed close to the lean. The heart fat shall be excluded.

🍁 In Canada, the veal breast only contains ribs 1 through 6.

313 Pecho de Ternera

El pecho deberá contener 11 costillas y consistir en la porción intacta del costillar y pecho del cuarto delantero. Es posible retirar el diafragma, pero si se deja, la porción membranosa deberá ser despellejada en forma muy próxima a la carne magra. Se deberá retirar la grasa del corazón.

🍁 En Canadá, el pecho de ternera solamente contiene las costillas 1ª a la 6ª.

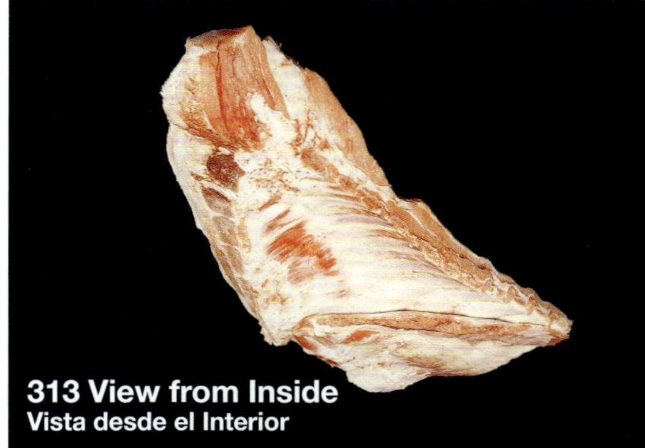

314 Veal Breast with Pocket

This item is prepared from Item No. 313. A pocket shall be formed by cutting through the flesh along the rack edge adjacent to the ribs, leaving not less than 1.0 inch (2.5 cm) or more than 1.5 inches (3.8 cm) of lean intact along the chuck edge, the belly edge, and the flank edge of the breast. There shall be no scores through the outside muscles covering the pocket.

314 Pecho de Ternera con Bolsillo

Esta pieza se prepara con la pieza número 313. Se formará un bolsillo cortando la carne a lo largo del borde del costillar adyacente a las costillas, y se dejará no menos de 2.5 cm (1.0 pulgada) o más de 3.8 cm (1.5 pulgadas) de carne magra intacta a lo largo del borde de la paleta, el borde de la barriga y el borde de la falda del pecho. No deberá haber incisiones profundas a través de los músculos externos que cubren el bolsillo.

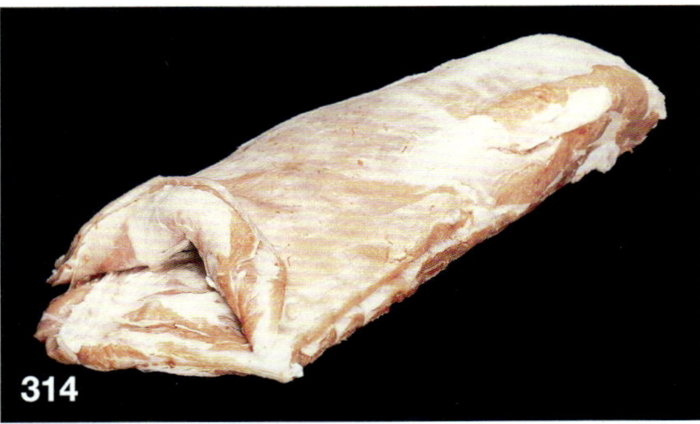

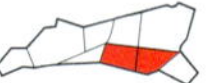

323 — Veal Short Ribs

This item is derived from the rib section of any rack and/or breast item. The short rib item shall contain at least one rib including the intercostal meat and lean together with the *serratus ventralis* muscle continuous across the cut surface on at least one side.

323 — Costillas Cortas (Costilla Cargada) de Ternera

Esta pieza proviene de la sección de las costillas de cualquier pieza de costillar y/o pecho. La pieza de costillas cortas deberá contener al menos una costilla que incluya la carne intercostal y la carne magra conjuntamente con el músculo *serratus ventralis* en forma continua a través de la superficie de corte por lo menos en un lado.

331

331 — Veal Loins

The loins are that portion remaining after the legs have been removed from Item No. 330 Hindsaddle. The legs shall be removed by a straight cut perpendicular to the back bone through a point immediately before the hip bone so that no part of the hip bone cartilage remains on the loins. Purchaser may specify they be split.

331 — Lomos de Ternera

Los lomos son las porciones restantes después de haberse extraído las piernas de la pieza número 330, Cuarto trasero, 2 Costillas - Mitad Trasera. Las piernas se extraerán mediante un corte recto perpendicular a la espina dorsal, hasta un punto inmediatamente anterior al hueso de la cadera, a fin de evitar que queden restos del cartílago de dicho hueso en los lomos. El comprador debe especificar si deben entregarse divididos.

332 View from Rack End, Split
Vista desde el Extremo del Costillar, Dividido

332 — Veal Loins, Trimmed

The trimmed loins are as described in Item No. 331, except the flank portions shall be excluded by a straight cut that is not more than 4.0 inches (10.0 cm) from the outer tip of the loin eye muscle (*longissimus dorsi*). The kidneys and kidney knobs shall also be excluded. The lumbar fat shall be trimmed so that it does not exceed 0.5 inch (13 mm) in thickness at the leg end. From the leg end, the fat shall be tapered down to the lean surface at a point not beyond 3/4ths of the length of the loin. Purchaser may specify they be split.

332 — Lomos de Ternera, Recortados de Grasa y Limpios

Los lomos recortados de grasa están descritos en la pieza número 331, salvo que se deberán eliminar las porciones de falda mediante un corte recto que no supere los 10.0 cm (4.0 pulgadas) desde la punta exterior del ojo del lomo del músculo (*longissimus dorsi*). Los riñones y la grasa circundante (riñonada) también deberán quitarse. Se deberá recortar la grasa lumbar a fin de que no exceda los 13 mm (0.5 pulgadas) de grosor en el extremo de la pierna. Desde el extremo de la pierna, se deberá nivelar la grasa hacia la parte magra a un punto que no supere las 3/4 partes de la longitud del lomo. El comprador debe especificar si deben entregarse divididos.

332A — Veal Loins, Block-Ready, Trimmed

This item is as described in Item No. 332 except that the flank portions shall be excluded by a straight cut that is not more than 1 inch (2.5 cm) from the *longissimus dorsi* on the rib and hip ends. The lumbar fat shall be removed entirely.

332A — Lomos de Ternera, Listos para Tablajear, Recortados de Grasa y Limpios

Esta pieza se describe en la pieza número 332, salvo que se deberán eliminar las porciones del flanco (falda) mediante un corte recto que no supere los 2.5 cm (1 pulgada) desde el *longissimus dorsi* en los extremos del costillar y la cadera. Se deberá eliminar completamente la grasa lumbar.

332A

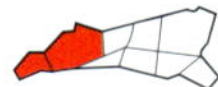

334 — Veal Legs

The legs are that portion of the Hindsaddle remaining after the removal of Item No. 331. The legs are split and sold as single legs, unless otherwise specified by the purchaser.

334 — Piernas de Ternera

Las piernas son la porción del cuarto trasero que quedan después de la extracción de la pieza número 331. Las piernas se separan y se venden en forma unitaria, a menos que el comprador especifique lo contrario.

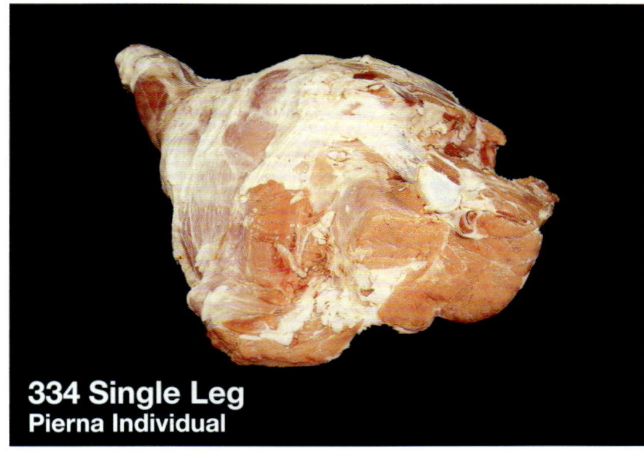
334 Single Leg
Pierna Individual

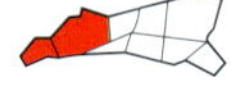

335 — Veal Leg, Boneless

This item is prepared from a single leg. The round bone shall be removed by a cut through the natural seam between the top round and the sirloin tip (knuckle). The flank, practically all cod or udder fat, and any surface fat in excess of 0.5 inch (13 mm) in thickness shall be excluded. All the bones, cartilage, lean and fat overlying the aitch bone, *sacrosciatic* ligament, gambrel cord, and the heavy connective tissue surrounding the kneecap shall also be excluded. When specified by the purchaser this item may be made into smaller pieces and netted or tied as roasts. If specified as roasts, the shank meat shall either be folded into the femur bone cavity of a roast or left as a separate portion.

335 — Pierna de Ternera, Deshuesada

Esta pieza se prepara a partir de una sola pierna. Se deberá extraer el hueso de la pierna (fémur) mediante un corte a través de la veta natural entre la pulpa negra y la pulpa bola. Se deberá eliminar la falda, prácticamente toda la grasa del escroto o la ubre, y la cubierta de grasa que exceda los 13 mm (0.5 pulgadas) de grosor. También se deberán eliminar todos los huesos, cartílagos, la carne magra y la grasa que recubren el hueso de la cadera, el ligamento *sacrociático*, el tendón de Aquiles y el tejido conectivo grueso que rodea la rótula. Cuando el comprador lo especifique, esta pieza puede presentarse en trozos más pequeños y colocarse en una malla o amarrarse como trozos rosbifs. Si se especifica la presentación de trozo rosbif, se deberá plegar la carne del chamberete dentro de la cavidad que deja el hueso del fémur de un rosbif o dejarla como una porción separada.

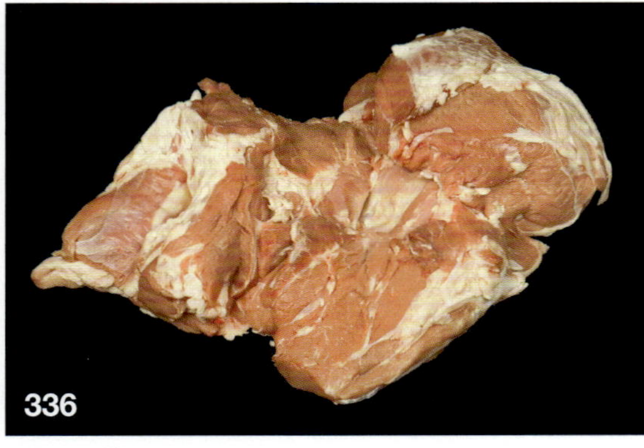

336

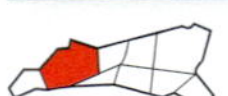

336 — Veal Leg, Shank Off, Boneless

This item is prepared to the same specifications as Item No. 335 with the additional requirement that the shank meat shall be excluded. This shall be accomplished by a cut through the stifle joint that follows the natural seam between the shank and the heel. If specified by the purchaser, this item may be made into smaller pieces and netted or tied as roasts.

336 — Pierna de Ternera, sin Chamberete, Deshuesada

Esta pieza se prepara bajo las mismas especificaciones que las de la pieza número 335, con el requisito adicional de que se deberá excluir la carne de chamberete. Esto se llevará a cabo mediante un corte a través de la articulación de la rodilla que sigue la veta natural entre el chamberete y el talón. Si el comprador lo especifica, esta pieza puede presentarse en trozos más pequeños y colocarse en una red o amarrarse como trozos rosbifs.

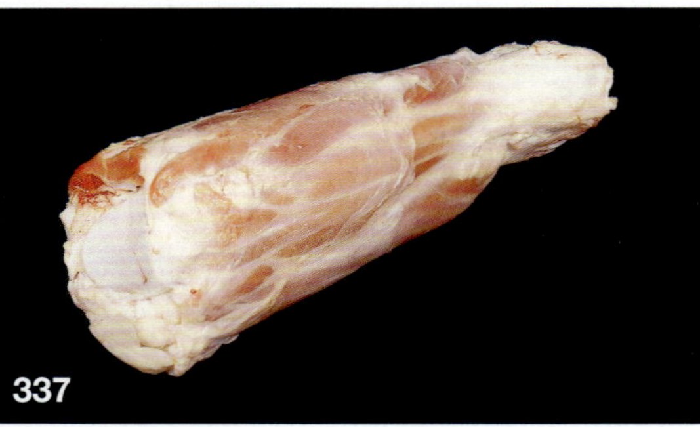

337

337 — Veal Hindshank

This item is prepared from Item No. 334. The shank bone with its meat attached shall be separated from the leg by a cut through the stifle joint that follows the natural seam between the shank and the heel. All hock bones and the gambrel cord shall be excluded.

337 — Chamberete Trasero de Ternera

Esta pieza se prepara con la pieza número 334. El hueso del chamberete con su carne incluida deberá ser separado de la pierna mediante un corte a través de la articulación de la rodilla, que siga la veta natural entre el chamberete y el talón. Se deberán excluir todos los huesos del chamberete trasero y el tendón de Aquiles.

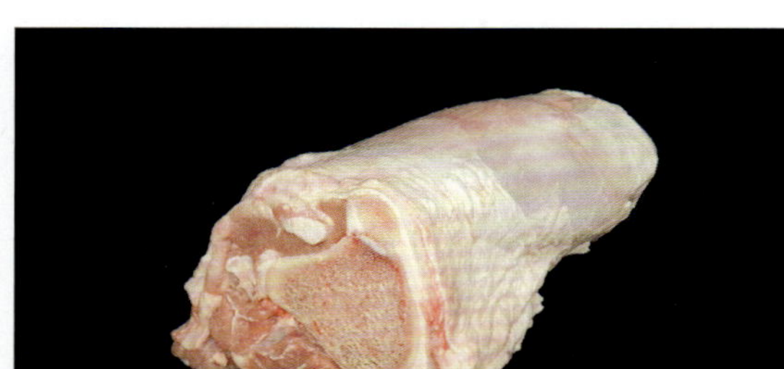

337A

337A — Veal Hindshank, Center-Cut

This item is prepared from Item No. 337 by straight cuts across the tibia and fibula bones at the dorsal and ventral ends of the hindshank so that the only portion of the hindshank remaining shall display both the tibia and fibula bones on both ends of the item.

🍁 In Canada, center-cut is not an approved modifier. See pg. xxv for more information.

337A — Chamberete Trasero de Ternera, Corte del Centro

Esta pieza se prepara con la pieza número 337 mediante cortes transversales en los huesos de la tibia y el peroné, en los extremos dorsal y ventral del chamberete trasero, de forma que la única porción del chamberete trasero que permanece mostrará tanto la tibia como el peroné en ambos extremos de la pieza.

🍁 En Canadá, "corte central" no es un modificador aprobado. Consulte la página xxv para obtener más información.

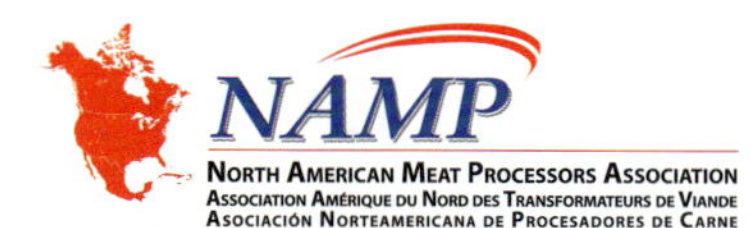

341 — Veal Back, Trimmed

This item consists of the racks and loins attached. The legs are removed by a straight cut perpendicular to the back bone through a point immediately anterior to the hip bone, leaving no part of the hip bone cartilage on the loin. The plates and flanks are removed by a straight cut that is not more than 4.0 inches (10.0 cm) from the outer tip of the eye muscle (*longissimus dorsi*). The kidneys and kidney knobs shall be removed, and the lumbar fat shall be trimmed so that it does not exceed 0.5 inch (13 mm) in thickness at the leg end. The lumbar fat shall be tapered down to the lean surface at a point not beyond 75 percent of the length of the loin portion.

Purchaser may specify one of the following options. If none is selected, Style A will apply.

Style A: The chucks removed by a straight cut between the 4th and 5th ribs to produce a Veal Back, 9 Ribs, Trimmed.

Style B: The chucks removed by a straight cut between the 5th and 6th ribs to produce a Veal Back, 8 Ribs, Trimmed.

341 — Espaldar de Ternera, Recortado de grasa y Limpio

Esta pieza consiste en los costillares y los lomos anexos. Las piernas se extraen mediante un corte recto perpendicular a la espina dorsal, hasta un punto inmediatamente anterior al hueso de la cadera; de esta manera, se evita que queden restos del cartílago del hueso de la cadera en el lomo. Los costillares y flancos (las faldas) se extraen mediante un corte recto de no más de 10.0 cm (4.0 pulgadas) desde la punta externa del ojo del músculo (*longissimus dorsi*). Se eliminarán los riñones y la grasa circundante (riñonada), y se recortará la grasa lumbar de manera que no exceda los 13 mm (0.5 pulgadas) de grosor en el extremo de la pierna. Se deberá afinar la grasa lumbar hacia la superficie magra a un punto que no supere el 75% de la longitud de la porción del lomo.

Es posible que el comprador especifique una de las siguientes opciones. Si no se elige ninguna opción, se aplicará el Estilo A.

Estilo A: Las paletas extraídas por corte recto entre las costillas 4ª y 5ª para producir un Espaldar de Ternera, 9 Costillas, Recortado de Grasa y Limpio.

Estilo B: Las paletas extraídas por corte recto entre las costillas 5ª y 6ª para producir un Espaldar de Ternera, 8 Costillas, Recortado de Grasa y Limpio.

344 — Veal Loin, Strip Loin, Boneless

This item is prepared from a Veal Loin as described in Item No. 331 or 332. The flank edge shall be excluded by a straight cut that is not more than 1.0 inch (2.5 cm) from the outer tip of the loin eye (*longissimus dorsi*) muscle. The tenderloin and all bones and cartilages shall also be excluded. Surface fat shall not exceed 0.5 inch (13 mm) at any point.

344 — Lomo de Ternera, Strip Loin, Deshuesado

Esta pieza se prepara con un lomo de ternera, como se describe en la pieza número 331 o 332. El borde del flanco (la falda) deberá extraerse mediante un corte recto que no exceda los 2.5 cm (1.0 pulgada) desde la punta exterior del ojo del lomo (músculo *longissimus dorsi*). También deberán excluirse el filete y todos los huesos y cartílagos. La cubierta de grasa no deberá superar los 13 mm (0.5 pulgadas) en ningún punto.

344

344A PSO 1

344A — Veal Loin, Strip Loin, Boneless, Skinned, 0 x 0

This item is as described in Item No. 344 except that the flank is removed adjacent to the *longissimus dorsi*. The fat covering and the thick opaque membranous "skin" surface of the major eye muscles shall be removed, leaving a smooth surface on the boneless strip loin.

PSO: 1 – *Multifidus dorsi* muscle shall be removed

344A — Lomo de Ternera, Strip Loin, Deshuesado, Despellejado, 0x0

Esta pieza está descrita en la pieza número 344, salvo que se debe extraer el flanco (la falda) adyacente al *longissimus dorsi*. Se deberá extraer la cubierta de grasa y la superficie "de piel" membranosa, gruesa y opaca de los músculos principales del ojo, lográndose una superficie pareja sobre el strip loin deshuesado.

PSO: 1 – El *Multifidus dorsi* deberá extraerse.

346

346 — Veal Leg, Butt Tenderloin, Trimmed

This item is that portion of the tenderloin separated from any type Item No. 334 leg. It shall consist of the *psoas major, psoas minor,* and *iliacus* muscles. The butt tender shall be practically free of all fat.

346 — Pierna de Ternera, Cabeza de Filete, Recortado de Grasa y Limpio

Esta pieza es la porción del filete que se separa de cualquier tipo de pierna de la pieza número 334. Estará conformada por los músculos *psoas mayor, psoas menor* e *iliacus*. La cabeza del filete deberá estar prácticamente libre de grasa.

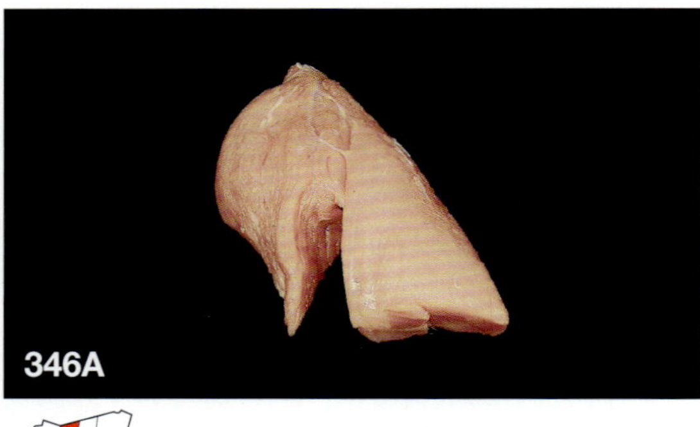
346A

346A — Veal Leg, Butt Tenderloin, Skinned

This item is the same as Item No. 346, except the *psoas minor* and the principal membranous tissue over the *psoas major* shall be excluded.

346A — Pierna de Ternera, Cabeza de Filete, Despellejado

Esta pieza es la misma que la número 346, salvo que se eliminará el *psoas menor* y el principal tejido membranoso sobre el *psoas mayor*.

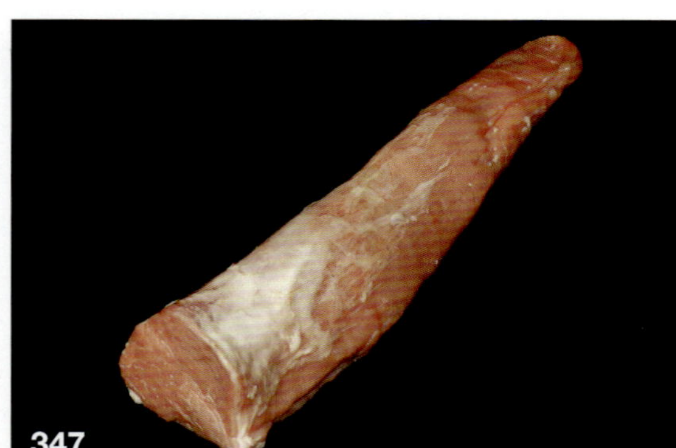
347

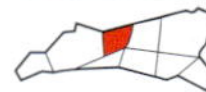

347 — Veal Loin, Short Tenderloin

This item is that portion of the tenderloin removed from Item No. 331 or 332. Practically all fat and the *psoas minor* shall be excluded.

347 — Lomo de Ternera, Filete Corto

Esta pieza es la porción del filete extraída de la pieza número 331 o 332. Se deberá excluir prácticamente toda la grasa y el *psoas menor*.

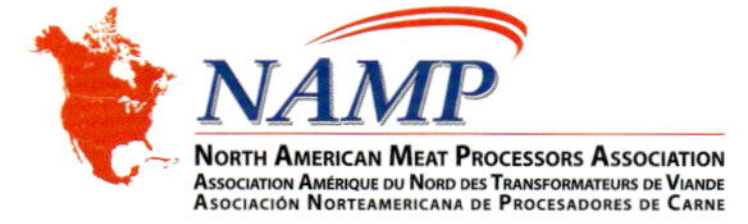

348   Veal Tenderloin

This item is derived from Item No. 330A hindquarter prior to separation of the leg from the loin and shall include the *psoas major* and *illiacus* (wing). The *psoas minor* (side muscle) and *sartorius* shall be excluded.

Picture shown is Fat Limitation Option 5, Peeled/Denuded (remaining fat shall not exceed 1.0 inch (2.5 cm) in any dimension). See page 139 for other FLO options.

348   Filete de Ternera

Esta pieza proviene de la pieza número 330A: "Cuarto Trasero, 2 Costillas", antes de la separación de la pierna y el lomo, y deberá incluir el *psoas mayor* y el *illiacus* ("ala del filete"). El *psoas menor* (músculo lateral) y el *sartorius* deberán excluirse.

La ilustración muestra la opción 5 para limitar la grasa: "Desprovisto de grasa/Prácticamente desnudo de grasa" [la grasa que queda no podrá exceder los 2.5 cm (1.0 pulgada) en ninguna dimensión]. Consulte la página 137 para ver otras opciones para limitar la grasa.

349   Veal Leg, Top Round (Inside), Cap On

The top round is prepared from any leg item, such as Item Nos. 334, 335, or 336, that meets the end requirements of this item. The item shall consist of the *semimembranosus, adductor, gracilis,* and the firmly attached *pectineus, iliopsoas,* and *sartorius* muscles. The top round is separated from the outside and sirloin tip (knuckle) portions of the leg along the natural seams.

The photo shown is Fat Limitation Option 1, Untrimmed, which is also known as "Commodity Drop".

This Cap On item may also be requested FLO 4, practically free of fat (75% lean/seam surface exposed). See pg. 139 for FLO options.

349   Pierna de Ternera, Pulpa Negra (Cara/Centro de Pierna), con Tapa

La pulpa negra se prepara a partir de cualquier pieza de pierna, como las piezas número 334, 335 o 336, que cumplen con los requisitos finales de esta pieza. Esta pieza estará compuesta por los músculos *semimembranosus, adductor y gracilis,* y los firmemente unidos *pectineus, iliopsoas* y *sartorius*. La pulpa negra se separa de las porciones del lado externo y de la bola de la pierna, a lo largo de las vetas naturales.

La fotografía muestra la opción 1 para limitar la grasa: "recorte de grasa y limpieza tipo commodity", que también se conoce como "Commodity Drop" (materia prima con menos procesamiento).

Esta pieza con tapa puede también solicitarse bajo la opción 4 para limitar la grasa: "Prácticamente libre de grasa (75% de la superficie expuesta es magra/superficie muscular descubierta por la disección)". Consulte la página 137 para analizar las opciones de especificación del comprador.

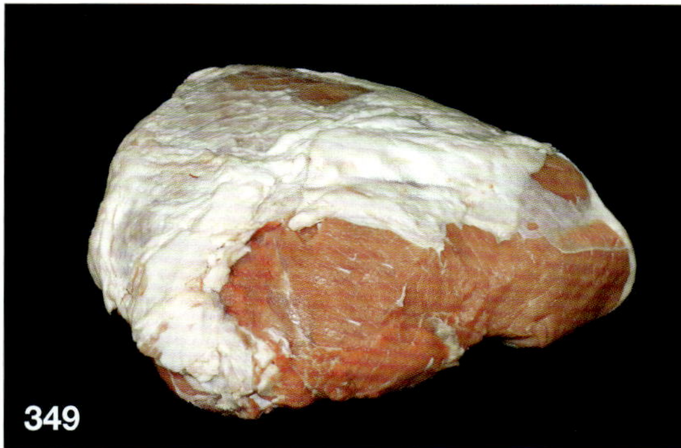

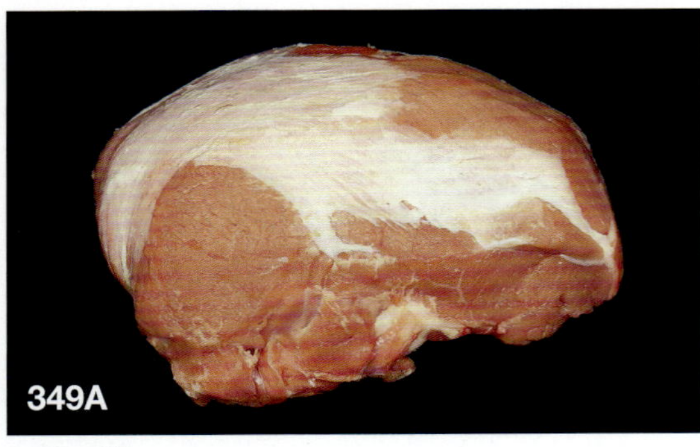

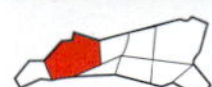

349A Veal Leg, Top Round, Cap Off

As described in Item No. 349, this item is further prepared by excluding the cap (*gracilis*) muscle and *gracilis* membrane.

PSO: 1 – In addition the purchaser may specify that the minor muscles (*pectineus*, *ilio psoas*, and *sartorius*) shall also be excluded together with the *gracilis* by cutting through the natural seams.

Picture shown is Fat Limitation Option (FLO) 5, Peeled/Denuded (remaining fat shall not exceed 1.0 inch (2.5 cm) in any dimension). See page 139 for other FLO options.

349A Pierna de Ternera, Pulpa Negra (Cara/Centro de Pierna), sin Tapa

Según la descripción en la pieza número 349, esta pieza recibe una preparación adicional; se extrae la tapa del músculo *gracilis* y la membrana *gracilis*.

PSO: 1 – Además, el comprador puede especificar que los músculos menores *pectineus*, *ilio psoas* y *sartorius* también sean excluidos conjuntamente con el *gracilis*, cortando por las vetas naturales.

La ilustración muestra la opción 5 para limitar la grasa: "Desprovisto de grasa/Prácticamente desnudo de grasa" [la grasa que queda no podrá exceder los 2.5 cm (1.0 pulgada) en ninguna dimensión]. Consulte la página 137 para ver otras opciones para limitar la grasa.

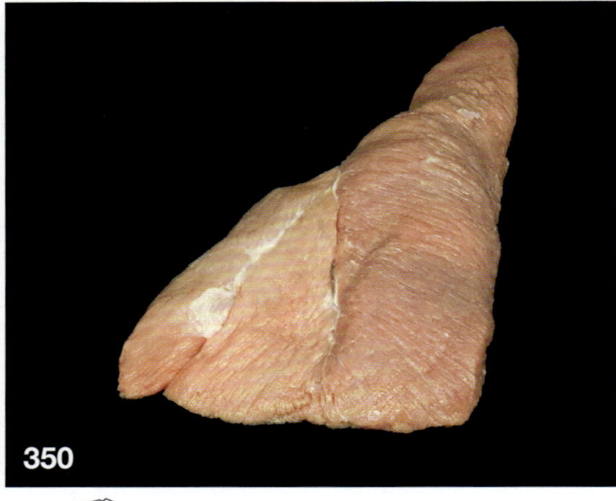

350 Veal Leg, Bottom (Gooseneck), Heel Out

This item may be prepared from the outside (*biceps femoris*, *biceps femoris ishiatic head*, and *semitendinosus*) portion of any boneless leg item. The heel (*gastrocnemius* and *super digital flexor* muscles), *sacrosciatic* ligament, and *popliteal* lymph gland shall be removed by cutting through the natural seam.

Picture shown is Fat Limitation Option (FLO) 6, Peeled/Denuded, Surface Membrane Removed (90 percent lean exposed). See page 139 for other FLO options.

350 Pierna de Ternera, Pulpa Blanca y Cuete, sin Chamberete, Deshuesada

Esta pieza puede prepararse con la porción de contracara (*biceps femoris*, *cabeza isquiática del biceps femoris* y *semitendinosus*) de cualquier pieza de pierna deshuesada. El talón (músculos *gastrocnemius* y *flexor digital superficial*), el ligamento *sacrociático* y los ganglios linfáticos *poplíteos* deberán quitarse realizándose un corte a través de la veta natural.

La ilustración muestra la opción 6 para limitar la grasa: "Desprovisto de grasa/Prácticamente desnudo de grasa, Membrana superficial retirada (90% de la superficie expuesta es magra)". Consulte la página 137 para ver otras opciones para limitar la grasa.

351A — Veal Leg, Sirloin Tip (Knuckle), Cap Off, Trimmed

This boneless item shall be prepared from a sirloin tip (knuckle) of any boneless leg item after the sirloin tip (knuckle) has been separated from the top (inside) and bottom (outside) portions along the natural seams and shall consist only of the *vastus lateralis, vastus medialis, rectus fermoris,* and *vastus intermedius* muscles. Any other attached muscles, bones, cartilages, silver skin, flap, and tendinous ends shall be removed. If purchasers desire a Cap On Sirloin Tip (Knuckle) they should request Item No. 351.

Picture shown is Fat Limitation Option (FLO) 6, Peeled/Denuded, Surface Membrane Removed (90 percent lean exposed). See page 139 for other FLO options.

351A — Pierna de Ternera, Pulpa Bola, sin Tapa, Recortada de Grasa y Limpia

Esta pieza deshuesada deberá prepararse a partir de una pulpa bola de cualquier pieza de pierna deshuesada después de separar la cara o centro de las porciones de la contracara siguiendo las vetas naturales, y se conformará únicamente por los músculos *vastus lateralis, vastus medialis, rectus fermoris* y *vastus intermedius*. Los demás músculos adheridos, así como los huesos, cartílagos, piel plateada, tapa y extremos tendinosos deberán retirarse. Si los compradores desean una Pulpa Bola con Tapa, deberán solicitar la pieza número 351.

La ilustración muestra la opción 6 para limitar la grasa: "Desprovisto de grasa/Prácticamente desnudo de grasa, Membrana superficial retirada (90% de la superficie expuesta es magra)". Consulte la página 137 para ver otras opciones para limitar la grasa.

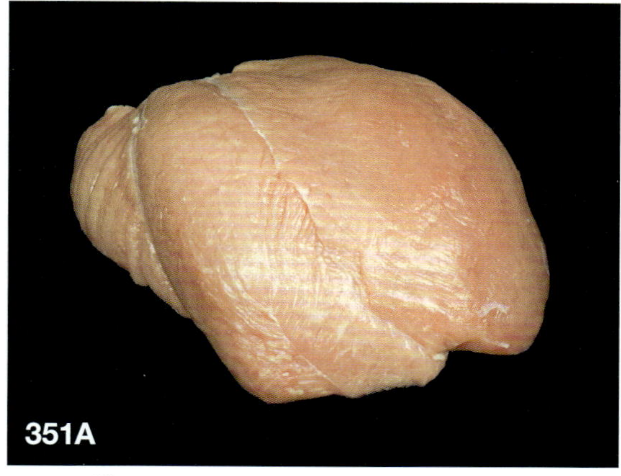

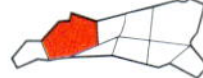

352A — Veal Leg, Hip, Cap Off, Boneless

The boneless hip is the top sirloin portion of the leg and shall consist of the *gluteus medius, gluteus accessorius,* and *gluteus profundus.* The cap muscle (*biceps femoris*) and the tri-tip (*tensor fasciae latae*) are removed. This item is sometimes referred to as the veal top sirloin or rump.

PSO: 1 – Purchaser may request that the *gluteus accessorius* and *gluteus profundus* muscles be removed.

Picture shown is Fat Limitation Option (FLO) 6, Peeled/Denuded, Surface Membrane Removed (90 percent lean exposed). See page 139 for other FLO options.

352A — Pierna de Ternera, Cadera, sin Tapa, Deshuesada

La cadera deshuesada es la porción de aguayón superior (top sirloin) de la pierna y consistirá en el *gluteus medius*, el *gluteus accessorius* y el *gluteus profundus.* Se extrae el músculo de la tapa (*biceps femoris*) y el del empuje (la punta triangular) (tensor de la fascia lata). Algunas veces, esta pieza es llamada "top sirloin" (aguayón superior) de ternera o "rump" (tajo anterior de la pulpa blanca).

PSO: 1 – El comprador puede solicitar que se extraigan los músculos *gluteus accessorius* y *gluteus profundus*.

La ilustración muestra la opción 6 para limitar la grasa: "Desprovisto de grasa/Prácticamente desnudo de grasa, Membrana superficial retirada (90% de la superficie expuesta es magra)". Consulte la página 137 para ver otras opciones para limitar la grasa.

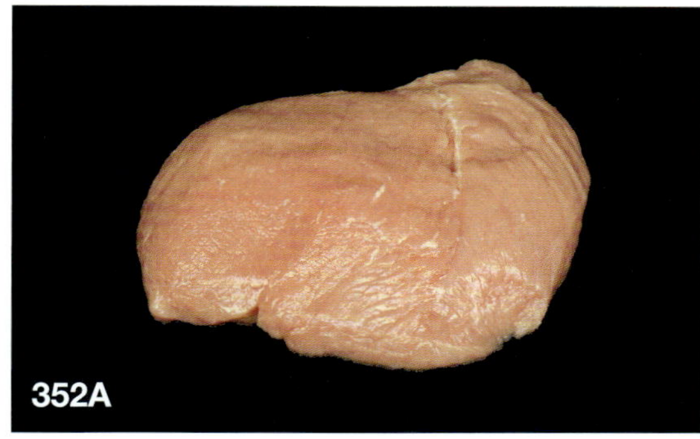

353

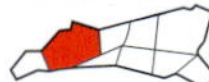

353 — Veal Leg, Eye of Round (Leg)

This item may be prepared from any leg item that meets the end requirements described. The eye shall consist of only of the *semitendinosus* muscle that has been separated along the natural seam from the *biceps femoris* and other leg muscles. It shall not be severed on either end.

Picture shown is Fat Limitation Option (FLO) 6, Peeled/Denuded, Surface Membrane Removed (90 percent lean exposed). See page 139 for other FLO options.

353 — Pierna de Ternera, Cuete

Esta pieza puede prepararse a partir de cualquier pieza de pierna que cumpla con los requisitos finales descritos. El cuete deberá consistir únicamente en el músculo *semitendinosus* que ha sido separado del *biceps femoris* así como de otros músculos de la pierna siguiendo las vetas naturales. No deberá cortarse en ninguno de los dos extremos.

La ilustración muestra la opción 6 para limitar la grasa: "Desprovisto de grasa/Prácticamente desnudo de grasa, Membrana superficial retirada (90% de la superficie expuesta es magra)". Consulte la página 137 para ver otras opciones para limitar la grasa.

363 — Veal Leg, TBS, 4 Parts

This boneless item is comprised of Item No. 349, 350, 351, Veal Leg, Sirloin Tip (Knuckle), and Item No. 352, Hip (Top Sirloin Butt), Cap Off. All bone, cartilage, silver skin, ligament, *popliteal* or other exposed lymph glands, heavy connective tissue or tendinous ends, and flap muscle are excluded. (The muscle names and specific preparation for Item Nos. 351 and 352 may be found in IMPS definitions.) Each portion shall be individually packaged and included in the same container.

363 — Pierna de Ternera, Deshuesada, 4 Piezas

Esta pieza deshuesada está compuesta por las piezas números 349, 350, 351, Pierna de Ternera, Pulpa Blanca y Pulpa Bola, y la pieza número 352, Cadera, Pulpa del Aguayón Superior/Top Sirloin sin Tapa. Se excluyen todos los huesos, cartílagos, membrana plateada ("espejo"), ligamentos, ganglios *poplíteos* u otros ganglios linfáticos expuestos, tejido conectivo grueso o extremos tendinosos y músculo de tapa. (Es posible encontrar los nombres de los músculos y la preparación específica de las piezas números 351 y 352 en las definiciones de IMPS (Especificaciones Institucionales de Compra de Carne, por sus siglas en inglés). Cada porción deberá ser empacada individualmente e incluida en el mismo recipiente.

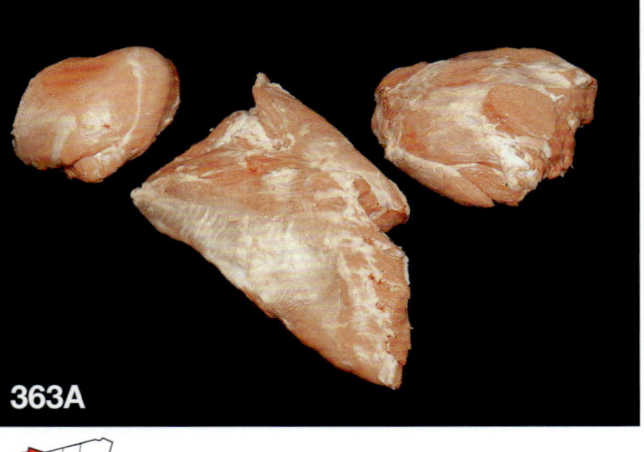

363A

363A — Veal Leg, TBS, 3 Parts

This boneless item has the same preparation and packaging requirements as Item No. 363 but excludes Item No. 352 Veal Leg, Hip, Cap Off, Tri-Tip Attached, Boneless.

363A — Pierna de Ternera, Deshuesada, 3 Piezas

Esta pieza deshuesada tiene los mismos requisitos de preparación y embalaje que la pieza número 363, salvo que excluye la pieza 352, Pierna de Ternera, Cadera, sin Tapa, con Empuje (Punta Triangular), Adherida, Deshuesada.

363B — Veal Leg, BHS, 3 Parts

This boneless item has the same preparation and packaging requirements as Item No. 363A; however, Item No. 349 (Top Round) is excluded and Item No. 352 (Hip or Top Sirloin) is included. Occasionally the Tri-Tip (*tensor fasciae latae*) is included on this item.

363B — Pierna de Ternera, Deshuesada, 3 Piezas

Esta pieza deshuesada tiene los mismos requisitos de preparación y embalaje que la pieza número 363A; no obstante, se excluye la pieza número 349 (Pulpa Negra) y se incluye la pieza número 352 (Cadera o Aguayón Superior/Top Sirloin). En ocasiones, se incluye el Empuje (Punta Triangular o *tensor de la fascia lata*) en esta pieza.

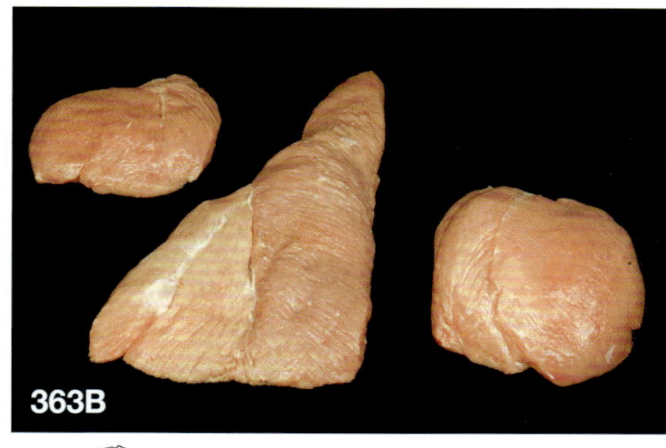
363B

388 — Veal Bones, Mixed

Mixed bones may include any combination of different types of bones from veal carcasses. Bones shall be sawed into sections or lengths to facilitate shipping and handling.

388 — Huesos de Ternera, Variados

Los Huesos de Ternera variados pueden incluir cualquier combinación de diferentes tipos de huesos provenientes de canales de ternera. Los huesos deberán cortarse con sierra en secciones o extensiones que faciliten el manejo y envío.

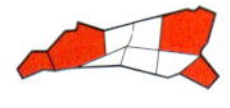

389 — Veal Bones, Marrow

Marrow bones shall be prepared from any combination of the shank, femur, or humerus bones of veal carcasses. The bones shall be sawed into sections or lengths to facilitate shipping and handling. Marrow shall be exposed on at least one end of each sawed section or length to qualify the bones as marrow bones.

389 — Huesos de Ternera, Tuétano

Los Huesos de Tuétano deberán prepararse a partir de cualquier combinación de chamberete, fémur o húmero de la canal de ternera. Los huesos deberán cortarse a sierra en secciones o extensiones que faciliten la manipulación y el traslado. La médula deberá estar expuesta en al menos uno de los extremos cortados a sierra para poder calificar como huesos de tuétano.

393 — Veal Flank, Flank Steak (IM)

This boneless item consists of the *rectus abdominis* muscle from the flank region of the carcass. The flank steak is located at the cod or udder end of flank. It is separated from the *transversus abdominis, obliquus abdominis internus, and obliquus abdominis externus* muscles through the natural seams. The item shall be prepared practically free of fat and membranous tissue.

PSO: 1 – Purchasers may request that the flank steak be further peeled to FLO 6 (see page 139) and cut square on both ends.

393 — Falda de Ternera, Concha (Bistec de Falda) (M. Rectus Abdominis)

Esta pieza deshuesada consiste en el músculo *rectus abdominis* de la región de la falda de la canal. El bistec de falda se ubica a nivel del canal inguinal o en el extremo de la ubre adyacente a la falda. Se separa de los músculos *transversus abdominis, obliquus abdominis internus y obliquus abdominis externus* a través de las vetas naturales. La pieza deberá prepararse de manera que quede prácticamente libre de grasa y del tejido membranoso.

PSO: 1 – Los compradores pueden solicitar que el recorte de grasa del bistec de falda sea mayor al indicado en la opción 6 especificada por el comprador (consulte la página 137) y que sea cortado cuadrado en ambos extremos.

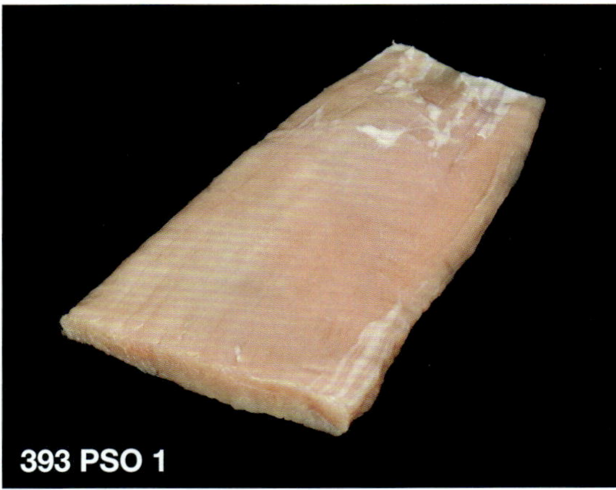
393 PSO 1

395 — Veal (or Calf) for Stewing

Diced veal or calf shall be prepared from any portion of the boneless carcass exclusive of shank and heel meat, provided that the end product meets the following requirements. The dices shall be free of bones, cartilages, heavy connective tissues, and lymph glands. At least 75 percent of the dices shall be of a size equivalent to a 0.75 inch (19 mm) to 1.5 inch (3.8 cm) cube. No individual surface on any dice shall be more than 2.5 inches (6.4 cm) in length, and must not exceed 0.125 inch (3 mm) fat thickness at any point. To facilitate dicing, the meat may be frozen and/or tempered once only.

395 — Trozos de Ternera para Cocer/Guisar

La carne de ternera o becerro troceada en cubos deberá prepararse a partir de cualquier porción de la canal deshuesada, salvo con la carne de chamberete y talón, siempre que el producto final cumpla con los siguientes requisitos: los cubos deberán estar libres de huesos, cartílagos, tejidos conectivos gruesos y ganglios linfáticos. Al menos el 75% de los cubos deberán tener un tamaño equivalente a un cubo de entre 19 mm (0.75 pulgadas) y 3.8 cm (1.5 pulgadas). Las superficies individuales de los cubos no deberán tener más de 6.4 cm (2.5 pulgadas) de longitud, ni exceder los 3 mm (0.125 pulgadas) de grosor de la grasa en ningún punto. Para facilitar el troceado, la carne puede estar congelada o atemperada, una sola vez.

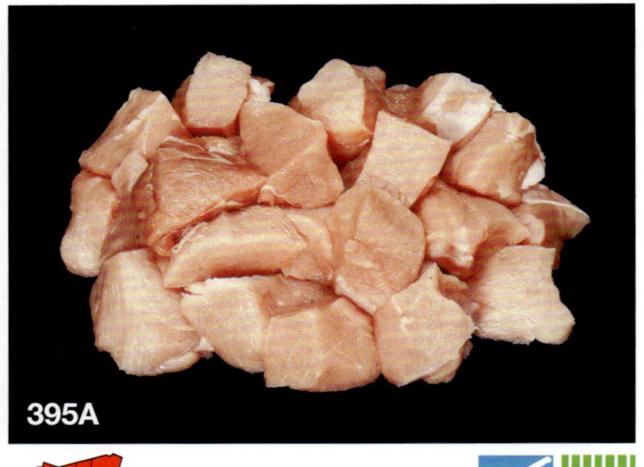

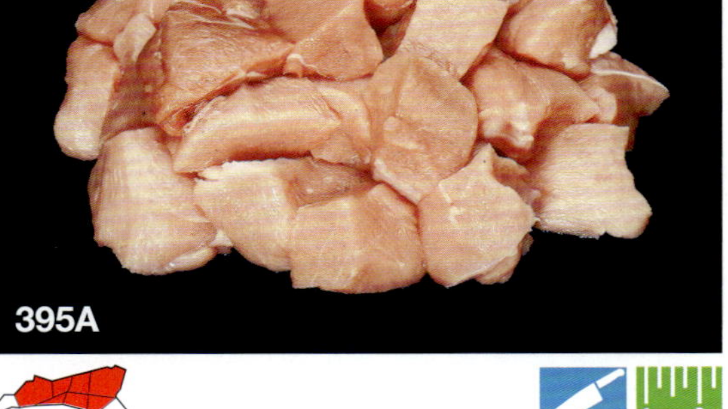

395A — Veal (or Calf) for Kabobs

In addition to the requirements of Item No. 395, the end product must be at least 90 percent within the size range with the exception that an individual surface may be no more than 3.0 inches (7.5 cm) in length. Purchaser, however, may specify other size and surface requirements.

395A — Trozos de Ternera para Brochetas

Además de los requisitos de la pieza número 395, el producto final debe estar al menos en un 90% dentro de la escala de tamaño, con la excepción de que una superficie individual no puede tener más de 7.5 cm (3.0 pulgadas) de longitud. El comprador, no obstante, puede especificar otros requisitos de tamaño y superficie.

396 Ground Veal

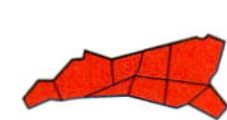

Ground veal or calf shall be prepared from any portion of boneless graded or ungraded carcasses. The meat shall be free of bones, cartilages, any type of gland, heavy connective tissue, and the tendinous ends of shanks and sirloin tip (knuckles) that are not exposed at least 75 percent lean on a cross-sectional cut. Unless otherwise specified by the purchaser, the finished product may be produced from previously certified boneless veal or calf that has been frozen and stock-piled. The purchaser may also specify the maximum quantity of such frozen meat that may be mixed with fresh-chilled meat prior to final grinding. Unless otherwise specified, the maximum fat content shall not exceed 15 percent. However, purchasers may specify a different fat content between 10 and 20 percent.

The boneless product shall be ground at least once through a plate having holes not larger than 1.0 inch (2.5 cm) in diameter. Alternatively, the product may be chopped or machine-cut by any method, provided the texture and appearance of the finished product is typical of product prepared by grinding alone. The product may be thoroughly blended one or more times prior to, but shall not be mixed again after, final grinding. The process of size reduction, blending, and final grinding shall be a continuous sequence. Unless specified differently by the purchaser, the final grind shall be made through a plate having holes 0.125 inch (3 mm) in diameter.

If the purchaser requests the product be coarse ground, the product shall include "Coarse Ground" in the label name and shall be ground only once through a plate having holes no larger than 1.0 inch (2.5 cm) and no smaller than 0.625 inch (16 mm) in diameter. A purchaser may request that a specific plate size in between these dimensions be used.

396 Carne Molida de Ternera

La carne molida de ternera o becerro deberá prepararse a partir de cualquier porción de canal deshuesada, clasificada por grados o sin clasificar. La carne no deberá tener huesos, cartílagos, ningún tipo de ganglios, tejido conectivo grueso ni los extremos tendinosos de chamberetes y pulpa bola que no se expongan al menos el 75% de carne magra en un corte transversal. A menos que el comprador especifique lo contrario, el producto terminado puede obtenerse a partir de ternera o becerro previamente certificados, deshuesados, que hayan sido congelados y almacenados. El comprador puede especificar la cantidad máxima de carne congelada que se puede mezclar con carne refrigerada en estado fresco antes de la molienda final. A menos que se especifique lo contrario, el contenido máximo de grasa no podrá exceder el 15%. Sin embargo, los compradores pueden especificar un contenido de grasa diferente, entre el 10 y el 20%.

El producto deshuesado deberá molerse pasándolo al menos una vez a través de una placa con orificios no mayores a 2.5 cm (1.0 pulgada) de diámetro. En forma alternativa, el producto puede picarse o cortarse a máquina por cualquier método, siempre que la textura y el aspecto del producto terminado sea típico del preparado únicamente mediante la molienda. El producto puede mezclarse perfectamente una o dos veces antes de la molienda final, pero no podrá ser mezclado de nuevo después de la misma. El proceso de reducción del tamaño, mezclado y molienda final deberá seguir una secuencia continua. A menos que el comprador especifique lo contrario, la molienda final deberá realizarse a través de una placa con orificios de 3 mm (0.125 pulgadas) de diámetro.

Si el comprador solicita que el producto sea molido grueso, su etiqueta deberá incluir la leyenda "Coarse Ground" (molido grueso) y deberá molerse una vez a través de una placa con orificios no mayores a 2.5 cm (1.0 pulgada) ni menores a 16 mm (0.625 pulgadas). Es posible que un comprador solicite que se use una placa específica cuya dimensión esté entre las dos anteriores.

Membership Information
Información sobre la membresía

Want your personal network to include the real decision-makers at the most successful meat & poultry processors and suppliers in North America?

THEN JOIN NAMP!

Founded in 1942, the North American Meat Processors Association (NAMP) is an international member-driven association of *progressive meat processors, distributors, center-of-the-plate specialists,* and suppliers selling primarily to the foodservice industry. NAMP provides exceptional value through high-caliber support programs and governmental representation to help ensure our members' success in the industry.

The Meat Buyer's Guide® is a NAMP publication. NAMP members can participate in the review/update process of each edition.

BENEFITS OF MEMBERSHIP

- 35% discount on *The Meat Buyers Guide®*
- A relaxed networking and learning environment at two major industry-wide meetings a year
- Learning opportunities at NAMP's 16+ food safety conferences and workshops: pay lower member fees
- NAMP's weekly report, *NewsLine,* which contains industry information and updates and NAMP's weekly Market Report, with complete up-to-date pricing information
- Unlimited free access to NAMP's College of Experts, our team of 34 Ph.D.-level consultants on 19 subjects important to your business
- A voice in government rulemaking: NAMP is a North American organization that effectively represents your interests to USDA-FSIS, USDA-AMS, and CFIA
- A cross-referenced *Member Resource Directory* for networking and enriching your business prospects
- Fast, on-line help from other members through NAMP's Listserve called "Bull Session"
- Exclusive technical/educational info on the Members Only section at www.namp.com

Members also enjoy toll-free access to NAMP's experienced staff and off-site consultants who are ready to help you with just about any problem, question or concern you may have. *It's like having your own team of experts without the added expense - an incredible value for your dues dollar!*

Membership in NAMP offers an unparalleled and unique opportunity to learn and network with your peers. Join today and you'll enrich your business prospects and benefit from other members' experiences. *It's what our long-time members call "The Magic of NAMP".*

WE INVITE YOU TO JOIN TODAY

To apply, go to www.namp.com or call +1 703.758.1900.

¿Quiere que su red personal incluya a quienes en verdad toman las decisiones y a los más exitosos procesadores y proveedores de carne roja y aves de América del Norte?

¡ENTONCES ÚNASE A NAMP!

La Asociación Norteamericana de Procesadores de Carne (NAMP), fundada en 1942, es una asociación internacional dedicada a sus integrantes, que incluyen *procesadores, distribuidores, especialistas en ingredientes principales del plato* y proveedores progresistas que venden principalmente a la industria de servicios de alimentación. NAMP ofrece un valor excepcional a través de programas de apoyo de gran nivel y representación en el gobierno para ayudar a garantizar el éxito de nuestros miembros en la industria.

La Guía para Compradores de Carne® es una publicación de NAMP. Los miembros de NAMP pueden participar en el proceso de revisión y actualización de cada edición.

BENEFICIOS DE LA MEMBRESÍA

- 35% de descuento en *La Guía para Compradores de Carne®*
- Un ambiente relajado para establecer contactos y aprender en dos grandes reuniones de toda la industria por año
- Oportunidades de aprendizaje en las conferencias y los talleres de inocuidad alimentaria de NAMP: pague tarifas más bajas para miembros
- Informe semanal de NAMP, *NewsLine,* que contiene información y actualizaciones de la industria, y el Informe de Mercado semanal de NAMP, con la información de precios completa y al día
- Acceso gratis ilimitado al colegio de expertos de NAMP, nuestro equipo de 34 con nivel de doctorado en 19 áreas importantes para su negocio
- Una voz en las normativas del gobierno: NAMP es una organización norteamericana que representa sus intereses de manera eficaz ante FSIS (Servicio de Inspección e Inocuidad Alimentaria) de USDA (Departamento de Agricultura de E.U.A.), AMS (Servicio de Mercadeo Agrícola) de USDA y la Agencia Canadiense de Inspección de Alimentos
- Un *Directorio de recursos de miembros* con referencia cruzada para establecer contactos y enriquecer las posibilidades de su negocio
- Ayuda rápida en Internet de otros miembros a través del Listserve de NAMP llamado "Bull Session"
- Información técnica y educativa exclusiva en la sección Members Only (sólo para miembros) de www.namp.com

Los miembros también disponen de acceso a través de un número telefónico sin cargo al experimentado personal de NAMP y a consultores descentralizados que están listos para ayudarle con prácticamente cualquier problema, consulta o inquietud que pueda tener. *Es como tener su propio equipo de expertos sin el gasto adicional ¡un increíble rendimiento por el valor de su suscripción!*

La membresía de NAMP ofrece una oportunidad única e incomparable de aprender y establecer contactos con sus colegas. Suscríbase hoy para enriquecer las posibilidades de su negocio y beneficiarse de la experiencia de otros miembros. *Es lo que nuestros miembros de muchos años llaman "La magia de NAMP".*

LO INVITAMOS A UNIRSE HOY

Para solicitar su inscripción, visite www.namp.com o llame al +1 703.758.1900.

Photo courtesy of The Beef Checkoff.
Fotografía cortesía del programa The Beef Checkoff.

Center of the Plate Training®

from the producers of
The Meat Buyer's Guide®

Course Specifics

Center of the Plate Training® offered by the North American Meat Processors Association (NAMP) is a first-hand look at how carcasses are converted into portioned items commonly traded in the foodservice and retail meat business. The course covers all the major center of the plate protein items: beef, veal, lamb, pork, and poultry (in some locations).

This course is held two to three times annually across North America. It spans two to three days of classroom learning, with presentations by industry experts. You also will receive a copy of the NAMP *Meat Buyer's Guide®*, which is used extensively in the course.

What You Will Learn From This Course

- The IMPS/NAMP numbering system, purchase specified options, and standards common to the industry.

- A knowledge of meat items as described by IMPS and by NAMP's *Meat Buyer's Guide®*.

- Where meat products originate and how this affects their final use.

- The importance of standards and how they keep products consistent, wholesome, and fair throughout the market.

- Common defects or inconsistencies in meat products that you should look for to prevent dissatisfied customers or unpleasant dining experiences.

- Current trends in the foodservice industry, new menu ideas and options.

- How value is determined for different meat products and how this is affected by quality parameters.

If you're involved in the buying and selling of meat products - from restaurants and supermarkets to foodservice distributors and meat companies - gain a competitive edge by applying the valuable information you'll learn from this course.

Visit www.namp.com for more information on specific courses, locations, and dates.

Visite www.namp.com para obtener información adicional sobre cursos específicos, sitios y fechas.

Capacitación en ingredientes principales del plato

de los realizadores de la Guía
para Compradores de Carne®

Detalles del curso

La Capacitación en ingredientes principales del plato que ofrece la Asociación Norteamericana de Procesadores de Carne (NAMP) es una mirada de primera mano a la forma en que las canales se convierten en piezas porcionadas comúnmente comercializadas en la industria de servicios de alimentación y los negocios minoristas de carne. El curso comprende las principales piezas proteicas que constituyen los ingredientes principales del plato: carne de res, ternera, cordero, cerdo y aves (en algunos lugares).

Este curso se dicta dos o tres veces al año en toda Norteamérica. Abarca de dos a tres días de aprendizaje en un salón de clase, con presentaciones a cargo de expertos de la industria. También recibirá una copia de *La Guía para Compradores de Carne®* de NAMP (Asociación Norteamericana de Procesadores de Carne, por sus siglas en inglés) que se utilizará exhaustivamente en el curso.

Qué aprenderá en este curso

- El sistema de numeración IMPS/NAMP, las opciones especificadas de compra y las normas comunes de la industria.

- Un conocimiento de las piezas de carne como se describen en las IMPS (Especificaciones Institucionales de Compra de Carne, por sus siglas en inglés) y en *La Guía para Compradores de Carne®* de NAMP.

- Dónde se originan los productos de carne y cómo afecta esto su uso final.

- La importancia de las normas y cómo logran que los productos sean uniformes, saludables y buenos en todo el mercado.

- Defectos o anomalías en los productos de carne que debería buscar para evitar clientes insatisfechos o que tengan experiencias desagradables en la mesa.

- Las tendencias actuales de la industria de servicios de alimentación, nuevas ideas y opciones para su menú.

- Cómo se determina el valor de diferentes productos de carne y cómo éste se ve afectado por los parámetros de calidad.

Si participa en la compra y venta de productos de carne, ya sea en restaurantes y supermercados o distribuidores de la industria de servicios de alimentación y empresas de carne, obtenga una ventaja competitiva aplicando la valiosa información que aprenderá en este curso.

Index/Índice

Veal & Calf Products and Weight Ranges
Productos de Ternera y Becerro y Escalas de Peso

PIEZA	PRODUCT NAME NOMBRE DE PRODUCTO	PG. PÁG.	Suggested Portion Weight Range Porción Sugerida Escala de Peso
1300	**Cubed Steak, Boneless** Bistec Suavizado (Ablandado por Machacado, Rayado), Deshuesado	168	3 – 8 oz. (85-226.8 gr)
1301	**Cubed Steak, Boneless, Special** Bistec Suavizado (Ablandado por Machacado, Rayado), Deshuesado, Especial	168	3 – 8 oz. (85-226.8 gr)
1302	**Veal Slices, Boneless** Tiras de Ternera, Deshuesadas	169	1 – 6 oz. (28.3-170.1 gr)
1306	**Rack, Rib Chops, 7 Rib** Costillar, Chuletas, de 7 Costillas	169	4 – 8 oz. (113.4-226.8 gr)
1306A	**Rack, Rib Chops, 6 Rib** Costillar, Chuletas, de 6 Costillas	169	4 – 8 oz. (113.4-226.8 gr)
1306B	**Rack, Rib Chops, Cap Off, 7 Rib** Costillar, Chuletas, sin Tapa, de 7 Costillas	170	4 – 8 oz. (113.4-226.8 gr)
1306C	**Rack, Rib Chops, Cap Off, 6 Rib** Costillar, Chuletas, sin Tapa, de 6 Costillas	170	4 – 8 oz. (113.4-226.8 gr)
1306D	**Rack, Rib Chops, Frenched, 7 Rib** Costillar, Chuletas, Estilo Francés, de 7 Costillas	170	4 – 8 oz. (113.4-226.8 gr)
1306E	**Rack, Rib Chops, Frenched, 6 Rib** Costillar, Chuletas, Estilo Francés, de 6 Costillas	171	4 – 8 oz. (113.4-226.8 gr)
1309	**Chuck, Shoulder Arm Chops** Paleta, Chuletas de Brazuelo	171	4 – 8 oz. (113.4-226.8 gr)
1309A	**Chuck, Shoulder Blade Chops** Paleta, Chuletas del 7	171	4 – 8 oz. (113.4-226.8 gr)
1312	**Osso Buco, Foreshank** Osobuco de Ternera, Chamberete de Mano	171	2 – 8 oz. (56.7-226.8 gr)
1332	**Loin Chops** Chuletas del Lomo	172	4 – 8 oz. (113.4-226.8 gr)
1336	**Cutlets, Boneless** Escalopas de Ternera, Deshuesadas	172	3 – 8 oz. (85-226.8 gr)
1337	**Osso Buco, Hindshank** Osobuco de Ternera, Chamberete Trasero	172	2 – 8 oz. (56.7-226.8 gr)
1349A	**Leg, Top Round (Inside), Cap Off, Cutlets, Boneless** Pierna (Cara/Centro), Sin Tapa, Escalopas, Deshuesadas	173	1 – 6 oz. (28.3-170.1 gr)
1396	**Ground Veal (or Calf) Patties** Ternera Molida para Hamburguesas	173	2 – 8 oz. (56.7-226.8 gr)
1396A	**Ground Veal (or Calf) and Soy Protein Product Patties** Carne de Ternera Molida y Hamburguesas con Producto Proteico Vegetal (PPV)	173	2 – 8 oz. (56.7-226.8 gr)

Información para hacer los pedidos

Tolerancias de peso y grosor de la porción*

El comprador especificará el peso y/o el grosor de la porción que desea. Para obtener ayuda en la especificación del peso, consulte las tablas de las escalas de peso. A menos que el comprador especifique otras tolerancias de peso y/o grosor, se deberán utilizar las tablas que aparecen a continuación. Cuando se especifique tanto el peso como el grosor, se recomienda que esos requisitos se limiten a piezas prensadas y/o rebanadas de forma mecánica.

Opciones para limitar la grasa

Chuletas

El comprador especificará uno de los siguientes grosores máximos de cubierta de grasa (en un punto cualquiera) en los bordes de la chuleta, a menos que se indiquen limitaciones precisas de grasa en la descripción detallada de la pieza. En caso de que no se especifique, el espesor de grasa no excederá los 6 mm (0.25 pulgadas) en ningún punto.

Chuletas	
Número de opción	**Grosor máximo de grasa en un punto cualquiera del corte en porciones***
1	6 mm (0.25 pulgadas)
2	3 mm (0.125 pulgadas)
3	Prácticamente libre de grasa [el 75% de la superficie expuesta es magra/superficie muscular descubierta por la disección y la grasa que queda no debe exceder los 3 mm (0.125 pulgadas)]
4	Desprovisto de grasa/Prácticamente desnudo de grasa [la grasa que queda no debe exceder los 2.5 cm (1.0 pulgada) en la dimensión más larga y/o 3 mm (0.125 pulgadas) de grosor]
5	Desprovisto de grasa/Prácticamente desnudo de grasa, Membrana superficial retirada [el 90% de la superficie expuesta es magra y la grasa que queda no debe exceder los 3 mm (0.125 pulgadas)]

* **Importante: cuando se especifiquen los grosores promedio de grasa en la descripción de la pieza, aplicará la limitación "Máximo en un punto cualquiera" correspondiente.**

Tolerancias de grosor de la porción		
Grosor especificado	**Tolerancia de grosor**	**Uniformidad de grosor**
2.5 cm (1.0 pulgada o menos)	± 5 mm (0.1875 pulgadas)	5 mm (0.1875 pulgadas)
Más de 2.5 cm (1.0 pulgada)	± 6 mm (0.25 pulgadas)	6 mm (0.25 pulgadas)

Tolerancia de peso de la porción		
Peso especificado	**Tolerancia de peso**	**Uniformidad de grosor**
Menor que 170 g (6.0 oz.)	± 7 g (0.25 oz.)	5 mm (0.1875 pulgadas)
170 g (6.0 oz.) o más	± 14 g (0.50 oz.)	6 mm (0.25 pulgadas)

Los compradores que tengan necesidades o especificaciones especiales deben comunicarse con sus proveedores.

* Las medidas de grosor no se aplican a 6 mm (0.25 pulgadas) del borde. Además, el valor que se indica en la uniformidad del grosor es la máxima diferencia admitida entre la medida más fina y la más gruesa de una chuleta o bistec individual.

Ordering Data

Portion-Cut Weight and Thickness Tolerances*

The purchaser shall specify the portion weight and/or thickness desired. For assistance in specifying weight, see weight range tables. Unless other portion weight and/or thickness tolerances are specified by the purchaser, the following tables shall be used. When both weight and thickness are specified, it is recommended that those requirements be limited to items that are mechanically pressed and/or sliced.

Fat Limitation Options (FLO)

Chops

The purchaser shall specify one of the following maximum (at any one point) thicknesses of surface fat on the edges of the chop unless definite fat limitations are indicated in the detailed Item Descriptions. If not specified, fat thickness shall not exceed 0.25 inch (6 mm) at any one point.

Chops	
Option No.	**Maximum Fat Thickness at Any One Point for Portion Cuts***
1	0.25 inch (6 mm)
2	0.125 inch (3 mm)
3	Practically free (75 percent lean/seam surface exposed and remaining fat shall not exceed 0.125 inch (3 mm))
4	Peeled/Denuded (remaining fat shall not exceed 1.0 inch (2.5 cm) in the longest dimension and/or 0.125 inch (3 mm) in thickness)
5	Peeled/Denuded, Surface Membrane Removed (90 percent lean exposed and remaining fat shall not exceed 0.125 inch (3 mm))

* Note: When average fat thicknesses are specified in Item Descriptions, the appropriate "Maximum at Any One Point" limitation shall apply.

Portion Thickness Tolerances		
Specified Thickness	**Thickness Tolerance**	**Thickness Uniformity**
1.0 inch (2.5 cm or less)	± 0.1875 inch (5 mm)	0.1875 inch (5 mm)
More than 1.0 inch (2.5 cm)	± 0.25 inch (6 mm)	0.25 inch (6 mm)

Portion Weight Tolerance		
Specified Weight	**Weight Tolerance**	**Thickness Uniformity**
Less than 6.0 oz. (170 g)	± 0.25 oz. (7 g)	0.1875 inch (5 mm)
6.0 oz. (170 g) or more	± 0.50 oz. (14 g)	0.25 inch (6 mm)

Purchasers with special needs or specifications should contact their suppliers.

* Thickness measurements not applicable with 0.25 inch (6 mm) of edge. Also, value listed under thickness uniformity is the maximum allowable difference between the thinnest and thickest measurement of an individual chop or steak.

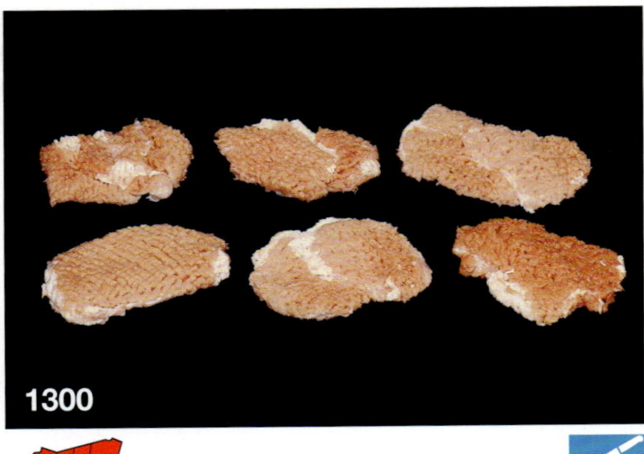

1300 — Veal Cubed Steak, Boneless

Cubed steaks shall be prepared from any portion of the boneless carcass excluding the shank and heel meat. The steaks shall be free of bones, cartilages, lymph glands, and heavy connective tissue. Unless otherwise specified, steaks shall be cubed no more than two times. Knitting together two or more pieces and folding the meat during cubing is permitted. After the cubing is completed, the surface and seam fat shall not exceed 15 percent of the total area on either side of the steak. Individual steaks shall remain intact when suspended from any point 0.5 inch (13 mm) from the outer edge.

1300 — Bistec de Ternera Suavizado (Ablandado por Machacado, Rayado), Deshuesado

Las escalopas suavizadas deberán ser preparadas a partir de cualquier porción de la canal deshuesada, sin incluir el chamberete y el talón. Los bistecs no deberán contener huesos, cartílagos, ganglios linfáticos ni tejido conectivo grueso. A menos que se especifique lo contrario, los bistecs no deberán suavizarse mecánicamente más de dos veces. Se permite unir dos o más piezas y plegar la carne al cortar. Cuando se termine de suavizar, la cubierta de grasa y las vetas de grasa intermuscular no deberán exceder el 15% del área total de ninguno de los lados del bistec. Los bistecs individuales deben permanecer intactos al suspenderse de cualquier punto a 13 mm (0.5 pulgadas) desde el borde exterior.

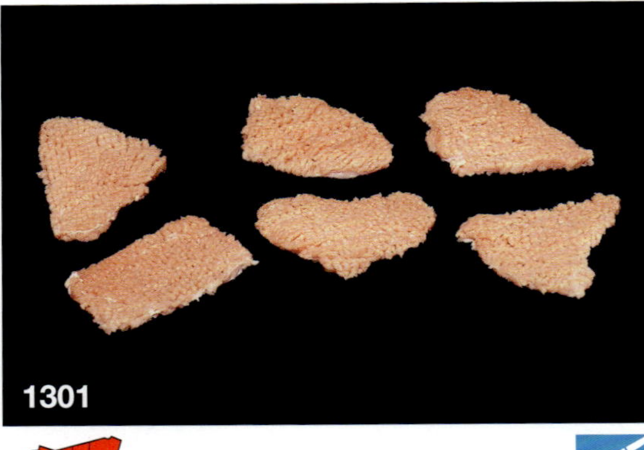

1301 — Veal Cubed Steak, Boneless, Special

This item shall be prepared only from any combination of lean from the leg excluding shank and heel meat, loin, rib, or square-cut chuck portions of the boneless carcass. Purchaser, however, may stipulate only certain allowed specific primal cuts, such as the leg, loin, rib, square-cut chuck, or combination, be used to prepare this item. The product shall then be labeled accordingly. No knitting or folding of the meat is permitted. All other requirements of Item No. 1300 shall apply.

1301 — Bistec de Ternera Suavizado (Ablandado por Machacado, Rayado), Deshuesado, Especial

Esta pieza deberá prepararse únicamente a partir de cualquier combinación de carne magra de la pierna, salvo porciones de carne de chamberete y talón, lomo, costilla o paleta de corte cuadrado, de la canal deshuesada. El comprador, sin embargo, puede estipular solamente determinados cortes primarios específicos, tales como pierna, lomo, costilla, paleta de corte cuadrado, o una combinación, para ser usados en la preparación de esta pieza. El producto deberá llevar la etiqueta correspondiente. No se permite unir ni plegar la carne. Se aplicarán todos los demás requisitos de la pieza número 1300.

1302 — Veal Slices, Boneless

The raw material and processing requirements of Item No. 1301 apply to this item. Further, if specified by the purchaser, either the raw materials or the prepared slices from the product shall be mechanically tenderized one time (pinned, paddled, or pounded). Surface and seam fat shall not exceed 0.25 inch (6 mm) in thickness at any point. As an alternative, purchaser may specify surface and seam fat limitations in terms of maximum surface area percentage.

1302 — Tiras de Ternera, Deshuesadas

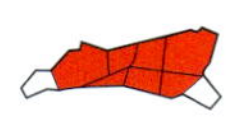

Para esta pieza, se aplican la materia prima y los requisitos de procesamiento descritos en la pieza número 1301. Asimismo, en caso de ser especificado por el comprador, tanto la materia prima como las tiras preparadas deberán someterse a un ablandamiento mecánico por una sola vez (alfilerazos/lancetado, golpes, machaques). La cubierta de grasa y las vetas de grasa intermuscular no deberán exceder un grosor de 6 mm (0.25 pulgadas) en ningún punto. Como alternativa, el comprador puede especificar límites a la cubierta de grasa y vetas de grasa intermuscular en términos de su porcentaje máximo del área de la superficie.

1306 — Veal Rack, Rib Chops, 7 Rib

The rib chops shall be prepared from one-half of Item No. 306. The protruding edge of the chine bone shall be excluded by a cut along the dorsal edge of the spinal cord groove that does not score the eye (*longissimus dorsi*) muscle. The tail length of the chop shall not be more than 3.0 inches (7.5 cm) from the ventral edge of the *longissimus dorsi* muscle unless purchaser specifies another option as described below.

PSO: 1 – 2.0 inches (5.0 cm)

    2 – 1.0 inch (2.5 cm)

    3 – 0.0 inch (0 mm)

1306 — Costillar de Ternera, Chuletas, de 7 Costillas

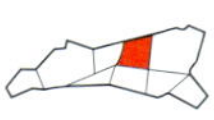

Las chuletas del costillar deberán prepararse a partir de una mitad de la pieza número 306. Se deberá extraer el borde protuberante del espinazo mediante un corte a lo largo del borde dorsal del canal raquídeo que no haga una incisión profunda en el músculo del ojo (*longissimus dorsi*). La longitud de la cola de la chuleta no deberá exceder los 7.5 cm (3.0 pulgadas) desde el borde ventral del músculo *longissimus dorsi* a menos que el comprador especifique otra opción de las que se describen a continuación.

PSO: 1 – 5.0 cm (2.0 pulgadas)

    2 – 2.5 cm (1.0 pulgadas)

    3 – 0 mm (0.0 pulgadas)

1306A — Veal Rack, Rib Chops, 6 Rib

Other than that the rib chops shall be prepared from one-half of a 6 rib Veal Rack meeting the requirements of Item No. 306A, all the other preparation and tail length requirements of Item No. 1306 apply.

1306A — Costillar de Ternera, Chuletas, de 6 Costillas

Salvo que las chuletas del costillar deben prepararse de un costillar de ternera de 6 costillas que cumpla con los requisitos de la pieza número 306A, se aplicarán los demás requisitos de preparación y longitud de la cola de la pieza número 1306.

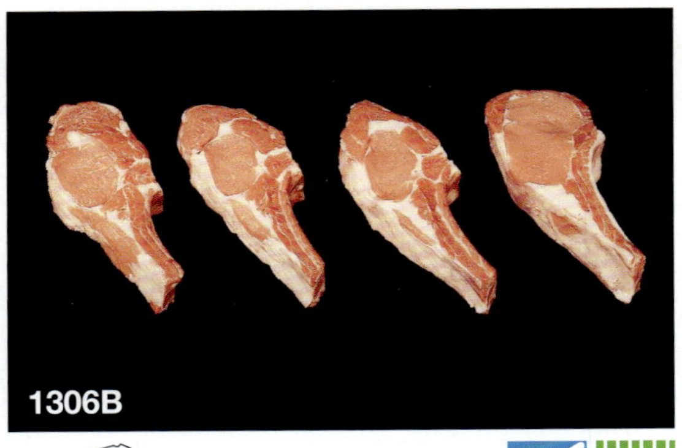

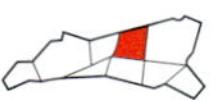

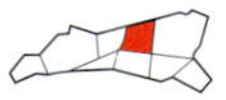

1306B Veal Rack, Rib Chops, Cap Off, 7 Rib

Other than that the rib chops shall be prepared from a 7 rib Veal Rack meeting the requirements of Item 306B, which imposes additional requirements regarding the exclusion of the cap meat, all the other preparation and tail length requirements of Item No. 1306 apply.

1306B Costillar de Ternera, Chuletas, sin Tapa, de 7 Costillas

Salvo que las chuletas del costillar deben prepararse de un costillar de ternera de 7 costillas que cumpla con los requisitos de la pieza número 306B, lo cual impone requisitos adicionales sobre la exclusión de carne de la tapa, se aplicarán los demás requisitos de preparación y longitud de la cola de la pieza número 1306.

1306C Veal Rack, Rib Chops, Cap Off, 6 Rib

Other than that the rib chops shall be prepared from a 6 rib Veal Rack meeting the requirements of Item No. 306C, which imposes additional requirements regarding the exclusion of the cap meat, all the other preparation and tail length requirements of Item No. 1306 apply.

1306C Costillar de Ternera, Chuletas, sin Tapa, de 6 Costillas

Salvo que las chuletas del costillar deben prepararse a partir de un costillar de ternera de 6 costillas que cumpla con los requisitos de la pieza número 306C, lo cual impone requisitos adicionales sobre la inclusión de carne de la tapa, se aplicarán los demás requisitos de preparación y longitud de la cola de la pieza número 1306.

1306D Veal Rack, Rib Chops, Frenched, 7 Rib

This item may be produced from product as described in Item Nos. 306B or 306D, except that the tail length shall not exceed 3.0 inches (7.5 cm) in length from the ventral edge of the *longissimus dorsi*. In preparing the item the breast side of the rib bones shall be Frenched. Frenching is accomplished by the exclusion of the intercostal meat and the lean and fat over the ribs. When completed the exposed portion of the rib bone shall not exceed 1.5 inches (3.8 cm) in length. A purchaser may alternatively specify the chop to be Frenched immediately ventral to the *longissimus dorsi*.

1306D Costillar de Ternera, Chuletas, Estilo Francés, de 7 Costillas

Esta pieza puede obtenerse a partir del producto descrito en las piezas números 306B o 306D, salvo que la longitud de la cola no deberá exceder los 7.5 cm (3.0 pulgadas) desde el borde ventral del *longissimus dorsi*. Al preparar la pieza, el lado del pecho de los huesos del costillar deberá ser Estilo francés. Este estilo se logra mediante la exclusión de la carne intercostal, la grasa y la carne magra que recubre las costillas. Al terminar, la porción expuesta del hueso del costillar no deberá exceder una longitud de 3.8 cm (1.5 pulgadas). Por otro lado, el comprador puede especificar que la chuleta adquiera el Estilo francés en una orientación inmediatamente ventral al *longissimus dorsi*.

1306E — Veal Rack, Rib Chops, Frenched, 6 Rib

Other than that the rib chops shall be prepared from a 6 rib Veal Rack meeting the end requirements of Item No. 306E, the other preparation and tail length requirements of Item No. 1306D apply.

1306E — Costillar de Ternera, Chuletas, Estilo Francés, de 6 Costillas

Salvo que las chuletas del espaldar deben prepararse de un costillar de ternera de 6 costillas que cumpla con los requisitos finales de la pieza número 306E, se aplicarán los demás requisitos de preparación y longitud de la cola de la pieza número 1306D.

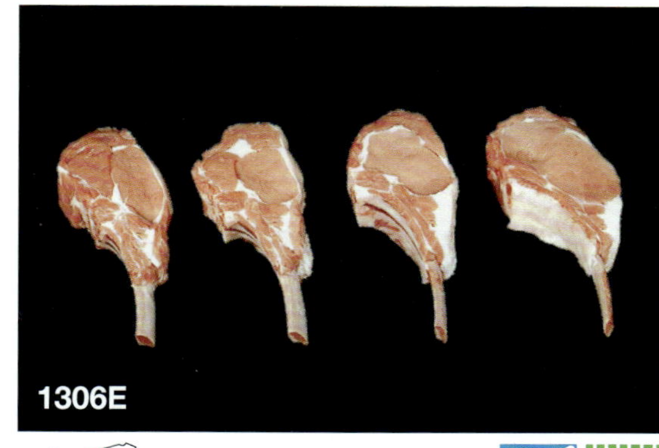

1306E

1309 — Veal Chuck, Shoulder Arm Chops

This item may be prepared from any single square-cut chuck such as described in Item Nos. 309 or 309A. The arm chops shall contain a cross section of the humerus and shall be cut approximately parallel to the shank side of the shoulder. All rib and blade bones and intercostal meat shall be excluded.

1309 — Paleta de Ternera, Chuletas de Brazuelo

Esta pieza puede prepararse de cualquier paleta de corte cuadrado como las descritas en las piezas números 309 o 309A. Las chuletas de brazuelo deberán mostrar un corte transversal del húmero y ser cortadas de forma aproximadamente paralelas al lado adyacente al chamberete de la espaldilla. Se deberán excluir todos los huesos de costillas y paleta, así como la carne intercostal.

1309A — Veal Chuck, Shoulder Blade Chops

This item may be prepared from any single square-cut chuck such a described in Item Nos. 309 or 309A. The blade chops must contain a portion of the blade bone and shall be cut approximately parallel to the rib bones.

1309A — Paleta de Ternera, Chuletas del 7

Esta pieza, llamada así por la forma del número 7 que adquiere el corte transversal del hueso de la paleta, puede prepararse de cualquier paleta de corte cuadrado como las descritas en las piezas números 309 o 309A. Las chuletas del 7 deben contener una porción de hueso de la paleta y deben ser cortadas de manera aproximadamente paralela a los huesos de las costillas.

1312 — Veal Osso Buco, Foreshank

This item shall be prepared from Item No. 312. The foreshanks shall be cut into the thickness specified by the purchaser. The slices shall be cut approximately perpendicular to the bone length so as to display a cross-section surface at least 75 percent lean on each side.

1312 — Osobuco de Ternera, Chamberete de Mano

Esta pieza se prepara con la pieza número 312. Los chamberetes de mano deberán cortarse al grosor especificado por el comprador. Las rebanadas deberán cortarse de forma aproximadamente perpendicular a la longitud del hueso, de forma que la superficie del corte transversal presente un 75% de carne magra en cada lado.

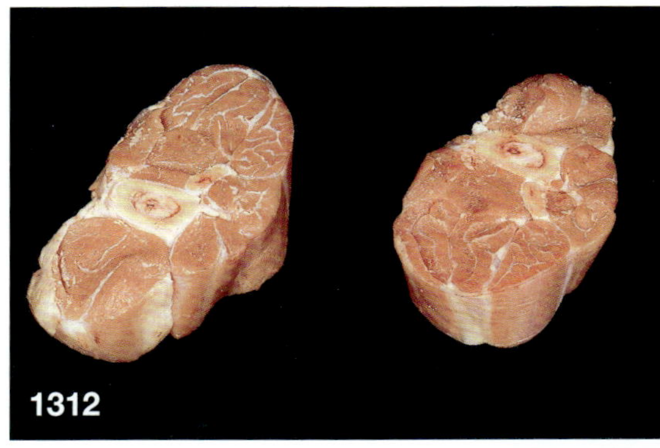

1312

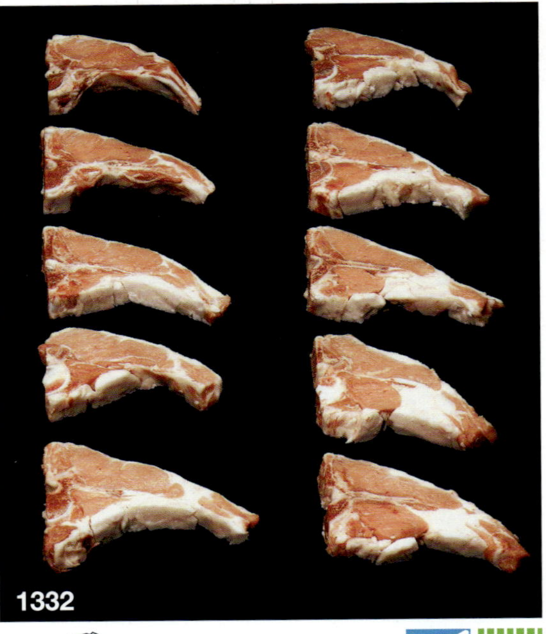

1332

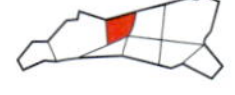

1332 — Veal Loin Chops

This item is prepared from a single veal loin meeting the end requirements of Item No. 332. Loin chops shall contain no portion of the hip bone or related cartilage. The tail length of the chop shall not be more than 3.0 inches (7.5 cm) from the ventral edge of the *longissimus dorsi* muscle unless purchaser specifies another option as described below.

PSO: 1 – 2.0 inches (5.0 cm)
     2 – 1.0 inch (2.5 cm)
     3 – 0.0 inch (0 mm)

1332 — Chuletas del Lomo de Ternera

Esta pieza se prepara de un lomo individual de ternera que cumpla con los requisitos finales de la pieza número 332. Las chuletas de lomo no deberán contener ninguna porción del hueso de la cadera ni del cartílago correspondiente. La longitud de la cola de la chuleta no deberá exceder los 7.5 cm (3.0 pulgadas) desde el borde ventral del músculo *longissimus dorsi*, a menos que el comprador especifique otra opción como las que se describen a continuación.

PSO: 1 – 5.0 cm (2.0 pulgadas)
     2 – 2.5 cm (1.0 pulgadas)
     3 – 0 mm (0.0 pulgadas)

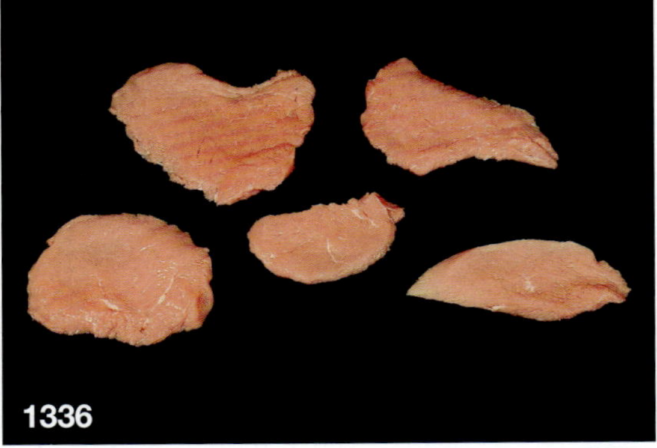

1336

1336 — Veal Cutlets, Boneless

This item shall be prepared from a veal leg that meets the end requirements of Item No. 336. The heel and any remaining shank meat, fat, and surface membranous tissue shall be excluded. The leg muscles may be split lengthwise and sliced across the grain to obtain the specified size cutlets. If specified by the purchaser, each cutlet shall be mechanically tenderized one time (pinned, paddled, or pounded) in such a manner that the portion shall retain its approximate original shape. Knitting of two or more pieces or folding of the meat is not allowed.

1336 — Escalopas de Ternera, Deshuesadas

Esta pieza deberá prepararse a partir de una pierna de ternera que cumpla con los requisitos de la pieza número 336. Se deberá excluir el talón y demás carne restante del chamberete, grasa y tejido membranoso superficial. Los músculos de la pierna pueden separarse longitudinalmente y cortarse en el sentido del grano para obtener las escalopas del tamaño especificado. Si lo especifica el comprador, las escalopas deberán someterse a un ablandamiento mecánico por una sola vez (alfilerazos/lanceteado, golpes, machaques) de forma que la porción mantenga su forma original aproximada. No se permite unir dos o más piezas ni plegar la carne.

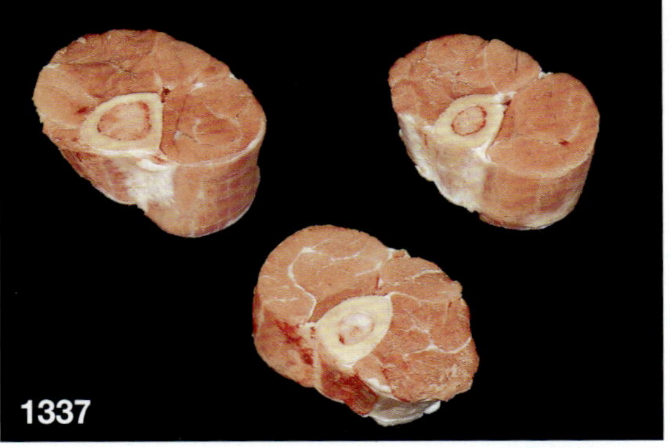

1337

1337 — Veal Osso Buco, Hindshank

This item shall be prepared from Item No. 337. The hindshank shall be cut into the thickness specified by the purchaser. The slices shall be cut approximately perpendicular to the bone length so as to display a cross-section surface at least 75 percent lean on each side.

1337 — Osobuco de Ternera, Chamberete Trasero

Esta pieza se prepara con la pieza número 337. El chamberete trasero deberá cortarse del grosor especificado por el comprador. Las rebanadas deberán cortarse de forma aproximadamente perpendicular a la longitud del hueso, de forma que la superficie del corte transversal presente un 75% de carne magra en cada lado.

1349A — Veal Leg, Top Round (Inside), Cap Off, Cutlets, Boneless

This cutlet shall be prepared from a top round (inside) item that meets the requirement of Item No. 349A. All fat and membranous surface tissue shall be excluded. If specified by the purchaser, each cutlet shall be cubed twice in such a manner that the portion shall retain its approximate original shape. Knitting of two or more pieces or folding of the meat is not allowed.

1349A — Pierna del Ternera (Cara/Centro), Sin Tapa, Escalopas, Deshuesadas

Esta escalopa deberá prepararse a partir de una pieza de cara/centro que cumpla con los requisitos de la pieza número 349A. Deberá eliminarse toda la grasa y el tejido membranoso superficial. Si el comprador lo especifica, cada escalopa deberá ser suavizada mecánicamente dos veces, de forma tal que la porción mantenga su forma original aproximada. No se permite unir dos o más piezas ni plegar la carne.

1396 — Ground Veal (or Calf) Patties

This item is prepared from product as described in Item No. 396. The ground meat shall be mechanically formed into patties of the shape and size specified by the purchaser. Patties shall be separated from each other by a means that will prevent them from sticking together when packaged. Patties shall be frozen unless specified fresh.

1396 — Ternera Molida para Hamburguesas

Esta pieza se prepara con producto según la descripción de la pieza número 396. La carne molida será procesada mecánicamente para elaborar hamburguesas de la forma y tamaño especificados por el comprador. Se deberán separar las hamburguesas entre sí de forma que no se peguen unas con otras al empaquetarse. Las hamburguesas deberán congelarse a menos que se especifique que se solicitan frescas.

1396A — Ground Veal (or Calf) and Soy Protein Product Patties

This item is prepared from ground product as described in IMPS Item No. 396A. The ground mixture includes soy protein product that is added to ground veal (or calf) Item No. 396. The patty processing requirements are the same as in Item No. 1396.

1396A — Carne de Ternera Molida y Hamburguesas con Producto Proteico Vegetal (PPV)

Esta pieza se prepara con producto molido según la descripción de IMPS (Especificaciones Institucionales de Compra de Carne, por sus siglas en inglés) para la pieza número 396A. La mezcla molida incluye producto proteico vegetal, que se agrega a la carne molida de ternera (o becerro) de la pieza número 396. Los requisitos de procesamiento de la hamburguesa son los mismos que los descritos en la pieza número 1396.

Membership Information
Información sobre la membresía

Want your personal network to include the real decision-makers at the most successful meat & poultry processors and suppliers in North America?

THEN JOIN NAMP!

Founded in 1942, the North American Meat Processors Association (NAMP) is an international member-driven association of *progressive meat processors, distributors, center-of-the-plate specialists,* and suppliers selling primarily to the foodservice industry. NAMP provides exceptional value through high-caliber support programs and governmental representation to help ensure our members' success in the industry.

The Meat Buyer's Guide® is a NAMP publication. NAMP members can participate in the review/update process of each edition.

BENEFITS OF MEMBERSHIP

- 35% discount on *The Meat Buyers Guide*®
- A relaxed networking and learning environment at two major industry-wide meetings a year
- Learning opportunities at NAMP's 16+ food safety conferences and workshops: pay lower member fees
- NAMP's weekly report, *NewsLine,* which contains industry information and updates and NAMP's weekly Market Report, with complete up-to-date pricing information
- Unlimited free access to NAMP's College of Experts, our team of 34 Ph.D.-level consultants on 19 subjects important to your business
- A voice in government rulemaking: NAMP is a North American organization that effectively represents your interests to USDA-FSIS, USDA-AMS, and CFIA
- A cross-referenced *Member Resource Directory* for networking and enriching your business prospects
- Fast, on-line help from other members through NAMP's Listserve called "Bull Session"
- Exclusive technical/educational info on the Members Only section at www.namp.com

Members also enjoy toll-free access to NAMP's experienced staff and off-site consultants who are ready to help you with just about any problem, question or concern you may have. *It's like having your own team of experts without the added expense - an incredible value for your dues dollar!*

Membership in NAMP offers an unparalleled and unique opportunity to learn and network with your peers. Join today and you'll enrich your business prospects and benefit from other members' experiences. *It's what our long-time members call "The Magic of NAMP".*

WE INVITE YOU TO JOIN TODAY

To apply, go to www.namp.com or call +1 703.758.1900.

¿Quiere que su red personal incluya a quienes en verdad toman las decisiones y a los más exitosos procesadores y proveedores de carne roja y aves de América del Norte?

¡ENTONCES ÚNASE A NAMP!

La Asociación Norteamericana de Procesadores de Carne (NAMP), fundada en 1942, es una asociación internacional dedicada a sus integrantes, que incluyen *procesadores, distribuidores, especialistas en ingredientes principales del plato* y proveedores progresistas que venden principalmente a la industria de servicios de alimentación. NAMP ofrece un valor excepcional a través de programas de apoyo de gran nivel y representación en el gobierno para ayudar a garantizar el éxito de nuestros miembros en la industria.

La Guía para Compradores de Carne® es una publicación de NAMP. Los miembros de NAMP pueden participar en el proceso de revisión y actualización de cada edición.

BENEFICIOS DE LA MEMBRESÍA

- 35% de descuento en *La Guía para Compradores de Carne*®
- Un ambiente relajado para establecer contactos y aprender en dos grandes reuniones de toda la industria por año
- Oportunidades de aprendizaje en las conferencias y los talleres de inocuidad alimentaria de NAMP: pague tarifas más bajas para miembros
- Informe semanal de NAMP, *NewsLine,* que contiene información y actualizaciones de la industria, y el Informe de Mercado semanal de NAMP, con la información de precios completa y al día
- Acceso gratis ilimitado al colegio de expertos de NAMP, nuestro equipo de 34 con nivel de doctorado en 19 áreas importantes para su negocio
- Una voz en las normativas del gobierno: NAMP es una organización norteamericana que representa sus intereses de manera eficaz ante FSIS (Servicio de Inspección e Inocuidad Alimentaria) de USDA (Departamento de Agricultura de E.U.A.), AMS (Servicio de Mercadeo Agrícola) de USDA y la Agencia Canadiense de Inspección de Alimentos
- Un *Directorio de recursos de miembros* con referencia cruzada para establecer contactos y enriquecer las posibilidades de su negocio
- Ayuda rápida en Internet de otros miembros a través del Listserve de NAMP llamado "Bull Session"
- Información técnica y educativa exclusiva en la sección Members Only (sólo para miembros) de www.namp.com

Los miembros también disponen de acceso a través de un número telefónico sin cargo al experimentado personal de NAMP y a consultores descentralizados que están listos para ayudarle con prácticamente cualquier problema, consulta o inquietud que pueda tener. *Es como tener su propio equipo de expertos sin el gasto adicional ¡un increíble rendimiento por el valor de su suscripción!*

La membresía de NAMP ofrece una oportunidad única e incomparable de aprender y establecer contactos con sus colegas. Suscríbase hoy para enriquecer las posibilidades de su negocio y beneficiarse de la experiencia de otros miembros. *Es lo que nuestros miembros de muchos años llaman "La magia de NAMP".*

LO INVITAMOS A UNIRSE HOY

Para solicitar su inscripción, visite www.namp.com o llame al +1 703.758.1900.

pork / cerdo

406 Pork Shoulder, Boston Butt, Bone In / Paleta (Espaldilla), Cabeza de Lomo, con Hueso

406A Pork Shoulder, Boston Butt, Boneless / Paleta (Espaldilla), Cabeza de Lomo, Deshuesada

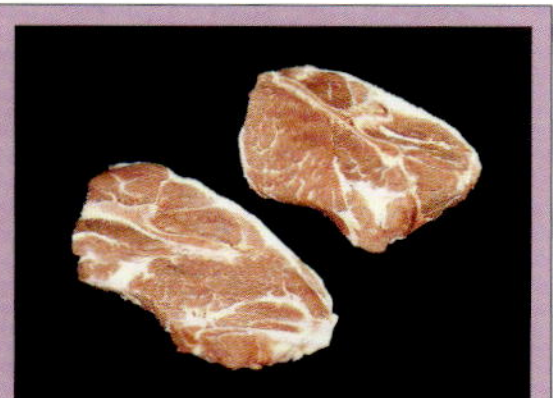

1406 Pork Boston Butt Steaks
Escalopas de Cabeza de Lomo, Con Hueso

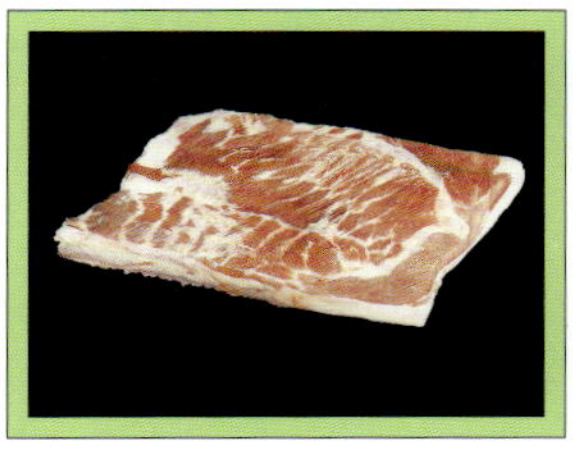

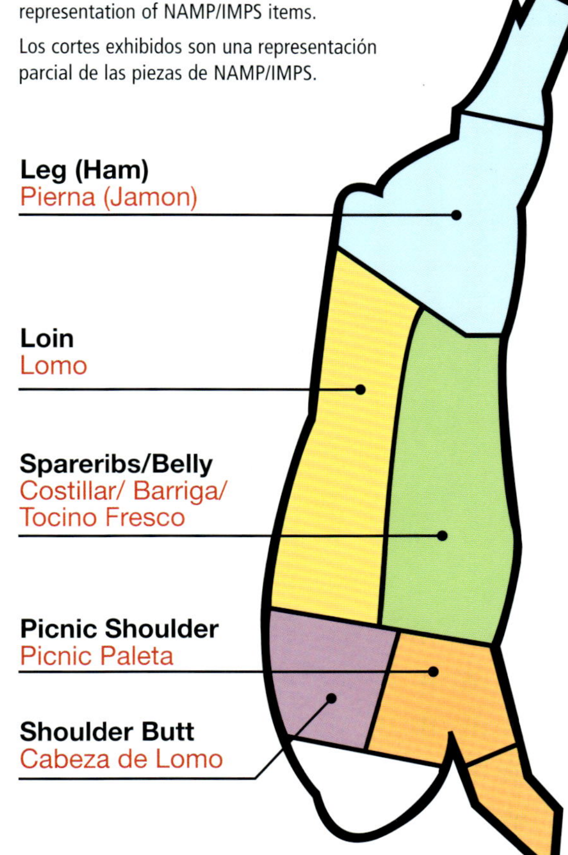

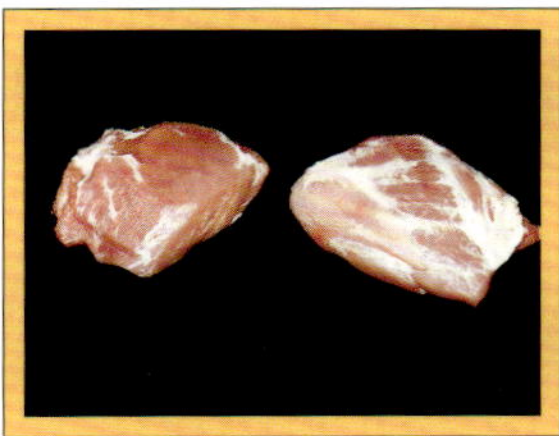

408 Pork Belly
Barriga/Tocino Fresco

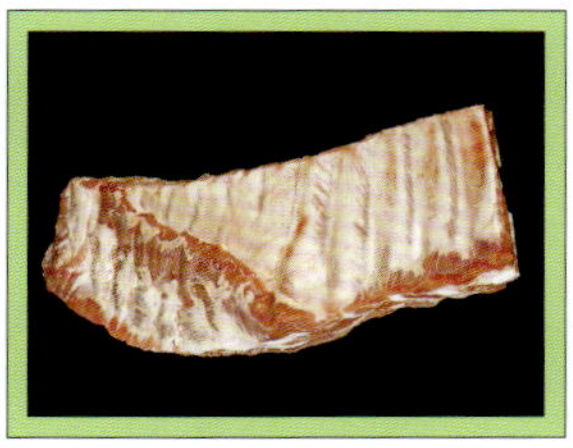

416A Pork Spareribs, St. Louis Style / Costillar, Costillas Estilo San Luis

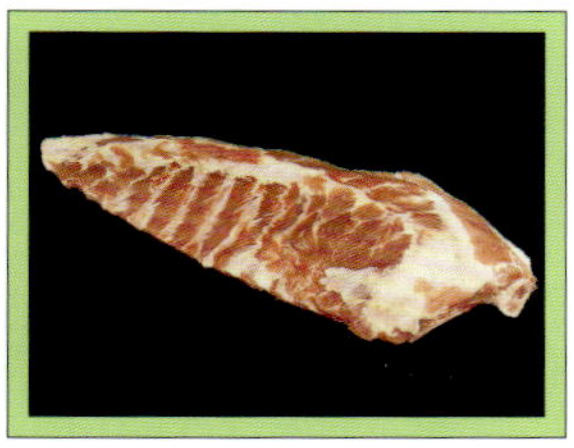

416 Pork Spareribs
Costillar

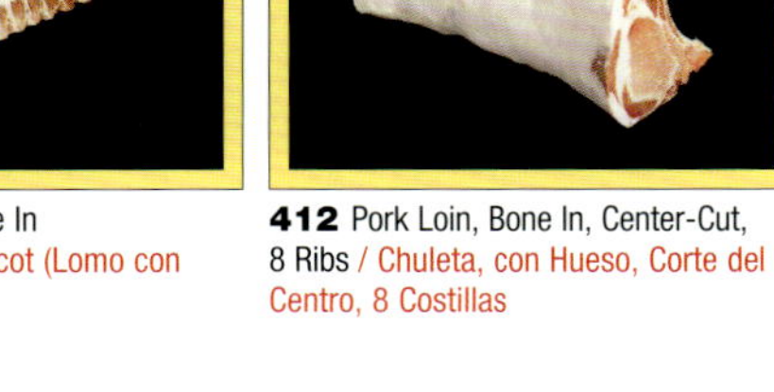

405B Pork Shoulder, Picnic, Cushion, Boneless / Paleta, Picnic (Espaldilla), Cojín (Cushion), Deshuesados

410 Pork Loin, Bone In
Chuleta Natural/Entrecot (Lomo con Hueso)

412 Pork Loin, Bone In, Center-Cut, 8 Ribs / Chuleta, con Hueso, Corte del Centro, 8 Costillas

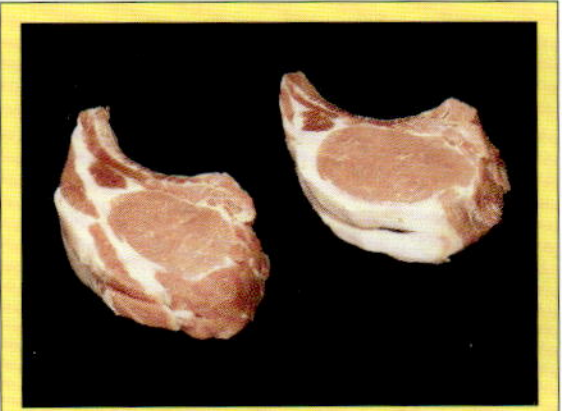

1410A Pork Loin, Rib Chips
Chuletas, Tajadas del Costillar

412E PSO 3 Pork Loin, Boneless, Center-Cut, 11 Ribs Chuleta (Lomo) Deshuesado, Corte del Centro, 11 Costillas

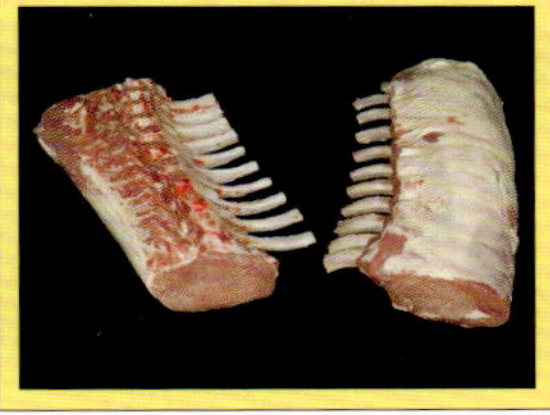

412G Pork Loin, Center-Cut, Rib End (Rack) / Chuleta, Corte del Centro, Extremo Adyacente al Costillar

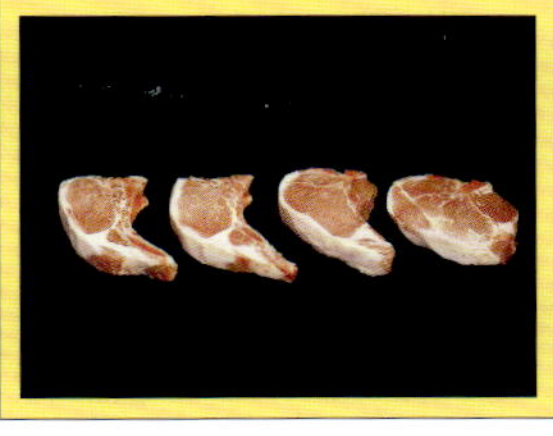

1412 Pork Loin Chops, Center-Cut / Chuletas de Lomo, Corte del Centro

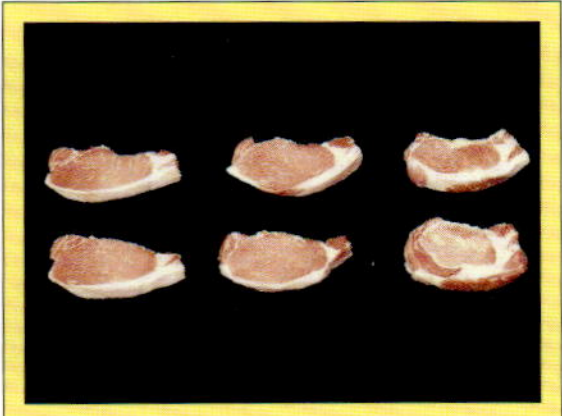

1412B Pork Loin Chops, Center-Cut, Boneless
Chuletas de Lomo, Corte del Centro, Deshuesadas

413A Pork Loin, Boneless, Roast
Chuleta (Lomo), Deshuesado, Rollo Amarrado

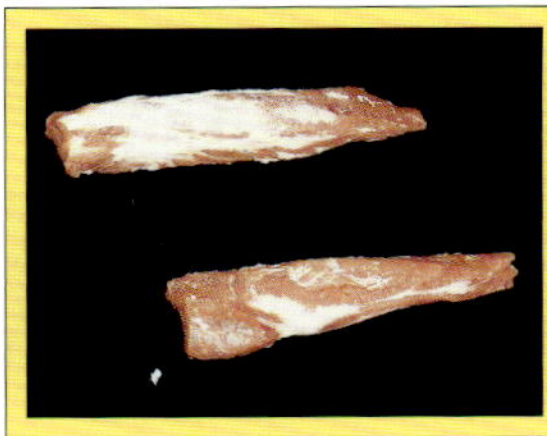

415 Pork Tenderloin
Filete de Cerdo

422 Pork Loin, Back Ribs
Chuleta, Costillas del Espaldar/Chuleta

424 Pork Loin, Riblet
Chuleta, Costelitas (Riblets)

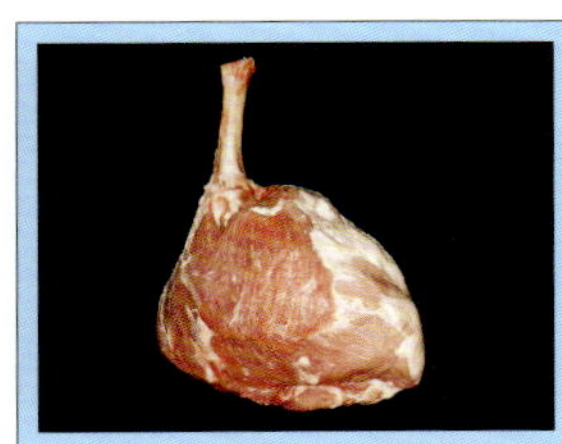

401E Pork Leg (Fresh Ham), Semi-Boneless, Handle On Pierna de Cerdo (Jamon Fresco), Semideshuesada, con Caña (Mango)

1495 Coarse Chopped Pork
Cortadillo de Cerdo

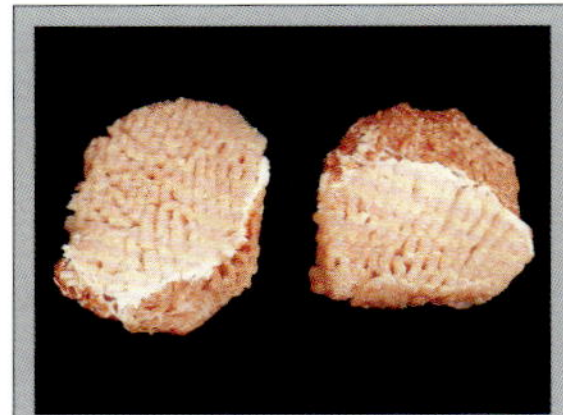

1400 Pork Steaks Cubed
Escalopas Suavizadas (Ablandada por Machacado, Rayado)

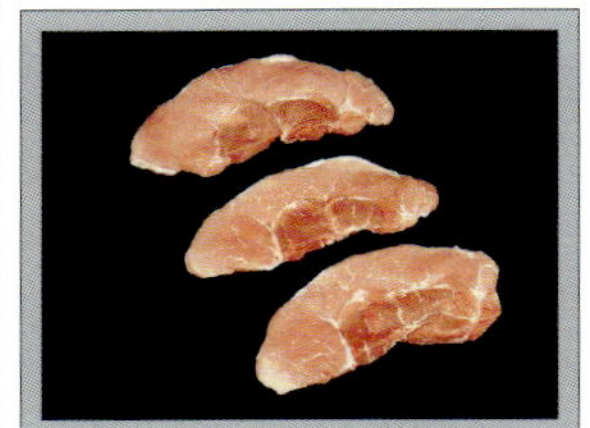

1402 Pork Cutlets
Escalopas de Cerdo

402B Pork Leg (Fresh Ham), Boneless / Pierna (Jamon Fresco), Deshuesada

Guía de colores de chuletas de cerdo cocidas

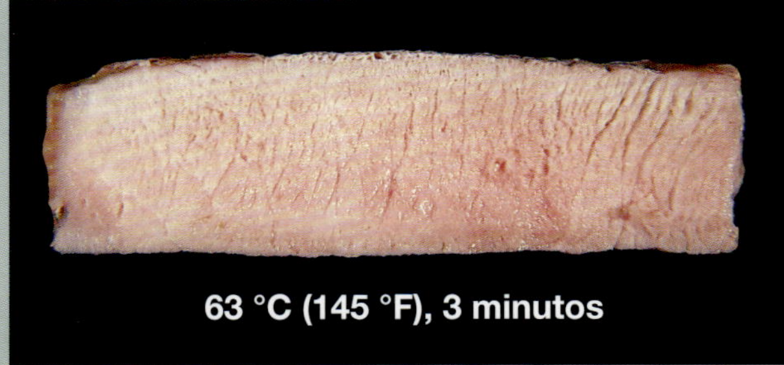

63 °C (145 °F), 3 minutos

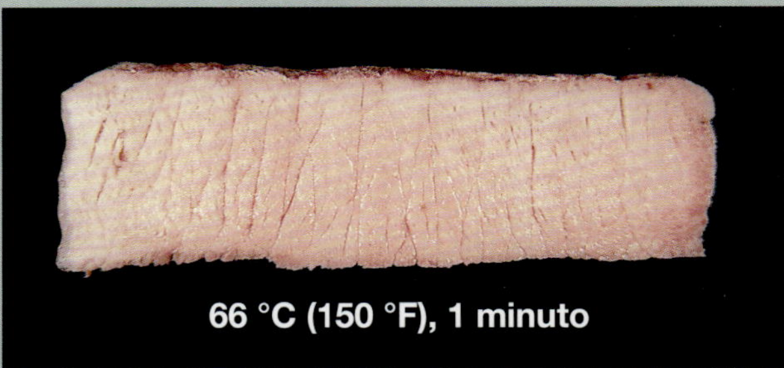

66 °C (150 °F), 1 minuto

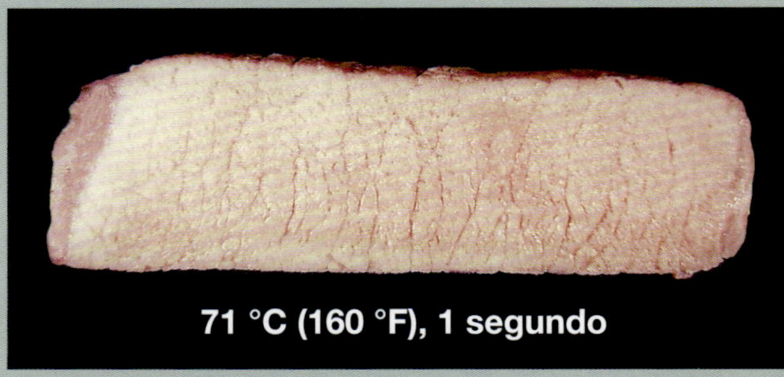

71 °C (160 °F), 1 segundo

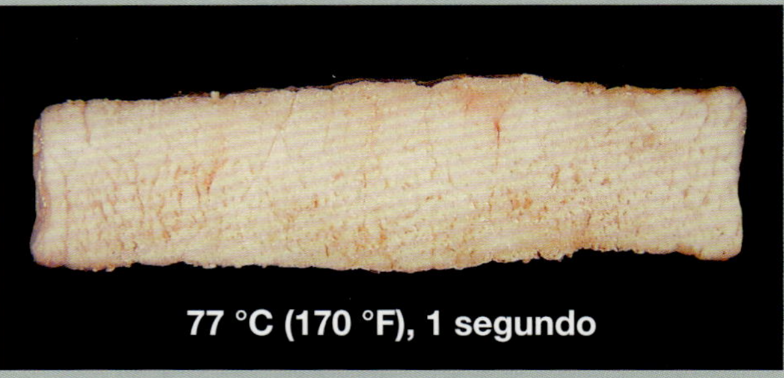

77 °C (170 °F), 1 segundo

Las imágenes anteriores muestran chuletas de lomos de un color típico, pH (5.6–5.8), cocidas desde el estado descongelado hasta las cuatro combinaciones finales de tiempo/temperatura (Código de Alimentos de la FDA). Las chuletas cocidas hasta la temperatura final más baja tendrán un color ligeramente rosa pero serán más jugosas y tiernas, y tendrán más sabor que las chuletas cocidas a 77 °C o más. Las chuletas con una solución de sal y fosfato tienen un color similar al de las chuletas sin agregados.

Rasgos de calidad del lomo crudo pálido, blando y exudativo

Rasgos de calidad del lomo crudo oscuro, firme y seco (DFD, por sus siglas en inglés)

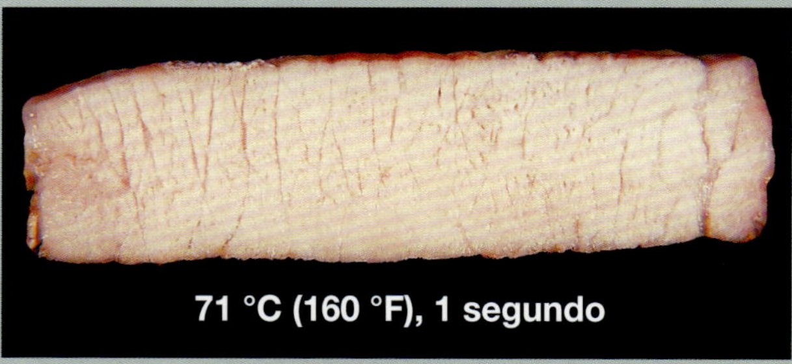

71 °C (160 °F), 1 segundo

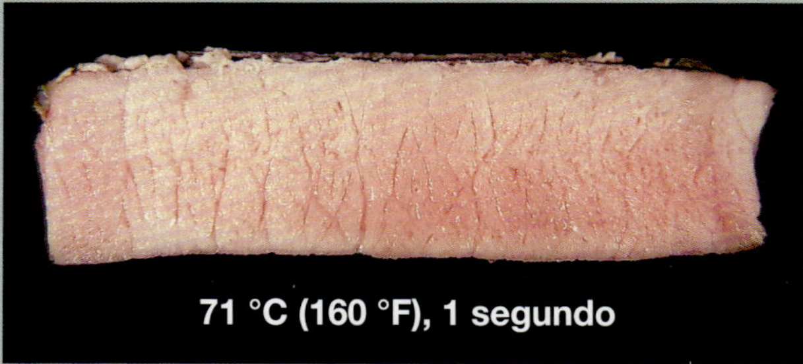

71 °C (160 °F), 1 segundo

El color del interior de las chuletas cocidas puede variar según la calidad del cerdo, el color del pigmento y otros factores. Estas imágenes muestran la variación de color en el interior de las chuletas. Las chuletas PSE (pH 5.3) son menos rosa y las chuletas DFD (pH 6.6) tienen un color rosa más oscuro que las chuletas normales cuando se cocinan hasta un grado de cocción medio (71 °C).

Termine con las dudas a la hora de asar.

S. A. Hawthorne, R. Lien, M. C. Hunt, y D. H. Kropf, Departamento de Ciencia Animal y de los Alimentos, Universidad Estatal de Kansas, Weber Hall, Manhattan, Kansas 66506

Publicado por K-State Research and Extension (Estación Experimental Agrícola y Servicio de Extensión Cooperativo de la Universidad Estatal de Kansas) y National Pork Board (Junta Nacional del Cerdo), Des Moines, IA. Este mensaje es patrocinado por el programa America's Pork Checkoff.

Pork Chop Cooked Color Guide

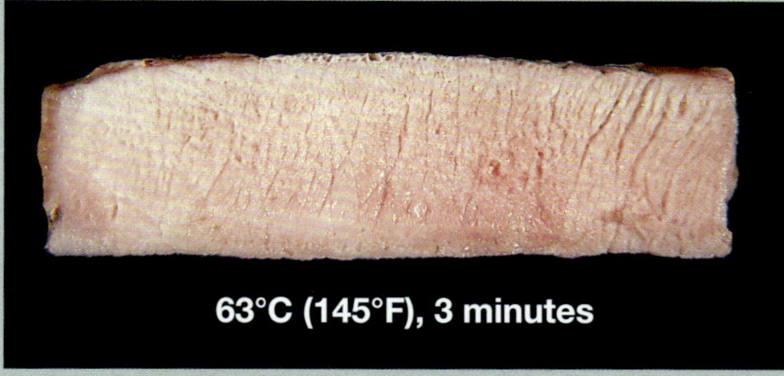

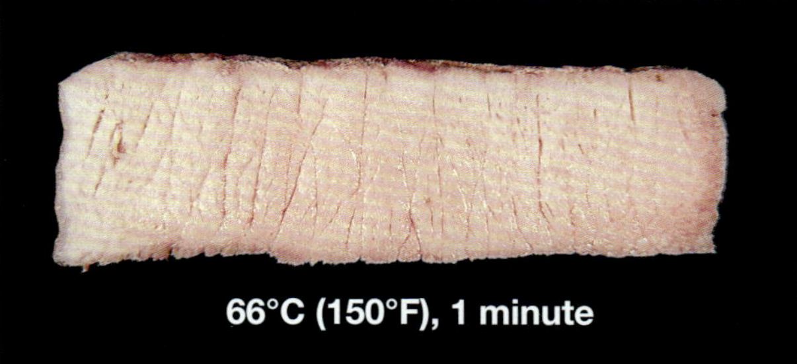

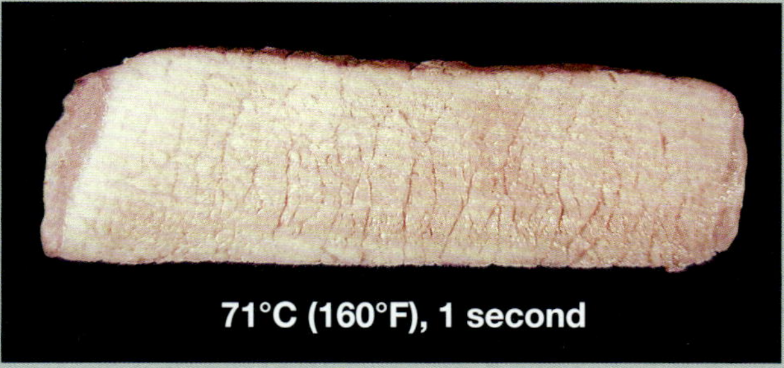

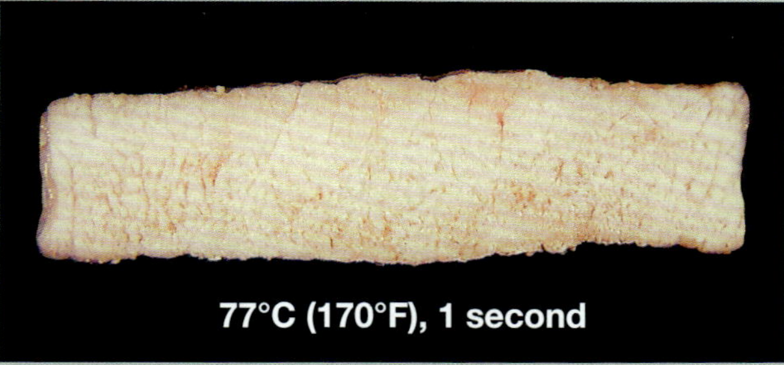

Shown above are chops from loins that were typical in color, pH (5.6–5.8), and exudativeness cooked from the thawed state to four safe endpoint time/temperature combinations (FDA Food Code). Chops cooked to the lower endpoint temperatures will be slightly pink but will be more juicy, tender, and flavorful than chops cooked to 77°C or higher. Chops enhanced with a phosphate-salt solution had similar cooked colors of non-enhanced chops.

Raw Loin Quality Traits
Pale, Soft, and Exudative (PSE)

Raw Loin Quality Traits
Dark, Firm, and Dry (DFD)

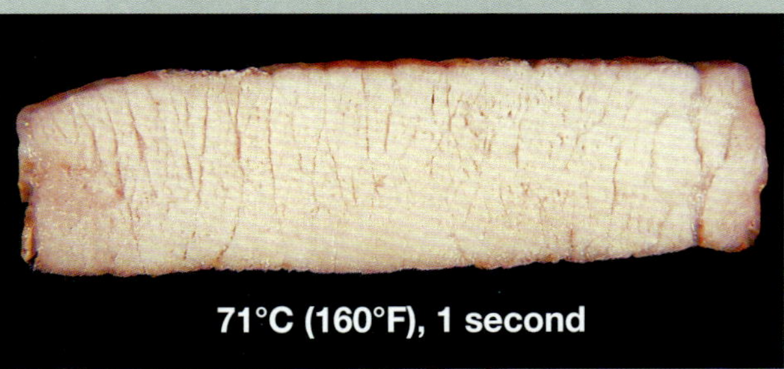

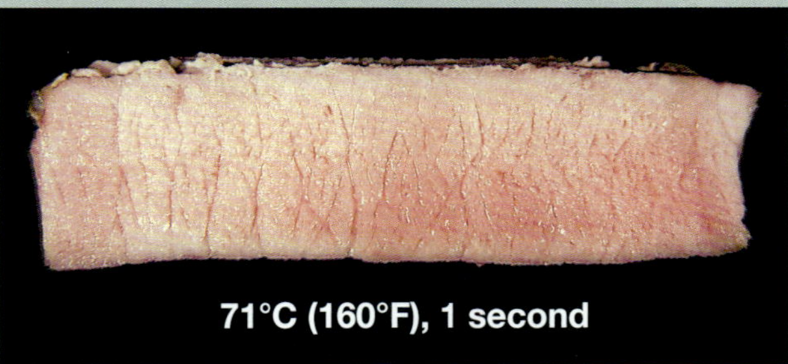

Chops can vary in internal cooked color depending on pork quality, pigment color, and other factors. These chops show the color range in the chop interior, PSE chops (pH 5.3) are less pink and DFD chops (pH 6.6) are darker pink than normal chops, when cooked to a medium degree of doneness (71°C).

Take the guesswork out of grilling.

S. A. Hawthorne, R. Lien, M. C. Hunt, and D. H. Kropf, Department of Animal Sciences and Industry, Kansas State University, Weber Hall, Manhattan, Kansas 66506

Published by K-State Research and Extension and the National Pork Board, Des Moines, IA. This message partially funded by America's Pork Checkoff program.

Pork Skeletal Chart / Diagrama de estructura esquelética del cerdo

Location, Structure, and Names of Bones
Ubicación, estructura y nombres de los huesos

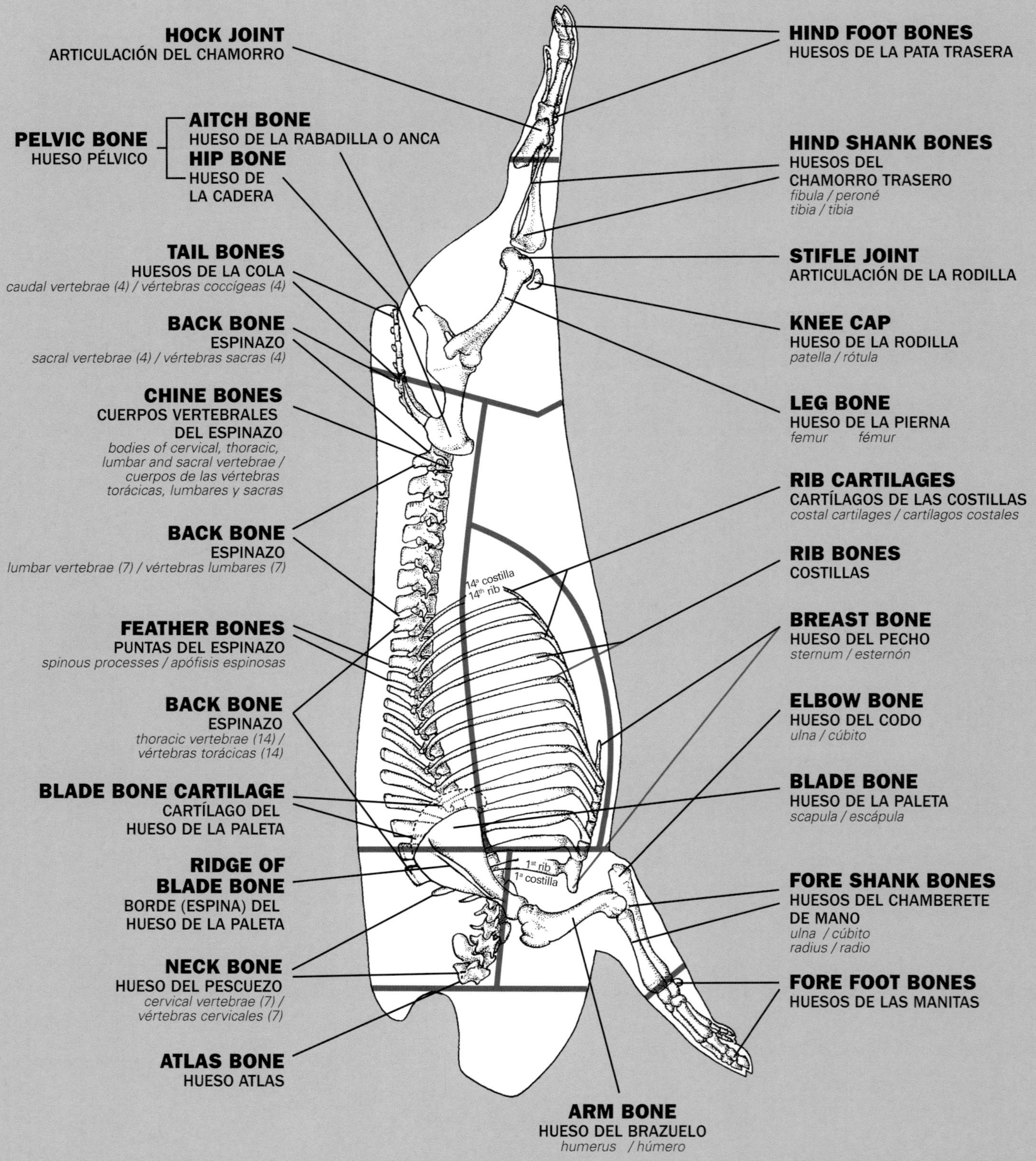

Courtesy of the American Meat Science Association. / Cortesía de la Asociación Americana de Ciencia de la Carne.

Pork Primal Cuts / Cortes Primarios de Cerdo

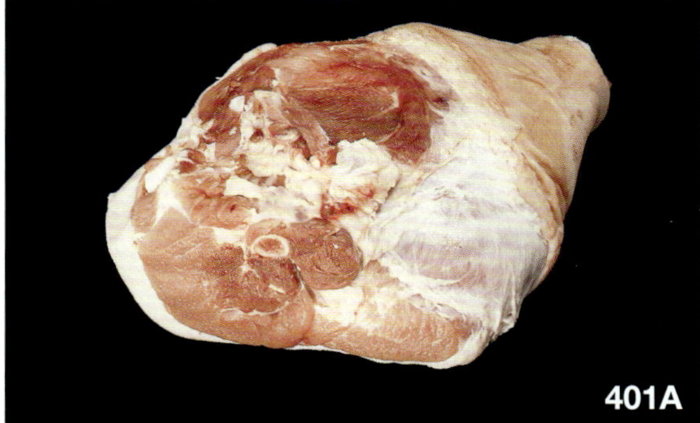

Pork Leg (Fresh Ham)

Pierna con Lonja (Jamón Fresco), de Chamorro Corto

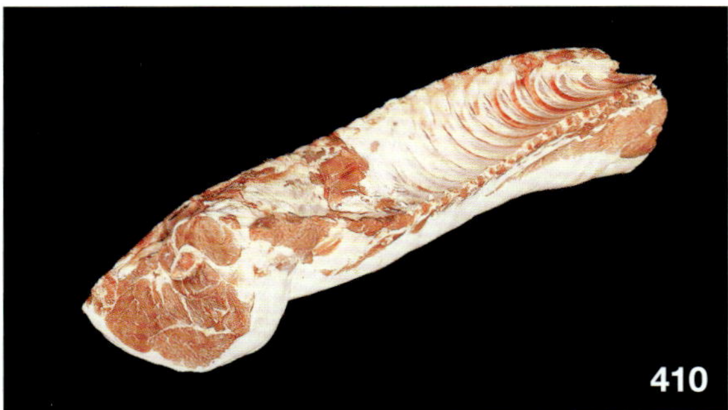

Pork Loin, Regular

Chuleta Natural/Entrecot de Cerdo,
(Lomo con Hueso)

Pork Shoulder, Boston Butt

Paleta (Espaldilla) de Cerdo, Cabeza de Lomo

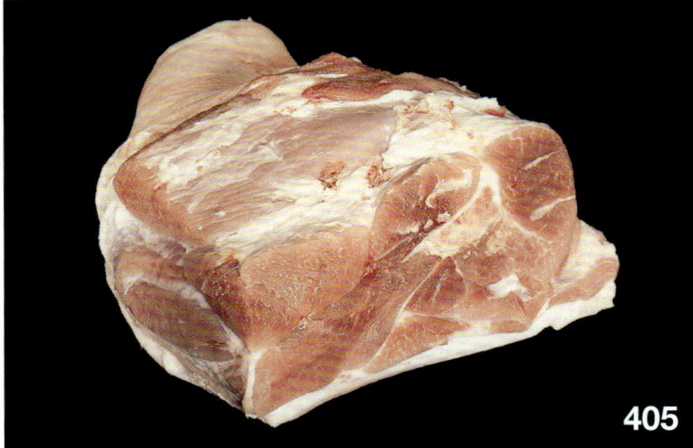

Pork Shoulder, Picnic

Paleta (Espaldilla) de Cerdo, Picnic (Brazuelo),
sin Cabeza de Lomo

Loin-Leg (Ham) Separation
Separación Lomo-Pierna (Jamón)

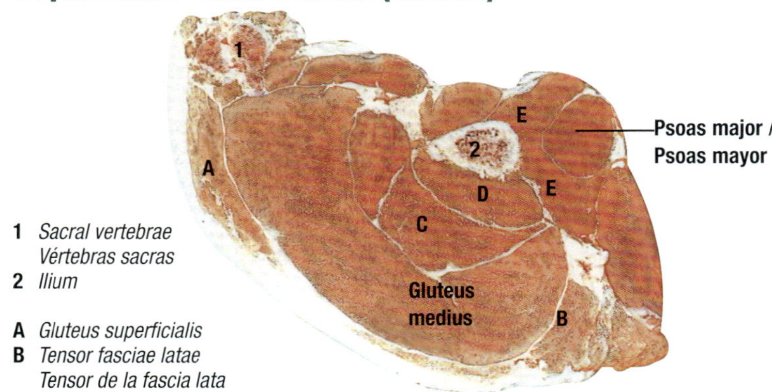

1 Sacral vertebrae
   Vértebras sacras
2 Ilium

A Gluteus superficialis
B Tensor fasciae latae
   Tensor de la fascia lata
C Gluteus accessorius
D Gluteus profundus
E Iliacus

Loin-Shoulder Separation
Separación lomo-paleta

A Trapezius
B Pectorales profundi
C Rhomboideus
D Splenius
E Semispinalis capitis
F Infraspinatus
G Triceps brachii
H Longissimus
I Subcapularis
J Supraspinatus

1 Scapula / Escápula
2 Thoracic vertebrae
   Vértebras torácicas
3 Rib / Costilla

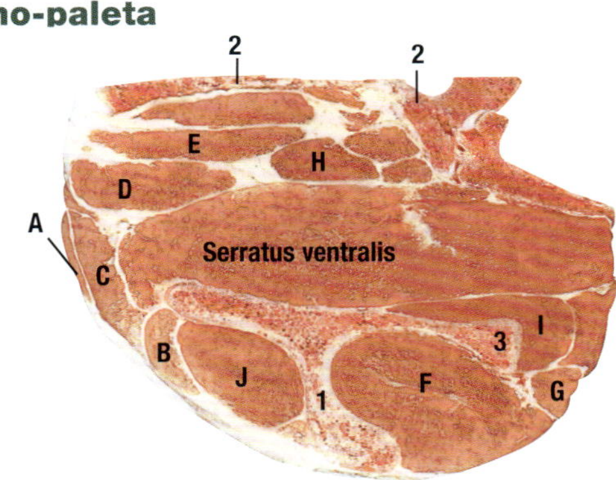

Butt-Picnic Separation
Separación Cabeza de Lomo-Picnic (Brazuelo)

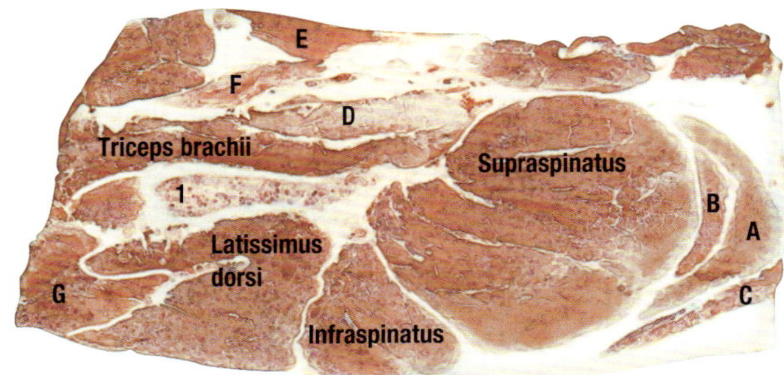

A Cutaneous faciei
B Pectorales profundus
C Semispinalis capitis
D Infraspinatus
E Deltoideus

F Teres minor / Teres menor
G Pectorales profundus

1 Scapula / Escápula

Index / Índice

Pork Products and Weight Ranges
Productos de cerdo y escalas de peso

ITEM PIEZA	PRODUCT NAME / NOMBRE DE PRODUCTO	PG. PÁG.	Weight Ranges (Pounds) / Escalas de peso (libras/kg)		
			A	B	C
400	**Carcass** Canal	184	150-190 (68-86.2)	190-230 (86.2-104.3)	230-up (Más de 104.3)
400A	**Roasting Pig** Lechón para Rostizar	184	30-50 (13.6-22.7)	50-70 (22.7-31.8)	70-up (Más de 31.8)
401	**Leg (Fresh Ham)** Pierna con Lonja (Jamón Fresco con Piel/Cuero)	185	17–20 (7.7-9.1)	20–28 (9.1-12.7)	28-up (Más de 12.7)
401A	**Leg (Fresh Ham), Short Shank** Pierna con Lonja (Jamón Fresco), de Chamorro Corto	185	17–20 (7.7-9.1)	20–28 (9.1-12.7)	28-up (Más de 12.7)
401C	**Leg (Fresh Ham), Semi-Boneless** Pierna (Jamón Fresco), Semideshuesada	186	16–18 (7.3-8.2)	18-20 (8.2-9.1)	20-up (Más de 9.1)
401D	**Leg, Hind Shank** Pierna (Jamón Fresco), Chamorro Trasero	186	1.5-down (Menos de 0.68)	1.5-2 (0.68-0.90)	2-up (Más de 0.90)
401E	**Leg (Fresh Ham), Semi-Boneless, Handle On** Pierna de Cerdo (Jamón Fresco), Semideshuesada, con Caña (Mango)	186	14-16 (6.4-7.3)	16-19 (7.3-8.6)	19-up (Más de 8.6)
402	**Leg (Fresh Ham), Skinned** Pierna de Cerdo (Jamón Fresco), Semidescuerado (sin Lonja)	187	17–20 (7.7-9.1)	20–28 (9.1-12.7)	28-up (Más de 12.7)
402A	**Leg (Fresh Ham), Skinned, Short Shank** Pierna de Cerdo (Jamón Fresco), Semidescuerado (sin Lonja), de Chamorro Corto	187	17–20 (7.7-9.1)	20–28 (9.1-12.7)	28-up (Más de 12.7)
402B	**Leg (Fresh Ham), Boneless** Pierna (Jamón Fresco), Deshuesada	187	8-10 (3.6–4.5)	10 – 14 (4.5-6.4)	14-up (Más de 6.4)
402C	**Leg (Fresh Ham), Boneless, Short Shank, Trimmed** Pierna (Jamón Fresco), Deshuesada, de Chamorro Corto, Recortada de Grasa y Limpia	188	8-10 (3.6–4.5)	10 – 14 (4.5-6.4)	14-up (Más de 6.4)
402D	**Leg (Fresh Ham), Outside** Pierna (Jamón Fresco), Pulpa Blanca	188	4–5 (1.8-2.3)	5 – 7 (2.3-3.2)	7-up (Más de 3.2)
402E	**Leg (Fresh Ham), Outside, Trimmed, Shank Removed** Pierna (Jamón Fresco), Pulpa Blanca, Recortada de Grasa y Limpia, Sin Chamorro	188	3-4 (1.4-1.8)	4-6 (1.8-2.7)	6-up (Más de 2.7)
402F	**Leg (Fresh Ham), Inside** Pierna (Jamón Fresco), Pulpa Negra	189	3-4 (1.4-1.8)	4-6 (1.8-2.7)	6-up (Más de 2.7)
402G	**Leg (Fresh Ham), TBS, 3-Way, Boneless** Pierna (Jamón Fresco), TBS, 3 Piezas, Deshuesada	189	14–16 (6.4-7.3)	16–20 (7.3-9.1)	20-up (Más de 9.1)
402H	**Leg (Fresh Ham), Tip** Pierna (Jamón Fresco), Pulpa Bola	189	2-2.5 (0.9-1.1)	2.5-3 (1.1-1.4)	3-up (Más de 1.4)
402J	**Leg (Fresh Ham), Inside Cap (IM)** Pierna (Jamón Fresco), Tapa del Centro de Pierna (MI)	190	Amount as Specified / Cantidad según lo especificado		
403	**Shoulder** Paleta (Espaldilla)	190	12–16 (5.4-7.3)	16–22 (7.3-10)	22-up (Más de 10)
403B	**Shoulder, Outside** Paleta (Espaldilla), Contracara	191	12-16 (5.4-7.3)	16-22 (7.3-10)	22-up (Más de 10)
403C	**Shoulder, Inside, Boneless** Paleta (Espaldilla), Cara, Deshuesada	191	3-5 (1.4-2.3)	5-8 (2.3-3.6)	8-up (Más de 3.6)
404	**Shoulder, Skinned** Paleta (Espaldilla), Semidescuerada (sin Lonja)	192	12–16 (5.4-7.3)	16–22 (7.3-10)	22-up (Más de 10)
405	**Shoulder, Picnic** Paleta (Espaldilla), Picnic (Brazuelo), sin Cabeza de Lomo	192	6–8 (2.7-3.6)	8-11 (3.6-5)	11-up (Más de 5)
405A	**Shoulder, Picnic, Boneless** Paleta (Espaldilla), Picnic (Brazuelo), Deshuesada	193	4–6 (1.8-2.7)	6–9 (2.7-4.1)	9-up (Más de 4.1)
405B	**Shoulder, Picnic, Cushion, Boneless** Paleta (Espaldilla), Picnic (Brazuelo), Maciza "Cojín" (Cushion), Deshuesada	193	Amount as Specified / Cantidad según lo especificado		
405C	**Shoulder, Pectoral Meat (IM)** Paleta (Espaldilla), Carne de Pectoral (MI)	193	1.5-down (Menos de 0.68)	1.5-2 (0.68-0.90)	2-up (Más de 0.90)
406	**Shoulder, Boston Butt, Bone In, Shoulder Blade** Paleta (Espaldilla), Cabeza de Lomo, con Hueso de Paleta ♣ Shoulder Blade	193	6-8 (2.7-3.6)	8-11 (3.6-5)	11-up (Más de 5)
406A	**Shoulder, Boston Butt, Boneless** Paleta (Espaldilla), Cabeza de Lomo, Deshuesada	194	4-7 (1.8-3.2)	7-10 (3.2-4.5)	10-up (Más de 4.5)
406B	**Shoulder, Boston Butt, Boneless, Special** Paleta (Espaldilla), Cabeza de Lomo, Deshuesada, Especial	194	4–6 (1.8-2.7)	6-10 (2.7-4.5)	10-up (Más de 4.5)
407	**Shoulder Butt, Cellar Trimmed, Boneless** Cabeza de Lomo, Sin Hueso de Paleta y Recortada de Grasa y Limpia, Deshuesada	194	3-5 (1.4-2.3)	5-9 (2.3-4.1)	9-up (Más de 4.1)
408	**Belly** Barriga/Tocino Fresco	195	12-16 (5.4-7.3)	16-20 (7.3-9.1)	20-up (Más de 9.1)
408A	**Fat Back** Lonja sin Cuero de la Chuleta (Grasa del Espaldar)	195	Not Applicable / No corresponde		
409	**Belly, Skinless** Barriga/Tocino Fresco, Descuerada(o)	196	9-12 (4.1-5.4)	12-15 (5.4-6.8)	15-up (Más de 6.8)
409A	**Belly, Single Ribbed, Skinless** Barriga/Tocino Fresco, sin Costillas, Descuerada(o)	196	12-16 (5.4-7.3)	16-20 (7.3-9.1)	20-up (Más de 9.1)
409B	**Belly, Center-Cut, Skinless** Barriga/Tocino Fresco, Corte Rectangular del Centro, Descuerada(o)	196	9–11 (4.1-5)	11-14 (5-6.4)	14-up (Más de 6.4)

ITEM PIEZA	PRODUCT NAME NOMBRE DE PRODUCTO	PG. PÁG.	Weight Ranges (Pounds) / Escalas de peso (libras/kg)		
			A	B	C
410	Loin, Bone In Chuleta Natural/Entrecot (Lomo con Hueso)	197	14–18 (6.4-8.2)	18–24 (8.2-10.9)	24-up (Más de 10.9)
410A	Loin, Leg (Sirloin) End, Bone In Chuleta, Extremo Adyacente a la Pierna (Sirloin), con Hueso	198	4–6 (1.8-2.7)	6–8 (2.7-3.6)	8-up (Más de 3.6)
410B	Loin, Rib End, Bone In Chuleta, Extremo Adyacente al Costillar, con Hueso	199	4.5–5.5 (2-2.5)	5.5–6.5 (2.5-3)	6.5-up (Más de 3)
411	Loin, Bone In, Bladeless Chuleta, con Hueso, Excepto Hueso de la Paleta	199	14–18 (6.4-8.2)	18–24 (8.2-10.9)	24-up (Más de 10.9)
412	Loin, Bone In, Center-Cut, 8 Ribs Chuleta, con Hueso, Corte del Centro, 8 Costillas	200	6–8 (2.7-3.6)	8–11 (3.6-5)	11-up (Más de 5)
412A	Loin, Bone In, Center-Cut, 8 Ribs, Chine Bone Off Chuleta, con Hueso, Corte del Centro, 8 Costillas, con Espinazo Rebajado	201	5 – 7 (2.3-3.2)	7 – 10 (3.2-4.5)	10-up (Más de 4.5)
412C	Loin, Bone In, Center-Cut, 11 Ribs Chuleta, con Hueso, Corte del Centro, 11 Costillas	201	7–9 (3.2-4.1)	9–12 (4.1-5.4)	12-up (Más de 5.4)
412D	Loin, Bone In, Center-Cut, 11 Ribs, Chine Bone Off Chuleta, con Hueso, Corte del Centro, 11 Costillas, con Espinazo Rebajado	202	6–8 (2.7-3.6)	8–11 (3.6-5)	11-up (Más de 5)
412E	Loin, Boneless, Center-Cut, 11 Ribs Chuleta (Lomo), Deshuesado, Corte del Centro, 11 Costillas	202	5–6 (2.3-2.7)	6–8 (2.7-3.6)	8-up (Más de 3.6)
412G	Loin, Center-Cut, Rib End (Rack) Chuleta, Corte del Centro, Extremo Adyacente al Costillar	203	7.5-down (Menos de 3.4)	7.5–10 (3.4-4.5)	10-up (Más de 4.5)
413	Loin, Boneless Chuleta (Lomo), Deshuesado	204	8-10 (3.6–4.5)	10–13 (4.5-5.9)	13-up (Más de 5.9)
413A	Loin, Boneless, Roast Chuleta (Lomo), Deshuesado, Rollo Amarrado	205	8-10 (3.6–4.5)	10–13 (4.5-5.9)	13-up (Más de 5.9)
413B	Loin, Boneless, Special Chuleta (Lomo), Deshuesado, Rollo Amarrado, Especial	205	8-10 (3.6–4.5)	10–13 (4.5-5.9)	13-up (Más de 5.9)
413C	Loin, Loin Eye Chuleta (Lomo), Ojo del Lomo	206	5–8.5 (2.3-3.9)	8.5–11 (3.9-5)	11-up (Más de 5)
414	Loin, Canadian Back Chuleta (Lomo), Estilo Canadiense	206	4–5 (1.8-2.3)	5 – 7 (2.3-3.2)	7-up (Más de 3.2)
415	Tenderloin Filete de Cerdo	206	1 – 1.5 (0.45-0.68)	1.5–2 (0.68-0.90)	2-up (Más de 0.90)
415A	Tenderloin, Side Muscle Off Filete, sin Músculo de al Lado	207	1 – 1.5 (0.45-0.68)	1.5–2 (0.68-0.90)	2-up (Más de 0.90)
416	Spareribs, Side Ribs Costillar, Costillas de la Media Canal 🍁 Side Ribs	210	2–4 (0.9-1.8)	4–6 (1.8-2.7)	6-up (Más de 2.7)
416A	Spareribs, St. Louis Style, Side Rib, Centre Cut Costillar, Costillas de Media Canal estilo San Luis, Corte del Centro 🍁 Side Ribs, Centre Cut	211	2–3 (0.90-1.4)	3–4 (1.4-1.8)	4-up (Más de 1.8)
416B	Spareribs, Brisket Bones Costillar, Huesos del Pecho	211	0.33–0.5 (0.15-0.23)	0.5–1 (0.23-0.45)	1-up (Más de 0.45)
416C	Spareribs, Breast Off Costillar, sin Pecho	211	2–4 (0.9-1.8)	4–6 (1.8-2.7)	6-up (Más de 2.7)
416D	Breast Bones Pecho, Huesos	211	1 – 1.5 (0.45-0.68)	1.5–2 (0.68-0.90)	2-up (Más de 0.90)
417	Shoulder Hocks Chamorros de Paleta	207	0.75–1.25 (0.34-0.57)	1.25–2 (0.57-0.90)	2-up (Más de 0.90)
417A	Leg (Fresh Ham) Hocks Pierna (Jamón Fresco), Chamorros	207	Not Applicable / No corresponde		
418	Trimmings Recortes	208	Not Applicable / No corresponde		
419	Jowl Papada	208	Not Applicable / No corresponde		
420	Pig's Feet, Front Manitas	209	Not Applicable / No corresponde		
421	Neck Bones Huesos del Pescuezo	209	Amount as Specified / Cantidad según lo especificado		
422	Loin, Back Ribs Chuleta, Costillas del Espaldar/Chuleta	209	1.5–1.75 (0.68-0.79)	1.75–2.25 (0.79-1)	2.25-up (Más de 1)
423	Loin, Country-Style Ribs Chuleta, Costillas Estilo Campestre	212	3–3.5 (1.4-1.6)	3.5–4 (1.6-1.8)	4-up (Más de 1.8)
424	Loin, Riblet Chuleta, Costelitas (Riblets)	212	Not Applicable / No corresponde		
435B	Pork for Kabobs Trozos para Brochetas	213	Amount as Specified / Cantidad según lo especificado		
496	Ground Pork Carne Molida de Cerdo	214	Amount as Specified / Cantidad según lo especificado		

Información para hacer los pedidos

Opciones especificadas por el comprador (PSO)

Los compradores pueden especificar varias opciones diferentes en los productos que desean comprar. Estas opciones incluyen, entre otras, una combinación del grado de calidad, estado de refrigeración, mediciones sobre límites de grasa e instrucciones de procesamiento. Las piezas que se enumeran en el texto pueden incluir opciones específicas. Algunas de estas opciones se explican más detalladamente en la sección introductoria al comienzo de la *Guía para Compradores de Carne*, o más adelante en esta sección o en la descripción de la pieza correspondiente. Los compradores que tengan necesidades o especificaciones especiales deben comunicarse con sus proveedores.

Estado de refrigeración

A **FRESCO**	−2.2 °C (28 °F) o mayor
B **CONGELADO**	−2.2 °C (28 °F) o menor
C **OPCIÓN ESPECIFICADA POR EL COMPRADOR**	−17.8 °C (0 °F) o menor

El producto se puede pedir fresco o congelado. El término *refrigerado en estado fresco* es utilizado por el Servicio de Mercadeo Agrícola del Departamento de Agricultura de E.U.A. para describir los productos que no han sido congelados anteriormente.

Grado

En E.U.A., las canales de cerdo se clasifican en grados por (a) la clase en sí, según la condición sexual aparente del animal al momento del sacrificio, y (b) el grado de clasificación, que refleja la calidad y el rendimiento esperado de los cortes magros de la canal.

Las cinco clases de canales de cerdo son cerdo joven castrado, cerda primeriza, cerda hembra, cerdo padrote y verraco.

Los cinco grados son U.S. Nº 1, U.S. Nº 2, U.S. Nº 3, U.S. Nº 4 y U.S. Utilitario. Estos grados, sin embargo, no se aplican a las canales de cerdos padrotes y verracos. Por lo general no es necesario especificar el grado para piezas diferentes a la pieza número 400, ya que los requisitos de la descripción de las piezas y/o los límites de grasa especificados generalmente se aplican. El comprador puede, sin embargo, especificar las piezas que se prepararán de un solo grado o de una combinación de grados E.U.A. para canales de cerdos jóvenes castrados o hembras primerizas en caso de que lo deseen.

No existe un sistema federal de clasificación por grados para cerdos en Canadá. La clasificación podrá obtenerse de la Autoridad de Clasificación de Cerdos de Ontario.

Todas las piezas deben cumplir con los REQUISITOS DE MATERIALES como se describe en la sección introductoria de esta guía. La sección de calidad de la carne magra describe el producto típico de la carne derivada de cerdos jóvenes castrados o hembras primerizas.

La carne magra debe contener un color brillante razonablemente uniforme que varíe desde el rosa claro hasta el rojo claro, y se permite un color que contenga levemente dos tonos.

Opciones para limitar la grasa (FLO)

Cortes y piezas

El comprador podrá especificar uno de los siguientes grosores promedio máximos de cubierta de grasa cuando la limitación de grasa que se indica en la descripción detallada de la pieza no sea la deseada.

Cortes y piezas

Número de opción	Grosor promedio máximo	Máximo en un punto cualquiera
1	19 mm (0.75 pulgadas) con recorte de grasa y limpieza tipo commodity	25 mm (1.0 pulgada)
2	6 mm (0.25 pulgadas)	13 mm (0.5 pulgadas)
3	3 mm (0.125 pulgadas)	6 mm (0.25 pulgadas)
4	Prácticamente libre de grasa (el 75% de la superficie expuesta es magra/desgrasada)	3 mm (0.125 pulgadas)
5	Desprovisto de grasa/Prácticamente desnudo de grasa* [la grasa que queda no debe exceder los 2.5 cm (1.0 pulgada) en la dimensión más larga y/o 3 mm (0.125 pulgadas) de grosor]	3 mm (0.125 pulgadas)
6	Desprovisto de grasa/Prácticamente desnudo de grasa, Membrana superficial retirada** (el 90% de la superficie expuesta es magra)	3 mm (0.125 pulgadas)

*/** – consulte la definición en la página xlii

Importante: cuando se especifiquen los grosores promedio de grasa en la descripción de la pieza, aplicará la limitación "Máximo en un punto cualquiera" correspondiente. Cuando se especifiquen las opciones 3–6 para las piezas de paleta y lomo, se deberá quitar toda la carne magra falsa.

Es posible obtener información sobre la nomenclatura de la musculatura porcina en el sitio web de la Universidad de Nebraska: http://porcine.unl.edu

Ordering Data

Purchaser Specified Options (PSO)

Purchasers may specify a number of different options on the products they wish to purchase. These options (PSO) include among others, a combination of grade, state of refrigeration, fat limitation measurements, and processing instructions. Items listed in the text may also include specific choices. Some of these options are explained in more detail in the Introductory Section at the front of *The Meat Buyer's Guide*, or later in this section, or in the appropriate Item Description. Purchasers who have special needs or specifications should contact their suppliers.

State of Refrigeration

A **FRESH**	28°F (−2.2°C) or higher
B **FROZEN**	28°F (−2.2°C) or lower
C **PSO**	0°F (−17.8°C) or lower

Product may be ordered fresh or frozen. The term *fresh chilled* is used by the USDA Agricultural Marketing Service to describe product that has not been previously frozen.

Grade

In the U.S., pork carcasses are graded by (a) class, as determined by the apparent sex condition of the animal at the time of slaughter, and (b) grade, which reflects quality and the expected yield of lean cuts in the carcass.

The five classes of pork carcasses are barrow, gilt, sow, stag, and boar.

The five grades are U.S. No. 1, U.S. No. 2, U.S. No. 3, U.S. No. 4, and U.S. Utility. These grades, however, do not apply to stag and boar carcasses. It is usually not necessary to specify a grade other than for Item No. 400 as the requirements of the Item Description and/or specified fat limitation generally apply. The purchaser, may, however, specify items to be derived from one or a combination of the U.S. grades for barrow or gilt carcasses if they so desire.

There is no federal grading system for pork in Canada. Grading may be provided by the Ontario Pork Grading Authority.

All items shall comply with the MATERIAL REQUIREMENTS as described in the front section of this Guide. The lean quality section describes product that is typical of meat derived from barrows or gilts.

The lean must possess a bright reasonably uniform color ranging from light pink to light red, and a slight two-toned color is permissible.

Fat Limitation Options (FLO)

Cuts and Roasts

The purchaser may specify one of the following maximum average thicknesses of surface fat when the fat limitation indicated in the detailed Item Descriptions are not desired.

Cuts and Roasts		
Option No.	Maximum Average Thickness	Maximum at Any One Point
1	0.75 inch (19 mm) "Commodity Trim"	1.0 inch (25 mm)
2	0.25 inch (6 mm)	0.5 inch (13 mm)
3	0.125 inch (3 mm)	0.25 inch (6 mm)
4	Practically free (75 percent lean/seam surface exposed)	0.125 inch (3 mm)
5	Peeled/Denuded* (remaining fat shall not exceed 1.0 inch (2.5 cm) in the longest dimension and/or 0.125 inch (3 mm) in thickness)	0.125 inch (3 mm)
6	Peeled/Denuded, Surface Membrane Removed** (90 percent lean exposed)	0.125 inch (3 mm)

*/** – see page xvi for definition

Note: When average fat thicknesses are specified in Item Descriptions, the appropriate "Maximum at Any One Point" limitation shall apply. When Options 3–6 are specified for shoulder and loin items, all false lean shall be removed.

Information on Pork muscle nomenclature may be found on the University of Nebraska website, http://porcine.unl.edu

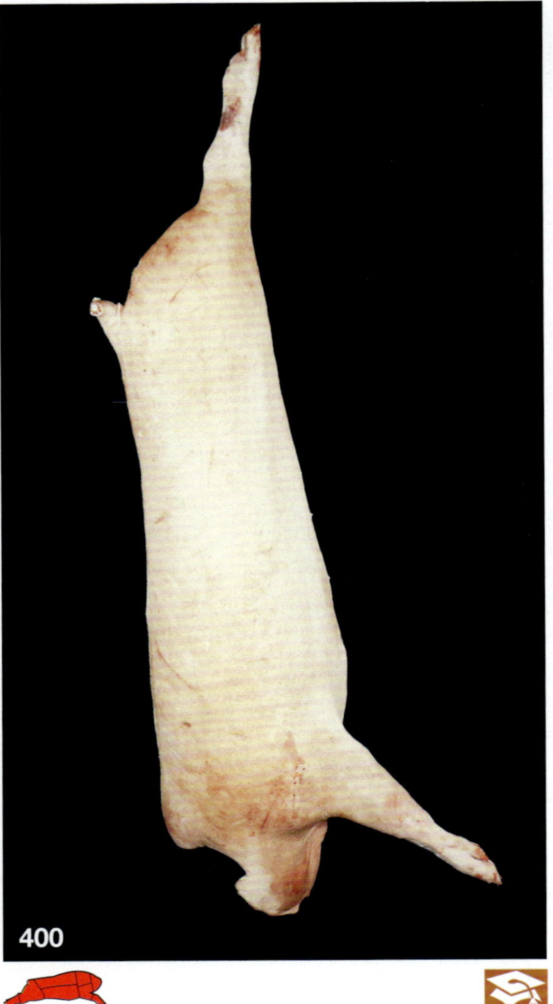

400

400   Pork Carcass

The carcass shall be dressed without the head and kidneys and be practically free of internal fat. Carcasses with a "stuck" shoulder are not acceptable. In addition, no other objectionable scores shall appear on the outside of the carcass. Unless otherwise specified, the carcass shall be skin-on. It shall be split into reasonably uniform sides by cutting lengthwise through the backbone so that the major muscles of the loin and shoulder are not scored and so that the spinal cord groove is evident on at least 75 percent of both sides of the back bone. Mutilated feet shall be removed either at the hock or upper knee joint. The membranous portion of the diaphragm shall be excluded close to the lean, although the lean portion and the membrane surrounding it may remain, if firmly attached to the carcass. The jowl may remain intact with each carcass side. Minor trimming of the jowl is acceptable for removal of bloody portions and ragged edges. Excessively trimmed or mutilated jowls, however, shall be excluded by a reasonably straight cut perpendicular to the length of the carcass that is not more than 1.0 inch (2.5 cm) anterior to the ear dip.

400   Canal de Cerdo

La canal deberá prepararse de forma que quede sin cabeza, riñones y prácticamente libre de grasa interna. No se aceptarán canales con una paleta "atascada". Además, no deberá aparecer ninguna otra marca objetable en el exterior de la canal. A menos que se especifique lo contrario, la canal deberá tener piel. Se deberá dividir en medias canales razonablemente uniformes mediante cortes longitudinales a través de los huesos del espinazo, de modo que los músculos principales del lomo y la paleta no se sufran incisiones y que el canal raquídeo sea evidente al menos en un 75% de ambos lados de los huesos del espinazo. Las patas mutiladas deberán quitarse en la articulación de la rodilla o la articulación superior de la rodilla. La porción membranosa del diafragma deberá despellejarse hasta descubrir la carne magra, aunque la porción de carne magra y la membrana que la recubre podrán permanecer si se encuentran firmemente unidas a la canal. La papada podrá quedar intacta en cada media canal. Se acepta un recorte menor de la papada para quitar las porciones sanguinolentas y los bordes irregulares. Sin embargo, las papadas excesivamente recortadas o mutiladas deberán quitarse mediante un corte razonablemente recto y perpendicular a la longitud de la canal, anterior a la depresión de la oreja, a no más de 2.5 cm (1.0 pulgada) de distancia de ella.

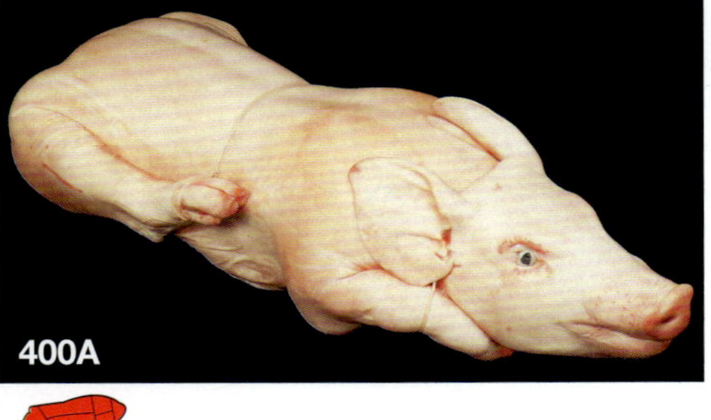

400A

400A   Pork Roasting Pig

The whole unsplit roasting pig has the head on, and may include the internal fat and the membranous portion of the diaphragm. If applicable other requirements of Item No. 400 also apply.

400A   Lechón para Rostizar

El Lechón para Rostizar entero tiene la cabeza, y puede incluir la grasa interna y la porción membranosa del diafragma. Si corresponde, los otros requisitos de la pieza número 400 también se aplican.

401 — Pork Leg (Fresh Ham)

The pork leg, or fresh ham as it is commonly known, is separated from a pork side by a straight cut approximately perpendicular to a line parallel to the shank bones. The cut passes through a point which is not less than 1.5 inches (3.8 cm) and not more than 3.5 inches (8.8 cm) from the anterior edge of the aitch bone. The foot shall be excluded at or slightly above the hock joint. The tail, vertebrae, flank muscle (*rectus abdominis*), *cutaneous trunci*, prefemoral lymph gland, and any other exposed lymph glands shall be removed. The skin and collar fat over the cushion (*semimembranosus*) shall be smooth and well rounded such that the innermost curvature of the skin is trimmed back at least half the distance from the stifle joint to the posterior edge of the aitch bone. The skin overlying the medial side (inside) of the *quadriceps femoris* and fat close to the lean overlying the *quadriceps femoris* and pelvic area shall be excluded. The fat thickness beneath the leg face measured at the skin edge and directly under the bone shall not exceed that indicated in the accompanying schedule:

See page 179 for muscle identification.

Weight Range of Leg (pounds)	Maximum Fat Thickness (inches)
A. 17-20	1.50
(7.7-9.1 kg)	(3.8 cm)
B. 20-28	1.75
(9.1-12.7 kg)	(4.3 cm)
C. 28-up	2.00
(12.7 kg up)	(5.0 cm)

401 — Pierna de Cerdo con Lonja (Jamón Fresco con Piel/Cuero)

La pierna de cerdo, o jamón fresco como se le llama comúnmente, se separará de la media canal del cerdo mediante un corte recto aproximadamente perpendicular a una línea paralela a los huesos del chamorro. El corte debe pasar a través de un punto que no se encuentre a menos de 3.8 cm (1.5 pulgadas) ni a más de 8.8 cm (3.5 pulgadas) del borde anterior del hueso de la cadera. La pata se quitará en la articulación del chamorro o levemente por encima de ella. Se deberán quitar la cola, las vértebras, el músculo de la falda (*rectus abdominis*), el *cutaneous trunci*, los ganglios linfáticos prefemorales y cualquier otro ganglio linfático expuesto. El collar de piel y la grasa del collar que recubre la maciza "cojín" (*semimembranosus*) deberán ser suaves y redondeados de modo que la curvatura interna de la piel se recorte de grasa hacia atrás al menos la mitad de la distancia desde la articulación de la rodilla hasta el borde posterior del hueso de la cadera. Se deberá quitar la piel que recubre el lado medial (interno) del *quadriceps femoris* y la grasa cercana a la carne magra que recubre el *quadriceps femoris* y el área pélvica. El grosor de grasa debajo de la cara de la pierna, medido en el borde de la piel y directamente debajo del hueso, no excederá lo indicado en la siguiente tabla:

Consulte la página 179 para ver la identificación de los músculos.

Escala de peso de jamón (kg)	Grosor máximo de grasa (cm)
A. 7.7-9.1 kg	3.8 cm
(17-20 libras)	(1.50 pulgadas)
B. 9.1-12.7 kg	4.3 cm
(20-28 libras)	(1.75 pulgadas)
C. 12.7 kg y más	5.0 cm
(28 libras y más)	(2.00 pulgadas)

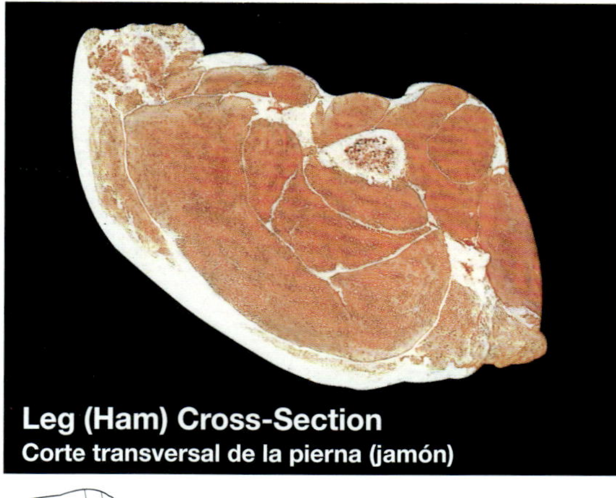

Leg (Ham) Cross-Section
Corte transversal de la pierna (jamón)

401A — Pork Leg (Fresh Ham), Short Shank

This item is as described in Item No. 401, except the shank shall be excluded by a straight cut made at an approximate right angle to the shank bones exposing a cross section of the heel (*gastrocnemius*).

401A — Pierna con Lonja (Jamón Fresco), de Chamorro Corto

Esta pieza es igual a la pieza que se describe en el número 401, excepto que se deberá retirar el chamorro mediante un corte recto aproximadamente perpendicular a los huesos del chamorro que exponga un corte transversal del talón (*gastrocnemius*).

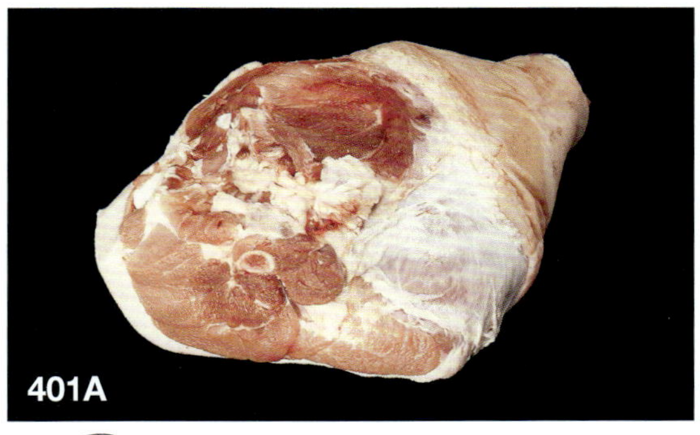

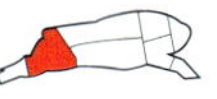

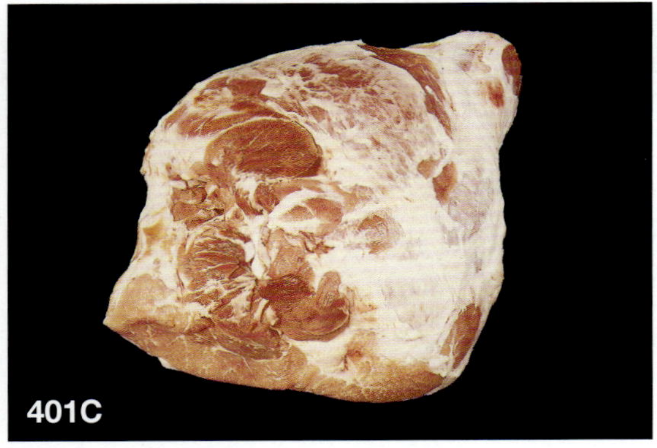

401C

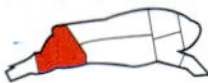

401C — Pork Leg (Fresh Ham), Semi-Boneless

This item is as described in Item No. 401A, except in addition, the pelvic or hip bone (aitch bone) including the fat and lean above it (oyster), the vertebrae, flank, and *ilio psoas* muscles are excluded. Unless specified otherwise all skin shall also be excluded.

401C — Pierna de Cerdo (Jamón Fresco), Semideshuesada

Esta pieza es igual a la pieza número 401A, excepto que además se deberá retirar el hueso pélvico (de la cadera), incluyendo la grasa y la carne magra que se encuentran sobre él (ostra de la cadera), las vértebras, la falda y los músculos *ilio psoas*. A menos que se especifique lo contrario, también se deberá quitar toda la piel.

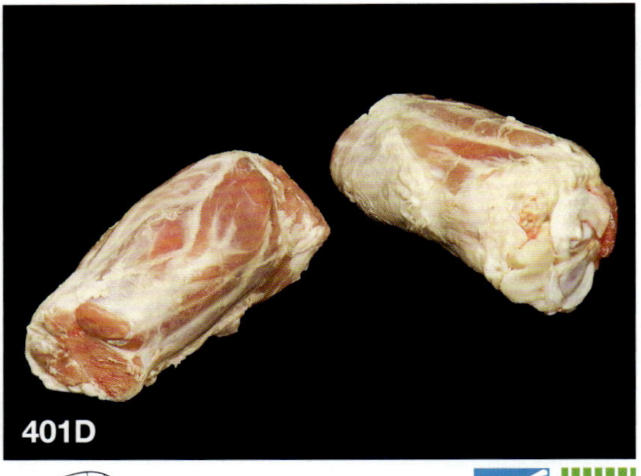

401D

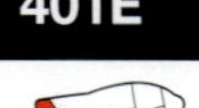

401D — Pork Leg, Hind Shank

This item will consist of the skinless hind shank of the pork leg. It is separated from the leg by straight cut passing through the stifle joint. The foot will be removed at or slightly above the hock joint.

PSO: 1 – Item frenched by removing the lean and fat from the distal (hock joint) end so that the shank bone is exposed for the distance of 1.0 inch (2.5 cm).

401D — Pierna de Cerdo (Jamón Fresco), Chamorro Trasero

Esta pieza consistirá en el chamorro trasero descuerado de la pata de cerdo. Se separará de la pierna mediante un corte recto que pase a través de la articulación de la rodilla. La pata se quitará en la articulación del chamorro o un poco por encima de ella.

PSO: 1 – Pieza preparada al estilo francés mediante la extracción de la carne magra y la grasa del extremo distal (articulación del chamorro) de modo que el hueso del chamorro quede expuesto por una distancia de 2.5 cm (1.0 pulgada).

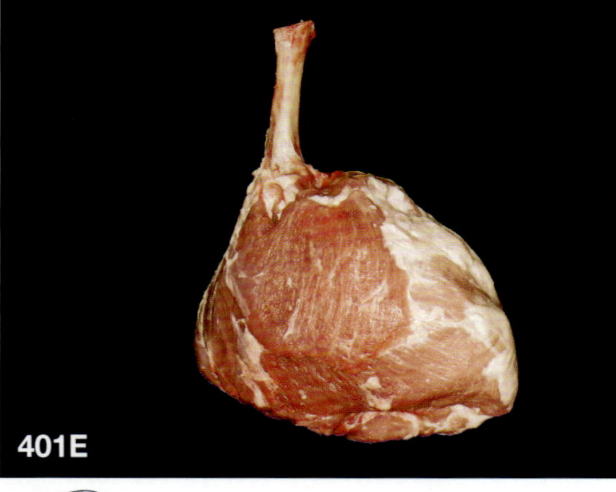

401E

401E — Pork Leg (Fresh Ham), Semi-Boneless, Handle On

This item is as described in Item No. 401, except that the pelvic bone (aitch or hip), fat and lean above the pelvic bone (oyster), vertebrae, flank, and *ilio psoas* muscles are excluded. The leg shall be "faced" by a straight cut that exposes the *semitendinosus*, and a cross section of the ball of the femur. This cut may sever the *quadriceps* group. Further, the shank and heel meat shall be excluded from the tibia (shank bone) by a straight cut perpendicular to the ventral edge of the leg leaving no less than 3.5 inches (8.8 cm) of the shank bone exposed. The fibula shall be completely removed, minimizing scoring to adjacent lean. The exposed shank bone shall be trimmed practically free of lean. Unless otherwise specified, all skin shall be removed. A commonly used name to describe this item is "Steamship Leg of Pork".

401E — Pierna de Cerdo (Jamón Fresco), Semideshuesada, con Caña (Mango)

Esta pieza es igual a la pieza que se describe en el número 401, excepto que se quitarán el hueso pélvico (coxal o cadera), la grasa y la carne magra que se encuentran precubriendo el hueso pélvico (ostra de la cadera), las vértebras, la falda y los músculos *ilio psoas*. Se le aplicará a la pierna un corte recto que exponga el músculo *semitendinosus* y un corte transversal de la cabeza del fémur. Este corte puede separar el grupo de *quadriceps*. Además, se deberán excluir de la tibia (hueso del chamorro), las carnes del chamorro y del talón mediante un corte recto perpendicular al borde ventral de la pierna que deje expuestos no menos de 8.8 cm (3.5 pulgadas) del hueso del chamorro. El peroné deberá quitarse totalmente, minimizando cualquier incisión en la carne magra adyacente. El hueso expuesto del chamorro deberá limpiarse hasta que quede prácticamente libre de carne magra. A menos que se especifique lo contrario, se deberá quitar toda la piel. Al estilo de esta Pierna de Cerdo se le denomina comúnmente "Steamship" en los EUA.

402 — Pork Leg (Fresh Ham), Skinned

In addition to meeting the requirement of Item No. 401, the skin and fat on the outside of the leg must be trimmed. The skin shall be excluded anterior to a straight line parallel to the leg face, which starts at a point that does not exceed 25 percent of the distance from the stifle joint to the leg face. The fat that is exposed shall be trimmed so as not to exceed 0.5 inch (13 mm) in depth at any point that is 1.5 inches (3.8 cm) or more from the skin edge, except at the tail end of the pelvic area, where the fat thickness shall not exceed 1.0 inch (2.5 cm).

402 — Pierna de Cerdo (Jamón Fresco), Semidescuerado (sin Lonja)

Además de cumplir con los requisitos de la pieza número 401, se deberá recortar la piel y la grasa exterior de la pierna. Se deberá quitar la piel desde el lado anterior a una línea recta paralela a la cara de la pierna, que comience en un punto que no esté a más del 25% de la distancia desde la articulación de la rodilla hasta la cara de la pierna. La grasa expuesta deberá recortarse de forma que no exceda los 13 mm (0.5 pulgadas) de profundidad en ningún punto que se encuentre a 3.8 cm (1.5 pulgadas) o más desde el borde de la piel, excepto en el extremo de la cola en el área pélvica, donde el grosor de la grasa no deberá exceder los 2.5 cm (1.0 pulgada).

402A — Pork Leg (Fresh Ham), Skinned, Short Shank

This bone in leg item is as described in Item No. 402, except the shank shall be excluded as described in Item No. 401A.

402A — Pierna de Cerdo (Jamón Fresco), Semidescuerado (sin Lonja), de Chamorro Corto

Esta pieza con hueso es igual a la pieza que se describe en el número 402, excepto que se quitará el chamorro como se describe en la pieza número 401A.

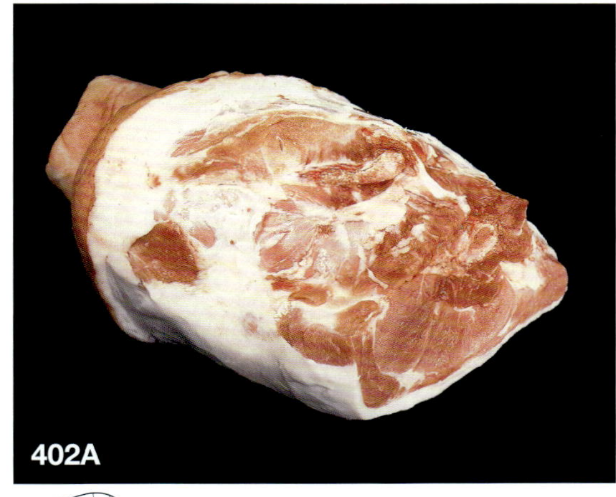

402A

402B — Pork Leg (Fresh Ham), Boneless

This item is prepared from Item No. 401. All bones, cartilages, skin, flank muscle (*rectus abdominis*), *cutaneous trunci*, fat and lean above the aitch bone, and exposed lymph glands shall be excluded. The tendinous ends of shanks shall be excluded so that the cross-sectional cut exposes not less than 75 percent lean. The loin end shall be exposed by a straight cut anterior to the *quadriceps femoris*. The cut shall not be less than 1.0 inch (2.5 cm) and not more than 3.0 inches (7.5 cm) from the anterior end of the femur pocket. Shank meat that is firmly attached may remain and shall be folded into the femur cavity. Unless specified otherwise by the purchaser this item shall be netted or tied, often referred to as BRT (boned, rolled, and tied).

402B — Pierna de Cerdo (Jamón Fresco), Deshuesada

Esta pieza se prepara con la pieza número 401. Se deberán quitar todos los huesos, cartílagos, piel, músculo de la falda (*rectus abdominis*), músculo *cutaneous trunci*, la grasa y la carne magra sobre el hueso de la cadera y los ganglios linfáticos expuestos. Se retirarán los extremos tendinosos de los chamorros, de forma que el corte transversal exponga al menos un 75% de carne magra. El extremo posterior quedará expuesto mediante un corte recto anterior al *quadriceps femoris*. Los cortes no estarán a menos de 2.5 cm (1.0 pulgada) ni a más de 7.5 cm (3.0 pulgadas) de distancia desde el extremo anterior de la cavidad del fémur. La carne del chamorro que se encuentre firmemente unida podrá permanecer y se plegará hacia adentro de la cavidad del fémur. A menos que el comprador especifique lo contrario, esta pieza se atará o colocará en una malla, lo que generalmente se llama DEA (deshuesado, enrollado y enmallado).

402B

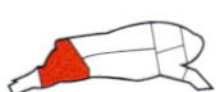

402C — Pork Leg (Fresh Ham), Boneless, Short Shank, Trimmed

This item is as described in Item No. 402B, except the *popliteal* lymph gland and surrounding (star) fat in excess of 0.25 inch (6 mm) shall be excluded. Additional shank meat shall be eliminated from this item by a straight cut made at an approximate right angle to the length of the shank exposing the *gastrocnemius* muscle. Unless specified otherwise by the purchaser this item shall be netted or tied.

402C — Pierna de Cerdo (Jamón Fresco), Deshuesada, de Chamorro Corto, Recortada de Grasa y Limpia

Esta pieza es igual a la pieza que se describe en el número 402B, excepto que se deberán quitar los ganglios linfáticos *poplíteos* y la grasa circundante que supere los 6 mm (0.25 pulgadas). La carne adicional del chamorro se eliminará de esta pieza mediante un corte recto y aproximadamente perpendicular a la longitud del chamorro que exponga el músculo *gastrocnemius*. A menos que el comprador especifique lo contrario, esta pieza se atará o colocará en una malla.

402D — Pork Leg (Fresh Ham), Outside

This boneless item shall consist of the outside muscles (*biceps femoris* and *semitendinosus*) from the leg. The inner shank (*gastrocnemius*) may remain. However, the *flexor digitorum superficialis* muscle, or mouse as it is often referred to, shall be excluded. The *popliteal* lymph gland and surrounding fat in excess of 0.25 inch (6 mm) in depth shall also be excluded. The purchaser may specify outsides from two legs be reversed and netted or tied so that the boned surfaces when placed together produce a uniformly thick roast. If this option is specified, the purchaser may also request the item to be divided into approximately equal portions by a straight cut(s) at a right angle to the length of the item.

402D — Pierna de Cerdo (Jamón Fresco), Pulpa Blanca

Esta pieza deshuesada consiste en los músculos de la pulpa blanca (*biceps femoris* y *semitendinosus*) de la pierna. Podrá permanecer la parte interna del chamorro (*gastrocnemius*). Sin embargo, se deberá quitar el músculo *flexor digitorum superficialis*, o ratón, como se denomina comúnmente. También se deberán quitar los ganglios linfáticos *poplíteos* y la grasa circundante que supere los 6 mm (0.25 pulgadas) de profundidad. El comprador puede especificar que dos porciones de pulpa blanca se inviertan y aten o coloquen en una malla, de manera que cuando las superficies deshuesadas se coloquen juntas formen un rollo de grosor uniforme. Si se especifica esta opción, el comprador también podrá solicitar que la pieza se divida en porciones aproximadamente iguales mediante corte(s) recto(s) perpendicular(es) a la longitud de la pieza.

402E
Outside
Pulpa Blanca

402E — Pork Leg (Fresh Ham), Outside, Trimmed, Shank Removed

This boneless item is as described in Item No. 402D, except both the inner shank and *flexor digitorum superficialis* (mouse) shall be excluded by a cut through the natural seam. The purchaser may also request the preparation options described for this item.

402E — Pierna de Cerdo (Jamón Fresco), Pulpa Blanca, Recortada de Grasa y Limpia, Sin Chamorro

Esta pieza es igual a la pieza que se describe en la número 402D, excepto que la parte interna del chamorro y el *flexor digitorum superficialis* (ratón) deberán quitarse mediante un corte a través de la veta natural. El comprador también podrá solicitar las opciones de preparación descritas para esta pieza.

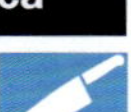

402F Pork Leg (Fresh Ham), Inside

This boneless item consists of the *semimembranosus* and related muscles of the inside portion of the leg remaining after separation from the outside and leg tip (knuckle) portions of the leg along the natural seam. All bones, cartilage, exposed heavy (opaque) connective tissue, lean and fat overlying the aitch bone (oyster), and the *gracilis* membrane (opaque portion) shall be excluded. The purchaser may specify insides from two legs be reversed and netted or tied so that the boned surfaces when placed together produce a uniformly thick roast.

402F Pierna de Cerdo (Jamón Fresco), Pulpa Negra

Esta pieza deshuesada consiste en el músculo *semimembranosus* y los músculos asociados de la porción de pulpa negra que quedan después de la separación de las porciones de pulpa blanca y pulpa bola de la pierna a lo largo de la veta natural. Se deberán quitar todos los huesos, los cartílagos, el tejido conectivo grueso (opaco) y expuesto, la carne magra y la grasa que recubren el hueso de la cadera (ostra de la cadera) y la membrana del músculo *gracilis* (porción opaca). El comprador puede especificar que dos porciones de pulpa negra se inviertan y aten o coloquen en una malla, de manera que cuando las superficies deshuesadas se coloquen juntas formen un rollo de grosor uniforme.

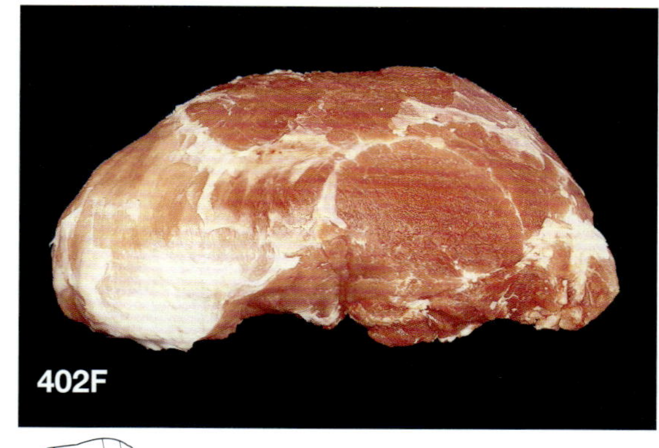

402G Pork Leg (Fresh Ham), TBS, 3-Way, Boneless

This item shall consist of inside (Item No. 402F), outside (Item No. 402E), and leg tip (knuckle) (Item No. 402H) portions of the pork leg individually packaged and placed into the same container. The leg tip (knuckle) portion shall consist of the *tensor fasciae latae* and *quadriceps* group. All bones and cartilage shall be removed. The purchaser may specify the packaging of individual roasts such as described in Item Nos. 402F (2 Insides) and 402E (2 Trimmed Outsides) and 402H (2 leg tips (knuckles)) from two No. 402G Pork Leg items, be placed into the same container.

402G Pierna de Cerdo (Jamón Fresco), TBS, 3 Piezas, Deshuesada

Esta pieza consistirá en las porciones de pulpa negra (pieza número 402F), pulpa blanca (pieza número 402E) y pulpa bola (pieza número 402H) de la pierna de cerdo, empaquetadas de forma individual y colocadas en el mismo envase. La porción de pulpa bola consistirá en el *tensor de la fascia lata* y el grupo de *quadriceps*. Se deberán quitar todos los huesos y cartílagos. El comprador podrá especificar que se coloquen en el mismo envase las piezas individuales como las que se describen en las piezas número 402F (2 pulpas negras) y 402E (2 pulpas blancas recortadas de grasa) y 402H (2 pulpas bola) de dos piezas número 402G, Pierna de Cerdo.

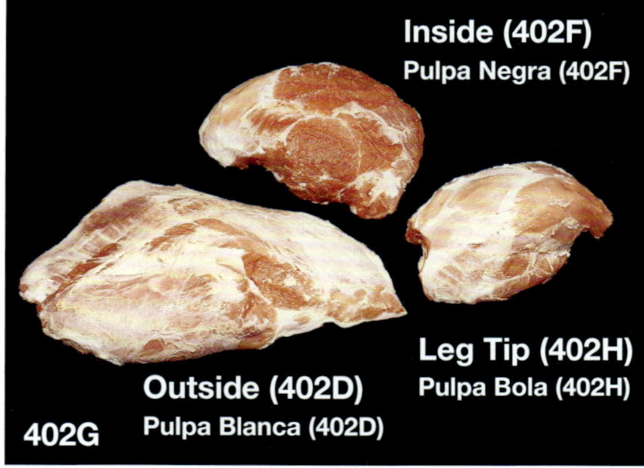

402H Pork Leg (Fresh Ham), Tip

This item shall consist of the leg tip (knuckle) portion of the leg (the *tensor fasciae latae* and *quadriceps* group).

PSO: 1 – The purchaser may specify the removal of the *tensor fasciae latae* from the *quadriceps* group through the natural seam. The remaining item is sometimes referred to as a "Pocket Roast".

402H Pierna de Cerdo (Jamón Fresco), Pulpa Bola

Esta pieza consistirá en la porción de pulpa bola de la pierna (el *tensor de la fascia lata* y el grupo de *quadriceps*).

PSO: 1 – El comprador puede especificar la extracción del *tensor de la fascia lata* del grupo de *quadriceps* mediante un corte a través de la veta natural. A la pieza que queda se le llama en ocasiones Pulpa bola sin Empuje (M. tensor de la fascia lata).

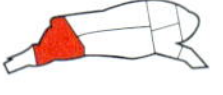

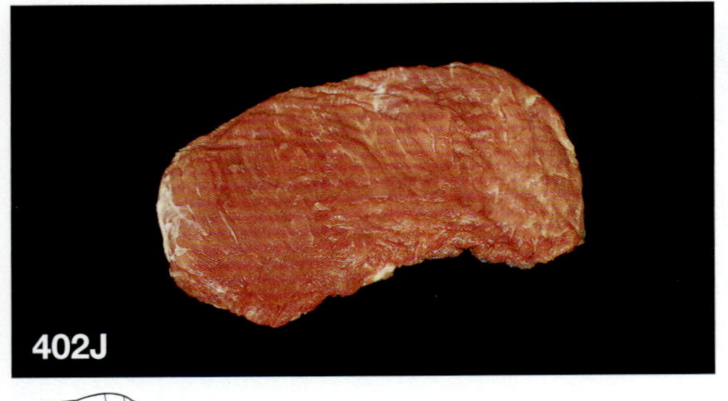

402J

402J Pork Leg (Fresh Ham), Inside Cap (IM)

This item shall consist of the *gracilis* muscle that is separated from the inside leg by cutting through the natural seams.

402J Pierna de Cerdo (Jamón Fresco), Tapa del Centro de Pierna (MI)

Esta pieza consistirá en el músculo *gracilis* que se separa de la pulpa negra cortando a través de las vetas naturales.

403

403 Pork Shoulder

The shoulder is separated from the side by a straight cut that is approximately perpendicular to the length of the side. The cut shall be made posterior to (so as not to expose) the elbow, but not more than 1.0 inch (2.5 cm) from the tip of the elbow. The outer tip of the *subscapularis* muscle shall not extend past the dorsal edge of the base of the medial ridge of the blade bone. The foot shall be excluded at or slightly above the upper knee joint by a straight cut approximately perpendicular to the shank bones. The jowl shall be excluded by a straight cut approximately parallel with the loin side that is anterior to, but not more than 1.0 inch (2.5 cm) from, the innermost curvature of the ear dip. The neck bones, ribs, breast bones, associated cartilage, and breast flap (through the major crease) shall also be excluded. The fat and skin shall be beveled to meet the lean on the dorsal edge. The exterior fat thickness at the dorsal skin edge, measured at the center of the cut, shall not exceed that indicated in the following schedule:

Weight Range of Shoulder (pounds)	Maximum Fat Thickness (inches)
A. 12-16 (5.4-7.3 kg)	1.25 (3.1 cm)
B. 16-22 (7.3-10 kg)	1.50 (3.8 cm)
C. 22 & up (10 kg & up)	2.0 (5.0 cm)

403 Paleta (Espaldilla) de Cerdo

La espaldilla se separa de la media canal mediante un corte recto aproximadamente perpendicular a la longitud de la media canal. El corte debe hacerse por la parte posterior del codo (para no exponerlo) pero a no más de 2.5 cm (1.0 pulgada) de la punta del codo. El extremo exterior del músculo *subscapularis* no deberá extenderse más allá del borde dorsal de la base del borde óseo (espina) del hueso de la paleta. Se quitará la pata delantera en la articulación superior de la rodilla o un poco por encima de ella mediante un corte recto aproximadamente perpendicular a los huesos del chamorro. La papada se quitará mediante un corte recto aproximadamente paralelo con el lado correspondiente al lomo, anterior a la curvatura más profunda de la depresión de la oreja, pero a no más de 2.5 cm (1.0 pulgada) de ella. También se deberán quitar los huesos del pescuezo, las costillas, los huesos del pecho, los cartílagos asociados y el colgajo del pecho (a través del primer pliegue). La piel y la grasa deberán emparejarse hasta nivelarse con la carne magra en el borde dorsal. El grosor de la grasa exterior en el borde de la piel del extremo dorsal, medido en el centro del corte, no deberá exceder el grosor indicado en la siguiente tabla:

Escala de peso de espaldilla (kg)	Grosor máximo de grasa (cm)
A. 5.4-7.3 kg (12-16 libras)	3.1 cm (1.25 pulgadas)
B. 7.3-10 kg (16-22 libras)	3.8 cm (1.50 pulgadas)
C. 10 kg y más (22 libras y más)	5.0 cm (2.0 pulgadas)

403B — Pork Shoulder, Outside

This item shall consist of the shank, humerus, and blade bone and associated outside muscles of the shoulder as described in Item No. 403. It may be prepared directly from the carcass prior to the separation of the loin and belly by cutting through the breast flap and *pectoralis superficialis* and following the natural seam to a point immediately medial to the blade cartilage. The shank shall be excluded at or above the knee joint. The thick or arm end shall include the shank and humerus bones and the overlying lean (*latissimus dorsi, triceps brachii* group [cushion]) and minor muscles associated with the humerus. The thin or shoulder (blade) end shall consist of the blade bone and muscles overlying the blade bone (*supraspinatus, infraspinatus, latissimus dorsi,* and may contain the *subscapularis* and *teres major*). All sides shall be trimmed following the natural curvature of the major muscles and the scapula. The purchaser may specify all skin to be excluded.

403B — Paleta (Espaldilla) de Cerdo, Contracara

Esta pieza consistirá en el chamorro, el húmero y el hueso de la paleta y los músculos exteriores asociados de la paleta (espaldilla) como se describe en la pieza número 403. Puede prepararse directamente con la canal, previa separación del lomo y la barriga mediante un corte a través del colgajo del pecho y el *pectoralis superficialis* siguiendo la veta natural hasta un punto inmediatamente medial al cartílago de la paleta. El chamorro se quitará en la articulación de la rodilla o por encima de ella. El extremo grueso o del brazuelo incluirá los huesos del chamorro, y el húmero y la carne magra que los recubren [grupo *latissimus dorsi, triceps brachii* (maciza "cojín")] y los músculos menores asociados con el húmero. El extremo delgado o adyacente de la espaldilla consistirá en el hueso de la paleta y los músculos que lo recubren (*supraspinatus, infraspinatus, latissimus dorsi,* y puede contener el *subscapularis* y el *teres mayor*). Todos los lados serán recortados de grasa siguiendo la curvatura natural de los músculos principales y el hueso de la paleta (la escápula). El comprador podrá especificar que se quite toda la piel.

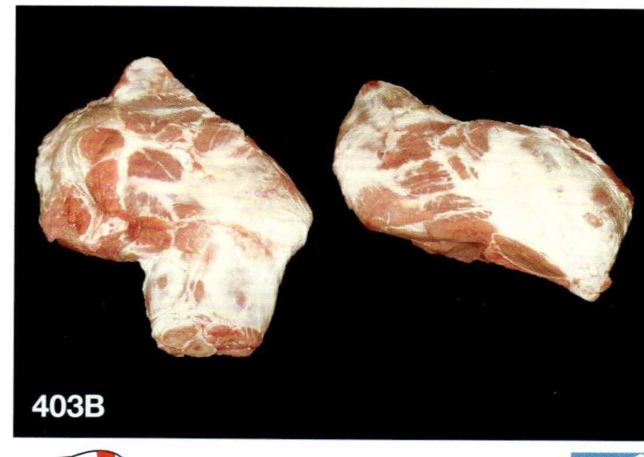

403B

403C — Pork Shoulder, Inside, Boneless

This item is prepared from the remaining portion of the shoulder after the removal of the outside shoulder as described in Item No. 403B. The loin shall have been removed so that the *longissimus* is equal to or larger than the *spinalis dorsi*. All false lean (*trapezius*) shall be excluded. The ventral edge shall have been made by a straight cut perpendicular to the loin end that does not exceed 2.0 inches (5.0 cm) from the *longissimus*. The anterior end is trimmed so that there is no evidence of the ear dip. All bones and cartilage shall be excluded.

403C — Paleta (Espaldilla) de Cerdo, Cara, Deshuesada

Esta pieza se prepara con la porción restante de la paleta (espaldilla) después de quitar la contracara de la paleta, como se describe en la pieza número 403B. El lomo deberá quitarse de modo que el *longissimus* sea igual o más grande que el *spinalis dorsi*. Toda la carne magra falsa (*trapezius*) deberá quitarse. El borde ventral deberá haberse realizado mediante un corte recto perpendicular al extremo adyacente al lomo que no exceda los 5.0 cm (2.0 pulgadas) desde el *longissimus*. El extremo anterior estará recortado de grasa y limpio, de modo que no queden rastros de la depresión de la oreja. Se quitarán todos los huesos y cartílagos.

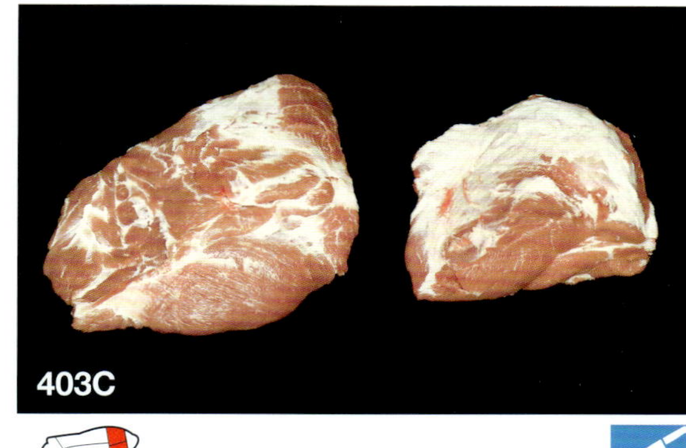

403C

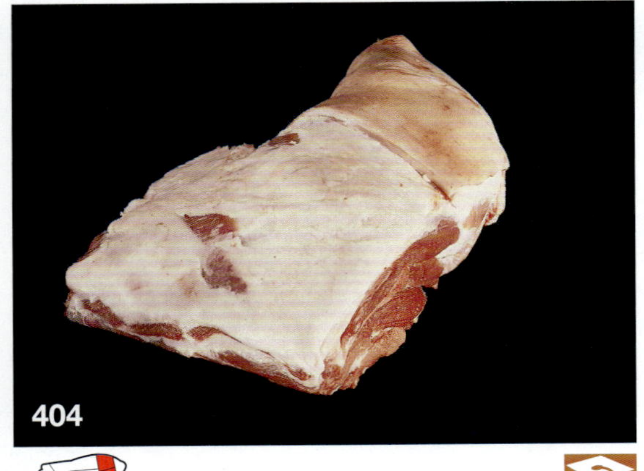

404 Pork Shoulder, Skinned

The shoulder is as described in Item No. 403, except the skin and fat on the outside of the shoulder shall be trimmed. The skin dorsal to a straight line parallel to the dorsal side, which starts at a point that does not exceed 25 percent of the distance from the elbow joint to the dorsal side, shall be excluded. The fat exposed by the elimination of the skin shall be trimmed not to exceed 0.5 inch (13 mm) in depth at any point 1.5 inches (3.8 cm) or more from the edge of the skin collar. Traces of the false lean shall be visible.

404 Paleta (Espaldilla) de Cerdo, Semidescuerada (sin Lonja)

La paleta (espaldilla) es igual a la descripción de la pieza número 403, excepto que se recortará la piel y la grasa en la contracara de la paleta. Se quitará la piel dorsal con respecto a una línea recta paralela al lado dorsal, que comience en un punto que no exceda el 25% de la distancia desde la articulación del codo hasta el lado dorsal. La grasa expuesta a causa de la eliminación de la piel deberá recortarse de forma que no exceda los 13 mm (0.5 pulgadas) de profundidad en ningún punto que se encuentre a 3.8 cm (1.5 pulgadas) o más desde el borde del collar de piel. Los rastros de carne magra falsa deben estar visibles.

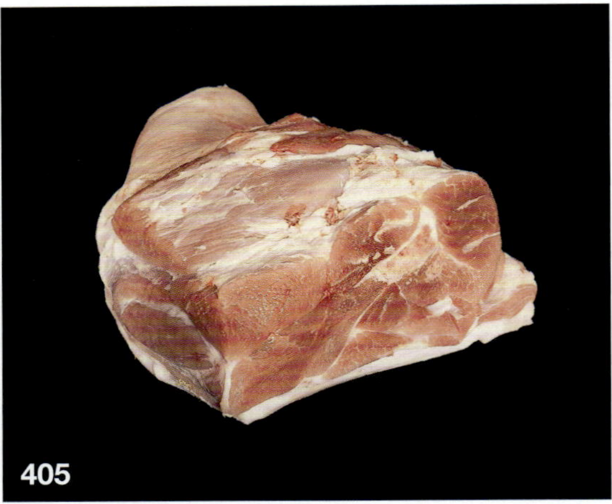

405 Pork Shoulder, Picnic

This item is prepared from Item No. 403. The butt shall be excluded by a straight cut, dorsal to the shoulder joint, at an approximate right angle with the belly side. The jowl shall be excluded by a straight cut approximately parallel with the belly side, which is not more than 1.0 inch (2.5 cm) anterior from the half moon muscle (*pectoralis profundi*), measured on the butt side. The fat and skin shall be beveled to meet the lean on the dorsal edge. The fat thickness, measured at the center of the butt side, shall not exceed that indicated in the following schedule:

Weight Range of Shoulder Picnic (lbs.)	Maximum Fat Thickness (inches)
A. 6-8 (2.7-3.6 kg)	0.625 (16 mm)
B. 8-11 (3.6-5 kg)	0.75 (19 mm)
C. 11 & up (5 kg & up)	1.25 (3.1 cm)

405 Paleta (Espaldilla) de Cerdo, Picnic (Brazuelo), sin Cabeza de Lomo

Esta pieza se prepara con la pieza número 403. La cabeza de lomo deberá quitarse mediante un corte recto, dorsal a la articulación de la paleta, aproximadamente en ángulo recto respecto al lado de la barriga. Se deberá quitar la papada mediante un corte recto, aproximadamente paralelo al lado de la barriga, anterior al músculo media luna (*pectoralis profundi*), a no más de 2.5 cm (1.0 pulgada) de distancia, medida del lado de la cabeza de lomo. La piel y la grasa deberán emparejarse hasta nivelarse con la carne magra en el borde dorsal. El grosor de la grasa, medido en el centro del lado de la cabeza de lomo, no deberá exceder el indicado en la siguiente tabla:

Escala de peso de picnic de paleta (kg)	Grosor máximo de grasa (cm)
A. 2.7-3.6 kg (6-8 libras)	16 mm (0.625 pulgadas)
B. 3.6-5 kg (8-11 libras)	19 mm (0.75 pulgadas)
C. 5 kg y más (11 libras y más)	3.1 cm (1.25 pulgadas)

405A — Pork Shoulder, Picnic, Boneless

This item is prepared from Item No. 405. All bones, cartilage and skin shall be excluded. The belly side of the picnic shall expose a cross section of the cushion (*triceps brachii* group). The butt side shall expose a full cross section of the *supraspinatus* with no more than a slight enlargement of tendons. The jowl shall be excluded by a cut that is not more than 1.0 inch (2.5 cm) anterior from the half moon muscle (*pectoralis profundi*), measured on the butt side. The tendinous ends of the shank shall be excluded to a point where a cross-sectional cut exposes at least 75 percent lean.

405A — Paleta (Espaldilla) de Cerdo, Picnic (Brazuelo), Deshuesada

Esta pieza se prepara con la pieza número 405. Se deberán quitar todos los huesos, cartílagos y piel. El lado de la barriga pegado al picnic (brazuelo) deberá exponer un corte transversal del cojín (grupo de *triceps brachii*). El lado de la cabeza de lomo debe exponer un corte transversal completo del *supraspinatus* que no tenga más que un ligero agrandamiento de los tendones. La papada debe quitarse mediante un corte anterior a la media luna (*pectoralis profundi*), que no se encuentre a más de 2.5 cm (1.0 pulgada) de distancia, medida del lado de la cabeza de lomo. Los extremos tendinosos del chamorro deberán quitarse hasta un punto donde el corte transversal muestre al menos un 75% de carne magra.

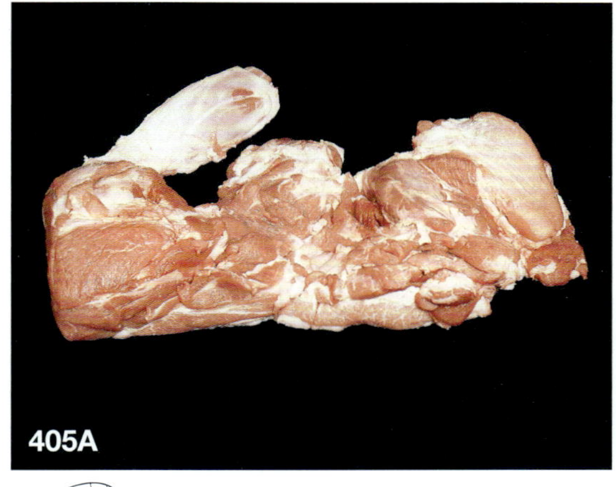
405A

405B — Pork Shoulder, Picnic, Cushion, Boneless

This item shall consist of the *triceps brachii* muscles from Item No. 405A and shall be practically free of fat. Tendons shall be trimmed flush with the lean.

405B — Paleta (Espadilla) de Cerdo, Picnic (Brazuelo), Mazica "Cojín" (Cushion), Deshuesada

Esta pieza consiste en los músculos *triceps brachii* de la pieza 405A y deberá estar prácticamente libre de grasa. Los tendones se recortarán de grasa al mismo nivel que la carne magra.

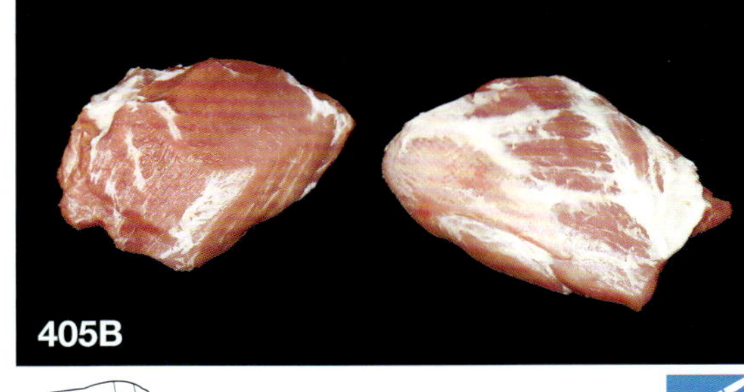
405B

405C — Pork Shoulder, Pectoral Meat (IM)

This item will consist of the *pectoralis profundis* muscle that is removed from the shoulder by cutting through the natural seams.

405C — Paleta (Espaldilla) de Cerdo, Carne de Pectoral (MI)

Esta pieza consistirá en el músculo *pectoralis profundis* que se separará de la paleta (espaldilla) mediante un corte a través de las vetas naturales.

405C

406 — Pork Shoulder, Boston Butt, Bone In

This item is as described in Item No. 403, except that the picnic is excluded as described in Item No. 405. Skin, neck bones, and related cartilage shall also be excluded. Traces of false lean shall be visible.

* In Canada, this item is referred to as the Shoulder Blade.

406 — Paleta (Espaldilla) de Cerdo, Cabeza de Lomo, con Hueso de Paleta

Esta pieza es igual a la pieza que se describe en el número 403, excepto que se debe quitar el picnic (brazuelo) como se describe en la pieza número 405. La piel, los huesos del pescuezo y los cartílagos asociados también deben quitarse. Los rastros de carne magra falsa deben estar visibles.

* En Canadá, esta pieza se llama "Shoulder Blade".

406

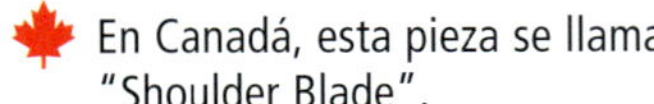

NAMP
NORTH AMERICAN MEAT PROCESSORS ASSOCIATION
ASSOCIATION AMÉRIQUE DU NORD DES TRANSFORMATEURS DE VIANDE
ASOCIACIÓN NORTEAMERICANA DE PROCESADORES DE CARNE

406A

406A Pork Shoulder, Boston Butt, Boneless

This item is prepared from Item No. 406. All bones, cartilages, and skin shall be removed. The loin side of the butt shall expose the *longissimus* equal to or larger than the combined areas of the *splenius* and *semispinalis capitis*. The picnic side shall expose a cross section of the *supraspinatus* with no more than a slight enlargement of tendons. The jowl shall be removed by a straight cut, approximately parallel with the loin side, which is not more than 1.0 inch (2.5 cm) anterior to the half moon muscle (*pectoralis profundi*), measured on the picnic side. Traces of false lean shall be visible. The lean and fat overlying the blade shall remain firmly attached. Purchaser may specify the boneless butt be netted or tied.

406A Paleta (Espaldilla) de Cerdo, Cabeza de Lomo, Deshuesada

Esta pieza se prepara con la pieza número 406. Se deberán quitar todos los huesos, cartílagos y piel. El lado del lomo de la cabeza de lomo deberá exponer el *longissimus* de igual o mayor tamaño que las áreas combinadas del *splenius* y el *semispinalis capitis*. El lado del picnic (brazuelo) debe exponer un corte transversal del *supraspinatus* que no tenga más que un ligero agrandamiento de los tendones. Se deberá quitar la papada mediante un corte recto, aproximadamente paralelo al lado correspondiente al lomo, anterior al músculo media luna (*pectoralis profundi*), a no más de 2.5 cm (1.0 pulgada) de distancia, medida del lado del picnic (brazuelo). Los rastros de carne magra falsa deben estar visibles. La carne magra y la grasa que recubren a la paleta deberán permanecer firmemente unidas. El comprador puede especificar que la cabeza de lomo deshuesada se ate o coloque en una malla.

406B Pork Shoulder, Boston Butt, Boneless, Special

This item is as described in Item No. 406A, except the false lean (*trapezius*) and underlying fat shall be excluded. The remaining roast shall be trimmed practically free of surface fat.

406B Paleta (Espaldilla) de Cerdo, Cabeza de Lomo, Deshuesada, Especial

Esta pieza es igual a la pieza que se describe en el número 406A, excepto que se deberá quitar la carne magra falsa (*trapezius*) y la grasa subyacente. El rollo amarrado debe recortarse para que quede prácticamente libre de cubierta de grasa.

407

407 Pork Shoulder Butt, Cellar Trimmed, Boneless

The butt is as described in Item No. 406A, except the lean and fat immediately overlying the blade shall be excluded.

407 Cabeza de Lomo de Cerdo, sin Hueso de Paleta y Recortada de Grasa y Limpia, Deshuesada

La cabeza de lomo es igual a la pieza que se describe en el número 406A, excepto que se deberá quitar la carne magra y la grasa que recubren la paleta.

408 — Pork Belly

The belly is prepared from the side after removal of the leg, shoulder, loin, fat back, and spareribs. All bones and cartilages, and practically all leaf fat, shall be excluded. The fat back shall also be excluded by a straight cut not more than 1.5 inches (3.8 cm) from the outermost dorsal curvature of scribe line. The anterior (shoulder) and posterior (leg) ends of the belly shall be reasonably straight and parallel. No side of the belly shall be more than 2.0 inches (5.0 cm) longer than its opposing side. The width of the flank muscle (*rectus abdominis*) shall be at least 25 percent of the width of the belly on the leg (sirloin) end. The fat on the ventral side of the belly and adjacent to the flank shall be trimmed to within 0.75 inch (19 mm) from the lean. The area ventral to the scribe line shall be free of scores and "snowballs" (exposed areas of fat) that measure 3.0 square inches (19.4 sq cm) or more. The belly shall be free of enlarged, soft, porous, dark, or seedy mammary tissue. The scribe line is not considered a score but shall not be more than 0.25 inch (6 mm) in depth at any point.

408 — Barriga/Tocino Fresco de Cerdo

La barriga se prepara de la media canal una vez que se quita la pierna, la paleta (espaldilla), el lomo, la lonja sin piel de la chuleta y el costillar. Se deberán quitar todos los huesos y cartílagos, y prácticamente toda la tela de grasa visceral (omental). También se deberá quitar la lonja sin piel de la chuleta mediante un corte recto dorsal a no más de 3.8 cm (1.5 pulgadas) desde la curvatura exterior de la línea de trazado. Los extremos anterior (adyacente a la paleta) y posterior (adyacente a la pierna) de la barriga deberán estar razonablemente rectos y paralelos. Ningún lado de la barriga podrá ser 5.0 cm (2.0 pulgadas) más largo que su lado opuesto. El ancho del músculo de la falda (*rectus abdominis*) deberá alcanzar al menos el 25% del ancho de la barriga en el extremo adyacente a la pierna (sirloin). La grasa del lado ventral de la barriga y adyacente a la falda deberá recortarse hasta alcanzar los 19 mm (0.75 pulgadas) desde la carne magra. El área ventral a la línea de trazado del corte deberá estar libre de incisiones y "bolas de nieve" (áreas expuestas de grasa) que midan 19.4 cm cuadrados (3.0 pulgadas cuadradas) o más. La barriga deberá estar libre de tejido mamario granuloso, oscuro, poroso, blando o exagerado en tamaño. La línea de trazado del corte no se considera una incisión pero no podrá exceder los 6 mm (0.25 pulgadas) de profundidad en ningún punto.

408A — Pork Fat Back

The fat back as referred to in the specifications for Item No. 408 shall be produced as described and shall be 0.5 inch (13 mm) thick on the average.

PSO: 1 – Purchaser may request this item skinless.

408A — Lonja sin Cuero de la Chuleta de Cerdo (Grasa del Espaldar)

La lonja sin piel de la chuleta, como se le llama en las especificaciones para la pieza número 408, deberá obtenerse como se describe y tendrá un grosor promedio de 13 mm (0.5 pulgadas).

PSO: 1 – El comprador puede solicitar que esta pieza se prepare sin piel.

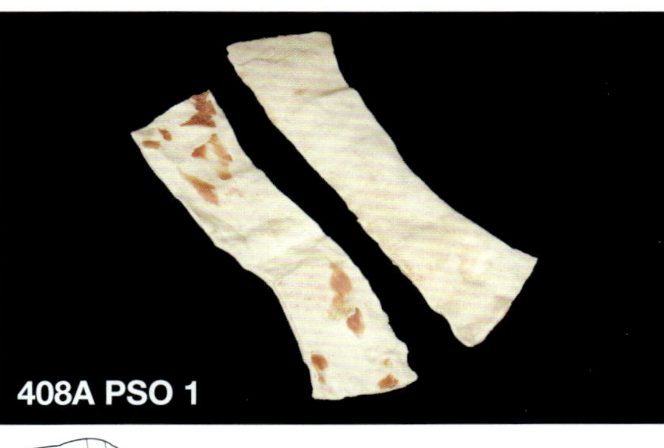

409 — Pork Belly, Skinless

The skinless belly is as described in Item No. 408, except the skin is removed leaving a smooth-skinned surface that is practically free of hair roots and scores.

409 — Barriga/Tocino Fresco de Cerdo, Descuerada(o)

La barriga descuerada es igual a la pieza que se describe en el número 408, excepto que se quita la piel dejando una superficie suave prácticamente libre de raíces de pelos e incisiones.

409A

409A — Pork Belly, Single Ribbed, Skinless

This item is as described in Item No. 409, except the rib bones are excluded by individually removing them, leaving the intercostal meat (rib fingers), costal cartilages, sternum, and *transversus abdominis* muscle intact.

PSO: 1 – The purchaser may specify that skin may remain and that the costal cartilages and/or sternum be excluded.

409A — Barriga/Tocino Fresco de Cerdo, sin Costillas, Descuerada(o)

Esta pieza es igual a la pieza que se describe en el número 409, excepto que las costillas se quitan de forma individual, dejando la carne intercostal (tiras de entrecostillas), los cartílagos costales, el esternón y el músculo *transversus abdominis* intactos.

PSO: 1 – El comprador puede especificar que se conserve la piel y que se excluyan los cartílagos costales y/o el esternón.

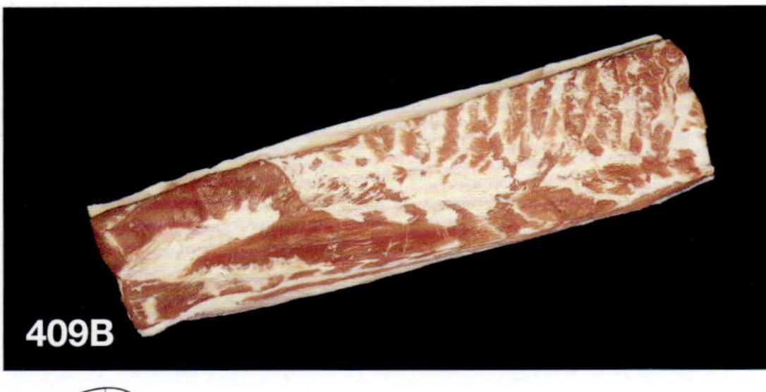

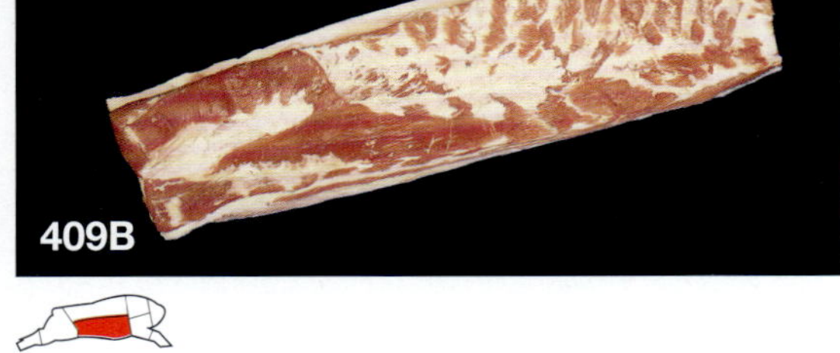

409B

409B — Pork Belly, Center-Cut, Skinless

This item is as described in Item No. 409, except the fat back shall be excluded by a straight cut no more than 0.5 inch (13 mm) dorsal to the outermost curvature of the scribe line. The fat and teat line on the ventral edge shall be eliminated by a straight cut immediately ventral to lean edge.

409B — Barriga/Tocino Fresco de Cerdo, Corte Rectangular del Centro, Descuerada(o)

Esta pieza es igual a la pieza que se describe en el número 409, excepto que se quita la lonja sin piel de la chuleta mediante un corte recto, dorsal a la curvatura exterior de la línea de trazado del corte, a no más de 13 mm (0.5 pulgadas) de distancia. La grasa y la línea de las tetillas en el borde ventral deberán quitarse mediante un corte recto inmediatamente ventral al borde magro.

410 — Pork Loin, Bone In

The loin is that portion of the side remaining after removal of the shoulder, leg, belly, and fat back, leaving a portion of the blade bone and its overlying lean and fat. There shall be not less than two sacral, but no caudal, vertebrae left remaining on the loin. The shoulder and leg shall be separated from the loin by straight cuts that are reasonably perpendicular to the split surface of the backbone. The outer tip of *subscapularis* muscle shall not extend past the center of the base of the medial ridge of the blade bone. The belly side shall be removed by a straight cut (a slight dorsal curvature is acceptable) that extends from a point that is ventral to, but not more than 3.0 inches (7.5 cm) from, the *longissimus* on the shoulder end to a point on the leg (sirloin) end ventral to, but not more than 0.5 inch (13 mm) from, the tenderloin. Surface fat shall be trimmed to an average of 0.25 inch (6 mm) in depth or less except in the hip bone area. The hip bone area is defined as the area contained within two parallel lines, 2.0 inches (5.0 cm) on either side of the anterior end of the hip bone and associated cartilage. Fat in the hip bone area shall be trimmed to the same contour as the rest of the trimmed fat surface of the loin. At least 2.0 inches (5.0 cm) of the false lean shall be exposed. Lumbar and pelvic fat shall be trimmed to 0.5 inch (13 mm) or less in depth. The tenderloin shall remain intact. The diaphragm and hanging tender shall be excluded. The spinal cord groove shall be evident on at least 75 percent of the vertebrae.

410 — Chuleta Natural/ Entrecot de Cerdo, (Lomo con Hueso)

El lomo es la porción de la media canal que queda después de extraer la paleta (espaldilla), la pierna, la barriga y la lonja sin piel de la chuleta, dejando una porción del hueso de la paleta, la carne magra y la grasa que lo recubren. Deben quedar al menos dos vértebras sacras, pero no coccígeas, en el lomo. La paleta (espaldilla) y la pierna deben separarse del lomo mediante cortes rectos razonablemente perpendiculares a la superficie de división del espinazo. El extremo exterior del músculo *subscapularis* no deberá extenderse más allá del centro de la base del borde óseo (espina) del hueso de la paleta. El lado de la barriga se quitará mediante un corte recto (aunque se aceptará una leve curvatura dorsal) que se extienda desde un punto ventral al *longissimus*, pero a no más de 7.5 cm (3.0 pulgadas) de distancia, en el extremo adyacente a la paleta (espaldilla), hasta un punto del extremo adyacente a la pierna (sirloin) ventral al filete, a no más de 13 mm (0.5 pulgadas) de distancia. La cubierta de grasa deberá recortarse hasta un promedio de 6 mm (0.25 pulgadas) de profundidad o menos, excepto en el área del hueso de la cadera. El área del hueso de la cadera se define como el área contenida dentro de dos líneas paralelas, a 5.0 cm (2.0 pulgadas) de distancia a ambos lados del extremo anterior del hueso de la cadera y el cartílago asociado. La grasa en el área de la cadera debe recortarse con el mismo contorno que el resto de la cubierta de grasa recortada del lomo. Deberán quedar expuestos al menos 5.0 cm (2.0 pulgadas) de carne magra falsa. La grasa lumbar y pélvica deberá recortarse hasta alcanzar los 13 mm (0.5 pulgadas) o menos de profundidad. El filete deberá permanecer intacto. El diafragma y la falda deberán quitarse. El canal raquídeo deberá verse por lo menos en el 75% de las vértebras.

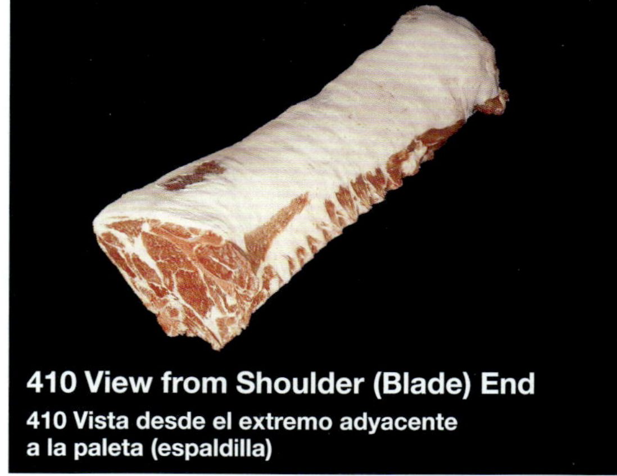

410 View from Shoulder (Blade) End
410 Vista desde el extremo adyacente a la paleta (espaldilla)

410 View from Leg (Sirloin) End
410 Vista desde el extremo adyacente a la pierna (sirloin)

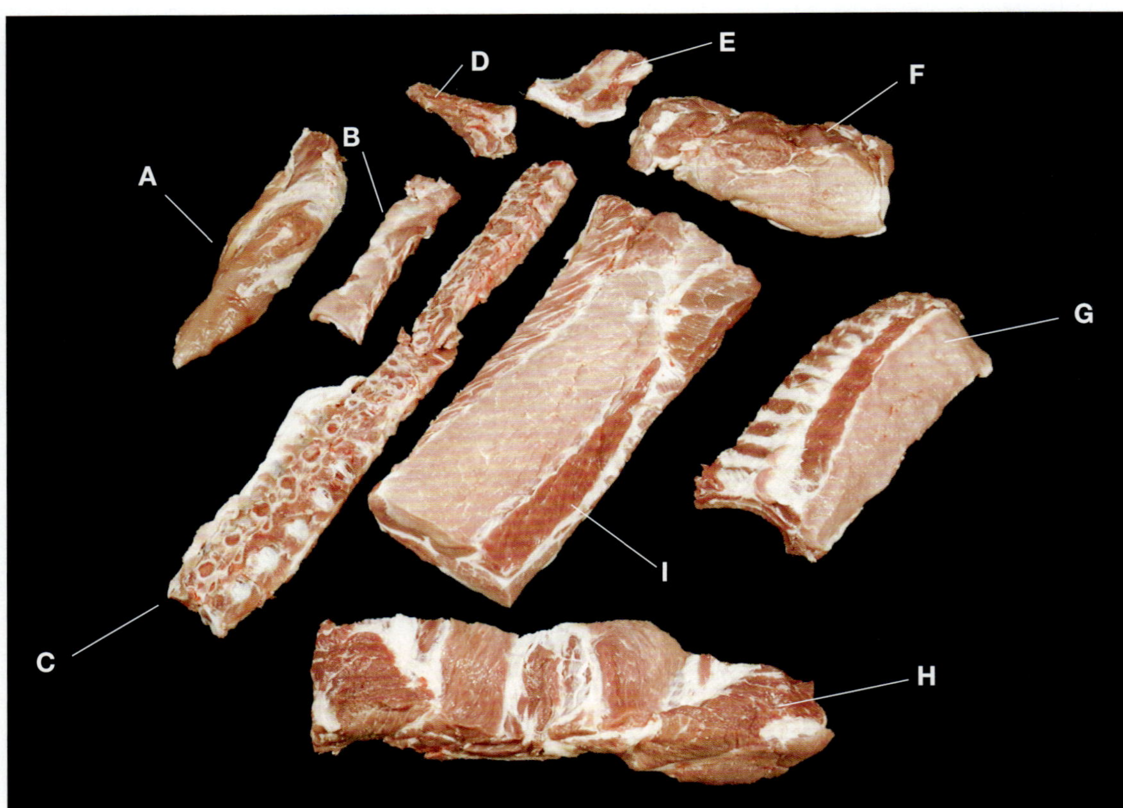

Pork Loin, Components
Lomo de Cerdo, Componentes

A 415 Tenderloin
415 Filete

B 424 Riblets
424 Costelitas

C Backbone
Huesos del espinazo

D Sacral and Caudal Vertebrae
Vértebras sacras y caudales

E Hip Bone
Hueso de la cadera

F Leg (Sirloin) End
Extremo adyacente de la pierna (Sirloin)

G 422 Back Ribs
422 Costillas del Espaldar

H 423 Country Style Ribs
423 Costillas Estilo Campestre

I 412B 8 Rib Center-Cut
412B Corte del Centro con 8 Costillas

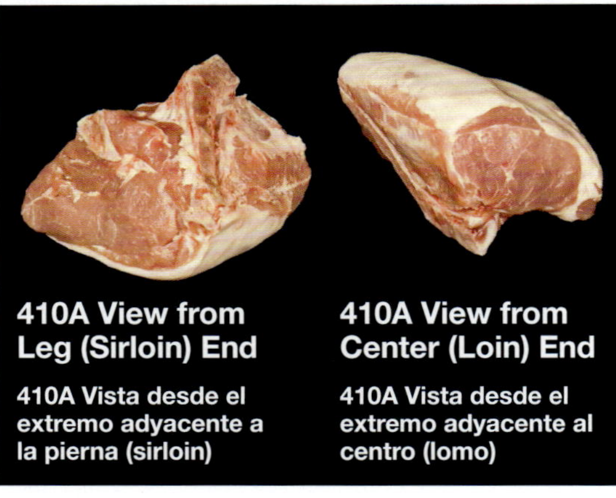

410A View from Leg (Sirloin) End

410A View from Center (Loin) End

410A Vista desde el extremo adyacente a la pierna (sirloin)

410A Vista desde el extremo adyacente al centro (lomo)

410A Pork Loin, Leg (Sirloin) End, Bone In

This item is prepared from Item No. 410 and as described in Item No. 412 for the preparation of a Bone In, Center-Cut, Pork Loin wherein the Leg (Sirloin) End, Bone In is removed anterior to the hip bone and associated cartilage, exposing the *gluteus medius.* Unless otherwise specified, a portion of the tenderloin may remain.

PSO: 1 – Pork Loin, Leg (Sirloin) End, Boneless is prepared by removing all bone, cartilage, surface fat, and remaining tenderloin, if any.

410A Chuleta de Cerdo, Extremo Adyacente a la Pierna (Sirloin), con Hueso

Esta pieza se prepara con la pieza número 410 y de la misma forma que se describe en la pieza número 412 para la preparación de una Chuleta de Lomo de Cerdo, Corte del Centro, con Hueso, donde el Extremo Adyacente a la Pierna (Sirloin), con Hueso, se quita en un punto anterior al hueso de la cadera y al cartílago asociado para exponer el *gluteus medius.* A menos que se especifique lo contrario, deberá quedar una porción del filete.

PSO: 1 – La pieza Chuleta de Lomo de Cerdo, Extremo Adyacente a la Pierna (Sirloin), Deshuesada, se prepara quitando todos los huesos, los cartílagos, la cubierta de grasa y el resto de filete, si es que queda.

410B — Pork Loin, Rib End, Bone In

This item is prepared from Item No. 410 and as described in Item No. 412 for the preparation of a Bone In, Center-Cut, Pork Loin wherein the Rib End, Bone In is separated from the Pork Loin so that the rib end shall have no less than two bones nor more than six bones.

410B — Chuleta de Cerdo, Extremo Adyacente al Costillar, con Hueso

Esta pieza se prepara con la pieza número 410 y de la misma forma que se describe en la pieza número 412 para la preparación de una Chuleta de Lomo de Cerdo, Corte del Centro, con Hueso, donde el Extremo Adyacente al Costillar, con Hueso, se separa del Lomo de Cerdo de forma que el extremo adyacente al costillar no tenga menos de dos huesos ni más de seis.

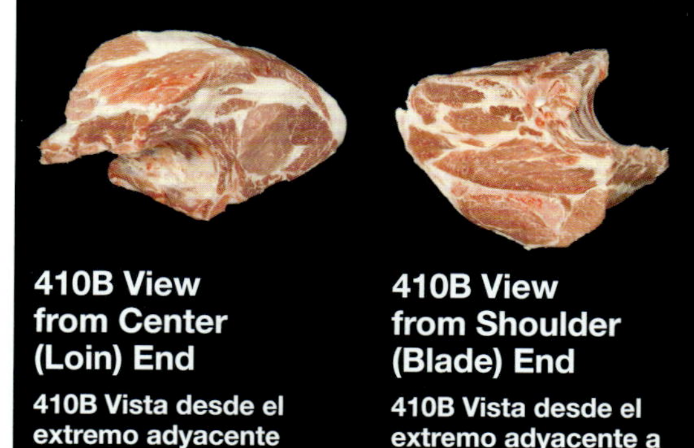

410B View from Center (Loin) End

410B Vista desde el extremo adyacente al centro (lomo)

410B View from Shoulder (Blade) End

410B Vista desde el extremo adyacente a la paleta (espaldilla)

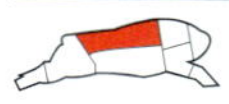

411 — Pork Loin, Bone In, Bladeless

The loin is as described in Item No. 410, except the blade bone, associated cartilage, and associated overlying lean and fat shall be removed. On the shoulder (blade) end, the *longissimus* shall be equal to or larger than the combined areas of the *splenius* and *semispinalis capitis*.

411 — Chuleta de Cerdo, con Hueso, Excepto Hueso de la Paleta

El lomo es igual a la pieza descrita en el número 410, excepto que se deberá quitar el hueso de la paleta, el cartílago asociado, así como la grasa y la carne magra que lo recubren. En el extremo adyacente a la paleta (espaldilla), el *longissimus* deberá ser igual o mayor a las áreas combinadas del *splenius* y el *semispinalis capitis*.

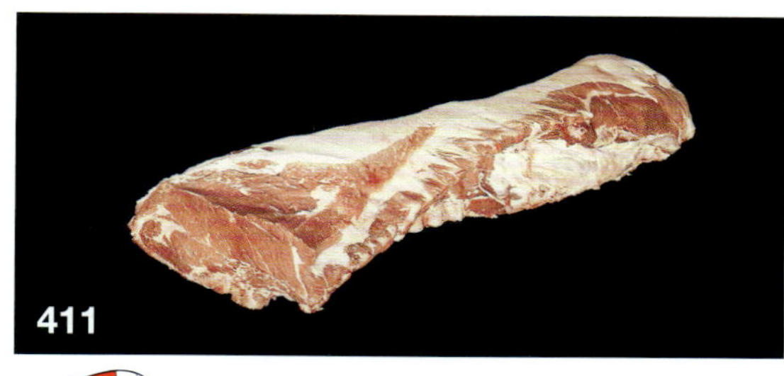

412 View from Leg (Sirloin) End

412 Vista desde el extremo adyacente a la pierna (sirloin)

412 View from Shoulder (Blade) End

412 Vista desde el extremo adyacente a la paleta (espaldilla)

412 — Pork Loin, Bone In, Center-Cut, 8 Ribs

This item is prepared from Item No. 410. The blade and the sirloin portions are eliminated by straight cuts made approximately perpendicular to the split surface of the backbone and the length of the loin. The sirloin is removed anterior to the hip bone and associated cartilage exposing the *gluteus medius.* The blade portion shall be removed to leave not more than eight ribs present. Floating rib(s) that do not show a cross-section at the belly side are exempt. The belly shall be removed by a straight cut (a slight dorsal curvature is acceptable) from a point that is ventral to, but not more than 4.0 inches (10.0 cm) from, the *longissimus* at the shoulder (blade) end to a point on the leg (sirloin) end that is ventral to, but not more than 3.0 inches (7.5 cm) from, the *longissimus*. Surface fat shall be trimmed to an average of 0.25 inch (6 mm) in depth. Lumbar fat shall be trimmed not to exceed 0.5 inch (13 mm) in depth. The tenderloin shall remain intact. The spinal cord groove shall be evident on at least 75 percent of the vertebrae.

412 — Chuleta de Cerdo, con Hueso, Corte del Centro, 8 Costillas

Esta pieza se prepara con la pieza número 410. Las porciones de paleta y sirloin se quitan mediante cortes rectos aproximadamente perpendiculares a la superficie de separación del hueso del espaldar y la longitud del lomo. El sirloin se quita por delante del hueso de la cadera y el cartílago asociado para exponer el *gluteus medius.* Se quitará la porción de paleta y no se dejarán más de ocho costillas. La(s) costilla(s) flotante(s) que no muestren un corte transversal del lado de la barriga no se incluirán en el corte. La barriga se quitará mediante un corte recto (aunque se aceptará una leve curvatura dorsal) desde un punto ventral al *longissimus*, pero a no más de 10.0 cm (4.0 pulgadas) de distancia, en el extremo adyacente a la espaldilla (paleta), hasta un punto del extremo adyacente a la pierna (sirloin) ventral al *longissimus*, a no más de 7.5 cm (3.0 pulgadas) de distancia. La cubierta de grasa se recortará hasta alcanzar un promedio de 6 mm (0.25 pulgadas) de profundidad. La grasa lumbar también deberá recortarse de forma que no exceda los 13 mm (0.5 pulgadas) de profundidad. El filete deberá permanecer intacto. El canal raquídeo deberá verse por lo menos en el 75% de las vértebras.

The purchaser may specify the following options for all applicable pork loins in the 412 and 413 series. Option nos. 1-4 are belly strap removal options (ventral to the *longissimus*; shoulder (blade) end x leg (sirloin) end), Option no. 5 is for trim, and Option nos. 6-11 are muscle and/or rib count designations. More than one of these options may be specified for a single item number.

El comprador podrá especificar las siguientes opciones para todos los lomos de cerdo de las series 412 y 413. Las opciones 1-4 son opciones de retiro de la barriga [ventral al *longissimus*; extremo adyacente a la paleta (espaldilla) x extremo adyacente a la pierna (sirloin)], la opción número 5 es de recorte de grasa y limpieza, y las opciones 6-11 son designaciones de músculos y/o de cantidad de costillas. Se puede especificar más de una de estas opciones para una pieza individual.

Option Number	Description
1	2.0 in. (5.0 cm) x 1.0 in. (2.5 cm) (belly strap removal)
2	1.0 in. (2.5 cm) x 1.0 in. (2.5 cm) (belly strap removal)
3	0.0 in. x 0.0 in. (belly strap removal)
4	Other belly strap removal dimensions as specified by the purchaser
5	All false lean removed (*trapezius* and *latissimus dorsi*)
6	*Multifidus dorsi* (tiger) muscle shall be removed
7	Tenderloin, as described in Item No. 415, shall be removed
8	Eight (8) Rib End (Rack), Center-Cut
9	Nine (9) Rib End (Rack), Center-Cut
10	Ten (10) Rib End (Rack), Center-Cut
11	Eleven (11) Rib End (Rack), Center-Cut

Número de opción	Descripción
1	5.0 cm (2.0 pulgadas) x 2.5 cm (1.0 pulgada) (extracción de barriga)
2	2.5 cm (1.0 pulgada) x 2.5 cm (1.0 pulgada) (extracción de barriga)
3	0.0 cm x 0.0 cm (extracción de barriga)
4	Otras dimensiones de retiro de las especificadas por el comprador
5	Extracción de toda la carne magra falsa (*trapezius* y *latissimus dorsi*)
6	Se deberá quitar el músculo *multifidus dorsi* (músculo del tigre)
7	El filete, como se describe en la pieza número 415, deberá quitarse
8	Extremo del Costillar con Ocho (8) Costillas, Corte del Centro
9	Extremo del Costillar con Nueve (9) Costillas, Corte del Centro
10	Extremo del Costillar con Diez (10) Costillas, Corte del Centro
11	Extremo del Costillar con Once (11) Costillas, Corte del Centro

412A — Pork Loin, Bone In, Center-Cut, 8 Ribs, Chine Bone Off

This item is as described in Item No. 412. In addition the tenderloin and the protruding edge of the chine bone and most of the spinal groove shall be removed and excluded. The *longissimus* shall not be scored.

See Pork Loin Option Chart on pg. 200 for Purchaser Specified Options.

412A — Chuleta de Cerdo, con Hueso, Corte del Centro, 8 Costillas, con Espinazo Rebajado

Esta pieza es igual a la pieza que se describe en el número 412. Además, el filete y el borde sobresaliente de las puntas y cuerpos vertebrales del espinazo, así como la mayor parte del canal raquídeo deberán quitarse. El *longissimus* no deberá ser sujeto a ningún corte.

Consulte el diagrama de opciones de lomo de cerdo en la página 200 para ver las opciones especificadas por el comprador (PSO).

412C — Pork Loin, Bone In, Center-Cut, 11 Ribs

This item is prepared from Item No. 410. The blade and the sirloin portions are excluded by straight cuts made approximately perpendicular to the split surface of the backbone and the length of the loin. The sirloin is removed anterior to the hip bone and associated cartilage exposing the *gluteus medius*. The blade portion shall be removed to leave no more than 11 ribs present. Floating rib(s) that do not show a cross section at the belly side are exempt. The belly shall be excluded by a straight cut (though a slight dorsal curvature is acceptable) from a point that is ventral to, but not more than 3.0 inches (7.5 cm) from, the *longissimus* at the shoulder (blade) end to a point on the leg (sirloin) end ventral to, but not more than 3.0 inches (7.5 cm) from, the *longissimus*. The blade bone, related cartilage, and overlying lean and fat shall also be excluded. Lumbar fat shall be trimmed not to exceed 0.5 inch (13 mm) in depth. The tenderloin shall remain intact. The spinal groove shall be evident on at least 75 percent of the vertebrae.

See Pork Loin Option Chart on pg. 200 for Purchaser Specified Options.

412C — Chuleta de Cerdo, con Hueso, Corte del Centro, 11 Costillas

Esta pieza se prepara con la pieza número 410. Las porciones de paleta y sirloin se quitan mediante cortes rectos aproximadamente perpendiculares a la superficie de separación de los huesos del espinazo y la longitud del lomo. El sirloin se quita por delante del hueso de la cadera y su cartílago asociado para exponer el *gluteus medius*. Se quitará la porción de la paleta y se dejarán no más de 11 costillas. La(s) costilla(s) flotante(s) que no muestren un corte transversal del lado de la barriga no se incluirán en el corte. La barriga se quitará mediante un corte recto (aunque se aceptará una leve curvatura dorsal) desde un punto ventral al *longissimus*, pero a no más de 7.5 cm (3.0 pulgadas) de distancia, en el extremo adyacente a la paleta (espaldilla), hasta un punto del extremo adyacente a la pierna (sirloin) ventral al *longissimus*, a no más de 7.5 cm (3.0 pulgadas) de distancia. El hueso de la paleta, el cartílago asociado, y la carne magra y la grasa que lo recubren también deberán quitarse. La grasa lumbar también deberá recortarse de forma que no exceda los 13 mm (0.5 pulgadas) de profundidad. El filete deberá permanecer intacto. El canal raquídeo deberá verse en por lo menos el 75% de las vértebras.

Consulte el diagrama de opciones de lomo de cerdo en la página 200 para ver las opciones especificadas por el comprador (PSO).

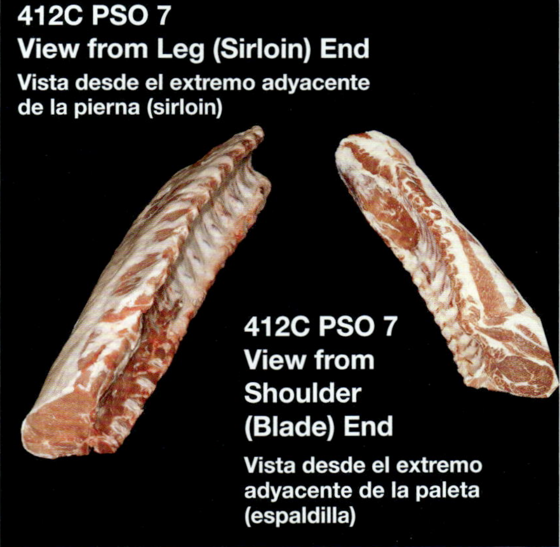

412D

412D — Pork Loin, Bone In, Center-Cut, 11 Ribs, Chine Bone Off

This item is as described in Item No. 412C. In addition the tenderloin and the protruding edge of the chine bone and most of the spinal groove shall be removed and excluded. The *longissimus* shall not be scored.

See Pork Loin Option Chart on pg. 200 for Purchaser Specified Options.

412D — Chuleta de Cerdo, con Hueso, Corte del Centro, 11 Costillas, con Espinazo Rebajado

Esta pieza es igual a la pieza que se describe en el número 412C. Además, el filete y el borde sobresaliente de las puntas y cuerpos vertebrales del espinazo, así como la mayor parte del canal raquídeo, deberán quitarse. El *longissimus* no deberá marcarse.

Consulte el diagrama de opciones de lomo de cerdo en la página 200 para ver las opciones especificadas por el comprador (PSO).

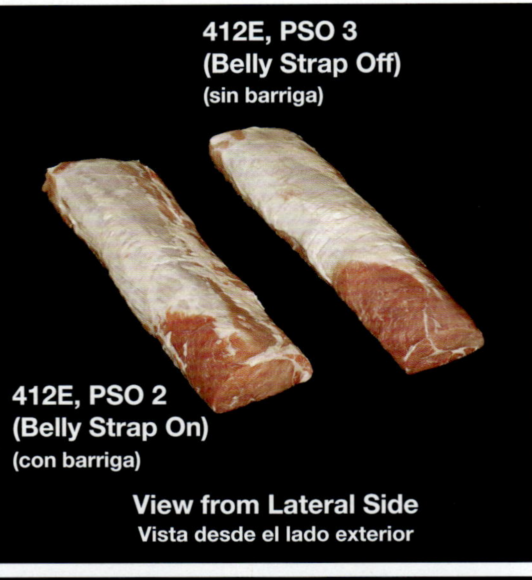

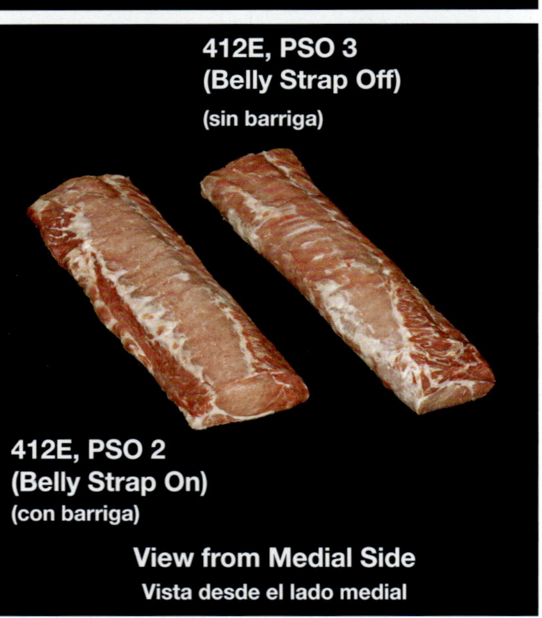

412E — Pork Loin, Boneless, Center-Cut, 11 Ribs

This item is prepared from Item No. 412C. The tenderloin and all bones and cartilages shall be excluded. On the shoulder (blade) end, the *longissimus* shall be approximately equal to or larger than the *spinalis dorsi,* and the *rhomboideus* shall not be present. The sirloin is eliminated anterior to the hip bone cartilage and shall expose the *gluteus medius.* The belly shall be excluded by a cut ventral to, but not more than 3.0 inches (7.5 cm) from, the *longissimus* at the shoulder (blade) end to a point on the leg (sirloin) end ventral to, but not more than 3.0 inches (7.5 cm) from, the *longissimus*.

See Pork Loin Option Chart on pg. 200 for Purchaser Specified Options.

412E — Chuleta (Lomo) de Cerdo, Deshuesado, Corte del Centro, 11 Costillas

Esta pieza se prepara con la pieza número 412C. El filete y todos los huesos y cartílagos deben quitarse. En el extremo adyacente a la paleta (espaldilla) el *longissimus* debe ser aproximadamente igual o más grande que el *spinalis dorsi,* y el *rhomboideus* no debe estar presente. El sirloin se retira mediante un corte anterior al cartílago del hueso de la cadera que deberá exponer al *gluteus medius.* La barriga se quitará mediante un corte ventral al *longissimus*, pero a no más de 7.5 cm (3.0 pulgadas) de distancia en el extremo adyacente a la paleta (espaldilla), hasta un punto del extremo adyacente a la pierna (sirloin) ventral al *longissimus*.

Consulte el diagrama de opciones de lomo de cerdo en la página 200 para ver las opciones especificadas por el comprador (PSO).

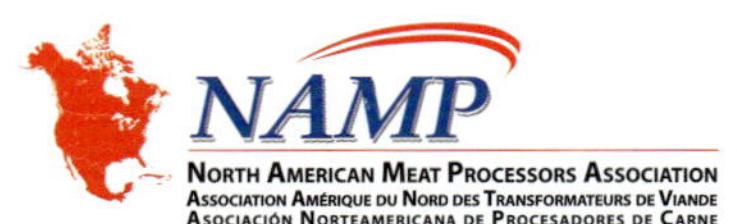

412G — Pork Loin, Center-Cut, Rib End (Rack)

This Center-Cut, Rib End, often referred to as a "Center-Cut Rack," is as described in Items No. 412A or 412D, except that the leg (sirloin) end shall be removed posterior to the last rib. To make the item roast ready, the purchaser may specify that the feather bones and the chine bones be removed.

Note: Purchaser may request that the ribs shall be Frenched by the exclusion of the intercostal meat and lean and fat between and over the ribs. The exposed portion of the rib bones shall not exceed 1.5 inches (3.8 cm), and the remaining intercostal meat and lean and fat over the rib bones shall not exceed 2.5 inches (6.3 cm) from the outer edge of the *longissimus* muscle.

See Pork Loin Option Chart on pg. 200 for Purchaser Specified Options.

412G — Chuleta de Cerdo, Corte del Centro, Extremo Adyacente al Costillar

El Corte del Centro, Extremo Adyacente al Costillar, con frecuencia denominado "Costillar del Centro", es igual a la pieza descrita en el número 412A o 412D, excepto que el extremo adyacente a la pierna (sirloin) debe quitarse en un punto posterior a la última costilla. Para preparar una pieza lista para asar, el comprador puede especificar que se quiten los cuerpos vertebrales del espinazo y las puntas del espinazo.

Importante: el comprador puede especificar que las costillas se preparen al Estilo Francés quitándoles la carne intercostal y la carne magra, así como la grasa entre y sobre las costillas. La porción de las costillas que queda expuesta no debe exceder los 3.8 cm (1.5 pulgadas) de longitud, y la carne intercostal, la grasa y la carne magra sobre las costillas no deben exceder los 6.3 cm (2.5 pulgadas) desde el borde exterior del músculo *longissimus*.

Consulte el diagrama de opciones de lomo de cerdo en la página 200 para ver las opciones especificadas por el comprador (PSO).

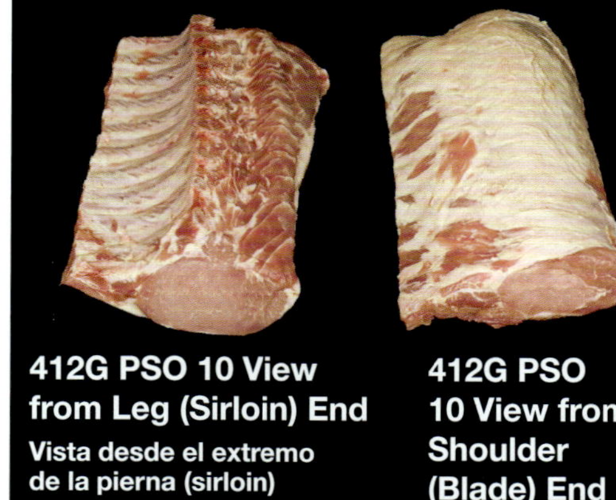

412G PSO 10 View from Leg (Sirloin) End
Vista desde el extremo de la pierna (sirloin)

412G PSO 10 View from Shoulder (Blade) End
Vista desde el extremo adyacente a la paleta (espaldilla)

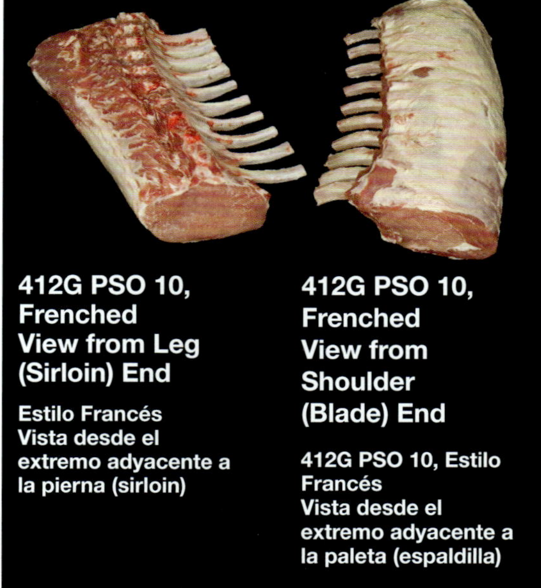

412G PSO 10, Frenched View from Leg (Sirloin) End
Estilo Francés Vista desde el extremo adyacente a la pierna (sirloin)

412G PSO 10, Frenched View from Shoulder (Blade) End
412G PSO 10, Estilo Francés Vista desde el extremo adyacente a la paleta (espaldilla)

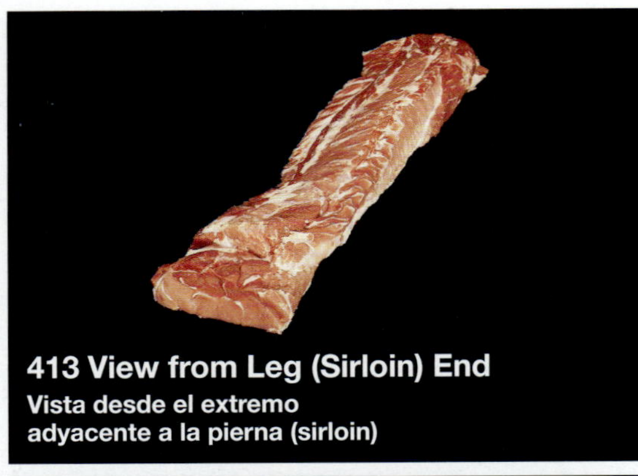

413 View from Leg (Sirloin) End
Vista desde el extremo
adyacente a la pierna (sirloin)

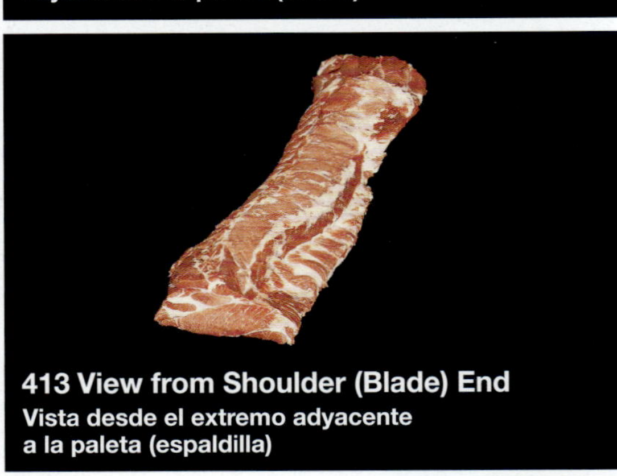

413 View from Shoulder (Blade) End
Vista desde el extremo adyacente
a la paleta (espaldilla)

413 — Pork Loin, Boneless

This item is prepared from Item No. 410. All skin, bones, cartilages, the tenderloin, and lean and fat overlying the blade bone shall be excluded. The leg (sirloin) end of the loin shall be exposed by a straight cut that shows no evidence of the *quadriceps femoris* nor the *longissimus*. The sirloin may be excluded immediately anterior to the hip bone pocket. In such cases, both the *longissimus* and *gluteus medius* shall be exposed on the leg (sirloin) end.

On the shoulder end, the *longissimus* shall be equal to or larger than the combined areas of the *splenius* and *semispinalis capitis.* The belly shall be removed by a cut that may display a slight dorsal curvature from a point ventral to, but not more than 2.0 inches (5.0 cm) from, the *longissimus* at the shoulder end to a point on the leg (sirloin) end no more than 1.0 inch (2.5 cm) ventral to the *longissimus* and/or *gluteus medius.* Surface fat shall not exceed 0.25 inch (6 mm) in depth, except in the hip pocket, which has no measurable fat requirement but shall be trimmed to the same contour as the rest of the trimmed fat surface. The hip bone area is defined as the area contained within two parallel lines, 1.0 inch (2.5 cm) on either side of the hip pocket area. To facilitate packaging, this item may be butterflied perpendicular to the length of the loin.

See Pork Loin Option Chart on pg. 200 for Purchaser Specified Options.

413 — Chuleta (Lomo) de Cerdo, Deshuesado

Esta pieza se prepara con la pieza número 410. Se deberá quitar toda la piel, los huesos, los cartílagos, el filete, y la carne magra y la grasa que recubren el hueso de la paleta. El extremo adyacente a la pierna (sirloin) deberá estar expuesto mediante un corte recto que no muestre la presencia del *quadriceps femoris* ni del *longissimus*. El sirloin puede quitarse en un punto inmediatamente anterior a la cavidad del hueso de la cadera. En esos casos, tanto el *longissimus* como el *gluteus medius* deberán estar expuestos en el extremo adyacente a la pierna (sirloin).

En el extremo adyacente a la paleta, el *longissimus* deberá ser igual o mayor a las áreas combinadas del *splenius* y el *semispinalis capitis.* La barriga deberá quitarse mediante un corte recto que puede presentar una leve curvatura dorsal desde un punto ventral al *longissimus*, pero a no más de 5.0 cm (2.0 pulgadas) de distancia, en el extremo de la espaldilla, hasta un punto del extremo adyacente a la pierna (sirloin) ventral al *longissimus* y/o *gluteus medius* que no se encuentre a más de 2.5 cm (1.0 pulgada). La cubierta de grasa no deberá exceder los 6 mm (0.25 pulgadas) de profundidad, excepto en la cavidad de la cadera, que no tiene requisitos de grasa medibles, pero deberá recortarse de grasa con el mismo contorno que el resto de la cubierta de grasa rebajada. El área del hueso de la cadera se define como el área contenida entre dos líneas paralelas, a 2.5 cm (1.0 pulgada) a cada lado del área de la cavidad de la cadera. Para facilitar el empaquetado, esta pieza puede abrirse por la mitad realizando un corte tipo mariposa perpendicular a la longitud del lomo.

Consulte el diagrama de opciones de lomo de cerdo en la página 200 para ver las opciones especificadas por el comprador (PSO).

413A Pork Loin, Boneless, Roast

The roast is prepared from a boneless loin as described in Item No. 413 that is further cut into two pieces of approximately equal length. These pieces shall be reversed with the boned surfaces positioned together so that the blade and sirloin portions are on opposite ends. The pieces shall be trimmed so that one piece of the boneless loin will not extend more than 1.0 inch (2.5 cm) in total length past its opposing piece. The boneless loin shall be netted or tied, often referred to as BRT (boned, rolled, and tied).

See Pork Loin Option Chart on pg. 200 for Purchaser Specified Options.

413A Chuleta (Lomo) de Cerdo, Deshuesado, Rollo Amarrado

El rollo amarrado se prepara con un lomo sin hueso como se describe en la pieza número 413, que luego se corta en dos piezas de aproximadamente igual tamaño. Estas piezas se deben invertir y las superficies deshuesadas se deben colocar juntas, de manera que las porciones de paleta y el sirloin estén en extremos opuestos. Las piezas deberán recortarse de modo que una pieza de lomo deshuesado no se extienda más de 2.5 cm (1.0 pulgada) de longitud total más allá de su pieza opuesta. El lomo deshuesado deberá atarse o colocarse en una malla, lo que generalmente se llama DEA (deshuesado, enrollado y enmallado).

Consulte el diagrama de opciones de lomo de cerdo en la página 200 para ver las opciones especificadas por el comprador (PSO).

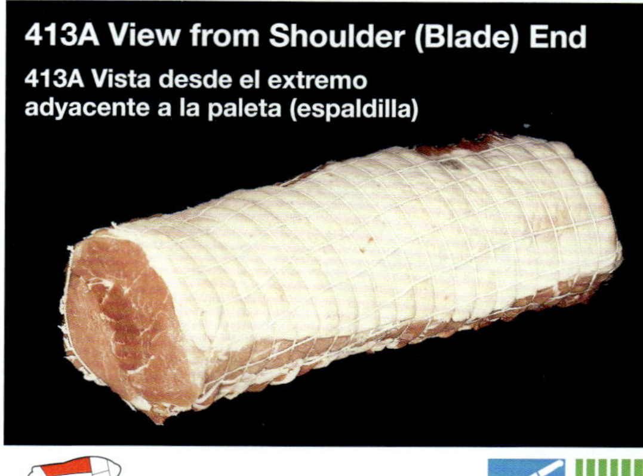

413A View from Leg (Sirloin) End
Vista desde el extremo adyacente a la pierna (sirloin)

413A View from Shoulder (Blade) End
413A Vista desde el extremo adyacente a la paleta (espaldilla)

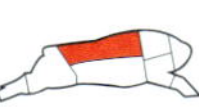

413B Pork Loin, Boneless, Special

This item is prepared as described in Item No. 413A, except the entire *infraspinatus, supraspinatus, latissimus dorsi,* and *trapezius* muscles shall be excluded. The belly shall be excluded immediately ventral to the *longissimus* and *gluteus medius*. The *iliocostalis* and the obliquus internus abdominis muscles shall also be excluded. Powdered wheat gluten or other binding agents may be used to bind the boned surface of each half of the netted or tied loin together. Purchaser may specify a type of binder to be used. The use of all binding agents and their application shall be in accordance with FSIS regulations. When binding agents other than wheat gluten are used, the product name shall be changed accordingly.

See Pork Loin Option Chart on pg. 200 for Purchaser Specified Options.

413B Chuleta (Lomo) de Cerdo, Deshuesado, Rollo Amarrado, Especial

Esta pieza se prepara como se describe en la pieza 413A, excepto que los músculos *infraspinatus, supraspinatus, latissimus dorsi* y *trapezius* deberán quitarse. La barriga deberá quitarse en un punto inmediatamente ventral al *longissimus* y al *gluteus medius*. El *iliocostalis* y los músculos obliquus internus abdominis también deberán quitarse. Se podrá utilizar gluten de trigo en polvo u otro agente aglutinante para unir las superficies deshuesadas de cada mitad del lomo atado o enmallado. El comprador puede especificar el tipo de aglutinante a utilizar. El uso de todos los agentes aglutinantes y su aplicación deberá cumplir con los reglamentos de FSIS (Servicio de Inspección e Inocuidad Alimentaria, por sus siglas en inglés). Cuando se utilicen agentes aglutinantes diferentes al gluten de trigo, el nombre del producto deberá cambiarse de acuerdo con ello.

Consulte el diagrama de opciones de lomo de cerdo en la página 200 para ver las opciones especificadas por el comprador (PSO).

413C — Pork Loin, Loin Eye

This item will consist of the *longissimus* and *multifidus dorsi* muscles.

An individual muscle (IM) item consisting only of the *longissimus* may be specified by requesting PSO 6, as shown in photo. See diagram Item No. 414.

413C — Chuleta (Lomo) de Cerdo, Ojo del Lomo

Esta pieza consistirá en los músculos *longissimus* y *multifidus dorsi*.

Se puede especificar que la pieza se prepare con un único músculo (IM) que consista en el *longissimus* solicitando la PSO 6, como se muestra en la imagen. Consulte el diagrama de la pieza 414.

414 View from Leg (Sirloin) End (Medial View)

Vista desde el extremo adyacente a la pierna (sirloin) (vista medial)

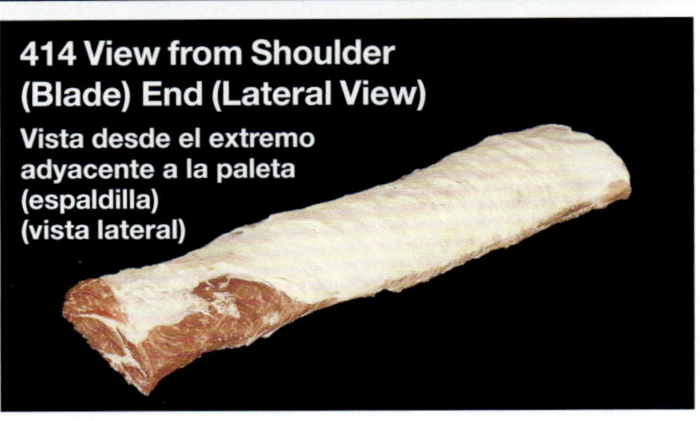

414 View from Shoulder (Blade) End (Lateral View)

Vista desde el extremo adyacente a la paleta (espaldilla) (vista lateral)

414 — Pork Loin, Canadian Back

This item is prepared from Item No. 410. All bones, catilages, tenderloin, and lean and fat overlying the blade bone shall be excluded. The shoulder (blade) and leg (sirloin) ends shall be excluded by straight cuts approximately parallel to each other. On the shoulder (blade) end, the *longissimus* shall be equal to or larger than the combined areas of the *splenius* and *semispinalis capitis*, and the sirloin shall be removed immediately anterior to the hip cartilage. The belly side shall be removed immediately ventral to the *longisimus*.

PSO: 1 – *Multifidus dorsi* (tiger) muscle shall be removed, as shown by dotted line in Medial View.

414 — Chuleta (Lomo) de Cerdo, Estilo Canadiense

Esta pieza se prepara con la pieza número 410. Se deberán quitar todos los huesos, cartílagos, el filete, y la carne magra y la grasa que recubren el hueso de la paleta. Los extremos adyacentes a la paleta (espaldilla) y la pierna (sirloin) deberán excluirse mediante cortes rectos aproximadamente paralelos uno con respecto al otro. En el extremo adyacente a la paleta (espaldilla), el (*longissimus* deberá ser igual o más grande que las áreas combinadas del *splenius* y el *semispinalis capitis*, y el sirloin deberá quitarse en un punto inmediatamente anterior al cartílago de la cadera. El lado de la barriga deberá quitarse en un punto inmediatamente ventral al *longissimus*.

PSO: 1– *El multifidus dorsi* (músculo del tigre) deberá retirarse como lo indica la línea punteada en la vista medial.

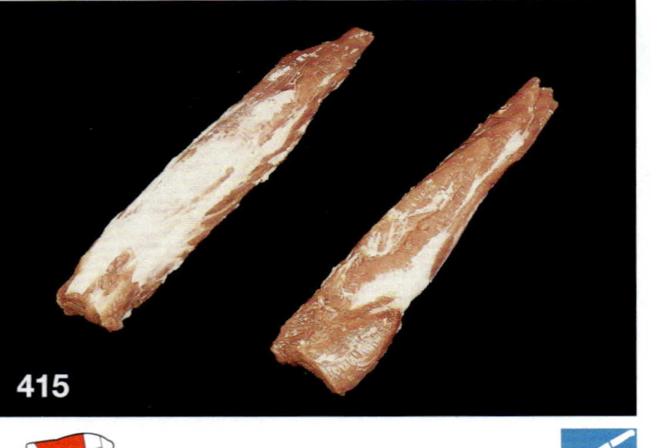

415 — Pork Tenderloin

This item is prepared from Item No. 410. The tenderloin shall be removed intact and shall consist of the *psoas major, psoas minor,* and *iliacus* only. The side muscle (*psoas minor*) shall be removed if not firmly attached. The anterior portion (tail end) shall be trimmed so that the tail is not split more than 1.0 inch (2.5 cm). The tenderloin shall be practically free of fat.

415 — Filete de Cerdo

Esta pieza se prepara con la pieza número 410. El filete deberá retirarse intacto y consistirá únicamente en los músculos *psoas mayor, psoas menor* e *iliacus*. El músculo de al lado (*psoas menor*) deberá quitarse si no se encuentra firmemente unido. La porción anterior (extremo de la cola) debe estar recortada de grasa y limpia de forma que la cola no esté fraccionada a más de 2.5 cm (1.0 pulgada). El filete debe estar prácticamente libre de grasa.

415A — Pork Tenderloin, Side Muscle Off

The tenderloin shall be as described in Item No. 415, except the side strip muscle (*psoas minor*) shall be removed.

See page 210-211 for Items 416–416D.

415A — Filete de Cerdo, sin Músculo de al Lado

El filete será igual a la pieza que se describe en la número 415, excepto que se deberá quitar el músculo de al lado *psoas menor*.

Consulte las páginas 210-211 para ver las piezas 416–416D.

417 — Pork Shoulder Hocks

Shoulder hocks shall be separated from the front feet at or above the upper knee joint. Shoulder hocks shall be at least 2.0 inches (5.0 cm) in length.

417 — Chamorros de Paleta de Cerdo

Los chamorros de paleta se separarán de las patas delanteras a nivel de la articulación o por encima de ella. Los chamorros de paleta deberán tener al menos 5.0 cm (2.0 pulgadas) de longitud.

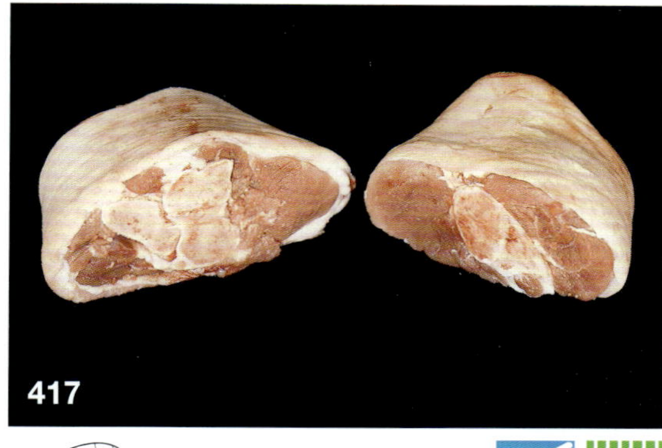

417A — Pork Leg (Fresh Ham) Hocks

The pork leg or fresh ham hocks shall be separated from the hind feet at or above the hock joint. The hocks shall be at least 2.0 inches (5.0 cm) in length.

417A — Pierna de Cerdo (Jamón Fresco), Chamorros

La pierna de cerdo o jamón fresco se separará de la pata trasera en la articulación del chamorro. Los chamorros deberán tener al menos 5.0 cm (2.0 pulgadas) de longitud.

418 Pork Trimmings

Trimmings shall be prepared from any portion of the carcass that yields product that will meet the end-item requirements. Trimmings shall be free of bones, cartilages, skin, seedy mammary tissue, exposed heavy tendons, and lymph glands including the *prefemoral, popliteal, prescapular* and any other exposed lymph glands. The tendinous ends of shanks shall be removed to a point where a cross-sectional cut exposes at least 75 percent lean.

Purchaser shall specify the fat content percentage desired. The fat percentage shall be verified by one of the following purchaser specified options. If not specified, the fat content shall be verified with PSO 2 requirements.

PSO: 1 – Fat content shall be declared on the product label

2 – Contractor shall submit documentation of fat analysis to purchaser

3 – Fat content certified by AMS (see Quality Assurance Provisions)

4 – Samples selected by AMS and sent to purchaser- designated laboratory

418 Recortes de Cerdo

Los recortes se prepararán con cualquier porción de la canal que dé como resultado un producto que cumpla con los requisitos de la pieza final. Los recortes deberán estar libres de huesos, cartílagos, piel, tejido mamario granuloso, tendones gruesos expuestos y ganglios linfáticos, incluyendo los ganglios linfáticos *prefemorales, los poplíteos, los prescapulares* y cualquier otro ganglio linfático expuesto. Los extremos tendinosos de los chamorros deberán quitarse hasta un punto donde el corte transversal muestre al menos un 75% de carne magra.

El comprador deberá especificar el porcentaje de contenido de grasa que desea. El porcentaje de grasa se verificará mediante una de las siguientes opciones especificadas por el comprador. En caso de que no se especifiquen, el contenido de grasa se verificará con los requisitos PSO 2.

PSO: 1 – El contenido de grasa deberá declararse en la etiqueta del producto

2 – El contratista deberá presentarle al comprador la documentación del análisis de grasa

3 – Contenido de grasa certificado por el Servicio de Mercadeo Agrícola (consulte las disposiciones de control de calidad)

4 – Muestras seleccionadas por el Servicio de Mercadeo Agrícola y enviadas al laboratorio designado por el comprador

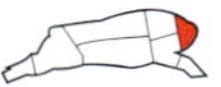

419 Pork Jowl

The jowl is removed from the shoulder as described in Item No. 403. Jowls shall be reasonably rectangular in shape and trimmed of loose tissue, bloody discoloration and other significant objectionable materials. Unless otherwise specified, the jowls shall have all skin removed.

419 Papada de Cerdo

La papada se separa de la paleta (espaldilla) como se describe en la pieza número 403. Las papadas deberán tener una forma razonablemente rectangular y se recortará el tejido suelto, la decoloración sanguinolenta y otros materiales objetables importantes. A menos que se especifique lo contrario, las papadas no deberán tener piel.

420 — Pork Pig's Feet, Front

The feet shall be removed at or above the upper knee joint of the front legs. All feet shall be trimmed practically free of hair and hair roots. Purchasers desiring Hind Feet should specify Item No. 420A.

420 — Manitas de Cerdo

Las manitas deberán separarse de las piernas delanteras en la articulación más superior de la rodilla o por encima de ella. Todas las manitas deberán ser recortadas de grasa hasta que estén prácticamente libres de pelos y raíces de pelos. Los compradores que deseen patas traseras deben especificar la pieza número 420A.

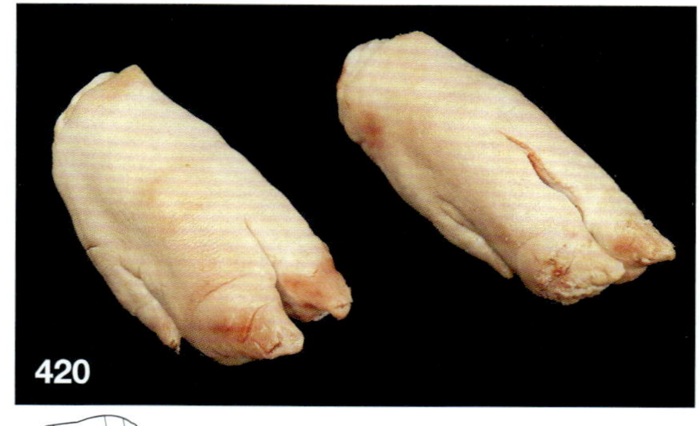

421 — Pork Neck Bones

The neck bones shall contain at least two cervical vertebrae and at least one, but not more than four, thoracic vertebrae, adjoining ribs, and intercostal lean.

421 — Huesos del Pescuezo de Cerdo

Los huesos del pescuezo deberán contener al menos dos vértebras cervicales y al menos una, pero no más de cuatro, vértebras torácicas, costillas adyacentes y carne magra intercostal.

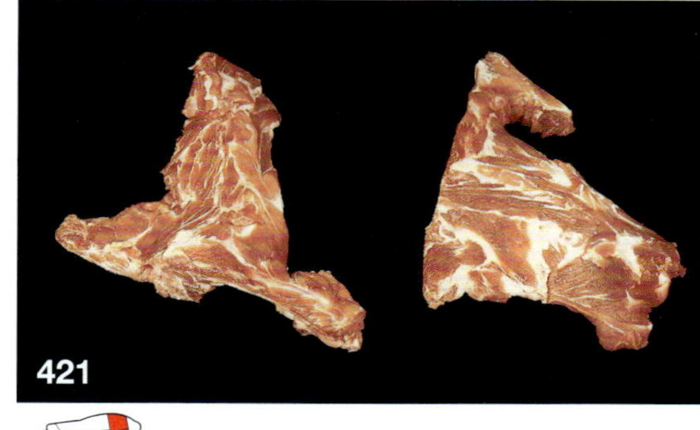

422 — Pork Loin, Back Ribs

The back ribs shall consist of at least eight ribs and related intercostal meat from a bone in pork loin. The back ribs section shall be intact, and the bodies of the thoracic vertebrae shall be removed except that small portions of the vertebrae may remain between the rib ends. When specified, the "skin" (*peritoneum*) shall be removed from the inside surface of the ribs and intercostal meat.

422 — Chuleta de Lomo de Cerdo, Costillas del Espaldar/Chuleta

Las costillas de espaldar consistirán en por lo menos ocho costillas y la carne intercostal asociada obtenidas a partir de un lomo de cerdo con hueso. La sección de las costillas del espaldar deberá estar intacta y el cuerpo de las vértebras torácicas deberá quitarse, excepto pequeñas porciones de las vértebras que podrán permanecer entre los extremos de las costillas. Cuando así se especifique, la "membrana" (*peritoneo*) deberá quitarse de la superficie interior de las costillas y la carne intercostal.

422 View from Fat Side
Vista desde el lado de la grasa

422 View from Bone Side
Vista desde el lado del hueso

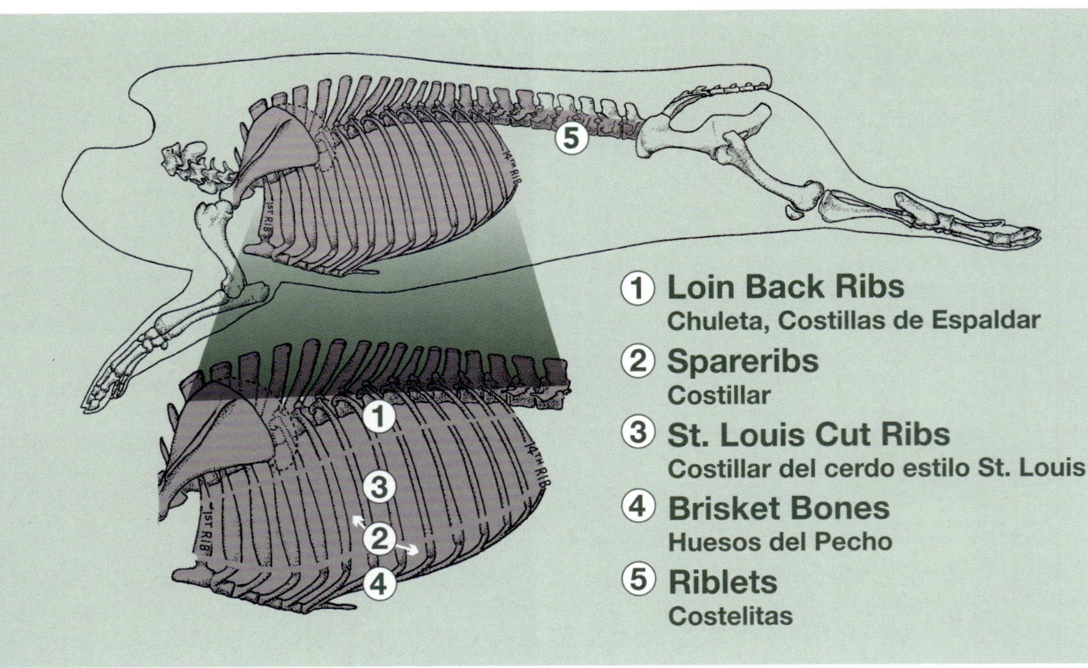

Pork Bone Structure Chart & Rib Guide

Diagrama de estructura esquelética y guía de costillas del cerdo

① **Loin Back Ribs**
Chuleta, Costillas de Espaldar

② **Spareribs**
Costillar

③ **St. Louis Cut Ribs**
Costillar del cerdo estilo St. Louis

④ **Brisket Bones**
Huesos del Pecho

⑤ **Riblets**
Costelitas

416 **Pork Spareribs**

Spareribs shall contain at least 11 ribs and associated costal cartilages and may include portions of the sternum and diaphragm. The membranous portion of the diaphragm close to the lean, and any portion of the diaphragm not firmly attached close to the inside surface of the ribs, shall be excluded. The lean shall not extend more than 2.0 inches (5.0 cm) past the curvature of the last rib and costal cartilage. Heart fat on the inside surface of the ribs shall not exceed 0.25 inch (6 mm) average depth. Leaf fat shall be trimmed practically free from the diaphragm and *transverse abdominis.*

Size references for Pork Spareribs can be found on page 183.

❦ In Canada, this item is referred to as Side Ribs.

416 **Costillar de Cerdo, Costillas de la Media Canal**

El costillar deberá contener al menos 11 costillas y los cartílagos costales asociados, y podrá incluir porciones del esternón y el diafragma. Se deberá quitar la porción membranosa del diafragma cercana a la carne magra, y cualquier porción del diafragma que no se encuentre firmemente unida cerca de la superficie interior de las costillas. La carne magra no podrá extenderse más de 5.0 cm (2.0 pulgadas) más allá de la curvatura de la última costilla y el cartílago costal. La grasa circundante al corazón que queda sobre la superficie interna de las costillas no deberá exceder los 6 mm (0.25 pulgadas) de profundidad promedio. La tela de grasa visceral debe limpiarse para que quede prácticamente libre del diafragma y el *transverse abdominis.*

Las referencias de tamaño para los costillares de cerdo se encuentran en la página 182.

❦ En Canadá, esta pieza se denomina "Side Ribs".

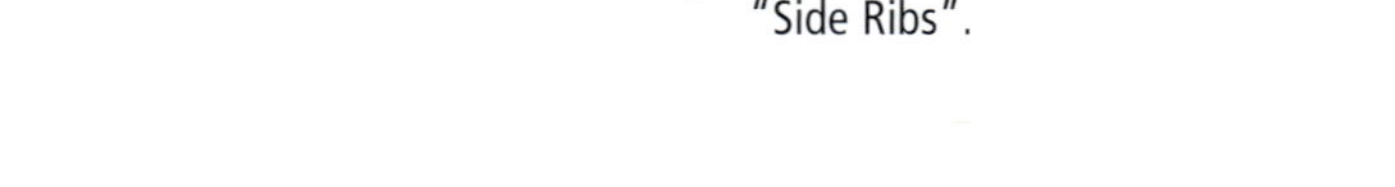

NAMP
NORTH AMERICAN MEAT PROCESSORS ASSOCIATION
ASSOCIATION AMÉRIQUE DU NORD DES TRANSFORMATEURS DE VIANDE
ASOCIACIÓN NORTEAMERICANA DE PROCESADORES DE CARNE

416A — Pork Spareribs, St. Louis Style

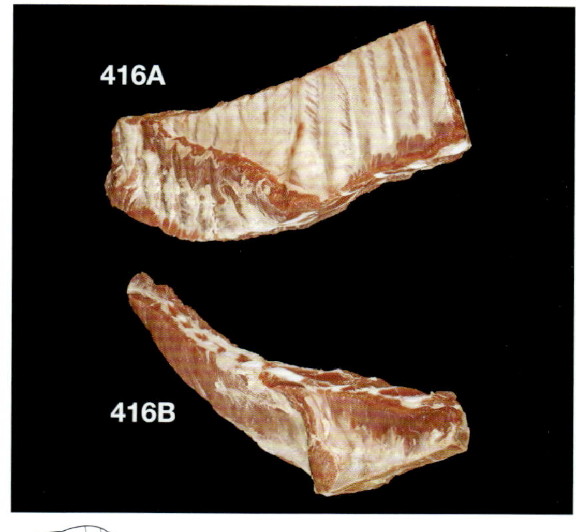

The spareribs shall be as described in Item No. 416, except the sternum and the ventral portion of the costal cartilages shall be excluded along with the flank portion. The breast shall be removed at a point that is dorsal to the curvature of the costal cartilages. If specified by the purchaser the diaphragm shall be excluded. Purchaser may also specify that the spareribs be separated into two approximate equal portions by a lengthwise cut.

🍁 In Canada, this item is referred to as Side Rib, Centre Cut.

416A — Costillar de Cerdo, Costillas de Media Canal estilo San Luis, Corte del Centro

El costillar es igual a la pieza descrita en el número 416, excepto que el esternón y la porción ventral de los cartílagos costales deberán quitarse junto con la porción de falda. El pecho deberá quitarse en un punto dorsal a la curvatura de los cartílagos costales. Si el comprador así lo especifica, se deberá quitar el diafragma. El comprador también podrá especificar que el costillar esté separado en dos porciones aproximadamente iguales mediante un corte longitudinal.

🍁 En Canadá, esta pieza se denomina "Side Rib, Centre Cut".

416B — Pork Spareribs, Brisket Bones

This item consists of the sternum, costal cartilages, and attached lean from Item No. 416 that was excluded when producing Item No. 416A.

416B — Costillar de Cerdo, Huesos del Pecho

Esta pieza consiste en el esternón, los cartílagos costales y la carne magra unida de la pieza número 416 que se excluyó cuando se obtuvo la pieza 416A.

416C — Pork Spareribs, Breast Off

This item is as described in Item No. 416, except the sternum is excluded.

416C — Costillar de Cerdo, sin Pecho

Esta pieza es igual a la pieza que se describe en la número 416, excepto que se debe quitar el esternón.

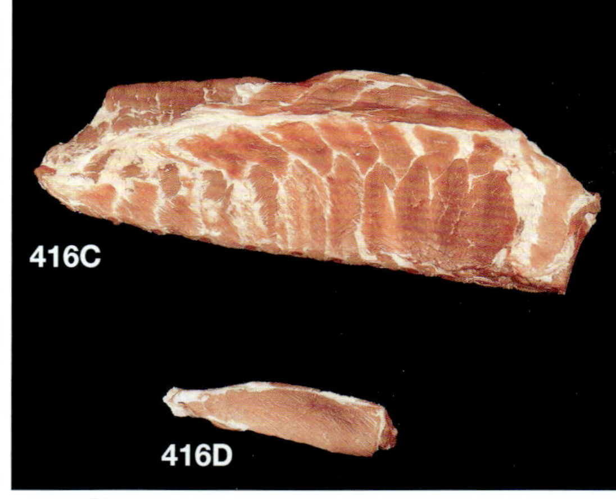

416D — Pork Breast Bones

This item shall consist of the breast (sternum) bone and associated lean and fat that was excluded when producing Item No. 416C.

416D — Pecho de Cerdo, Huesos

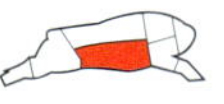

Esta pieza consiste en el hueso del pecho (esternón) y la carne magra y grasa asociada que fue retirada cuando se obtuvo la pieza 416C.

423 Alternative Option
423 Opción alternativa

423 — Pork Loin, Country-Style Ribs

This item shall be prepared from the shoulder (blade) end of a bone in pork loin and shall include not less than three or more than six ribs. The chine bone shall be excluded by a cut that exposes lean meat between the feather bones and ribs. Country-style ribs shall be divided into approximately equal portions by cutting through the flesh from the rib end (ventral) side to the feather bone side without severing the muscle cover (*trapezius*), leaving both portions attached. This cut leaves the blade bone and overlying lean and fat in one portion and the ribs and feather bones in the other.

As an alternative option, the chine bone as described above together with the blade bone, related cartilage, and overlying lean and fat shall be also be excluded. The country-style ribs shall also be separated into approximately equal portions by cutting through the flesh where the chine bones were removed. This cut leaves the ribs in one portion and the feather bones in the other. Both portions shall be packed into the same container. Unless the alternative option is specified, the first stated option applies.

423 — Chuleta de Cerdo, Costillas Estilo Campestre

Esta pieza se preparará con el extremo adyacente de la paleta (espaldilla) de un lomo de cerdo con hueso, e incluirá no menos de tres ni más de seis costillas. Se deberá excluir el espinazo a fin de exponer la parte magra entre las costillas y las puntas del espinazo. Las costillas estilo campestre se dividirán en porciones aproximadamente iguales mediante cortes a través de la carne desde el lado del extremo de las costillas (ventral) hacia el lado de la punta del espinazo, sin cortar la cobertura muscular (*trapezius*), dejando las dos porciones unidas. Este corte deja el hueso de la paleta y la carne magra y la grasa que lo recubren en una porción y las costillas y las puntas del espinazo en la otra.

Como opción alternativa, se quitará el espinazo como se describe anteriormente, junto con el hueso de la paleta, el cartílago asociado, la carne magra y la grasa que lo recubren. Las costillas estilo campestre también se separarán en porciones aproximadamente iguales realizando cortes a través de la carne donde se quitaron las puntas del espinazo. Este corte deja las costillas en una porción y las puntas del espinazo en la otra. Ambas porciones deberán empacarse en el mismo envase. A menos que se especifique la opción alternativa, se llevará a cabo la primera opción.

424

424 — Pork Loin, Riblet

This item is derived from the transverse processes (sometimes referred to as "paddle" or "finger" bones) and the associated lean from the lumbar vertebrae of any bone in pork loin item after the removal of the tenderloin and the loin eye. Riblets shall contain no less than four transverse processes, be held intact by the associated lean, and include no more than two rib bones. The item shall be trimmed practically free of surface fat.

 In Canada, Riblets refer to the rib portion of the neck bones.

424 — Chuleta de Cerdo, Costelitas (Riblets)

Esta pieza es un derivado de las apófisis transversas (en ocasiones llamadas "paletitas" o "huesecillos" tipo botana") y la carne magra asociada de las vértebras lumbares de cualquier pieza de lomo de cerdo con hueso, después de haber quitado el filete y el ojo del lomo. Las costelitas no deberán contener menos de cuatro apófisis transversas, deberán mantenerse intactas junto con su carne magra asociada y no deberán incluir más de dos costillas. La pieza debe limpiarse para que quede prácticamente libre de cobertura de grasa.

En Canadá las Costelitas hacen también referencia a la porción de costillas cerca de los huesos del pescuezo.

435B — Pork for Kabobs

This item shall be prepared from any portion of the carcass that yields product that meets the end-item requirements. Unless otherwise specified, the inner shank (heel portion of the leg), shank meat, and jowls shall be excluded. The Kabobs shall be free of bones, cartilages, skin, heavy connective tissue, seedy mammary tissue, and lymph glands. When the inner shank is allowed by the purchaser, the *flexor digitorum superficialis* (mouse muscle) shall be removed from the *gastrocnemius* through the natural seams. To facilitate processing, the meat may be frozen and/or tempered one time only. The meat shall be either hand or mechanically cut. Grinding is not permitted. Unless purchaser specifies otherwise, at least 90 percent by weight of the resulting Kabobs shall be of a size equivalent to not less than a 1.0 inch (2.5 cm) cube or not more than a 1.5 inches (3.8 cm) cube. No individual surface shall be more than 3.0 inches (7.5 cm) in length. The fat thickness of the surface and/or seam fat shall not exceed 0.125 inch (3 mm) at any point.

If purchaser desires Diced Pork, specify Item No. 435. Diced Pork has the same material requirements as Item No. 435B except for the size of the product dice. Unless otherwise specified, at least 75 percent by weight of the resulting dices shall be of a size equivalent to not less than 0.75 inch (19 mm) cube or not more than a 1.5 inches (3.8 cm) cube. No individual surface shall be more than 2.5 inches (6.3 cm) in length. The surface and/or seam fat shall not exceed 0.25 inch (6 mm) thickness at any point.

Purchaser also has the option to specify Item No. 435A, Pork for Stewing. The only specification difference between Item No. 435A and Item No. 435 is that at least 85 percent by weight of the dices shall meet the size requirements.

435B — Trozos de Cerdo para Brochetas

Esta pieza se preparará con cualquier porción de canal que dé como resultado un producto que cumpla con los requisitos de la pieza final. A menos que se especifique lo contrario, se quitará la parte interna del chamorro (porción del talón), la carne del chamorro y la papada. Los trozos para brochetas no deberán contener huesos, cartílagos, piel, tejido conectivo grueso, tejido mamario granuloso y ganglios linfáticos. Cuando el comprador permita que se conserve la parte interna del chamorro, el músculo *flexor digitorum superficialis* (ratón) deberá quitarse del *gastrocnemius* a través de las vetas naturales. Para facilitar el procesamiento, la carne puede congelarse y/o atemperarse solamente una vez. La carne se cortará a mano o a máquina. La molienda no está permitida. A menos que el comprador especifique lo contrario, al menos el 90% del peso de los trozos resultantes deberán tener un tamaño equivalente a un cubo de no menos de 2.5 cm (1.0 pulgada) y no más de 3.8 cm (1.5 pulgadas). Ninguna superficie individual debe ser mayor a 7.5 cm (3.0 pulgadas) de longitud. El grosor de la cubierta de grasa y/o las vetas de grasa intermuscular no deberá exceder los 3 mm (0.125 pulgadas) en ningún punto.

Si el comprador desea Carne de Cerdo Troceada, especifique la pieza número 435. La Carne de Cerdo Troceada tiene los mismos requisitos de material que la pieza número 435B, salvo el tamaño de los trozos de producto. A menos que se especifique lo contrario, por lo menos el 75% del peso de los trozos resultantes deberán tener un tamaño equivalente a un cubo de no menos de 19 mm (0.75 pulgadas) y no más de 3.8 cm (1.5 pulgadas). Ninguna superficie individual debe ser mayor a 6.3 cm (2.5 pulgadas) de longitud. La cubierta de grasa o las vetas de grasa intermuscular no deberán exceder los 6 mm (0.25 pulgadas) de grosor en ningún punto.

El comprador también tiene la opción de especificar la pieza número 435A, Trozos de Cerdo para Cocido/Guisado. La única especificación diferente entre la pieza número 435A y la pieza número 435 es que por lo menos el 85% del peso de los cubos deberá cumplir los requisitos de tamaño.

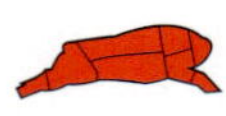

496 — Gound Pork

Material - Ground pork may be prepared from any portion of the carcass that will meet the end-item requirements. The meat shall be free of bones, cartilages, seedy mammary tissue, heavy exposed tendons, and exposed heavy (opaque) connective tissue. The prefemoral, popliteal, prescapular, and other exposed lymph glands shall be excluded. The tendinous ends of shanks shall be excluded so that a crosssectional cut exposes at least 75 percent lean. Unless otherwise specified, previously frozen product may be incorporated into the mixture. The quantity of frozen material may also be limited by the purchaser.

When specified by the purchaser, product labeled "lean finely textured pork" may also be combined with boneless pork meeting the above material requirements, provided it does not exceed 20 percent by weight of the combined finished product. Lean finely textured pork shall be produced and labeled in accordance with FSIS regulations.

Processing – The boneless meat shall be ground at least once through a plate having holes not larger than 1.0 inch (2.5 cm) in diameter. Alternatively, boneless pork may be chopped or machine cut by any method provided the texture and appearance of the product after final grinding is typical of ground pork prepared by grinding only. Unless otherwise specified, final grinding shall be through a plate having holes 0.1875 inch (5 mm) in diameter. When appropriate, a bone collector/extruder system may be used during the final grind. Pork may be thoroughly blended at least once prior to final grinding. However, the ground pork shall not be mixed after final grinding. Initial reduction in size, blending, final grinding, and packaging shall be a continuous sequence.

When coarse ground pork is specified, boneless meat shall be ground once through a plate having holes no larger than 1.0 inch (2.5 cm) and no smaller than 0.625 inch (16 mm) in diameter. Alternatively, the boneless meat may be ground twice, with the smallest plate having holes no larger than 1.0 inch (2.5 cm) and no smaller than 0.75 inch (19 mm) in diameter. Coarse ground meat may be blended after grinding or between grinds to assure uniformity of fat content. The term "coarse ground" shall appear in the product label.

Fat Content – Unless otherwise specified, the fat content shall not exceed 22 percent. Purchaser, however, may specify any fat content provided it does not exceed 30 percent.

Soy Protein Product (SPP) – Item No. 496A Ground Pork and Soy Protein is approved for use in Child Nutrition Programs under USDA Food and Nutrition Service (FNS) regulations. Item No. 496B is similar except that the SPP need not comply with FNS requirements and must be labeled Pork Patty Mix.

496 — Carne Molida de Cerdo

Material - La carne molida de cerdo puede prepararse a partir de cualquier porción de la canal que dé como resultado un producto que cumpla con los requisitos de la pieza final. La carne no debe contener huesos, cartílagos, tejido mamario granuloso, tendones gruesos expuestos ni tejido conectivo grueso (opaco). Se extraerán los ganglios linfáticos prefemorales, poplíteos, prescapulares y cualquier otro ganglio linfático expuesto. Se extraerán los extremos tendinosos de los chamorros, de modo que un corte de sección transversal presente al menos un 75% de carne magra. A menos que se especifique lo contrario, se podrá incorporar producto previamente congelado a la mezcla. El comprador también podrá limitar la cantidad de material congelado.

Cuando el comprador así lo especifique, el producto etiquetado como "carne magra de cerdo finamente texturizada" también puede combinarse con carne deshuesada de cerdo que cumpla con los requisitos especificados anteriormente, siempre que no exceda el 20% del producto combinado final. La carne magra de cerdo finamente texturizada deberá producirse y etiquetarse de acuerdo a las reglamentaciones de FSIS (Servicio de Inspección e Inocuidad Alimentaria, por sus siglas en inglés).

Procesamiento – La carne deshuesada deberá molerse al menos una vez a través de una placa con orificios que no superen los 2.5 cm (1.0 pulgada) de diámetro. De forma alternativa, la carne deshuesada puede picarse o cortarse a máquina mediante cualquier método, siempre y cuando la textura y la apariencia del producto después de la molienda final sean las típicas de la carne molida de cerdo preparada únicamente mediante molienda. A menos que se especifique lo contrario, la molienda final deberá realizarse a través de una placa con orificios de 5 mm (0.1875 pulgadas) de diámetro. Cuando corresponda, se podrá utilizar un sistema de extrusión/colector de huesos durante la molienda final. La carne de cerdo debe mezclarse muy bien al menos una vez antes de la molienda final. Sin embargo, la carne molida de cerdo no deberá mezclarse después de la molienda final. La disminución inicial en tamaño, el mezclado, la molienda final y el empaquetado seguirá una secuencia continua.

Cuando se especifica carne de cerdo molida gruesa, la carne de cerdo deshuesada debe molerse una vez a través de una placa con orificios que no superen los 2.5 cm (1.0 pulgada) ni sean inferiores a 16 mm (0.625 pulgadas) de diámetro. Al no especificarse lo anterior, la carne deshuesada puede molerse dos veces con la placa más pequeña de orificios que no superen 2.5 cm (1.0 pulgada) ni sean inferiores a 19 mm (0.75 pulgadas) de diámetro. La carne molida gruesa puede mezclarse después de la molienda o entre moliendas para asegurar la uniformidad del contenido de grasa. El término "Coarse Ground" (molido grueso) deberá aparecer en la etiqueta del producto.

Contenido de grasa – A menos que se especifique lo contrario, el contenido de grasa no excederá el 22%. Sin embargo, el comprador podrá especificar cualquier contenido de grasa, siempre que no exceda el 30%.

Producto Proteico Vegetal (PPV) Añadido Según La Normativa – La pieza número 496A, Carne Molida de Cerdo con Producto Proteico Vegetal, se encuentra aprobada para utilizarse en Programas de Nutrición Infantil regulados por el Servicio de Nutrición y Alimentos (FNS, por sus siglas en inglés) del Departamento de Agricultura de E.U.A. La pieza número 496B es similar, excepto que no es necesario que el PPV cumpla con los requisitos de FNS y debe etiquetarse como "Pork Patty Mix" (Mezcla para Hamburguesa de Cerdo).

Center of the Plate Training®

from the producers of The Meat Buyer's Guide®

Capacitación en ingredientes principales del plato

de los realizadores de la Guía para Compradores de Carne®

Course Specifics

Center of the Plate Training® offered by the North American Meat Processors Association (NAMP) is a first-hand look at how carcasses are converted into portioned items commonly traded in the foodservice and retail meat business. The course covers all the major center of the plate protein items: beef, veal, lamb, pork, and poultry (in some locations).

This course is held two to three times annually across North America. It spans two to three days of classroom learning, with presentations by industry experts. You also will receive a copy of the NAMP *Meat Buyer's Guide®*, which is used extensively in the course.

What You Will Learn From This Course

- The IMPS/NAMP numbering system, purchase specified options, and standards common to the industry.

- A knowledge of meat items as described by IMPS and by NAMP's *Meat Buyer's Guide®*.

- Where meat products originate and how this affects their final use.

- The importance of standards and how they keep products consistent, wholesome, and fair throughout the market.

- Common defects or inconsistencies in meat products that you should look for to prevent dissatisfied customers or unpleasant dining experiences.

- Current trends in the foodservice industry, new menu ideas and options.

- How value is determined for different meat products and how this is affected by quality parameters.

If you're involved in the buying and selling of meat products - from restaurants and supermarkets to foodservice distributors and meat companies - gain a competitive edge by applying the valuable information you'll learn from this course.

Visit www.namp.com for more information on specific courses, locations, and dates.

Visite www.namp.com para obtener información adicional sobre cursos específicos, sitios y fechas.

Detalles del curso

La Capacitación en ingredientes principales del plato que ofrece la Asociación Norteamericana de Procesadores de Carne (NAMP) es una mirada de primera mano a la forma en que las canales se convierten en piezas porcionadas comúnmente comercializadas en la industria de servicios de alimentación y los negocios minoristas de carne. El curso comprende las principales piezas proteicas que constituyen los ingredientes principales del plato: carne de res, ternera, cordero, cerdo y aves (en algunos lugares).

Este curso se dicta dos o tres veces al año en toda Norteamérica. Abarca de dos a tres días de aprendizaje en un salón de clase, con presentaciones a cargo de expertos de la industria. También recibirá una copia de *La Guía para Compradores de Carne®* de NAMP (Asociación Norteamericana de Procesadores de Carne, por sus siglas en inglés) que se utilizará exhaustivamente en el curso.

Qué aprenderá en este curso

- El sistema de numeración IMPS/NAMP, las opciones especificadas de compra y las normas comunes de la industria.

- Un conocimiento de las piezas de carne como se describen en las IMPS (Especificaciones Institucionales de Compra de Carne, por sus siglas en inglés) y en *La Guía para Compradores de Carne®* de NAMP.

- Dónde se originan los productos de carne y cómo afecta esto su uso final.

- La importancia de las normas y cómo logran que los productos sean uniformes, saludables y buenos en todo el mercado.

- Defectos o anomalías en los productos de carne que debería buscar para evitar clientes insatisfechos o que tengan experiencias desagradables en la mesa.

- Las tendencias actuales de la industria de servicios de alimentación, nuevas ideas y opciones para su menú.

- Cómo se determina el valor de diferentes productos de carne y cómo éste se ve afectado por los parámetros de calidad.

Si participa en la compra y venta de productos de carne, ya sea en restaurantes y supermercados o distribuidores de la industria de servicios de alimentación y empresas de carne, obtenga una ventaja competitiva aplicando la valiosa información que aprenderá en este curso.

Index / Índice

Pork Portion Cuts and Weight Ranges
Cortes porcionados de cerdo y escalas de peso

NAMP
NORTH AMERICAN MEAT PROCESSORS ASSOCIATION
ASSOCIATION AMÉRIQUE DU NORD DES TRANSFORMATEURS DE VIANDE
ASOCIACIÓN NORTEAMERICANA DE PROCESADORES DE CARNE

Información para hacer los pedidos

Ingredientes agregados

Si el comprador lo solicita, se pueden agregar ingredientes a cualquier porción cárnica de cerdo fresco a fin de mejorar el desempeño del producto. Los ingredientes pueden agregarse mediante inmersión o inyección y deben limitarse a agua, jugo de limón y fosfatos, a menos que el comprador lo solicite de otro modo. El comprador puede especificar cualquiera de los siguientes niveles de ingredientes agregados dentro de la orden de compra:

Número de opción	Porcentaje máximo de ingredientes agregados
1	7%
2	10%
3	12%
4	15%

Los ingredientes utilizados, el método de adición y el etiquetado del producto con los ingredientes agregados deben cumplir con las reglamentaciones del FSIS (Servicio de Inspección e Inocuidad Alimentaria, por sus siglas en inglés).

Calidad muscular de la carne fresca del cerdo

Los jamones frescos, paletas, paletas picnic, cabezas de lomo y lomos deben tener al menos un grado cárnico moderado, según un conjunto de evaluaciones de la muscularidad y de las cantidades de grasa intermuscular y externa.

Las barrigas deben presentar al menos una proporción levemente alta de carne magra en relación con la grasa y presentar una distribución uniforme de las capas de grasa y carne magra. Las barrigas pueden variar en grosor desde levemente gruesas a moderadamente gruesas, pero deben ser moderadamente uniformes en grosor, así como moderadamente largas en relación con su ancho.

Calidad esquelética de los productos de cerdo con hueso

Los huesos no deben estar osificados a un grado tal que no se observen cartílagos en las regiones pélvica, del espinazo y escapular. Las puntas del espinazo (apófisis espinosas) y las secciones transversales de los cuerpos vertebrales deben ser porosas. El color de los huesos debe variar de rojo a rosa intenso. Las superficies exteriores de las costillas deben mostrar al menos algo de color rojo.

Los cortes de cerdo con hueso deben estar libres de coyunturas dislocadas o exageradas, u otras malformaciones de la estructura ósea. Sin embargo, los cortes con los huesos quebrados durante el procesamiento son aceptables siempre que los huesos no estén astillados al punto que la carne magra alrededor de la fractura se encuentre afectada.

Opciones para limitar la grasa (FLO)

Cortes Porcionados

El comprador especificará uno de los siguientes grosores promedio máximos (en un punto cualquiera) de cubierta de grasa cuando las limitaciones de grasa que se indican en la descripción detallada de la pieza no son las deseadas.

Número de opción	Grosor máximo de grasa en un punto cualquiera del corte
1	6 mm (0.25 pulgadas)
2	3 mm (0.125 pulgadas)
3	Prácticamente libre de grasa [el 75% de la superficie muscular descubierta por la disección es magra y la grasa que queda no debe exceder los 3 mm (0.125 pulgadas)]
4	Desprovista de grasa/Prácticamente desnuda de grasa* [la grasa que queda no debe exceder los 2.5 cm (1.0 pulgada) en la dimensión más larga y/o 3 mm (0.125 pulgadas) de grosor]
5	Desprovista de grasa/Prácticamente desnuda de grasa** [el 90% de la superficie expuesta es magra y la grasa que queda no debe exceder los 3 mm (0.125 pulgadas)]

*/** – consulte la definición en la página xlv.

Tolerancias de peso y grosor de la porción*

El comprador especificará el peso y/o el grosor que desea. Para obtener asistencia en la especificación del peso, consultar las tablas de escalas de peso. Cuando se especifique tanto el peso como el grosor, se recomienda que esos requisitos se limiten a piezas prensadas y/o rebanadas de forma mecánica.

Tolerancias de grosor de la porción

Grosor especificado	Tolerancia de grosor	Uniformidad de grosor
2.5 cm (1.0 pulgada) o menos	± 5 mm (0.1875 pulgadas)	5 mm (0.1875 pulgadas)
Más de 2.5 cm (1.0 pulgada)	± 6 mm (0.25 pulgadas)	6 mm (0.25 pulgadas)

Tolerancia de peso de la porción

Peso especificado	Tolerancia de peso	Uniformidad de grosor
Menos de 170 g (6.0 onzas)	± 7 g (0.25 onzas)	5 mm (0.1875 pulgadas)
170 g (6.0 onzas) hasta 340 g (12.0 onzas)	± 14 g (0.50 onzas)	6 mm (0.25 pulgadas)
341 g (12.01 onzas) o más	± 21 g (0.75 onzas)	6 mm (0.25 pulgadas)

* Las medidas de espesor no se aplican con un borde de 6 mm (0.25 pulgadas). Además, el valor que se indica en la uniformidad de grosor es la máxima diferencia admitida entre la medición más fina y la más gruesa de una chuleta o tajada individual.

Los compradores que tengan necesidades o especificaciones especiales deben comunicarse con sus proveedores.

Ordering Data

Added Ingredients

If requested by the purchaser, ingredients may be added to any fresh pork item in order to enhance product performance. Ingredients may be added by immersion or injection and shall be limited to water, lemon juice, and phosphate unless otherwise specified by the purchaser. The purchaser may specify any one of the following levels of added ingredients within a purchase order:

Option No.	Maximum Percentage of Added Ingredients
1	7%
2	10%
3	12%
4	15%

The ingredients used, method of addition, and the labeling of the product with added ingredients shall be in accordance with FSIS regulations.

Muscle Quality of Fresh Pork

Fresh hams, shoulders, shoulder picnics, Boston butts, and loins must have at least a moderate degree of meatiness, based on a composite evaluation of thickness of muscling and quantity of intermuscular and external fat.

Bellies must indicate at least a slightly high ratio of lean to fat and have uniform distribution of fat and lean layers. The bellies may vary in thickness from slightly thick to moderately thick but must be moderately uniform in thickness throughout as well as moderately long in relationship to their width.

Skeletal Quality of Bone In Pork Products

Bones must not be ossified to a degree that cartilage is not evident in the pelvic, spinal, and scapular sections. The split chine bones, spinous processes, and cross-cut sections of bones must be porous. The color of the bones must range from red to deep pink. The exterior surfaces of the rib bones must show at least some redness.

Bone in pork cuts shall be free of dislocated or enlarged joints or other malformations of the skeletal structure. However, cuts with bones broken during processing are acceptable if the bones are not splintered to the extent that the lean around the fracture is affected.

Fat Limitation Options (FLO)

Portion Cuts

The purchaser shall specify one of the following maximum (at any one point) thicknesses of surface fat when the fat limitations indicated in the detailed Item Descriptions are not desired.

Option No.	Maximum Fat Thickness at Any One Point for Portion Cuts
1	0.25 inch (6 mm)
2	0.125 inch (3 mm)
3	Practically free (75 percent lean/seam surface exposed and remaining fat shall not exceed 0.125 inch (3 mm))
4	Peeled/Denuded* (remaining fat shall not exceed 1.0 inch (2.5 cm) in the longest dimension and/or 0.125 inch (3 mm) in thickness)
5	Peeled/Denuded, Surface Membrane Removed** (90 percent lean exposed and remaining fat shall not exceed 0.125 inch (3 mm))

*/** – see page xvi for definition.

Portion-Cut Weight and Thickness Tolerances*

The purchaser shall specify the portion weight and/or thickness desired. For assistance in specifying weight, see weight range tables. When both weight and thickness are specified, it is recommended that those requirements be limited to items that are mechanically pressed and/or sliced.

Portion Thickness Tolerances

Specified Thickness	Thickness Tolerance	Thickness Uniformity
1.0 inch (2.5 cm) or less	± 0.1875 inch (5 mm)	0.1875 inch (5 mm)
More than 1.0 inch (2.5 cm)	± 0.25 inch (6 mm)	0.25 inch (6 mm)

Portion Weight Tolerance

Specified Weight	Weight Tolerance	Thickness Uniformity
Less than 6.0 oz. (170 g)	± 0.25 oz. (7 g)	0.1875 inch (5 mm)
6.0 oz. (170 g) to 12.0 oz. (340 g)	± 0.50 oz. (14 g)	0.25 inch (6 mm)
12.01 oz. (341 g) or more	± 0.75 oz. (21 g)	0.25 inch (6 mm)

* Thickness measurements not applicable with 0.25 inch (6 mm) of edge. Also, value listed under thickness uniformity is the maximum allowable difference between the thinnest and thickest measurement of an individual chop or steak.

Purchasers with special needs or specifications should contact their suppliers.

1400 — Pork Steaks, Cubed

Cubed steaks shall be prepared from any portion of the carcass, except the shank or inner shank meat, that yields product that meets the end-item requirements. The unfrozen steaks shall be cubed twice, unless otherwise specified, at approximate right angles. Knitting of two or more pieces and folding the meat when cubing is permissible. After cubing, surface and seam fat shall not exceed 15 percent of the total area on either side of the steak. Individual steaks shall remain intact when suspended 0.5 inch (13 mm) from the outer edge. The steaks shall be free of heavy connective tissue, bones, cartilages, and lymph glands.

1400 — Escalopas de Cerdo Suavizadas (Ablandadas por Machacado, Rayado)

Las tajadas suavizadas deberán prepararse a partir de cualquier porción de la canal, salvo de la carne del chamorro y la parte interna del chamorro, que dé como resultado un producto que cumpla con los requisitos de la pieza final. Las tajadas no congeladas deberán cubicarse dos veces, a menos que se especifique de otro modo, en ángulos aproximadamente rectos. Se permite unir dos o más piezas y plegar la carne al cortarla en cubos. Después de trocearse en cubos, la cubierta de grasa y las vetas de grasa intermuscular no deberán exceder el 15% del área total en ambos lados de la tajada. Las tajadas individuales deben permanecer intactas al suspenderse a 13 mm (0.5 pulgadas) del borde externo. Las tajadas deberán estar libres de tejido conectivo grueso, huesos, cartílagos y ganglios linfáticos.

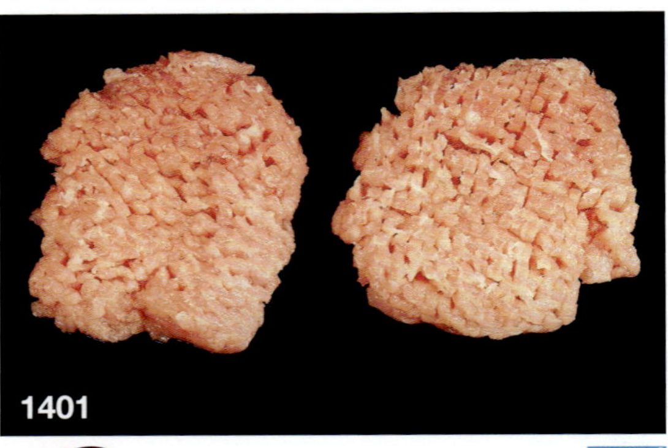

1401 — Pork Steaks, Cubed, Special

This item is as described in Item No. 1400, except the steaks shall be prepared from any combination of lean from the leg from the leg (excluding the shank and inner shank meat), sirloin, loin, and shoulder sections of the carcass. Knitting of two or more pieces and folding the meat when cubing is not permissible.

1401 — Escalopas de Cerdo Suavizadas (Ablandadas por Machacado, Rayado), Especial

Esta pieza es igual a la pieza que se describe en el número 1400, excepto que las tajadas deben prepararse a partir de cualquier combinación de carne magra de las secciones de la pierna (excluyendo la carne del chamorro y de la parte interna del chamorro), sirloin, lomo y paleta de la canal. No está permitido unir dos o más piezas ni plegar la carne al trocearla en cubos.

1401D — Pork Osso Bucco, Hind Shank

This item shall be prepared from Item No. 401D. The hind shank portions shall be cut to a thickness as specified by the purchaser, and approximately perpendicular to the bone length. The resulting cross section surfaces (both sides) shall display at least 75% exposed lean.

1401D — Osobuco de Cerdo, Chamorro Trasero

Esta pieza se prepara con la pieza número 401D. Las porciones de chamorro trasero deben cortarse del grosor especificado por el comprador, y aproximadamente perpendiculares a la longitud del hueso. Las superficies de los cortes transversales resultantes (ambos lados) deben presentar al menos un 75 % de carne magra.

1402 — Pork Cutlets

Cutlets shall be prepared from any combination of lean from the leg, excluding the shank and inner shank meat, loin, sirloin, or shoulder sections of the carcass that yields product that meets the end-item requirements. If a purchaser desires cutlets prepared only from the Pork Leg, then specify Item No. 1402G, which must meet the material requirements of Item No. 402G, as well as the preparation requirements contained in this item description. The cutlets shall be free of heavy (opaque) connective tissue, bones, cartilages, and lymph glands. When specified, the raw materials or the cutlets shall be mechanically tenderized not more than one time by using the multiple probe method (pinning). Pressing, knitting, or folding two pieces of meat together is not permissible. Surface and seam fat shall not exceed an average of 0.125 inch (3 mm) in thickness, and the thickness at any one point shall not exceed 0.25 inch (6 mm). Surface fat, measuring 0.1 inch (2 mm) or more in thickness, shall not exceed 50 percent of the circumference of the cutlet. Individual cutlets shall remain intact when suspended 0.5 inch (13 mm) from the outer edge. Alternatively, the purchaser may specify surface and seam fat limitations in terms of maximum surface area percentage. Both surface and seam fat of the total cut surface on either side of the cutlet shall not exceed the percentage specified by the purchaser.

1402 — Escalopas de Cerdo

Las escalopas se prepararán a partir de cualquier combinación de carne magra de las secciones de la pierna, excluyendo la carne del chamorro y la parte interna del chamorro, lomo, sirloin o paleta de la canal que dé como resultado un producto que cumpla con los requisitos de la pieza final. Si un comprador desea que las escalopas se preparen con la Pierna de Cerdo, deberán especificar la pieza número 1402G, que debe cumplir con los requisitos materiales de la pieza 402G, así como los requisitos de preparación que se indican en la descripción de la pieza. Las escalopas deberán estar libres de tejido conectivo grueso (opaco), huesos, cartílagos y ganglios linfáticos. Cuando se especifique, la materia prima o las escalopas deben suavizarse mecánicamente, no más de una vez, utilizando un método de múltiples vástagos puntiagudos, lancetas o puntas. No está permitido prensar, unir ni plegar dos piezas de carne entre sí. La cubierta de grasa y las vetas de grasa intermuscular no deberán exceder los 3 mm (0.125 pulgadas) de espesor como promedio, y el espesor en ningún punto deberá exceder los 6 mm (0.25 pulgadas). La cubierta de grasa, de un espesor de 2 mm (0.1 pulgada) o más, no deberá exceder el 50% de la circunferencia de la escalopa. Las escalopas individuales deben permanecer intactas al suspenderse a 13 mm (0.5 pulgadas) del borde externo. Asimismo, el comprador puede especificar limitaciones sobre cubierta de grasa y vetas de grasa intermuscular en términos del máximo porcentaje de área cubierta. Tanto la cubierta de grasa como las vetas de grasa intermuscular sobre la superficie total del corte en cada lado de la escalopa no deberán exceder el porcentaje especificado por el comprador.

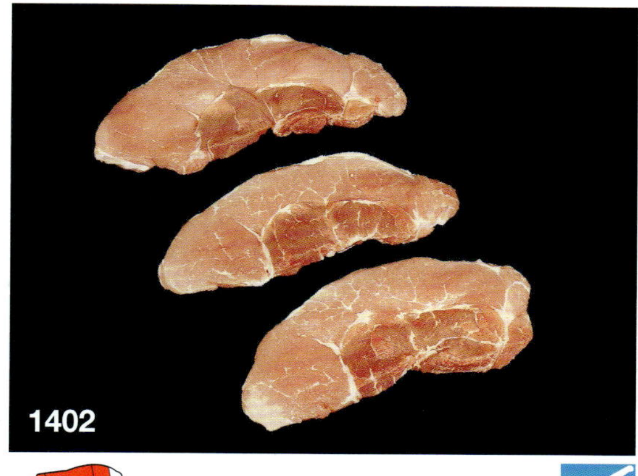

1406 — Pork Boston Butt Steaks

The steaks are prepared from Item No. 406. The slicing of steaks shall start on the loin side of the butt.

1406 — Escalopas de Cabeza de Lomo de Cerdo, con Hueso

Las escalopas se preparan con la pieza número 406. Los cortes de las tajadas de la cabeza de lomo deben comenzar en el lado adyacente al lomo.

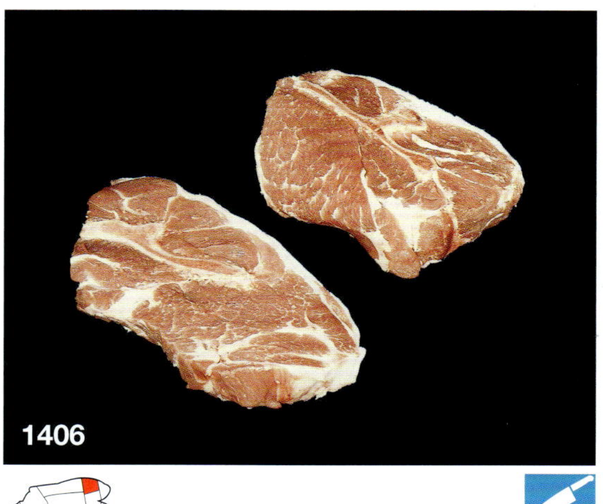

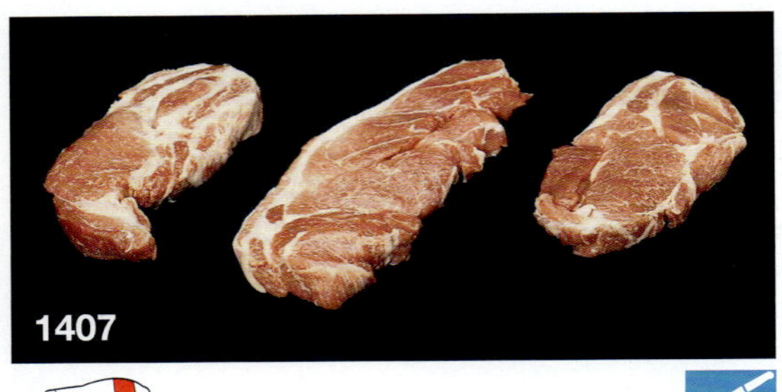

1407 — Pork Shoulder Butt Steaks, Boneless

The steaks are prepared from Item No. 407. The slicing of steaks shall start on the loin side of the butt.

1407 — Escalopas de Cabeza de Lomo, Deshuesadas

Las tajadas se preparan con la pieza número 407. Las rebanadas de tajadas de la cabeza de lomo deben comenzar en el lado adyacente al lomo.

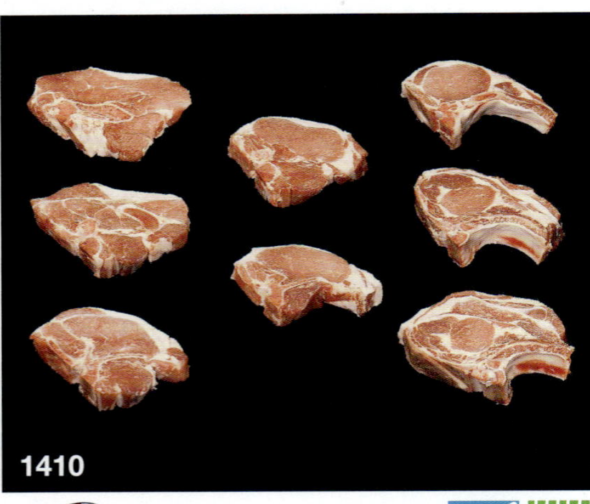

1410 — Pork Loin Chops

The chops are prepared from Item No. 410.

For all pork loin portion cut items, the purchaser may specify the following options:

PSO: *Tail length* - if not specified, the tail length will not exceed 1.0 inch (2.5 cm) from the *longissimus*. Distance from *longissimus*

PSO: 1 – 3.0 inches (7.5 cm)

2 – 2.0 inches (5.0 cm)

3 – 1.0 inch (2.5 cm)

4 – No tail (trimmed to meet specified fat trim)

5 – Other

1410 — Chuletas de Lomo de Cerdo

Las chuletas se preparan con la pieza número 410.

Para todas las piezas de lomo de cerdo, el comprador podrá especificar las siguientes opciones:

PSO: *Longitud de la cola*: si no se especifica, la longitud de la cola no excederá los 2.5 cm (1.0 pulgada) desde el *longissimus*. Distancia desde el *longissimus*

PSO: 1 – 7.5 cm (3.0 pulgadas)

2 – 5.0 cm (2.0 pulgadas)

3 – 2.5 cm (1.0 pulgada)

4 – Sin cola (recortado hasta alcanzar el recorte de grasa especificado)

5 – Otro

NAMP
NORTH AMERICAN MEAT PROCESSORS ASSOCIATION
ASSOCIATION AMÉRIQUE DU NORD DES TRANSFORMATEURS DE VIANDE
ASOCIACIÓN NORTEAMERICANA DE PROCESADORES DE CARNE

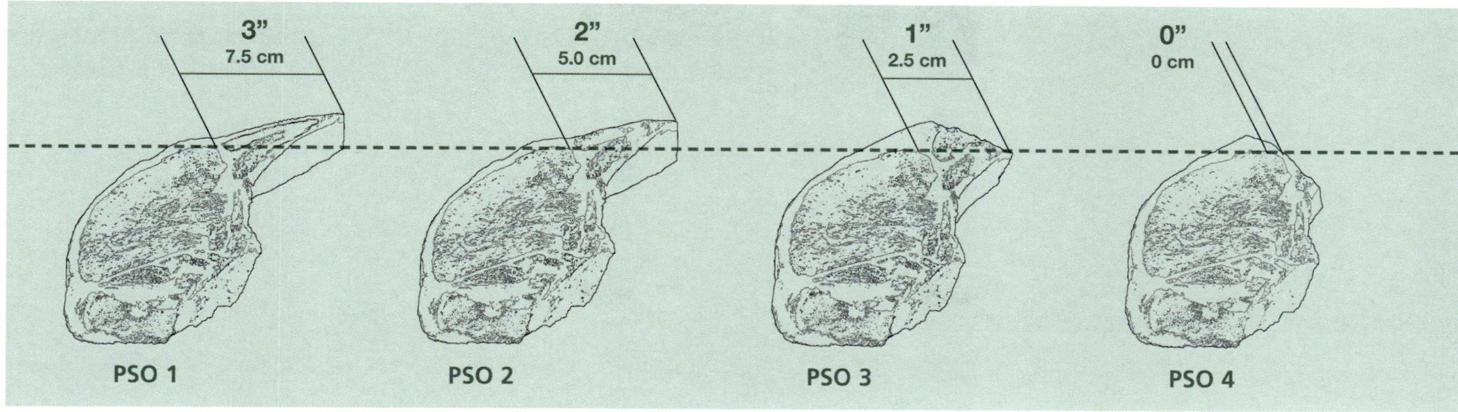

Graphic illustration of the length of tail difference on Pork Loin Chops.
Ilustración gráfica de diferencias en longitud de cola en Chuletas de Lomo de Cerdo.

1410A — Pork Loin, Rib Chops

This item is prepared from the rib portion of any bone in, Center-Cut 8, 9, 10, or 11 Rib Item in the No. 412 series. Each chop shall consist of at least one rib.

Pockets - When specified by the purchaser for pork loin portion items in the 1410A, 1412, and 1413 series, the pocket shall be made by a cut into the *longissimus*, leaving no less than 0.25 inch (6 mm) and not more than 0.5 inch (13 mm) of intact lean from the edge to the innermost point of the pocket. The cut shall not puncture either surface containing the cross section of the *longissimus*.

Note: Purchaser may request that the ribs shall be Frenched by the exclusion of the intercostal meat and lean and fat between and over the ribs. The exposed portion of the rib bones shall not exceed 1.5 inches (3.8 cm), and the remaining intercostal meat and lean and fat over the rib bones shall not exceed 2.5 inches (6.3 cm) from the outer edge of the *longissimus* muscle.

1410A — Chuletas de Cerdo, Tajadas del Costillar

Esta pieza se prepara con la porción del costillar de cualquier pieza con hueso, corte del centro, con 8, 9, 10 u 11 costillas de la serie 412. Cada chuleta debe consistir en al menos una costilla.

Cavidades: cuando el comprador lo especifique para las piezas de lomo de cerdo de las series 1410A, 1412 y 1413, la cavidad debe realizarse mediante un corte en el *longissimus* que no deje menos de 6 mm (0.25 pulgadas) ni más de 13 mm (0.5 pulgadas) de carne magra intacta desde el borde hasta el punto más interno de la cavidad. El corte no debe perforar ninguna superficie que contenga la sección transversal del *longissimus*.

Importante: el comprador puede especificar que las costillas se preparen al Estilo Francés quitándoles la carne intercostal y la carne magra así como la grasa entre y sobre las costillas. La porción de las costillas que queda expuesta no debe exceder los 3.8 cm (1.5 pulgadas) de longitud, y la carne intercostal, la grasa y la carne magra sobre las costillas no deben exceder los 6.3 cm (2.5 pulgadas) desde el borde exterior del músculo *longissimus*.

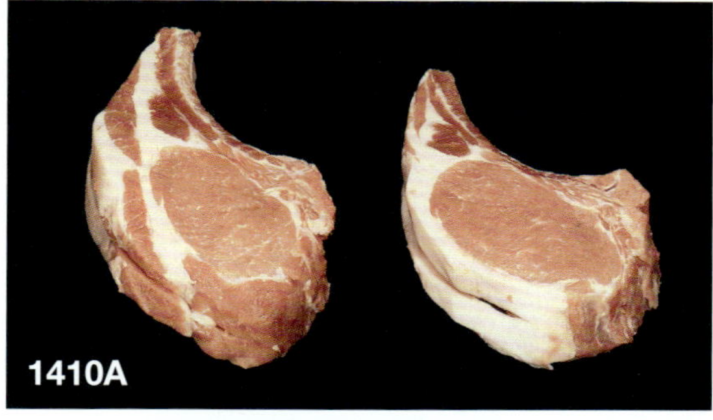

1410A

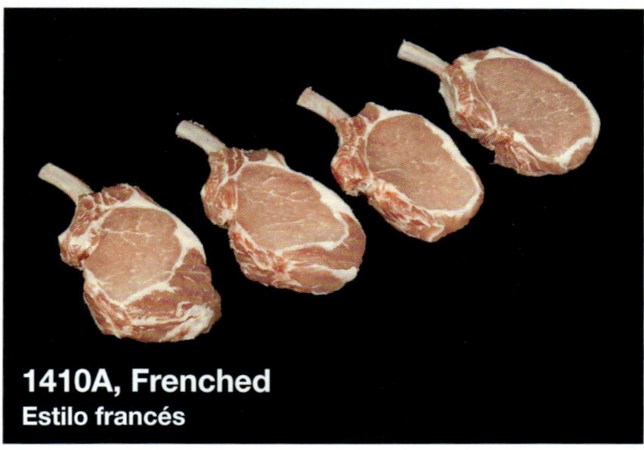

1410A, Frenched
Estilo francés

1410B — Pork Loin, End Chops

Pork end chops may be derived from the blade and sirloin portions of any pork loin.

1410B — Chuletas de Cerdo, Chuletas de los Extremos Adyacentes al Lomo

Las chuletas de cerdo pueden prepararse con las porciones de paleta y sirloin de cualquier lomo.

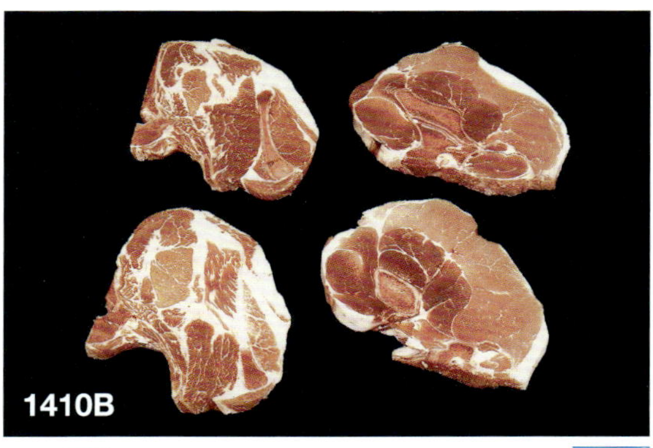

1410B

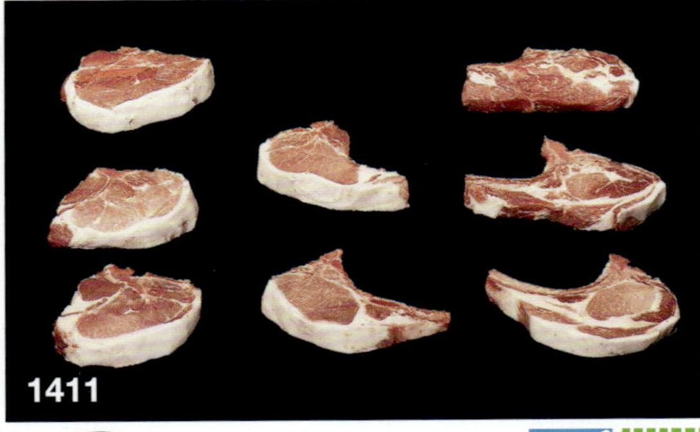

1411 — Pork Loin Chops, Bladeless

The chops are prepared from Item No. 411.

1411 — Chuletas de Lomo de Cerdo, Sin Hueso de la Paleta

Las chuletas se preparan con la pieza número 411.

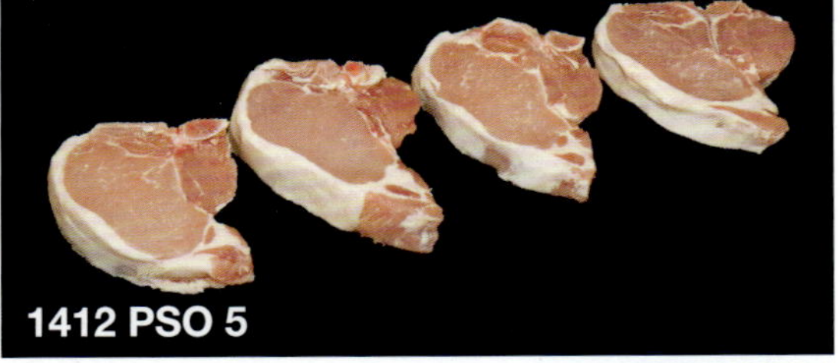

1412 — Pork Loin Chops, Center-Cut

The chops are prepared from Item Nos. 412 or 412C.

PSO: 5 – Purchaser may request only the "Porterhouse Chops" from the pork loin. The pork tenderloin shall be plainly evident on both sides of the "Porterhouse Chop."

1412 — Chuletas de Lomo de Cerdo, Corte del Centro

Las chuletas se preparan con la pieza número 412 o 412C.

PSO: 5 – El comprador puede solicitar únicamente las "Chuletas Porterhouse" del lomo de cerdo. El filete de cerdo debe verse claramente en ambos lados de las "Chuletas Porterhouse".

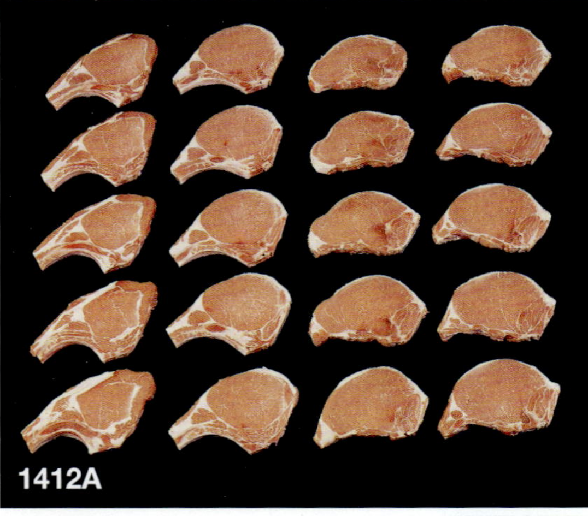

1412A — Pork Loin Chops, Center-Cut, Chine Bone Off

The chops are prepared from Item Nos. 412A or 412D.

The photo depicts chops cut from a 412D. The second, third, and fourth columns would be representative of chops cut from a 412A.

1412A — Chuletas de Lomo de Cerdo, Corte del Centro, con Espinazo Rebajado

Las chuletas se preparan con la pieza número 412A o 412D.

La fotografía muestra chuletas cortadas de una pieza 412D. La segunda, tercera y cuarta columna serían representativas de las chuletas cortadas de una pieza 412A.

1412B — Pork Loin Chops, Center-Cut, Boneless

The chops are prepared from Item Nos. 412B or 412E.

The photo depicts chop cut from a 412E. With the exception of the chop in the bottom right corner, all chops pictured would also be representative of chops cut from a 412B.

1412B — Chuletas de Lomo de Cerdo, Corte del Centro, Deshuesadas

Las chuletas se preparan con la pieza número 412B o 412E.

La fotografía muestra una chuleta cortada de una pieza 412E. Excepto la chuleta que se encuentra en la esquina inferior derecha, todas las chuletas fotografiadas también serían representativas de las chuletas preparadas con una pieza 412B.

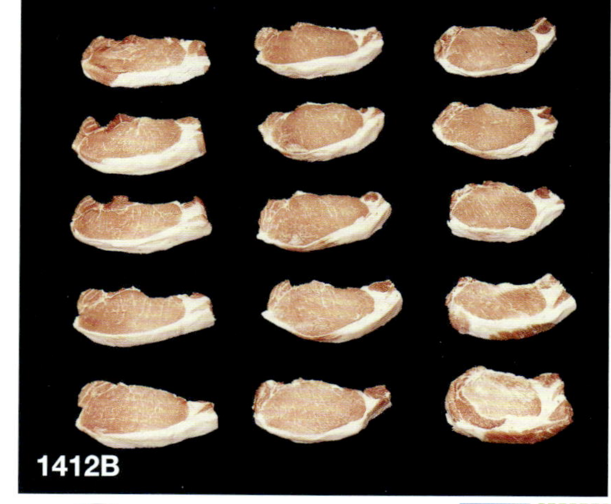

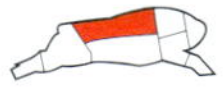

1412E — Pork Loin Chops, Center-Cut, One Muscle, Boneless

This item may be prepared from Item Nos. 412B or 412E, except that the sirloin shall be excluded at a point approximately 1.5 inches (3.8 cm) anterior to the hip cartilage so that the *longissimus* appears as one muscle. All muscles other than the *longissimus* and the *multifidus dorsi* shall be excluded. This item shall be practically free of fat and sliced at the thickness and/or portion weight specified by the purchaser. This item may be referred to as "America's Cut" when sliced to a thickness of not less than 1.25 inches (3.2 cm) or not more than 1.5 inches (3.8 cm).

1412E — Chuletas de Lomo de Cerdo, Corte del Centro, de un Solo Músculo, Deshuesadas

Esta pieza puede prepararse con las piezas número 412B o 412E, excepto que se deberá quitar el sirloin en un punto anterior al cartílago de la cadera, aproximadamente a 3.8 cm (1.5 pulgadas) de él, de modo que el *longissimus* aparezca como un solo músculo. Se quitará todo músculo que no sea el *longissimus* o el *multifidus dorsi*. Esta pieza deberá estar prácticamente libre de grasa y se rebanará en porciones del grosor y/o peso especificados por el comprador. A esta pieza se le puede llamar "Corte Americano" cuando se rebana con un grosor no menor a 3.2 cm (1.25 pulgadas) y no mayor a 3.8 cm (1.5 pulgadas).

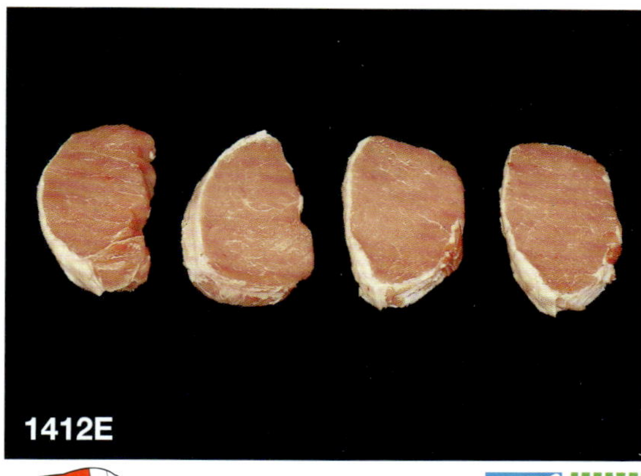

1413 — Pork Loin Chops, Boneless

The chops are prepared by cutting Item No. 413.

1413 — Chuletas de Lomo de Cerdo, Deshuesadas

Las chuletas se preparan cortando la pieza número 413.

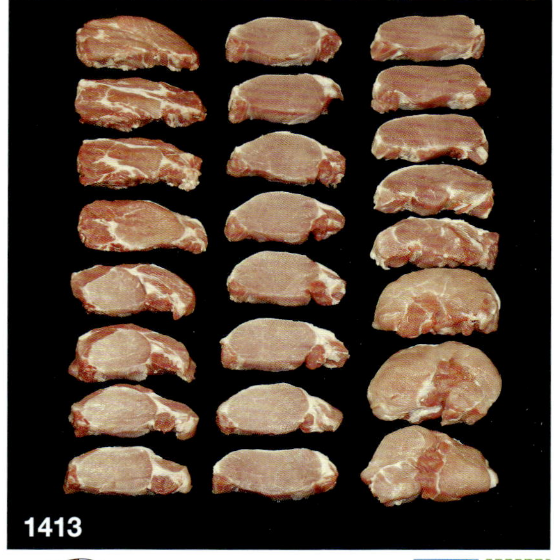

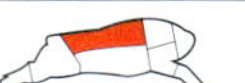

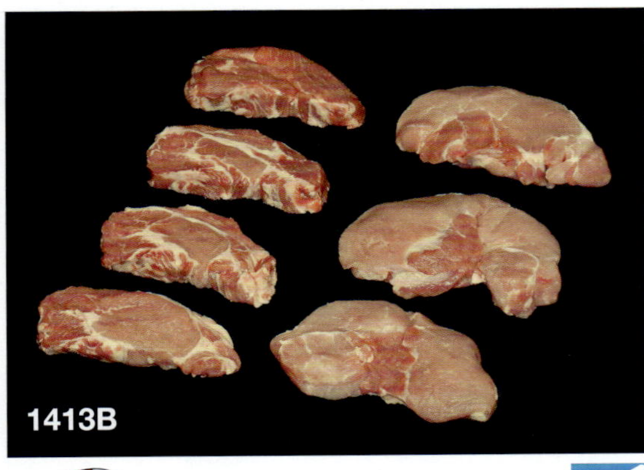

1413B — **Pork Loin, End Chops, Boneless**

The boneless pork chops may be derived from the blade and sirloin portions of any boneless loin.

1413B — **Chuletas de Lomo, de los Extremos Adyacentes al Lomo, Deshuesadas**

Las chuletas de cerdo deshuesadas pueden prepararse con las porciones de paleta y sirloin de cualquier lomo deshuesado.

1438 — **Pork Steaks, Flaked and Formed, Frozen**

The steaks shall be prepared from boneless pork that complies with the material requirements of Item No. 496 and shall be flaked and formed. Grinding is not permitted. The flaking and forming processes shall be in compliance with FSIS regulations. Product shall comply with fat content requirements of Item No. 496. The purchaser shall specify shape and weight of steaks. When specified, the flaked and formed steaks may be cubed and the term "cubed" may be included in the product label. When specified, the steaks shall be breaded and labeled appropriately. The breading and its application shall be in accordance with FSIS regulations.

1438 — **Escalopas de Cerdo, Finamente Rebanadas y Moldeadas, Congeladas**

Las escalopas deberán prepararse con cerdo deshuesado que cumpla con los requisitos materiales de la pieza número 496 y deberán rebanarse finamente y moldearse. La molienda no está permitida. Los procesos de rebanado fino y moldeado deberán cumplir con las reglamentaciones del FSIS (Servicio de Inspección e Inocuidad Alimentaria, por sus siglas en inglés). El producto deberá cumplir con los requisitos de contenido de grasa de la pieza número 496. El comprador especificará la forma y el peso de las tajadas. Cuando se especifique, las tajadas rebanadas finamente y moldeadas podrían suavizarse por machacado/rayado y el término "cubed" (suavizados mecánicamente) podrá aparecer en la etiqueta del producto. Cuando se especifique, las tajadas deberán empanizarse y etiquetarse adecuadamente. El empanizado y su proceso deberán realizarse de acuerdo con la reglamentación del FSIS (Servicio de Inspección e Inocuidad Alimentaria, por sus siglas en inglés).

1438A — Pork Sandwich Steaks, Flaked, Chopped, Formed, and Wafer Sliced, Frozen

1438A — Escalopas de Cerdo para Emparedados, Finamente Rebanadas, Picadas, Moldeadas y Rebanadas Como Obleas, Congeladas

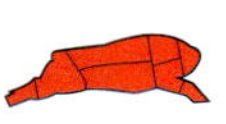 

The steaks shall be prepared from boneless pork that complies with the material requirements of Item No. 496. The flaking, chopping, forming, and slicing processes shall be in compliance with FSIS regulations and shall produce steaks that are moderately fine textured. Product shall comply with fat content requirements of Item No. 496. Each steak shall consist of two or more thin slices weighing approximately 1.0 oz. (28 g) each. No more than a minor amount of green/brown/gray rings shall be present. Steaks shall be packaged with paper separators between each steak. Unless otherwise specified, slices shall be approximately 4.75 x 7.5 inches (11.9 x 18.8 cm). The purchaser shall specify weight and/or number of slices per pound.

Purchasers who desire a Pork Steak, Sliced and Formed, Frozen prepared from boneless pork as described in Item No. 418 should specify Item No. 1438B. Ingredients may be added for the purpose of tenderizing and binding. The slicing, forming, use, and labeling of ingredients shall be in accordance with FSIS regulations. Purchaser shall specify weight, shape, and/or thickness of the steaks requested.

Las tajadas deberán prepararse con una carne deshuesada de cerdo que cumpla con los requisitos materiales de la pieza 496. Los procesos de rebanado fino, picado, moldeado y rebanado en obleas deberán realizarse de acuerdo a la reglamentación del FSIS (Servicio de Inspección e Inocuidad Alimentaria), y deberán producir tajadas finamente texturizadas. El producto deberá cumplir con los requisitos de contenido de grasa de la pieza número 496. Cada tajada consistirá en dos o más rebanadas finas que pesen aproximadamente 28 g (1.0 onza) cada una. No podrá haber más que una mínima cantidad de anillos verdes, marrones o grises. Las tajadas deberán empacarse con separadores de papel entre ellos. A menos que se especifique de otro modo, las tajadas deberán tener aproximadamente 11.9 x 18.8 cm (4.75 x 7.5 pulgadas). El comprador deberá especificar el peso y/o la cantidad de rebanadas por libra.

Los compradores que deseen Tajadas de Cerdo, Rebanadas y Moldeadas, Congeladas preparados con carne deshuesada de cerdo tal como se describe en la pieza número 418 deberán especificar la pieza número 1438B. Se podrán agregar ingredientes para suavizar y aglutinar. El rebanado, moldeado, uso y etiquetado de los ingredientes deberán realizarse de acuerdo con las regulaciones del FSIS (Servicio de Inspección e Inocuidad Alimentaria, por sus siglas en inglés). El comprador deberá especificar el peso, la forma y/o el grosor de las tajadas solicitadas.

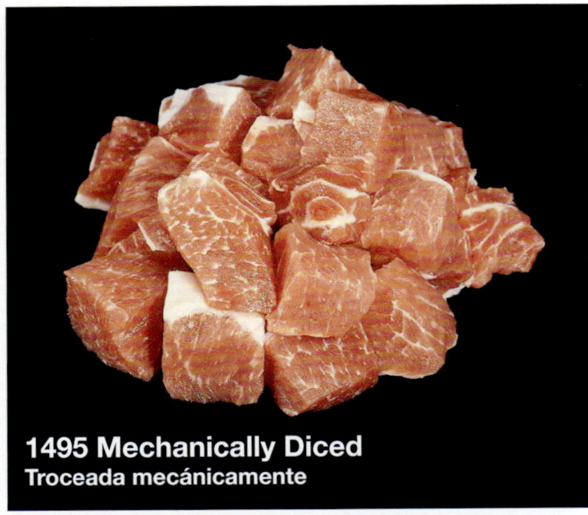

1495 Mechanically Diced
Troceada mecánicamente

1495 Hand Diced
Troceada a mano

1495 — Coarse Chopped Pork

This item shall be prepared from any portion of the carcass, excluding the shank meat and jowls, which yields product meeting the end-item requirements. In addition all skin, bones, cartilages, heavy connective tissue, and the *prefemoral, popliteal, prescapular* lymph glands, and any other exposed lymph glands, and all surface and seam fat in excess of 0.125 inch (3 mm) shall be excluded. The boneless meat shall be ground once through a plate with holes measuring 0.75 inch (19 mm). Alternatively, the boneless meat may be chopped or machine-cut by any method that yields equivalent results. If specified by the purchaser, the meat can be hand-diced to the desired size.

1495 — Cortadillo de Cerdo

Esta pieza se preparará con cualquier porción de la canal, excepto la carne de chamorros y papada, que dé como resultado un producto que cumpla con los requisitos de la pieza final. Además, se deberá quitar en su totalidad, la piel, huesos, cartílagos, tejido conectivo grueso, ganglios linfáticos *prefemorales, poplíteos y prescapulares*, y cualquier otro ganglio linfático expuesto, y toda cubierta de grasa y vetas de grasa intermuscular que exceda los 3 mm (0.125 pulgadas). La carne deshuesada deberá molerse una vez a través de una placa con orificios que midan 19 mm (0.75 pulgadas). De forma alternativa, la carne puede picarse o cortarse·a máquina mediante cualquier método que produzca un resultado equivalente. Si el comprador lo especifica, la carne puede trocearse a mano en cubos del tamaño que se requiera.

1496 — Ground Pork Patties

This item shall be prepared from Item No. 496. The ground pork shall be mechanically formed into patties of the size and shape specified by the purchaser. Unless specified otherwise, the patties shall be frozen. Patties shall be packaged and separated from each other by a means to prevent them from sticking together.

Purchasers desiring patties prepared from Ground Pork and Soy Protein Product (SPP) may specify Item No. 1496A for patties meeting FCS requirements. For patties that need not meet FCS SPP requirements, specify Item No. 1496B.

1496 — Hamburguesas de Cerdo

Esta pieza se prepara con la pieza número 496. La carne molida de cerdo será moldeada mecánicamente para elaborar hamburguesas de la forma y el tamaño especificados por el comprador. A menos que se especifique de otro modo, las hamburguesas deberán congelarse. Se deberán separar las hamburguesas entre sí de forma que no se peguen unas con otras al empacarse.

Los compradores que deseen hamburguesas preparadas con Carne Molida de Cerdo con Producto Proteico Vegetal (PPV) pueden especificar la pieza número 1496A para aquellas hamburguesas que deban cumplir con los requisitos de FCS (Servicio al Consumidor y de Alimentos, por sus siglas en inglés). Para las hamburguesas que no necesitan cumplir con los requisitos PPV del Servicio al Consumidor y de Alimentos, especifique la pieza 1496B.

NAMP
NORTH AMERICAN MEAT PROCESSORS ASSOCIATION
Association Amérique du Nord des Transformateurs de Viande
Asociación Norteamericana de Procesadores de Carne

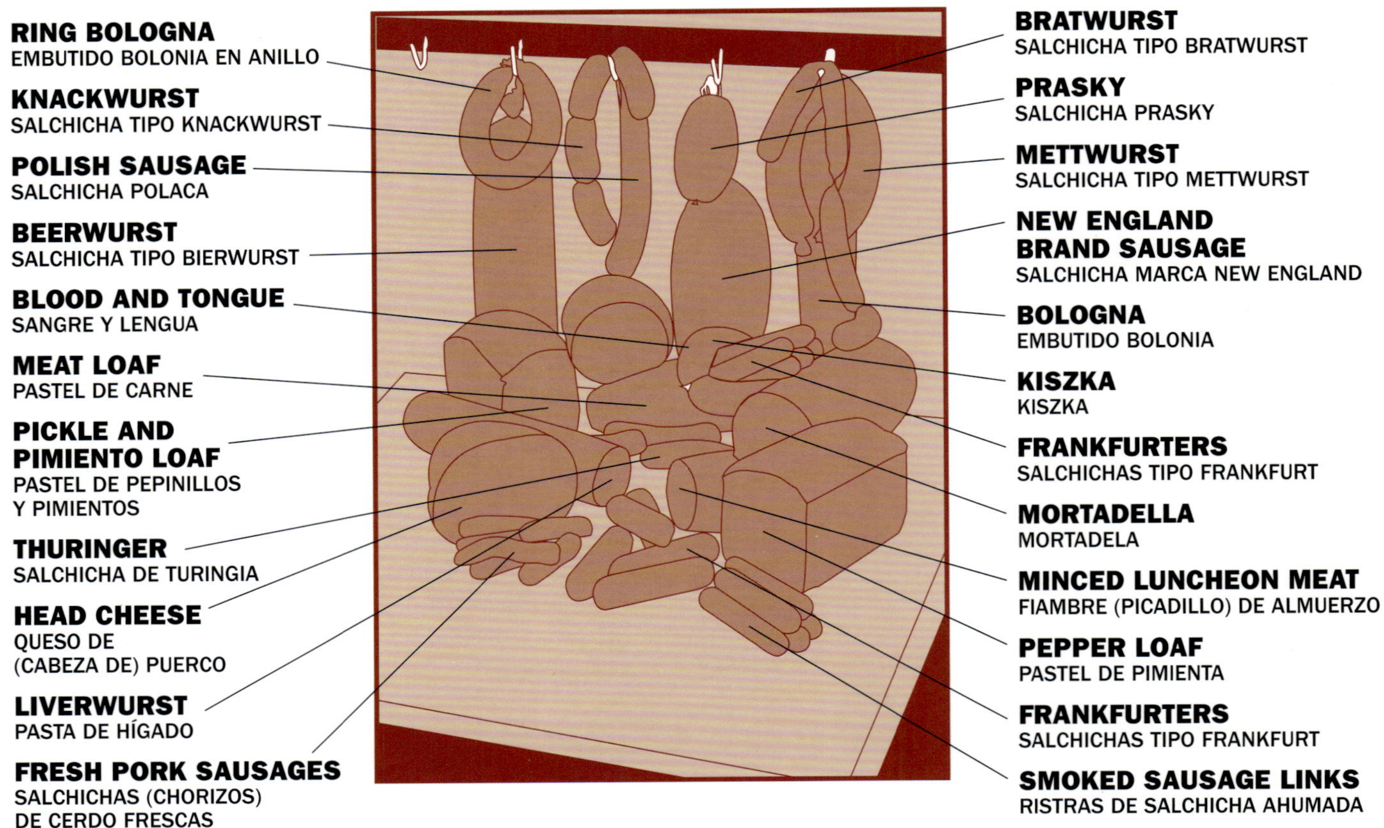

Index/Índice

Further-Processed/By-Products
Productos ya Procesados/Coproductos

Index/Índice

Cured, Cured and Smoked, and Fully-Cooked Pork Items
Piezas de cerdo curado, curado y ahumado, y completamente cocido

ITEM PIEZA	PRODUCT NAME / NOMBRE DEL PRODUCTO	PG. PÁG.	Weight Ranges (Pounds) / Escalas de peso (libras/kg)			
			A	B	C	D
501	Ham, Short Shank (Cured and Smoked) Jamón, de Chamorro Corto (Curado y Ahumado)	238	14 – 17 (6.4-7.7)	17–20 (7.7-9.1)	20–26 (9.1-11.8)	26–up (Más de 11.8)
503	Ham, Short Shank, Skinned (Cured and Smoked), Fully Cooked Jamón, de Chamorro Corto, Sin Piel/Lonja (Curado y Ahumado), Completamente Cocido	239	10 – 14 (4.5-6.4)	14 – 17 (6.4-7.7)	17–20 (7.7-9.1)	20–up (Más de 9.1)
505	Ham, Boneless, (Cured and Smoked), Fully Cooked Jamón, Deshuesado (Curado y Ahumado), Completamente Cocido	240	10 – 14 (4.5-5)	14–18 (6.4-8.2)	18–22 (8.2-10)	22–up (Más de 10)
508	Ham, Boiled, Boneless (Cured), Fully Cooked Jamón, Hervido, Deshuesado (Curado), Completamente Cocido	240	8 – 10 (3.6-4.5)	10 – 12 (4.5-5.4)	12 – 14 (5.4-6.4)	14–up (Más de 6.4)
509	Ham, Boneless (Cured and Smoked), Fully Cooked, Special Jamón, Deshuesado (Curado y Ahumado), Completamente Cocido, Especial	241	5 – 11 (2.3-5)	11–16 (5-7.3)		
510	Ham, Honey-Cured (Smoked), Partially Boned, Spiral Cut Jamón, Curado con Miel (Ahumado), Deshuesado Parcial, Corte en Espiral	242	8 – 10 (3.6-4.5)	10 – 12 (4.5-5.4)	12 – 14 (5.4-6.4)	14–up (Más de 6.4)
511	Ham, Chunked and Formed (Cured), Fully Cooked Jamón, Troceado y Moldeado (Curado), Completamente Cocido	242	8 – 10 (3.6-4.5)	10 – 12 (4.5-5.4)	12 – 14 (5.4-6.4)	14–up (Más de 6.4)
511A	Ham, Chunked and Formed (Cured and Smoked), Fully Cooked Jamón, Troceado y Moldeado (Curado y Ahumado), Completamente Cocido	243	8 – 10 (3.6-4.5)	10 – 12 (4.5-5.4)	12 – 14 (5.4-6.4)	14–up (Más de 6.4)
512A	Ham, Diced, (Cured and Smoked) Jamón, Troceado en Cubos (Curado y Ahumado)	243	As Specified by Purchaser (Según especificación del comprador)			
530	Pork Shoulder Butt, Cellar Trimmed, Boneless (Cured and Smoked) Cabeza de Lomo, Recortada de Grasa sin Hueso de Paleta, Deshuesada (Curada y Ahumada)	244	3 & down (Menos de 1.4)	3–5 (1.4-2.3)	5–7 (2.3-3.2)	7–up (Más de 3.2)
538	*Bacon, Slab, Center-Cut (Cured and Smoked), Skinless, Formed Tocino, Trozo de Panceta (Barriga), Corte del Centro (Curado y Ahumado), Sin Piel/Lonja, Moldeado	244	8 – 10 (3.6-4.5)	10 – 12 (4.5-5.4)	12 – 14 (5.4-6.4)	14–up (Más de 6.4)
539	*Bacon, Sliced (Cured and Smoked), Skinless Tocino, Rebanado (Curado y Ahumado), Sin Piel/Lonja	245	Cantidad de rebanadas por lb. según se especifique			
540	*Bacon, Sliced, Fully Cooked (Cured and Smoked), Skinless Tocino, Rebanado, Completamente Cocido (Curado y Ahumado), Sin Piel/Lonja	246	As Specified by Purchaser (Según especificación del comprador)			
547	Pork Center Loin, 11 Ribs (Cured and Smoked) Chuleta de Cerdo, 11 costillas (Curada y Ahumada)	247	5–7 (2.3-3.2)	7 – 10 (3.2-4.5)	10 – 12 (4.5-5.4)	12–up (Más de 5.4)
547A	Pork Center Loin (Cured and Smoked), Boneless Chuleta (Lomo del Centro) de Cerdo (Curado y Ahumado), Deshuesada	247	3–5 (1.4-2.3)	5–7 (2.3-3.2)	7 – 10 (3.2-4.5)	10–up (Más de 4.5)
550	Canadian Style Bacon (Cured and Smoked), Unsliced Lomo, Estilo Canadiense (Curado y Ahumado) sin Rebanar	248	3 & down (Menos de 1.4)	3–5 (1.4-2.3)	5–7 (2.3-3.2)	7–up (Más de 3.2)
550A	Canadian Style Bacon (Cured and Smoked), Sliced Lomo, Estilo Canadiense (Curado y Ahumado), Rebanado	248	5 & 10 Pound Containers as Specified (Recipientes de 5 y 10 libras según se especifique)			
558	*Spareribs, Fully Cooked Costillar de Cerdo, Completamente Cocido	249	3 & down (Menos de 1.4)	3–5 (1.4-2.3)	5–up (Más de 2.3)	
559A	*Costillar de Cerdo, Completamente Cocido, Estilo San Luis Costillar de Cerdo, Completamente Cocido, Cortado al Estilo San Luis	249	2 & down (Menos de 0.90)	2–3 (0.90-1.4)	3–up (Más de 1.4)	
561	*Hocks, Shoulder (Cured and Smoked) Chamorros, de Paleta/Espaldilla (Curados y Ahumados)	250	1 & down (Menos de 0.45)	1–1.5 (0.45-0.68)	1.5–up (Más de 0.68)	
1531	Ham Steaks (Cured and Smoked), Boneless Rodajas de Jamón (Curadas y Ahumadas), Deshuesadas	250	5–12 oz. as Specified by Purchaser (141.7-340.2 gr según especificación del comprador)			
1547	Pork Loin Chops, Center-Cut (Cured and Smoked) Chuletas de Lomo de Cerdo, Corte del Centro (Curadas y Ahumadas)	251	4 – 10 oz. as Specified by Purchaser (113.4-283.5 gr según especificación del comprador)			
1548	Pork Chops, Boneless, Center-Cut (Cured and Smoked) Chuletas de Lomo de Cerdo, Deshuesadas, Corte del Centro (Curadas y Ahumadas)	251	3 – 8 oz. as Specified by Purchaser (85-226.8 gr según especificación del comprador)			

Definición de términos

En la Serie 500 de las Especificaciones de Compras Institucionales de Carne (IMPS) para productos de cerdo curados, curados y ahumados y completamente cocidos, se utilizan varios términos específicos o descripciones del mercado para describir los distintos productos. Los compradores deben familiarizarse con sus significados, dado que en muchos casos éstos identifican la composición y las características del producto. Consulte la descripción de la pieza específica de cada producto para obtener más información. Las declaraciones que forman parte de la información contenida en las etiquetas reales en el producto también resultan útiles. En algunos casos, ciertos identificadores de productos (por ejemplo, carne magra o ligera en grasa, cuando se utilizan) deben cumplir con los requisitos nutrimentales específicos que exigen los reglamentos de etiquetado nutrimental del Servicio de Inspección e Inocuidad Alimentaria (FSIS). Otros requisitos relativos al contenido, procesamiento o etiquetado del producto también pueden regirse por los reglamentos o memorandos de políticas del Servicio de Inspección e Inocuidad Alimentaria. Las siguientes son definiciones de algunos términos frecuentemente utilizados. Otras definiciones adicionales que corresponden a esta serie se pueden encontrar en el propio documento de las IMPS. Si desea obtener más información acerca del producto que desea comprar, consulte a su proveedor.

Tocino: no puede contener sustancias agregadas, y el peso final del producto, después del curado y el ahumado, no debe sobrepasar su peso crudo, antes del curado. No hay requisitos de Proteína Libre de Grasa (PFF, por sus siglas en inglés).

Jamón picado: puede tener hasta un 15% de carne de chamorro. Esto es un 3% más de carne de chamorro de lo normal en un jamón entero.

Estilo campestre: significa que el producto es curado en seco y ahumado.

Curado: carne sumergida o inyectada con una solución de salmuera para extender la vida útil y/o conferir los sabores de los agentes de curado.

Curado en seco: curado sin inmersión o inyección.

Declaraciones de la etiqueta de porcentaje libre de grasa: un producto puede indicar que no tiene grasa en determinado porcentaje, describiéndolo como "95% libre de grasa", siempre y cuando la declaración también indique la cantidad exacta de grasa que contiene el producto, como en este ejemplo que contiene 5% de grasa. La declaración está relacionada únicamente con el contenido relativo de grasa en el producto final, no con la cantidad total de carne magra del producto, dado que éste también puede contener agua y condimentos.

Completamente cocido: para que se considere completamente cocido, el producto debe haber alcanzado, por lo general, una temperatura interna mínima de 64.4 °C (148 °F) y mostrar características propias de un producto cocido: separación parcial del hueso, color, textura, sabor, etc.

"Jamón", "Jamón con jugos naturales", "Jamón, adicionado con agua", "Producto de jamón y agua": las etiquetas de estos productos indican, en el mismo orden en que se listan, la cantidad de agua que queda en el jamón después de su procesamiento final. Una etiqueta que diga "solo JAMÓN" en mayúsculas (HAM, por su nombre en inglés) significa que no tiene agua, o que queda únicamente una cantidad de agua mínima que se produce de forma natural.

Jamón, Hervido: un producto completamente cocido y deshuesado que se debe cocer en agua. Se puede procesar en una lata o un envoltorio.

Jamón, Picado: no se debe confundir con JAMÓN PICADO. Aunque el producto es similar, puede contener hasta un máximo de 37% de carne de chamorro, que es 25% más de lo que se encuentra normalmente en un jamón.

Jamón, Troceado y Moldeado, o Jamón, Molido y Formado: un producto que se ha procesado con medios mecánicos para que la apariencia de su superficie de corte sea sustancialmente diferente de la que se espera ver en el producto habitual del jamón.

Curado con Miel: la miel se debe utilizar en cantidades suficientes para darle sabor y/o afectar la apariencia del producto final.

PFF (Proteína Libre de Grasa, por sus siglas en inglés): como el agua agregada diluye el contenido natural de proteínas del producto, el Servicio de Inspección e Inocuidad Alimentaria exige porcentajes mínimos de PFF para los jamones y otros productos curados de cerdo que se procesan con el agregado de otros ingredientes y distintas cantidades de agua, excepto el tocino. El producto con la menor cantidad de agua tiene el requisito de porcentaje de PFF más alto.

Estilo Pullman (Pullman Style): se refiere a un producto cárnico envasado en un envase grande generalmente rectangular o cuadrado en sus extremos.

Sin Lonja versus Descuerado: sin lonja significa que se debe quitar una cantidad especificada o un área especificada de piel. Descuerado significa que se ha quitado toda la piel.

Ahumado: el proceso por el cual los cortes de carne se han expuesto al humo seco de maderas, o se les ha aplicado externamente un saborizante ahumado líquido que se transmite al producto por transferencia térmica, o bien se les ha inyectado humo líquido junto con una solución de salmuera. Si se inyecta, la pieza se debe etiquetar como "Sabor Ahumado Agregado".

Rebanado en Espiral: un método de rebanar mecánicamente un jamón dejando siempre el jamón adherido al hueso.

Tono Bicolor: una variación, más que leve, de color, entre dos o más músculos diferentes en una misma superficie rebanada.

Definition of Terms

Within the Institutional Meat Purchase Specifications (IMPS) Series 500 for Cured, Cured and Smoked, and Fully Cooked Pork Products, a number of specific terms or marketplace descriptions are used to describe the various products. Purchasers should acquaint themselves with their meanings for in many cases they identify the composition and character of the product. Review the specific item description of each product for additional information. Actual label declarations on the product are also helpful. In some cases certain product identifiers – for example, lean or light, when used – must meet specific nutritional requirements as required by the Food Safety and Inspection Service (FSIS) nutritional labeling regulations. Other requirements as to product content, processing, or labeling may also be governed by FSIS regulations or policy memos. The following are the definitions of some commonly used terms. Additional ones applicable to this series may be found in the IMPS document itself. If you desire more information about the product you wish to purchase, please consult your supplier.

Bacon – May contain no added substances and the finished weight of the product may not exceed its raw, uncured weight after curing and smoking. There are no Protein Fat Free (PFF) requirements.

Chopped Ham – May have up to 15 percent shank meat. This is 3 percent more shank meat than normal in a whole ham.

Country Style – Means the product is dry cured and smoked.

Cured – Meat soaked or injected with a brine solution to extend shelf life and/or to impart the flavors of the curing agents.

Dry Cured – Cured without soaking or by injection.

Fat Free Percent Label Declarations – A product may state that it is a certain percent fat free, such as "95 percent Fat Free," provided the declaration also states the exact amount of fat the product contains, as in this example it contains 5 percent fat. The statement only relates to the fat content, not the total amount of lean in the product, since the product may also contain water and seasonings.

Fully Cooked – To be considered fully cooked the product generally must have reached a minimum internal temperature of 148°F and show product characteristics typical of a cooked product: partial bone separation, color, texture, flavor, etc.

"Ham," "Ham with Natural Juices," "Ham, Water Added," "Ham and Water Product" – These product labels in the order listed above indicate how much water remains in the ham after its final processing. A "HAM" only label means no water, or only a minimal naturally occurring amount of water remaining.

Ham, Boiled – A fully cooked, boneless product that must be cooked in water. May be processed either in a can or a casing.

Ham, Chopped – Not to be confused with CHOPPED HAM. Though the product is similar, it may contain up to a maximum of 37 percent shank meat, which is 25 percent more than normally present in a ham.

Ham, Chunked and Formed, or Ham, Ground and Formed – A product that has been processed by mechanical means so that its cut surface appearance is substantially different from that expected to be seen in the usual ham product.

Honey Cured – Honey shall be used in sufficient amounts to flavor and/or affect the appearance of the finished product.

PFF (Protein Fat Free) – Because added water dilutes the natural protein content of the product, FSIS requires minimum PFF percentages for hams and other cured pork products processed with the addition of added ingredients and differing amounts of water, except bacon. The product with the least water has the highest PFF percentage requirement.

Pullman Style – Refers to a meat product packed into a long container usually either rectangular or square shaped on its ends.

Skinned vs. Skinless – Skinned means that a specified amount or specified area of skin shall be removed. Skinless means that all the skin has been removed.

Smoked – The process by which meat cuts have been exposed to the dry smoke of hardwoods, or which have had externally applied liquid smoke flavor transmitted to the product by heat transfer, or which has had liquid smoke injected into the product along with a brine solution. If injected, the item must be labeled "Smoke Flavor Added."

Spiral Sliced – A method of mechanically slicing a ham while leaving the ham attached to the bone.

Two-Toned Color – More than a slight color variation between two or more different muscles within a single sliced surface.

Información para hacer los pedidos

Lo especificará el comprador

A los compradores se les ofrece una variedad de opciones diferentes con las que pueden seleccionar el producto que mejor se ajuste a sus necesidades. Algunas de estas opciones son técnicas, y otras son cuestión de gusto. En algunos casos en los que el comprador no elija, se especificará por omisión una opción predeterminada. En otros casos, el vendedor puede ejercer su propia opción. Cuando existen opciones, los compradores y vendedores deben llegar a un acuerdo mutuo con respecto a las especificaciones, la información para hacer los pedidos y los requisitos materiales de los productos objeto de transacción.

A continuación se incluye un breve resumen de algunos ejemplos de información para hacer los pedidos y requisitos materiales correspondientes a la Serie 500 de IMPS (Especificaciones de Compras Institucionales de Carne, por sus siglas en inglés) para productos de cerdo curado, curado y ahumado, y completamente cocido.

Estado de refrigeración

A **FRESCO**	−2.2 °C (28 °F) o mayor	
B **CONGELADO**	−2.2 °C (28 °F) o menor	
C **OPCIÓN ESPECIFICADA POR EL COMPRADOR**	−17.8 °C (0 °F) o menor	

Si no se selecciona, el producto se entregará como la opción A.

Tolerancias de peso y grosor de la porción

Peso*	Variación de porciones
Menos de 170 g (6.0 oz.)	± 7 g (0.25 oz.)
Más de 170 g (6.0 oz.)	± 14 g (0.50 oz.)

Grosor*	Variación de rebanadas
Menos de 2.5 cm (1.0 pulgada)	± 5 mm (0.1875 pulgadas)
Más de 2.5 cm (1.0 pulgada)	± 6 mm (0.25 pulgadas)

* En todos los casos, ya sea por peso o grosor, el grosor de las porciones o rebanadas no podrá variar de un extremo de la pieza al otro en más de 5 mm (0.1875 pulgadas) en su tamaño más pequeño, o 6 mm (0.25 pulgadas) en su mayor tamaño.

Estilos

Estilos	Nombre de IMPS	Ingredientes agregados			
		Jugos naturales	Agua	X% del peso son ingredientes agregados	Proteína de soya aislada
A	•				
B	•	•			
C	•		•		
D	•		•	•	
E	•		•		•
F	•		•	•	•

Salvo por la exclusión de ciertas piezas, el comprador puede decidir si desea que un producto incluya jugos naturales, agua o proteína de soya aislada. Las piezas excluidas se marcarán con un asterisco (*) en el índice de la Serie 500.

Si el comprador no identifica el estilo del producto deseado cuando corresponda indicar una opción, el estilo predeterminado por omisión es el Estilo B, "Nombre de IMPS", con Jugos Naturales.

Ordering Data

To Be Specified by the Purchaser

Purchasers are provided with a number of different options by which they may select the product best suited to their needs. Some of these options are technical, and others are a matter of choice. In some cases where the purchaser fails to make a choice, a default is specified. In other cases, the seller may exercise its own option. When options exist, buyers and sellers should reach an agreement between themselves with respect to the specifications, ordering data, and material requirements of the products expected to be purchased.

A brief summary of some Ordering Data and Material Requirements applicable to IMPS Series 500 for Cured, Cured and Smoked, and Fully Cooked Pork Products follows.

State of Refrigeration

A FRESH	28°F (−2.2°C) or higher
B FROZEN	28°F (−2.2°C) or lower
C PSO	0°F (−17.8°C) or lower

If not selected, product will be delivered as Option A.

Portion-Cut Weight and Thickness Tolerances

Weight*	Portion Variance
Less than 6.0 oz. (170 g)	± 0.25 oz. (7 g)
Over 6.0 oz. (170 g)	± 0.50 oz. (14 g)

Thickness*	Slice Variance
Less than 1.0 inch (2.5 cm)	± 0.1875 inch (5 mm)
More than 1.0 inch (2.5 cm)	± 0.25 inch (6 mm)

* In all instances whether by weight or thickness, the portions or slices may not vary in thickness from one end of the piece to the other by more than 0.1875 inch (5 mm) at the smaller size or 0.25 inch (6 mm) at the larger size.

Styles

		Ingredients Added			
Styles	IMPS Name	Natural Juices	Water	X% of Weight is Added Ingred.	Isolated Soy Protein
A	•				
B	•	•			
C	•		•		
D	•		•	•	
E	•		•		•
F	•		•	•	•

Except for the exclusion of certain items, the purchaser has a choice as to whether the product may be ordered to include natural juices, water, or isolated soy protein. The excluded items will be marked with an asterisk (*) in the Series 500 Table of Contents.

If the purchaser fails to identify the style of product desired when a choice is appropriate, the default is Style B, "IMPS Name," with Natural Juices.

Requisitos materiales

Varios requisitos materiales se aplican a los productos incluidos en la Serie 500 de IMPS (Especificaciones de Compras Institucionales de Carne, por sus siglas en inglés). Los reglamentos del Servicio de Inspección e Inocuidad Alimentaria establecen algunas de ellas y el proceso de certificación de AMS, (Servicio de Mercadeo Agrícola, por sus siglas en inglés) impone otras condiciones. A continuación se proporciona una breve lista.

Procedimientos de proteína libre de grasa

Se aplica cuando corresponda. Consulte la definición de los términos.

Aspectos de calidad

Estos se refieren al carácter de los cortes utilizados e incluyen referencias en cuanto a la carnosidad, la magrez, el grosor de la grasa, la textura, el color, la ausencia de hematomas y huesos quebrados, y la condición del esqueleto.

Colocar en una red o amarrar

Los términos se consideran intercambiables y a menos que el comprador solicite lo contrario de forma específica, el producto se colocará (enmallado) en una red.

Requisitos del envoltorio

Si se utilizan envoltorios artificiales, los materiales deben ser adecuados para evitar rasgaduras, agujeros y fisuras, y para conservar el alto vacío, si corresponde, y deben ser lo suficientemente fuertes como para contener el producto.

Requisitos de corte y limpieza

Estos requisitos indican en cierto detalle los procedimientos que se deben emplear para cortar y recortar la grasa de las piezas descritas en esta Serie de IMPS (Especificaciones de Compras Institucionales de Carne, por sus siglas en inglés). A menos que se describa lo contrario, el corte se debe realizar en una línea recta perpendicular a la superficie exterior. Los procedimientos de recorte de grasa varían en función de la pieza en cuestión. Se indica que el grosor de grasa promedio máximo debe ser de 6 mm (0.25 pulgadas) y el grosor de grasa máximo en cualquier punto debe ser de 13 mm (0.5 pulgadas). La definición de prácticamente desprovista de grasa (75% de carne magra expuesta) permite un máximo de 6 mm (0.25 pulgadas) de grasa. Los requisitos que se indican en las descripciones de las piezas tienen prioridad.

Requisitos de peso escurrido

A menos que el comprador especifique lo contrario, las piezas enlatadas y las piezas cocidas sin ahumar en bolsas plásticas para cocinar, además de cumplir con los porcentajes de PFF (Proteína Libre de Grasa, por sus siglas en inglés), también deben cumplir con los siguientes requisitos de peso escurrido.

Latas Pullman (forma cuadrada): el peso escurrido no debe ser inferior al 97% del peso neto marcado.

Latas con forma de pera: no menos de 95% como se indica anteriormente.

Bolsas plásticas para cocinar: no menos de 99% como se indica anteriormente.

Productos de proteína de soya

Describe los requisitos de PFF (Proteína Libre de Grasa, por sus siglas en inglés) para los Estilos E y F y otros procedimientos aplicables cuando se utiliza proteína de soya.

Programa de Nutrición Infantil (CN, por sus siglas en inglés)

Describe los procedimientos y los requisitos de etiquetado que se aplican a los productos del Programa de Nutrición Infantil.

Material Requirements

A number of material requirements apply to the products included in the IMPS 500 Series. Some of these are established by FSIS regulations and others are conditions imposed under the AMS certification process. A brief listing follows.

Protein Fat Free Procedures

Applied when appropriate. See Definition of Terms.

Quality Aspects

These refer to the character of the cuts used and include references to meatiness, leanness, fat thicknesses, texture, color, absence of bruises and broken bones, and skeletal condition.

Netting or Tying

The terms are considered to be interchangeable and unless specifically requested otherwise by the purchaser the product will be netted.

Casing Requirements

If artificial casings are used, the materials shall be adequate to prevent tears, holes, and splits, as well as to maintain a vacuum if applicable, and strong enough to contain the product.

Cutting and Trimming Requirements

These requirements spell out in some detail the procedures that are to be used to cut and trim the items described in this IMPS Series. Unless otherwise described, cutting shall be made in a straight line perpendicular to the outer surface. Trimming procedures vary depending on the item involved. The maximum average fat thickness is described to be 0.25 inch (6 mm) with a maximum fat thickness at any one point to be 0.5 inch (13 mm). The Practically Free (75 percent lean exposed) definition allows a maximum of 0.25 inch (6 mm) fat. Requirements stated in the item descriptions take precedence.

Drained-Weight Requirements

Unless a purchaser would specify differently, canned items and non-smoked cooked items in plastic cooking bags, in addition to meeting PFF percentages, must also meet the following drained-weight requirements.

> Pullman Cans: Drained weight not less than 97 percent of the marked net weight.
>
> Pear-Shaped Cans: Not less than 95 percent as above.
>
> Plastic Cooking Bags: Not less than 99 percent as above.

Soy Protein Products

Describes the PFF requirements for Styles E and F and other procedures applicable when soy protein is used.

Child Nutrition Program (CN)

Describes the procedures and labeling requirements applicable to CN products.

501 — Ham, Short Shank, (Cured and Smoked)

This ham is a cured and smoked product produced from a Pork Leg (fresh ham) meeting the material requirements of Item No. 401A. The ham has been separated from the side by a straight cut approximately perpendicular to a line parallel to the shank bones that is not less than 1.5 inches (3.8 cm) or more than 3.5 inches (8.9 cm) from the anterior edge of the aitch bone. Approximately one half or more of the shank has also been removed by a straight cut at a right angle to the shank bones. The tail, vertebrae, membrane, flank muscle, and any exposed lymph glands are removed. The skin and collar fat over the cushion shall be smooth and well rounded. The innermost curvature of the skin is trimmed back at least half the distance from the stifle joint to the posterior edge of the aitch bone. Additional skin and fat shall also be removed close to the lean in the knuckle and pelvis areas. Each ham shall be individually wrapped in moisture and grease-resistant wax paper or plastic. Unless otherwise specified by the purchaser, fat thickness beneath the ham face measured at the skin edge directly under the bone shall not exceed the measurements in the table below.

Weight Range of Ham	Max. Fat Thickness
14 to 17 pounds (6.4 to 7.7 kg)	0.50 inch (1.3 cm)
17 to 20 pounds (7.7 to 9.1 kg)	0.75 inch (1.9 cm)
20 to 26 pounds (9.1 to 11.8 kg)	1.00 inch (2.5 cm)
26 pounds and up (11.8 kg and up)	1.25 inches (3.2 cm)

501 — Jamón, de Chamorro Corto (Curado y Ahumado)

Este jamón es un producto curado y ahumado que se fabrica con una pierna de cerdo (jamón fresco) que cumple con los requisitos materiales de la pieza número 401A. La pierna se separa del lado con un corte recto aproximadamente perpendicular a una línea paralela a los huesos del chamorro que no se encuentre a menos de 3.8 cm (1.5 pulgadas) ni a más de 8.9 cm (3.5 pulgadas) del borde anterior del hueso de la cadera. También se quita aproximadamente la mitad o algo más del chamorro con un corte recto en ángulo recto con los huesos del chamorro. Se quita la cola, las vértebras, la membrana, el músculo de la falda y todos los ganglios linfáticos expuestos. El collar de piel y grasa que queda sobre el "cojín muscular" debe ser suave y bien redondeado. La curvatura más interior de la piel se vuelve a recortar como mínimo a la mitad de la distancia desde la articulación de la rodilla hasta el borde posterior del hueso de la cadera. También se debe quitar más piel y grasa hasta llegar casi a la carne magra en las áreas de la pulpa bola y la pelvis. Cada jamón se debe envolver individualmente en papel de cera o plástico resistente a la humedad y la grasa. A menos que el comprador especifique lo contrario, el grosor de la grasa debajo de la cara del jamón, medida en el borde de piel, directamente debajo del hueso, no debe superar las medidas de la siguiente tabla.

Escala de peso del jamón	Máx. grosor de la grasa
6.4 a 7.7 kg (14 a 17 libras)	1.3 cm (0.50 pulgadas)
7.7 a 9.1 kg (17 a 20 libras)	1.9 cm (0.75 pulgadas)
9.1 a 11.8 kg (20 a 26 libras)	2.5 cm (1.00 pulgada)
11.8 kg y más (26 libras y más)	3.2 cm (1.25 pulgadas)

503 — Ham, Short Shank, Skinned (Cured and Smoked), Fully Cooked

503 — Jamón, de Chamorro Corto, Sin Piel/Lonja (Curado y Ahumado), Completamente Cocido

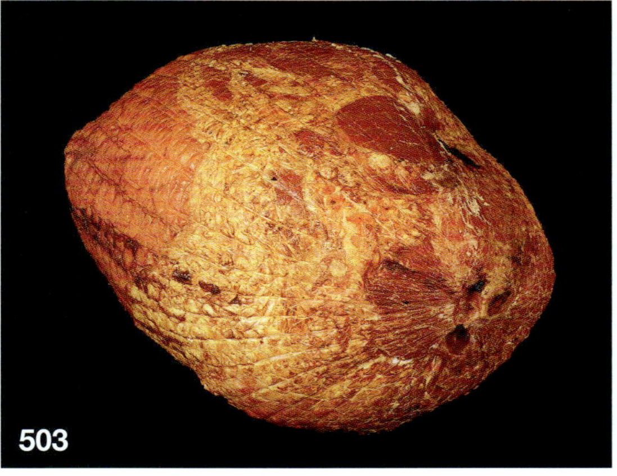

503

The ham is separated from the carcass with parallel cuts not more than 3.0 inches (7.5 cm) or less than 1.5 inches (3.8 cm) from the front of the aitch bone and between the stifle joint and the achilles tendon so that at least half of the shank has been removed. The tail, vertebrae, flank muscle and exposed lymph gland shall be removed. The skin shall be removed at least to the stifle joint and the skin collar well rounded with the fat remaining on the skinned area not over 0.25 inch (6 mm) average depth with a maximum of 0.5 inch (13 mm) at any point within 1.5 inches (3.8 cm) or more from the edge of the skin collar. The fat along the butt end shall be neatly beveled to meet the lean. In addition to curing, any further trimming, skinning, or defatting must be completed prior to smoking so that the finished product is smoothly trimmed and uniformly smoked on its entire surface. Promptly after cooking using a dry-heat method, the Fully Cooked smoked ham, if necessary, shall have any rendered surface fat or extraneous matter removed. It shall then be properly chilled to between 28 and 40°F prior to individually wrapping it in a suitable moisture- and grease-resistant plastic or paper.

La pierna (jamón fresco) se separa de la canal con dos cortes paralelos, uno de no más de 7.5 cm (3.0 pulgadas) ni menos de 3.8 cm (1.5 pulgadas) delante del hueso de la cadera y otro entre la articulación de la rodilla y el tendón de Aquiles, para quitar al menos la mitad del chamorro. Se deben quitar la cola, las vértebras, el músculo de la falda y los ganglios linfáticos expuestos. La piel se debe quitar al menos hasta la articulación de la rodilla, dejando un collar de piel bien redondeado y una cubierta de grasa remanente sobre el área sin piel que no debe superar una profundidad promedio de 6 mm (0.25 pulgadas) con un máximo de 13 mm (0.5 pulgadas) en cualquier punto ubicado a una distancia de 3.8 cm (1.5 pulgadas) o más del borde del collar de piel. La grasa a lo largo del extremo adyacente a la cabeza del filete se debe emparejar hasta nivelarse con la carne magra. Además del curado, se debe completar cualquier recorte o limpieza de grasa antes del ahumado para que el producto final quede suavemente limpio de grasa y uniformemente ahumado en toda su superficie. Si es necesario, inmediatamente después de la cocción mediante un método de calor seco, se deberá eliminar de la superficie del jamón completamente cocido y ahumado cualquier grasa derretida o sustancia o material extraño que se presente. Luego se deberá refrigerar adecuadamente a temperaturas entre -2.2 y 4 °C (28 y 40 °F) antes de envolverlo individualmente en un papel o plástico adecuado resistente a la humedad y a la grasa.

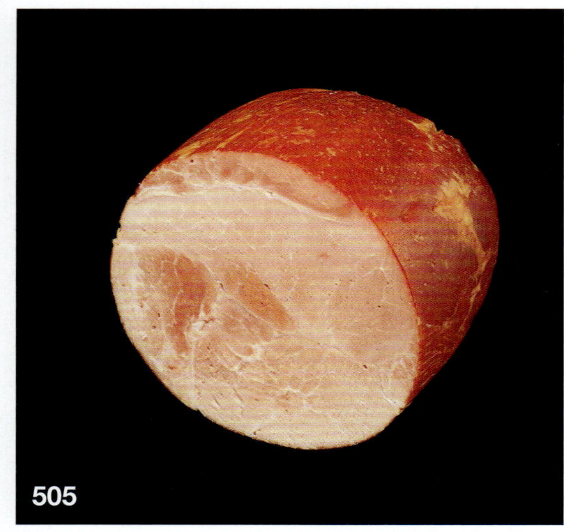

505

Ham, Boneless, (Cured and Smoked), Fully Cooked

The boneless ham represented by this description conforms to the requirements of Item No. 503, except that in addition to it being completely boneless and skinless, it shall also be free of the *popliteal* and all exposed lymph glands and any exposed heavy (opaque) connective tissue. In addition, any surface fat in excess of 0.25 inch (6 mm) depth at any point shall be removed. The femur, aitch bone, and shank bones shall be closely removed without undue scoring or damage to the ham. Prior to smoking and cooking, the ham shall be placed in a casing so that the major muscle fibers run lengthwise with the casing so as to permit slicing at approximately right angles to the long axis of the ham. The finished product shall be smooth and compact and free of pockets of air, moisture, or rendered fat. The ham may be cylindrical, oval, or elliptical in shape. Purchasers who prefer this product netted or string tied, but not in an artificial casing, should specify Item No. 505A.

505

Jamón, Deshuesado (Curado y Ahumado), Completamente Cocido

El jamón deshuesado que representa esta descripción se ajusta a los requisitos de la pieza número 503, con la diferencia de que además de ser completamente deshuesado y sin piel (lonja), no debe tener expuesto el ganglio *poplíteo* ni ningún tejido conectivo grueso (opaco). Además, se debe quitar toda la cubierta de grasa que supere los 6 mm (0.25 pulgadas) de profundidad en cualquier punto. El fémur, el hueso de la cadera y los huesos del chamorro se deben eliminar cuidadosamente sin dejar incisiones profundas indebidas ni algún otro daño al jamón. Antes del ahumado y la cocción, el jamón se debe colocar en un envoltorio de modo que las fibras musculares principales queden longitudinalmente alineadas con respecto al envoltorio para permitir el rebanado en ángulos aproximadamente rectos al eje longitudinal del jamón. El producto final debe ser de formas suaves y compacto, y no debe tener cavidades llenas de aire, humedad o de grasa derretida. El jamón puede tener una forma cilíndrica, ovalada o elíptica. Los compradores que prefieran este producto atado con cuerda o enmallado con una red, pero no en un envoltorio artificial, deben especificar la pieza número 505A.

508

Ham, Boiled, Boneless (Cured), Fully Cooked

This item may be prepared from any portion or portions of one or more hams that have been trimmed practically free of fat and heavy (opaque) connective tissue. Shank meat, if ground or chopped, only may be used as a binder up to an amount allowed by FSIS. The finished product may be requested in a pullman or pear shape, packaged either in a plastic-lined can or close fitting heat-sealed plastic-type bag free from gelatinous material, fat, or other matter on the exterior of the ham. If desired, smoke flavoring may be added and the product so labeled.

508

Jamón, Hervido, Deshuesado (Curado), Completamente Cocido

Esta pieza se puede preparar con cualquier porción o porciones de una o más piernas a las que se haya recortado prácticamente toda la grasa y el tejido conectivo grueso (opaco). La carne del chamorro, si se llega a moler o picar, sólo se puede utilizar como aglutinante en la cantidad permitida por el Servicio de Inspección e Inocuidad Alimentaria. El producto final se debe solicitar en forma de pera o al estilo pullman (forma cuadrada), envasado en una lata revestida de plástico o bien ajustado dentro de una bolsa plástica sellada con calor sin contener material gelatinoso, grasa o cualquier otra sustancia extraña en el exterior del jamón. Si se desea, se pueden agregar saborizantes ahumados, y el producto se debe etiquetar como corresponde.

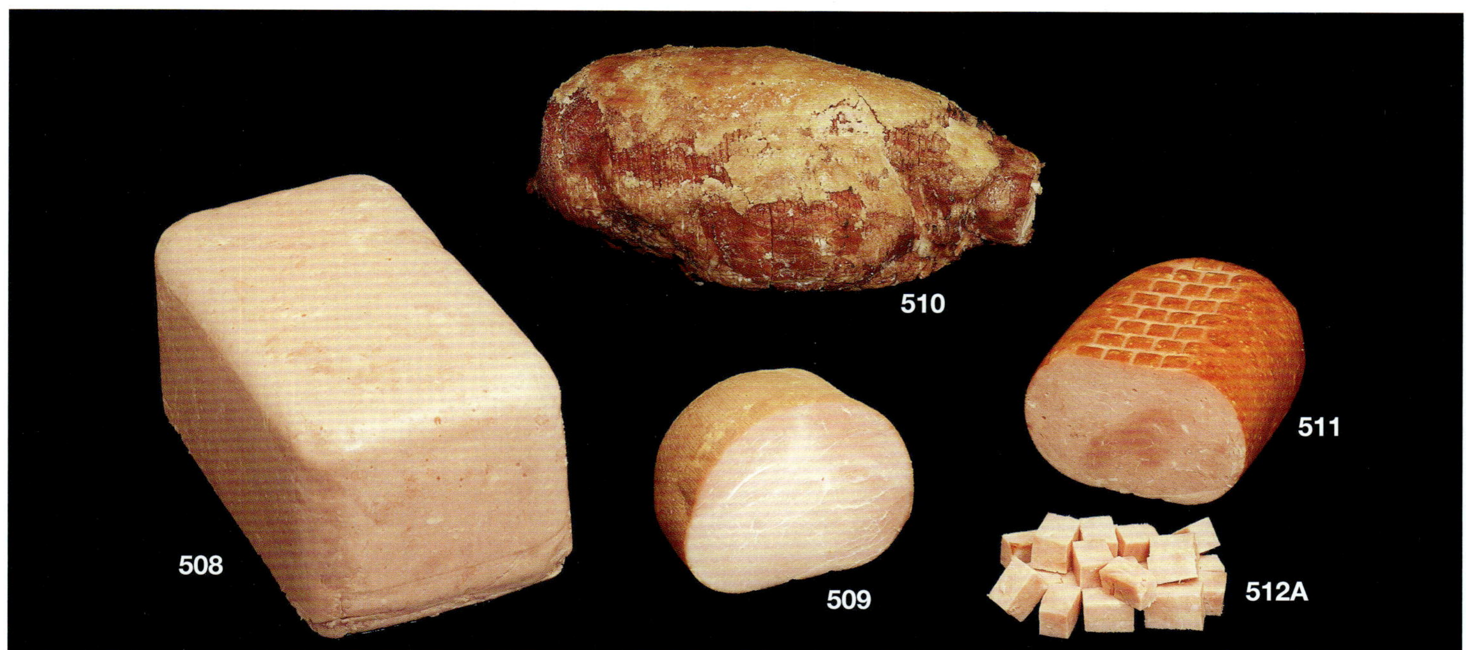

509 — Ham, Boneless (Cured and Smoked), Fully Cooked, Special

This product is prepared from either one or a combination of the inside or outside muscle portions of a ham. Any remaining portion of the ham may only be used if ground or chopped and used as a binder up to an amount allowed by FSIS. The lean muscle shall be trimmed of all fat including seam fat and shall be practically free from exposed heavy (opaque) connective tissue. A cross section of the item shall not show more than the appearance of four whole muscle systems (excluding binder) and shall be uniform in color without any two-tone effect across the entire cut surface.

509 — Jamón, Deshuesado (Curado y Ahumado), Completamente Cocido, Especial

Este producto se prepara con una porción o con la combinación de porciones de músculos de la cara o contracara de la pierna. Cualquier porción restante del jamón sólo se puede utilizar si ésta se muele o se pica y se utiliza como aglutinante hasta la cantidad que permite el Servicio de Inspección e Inocuidad Alimentaria. Al músculo magro se le debe recortar todas las grasas, incluidas las vetas de grasa intermuscular, y debe estar prácticamente desprovisto de tejido conectivo grueso (opaco) expuesto. Un corte transversal de la pieza no deberá mostrar más que la apariencia de cuatro sistemas musculares completos (excluido el aglutinante muscular) y debe tener un color uniforme sin efecto alguno de tono bicolor en toda la superficie de corte.

510 — Ham, Honey-Cured (Smoked), Partially Boned, Spiral Cut

This product is produced from a completely skinless ham that has had honey included in its curing process prior to smoking. The shank shall be removed from the ham through the natural seam that separated the shank from the heel. The aitch bone and overlying flesh and the shank bones shall be removed without undue scoring or other damage to the ham while leaving the femur bone intact. All surface fat in excess of 0.25 inch (6mm) average depth and 0.5 inch (13mm) at any point shall be removed. The ham shall be spiral sliced to the thickness specified by the purchaser so that the slices remain firmly attached to the femur bone. The smooth, plumb, elongated, oval-shaped, spiral-sliced ham shall be vacuum packaged in a close-fitting polyethylene plastic bag. Though not designated as such by this item number, the spiral cut ham may also be specified by the purchaser to be fully cooked by the dry heat method. (*Pictured on page 241.*)

510 — Jamón, Curado con Miel (Ahumado), Deshuesado Parcial, Corte en Espiral

Este producto se produce con una pierna completamente sin piel (lonja) cuyo proceso de curado incluye el agregado de miel antes de proceder al ahumado. Se debe quitar el chamorro del jamón a través del surco natural que separa el chamorro del talón. Se debe quitar el hueso de la cadera y la carne que lo recubre, así como los huesos del chamorro, sin producir incisiones profundas indebidos ni otro daño al jamón, y también se debe dejar el hueso del fémur intacto. Se debe quitar toda la cubierta de grasa que supere los 6 mm (0.25 pulgadas) de profundidad promedio y los 13 mm (0.5 pulgadas) en cualquier punto. El jamón se debe rebanar en espiral con el grosor que especifique el comprador cuidando que las rebanadas permanezcan firmemente adheridas al hueso del fémur. El jamón de forma suave, bien aplomado, alargado, con silueta ovalada y rebanado en espiral se debe envasar al vacío, bien ajustado, en una bolsa plástica de polietileno. Aunque no se designe como tal en este número de pieza, el comprador también puede especificar que el jamón con corte en espiral esté completamente cocido con el método de calor seco. (*Ilustración en la página 241*).

511 — Ham, Chunked and Formed (Cured), Fully Cooked

This ham may be prepared from any portion of a ham that will meet the end-item description for this product. Shank meat, however, may only be used if it is ground or chopped and used as a binder in accord with FSIS regulations. The ham itself shall be free from bones, cartilage, skin, heavy connective tissue, air or gelatin pockets, and lymph glands. A cross-section cut of this item will show a definition of various muscle groups as you would expect to see of chunks of ham that are held together with a binder of finely ground ham trimmings or finely ground shank meat. Purchaser may order this item either in an artificial casing or in a can. If ordered canned, the ham shall be fully enclosed in a polyethylene liner and unless otherwise specified shall be pullman style. (*Pictured on page 241.*)

511 — Jamón, Troceado y Moldeado (Curado), Completamente Cocido

Este jamón se puede preparar con cualquier porción de la pierna que cumpla con la descripción de pieza final para este producto. Sin embargo, la carne del chamorro sólo se puede utilizar si es molida o picada y se usa como aglutinante, de acuerdo con los reglamentos del Servicio de Inspección e Inocuidad Alimentaria. El jamón en sí mismo no debe incluir huesos, cartílagos, piel, tejido conectivo grueso, cavidades de gelatina o de aire, ni ganglios linfáticos. Un corte transversal de esta pieza mostrará una definición de varios grupos musculares como se esperaría ver cuando los trozos de jamón se mantienen pegados con un aglutinante compuesto por recortes de jamón finamente molidos o por carne de chamorro finamente molida. El comprador podrá pedir esta pieza en una envoltura artificial o en una lata. Si se pide en lata, el jamón se deberá envolver completamente en un forro de polietileno y, a menos que se especifique lo contrario, deberá seguir el estilo pullman (de forma cuadrada). (*Ilustración en la página 241*).

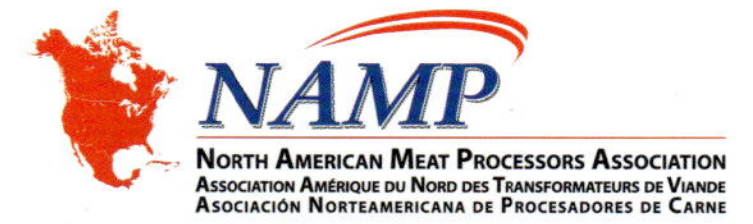

511A — Ham, Chunked and Formed (Cured and Smoked), Fully Cooked

This item may be prepared from any portion of the ham excluding shank meat unless the shank meat is ground or chopped and used as a binder in accordance with federal regulations. The ham shall be free from bones, cartilage, skin, heavy connective tissue, air or gelatin pockets, and lymph glands. A cross-section view of the ham will show chunks of ham held together with a binder of finely ground or chopped shank meat or ham trimmings. The cured ham shall be stuffed into an artificial casing and smoked. The use of artificial smoke flavoring is not allowed.

511A — Jamón, Troceado y Moldeado (Curado y Ahumado), Completamente Cocido

Esta pieza se puede preparar con cualquier porción de la pierna (jamón) excluyendo la carne de chamorro, a menos que se muela o pique la carne de chamorro y se utilice como aglutinante de acuerdo con los reglamentos federales. El jamón no debe incluir huesos, cartílagos, piel, tejido conectivo grueso, cavidades de gelatina o aire, ni ganglios linfáticos. Una sección transversal del jamón mostrará trozos de jamón pegados con un aglutinante de carne de chamorro finamente molida o picada, o recortes de jamón. El jamón curado debe estar envasado en una envoltura artificial y ahumado. No está permitido el uso de saborizantes para impartir artificialmente el sabor a ahumado.

512A — Ham, Diced (Cured and Smoked)

Product for this item shall come from ham that is cured, smoked, and fully cooked prior to dicing. All trimming, skinning, or defatting as required may be done either before or after curing but must be completed prior to smoking or dicing. The use of smoke flavoring is not permitted in this product. Any appropriate Series 500 ham or portions thereof may be used or specified by the purchaser to meet the end requirements of this item. Dices shall be practically free from shank and heel meat (innershank), fat, bones, cartilage, skin, connective tissue, and lymph glands. The meat may be either hand or mechanically diced but grinding or chopping is not allowed. To facilitate dicing, the product may be frozen and/or tempered one time prior to dicing. The size of both the dice and package must be specified by the purchaser. *(Pictured on page 241.)*

512A — Jamón, Troceado en Cubos (Curado y Ahumado)

El producto para esta pieza debe ser de un jamón que esté curado, ahumado y completamente cocido antes del troceado en cubos. Se pueden realizar todos los recortes, despellejes o extracciones de grasa que se requieran antes o después del curado, pero esta limpieza se debe completar antes de proceder al ahumado o troceado en cubos. En este producto no se permite el uso de saborizantes de ahumado. Se puede utilizar cualquier jamón adecuado de la Serie 500 o porciones del mismo, o bien, el comprador lo puede especificar para que cumpla con los requisitos finales de esta pieza. Los trozos en cubos deberán estar prácticamente libres de carne de chamorro y talón (chamorro interno), grasa, huesos, cartílago, piel, tejido conectivo y ganglios linfáticos. La carne se puede trocear a mano o mecánicamente, pero no se permite molerla ni picarla. Para facilitar el troceado en cubos, el producto se puede congelar y/o atemperar por una vez antes del troceado. El comprador debe especificar el tamaño del cubo y del envase. *(Ilustración en la página 241).*

530 — Pork Shoulder Butt, Cellar Trimmed, Boneless (Cured and Smoked)

In addition to meeting the material requirements of Item No. 407, this item shall be trimmed so that any surface fat in excess of 0.25 inch (6 mm) is excluded. The trimmed, boneless shoulder butt shall be cured and stuffed into a close, smooth-fitting artificial casing, either prior to or after smoking. Dissolved clear gelatin may be used to momentarily dip the product to facilitate stuffing into the casing. Promptly after smoking, the finished product shall have all grease and extraneous matter removed.

If the purchaser desires that this item be further trimmed to remove the false lean and additional fat from the meat surface, so that the surface is at least 75 percent practically free from fat with no other fat in excess of 0.25 inch (6 mm) remaining, then the purchaser should specify Item No. 531, Pork Boston Butt, Boneless (Cured and Smoked), Special.

530 — Cabeza de Lomo, Recortada de Grasa sin Hueso de Paleta, Deshuesada (Curada y Ahumada)

Además de cumplir con los requisitos materiales de la pieza número 407, se deberá recortar la grasa de esta pieza para excluir toda la cubierta de grasa que supere los 6 mm (0.25 pulgadas). La cabeza de lomo recortada de grasa y deshuesada se deberá curar y embutir en una tripa artificial ajustada suavemente, antes o después del ahumado. Se puede usar gelatina transparente disuelta para remojar momentáneamente el producto para facilitar el embutido en la tripa. Inmediatamente después del ahumado, se deberá eliminar toda la grasa y el material extraño al producto final.

Si el comprador desea un recorte adicional de esta pieza para quitar la carne magra falsa y más grasa de la cubierta de la carne, para que la superficie sea al menos un 75% libre de grasa con ningún otro exceso de grasa que los 6 mm (0.25 pulgadas) restantes, debe especificar la pieza número 531, Cabeza de Lomo de Cerdo, Deshuesada (Curada y Ahumada), Especial.

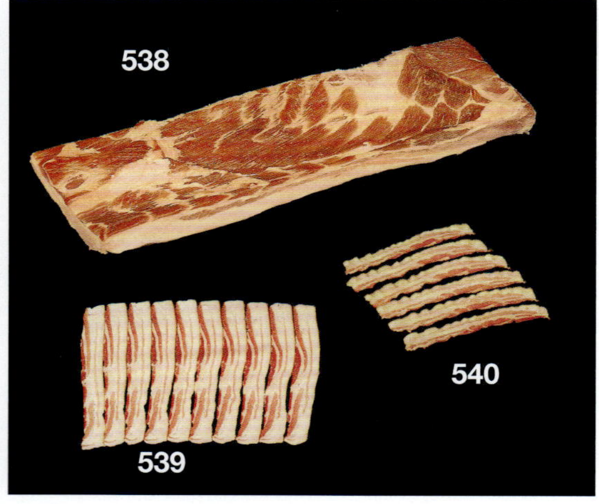

538 — Bacon, Slab, Center-Cut (Cured and Smoked), Skinless, Formed

The slab bacon meeting this item description is produced from a cured and smoked belly that is square on all edges with approximately straight and parallel sides and ends, which will have been pressed and formed skinless after smoking and cooling. The fat back will have been removed by a straight cut dorsal to, but not exceeding 0.5 inch (13 mm) of the outermost curvature of the scribe line. The ventral portion of the belly shall have been removed by a straight cut dorsal to the teat line. The belly from which this item is produced will have no bone or cartilage, and will be practically free of leaf fat. It shall also be free of enlarged, soft, porous, or seedy mammary tissue; pizzle recesses; scores; or other damage. The skin shall have been removed either before or after curing but before smoking, leaving a smoothly skinned surface free of hair roots. The maximum thickness of the formed slab shall not exceed 2.25 inches (5.6 cm). The minimum thickness of the slab shall not be less than 0.75 inch (19 mm). There shall be no area of exposed fat on the face side of the belly that exceeds 4.0 square inches (25 sq. cm).

538 — Tocino, Trozo de Panceta (Barriga), Corte del Centro (Curado y Ahumado), Sin Piel/Lonja, Moldeado

El trozo de panceta que cumple con la descripción de esta pieza se produce con una barriga curada y ahumada que es cuadrada en todos los bordes con lados y extremos aproximadamente rectos y paralelos, que deberá haber sido prensada y moldeada sin lonja después del ahumado y enfriamiento. La lonja sin piel de la chuleta se quitará con un corte dorsal recto a 13 mm (0.5 pulgadas) como máximo de la curvatura exterior de la línea de trazado del corte. La porción ventral de la barriga se deberá haber quitado con un corte dorsal recto en la línea de las tetillas. La barriga de la cual se produce esta pieza no deberá tener huesos ni cartílagos, y estará prácticamente libre de la tela de grasa visceral. Además, no deberá tener tejido mamario agrandado, suave, poroso ni de mal aspecto (granuloso), restos ocultos penianos, cortes profundos, ni algún otro daño. La piel se deberá haber quitado antes o después del curado pero siempre antes del ahumado, dejando una superficie suave sin raíces de pelo. El grosor máximo del trozo de panceta formado no deberá superar los 5.6 cm (2.25 pulgadas). El grosor mínimo del trozo de panceta no deberá ser inferior a 19 mm (0.75 pulgadas). No deberá tener un área de grasa expuesta en el lado frontal de la barriga mayor a 25 cm² (4.0 pulgadas cuadradas).

539 Bacon, Sliced (Cured and Smoked), Skinless

Sliced bacon meeting this item description may be produced from any Series 500 skinless slab bacon such as the Item No. 538 illustrated. Individual slices in each package or container shall at least be reasonably uniform in length, width, and thickness, and range from 8 to 10 inches (20 to 25 cm) in length without underfolding. The surface lean on the face of the slice shall extend at least 75 percent of the length of the slice. Unsliced pieces or slices showing hanger comb marks, product residue, punctured or mutilated sections, bruises, or severe muscle separation shall be excluded. Any slices with breaks extending more than half the width of the slice, or those cut on an appreciable slant or bias, or which have any bone, cartilage, skin, or hair roots or other belly defects or serious damage shall also be excluded. If necessary, one part slice may be used in each package or container to make the declared exact weight. The part slice shall not be considered when determining defects. The bacon package or container shall contain the number of slices per pound as specified according to the weight range table. *(Pictured on page 244.)*

Number of Slices Per Pound

12–14, 14–18, 18–22, 22–26, 26–30, 28–32, or as specified.

Packaging Options

Purchasers must specify the packaging option they desire either in individual one-pound packages or bulk packaged as follows:

1. **Laid out** – Laid out bacon is a product that is packaged as individually spaced slices placed adjacent to each other on grease- and/or heat-resistant paper.

2. **Shingle** – Shingled bacon is a product wherein the slices overlap one another and are packaged on grease-resistant paper or board.

3. **Stack** – Stacked bacon has slices packaged on edge in their sequence of slicing on grease resistant paper or board.

Packaged bacon will be made available in suitable boxes in quantities ordinarily weighing from 12 to 24 pounds. Depending on the option chosen the sliced bacon may also be available or specified in sealed one-pound packages, vacuum packed or gas flushed or in laminated plastic pouches. Purchasers may also request chemical analyses for fat, moisture, and the salt content of bacon. The analysis may be specified for one or all of the above. Unless otherwise specified the fat content shall not exceed 61 percent, the salt content 2.5 percent, and the moisture content 3.0 percent by calculation as determined in accordance with the official methods of the Association of Analytical Chemists at an FSIS-approved laboratory designated by the vendor.

539 Tocino, Rebanado (Curado y Ahumado), Sin Piel/Lonja

El tocino rebanado que cumple con la descripción de esta pieza se puede producir con cualquiera de los trozos de panceta sin lonja de la serie 500, como la pieza número 538 que se muestra en la ilustración. Las rebanadas individuales de cada paquete o recipiente deberán tener un largo, ancho y grosor razonablemente uniformes, y el largo podrá variar entre 20 y 25 cm (8 a 10 pulgadas) sin plegarse. La carne magra que queda en la superficie de la cara de la rebanada deberá extenderse al menos un 75% a lo largo de la rebanada. Se deberán excluir las piezas sin rebanar o rebanadas que presenten marcas de ganchos, residuos del producto, secciones perforadas o mutiladas, hematomas o despegamiento en exceso de sus hebras musculares. También se deberán excluir todas las rebanadas con quiebres que se extiendan más allá de la mitad del ancho de la rebanada, o las que se hayan cortado con sesgo o desviación apreciable, o que contengan hueso, cartílago, piel o raíces de pelos o cualquier otro defecto o daño grave en la barriga. Si es necesario, una parte de la rebanada se puede utilizar en cada paquete o recipiente para lograr el peso exacto declarado. La rebanada parcial no se deberá tener en cuenta para determinar los defectos. El paquete o recipiente del tocino debe contener la cantidad de rebanadas por libra que se especifica, de acuerdo con la tabla de escalas de peso *(ilustración en la página 244).*

Cantidad de rebanadas por libra

12 – 14, 14 – 18, 18 – 22, 22 – 26, 26 – 30, 28 – 32, o según se especifique.

Opciones de envasado

Los compradores deben especificar la opción de envasado que desean, ya sea en paquetes individuales de una libra o envasado a granel como se indica a continuación:

1. **Extendido en Filas**: el tocino cuando se presenta extendido en filas es un producto que se envasa con rebanadas individualmente separadas unas de las otras, pero colocadas de forma adyacente y consecutiva sobre papel resistente a la grasa y/o al calor.

2. **Superpuesto**: cuando el tocino se presenta superpuesto es un producto en el que las rebanadas se colocan unas sobre otras y se envasan sobre papel o cartón resistente a la grasa.

3. **Apilado en Serie**: cuando el tocino se presenta apilado en serie tiene las rebanadas tocándose unas con otras por sus bordes en la secuencia original del rebanado del tocino y colocadas sobre papel o cartón resistente a la grasa.

El tocino empacado se ofrecerá envasado en las cajas adecuadas, en cantidades que generalmente pesan entre 12 y 24 libras. En función de la opción seleccionada, el tocino rebanado también puede estar disponible o especificado en paquetes de una libra sellados y envasados al vacío o en atmósferas controladas o en bolsas plásticas multilaminadas. Los compradores también pueden solicitar análisis químicos de grasa, humedad y contenido de sal del tocino. El análisis se puede especificar para uno o todos los componentes químicos mencionados anteriormente. A menos que se especifique lo contrario, el contenido de grasa no deberá superar el 61%, el contenido de sal el 2.5% y el contenido de humedad el 3.0% según el cálculo proximal realizado de acuerdo con los métodos oficiales de la Asociación de Químicos Analíticos (Association of Analytical Chemists) en un laboratorio aprobado por el Servicio de Inspección e Inocuidad Alimentaria a designar por el proveedor.

540 — Bacon, Sliced, Fully Cooked (Cured and Smoked), Skinless

The fully cooked sliced bacon shall be prepared from a bacon belly that meets all the requirements necessary to produce Item No. 539. After cooking, the yield of the finished product must not exceed 40 percent. In addition, the slices shall be uniform in appearance and not less than 5.0 inches (12.5 cm) or more than 7.0 inches (17.5 cm) long. The slices shall not be cut or torn for more than one-half the width of the slice and shall not be overcooked or have any burnt edges or areas measuring more than 0.3 inch (7.6 mm) in any dimension. The slices shall not break or crack when the ends are brought together. There shall be no evidence of any off-odors or flavor. The finished product shall also adhere to all required standard of identity requirements such as antioxidants, salt, moisture, and protein content.

Packaging shall consist of 15 slices laid out on parchment-type paper. Purchasers may specify the product to be delivered in cartons, pouches, or cans of up to 300 slices. Pouches and cans shall be properly cartoned. As an option, the purchaser may specify the cooked bacon in a round slice shape appropriate for sandwich bun use. If so, certain requirements listed above such as length and packaging may not be applicable and are subject to agreement between the purchaser and supplier. *(Pictured on page 244.)*

540 — Tocino, Rebanado, Completamente Cocido (Curado y Ahumado), Sin Piel/Lonja

El tocino rebanado completamente cocido se debe preparar con una barriga de tocino que cumpla con todos los requisitos necesarios para producir la pieza número 539. Después de cocido, el rendimiento del producto final no debe superar el 40%. Además, las rebanadas deberán tener una apariencia uniforme y no podrán tener menos de 12.5 cm (5.0 pulgadas) o más de 17.5 cm (7.0 pulgadas) de largo. Las rebanadas no se deberán cortar o romper en más de la mitad del ancho de la rebanada, y no se deberán cocer excesivamente ni deberán tener bordes chamuscados o áreas que midan más de 7.6 mm (0.3 pulgadas) en ninguna dimensión. Las rebanadas no se deben romper ni agrietar cuando se juntan los extremos. No deben existir indicios de ningún olor o sabor de mal estado. El producto final también deberá cumplir con todos los estándares exigidos de requisitos de identidad como antioxidantes, sal, humedad y contenido proteico.

El envasado deberá consistir en 15 rebanadas colocadas sobre papel tipo pergamino. Los compradores pueden especificar que se entregue el producto en cajas, estuches o latas de hasta 300 rebanadas. Los estuches o latas deberán colocarse correctamente en cajas. De forma alternativa, el comprador puede especificar el tocino cocido en una rebanada redonda adecuada para el uso en panes de emparedados. De ser así, es posible que ciertos requisitos que se indican anteriormente, como el largo y el envasado, no correspondan y estarán sujetos a un acuerdo entre el comprador y el proveedor. *(Ilustración en la página 244).*

547 — Pork Center Loin, 11 Ribs (Cured and Smoked)

This item is prepared from an Item No. 545 Pork Loin (Cured and Smoked). The line of separation of the loin from the belly shall be a reasonably straight line that is not more than 3.0 inches (7.5 cm) from the belly to the *longissimus dorsi* muscle on the shoulder end, that extends to a point on the ham end, which is not more than 0.5 inch (13 mm) from the tenderloin, excluding some allowance for curvature. The tenderloin must be intact. The shoulder end separation shall be made from a point that leaves not more than 11 ribs on the loin. Floating rib(s) not visible in the cross-section cut at the belly end are not counted. The ham or hip end of the loin shall be removed immediately anterior to the hip bone together with any related cartilage so as to expose the *gluteus medius* muscle. Surface fat shall be trimmed to an average depth of 0.25 inch (6 mm) and may not exceed 0.5 inch (13 mm) at any point. Loins with broken bones or that have had more than a slight amount of lean removed are not acceptable. The diaphragm and hanging tender shall have been removed and the cleaned spinal cord groove visible on at least 75 percent of the vertebrae. *(Also pictured on page 248.)*

547 — Chuleta de Cerdo, 11 costillas (Curada y Ahumada)

Esta pieza se prepara con la pieza número 545, Lomo de Cerdo (Curado y Ahumado). La línea de separación del lomo de la barriga deberá ser una línea razonablemente recta que no se encuentre a más de 7.5 cm (3.0 pulgadas) desde la barriga hasta el músculo *longissimus dorsi* en el extremo adyacente a la paleta, que se extienda hasta un punto en el extremo adyacente a la pierna (jamón), que no se encuentre a más de 13 mm (0.5 pulgadas) del filete, permitiendo cierto margen por la curvatura. El filete debe preservarse íntegro. La separación del extremo adyacente a la paleta se deberá hacer desde un punto que deje no más de 11 costillas sobre el lomo. Las costillas flotantes no visibles en el corte transversal en el extremo de la barriga no se cuentan. El extremo del lomo adyacente a la pierna (jamón) o cadera se deberá retirar inmediatamente antes del hueso de la cadera junto con cualquier cartílago relacionado para exponer el músculo *gluteus medius*. Se deberá recortar la cubierta de grasa hasta una profundidad promedio de 6 mm (0.25 pulgadas) y no podrá superar los 13 mm (0.5 pulgadas) en ningún punto. No se aceptan los lomos con huesos quebrados o a los que se les haya quitado más que una pequeña cantidad de carne magra. Se deberá haber quitado el diafragma y la arrachera gallo (arrachera colgante del lomo) y deberá estar visible el surco (canal raquídeo) limpio de médula espinal en al menos un 75% de las vértebras. *(También ilustrado en la página 248).*

547A — Pork Center Loin (Cured and Smoked), Boneless

The product described as this item shall meet the requirements of Item No. 547 and shall in addition be completely boneless with all cartilages and the tenderloin removed. Further, on the blade end of the boneless loin the exposed *longissimus dorsi* shall be at least 2.0 inches (5 cm) in diameter, and the cut that separated the loin from the belly shall be a straight line that is no longer from the *longissimus dorsi* at either end of the boneless loin than 3.0 inches (7.5 cm). In the event the finished product is encased in an artificial casing, the product may be dipped in a dissolved clear gelatin only to the extent necessary to facilitate stuffing into the casing. *(Pictured on page 248.)*

547A — Chuleta (Lomo del Centro) de Cerdo (Curado y Ahumado), Deshuesada

El producto que se describe como esta pieza deberá cumplir con los requisitos de la pieza número 547 y además deberá estar completamente deshuesado y libre de todos los cartílagos y el filete. Además, en el extremo del lomo deshuesado adyacente a la paleta, el *longissimus dorsi* expuesto deberá tener un diámetro de al menos 5 cm (2.0 pulgadas) y el corte que separó el lomo de la barriga deberá ser en una línea recta que no supere los 7.5 cm (3.0 pulgadas) de largo desde el *longissimus dorsi* en cualquier extremo del lomo deshuesado. En caso de que el producto final se envase en un envoltorio artificial, el producto puede sumergirse en gelatina transparente disuelta sólo en la medida necesaria para facilitar el envasado. *(Ilustración en la página 248).*

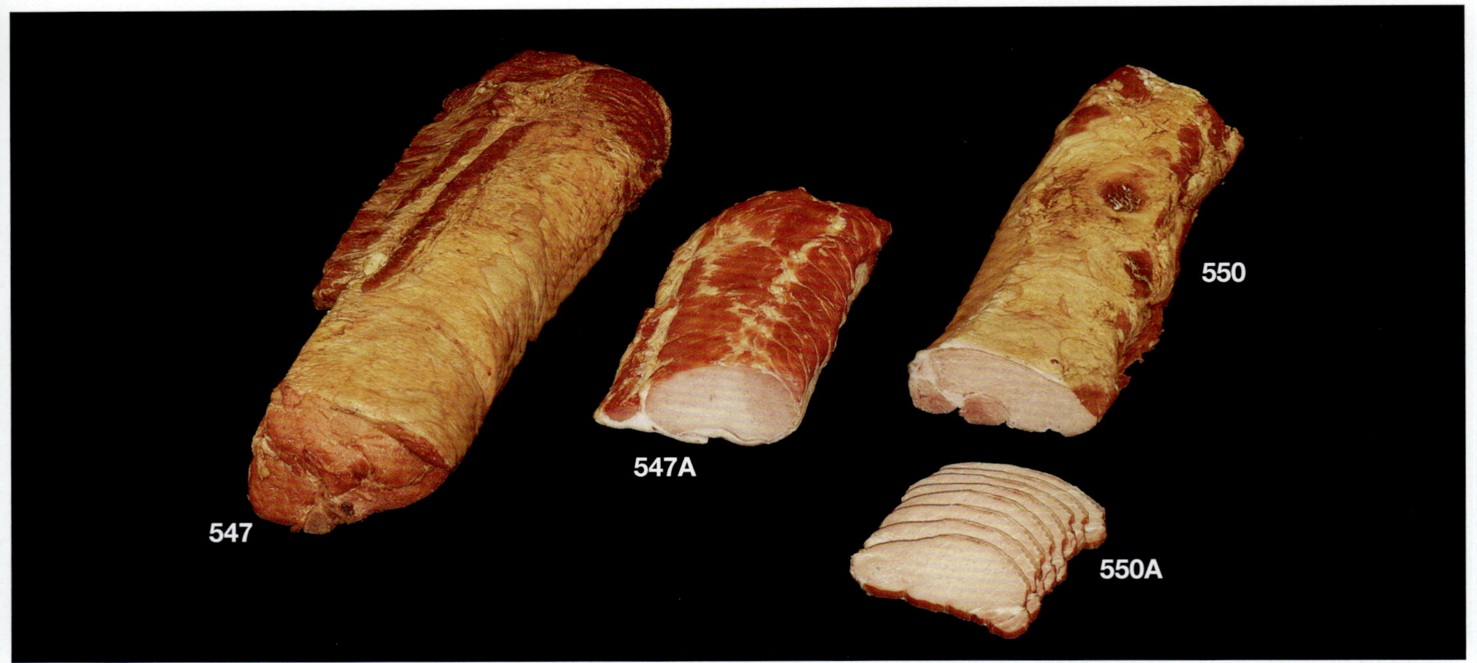

550 — Canadian Style Bacon (Cured and Smoked), Unsliced

This item, also referred to as a "Canadian Back," must meet all the requirements necessary to produce a Boneless Center-Cut Pork Loin as described in Item No. 547A but that in addition has been further trimmed of all surface fat and the end-to-end straight-line cut modified so that only the *longissimus dorsi, spinalis dorsi, multifidus dorsi, complexus,* and *gluteus medius* muscles remain. The end product may also be encased in an artificial casing as described in Item No. 547A.

550 — Lomo, Estilo Canadiense (Curado y Ahumado) sin Rebanar

Esta pieza, también denominada "Espaldar Estilo Canadiense", debe cumplir con todos los requisitos necesarios para producir un lomo de cerdo, corte del centro, deshuesado tal como se describe en la pieza número 547A, pero del que además se le ha recortado toda la cubierta de grasa y se ha modificado el corte en línea recta de un extremo al otro para que sólo queden los músculos *longissimus dorsi, spinalis dorsi, multifidus dorsi, complexus* y *gluteus medius*. El producto final también se podrá embalar con un envoltorio artificial como se describe en la pieza número 547A.

550A — Canadian Style Bacon (Cured and Smoked), Sliced

This item is the end product derived by slicing Item No. 550. The slices shall be uniform in thickness and diameter and may not include any slices that show string or hanger marks, slices from small or irregular end sections, or slices that have been mutilated or have an appearance of being a scrap machine piece. The slice thickness may range from 7 to 9 slices per linear inch. Slicing shall be done at an approximate right angle to the major muscle and shall be packaged in so far as practical in the same sequence in which the slices were produced. Purchaser may specify packaging in layers, 1 lb., or bulk containers.

550A — Lomo, Estilo Canadiense (Curado y Ahumado), Rebanado

Esta pieza es el producto final derivado del rebanado de la pieza número 550. Las rebanadas deben tener un grosor y un diámetro uniformes y no pueden incluir ninguna rebanada que muestre marcas de cuerdas ni ganchos, rebanadas de secciones de extremos pequeños o irregulares ni rebanadas que hayan sido mutiladas o tengan una apariencia de ser residuo de máquina de recorte. El grosor de las rebanadas puede variar entre 7 y 9 rebanadas por pulgada lineal. El rebanado se debe realizar con un ángulo aproximadamente recto con respecto al músculo principal y debe envasarse prácticamente en la misma secuencia en que se produjeron las rebanadas. El comprador puede especificar el envasado en capas, de 1 lb., o en recipientes a granel.

558 — Spareribs, Fully Cooked

These fully cooked spareribs shall have at least 11 ribs and may include portions of the costal cartilages with or without portions of the sternum and diaphragm. Both the membranous portion of the diaphragm or any portion of it not firmly attached shall be removed close to the lean. The lean shall not extend more than 2.0 inches (5 cm) past the curvature of the last rib and costal cartilage. Heart fat on the inside surface of the ribs shall not exceed 0.25 inch (6 mm) average depth, and the diaphragm and *transverse abdominis* shall be trimmed practically free of leaf fat. (If desired, the purchaser may order this item cured and smoked instead of fully cooked, by specifying Item No. 559 Spareribs (Cured and Smoked).

558 — Costillar de Cerdo, Completamente Cocido

Estos costillares de cerdo completamente cocidos deben tener al menos 11 costillas y pueden incluir porciones de los cartílagos costales con o sin partes del esternón y del diafragma. La porción membranosa del diafragma o cualquier otra porción de la misma que no esté firmemente adherida se deberá retirar hasta casi llegar a la carne magra. La carne magra no podrá extenderse más de 5 cm (2.0 pulgadas) más allá de la curvatura de la última costilla y su cartílago costal. La grasa del corazón en la superficie interior de las costillas no debe superar una profundidad promedio de 6 mm (0.25 pulgadas), y el diafragma y el *transverse abdominis* se deben recortar de grasa hasta que prácticamente no quede tela de grasa visceral (si se desea, el comprador puede pedir esta pieza curada y ahumada en lugar de completamente cocida, si se especifica la pieza número 559, Costillar de Cerdo (Curado y Ahumado).

558

559A — Pork Spareribs, Fully Cooked, St. Louis Style

Product meeting this description shall be prepared from spareribs that conform to fresh pork Item No. 416A Pork Spareribs, St. Louis Style, which requires there be at least 11 ribs and that the sternum (breast bone), costal cartilages, and flank portion be removed. When specified the diaphragm shall also be removed. Purchasers may specify a weight range desired and request that the spareribs be separated into two approximately equal portions by a lengthwise cut. If preferred the product may instead be cured and smoked and specified as Item No. 559B, Pork Spareribs, Cured and Smoked, St. Louis Style.

559A — Costillar de Cerdo, Completamente Cocido, Estilo San Luis

El producto que cumple con esta descripción se debe preparar con un costillar de cerdo que cumpla con la pieza de cerdo fresco número 416A, Costillar de Cerdo, Estilo San Luis, que requiere que haya al menos 11 costillas y que se quite el esternón (hueso del pecho), los cartílagos costales y la porción de la falda. Cuando se especifique, el diafragma también se deberá quitar. Los compradores pueden especificar un rango de peso deseado y solicitar que el costillar se separe en dos porciones aproximadamente iguales con un corte longitudinal. Si se prefiere, el producto se puede curar y ahumar, especificándolo como la pieza número 559B, Costillar de Cerdo, Curado y Ahumado, Estilo San Luis.

559A

561 — Hocks, Shoulder (Cured and Smoked)

Hocks may be prepared from either the pork shoulder or picnic. The hock shall be separated from the front feet at or slightly above the upper knee joint toward the elbow, and shall be at least 2.0 inches (5 cm) in length.

Purchasers may request hocks prepared from a ham. Ham hocks shall be separated from the hind foot by a cut at or above the hock joint toward the ham, and shall be at least 2.0 inches (5 cm) in length.

A visible difference between a shoulder and a ham hock (Item 560, Hocks, Ham (Cured and Smoked)), is that the shoulder hock will not exhibit the Achilles tendon.

561 — Chamorros, de Paleta/ Espaldilla (Curados y Ahumados)

Los chamorros se pueden preparar con la espaldilla o el brazuelo picnic del cerdo. El chamorro se debe separar de las patas delanteras en la articulación superior, o levemente por encima de ella hacia el codo, y deberá tener un largo de al menos 5 cm (2.0 pulgadas).

Los compradores pueden solicitar chamorros preparados a partir de la pierna (jamón). Los chamorros de la pierna (jamón) se deben separar de la pata trasera por medio de un corte en la articulación del chamorro, o por encima de ella hacia la pierna, y deberán tener un largo de al menos 5 cm (2.0 pulgadas).

Una visible diferencia entre un chamorro de paleta y un chamorro de pierna [pieza 560, Chamorros, de Jamón (Curados y Ahumados)], es que el chamorro de paleta no presentará el tendón de Aquiles.

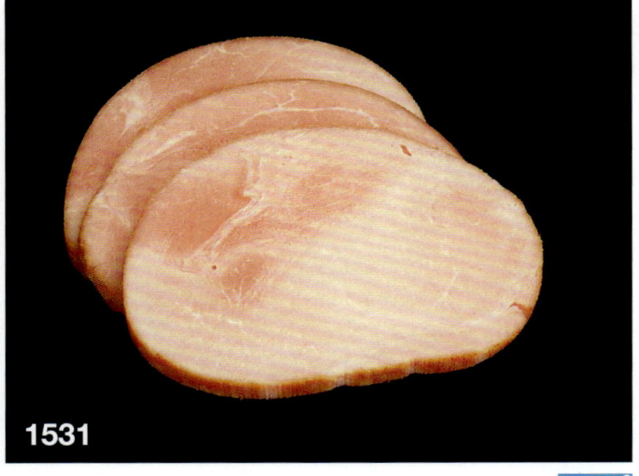

1531 — Ham Steaks (Cured and Smoked), Boneless

This item may be prepared from a ham meeting the requirements of Item Nos. 505, 508, or 509. The steaks shall be sliced perpendicular to the long axis of the ham. The slices shall be portioned as requested by the purchaser. All slices shall exhibit a cured and smoked appearance and be approximately uniform in shape depending on the ham item selected for use. Though a slightly two-toned or iridescent color is permissible, the lean meat shall have a fine, smooth texture and should display a uniform and bright color. The ham steaks shall be free from all skin, bruises, blood clots, lymph glands, bone cartilage, and surface fat. Excessive trimming of the steak for any reason is prohibited.

1531 — Rodajas de Jamón (Curadas y Ahumadas), Deshuesadas

Esta pieza se puede preparar con un jamón que cumpla los requisitos de las piezas número 505, 508 o 509. Los bistecs deben rebanarse de forma perpendicular al eje largo del jamón. Las rebanadas deberán estar porcionadas según lo solicite el comprador. Todas las rebanadas deberán exhibir una apariencia curada y ahumada, y pueden tener una forma aproximadamente uniforme en función de la pieza de jamón seleccionada. Aunque se permite un leve tono bicolor o una apariencia iridiscente, la carne magra deberá tener una textura suave y fina, y deberá presentar un color vivo uniforme. Los bistecs de jamón no deben tener piel, hematomas, coágulos de sangre, ganglios linfáticos, cartílago de huesos ni cubierta de grasa. Está prohibido el recorte excesivo de la rodaja por cualquier motivo.

1547 Pork Loin Chops, Center-Cut (Cured and Smoked)

The center-cut chops meeting this requirement may be cut from Item No. 547 or prepared and cut from Item No. 545. Surface fat shall not exceed 0.25 inch (6 mm) at any point. Chops shall be cut at an approximate right angle to length of the loin and be practically free from fractures, tag ends, bruises or blood clots, and knife scores. If desired, chops may also be ordered cut from end to end using the entire Item No. 545, in which case they should be specified as Item No. 1545 Pork Loin Chops.

1547 Chuletas de Lomo de Cerdo, Corte del Centro (Curadas y Ahumadas)

Las chuletas del centro que cumplen con este requisito se pueden cortar de la pieza número 547 o prepararse y cortarse de la pieza número 545. La cubierta de grasa no debe superar los 6 mm (0.25 pulgadas) en cualquier punto. Las chuletas se deben cortar en un ángulo aproximadamente recto longitudinalmente con respecto al lomo, y prácticamente no deben tener ninguna fractura, extremos rasgados, hematomas o coágulos de sangre, ni cortes profundos de cuchillos. Si se desea, las chuletas también se pueden pedir cortadas de un extremo a otro utilizando la pieza número 545, en cuyo caso se deberán especificar como pieza número 1545 Chuletas de Lomo de Cerdo.

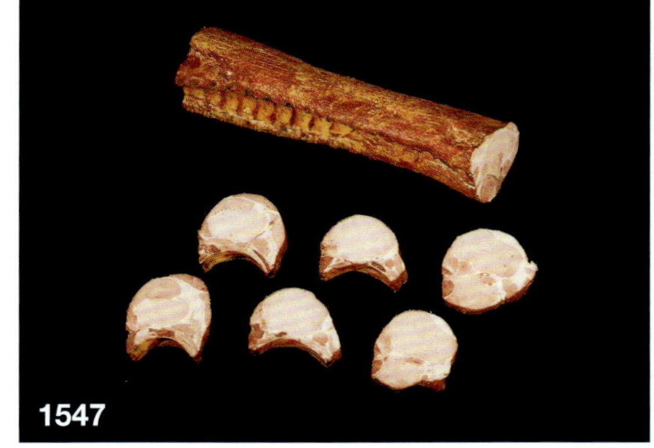

1548 Pork Chops, Boneless, Center-Cut (Cured and Smoked)

The chops may be cut from either an Item No. 548A, 8 Rib Boneless Center Loin or prepared and cut from an Item No. 547A, 11 Rib Boneless Center Loin. Surface fat shall not exceed 0.25 inch (6 mm) at any point. Chops shall be cut at an approximate right angle to length of the loin and be practically free from bones or cartilage, fractures, tag ends, bruises or blood clots, and knife scores. If desired, chops may also be ordered cut from end to end using the entire Item No. 547A, in which case they should be specified as Item No. 1547A Pork Loin Chops.

1548 Chuletas de Lomo de Cerdo, Deshuesadas, Corte del Centro (Curadas y Ahumadas)

Las chuletas se pueden cortar de una pieza número 548A, Chuleta, Lomo Deshuesado, Corte del Centro, 8 Costillas o se pueden preparar y cortar de una pieza número 547A, Chuleta, Lomo Deshuesado, Corte del Centro, 11 Costillas. La cubierta de grasa no debe superar los 6 mm (0.25 pulgadas) en cualquier punto. Las chuletas se deben cortar en un ángulo aproximadamente recto longitudinalmente con respecto al lomo y prácticamente no deben tener ningún hueso o cartílago, fracturas, extremos rasgados, hematomas o coágulos de sangre, ni cortes profundos de cuchillos. Si se desea, las chuletas también se pueden pedir cortadas de un extremo a otro utilizando la pieza número 547A, en cuyo caso se deberán especificar como pieza número 1547A Chuletas de Lomo de Cerdo.

Información para hacer los pedidos

Lo especificará el comprador

En algunos casos, los compradores podrán tener la oportunidad de variar las especificaciones o seleccionar opciones que correspondan a los productos descritos en la Serie 600 de IMPS (Especificaciones de Compras Institucionales de Carne, por sus siglas en inglés), productos de carne de res curados, secos, ahumados y completamente cocidos. Cuando se pueda seleccionar una opción de compra, pero no se señale ninguna selección, procederá una opción predeterminada por la omisión. El comprador y el vendedor deben llegar a un acuerdo mutuo con respecto a los cambios de las especificaciones.

Estado de refrigeración

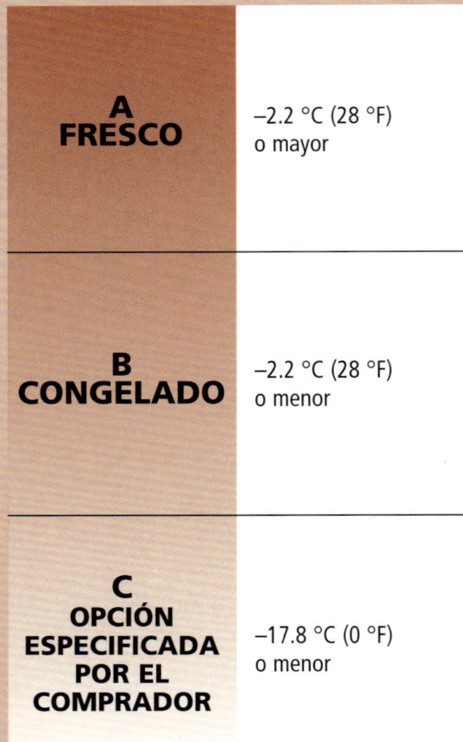

A FRESCO	−2.2 °C (28 °F) o mayor
B CONGELADO	−2.2 °C (28 °F) o menor
C OPCIÓN ESPECIFICADA POR EL COMPRADOR	−17.8 °C (0 °F) o menor

Si no se selecciona, el producto se entregará como la opción A.

ESTILOS

A menos que se especifique lo contrario, cualquier pieza de esta serie se puede pedir rebanada. Si no se selecciona ningún estilo cuando hayan opciones disponibles, el producto se entregará entero.

Los compradores deben especificar el grosor deseado de la rebanada, pero no deberían señalar especificaciones de peso para porciones, excepto para aquellas piezas que se hayan sometido a prensado y moldeado.

Ordering Data

North American Meat Processors Association
Association Amérique du Nord des Transformateurs de Viande
Asociación Norteamericana de Procesadores de Carne

To Be Specified by the Purchaser

Purchasers in some instances may have an opportunity to vary the specifications or select options applicable to the products described in IMPS Series 600 Cured, Dried, Smoked and Fully Cooked Beef Products. When a purchase option may be selected and a choice is not made, a default is specified. Buyer and seller should reach agreement between themselves with respect to changes in specifications.

State of Refrigeration

A FRESH	28°F (−2.2°C) or higher
B FROZEN	28°F (−2.2°C) or lower
C PSO	0°F (−17.8°C) or lower

If not selected, product will be delivered as Option A.

STYLES

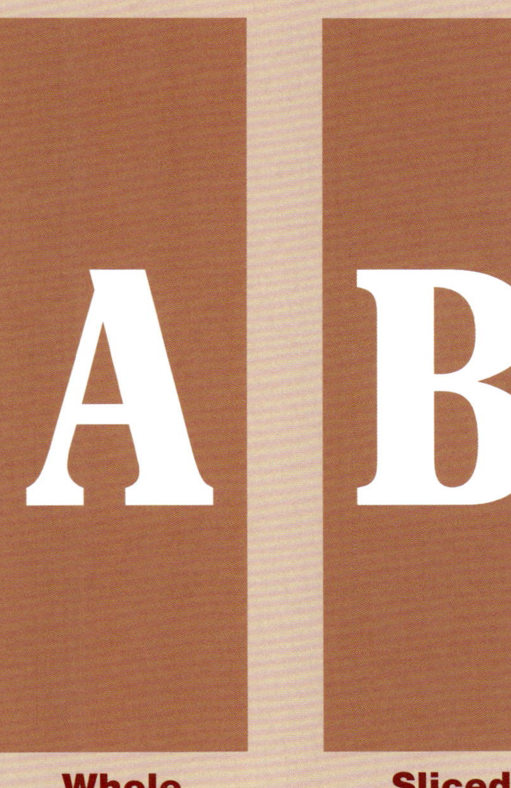

Unless otherwise specified, any item in this series may be ordered sliced. If no style is selected when an option is applicable, the product will be delivered whole.

Purchasers shall specify the slice thickness desired and should avoid specifying a portion weight except for those items that have been pressed and formed.

Requisitos materiales

Además de todos los requisitos de la descripción de la pieza, los productos deberán tener al menos un grado moderado de carnosidad o en grosor muscular con relación a la grasa interior o exterior. La carne debe estar prácticamente libre de hematomas, coágulos de sangre, tejidos sanguinolentos, decoloración, cortes profundos, cortes incorrectos, marcas de ganchos, polvo de huesos o cualquier otro defecto que pueda afectar negativamente el uso del producto.

El producto final debe cumplir con todos los requisitos de compra correspondientes. Si se ordena refrigerado, no debe presentar evidencia alguna de congelación, descongelación o mal manejo. Todos los productos deberán estar libres de mal olor u olores extraños. La grasa amarillenta o excesivamente aceitosa tampoco es aceptable.

Grosor de la grasa

A menos que se especifique lo contrario, el grosor de la cubierta de grasa para todos los productos de carne de res curada con sal, completamente cocida y ahumada no deberá superar una profundidad promedio de 6 mm (0.25 pulgadas) ni los 12 mm (0.5 pulgadas) en cualquier punto. No se permite que sólo se hagan cortes en bisel a los bordes. Cuando haya una depresión natural en el músculo, la cubierta de grasa de la depresión no debe superar los 19 mm (0.75 pulgadas) de largo (consulte las explicaciones anteriores de transición y planificación). Todos los productos de carne seca de res deberán estar prácticamente libres de cubierta de grasa y no deberán tener más que una pequeña cantidad de grasa interna. Cualquier especificación de grasa que indique "prácticamente libre" significa que incluye un 75% de carne magra expuesta con un máximo de grasa en cualquier punto de 6 mm (0.25 pulgadas). Una especificación de "limpio de grasa" significa que incluye un 90% de carne magra expuesta con un máximo de grasa en cualquier punto de 3 mm (0.125 pulgadas).

Requisitos de corte y limpieza

Los cortes musculares individuales de carne de res que se utilicen para cumplir con los requisitos de la Serie 600 de IMPS (Especificaciones de Compras Institucionales de Carne, por sus siglas en inglés) deben aproximarse bastante a las especificaciones de la Serie 100 de las IMPS para esa pieza. Una variación de peso del 4% de músculo magro agregado o extraído es aceptable. Sin embargo, una limpieza excesiva para cumplir con la especificación de peso no es aceptable. Después del curado se podrán realizar recortes y limpiezas sólo de carácter menor; pero después de la cocción o el ahumado, para evitar la contaminación microbiana, no se permitirá realizar una limpieza ulterior del producto. Los cortes deberán ser perpendiculares a la superficie exterior y sin incisiones objetables a la carne magra. Se deberán quitar todos los bordes irregulares.

En malla o amarrado

Los términos se deberán considerar intercambiables, y a menos que el comprador solicite lo contrario de forma específica, el producto se colocará en una red.

Productos que contienen soluciones agregadas

Los productos que contienen ingredientes agregados deben cumplir con todos los reglamentos del FSIS (Servicio de Inspección e Inocuidad Alimentaria, por sus siglas en inglés). A menos que el comprador especifique lo contrario en un acuerdo con el vendedor, los productos finales cocidos o cocidos y curados no podrán exceder el peso del producto fresco sin curar. Si el comprador opta por especificar un nivel de soluciones que permitan aumentar el peso, se deberá exigir una declaración impresa adjunta al nombre del producto que indique el porcentaje de soluciones agregadas. Todas las etiquetas deben cumplir con los reglamentos del Servicio de Inspección e Inocuidad Alimentaria.

Además, los productos de carne de res curados o curados con sal se curarán de manera completa pero ligera, nunca excesiva. La superficie del corte será uniforme y con un color vivo, y salvo por un leve tono bicolor o una apariencia iridiscente, no se permitirá ningún tono verdoso, veteado u otra decoloración.

Las lenguas ahumadas exhibirán el aroma y apariencia característicos de los productos correctamente ahumados. La superficie exterior estará adecuadamente seca pero no de forma excesiva, ni chamuscada, y el producto quedará uniformemente seco y firme en su totalidad.

Los productos procesados de carne de res seca, además de ahumarse y cocerse completamente, deberán estar prácticamente libres de agujeros de aire, cavidades de humedad, grasa derretida o material gelatinoso. Cualquier grano de sal incrustado, sustancia extraña o residuo del ahumadero se deberá extraer cuidadosamente mediante un cepillado suave o con un paño, sin lavar para no dañar el producto. Las mallas, cuerdas y dispositivos similares para colgar el producto deberán eliminarse por completo. El secado se realizará de acuerdo con los reglamentos del Servicio de Inspección e Inocuidad Alimentaria.

Material Requirements

In addition to any requirements in the Item Description, products shall have at least a moderated degree of meatiness or thickness of muscling in relation to interior or exterior fat. The meat shall be practically free from bruises, blood clots, bloody tissue or discoloration, scores, miscuts, hook marks, bone dust, or any other condition that would negatively affect the use of the product.

The finished product shall meet all applicable purchase requirements. If ordered chilled, there shall be no evidence of freezing, defrosting, or mishandling. All products will be free of any "off" or foreign odors. Yellow-colored or excessively oily fat is also not acceptable.

Fat Thickness

Unless otherwise specified, surface fat thickness for all corned, fully cooked, and smoked beef products shall not exceed 0.25 inch (6 mm) average depth or 0.5 inch (12 mm) at any one point. Beveling only the edges is not allowed. When a natural depression occurs in the muscle, only that surface fat above a depression no more than 0.75 inch long (19 mm) is considered. (See previous explanations of bridging and planing.) All dried beef products shall be practically free of surface fat and shall have no more than a small amount of internal fat. Any fat specification that calls for "Practically Free" means that there is 75 percent lean exposed with a maximum fat at any one point of 0.25 inch (6 mm). A "Defatted" specification means there is 90 percent lean exposed with a maximum fat at any one point of 0.125 inch (3 mm).

Cutting and Trimming Requirements

Individual beef muscle cuts used to meet the IMPS Series 600 requirements should closely approximate the specifications found for that item in the IMPS Series 100. A 4 percent weight variation of added or removed lean muscle is acceptable. However, excessive trimming to meet a weight specification is not acceptable. Only minor trimming may be done after curing, but in order to prevent microbial contamination, no further trimming is allowed after cooking or smoking the product. Cuts are to be made perpendicular to the outer surface and without objectionable scores to the lean. All ragged edges are to be removed.

Netting or Tying

The terms are considered to be interchangeable and unless specifically requested otherwise by the purchaser the product will be netted.

Products Containing Added Solutions

Products containing added ingredients shall comply with all FSIS regulations. Unless otherwise specified by the purchaser in an agreement with the seller, cooked or cooked and cured finished products may not exceed the weight of the fresh uncured product. If a purchaser elects to specify a level of solutions that would allow the weight to be greater, a declaration is required to be printed adjacent to the product name indicating the percent of added solutions. All labels must conform to FSIS regulations.

In addition, cured or corned beef products shall be mildly and thoroughly but not excessively cured. The cut surface shall be uniform and bright in color, and except for a slightly two-toned or iridescent appearance, no greening, streaking, or other discoloration is permissible.

Smoked tongues shall exhibit the characteristic aroma and appearance of well-smoked products. The exterior surface will be fairly but not excessively dry or scorched and the entire product of uniform dryness and firmness throughout.

Processed dried beef products, in addition to being thoroughly smoked and cooked, shall be practically free from air holes, pockets of moisture, rendered fat, or gelatinous material. Any encrusted salt, extraneous matter, or smokehouse residue shall be closely removed either by light brushing or wiping and without washing so as not to damage the product. Stockinettes, strings, and similar hanging devices shall be completely eliminated. Drying shall be done in accordance with FSIS regulations.

Index/Índice

Cured, Dried, Cooked and Smoked Beef Products
Productos de Carne de Res, Curados, Secos, Cocidos y Ahumados

ITEM PIEZA	PRODUCT NAME / NOMBRE DEL PRODUCTO	PG. PÁG.	Weight Ranges (Pounds) / Escalas de peso (libras/kg)			
			A	B	C	D
601	**Brisket, Boneless, Deckle-Off, Corned** Pecho, Deshuesado, sin Grasa Endurecida ni Cartílagos, Curado con Sal	257	9 & down (Menos de 4.1)	9 – 14 (4.1-6.4)	14–up (Más de 14)	
604	**Beef Top (Inside) Round, Corned** Pulpa Negra (Cara/Centro de Pierna), Curada con Sal	257	16 & down (Menos de 7.3)	16 – 27 (7.3-12.2)	27–up (Más de 12.2)	
604A	**Beef Top (Inside) Round, Cap Off, Corned** Pulpa Negra (Cara/Centro de Pierna), sin su Tapa, Curada con Sal	258	12 & up (Más de 5.4)			
608	**Beef Outside Round, Corned (Flat)** Pulpa Blanca, Curada con Sal	258	11 & down (Menos de 5)	11 – 18 (5-8.2)	18–up (Más de 8.2)	
608A	**Beef Round, Eye of Round, Corned** Pierna, Cuete de Res, Curado con Sal	258	3 & down (Menos de 1.4)	3 – 5 (1.4-2.3)	5–up (Más de 2.3)	
611	**Beef Pastrami** Pastrami (Pastrón) de Res	259	As Specified by Purchaser (Según especificación del comprador)			
612	**Beef Fajita Strips** Tiras de Fajita de Res	259	0.25 lb. (0.11 kg)	0.5 lb. (0.23 kg)	1 lb. (0.45 kg)	Bulk (A granel)
613	**Beef Tongue, Cured, Trimmed** Lengua de Res, Curada, Limpia	260	3 & up (Más de 1.4)			
614	**Beef Tongue, Cured and Smoked, Trimmed** Lengua de Res, Curada y Ahumada, Limpia	260	3 – 5 (1.4-2.3)	5–up (Más de 2.3)		
618	**Sliced Processed Dried Beef** Carne Seca de Res, Procesada, Rebanada	260	.25 lb. (0.11 kg)	.5 lb. (0.23 kg)	1 lb. (0.45 kg)	A granel
619	**Sliced Dried Beef** Carne Seca de Res, Rebanada	261	.25 lb. (0.11 kg)	.5 lb. (0.23 kg)	1 lb. (0.45 kg)	Bulk (A granel)
623	**Beef Top (Inside) Round, Fully Cooked** Pulpa Negra (Cara/Centro de Pierna), Completamente Cocida	261	14 – 17 (6.4-7.7)	17 – 20 (7.7-9.1)	20 – 23 (9.1-10.4)	23–up (Más de 10.4)
623A	**Beef Top (Inside) Round, Cap Off, Fully Cooked** Pulpa Negra (Cara/Centro de Pierna), Sin Su Tapa, Completamente Cocida	262	12 & up (Más de 5.4)			
624	**Beef Outside Round, Fully Cooked** Pulpa Blanca, Completamente Cocida	262	10 & down (Menos de 4.5)	10 – 16 (4.5-7.3)	16–up (Más de 7.3)	
624A	**Beef Round, Eye of Round, Fully Cooked** Pierna, Cuete de Res, Completamente Cocido	262	2 & up (Más de 0.90)			
625	**Beef Brisket, Boneless, Deckle-Off, Corned, Fully Cooked** Pecho de Res, Deshuesado, sin Grasa Endurecida ni Cartílagos, Curado con Sal, Completamente Cocido	263	9 & down (Menos de 4.1)	9 – 12 (4.1-5.4)	12–up (Más de 5.4)	
630	**Beef Rib, Ribeye Roll, Fully Cooked** Chuletón, Rollo de Ribeye (Ojo del Chuletón Arrollado), Completamente Cocido	263	8 & down (Menos de 3.6)	8 – 10 (3.6-4.5)	10 – 12 (4.5-5.4)	12–up (Más de 5.4)
630A	**Beef Rib, Ribeye Roll, Lip-On, Fully Cooked** Chuletón, Rollo de Ribeye (Ojo del Chuletón Arrollado), Sin Cordón, Completamente Cocido	263	12 & up (Más de 5.4)			

601   Brisket, Boneless, Deckle-Off, Corned

Corned beef briskets shall be produced from beef briskets that conform to Item No. 120, Beef Brisket, DeckleOff, Boneless, and have flesh that is at least moderately thick and firmly textured with a plump appearance. Any remaining fat shall be at least moderately firm and smooth, and unless otherwise specified not exceed 0.25 inch (6 mm) average depth or 0.5 inch (13 mm) at any one point. The surface from which the deckle has been removed shall be practically free from fat and the thin edge of the web muscle must be trimmed so as to expose the lean. The finished product shall have a uniform bright color ranging from pink to medium red although a slight two-toned or iridescent appearance is permissible. The packaged product may or may not contain curing spices. A declaration is required on the label indicating the percent of solution added if the added level exceeds 20 percent.

601   Pecho, Deshuesado, sin Grasa Endurecida ni Cartílagos, Curado con Sal

El pecho de res curado con sal se debe producir con pecho de res que se ajuste a la pieza número 120, Pecho de Res, sin Grasa Endurecida ni Cartílagos, Deshuesado y tener carne que sea al menos moderadamente gruesa y con una textura firme y una apariencia de estar entrando en carnes. Toda la grasa restante debe ser moderadamente firme y suave, y, a menos que se especifique lo contrario, no deberá superar la profundidad promedio de 6 mm (0.25 pulgadas) ni los 13 mm (0.5 pulgadas) en ningún punto. La superficie de la cual se ha quitado la grasa dura y los cartílagos prácticamente no deberá tener grasa, y se debe recortar la grasa del borde delgado del tejido muscular para (músculo de la tela) que quede la carne magra expuesta. El producto final deberá tener un color vivo uniforme que va del rosado al rojo medio, aunque se permite un leve tono bicolor o una apariencia iridiscente. El producto envasado puede contener o no especias de curado. Se exige una declaración en la etiqueta que indique el porcentaje de solución agregada si el nivel agregado supera el 20%.

604   Beef Top (Inside) Round, Corned

Corned top rounds shall be produced from insides that conform to Item No. 169, Beef Round, Top (Inside). If requested, smaller roasts may be fabricated by splitting the item no more than twice lengthwise and then if desired, girthwise, into approximate equal portions. The color and general appearance of this item shall be the same as that described in Item No. 601 but may not contain more than 10 percent added solutions, unless a lower amount is specified. The fat cover, unless otherwise specified, shall not exceed 0.25 inch (6 mm) average depth or 0.5 inch (13 mm) at any one point.

604   Pulpa Negra (Cara/Centro de Pierna), Curada con Sal

La pulpa negra curada con sal se debe producir con la cara/centro de pierna que se ajuste a la pieza número 169, Pierna (Piña), Pulpa Negra (Cara/Centro). Si se solicita, se pueden fabricar rosbifs más pequeños dividiendo la pieza longitudinalmente en dos partes como máximo, y luego si se desea circunferencialmente, en porciones aproximadamente iguales. El color y la apariencia general de esta pieza debe ser igual a la que se describe en la pieza número 601, pero no puede contener más del 10% de soluciones agregadas, a menos que se especifique una cantidad inferior. A menos que se especifique lo contrario, la cubierta de grasa no deberá superar la profundidad promedio de 6 mm (0.25 pulgadas) ni los 13 mm (0.5 pulgadas) en ningún punto.

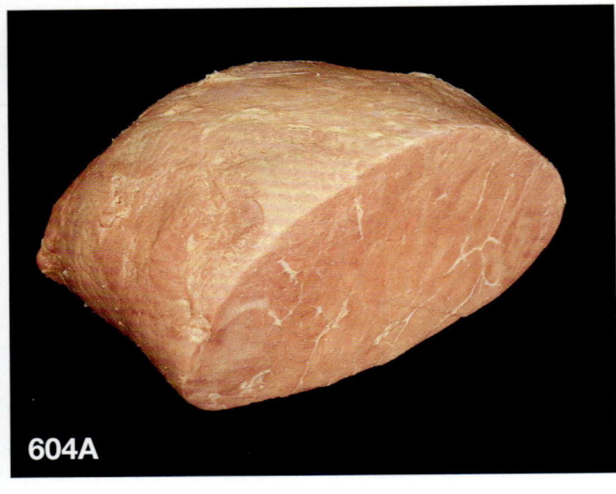
604A

604A Beef Top (Inside) Round, Cap Off, Corned

This item shall be prepared from product meeting the end item description of Item No. 169A. The only difference between this item and Item No. 604 is that the entire *gracilis* muscle as well as the loose side *pectineus* and *sartorius* muscles shall be separated and excluded from this item through the natural seams.

604A Pulpa Negra (Cara/Centro de Pierna), sin su Tapa, Curada con Sal

Esta pieza se debe preparar con un producto que cumpla con la descripción de la pieza final de la pieza número 169A. La única diferencia entre esta pieza y la pieza número 604 es que el músculo *gracilis* completo y el lado suelto de los músculos *pectineus* y *sartorius* se deben separar y excluir de esta pieza a través de las vetas naturales.

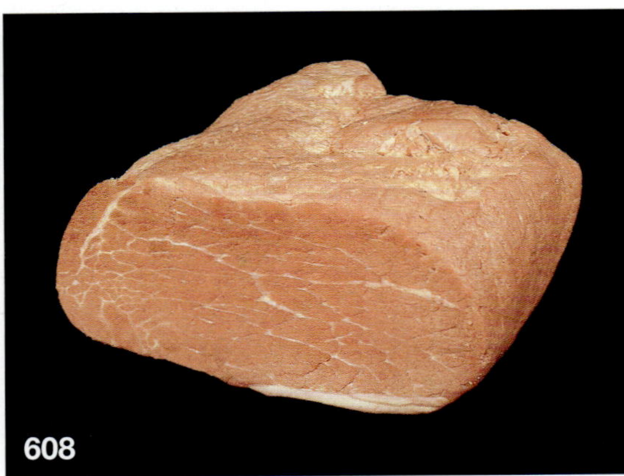
608

608 Beef Outside Round, Corned (Flat)

This corned outside round shall consist of the *biceps femoris* muscle and may contain the *gluteus medius*, *gluteus accessorius*, and *gluteus profundus* muscles. If the *gluteus medius* muscle is present, then the exposed *biceps femoris* muscle at the loin end shall be equal to or larger in size than the *gluteus medius* muscle face. The outside round is separated from the top round, sirloin tip (knuckle), heel, and *semitendinosus* or eye of the round, between the natural muscle seams. All bones, cartilages, *sacrosciatic* ligament, and the lean and fat that overlaid the ligament, the opaque heavy connective tissue or silver skin along the ventral side as well as the *popliteal* lymph gland, shall be removed from this product. The fat cover, unless otherwise specified, shall not exceed 0.25 inch (6 mm) average depth or 0.5 inch (13 mm) at any one point.

608 Pulpa Blanca, Curada con Sal

Esta pulpa blanca curada con sal consiste en el músculo *biceps femoris* y puede contener los músculos *gluteus medius*, *gluteus accessorius* y *gluteus profundus*. Si está presente el músculo *gluteus medius*, el músculo expuesto *biceps femoris* en el extremo posterior debe ser igual o de mayor tamaño que la cara del músculo *gluteus medius*. La pulpa blanca se separa de la pulpa negra, de la pulpa bola, del talón y del *semitendinosus* o cuete de res, entre las vetas naturales de los músculos. Se deberán quitar de este producto todos los huesos, los cartílagos, el ligamento *sacrociático* y la grasa y carne magra que recubren el ligamento, el tejido conectivo opaco grueso o piel plateada a lo largo del lado ventral, y el ganglio linfático *poplíteo*. A menos que se especifique lo contrario, la cubierta de grasa no deberá superar la profundidad promedio de 6 mm (0.25 pulgadas) ni los 13 mm (0.5 pulgadas) en ningún punto.

608A

608A Beef Round, Eye of Round, Corned

This boneless corned item consists solely of the *semitendinosus* muscle (eye of round) and shall not be severed on either end. Further, the items shall be separated from the top round, outside round, and the heel between the natural muscle seams. In addition, this item shall be skinned of all surface fat and external facia membrane.

608A Pierna, Cuete de Res, Curado con Sal

Esta pieza deshuesada curada con sal consiste únicamente en el músculo *semitendinosus* (cuete de res) y no deberá separarse de ningún extremo. Asimismo, las piezas deberán separarse de la pulpa negra, de la pulpa blanca y del talón entre las vetas naturales de los músculos. Además, esta pieza se debe limpiar de toda la cubierta de grasa y la membrana externa.

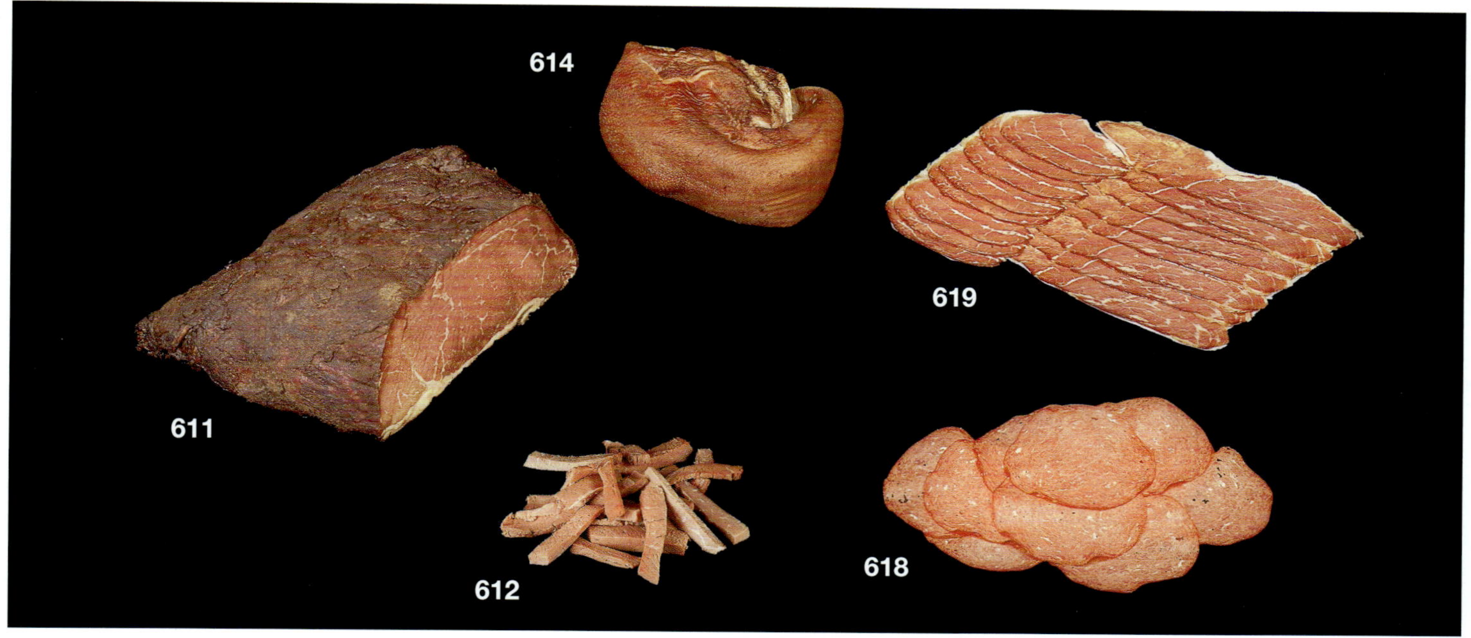

611 Beef Pastrami

A product meeting this description may be prepared from any raw skeletal portion of the beef carcass such as a plate, top, flat, or eye of the round as specified by the purchaser except the cutaneous, shank, and heel meat portions. The raw materials used must meet all the end-item requirements for that beef cut and be practically free of surface and seam fat. Unless specified otherwise, the pieces used shall not be less than 8.0 square inches (20 sq. cm) on one side, nor less than 0.5 inch (13 mm) thick at any point. The finished product shall have been cured, smoked, and fully cooked. Unless otherwise specified, smoke flavoring may be used in lieu of actual smoking.

611 Pastrami (Pastrón) de Res

Un producto que cumple con esta descripción se puede preparar con cualquier porción muscular derivada de la canal de res como un costillar, pulpa negra, pulpa blanca o cuete de res según lo especifique el comprador, excepto las porciones cárnicas cutáneas, del chamberete y del talón. Las materias primas usadas deben cumplir con los requisitos de pieza final para ese corte de res y prácticamente no deben tener cubierta de grasa ni vetas de grasa intermuscular. A menos que se especifique lo contrario, las piezas utilizadas deberán tener un grosor que no sea inferior a 20 cm² (8.0 pulgadas cuadradas) en un lado, ni deberán tener un grosor inferior a 13 mm (0.5 pulgadas) en ningún punto. El producto final deberá haberse curado, ahumado y cocido completamente. A menos que se especifique lo contrario, se pueden utilizar saborizantes para impartir el sabor a ahumado en lugar del ahumado real.

612 Beef Fajita Strips

Fajita strips may be produced from any raw skeletal portion of the beef carcass specified by the purchaser with the exception of the cutaneous, shank, and heel meat portions. The meat shall be practically free of fat and shall be seasoned, or marinated as requested, and then fully cooked. The beef shall be mechanically diced 0.5 x 0.5 x 1.0 inch (13 mm x 13 mm x 2.5 cm) long, or 0.5 x 0.5 x 2.5 inches (13 mm x 13 mm x 6.4 cm) long, or to any other size specified by the purchaser. A product size option must be specified by the purchaser. At least 75 percent of the resulting product by weight must conform to the size requirement. Grinding is not permitted. To facilitate dicing, the beef may be frozen and/or tempered one time only prior to it being diced. Purchaser shall also specify how it desires the finished product packaged.

612 Tiras de Fajita de Res

Las tiras de fajita se pueden producir de cualquier porción muscular cruda de la canal de res que especifique el comprador, con excepción de las porciones cárnicas cutáneas, del chamberete y del talón. La carne deberá estar prácticamente libre de grasa y se deberá condimentar, o marinar según se solicite, y luego cocer completamente. La carne de res se deberá trocear en cubos de forma mecánica de 13 mm x 13 mm x 2.5 cm (0.5 x 0.5 x 1.0 pulgadas) de largo, o 13 mm x 13 mm x 6.4 cm (0.5 x 0.5 x 2.5 pulgadas) de largo, o en cualquier otra medida que especifique el comprador. El comprador debe especificar una opción de tamaño del producto. Al menos el 75% del producto resultante en peso debe cumplir con el requisito de tamaño. La molienda no está permitida. Para facilitar el corte de trozos en cubos, la carne de res se puede congelar y/o atemperar una única vez antes de cortarla. El comprador también deberá especificar cómo desea que se envase el producto final.

613 — Beef Tongue, Cured, Trimmed

This item shall be prepared from a beef tongue meeting the end-item requirements of Item No. 1710, Style 06, described in the Series 700 section of this guide.

613 — Lengua de Res, Curada, Limpia

Esta pieza se debe preparar con una lengua de res que cumpla con los requisitos de pieza final de la pieza número 1710, Estilo 06, descrita en la Serie 700 de esta guía.

614 — Beef Tongue, Cured and Smoked, Trimmed

This item shall be prepared from a cured beef tongue as described in Item No. 613. The tongue shall be thoroughly smoked and shall be practically free of encrusted salt, extraneous matter, and smokehouse residue. *(Pictured on page 259.)*

614 — Lengua de Res, Curada y Ahumada, Limpia

Esta pieza se debe preparar con una lengua de res curada como se describe en la pieza número 613. La lengua debe ahumarse completamente y estar prácticamente libre de granos de sal incrustados, sustancias extrañas o residuos del ahumadero. *(Ilustración en la página 259).*

618 — Sliced Processed Dried Beef

This product is sliced from a coarsely ground, cured, smoked and fully cooked processed dried beef that has been stuffed in casings or mechanically formed and dried. Drying shall be done in accordance with FSIS regulations. The finished product shall be practically free from air holes, pockets of moisture, rendered fat, and gelatinous material. The raw materials used to prepare the dried beef for slicing may come from any skeletal portion of the beef carcass specified by the purchaser with the exception of the cutaneous, shank, and heel meat portions. The slices shall be uniform in thickness and number 24 or more slices per inch (2.5 cm). Slices shall be fairly intact, and no more than 40 percent of the sample unit may be composed of broken slices of two or more pieces. No extremely frayed, shredded, small or scrap pieces, or product residue shall be included. All dried beef products shall be practically free of surface fat and shall have no more than a small amount of inter and intramuscular fat. If purchasers should desire to order this product unsliced, specify Item No. 617, Processed Dried Beef. *(Pictured on page 259.)*

618 — Carne Seca de Res, Procesada, Rebanada

Este producto se rebana de una carne seca de res procesada, molida gruesa, curada, ahumada y completamente cocida que se ha embutido en tripas o se ha moldeado mecánicamente y se ha secado. El secado se realizará de acuerdo con los reglamentos del Servicio de Inspección e Inocuidad Alimentaria. El producto final deberá estar prácticamente libre de agujeros de aire, cavidades de humedad, grasa derretida y material gelatinoso. Las materias primas utilizadas para preparar la carne seca de res para rebanar pueden extraerse de cualquier porción ósea de la canal de res que el comprador especifique, con excepción de las porciones de carne del chamberete, del talón y cutánea. Las rebanadas deben tener un grosor uniforme y deben ser no menos de 24 rebanadas por pulgada (2.5 cm). Las rebanadas deben estar prácticamente intactas, y no más del 40% de la muestra puede estar compuesta por rebanadas quebradas en dos o más piezas. No se deben incluir piezas extremadamente deterioradas, desmenuzadas, pequeñas o recortadas, ni los residuos del producto. Todos los productos de carne seca de res deben estar prácticamente libres de cubierta de grasa y no deberán tener más que una pequeña cantidad de grasa intermuscular e intramuscular. Si los compradores desean pedir este producto sin rebanar, especifique la pieza número 617, Carne Seca de Res, Procesada. *(Ilustración en la página 259).*

619 — Sliced Dried Beef

Product meeting this description may come from dried Item Nos. 603, Beef Knuckle, Peeled, Dried; or 605, Beef Top (Inside) Round, Dried; or 607, Beef Bottom (Gooseneck) Round, Heel-Out, Dried. Full descriptions of these raw material items may be found in the Institutional Meat Purchase Specifications (IMPS) Series 600 for Cured, Dried, Smoked and Fully Cooked Beef Products. Purchasers may specify the product from which they wish Item No. 619 to be sliced. The unsliced dried items must conform to FSIS regulations and exhibit the same finished product quality characteristics as noted in Item No. 618. The slices shall be uniform in thickness and number 40 or more slices per inch (2.5 cm). Slices shall be a minimum of 75 percent intact, so that no more than 25 percent of the sample unit may be composed of broken slices of two or more pieces. No extremely frayed, shredded, small end piece slices, scrap pieces, or product residue shall be included. Slices showing string or hanger marks shall also be excluded. All dried beef products shall be practically free of surface fat and shall have no more than a small amount of inter and intramuscular fat. *(Pictured on page 259.)*

619 — Carne Seca de Res, Rebanada

El producto que cumple con esta descripción puede producirse seco con las piezas número 603, Pulpa Bola de Res, Limpia (de Grasa y Pellejo), Seca, o 605, Pulpa Negra (Cara/Centro de pierna), Seca, o 607, Contracara con Cuete, sin Talón, Seca. Las descripciones completas de estas piezas de materia prima se pueden encontrar en las Especificaciones de Compras Institucionales de Carne (IMPS, por sus siglas en inglés) Serie 600 para productos de carne de res curados, secos, ahumados y cocidos completamente. Los compradores pueden especificar el producto del que deseen que se rebane la pieza número 619. Las piezas secas sin rebanar deben cumplir con los reglamentos del Servicio de Inspección e Inocuidad Alimentaria y exhibir las mismas características de calidad del producto final que se indica en la pieza número 618. Las rebanadas deben tener un grosor uniforme, y su número no debe ser inferior a 40 rebanadas por cada 2.5 cm (1 pulgada). Las rebanadas deben estar íntegras en un 75% como mínimo y no más del 25% de las unidades de muestra pueden estar compuestas por rebanadas quebradas en dos o más piezas. No se deben incluir piezas extremadamente deterioradas, desmenuzadas, pequeñas (por venir de los extremos) o recortadas, o derivadas de los residuos del producto. También se deben excluir las rebanadas que presenten marcas de cuerdas o ganchos. Todos los productos de carne seca de res deben estar prácticamente libres de cubierta de grasa y no deberán tener más que una pequeña cantidad de grasa intermuscular e intramuscular. *(Ilustración en la página 259).*

623 — Beef Top (Inside) Round, Fully Cooked

The fully cooked top round shall be produced from insides that conform to Item No. 169, Beef Round, Top (Inside). The item shall be netted or tied and fully cooked to the degree of doneness specified by the purchaser in conformity with applicable FSIS regulations. When smaller size roasts are specified, the fully cooked top round shall be split by no more than two lengthwise cuts. If necessary, smaller pieces may then be made by girthwise cuts so that all portions are of approximate equal size. The fat cover, unless otherwise specified, shall not exceed 0.25 inch (6 mm) average depth or 0.5 inch (13 mm) at any one point.

623 — Pulpa Negra (Cara/Centro de Pierna), Completamente Cocida

La pulpa negra completamente cocida se debe producir con la cara/centro de pierna que se ajuste a la pieza número 169, Pierna (Piña), Pulpa Negra (Cara/Centro). La pieza se debe atar o colocar en una red y se debe cocer completamente hasta el grado de cocción que especifique el comprador, de conformidad con los reglamentos aplicables del Servicio de Inspección e Inocuidad Alimentaria. Cuando se especifican rosbifs más pequeños, la pulpa negra completamente cocida se puede dividir en no más de dos cortes longitudinales. Si es necesario, las piezas más pequeñas se pueden obtener con cortes circunferenciales para que todas las porciones tengan aproximadamente el mismo tamaño. A menos que se especifique lo contrario, la cubierta de grasa no deberá superar la profundidad promedio de 6 mm (0.25 pulgadas) ni los 13 mm (0.5 pulgadas) en ningún punto.

623A — Beef Top (Inside) Round, Cap Off, Fully Cooked

This item shall be prepared from a cap off top round meeting the end-item requirements of Item No. 604A. The item shall be fully cooked to the degree of doneness specified by the purchaser in conformity with applicable FSIS regulations.

623A — Pulpa Negra (Cara/Centro de Pierna), Sin Su Tapa, Completamente Cocida

Esta pieza se debe preparar con una pulpa negra sin su tapa que cumpla los requisitos de pieza final de la pieza número 604A. La pieza se debe cocer completamente hasta el grado de cocción que especifique el comprador,de conformidad con los reglamentos aplicables del Servicio de Inspección e Inocuidad Alimentaria.

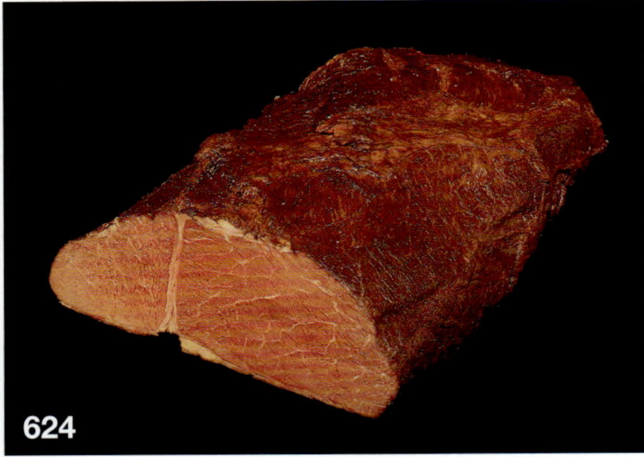

624

624 — Beef Outside Round, Fully Cooked

The fully cooked outside round shall be produced from an outside round suitable to produce Item No. 171B, Beef Round, Outside Round (Flat). This is the same raw material specification used to produce Item No. 608, Beef Outside Round, Corned; except in this instance the item is not corned but fully cooked. The item shall be fully cooked to the degree of doneness specified by the purchaser in conformity with applicable FSIS regulations. The fat cover, unless otherwise specified, shall not exceed 0.25 inch (6 mm) average depth or 0.5 inch (13 mm) at any one point.

624 — Pulpa Blanca, Completamente Cocida

La pulpa blanca completamente cocida se debe producir con una pulpa blanca adecuada para producir la pieza número 171B, Pierna (Piña), Contracara, Pulpa Blanca. Esta es la misma especificación de materia prima utilizada para producir la pieza número 608, Pulpa Blanca, Curada con Sal, con la diferencia de que en este caso la pieza no está curada sino completamente cocida. La pieza se debe cocer completamente hasta el grado de cocción que especifique el comprador, de conformidad con los reglamentos aplicables del Servicio de Inspección e Inocuidad Alimentaria. A menos que se especifique lo contrario, la cubierta de grasa no deberá superar la profundidad promedio de 6 mm (0.25 pulgadas) ni los 13 mm (0.5 pulgadas) en cualquier punto.

624A — Beef Round, Eye of Round, Fully Cooked

This item shall be prepared from product that meets the raw material requirements of Item No. 171C, which are those described in Item No. 608A. The item shall be fully cooked to the degree of doneness specified by the purchaser in conformity with applicable FSIS regulations.

624A — Pierna, Cuete de Res, Completamente Cocido

Esta pieza se debe preparar con productos que cumplan con los requisitos de materia prima de la pieza número 171C, que son los que se describen en la pieza número 608A. La pieza se debe cocer completamente hasta alcanzar el grado de cocción que especifique el comprador, de conformidad con los reglamentos aplicables del Servicio de Inspección e Inocuidad Alimentaria.

625 — Beef Brisket, Boneless, Deckle-Off, Corned, Fully Cooked

The fully cooked brisket shall be produced from beef briskets that conform to Item No. 120, Beef Brisket, Deckle-Off, Boneless. This is the same raw material specification used to produce Item No. 601, Brisket, Boneless, Deckle Off, Corned; except in this instance the item is not corned but fully cooked. The item shall be fully cooked to the degree of doneness specified by the purchaser in conformity with applicable FSIS regulations. The fat cover, unless otherwise specified, shall not exceed 0.25 inch (6 mm) average depth or 0.5 inch (13 mm) at any one point.

625 — Pecho de Res, Deshuesado, sin Grasa Endurecida ni Cartílagos, Curado con Sal, Completamente Cocido

El pecho cocido se debe producir de pechos de res que se ajusten a la pieza número 120, Pecho de Res, Sin Grasa Endurecida ni Cartílagos, Deshuesado. Esta es la misma especificación de materia prima utilizada para producir la pieza número 601, Pecho de Res, Deshuesado, sin Grasa Endurecida ni cartílagos, Curado con sal, con la diferencia de que en este caso la pieza no está curada con sal sino cocida. La pieza se debe cocer completamente hasta el grado de cocción que especifique el comprador, de conformidad con los reglamentos aplicables del Servicio de Inspección e Inocuidad Alimentaria. A menos que se especifique lo contrario, la cubierta de grasa no deberá superar la profundidad promedio de 6 mm (0.25 pulgadas) ni los 13 mm (0.5 pulgadas) en ningún punto.

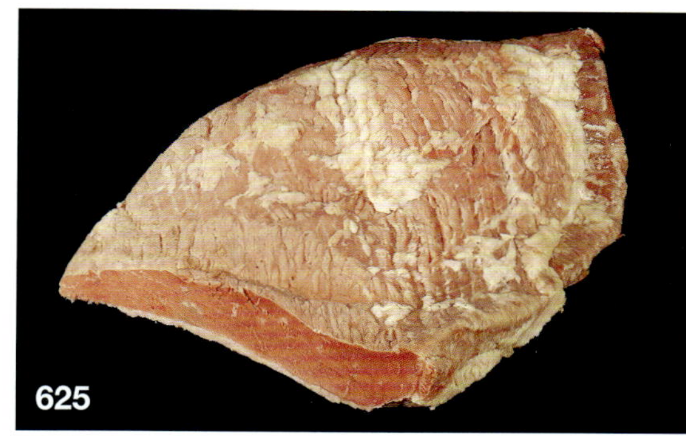

625

630 — Beef Rib, Ribeye Roll, Fully Cooked

This boneless fully cooked item shall be prepared from product meeting the end requirements of Item No. 112. The item shall be fully cooked to the degree of doneness specified by the purchaser in conformity with applicable FSIS regulations.

630 — Chuletón, Rollo de Ribeye (Ojo del Chuletón Arrollado), Completamente Cocido

Esta pieza deshuesada y completamente cocida se debe preparar con productos que cumplan con los requisitos finales de la pieza número 112. La pieza se debe cocer completamente hasta el grado de cocción que especifique el comprador, de conformidad con los reglamentos aplicables del Servicio de Inspección e Inocuidad Alimentaria.

630

630A — Beef Rib, Ribeye, Lip-On, Fully Cooked

This boneless fully cooked item shall be prepared from product meeting the end requirements of Item No. 112A. The item shall be fully cooked to the degree of doneness specified by the purchaser in conformity with applicable FSIS regulations.

630A — Chuletón, Rollo de Ribeye (Ojo del Chuletón Arrollado), Con Cordón, Completamente Cocido

Esta pieza deshuesada y completamente cocida se debe preparar con productos que cumplan con los requisitos finales de la pieza número 112A. La pieza se debe cocer completamente hasta el grado de cocción que especifique el comprador, de conformidad con los reglamentos aplicables del Servicio de Inspección e Inocuidad Alimentaria.

Información para hacer los pedidos

Lo especificará el comprador

En algunos casos, los compradores podrán tener la oportunidad de variar las especificaciones o seleccionar opciones que corresponden a los productos descritos en la Serie 700 de IMPS Variedades cárnicas y coproductos. El comprador y el vendedor deben llegar a un acuerdo en cuanto al producto deseado cuando sus opciones estén disponibles. En el caso de que no se decidan por ninguna opción, prevalecerá la descripción de la pieza.

Estado de refrigeración

A FRESCO	−2.2 °C (28 °F) o mayor
B CONGELADO	−2.2 °C (28 °F) o menor
C OPCIÓN ESPECIFICADA POR EL COMPRADOR	−17.8 °C (0 °F) o menor

En muchos casos, debido al carácter perecedero y la naturaleza del producto, o al modo en que se debe procesar, es posible que no se pueda optar por recibir el producto fresco o congelado. Sin embargo, si no se selecciona, el producto se entregará fresco si es posible.

Tolerancias de peso y grosor de la porción

Peso*	Variación de porciones
Menos de 170 g (6.0 oz.)	± 7 g (0.25 oz.)
Más de 170 g (6.0 oz.)	± 14 g (0.50 oz.)

Grosor*	Variación de rebanadas
Menos de 2.5 cm (1.0 pulgada)	± 5 mm (0.1875 pulgadas)
Más de 2.5 cm (1.0 pulgada)	± 6 mm (0.25 pulgadas)

* En todos los casos, ya sea por peso o grosor, el grosor de las porciones o rebanadas no podrá variar de un extremo al otro de la pieza en más de 5 mm (0.1875 pulgadas) en la medida menor o 6 mm (0.25 pulgadas) en la medida mayor.

Requisitos materiales

Las descripciones de las piezas para las variedades cárnicas y coproductos contienen los requisitos básicos de cada producto. Además, el producto deberá estar completamente limpio, escurrido y prácticamente libre de cubierta de grasa (75% de carne magra expuesta) a menos que la descripción de la pieza indique otra cosa. No se permitirá ninguna condición del producto que afecte negativamente su uso. Se aceptará el hígado que ha sido "despuntado" quitando una delgada tira de carne de la punta del lóbulo izquierdo, para drenar el exceso de sangre. Los corazones que presentan incisiones (cortes profundos) que se han realizado con motivo de inspecciones del Servicio de Inspección e Inocuidad Alimentaria también se aceptarán, siempre y cuando el corte no sea excesivo. Los requisitos de corte y limpieza que corresponden a estos productos son similares a los de otras series de IMPS.

Ordering Data

To Be Specified by the Purchaser

Purchasers in some instances may have an opportunity to vary the specifications or select options applicable to the products described in IMPS Series 700 Variety Meats and By-Products. Buyer and seller should reach agreement between themselves as to the product desired when such choices are available. In the event choices are not made, the Item Description shall prevail.

State of Refrigeration

A FRESH	28°F (−2.2°C) or higher
B FROZEN	28°F (−2.2°C) or lower
C PSO	0°F (−17.8°C) or lower

In many instances, because of the perishability and nature of the product, or the manner in which it must be processed, a choice of receiving either fresh or frozen product may not be available. If not selected, however, product will be delivered fresh if this is possible.

Portion Weight and Thickness Tolerances

Weight*	Portion Variance
Less than 6.0 oz. (170 g)	± 0.25 oz. (7 g)
Over 6.0 oz. (170 g)	± 0.50 oz. (14 g)
Thickness*	**Slice Variance**
Less than 1.0 inch (2.5 cm)	± 0.1875 inch (5 mm)
More than 1.0 inch (2.5 cm)	± 0.25 inch (6 mm)

* In all instances whether by weight or thickness, the portions or slices may not vary in thickness from one end of the piece to the other by more than 0.1875 inch (5 mm) at the smaller size or 0.25 inch (6 mm) at the larger size.

Material Requirements

The Item Descriptions for Variety Meats and By-Products contain the basic requirements for each product. In addition, product shall be thoroughly cleaned, drained, and be practically free (75 percent lean exposed) of surface fat unless the Item Description states differently. A condition of product that would negatively affect its use is not allowed. Liver that has been "tipped" by removing a thin strip of meat from the tip of the left lobe, in order to drain excess blood, is acceptable. Hearts that have been incised (scored) for FSIS inspection purposes are also acceptable provided the scoring is not excessive. Cutting and trimming requirements as applicable to these products are similar to those in other IMPS series.

Index/Índice

Variety Meats and Edible By-Products
Variedades Cárnicas y Coproductos Comestibles

1710 — Style 06: Beef Tongue, Swiss-Cut

A Swiss-cut beef tongue is a tongue that has had the U-shaped hyoid bones removed and has been trimmed to remove all glands, root, and underside blade meat. It shall be almost entirely free from fat. A beef tongue has a well defined humplike prominence on its topside marked by a groove toward the front end. The color of tongues vary, but are generally light and white, though some may show black pigmentation.

1710 — Lengua de Res, Estilo 06, Corte Suizo

La lengua de res con corte suizo es una lengua a la que se le han extraído los huesos hioides con forma de U y se ha limpiado para quitar todas las glándulas, la raíz y la carne que rodea al hueso de la paleta. La grasa se debe eliminar casi completamente. La lengua de res tiene una protuberancia bien definida en su lado superior, parecida a una giba, marcada con un surco que recorre la superficie hacia el extremo frontal. El color de las lenguas puede variar, pero generalmente son claras y blancas, aunque algunas pueden presentar una pigmentación negra.

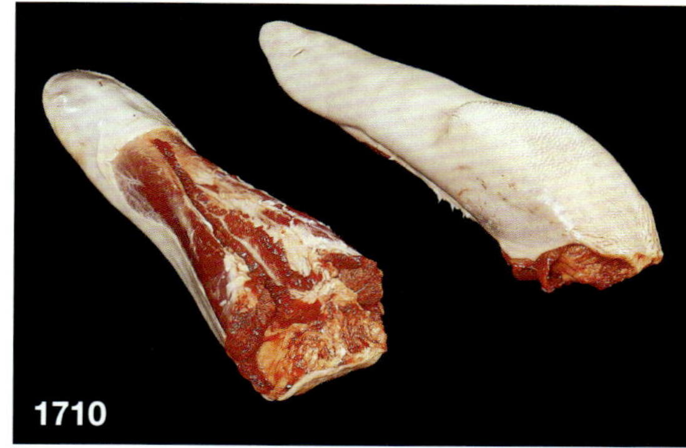

1710

1724 — Beef Liver

Beef livers are smooth, rounded, and somewhat rectangular in shape. They have a thin membrane or skin covering. The liver consists of two lobes of substantially different size. The color of livers in young animals are light to dark brown with reddish shades predominating. All ducts, blood vessels, lymph nodes, and connective tissue are to be trimmed even with the liver's surface.

1724 — Hígado de Res

Los hígados de res son suaves, redondeados y con una forma algo rectangular. Tienen una membrana o piel delgada que los recubre. El hígado consiste en dos lóbulos de tamaños sustancialmente diferentes. El color de los hígados en animales jóvenes varía entre marrón claro y oscuro con tonos rojizos que predominan. Todos los conductos, vasos sanguíneos, nódulos linfáticos y tejidos conectivos deberán recortarse para uniformizar la superficie del hígado.

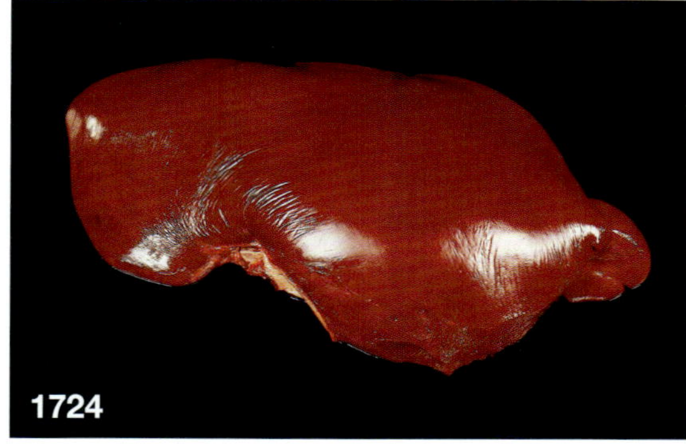

1724

1724 — Style 17: Beef Liver, Skinned

When a beef liver is ordered to this specification, it shall have the rear small lobe removed even with the surface of the larger lobe. In addition, the membrane or skin covering the liver shall be almost completely removed by means of a mechanical device.

1724 — Hígado de Res, Estilo 17, Limpio de Membranas

Cuando se pide un hígado de res con esta especificación, se debe quitar el lóbulo pequeño trasero a ras de la superficie del lóbulo mayor para que sea uniforme. Además, la membrana o piel que recubre el hígado se debe quitar casi completamente con un dispositivo mecánico.

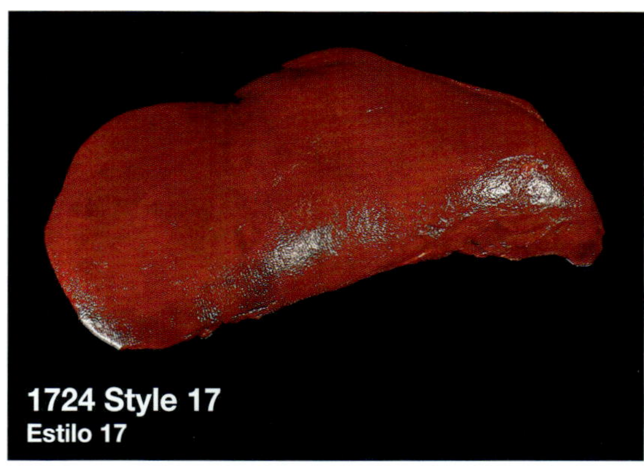

1724 Style 17
Estilo 17

1724 Style 17, PSO B and PSO C
Estilo 17, PSO B y PSO C

1724 Style 17 PSO B: Beef Liver, Skinned and Sliced as Specified

Style 17 PSO C: Beef Liver, Skinned and Portion Cut as Specified

A purchaser may order this item either sliced to a desired thickness, generally 0.25 inch (6 mm) or larger, or portion cut to an approximate specified weight, generally 4 oz. (114 g). Larger or smaller portion sizes are processed in approximate 1 oz. (28.35 g) increments. Whether ordered sliced or portioned, the product should be approximately uniform in thickness throughout.

The liver may be molded, frozen, and tempered to facilitate the slicing or portioning process. Product may be packaged intact similar to a loaf or spaced on separators between the layers.

1724 Hígado de Res, Estilo 17 PSOB, Limpio de Membranas y Rebanado Según se Especifique

Hígado de Res, Estilo 17 PSO C, Limpio de Membranas y en Cortes Porcionados según se especifique

Un comprador puede pedir esta pieza rebanada con el grosor deseado, generalmente 6 mm (0.25 pulgadas) o mayor, o en cortes porcionados de un peso específico aproximado, generalmente de 114 g (4 oz.). Los tamaños más grandes o más pequeños de las porciones se procesan en incrementos de aproximadamente 28.35 g (1 oz.). Ya sea que se solicite rebanado o porcionado, el producto debe tener un grosor general aproximadamente uniforme.

El hígado se puede moldear, congelar y atemperar para facilitar el proceso de rebanado o porcionado. El producto se puede envasar íntegro del mismo modo que un pastel, o espaciado con separadores entre sus capas.

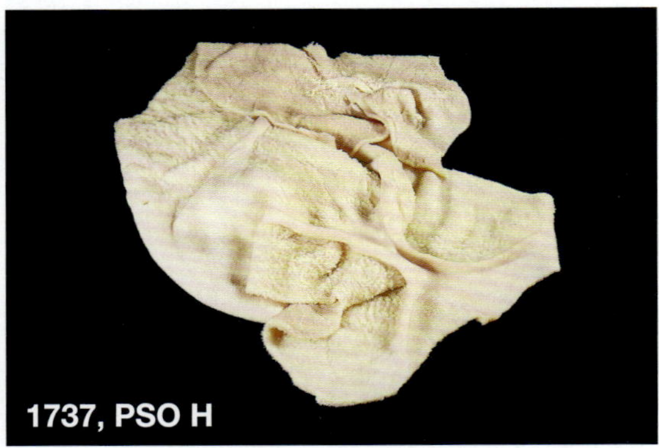

1737, PSO H

1737 Beef Paunch (Tripe), PSO H: Scalded and Bleached

The paunch or rumen is the first stomach in cattle and other ruminant animals. It is the largest of the four stomachs. It is lined with a thick layer of moist cells contained within muscular folds or pillars. It is whitish in color when scaled and bleached. Other purchase options are washed only, or scalded.

1737 Menudo (Panza o Mondongo) de Res, PSO H, Escaldado y Blanqueado

El menudo o panza es el primer estómago del ganado vacuno y otros rumiantes. Es el más grande de los cuatro estómagos. Está revestido con una capa gruesa de células húmedas contenidas en pliegues musculares o pilares. Tiene un color blanquecino cuando se realiza el escaldado y blanqueado. Otras opciones de compra son "Solamente lavado" o "Escaldado".

1739

1739 Beef Honeycomb Tripe

Honeycomb tripe is the tripe from the *reticulum* or second stomach of ruminant animals. It derives this name from the honeycomb appearance created by the numerous ridges that separate a network of cells in a compartment within the *reticulum*.

1739 Panalillo o Cacariso (Retículo/Bonete de Res)

El panalillo o cacariso es el mondongo del *reticulum* o segundo estómago de los rumiantes. Su nombre se deriva de la apariencia de un panal creada por la cantidad de surcos que separan un entrelazado de celdas en el compartimiento interior del *reticulum*.

1740 Beef Mountain Chain Tripe

Mountain chain tripe is the name given to the muscular folds or pillars seen in the rumen or paunch. These pillars or folds are more pronounced in older beef animals.

1740 Menudo Callo Grueso (Pilares de la Panza)

Menudo callo grueso es el nombre que se asigna a los pliegues musculares o pilares que se encuentran en el interior de la panza o barriga. Estos pilares o pliegues se ven más pronunciados en las reses de mayor edad.

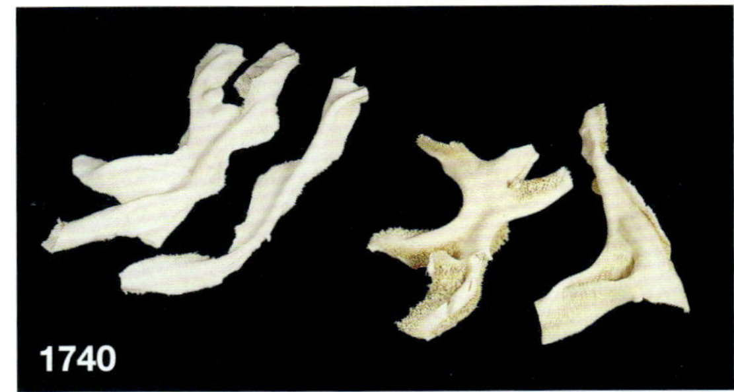
1740

1791 Beef Oxtail

The beef tail is usually referred to as an oxtail. It is removed from the carcass between the 2nd and 3rd *coccygeal* vertebrae. The last 2 or 3 vertebrae are also removed from the tip end of the tail. The surface fat is trimmed to a maximum of 0.25 inches (6 mm). The item may be purchased either whole or disjointed as Purchaser Specified Option D.

1791 Cola de Res

La cola de res generalmente se conoce como cola o rabo. Se extrae de la canal entre la segunda y la tercera vértebra *coccígea*. Las 2 o 3 últimas vértebras coccígeas también se extraen del extremo final de la cola. Se recorta la cubierta de grasa hasta un máximo grosor de 6 mm (0.25 pulgadas). La pieza se puede comprar completa o desarticulada como la Opción D especificada por el comprador.

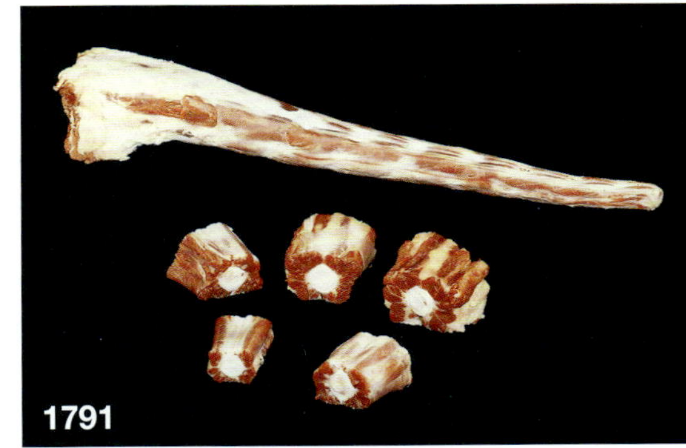
1791

2703 Lamb Cheek Meat

Cheek meat is derived from the jaw area and shall be trimmed of glandular material.

2703 Carne de Cachete de Cordero

La carne de cachete se deriva del área de la mandíbula y se le debe recortar todo el material glandular.

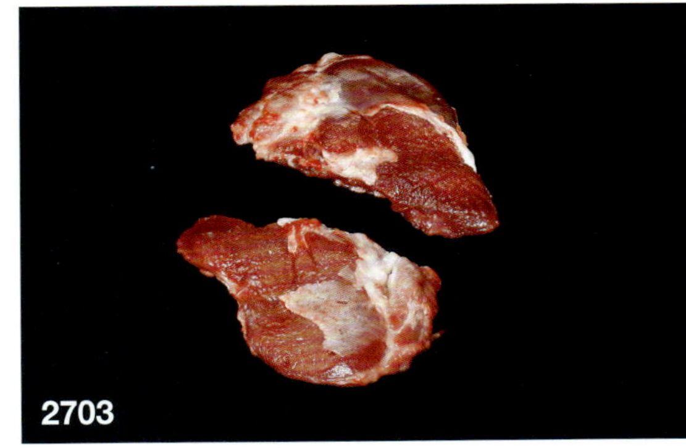
2703

2710 Lamb Tongue

The tongue is usually light in color but may show varying shades of black pigmentation. The tip has a two prong appearance with an indentation running towards a minor prominence on the top side. Tongues are harvested without bone, tonsils, glands, or root and there is little underlying base or blade meat attached.

2710 Lengua de Cordero

La lengua generalmente tiene un color claro, pero puede presentar tonos variados de pigmentación negra. La punta tiene una apariencia bífida con un surco que recorre el lado superior hacia una protuberancia menor. Las lenguas se obtienen sin hueso, amígdalas, glándulas ni raíz, y deben tener poca base subyacente o colgajos de carne que rodean el hueso a la paleta.

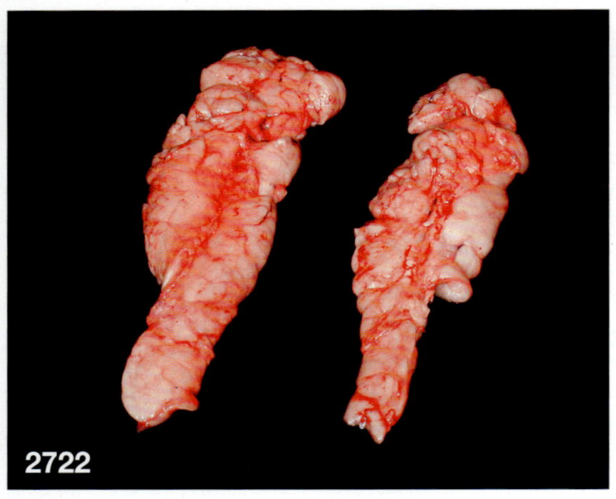

2722

2722 Lamb Sweetbreads

The sweetbread is the Thymus gland. Lamb sweetbreads are a white pinkish rather plump oblong shaped gland found in the neck area lying along the trachea.

2722 Mollejas (Timo) de Cordero

La molleja es la glándula timo. Las mollejas de cordero las constituye una glándula blanca con tonos rosa, bastante rellena y más larga que ancha, que yace en el área del cuello a lo largo de la tráquea.

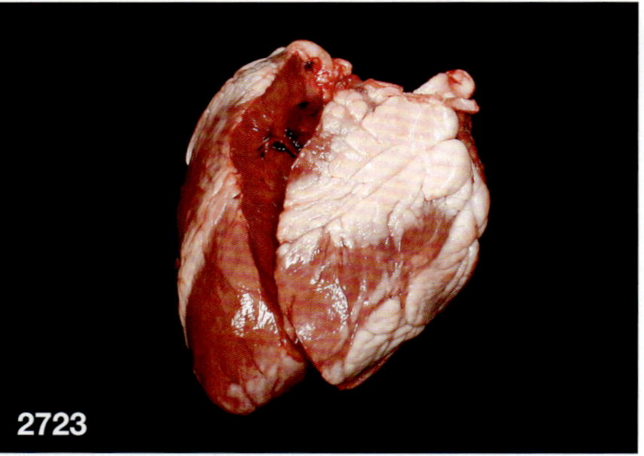

2723

2723 Lamb Heart

The heart is a muscular cone shaped organ located in the thorax region. The lamb heart is more pointed in appearance than those of other species, and the fat surrounding it is white and hard. The heart weighs approximately 8 ounces (230 g). The whole heart includes the cap with fat, arteries, and veins attached.

2723 Corazón de Cordero

El corazón es un órgano muscular cónico ubicado en la región del tórax. El corazón de cordero tiene un aspecto más puntiagudo que los de otras especies y la grasa que lo rodea es blanca y dura. El corazón pesa aproximadamente 230 g (8 onzas). El corazón entero incluye la tapa con grasa, arterias y venas conexas.

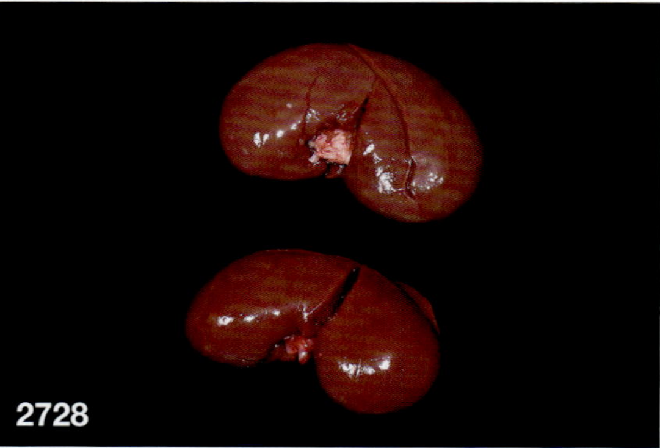

2728

2728 Lamb Kidney

The kidney is a bean shaped, smooth, firm, reddish-brown organ with a depression at the point of attachment to the blood vessels, pizzle cord, and ureter. These attachments and fat shall be trimmed close to the surface of the kidney.

2728 Riñón de Cordero

El riñón es un órgano con forma de frijol, suave, firme y marrón rojizo que tiene una depresión en el punto de conexión de los vasos sanguíneos, el cordón peniano y el uréter. Estas conexiones y la grasa deben recortarse hasta muy cerca de la superficie del riñón.

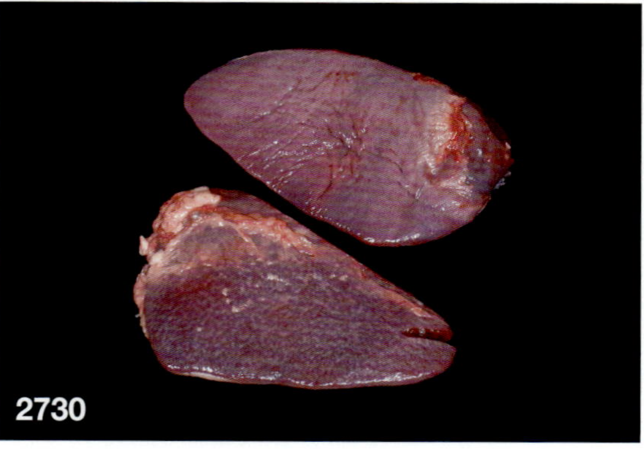

2730

2730 Lamb Spleen

The spleen is a triangular, somewhat pyramidal shaped organ with rounded edges. The spleen is blueish red in color and weighs approximately 4 ounces (100 g). It measures approximately 6 inches by 4 inches (15 by 10 cm), but may vary considerably both in dimensions and weight. It is part of the lymph system.

2730 Bazo de Cordero

El bazo es un órgano triangular y algo piramidal con bordes redondeados. El bazo tiene un color rojo azulado y pesa aproximadamente 100 g (4 onzas). Mide aproximadamente 15 cm por 10 cm (6 por 4 pulgadas), pero puede variar considerablemente tanto en tamaño como en peso. Forma parte del sistema linfático.

2772 — Lamb Caul Fat

This item is a soft, lacy, white, fat-like membrane harvested from the abdominal cavity of Item No. 200, Lamb Carcass. This item is sometimes referred to as "Lamb Veil".

2772 — Redaño (Grasa Omental) de Cordero

Esta pieza es una membrana suave, reticular, blanca y con aspecto de malla traslúcida de grasa que se extrae de la cavidad abdominal de la pieza número 200, Canal de Cordero. A veces a esta pieza también se le llama "Velo de cordero".

3701 — Veal Brains

The item is found in the frontal top area of the skull. The individual sections weigh approximately 8 ounces (227 g) when separated from the spinal cord. As pictured, the brains are shown intact and attached. Purchasers desiring only the individual sections should so specify.

3701 — Sesos de Ternera

La pieza se encuentra en el área frontal superior del cráneo. Las secciones individuales pesan aproximadamente 227 g (8 onzas) cuando se separan de la médula espinal. Como se muestra en la ilustración, los sesos se presentan intactos y unidos. Los compradores que deseen únicamente secciones individuales deben especificarlo.

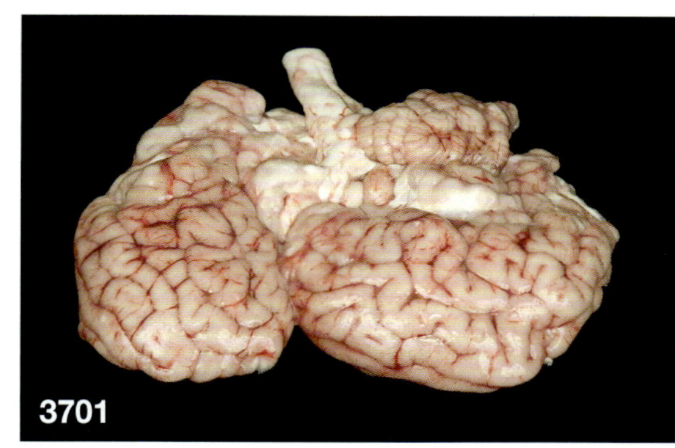

3701

3710 — Style 06 Veal Tongue, Swiss-Cut

A Swiss-cut veal tongue is a tongue that has had the U-shaped hyoid bones removed and has been trimmed to remove all glands, root, and underside blade meat. It shall be almost entirely free from fat. The veal tongue has a less defined humplike prominence on its topside, but otherwise is similar to a beef tongue, though much smaller in size and weight. Veal tongues are usually white in color.

3710 — Lengua de Ternera, Estilo 06, Corte Suizo

Una lengua de ternera con corte suizo es una lengua a la que se le han extraído los huesos hioides con forma de U y se ha limpiado para quitar todas las glándulas, la raíz y carne que rodea el hueso de la paleta. La grasa se debe eliminar casi completamente. La lengua de ternera tiene una protuberancia menos definida en su lado superior, pero es similar a la lengua de res, aunque mucho más pequeña y menos pesada. Las lenguas de ternera generalmente son de color blanco.

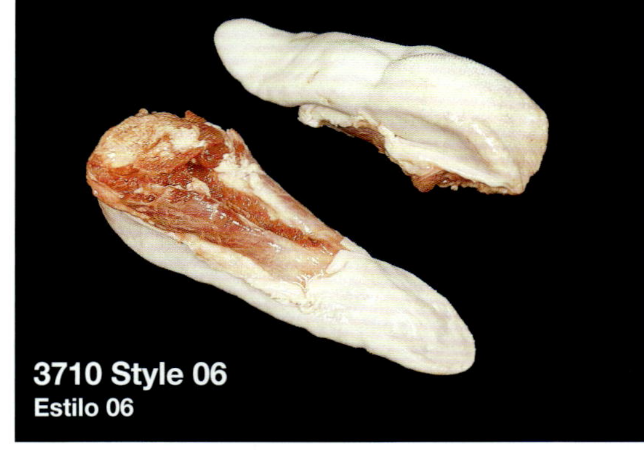

3710 Style 06
Estilo 06

3722 — Veal Sweetbreads

The sweetbread is the thymus gland. Veal sweetbreads are considered the most desirable. One side of the gland is plump and rounded and the other, or heart side, is more elongated and narrow. The sweetbreads have a membrane cover but otherwise are trimmed free of excess fat and tissues. When sold together in sets, they are referred to as pairs. Veal sweetbreads are pinkish white in color and multilobed in appearance.

3722 — Mollejas (Timo) de Ternera

La molleja es la glándula timo. Las mollejas de ternera se consideran las más deseadas. Un lado de la glándula es relleno y redondeado y el otro, o lado adyacente al corazón, es más alargado y delgado. Las mollejas pueden conservar una membrana que las recubre, pero se les recorta todo exceso de grasa y tejidos. Cuando se venden en conjuntos, se les refiere como "en pares". Las mollejas de ternera tienen un color blanco con tonos rosa y un aspecto con varios lóbulos.

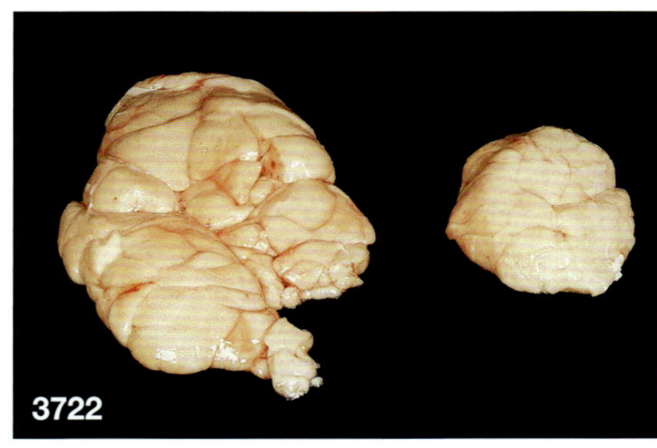

3722

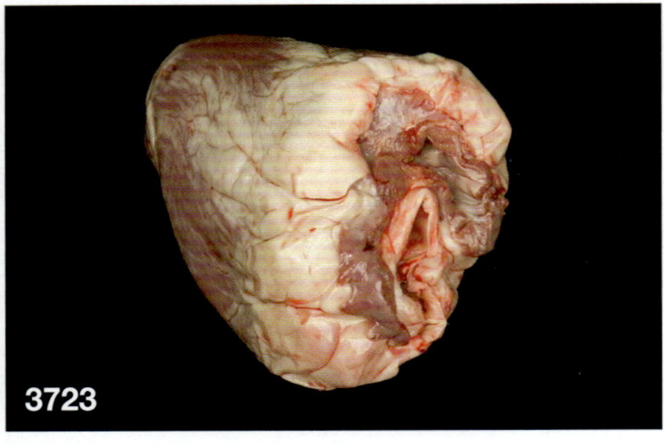

3723

3723 Veal Heart

A muscular, cone-shaped organ located in the thorax region of the veal carcass. It weighs approximately 2.5 pounds (1.1 kg). Purchasers desiring a special preparation of this item should request it from their supplier.

3723 Corazón de Ternera

Un órgano muscular cónico ubicado en la región torácica de la canal de ternera. Pesa aproximadamente 1.1 kg (2.5 libras). Los compradores que deseen una preparación especial de esta pieza deben solicitarla a su proveedor.

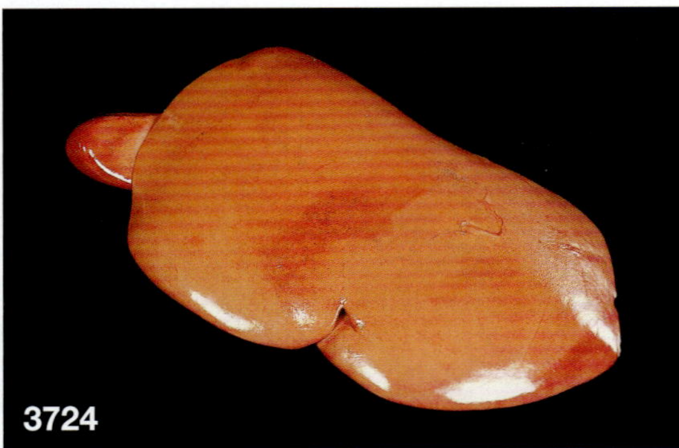

3724

3724 Veal Liver

The liver is a smooth, somewhat rounded and rectangular organ covered with a thin membrane or skin. Veal livers vary in color from light reddish tan to tan and have two lobes of substantially different sizes. Larger, heavier, and darker livers are generally called calf. Livers from special-fed or formula veal may also be quite large but are lighter in color. Veal and calf livers are not usually sold skinned.

3724 Hígado de Ternera

El hígado es un órgano suave, algo ovalado y rectangular recubierto con una membrana o cubierta delgada. El color de los hígados de ternera varía de café rojizo claro a café y tiene dos lóbulos de tamaños sustancialmente diferentes. Los hígados más grandes, más pesados y más oscuros generalmente se llaman hígados de becerro. Los hígados de ternera con una alimentación o fórmula especial también podrán ser bastante grandes pero de un color más claro. Los hígados de ternera y becerro generalmente no se venden limpios de membranas.

3724 Style 17, PSO B
Estilo 17, PSO B

3724 Style 17, PSO C
Estilo 17, PSO C

3724 Style 17 PSO B: Veal Liver, Sliced as Specified

Style 17 PSO C: Veal Liver, Portion Cut as Specified

A purchaser may order this item either sliced to a desired thickness, generally 0.25 inch (6 mm) or larger, or portion-cut to an approximate specified weight, generally 4 oz. (114 g). Larger or smaller portion sizes are processed in approximate 1 oz. (28.35 g) increments. Whether ordered sliced or portioned, the product should be approximately uniform in thickness throughout.

The liver may be molded, frozen, and tempered to facilitate the slicing or portioning process. Product may be packaged intact similar to a loaf, or spaced on separators between the layers.

3724 Hígado de Ternera, Estilo 17 PSO B, Rebanado según se especifique

Hígado de Ternera, Estilo 17 PSO C, Porcionado según se especifique

El comprador puede pedir esta pieza rebanada con el grosor deseado, generalmente 6 mm (0.25 pulgadas) o mayor, o en porciones, especificando un peso aproximado, generalmente de 114 g (4 oz.). Los tamaños de porciones más grandes o más pequeñas se procesan en incrementos de peso aproximadamente de 28.35 g (1 oz.). Ya sea que se solicite rebanado o porcionado, el producto debe tener un grosor general aproximadamente uniforme.

El hígado se puede moldear, congelar y atemperar para facilitar el proceso de rebanado o porcionado. El producto se puede envasar intacto del mismo modo que un pastel, o espaciado con separadores entre las capas.

3728 — Veal Kidney

The veal kidney is a rectangular, multilobed concave organ with a slight depression on the opposite side where the blood vessels and other connections to the body occur. Its color is reddish-tan. Kidneys are trimmed even to the surface on the depression side of excess fat and attachments to the body. The membrane that surrounds the kidney shall also be removed.

3728 — Riñón de Ternera

El riñón de ternera es un órgano rectangular, cóncavo, con varios lóbulos, que tiene una pequeña depresión del lado opuesto a la ubicación de los vasos sanguíneos y otras conexiones al cuerpo. Su color es pardo rojizo. Se recorta el exceso de grasa y las conexiones al cuerpo en el lado de la depresión de los riñones para uniformizar la superficie. La membrana que rodea al riñón también se debe quitar.

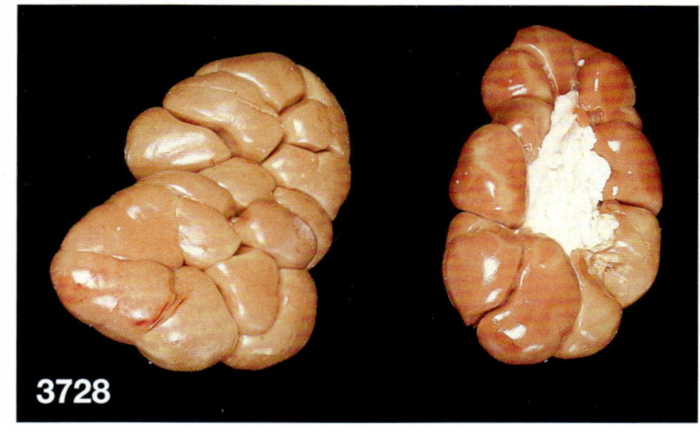
3728

3791 — Veal Tail

The veal tail is similar in appearance to the beef oxtail except it is smaller in overall size. It measures approximately 8 inches (20 cm) long and 0.75 inches (18 mm) in diameter. The veal tail is separated from the carcass in the same manner as described in Item No. 1791 Beef Oxtail. This item may be purchased whole or specified disjointed as Purchaser Specified Option D (Disjointed).

3791 — Cola de Ternera

La cola de ternera tiene un aspecto similar a la cola de res, excepto que el tamaño generalmente es más pequeño. Mide aproximadamente 20 cm (8 pulgadas) de largo y 18 mm (0.75 pulgadas) de diámetro. La cola de ternera se separa de la canal del mismo modo que se describe en la pieza número 1791, Cola de Res. Esta pieza se puede comprar entera o se puede especificar desarticulada como en la Opción especificada por el comprador D (Desarticulada).

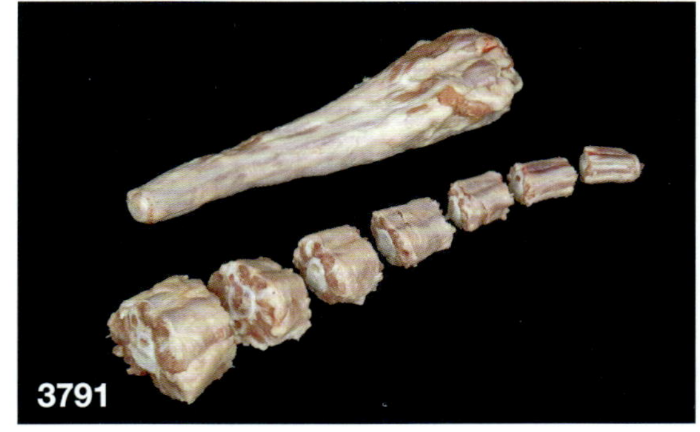
3791

4701 — Pork Brains

This item is located inside the front top skull, and weighs approximately 4 to 5 ounces (130 g). The brains are elongated and oval to somewhat bean shaped.

4701 — Sesos de Cerdo

Esta pieza está ubicada dentro de la parte frontal superior del cráneo y pesa aproximadamente 130 g (entre 4 y 5 onzas). Los sesos son alargados y ovalados con forma parecida a un frijol.

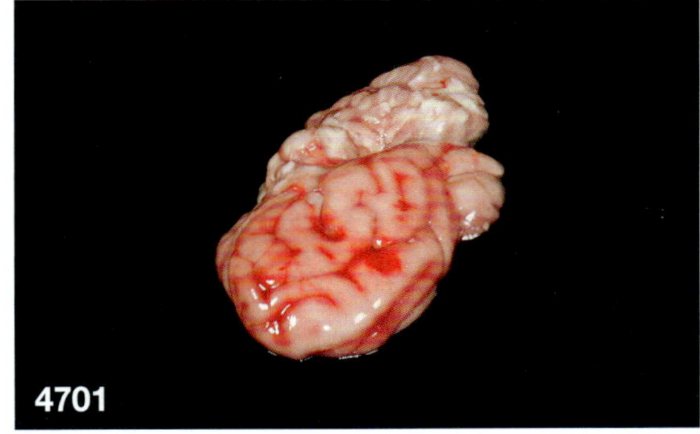
4701

4710 — Pork Tongue

The tongue is rather thin and has a pointed tip. The tongue is soft pink in color with a whitish pink membrane covering. All tongues are harvested with bone, root, and blade meat removed.

4710 — Lengua de Cerdo

La lengua es bastante delgada y tiene un extremo en punta. Tiene un color rosa suave y la recubre una membrana de color rosa blancuzco. Todas las lenguas se obtienen retirando el hueso, la raíz y la carne que rodea al hueso de la paleta.

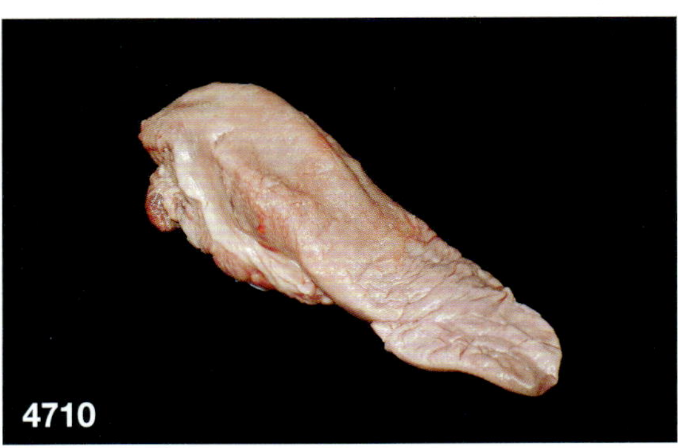
4710

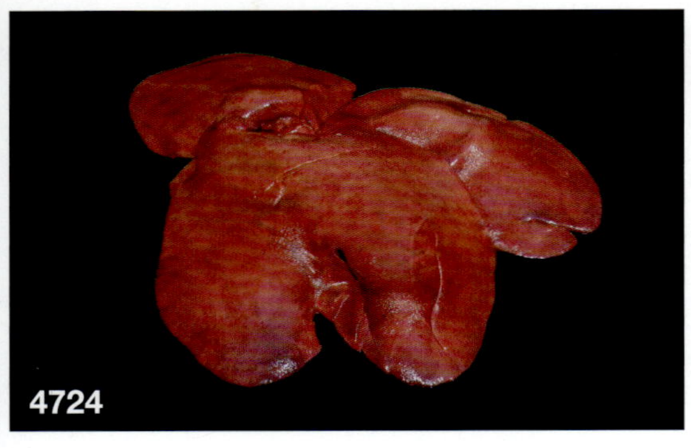
4724

4724 Pork Liver

Pork livers are smooth, irregular shaped, and covered with a thin membrane or skin. The liver consists of four lobes of varying size marked with notches and indentations. The liver has a reddish brown color, and the texture of the liver is more firm than other species. All ducts, blood vessels, lymph nodes and connective tissues are to be trimmed even with the surface of the liver.

4724 Hígado de Cerdo

Los hígados de cerdo son lisos, de forma irregular y recubiertos con una membrana o piel delgada. El hígado consiste en cuatro lóbulos de distintos tamaños marcados con muescas y surcos. El hígado tiene un color marrón rojizo y una textura más firme que la de otras especies. Todos los conductos, vasos sanguíneas, nódulos linfáticos y tejidos conectivos deberán recortarse para uniformizar la superficie del hígado.

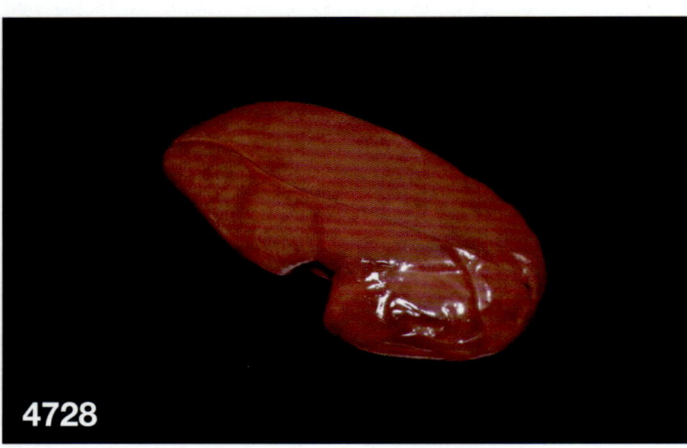
4728

4728 Pork Kidney

The pork kidney is flat, bean shaped, smooth, firm, reddish-brown organ with a depression at the point of attachment to the blood vessels, pizzle cord, and ureter. These attachments and fat shall be trimmed close to the surface of the kidney.

4728 Riñón de Cerdo

El riñón de cerdo es un órgano plano, con forma de frijol, de superficie lisa, textura firme y color marrón rojizo, que tiene una depresión en el punto de conexión de los vasos sanguíneos, el cordón peniano y el uréter. Estas estructuras anexas y la grasa deben recortarse hasta casi tocar la superficie del riñón.

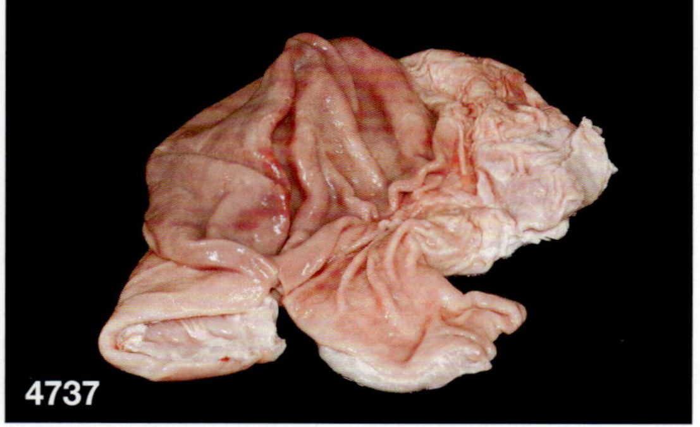
4737

4737 Pork Stomach

The pork paunch is referred to as the stomach or hog's maw. Pigs/hogs are a non-ruminant animals and have only one stomach to perform digestive functions. The different regions of the stomach are marked by numerous small folds and the regions vary in color from grayish white to deep red.

Purchaser Specified Options:
PSO F: Washed
PSO G: Scalded
PSO H: Scalded & Bleached

4737 Estómago (Buche) de Cerdo

La panza de cerdo se conoce como estómago o buche de cerdo. Los lechones/cerdos son animales no rumiantes y tienen un solo estómago para realizar las funciones digestivas. Las diferentes regiones internas del estómago están marcadas por numerosos pliegues pequeños y varían de color entre el blanco grisáceo y el rojo intenso.

Opciones Especificadas por el Comprador:
PSO F: Lavado
PSO G: Escaldado
PSO H: Escaldado y blanqueado

4744 — Pork Chitterlings (Large Intestine)

In pork, the large intestine is usually referred to as chitterlings. The large intestine connects to the small intestine and is continuous through to the rectum. It is about 10 to 15 feet long (3 to 4.5 m) and approximately 2 inches (5 cm) in diameter. Chitterlings are very moist and while they are tubular in shape when harvested, it is ordinarily processed and sold in approximately 12 inch long (30 cm) pieces.

4744 — Machitos, Tripas (Intestino Grueso) de Cerdo

En el cerdo, el intestino grueso generalmente se conoce como machitos o tripas. El intestino grueso está conectado con el intestino delgado y se continúa hasta el recto. Mide entre 3 y 4.5 m (10 y 15 pies) de largo y aproximadamente 5 cm (2 pulgadas) de diámetro. Los machitos o tripas son muy húmedos y si bien tienen una forma tubular cuando se extraen, generalmente se procesan y se venden en piezas aplanadas de aproximadamente 30 cm (12 pulgadas) de largo.

4772 — Pork Caul Fat

This item is a soft, lacy, white, fat-like membrane harvested from the abdominal cavity of Item No. 400, Pork Carcass.

4772 — Grasa Redaño de Cerdo

Esta pieza es una membrana suave, reticular, blanca y con aspecto de malla traslúcida que se extrae de la cavidad abdominal de la pieza número 400, Canal de Cerdo.

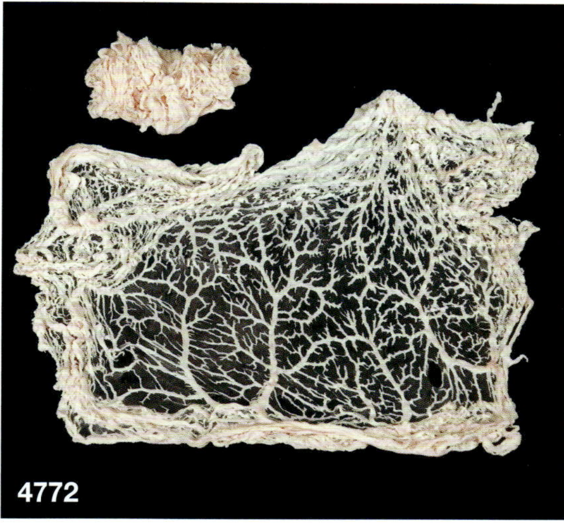

Membership Information
Información sobre la membresía

Want your personal network to include the real decision-makers at the most successful meat & poultry processors and suppliers in North America?

THEN JOIN NAMP!

Founded in 1942, the North American Meat Processors Association (NAMP) is an international member-driven association of **progressive meat processors, distributors, center-of-the-plate specialists,** and suppliers selling primarily to the foodservice industry. NAMP provides exceptional value through high-caliber support programs and governmental representation to help ensure our members' success in the industry.

The Meat Buyer's Guide® is a NAMP publication. NAMP members can participate in the review/update process of each edition.

BENEFITS OF MEMBERSHIP

- 35% discount on *The Meat Buyers Guide®*
- A relaxed networking and learning environment at two major industry-wide meetings a year
- Learning opportunities at NAMP's 16+ food safety conferences and workshops: pay lower member fees
- NAMP's weekly report, *NewsLine,* which contains industry information and updates and NAMP's weekly Market Report, with complete up-to-date pricing information
- Unlimited free access to NAMP's College of Experts, our team of 34 Ph.D.-level consultants on 19 subjects important to your business
- A voice in government rulemaking: NAMP is a North American organization that effectively represents your interests to USDA-FSIS, USDA-AMS, and CFIA
- A cross-referenced *Member Resource Directory* for networking and enriching your business prospects
- Fast, on-line help from other members through NAMP's Listserve called "Bull Session"
- Exclusive technical/educational info on the Members Only section at www.namp.com

Members also enjoy toll-free access to NAMP's experienced staff and off-site consultants who are ready to help you with just about any problem, question or concern you may have. *It's like having your own team of experts without the added expense - an incredible value for your dues dollar!*

Membership in NAMP offers an unparalleled and unique opportunity to learn and network with your peers. Join today and you'll enrich your business prospects and benefit from other members' experiences. *It's what our long-time members call "The Magic of NAMP".*

WE INVITE YOU TO JOIN TODAY

To apply, go to www.namp.com or call +1 703.758.1900.

¿Quiere que su red personal incluya a quienes en verdad toman las decisiones y a los más exitosos procesadores y proveedores de carne roja y aves de América del Norte?

¡ENTONCES ÚNASE A NAMP!

La Asociación Norteamericana de Procesadores de Carne (NAMP), fundada en 1942, es una asociación internacional dedicada a sus integrantes, que incluyen **procesadores, distribuidores, especialistas en ingredientes principales del plato** y proveedores progresistas que venden principalmente a la industria de servicios de alimentación. NAMP ofrece un valor excepcional a través de programas de apoyo de gran nivel y representación en el gobierno para ayudar a garantizar el éxito de nuestros miembros en la industria.

La Guía para Compradores de Carne® es una publicación de NAMP. Los miembros de NAMP pueden participar en el proceso de revisión y actualización de cada edición.

BENEFICIOS DE LA MEMBRESÍA

- 35% de descuento en *La Guía para Compradores de Carne®*
- Un ambiente relajado para establecer contactos y aprender en dos grandes reuniones de toda la industria por año
- Oportunidades de aprendizaje en las conferencias y los talleres de inocuidad alimentaria de NAMP: pague tarifas más bajas para miembros
- Informe semanal de NAMP, *NewsLine*, que contiene información y actualizaciones de la industria, y el Informe de Mercado semanal de NAMP, con la información de precios completa y al día
- Acceso gratis ilimitado al colegio de expertos de NAMP, nuestro equipo de 34 con nivel de doctorado en 19 áreas importantes para su negocio
- Una voz en las normativas del gobierno: NAMP es una organización norteamericana que representa sus intereses de manera eficaz ante FSIS (Servicio de Inspección e Inocuidad Alimentaria) de USDA (Departamento de Agricultura de E.U.A.), AMS (Servicio de Mercadeo Agrícola) de USDA y la Agencia Canadiense de Inspección de Alimentos
- Un *Directorio de recursos de miembros* con referencia cruzada para establecer contactos y enriquecer las posibilidades de su negocio
- Ayuda rápida en Internet de otros miembros a través del Listserve de NAMP llamado "Bull Session"
- Información técnica y educativa exclusiva en la sección Members Only (sólo para miembros) de www.namp.com

Los miembros también disponen de acceso a través de un número telefónico sin cargo al experimentado personal de NAMP y a consultores descentralizados que están listos para ayudarle con prácticamente cualquier problema, consulta o inquietud que pueda tener. *Es como tener su propio equipo de expertos sin el gasto adicional ¡un increíble rendimiento por el valor de su suscripción!*

La membresía de NAMP ofrece una oportunidad única e incomparable de aprender y establecer contactos con sus colegas. Suscríbase hoy para enriquecer las posibilidades de su negocio y beneficiarse de la experiencia de otros miembros. *Es lo que nuestros miembros de muchos años llaman "La magia de NAMP".*

LO INVITAMOS A UNIRSE HOY

Para solicitar su inscripción, visite www.namp.com o llame al +1 703.758.1900.

Index/Índice

Sausage Products
Productos Embutidos

Tabla de fórmulas

El comprador especificará la formulación del producto.

IMPORTANTE: el nombre de producto de las piezas formuladas con una combinación de carne roja y de aves se debe etiquetar de la siguiente forma:

Fórmula	Requisito de etiquetado
P	NOMBRE DE LA PIEZA (Salchichas Tipo Frankfurt, etc.) de carne de res y pavo
P1	NOMBRE DE LA PIEZA (Embutido Tipo Bolonia, etc.) de carne de res y pollo
P2	NOMBRE DE LA PIEZA (Salame, etc.) de carne de cerdo y pavo
P3	NOMBRE DE LA PIEZA (Salchichas Tipo Frankfurt, etc.) de carne de cerdo y pollo

Especias y condimentos

Cuando se requiera específicamente una especia o condimento en la descripción de la pieza individual, ese condimento o ingrediente en particular deberá indicarse individualmente en la etiqueta de ingredientes del fabricante.

Sólo ingredientes principales

A Carne de res y cerdo en cualquier combinación

A1 La fórmula A más leche en polvo descremada y/o leche en polvo desnatada reducida en calcio

B Carne de res, cerdo (res es predominante)

B1 La fórmula B más leche en polvo descremada y/o leche en polvo desnatada reducida en calcio

C Cerdo, carne de res (cerdo es predominante)

C1 La fórmula C más leche en polvo descremada y/o leche en polvo desnatada reducida en calcio

D Carne de res

D1 La fórmula D más leche en polvo descremada y/o leche en polvo desnatada reducida en calcio

L Fórmula (A, B, C, etc., según se especifique), con una formulación reducida en grasa. Los productos de formulación reducida en grasa están sujetos a los requisitos materiales indicados en IMPS (Especificaciones de Compras Institucionales de Carne, por sus siglas en inglés) para los productos embutidos de la serie 800

P Carne de res y pavo (res es predominante)

P1 Carne de res y pollo (res es predominante)

P2 Cerdo y pavo (cerdo es predominante)

P3 Cerdo y pollo (cerdo es predominante)

H Carne de res y cerdo en cualquier combinación más carne de corazón de res (consulte la pieza 804, Salchichón Tipo Salami, Cocido)

H1 Carne de res y cerdo en cualquier combinación más cualquier combinación de menudo (panza o mondongo) de res, carne de corazón de res, carne de corazón de cerdo, carne de lengua de res y carne de lengua de cerdo

H2 La fórmula H1 más leche en polvo descremada y/o leche en polvo desnatada reducida en calcio

H3 Carne de res, carne de corazón de res (res es predominante) (consulte la pieza número 808, Salami Seco)

H4 Carne de res, cerdo, carne de corazón de res (res es predominante) (consulte la pieza número 808, Salami Seco)

G Carne de cerdo

G1 La fórmula G más leche en polvo descremada y/o leche en polvo desnatada reducida en calcio

G2 Carne de cerdo, res, carne de corazón de cerdo (cerdo es predominante)

G3 La fórmula G2 más leche en polvo descremada y/o leche en polvo desnatada reducida en calcio

G4 Carne de cerdo, de res, ternera (cerdo es predominante)

G5 La fórmula G4 más leche en polvo descremada y/o leche en polvo desnatada reducida en calcio

G6 Carne de cerdo, ternera (cerdo es predominante)

G7 La fórmula G6 más leche en polvo descremada y/o leche en polvo desnatada reducida en calcio

V Hígados de cerdo, cerdo (hígado de cerdo es predominante)

V1 La fórmula V más leche en polvo descremada y/o leche en polvo desnatada reducida en calcio

V2 Hígados de cerdo, carne de cerdo con papadas ahumadas y/o extremos y trozos de tocino (hígado de cerdo es predominante)

V3 La fórmula V2 más leche en polvo descremada y/o leche en polvo desnatada reducida en calcio (consulte la pieza número 803 de la serie V)

X Carne de ternera

X1 La fórmula X más leche en polvo descremada y/o leche en polvo desnatada reducida en calcio

X2 Carne de ternera, cerdo (ternera es predominante)

X3 La fórmula X2 más leche en polvo descremada y/o leche en polvo desnatada reducida en calcio

Y Jamón

Y1 La fórmula Y más leche en polvo descremada y/o leche en polvo desnatada reducida en calcio

Table of Formulas

Product formulation shall be specified by the purchaser.

NOTE: The product name of combination red meat and poultry formulated sausage items must be labeled as follows:

Formula	Labeling Requirement
P	Beef and Turkey ITEM NAME (Frankfurter, etc.)
P1	Beef and Chicken ITEM NAME (Bologna, etc.)
P2	Pork and Turkey ITEM NAME (Salami, etc.)
P3	Pork and Chicken ITEM NAME (Frankfurter, etc.)

Spices and Seasonings

When a spice or seasoning is specifically required within the individual Item Description, that particular seasoning or ingredient shall be individually listed on the manufacturer's label of ingredients.

Major Ingredients Only

A Beef and pork in any combination

A1 Formula A plus nonfat dry milk and/or calcium-reduced dried skim milk

B Beef, pork (beef is predominant)

B1 Formula B plus nonfat dry milk and/or calcium-reduced dried skim milk

C Pork, beef (pork is predominant)

C1 Formula C plus nonfat dry milk and/or calcium-reduced dried skim milk

D Beef

D1 Formula D plus nonfat dry milk and/or calcium-reduced dried skim milk

L Formula (A, B, C, etc., as specified), lower fat formulation. Lower fat formulated products are subject to specific material requirements stated in the IMPS specifications for Sausage Products Series 800

P Beef and turkey (beef is predominant)

P1 Beef and chicken (beef is predominant)

P2 Pork and turkey (pork is predominant)

P3 Pork and chicken (pork is predominant)

H Beef and pork in any combination plus Beef Heart Meat (See Item 804 Salami, Cooked)

H1 Beef and pork in any combination plus any one or any combination of beef tripe, beef heart meat, pork heart meat, beef tongue meat, and pork tongue meat

H2 Formula H1 plus nonfat dry milk and/or calcium-reduced dried skim milk

H3 Beef, beef heart meat (beef is predominant) (see Item No. 808 Dry Salami)

H4 Beef, pork, beef heart meat (beef is predominant) (see Item No. 808 Dry Salami)

G Pork

G1 Formula G plus nonfat dry milk and/or calcium-reduced dried skim milk

G2 Pork, beef, pork heart meat (pork is predominant)

G3 Formula G2 plus nonfat dry milk and/or calcium-reduced dried skim milk

G4 Pork, beef, veal (pork is predominant)

G5 Formula G4 plus nonfat dry milk and/or calcium-reduced dried skim milk

G6 Pork, veal (pork is predominant)

G7 Formula G6 plus nonfat dry milk and/or calcium-reduced dried skim milk

V Pork livers, pork (pork liver is predominant)

V1 Formula V plus nonfat dry milk and/or calcium-reduced dried skim milk

V2 Pork livers, pork with smoked jowls and/or bacon ends and pieces (pork liver is predominant)

V3 Formula V2 plus nonfat dry milk and/or calcium-reduced dried skim milk (See Item No. 803 on V series)

X Veal

X1 Formula X plus nonfat dry milk and/or calcium-reduced dried skim milk

X2 Veal, pork (veal is predominant)

X3 Formula X2 plus nonfat dry milk and/or calcium-reduced dried skim milk

Y Ham

Y1 Formula Y plus nonfat dry milk and/or calcium reduced dried skim milk

Información para hacer los pedidos

Lo especificará el comprador

No es necesario que el comprador especifique todas las opciones de información que se indican a continuación para hacer sus pedidos. La mayoría de los productos de esta serie tienen "incorporadas" descripciones detalladas de la pieza, (por ejemplo: forma, estilo, etc.). Sin embargo, el comprador podrá especificar cualquier opción de compra alternativa en el contrato u orden de compra, incluidas las que se indican a continuación, siempre y cuando dichas opciones sean claras y concisas.

Estado de refrigeración

A **FRESCO**	–2.2 °C (28 °F) o mayor
B **CONGELADO**	–2.2 °C (28 °F) o menor
C **OPCIÓN ESPECIFICADA POR EL COMPRADOR**	–17.8 °C (0 °F) o menor

Clase

A– Ahumado (calor seco) – sólo Horneado

B– Sin ahumar (calor húmedo)

C–Dorado en aceite caliente

IMPORTANTE: a menos que el comprador lo autorice específicamente, no está permitido el uso de colorantes artificiales en la fabricación de cualquier pieza de salchichas.

Tolerancias de peso y grosor de las hamburguesas*

Tolerancias de grosor de la porción

Grosor especificado	Tolerancia de grosor - Uniformidad	Grosor
2.5 cm (1.0 pulgada) o menos	± 5 mm (0.1875 pulgadas)	5 mm (0.1875 pulgadas)
Más de 2.5 cm (1.0 pulgada)	± 6 mm (0.25 pulgadas)	6 mm (0.25 pulgadas)

Tolerancias de peso de la porción*

Peso especificado	Tolerancia de peso - Uniformidad	Grosor
Menor que 170 g (6.0 oz.)	± 7 g (0.25 oz.)	5 mm (0.1875 pulgadas)
170 g (6.0 oz.) o más	± 14 g (0.50 oz.)	6 mm (0.25 pulgadas)

* Las medidas de grosor no aplican a una distancia de 6 mm (0.25 pulgadas) medida desde el borde. Las tolerancias de peso y grosor de las porciones para las hamburguesas cocidas deben permitirse hacia el valor superior (por ej., +/– 0.50 oz., +/– 6 mm) para permitir variaciones de cocción.

Tipo

A - Sin rebanar

B - Rebanado (el comprador debe especificar una cantidad de rebanadas por libra)

C - Tortita/ Hamburguesa

D - Desmenuzado

E - En ristras

F - A granel

Forma

A - Rectangular

B - Redonda

Opciones de cocción

A - Horneado

B - Cocido

C - Fresco sin cocer (sin agregado de sales/ soluciones del curado)

D - Fermentado sin cocer (sales/soluciones del curado agregadas)

Estilo

A - Tripas artificiales (no comestibles)

B - Tripas de cerdo o cordero, en ristras (naturales)

B1 - Tripas de cerdo o cordero, sin ristras (naturales)

C - Sin cubierta (moldeadas mecánicamente)

D - Tripas de colágeno (comestibles)

E - Bolsas de tela

F - A granel

Ordering Data

To Be Specified by the Purchaser

Not all of the ordering data options listed below are required to be specified by the purchaser. Most of the items in this series have "built in" detailed Item Descriptions; (for example: shape, style, etc.). However, any alternative purchaser options, including those listed below, may be specified by the purchaser in the contract or purchase order as long as those options are clear and concise.

State of Refrigeration

A **FRESH**	28°F (–2.2°C) or higher
B **FROZEN**	28°F (–2.2°C) or lower
C **PSO**	0°F (–17.8°C) or lower

Class

A–Smoked (dry heat) – Baked only

B–Unsmoked (moist heat)

C–Browned in hot oil

NOTE: Unless specifically authorized by the purchaser, use of artificial colors in the manufacture of any sausage item shall not be permitted.

Patty Weight and Thickness Tolerances*

Portion Thickness Tolerances

Specified Thickness	Thickness Tolerance - Uniformity	Thickness
1.0 inch (2.5 cm) or less	± 0.1875 inch (5 mm)	0.1875 inch (5 mm)
More than 1.0 inch (2.5 cm)	± 0.25 inch (6 mm)	0.25 inch (6 mm)

Portion Weight Tolerances*

Specified Weight	Weight Tolerance - Uniformity	Thickness
Less than 6.0 oz. (170 g)	± 0.25 oz. (7 g)	0.1875 inch (5 mm)
6.0 oz. (170 g) or more	± 0.50 oz. (14 g)	0.25 inch (6 mm)

* Thickness measurements not applicable within 0.25 inch (6 mm) of the edge. Portion weight and thickness tolerances for cooked patties shall be allowed at the higher value (i.e., +/– 0.50 oz., +/– 0.25 inch) to allow for cooking variances.

Type

A - Unsliced

B - Sliced (purchaser must specify a slice count per pound)

C - Patty

D - Crumbles

E - Linked

F - Bulk

Shape

A - Rectangular

B - Round

Cooking Options

A - Baked

B - Cooked

C - Uncooked Fresh (no cure added)

D - Uncooked Fermented (cure added)

Style

A - Artificial casings (inedible)

B - Hog or sheep casings, linked (natural)

B1 - Hog or sheep casings, unlinked (natural)

C - Skinless (mechanically formed)

D - Collagen casings (edible)

E - Cloth bags

F - Bulk

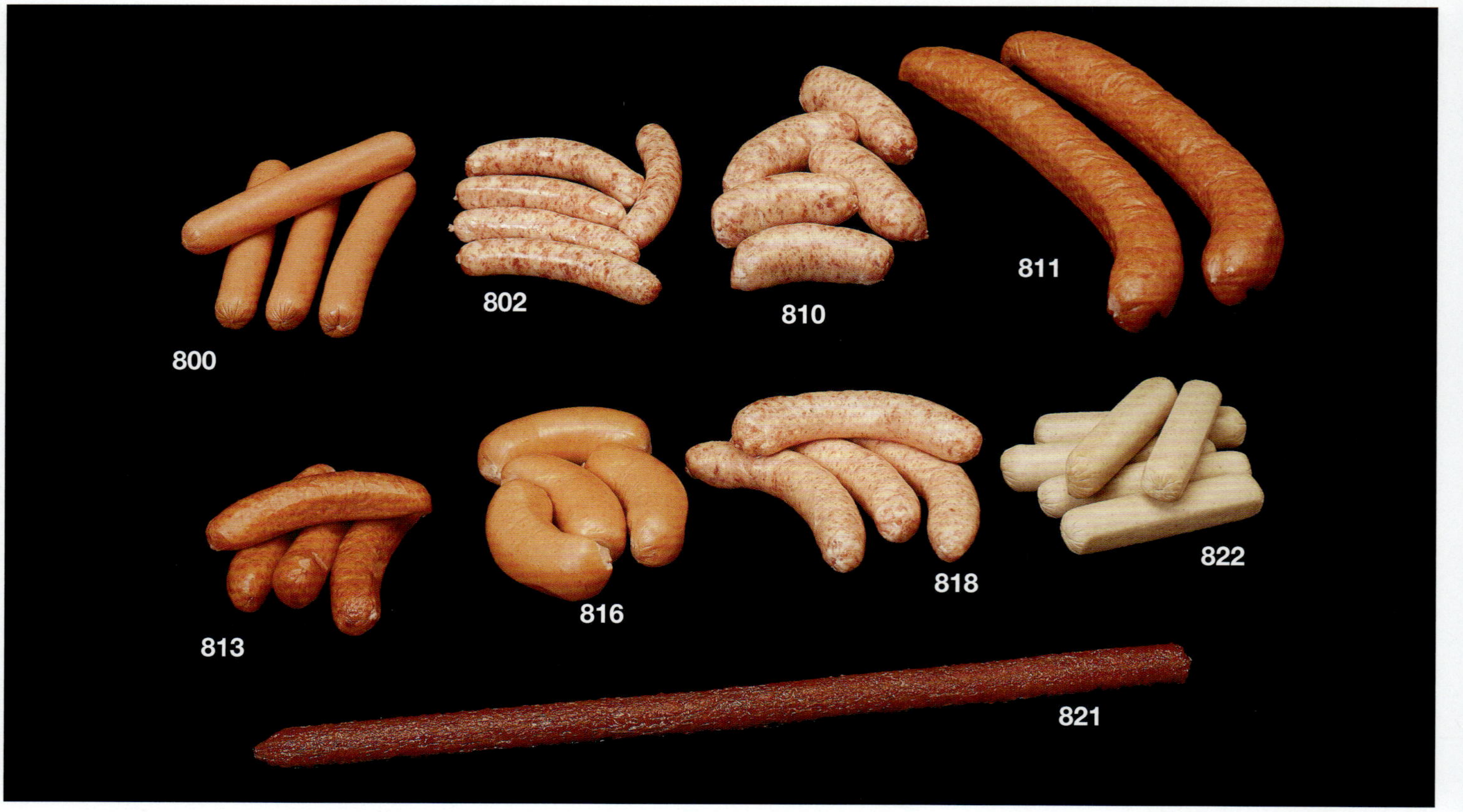

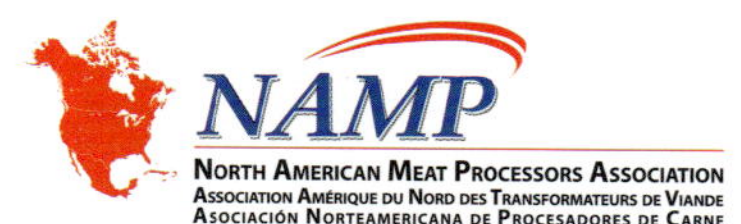

800 Frankfurters

Frankfurters are a smoked, cooked, linked sausage. They are either skinless, stuffed in sheep casing, or stuffed in collagen casings. They are uniform in length and diameter. Links shall be 5.0 to 6.0 inches (12.5 to 15 cm) in length. The finished links may be specified by number per lb. such as 4, 5, 6, 7, 10, 12 links per lb.

Product formulation shall be specified by the purchaser.

FORMULAS AVAILABLE (major ingredients only)
Note: Refer to Table of Formulas on page 279.

A, A1, B, B1, C, C1, D, L, P, P1, P2, P3

800 Salchichas Tipo Frankfurt

Las salchichas tipo Frankfurt son salchichas ahumadas y cocidas en ristras. Pueden presentarse sin cubierta, embutidas en tripas de cordero o embutidas en tripas de colágeno. Tienen un largo y un diámetro uniformes. Las salchichas en ristras deberán medir entre 12.5 y 15 cm (5.0 y 6.0 pulgadas) de largo. Las ristras terminadas se pueden especificar por cantidad por lb., por ejemplo 4, 5, 6, 7, 10 o 12 salchichas por lb.

El comprador especificará la formulación del producto.

FÓRMULAS DISPONIBLES (sólo ingredientes principales)
Importante: consulte la Tabla de fórmulas en la página 278.

A, A1, B, B1, C, C1, D, L, P, P1, P2, P3

801 Bologna

Bologna is a smoked, cooked sausage. The red meat or red meat and poultry components shall be very finely comminuted and stuffed into artificial or natural casings. If poultry is included in the formulation for this item, it may not exceed 50 percent of the total meat content. The interior cut surface is smooth, fine-textured, light to moderately dark pink in background color, and finely mottled with evenly distributed light to dark red flecks. Sticks shall have uniform diameter measuring from 4.0 to 5.0 inches (10 to 12.5 cm) and may weigh up to approximately 12 lbs. (5.4 kg). Ring style bologna shall weigh approximately 1.0 to 1.5 lbs. (0.5 to 0.7 kg).

Product formulation shall be specified by the purchaser. The formulas available (major ingredients only) are the same as those available to produce Item No. 800 Frankfurters. *(Pictured on page 283.)*

801 Embutido Tipo Bolonia

La Bolonia es un embutido ahumado y cocido. Los componentes de carne roja, o carne roja y ave, se deberán picar/moler muy finamente y se embutirán en tripas artificiales o naturales. Si se incluye carne de ave en la formulación de esta pieza, ésta no puede superar el 50% del contenido cárnico total. La superficie del corte hacia el interior es suave, con textura fina, color de fondo rosa, entre claro y moderadamente oscuro, y moteado con manchas finas uniformemente distribuidas de color rojo claro a oscuro. Las barras deben tener un diámetro uniforme que mida entre 10 y 12.5 cm (4.0 y 5.0 pulgadas) y pueden pesar hasta 5.4 kg (12 lb.) aproximadamente. La Bolonia con forma de aro deberá pesar entre 0.5 y 0.7 kg (1.0 y 1.5 lb.) aproximadamente.

El comprador especificará la formulación del producto. Las fórmulas disponibles (únicamente ingredientes principales) son las mismas que las disponibles para producir la pieza número 800, Salchichas Tipo Frankfurt. *(Ilustración en la página 283).*

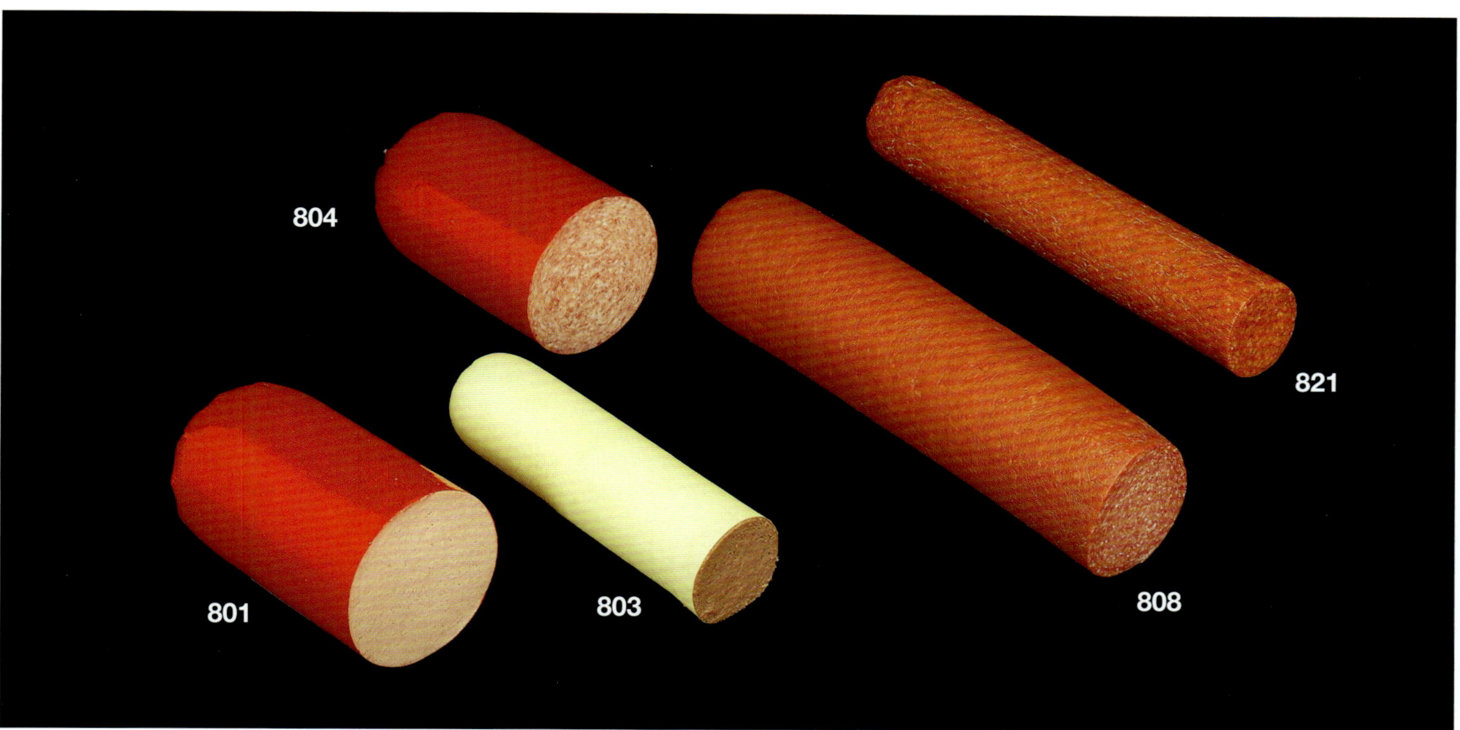

802 — Pork Sausage

Pork sausage is a fresh, all-pork product. The meat is chopped or ground to a moderately coarse texture and mixed with salt and spices. Pork sausage may be packed in bulk, formed mechanically, or stuffed in artificial or natural casings. The links, rolls, and bags are moderately uniform in length and diameter. For product in unlinked hogcasings, no more than one piece shall be less than 12 inches (30 cm) in length in a primary container. *(Pictured on page 282.)*

STYLE - Note refer to Ordering Data on page 281.
A, B, B1, C, D, E, F

SIZE - Links - 4 to 16 to the lb.
Rolls, Bags, or Units may be from 1 lb. to 10 lbs. each.

802 — Salchicha (Chorizo) de Cerdo

La salchicha (chorizo) de cerdo es un producto fresco puro de cerdo. La carne se pica o muele para lograr una textura moderadamente gruesa y se mezcla con sal y especias. La salchicha (chorizo) de cerdo se puede envasar a granel, moldeada mecánicamente o embutida en tripas artificiales o naturales. Las ristras, rollos y bolsas tienen un largo y diámetro moderadamente uniformes. Para el producto en unidades embutidas en tripas de cerdo, pero que no viene en ristras, en su envase primario no podrá haber más de una pieza con un largo menor a 30 cm (12 pulgadas). *(Ilustración en la página 282).*

ESTILO - Importante: consulte los datos de pedido de la página 280. A, B, B1, C, D, E, F

TAMAÑO - Ristras: 4 a 16 por lb.
Los rollos, bolsas o unidades pueden ser de 1 lb. a 10 lb. cada uno.

802A — Pork Sausage Patties

Patties meeting this item description are produced from product prepared to the material specifications described in Item No. 802. After being ground or chopped, the pork sausage is mechanically formed into patties of the approximate diameter specified by the purchaser. Unless one of the options listed below is specified, it is assumed that the purchaser desires a 4.0 inch (10 cm) patty. The suggested weight range of the patties is 2.5 to 3.0 ozs. (28 grams equal 1 oz.). The finished product in whatever size diameter ordered shall be uniform in weight and thickness. *(Pictured on page 286.)*

Patty diameter size options:

A - 2.0 inches (5 cm)
B - 2.5 inches (6.4 cm)
C - 3.0 inches (7.5 cm)
D - 3.5 inches (8.9 cm)
E - 4.0 inches (10 cm)

802A — Tortitas/Hamburguesas de Salchichas de Cerdo

Las tortitas/hamburguesas que cumplen con la descripción de esta pieza se fabrican con productos preparados según las especificaciones materiales descritas en la pieza número 802. Después de molida o picada, la carne condimentada de cerdo se moldea mecánicamente en tortitas/hamburguesas con un diámetro aproximado al que especifique el comprador. A menos que se especifique una de las opciones indicadas a continuación, se asume que el comprador desea una tortita/hamburguesa de 10 cm (4.0 pulgadas). La variación de peso sugerida para las tortitas/hamburguesas es de 70.8 a 85.0 gramos (2.5 a 3.0 oz.). El producto final en cualquier tamaño de diámetro que se pida debe tener un peso y un grosor uniformes. *(Ilustración en la página 286).*

Opciones de tamaño de diámetro de la tortita/hamburguesa:

A - 5 cm (2.0 pulgadas)
B - 6.4 cm (2.5 pulgadas)
C - 7.5 cm (3.0 pulgadas)
D - 8.9 cm (3.5 pulgadas)
E - 10 cm (4.0 pulgadas)

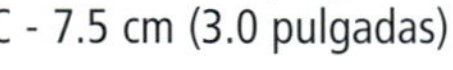

NAMP
NORTH AMERICAN MEAT PROCESSORS ASSOCIATION
ASSOCIATION AMÉRIQUE DU NORD DES TRANSFORMATEURS DE VIANDE
ASOCIACIÓN NORTEAMERICANA DE PROCESADORES DE CARNE

802B Pork Sausage, Cooked

Fully cooked items meeting this description are processed from pork sausage materials described in item Nos. 802 and 802A. The cooked product may be in bulk, link, patty, or crumble form as specified by the purchaser. In the case of cooked patties the specific diameter sizes stated in Item No. 802A do not apply but the product dimensions are required to be uniform in thickness and diameter. A cooked item type produced under this IMPS designation shall be purchased as Pork Sausage, Cooked, Patties (or Crumbles, Links, etc., as appropriate). The cooked weights of individual patties, the number of links per pound, or the weight of bulk packages shall be specified by the purchaser. *(Pictured on page 286.)*

802B Salchicha (Chorizo) de Cerdo, Cocida

Las piezas completamente cocidas que cumplen con esta descripción se procesan a partir de los materiales de salchicha (chorizo) de cerdo que se describen en las piezas número 802 y 802A. El producto cocido puede ofrecerse a granel, en ristras, en tortitas/hamburguesas o desmenuzado según la especificación del comprador. En el caso de tortitas/hamburguesas cocidas, no corresponden los tamaños de diámetro específicos indicados en la pieza número 802A, pero las dimensiones del producto deben tener un grosor y un diámetro uniformes. Un tipo de pieza cocida que se produce según esta designación de IMPS (Especificaciones de Compras Institucionales de Carne, por sus siglas en inglés) deberá comprarse como salchicha (chorizo) de cerdo, cocida, tortita/hamburguesa (o desmenuzado, en ristras, etc., según corresponda). El comprador deberá especificar los pesos cocidos de las tortitas/hamburguesas individuales, la cantidad de salchichas en ristras por libra o el peso de los paquetes a granel. *(Ilustración en la página 286).*

803 Liver Sausage (Braunschweiger)

Liver sausage is a cooked sausage with a smoked characteristic (a smoked characteristic may be imparted by smoking, by adding smoked meats to the formula, or a combination of both). The meat components consist of pork with smoked jowls and/or bacon ends included in some formulas. These are combined with pork livers, finely comminuted and stuffed in artificial or natural casings. Onion shall be included as a seasoning. Unless otherwise specified by the purchaser, sticks shall have a uniform diameter measuring from 2.0 to 3.0 inches (5 to 7.5 cm) and shall weigh from 5.0 to 8.0 pounds (2.3 to 3.6 kg). The interior cut surface is smooth, fine-textured, and light reddish-brown in color. *(Pictured on page 283.)*

FORMULAS AVAILABLE (major ingredients only)
Note: Refer to Table of Formulas on page 279.
V, V1, V2, V3

803 Embutido (Pasta) de Hígado (Tipo Braunschweiger)

El embutido (pasta) de hígado es una salchicha cocida con una característica de ahumado (la característica de ahumado se puede impartir mediante el proceso de ahumado, o agregando carnes ahumadas a la fórmula, o una combinación de ambas opciones). Los componentes cárnicos consisten en carne de cerdo con papadas ahumadas y/o extremos cortados de piezas de tocino que se incluyen en algunas fórmulas. Estos se combinan con hígados de cerdo finamente molidos y embutidos en tripas naturales o artificiales. Se deberá incluir cebolla como condimento. A menos que el comprador especifique lo contrario, los bastones deberán tener un diámetro uniforme que mida entre 5 y 7.5 cm (2.0 y 3.0 pulgadas) y deberán pesar entre 2.3 y 3.6 kg (5.0 y 8.0 libras). La superficie del corte hacia el interior tiene una textura fina y lisa, y un color marrón rojizo claro. *(Ilustración en la página 283).*

FÓRMULAS DISPONIBLES (sólo ingredientes principales)
Importante: consulte la Tabla de fórmulas en la página 278.
V, V1, V2, V3

804 Salami, Cooked

Cooked salami is a smoked, cooked sausage. The meat components consist of moderately coarse-cut pork and finely comminuted beef with finely comminuted beef heart meat included in some formulas. Alternatively, a moderately coarse-cut beef or red meat and poultry formulation may be specified. Seasonings, unless otherwise specified, shall include garlic and whole black peppercorns (at least a portion of a peppercorn shall be in evidence on either sliced surface). Salami is stuffed in artificial casings and has a uniform diameter measuring from 3.5 to 5.4 inches (8.9 to 11.4 cm), unless otherwise specified by the purchaser. Sticks shall weigh from 7 to 12 lbs. (3.2 to 5.4 kg) and shall be moderately uniform in length. The interior cut surface is moderately coarse in texture and light to dark reddish-brown in color. *(Pictured on page 283.)*

Product formulation shall be specified by the purchaser.

FORMULAS AVAILABLE (major ingredients only)
Note: Refer to Table of Formulas on page 279.
A, A1, B, C, D, H, L, P, P1, P2, P3

804 Salame, Cocido

El salame cocido es un embutido ahumado, cocido. Los componentes cárnicos consisten en carne de cerdo cortada moderadamente gruesa y carne de res finamente molida con carne de corazón de res finamente molida que se incluye en algunas fórmulas. De forma alternativa, se puede especificar una formulación de carne de res cortada moderadamente gruesa o con carne roja y carne blanca de aves. Los condimentos, a menos que se especifique lo contrario, deberán incluir ajo y granos de pimienta negra enteros (al menos una porción de los granos de pimienta deberán verse en cualquiera de las superficies de una rebanada). El salame está embutido en tripas artificiales y tiene un diámetro uniforme que mide entre 8.9 y 11.4 cm (3.5 y 5.4 pulgadas), a menos que el comprador especifique lo contrario. Los bastones deberán pesar entre 3.2 y 5.4 kg (7 y 12 lb.) y deberán tener un largo moderadamente uniforme. La superficie de corte interior tiene una textura moderadamente gruesa y un color marrón rojizo de claro a oscuro. *(Ilustración en la página 283).*

El comprador especificará la formulación del producto.

FÓRMULAS DISPONIBLES (sólo ingredientes principales)
Importante: consulte la Tabla de fórmulas en la página 278.
A, A1, B, C, D, H, L, P, P1, P2, P3

805 — Minced Luncheon Meat

Minced luncheon meat is a smoked, cooked sausage. The meat components consist of moderately coarse-cut pork and finely comminuted beef with pork heart meat included in some formulas. The product is stuffed in artificial casings. Stuffed round casings shall measure from 3.5 to 4.5 inches (8.9 to 11.4 cm) in uniform diameter unless otherwise specified by the purchaser. When the stuffed casings are formed into rectangular shapes by wire or metal molds, they shall measure from 3.0 to 4.0 inches (7.5 to 10 cm) in width and depth. Sticks shall weigh from 5 to 10 lbs. (2.3 to 4.5 kg). The interior cut surface is moderately fine-textured and light pink in color. *(Pictured on page 287.)*

FORMULAS AVAILABLE (major ingredients only)
Note: Refer to Table of Formulas on page 279.
C, C1, G2, G3

805 — Fiambre (Picadillo) de Almuerzo

El fiambre/picadillo de almuerzo es un embutido ahumado, cocido. Los componentes cárnicos consisten en carne de cerdo cortada moderadamente gruesa y carne de res finamente molida con carne de corazón de cerdo que se incluye en algunas fórmulas. El producto se embute en tripas artificiales. Los embutidos en tripas de forma redonda deben medir entre 8.9 y 11.4 cm (3.5 y 4.5 pulgadas) de diámetro uniforme a menos que el comprador especifique lo contrario. Cuando los tripas embutidos se moldean con formas rectangulares por medio de moldes de alambre o metal, deben medir entre 7.5 y 10 cm (3.0 y 4.0 pulgadas) de ancho y profundidad. Los bastones deben pesar entre 2.3 y 4.5 kg (5 y 10 lb.). La superficie del corte hacia el interior tiene una textura moderadamente fina y un color rosa claro. *(Ilustración en la página 287).*

FÓRMULAS DISPONIBLES (sólo ingredientes principales)
Importante: consulte la Tabla de fórmulas en la página 278.
C, C1, G2, G3

807 — Thuringer

Thuringer is a "semi-dry," smoked, uncooked, fermented sausage. Its principal meat component is usually beef, though several different meat formulations are also available. The meat shall be moderately coarse-cut and display a uniform overall dark reddish-brown color. The finished product has a characteristically sharp flavor. Thuringer is stuffed in artificial casings of uniform diameter measuring from 2.5 to 3.5 inches (6.4 to 8.9 cm), unless otherwise specified by the purchaser. The sticks shall weigh from 4 to 8 lbs. (1.8 to 3.6 kg). A very slight amount of naturally occurring dry mold may be present on the surface of the casing. No binders or extenders are permitted.

Product formulation shall be specified by the purchaser.

FORMULAS AVAILABLE (major ingredients only)
Note: Refer to Table of Formulas on page 279.
A, B, D, H, H3, H4

807 — Salchicha Tipo Turingia

La salchicha alemana tipo Turingia es una salchicha "semiseca", ahumada, sin cocer, fermentada. El componente cárnico principal generalmente es la carne de res, aunque también hay diversas formulaciones de carnes diferentes. La carne deberá estar cortada moderadamente gruesa y mostrar en general un color marrón rojizo uniforme. El producto final tiene un sabor característicamente fuerte. La salchicha tipo Turingia está embutida en tripas artificiales y tiene un diámetro uniforme que mide entre 6.4 y 8.9 cm (2.5 y 3.5 pulgadas), a menos que el comprador especifique lo contrario. Los bastones deben pesar entre 1.8 y 3.6 kg (4 y 8 lb.). Podrá presentar una cantidad muy pequeña de moho seco que se forma naturalmente en la superficie de la tripa. No se permiten aglutinantes ni espesantes.

El comprador especificará la formulación del producto.

FÓRMULAS DISPONIBLES (sólo ingredientes principales)
Importante: consulte la Tabla de fórmulas en la página 278.
A, B, D, H, H3, H4

808 — Dry Salami

Dry salami is a smoked, uncooked dry sausage. The meat components consist of moderately coarse-cut beef with moderately coarse-cut pork and/or beef heart meat included in some formulas. The product seasoning includes garlic. Dry salami is stuffed in artificial or natural casings measuring from 2.0 to 3.0 inches (5 to 7.5 cm) in diameter unless otherwise specified by the purchaser. The salami shall be uniform in diameter and processed so as to produce a firm, hard finished product. Sticks shall weigh from 2 to 5 lbs. (0.9 to 2.3 kg). The interior cut surface is firm, moderately coarse-textured with a uniform distribution of white fat particles throughout a medium to dark reddish-brown background color. A very slight amount of dry surface mold is natural on this product and may be present on this item. No binders or extenders are permitted. *(Pictured on page 283.)*

Product formulation shall be specified by the purchaser.

FORMULAS AVAILABLE (major ingredients only)
Note: Refer to Table of Formulas on page 279.
A, B, D, G, H, H3

808 — Salame Seco

El salame seco es un embutido seco ahumado sin cocer. Los componentes cárnicos consisten en carne de res cortada moderadamente gruesa con carne de cerdo cortada moderadamente grueso y/o carne de corazón de res que se incluye en algunas fórmulas. Los condimentos del producto incluyen ajo. El salame seco está embutido en tripas naturales o artificiales que miden entre 5 y 7.5 cm (2.0 y 3.0 pulgadas) de diámetro a menos que el comprador especifique lo contrario. El salame seco deberá tener un diámetro uniforme y se deberá procesar para lograr un producto final firme y duro. Los bastones deben pesar entre 0.9 y 2.3 kg (2 y 5 lb.). La superficie del corte hacia el interior es firme, con una textura moderadamente gruesa y una distribución uniforme de partículas de grasa blanca en un color de fondo marrón rojizo con un tono de medio a oscuro. Una cantidad muy pequeña de moho superficial seco es natural en este producto y puede estar presente en esta pieza. No se permiten extensores de carne ni aglutinantes. *(Ilustración en la página 283).*

El comprador especificará la formulación del producto.

FÓRMULAS DISPONIBLES (sólo ingredientes principales)
Importante: consulte la Tabla de fórmulas en la página 278.
A, B, D, G, H, H3

810   Breakfast Sausage

Breakfast sausage is a fresh product. The meat components consist of predominately pork, with smaller amounts of beef and/or veal. Alternatively, an all beef or red meat and poultry formulation may be specified. The meat is chopped or ground to a moderately coarse texture. Breakfast sausage may be packed in bulk or stuffed in collagen or hog casings. The links and rolls are moderately uniform in length and diameter. For product in unlinked hog or collagen casings, no more than one piece shall be less than 12 inches (30 cm) in length in a primary container. *(Pictured on page 282.)*

Ordering Data:

Styles and sizes are similar to those available for Item No. 802 Sausage.

810   Salchicha para Desayuno

La salchicha para desayuno es un producto fresco. Los componentes cárnicos consisten principalmente en cerdo, con pequeñas cantidades de carne de res y/o ternera. De forma alternativa, se puede especificar una formulación de pura carne de res o de carne roja con carnes blancas de aves. La carne se pica o muele para lograr una textura moderadamente gruesa. La salchicha para desayuno puede empacarse a granel o estar embutida en tripas de cerdo o de colágeno. Las ristras y los rollos tienen un largo y un diámetro moderadamente uniformes. Para el producto que no se produzca en ristras, que sea embutido en tripas de cerdo o de colágeno, no se aceptará en un envase primario más de una pieza con un largo menor a 30 cm (12 pulgadas). *(Ilustración en la página 282).*

Información para hacer los pedidos:

Los estilos y tamaños son similares a los disponibles para la pieza número 802 Salchicha (Chorizo) de Cerdo.

811   Smoked Sausage

Smoked sausage is a smoked, cooked, linked sausage. The meat components consist of all pork or pork and beef with beef tripe, beef and pork heart meat, and beef and pork tongue meat included in some formulas. The meat is chopped or ground to a moderately coarse texture. Smoked sausages are either skinless or stuffed in hog or collagen casings and are moderately uniform in length and diameter. The interior cut surface is moderately coarse in texture (formulas D and D1 may be moderately fine-textured). *(Pictured on page 282.)*

Smoked sausage is available in a variety of link sizes, including 48 to 51 per lb. It may also be ordered in rope style.

FORMULAS AVAILABLE (major ingredients only)
Note: Refer to Table of Formulas on page 279.
B, B1, C, C1, D, D1, G, H1, H2

811   Salchicha Ahumada

La salchicha ahumada es una salchicha ahumada y cocida en ristras. Los componentes cárnicos consisten en puro cerdo o carne de cerdo y de res con panza o mondongo de res, carne de corazón de res y cerdo, y carne de lengua de res y cerdo, incluidos en algunas fórmulas. La carne se pica o muele para lograr una textura moderadamente gruesa. Las salchichas ahumadas vienen sin cubierta o embutidas en tripas de cerdo o de colágeno y tienen un largo y un diámetro moderadamente uniformes. La superficie de corte interior tiene una textura moderadamente gruesa (las fórmulas D y D1 pueden tener una textura moderadamente fina). *(Ilustración en la página 282).*

La salchicha ahumada está disponible en una variedad de tamaños de ristra, que incluyen entre 48 y 51 unidades por lb. También se pueden pedir en el estilo de cuerda.

FÓRMULAS DISPONIBLES (sólo ingredientes principales)
Importante: consulte la Tabla de fórmulas en la página 278.
B, B1, C, C1, D, D1, G, H1, H2

812   New England Brand Sausage

New England Brand sausage is a smoked, cooked sausage. The meat components consist predominately of pork chunks with a small amount of finely comminuted beef. The product is stuffed in artificial or natural casings with a uniform diameter of between 3.5 to 4.5 inches (8.9 to 11.4 cm), unless otherwise specified by the purchaser. Individual sausages shall weigh from 5 to 10 lbs. (2.3 to 4.5 kg). The texture of the interior cut surface is variable, with 70 to 80 percent of the area comprised of pork chunks with the remainder of the surface being finely textured.

812   Salchicha Marca New England

La salchicha marca New England es una salchicha ahumada y cocida. Los componentes cárnicos consisten predominantemente en trozos de cerdo con una pequeña cantidad de carne de res finamente molida. El producto se embute en tripas naturales o artificiales con un diámetro uniforme que varía entre 8.9 y 11.4 cm (3.5 y 4.5 pulgadas), a menos que el comprador especifique lo contrario. Las salchichas individuales deben pesar entre 2.3 y 4.5 kg (5 y 10 lb.). La textura de la superficie del corte hacia el interior es variable, con un 70% u 80% del área compuesta por trozos de cerdo, y el resto de la superficie con una textura fina.

813   Polish Sausage

Polish sausage is a smoked, cooked, linked sausage. The meat components may consist of moderately coarse-cut pork, beef, or moderately coarse-cut pork with finely comminuted beef, or beef and veal combination. Alternatively, a moderately coarse-cut beef or pork and poultry formulation may be specified. Seasonings shall include garlic. The interior cut surface of the product is moderately coarse in texture with a uniform distribution of light-colored particles throughout a medium to dark reddish-brown background color. The product is stuffed in hog or equivalent-diameter collagen casings as specified by the purchaser. The finished links shall be moderately uniform in length and diameter and 3.0 to 5.0 inches (7.5 to 12.5 cm) long unless otherwise specified by the purchaser. This product is also available in sticks 11 to 13 inches (28 to 33 cm) long or in rope style. *(Pictured on page 282.)*

813   Salchicha Polaca

La salchicha polaca es una salchicha ahumada y cocida en ristras. Los componentes cárnicos pueden consistir en carne cortada moderadamente gruesa, de res o de cerdo o carne de cerdo cortada moderadamente gruesa con carne de res molida en partículas finas, o una combinación de res y ternera. De forma alternativa, se puede especificar una formulación con carne de res o cerdo cortada moderadamente gruesa, combinada con carne de aves. Los condimentos deberán incluir ajo. La superficie del corte hacia el interior del producto tiene una textura moderadamente gruesa con una distribución uniforme de partículas de colores claros en un color de fondo marrón rojizo con un tono entre medio y oscuro. El producto está embutido en tripas de cerdo o sus equivalentes en diámetro de colágeno, según lo especifique el comprador. Las salchichas en ristras finales deberán tener un largo y un diámetro moderadamente uniformes y deberán medir entre 7.5 y 12.5 cm (3.0 y 5.0 pulgadas) de largo a menos que el comprador especifique lo contrario. Este producto también está disponible en bastones de 28 a 33 cm (11 a 13 pulgadas) de largo o en un estilo de cuerda. *(Ilustración en la página 282).*

814 Meat Loaves

Meat Loaves are baked (dry heat) or cooked (moist heat) products as specified by the purchaser. They may be either rectangular or rounded in shape with a uniform diameter. The meat components of the loaf shall be finely comminuted. Loaves shall weigh between 4 to 8 lbs. (1.8 to 3.6 kg). The exterior surface of the meat loaf may be produced either smoked, unsmoked, or browned in hot oil. The interior cut surface is smooth, fine-textured, light pink in background color, and finely mottled with evenly distributed light to dark red flecks. The individual loaves are encased or wrapped in grease- and moisture-resistant paper or plastic film.

Product formulation shall be specified by the purchaser.

FORMULAS AVAILABLE (major ingredients only)
Note: Refer to Table of Formulas on page 279.
C, C1, D, D1, G, G1, G4, G5, G6, G7, X, X1, Y, Y1

814 Pasteles (Budines) de Carne

Los pasteles/budines de carne son productos horneados (por calor seco) o cocidos (por calor húmedo) según lo especifique el comprador. Pueden tener una forma rectangular o redonda con un diámetro uniforme. El componente cárnico del pastel deberá ser molido finamente. Los pasteles deberán pesar entre 1.8 y 3.6 kg (4 y 8 lb.). La superficie exterior del pastel/budín de carne se podrá producir ahumada, sin ahumar o dorada en aceite caliente. La superficie del corte hacia el interior es lisa, con textura fina, de color de fondo rosa claro y moteada con manchas uniformemente distribuidas de color rojo claro a oscuro. Los pasteles individuales deberán revestirse o envolverse con papel resistente a la grasa y la humedad o con una película plástica.

El comprador especificará la formulación del producto.

FÓRMULAS DISPONIBLES (sólo ingredientes principales)
Importante: consulte la Tabla de fórmulas en la página 278.
C, C1, D, D1, G, G1, G4, G5, G6, G7, X, X1, Y, Y1

815 Meat Food Product Loaves

Meat food product loaves are baked (dry heat) or cooked (moist heat) products. Beef, pork, and veal may be used singly or in any combination. Other ingredients, such as meat by-products, pickles, pimientos, cheese, nuts, etc., are added as applicable except that lungs, spleens, tripe, udders, blood, skin, cracklings, brains, lips, ears, snouts, kidneys, tongue trimmings, and meat and meat by-products from lamb, yearling mutton, mutton, and goats shall not be used in preparing the loaf. Nonfat dry milk and/or calcium-reduced dried skim milk may be added. Individual loaves shall weigh from 4 to 8 lbs. (1.8 to 3.6 kg). The exterior surface may be smoked, unsmoked, or browned in hot oil. The other ingredients, pimiento, pickles, olives, cheese, pepper, etc. (actual ingredients are to be identified and controlled by FSIS) as applicable, shall be of a quantity and size large enough to be easily distinguished from the cut surface and shall be reasonably well distributed throughout the item. Pimiento juice, pickle juice, olive juice, etc., shall not be substitutable for the fruit itself. The individual loaves shall be encased or wrapped in grease- and moisture-resistant paper or plastic film. The finished product shall be uniform in diameter. *(Pictured on page 287.)*

Meat food product loaves must be specified by name (for example: pickle loaf, ham and cheese loaf, etc.). Any meat food product loaf not listed below may be ordered. However, if the name is inadequate to appropriately identify the product, the purchaser may be requested to furnish additional information to establish a definite basis for identification.

CONDIMENTS (major ingredients)

A	Pimiento Loaf (sweet red peppers are not substitutable)
B	Pickle and Pimiento Loaf
C	Pickle Loaf
D	Olive Loaf (use of stuffed olives is not acceptable)
E	Pepper Loaf (contains cracked black pepper)
F	Cheese Loaf
G	Macaroni and Cheese Loaf
H	Liver Loaf
I	Pickle and Pimiento Loaf (sweet red peppers)

815 Pasteles de Carne y Otros Productos Alimenticios

Los pasteles de carne y otros productos alimenticios son productos horneados (calor seco) o cocidos (calor húmedo). Se puede utilizar la carne de res, cerdo y ternera en forma individual o combinada. Otros ingredientes, como coproductos cárnicos, pepinillos, pimientos, queso, nueces, etc., se agregan según corresponda, aunque para preparar el pastel, no se deberán utilizar los recortes de pulmones, bazos, menudo (panza o mondongo), ubres, sangre, piel, chicharrones, sesos, labios, orejas, hocicos, riñones o lengua, ni la carne o coproductos cárnicos de cordero, carnero añojo, carnero o de cabra. Se puede agregar leche en polvo descremada y/o leche en polvo desnatada reducida en calcio. Los pasteles individuales deberán pesar entre 1.8 y 3.6 kg (4 y 8 lb.). La superficie exterior podrá estar ahumada, sin ahumar o dorada en aceite caliente. El resto de los ingredientes, como pimiento, pepinillos, aceitunas, queso, pimienta, etc. (el Servicio de Inspección e Inocuidad Alimentaria identificará y controlará los ingredientes reales) según corresponda, deberán incluirse en cantidades y tamaños lo suficientemente grandes como para distinguirse fácilmente desde la superficie del corte hacia el interior y se deberán distribuir razonablemente por toda la pieza. El jugo de pimiento, el jugo del pepinillo, el jugo de las aceitunas, etc. no deberá ser sustituto del fruto mismo. Los pasteles individuales deberán revestirse o envolverse con papel resistente a la grasa y la humedad o con una película plástica. El producto final deberá tener un diámetro uniforme. *(Ilustración en la página 287).*

Los pasteles de carne y otros productos alimenticios se deberán especificar por nombre (por ejemplo: pastel de pepinillos, pastel de jamón y queso, etc.). Se puede realizar el pedido de cualquier otro pastel de carne y otros productos alimenticios que no se haya indicado en la lista que sigue. Sin embargo, si el nombre es inadecuado para identificar el producto correctamente, se le podrá solicitar al comprador que proporcione información adicional para establecer una base concreta para su debida identificación.

CONDIMENTOS (ingredientes principales)

A	Pastel de pimiento (los pimientos morrones no se podrán sustituir)
B	Pastel de pepinillos y pimientos
C	Pastel de pepinillos
D	Pastel de aceitunas (no se acepta el uso de aceitunas rellenas)
E	Pastel de pimienta (contiene pimienta negra molida)
F	Pastel de queso
G	Pastel de macarrones y queso
H	Pastel de hígado
I	Pastel de pepinillos y pimiento (pimientos morrones)

816 Knockwurst

Knockwurst is a smoked, cooked, linked sausage. The meat components consist of very finely comminuted beef, or a predominately beef and pork combination. Alternative formulations may include nonfat dry milk and/or calcium- reduced dried skim milk. Beef and poultry or pork and poultry combinations may also be specified. The interior cut surface of the finished product is smooth, finely textured, and light to moderately dark pink in color. Artificial color is not allowed. The knockwurst may be either skinless or stuffed into hog or collagen casing as specified by the purchaser. The finished links may be specified by number per lb. such as 4, 5, 6, or 8 links per lb. *(Pictured on page 282.)*

816 Salchicha Tipo Knockwurst

La salchicha tipo Knockwurst es una salchicha ahumada y cocida en ristras. Los componentes cárnicos consisten en carne de res molida muy fina o una combinación de cerdo y res, predominando la de res. Las formulaciones alternativas pueden incluir leche en polvo descremada y/o leche en polvo desnatada reducida en calcio. También se pueden especificar combinaciones de carne de res con la de aves, o de cerdo con aves. La superficie del corte hacia el interior del producto final es suave, con una textura fina y un color rosa entre claro y moderadamente oscuro. No se permiten colorantes artificiales. La salchicha tipo Knockwurst puede ser desprovista de cubierta o embutida en tripas de cerdo o colágeno según lo especifique el comprador. Las ristras finales se pueden especificar en cantidad por lb., por ejemplo, 4, 5, 6 u 8 salchichas en ristras por lb. *(Ilustración en la página 282).*

817 Breakfast Sausage, Cooked

Breakfast sausage is a cooked, linked sausage. The meat components consist of moderately coarse-cut pork and/or beef. Alternatively, a moderately coarse-cut red meat and poultry formulation may be specified. The interior cut surface of the finished product is moderately coarse in texture. The links shall either be skinless or stuffed into collagen casings as specified by the purchaser, and shall be uniform in length and diameter. After cooking the links shall number 19 to 21 per lb. *(Pictured on page 286.)*

817 Salchicha para Desayuno, Cocida

La salchicha para desayuno es una salchicha cocida en ristras. Los componentes cárnicos consisten en carne de cerdo y/o res cortada moderadamente gruesa. De forma alternativa, se puede especificar una formulación de carne roja y carne blanca de aves cortadas moderadamente gruesas. La superficie del corte hacia el interior del producto final tiene una textura moderadamente gruesa. Las salchichas en ristras se deberán presentar sin cubierta o embutidas en tripas de colágeno según lo especifique el comprador, y deberán tener un largo y un diámetro uniformes. Después de la cocción, las salchichas en ristras deberán incluir entre 19 y 21 salchichas por lb. *(Ilustración en la página 286).*

818 Italian Sausage

Italian sausage is a fresh, uncooked, product that is available in link, rope style, bulk, or patty form as specified by the purchaser. The meat components shall be chopped or ground to a moderately coarse texture displaying uniform color ranging from medium to dark reddish-brown with evenly distributed fat particles. The red meat formulations may consist of pork, beef, or combinations thereof. The use of nonfat dry milk and/or calcium-reduced dried skim milk and combinations of beef and poultry, or pork and poultry may also be specified. All spices used to produce a hot or sweet (mild) flavoring specified by the purchaser must meet USDA labeling requirements.

When processed as links, unless specified as skinless, or rope style, the product shall be stuffed into a natural hog or collagen casing. Links shall be moderately uniform in length and diameter and measure 5.0 to 6.0 inches (12.5 to 15 cm) in length. If the Italian sausage is produced in patty form, the patties in the size specified shall be uniform in diameter and thickness. The purchaser may specify that bulk finished product be cooked, for example, as Italian Sausage, Crumbled, Cooked. *(Pictured on page 282.)*

818 Salchicha Italiana

La salchicha italiana es un producto fresco sin cocer que está disponible en formato de ristras, en estilo de cuerda, a granel o en tortitas/hamburguesas, según lo especifique el comprador. Los componentes cárnicos se deberán picar o moler hasta lograr una textura moderadamente gruesa que muestre un color uniforme que puede variar entre el marrón rojizo medio y oscuro, con partículas de grasa distribuidas uniformemente. Las formulaciones de carne roja pueden consistir en carne de cerdo, res o combinaciones de ambas. También se puede especificar el uso de leche en polvo descremada y/o leche en polvo desnatada reducida en calcio y combinaciones de carne de res y aves o cerdo y aves. Todas las especias utilizadas para producir un sabor picante o dulce (suave) que especifique el comprador deben cumplir con los requisitos de etiquetado del USDA (Departamento de Agricultura de E.U.A., por sus siglas en inglés).

Cuando se procesa en ristras, a menos que se especifique sin cubierta o en estilo de cuerda, el producto deberá embutirse en tripas de cerdo naturales o de colágeno. Las salchichas en ristras deberán tener un largo y un diámetro moderadamente uniformes y medir entre 12.5 y 15 cm (5.0 y 6.0 pulgadas) de largo. Si la salchicha italiana se produce en forma de tortita/hamburguesa, las tortitas/hamburguesas deberán tener un diámetro y un grosor uniformes del tamaño que se especifique. El comprador puede especificar que el producto final a granel sea cocido, por ejemplo, como Salchicha Italiana, Desboronada, Cocida. *(Ilustración en la página 282).*

820 — Head Cheese

Head cheese is a cooked product. The meat components may consist of all pork head meats or predominately pork head meats with pork, cured pork, and/or other pork by-products included, except that ears, livers, and spleens are prohibited. The meat is coarse-cut to fine-cut. Onion shall be included as a seasoning. Head cheese may have gelatin added. The finished product is stuffed in artificial or natural casings, as specified by the purchaser, and shall weigh from 4 to 8 lbs. (1.8 to 3.6 kg) with a uniform diameter. The interior cut surface is resilient, and very coarse-textured with an even distribution of ingredients. *(Pictured on page 287.)*

820 — Queso de (Cabeza de) Puerco

El queso de (cabeza de) puerco es un producto cocido. Los componentes cárnicos pueden consistir en todas las carnes de la cabeza de cerdo o predominantemente carnes de cabeza de cerdo con carnes de la canal de cerdo, carne de cerdo curada y/u otros coproductos de cerdo que pueden ser incluidos, excepto las orejas, hígados y bazos, los cuales están prohibidos. La carne puede tener entre corte grueso y corte fino. Se debe incluir cebolla como condimento. El queso de (cabeza de) puerco puede tener gelatina agregada. El producto final se embute en tripas naturales o artificiales, según lo especifique el comprador, y deberá pesar entre 1.8 y 3.6 kg (4 y 8 lb.) con un diámetro uniforme. La superficie del corte hacia el interior tiene una cualidad elástica y con una textura muy gruesa, con una distribución uniforme de los ingredientes. *(Ilustración en la página 287).*

821 — Pepperoni

Pepperoni is moderately coarse-textured dry sausage prepared from pork and beef. The interior cut surface is moderately coarse in texture with a uniform color ranging from medium to dark brownish-red. Unless otherwise specified by the purchaser, the sticks shall have a moderately uniform diameter of 1.5 to 2.0 inches (3.8 to 5 cm). Pepperoni is generally processed so as to produce a firm, hard product in approximate uniform length sticks weighing 1 to 2 lbs. each (0.5 to 0.9 kg), though smaller link or larger diameter and weight styles are also available. A very slight amount of dry surface mold is natural on this product and may be present on this item. Pepperoni shall contain no extenders or binders. *(Pictured on page 282 and 283.)*

Product formulation shall be specified by the purchaser.

FORMULAS AVAILABLE (major ingredients only)
Note: Refer to Table of Formulas on page 279.
A, G

821 — Pepperoni

El pepperoni es un embutido seco con textura moderadamente gruesa preparada con carne de cerdo y de res. La superficie del corte hacia su interior tiene una textura moderadamente gruesa con una coloración uniforme que varía del rojo parduzco medio al oscuro. A menos que el comprador especifique lo contrario, los bastones tendrán un diámetro moderadamente uniforme de 3.8 a 5 cm (1.5 a 2.0 pulgadas). El Pepperoni generalmente se procesa para lograr un producto firme y duro en bastones con un largo aproximadamente uniforme que pesen entre 0.5 y 0.9 kg (1 y 2 lb.) cada uno, aunque también hay otros estilos disponibles con ristras de embutidos más pequeños o con diámetros mayores y distintos pesos. Una cantidad muy pequeña de moho superficial seco es natural en este producto y puede estar presente en la pieza. El Pepperoni no deberá contener extensores ni aglutinantes. *(Ilustración en la página 282 y 283).*

El comprador especificará la formulación del producto.

FÓRMULAS DISPONIBLES (sólo ingredientes principales)
Importante: consulte la Tabla de fórmulas en la página 278.
A, G

822 — Bratwurst

Bratwurst may be produced either uncooked or cooked as specified by the purchaser. The meat components may range from fine to slightly coarse comminuted pork, veal, beef, pork and beef, or veal and pork. Nonfat dry milk as well as turkey or chicken may also be included in some formulations provided the red meat ingredient is predominant. The interior cut surface of the uncooked product shall be light to pale pink in color and fairly smooth in texture, whereas the cooked color is light to pale gray. Spices shall include garlic. Links shall be uniform in length and diameter and may either be specified skinless or stuffed into a natural or collagen casing. Unless otherwise specified links shall measure 4.5 to 5.5 inches (11.4 to 14.0 cm) in length in the uncooked state. The finished links may be specified by number per lb. such as 4, 5, 6, or 8 links per lb. *(Pictured on page 282.)*

822 — Salchicha Tipo Bratwurst

La salchicha tipo Bratwurst puede producirse cocida o no, según las especificaciones del comprador. Los componentes cárnicos pueden triturarse y variar desde partículas finas a levemente gruesas con carne de cerdo, ternera, res, cerdo y res o ternera y cerdo. También se puede incluir leche en polvo descremada y pavo o pollo en algunas formulaciones, siempre y cuando predomine el ingrediente de carne roja. La superficie del corte hacia el interior del producto sin cocer tendrá un color rosado claro a pálido y una textura bastante suave, mientras que el color del producto cocido es gris claro a pálido. Las especias deberán incluir ajo. Las salchichas en ristras deberán tener un largo y un diámetro uniformes y se puede especificar que sean desprovistas de cubierta artificial o embutidas en tripa natural o de colágeno. A menos que se especifique lo contrario, las salchichas en ristras, sin cocer, medirán entre 11.4 y 14.0 cm (4.5 y 5.5 pulgadas) de largo. Las salchichas en ristras terminadas se podrán especificar en una cantidad por lb., por ejemplo 4, 5, 6 u 8 salchichas ristras por lb. *(Ilustración en la página 282).*

822A — Bratwurst Patty

A bratwurst patty may be produced either uncooked or cooked as specified by the purchaser. The meat component specifications are the same as those described in Item No. 822 Bratwurst. As noted in Item No. 802A, uncooked patty sizes may range from 2.0 to 4.0 inches in diameter (5 to 10 cm). Cooked patty specifications match those described in Item No. 802B.

822A — Tortita/Hamburguesa de Salchicha Tipo Bratwurst

La tortita/hamburguesa tipo Bratwurst puede producirse cocida o no, según las especificaciones del comprador. Las especificaciones del componente cárnico son las mismas que se describen en la pieza número 822 Salchicha Tipo Bratwurst. Tal como se indica en la pieza número 802A, el diámetro de las tortitas/hamburguesas sin cocer puede variar de 5 a 10 cm (2.0 a 4.0 pulgadas). Las especificaciones de las tortitas/hamburguesas cocidas coinciden con las que se describen en la pieza número 802B.

824 — Pork Rib Shape Patty

Fresh, uncured, boneless pork shall be ground one time only through a 0.25 inch (6 mm) plate, mixed with the appropriate seasonings (if specified), and mechanically formed to give the appearance, consistency, and texture of a natural rib slab with rib protrusions. Alternatively, the item may be produced using any FSIS-approved and labeled restructuring method that will yield an acceptable end item that exhibits the appearance, consistency, and texture of a natural rib slab. The texture of this item shall be moderately coarse and shall be light pink to light red in color. If desired, the purchaser may further specify the shape dimensions. The fat content shall not exceed 25 percent, which must be verified either by an FSIS-approved laboratory by the vendor or contractually by certification. This product may be purchased either cooked or uncooked. *(Pictured on page 286.)*

824 — Tortita/Hamburguesa en Forma de Costillar de Cerdo

La carne de cerdo fresca, sin curar y deshuesada debe molerse sólo una vez a través de una placa de 6 mm (0.25 pulgadas), mezclarse con los condimentos adecuados (si se especifican) y moldearse mecánicamente para proporcionar la apariencia, consistencia y textura de un costillar natural, imitando las protuberancias de las costillas. De forma alternativa, la pieza se puede producir utilizando cualquier método de reestructuración aprobado y etiquetado por el Servicio de Inspección e Inocuidad Alimentaria, que genere una pieza final aceptable que presente la apariencia, consistencia y textura de un costillar natural. La textura de esta pieza deberá ser moderadamente gruesa y deberá tener un color rosa claro a rojo claro. Si el comprador lo desea, puede especificar las dimensiones de la forma. El contenido de grasa no deberá superar el 25%, lo cual deberá ser verificado por el proveedor en un laboratorio aprobado por el Servicio de Inspección e Inocuidad Alimentaria, o certificado contractualmente. Este producto se podrá comprar cocido o sin cocer. *(Ilustración en la página 286).*

825 — Canned Luncheon Meat

The only meat ingredients to be used in producing this product shall be carcass pork and/or beef. Hearts, tongues, and other variety meats items shall not be allowed. Other ingredients, however, such as salt, curing ingredients, sweetening agents, spices, flavorings, etc., in accord with FSIS regulations are allowed. The salt content, however, unless otherwise specified, shall be not more than 1.5 percent. The filled cans shall be vacuum sealed and thermally processed. The cans used shall be a commercially acceptable, open-top style, coated with enamel (or other suitable material) on both inside and outside. The finished product shall have good cohesion and hold together as an intact unit when removed from the can. Cans may be specified either cylindrical or rectangular depending on the size desired. Unless otherwise specified the fat content of the product shall not exceed 25 percent. Further, fat shall not cover more than 10 percent of the outer core surface. Depending on the formulation, the product shall have uniform color, ranging from pink to reddish-brown (a slight color variation between internal and external surfaces is permitted). *(Pictured on page 287.)*

825 — Carne de Almuerzo Enlatada

Los únicos ingredientes cárnicos que se utilizarán para fabricar este producto deberán provenir de la canal de cerdo o de res. No se permitirán los corazones, lenguas ni otras piezas de variedades cárnicas. Sin embargo, se permiten otros ingredientes como sal, ingredientes del curado, agentes endulzantes, especias, saborizantes, etc., de acuerdo con los reglamentos del Servicio de Inspección e Inocuidad Alimentaria. No obstante, el contenido de sal, a menos que se especifique lo contrario, no deberá superar el 1.5%. Las latas llenas se sellarán al vacío y se procesarán térmicamente. Las latas utilizadas deberán ser comercialmente aceptables, con estilo de apertura en su tapa, revestidas con esmalte (u otro material adecuado) tanto en el interior como en el exterior. El producto final deberá tener una buena cohesión y mantenerse íntegro como una pieza intacta al extraerlo de la lata. Las latas se pueden especificar con forma cilíndrica o rectangular en función del tamaño deseado. A menos que se especifique lo contrario, el contenido de grasa del producto no deberá superar el 25%. Además, la grasa no deberá cubrir más del 10% de la superficie externa. En función de la formulación, el producto deberá tener un color uniforme, que va del rosa al marrón rojizo (se permite una pequeña variación de color entre las superficies interna y externa). *(Ilustración en la página 287).*

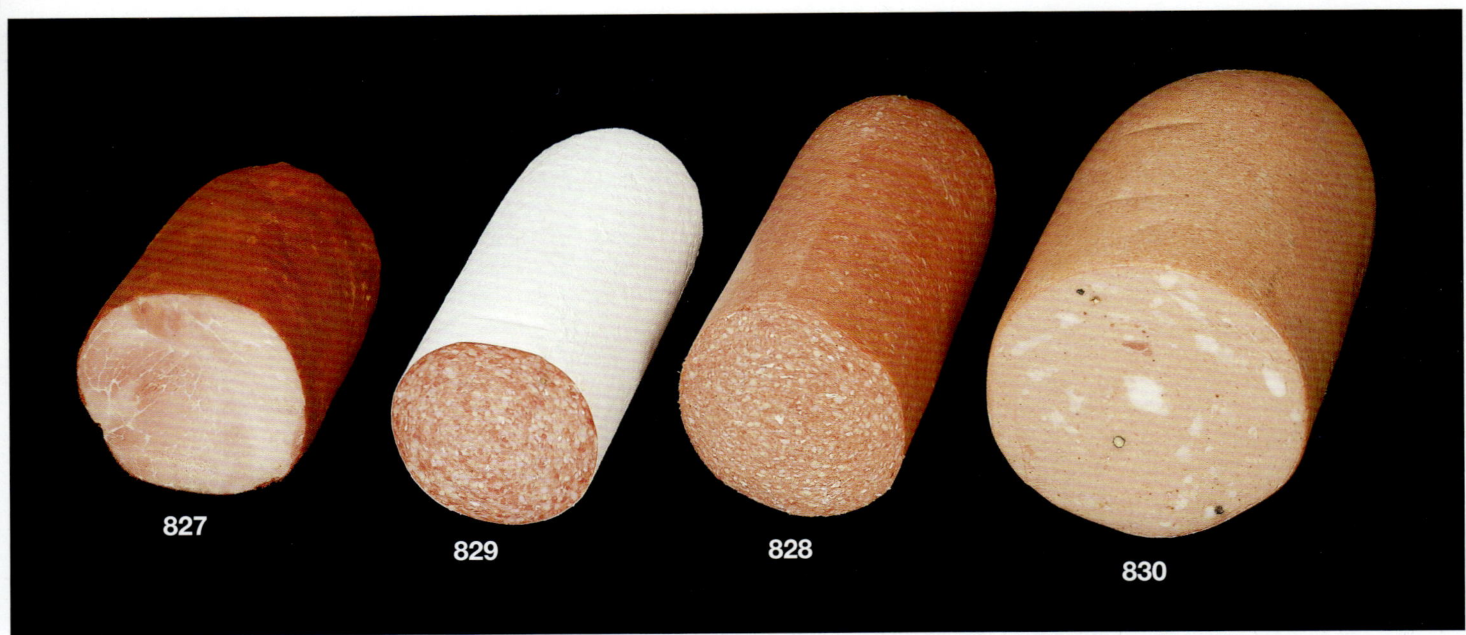

827 — Capacollo, Cooked

A cured and cooked product processed from a pork butt that meets the requirements for Item No. 407 Pork Shoulder Butt, Cellar Trimmed, Boneless. The curing process may be by dry curing, immersion curing, or pump curing. The cured product is coated with spices and paprika before cooking. This product shall always be labeled with "Cooked" as part of the product name. The product may be produced and labeled as a water-added product if desired. A number of different spellings exist for Capacollo.

827 — Capacolo, Cocido

Un producto curado y cocido procesado de la cabeza de lomo del cerdo que cumple con los requisitos de la pieza número 407, Cabeza de Lomo, Recortada de Grasa sin Hueso de Paleta, Deshuesada. El proceso de curado se puede realizar mediante curado en seco, curado por inmersión o curado por bombeo/inyección. El producto curado se debe recubrir con especias y pimentón antes de cocerse. Este producto siempre deberá etiquetarse como "Cocido" como parte del nombre del producto. El producto se puede fabricar y etiquetar como un producto con "agua añadida" si se desea. Existe una variedad de formas distintas de escribir Capacolo.

828 — Summer Sausage

Summer Sausage is a fanciful name given to a number of semi-dry or cooked sausages. The name derives from the fact that originally these sausages were prepared in the winter for use in the summer. It may be produced from a variety of meat and meat by-product ingredient formulas such as those allowed for other semi-dry or cooked products. By definition, however, Summer Sausage may also include extenders if so desired. Summer Sausage in many cases is a fermented product that displays product characteristics similar to Thuringer and Cervelat.

828 — Salchicha Veraniega

La salchicha veraniega es un nombre creativo para diversas salchichas semisecas o cocidas. El nombre se deriva del hecho de que originalmente estas salchichas se preparaban en invierno para su consumo en verano. Se pueden producir con una variedad de fórmulas de ingredientes cárnicos y coproductos cárnicos como los que se permiten para otros productos semisecos o cocidos. Sin embargo, por definición, la salchicha veraniega también puede incluir extensores de carne, si así se desea. En muchos casos, la salchicha veraniega es un producto fermentado que presenta características similares a las salchichas tipo Turingia y Cervelat.

829 — Genoa Salami

A type of fairly dry salami made primarily from finely chopped pork with some added pork fat, a small amount of beef, and seasonings. Genoa Salami has a higher moisture protein ratio than a dry or Italian Salami. This and similar types of salami usually display a covering of white mold. It comes in sticks measuring from 2.0 to 3.0. inches in diameter (5 to 7.5 cm), which weigh from 2.0 to 5.0 lbs. (0.9 to 2.3 kg).

829 — Salame Tipo Genovés

Un tipo de salame bastante seco producido principalmente de cerdo picado en trozos pequeños con algo de grasa de cerdo agregada, una pequeña cantidad de carne de res y condimentos. El salame tipo genovés tiene una proporción de humedad en relación con proteínas mayor que un salame seco o uno italiano. Este y otros tipos de salami similares generalmente presentan una cobertura de moho blanco. Viene en bastones que miden de 5 a 7.5 cm (2.0 a 3.0 pulgadas) de diámetro y pesan entre 0.9 y 2.3 kg (2.0 y 5.0 lb.).

830   Mortadella

Mortadella is a cooked and smoked sausage that is light in color and similar in texture to bologna. Mortadella is made from finely ground pork, beef, and chunks of pork fat. It is recognizable by large chunks of pork fat and pistachio nuts on its interior cut surface. Other condiments that may be included are sweet red peppers and whole black peppers. Sticks have a uniform diameter measuring from 4.0 to 5.0 inches (10 to 12.5 cm). Mortadella may also be produced as a dry or semi-dry product. It may be made with or without pork fat chunks. Mortadella also may be made from poultry and pork fat and may include extenders. *(Pictured on page 292.)*

830   Mortadela

La mortadela es una salchicha cocida y ahumada que tiene un color claro y una textura similar a la del embutido tipo Bolonia. La mortadela se produce a partir de carne finamente molida de cerdo y res, y trozos de grasa de cerdo. Se reconoce por los trozos relativamente grandes de grasa de cerdo y los pistachos en la superficie del corte hacia su interior. Otros condimentos que se pueden incluir son pimientos morrones y pimienta negra en granos. Las barras tienen un diámetro uniforme que mide de 10 a 12.5 cm (4.0 a 5.0 pulgadas). La mortadela también se podrá producir como un producto seco o semiseco. Puede producirse con o sin trozos de grasa de cerdo. La mortadela también podrá producirse con grasa de aves y cerdo y podrá incluir extensores de carne. *(Ilustración en la página 292).*

Course Specifics

Center of the Plate Training® offered by the North American Meat Processors Association (NAMP) is a first-hand look at how carcasses are converted into portioned items commonly traded in the foodservice and retail meat business. The course covers all the major center of the plate protein items: beef, veal, lamb, pork, and poultry (in some locations).

This course is held two to three times annually across North America. It spans two to three days of classroom learning, with presentations by industry experts. You also will receive a copy of the NAMP *Meat Buyer's Guide®*, which is used extensively in the course.

What You Will Learn From This Course

- The IMPS/NAMP numbering system, purchase specified options, and standards common to the industry.

- A knowledge of meat items as described by IMPS and by NAMP's *Meat Buyer's Guide®*.

- Where meat products originate and how this affects their final use.

- The importance of standards and how they keep products consistent, wholesome, and fair throughout the market.

- Common defects or inconsistencies in meat products that you should look for to prevent dissatisfied customers or unpleasant dining experiences.

- Current trends in the foodservice industry, new menu ideas and options.

- How value is determined for different meat products and how this is affected by quality parameters.

If you're involved in the buying and selling of meat products - from restaurants and supermarkets to foodservice distributors and meat companies - gain a competitive edge by applying the valuable information you'll learn from this course.

Visit www.namp.com for more information on specific courses, locations, and dates.

Visite www.namp.com para obtener información adicional sobre cursos específicos, sitios y fechas.

Detalles del curso

La Capacitación en ingredientes principales del plato que ofrece la Asociación Norteamericana de Procesadores de Carne (NAMP) es una mirada de primera mano a la forma en que las canales se convierten en piezas porcionadas comúnmente comercializadas en la industria de servicios de alimentación y los negocios minoristas de carne. El curso comprende las principales piezas proteicas que constituyen los ingredientes principales del plato: carne de res, ternera, cordero, cerdo y aves (en algunos lugares).

Este curso se dicta dos o tres veces al año en toda Norteamérica. Abarca de dos a tres días de aprendizaje en un salón de clase, con presentaciones a cargo de expertos de la industria. También recibirá una copia de *La Guía para Compradores de Carne®* de NAMP (Asociación Norteamericana de Procesadores de Carne, por sus siglas en inglés) que se utilizará exhaustivamente en el curso.

Qué aprenderá en este curso

- El sistema de numeración IMPS/NAMP, las opciones especificadas de compra y las normas comunes de la industria.

- Un conocimiento de las piezas de carne como se describen en las IMPS (Especificaciones Institucionales de Compra de Carne, por sus siglas en inglés) y en *La Guía para Compradores de Carne®* de NAMP.

- Dónde se originan los productos de carne y cómo afecta esto su uso final.

- La importancia de las normas y cómo logran que los productos sean uniformes, saludables y buenos en todo el mercado.

- Defectos o anomalías en los productos de carne que debería buscar para evitar clientes insatisfechos o que tengan experiencias desagradables en la mesa.

- Las tendencias actuales de la industria de servicios de alimentación, nuevas ideas y opciones para su menú.

- Cómo se determina el valor de diferentes productos de carne y cómo éste se ve afectado por los parámetros de calidad.

Si participa en la compra y venta de productos de carne, ya sea en restaurantes y supermercados o distribuidores de la industria de servicios de alimentación y empresas de carne, obtenga una ventaja competitiva aplicando la valiosa información que aprenderá en este curso.

NAMP
NORTH AMERICAN MEAT PROCESSORS ASSOCIATION
ASSOCIATION AMÉRIQUE DU NORD DES TRANSFORMATEURS DE VIANDE
ASOCIACIÓN NORTEAMERICANA DE PROCESADORES DE CARNE

Clases de aves comúnmente ofrecidas por los proveedores de la industria de servicios de alimentación

Pollo

El pollo tiene carne blanca y oscura, y tiene poca grasa cuando se prepara sin piel. Es adaptable, económico, se encuentra a disposición inmediata fresco o congelado y puede prepararse de diferentes formas.

- **Clases:**
  Pollo/Pollo de engorde
  Capón
  Gallina Cornish
  Gallina (para cocinar o para hornear)
  Gallo
  Pollito

Pavo

El pavo tiene carne blanca y oscura, y tiene poca grasa cuando se prepara sin piel. Es económico y adaptable a diferentes métodos de cocción.

- **Clases:**
  Macho/Hembra Joven

Pato

El pato es un ave de carne oscura. En la preparación comercial se utilizan dos variedades comunes. El pato de Pekín es el pato que se encuentra disponible más comúnmente. El pato que se prepara más comúnmente es el pato joven para asar o de engorde. El pato tiene un alto porcentaje de huesos y grasa en relación con la carne. Generalmente, un ave de 1.8 kg (4 libras) solamente tiene carne para alimentar a dos personas.

- **Clases:**
  Pato entero
  Pato para rostizar
  Pato maduro

Ganso

El ganso es un ave de carne muy grasosa y oscura. Generalmente se prepara rostizado.

- **Clases:**
  Joven
  Maduro

Aves de Caza

- **Aves de Caza Domésticas**

Las aves de caza se procesan mediante la misma inspección general que la carne y las aves domesticadas. Debido al pequeño tamaño de la mayoría de las aves de caza, éstas no se procesan en varias partes.

- **Aves de Caza Importadas**

El Departamento de Agricultura de E.U.A. (USDA, por sus siglas en inglés) y la Administración de Alimentos y Medicamentos (FDA, por sus siglas en inglés) trabajan para asegurar la salubridad de las aves de caza importadas. Únicamente los países aprobados por USDA tienen permiso para exportar aves de caza a los Estados Unidos. Los cargamentos de aves de caza están sujetos a inspecciones del Departamento de Agricultura de E.U.A.

Gallina de Guinea

La gallina de guinea es un ave de caza domesticada. Tiene carne clara y oscura con poca grasa. Es más popular en Europa que en América del Norte.

- **Clases:**
  Cría
  Madura

Pichón

El pichón es una de las aves más antiguamente conocidas por los humanos. La forma comestible que se encuentra más comúnmente en los Estados Unidos es el palomino. El palomino tiene carne oscura y tierna con poca grasa.

- **Clases:**
  Palomino
  Pichón

Perdiz

Las perdices se crían extensamente en reservas de caza y granjas para uso comercial. No existen variedades nativas. La carne tiende a ser de textura gruesa. Se recomienda la cocción al vapor.

Faisán

El faisán es el ave de caza más popular. Las aves criadas en granjas se encuentran disponibles frescas o congeladas. La carne tiene un sabor suave y la hembra es más tierna que el macho.

Codorniz

La codorniz es el ave de caza que se encuentra disponible más comúnmente y está relacionada con el faisán. Las especies populares de codorniz europea y codorniz de California se crían en granjas. Son aves pequeñas y magras.

Classes of Poultry Commonly Available from Foodservice Suppliers

Chicken

Chicken has white and dark meat and when prepared without its skin has little fat. It is adaptable, economical, readily available fresh or frozen, and can be prepared in a variety of ways.

- **Classes:**
  Broiler/Fryer
  Capon
  Cornish Game Hen
  Fowl (stewing hens or baking hens)
  Rooster
  Poussin

Turkey

Turkey has white and dark meat and when prepared without its skin has little fat. It is economical and is adaptable to many cooking methods.

- **Classes:**
  Young Tom/Hen

Duck

Duck is a dark meat bird. There are two common varieties used in commercial preparation. The most widely available is the pekin duck. The most commonly prepared is the broiler or roaster duckling. Duck has a high percentage of bone and fat to meat. Generally, a four-pound bird will feed only two people.

- **Classes:**
  Duckling (Broiler/Fryer)
  Roaster
  Mature

Goose

Goose is a very fatty dark meat bird. It is usually roasted.

- **Classes:**
  Young
  Mature

Game Birds

- **Domestic Game Birds**

Game birds are processed under the same federal inspection as domesticated meat and poultry. Due to the small size of most game birds they are not processed into many parts.

- **Imported Game Birds**

The United States Department of Agriculture (USDA) and the Food and Drug Administration (FDA) work to ensure the wholesomeness of imported game birds. Only USDA-approved countries have permits to export game birds into the United States. Game bird shipments are subject to USDA or FDA import inspections.

Guinea Fowl/Guinea Hen

A guinea is a domesticated game bird. It has tender light and dark meat with little fat. It is more popular in Europe than in North America.

- **Classes:**
  Baby
  Mature

Pigeon

The pigeon is one of the oldest birds known to humans. The most common edible form found in the United States is squab. Squab has dark, tender meat with little fat.

- **Classes:**
  Squab
  Pigeon

Partridge

Partridges are widely raised on game preserves and farms for commercial use. There are no native varieties. The meat tends to be coarse textured. Moist cooking is recommended.

Pheasant

Pheasant is the most popular game bird. Farm-raised birds are available fresh or frozen. The meat is mildly flavored and the hen is more tender than the cock.

Quail

The quail is the most commonly available game bird and is related to the pheasant. The popular European and California species are farm-raised. They are small, lean birds.

Opciones especificadas por el comprador

En Estados Unidos, además de poder solicitar cortes de aves crudos y preparados, la mayoría de los procesadores ofrecen una amplia variedad de opciones especificadas por el comprador (PSO, por sus siglas en inglés). A solicitud, muchos productos pueden prepararse de forma personalizada. Por ejemplo, el producto puede comprarse fresco o congelado, con huesos o deshuesado, con piel o sin piel, crudo o cocido mediante diferentes procesos, o preparado en porciones de diferentes tamaños. Los productos también pueden prepararse o cortarse según diferentes especificaciones. Pueden existir opciones no disponibles en algunas especies o para algunas partes de la canal. Hemos identificado las opciones especificadas por el comprador (PSO) con este ícono.

Aquí se incluye una lista de las opciones especificadas por el comprador. Por favor verifique la disponibilidad con su procesador.

- **General**

  Predeterminado: A menos que se especifique, el producto se entregará fresco, con piel y con huesos.
  Sin piel
  Entero
  Dividido
  Tamaño de la porción, a menos que se especifique en la descripción de la pieza
  Deshuesado

- **Tipo de refrigeración o estado, o tipo de procesamiento**

  Refrigerado en fresco
  Congelado - A granel
  Congelado - CRI (congelado rápido individual) o CI (congelado individual)
  Helado
  CO_2
  Irradiado

- **Estilo**

  Predeterminado: Listo para Comer
  Asado a la Parrilla
  Horneado
  Escaldado
  Asado
  Frito
  Rostizado
  Ahumado

- **Baños o Inmersión (sujeto a los requisitos de etiquetado del Servicio de Inspección e Inocuidad Alimentaria)**

  Predeterminado: Listo para cocer (RTC, por sus siglas en inglés)
  Bañado
  Rebozado
  Empanizado
  Inyectado
  Marinado
  Condimentado
  Otros: Puede incluir combinaciones especificadas por el comprador.

- **Opciones de envasado**

  A granel
  CVP (las partes se envasan a granel con diferentes pesos, en bolsas selladas al vacío)
  Envuelto de forma individual
  Colocado en una caja en forma individual
  Paquetes individuales en un envase
  Empaquetado con atmósfera modificada
  Separado por capas
  Envasado al vacío

Evaluación

El Departamento de Agricultura de E.U.A. (USDA, por sus siglas en inglés) a través del Servicio de mercadeo agrícola (AMS, por sus siglas en inglés) y sus Programas de Aves ofrece un servicio voluntario con cargo por la de evaluación de la calidad de las aves. Todas las aves deben ser inspeccionadas por el Servicio de Inspección e Inocuidad Alimentaria de USDA para evaluar su salubridad antes de la calificación. Para obtener más información sobre la calificación de las aves tanto en Estados Unidos, Canadá como en Mexico, consulte la sección introductoria de *la Guía*.

Purchaser Specified Options (PSO)

In the U.S., in addition to ordering raw and prepared cuts of poultry, most meat processors offer a wide variety of purchaser specified options (PSO). Upon request, many products can be custom prepared. For example, product may be purchased fresh or frozen, bone-in, boneless, skin-on, skinless, raw or cooked by different processes, or manufactured in random portion sizes. Products may also be produced or cut according to specifications. All options may not be available in some species and for some carcass parts. We have identified specific PSOs in this book with this icon.

Here is a list of purchaser specified options.
Please check with your processor for availability.

- **General**

  Default: Unless specified, product will be delivered fresh, skin-on, and bone-in.
  Skinless
  Whole
  Split
  Portion-sized, unless specified in Item Description
  Boneless

- **Type of Refrigeration or Condition, or Type of Processing**

  Fresh/chilled
  Frozen-Bulk
  Frozen-IQF or IF
  Iced
  CO_2
  Irradiated

- **Style**

  Default: Ready to Eat
  Barbequed
  Baked
  Blanched
  Broiled
  Fried
  Roasted
  Smoked

- **Coatings or Immersion (subject to FSIS labeling requirements)**

  Default: Ready to Cook (RTC)
  Basted
  Battered
  Breaded
  Injected
  Marinated
  Seasoned
  Other: May include combinations specified by purchaser.

- **Packaging Options**

  Bulk
  CVP (parts are bulk packed in various weights in bags and vacuum sealed)
  Individually wrapped
  Individually boxed
  Individual packages in a container
  Modified atmosphere packaged
  Separated in layers
  Vacuum packed

Grading

The United States Department of Agriculture (USDA) through its Agricultural Marketing Service (AMS) and its Poultry Programs offers voluntary, fee-for-service, quality grading for poultry. All poultry must be inspected for wholesomeness by the USDA's Food Safety and Inspection Service prior to grading. For more information on poultry grading in both the United States, Canada and Mexico, see the front section of *The Guide*.

Sistema numérico

El sistema numérico que se utiliza para etiquetar las especies y los cortes listados en la *Guía de Carnes para el Comprador* fue desarrollado en 1999. La Asociación Norteamericana de Procesadores de Carne (NAMP, por sus siglas en inglés) y el Departamento de Agricultura de Estados Unidos tienen una larga historia de trabajo conjunto en la identificación de los diferentes cortes de carne y aves. El sistema numérico es esencial para estandarizar los cortes. El sistema fue desarrollado para que los cortes nuevos pudieran ser incluidos de forma lógica. Esta página ofrece una explicación del sistema numérico.

Los primeros y los segundos dígitos identifican conjuntamente el número de serie, el tipo y la clase de ave (por ej., pavo, joven, maduro).

Identifica una parte específica, por ejemplo, ala, pierna, cuarto.

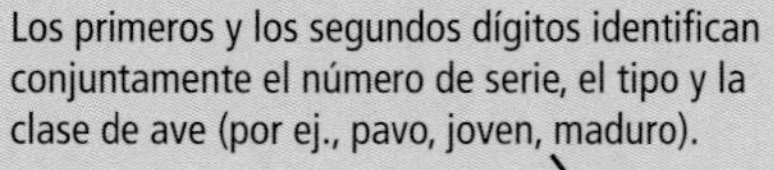

Designa a las aves, para evitar confución con los números de carnes rojas.

Los primeros y los segundos dígitos identifican conjuntamente el número de serie, tipo y clase de ave (por ej., pavo, joven, maduro).

EJEMPLO:

Pavo, Cuarto de Pierna

P2030

Pavo **Cuarto de pierna**

Código numérico

Código para identificar aves, 1º y 2º dígito.

P10	Pollo/Pollo de engorde
P11	Pollo para rostizar
P12	Capón
P13	Gallina (generalmente no disponible)
P14	Pollo, cría
P15	Gallina Rock Cornish
P20	Pavo
P21	Macho
P22	Gallina
P23	Maduro (generalmente no disponible)
P24	Macho reproductor (generalmente no disponible)
P25	Gallina reproductora (generalmente no disponible)
P26	Pavo salvaje
P30	Pato joven
P31	Pato joven para rostizar
P32	Pato maduro (generalmente no disponible)
P40	Ganso joven
P41	Ganso maduro (generalmente no disponible)
P50	Gallina de Guinea
P60	Palomino
P61	Palomino (generalmente no disponible)
P70	Codorniz
P71	Codorniz faraona
P72	Faisán
P73	Faisán, cría
P74	Perdiz
P75	Perdiz de Chukar

Código para identificar aves, 3º y 4º dígito

00	Canal entera	31	Pierna
01	Canal con menudencias	32	Pierna semi deshuesada
02	Canal sin menudencias	33	Muslo
03	Mitad delantera	34	Muslo con porción trasera
04	Porción inferior	35	Pierna
05	Ocho (8) piezas – sin menudencias	36	Ala entera
06	Nueve (9) piezas – sin menudencias	37	Alón
07	Diez (10) piezas – sin menudencias	38	Trozo plano
08	Mitades (media canal)	39	Punta
09	Cuarto	40	Ala tipo V
10	Cuarto de pechuga	40C	Ala
11	Cuarto de pechuga sin ala	41	Espalda
12	Pechuga entera con costillar	42	Cuello
13	Pechuga entera sin costillar	43	Menudencias
14	Media pechuga con costillar	44	Molleja
15	Media pechuga sin costillar	45	Hígado
16	Pechuga para aerolínea (estilo aerolínea)	46	Paté de hígado
17	Filete, entero	47	Patas
18	Filete, recortado	48	Garras
19	Carne de la escápula	49	Huesos
30	Cuarto de pierna	50	Lengua
		51	Testículos (fritos)
		52	Corazón
		53–99	Reservado para uso futuro

Numbering System

The numbering system used to label each individual species and cut listed in *The Meat Buyer's Guide* was developed in 1999. NAMP and the United States Department of Agriculture have a long history of working together to identify the various cuts of meat and poultry. A numbering system is essential for standardizing cuts. The system was developed so that new cuts may be logically inserted. This page provides an explanation of the numbering system.

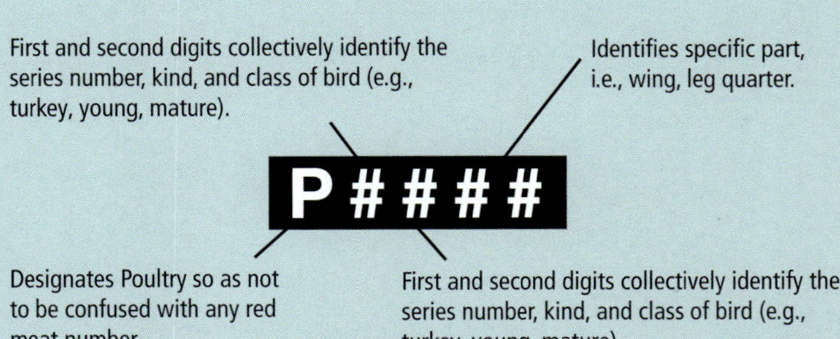

Number Key

Key to Identify Birds
1st and 2nd Digit

P10	Broiler/Fryer
P11	Roaster chicken
P12	Capon
P13	Fowl (not commonly available)
P14	Poussin
P15	Rock cornish game hen
P20	Young turkey
P21	Tom
P22	Hen
P23	Mature (not commonly available)
P24	Breeder tom (not commonly available)
P25	Breeder hen (not commonly available)
P26	Wild turkey
P30	Duckling
P31	Roaster duckling
P32	Mature duck (not commonly available)
P40	Young goose
P41	Mature goose (not commonly available)
P50	Guinea fowl
P60	Squab
P61	Pigeon (not commonly available)
P70	Quail
P71	Pharaoh quail
P72	Pheasant
P73	Baby pheasant
P74	Partridge
P75	Chukar (partridge)

Key to Identify Birds
3rd and 4th Digit

00	Whole carcass
01	Carcass with giblets
02	Carcass without giblets (WOG)
03	Front half
04	Lower portion
05	Eight (8) piece cut – (WOG)
06	Nine (9) piece cut – (WOG)
07	Ten (10) piece cut – (WOG)
08	Halves (half carcass)
09	Quarter
10	Breast quarter
11	Breast quarter without wing
12	Whole breast with ribs
13	Whole breast without ribs
14	Breast half with ribs
15	Breast half without ribs
16	Airline breast (airline style)
17	Tenderloin, Whole
18	Tenderloin, Clipped
19	Scapula Meat
30	Leg quarter

31	Leg
32	Semi-boneless leg
33	Thigh
34	Thigh with back portion
35	Drumstick
36	Whole wing
37	Wing drummette
38	Wing Mid Joint (Flat or Paddle)
39	Wingtip (Tip)
40	V-Wing
40C	Cut Wing
41	Back
42	Neck
43	Giblets
44	Gizzard
45	Liver
46	Foie gras
47	Feet
48	Paws
49	Bones
50	Tongue
51	Testicles (Fries)
52	Heart
53–99	Reserved for future use

Anatomy of a Bird / Anatomía del ave

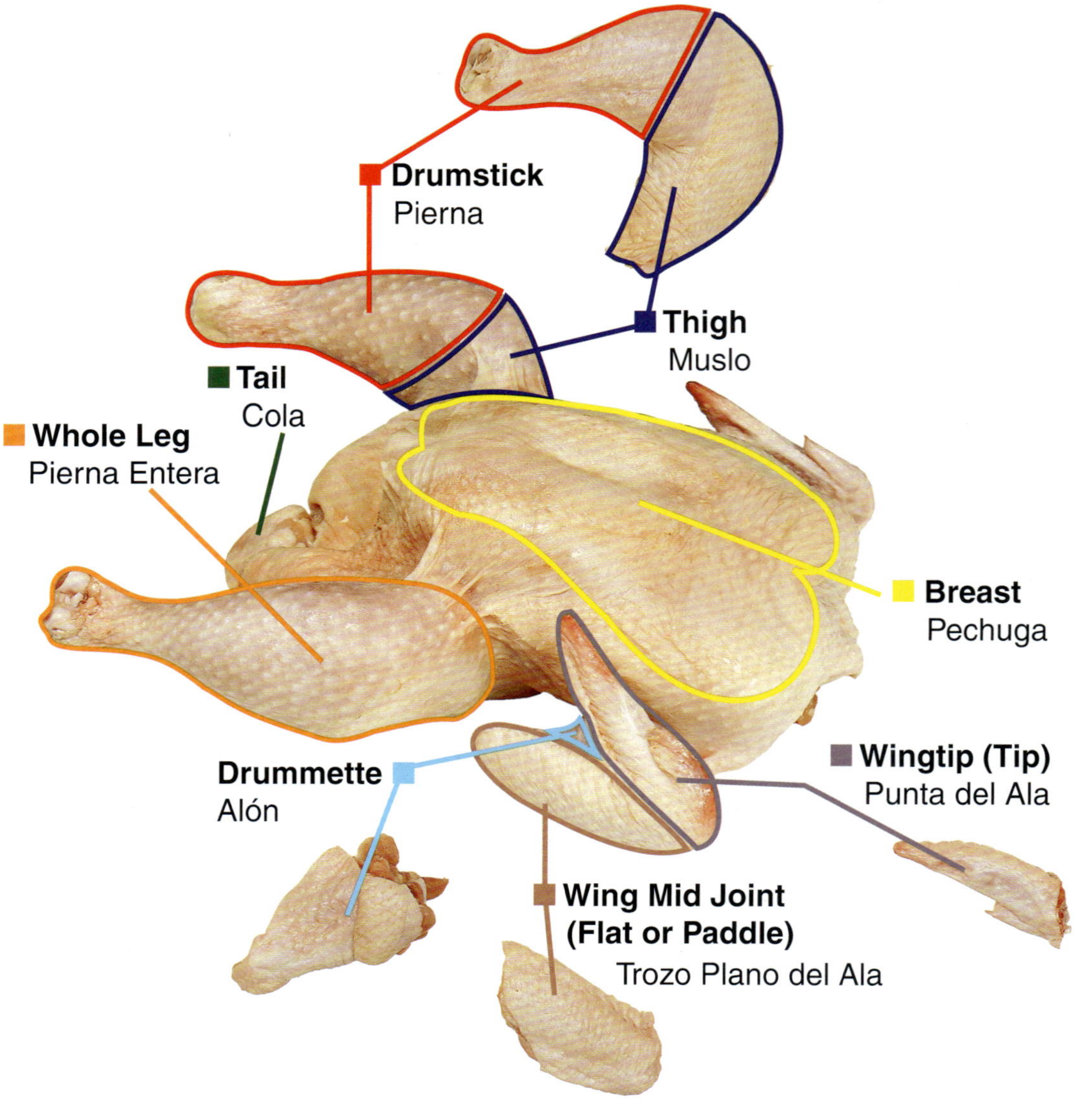

Yellow Chickens versus White Chickens
Comparación entre pollos amarillos y pollos blancos

Chicken skin color varies from cream-colored to yellow. Skin color is a result of the type of feed the chicken ate, not a measure of nutritional value, flavor, tenderness, or fat content. Color preferences vary in different sections of the country so growers use the type of feed that produces the desired color.

El color de la piel del pollo varía de color crema a amarillo. El color de la piel es consecuencia del tipo de alimentación del pollo, no una medida del valor nutricional, el sabor, la ternura o el contenido de grasa. Las preferencias de color varían en las diferentes secciones del país, por lo que los criadores utilizan el tipo de ración que produce el color deseado.

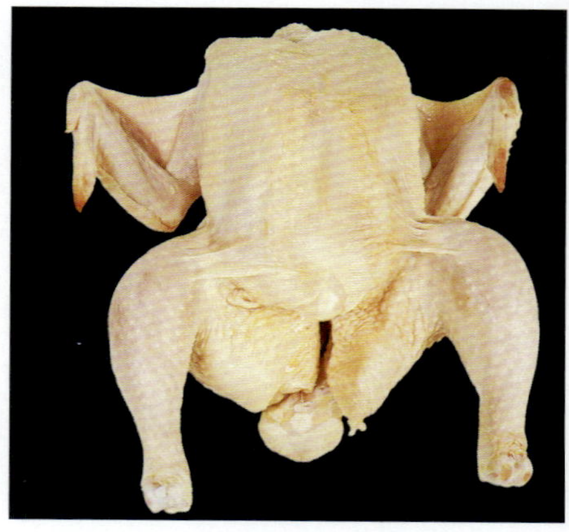

The term "white chicken" also applies to chicken whose skin has been scalded to 135° F, which removes the cuticle for better breading and battering.

El término "pollo blanco" también se aplica a pollos cuya piel haya sido escaldada a 57 °C (135 °F), lo que quita la capa externa de la piel para un mejor empanizado y rebozado.

P1000

Broiler
Pollo entero

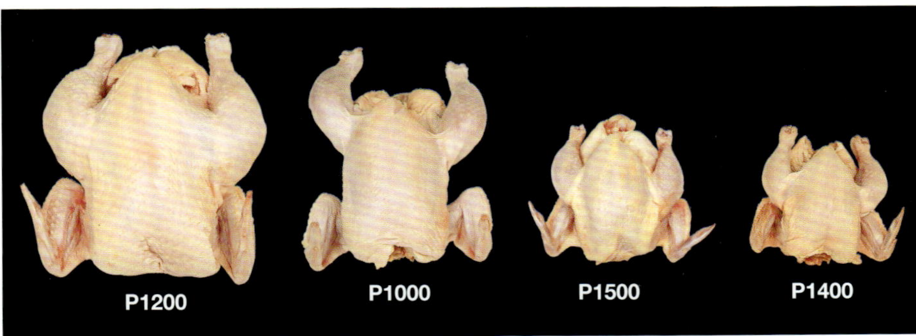

P1200 **P1000** **P1500** **P1400**

Capon, Broiler, Cornish, Poussin
Capón, Pollo, Gallina Cornish, Cría

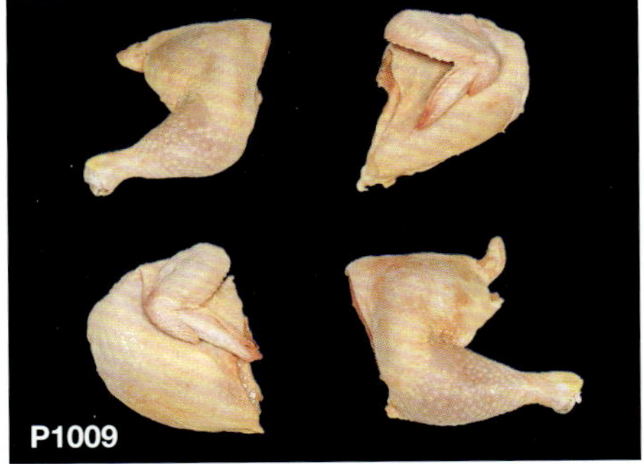

P1009

Broiler, Quartered
Pollo, Cuartos

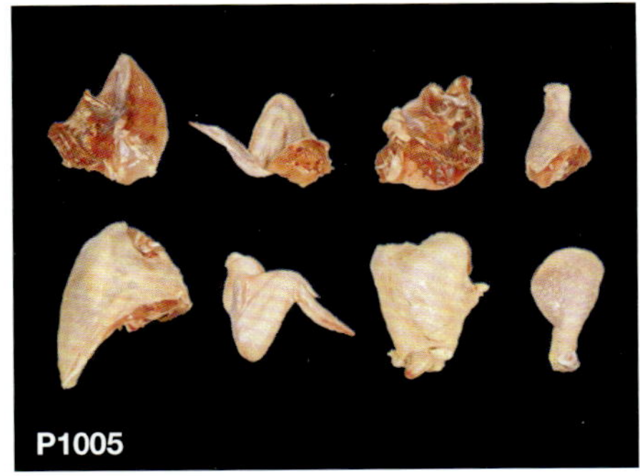

P1005

Eight-Piece Broiler
Pollo, Corte Ocho Piezas

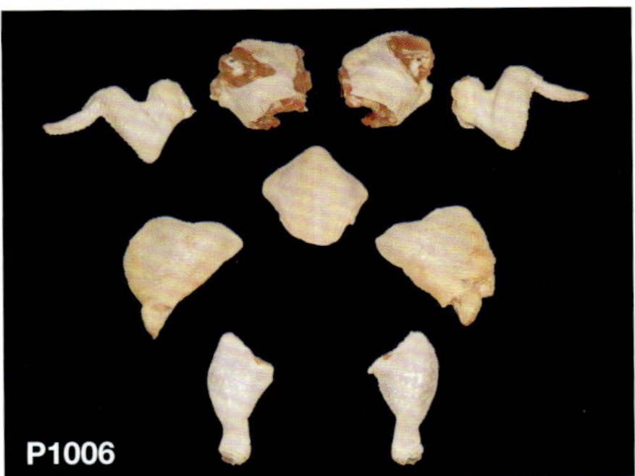

P1006

Nine-Piece Broiler
Pollo, Corte Nueve Piezas

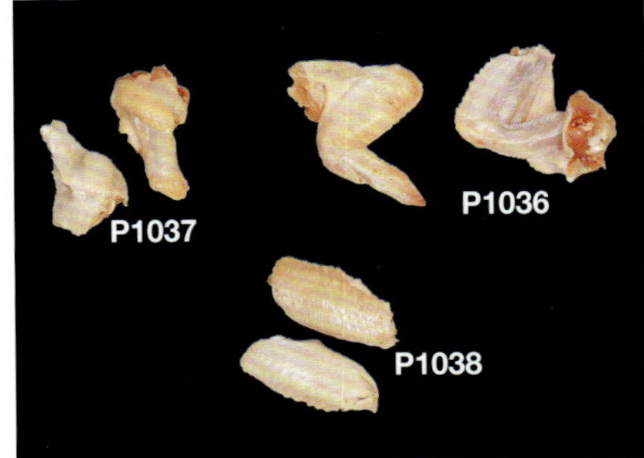

Wings
Alas

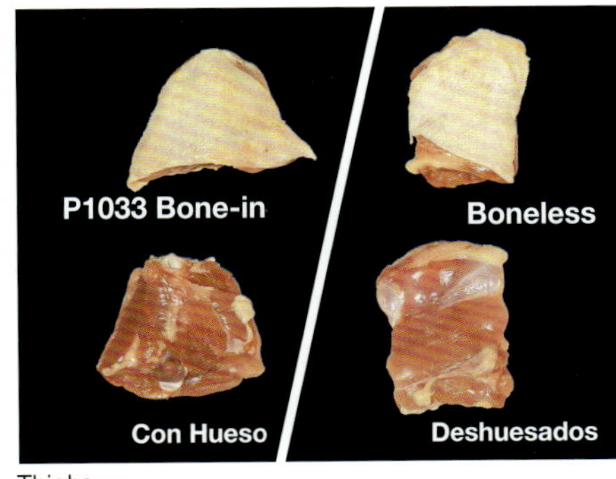

Thighs
Muslos

Boneless Breasts
Pechugas Deshuesadas

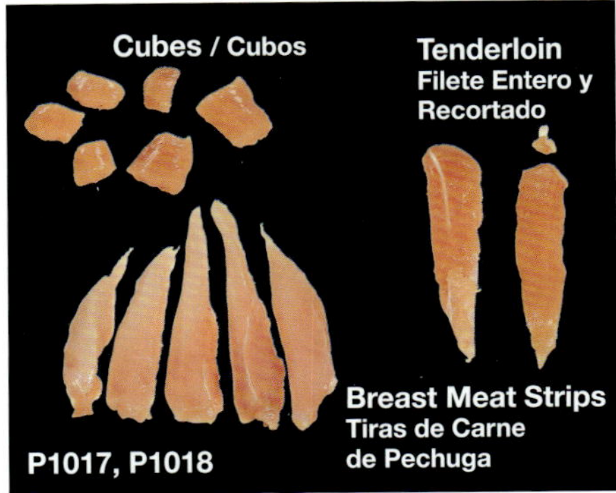

Breast Meat
Carne de Pechuga

Portion-Controlled Breast Meat
Carne de Pechuga en Porciones Controladas

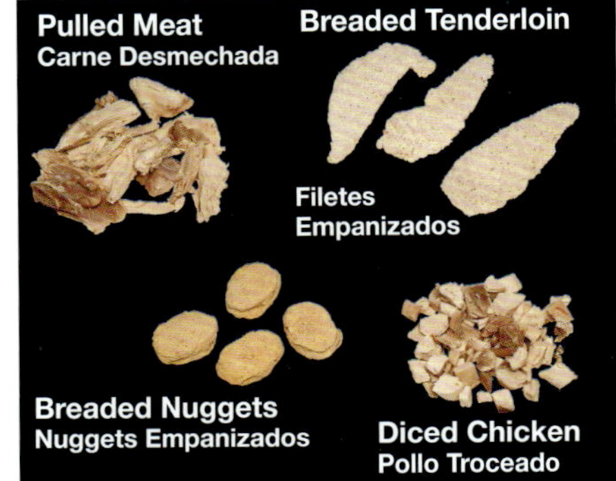

Value-Added Chicken
Pollo con Valor Agregado

Index/Índice

Chicken Products
Productos de Pollo

Many of the chicken and turkey products shown in the poultry section of *The Meat Buyer's Guide* are also illustrated and referenced in the U.S. Trade Descriptions for Poultry (USTDs), which are maintained by the United States Department of Agriculture, Agricultural Marketing Service, Poultry Programs. The following is a cross reference of products to assist buyers and sellers who use both *The Meat Buyer's Guide* and USTDs when buying and selling poultry.

Muchos de los productos de pollo y pavo que aparecen en la sección de aves de La Guía para Compradores de Carne también se ilustran y detallan en las Descripciones de Comercio de E.U.A. para la carne de ave (USTD, por sus siglas en inglés), que se sustentan mediante los Programas de Aves del Servicio de Mercadeo Agrícola (AMS, por sus siglas en inglés), Departamento de Agricultura de E.U.A. (USDA, por sus siglas en inglés). A continuación se presenta una referencia cruzada de los productos para ayudar a los compradores y vendedores que utilizan tanto La Guía para Compradores de Carne como las Descripciones de Comercio de E.U.A en la compra y venta de carne de ave.

ITEM PIEZA	PRODUCT NAME / NOMBRE DEL PRODUCTO	USTD STYLE NUMBER	PG. PÁG.
P1001	Whole Broiler with Giblets / Pollo Entero con Menudencias	70101	307
P1002	Whole Broiler without Giblets (WOG) / Pollo Entero sin Menudencias	70102	307
P1003	Broiler, Front Half / Pollo – Mitad Delantera	70301	307
P1004	Broiler, Lower Portion / Pollo – Parte Inferior	70401	308
P1005	Eight (8) Piece Cut Broiler – WOG / Pollo – Corte Ocho (8) Piezas – Sin Menudencias	70204	308
P1006	Nine (9) Piece Cut Broiler – WOG / Pollo – Corte Nueve (9) Piezas - Sin Menudencias	70206	308
P1007	Ten (10) Piece Cut Broiler – WOG / Pollo – Corte Diez (10) Piezas - sin Menudencias	70208	308
P1008	2 Broiler Halves (Half Carcass) / Pollo – Mitades (Media Canal)	70201	309
P1009	Broiler Quarters / Pollo – Cuartos	70202	309
P1010	Broiler Breast Quarter / Pollo – Cuarto de Pechuga	70501	309
P1011	Broiler Breast Quarter without Wing / Pollo – Cuarto de Pechuga sin Ala	70502	309
P1012	Broiler Breast with Ribs / Pollo – Pechuga – con Costillar	70601	310
P1013	Broiler Breast without Ribs / Pollo – Pechuga - sin Costillar / ♣ Trimmed Breast / Pechuga Limpio		310
P1014	Broiler Breast Half With Ribs / Pollo– Media Pechuga – con Costillar	70701	310
P1015	Broiler Breast Half without Ribs / Pollo – Media Pechuga – sin Costillar		310
P1016	Broiler Airline Breast / Pollo – Pechuga para Aerolínea	70705	311
P1017	Broiler Tenderloin, Whole / Pollo – Filete, Entero	70801	311
P1018	Broiler Tenderloin, Clipped / Pollo – Filete, Recortado	70802	311
P1030	Broiler Leg Quarter / Pollo - Cuarto de Pierna / ♣ Hind Quarter or Leg, Back Attached / Cuarto Trasero o de Pierna - con Espaldar	70901	311
P1031	Broiler Leg / Pollo – Pierna	71001	311
P1033	Broiler Thigh / Pollo – Muslo	71101	312
P1034	Broiler Thigh with Back Portion / Pollo – Muslo con Porción Trasera	71102	312
P1035	Broiler Drumstick / Pollo – Pierna	71201	312
P1036	Broiler Wing / Pollo – Ala	71301	312
P1037	Broiler Wing Drummette / Pollo – Ala – "Alón"	71304	313
P1038	Broiler Wing Mid Joint (Flat or Paddle) / Pollo – Ala – Trozo Plano	71305	313
P1039	Broiler Wingtip (Tip) / Pollo – Ala – Punta	71306	313
P1040	Broiler V-Wing / Pollo – Ala tipo V / ♣ Winglet / Alita	71303	313
P1040C	Broiler Cut Wing / Pollo – Ala	71302	313
P1041	Broiler Back / Pollo – Espalda	71403	314
P1042	Broiler Neck / Pollo – Cuello	71601	314
P1043	Broiler Giblets / Pollo – Menudencias	74002	314
P1044	Broiler Gizzard / Pollo– Molleja	71901	315
P1045	Broiler Liver / Pollo – Hígado	72001	315
P1047	Broiler Feet / Pollo – Patas	71801	315
P1048	Broiler Paws / Pollo – Garras	71803	315
P1049	Broiler Bones / Pollo – Huesos		315
P1052	Broiler Heart / Pollo – Corazón	72101	315

General Size Comparison / Comparación de tamaño general

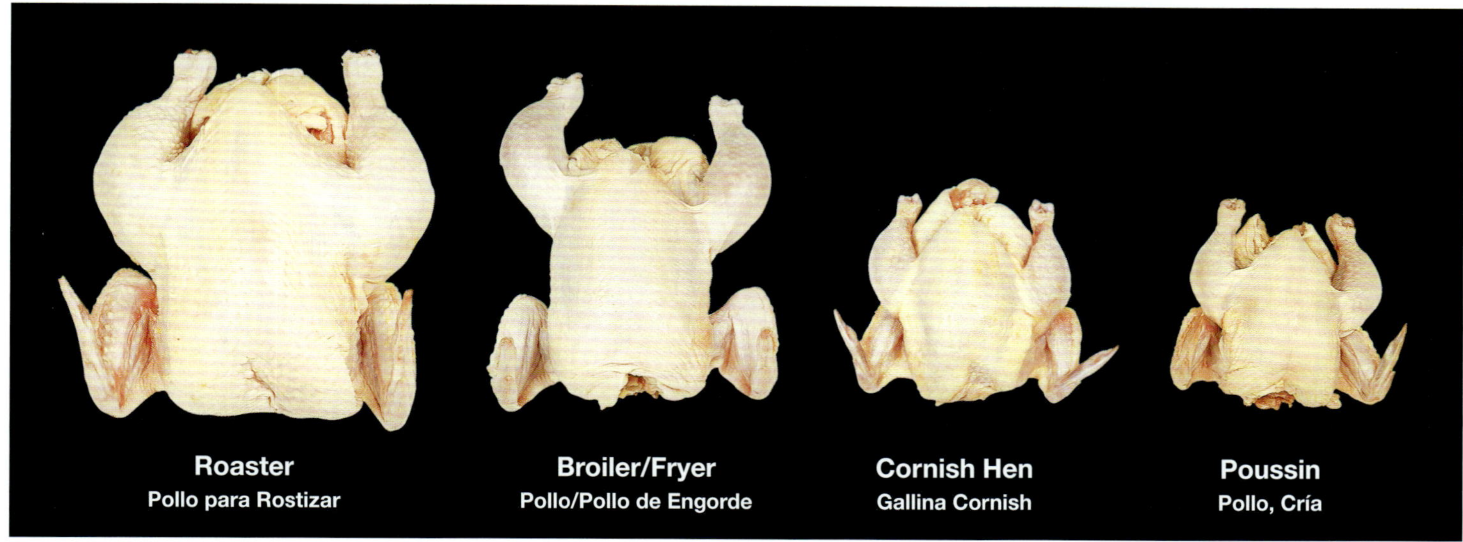

Capons are of similar size to roasters. / Los capones tienen un tamaño similar a los pollos para rostizar.

Classes Of Chicken / Tipos de pollo

P1000 Broiler

The terms *broiler* and *fryer* are interchangeable within the industry. The term *broiler* is more common, and for simplification, all descriptions will refer to items only as broilers.

P1000 Pollo

Los términos *pollo* y *pollo de engorde* se utilizan indistintamente dentro de la industria. El término *pollo* es más común y, a modo de simplificación, todas las descripciones se referirán únicamente a las piezas como pollos.

P1100 Roaster or Roasting Chicken

The parts descriptions for Item No. P1100 roaster chicken are the same as those for Item No. P1000 Broiler.

P1100 Pollo para Asar u Hornear

La descripción de la pieza número P1100, Pollo para Asar, es igual a la de la pieza número P1000, Pollo.

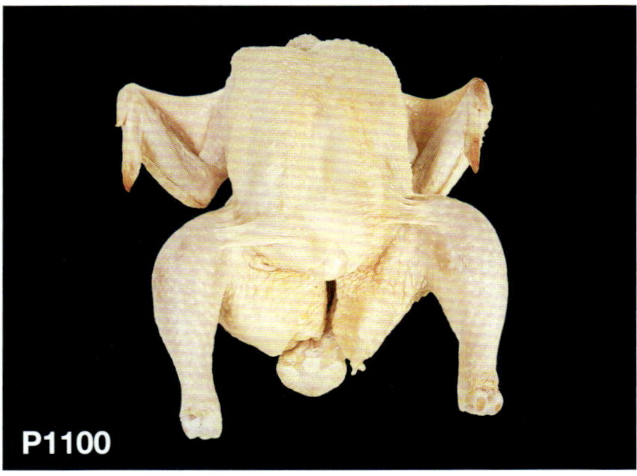

P1200

P1200 Capon

Capons are castrated roosters. The parts descriptions for Item No. P1200 capon are the same as those for Item No. P1000 Broiler. Whole capon with giblets (P1201) normally is a stock item but some of the other parts may not be as readily available. Customers with special needs should discuss the availability of such items with their supplier.

P1200 Capón

Los capones son gallos castrados. La descripción de la pieza número P1200, Capón, es igual a la de la pieza número P1000, Pollo. Generalmente hay existencias de capón entero con menudencias (P1201), pero algunas de las otras partes pueden no conseguirse tan fácilmente. Los clientes con necesidades especiales deben consultar la disponibilidad de estos productos con sus proveedores.

P1300 Fowl (Stewing Hen or Baking Hen)

The parts descriptions for Item No. P1300 Fowl are the same as those for Item No. P1000 Broiler. Whole fowl or hens or baking or stewing hens with giblets (Item No. P1301) normally is a stock item but some of the other parts may not be as readily available. Customers with special needs should discuss the availability of such items with their supplier. The parts from spent fowl are normally unavailable since the carcass meat from such birds is primarily used in making further-processed products.

P1300 Aves (Gallina para Cocinar o para Hornear)

La descripción de la pieza número P1300, Gallina, es igual a la de la pieza número P1000, Pollo. Generalmente hay existencias de gallinas para cocinar o para hornear con menudencias (pieza número P1301) pero algunas de las otras partes pueden no conseguirse tan fácilmente. Los clientes con necesidades especiales deben consultar la disponibilidad de estos productos con sus proveedores. Las partes de una gallina usada normalmente no están disponibles, ya que la carne de las canales de estas aves se utiliza fundamentalmente para realizar productos con procesamiento adicional.

P1400 Poussin

Poussin chickens are very small, young, immature birds. They normally are available only as whole birds with giblets (Item No. P1401), or as a boneless or semi-boneless whole-bird specialty item.

P1400 Pollo, Cría

Las crías de pollo son aves muy pequeñas, jóvenes e inmaduras. Generalmente se encuentran disponibles únicamente como aves enteras con menudencias (pieza número P1401), o como una pieza especial de ave entera deshuesada o semi deshuesada.

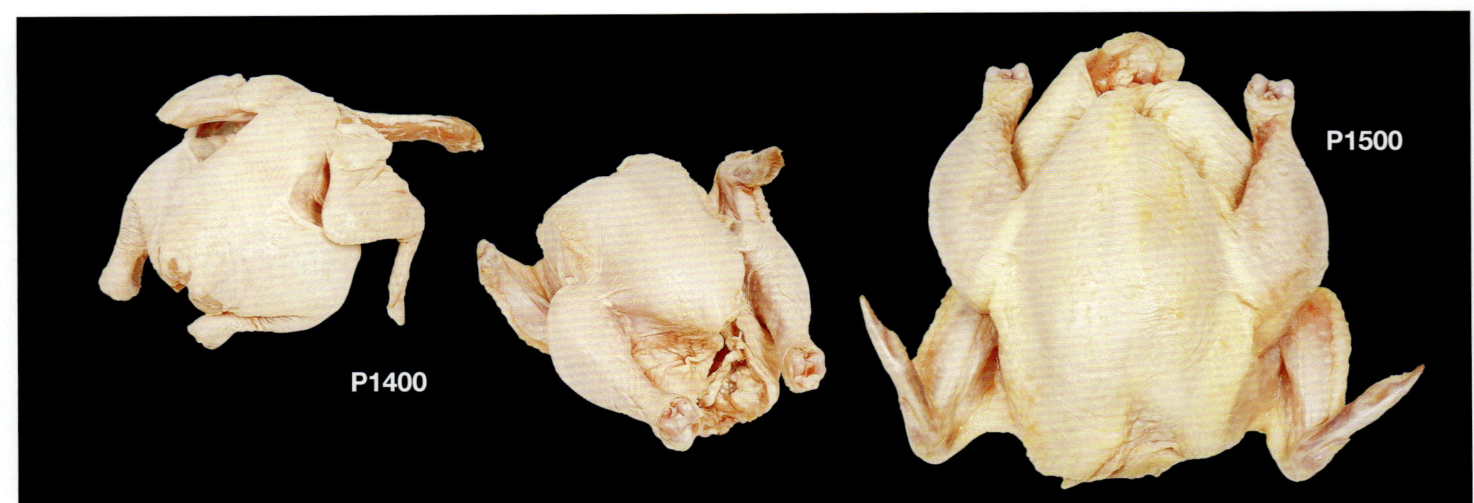

P1400

P1500

P1500 — Rock Cornish Game Hen or Cornish Game Hen

Game hens are young, special breed, immature birds that are older and larger than poussin chickens. They are normally available only as whole birds with giblets (Item No. P1501), or as a boneless or semi-boneless whole-bird specialty item. *(Pictured on page 306.)*

P1500 — Gallinas Rock Cornish o Gallinas Cornish

Las gallinas cornish son aves jóvenes, inmaduras y de cría especial que tienen un tamaño mayor y más edad que las crías de pollo. Generalmente se encuentran disponibles únicamente como aves enteras con menudencias (pieza número P1501), o como una pieza especial de ave entera deshuesada o semi deshuesada. (Ilustración en la página 306).

P1001 — Whole Broiler with Giblets

This item consists of the whole carcass with the giblets and neck normally wrapped or bagged in parchment paper or plastic material. The giblets, which are comprised of the gizzard, heart, and liver, are usually stuffed inside the body cavity together with the neck and are included in the broiler's net weight. Due to processing procedures the included giblets or neck or parts thereof are not from the original carcass.

P1001 — Pollo Entero con Menudencias

Esta pieza consiste en la canal entera con las menudencias y el cuello normalmente envueltos o embolsados en papel pergamino o plástico. Las menudencias, que se componen de la molleja, el corazón y el hígado, se ubican dentro de la cavidad del cuerpo junto con el cuello y se incluyen en el peso neto del pollo. Debido a los procedimientos de procesamiento, las menudencias, el cuello o parte de los mismos no son de la canal original.

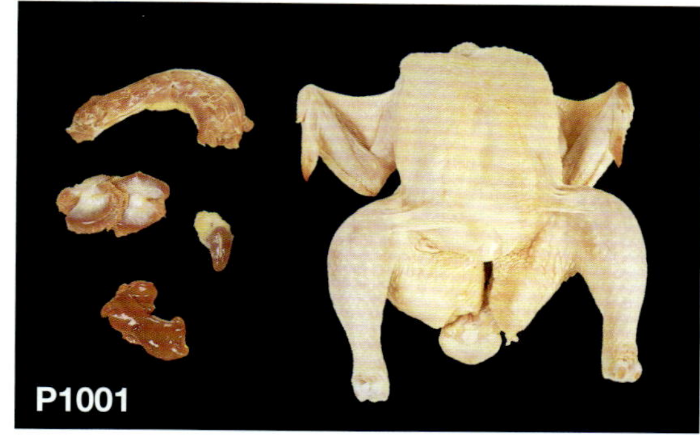

P1001

P1002 — Whole Broiler without Giblets (WOG)

This item is the net weight whole carcass without the giblets or neck. The item is commonly referred to as a WOG.

P1002 — Pollo Entero sin Menudencias

Esta pieza consiste en el peso neto de la canal entera sin las menudencias ni el cuello. La pieza se denomina comúnmente WOG (sin menudencias, por sus siglas en inglés).

Whole Broiler, Cut Up

Purchasers may specify that cut up chicken be produced from broilers either with or without giblets. The cut up chicken may be processed according to purchaser's specifications in a variety of different ways such as into halves, quarters, breasts, legs, thighs, drumsticks, 8-, 9-, or 10-piece chicken, etc. Ask your supplier to assist you in making your selection.

Pollo Entero, Cortes

Los compradores pueden especificar que los cortes de pollo se preparen con pollos con o sin menudencias. Los cortes de pollo se procesarán de acuerdo a las especificaciones del comprador de diferentes maneras como mitades, cuartos, pechugas, piernas, muslos, patas, 8, 9 o 10 piezas, etc. Pídale a su proveedor que le ayude a realizar su selección.

P1003 — Broiler, Front Half

This item is produced from a whole carcass by separating the whole breast and wings intact in one piece from the carcass by a cut made perpendicular to the backbone.

P1003 — Pollo, Mitad Delantera

Esta pieza se produce con una canal entera, separando de la canal la pechuga entera y las alas intactas en una pieza mediante un corte perpendicular al espinazo.

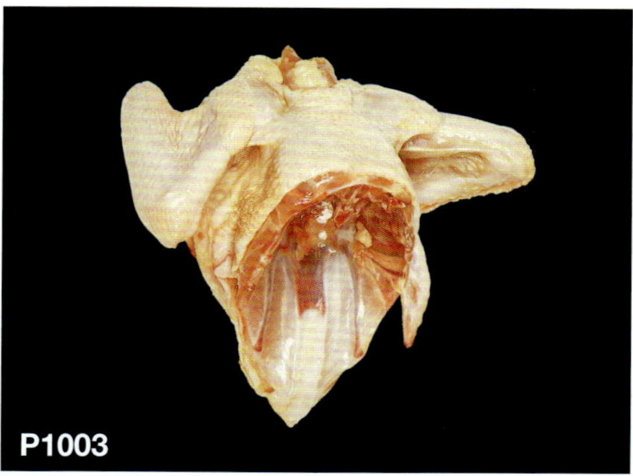

P1003

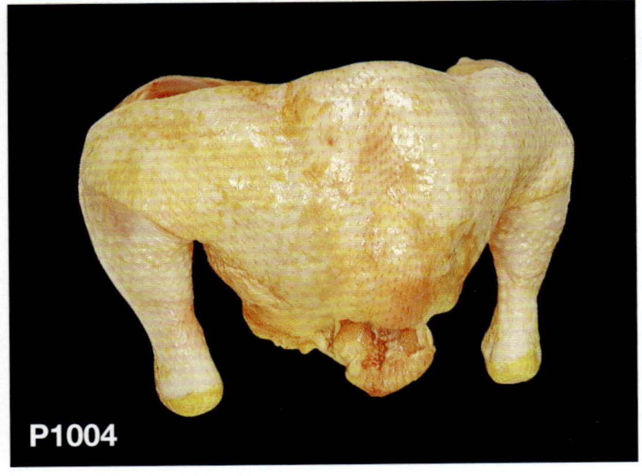

P1004

P1004 — Broiler, Lower Portion

This item is produced from a whole carcass by separating the rear portion of the carcass, which contains the whole legs, tail, and backbone in one piece, from the front half of the carcass by a cut made perpendicular to the backbone. This item is sometimes referred to as the "saddle".

P1004 — Pollo, Parte Inferior

Esta pieza se prepara con la canal entera, separando de la mitad delantera la porción trasera de la canal que contiene las piernas enteras, la cola y el espinazo en una sola pieza, mediante un corte perpendicular al espinazo. Esta pieza con frecuencia se llama "lomo".

P1005

P1005 — Eight (8) Piece Cut Broiler, WOG

The eight (8) piece chicken, as the item is normally called, is produced by separating the whole carcass into two (2) whole wings, two (2) breast halves that include the ribs and back portion, two (2) thighs with back portion and tail attached, and two (2) drumsticks. Purchasers may specify that the back portion and tail be excluded.

P1005 — Pollo, Corte Ocho (8) Piezas, Sin Menudencias

El pollo de ocho (8) piezas, como se denomina comúnmente este artículo, se prepara separando la canal entera en dos (2) alas enteras, dos (2) medias pechugas que incluyen las costillas y la porción trasera, dos (2) muslos con la porción trasera y la cola unidas, y dos (2) piernas. Los compradores pueden especificar que la porción trasera y la cola se excluyan.

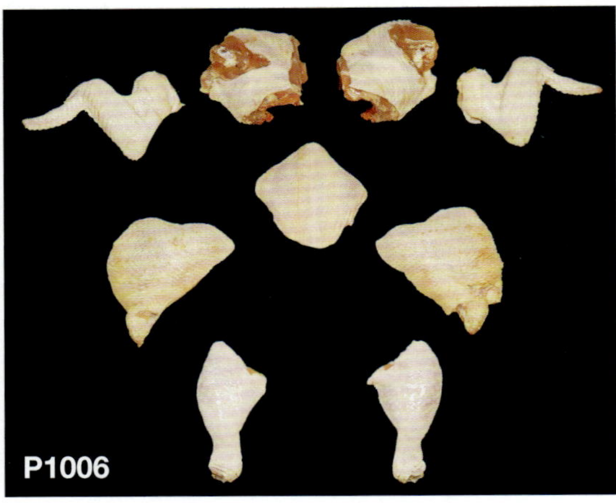

P1006

P1006 — Nine (9) Piece Cut Broiler, WOG

The nine (9) piece chicken, as the item is normally called, is produced by separating the whole carcass into two (2) whole wings, (1) wishbone segment made by cutting across the whole breast at a point approximately halfway between the end of the wishbone (*hypocledium*) and the point where the wing is separated from the breast, two (2) breast half portions with rib and back remaining after the removal of the wishbone segment, two (2) thighs with back portion and tail attached, and two (2) drumsticks. Purchasers may specify that the back portion and tail be excluded.

P1006 — Pollo, Corte Nueve (9) Piezas, Sin Menudencias

El pollo de nueve (9) piezas, como se denomina comúnmente este artículo, se prepara separando la canal entera en dos (2) alas enteras, un (1) segmento del hueso de la suerte realizado mediante un corte a través de la pechuga en un punto medio aproximado entre el extremo del hueso de la suerte (*fúrcula*) y el punto donde el ala se separa de la pechuga, dos (2) medias pechugas que incluyen las costillas y la espalda que quedan después de quitar el segmento del hueso de la suerte, dos (2) muslos con la porción trasera y la cola unidas, y dos (2) piernas. Los compradores pueden especificar que la porción trasera y la cola se excluyan.

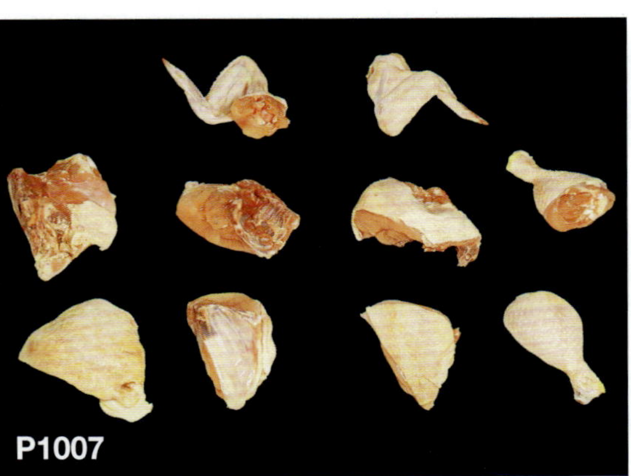

P1007

P1007 — Ten (10) Piece Cut Broiler, WOG

The ten (10) piece chicken is produced by separating the whole carcass into an eight (8) piece and then splitting each of the breast halves diagonally from the back to keep bone to produce four (4) approximately equal breast portions. Purchasers may specify that the lower portion and tail be excluded.

P1007 — Pollo, Corte Diez (10) Piezas, Sin Menudencias

El pollo de diez (10) piezas se obtiene dividiendo la canal entera en (8) piezas y luego dividiendo cada una de las medias pechugas diagonalmente desde la espalda, a fin de conservar el hueso para producir cuatro (4) porciones de pechuga aproximadamente iguales. Los compradores pueden especificar que la porción inferior de la cola se excluya.

P1008 — Broiler Halves (Half Carcass)

Halves may be produced from eviscerated carcasses that include the giblets and neck or from those without giblets (WOG). They may also be sold net weight as individual halves. Purchasers must specify their preference. The halves are prepared by splitting the carcass from end to end through the back and breast so as to produce approximately equal right and left sides.

 In Canada, broiler halves shall exclude the neck.

P1008 — Pollo en Mitades (Media Canal)

Las mitades pueden prepararse con canales sin vísceras que incluyan las menudencias y el cuello o con canales que no tengan menudencias. También pueden venderse por peso neto como mitades individuales. Los compradores deben especificar su preferencia. Las mitades se preparan dividiendo la canal de cabo a rabo a través de la espalda y de la pechuga, de modo que el lado derecho y el lado izquierdo queden aproximadamente iguales.

En Canadá, las medias canales de pollo deben excluir el cuello.

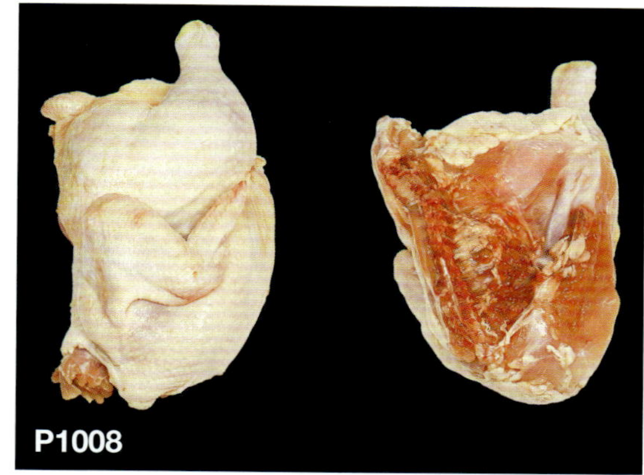

P1008

P1009 — Broiler Quarters

Quarters are produced from eviscerated whole carcasses that may include the giblets but not the neck or from carcasses without giblets (WOG). The carcass must be cut into four equal parts.

P1009 — Pollo, Cuartos

Los cuartos se preparan con canales enteras sin vísceras que pueden incluir las menudencias pero no el cuello, o con canales sin menudencias. La canal debe cortarse en cuatro partes iguales.

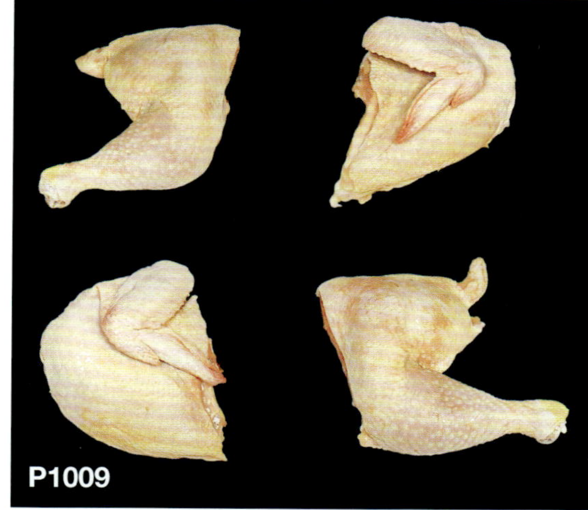

P1009

P1010 — Broiler Breast Quarter

The breast quarter is the front quarter of the broiler carcass and consists of a half breast, wing, and back portion attached in one piece.

P1010 — Pollo, Cuarto de Pechuga

El cuarto de pechuga es el cuarto delantero de la canal de pollo y consiste en las porciones de media pechuga, ala y porción trasera unidas en una pieza.

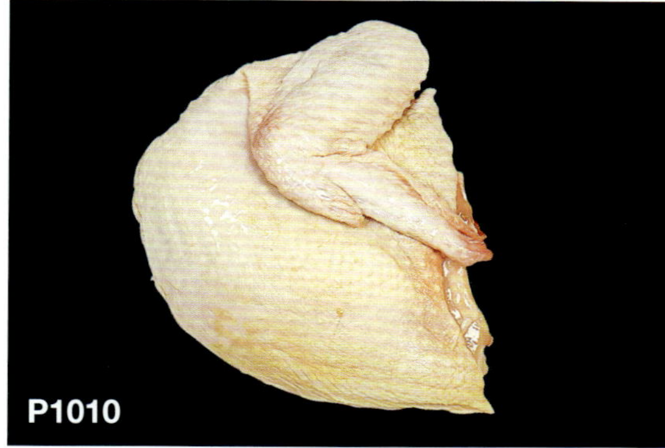

P1010

P1011 — Broiler Breast Quarter without Wing

The breast quarter without a wing is the same as Item No. P1010 except that the wing portion is excluded.

P1011 — Pollo, Cuarto de Pechuga, sin Ala

El cuarto de pechuga sin ala es igual a la pieza número P1010, excepto que se quita la porción de ala.

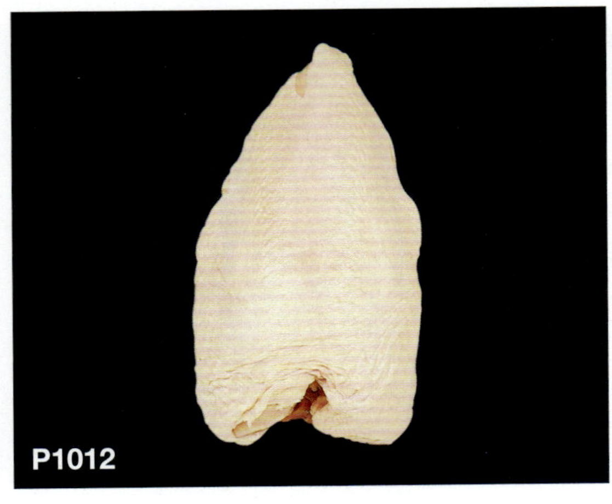

P1012

P1012 — Broiler Breast with Ribs

The whole breast with ribs attached is separated from the back of the carcass starting at the shoulder joint and proceeding toward the tail and then downward from the point of the junction of the last vertebral and sternal ribs. The neck skin will be excluded. Unless requested by the purchaser that it be excluded, or separated and included, the wishbone portion (see glossary) is left attached. Purchasers may specify that the whole breast be split into approximate equal halves. Purchasers may also specify the wishbone be removed prior to splitting and included as a separate piece.

P1012 — Pollo, Pechuga, con Costillar

La pechuga entera con costillar se separa de la espalda de la canal comenzando en la articulación de la espaldilla, continuando hacia la cola y luego hacia abajo desde el punto de unión de las últimas costillas vertebrales y del esternón. Se quitará la piel del cuello. A menos que el comprador solicite que se quite, o que se separe y que se incluya, la porción de la espoleta (ver glosario) se dejará unida. Los compradores podrán especificar que la pechuga entera se divida en mitades aproximadamente iguales. Los compradores también podrán especificar que se quite el hueso de la suerte antes de la división y que se incluya como una pieza por separado.

P1013 — Broiler Breast without Ribs

This item is the same as described in Item No. P1012 except that the rib bones are excluded.

🍁 In Canada, this item is referred to as a Trimmed Breast.

P1013 — Pollo, Pechuga, sin Costillar

Esta pieza es igual a la pieza que se describe en el número P1012, excepto que se quitan las costillas.

🍁 En Canadá, a esta pieza se le denomina Pechuga Limpia.

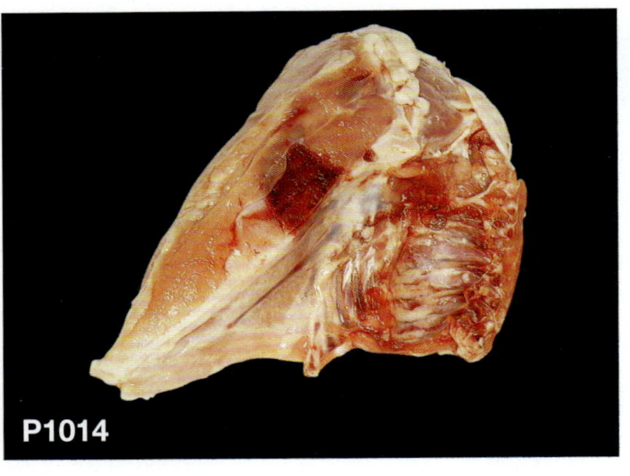

P1014

P1014 — Broiler Breast Half with Ribs

The breast half with rib bones attached is produced by cutting through the breastbone (keel) so that the whole breast as described in Item No. P1012 is divided into two approximately equal portions.

P1014 — Pollo, Media Pechuga, con Costillar

La media pechuga con costillar se obtiene mediante un corte a través del esternón (quilla), de modo que toda la pechuga como se describe en la pieza P1012 se divida en dos porciones aproximadamente iguales.

P1015

P1015 — Broiler Breast Half without Ribs

The breast half without rib bones is produced by cutting through the breast bone (keel) so that the whole breast as described in Item No. P1013 is divided into two approximately equal portions.

P1015 — Pollo, Media Pechuga, sin Costillar

La media pechuga sin costillar se obtiene mediante un corte a través del esternón (quilla), de forma que toda la pechuga como se describe en la pieza P1013 se divida en dos porciones aproximadamente iguales.

P1016 — Broiler Airline Breast

This item is a boneless, skin-on half breast, with the first wing joint attached. The airline style is also available in a boneless, skin-on "double breast" with the first wing joint attached on each side.

P1016 — Pollo, Pechuga para Aerolínea

Esta pieza es una media pechuga deshuesada, con piel y con la coyuntura de la primera ala unida. El estilo para aerolínea también está disponible en una "pechuga doble", deshuesada, con piel, con la coyuntura de la primera ala unida a cada lado.

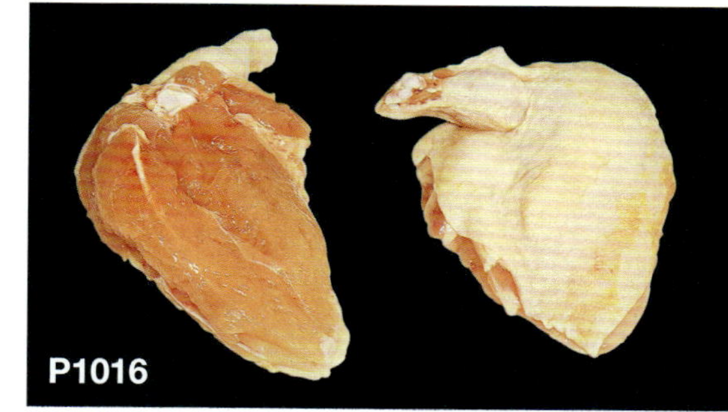

P1017 — Broiler Tenderloin, Whole

A tenderloin is produced by separating the inner pectoral muscle from the breast and the sternum. The tenderloin consists of a single intact muscle with the embedded tendon.

P1017 — Pollo, Filete, Entero

El filete se obtiene mediante la separación del músculo pectoral interno de la pechuga y el esternón. El filete consiste en un músculo único intacto con el tendón incorporado.

P1018 — Broiler Tenderloin, Clipped

A clipped tenderloin is produced by separating the inner pectoral muscle from the breast and the sternum. The protruding portion of the tendon is removed. The tenderloin with tendon clipped consists of a single intact muscle.

P1018 — Pollo, Filete, Recortado

El filete recortado se obtiene al separar el músculo pectoral interno de la pechuga y el esternón. Se quita la porción sobresaliente del tendón. El filete con el tendón recortado consiste en un músculo único intacto.

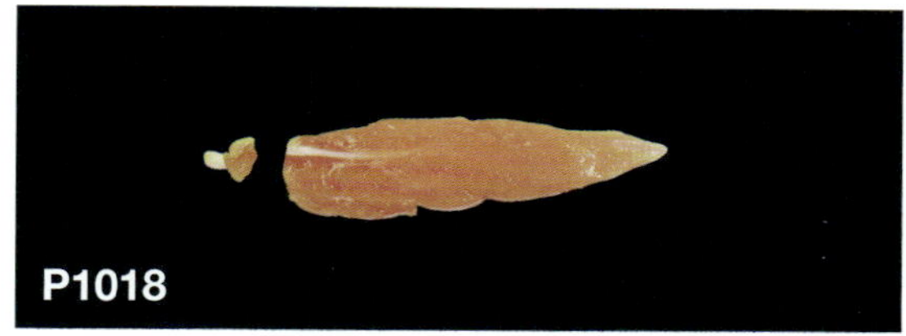

P1030 — Broiler Leg Quarter

The leg quarter consists of the drumstick, thigh, and back portion attached in one piece. The part may also include a portion of the tail, abdominal fat, and up to two ribs.

PSO Item may be requested boneless.

In Canada, this item is also referred to as a Hind Quarter or as a Leg, Back Attached.

P1030 — Pollo, Cuarto de Pierna

El cuarto de pollo consiste en la pierna, el muslo y una porción trasera unidos en una pieza. La pieza también puede incluir una porción de la cola, grasa abdominal y hasta dos costillas.

PSO La pieza puede solicitarse deshuesada.

En Canadá, esta pieza se denomina Cuarto Trasero o de Pierna, con Espaldar.

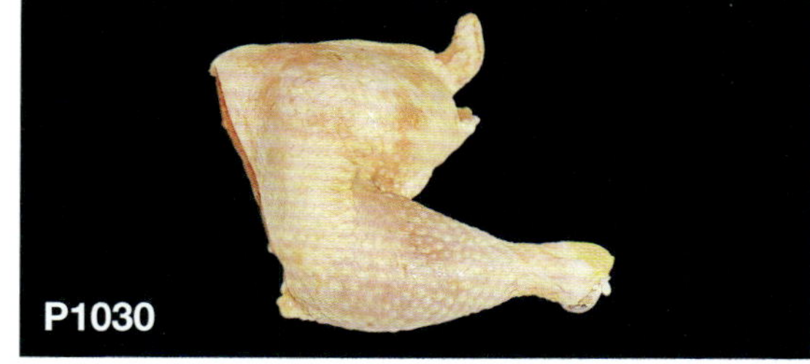

P1031 — Broiler Leg

The leg consists of the drumstick and thigh attached in one piece with the back and pelvic bone excluded. Purchasers may specify that the leg be disjointed.

PSO Item may be requested boneless.

P1031 — Pollo, Pierna

La pieza consiste en la pierna y el muslo unidos en una sola pieza, sin la porción trasera ni el hueso pélvico. Los compradores pueden especificar que la pierna se desarticule.

PSO La pieza puede solicitarse deshuesada.

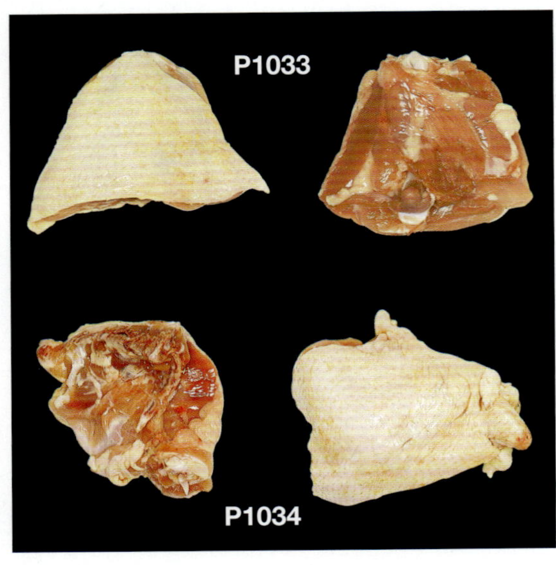

P1033 — Broiler Thigh

The thigh is the upper portion of the leg that remains after the drumstick is excluded.

P1033 — Pollo, Muslo

El muslo es la porción superior de la pierna que queda después de que se quita la parte inferior de la misma.

P1034 — Broiler Thigh with Back Portion

The thigh with back portion is the portion of the leg quarter that remains after the drumstick is excluded. The part may also include associated abdominal fat and up to two ribs.

P1034 — Pollo, Muslo con Porción Trasera

El muslo con porción trasera es la porción del cuarto que queda después de quitar la pierna. Esta porción también puede incluir la grasa abdominal asociada y hasta dos costillas.

P1035 — Broiler Drumstick

The drumstick is the lower portion of the leg. It is separated from the thigh at the point where the *femur*, *fibula*, and *tibiotarus* bones are joined.

P1035 — Pollo, Pierna

Este corte es la parte inferior de la pierna. Se encuentra separada del muslo en un punto donde se juntan los huesos *fémur*, *fíbula* y *tibio tarso*.

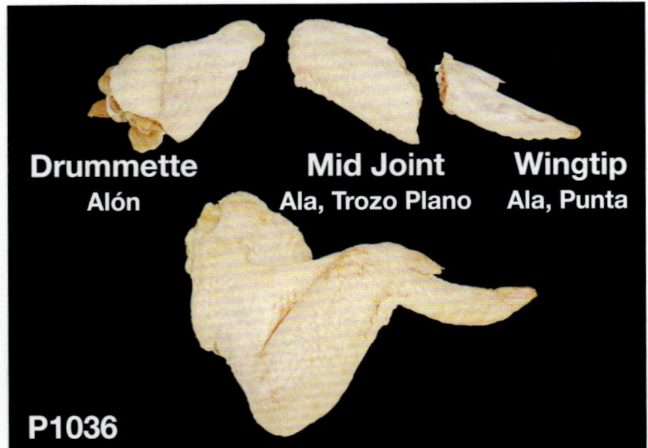

P1036 — Broiler Wing

The whole wing consists of three joints or segments. The wing will have all the muscle and skin intact. It is separated from the carcass at the point where it joins the shoulder or *scapula* bone. The first joint of the wing contains the *humerus* bone, the second joint includes the *ulna* and *radius* bones, and the third is the wingtip. Sellers may provide whole wings with or without the wingtip attached, unless requested otherwise by the purchaser. (See page 302, Anatomy of a Bird, for enlarged Broiler Wing detail.)

P1036 — Pollo, Ala

El ala entera consiste en tres articulaciones o segmentos. El ala tendrá todos los músculos y la piel intacta. Se separa de la canal en el punto donde se une con la espaldilla o la *escápula*. La primera articulación del ala contiene el *húmero*, la segunda articulación incluye el *cúbito* y el *radio*, y la tercera es la punta del ala. Los vendedores pueden proporcionar alas enteras con o sin la punta unida, a menos que el comprador lo solicite de otro modo (consulte la página 302, Anatomía del ave, para ver un detalle aumentado del Ala de Pollo).

P1037 — Broiler Wing Drummette

The drumette is the first joint or segment of the whole wing and consists of the *humerus* bone, which has been separated from the carcass at the shoulder and from the second wing joint. The muscle and skin will be intact.

P1037 — Pollo, Ala, Alón

El alón es la primera articulación o segmento de toda el ala y consiste en el *húmero*, que ha sido separado de la canal en la espaldilla y de la segunda articulación del ala. El músculo y la piel permanecerán intactos.

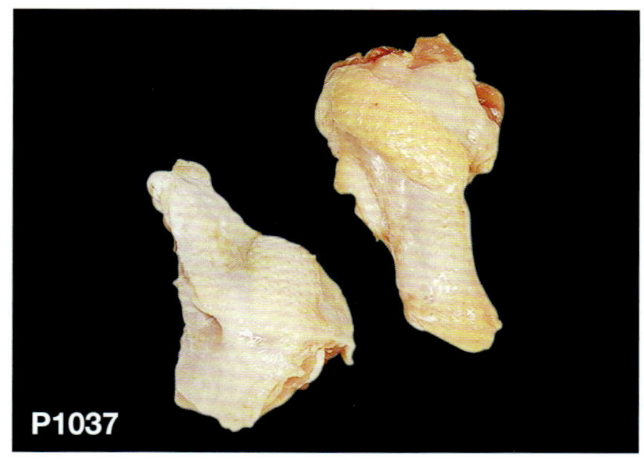
P1037

P1038 — Broiler Mid Joint (Flat or Paddle)

The mid joint or flat is the second joint or segment of the whole wing. It is the portion that remains after the drummette and the tip joint are removed leaving the *ulna* and *radius* bones attached to each other with the muscle and skin intact.

P1038 — Pollo, Ala, Trozo Plano

La parte media del ala o trozo plano es la segunda articulación o segmento del ala. Es la porción que permanece después de que se quitaron el alón y la punta, dejando el *cúbito* y el *radio* unidos por medio del músculo y la piel intacta.

P1038

P1039 — Broiler Wingtip (Tip)

The wingtip is the third joint or segment of the whole wing. It is the portion that remains after the wing flat is removed.

P1039 — Pollo, Ala, Punta

La punta es la tercera articulación o segmento del ala. Es la porción que permanece después de que se quita el trozo plano.

P1040 — Broiler V-Wing

The V-Wing is comprised of the second (mid joint) and third (wingtip) joints of the whole wing in one piece. At times the second segment or mid joint is substituted for this item.

 In Canada, this item is also referred to as a Winglet.

P1040 — Pollo, Ala tipo V

El Ala tipo V se compone de la segunda (trozo plano) y la tercera (punta) articulación del ala en una sola pieza. En ocasiones, el segundo segmento o trozo plano se sustituye por esta pieza.

 En Canadá, esta pieza también se denomina Alita.

P1040C — Broiler Cut Wing

The Cut Wing consists of the first and second segments (Drummette and Mid Joint) separated and packaged together to include approximate equal numbers. The wingtip is not included. This item is also commonly called the "Party Wing".

P1040C — Pollo, Ala

El Ala consiste en el primer y segundo segmento (alón y trozo plano) separados y empaquetados juntos para incluir aproximadamente cantidades iguales. La punta del ala no se incluye. Esta pieza también se denomina comúnmente "Party Wing".

Purchasers may request other variations in wing cuts and should be clear in their specifications with regard to the exact joints, cut, size, and packaging desired.

Los compradores pueden solicitar otras variantes de cortes de ala y deberían ser claros en las especificaciones respecto a las articulaciones exactas, corte, tamaño y empaque que se desean.

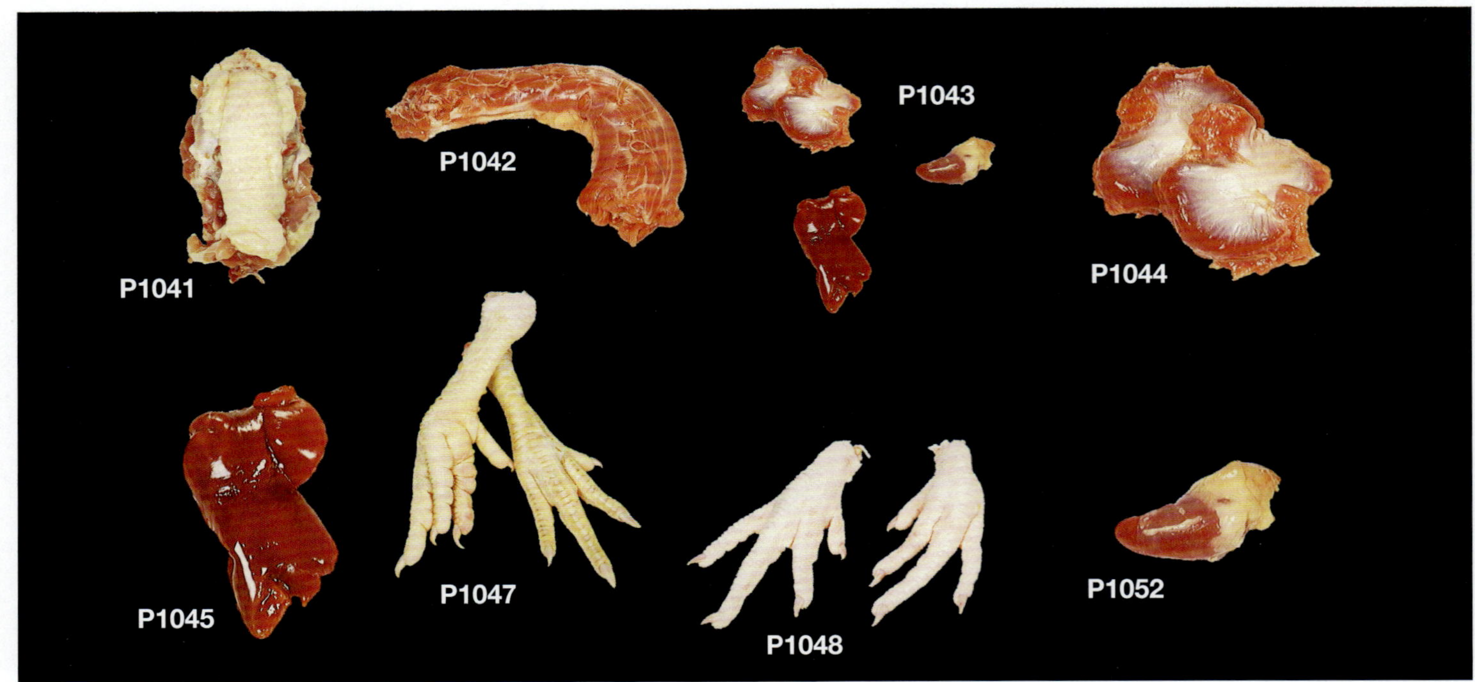

P1041 Broiler Back

The back consists of all the *vertebrae* posterior to the shoulder joint and includes the pelvic bones. It may also include the *vertebral* ribs and *scapula* bones. The skin will be substantially intact with any meat remaining on the pelvic bones left attached.

P1041 Pollo, Espalda

La espalda consiste en todas las *vértebras* posteriores a la articulación de la espaldilla e incluye los huesos pélvicos. También puede incluir las costillas *vertebrales* y los huesos de la *escápula*. La piel permanecerá sustancialmente intacta y se dejará unida la carne que quede en los huesos pélvicos.

P1042 Broiler Neck

The neck is separated from the carcass at the shoulder joint and may or may not have neck skin attached.

P1042 Pollo, Cuello

El cuello está separado de la canal en la articulación de la espaldilla y puede o no tener la piel del cuello adherida.

P1043 Broiler Giblets

The term *giblets* is used to describe an item that consists of hearts, gizzards, and livers. Giblet packages should contain approximately equal numbers of each of these parts, though in processing whole carcasses with giblets, a piece of a part or a part itself may be missing.

P1043 Pollo, Menudencias

El término *menudencias* se utiliza para describir una pieza que consiste en corazones, mollejas e hígados. Los paquetes de menudencias deben contener aproximadamente cantidades iguales de cada una de estas partes, aunque al procesar las canales enteras con menudencias pueda faltar un trozo de una parte o una parte entera.

P1044 — Broiler Gizzard

The gizzard is a brownish, dark colored muscular organ in the bird that functions in the same fashion as a stomach. Purchasers may specify that the gizzard be split open, cleaned, and the fat excluded.

P1044 — Pollo, Molleja

La molleja es un órgano muscular del ave con tono café oscuro que funciona de la misma forma que el estómago. Los compradores pueden especificar que la molleja se abra por la mitad, se limpie y se le quite la grasa.

P1045 — Broiler Liver

The liver is a smooth two-lobed organ covered with a thin membrane. The lobes are of approximately equal size. It is brownish to reddish in color. Though usually sold separately, some processors may sell them mixed together with hearts.

P1045 — Pollo, Hígado

El hígado es un órgano blando, de dos lóbulos, que se encuentra recubierto con una fina membrana. Los lóbulos son aproximadamente del mismo tamaño. Su color es de café a rojizo. Aunque por lo general se venden por separado, algunos procesadores pueden venderlos mezclados con corazones.

P1047 — Broiler Feet

The feet are the portions of leg that have been separated from the carcass at the hock joint.

P1047 — Pollo, Patas

Las patas son las porciones de pierna que han sido separadas de la canal en la articulación de la parte inferior de la pierna.

P1048 — Broiler Paws

The paws are the portions of the feet that contain the claws and that have been separated from the feet at the approximate location of the first *metatarsal* (spur).

P1048 — Pollo, Garras

Las garras son las porciones de la pata que contienen las púas y que han sido separadas de la pata aproximadamente en la primera espuela del *metatarso*.

P1049 — Broiler Bones

Bones include any type of bone from the carcass. They may or may not include skin and tissue.

P1049 — Pollo, Huesos

Los huesos incluyen cualquier tipo de hueso de la canal. Pueden o no incluir piel y tejido.

P1052 — Broiler Heart

This is a dark reddish colored muscular organ located within the rib section of the bird.

P1052 — Pollo, Corazón

Este es un órgano muscular de color rojizo oscuro ubicado dentro de la sección del costillar del ave.

Further-Processed Chicken Products / Productos de Pollo ya Procesados

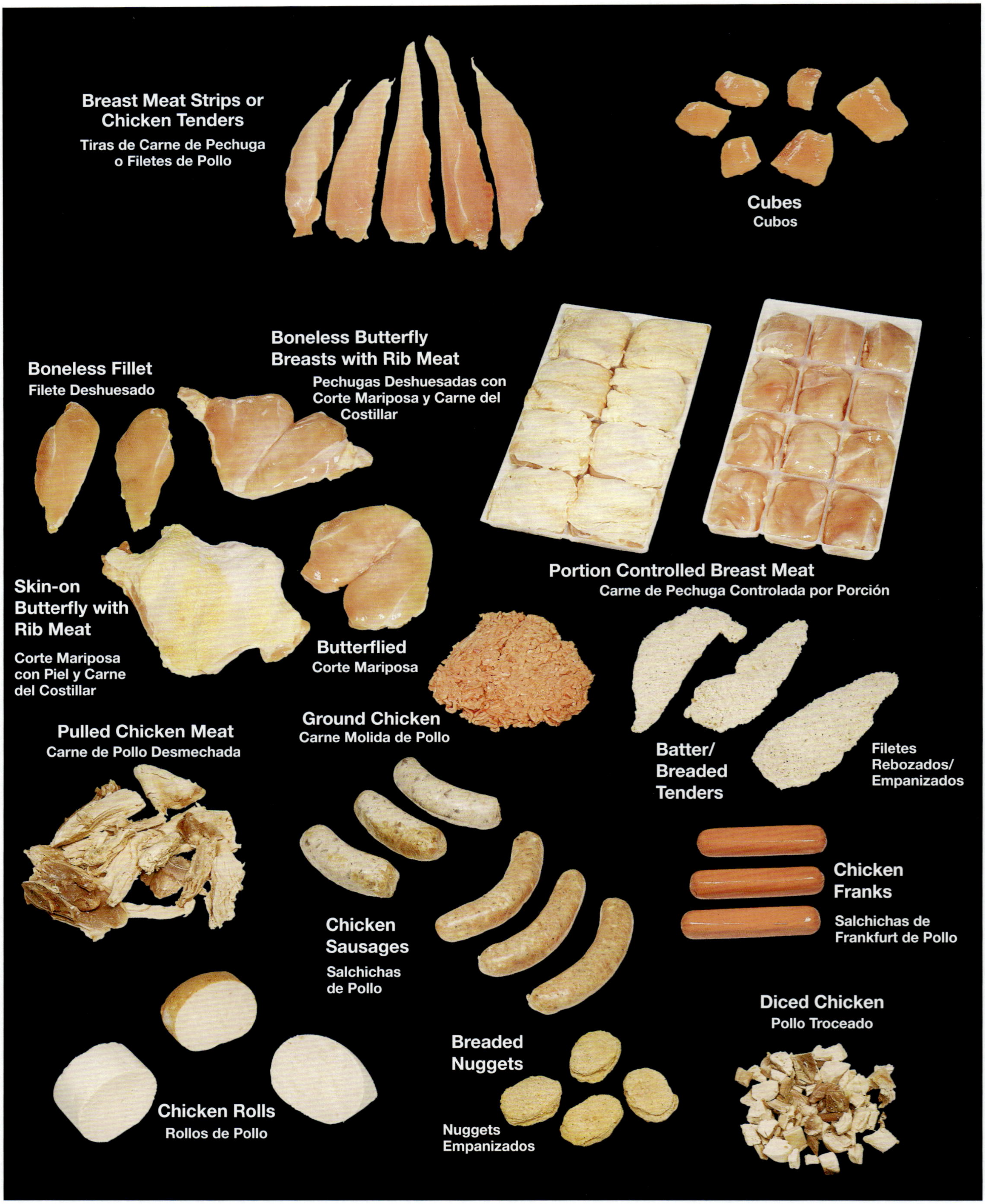

Breast Meat Strips or Chicken Tenders
Tiras de Carne de Pechuga o Filetes de Pollo

Cubes
Cubos

Boneless Fillet
Filete Deshuesado

Boneless Butterfly Breasts with Rib Meat
Pechugas Deshuesadas con Corte Mariposa y Carne del Costillar

Portion Controlled Breast Meat
Carne de Pechuga Controlada por Porción

Skin-on Butterfly with Rib Meat
Corte Mariposa con Piel y Carne del Costillar

Butterflied
Corte Mariposa

Batter/ Breaded Tenders
Filetes Rebozados/ Empanizados

Pulled Chicken Meat
Carne de Pollo Desmechada

Ground Chicken
Carne Molida de Pollo

Chicken Sausages
Salchichas de Pollo

Chicken Franks
Salchichas de Frankfurt de Pollo

Diced Chicken
Pollo Troceado

Chicken Rolls
Rollos de Pollo

Breaded Nuggets

Nuggets Empanizados

Further-Processed Chicken Products
Productos de Pollo ya Procesados

- **Chicken Rolls – Ready-to-Eat**
  All White
  White Combo (white predominant)
  Dark Combo (dark predominant)
  All Dark

- **Chicken Breast/ White Meat Items – Ready-to-Eat**
  Whole Muscle Items
  Chunk and Formed Items
  Chopped and Formed Items

- **Chicken Dark Meat Items – Ready-to-Eat**
  Whole Muscle Items
  Chunk and Formed Items
  Chopped and Formed Items

- **Other Chicken Luncheon Meats – Ready-to-Eat (may be of various formulas and composition)**
  Bologna
  Luncheon Loaf
  Smoked Sausage
  Sausage with Seasonings

- **Chicken Franks – Ready-to-Eat**
  Regular Franks (8-1, 10-1, dinner or foot long, etc.)
  Cheese Franks (8-1, etc.)
  Corndogs
  Chili Franks

- **Batter/Breaded (Raw or Cooked) Chicken Products**
  Nuggets
  Sticks or Fingers
  Patties
  Tenders, etc.

- **Diced Chicken (Raw or Cooked)**
  White
  Combo
  Dark

- **Pulled Chicken (Raw or Cooked)**
  White
  Dark

- **Ground Chicken Products – Raw**
  Ground Chicken
  Ground Chicken Patties
  Seasoned Ground Chicken (bulk or patties)
  Chicken Sausage (links or patties)

- **Other Fabricated Boneless Raw Chicken Parts**
  Breast Slices/Steaks/Cutlets
  Dark Slices/Steaks/Cutlets
  Chicken Tenders (from any portion of the Breast)

- **Cooked Chicken**
  Whole Cooked Broiler
  Various other

- **Rollos de pollo - Listos para Comer**
  Solo Carne Blanca
  Carne Combinada Blanca (predominantemente blanca)
  Carne Combinada Oscura (predominantemente oscura)
  Solo Carne Oscura

- **Pechuga de Pollo/ Piezas de Carne Blanca – Listas para Comer**
  Piezas de Músculos Enteros
  Piezas Troceadas y Moldeadas
  Productos Picados y Moldeados

- **Piezas de Carne Oscura – Listas para Comer**
  Piezas de Músculos Enteros
  Piezas Troceadas y Moldeadas
  Productos Picados y Moldeados

- **Otras Carnes de Pollo para el Almuerzo – Listas para Comer (pueden tener diferentes fórmulas y composiciones)**
  Embutido Boloña
  Pastel de Almuerzo
  Salchicha Ahumada
  Salchicha con Condimentos

- **Salchichas de Frankfurt de Pollo – Listas para Comer**
  Salchichas de Frankfurt Regulares (8-1, 10-1, de un pie de largo o tamaño cena, etc.)
  Salchichas de Frankfurt, de Queso (8-1, etc.)
  Banderillas de Salchicha
  Salchichas de Frankfurt, de Chili

- **Productos de Pollo Rebozados o Empanizados (Crudos o Cocidos)**
  Nuggets
  Bastones o Palitos
  Hamburguesas
  Filetes, etc.

- **Pollo Troceado (Crudo o Cocido)**
  Carne Blanca
  Carne Combinada
  Carne Oscura

- **Pollo Desmechado (Crudo o Cocido)**
  Carne Blanca
  Carne Oscura

- **Productos de Carne Molida de Pollo – Crudos**
  Carne Molida de Pollo
  Hamburguesas de Carne Molida de Pollo
  Carne Molida de Pollo Condimentada (a granel o hamburguesas)
  Salchicha de Pollo (ristras o hamburguesas)

- **Otras Partes Crudas y Deshuesadas Fabricadas con Pollo**
  Rebanadas/Bistecs/Escalopines de Pechuga
  Rebanadas/Bistecs/Escalopines de Carne Oscura
  Filetes de Pollo (de cualquier porción de la Pechuga)

- **Pollo Cocido**
  Pollo Entero Cocido
  Otros varios

Membership Information
Información sobre la membresía

Want your personal network to include the real decision-makers at the most successful meat & poultry processors and suppliers in North America?

THEN JOIN NAMP!

Founded in 1942, the North American Meat Processors Association (NAMP) is an international member-driven association of *progressive meat processors, distributors, center-of-the-plate specialists,* and suppliers selling primarily to the foodservice industry. NAMP provides exceptional value through high-caliber support programs and governmental representation to help ensure our members' success in the industry.

The Meat Buyer's Guide® is a NAMP publication. NAMP members can participate in the review/update process of each edition.

BENEFITS OF MEMBERSHIP

- 35% discount on *The Meat Buyers Guide®*
- A relaxed networking and learning environment at two major industry-wide meetings a year
- Learning opportunities at NAMP's 16+ food safety conferences and workshops: pay lower member fees
- NAMP's weekly report, *NewsLine,* which contains industry information and updates and NAMP's weekly Market Report, with complete up-to-date pricing information
- Unlimited free access to NAMP's College of Experts, our team of 34 Ph.D.-level consultants on 19 subjects important to your business
- A voice in government rulemaking: NAMP is a North American organization that effectively represents your interests to USDA-FSIS, USDA-AMS, and CFIA
- A cross-referenced *Member Resource Directory* for networking and enriching your business prospects
- Fast, on-line help from other members through NAMP's Listserve called "Bull Session"
- Exclusive technical/educational info on the Members Only section at www.namp.com

Members also enjoy toll-free access to NAMP's experienced staff and off-site consultants who are ready to help you with just about any problem, question or concern you may have. *It's like having your own team of experts without the added expense - an incredible value for your dues dollar!*

Membership in NAMP offers an unparalleled and unique opportunity to learn and network with your peers. Join today and you'll enrich your business prospects and benefit from other members' experiences. *It's what our long-time members call "The Magic of NAMP".*

WE INVITE YOU TO JOIN TODAY

To apply, go to www.namp.com or call +1 703.758.1900.

¿Quiere que su red personal incluya a quienes en verdad toman las decisiones y a los más exitosos procesadores y proveedores de carne roja y aves de América del Norte?

¡ENTONCES ÚNASE A NAMP!

La Asociación Norteamericana de Procesadores de Carne (NAMP), fundada en 1942, es una asociación internacional dedicada a sus integrantes, que incluyen *procesadores, distribuidores, especialistas en ingredientes principales del plato* y proveedores progresistas que venden principalmente a la industria de servicios de alimentación. NAMP ofrece un valor excepcional a través de programas de apoyo de gran nivel y representación en el gobierno para ayudar a garantizar el éxito de nuestros miembros en la industria.

La Guía para Compradores de Carne® es una publicación de NAMP. Los miembros de NAMP pueden participar en el proceso de revisión y actualización de cada edición.

BENEFICIOS DE LA MEMBRESÍA

- 35% de descuento en *La Guía para Compradores de Carne®*
- Un ambiente relajado para establecer contactos y aprender en dos grandes reuniones de toda la industria por año
- Oportunidades de aprendizaje en las conferencias y los talleres de inocuidad alimentaria de NAMP: pague tarifas más bajas para miembros
- Informe semanal de NAMP, *NewsLine,* que contiene información y actualizaciones de la industria, y el Informe de Mercado semanal de NAMP, con la información de precios completa y al día
- Acceso gratis ilimitado al colegio de expertos de NAMP, nuestro equipo de 34 con nivel de doctorado en 19 áreas importantes para su negocio
- Una voz en las normativas del gobierno: NAMP es una organización norteamericana que representa sus intereses de manera eficaz ante FSIS (Servicio de Inspección e Inocuidad Alimentaria) de USDA (Departamento de Agricultura de E.U.A.), AMS (Servicio de Mercadeo Agrícola) de USDA y la Agencia Canadiense de Inspección de Alimentos
- Un *Directorio de recursos de miembros* con referencia cruzada para establecer contactos y enriquecer las posibilidades de su negocio
- Ayuda rápida en Internet de otros miembros a través del Listserve de NAMP llamado "Bull Session"
- Información técnica y educativa exclusiva en la sección Members Only (sólo para miembros) de www.namp.com

Los miembros también disponen de acceso a través de un número telefónico sin cargo al experimentado personal de NAMP y a consultores descentralizados que están listos para ayudarle con prácticamente cualquier problema, consulta o inquietud que pueda tener. *Es como tener su propio equipo de expertos sin el gasto adicional ¡un increíble rendimiento por el valor de su suscripción!*

La membresía de NAMP ofrece una oportunidad única e incomparable de aprender y establecer contactos con sus colegas. Suscríbase hoy para enriquecer las posibilidades de su negocio y beneficiarse de la experiencia de otros miembros. *Es lo que nuestros miembros de muchos años llaman "La magia de NAMP".*

LO INVITAMOS A UNIRSE HOY

Para solicitar su inscripción, visite www.namp.com o llame al +1 703.758.1900.

turkey / pavo

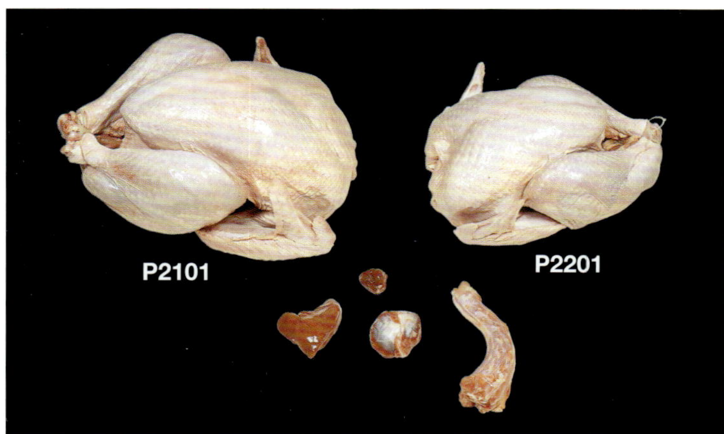

Whole Tom and Hen Turkeys
Pavo Entero – Macho y Hembra

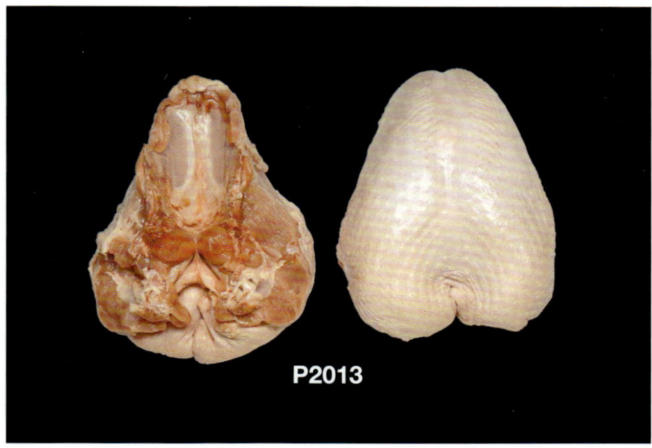

Breast without Ribs
Pechuga sin Costillar

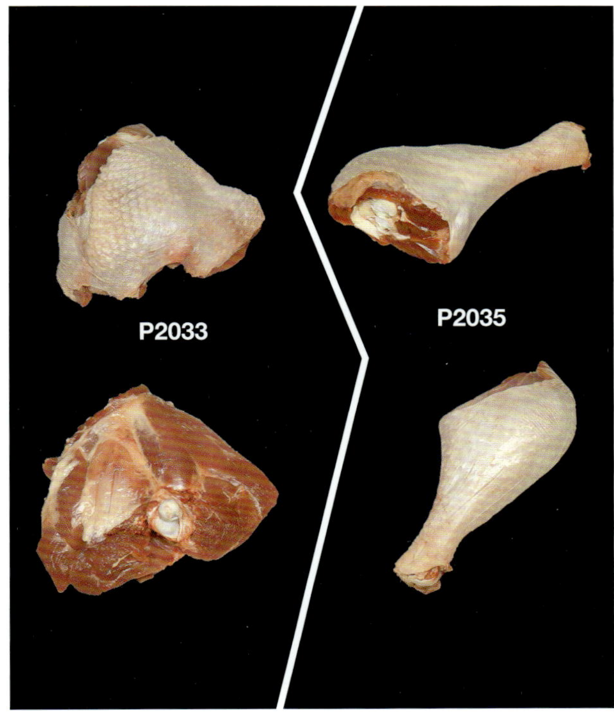

Thighs
Muslos

Drumsticks
Piernas

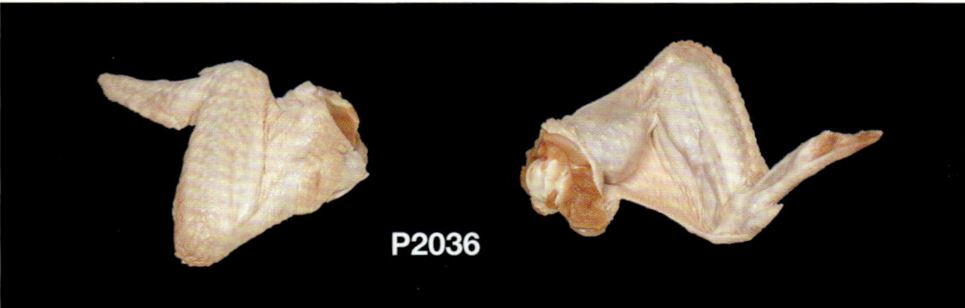

Wings
Alas

Skin-On Boneless Breast
with Rib Meat
Pechuga Deshuesada – con Carne
de Costilla y Piel

Skin-On Boneless Breast
Boneless Skinless Breast
Pechuga Deshuesada, sin Piel

Index/Índice

Turkey Products
Productos de Pavo

Many of the chicken and turkey products shown in the poultry section of *The Meat Buyer's Guide* are also illustrated and referenced in the U.S. Trade Descriptions for Poultry (USTDs), which are maintained by the United States Department of Agriculture, Agricultural Marketing Service, Poultry Programs. The following is a cross reference of products to assist buyers and sellers who use both *The Meat Buyer's Guide* and USTDs when buying and selling poultry.

Muchos de los productos de pollo y pavo que aparecen en la sección de aves de La Guía para Compradores de Carne también se ilustran y detallan en las Descripciones de Comercio de E.U.A. para la carne de ave (USTD, por sus siglas en inglés), que se sustentan mediante los Programas de Aves del Servicio de Mercadeo Agrícola (AMS, por sus siglas en inglés) del Departamento de Agricultura de E.U.A. (USDA, por sus siglas en inglés). A continuación se presenta una referencia cruzada de los productos para ayudar a los compradores y vendedores que utilizan tanto La Guía para Compradores de Carne como las Descripciones de Comercio de E.U.A en la compra y venta de la carne de ave.

ITEM PIEZA	PRODUCT NAME NOMBRE DEL PRODUCTO	USTD STYLE NUMBER	PG. PÁG.
P2001	**Whole Young Turkey with Giblets** Pavo Entero – Cría – con Menudencias	710101	322
P2001	**Whole Young Turkey Cut Up** Pavo Entero – Cría - Cortes	710101	322
P2003	**Young Turkey Front Half** Pavo – Mitad Delantera	710601	322
P2008	**Young Turkey Halves (Half Carcass)** Pavo – Mitades (Media Canal)		322
P2010	**Young Turkey Breast Quarter** Pavo – Cuarto de Pechuga		322
P2011	**Young Turkey Breast Quarter without Wing** Pavo – Cuarto de Pechuga Sin Ala	710704	324
P2012	**Young Turkey Whole Breast with Ribs** Pavo – Pechuga Entera con Costillar	710604	324
P2013	**Young Turkey Whole Breast without Ribs** Pavo – Pechuga Entera sin Costillar ❧ Trimmed Breast / Pechuga Limpia	710614	324
P2014	**Young Turkey Breast Half with Ribs** Pavo – Media Pechuga con Costillar	710701	324
P2015	**Young Turkey Breast Half without Ribs** Pavo – Media Pechuga sin Costillar	710705	324
P2017	**Young Turkey Tenderloin, Whole** Pavo – Filete, Entero	710801	325
P2018	**Young Turkey Tenderloin, Clipped** Pavo – Filete, Recortado	710802	325
P2019	**Young Turkey Scapula Meat** Pavo – Carne de la Escápula	**716011**	325
P2030	**Young Turkey Leg Quarter** Pavo – Cuarto de Pierna ❧ Hind Quarter or Leg, Back Attached / Cuarto Trasero o de Pierna - con Espaldar	710901	325
P2031	**Young Turkey Leg** Pavo – Pierna	711001	325
P2033	**Young Turkey Thigh** Pavo – Muslo	711103	325
P2035	**Young Turkey Drumstick** Pavo – Pierna	711201	326
P2036	**Young Turkey Whole Wing** Pavo – Ala Entera	711301	326
P2040	**Young Turkey V-Wing** Pavo – Ala tipo V ❧ Winglet / Alita	**81303**	326
P2042	**Turkey Neck** Pavo – Cuello	711601	326
P2043	**Young Turkey Giblets** Pavo – Menudencias		326
P2051	**Turkey Testicles (Fries)** Testiculos (fries)	712201	326

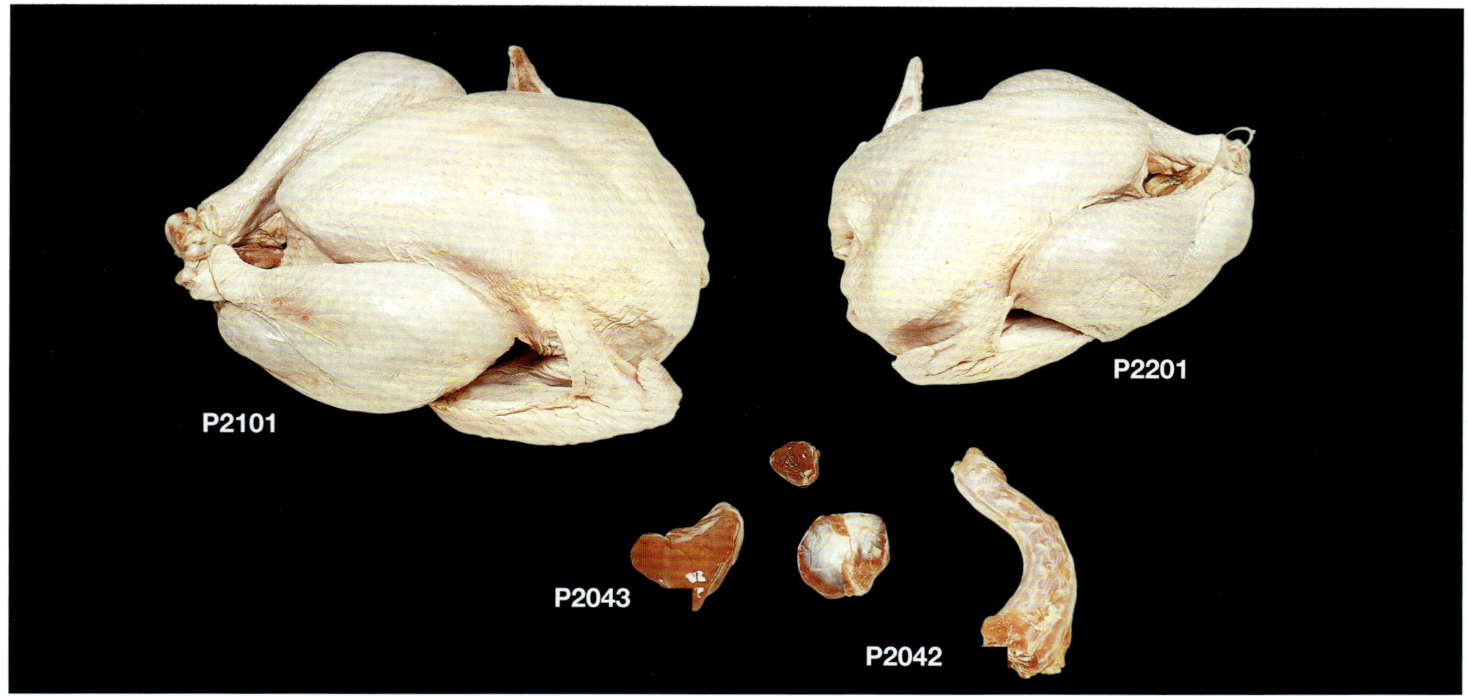

P2000 Young Turkey

Turkeys are generally ordered by weight. Young turkeys are the most commonly available for foodservice. Turkeys are generally between 8 pounds and 24 pounds and are ordered in 2-pound increments.

When specifically ordering a young tom ask for Item No. P2101. When specifically ordering a young hen ask for Item No. P2201.

Young tom Item No. P2101 weight range in pounds:

16–18
18–20
20–22
22–24
24 and up: ask your processor for availability

Young hen Item No. P2201 weight range in pounds:

8–10
10–12
12–14
14–16

P2000 Pavo

Los pavos generalmente se ordenan por peso. Los pavos jóvenes son los más comunes en la industria de los servicios de alimentación. Los pavos generalmente pesan entre 3.5 y 11 kg (8 y 24 libras) y se ordenan por rangos de 1 kg (2 libras).

Cuando pida específicamente un pavo joven macho, solicite una pieza número P2101. Cuando pida específicamente un pavo joven hembra, solicite una pieza número P2201.

Escalas de peso en kg de la pieza número P2101, pavo joven macho:

7–8 kg (16-18 libras)
8–9 kg (18-20 libras)
9–10 kg (20–22 libras)
10–11 kg (22–24 libras)
11 kg (24 libras) y más: consulte la disponibilidad con su procesador

Escalas de peso en kg de la pieza número P2201, pavo joven hembra:

3.5–4.5 kg (8–10 libras)
4.5–5.5 kg (10-12 libras)
5.5–6.5 kg (12-14 libras)
6.5–7.5 (14-16 libras)

P2001 — Whole Young Turkey with Giblets

This item consists of the whole carcass with the giblets and neck normally wrapped or bagged in parchment paper or plastic material. The giblets, which are comprised of the gizzard, heart, and liver, are usually placed inside the crop cavity. The neck is inserted into the body cavity, and the giblets are included in the turkey's net weight.

Whole Young Turkey – Cut Up

Purchasers may request that any amount of whole carcasses be cut up into halves, quarters, front or lower portion, or individual parts. Giblets are included unless specified otherwise.

P2003 — Young Turkey Front Half

This item is produced from a whole carcass by separating intact, from the carcass including the keel and back bones, and a whole or partial wing(s) in one piece by a cut made perpendicular to the backbone. This cut may also be referred to as a hotel breast.

P2008 — Young Turkey Halves (Half Carcass)

Halves may be produced from eviscerated carcasses that include the giblets and neck or from those without giblets (WOG). The halves are also sold individually net weight when requested. Purchasers must specify their preference. The halves are prepared by splitting the carcass from end to end through the back and breast so as to produce approximately equal right and left sides.

- In Canada, young turkey halves shall exclude the neck.

P2010 — Young Turkey Breast Quarter

The breast quarter is the front quarter of the young turkey carcass and consists of a half breast, wing, and back portion attached in one piece.

P2001 — Pavo Entero, Cría, con Menudencias

Esta pieza consiste en la canal entera con las menudencias y el cuello normalmente envueltos o embolsados en papel pergamino o plástico. Las menudencias, que se componen de la molleja, el corazón y el hígado, generalmente se colocan dentro de la cavidad del buche. El cuello se inserta en la cavidad del cuerpo y las menudencias se incluyen en el peso neto del pavo.

Pavo Entero, Cría – Cortes

Los compradores pueden solicitar que cualquier cantidad de canales enteras se corten en mitades, cuartos, porciones delanteras y traseras o porciones individuales. Las menudencias se incluyen a menos que se especifique lo contrario.

P2003 — Pavo, Mitad Delantera

Esta pieza se prepara con una canal entera, separándola de la canal mediante un corte perpendicular al espinazo de forma que incluya la quilla y el espinazo, y un ala entera o parcial. Este corte también puede denominarse como pechuga de hotel.

P2008 — Pavo en Mitades (Media Canal)

Las mitades pueden prepararse con canales sin vísceras que incluyan las menudencias y el cuello o con canales que no tengan menudencias. Las mitades también se venden individualmente por peso neto cuando se solicita. Los compradores deben especificar su preferencia. Las mitades se preparan dividiendo la canal de cabo a rabo a través de la espalda y de la pechuga, de forma que el lado derecho y el lado izquierdo queden aproximadamente iguales.

- En Canadá, las medias canales de pavo deben excluir el cuello.

P2010 — Pavo, Cuarto de Pechuga

El cuarto de pechuga es el cuarto delantero de la canal de pavo joven y consiste en las porciones de media pechuga, ala y porción trasera unidas en una pieza.

General Purchaser Specified Options (PSO) for Turkey
Opciones generales para pavo especificadas por el comprador

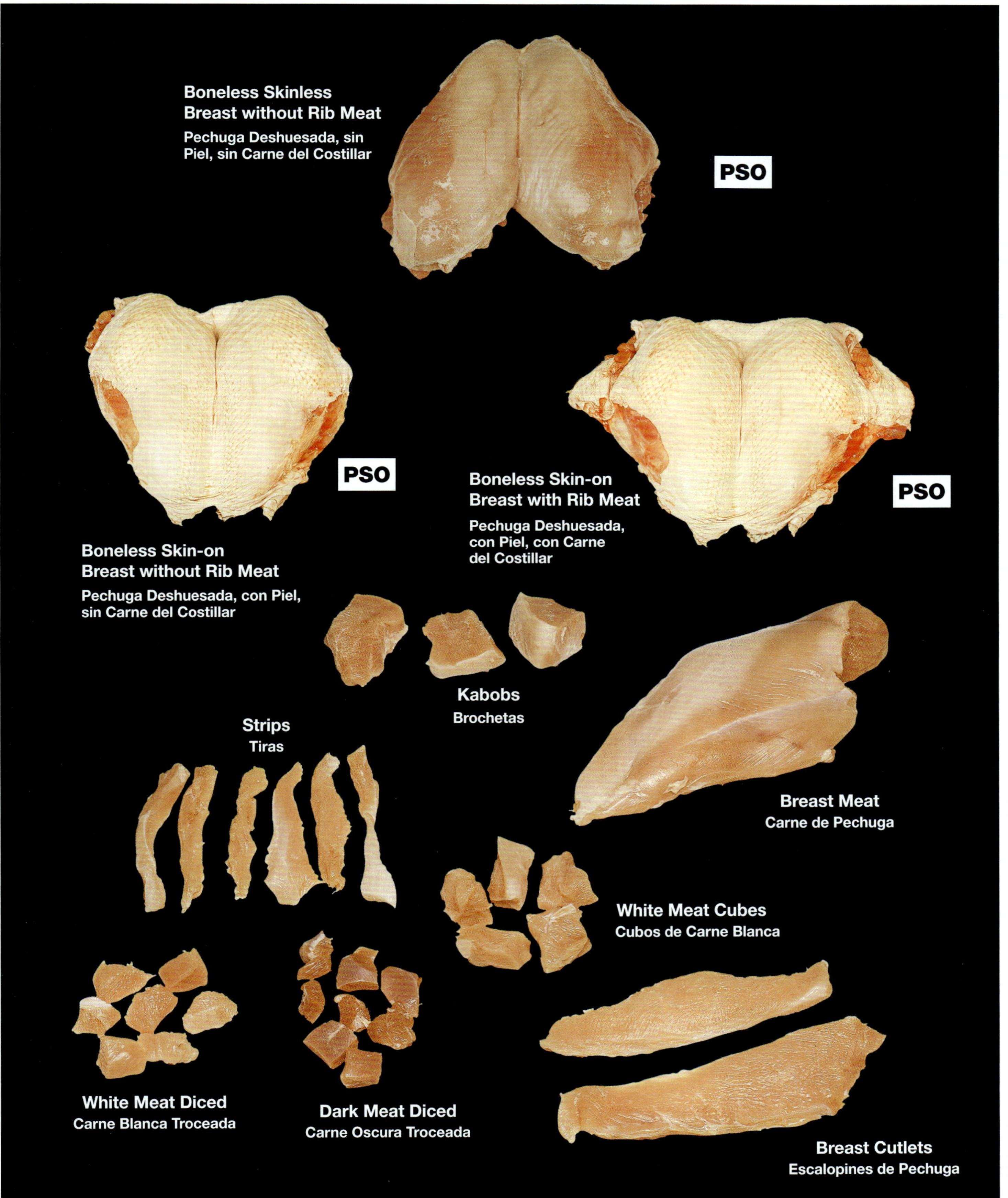

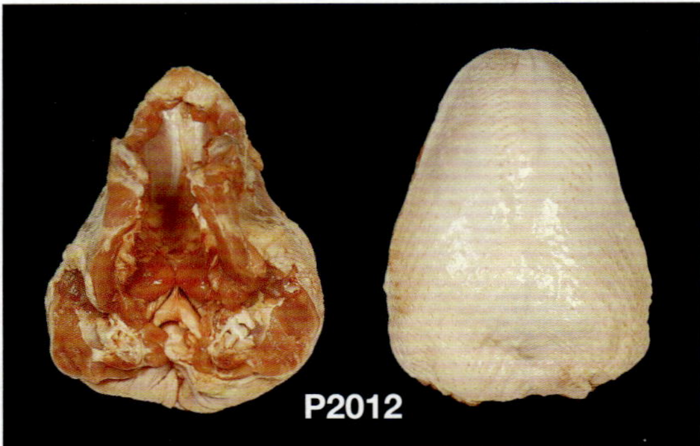

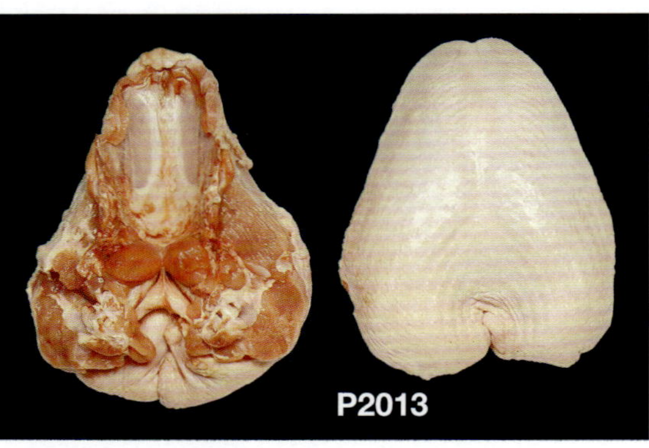

P2011 — Young Turkey Breast Quarter without Wing

The breast quarter without a wing is the same as Item No. P2010 except that the wing portion is excluded.

P2011 — Pavo, Cuarto de Pechuga sin Ala

El cuarto de pechuga sin ala es igual a la pieza número P2010, excepto que se quita la porción del ala.

P2012 — Young Turkey Whole Breast with Ribs

The whole breast with ribs attached is separated from the back of the carcass starting at the shoulder joint and proceeding toward the tail and then downward from the point of the junction of the last *vertebral* and *sternal* ribs. The neck skin will be trimmed below the waddles and may be included up to the whisker. Unless requested by the purchaser that it be excluded, or separated and included, the wishbone portion (see glossary) is left attached. Purchasers may specify the whole breast be split into approximately equal halves.

P2012 — Pavo, Pechuga Entera con Costillar

La pechuga entera con costillar se separa de la espalda de la canal a partir de la articulación de la espaldilla, continuando hacia la cola, y luego hacia abajo desde el punto de unión de las últimas costillas *vertebrales* y del *esternón*. La piel del cuello debe limpiarse debajo de la papada y puede incluirse hasta el bigote. A menos que el comprador solicite que se quite, o que se separe y que se incluya, la porción del hueso de la suerte (ver glosario) se dejará unida. Los compradores podrán especificar que la pechuga entera se divida en mitades aproximadamente iguales.

P2013 — Young Turkey Whole Breast without Ribs

This item is the same as described in Item No. P2012 except that the rib bones are excluded.

* In Canada, this item is referred to as a Trimmed Breast.

P2013 — Pavo, Pechuga Entera sin Costillar

Esta pieza es igual a la pieza que se describe en el número P2012, excepto que se quitan las costillas.

* En Canadá a esta pieza se le denomina Pechuga Limpia.

P2014 — Young Turkey Breast Half with Ribs

The breast half with rib bones attached is produced by cutting through the breastbone (keel) so that the whole breast as described in Item No. P2012 is divided into two approximately equal portions.

P2014 — Pavo, Media Pechuga, con Costillar

La pechuga con el costillar unido se obtiene mediante un corte a través del esternón (quilla), de modo que la pechuga entera como se describe en la pieza número P2012, se divida en dos porciones aproximadamente iguales.

P2015 — Young Turkey Breast Half without Ribs

The half breast without rib bones is produced by cutting through the breastbone (keel) so that the whole breast as described in Item No. P2013 is divided into two approximately equal portions.

P2015 — Pavo, Media Pechuga, sin Costillar

La media pechuga sin costillar se obtiene mediante un corte a través del esternón (quilla), de modo que toda la pechuga como se describe en la pieza P2013, se divida en dos porciones aproximadamente iguales.

P2017 — Young Turkey Tenderloin, Whole

A tenderloin is produced by separating the inner pectoral muscle from the breast and the sternum. The tenderloin consists of a single intact muscle with the embedded tendon.

P2017 — Pavo, Filete, Entero

El filete se obtiene mediante la separación del músculo pectoral interno de la pechuga y el esternón. El filete consiste en un músculo único intacto con el tendón incorporado.

P2018 — Young Turkey Tenderloin, Clipped

A clipped tenderloin is produced by separating the inner pectoral muscle from the breast and the sternum. The protruding portion of the tendon is removed. The tenderloin with tendon clipped consists of a single intact muscle.

P2018 — Pavo, Filete, Recortado

El filete recortado se obtiene al separar el músculo pectoral interno de la pechuga y el esternón. Se quita la porción sobresaliente del tendón. El filete con el tendón recortado consiste en un músculo único intacto.

P2019 — Young Turkey Scapula Meat

Scapula Meat is produced by removing the meat attached to the scapula bone (shoulder blade). The scapula meat consists of boneless white meat.

P2019 — Pavo, Carne de la Escápula

La Carne de la Escápula se obtiene quitando la carne adherida al hueso de la escápula (espaldilla). La carne de la escápula consiste en carne blanca deshuesada.

P2030 — Young Turkey Leg Quarter

The leg quarter is the rear quarter of the young turkey carcass that consists of the drumstick, thigh, and back portion attached in one piece. The part may also include a portion of the tail, abdominal fat, and a section of ribs.

 In Canada, this item is also referred to as a Hind Quarter or as a Leg, Back Attached.

P2030 — Pavo, Cuarto de Pierna

El cuarto de pierna es el cuarto trasero de la canal de pavo que consiste en la pierna, el muslo y una porción trasera unidas en una pieza. La pieza también puede incluir una porción de la cola, grasa abdominal y una sección de costillas.

 En Canadá, esta pieza se denomina Cuarto Trasero o de Pierna, con Espaldar.

P2031 — Young Turkey Leg

The leg consists of the drumstick and thigh attached in one piece with the back and pelvic bone excluded. Purchasers may specify that the leg be disjointed.

PSO Item may be requested boneless.

P2031 — Pavo, Pierna

La pieza consiste en la pierna y el muslo unidos en una sola pieza, sin la porción trasera ni el hueso pélvico. Los compradores pueden especificar que la pierna se desarticule.

PSO La pieza puede solicitarse deshuesada.

P2031

P2033 — Young Turkey Thigh

The thigh is the upper portion of the leg that remains after the drumstick is excluded.

PSO Item may be requested boneless.

P2033 — Pavo, Muslo

El muslo es la porción superior de la pierna que queda después de que se quita la parte inferior de la misma.

PSO La pieza puede solicitarse deshuesada.

P2033

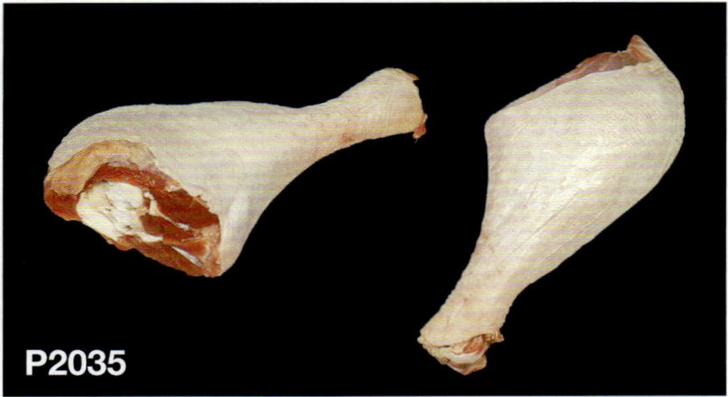

P2035

P2036

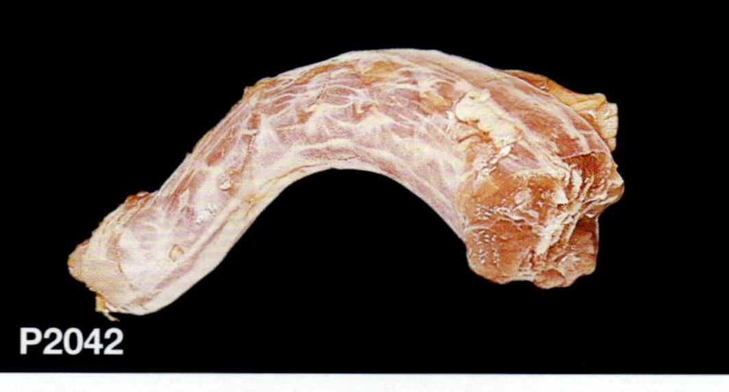

P2042

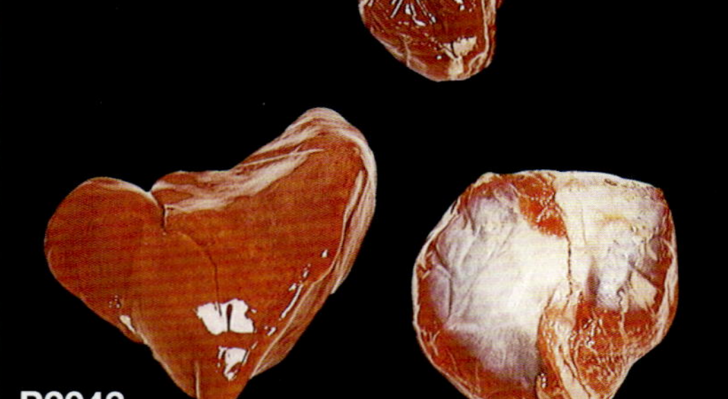

P2043

P2035 — Young Turkey Drumstick

The drumstick is the lower portion of the leg. It is separated from the thigh at the point where the *femur, fibula,* and *tibiotarsus* bones are joined.

P2035 — Pavo, Pierna

Este corte es la parte inferior de la pierna. Se encuentra separada del muslo en un punto donde se juntan los huesos *fémur, fíbula* y *tibio tarso.*

P2036 — Young Turkey Whole Wing

The whole wing consists of three joints or segments. The wing will have all the muscle and skin intact. It is separated from the carcass at the point where it joins the shoulder or *scapula* bone. The first joint of the wing contains the *humerus* bone, the second joint (V-Wing) includes the *ulna* and *radius* bones, and the third is the wingtip. Sellers may provide whole wings with or without the wingtip attached, unless requested otherwise by the purchaser.

P2036 — Pavo, Ala Entera

El ala entera consiste en tres articulaciones o segmentos. El ala tendrá todos los músculos y la piel intacta. Se separa de la canal en el punto donde se une con la espaldilla o la *escápula.* La primera articulación del ala contiene el *húmero,* la segunda articulación (Ala tipo V) incluye el *cúbito* y el *radio,* y la tercera es la punta del ala. Los vendedores pueden proporcionar alas enteras con o sin la punta unida, a menos que el comprador lo solicite de otro modo.

P2040 — Turkey V-Wing

The V-wing is comprised of the second (flat) and third (tip) joints of the whole wing in one piece.

 In Canada, this item is also referred to as a Winglet.

P2040 — Pavo, Ala tipo V

El Ala tipo V se compone de la segunda (trozo plano) y la tercera (punta) articulación del ala en una sola pieza.

 En Canadá, esta pieza también se denomina Alita.

P2042 — Turkey Neck

The neck is separated from the carcass at the shoulder joint and may or may not have neck skin attached.

P2042 — Pavo, Cuello

El cuello está separado de la canal en la articulación de la espaldilla y puede o no tener la piel del cuello adherida.

P2043 — Young Turkey Giblets

The term *giblets* is used to describe an item that consists of hearts, gizzards, and livers. Giblet packages should contain approximately equal numbers of each of these parts, though in processing whole carcasses with giblets a piece from a part or one of the parts itself may be missing from the package.

P2043 — Pavo, Menudencias

El término *menudencias* se utiliza para describir una pieza que consiste en corazones, mollejas e hígados. Los paquetes de menudencias deben contener aproximadamente cantidades iguales de cada una de estas partes, aunque al procesar las canales enteras con menudencias pueda faltar un trozo de una parte o una parte entera en el paquete.

P2051 — Testicles (Fries)

The testicles, which come from male birds, are commonly referred to as *fries.*

P2051 — Testículos (Fritos)

Los testículos, que provienen de las aves macho, se denominan comúnmente *fritos.*

Further-Processed Turkey Products / Productos de Pavo ya Procesados

- **Other Turkey Luncheon Meats – Ready-to-Eat (may be of various formulas and composition)**
  Pastrami
  Salami
  Cooked (Cotto) Salami
  Bologna
  Luncheon Loaf
  Smoked Sausage
  Summer Sausage
  Polish Sausage
  Braunschweiger, etc.

- **Turkey Franks – Ready-to-Eat**
  Regular Franks
  Cheese Franks
  Corndogs
  Chili Franks

- **Batter/Breaded (Raw or Cooked) Turkey Products**
  Nuggets, Sticks or Fingers, Patties, etc.

- **Diced Turkey (Raw or Cooked)**
  White
  Combo
  Dark

- **Ground Turkey Products – Raw**
  Ground Turkey
  Ground Turkey Patties
  Seasoned Ground Turkey (bulk or patties)
  Turkey Sausage (links or patties)

- **Other Fabricated Boneless Raw Turkey Parts**
  Breast Slices/Steaks/Cutlets
  Dark Slices/Steaks/Cutlets
  Turkey Tenders (from any portion of the Breast)

- **Otras Carnes de Pavo para el Almuerzo – Listas para Comer (pueden tener diferentes fórmulas y composiciones)**
  Pastrami
  Salami
  Salami Cocido (Cotto)
  Embutido Boloña
  Pastel de Almuerzo
  Salchicha Ahumada
  Salchicha de Verano
  Salchicha Polaca
  Braunschweiger, etc.

- **Salchichas de Frankfurt de Pavo – Listas para Comer**
  Salchichas de Frankfurt, Regulares
  Salchichas de Frankfurt, de Queso
  Banderillas de Salchicha
  Salchichas de Frankfurt, de Chili

- **Productos de Pavo Rebozados o Empanizados (Crudos o Cocidos)**
  Nuggets, Bastones o Palitos, Hamburguesas, etc.

- **Pavo Troceado (Crudo o Cocido)**
  Carne Blanca, Carne Combinada, Carne Oscura

- **Productos de Carne Molida de Pavo – Crudos**
  Carne Molida de Pavo
  Hamburguesas de Carne Molida de Pavo
  Carne Molida de Pavo Condimentada (a granel o hamburguesas)
  Salchicha de Pavo (ristras o hamburguesas)

- **Otras partes Crudas y Deshuesadas Fabricadas con Pavo**
  Rebanadas/Bistecs/Escalopines de Pechuga
  Rebanadas/Bistecs/Escalopines de Carne Oscura
  Filetes de Pavo (de cualquier porción de la Pechuga)

Further-Processed Turkey Products / Productos de Pavo ya Procesados

Smoked Turkey
Pavo Ahumado

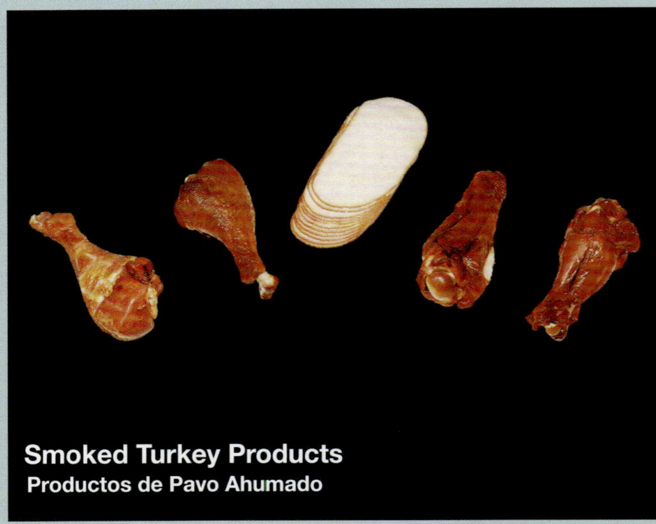

Smoked Turkey Products
Productos de Pavo Ahumado

- **Turkey Roasts – Available Raw or Cooked**

  Natural Shape
  Natural Slab
  Rolled
  Netted
  Breast with skin
  All White with skin
  White Combo (white predominant)
  White and Dark in Natural Proportions
  Dark Combo (dark predominant)
  All Dark
  Seasoned

- **Turkey Rolls – Ready-to-Eat**

  All White
  White Combo (white predominant)
  Dark Combo (dark predominant)
  All Dark

- **Turkey Breast/White Meat Items – Ready-to-Eat**

  Whole Muscle Items
  Chunk and Formed Items
  Chopped and Formed Items

- **Turkey Dark Meat Items – Ready-to-Eat**

  Whole Muscle Items
  Chunk and Formed Items
  Chopped and Formed Items

- **Turkey Ham – Ready-to-Eat**

  Whole Muscle
  Chunk and Formed
  Chopped and Formed
  Smoked
  Water Added

- **Rosbifs de Pavo – Disponibles Crudos o Cocidos**

  Forma Natural
  Trozo Natural
  Enrollados
  En Malla
  Pechuga con Piel
  Solo Carne Blanca con Piel
  Carne Combinada Blanca (predominantemente blanca)
  Carne Blanca y Carne Oscura en Proporciones Naturales
  Carne Combinada Oscura (predominantemente oscura)
  Solo Carne Oscura
  Condimentados

- **Rollos de Pavo – Listos para Comer**

  Solo Carne Blanca
  Carne Combinada Blanca (predominantemente blanca)
  Carne Combinada Oscura (predominantemente oscura)
  Solo Carne Oscura

- **Pechuga de Pavo/ Piezas de Carne Blanca – Listas para Comer**

  Piezas de Músculos Enteros
  Piezas Troceadas y Moldeadas
  Productos Picados y Moldeados

- **Piezas de Carne Oscura de Pavo – Listas para Comer**

  Piezas de Músculos Enteros
  Piezas Troceadas y Moldeadas
  Productos Picados y Moldeados

- **Jamón de Pavo – Listo para Comer**

  Músculo Entero
  Troceado y Moldeado
  Picado y Moldeado
  Ahumado
  Adicionado con agua

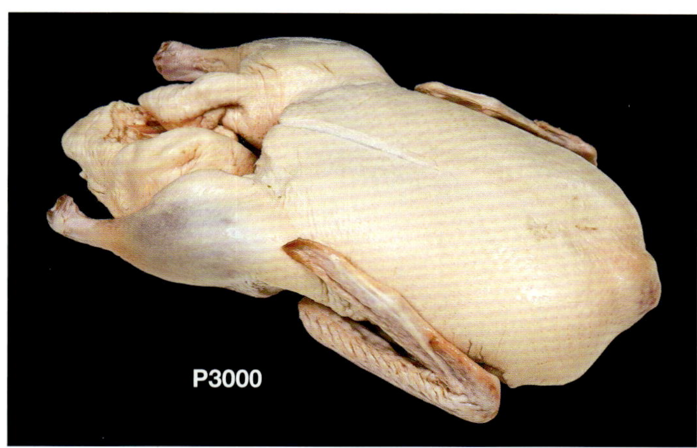

Whole Duck
Pato Entero

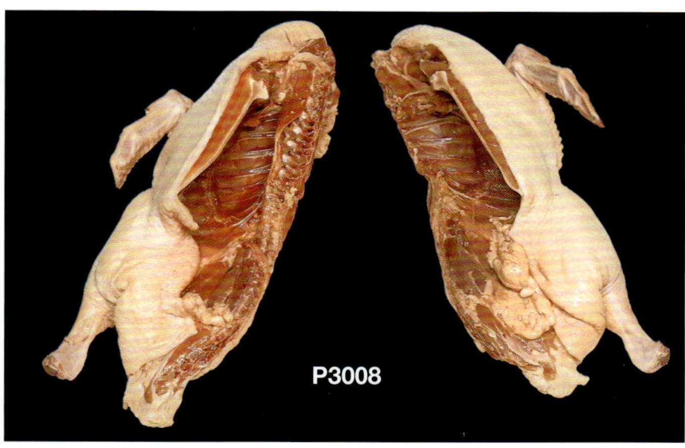

Duck Half
Pato Joven - en Mitades

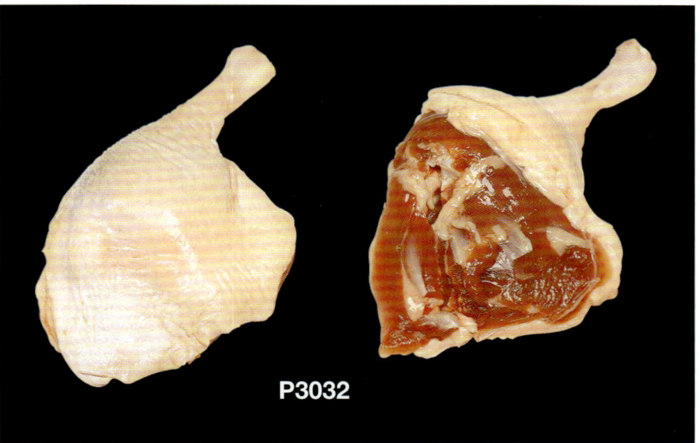

Semi-Boneless Duck Leg
Pato Joven - Pierna Semi Deshuesada

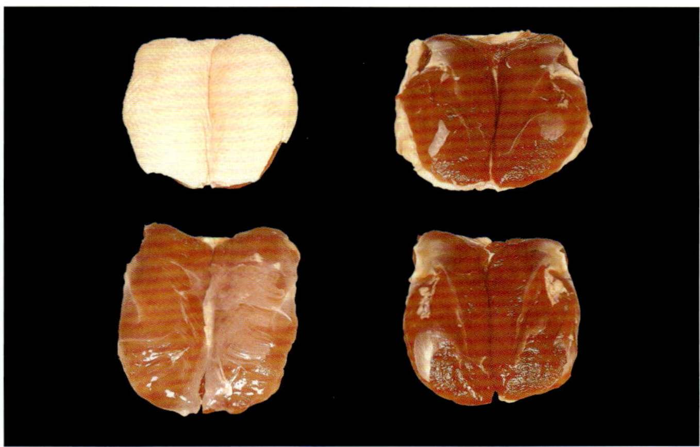

Boneless Duck Breast Meat
Carne de Pechuga de Pato Deshuesada

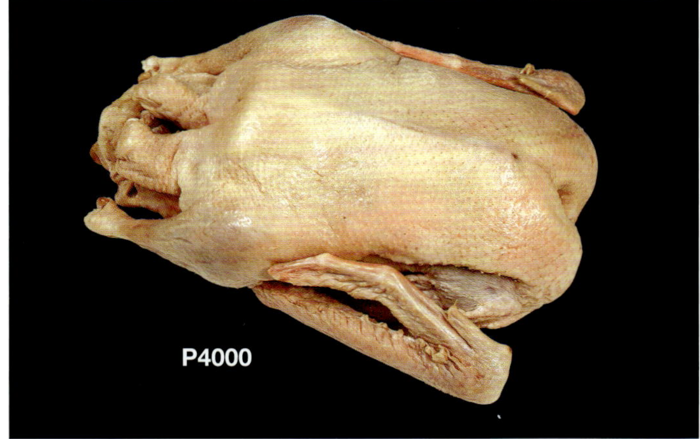

Whole Goose
Ganso Entero

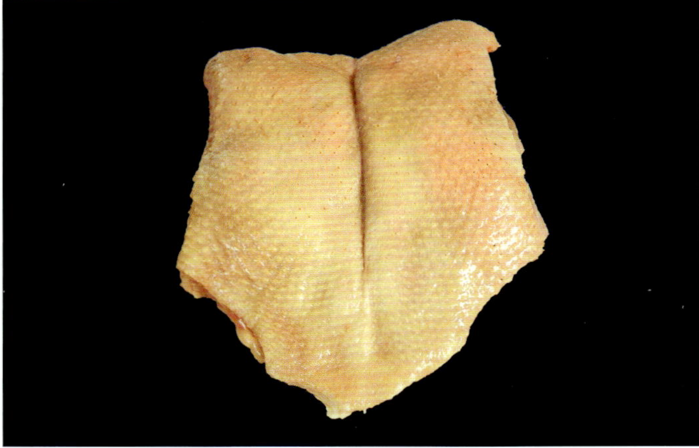

Boneless Skin On Goose Breast
Pechuga de Ganso Deshuesada Con Piel

Classes of Duck / Tipos de pato

P3000 — Duckling (Broiler/Fryer)

P3000 — Pato Joven

The term *duckling* is used in describing younger, tender meat-type ducks. A duckling may be of either sex and usually is between 6 and 8 weeks old. The ready-to-cook (RTC) weight of young ducklings, or broiler ducklings as they are occasionally referred to, range from 3 to 6 pounds. They are primarily produced from strains of the white pekin breed, which were originally imported from China. Though now raised for the most part in the Midwest and the western parts of the United States, early on the production of pekin duck occurred on Long Island, New York, from which the name Long Island Duckling originated. Only ducks from this region may be labeled as such.

Other young ducklings are also produced in limited numbers from domesticated muscovy, mallard, and other imported breeds. Muscovy ducks are originally from South America. Their skin is somewhat pink/white rather than yellowish, and they have fuller-fleshed breasts. Males are larger than females. Pekin and muscovy strains are sometimes crossbred and are called mullard ducks.

El término *pato joven* se utiliza para describir a los patos más jóvenes, con carne más tierna. Un pato joven puede ser de cualquier sexo y generalmente tiene entre 6 y 8 semanas de edad. El peso listo para cocer (RTC) de los patos jóvenes, o patos jóvenes de engorde como se les llama ocasionalmente, varía de 1.4 a 2.7 kilogramos (3 a 6 libras). Se producen principalmente a partir de la raza de patos blancos de Pekín importados originalmente de China. Aunque hoy en día los patos de Pekín se crían fundamentalmente en las regiones norte-centro y occidental del país, anteriormente se criaban en Long Island, Nueva York, de donde se origina el nombre "patos jóvenes Long Island". Solamente los patos de esta región podrán etiquetarse como tales.

También se producen otros patos jóvenes en cantidades limitadas, como el muscovy domesticado, el mallard y otras razas importadas. Los patos muscovy son originarios de América del Sur. Su piel es rosa/blancuzca en vez de amarillenta, y tienen pechugas más carnosas. Los machos son más grandes que las hembras. En ocasiones las razas de patos de Pekín y muscovy se cruzan, y se les llama mullard.

P3100 Roaster Duckling

A roaster duckling is a somewhat older duckling with characteristics similar to those of younger ducklings. They are usually less than 16 weeks old and are of either sex. They have a ready-to-cook weight ranging from 4 to 7 pounds.

P3100 Pato Joven para Asar

Un pato joven para asar es un pato un poco mayor con características similares a la de los patos jóvenes. Generalmente tienen menos de 16 semanas de edad y son de cualquier sexo. Tienen un peso listo para cocer que varía entre 1.8 y 3.2 kilogramos (4 a 7 libras).

P3200 Mature Duck

These are referred to as mature or old duck. They may be of either sex and are normally more than 6 months of age. Their meat is tough in comparison to that from young ducklings and is most often used in processed products.

P3200 Pato Maduro

A estos patos se les llama patos maduros o viejos. Pueden ser de cualquier sexo y generalmente tienen más de 6 meses de edad. Su carne es dura en comparación con la de los patos jóvenes, y se utiliza con frecuencia en productos procesados.

P3001 Whole Ducklings with Giblets

This item consists of the whole carcass with the giblets and neck normally wrapped or bagged in parchment paper or plastic material. The giblets, which are comprised of the gizzard, heart, and liver, are usually stuffed inside the body cavity together with the neck and are included in the duckling's net weight. Due to processing procedures the included giblets or neck or parts thereof are not from the original bird.

P3001 Pato Joven Entero con Menudencias

Esta pieza consiste en la canal entera con las menudencias y el cuello normalmente envueltos o embolsados en papel pergamino o plástico. Las menudencias, que se componen de la molleja, el corazón y el hígado, se ubican dentro de la cavidad del cuerpo junto con el cuello y se incluyen en el peso neto del pato. Debido a los procedimientos de procesamiento, las menudencias, el cuello o parte de los mismos no son del ave original.

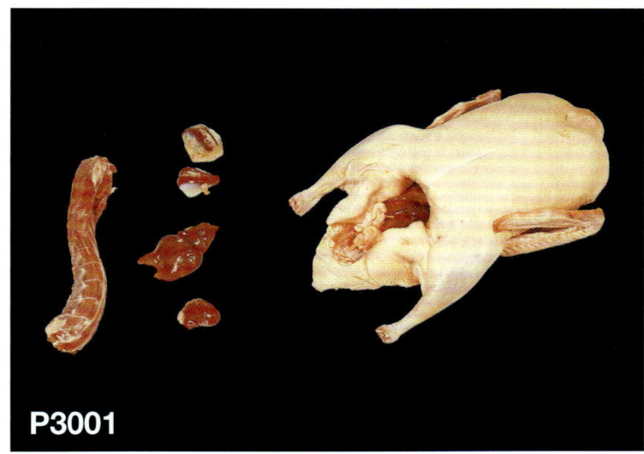

P3001

P3002 Whole Ducklings without Giblets (WOG)

This item is the net weight whole bird without the giblets or neck. The item is frequently referred to as WOG.

Whole Ducklings – Cut Up

Purchasers may specify that the cut up ducklings be produced from birds with or without giblets and necks included. Whole birds may be cut up into halves, quarters, etc. as specified by the purchaser.

P3002 Pato Joven Entero sin Menudencias

Esta pieza consiste en el peso neto del ave entera sin las menudencias ni el cuello. La pieza se denomina comúnmente WOG (sin menudencias, por sus siglas en inglés).

Pato Joven Entero – Cortes

Los compradores pueden especificar que los cortes de pato se preparen con aves con o sin menudencias y cuello incluidos. Las aves enteras pueden cortarse en mitades, cuartos, etc., según lo especifique el comprador.

P3002

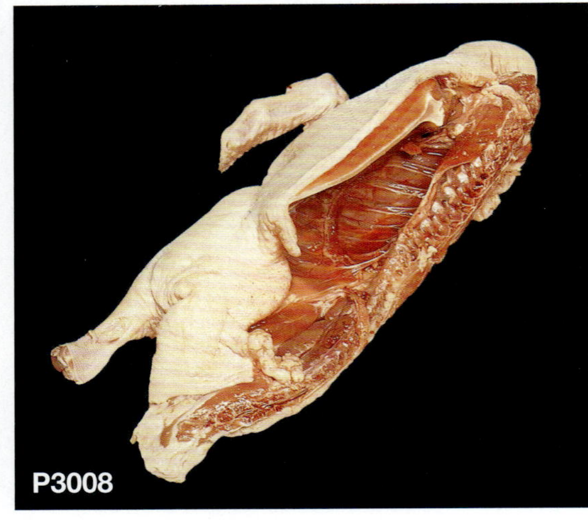

P3008

P3008 Duckling Halves (Half Carcass)

Halves may be produced from eviscerated carcasses that include the giblets and neck or from those without giblets (WOG). They may also be sold net weight as individual halves. Purchasers must specify their preference. The halves are prepared by splitting the carcass from end to end through the back and breast so as to produce approximately equal right and left sides.

P3008 Pato Joven en Mitades (Media Canal)

Las mitades pueden prepararse con canales sin vísceras que incluyan las menudencias y el cuello o con canales que no tengan menudencias. También pueden venderse por peso neto como mitades individuales. Los compradores deben especificar su preferencia. Las mitades se preparan dividiendo la canal de cabo a rabo a través de la espalda y de la pechuga, de modo que el lado derecho y el lado izquierdo queden aproximadamente iguales.

P3009 Duckling Quarters

Quarters are produced from eviscerated whole carcasses that may include the giblets but not the neck or from carcasses without giblets (WOG). The carcass must be cut into four equal parts.

P3009 Pato Joven, Cuartos

Los cuartos se preparan con canales enteras sin vísceras que pueden incluir las menudencias pero no el cuello, o con canales sin menudencias. La canal debe cortarse en cuatro partes iguales.

P3010 Duckling Breast Quarter

The breast quarter is the front quarter of the duckling carcass and consists of a half breast, wing, and back portion attached in one piece.

P3010 Pato Joven, Cuarto de Pechuga

El cuarto de pechuga es el cuarto delantero de la canal de pato y consiste en las porciones de media pechuga, ala y porción trasera unidas en una pieza.

P3011 Duckling Breast Quarter without Wing

The breast quarter without a wing is the same as Item No. P3010 except that the wing portion is excluded.

P3011 Pato Joven, Cuarto de Pechuga sin Ala

El cuarto de pechuga sin ala es igual a la pieza número P3010, excepto que se quita la porción de ala.

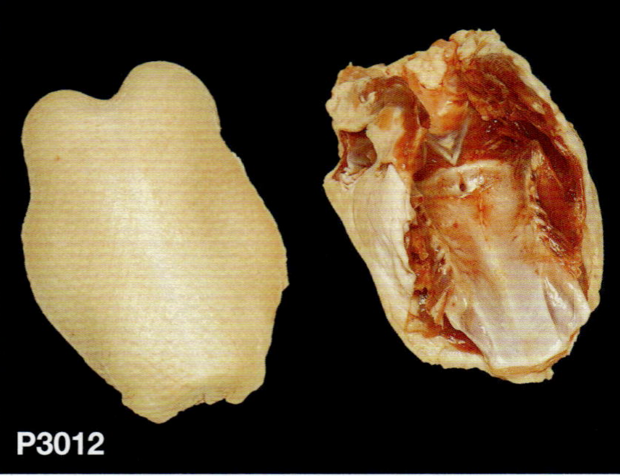

P3012

P3012 Duckling Whole Breast with Ribs

The whole breast with ribs attached is separated from the back of the carcass starting at the shoulder joint and proceeding toward the tail and then downward from the point of the junction of the last *vertebral* and *sternal* ribs. The neck skin will be excluded. Unless requested by the purchaser that it be excluded, or separated and included, the wishbone portion (see glossary) is left attached. Purchasers may also specify the wishbone be removed prior to splitting and included as a separate piece. Purchasers may specify the whole breast be split into approximately equal halves.

P3012 Pato Joven, Pechuga Entera, con Costillar

La pechuga entera con costillar se separa de la espalda de la canal comenzando en la articulación de la espaldilla, continuando hacia la cola, y luego hacia abajo desde el punto de unión de las últimas costillas *vertebrales* y del *esternón*. Se quitará la piel del cuello. A menos que el comprador solicite que se quite, o que se separe y que se incluya, la porción de la espoleta (ver glosario) se dejará unida. Los compradores también podrán especificar que se quite el hueso de la suerte antes de la división y que se incluya como una pieza por separado. Los compradores podrán especificar que la pechuga entera se divida en mitades aproximadamente iguales.

P3013 — Duckling Whole Breast without Ribs

This item is the same as described in Item No. P3012 except that the rib bones are excluded.

P3013 — Pato Joven, Pechuga Entera, sin Costillar

Esta pieza es igual a la pieza que se describe en el número P3012, excepto que se quitan las costillas.

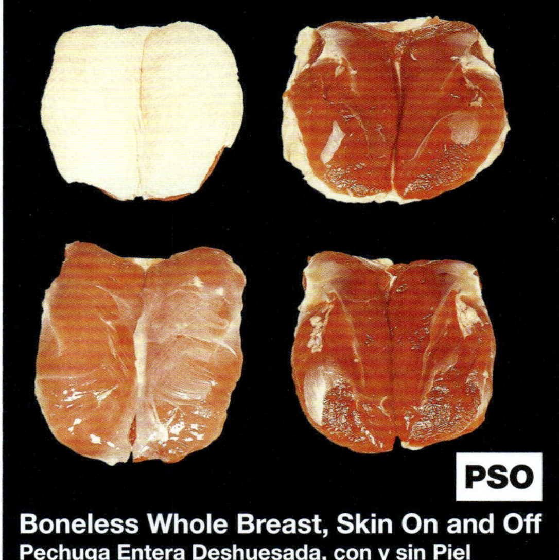
Boneless Whole Breast, Skin On and Off
Pechuga Entera Deshuesada, con y sin Piel

P3014 — Duckling Breast Half with Ribs

The half breast with rib bones attached is produced by cutting through the breastbone (keel) so that the whole breast as described in Item No. P3012 is divided into two approximately equal portions.

P3014 — Pato Joven, Media Pechuga, con Costillar

La media pechuga con costillar se obtiene mediante un corte a través del esternón (quilla) de modo que la pechuga entera como se describe en la pieza P3012, se divida en dos porciones aproximadamente iguales.

P3015 — Duckling Breast Half without Ribs

The half breast without rib bones is produced by cutting through the breastbone (keel) so that the whole breast as described in Item No. P3013 is divided into two approximately equal portions.

P3015 — Pato Joven, Media Pechuga, sin Costillar

La media pechuga sin costillar se obtiene mediante un corte a través del esternón (quilla) de modo que la pechuga entera como se describe en la pieza número P3013, se divida en dos porciones aproximadamente iguales.

P3030 — Duckling Leg Quarter

The leg quarter is the rear quarter of the duckling carcass, which consists of the drumstick, thigh, and back portion attached in one piece. The part may also include a portion of the tail, abdominal fat, and up to two ribs.

P3030 — Pato Joven, Cuarto de Pierna

El cuarto de pierna es el cuarto trasero de la canal de pato que consiste en la pierna, el muslo y una porción trasera unidas en una pieza. La pieza también puede incluir una porción de la cola, grasa abdominal y hasta dos costillas.

P3031 — Duckling Leg

The leg consists of the drumstick and thigh attached in one piece with the back and pelvic bone excluded. Purchasers may specify that the leg be disjointed.

P3031 — Pato Joven, Pierna

La pieza consiste en la pierna y el muslo unidos en una sola pieza, sin la porción trasera ni el hueso pélvico. Los compradores pueden especificar que la pierna se desarticule.

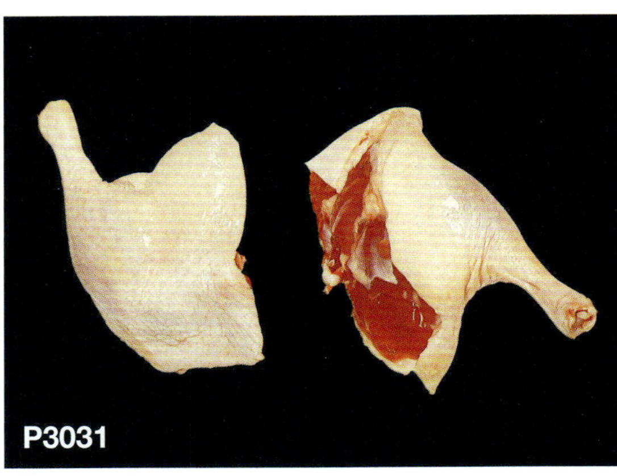

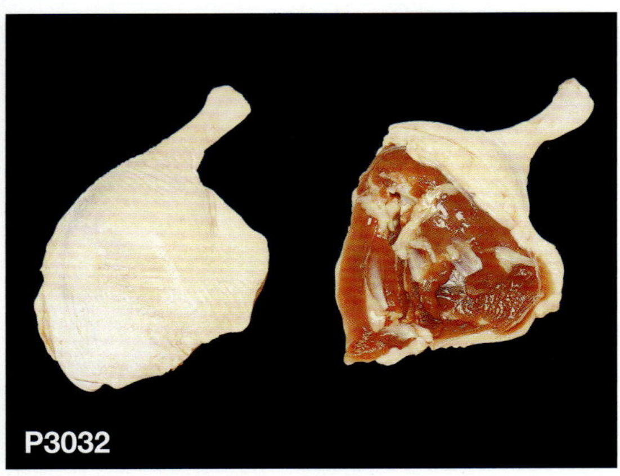

P3032

P3032 Semi-Boneless Duckling Leg

A semi-boneless duckling leg is fabricated from an Item No. P3031 Duckling Leg by removing the *femur* bone and connective cartilage at the knee joint so as to leave the boneless thigh meat firmly attached to the duckling drumstick.

P3032 Pato Joven, Pierna Semi Deshuesada

La pierna semi deshuesada de pato se prepara con la pieza número P3031, Pato Joven, Pierna, quitando el *fémur* y el cartílago conectivo en la articulación de la rodilla a fin de dejar la carne del muslo sin hueso firmemente unida a la pierna del pato.

P3033 Duckling Thigh

The thigh is the upper portion of the leg that remains after the drumstick is excluded.

P3033 Pato Joven, Muslo

El muslo es la porción superior de la pierna que queda después de que se quita la parte inferior de la misma.

PSO

Boneless Duckling Leg
Pato Joven, Pierna Deshuesada

P3035 Duckling Drumstick

The drumstick is the lower portion of the leg. It is separated from the thigh at the point where the *femur*, *fibula*, and *tibiotarus* bones are joined.

P3035 Pato Joven, Pierna

Este corte es la parte inferior de la pierna. Se encuentra separada del muslo en un punto donde se juntan los huesos *fémur*, *fíbula* y *tibio tarso*.

P3036 Duckling Whole Wing

The whole wing consists of three joints or segments. The wing will have all the muscle and skin intact. It is separated from the carcass at the point where it joins the shoulder or *scapula* bone. The first joint of the wing contains the *humerus* bone, the second joint includes the *ulna* and *radius* bones, and the third is the wingtip. Sellers may provide whole wings with or without the wingtip attached, unless requested otherwise by the purchaser.

P3036 Pato Joven, Ala Entera

El ala entera consiste en tres articulaciones o segmentos. El ala tendrá todos los músculos y la piel intacta. Se separa de la canal en el punto donde se une con la espaldilla o la *escápula*. La primera articulación del ala contiene el *húmero*, la segunda articulación incluye el *cúbito* y el *radio*, y la tercera es la punta del ala. Los vendedores pueden proporcionar alas enteras con o sin la punta unida, a menos que el comprador lo solicite de otro modo.

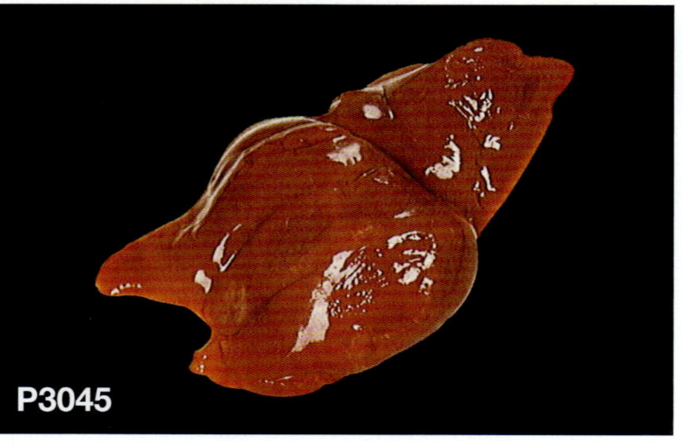

P3045

P3045 Duckling Liver

The liver is a smooth two-lobed organ covered with a thin membrane. One lobe is somewhat larger than the other. It is brownish to reddish or mahogany in color. Though usually sold separately, some processors may sell them mixed together with hearts.

P3045 Pato Joven, Hígado

El hígado es un órgano blando, de dos lóbulos, que se encuentra recubierto con una fina membrana. Un lóbulo es algo más grande que el otro. Su color es café a rojizo o caoba. Aunque por lo general se venden por separado, algunos procesadores pueden venderlos mezclados con corazones.

Duck Specialty Products / Productos especiales de pato

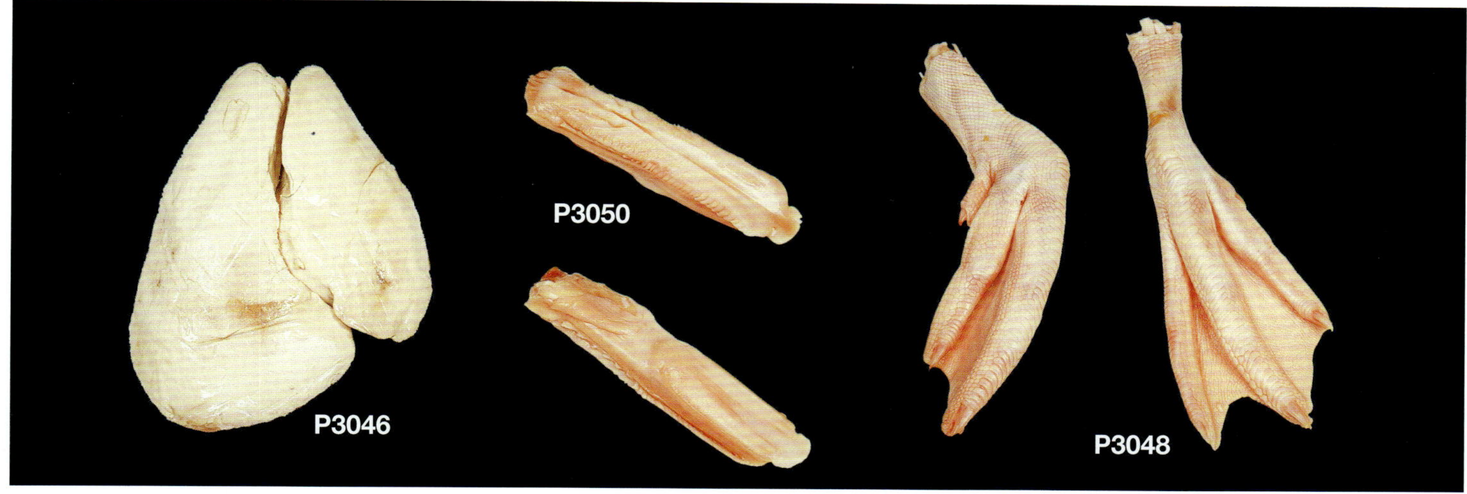

P3046 — Duck Foie Gras

Fat livers of this type are specially produced by force feeding ducklings with a fattening corn-based mixture. The activity of the ducklings is also kept limited so that the livers become enlarged. Their color is beige compared to the livers described in item P3045. The membrane and vein between the two lobes is ordinarily removed. The texture is quite smooth.

P3046 — Pato, Paté de Hígado

Los hígados de este tipo se producen especialmente alimentando a la fuerza a los patos jóvenes con una mezcla de ración de engorde a base de maíz. La actividad de los patos también se restringe para que los hígados se agranden. Su color es beige en comparación con los hígados que se describen en la pieza número P3045. La membrana y la vena entre los dos lóbulos normalmente se quita. La textura es bastante suave.

P3048 — Duckling Paws

The paws are the portions of the feet that contain the claws and webbing between the toes.

P3048 — Pato Joven, Garras

Las garras son las porciones de la pata que contienen las púas y la membrana entre los dedos.

P3050 — Duckling Tongue

The tongue is a very small, light colored muscle in the head of the bird that is attached at the beginning of the *trachea* and *esophagus* area.

P3050 — Pato Joven, Lengua

La lengua es un músculo muy pequeño, de color claro, que se encuentra en la cabeza del ave y está unido al comienzo de la zona de la *tráquea* y el *esófago*.

Further-Processed Items
Piezas ya procesadas

A wide variety of specialty products are made from duckling. Check with your processor for availability and special formulations. The items above represent just two of the many products available.

Una gran variedad de productos especiales se realizan con pato joven. Consulte la disponibilidad y las formulaciones especiales con su procesador. Las piezas que se describen anteriormente son sólo dos de los muchos productos disponibles.

Classes of Geese / Tipos de ganso

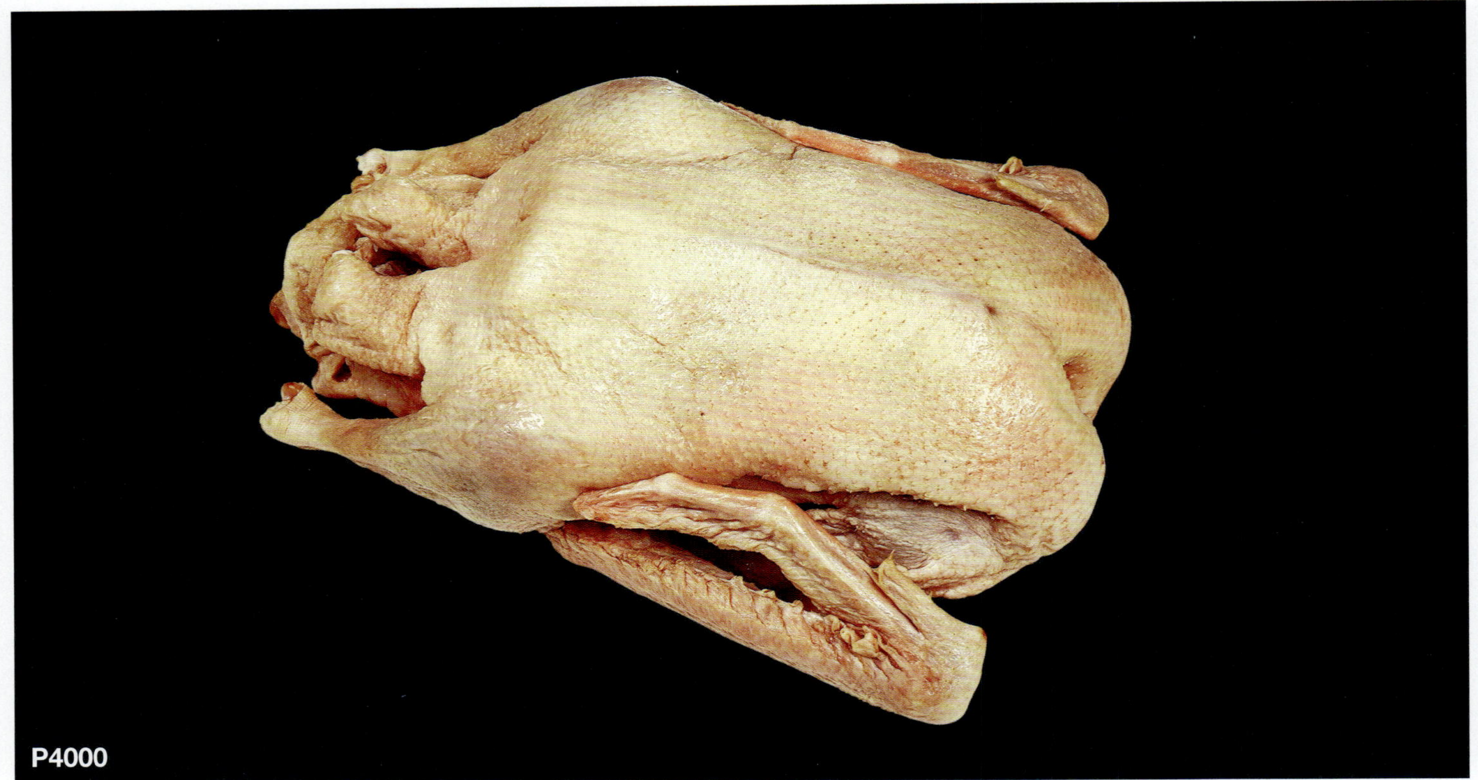

P4000 — Young Goose

A young goose or gosling may be of either sex and usually is from 10 to 16 weeks of age at time of slaughter. Geese are still considered young at 18 to 22 weeks of age. In young geese the windpipe may be easily dented. The most desirable carcasses are well fleshed, tender-meated, not overly fat, uniform in breadth throughout their entire length, and weigh in the range of 10 to 14 pounds. Lighter and heavier weights are also available. Geese are normally available sized in 2-pound increments such as 8 to 10 pounds, 10 to 12 pounds, etc. When frozen at very low temperatures and/or by means of moving air, the skin color is whiter in appearance than if fresh or frozen at usual freezer temperature.

P4000 — Ganso Joven

Un ganso joven puede ser de cualquier sexo y generalmente tiene entre 10 y 16 semanas de edad al momento del sacrificio. Los gansos aún se consideran jóvenes a la edad de 18 a 22 semanas. En los gansos jóvenes la tráquea se puede cortar fácilmente. Las canales más deseables tienen mucha carne tierna y sin mucha grasa, tienen un ancho uniforme a través de todo el largo y pesan entre 4.5 y 6.5 kg (10 a 14 libras). También se encuentran disponibles canales con mayor y menor peso. Los gansos se encuentran disponibles en rangos de 1 kg (2 libras) como por ejemplo de 3.5 a 4.5 kg (8 a 10 libras), de 4.5 a 5.5 kg (10 a 12 libras), etc. Cuando están congelados a muy bajas temperaturas y/o por medio de aire en movimiento, el color de la piel es más blanco que en estado fresco o congelado a una temperatura de congelamiento normal.

P4100 — Mature Goose

A mature or old goose may be of either sex and is usually 25 weeks of age or older. The flesh has toughened and the windpipe has hardened. Much of the added weight is in the form of fat. Larger weights in geese, however, are not necessarily a sign of age, but may be due to how the geese were fed. Mature geese are usually exported as whole carcass or the flesh further processed into specialty products.

P4100 — Ganso Adulto

Un ganso maduro o viejo puede ser de cualquier sexo y en general tiene 25 semanas o más de edad. La carne y la tráquea son más duras. Una gran parte del peso agregado se encuentra en forma de grasa. Sin embargo, un mayor peso en los gansos no necesariamente es un signo de edad, sino que puede deberse a la forma en que el ganso fue alimentado. Los gansos maduros generalmente se exportan como canales enteras o la carne se procesa en productos especiales.

P4001 — Whole Goose with Giblets

This item consists of the whole carcass with the giblets and neck normally wrapped or bagged in parchment paper or plastic material. The giblets, which are comprised of the gizzard, heart, and liver, are usually stuffed inside the body cavity together with the neck and are included in the goose's net weight. Due to processing procedures the included giblets or neck or parts thereof are not from the original bird.

P4001 — Ganso Entero con Menudencias

Esta pieza consiste en la canal entera con las menudencias y el cuello normalmente envueltos o embolsados en papel pergamino o plástico. Las menudencias, que se componen de la molleja, el corazón y el hígado, se ubican dentro de la cavidad del cuerpo junto con el cuello, y se incluyen en el peso neto del ganso. Debido a los procedimientos de procesamiento, las menudencias, el cuello o parte de los mismos no son del ave original.

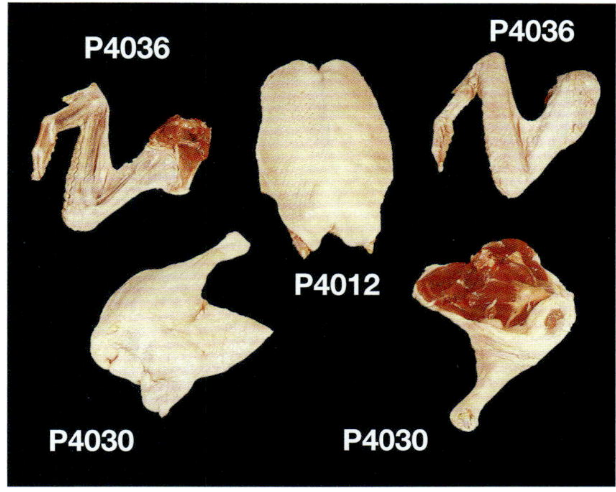

Goose, Cut Up

Purchasers may request that whole birds be cut up into halves, quarters, front or back halves, etc. Giblets are included unless otherwise specified.

Ganso, Cortes

Los compradores pueden solicitar que las aves enteras se corten en mitades, cuartos, mitades delanteras o posteriores, etc. Las menudencias se incluyen a menos que se especifique lo contrario.

P4003 — Goose, Front Half

This item is produced from a whole carcass by separating the whole breast and wings intact in one piece from the carcass by a cut made perpendicular to the backbone. Giblets are excluded.

P4003 — Ganso, Mitad Delantera

Esta pieza se produce con una canal entera separando de la canal la pechuga entera y las alas intactas en una pieza mediante un corte perpendicular al espinazo. Las menudencias se excluyen.

P4004 — Goose, Lower Portion

This item is produced from a whole carcass by separating the rear portion of the carcass, which contains the whole legs, tail, and backbone in one piece, from the front half of the carcass by a cut made perpendicular to the backbone. Giblets are excluded.

P4004 — Ganso, Parte Inferior

Esta pieza se prepara con la canal entera, separando de la mitad delantera la porción trasera de la canal que contiene las piernas enteras, la cola y el espinazo en una sola pieza, mediante un corte perpendicular al espinazo. Las menudencias se excluyen.

P4008 — Goose Halves (Half Carcass)

Halves may be produced from eviscerated carcasses that include the giblets and neck or from those without giblets (WOG). They may also be sold net weight as individual halves. Purchasers must specify their preference. The halves are prepared by splitting the carcass from end to end through the back and breast so as to produce approximately equal right and left sides.

P4008 — Ganso en Mitades (Media Canal)

Las mitades pueden prepararse con canales sin vísceras que incluyan las menudencias y el cuello o con canales que no tengan menudencias. También pueden venderse por peso neto como mitades individuales. Los compradores deben especificar su preferencia. Las mitades se preparan dividiendo la canal de cabo a rabo a través de la espalda y de la pechuga, de modo que el lado derecho y el lado izquierdo queden aproximadamente iguales.

P4009 — Goose Quarters

Quarters are produced from eviscerated whole carcasses that may include the giblets but not the neck or from carcasses without giblets (WOG). The carcass must be cut into four equal parts.

P4009 — Ganso, Cuartos

Los cuartos se preparan con canales enteras sin vísceras que pueden incluir las menudencias pero no el cuello, o con canales sin menudencias. La canal debe cortarse en cuatro partes iguales.

P4010 — Goose Breast Quarter

The breast quarter is the front quarter of the young goose carcass and consists of a half breast, wing, and back portion attached in one piece.

P4010 — Ganso, Cuarto de Pechuga

El cuarto de pechuga es el cuarto delantero de la canal de ganso joven y consiste en las porciones de media pechuga, ala y porción trasera unidas en una pieza.

P4011 — Goose Breast Quarter without Wing

The breast quarter without a wing is the same as Item No. P4010 except that the wing portion is excluded.

P4011 — Ganso, Cuarto de Pechuga sin Ala

El cuarto de pechuga sin ala es igual a la pieza número P4010, excepto que se quita la porción de ala.

P4012 — Goose Whole Breast with Ribs

The whole breast with ribs attached is separated from the back of the carcass starting at the shoulder joint and proceeding toward the tail and then downward from the point of the junction of the last *vertebral* and *sternal* ribs. The neck skin will be excluded. Unless requested by the purchaser that it be excluded, or separated and included, the wishbone portion (see glossary) is left attached. Purchasers may specify the whole breast be split into approximately equal halves. Purchasers may also specify the wishbone be removed prior to splitting and included as a separate piece.

P4012 — Ganso, Pechuga Entera con Costillar

La pechuga entera con costillar se separa de la porción trasera de la canal a partir de la articulación de la espaldilla, continuando hacia la cola, y luego hacia abajo desde el punto de unión de las últimas costillas *vertebrales* y del *esternón*. Se quitará la piel del cuello. A menos que el comprador solicite que se quite, o que se separe y que se incluya, la porción de la espoleta (ver glosario) se dejará unida. Los compradores podrán especificar que la pechuga entera se divida en mitades aproximadamente iguales. Los compradores también podrán especificar que se quite el hueso de la suerte antes de la división y que se incluya como una pieza por separado.

P4013 — Goose Whole Breast without Ribs

This item is the same as described in Item No. P4012 except that the rib bones are excluded.

P4013 — Ganso, Pechuga Entera sin Costillar

Esta pieza es igual a la pieza que se describe en el número P4012, excepto que se quitan las costillas.

Goose Breast, Boneless, Skin On
Ganso, Pechuga, Deshuesada, con Piel

4014 — Goose Breast Half with Ribs

The half breast with rib bones attached is produced by cutting through the breastbone (keel) so that the whole breast as described in Item No. P4012 is divided into two approximately equal portions.

4014 — Ganso, Media Pechuga, con Costillar

La media pechuga con costillar se obtiene mediante un corte a través del esternón (quilla), de modo que toda la pechuga como se describe en la pieza P4012 se divida en dos porciones aproximadamente iguales.

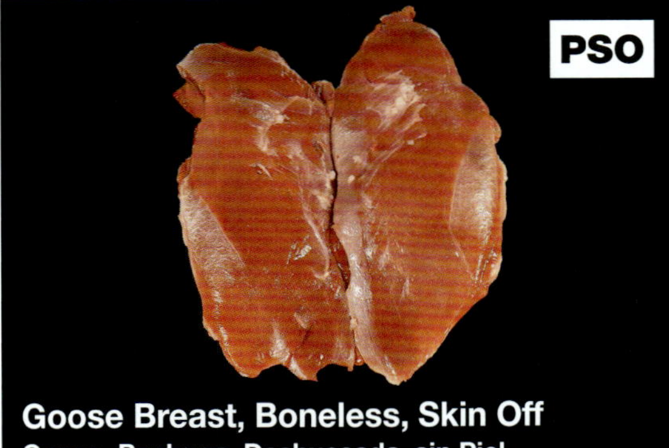

Goose Breast, Boneless, Skin Off
Ganso, Pechuga, Deshuesada, sin Piel

P4015 — Goose Breast Half without Ribs

The half breast without rib bones is produced by cutting through the breastbone (keel) so that the whole breast as described in Item No. P4013 is divided into two approximately equal portions.

P4015 — Ganso, Media Pechuga, sin Costillar

La media pechuga sin costillar se obtiene mediante un corte a través del esternón (quilla) de modo que la pechuga entera como se describe en la pieza número P4013 se divida en dos porciones aproximadamente iguales.

P4030 — Goose Leg Quarter

The leg quarter is the rear quarter of the young goose carcass, which consists of the drumstick, thigh, and back portion attached in one piece. The part may also include a portion of the tail, abdominal fat, and up to two ribs.

P4030 — Ganso, Cuarto de Pierna

El cuarto de pierna es el cuarto trasero de la canal de ganso que consiste en la pierna, el muslo y una porción trasera unidas en una pieza. La pieza también puede incluir una porción de la cola, grasa abdominal y hasta dos costillas.

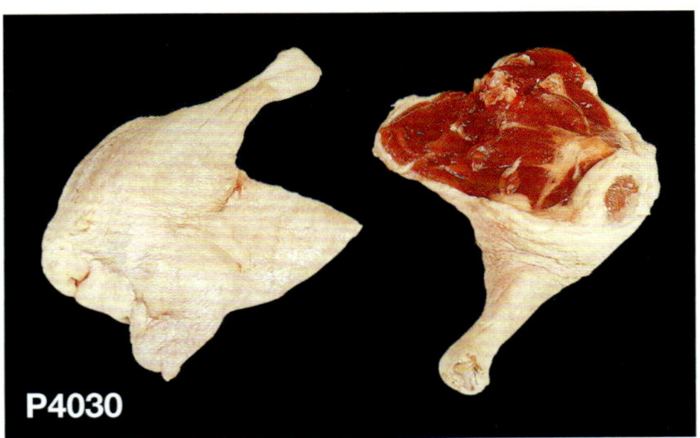

P4031 — Goose Leg

The leg consists of the drumstick and thigh attached in one piece with the back and pelvic bone excluded. Purchasers may specify that the leg be disjointed.

P4031 — Ganso, Pierna

La pieza consiste en la pierna y el muslo unidos en una sola pieza, sin la porción trasera ni el hueso pélvico. Los compradores pueden especificar que la pierna se desarticule.

P4033 — Goose Thigh

The thigh is the upper portion of the leg that remains after the drumstick is excluded.

P4033 — Ganso, Muslo

El muslo es la porción superior de la pierna que queda después de que se quita la parte inferior de la misma.

P4035 — Goose Drumstick

The drumstick is the lower portion of the leg. It is separated from the thigh at the point where the *femur, fibula, and tibiotarus* bones are joined.

P4035 — Ganso, Pierna

Esta pieza es la porción inferior de la pierna. Se encuentra separada del muslo en un punto donde se juntan los huesos *fémur, fíbula y tibio tarso*.

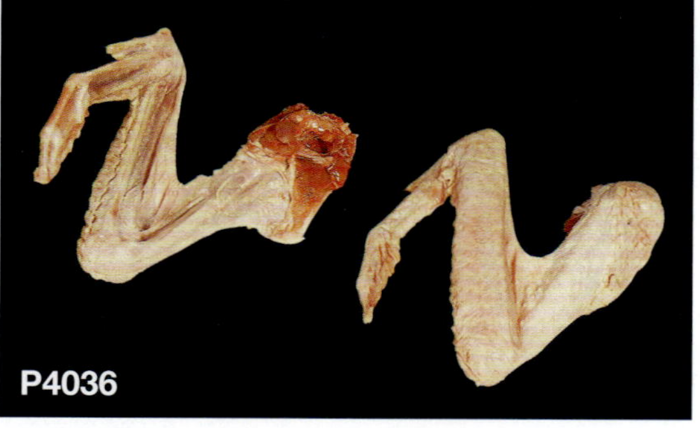

P4036

P4036 — Goose Wing

The whole wing consists of three joints or segments. The wing will have all the muscle and skin intact. It is separated from the carcass at the point where it joins the shoulder or *scapula* bone. The first joint of the wing contains the *humerus* bone, the second joint includes the *ulna* and *radius* bones, and the third is the wingtip. Sellers may provide whole wings with or without the wingtip attached, unless requested otherwise by the purchaser.

P4036 — Ganso, Ala

El ala entera consiste en tres articulaciones o segmentos. El ala tendrá todos los músculos y la piel intacta. Se separa de la canal en el punto donde se une con la espaldilla o la *escápula*. La primera articulación del ala contiene el *húmero*, la segunda articulación incluye el *cúbito* y el *radio*, y la tercera es la punta del ala. Los vendedores pueden proporcionar alas enteras con o sin la punta unida, a menos que el comprador lo solicite de otro modo.

P4043 — Goose Giblets

The term *giblets* is used to describe an item that consists of hearts, gizzards, and livers. Giblet packages should contain approximately equal numbers of each of these parts, though in processing whole carcasses with giblets a piece of a part or a part itself may be missing.

P4043 — Ganso, Menudencias

El término *menudencias* se utiliza para describir una pieza que consiste en corazones, mollejas e hígados. Los paquetes de menudencias deben contener cantidades aproximadamente iguales de cada una de estas partes, aunque al procesar las canales enteras con menudencias pueda faltar un trozo de una parte o una parte entera.

P4045 — Goose Liver

The liver is a smooth two-lobed organ covered with a thin membrane. The lobes are of approximately equal size. It is brownish to reddish in color. Though usually sold separately, some processors may sell them mixed together with hearts.

P4045 — Ganso, Hígado

El hígado es un órgano blando, de dos lóbulos, que se encuentra recubierto con una fina membrana. Los lóbulos son aproximadamente del mismo tamaño. Su color va del café al rojizo. Aunque por lo general se venden por separado, algunos procesadores pueden venderlos mezclados con corazones.

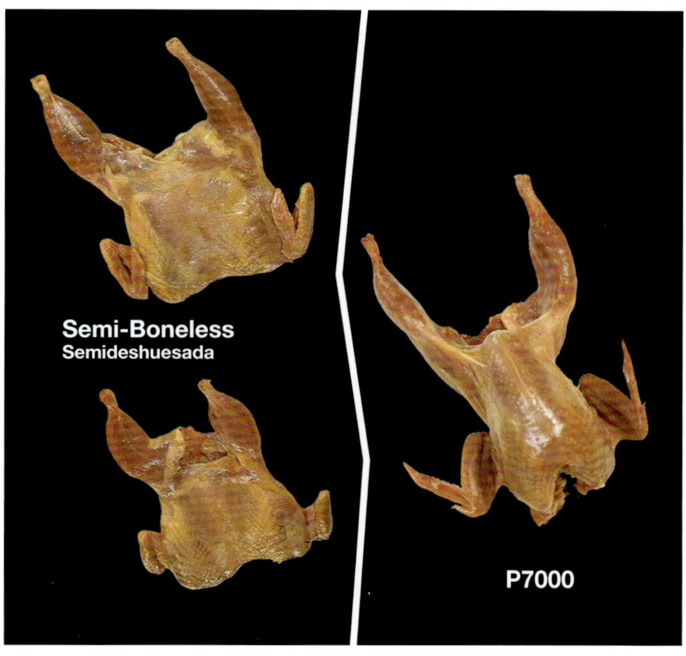

Whole Quail
Codorniz Entera

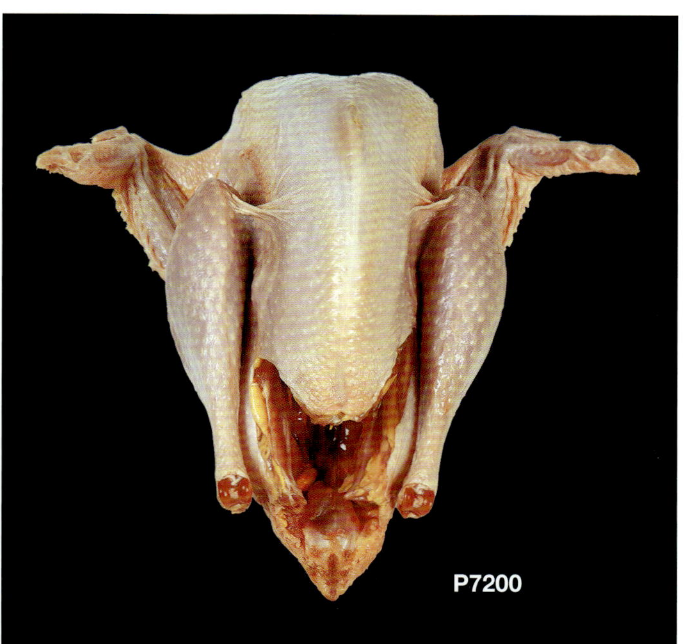

Whole Pheasant
Faisán Entero

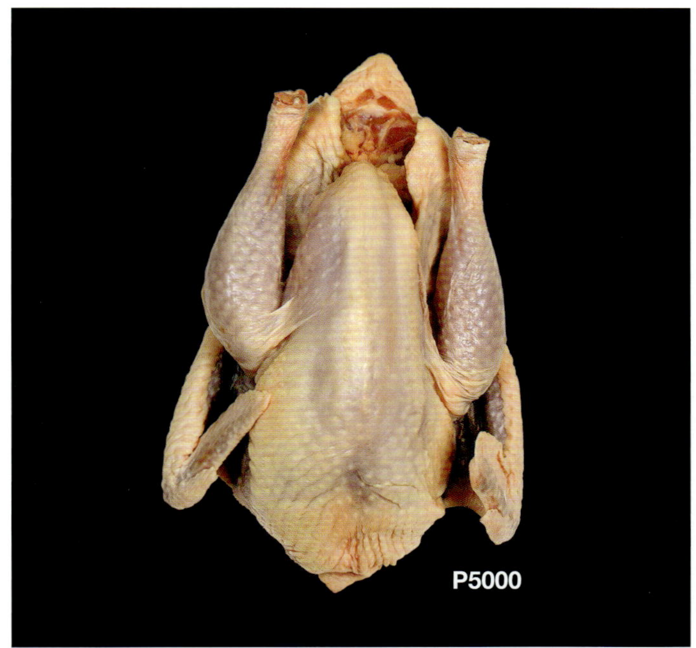

Whole Guinea Fowl
Gallina de Guinea Entera

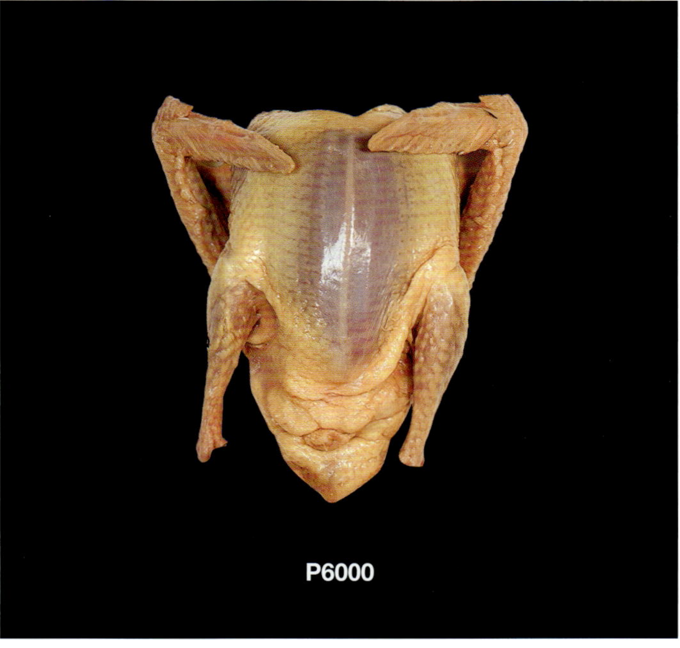

Whole Squab
Palomino (Pichón) Entero

Domesticated Game Birds

There are numerous birds used for food and hunting purposes found in the North America. Some remain in the wild state while some though wild have been domesticated and are farm raised for food or for use on hunting preserves. In many parts of the world almost any variety of bird is used for food.

The terminology noted on the following pages and the carcass parts when available or desired by the meat purchaser may be identified by the same part number and/or options specified for other poultry species in *The Meat Buyer's Guide*.

Aves de Caza Domesticadas

En América del Norte existen diversas aves utilizadas como alimento y para la caza. Algunas permanecen en estado salvaje mientras que otras, si bien salvajes, han sido domesticadas y se crían en granjas como alimento y para uso en reservas de caza. En muchas partes del mundo casi todas las variedades de aves se utilizan como alimento.

La terminología que se utiliza en las páginas siguientes y las partes de la canal cuando se encuentran disponibles o las desea el comprador pueden identificarse mediante el mismo número de parte y/u opciones especificadas para otras especies de aves en *La Guía para Compradores de Carne*.

P5000 — Young Guinea Fowl

Guinea fowl are also referred to as guinea hen or African pheasant. The species originated in western Africa and was later domesticated in other countries. A young guinea fowl may be of either sex and is usually about 11 weeks old.

P5000 — Gallina de Guinea Joven

La gallina de guinea también se denomina ave de guinea o faisán africano. La especie se originó en el oeste de África y luego se domesticó en otros países. Una gallina de guinea joven puede ser de cualquier sexo y generalmente tiene 11 semanas de edad.

P5001 — Whole Young Guinea Fowl with Giblets

This item consists of the whole carcass packaged with the giblets and neck normally wrapped or bagged in parchment paper or plastic material and stuffed inside the body cavity. Due to processing procedures the included giblets or neck or parts thereof are not necessarily from the same bird. A ready-to-cook guinea fowl weighs 2 to 3 pounds, including the gizzard, heart, liver, and neck. The skin is a mottled whitish gray color and the flesh is light red.

Due to their small size, guinea fowl are generally sold as whole carcasses and are normally not processed into parts like chicken and turkey.

P5001 — Gallina de Guinea Joven, Entera, con Menudencias

La pieza consiste en una canal entera empaquetada con los menudencias y el cuello envueltos o embolsados en papel de pergamino o plástico, y ubicados dentro de la cavidad del cuerpo. Debido a los procedimientos de procesamiento, las menudencias, el cuello o parte de los mismos no son necesariamente de la misma ave. Una gallina de guinea lista para cocinar pesa entre 0.9 y 1.35 kilogramos (2 a 3 libras), incluyendo la molleja, el corazón, el hígado y el cuello. La piel es de color gris blancuzco manchada y la carne de color rojo claro.

Debido a su pequeño tamaño, las gallinas de guinea generalmente se venden como canales enteras y generalmente no se procesan en partes como el pollo y el pavo.

P5000

Young Guinea Fowl – 5-Piece Cut-Up
Gallina de Guinea Joven – 5 piezas

P5016 — Guinea Fowl Airline Breast

This item is a boneless half breast skin on with the first wingjoint attached. It weighs 6 to 9 ounces. The airline style is also available in a "double breast" with the first wing joint attached on each side.

P5016 — Gallina de Guinea, Pechuga para Aerolínea

Esta pieza es una media pechuga deshuesada, con piel, y con la coyuntura de la primera ala unida. Pesa entre 170 y 250 gramos (6 a 9 onzas). El estilo para aerolínea también está disponible en una "pechuga doble", con la coyuntura de la primera ala unida a cada lado.

P5030 — Guinea Fowl Leg Quarter

The leg quarter is the rear quarter of the guinea fowl carcass that consists of the drumstick, thigh, and back portion attached in one piece. The part may also include a portion of the tail, abdominal fat, and up to two ribs.

P5030 — Gallina de Guinea, Cuarto de Pierna

El cuarto de pierna es el cuarto trasero de la canal de la gallina de guinea que consiste en la pierna, el muslo y una porción trasera unidas en una pieza. La pieza también puede incluir una porción de la cola, grasa abdominal y hasta dos costillas.

P6001

P6000 Squab (Young Pigeon)

Squab are young pigeons and are approximately 28 to 30 days old when processed. They may be of either sex. The species originated in the Middle East and Asia and is one of the oldest birds known to humans. In the United States most of the available squab is from domesticated stock. They are commercially raised and have never flown.

P6000 Palomino (Pichón)

Los palominos son ejemplares jóvenes que tienen aproximadamente 28 a 30 días cuando son procesados. Pueden ser de cualquier sexo. La especie originada en Oriente Medio y Asia es una de las aves más antiguamente conocidas por los humanos. En Estados Unidos, la mayoría de los palominos disponibles provienen de existencias domesticadas. Son criados comercialmente y nunca han volado.

P6001 Whole Squab (Young Pigeon) with Giblets

The item is sold with the giblets wrapped or bagged and stuffed inside the body cavity or as a whole carcass. A ready-to-cook squab weighs 12 to 16 ounces, including the gizzard, heart, liver, and neck. The skin is a mottled whitish color, and the flesh is tender and dark in color.

Normally, the most commonly available part is a partially boneless, skin-on whole carcass with attached wings and all bones other than the *femur* bones excluded. Partially boneless carcasses weigh 9 to 14 ounces.

P6001 Palomino Entero (Pichón) con Menudencias

La pieza se vende con las menudencias envueltas o embolsadas ubicadas dentro de la cavidad del cuerpo o como una canal entera. Un palomino listo para cocinar pesa entre 350 y 450 gramos (12 a 16 onzas), incluyendo la molleja, el corazón, el hígado y el cuello. La piel es de color blanco manchado y la carne es tierna y de color oscuro.

Generalmente, la parte que se encuentra disponible más comúnmente es una canal entera deshuesada y con piel, con las alas unidas y sin ningún hueso, a excepción de los huesos del *fémur*. Las canales parcialmente deshuesadas pesan entre 250 y 400 gramos (9 a 14 onzas).

P6016 Squab Airline Breast

This item is a boneless half breast skin on with the first wing joint attached. It is also available in a "double breast" with the first wing joint attached on each side.

P6016 Palomino, Pechuga para Aerolínea

Esta pieza es una media pechuga deshuesada, con piel y con la coyuntura de la primera ala unida. También está disponible en una "pechuga doble" con la coyuntura de la primera ala unida a cada lado.

P7000 Quail

Quail is one of the more popular game birds eaten in the United States. In some instances the names *quail* and *partridge* are used interchangeably, but primarily the term quail is used to identify the species. (For more information on partridge, see Item No. P7400 Partridge). The common quail originated in Europe and seasonally migrates into Africa and India. There are now a number of other varieties of quail found and identified around the world.

P7000 Codorniz

La codorniz es una de las aves de caza que más se come en Estados Unidos. En algunos casos, los nombres *codorniz* y *perdiz* se utilizan de forma indistinta, pero fundamentalmente se utiliza el término codorniz para identificar la especie. (Para obtener más información sobre la perdiz, vea la pieza número P7400, Perdiz). La codorniz común es originaria de Europa y migra por temporadas a África e India. Existen actualmente otras variedades de codorniz que se encuentran e identifican en todo el mundo.

P7001 — Whole Quail

This item consists of the whole carcass packaged with the giblets and neck normally wrapped or bagged in parchment paper or plastic material and stuffed inside the body cavity. Due to processing procedures the included giblets or neck or parts thereof are not necessarily from the same bird. The skin is whitish in color. A ready-to-cook quail weighs approximately 3 to 7 ounces, including the gizzard, heart, liver, and neck.

P7001 — Codorniz Entera

La pieza consiste en una canal entera empaquetada con los menudencias y el cuello envueltos o embolsados en papel de pergamino o plástico, y ubicados dentro de la cavidad del cuerpo. Debido a los procedimientos de procesamiento, las menudencias, el cuello o parte de los mismos no son necesariamente de la misma ave. La piel es de color blancuzco. Una codorniz lista para cocinar pesa entre 85 y 200 gramos (3 a 7 onzas) aproximadamente, incluyendo la molleja, el corazón, el hígado y el cuello.

P7001 Whole Quail
Codorniz Entera

P7100 — Pharoah Quail

The Pharoah species was imported from Europe and has been scientifically bred to produce consistent quality and has a mixture of white and dark meat. Today the European variety is the one most widely found in the United States.

P7100 — Codorniz Faraona

La especie faraona se importó de Europa y se crió científicamente para producir una calidad constante. Tiene una mezcla de carne blanca y oscura. Hoy en día, la variedad europea es la que se encuentra más comúnmente en Estados Unidos.

Quail Specialty Items

Semi-Boneless (European Style) Quail

This item, also referred to as sleeve-boned, is a partially boneless, skin-on whole carcass with attached wings and all bones other than the femur bones excluded.

PSO Boneless Quail Breast

Check with your supplier for availability.

Piezas especiales de codorniz

Codorniz (Estilo Europeo) Semi Deshuesada

Esta pieza, también llamada funda semi deshuesada, es una canal entera, semi deshuesada, con piel, con las alas unidas y todos los huesos, a excepción de los huesos del fémur.

PSO Codorniz - Pechuga Deshuesada

Consulte la disponibilidad con su proveedor.

Semi-Boneless (European Style) Quail
Codorniz (Estilo Europeo) Semi Deshuesada

P7200 — Pheasant

The species was first found in the Far East but is now quite common worldwide. It was originally wild or home raised. It is still found in the wild but in the United States most pheasant are domestically raised either for the food industry or for use on hunting preserves. Pheasants are classified as young or mature by their age. There are presently more than 50 different breeds of pheasant.

P7200 — Faisán

La especie fue encontrada por primera vez en el Extremo Oriente, pero ahora es bastante común en todo el mundo. Originalmente era salvaje o se criaba domésticamente. Todavía se encuentran en estado salvaje, pero en Estados Unidos la mayoría de los faisanes se crían de forma doméstica, ya sea para la industria de la alimentación o para su uso en las reservas de caza. Los faisanes se clasifican como jóvenes o maduros según su edad. En la actualidad, hay más de 50 razas diferentes de faisán.

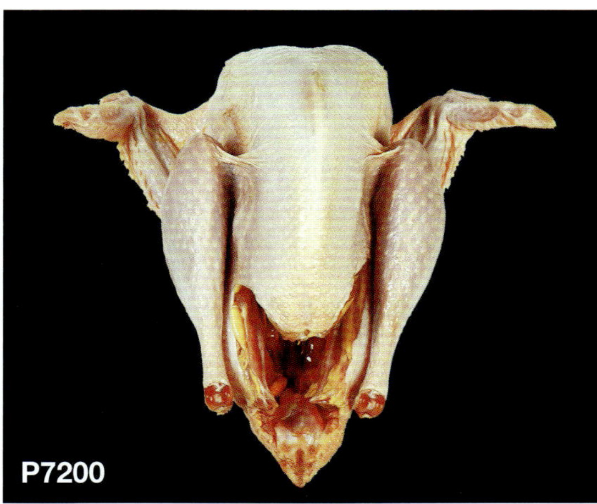

P7200

P7202 Whole Pheasant

Pheasants are sold both as whole carcasses or processed into various parts. A ready-to-cook pheasant weighs 1.75 to 4 pounds. The breast meat is white and leg meat is dark colored. The breast meat is the most popular portion since the pheasant legs, unlike those of the guinea fowl, have tendons.

P7202 Faisán Entero

Los faisanes se venden tanto en canales enteras como procesados en varias partes. Un faisán listo para cocinar pesa entre 0.8 y 1.8 kg (1.75 a 4 libras). La carne de la pechuga es blanca y la de la pierna es oscura. La carne de la pechuga es la porción más popular, ya que las piernas de faisán, a diferencia de las de la gallina de guinea, tienen tendones.

P7300 Baby Pheasant

Baby pheasant are normally 12 to 16 weeks of age and weigh approximately 14 to 20 ounces. Pheasant produced especially for the foodservice or retail marketplace have been bred so as to provide larger breasts and clearer flesh.

P7300 Faisán, Cría

Las crías de faisán normalmente tienen de 12 a 16 semanas de edad y pesan aproximadamente de 400 a 600 gramos (14 a 20 onzas). El faisán producido especialmente para la industria de servicios de alimentación o el mercado minorista ha sido criado para proporcionar pechugas más grandes y una carne más clara.

P7316 Pheasant Airline Breast

This item is a boneless half breast skin on with the first wing joint attached. It weighs 6 to 10 ounces. The airline style is also available in a "double breast" with the first wing joint attached on each side.

P7316 Faisán, Pechuga para Aerolínea

Esta pieza es una media pechuga deshuesada, con piel y con la coyuntura de la primera ala unida. Pesa entre 170 y 280 gramos (6 a 10 onzas). El estilo para aerolínea también está disponible en una "pechuga doble", con la coyuntura de la primera ala unida a cada lado.

P7316

P7400 — Partridge

There are no native partridge species in the United States, though other species, some nearly extinct, including the grouse, are substituted as partridge when available. The terms *partridge* and *quail* are sometimes interchangeable. Most partridge available in the market are derived from European or African varieties. Partridge are identified as young up to a year and are considered mature once they are more than 15 months old. Due to their small size, partridge are generally sold as whole carcasses and are not processed into parts like chicken and turkey.

P7400 — Perdiz

No existen especies nativas de perdices en Estados Unidos, sin embargo otras especies, algunas casi extintas, incluyendo el urogallo, sustituyen a la perdiz cuando están disponibles. Los términos *perdiz* y *codorniz* son intercambiables en ocasiones. La mayoría de las perdices disponibles en el mercado se derivan de variedades europeas o africanas. Las perdices se identifican como jóvenes hasta el primer año y se consideran maduras una vez que tienen más de 15 meses de edad. Debido a su pequeño tamaño, las perdices generalmente se venden como canales enteras y no se procesan en partes como el pollo y el pavo.

P7400 — Common or Grey Partridge

This is a European species found as far away as the Middle East. Many were imported from Hungary and raised in England and are of the same species as the common or grey partridge. This variety is also sometimes referred to as *Hungarian partridge.*

P7400 — Perdiz Común o Gris

Esta es una especie europea que se encuentra incluso hasta en el Medio Oriente. Muchas fueron importadas de Hungría y criadas en Inglaterra y son de la misma especie que la perdiz común o gris. En ocasiones, a esta variedad también se le llama *perdiz húngara.*

P7500 — Chukar

This partridge species is found from Asia minor to China and in the mountains of India. The various partridge of the species are different in size and plumage depending on the climate in which they were found.

P7500 — Perdiz de Chukar

Esta especie de perdiz se encuentra desde Asia Menor hasta China y en las montañas de India. Las diferentes perdices de esta especie varían en tamaño y plumaje, dependiendo del clima en el que se encuentren.

Glossary

Note: All Item Nos. refer to the NAMP *The Meat Buyer's Guide*.

A

Aging – A process by which beef is held under controlled temperatures for a period of time. This allows enzymatic activity to degrade complex proteins, changing flavor and tenderness. See also Dry Aging and Wet Aging.

AMS – Agricultural Marketing Service, USDA.

Anterior to – Toward the front of the carcass, or forward of.

Asian Style – This item, also referred to as traditional Asian Style refers most commonly to ducklings and is a carcass processed as a whole animal except that the head and feet are left intact.

A.P. (As-Purchased) – The condition or cost of an item as it is purchased or received from a supplier.

A.S. (As-Served) – The weight or size of a food item as sold or served after processing or cooking.

B

Baby Back Ribs – Smaller sizes of back ribs from pork loins.

Backstrap – The elastic yellowish color connective tissue running from the neck through the rib region of beef, veal, and lamb.

Bake – To cook by dry heat. When applied to meat, it is called roasting.

Ball Tip – Also referred to as Ball or Butcher's Heart. See Item No. 185B.

Barbecue – To roast meat slowly on a grill, spit, or over coals. While cooking, meat is usually basted with a sauce.

Baron of Beef – A descriptive name of bone in beef round items from Item Nos. 160 to 166B that are generally of large size and used for roasting. Also referred to as Steamship Round.

Bar Round – Boneless rump, shank, and heel-off round tied girthwise and lengthwise.

Baseball Cut – The dorsal side of the center cut beef sirloin top butt. See Item No. 184F. The steak from this cut may be called a baseball steak or filet style steak. See Item No. 1184F.

Baste – To moisten meat with a liquid while cooking, to add flavor and to prevent drying of the surface.

BBQ Ribs – Ribs from all species prepared by barbecuing.

Binders – Approved edible substances used for stabilizing, binding, and changing texture and shape of food.

Blade Meat – The lean meat overlying the ribeye and rib portion of the primal rib. Also referred to as false meat, rib lifter meat, cap meat, or wedge meat. See Item No. 109B.

Blast Frozen – Products are frozen rapidly at extremely low temperatures (–10° F or lower) in conjunction with high-velocity air movement around the product.

Block Ready – A cut that is sold ready for further processing or portioning.

Bob Veal, Bobby – Meat of very young (usually less than 21 days) beef and dairy animals.

Boil – To cook in water or other liquid, in which bubbles rise continually and break on the surface.

Boned Breasts (Poultry) – Sometimes labeled cutlets. One hundred percent edible light meat. Boneless breasts may or may not include skin; cutlets normally are sold without skin.

Braise – To brown meat in a small amount of fat, then cook slowly in a covered utensil in a small amount of liquid.

Breaded – Product that is coated with less than 30 percent of an edible substance, usually flour or bread crumbs. Product may first be dipped in a batter to enhance the adherence of the breading.

Breaded and Pre-browned (Breading Set in Hot Oil) – Uncooked breaded products with the breading set in hot oil must state "ready to cook" or some other term to indicate the product is not cooked or show cooking instructions on the label.

Brochette Meat – Cubes of meat (beef, veal, pork, lamb) ordinarily put on a skewer and cooked by broiling. Also referred to as Kabob Meat.

Broil – To cook by direct heat. Grill.

Broilers – Young chickens produced for meat. The terms broilers and fryers are interchangeable.

Broilers for Deboning – Six to eight pounds ready-to-cook weight basis, that are hand-deboned for nuggets, patties, strips, and similar boneless products.

BRT – Boned, rolled, and tied (or netted).

Buffalo Wings – Deep-fried chicken wings typically served with a hot sauce and a blue cheese dressing. The wing is prepared by separating the drummette and midjoint and removing the wing tip.

Butcher's Heart – See Ball Tip.

Butterfly – To split steaks, chops, cutlets, and roasts in half, leaving halves hinged on one side.

Button – Soft white tips of cartilage on the dorsal end of the vertical spinous processes (feather bones) in younger animals. Mineral is deposited in the buttons as the animal grows older, and the buttons take on an appearance similar to the hard bone.

C

Cafeteria Round – Any one of a variety of beef rounds that may be used for carving on a buffet line. May be bone in or boneless and may have a handle on or off as specified by purchaser. See Baron of Beef.

glossary

Calf – In the U.S., calf is differentiated from veal on the basis of lean color. Calf has a grayish red to moderately red lean color, while veal is usually grayish pink. The darker color is a result of maturity as calf is marketed at 5 to 10 months while most veal is marketed prior to 20 weeks of age.

Cap Meat – See Blade Meat. May also be the fat cover and lean of a beef rib, veal rack, lamb rack, pork loin, or any other meat cut where the term applies, such as a knuckle, top sirloin, or leg.

Capon – Six to 10 pounds ready-to-cook, surgically unsexed male broiler.

Carcass – The dressed, slaughtered animal, containing two "sides."

Center Cut – Term used to indicate the interior portion of different cuts of meat after removal of outer edges or ends to create a more desirable portion that may be more uniform in appearance.

CFIA – Canadian Food Inspection Agency

Chain – The side muscle of a tenderloin.

Channel Fat – Fat located over the vertebrae on the inside surface of beef chucks, ribs, and loins. Also on the inside surface of pork loins.

Chateaubriand – The center cut portion of the whole completely trimmed tenderloin, which has the same size diameter on both cut ends and is reasonably uniform in girth with a minimum of tapering. Cooked and served as one piece.

Chicken Paws – The lower portion of the chicken foot remaining after cutting the chicken leg into two parts just below the spurpoint.

Chilled – A temperature-related term generally used to describe fresh product.

Chine bone – A part of the backbone that remains after the carcass is split.

Chuck Tender – *Supraspinatus* muscle. See Item No. 116B. Also referred to as Mock Tender and Scotch Tender.

Chunked and Formed – A meat product that consists of meat chunks (approximately 1.0 inch (2.5 cm) square) formed into a desired shape. The meat chunks are usually produced by coarse grinding or dicing. The chunks are massaged (tumbled) prior to forming.

Clod Heart – A name given to the *triceps brachii long head* muscle. Also referred to as the Shoulder Center. See Item No. 114E.

Close Trim – Trimming more surface or cover fat from a product than is generally industry specifications. Close trim is regarded as 0.25 inch or less.

Club Steak – Historically a steak from the rib end portion of the beef short loin. Considered as any beef steak from the rib or loin, primarily used for grilling.

Cock – A male chicken also called a rooster. Neither the whole bird nor the parts from the cock are normally available since the carcass meat is primarily used for further-processed products.

Cod/Udder Fat – A smooth deposit of fat in the udder region of heifers and cows. Cod fat in steers is a rough and irregular-shaped fat deposit in the scrotal region.

Comb – A fleshy or cartilaginous variable serrated-shaped appendage on the head of the bird.

Comminuted – Reduction of meat particle size, using such methods as grinding, dicing, and chopping.

Corner Piece – A portion of the short plate that includes the 6th, 7th, and 8th rib portions but does not include costal cartilage.

Cornish Game Hens – A ready-to-cook hen that is about 14–22 ounces (sometimes referred to as Rock Cornish Hen).

Cowboy Steak – A name given to Frenched single-bone rib steak. See Item No. 1103B. Sometimes this term is also applied to a frenched split-bone rib steak.

Crown Roast – A roast prepared from either a lamb rack or pork rib end or rack, usually Frenched, and several pieces tied into a round shape resembling a crown.

Cryogenic Freezing – This is the most rapid freezing method for meat. Liquid nitrogen and liquid carbon dioxide are the most common condensed gases that serve as the refrigerant in cryogenic systems.

Cubed – Refers to a process of mechanical tenderization using a machine with two sets of sharp pointed disks that score or cut muscle fibers without tearing. Irregular pieces of meat can be shaped and "knitted" together with this machine.

Cube Meat – Any meat that has been cut into uniform pieces. See Kabob and Brochette Meat.

Coulotte – A term used to refer to the flat, triangular-shaped muscle (*biceps femoris*) that lies immediately beneath the surface fat of the top butt. It can be cut into steaks or cooked in one piece. It is sold fat-on and defatted. See Item No. 184D.

Cured – Meat products that have been infused with special saline solutions and ingredients to enhance flavor and color, and extend shelf life. Commonly called "corned" when referring to a cured beef item (e.g., Corned Beef).

Cutlet, Poultry – Cutlets may be either slices from a whole muscle or they may be fabricated. In either instance the labeling for the cutlet must properly describe it, e.g., poultry cutlet chopped and formed.

D

Dark Meat – Drumstick, thigh, thigh trim meat, and dark trim meat of chickens and turkeys.

Deckle – Fat and lean lying between bone and the main muscle of the brisket.

Delmonico Steak – A boneless steak cut from the beef rib (lip on or lip off).

Denuded – Meat cuts that have had practically all surface fat removed. Also referred to as Peeled.

Denver Ribs – The name given to the lamb spareribs specially prepared from Item No. 209.

Diaphragm – The muscle that supports the viscera (inner organs) of an animal and is commonly referred to in beef as an outside skirt. See Item No. 121C.

Diced – See Cube Meat.

Dorsal to – Toward the back of the carcass, upper or top line.

Dressed Poultry – The cleaned, defeathered and eviscerated poultry that is ready for sale. Also termed ready-to-cook (RTC).

Dry Aged – Fresh meat cuts that have been stored (without vacuum packaging) for various periods of time under controlled temperatures, humidity, and air flow to avoid spoilage and ensure flavor enhancement, tenderness, and palatability. Prior to cutting or trimming, a dry-aged product will customarily have a firm, hard surface on exposed edible tissue.

Duck Press – A cooking tool that uses pressure to extract the juices from the carcass of fowl.

E

Edible By-Products – The edible organs, fat, and glands of a meat animal. Included are heart, tongue, liver, pancreas, thymus (beef and veal sweetbreads), kidney, spleen (melt), brains, stomach walls (tripe), hog intestines (chitterlings), and testicles (fries). See Variety Meats.

End Cuts – Cuts made from the ends of primal or subprimal cuts. Ends often lack the uniformity of the adjacent cuts.

End to End – A requirement that includes all cuts made from the primal or sub-primal cut being sliced.

Enzyme – A complex protein compound produced by animals and plants that has the ability to accelerate organic reactions.

Establishment Number – Number granted an establishment or plant when it complies with all requirements for federal or state inspection, and which identifies the processing plant wherever found.

Evisceration – The process of removing the internal organs.

Export Rib – A commonly used industry term for a bone in, lip-on beef rib eye. Sometimes referred to as BILO Rib.

F

Fabricated Cuts – Cuts made from primal and sub-primal cuts. Fabricated cuts can be boneless or bone in.

Fajitas – Boneless meat, sliced into narrow irregular strips from 1.0 inch (2.5 cm) to 3.0 inches (7.5 cm) in length. Usually cut from extra-lean, more tender beef and chicken. It can also be marinated. It is a common ingredient in Tex-Mex dishes.

False Lean – The cutaneous muscle imbedded in the fat overlying the shoulder area of a pork or beef side. It is exposed when the loin is closely trimmed.

FCS – Food and Consumer Service, USDA (formerly Food and Nutrition Service).

Feather – The horny type structures covering the body of the bird. They are removed from the carcass at the first stage of processing.

Fillets – Boneless slices of lean meat that form portion cuts of uniform size and shape. May be cubed mechanically if specified.

Filet Mignon – A steak cut from a beef tenderloin.

Finger Meat – Intercostal meat between the ribs. Also referred to as Rib Fingers.

Flanken – Kosher or non-Kosher beef used for soup meat or boiled beef. It is usually cut from the plate, brisket, chuck, short ribs, or corner piece from a fabricated rib.

Flap – See Item No. 185A. See also Item No. 116G.

Flat – See Item No. 171B.

Flat Iron – A name given to the *infraspinatus* muscle of the Clod after the connective tissue or shoulder tendon has been removed. See Item No. 114D. See also Item No. 1114D.

FLO – Fat Limitation Options.

Foie Gras – Any fattened fowl liver, most common varieties are duck and goose.

Forequarter – The anterior portion of a beef side, including ribs 1 through 12.

Foresaddle – Unsplit forequarter of a veal or lamb carcass.

Formed, Molded, Pressed – Chunks of meat, including sections, may be formed, molded, and pressed to make roasts, rolls, logs, etc.

Formula-Fed Veal – See Special-Fed Veal.

Free Range – Chickens or turkeys that are raised with access to the area outside the grow-out houses.

Freezer Burn – Discoloration due to loss of moisture and oxidation in freezer-stored meats.

Frenched – The process by which the bone is exposed after removing the intercostal meat (the meat between the bones), and/or the lean and fat surrounding it to provide a decorative appearance.

Fresh – Refers to meats that have not been canned, cured, smoked, or cooked. In order for poultry to qualify as fresh, however, in addition to the above, the product must never have been frozen.

Frozen – Refers to meat that has been reduced in temperature to below the freezing temperature of meat (<28°F).

Fry – To cook in fat or oil. Applied especially (1) to cooking in a small amount of fat, also called pan-frying; and (2) to cooking in a deep layer of fat, also called deep-fat frying.

Fryer – A young chicken produced for meat. A term often used interchangeably with "broiler."

FSIS – Food Safety and Inspection Service, USDA.

Further-Processed Poultry Products – Poultry products prepared by cooking, smoking, grinding, deboning, dehydrating, or otherwise processing beyond the cut-up stage so as to change form, appearance, texture, or to keep quality. Further-processed products include nuggets, patties, hot dogs, pot pies, and hundreds of other products.

G

Giblets – The liver, heart, and gizzard of a poultry carcass. Although often packaged with them, the neck of a bird is not a giblet.

Gizzard – A bird's second stomach.

Grade – USDA or CFIA designation that indicates quality or yield of meat. See Quality Grade and Yield Grade.

Gristle – Inedible tough elastic tissue or cartilage.

Gross Weight – Refers to the weight of products plus their packaging and packing materials, including the shipping container and closure materials such as strapping.

glossary

Grow-Out House – Building used for brooding and raising broilers and turkeys.

H

HACCP – Acronym for Hazard Analysis and Critical Control Points (pronounced "hassup"). Meat, poultry, and seafood companies operate under this science-based food safety system. An explanation of the system is found in the front section of the *Guide*.

Halal and Zabiah Halal – Meat and poultry products slaughtered and prepared in accordance with Islamic law.

Ham – Meat from the hind leg of pork that has been cured and smoked.

Ham, "Country Style" – A dry-cured, smoked ham. Called "country ham" when produced in a rural area, and called "country-style ham" if produced elsewhere.

Ham, Fresh – See Item No. 401.

Ham, Water Added – Cooked ham with a minimum protein fat-free (PFF) value of 17.0. (Typically 10 percent or less water added.)

Hanging Tender – The portion of the diaphragm muscle that is attached to the back region of the last rib. See Item No. 140.

Hatchery – A facility housing large egg incubators in which baby chicks are hatched.

Heel – A group of small muscles located in the lower portion of the outside round (adjacent to the femur bone). Also known as horseshoe. The mouse is one of the muscle groups that makes up the heel. See Mouse.

Hen – The adult female of several species of poultry.

Hindquarter – The posterior portion of the beef side remaining after severance from the 12th rib forequarter.

Hindsaddle – Unsplit hindquarter of a veal or lamb carcass.

Hip – Sirloin portion of the hindquarter. See Item No. 181.

HRI – Hotels, Restaurants, and Institutions. Used as a synonym for the foodservice industry.

Hump Meat – The dorsal portion of the *rhomboideus* muscle of the beef chuck. Most prominent in *Bos Indicus* breeds of cattle.

I

IM – When "IM" appears with the name of an item, it designates that the roast or steak is composed of one muscle. Variation of quality will be eliminated since IM cuts will yield highly uniform slices as compared to multiple muscle cuts. When portioning IM cuts, they should be sliced at an approximate right angle to the grain (direction of muscle fibers).

Injected – Meat cuts that have had solutions introduced throughout the muscles by injection or pumping. Also referred to as Pumped or "Processed With."

Inspection Mark of Meat Products – Official stamp on federally or state-inspected and/or labeled meat products. Each inspected meat product, or its immediate container, shall bear the mark of inspection and the number of the establishment where it was last processed. See Establishment Number.

IQF – Individually quick frozen. Refers to cuts that have been individually frozen at extremely low temperatures immediately after processing.

J-K

Japanese Quail – A type of quail that are prolific egg producers and raised primarily for this purpose.

Kabob – Boneless dices of meat that are generally placed on skewers and grilled. Also referred to as Brochette Meat and Cube Meat.

Kansas City Steak – Strip loin steak. Can be either bone in or boneless. Also referred to as a New York Steak. See Item Nos. 1179, 1180B.

Kassler Rib – Smoked bone in pork loin.

Kosher – Meat from animals slaughtered under Rabbinical supervision.

Kosher Style – Used in reference to pure beef sausage and corned beef that is seasoned with garlic and spices, imparting a flavor similar to real Kosher products. This term is illegal for use in advertising or product description in a number of states.

L

Laid-Out Pack – A portion, single thickness on separating sheets or boards.

Leaf Fat – A high-quality fat lining from the abdominal wall in pork, commonly called kidney fat in beef and lamb.

Lifter Meat – See Blade Meat.

Liquid Tenderization – To use any enzymatic solutions to tenderize meat cuts.

Live Weight – Weight of the live animal.

Loin End – See Hip.

London Broil – Applies to a variety of beef cuts, usually boneless that can be broiled and then thinly sliced.

Long Island Duckling – Early production of ducklings in the United States originated on Long Island and the ducklings came to be identified as those from this region. They were produced from strains of white pekin ducks that were imported from China. The designation Long Island Duckling is geographically restricted to ducklings that have been raised on Long Island, New York. Today, white pekin ducklings are primarily raised in the Midwest and Western sections of the country and may sometimes be referred to as Long Island Style Ducklings.

M

Marbling – Intramuscular fat; flecks of fat within the lean. It is an important factor affecting quality in meat. Marbling enhances palatability by increasing juiciness and flavor.

Marinate – To be labeled "marinated," a product must use a marinade that is a mixture in which food is either soaked, massaged, tumbled, or injected in order to enhance taste, tenderness, or other sensory attributes such as color or juiciness.

Market Weight (Poultry) – The weight of the chicken after it has been processed (defeathered, eviscerated, and cleaned). Also termed dressed weight or ready-to-cook (RTC) weight.

Marrow – An edible, fatty substance found in the center of bones.

Marrow Bones – Refers to the large round bones and shank bones of the round and chuck (excluding knuckle bones), which contain significant amounts of marrow. The bones are usually cut into shorter pieces to expose the marrow.

Medallion – Usually small, round slices of meat. Also referred to as Tournedos when cut from beef tenderloins.

Medial – Toward the median plane that divides the carcass vertically into left and right sides.

Milk-Fed Veal – See Special-Fed Veal.

Mock Tender – See Chuck Tender.

Mouse – *Digital flexor* muscles found in the heel.

MSP – Mechanically separated poultry. This refers to poultry raw materials or food products made by mechanically separating bone from muscle tissue of carcasses and parts of poultry carcasses. MSP must be declared as mechanically separated chicken or turkey on the label.

Mutton – Meat removed from sheep carcasses that are considered physiologically mature (absence of break joints).

N

Nature-Fed Veal – See Special-Fed Veal.

Navel – Short plate. See Item No. 121.

Necks of Beef – The portion of chuck located above the 1st rib bone, blade, and arm bones.

Needled, Needling – A tenderizing process involving penetration of muscles by closely spaced thin blades with sharpened ends that cut muscle fibers into short segments. Also referred to as Pinned.

Net Weight – Weight of the contents of a container after the weight of packaging and packing materials has been deducted.

New York Steak – Different regions of the country use the term "New York" to refer to either bone in or boneless beef strip loins or steaks. See Kansas City Steak.

New York-Dressed – Fowl with only the blood and feathers removed. Does not apply to turkeys.

New York Style Round – Primal round with the sirloin tip (knuckle) removed.

No Roll – Refers to beef carcasses and cuts that have not been officially graded and identified by USDA. The quality grade is usually lower than Select.

Notched – Generally, notch cutting is made on rack, loin, and sirloin portions of lamb, veal, and pork. Starting on the split surface of the chine bone, saw cuts shall be made between vertebrae junctures to a point into the lean so that the rack, loin or sirloin items are left intact and the user may slice items into portions with a knife before or after roasting.

O-P

Off Condition – Meat and/or meat products that are unwholesome.

Onglet Steak – Another name for the Hanging Tender Steak. See Item No. 1140.

Paddle Bones – The transverse processes of the lumbar vertebrae of pork loins. See Item No. 424. The transverse processes are also referred to as finger bones in pork and other species.

Panbroil – To cook uncovered in a frying pan. The fat is poured off as it accumulates.

Panfry – To cook in a small amount of fat.

Papain – Enzyme obtained from juice of the papaya. Its enzymatic action breaks down the protein in meat and creates a tenderizing effect.

Parts (Poultry) – Ready-to-cook chicken legs (thighs and drumsticks), breasts, or wings.

Pectoral Meat – Those various muscles usually associated with the beef brisket and plate and also found in the pork shoulder.

Peeled – See Denuded.

Peeled Tender of Beef (Wedge Fat In) – See Item No. 189B.

Petite Tender – The *teres major* muscle of the clod. See Item No. 114F.

PFF – Protein, Fat-Free. Refers to a formula used by USDA to calculate the amount of added moisture in cured meat products.

Pickled – See Cured.

Pigeon – A mature squab. Not readily available for foodservice. The meat is tough, and the skin is coarse textured.

Pinned – See Needled.

Plate Piece – See Corner Piece.

Pork Breast – See Item No. 405C.

Porterhouse Tails – Portions of the flank muscles trimmed from short loins or strips. Also referred to as Steak Tails.

Portion Control Cuts – Items that have been cut, sliced, or formed to specified weights or thicknesses.

Posterior to – Toward the rear of the carcass, behind.

Poussin – A baby chicken raised on grain products.

glossary

Practically Free of Fat – Terminology used to describe a meat cut on which there is no practically trimmable fat present.

Precooked – Products that have been cooked but may require reheating or additional cooking prior to eating.

Primal Cuts – Basic major cuts into which carcasses and sides are separated.

"Prime" Rib – This term refers to a beef rib roast and does not refer to the quality grade of that roast. It is a generic description.

Protein – A nutrient. Foods of animal origin are the best source of high biological quality, complete protein because they contain the 8 essential amino acids in the proportions necessary to build, maintain, and repair the body tissues and strengthen its defense mechanism against infection and disease.

P.S.E – Pale, Soft, and Exudative pork. This pork yields undesirable-looking fresh and cured cuts. When detected, PSE meat is usually processed into sausage.

PSMO – Peeled beef tender, side muscle on. See Item Nos. 189A, 189B. Term should always be clarified between buyer and seller.

PSO – Purchaser Specified Option.

Pullman Style – Usually refers to a meat product packed into a long container (usually rectangular or square).

Pullet – A young female chicken before she begins to lay eggs.

Pumped – See Injected.

Purge – The juices exuded from fresh, cooked, and cured meat cuts after they are packaged and which remain in the package at the time of opening.

Q-R

Quality Grade – Each grade denotes a specific level of quality as determined by the USDA or CFIA.

Ranch Steak – A name given to the clod heart when prepared into steaks. See Item No. 1114E.

Ratite – A large flightless bird having a flat breastbone. Common ratites are ostriches, emus, and rheas. Since these birds are slaughtered and processed like livestock, they are designated as livestock by the USDA but not included in this publication.

Ready-to-Cook (RTC) – Dressed, whole-bodied carcass or parts ready for the consumer to cook.

Rib Fingers – See Finger Meat.

Riblets – Associated with pork (see Item No. 424), but may also be harvested from other species. The term *riblets* is sometimes used by foodservice operators to describe items harvested from other species.

Rooster – See Cock.

S

Sausage – Comminuted meat products prepared with meat or meat by-products and seasoned with spices (salt, pepper, etc.) in small amounts. Sausage products may be cooked or uncooked and smoked or unsmoked.

Sauté – A method of cooking meat in a skillet or pan while in the presence of a small amount of cooking oil. Meat pieces should be tender and cut very thin because cooking time is short.

Scotch Tender – See Chuck Tender.

Sear – To brown surface of meat by brief application of intense heat.

Sectioned and Formed – A meat product that consists of entire muscles (or muscle systems) that are closely trimmed, massaged, and then formed into a desired shape. Sectioned and formed hams are an example of this product type.

Shell Loin – Bone-in strip loin. See Item Nos. 175, 179.

Shell Steak – Steak made from one of the shell loins or bone in strip loin.

Shin, Shins of Beef – Hindshank and/or foreshank. The hock bones shall be removed.

Shoulder Rose – The *cutaneous* muscle of the clod. See Item No. 114.

Shrink – This term refers to the weight loss from meat/meat products that may occur throughout the product's life (slaughter to consumer).

Shrink Wrap – Using plastic self-adhering wrapping material to tightly conform to the shape of meat or cartons.

Side – One matched forequarter and hindquarter or one half of a meat animal carcass.

Simmer – To cook in liquid at a temperature of approximately 185°F. Bubbles form slowly and break below the surface.

Sirloin – That portion of the beef hindquarter remaining after the round, short loin, and flank are removed. Steaks cut from this item are called sirloin steaks. Also referred to as Hip.

Sirloin Tip – Beef knuckle. See Items Nos. 167 and 167A.

Sirloin Tip Steak – Refers to a steak cut from the sirloin tip (knuckle). See Item Nos. 1167, 1167A.

Smoke – The process of treating or curing meat with smoke as both a flavoring and a preservative.

Smoked – Meat cuts that have been exposed to the dry smoke of hardwoods, or that have had liquid smoke applied externally or as a cure ingredient.

Snude – The fleshy or cartilaginous variable serratedshaped appendage on the head of a turkey.

Soy Added – Refers to the addition of hydrated soy protein to a meat product.

Special-Fed Veal – Beef/dairy animals that are fed scientifically controlled liquid diets that produce pale fine-textured meat. Generally slaughtered at 15 to 20 weeks of age. Also referred to as Formula-Fed, Milk-Fed, or Nature-Fed Veal.

SRM – The acronym for Specified Risk Materials. An explanation of the term appears in the front section of the Guide.

Steak-Ready – A primal or sub-primal cut that has been trimmed in such a manner that steaks may be portioned from it without substantial further trimming.

Steak Tails – See Item No. 176.

Steamboat Round, Steamship Round – See Cafeteria Round and Baron of Beef.

Stir Fry – A method of cooking small pieces of meat in a small amount of cooking oil over intense heat, usually in a wok. The meat is stirred constantly during cooking and is cooked for a brief time.

St. Louis Style Spare Ribs – Spareribs with the brisket bone removed. See Item No. 416A.

Sub-Primal Cuts – Smaller cuts derived from primal cuts.

T

Tenderloin (Chicken) – The inner pectoral muscle that lies adjacent to the rib cage parallel to the breast bone.

Texas Ribs – Beef back ribs. See Item No. 124.

Tiger Muscle – The *multfidus dorsi* muscle found on the dorsal side of the boneless pork loin. See Item Nos. 413C, 414.

Top Sirloin Butt (Bone In) – Item No. 184 with the bone remaining.

Tournedos – See Medallion.

Tri-Tip – Also known as the triangle. See Item Nos. 185C, 185D.

Trichinae Certified Pork – Pork that has been specially processed to be certified by USDA as being trichinae-free.

Trimmed Corner Piece – See Corner Piece. This cut is prepared from a corner piece by removing the fat cover and first layer of lean.

TSP – Trisodium phosphate, a solution permitted as use for an antimicrobial agent on poultry.

U-V

UPC – The acronym for Universal Product Code. A bar code and numbering codification system used to identify products by electronic devices for inventory control and pricing.

USDA – United States Department of Agriculture.

USDA Grade A – A symbol applied to chickens or turkeys that have passed inspection by U.S. Department of Agriculture officials and meet certain high standards of quality, size, and appearance criteria.

Vacuum Aging – Aging in plastic packaging from which air has been removed.

Vacuum Packed – Refers to the process of encasing meat cuts in bags or pouches fabricated from laminated plastic, evacuating air from the bags and sealing them for extended refrigerated storage.

Variety Meats – See Edible By-Products.

Veal – See Calf.

Vein Steak – Steak cut from the hip end of the sirloin strip or short loin showing a piece of connective tissue separating the loin eye (*longissimus dorsi*) from the small muscle (*gluteus medius*), which lies immediately beneath the surface fat. The connective tissue forms an irregular half-moon shape. Also referred to as Veiny.

Ventral to – Toward the lower surface of the carcass, away from the back.

W

Water Added – USDA labeling term that identifies a meat cut that has been injected with cure solution in excess of the amount lost during the curing and smoking process, thus yielding a cut that weighs more than the original uncured weight. There are differences in label requirements from various other products to which water has been added.

Wet Aging – See Vacuum Aging.

White Meat – Meat from the breast, wing, or scapula of turkeys and chickens. No skin is included.

Whole Chicken – Ready-to-cook chicken that is not cut-up, includes giblets and meat.

Wild Duck – Wild ducks, such as Mallard, Canvasback, Teal, Widgeon, etc., are protected by law under international migratory bird treaties.

Wild Goose – Wild geese such as those from Canada are protected by law under international migratory bird treaties.

Wishbone Portion (Pulley Bones) – The wishbone portion consists of the pulley bones together with their covering muscle and skin excluding the neck skin. The portion may be produced from any whole breast. The portion includes the *hypocledium* end of the wishbone, and the separation occurs along a line approximately halfway between the wishbone and the *sternal spine* to the point where the wishbone joins the shoulder.

WOG – Term given to broilers sold without giblets and neck.

X-Z

Yield Grade – These grades are designed to identify carcasses for differences in cutability or yield and are applied by the USDA Grading Service.

Young Meat Chickens – Although usually referring to broilers, this category includes broilers (more than 90 percent of the young meat chickens category), young roasters, Cornish game hens, capons, and certain other special types of young poultry meat.

Young Roaster Chicken – A broiler that is 6 to 8 pounds, ready-to-cook, sold fresh or frozen through grocery retail. The broiler is sold either whole or cut-up.

Membership Information
Información sobre la membresía

Want your personal network to include the real decision-makers at the most successful meat & poultry processors and suppliers in North America?

THEN JOIN NAMP!

Founded in 1942, the North American Meat Processors Association (NAMP) is an international member-driven association of *progressive meat processors, distributors, center-of-the-plate specialists,* and suppliers selling primarily to the foodservice industry. NAMP provides exceptional value through high-caliber support programs and governmental representation to help ensure our members' success in the industry.

The Meat Buyer's Guide® is a NAMP publication. NAMP members can participate in the review/update process of each edition.

BENEFITS OF MEMBERSHIP

- 35% discount on *The Meat Buyers Guide*®
- A relaxed networking and learning environment at two major industry-wide meetings a year
- Learning opportunities at NAMP's 16+ food safety conferences and workshops: pay lower member fees
- NAMP's weekly report, *NewsLine,* which contains industry information and updates and NAMP's weekly Market Report, with complete up-to-date pricing information
- Unlimited free access to NAMP's College of Experts, our team of 34 Ph.D.-level consultants on 19 subjects important to your business
- A voice in government rulemaking: NAMP is a North American organization that effectively represents your interests to USDA-FSIS, USDA-AMS, and CFIA
- A cross-referenced *Member Resource Directory* for networking and enriching your business prospects
- Fast, on-line help from other members through NAMP's Listserve called "Bull Session"
- Exclusive technical/educational info on the Members Only section at www.namp.com

Members also enjoy toll-free access to NAMP's experienced staff and off-site consultants who are ready to help you with just about any problem, question or concern you may have. *It's like having your own team of experts without the added expense - an incredible value for your dues dollar!*

Membership in NAMP offers an unparalleled and unique opportunity to learn and network with your peers. Join today and you'll enrich your business prospects and benefit from other members' experiences. *It's what our long-time members call "The Magic of NAMP".*

WE INVITE YOU TO JOIN TODAY

To apply, go to www.namp.com or call +1 703.758.1900.

¿Quiere que su red personal incluya a quienes en verdad toman las decisiones y a los más exitosos procesadores y proveedores de carne roja y aves de América del Norte?

¡ENTONCES ÚNASE A NAMP!

La Asociación Norteamericana de Procesadores de Carne (NAMP), fundada en 1942, es una asociación internacional dedicada a sus integrantes, que incluyen *procesadores, distribuidores, especialistas en ingredientes principales del plato* y proveedores progresistas que venden principalmente a la industria de servicios de alimentación. NAMP ofrece un valor excepcional a través de programas de apoyo de gran nivel y representación en el gobierno para ayudar a garantizar el éxito de nuestros miembros en la industria.

La Guía para Compradores de Carne® es una publicación de NAMP. Los miembros de NAMP pueden participar en el proceso de revisión y actualización de cada edición.

BENEFICIOS DE LA MEMBRESÍA

- 35% de descuento en *La Guía para Compradores de Carne*®
- Un ambiente relajado para establecer contactos y aprender en dos grandes reuniones de toda la industria por año
- Oportunidades de aprendizaje en las conferencias y los talleres de inocuidad alimentaria de NAMP: pague tarifas más bajas para miembros
- Informe semanal de NAMP, *NewsLine*, que contiene información y actualizaciones de la industria, y el Informe de Mercado semanal de NAMP, con la información de precios completa y al día
- Acceso gratis ilimitado al colegio de expertos de NAMP, nuestro equipo de 34 con nivel de doctorado en 19 áreas importantes para su negocio
- Una voz en las normativas del gobierno: NAMP es una organización norteamericana que representa sus intereses de manera eficaz ante FSIS (Servicio de Inspección e Inocuidad Alimentaria) de USDA (Departamento de Agricultura de E.U.A.), AMS (Servicio de Mercadeo Agrícola) de USDA y la Agencia Canadiense de Inspección de Alimentos
- Un *Directorio de recursos de miembros* con referencia cruzada para establecer contactos y enriquecer las posibilidades de su negocio
- Ayuda rápida en Internet de otros miembros a través del Listserve de NAMP llamado "Bull Session"
- Información técnica y educativa exclusiva en la sección Members Only (sólo para miembros) de www.namp.com

Los miembros también disponen de acceso a través de un número telefónico sin cargo al experimentado personal de NAMP y a consultores descentralizados que están listos para ayudarle con prácticamente cualquier problema, consulta o inquietud que pueda tener. *Es como tener su propio equipo de expertos sin el gasto adicional ¡un increíble rendimiento por el valor de su suscripción!*

La membresía de NAMP ofrece una oportunidad única e incomparable de aprender y establecer contactos con sus colegas. Suscríbase hoy para enriquecer las posibilidades de su negocio y beneficiarse de la experiencia de otros miembros. *Es lo que nuestros miembros de muchos años llaman "La magia de NAMP".*

LO INVITAMOS A UNIRSE HOY

Para solicitar su inscripción, visite www.namp.com o llame al +1 703.758.1900.

Glosario

Importante: todos los números de piezas hacen referencia a la Guía para Compradores de Carne de la Asociación Norteamericana de Procesadores de Carne o NAMP.

A

A.P. (As-Purchased) Como fue comprado – La condición o el costo de una pieza tal como se compró o se recibió de un proveedor.

A.S. (As-Served) Como fue servido – El peso o tamaño de una pieza de comida al venderse o servirse después del procesamiento o cocción.

Ablandamiento líquido – Uso de soluciones enzimáticas para suavizar los cortes de carne.

Adicionado con agua – Término en la etiqueta del Departamento de Agricultura de E.U.A. (USDA, por sus siglas en inglés) que identifica un corte magro al que se le ha inyectado una solución para curado en mayor cantidad que la perdida durante el proceso de curado y ahumado, produciendo así un corte que pesa más que el original sin curar. Existen diferencias en los requisitos de etiquetado por parte de otros productos a los que se les ha agregado agua.

Adicionado con soya – Se refiere a la adición de proteína de soya hidratada a un producto cárnico.

Adobada, Encurtida – Ver "Curado".

Aglutinantes – Sustancias comestibles aprobadas, usadas para estabilizar, aglutinar y cambiar la textura y forma del alimento.

Ahumado – Proceso de tratamiento o curado de la carne con humo, con fines de impartir sabor y mejorar su conservación.

Ahumados – Cortes de carne que han sido expuestos al humo seco de maderas duras, o que se les ha aplicado externamente humo líquido o como un ingrediente de curado.

Alas Búfalo – Alas de pollo fritas en abundante aceite, en general servidas con salsa picante y aderezo de queso azul. El ala se prepara separando el alón (drummette) y el ala intermedia y quitando el extremo del ala.

Alfilerazo – Ver "punción".

AMS (Agricultural Marketing Service, USDA) – Servicio de Mercadeo Agrícola, Departamento de Agricultura de E.U.A.

Anterior a – Hacia el frente de la canal, o más adelante.

Arrachera Gallo, Pilar – La porción del músculo del diafragma que se une a la región posterior de la última costilla. Ver pieza número 140.

Asado Londinense (London Broil) – Se aplica a una variedad de cortes de carne de res, en general deshuesados que pueden asarse y luego cortarse en rodajas finas.

Asar – Cocer directamente al fuego. Cocer en la parrilla.

Asar a la Sartén – Cocer sin tapar en una sartén. Se quita la grasa a medida que se acumula.

Ave no voladora – Ave de gran tamaño con esternón plano. Las aves comunes de esta especie son las avestruces, los emúes y los ñandúes. Debido a que estas aves son sacrificadas y procesadas como ganado, así son designadas por el Departamento de Agricultura de E.U.A. (USDA, por sus siglas en inglés) pero no son incluidas en esta publicación.

Aves Limpias – Las aves limpias, desplumadas y sin vísceras, listas para la venta. También llamadas "listas para cocer" (RTC, ready-to-cook).

B

Bañar – Humedecer la carne con un líquido mientras se está cociendo para agregar sabor y evitar que se seque la superficie.

Banda ligamentosa – El tejido conjuntivo elástico amarillento que va desde el cuello (ligamento de la nuca) hasta la región del espaldar de la canal de res, ternera y cordero.

Bar Round ("Pierna tipo Bar") – Cadera, pata y pierna sin talón, deshuesados y atados circunferencial y longitudinalmente.

Barbecue – Asar la carne lentamente sobre una parrilla, asador o sobre brasas. Durante el cocimiento, la carne por lo general se baña con una salsa.

Barón de la Carne – Nombre descriptivo de piezas redondas de hueso de carne de res que comprende las piezas número 160 a 166B, que generalmente son de gran tamaño y se usan para asado. También se llaman Piernas tipo "Steamship".

Becerro – En los EE.UU., "Becerro" se diferencia de "Ternera" sobre la base de la carne magra. La carne magra del becerro tiene un color rojo grisáceo a moderadamente rojo, mientras que la de la ternera por lo general es rosa grisácea. El color más oscuro es resultado de la madurez, ya que el becerro se comercializa de los cinco a diez meses mientras que la ternera, antes de las 20 semanas de edad.

Bistec "Onglet" – Otro nombre en inglés para Bistec de Arrachera Gallo (Arrachera Colgante del Lomo). Ver pieza número 1140.

Bistec con Veta – Bistec cortado del extremo de la cadera de la tira de Sirloin (aguayón) o lomo, mostrando una parte del tejido conjuntivo (nervio) que separa el ojo del lomo (m. longissimus dorsi) del pequeño músculo (m. gluteus medius) acompañante, y que se encuentra inmediatamente debajo de la cubierta de grasa. El tejido conjuntivo forma una media luna de forma irregular. También llamado bistec "veteado".

Bistec de Cola de falda – Ver pieza número 176.

Bistec de punta de Sirloin – Se refiere a un bistec cortado de la punta de Sirloin (porción de pulpa bola). Ver piezas números 1167, 1167A.

Bistec estilo New York – Regiones diferentes del país usan el término "New York" para denominar a los bistecs del lomo (strip loin), con o sin hueso. Ver Bistec estilo "Kansas City".

Bombeado – Ver "inyectado".

Bistec del Vaquero (Cowboy) – Nombre asignado a un bistec al estilo francés, con un solo hueso de la costilla dividido. Ver pieza número 1103B. Algunas veces este término se aplica también a un bistec el estilo francés con hueso dividido.

Bistec Delmonico – Bistec deshuesado extraído del espaldar (chuletón) de res (con y sin cordón).

Botones – Puntas blancas suaves de cartílago en el extremo dorsal (punta) de las apófisis espinosas (puntas del espinazo) en los animales más jóvenes. El mineral se deposita en los botones conforme el animal crece, y los botones se van calcificando tomando una apariencia similar a la del hueso duro.

Brasear – Dorar la carne en una pequeña cantidad de grasa, después cocer lentamente en un utensilio tapado en una pequeña cantidad de líquido.

Butcher's Heart – Ver Punta de Pulpa Bola.

C

Cadena – Músculo lateral de un filete.

Canal – El animal sacrificado y faenado, compuesto por dos "lados".

Capón – Rostizado, macho, capado quirúrgicamente, listo para asar, de seis a 10 libras.

Carne blanca – Carne del pecho, ala o escápula de pavos y pollos. No incluye la piel.

Carne del pectoral – Los distintos músculos generalmente asociados con el pecho y costillar de carne de res y también encontrados en la espaldilla de cerdo.

Carne de la Giba – Porción dorsal del músculo romboides de la paleta de la carne de res. Más prominente en las razas Bos Indicus (cebuínas) de ganado.

Carne de paleta – La carne magra que recubre el ribeye y la parte de las costillas del espaldar (chuletón) primario. También llamada Carne Falsa, Tapa del Costillar, Tapa o Carne Encalzada. Ver pieza número 109B.

Carne en trozos – Cualquier carne que haya sido cortada en piezas uniformes. Ver Trozos de Res para Brocheta o Kabob.

Carne entrecostilla – Carne intercostal que se intercala entre las costillas. También llamada "tiras de entrecostillas".

Carne magra falsa – El músculo subcutáneo incorporado en la grasa que se encuentra sobre el área de la paleta del cerdo o media canal de res. Queda expuesta cuando la grasa del lomo se recorta a fondo.

Carne oscura – Pata, muslo, carne limpia de muslo y carne oscura limpia de pollos y pavos.

Carne para Brocheta – Cubos de carne (de res, ternera, cerdo, cordero) que generalmente se colocan en brochetas y se asan a la parrilla. También llamada carne para Kabob.

Carnero – La carne derivada de las canales de ovinos que se consideran fisiológicamente maduros o adultos (ausencia de coyunturas de quiebre).

Cerdo certificado libre de triquina – Cerdo que ha sido especialmente procesado para obtener la certificación del Departamento de Agricultura de E.U.A. (USDA, por sus siglas en inglés) como libre de triquina.

CFIA (Canadian Food Inspection Agency) – Agencia Canadiense de Inspección de Alimentos

Chateaubriand – La porción del centro del filete entero completamente limpio; que tiene el mismo tamaño de diámetro en ambos extremos de la pieza y su circunferencia es razonablemente uniforme con un mínimo de forma de cono. Cocido y servido como una sola pieza.

Club Steak – Históricamente, un bistec de carne de res de la porción extrema más aproximada al costillar del lomo corto (short loin). Considerado como cualquier bistec de carne de res del espaldar (chuletón) o lomo, usado fundamentalmente para asar a la parrilla.

Cocimiento a fuego lento – Cocer en líquido a una temperatura de aproximadamente 185°F (85°C). Las burbujas se forman lentamente y rompen debajo de la superficie.

Codorniz japonesa – Tipo de codorniz que es prolífica productora de huevos y se cría fundamentalmente a tales fines.

Congelación criogénica – Se trata del método de congelamiento más rápido para la carne. El nitrógeno líquido y el dióxido de carbono líquido son los gases condensados más comunes que sirven como refrigerantes en los sistemas criogénicos.

Congelación instantánea – Los productos se congelan rápidamente a temperaturas extremadamente bajas (−10° F [-23.3°C] o menos) junto con un movimiento de aire a gran velocidad alrededor del producto.

Congelado – Se refiere a la carne que ha sido sometida a una reducción de temperatura por debajo del grado de congelamiento de la carne (<28°F o <2.2°C).

Contracara – Ver pieza número 171B.

Coproductos comestibles – Los órganos comestibles, la grasa y las glándulas de un animal de carne. Entre ellas, se hallan el corazón, la lengua, hígado, páncreas, timo (mollejas bovinas y de ternera), riñón, bazo, sesos, paredes gástricas (callos), intestinos (menudencias), y testículos ("criadillas"). Ver "variedades cárnicas".

Corazón de planchuela – Nombre asignado a la cabeza larga del músculo tríceps braquial (en latín: triceps brachii). También llamada "Centro de Paleta". Ver pieza número 114E.

Corte del Centro – Término usado para indicar la porción interior de los diferentes cortes de carne después de haber quitado los bordes o extremos para crear una porción más deseable que tendrá una apariencia más uniforme.

Corte mariposa – Abrir por la mitad los bistecs, chuletas, escalopas y carne para asar, dejando las mitades unidas por un lado.

Corte Pelota de Béisbol (porción dorsal del Aguayón) – El lado dorsal del corte del centro del Bistec de Aguayón sin Tapa. Ver pieza número 184F. El bistec de este corte puede llamarse "Bistec Pelota de Béisbol" o "Bistec estilo Filet". Ver pieza número 1184F.

Corte de muesca – Generalmente, el corte de muesca se realiza en las porciones de costillar, lomo y sirloin de cordero, ternera y cerdo. Comenzando desde la superficie dividida del espinazo, se harán cortes a sierra entre las vértebras hasta un punto de la carne magra tal que el costillar, lomo y sirloin queden intactos y el usuario pueda cortar las piezas en porciones con un cuchillo antes o después de asadas.

Cortes de Puntas – Cortes hechos de los extremos o puntas de los cortes primarios o subprimarios. Las puntas en general carecen de la uniformidad de tamaño y forma de los cortes adyacentes originarios.

Cortes fabricados – Cortes o piezas derivados a partir de los cortes primarios y subprimarios. Los cortes fabricados pueden ser deshuesados o con hueso.

Cortes porcionados bajo control – Piezas que han sido cortadas, rebanadas o formadas según pesos o grosores especificados.

Cortes primarios – Cortes básicos principales, mayoristas, derivados de las canales y sus lados.

Cortes subprimarios – Cortes ulteriores más pequeños derivados de los cortes primarios.

Costillar en Corona – Trozo de carne preparado de un costillar de cordero o con un extremo del costillar de cerdo, generalmente al estilo francés, con varias piezas amarradas en forma circular, parecida a una corona.

Costelitas (Riblets, en inglés) – Asociadas con el cerdo (ver pieza número 424), pero que también puede obtenerse de otras especies. El término "riblets" se usa algunas veces en la industria de servicios de alimentación para describir piezas obtenidas de otras especies.

Costillar estilo San Luis – Costillar sin el hueso del pecho. Ver pieza número 416A.

Costillas Tejanas – Costillas del espaldar de res. Ver pieza número 124.

Costillas Baby Back – Porciones más pequeñas de las costillas cercanas a las vértebras torácicas del espaldar del cerdo.

Costillas BBQ – Costillas de todos los tipos preparadas para hacer parrilla (barbecue).

Costillas Denver – Nombre otorgado al costillar del cordero especialmente preparado para la pieza número 209.

Coulotte – Término utilizado para referirse al músculo aplanado, de forma triangular (bíceps femoris) que se encuentra inmediatamente por debajo de la cubierta de grasa de la pulpa del aguayón. Puede cortarse en bistecs o cocinarse en una pieza. Se vende tanto con grasa como sin grasa. Ver pieza número 184D.

Cresta – Apéndice carnoso o cartilaginoso de forma dentada variable que se encuentra en la cabeza del ave.

Criadero – Establecimiento que contiene grandes incubadoras de huevos en las que se empollan las aves pequeñas.

Crianza a campo abierto – Pollos o pavos que son criados con acceso al área exterior a la de los galpones de crianza.

Cuarto delantero – Porción anterior de una media canal de res que incluye de la costilla 1 a la 12.

Cuarto delantero en silla de montar – Cuarto delantero sin dividir a lo largo del espinazo, de una canal de ternera o cordero.

Cuarto posterior en silla de montar – Cuarto trasero sin dividir el espinazo de una ternera o canal de cordero.

Cuarto trasero – La porción posterior de la media canal que queda después del corte transversal del cuarto delantero en la 12ª costilla.

Curado – Productos de carne que han sido inyectados con soluciones e ingredientes especiales para mejorar el sabor y el color, y preservar los productos para prolongar su vida en los anaqueles o vitrinas. Comúnmente llamados "corned" (curado con sal) al referirse a una pieza de carne de res curada con sal.

D

DEA – deshuesado, enrollado y amarrado (o en malla).

De punta a punta – Requerimiento que incluye todos los cortes hechos del corte primario o subprimario que se rebanan.

Desjugue – Líquidos de apariencia sanguinolenta exudados de los cortes de carne fresca, cocida y curada, después de que se empaquetan y que están presentes en el empaque en el momento de abrirlo.

Desprovisto de grasa – Ver "prácticamente desnudo de grasa".

Diafragma – Músculo que sostiene las vísceras (órganos internos) de un animal y comúnmente es llamado en la carne de res como arrachera delgada regular. Ver pieza número 121C.

Dorsal a – Hacia el espaldar de la canal, por encima o a la línea tope o superior.

E

Empacado al vacío – Hace referencia al proceso de colocar cortes de carne en bolsas de plástico laminado, evacuando el aire de las mismas y selladas herméticamente para prolongar el almacenamiento en refrigeración.

Empanizado – Producto que está recubierto con menos de 30 por ciento de una sustancia comestible, generalmente harina o pan molido. El producto debe primero remojarse en una mezcla para mejorar la adherencia del empanizado.

Empanizado y predorado (empanizado en aceite caliente) – Los productos empanizados sin cocer empanizados en aceite caliente (sofreídos) deben lucir la inscripción "ready to cook" (listo para cocinar) o similar para indicar que el producto no está cocido, o debe contener instrucciones de cocción en la etiqueta.

Empaque Multicapa de Pieza Rebanada – Una porción en rebanadas de espesor uniforme colocadas sobre láminas o tablas para su separación.

Empuje – También conocido como punta triangular. Ver piezas números 185C, 185D.

En malas condiciones (deteriorada, echada a perder) – Carne o productos cárnicos que no están en buen estado.

Envoltura Encogible – Material plástico autoadherente para envolver, que se ajusta firmemente a la forma de la carne o las cajas.

Enzima – Fermento cuya estructura química compleja corresponde a un compuesto proteico producido por animales y plantas que tienen la habilidad de acelerar reacciones orgánicas.

Escalopines, aves – Los Escalopines pueden ser rodajas de la totalidad de un músculo o pueden ser fabricados. En ambas instancias, el etiquetado del escalopín debe describirlo correctamente; por ej., escalopín de ave, picado y formado.

Espaldar (Chuletón) para exportación – Término comúnmente usado en la industria para un corte de ribeye de carne de res con hueso y con cordón. Algunas veces llamado Costilla BILO.

Estilo asiático – Esta pieza, también llamada "estilo asiático tradicional", se refiere más comúnmente a patos jóvenes. Esta pieza es una canal procesada como un animal completo, excepto que la cabeza y las patas se dejan intactas.

Estilo francés – Proceso por el que el hueso de la costilla queda expuesto cuando se extrae la carne intercostal (carne entre costillas), y/o la carne magra y grasa que la rodea; se trabaja con fines decorativos.

Estilo Kosher – Se usa en referencia a embutidos de pura carne de res y carne de res curada con sal, condimentada con ajo y especias, lo que imparte un sabor similar a los productos Kosher verdaderos. El uso de este término es ilegal en publicidad o en la descripción del producto en varios estados de E.U.A.

Estilo Pullman – Generalmente se refiere a un producto cárnico empacado en un recipiente largo (usualmente rectangular o cuadrado).

Evisceración – Proceso de extracción de los órganos internos.

Extremo adyacente al lomo – Ver "Hip" (cadera).

Fajitas – Carne deshuesada, cortadas en tiras angostas irregulares, de 1.0 pulgada (2.5 cm) a 3.5 pulgadas (7.5 cm) de longitud. Generalmente se cortan de la carne más tierna extra magra, de res o de pollo. También se pueden marinar. Es un ingrediente cárnico común en los platos Tex-Mex.

Falda – Ver pieza número 185A. Ver también pieza número 116G.

FCS (Food and Consumer Service, USDA) – Servicio al Consumidor y de Alimentos, Departamento de Agricultura de los E.U.A. (ex Servicio de Nutrición y Alimentos).

Filete miñón – Un corte de bistec proveniente del filete de carne de res entero sin cuerda.

Filetes – Rebanadas de carne magra deshuesada que forman cortes porcionados con tamaño y forma uniformes. Pueden suavizarse mecánicamente si se especifica.

Filete (Pollo) – El músculo pectoral interno que se ubica adyacente a la caja torácica, paralelo al esternón.

Flanken – Carne de res producida o no bajo el ritual Kosher usada como carne para sopas o guisada. Generalmente se corta del costillar, pecho, paleta, costillas cortas (costilla cargada) o pieza angular (corner piece) de un espaldar fabricado.

FLO (Fat Limitation Options) – Opciones para limitar la grasa.

Freír – Cocer en grasa (manteca) o aceite. Se refiere especialmente a (1) cocer en una pequeña cantidad de grasa, también llamada freír en sartén; y (2) cocer la carne inmersa en una capa más profunda de grasa, también llamada freír en abundante grasa.

Freír o Sofreír a la Sartén – Cocer en una cantidad pequeña de grasa en una cacerola o sartén.

Fresco – Se refiere a carnes que no han sido enlatadas, curadas, ahumadas ni cocidas. A fin de que las aves se consideren frescas, sin embargo, además de lo anterior, el producto no debe haber sido nunca congelado.

FSIS (Food Safety and Inspection Service, USDA) – Servicio de Inspección e Inocuidad Alimentaria, Departamento de Agricultura de los E.U.A.

Gallina – Hembra adulta de diversas especies de aves.

Gallina joven – gallina de menos de un año, antes de comenzar a poner huevos.

Gallo – Un pollo macho. Ni la totalidad del ave ni las partes del gallo se ofrecen a la venta ya que la carne de la canal se usa fundamentalmente para productos ya procesados.

Galpón de crianza – Construcción utilizada para incubar y criar pollos de engorde y pavos.

Garras de Pollo – La porción inferior de la pata del pollo que queda una vez cortada la pierna en dos partes, justo por debajo del espolón.

Grado – Designación del Departamento de Agricultura de los E.U.A. o de la Agencia Canadiense de Inspección de Alimentos que indica la calidad o el rendimiento en cortes de la canal. Ver "grado de calidad" y "grado de rendimiento".

Ganso Silvestre – El ganso silvestre tal como los de Canadá están legalmente protegidos por los tratados internacionales de las aves migratorias.

Grado de calidad – Cada grado clasificatorio denota un nivel específico de calidad según lo determinado por el Departamento de Agricultura de E.U.A. (USDA, por sus siglas en inglés) o la Agencia Canadiense de Inspección de Alimentos (CFIA, por sus siglas en inglés).

Grado de rendimiento – Estos grados se designan para identificar diferencias de posibilidad de cortes o de rendimientos de canales, y se aplican por parte del servicio de clasificación del Departamento de Agricultura de E.U.A. (USDA, por sus siglas en inglés).

Grasa acanalada – Grasa localizada sobre las vértebras en la parte interna de las paletas, espaldares (chuletones) y lomos de res. También en la superficie interna de los lomos de cerdo.

Grasa de escroto/ubre – Depósito uniforme de grasa en la región de la ubre en las vaquillas y vacas. La grasa del escroto en los novillos es un depósito de grasa áspero y de forma irregular en la región escrotal.

Grasa endurecida – Grasa y carne magra entre el hueso y el músculo principal del pecho.

H

HACCP (Hazard Analysis and Critical Control Points) – Análisis de Riesgos y Puntos Críticos de Control (en inglés, la sigla se pronuncia "hassup"). Las empresas de carnes rojas, avícolas y de mariscos funcionan bajo este sistema de seguridad de alimentos con base científica. La sección al frente de esta Guía contiene una explicación del sistema.

Halal y Zabiah Halal – Productos cárnicos y avícolas sacrificados y preparados conforme a la ley Islámica.

Hervir – Cocer en agua u otro líquido, en donde las burbujas suben continuamente y rompen en la superficie.

Hip (Cadera) – Porción de sirloin (aguayón) del cuarto trasero. Ver pieza número 181.

Hornear – Cocer mediante calor seco. Cuando se aplica a la carne, también se llama asado.

HRI (Hotels, Restaurants, and Institutions) – Hoteles, restaurantes e instituciones. Usado como sinónimo para la industria de servicios de alimentación (industria restaurantera y de comedores industriales).

Hueso del Espinazo – Parte de la columna vertebral que permanece una vez que se divide la canal en lados.

Huesos de Tuétano – Se refiere a los huesos grandes de la pierna y a los huesos del chamberete (excluyendo los nudillos) que contienen cantidades importantes de médula ósea. Los huesos generalmente se cortan en piezas más pequeñas para dejar expuesta la médula.

I

Inyectados – Cortes de carne en los que se han introducido salmueras a través de los músculos por inyección o bombeo. También conocidos como "Bombeados" o "Procesados con".

IQF (Individually quick frozen) – CRI, congelado rápido individual. Se refiere a los cortes que se han congelado individualmente a temperaturas extremadamente bajas inmediatamente después de procesados.

J-K

Jamón – Carne de la pierna trasera del cerdo que ha sido curada y ahumada.

Jamón, "al estilo campestre" – Jamón curado en seco y ahumado. Llamado "jamón campestre" cuando se produce en un área rural, y llamado "jamón al estilo campestre" si es producido en otro lugar.

Jamón, Con Agua Añadida – Jamón cocido con un valor mínimo de proteína libre de grasa (PFF, por su sigla en inglés) de 17.0. (Generalmente, adicionado con un 10% o menos de agua.)

Jamón, Fresco – Ver pieza número 401.

Juil – Músculo Supraspinatus. Ver pieza número 116B. También llamado en inglés Mock Tender y Scotch Tender.

Kabob, Trozos de Res para Brocheta – Trozos de carne deshuesada que generalmente se colocan en brochetas y se asan a la parrilla. También llamada "carne para brocheta" y "carne en trozos" o "carne en cubos".

Kansas City Steak – Bistec Strip Loin estilo Kansas City. Puede ser con o sin hueso. También es conocido como "Bistec Strip Loin (New York)". Ver piezas números 1179, 1180B.

Kassler Rib – Lomo de cerdo ahumado con hueso.

Kosher – Carne de animales sacrificados según el ritual judío bajo la supervisión de un Rabino.

L

Lado – Un cuarto delantero y un cuarto trasero juntos o la mitad de un animal en canal.

Limpieza a fondo – Quitar más cubierta de grasa de un producto de lo que generalmente indican las especificaciones de la industria. Se considera limpiar a fondo como 0.25 pulgadas o menos.

Limpio al estilo New York – Aves a las que solamente se les ha quitado la sangre y las plumas. No se aplica a los pavos.

Listo para cocinar (RTC) – Canal entera o sus partes limpias, listas para que los consumidores las sometan a cocción.

Listo para cortar bistecs (Steak Ready, en inglés) – Corte primario o subprimario listo para cortar en bistecs, que ha sido recortado de grasa de manera tal que es posible que los bistecs puedan cortarse en porciones sin tener que volver a recortar la grasa.

Listo para tablajear o procesar (Block Ready, en inglés) – Corte que se vende listo para su posterior procesamiento o corte en porciones.

MI (Músculo individual) – Cuando aparece "MI" con el nombre de una pieza, significa que el rosbif o bistec se compone de un solo músculo. De esta manera se eliminará la variación en calidad ya que los cortes MI rendirán rebanadas sumamente uniformes en comparación con los cortes multi-musculares. Al hacer porciones de cortes MI, se deben rebanar en un ángulo recto aproximado al grano (dirección de las fibras del músculo).

Maduración – Proceso mediante el cual se mantiene la carne de res bajo temperatura controlada durante determinado período de tiempo. Esto permite que la actividad enzimática degrade las proteínas complejas, cambiando el sabor y la suavidad. Consultar también "maduración en seco" y "maduración húmeda".

Maduración al vacío – Maduración de la carne que ocurre una vez empacadas al alto vacío en bolsas plásticas impermeables al oxígeno.

Maduración en seco – Cortes de carne fresca que han sido almacenados (sin ser envasados al vacío) por varios períodos de tiempo bajo temperaturas, humedad, y flujo de aire controlados, para evitar que se echen a perder y asegurar la mejora del sabor, suavidad y gusto. Antes del corte o limpieza, un producto sometido a una maduración en seco habitualmente tendrá una superficie firme y dura del tejido comestible expuesto.

Maduración húmeda – Ver "maduración al vacío".

Marinado – Para poder ser etiquetado como "marinado", un producto debe usar una marinada o adobo que sea una mezcla en la que el alimento sea dejado en remojo, masajeado, revuelto, o inyectado a fin de mejorar el sabor, la suavidad u otros atributos sensoriales tales como color o jugosidad.

Marmoleado, también conocido como marmoleo o marmorización – Grasa intramuscular; veteado de grasa dentro de la carne magra. Constituye un factor importante que afecta favorablemente la calidad de la carne. El marmoleado mejora lo paladeable de la carne cocida ya que aumenta la cantidad de jugo y el gusto.

Medallón – Generalmente se refiere a rebanadas pequeñas y delgadas de carne de filetes de res. También llamados "tournedos".

Medial – Hacia el plano medio que divide la canal en forma vertical en los lados izquierdo y derecho.

Menudencias – Hígado, corazón y molleja de una canal de ave. Si bien a menudo se empaca con el pollo, el cuello no se considera menudencia.

Mock Tender – Ver "Juil".

Molida – Reducción del tamaño de la partícula de la carne, usando métodos tales como molienda, troceado (cubicado) y triturado.

Molleja – Segundo estómago del ave.

Mouse (ratón) – Músculos flexores digitales que se encuentran en el talón.

MSP (Mechanically separated poultry) – Carne de aves separadas mecánicamente, también conocida como "pasta de aves". Se refiere a materia prima avícola o productos alimenticios confeccionados por la separación mecánica de huesos y tejido muscular de canales y partes de canales de aves. La etiqueta del pollo o pavo debe contener la sigla MSP que indique la aplicación de la separación mecánica.

Músculo del Tigre – Músculo multifidus dorsi del lado dorsal del lomo de cerdo deshuesado. Ver piezas números 413C, 414.

Navel – Costillar corto. Ver pieza número 121.

Número de establecimiento – Número otorgado a un establecimiento o planta cuando cumple con todos los requisitos para la inspección federal o estatal, y que identifica el origen de la planta de procesamiento donde ésta se encuentre.

P.S.E (Pale, Soft, and Exudative pork) – Carne de Cerdo Pálida, Fofa y Exudativa. Esta condición de la carne de rinde cortes frescos y curados de aspecto poco atractivo. Al ser detectada, la carne PSE generalmente se usa para procesar embutidos.

Paletitas vertebrales – Apófisis transversas de las vértebras lumbares de los lomos de cerdo. Ver pieza número 424. Las apófisis transversas también son llamadas "huesecillos" tipo botana en el caso del cerdo (ver Costelitas) y otras especies.

Paletilla California sin nervio – Nombre otorgado al músculo infraspinatus de la planchuela una vez retirado el tejido conectivo o tendón de la paleta. Ver pieza número 114D. Ver también pieza número 1114D.

Papaína – Enzima obtenida del jugo de la papaya. Su acción enzimática rompe la estructura de la proteína de la carne y crea un efecto suavizante.

Partes (aves) – Piernas de pollo listas para cocer (muslos y patas), pechugas o alas.

Pato Silvestre – Los patos silvestres, tales como los Mallard, Canvasback, Teal, Widgeon, etc., están legalmente protegidos por los tratados internacionales de las aves migratorias.

Paté o pasta de hígado – Confeccionado de hígado de aves engordadas; las variedades más comunes son pato y ganso.

Pato joven Long Island – Las primeras producciones de patos jóvenes en los Estados Unidos se originaron en Long Island y los animales tomaron la identificación de dicha región. Fueron producidos a partir de razas de patos blancos de Pekín importados de China. La designación de "Pato joven Long Island" está geográficamente restringida a los animales criados en Long Island, Nueva York. Hoy en día, los patos jóvenes blancos de Pekín son fundamentalmente criados en las regiones norte-centro y occidental del país y es posible que algunas veces se los llame "patos jóvenes Long Island".

Pecho de cerdo – Ver pieza número 405C.

Pechugas sin Hueso (Aves) – Algunas veces llamadas Escalopines. Carne 100% magra y comestible. Las pechugas deshuesadas pueden, o no, incluir la piel; en general, los escalopines se venden sin piel.

Pérdida de peso (merma) – Este término se refiere a la disminución de peso que sufre la carne o los productos cárnicos durante la vida de los mismos (desde el sacrificio del animal a su consumo).

Pescuezos de res – Porción del cuello del cuarto delantero, pegado al diezmillo, ubicada por arriba del hueso de la primera costilla, el hueso de la paleta y del brazuelo.

Peso bruto – Se refiere al peso de los productos más su empaque y los materiales de envoltorio, inclusive el recipiente para el traslado y los materiales para cerrarlo tal como correas.

Peso de mercado (aves) – Peso del pollo una vez procesado (desplumado, sin vísceras y limpio). También llamado "peso limpio" o "peso listo para cocer (RTC)".

Peso en vivo – Peso del animal vivo (en pie).

Peso neto – Peso del contenido de un recipiente después de restar el peso de los materiales de embalaje y empaque.

PFF – Proteína, libre de grasa. Hace referencia a una fórmula usada por el USDA (Departamento de Agricultura de E.U.A, por sus siglas en inglés) para calcular la cantidad de humedad incorporada en los productos cárnicos curados.

Pichón – Palomino maduro. No se encuentra a disposición inmediata para la industria de servicios de alimentación. La carne es dura y la piel es de textura gruesa.

Pierna estilo New York – Pierna primaria sin la punta de sirloin (parte de la pulpa bola).

Pierna tipo Cafetería – Cualquiera de las variedades de piernas de carne de res que se usarán para trinchar en una línea de buffet. Pueden ser con hueso o sin hueso y pueden tener o no un mango (4 pulgadas de hueso) conforme lo especifique el comprador. Ver Barón de la Carne.

Pierna tipo "Steamboat", Pierna tipo "Steamship" – Ver Pierna tipo Cafetería y Barón de carne de res.

Pieza angular – Una parte del costillar corto que incluye las porciones de la 6ª, 7ª y 8ª costilla pero no incluye el cartílago costal.

Pieza angular recortada de grasa – Ver pieza angular. Este corte está preparado a partir de una pieza angular o "corner piece", quitando la capa de grasa y la primera capa de carne magra.

Plate Piece ("Pieza Costillar") – Ver pieza angular.

Pluma – Estructuras de tipo calloso que cubren el cuerpo del ave. Se retiran de la canal en la primera etapa del procesamiento.

Pollito – Pichón de pollo que es alimentado con productos de grano.

Pollito rosticero – Pollo joven de 6 a 8 libras, listo para cocer, vendido fresco o congelado a través del negocio minorista. El pollo de engorde se vende tanto entero como en trozos.

Pollito tierno "Cornish" – Pollito listo para cocer de alrededor de 14 a 22 libras (algunas veces llamados Pollitos tiernos "Rock Cornish").

Pollitos para carne – Si bien en general se refiere a los pollos de engorde, esta categoría incluye pollos de engorde (categoría de más del 90% de los pollos para carne), pollos rosticeros, pollitos tiernos "Rock Cornish, capones y algunos otros tipos de aves jóvenes para carne.

Pollo de engorde – Un pollo joven producido para carne. Término generalmente usado en forma intercambiable con "broiler".

Pollos de engorde – Pollos producidos para carne. Los términos "para asar" (broiler) y "para freír" (fryer) son intercambiables.

Pollos de engorde para deshuesar – Se parte de un peso listo para cocer de seis a ocho libras, que se deshuesa a mano para nuggets, hamburguesas, tiras, y productos deshuesados similares.

Pollo entero – Pollo listo para cocer que no está cortado; incluye menudencias y carne.

Porción del hueso de la suerte (clavícula) – La porción del hueso de la suerte consiste en la clavícula conjuntamente con su músculo que las cubre y la piel, excluyendo la piel del pescuezo. La porción puede producirse a partir de cualquier pecho entero. La porción incluye el extremo del hipocledium del hueso de la suerte, y la separación tiene lugar a lo largo de una línea aproximadamente a medio camino entre el hueso de la suerte y la columna del esternón hasta el punto en que el hueso de la suerte se une a la espaldilla.

Porterhouse Tails – Porciones de los músculos laterales recortados de lomos cortos o tiras. También llamados "Steak Tails".

Posterior hacia – Hacia el lado posterior del canal, por detrás.

Prácticamente desnudo de grasa – Cortes de carne a las que se le ha quitado prácticamente toda la cubierta de grasa. También se les refiere como "desprovistos de grasa".

Prácticamente libre de grasa – Terminología utilizada para describir un corte de carne en el que prácticamente no queda grasa que recortar.

Precocinado – Productos que han sido cocidos pero que pueden requerir recalentamiento o cocido adicional antes de ingerirlos.

Prensa para Patos – Una herramienta de cocina que se vale de la presión para extraer los jugos de la canal de las aves.

Prime rib – Este término se refiere a un rosbif del espaldar de res y, contrario a lo que se piensa, no determina el grado de calidad del rosbif. Se trata de una descripción genérica.

Productos avícolas ya procesados – Los productos avícolas preparados por cocimiento, ahumado, molido, deshuesado, deshidratado u otro tipo de procesamiento más allá de la etapa de corte para cambiar la forma, el aspecto, la textura o para mantener la calidad. Los productos con procesamiento adicional incluyen nuggets, hamburguesas, perros calientes, pasteles y cientos de otros productos.

Proteína – Un nutrimento. Los alimentos de origen animal son la mejor fuente de proteína completa y de alta calidad biológica, ya que contienen los ocho aminoácidos esenciales en las proporciones necesarias para generar, mantener y reparar los tejidos del cuerpo así como fortalecer su mecanismo de defensa contra infecciones y enfermedades.

PSMO – Filete de carne de res desprovisto de grasa, con cuerda lateral. Ver piezas números 189A, 189B. El término debe ser aclarado siempre entre el comprador y el vendedor.

PSO (Purchaser Specified Option) – Opción especificada por el comprador.

Pulpa del Aguayón Superior (con hueso) – Pieza número 184 conservando el hueso.

Punción, puncionado, lanceteado – Proceso de ablandamiento que implica la penetración de los músculos con cuchillas delgadas sumamente juntas con puntas afiladas que cortan las fibras musculares en pequeños segmentos. También llamado alfilerazo.

Punta de Pulpa Bola – También llamada Bola o Butcher's Heart ("Corazón del Carnicero"). Ver pieza número 185B.

Punta de Sirloin – Pulpa bola de carne de res remanente en el sirloin. Ver piezas número 167 y 167A.

Q-R

Quemado por congelación – Decoloración debida a la pérdida de humedad y a la oxidación en carnes almacenadas en congelación.

Ranch Steak (Bistec ranchero) – Nombre dado al corazón de planchuela cuando se lo prepara en bistecs. Ver pieza número 1114E.

Reformado, moldeado, prensado – Trozos de carne, inclusive secciones, que pueden ser reformadas, moldeadas y prensadas para hacer rosbifs, rollos, embutidos, etc.

Refrigerado – Término relacionado con la temperatura, generalmente usado para describir productos fríos.

S

Salchicha – Productos de carne picada preparados con carne o con subproductos de la carne y sazonados con especias (sal, pimienta, etc.) en pequeñas cantidades. Los productos embutidos pueden estar cocidos o no, y ahumados o no.

Salteado en tiras – Método de cocción de pequeñas tiras de carne con una pequeña cantidad de aceite de cocina en calor intenso, generalmente en una sartén chica. La carne se revuelve continuamente durante su cocción y ésta es rápida.

Saltear – Método de cocción de carne en un sartén o cacerola con un poco de aceite. Las piezas de carne deben ser suaves y estar en cubos pequeños ya que el tiempo de cocción es corto.

Scotch Tender – También conocido como "Mock Tender" o "Chuck Tender". Se refiere al músculo supraspinatus. Ver Juil.

Sello de inspección de los productos de carne – Sello oficial colocado en productos cárnicos inspeccionados o etiquetados a nivel federal o estatal. Cada producto de carne inspeccionado, o su envase inmediato, debe llevar el sello de inspección y el número del último establecimiento que lo procesó. Ver "número de establecimiento".

Shell Loin – Strip loin, con hueso. Ver piezas números 175, 179.

Shell Steak – Bistec tipo Shell (de concha) hecho de uno de los cortes del Lomo tipo Shell (Lomo de Concha) Loin o Strip Loin con hueso.

Shins, Shins de la pierna de res – Nombre en inglés que se le da al Chamberete trasero o chamberete de mano. Se extraerán los huesos del chamberete.

Sin Sello (No Clasificada) – Se refiere a canales y cortes de carne de res que no han sido oficialmente clasificados e identificados por el Departamento de Agricultura de E.U.A. con su grado oficial de calidad. El grado de calidad de las Carnes Sin Sello es, en general, inferior al grado de calidad USDA "Select".

Sirloin – Sirloin o Aguayón es esa porción del cuarto trasero de la canal bovina que queda después de haber quitado la pierna, el lomo y la falda. Los bistecs cortados de esta pieza reciben el nombre de bistecs del Sirloin. También llamado "hip (cadera).

SRM (Specified Risk Materials) – Sigla que significa materiales (tejidos comestibles) especificados de riesgo con respecto a la Encefalopatía Espongiforme Bovina. La sección al frente de esta Guía contiene una explicación del término.

Suadero – El músculo cutáneo de la planchuela. Ver pieza número 114.

Suavizado – Se refiere a un proceso de ablandamiento mecánico en el que se usa una máquina con dos juegos de discos de puntas afiladas que marcan o cortan las fibras musculares sin desgarrarlas. Con esta máquina, es posible dar forma y "entretejer" piezas irregulares de carne.

T

Talón – Grupo de músculos pequeños ubicados en la parte inferior del contracuete (adyacente al hueso del fémur). También conocido en inglés como "horseshoe" (herradura). El llamado "mouse" (ratón, en inglés) es uno de los grupos musculares que forman el talón. Ver "Mouse" (ratón).

Tapa – Ver Carne de paleta. Puede ser también la cubierta de grasa y la superficie magra del costillar de carne de res, ternera, cordero, lomo de cerdo o cualquier otro corte de carne en el que se aplique el término, tal como bola, top sirloin o pierna.

Tapa del costillar – Ver "Carne de paleta".

Tela de Grasa Visceral – Recubrimiento de grasa de alta calidad que proviene de la pared abdominal del cerdo, generalmente llamado grasa de riñonada en la carne de res y de cordero.

Teres filé desprovisto de grasa (con grasa intercalada) – Ver pieza número 189B.

Teres filé – El músculo teres o redondo mayor de la planchuela. Ver pieza número 114F.

Ternera – Ver "becerro".

Ternera alimentada naturalmente – Ver "Ternera con alimentación especial".

Ternera alimentada con fórmula – Ver "ternera con alimentación especial".

Ternera alimentada con leche – Ver "ternera con alimentación especial".

Ternera con alimentación especial – Becerros de Ganado de leche que son alimentados mediante dietas científicamente controladas que producen una carne pálida de textura fina. En general se sacrifican a las 15 o 20 semanas de edad. También llamadas terneras alimentadas a fórmula, alimentadas a leche o alimentadas naturalmente.

Ternera lechal – Carne de res muy joven (generalmente de menos de 21 días) y de animales lecheros.

Ternilla (cartílago o ligamento) – Tejido elástico y duro no comestible.

Tostar – Dorar la superficie de la carne mediante la breve aplicación de intenso calor.

Tournedos – Ver "Medallón".

Troceada – Ver "carne en trozos".

Troceada y moldeada – Un producto cárnico que consiste en trozos de carne (de aproximadamente 1.0 pulgada cuadradas, o 2.5 cm) con una forma determinada. Los trozos de carne generalmente se producen mediante molienda o cubicado grueso. Los trozos se amasan (revuelven) antes de moldearse.

Troceado y moldeado – Producto cárnico que consiste en músculos enteros (o sistemas musculares) que se recortan de grasa al máximo, se masajean y luego se les da la forma de la figura deseada. Los jamones troceados y moldeados son un ejemplo de este tipo de producto.

TSP (Trisodium phosphate) – Fosfato trisódico, solución permitida para su uso como agente antimicrobiano en productos avícolas.

Tuétano – Es la médula ósea, sustancia grasosa, comestible, que se encuentra en el centro de los huesos.

U-Z

UPC (Universal Product Code) – Sigla que significa Código universal de productos. Sistema de código de barras y numeración usado para identificar productos mediante mecanismos electrónicos a efectos de control de inventario y marcado de precios.

USDA (United States Department of Agriculture) – Departamento de Agricultura de Estados Unidos.

USDA Grado A – Símbolo aplicado a pollos o pavos que han pasado la inspección de los funcionarios del Departamento de Agricultura de E.U.A. y que cumplen determinadas normas exigentes de calidad, tamaño y aspecto.

Variedades cárnicas – Ver "variedades cárnicas y coproductos comestibles".

Ventral hacia – Hacia la superficie inferior del canal, alejado del espaldar.

WOG – Término dado a los pollos de engorde sin menudencias ni pescuezo.

Esperamos que considere que la sección de información sobre nutrición constituye una ayuda valiosa en la planificación del menú y para responder a las consultas sobre nutrición de los clientes.

Debido a que los tamaños de las porciones varían según los requisitos de costos o de menú del cliente, la información nutricional se expresa en formato de 1.0 onza cocida. Esto facilitará la conversión de los datos a las porciones de la industria de servicios de alimentación. Hemos escogido datos de productos cocidos en vez de crudos debido a que se anticipa que los usuarios de la Guía para Compradores de Carne preferirá informar a sus clientes en función del perfil nutricional del producto como se lo sirve, más que como se lo compra. Ya que en las porciones servidas pueden existir variaciones en el recorte o en la grasa interna, se suministra la información con un criterio de carne magra separable. Sin embargo, los datos detallados no tienen en cuenta ningún ingrediente, sazón, ni salsa agregados, que puedan usarse en la preparación o presentación de los productos cárnicos descritos.

Como orientación, a fin de aproximarse al peso cocido de la porción cruda, multiplicar el peso en onzas crudas por 0.75 (75%) para obtener el peso cocido. (Es posible que se noten algunas variaciones debido a los tiempos y temperaturas de cocción.) Luego, simplemente multiplique los datos nutricionales de 1.0 onza por el peso cocido de su porción para obtener la información para esa pieza del menú.

Como ayuda para los usuarios de la Guía para Compradores de Carne, la Asociación Norteamericana de Procesadores de Carne (NAMP, por sus siglas en inglés) se complace en incluir la siguiente información sobre nutrición.

La nutrición se ha convertido en una importante consideración tanto para los proveedores como para los usuarios finales. La Administración de Alimentos y Medicamentos (FDA, por sus siglas en inglés) del Departamento de Salud y Servicios Humanos así como el Servicio de Inspección e Inocuidad Alimentaria (FSIS, por sus siglas en inglés) del Departamento de Agricultura de E.U.A. han puesto en marcha reglamentaciones sobre etiquetado de nutrición en comercios de venta al por menor, para ofrecer información nutricional comprensible y con sentido.

La información de esta sección proviene de la Serie N° 8 del Manual de Agricultura, publicada por el Departamento de Agricultura de E.U.A y su Servicio de Información sobre Nutrición Humana, perteneciente a los Servicios al Consumidor y sobre Alimentos.

Esta sección se propone ser usada como guía. En algunas circunstancias, los productos de la industria de servicios de alimentación descritos en las Especificaciones institucionales de compra de carne, sobre las que se basa la Guía para Compradores de Carne, no se correlacionan directamente con las descripciones de los comercios al por menor de los productos usados en el Manual de Agricultura. De igual manera, es posible que haya algunas variaciones en los perfiles de nutrientes de los productos contenidos en este documento, pero no deberían ser suficientemente importantes como para afectar la aplicación general de la información.

Ahora, la información publicada en el Manual 8 se mantiene actualizada en la Base nacional de datos de nutrientes de USDA como referencia estándar. Esta referencia se actualiza en forma constante y proporciona acceso a la más reciente información en más de 7,000 alimentos. Se proporciona una función de búsqueda por Internet.

Para ingresar a la base de datos nacional de nutrientes de referencia estándar del Departamento de Agricultura de E.U.A., visite:

http://www.nal.usda.gov/fnic/foodcomp/search

Nuestros perfiles incluyen los minerales hierro, zinc, sodio y calcio, así como las vitaminas riboflavina y tiamina. Los lípidos y ácidos grasos incluidos son saturados, monosaturados, poliinsaturados y colesterol. No se incluyeron los carbohidratos y las vitaminas A y C debido a que sus cantidades no difieren demasiado de cero en el caso de la carne fresca. Se proporciona una explicación de términos y abreviaciones en el reverso de la página.

Ejemplo

1180A Lomo, Bistec Strip Loin (New York), 12.0 oz. crudo

Convertir peso crudo a peso cocido: 12.0 oz. x 0.75 oz. = 9.0 oz.

De las tablas: 9.0 oz. x 59 calorías totales por oz. = 531 calorías totales para esta porción

We hope you will find the Nutrition Information Section to be a valuable aid in menu planning and in responding to customers' nutrition questions.

Since portion sizes vary accordingly to a customer's cost or menu requirements, the nutrition information is expressed in a 1.0 oz cooked format. This should make it easier to convert the data to foodservice portions. We have chosen to use cooked rather than raw product data because it is anticipated that users of The Meat Buyer's Guide would wish to inform their customers based upon the nutrient profile of the product as served rather than as purchased. Since variations may exist in the trim or internal fat in served portions, the information is provided on a separable lean basis. The data listed, however, does not account for any added ingredients, seasonings, or sauces that may be used in the preparation or presentation of the meat products described.

As a guideline, in order to approximate the cooked weight of your raw serving, multiply the raw ounces weight by 0.75 (75 percent) to obtain the cooked weight. (Some variations may occur due to cooking times and temperatures.) Then simply multiply the 1.0 oz. nutrient data in the tables by the cooked weight of your portion to obtain the information for that particular menu item.

As an aid to users of *The Meat Buyer's Guide*, the North American Meat Processors Association (NAMP) is pleased to include this section on nutrition information.

Nutrition has become an important consideration for providers and end-users alike. The Food and Drug Administration (FDA) of the Department of Health and Human Services and the Food Safety and Inspection Service (FSIS) of the Department of Agriculture, have implemented nutrition labeling regulations in retail stores to provide meaningful as well as understandable nutritional information.

The information in this section comes from the Agriculture Handbook No. 8 Series, published by the United States Department of Agriculture and its Food and Consumer Services' Human Nutrition Information Service.

This section is intended to be used as a guide. In some instances, the foodservice products described in the Institutional Meat Purchase Specifications, upon which The Meat Buyer's Guide is based, do not correlate directly with the retail descriptions of the products used in the Agriculture Handbook. Accordingly, there may be some variations in the nutrient profiles of the products contained herein, but they should not be significant enough to affect the general application of the information.

The information published in Handbook 8 is now kept up to date in the USDA National Nutrient Database for Standard Reference. This reference is continually updated and provides access to the most up-to-date information on more than 7,000 foods. An online search function is provided.

To access the USDA National Nutrient Database for Standard Reference, go to:

http://www.nal.usda.gov/fnic/foodcomp/search

Included in our profiles are the minerals iron, zinc, sodium, and calcium, and the vitamins riboflavin and thiamin. Lipids or fatty acids included are saturated, mono-unsaturated, polyunsaturated, and cholesterol. Carbohydrates and vitamins A and C were not included because their amounts are not significantly different from zero for fresh meat. An explanation of terms and abbreviations is offered on the adjacent page.

Example

1180A Beef Strip Loin Steak, 12.0 oz. raw

Convert raw to cooked weight: 12.0 oz. x 0.75 oz. = 9.0 oz.

From the tables: 9.0 oz. x 59 total calories per oz. = 531 total calories for this portion

Explicación acerca de la sección de nutrición

Términos y abreviaciones

Unidades de Medida

1.0 oz.	=	28.35 gramos
1.0 lb.	=	453.6 gramos
oz.	=	onza
lb.	=	libra (16.0 oz.)
g	=	gramo
mg	=	miligramo (1/1000 de un gramo)

Lípidos o ácidos grasos*

SFA	=	ácido graso saturado
MUFA	=	ácido graso monoinsaturado
PUFA	=	ácido graso poliinsaturado
CHOL	=	colesterol
Grasa total	=	El total de grasa representa todos los ácidos grasos, inclusive las grasas no listadas en forma individual.
1 g de grasa total	=	9 calorías

*Para simplificar, es posible referirse a los ácidos grasos como grasa.

AH   Manual de Agricultura, publicado por los Servicios al Consumidor y de Nutrición y Alimentos del Departamento de Agricultura de E.U.A.

AH8   La serie número 8 del Manual de Agricultura informa acerca de la composición de alimentos. Se cubren veintidós grupos distintos de alimentos. Cada grupo de alimentos es designado por un número determinado. Los productos de carne de res, por ejemplo, se detallan bajo AH 8-13; por productos porcinos, bajo AH 8-10 y los productos de cordero, ternera y animales de caza, bajo AH 8-17.

Cortes combinados   Los datos de nutrientes correspondientes a combinaciones de cortes de carne de res, cordero, ternera y cerdo se basan en el perfil de nutriente de la canal entera. Los perfiles de nutrientes de los cortes individuales pueden diferir en algún grado de la canal.

IMPS   Especificaciones Institucionales de Compra de Carne, preparadas por el Programa de Ganado y Granos, Sucursal de Estandarización, del Servicio de Mercadeo Agrícola (AMS). La Guía para Compradores de Carne, publicada por la Asociación Norteamericana de Procesadores de Carne (NAMP), es una representación pictórica de las piezas de las Especificaciones Institucionales de Compra de Carne o IMPS.

Las designaciones numéricas que aparecen bajo las columnas de IMPS en cada tabla constituyen los números de identificación de los cortes de carne descritos. A menudo, al referirse a los diversos cortes de carne, se hace referencia a este número de IMPS o NAMP.

USDA   Departamento de Agricultura de Estados Unidos.

Explanation of the Nutrition Section

Terms and Abbreviations

Units of Measure

1.0 oz.	=	28.35 grams
1.0 lb.	=	453.6 grams
oz.	=	ounce
lb.	=	pound (16.0 oz.)
g	=	gram
mg	=	milligram (1/1000 of a g)

Lipids or Fatty Acids*

SFA	=	saturated fatty acid
MUFA	=	monounsaturated fatty acid
PUFA	=	polyunsaturated fatty acid
CHOL	=	cholesterol
Total Fat	=	total Fat represents all fatty acids including fats not individually listed.
1 g Total Fat	=	9 Calories

*For simplification, fatty acids may be referred to as fat.

AH — Agriculture Handbook, published by the USDA's Food Nutrition and Consumer Services.

AH8 — The Composition of Foods is reported in the Agriculture Handbook No. 8 Series. Twenty-two various food groups are covered. Each food group is designated by a certain number. Beef Products, for example, are listed in AH 8-13, Pork Products in AH 8-10, and Lamb, Veal, and Game Products in AH 8-17.

Composite — The composite nutrient data for beef, lamb, veal, and pork are based on the nutrient profile of the entire carcass. Nutrient profiles of individual cuts may differ somewhat from that of the carcass.

IMPS — Institutional Meat Purchase Specifications, prepared by the Livestock and Seed Program, Standardization Branch, of the USDA's Agricultural Marketing Service (AMS). The Meat Buyer's Guide, published by the North American Meat Processors Association (NAMP), is a pictorial representation of items in the IMPS.

The numeric designations appearing under the IMPS column on each chart are the identifying numbers for the meat cuts described. The various meat cuts are often referred to by this IMPS or NAMP number.

USDA — United States Department of Agriculture.

beef nutrition information

IMPS	Description / Descripción	USDA AH 8-13 Page / Página	Total Calories Calorías totales	Calories from Total Fat Calorías de la grasa total
100	**Composite Cooked** Cortes Combinados Cocidos	60	61	25
112A	**Beef Ribeye Roll, Lip-On, Eye, Loin end, 0 inch trim, Choice, Broiled** Rollo de Ribeye, con Cordón, Ojo de la Chuleta, Punta de lomo, Recortado a 0 pulgadas de Grasa, Choice, Asado	144	64	30
114A	**Beef Chuck, Shoulder Clod Roast, Braised** Paleta de Res, Rosbif de Planchuela de Paleta, Estofado	96	61	21
120	**Beef Brisket, Boneless, Deckle-Off, Whole, Braised** Pecho de res, Deshuesado, Sin Grasa Endurecida ni Carne Intercostal, Entero, Estofado	75	69	33
123A	**Beef Short Plate, Short Ribs, Choice, Braised** Costillar de res, Costilla Cargada, Costillas (Agujas) Cortas,, Choice, Estofado	199	84	46
135A	**Beef for Stewing, Beef Composite** Trozos de Res en Cubos para Cocido/Guisado, Cortes Combinados de Carne de Res	60	61	25
136	**Ground Beef-80/20 Broiled, Medium (From Nutrient Values of Muscle Foods)** Carne Molida de Res-80/20 Asada, Término Medio (según Valores de Nutrientes de Alimentos Musculares)		76	46
136	**Ground Beef-85/15 Broiled, Medium (From Nutrient Values of Muscle Foods)** Carne Molida de Res-85/15 Asada, Término Medio (según Valores de Nutrientes de Alimentos Musculares)		68	37
136	**Ground Beef-90/10 Broiled, Medium (Extrapolated from Handbook 8-13)** Carne Molida de Res-90/10 Asada, Término Medio (Extrapolado del Manual 8-13)		56	27
	Combinations of beef with carrageenan, oat bran, or other vegetable proteins are also available También se dispone de combinaciones de carne de res con carragenato, salvado de avena u otras proteínas vegetales			
167A	**Beef Round, Sirloin Tip (Knuckle), Peeled, Roasted** Pierna (Piña) de Res, Punta de Sirloin (Pulpa Bola), Rostizada	259	52	18
168	**Beef Round, Top Inside, Broiled** Pierna (Piña) de Res, Pulpa Negra (Cara/Centro), Asada	283	51	13
171B	**Beef Round, Outside, Bottom Round, Braised** Pierna (Piña) de Res, Contracara, Pulpa Blanca, Estofado	221	59	21
171C	**Beef Round, Eye of Round, Roasted** Pierna (Piña) de Res, Contracara, Cuete, Rostizado	242	48	13
184	**Beef Loin Top Sirloin Butt, Broiled No roasted data available** Lomo de Res, Pulpa del Aguayón Superior/Top Sirloin, Aguayón con Tapa, Asado No se dispone de datos de rostizado	355	55	18
193	**Flank Steak, Choice, 0 inch trim, Broiled** Concha de Falda, Choice, Recortada a 0 pulgadas de Grasa, Asada	121	59	26
1112	**Beef Rib, Ribeye Roll Steak, Eye, Loin end, Choice, 0 inch trim, Broiled** Chuletón (Espaldar) de Res, Bistec de Rollo de Ribeye, Ojo de la Chuleta, Extremo Adyacente al Lomo, Choice, Recortado a 0 pulgadas de Grasa, Asada	144	64	30
1174	**Beef Loin, T-Bone Steak, Short-Cut, Choice, Broiled** Lomo de Res, Bistec T-Bone, Lomo Corto, Choice, Asado	300	61	26
1180A	**Beef Loin, Strip Loin Steak, Extra Short-Cut, Boneless, Broiled** Lomo de Res, Bistec Strip Loin (New York), Lomo Extra Corto, Deshuesado, Asado	312	59	24
1184B	**Beef Loin, Top Sirloin Butt Steak, Center Cut, Boneless, Broiled** Lomo de Res, Bistec de Pulpa del Aguayón Superior/Top Sirloin, sin Tapa, Corte del Centro, Deshuesado, Asado	355	55	18
1189A	**Beef Loin, Tenderloin Steak, Side Muscle On, Defatted, Broiled** Lomo de Res, Medallón de Filete, con Cuerda (Psoas Menor), Limpio de Grasa, Asado	334	60	26
1190A	**Beef Loin, Tenderloin Steak, Side Muscle Off, Skinned, Broiled** Lomo de Res, Medallón de Filete, sin Cuerda (Psoas Menor), Despellejado, Asado	335	58	24

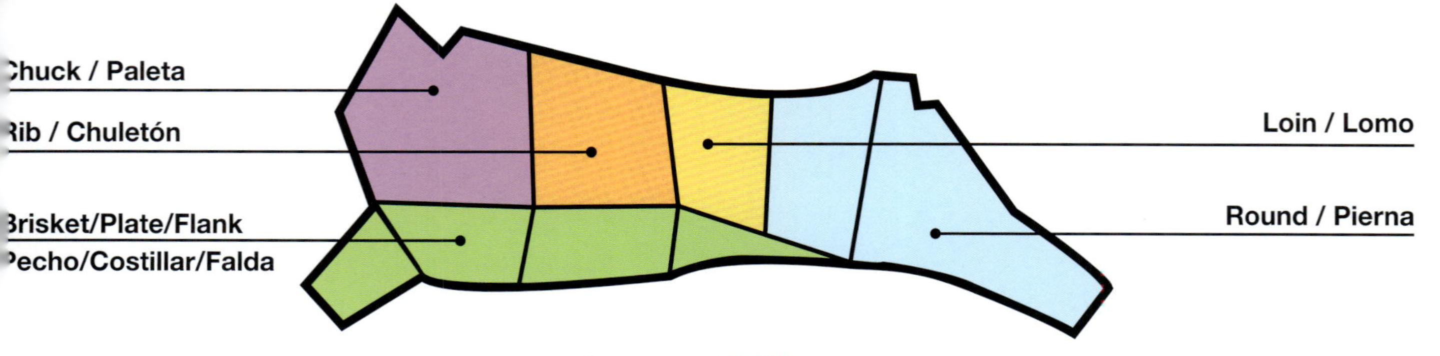

Total Fat g / Total de grasa g	SFA g	MUFA g	PUFA g	Chol mg	Protein / Proteína g	Calcium / Calcio mg	Iron / Hierro mg	Sodium / Sodio mg	Zinc mg	Riboflavin / Riboflavina mg	Thiamin / Tiamina mg	IMPS
2.81	1.07	1.18	0.10	24	8.38	2.33	0.85	19	1.96	0.07	0.03	100
3.31	1.34	1.40	0.09	23	7.94	3.67	0.73	20	1.98	0.06	0.03	112A
2.35	0.85	0.98	0.09	29	9.36	2.67	1.07	19	2.45	0.08	0.02	114A
3.62	1.29	1.66	0.11	26	8.43	1.67	0.80	20	1.95	0.06	0.02	120
5.14	2.19	2.26	0.16	26	8.71	3.00	0.95	17	2.21	0.06	0.02	123A
2.81	1.07	1.18	0.10	24	8.38	2.33	0.85	19	1.96	0.07	0.03	135A
5.06	1.99	2.22	0.19	25	7.12	3.00	0.63	22	1.54	0.06	0.01	136
4.07	1.60	1.78	0.15	24	7.36	3.00	0.67	22	1.56	0.07	0.02	136
3.04	1.22	1.32	0.13	23	7.27	2.00	0.72	22	1.61			136
— No comparable data available / No existen datos comparativos												
1.95	0.68	0.78	0.08	23	8.13	1.33	0.83	18	2.00	0.08	0.03	167A
1.39	0.48	0.54	0.06	24	8.98	1.67	0.82	17	1.58	0.08	0.03	168
2.32	0.78	1.02	0.09	27	8.95	1.33	0.98	14	1.55	0.07	0.02	171B
1.39	0.50	0.59	0.04	20	8.21	1.33	0.55	18	1.34	0.05	0.02	171C
2.04	0.79	0.87	0.08	25	8.60	3.00	0.95	19	1.85	0.08	0.04	184
2.87	1.23	1.15	0.11	19	7.67	2.00	0.73	23	1.36	0.05	0.03	193
3.31	1.34	1.40	0.09	23	7.94	3.67	0.73	20	1.98	0.06	0.03	1112
2.94	1.18	1.18	0.11	23	7.97	2.00	0.85	19	1.53	0.07	0.03	1174
2.66	1.02	1.07	0.09	22	8.11	2.33	0.70	19	1.48	0.06	0.03	1180A
2.04	0.79	0.87	0.08	25	8.60	3.00	0.95	19	1.85	0.08	0.04	1184B
2.85	1.06	1.07	0.11	24	8.00	2.00	1.01	18	1.58	0.08	0.04	1189A
2.69	1.01	1.02	0.10	24	8.00	2.00	1.01	18	1.58	0.08	0.04	1190A

The above Data are for a 1.0 oz. portion, cooked, separable lean only. Computed on an all grades basis using the most recent USDA Handbook 8-13 data for separable lean only (0.25 inch fat trim except where otherwise noted).

The all grades basis is a combination of Prime, Choice, and Select USDA quality grades weighted by their market proportions.

Los datos que anteceden corresponden a una porción de 1.0 oz., cocida, de sólo carne magra separable. Contabilizado en la base de todos los grados usando los datos más recientes del Manual 8-13 del Departamento de Agricultura de E.U.A. para sólo la carne magra separable (recorte de 0.25 pulgadas salvo que se indique de otro modo).

La base de todos los grados es una combinación de todos los grados de calidad "Prime" (excelente), "Choice" (preferencia), y "Select" (selecta) del Departamento de Agricultura de E.U.A., sopesados por sus proporciones de mercado.

To access the USDA National Nutrient Database for Standard Reference, go to www.nal.usda.gov/fnic/foodcomp/search

Para ingresar a la base de datos nacional de nutrientes de referencia estándar del Departamento de Agricultura de E.U.A., visite: www.nal.usda.gov/fnic/foodcomp/search

lamb nutrition information

IMPS	Description / Descripción	USDA AH 8-13 Page / Página	Total Calories Calorías totales	Calories from Total Fat Calorías de la grasa total
00	Composite, Cooked Cortes Combinados, Cocidos	34	58	24
08	Shoulder, Square-Cut, Boneless, Tied, Roasted Paleta (Espaldilla), Corte Cuadrado, Deshuesada, Amarrada, Rostizada	72	58	27
10	Foreshank, Braised Chamberete de Mano, Estofado	40	53	15
234	Leg, Boneless, Tied, Roasted Pierna, Deshuesada, Amarrada, Rostizada	44	54	20
295A	Lamb for Kabobs Cubed for Stew or Kabob, Leg and Shoulder, Broiled Trozos de Cordero para Brochetas o Guisado, Ablandado para Guisado o Kabob, Pierna y Paleta, Asado	91	53	19
296	Ground Lamb, Broiled Carne Molida de Cordero, Asada	93	80	50
245	Sirloin, Boneless, Roasted Aguayón (Sirloin), Deshuesado, Asado	52	58	23
204C	Rib Chops, Frenched, Broiled Chuletas del Espaldar, Estilo Francés, Asadas	63	67	33
207	Shoulder Chops, Broiled Chuletas de Brazuelo y Paleta (Chuletas del 7), Asadas	71	60	27
232A	Loin Chops, Broiled Chuletas de Lomo, Asadas	57	61	25

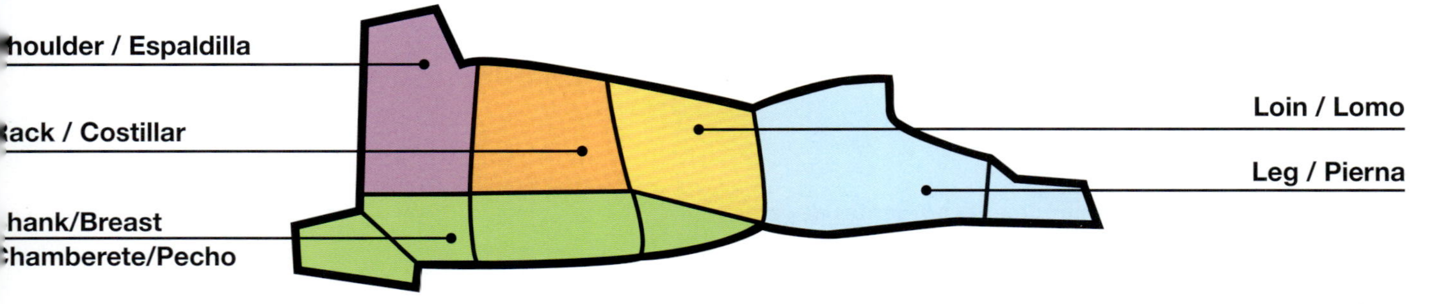

Total Fat g / Total de grasa g	SFA g	MUFA g	PUFA g	Chol mg	Protein Proteína g	Calcium Calcio mg	Iron Hierro mg	Sodium Sodio mg	Zinc mg	Riboflavin Ribo-flavina mg	Thiamin Tiamina mg	IMPS
2.70	0.96	1.18	0.18	26	8.00	4.33	0.58	21	1.49	0.08	0.03	200
3.05	1.16	1.24	0.27	25	7.07	5.33	0.60	19	1.71	0.07	0.03	208
1.71	0.61	0.75	0.11	30	8.79	5.67	0.64	21	2.45	0.05	0.01	210
2.19	0.78	0.96	0.14	25	8.02	2.33	0.60	19	1.40	0.08	0.03	234
2.08	0.74	0.84	0.19	26	7.95	3.67	0.66	22	1.63	0.08	0.03	295A
5.57	2.30	2.36	0.40	27	7.01	6.33	0.51	23	1.32	0.07	0.03	296
2.60	0.93	1.14	0.17	26	8.03	2.33	0.62	20	1.37	0.09	0.03	245
3.67	1.32	1.48	0.34	26	7.86	4.67	0.63	24	1.49	0.07	0.03	1204C
2.97	1.10	1.20	0.27	26	7.68	5.67	0.62	23	1.87	0.08	0.03	1207
2.76	0.98	1.21	0.18	27	8.50	5.33	0.57	24	1.17	0.08	0.03	1232A

The above Data are for a 1.0 oz. portion, cooked, separable lean only. Computed using data from USDA Handbook 8-17 (1989), from USDA Choice grade domestic lamb weighted by the proportion of the market share for each yield grade. Surface fat trimmed to 0.25 inch.

Los datos que anteceden corresponden a una porción de 1.0 oz., cocida, de sólo carne magra separable. Contabilizados con datos extraídos del Manual 8-17 (1989) del Departamento de Agricultura de E.U.A., del cordero doméstico grado "Choice" de dicho Departamento, sopesado según la proporción de la participación de mercado de cada grado de rendimiento. Recortado a 0.25 pulgadas de la cubierta de grasa.

To access the USDA National Nutrient Database for Standard Reference, go to www.nal.usda.gov/fnic/foodcomp/search

Para ingresar a la base de datos nacional de nutrientes de referencia estándar del Departamento de Agricultura de E.U.A., visite: www.nal.usda.gov/fnic/foodcomp/search

veal nutrition information

MPS	Description / Descripción	USDA AH 8-13 Page / Página	Total Calories Calorías totales	Calories from Total Fat Calorías de la grasa total
300	Composite, Cooked Cortes Combinados, Cocidos	123	55	17
310B	Veal Chuck, Shoulder Clod Roast, Roasted Paleta de Ternera, Rosbif de Planchuela de Paleta, Rostizada	159	46	15
349A	Veal Leg, Top Round, Cap Off, Roasted Pierna de Ternera, Pulpa Negra (Cara/Centro de Pierna), sin Tapa, Rostizada	135	43	9
395	Veal for Stewing, Cubed for Stew, Leg and Shoulder, Braised Trozos de Ternera para Cocer/Guisar, Ablandada para Guisar, Pierna y Paleta (Espaldilla), Estofada	173	53	11
396	Ground Veal, Broiled Carne Molida de Ternera, Asada	175	49	19
1306A	Veal Rack, Rib Chops, Frenched, Rib, Roasted Costillar de Ternera, Chuletas del Costillar, Estilo Francés, Costilla, Rostizado	147	50	19
1332	Veal Loin, Loin Chops, Loin, Roasted Lomo de Ternera, Chuletas de Lomo, Lomo, Rostizado	141	50	18
1336	Veal Cutlets, Leg, Not Breaded, Pan-Fried Escalopas de Ternera, Pierna, sin Empanizar, Fritas en Sartén	134	52	12

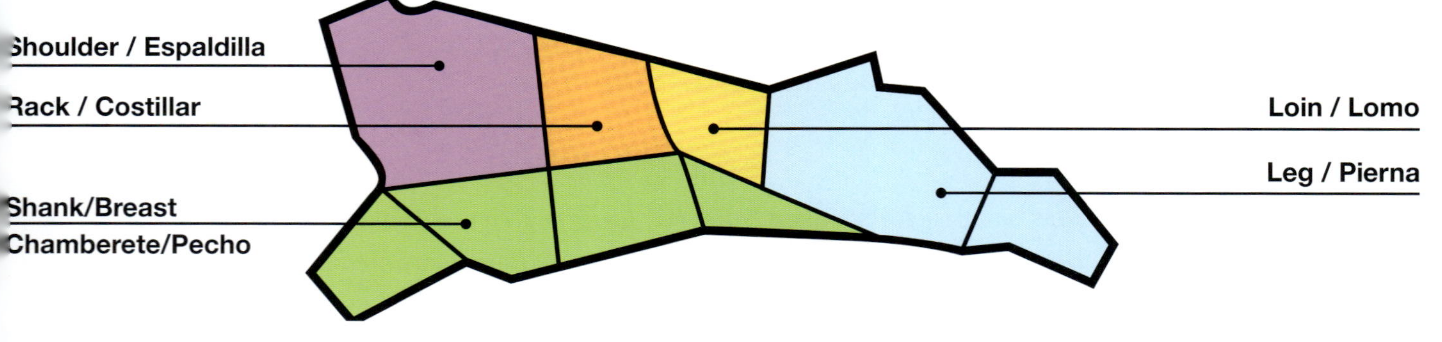

NAMP
NORTH AMERICAN MEAT PROCESSORS ASSOCIATION
ASSOCIATION AMÉRIQUE DU NORD DES TRANSFORMATEURS DE VIANDE
ASOCIACIÓN NORTEAMERICANA DE PROCESADORES DE CARNE

Total Fat g / Total de grasa g	SFA g	MUFA g	PUFA g	Chol mg	Protein Proteína g	Calcium Calcio mg	Iron Hierro mg	Sodium Sodio mg	Zinc mg	Riboflavin Ribo-flavina mg	Thiamin Tiamina mg	IMPS
1.86	0.52	0.67	0.17	33	9.04	6.67	0.33	25	1.44	0.10	0.02	300
1.65	0.65	0.61	0.12	31	7.40	7.67	0.33	26	1.22	0.09	0.02	310B
0.96	0.35	0.34	0.08	29	7.95	1.67	0.26	19	0.87	0.09	0.02	349A
1.22	0.37	0.39	0.13	41	9.90	8.00	0.41	26	1.70	0.11	0.02	395
2.14	0.86	0.80	0.16	29	6.91	4.67	0.28	23	1.10	0.08	0.02	396
2.11	0.59	0.75	0.19	32	7.30	3.33	0.27	27	1.27	0.08	0.02	1306A
1.97	0.73	0.71	0.16	30	7.46	6.00	0.24	27	0.92	0.09	0.02	1332
1.31	0.37	0.47	0.12	30	9.40	2.00	0.25	22	0.96	0.10	0.02	1336

The above Data are for a 1.0 oz. portion, cooked, separable lean only computed using data from USDA Handbook 8-17 (1989). Surface fat is minimal in most cases. The information was derived from averaging USDA Choice grade special-fed veal with an equal number of USDA Good grade bob veal calves. Due to the weight differences in the two types of animals, the data was computed by weighting the average to reflect 85 percent special-fed and 15 percent bob veal.

Los datos que anteceden corresponden a porciones de 1.0 oz. cocidas, con sólo carne magra separable, contabilizados mediante datos del Manual 8-17 (1989) del Departamento de Agricultura de E.U.A. En la mayoría de los casos, la cubierta de grasa es mínima. La información surgió de promediar datos de la ternera con alimentación especial de grado "Choice" según el Departamento de Agricultura de E.U.A. con una cantidad equivalente de terneras lechales de grado "Bueno" según dicho Departamento. Debido a las diferencias de peso en los dos tipos de animales, los datos se contabilizaron pesando el promedio, a fin de reflejar el 85% de alimentación especial y el 15% de terneras lechales.

To access the USDA National Nutrient Database for Standard Reference, go to www.nal.usda.gov/fnic/foodcomp/search

Para ingresar a la base de datos nacional de nutrientes de referencia estándar del Departamento de Agricultura de E.U.A., visite: www.nal.usda.gov/fnic/foodcomp/search

IMPS	Description / Descripción	USDA AH 8-13 Page / Página	Total Calories Calorías totales	Calories from Total Fat Calorías de la grasa total
400	**Composite, Cooked** Cortes Combinados, Cocidos	27	60	24
402C	**Pork Fresh Ham, Boneless, Trimmed, Tied, Leg (Ham) Whole, Roasted** Pierna (Jamón Fresco) de Cerdo, Deshuesada, Recortada de Grasa, Amarrada, Pierna (Jamón), Entera, Rostizada	39	60	24
414	**Pork Loin, Canadian Back, Loin, Whole, Roasted** Chuleta (Lomo) de Cerdo, Estilo Canadiense, Lomo, Entero, Rostizado	55	59	25
415A	**Pork Tenderloin, Side Muscle Off, Roasted** Filete de Cerdo, sin Músculo de al Lado, Rostizado	125	46	12
416A	**Pork Spareribs, St. Louis Style, Separable Lean and Fat, Braised** Costillar de Cerdo, Estilo San Luis, Carne Magra y Grasa Separables, Estofado	157	113	77
422	**Pork Loin, Back Ribs, Separable Lean and Fat, Roasted** Chuleta de Cerdo, Costillas de Espaldar, Carne Magra y Grasa Separables, Rostizado	57	105	75
435	**Diced Pork, Composite Cooked** Cerdo Troceado, Corte Combinado, Cocido	27	60	24
496	**Ground Pork, Cooked** Carne Molida de Cerdo, Cocida	159	84	53
1412A	**Pork Loin Chops, Center-Cut, Chine Bone Off, Broiled** Chuletas de Lomo de Cerdo, Corte del Centro, Espinazo Rebajado, Asadas	75	57	21
1412B	**Pork Chops, Center-Cut, Boneless, Broiled** Chuletas de Lomo de Cerdo, Corte del Centro, Deshuesado, Asadas	135	58	20

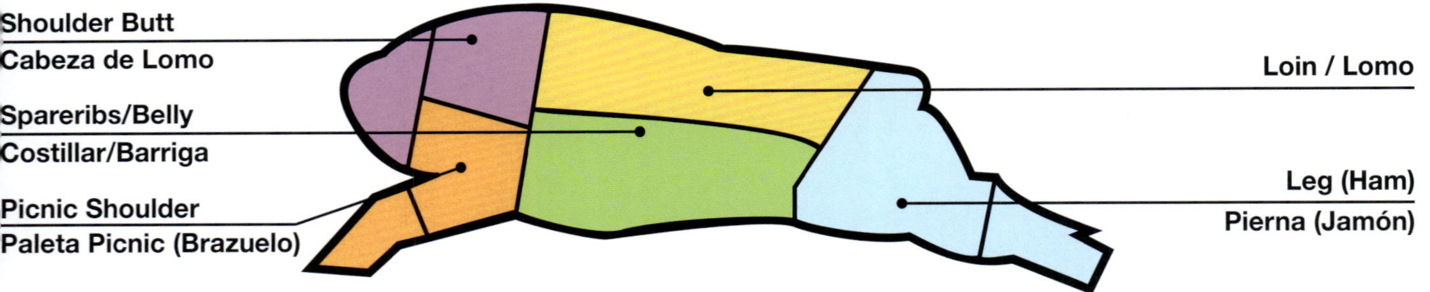

Total Fat g / Total de grasa g	SFA g	MUFA g	PUFA g	Chol mg	Protein / Proteína g	Calcium / Calcio mg	Iron / Hierro mg	Sodium / Sodio mg	Zinc mg	Riboflavin / Ribo-flavina mg	Thiamin / Tiamina mg	IMPS
2.74	0.97	1.23	0.21	24	8.29	6.0	0.31	17	0.84	0.10	0.24	400
2.67	0.93	1.26	0.24	27	8.33	2.0	0.32	18	0.92	0.10	0.20	402C
2.73	0.99	122	0.22	23	8.11	5.0	0.31	15	0.72	0.09	0.21	414
1.36	0.47	0.55	0.12	22	7.97	1.7	0.42	16	0.74	0.11	0.27	415A
8.58	3.15	3.82	0.77	34	8.23	13.3	0.52	26	1.30	0.11	0.12	416A
8.38	3.11	3.81	0.66	33	6.87	12.7	0.39	28	0.95	0.06	0.12	422
2.74	0.97	1.23	0.21	24	8.29	6.0	0.31	17	0.84	0.10	0.24	435
5.88	2.19	2.62	0.53	27	7.28	6.3	0.37	21	0.91	0.06	0.20	496
2.29	0.84	1.03	0.16	23	8.55	8.7	0.24	17	0.67	0.09	0.33	1412A
2.20	0.77	1.02	0.14	23	8.82	8.7	0.23	18	0.67	0.09	0.25	1412B

The above Data are for a 1.0 oz. portion, cooked, separable lean only. The nutrients were computed using data from USDA Handbook 8–10 (1992).

Los datos que anteceden corresponden a porciones de 1.0 oz. cocidas, con sólo carne magra separable. Los nutrientes fueron contabilizados usando datos del Manual 8-10 (1992) del Departamento de Agricultura de E.U.A.

To access the USDA National Nutrient Database for Standard Reference, go to www.nal.usda.gov/fnic/foodcomp/search

Para ingresar a la base de datos nacional de nutrientes de referencia estándar del Departamento de Agricultura de E.U.A., visite: www.nal.usda.gov/fnic/foodcomp/search

Further Processed/By-Products / Productos ya Procesados/Coproductos

IMPS	Description / Descripción	USDA AH 8 Page / Página	Total Calories Calorías totales	Calories from Total Fat Calorías de la grasa total
510	Ham, Honey Cured (Smoked), Partially Boned, Spiral Cut Jamón, Curado con Miel (Ahumado), Deshuesado Parcial, Corte en Espiral	AH 8-7 39	37	13
539	Pork Belly, Cured and Smoked, Bacon, Sliced, Broiled or Pan-Fried Barriga de Cerdo, Curada y Ahumada, Tocino, Rebanado, Asado o Frito en Sartén	AH 8-10 190	163	126
550A	Canadian Style Bacon, Cured and Smoked, Sliced, Grilled Lomo Estilo Canadiense, Curado y Ahumado, Rebanado, Asado a la Parrilla	AH 8-10 194	52	22
623	Roast Beef, Top Round, Cooked, Choice 0.25 inch trim, separable lean only Rosbif, Cara/Centro Pierna, Cocida, Choice, Recortado a 0.25 pulgadas de Grasa, Solo Carne Magra Separable	AH 8-13 284	60	17
625	Brisket, Boneless, Deckle Off, Corned, Cooked Pecho, Deshuesado, sin Grasa Endurecida, Curado, Cocido	AH 8-13 412	71	48
703	Beef Liver, Portion Cut, Braised Hígado de Res, Cortado en Porciones, Estofado	AH 8-13 393	46	13
705	Calf Liver, Portion Cut, Pan Fried Hígado de Becerro, Cortado en Porciones, Frito en Sartén	AH 8-17 232	69	29
716	Beef Tongue, Cooked, Simmered Lengua de Res, Hervida a Fuego Lento	AH 8-13 407	80	53
800	Frankfurters, Beef and Pork Salchichas Tipo Frankfurt, Carne de Res y de Cerdo	AH 8-7 33	91	74
801	Bologna, Beef and Pork Embutido Tipo Bolonia, Carne de Res y de Cerdo	AH 8-7 20	89	72
802	Pork Sausage, Cooked Salchicha (Chorizo) de Cerdo, Cocido	AH 8-7 75	105	79
803	Liver Sausage, Braunschweiger Embutido (Pasta de Hígado), Braunschweiger	AH 8-7 24	102	82
804	Salami, Cooked, Beef Salame, Cocido, Carne de Res	AH 8-7 77	72	51
808	Dry Salami, Beef and Pork Salame Seco, Carne de Res y de Cerdo	AH 8-7 81	119	88
816	Knockwurst Salchicha Tipo Knockwurst	AH 8-7 50	87	71

Total Fat g Total de grasa g	SFA g	MUFA g	PUFA g	Chol mg	Protein Proteína g	Calcium Calcio mg	Iron Hierro mg	Sodium Sodio mg	Zinc mg	Riboflavin Ribo-flavina mg	Thiamin Tiamina mg	IMPS
1.41	0.46	0.67	0.14	13	5.48	2.00	0.22	405	0.55	0.06	0.26	510
13.96	4.94	6.72	1.65	24	8.63	3.35	0.46	452	0.92	0.08	0.20	539
2.39	0.81	1.14	0.23	16	6.88	2.65	0.23	439	0.48	0.06	0.23	550A
1.84	0.63	0.72	0.08	25	10.24	1.00	0.94	13	1.29	0.07	0.02	623
5.38	1.80	2.61	0.19	28	5.15	2.33	0.53	321	1.30	0.05	0.01	625
1.39	0.54	0.18	0.30	110	6.91	2.00	1.92	20	1.72	1.16	0.06	703
3.23	1.20	0.70	0.51	93	8.43	3.33	1.48	37	2.23	0.95	0.07	705
5.88	2.53	2.68	0.22	30	6.23	2.00	0.96	17	1.36	0.10	0.01	716
8.26	3.05	3.88	0.77	14	3.20	3.06	0.33	318	0.52	0.03	0.06	800
8.01	3.03	3.80	0.68	16	3.31	3.31	0.43	289	0.55	0.04	0.05	801
8.83	3.06	3.94	1.08	24	5.57	8.94	0.35	367	0.71	0.07	0.21	802
9.10	3.09	4.23	1.06	44	3.83	2.00	2.65	324	0.80	0.43	0.07	803
5.70	2.39	2.64	0.25	17	4.17	2.00	0.57	328	0.61	0.07	0.04	804
9.75	3.46	4.85	0.91	22	6.48	2.12	0.43	527	0.92	0.08	0.17	808
7.87	2.89	3.63	0.83	16	3.37	3.00	0.26	286	0.47	0.04	0.10	816

The above data are for a 1.0 oz. portion, cooked or prepared as noted.

Los datos que anteceden corresponden a una porción de 1.0 oz. cocida o preparada según se especifica.

To access the USDA National Nutrient Database for Standard Reference, go to www.nal.usda.gov/fnic/foodcomp/search

Para ingresar a la base de datos nacional de nutrientes de referencia estándar del Departamento de Agricultura de E.U.A., visite: www.nal.usda.gov/fnic/foodcomp/search

Chicken / Pollo

Description / Descripción	Serving Size Tamaño de la porción	Calories Per 100 Grams Calorías por 100 gramos	Total Fat Total de grasa g	Protein Proteína g	Vitamin Vitamina A IU	Vitamin Vitamina C mg	Calcium Calcio mg	Iron Hierro mg
Chicken, broilers, dark meat only, cooked, roasted Pollo, pollos de engorde, carne oscura solamente, cocida, rostizada	100 grams / gramos	205	9.73	27.37	72	0	15	1.33
Chicken, broilers, light meat only, cooked, roasted Pollo, pollos de engorde, carne clara solamente, cocida, rostizada	100 grams / gramos	173	4.5	30.9	29	0	15	1.06
Chicken, broilers, dark meat and skin, cooked, roasted Pollo, pollos de engorde, carne y piel oscuras, cocida, rostizada	100 grams / gramos	253	15.78	25.97	201	0	15	1.36
Chicken, broilers, light meat and skin, cooked, roasted Pollo, pollos de engorde, carne y piel claras, cocida, rostizada	100 grams / gramos	222	10.85	29.02	110	0	15	1.14
Chicken, broilers, meat only, roasted Pollo, pollos de engorde, carne solamente, rostizada	100 grams / gramos	190	7.4	28.93	53	0	15	1.2
Chicken, broilers, meat and skin, cooked, roasted Pollo, pollos de engorde, carne y piel, cocida, rostizada	100 grams / gramos	239	13.6	27.3	161	0	15	1.26
Chicken, Cornish game hens, meat only, cooked, roasted Pollo, pollito tierno "Cornish", carne solamente, cocida, rostizada	100 grams / gramos	134	3.87	23.3	65	.6	13	.77
Chicken, Cornish game hens, meat and skin, cooked, roasted Pollo, pollito tierno "Cornish", carne y piel, cocidas, rostizadas	100 grams / gramos	260	18.21	22.27	106	.5	13	.91
Chicken, Capon, meat and skin, cooked, roasted Pollo, capón, carne y piel, cocidos, rostizados	100 grams / gramos	229	11.65	28.96	68	0	14	1.49

NAMP
NORTH AMERICAN MEAT PROCESSORS ASSOCIATION
ASSOCIATION AMÉRIQUE DU NORD DES TRANSFORMATEURS DE VIANDE
ASOCIACIÓN NORTEAMERICANA DE PROCESADORES DE CARNE

Other Poultry / Otras Aves

Description / Descripción	Serving Size Tamaño de la porción	Calories Per 100 Grams Calorías por 100 gramos	Total Fat Total de grasa g	Protein Proteína g	Vitamin A Vitamina A IU	Vitamin C Vitamina C mg	Calcium Calcio mg	Iron Hierro mg
Turkey, dark meat, cooked, roasted Pavo, carne oscura, cocido, rostizado	100 grams / gramos	187	7.22	28.57	0	0	32	2.33
Turkey, light meat, cooked, roasted Pavo, carne clara, cocido, rostizado	100 grams / gramos	157	3.22	29	0	0	19	1.35
Turkey, dark meat and skin, cooked, roasted Pavo, carne y piel oscuras, cocido, rostizado	100 grams / gramos	221	11.54	27.49	0	0	33	2.27
Turkey, light meat and skin, cooked, roasted Pavo, carne y piel claras, cocido, rostizado	100 grams / gramos	197	8.33	28.57	0	0	21	1.41
Duck, meat only, cooked, roasted Pato, carne solamente, cocido, rostizado	100 grams / gramos	201	11.2	23.48	77	0	12	2.7
Duck, meat and skin, cooked, roasted Pato, carne y piel, cocido, rostizado	100 grams / gramos	337	28.35	18.99	210	0	11	2.7
Goose, meat only, cooked, roasted Ganso, carne solamente, cocido, rostizado	100 grams / gramos	238	12.67	28.97	40	0	14	2.87
Goose, meat and skin, cooked, roasted Ganso, carne y piel, cocido, rostizado	100 grams / gramos	305	21.92	25.16	70	0	13	2.83
Pheasant, meat only, raw Faisán, carne solamente, crudo	100 grams / gramos	133	3.64	23.57	165	6	13	1.15
Pheasant, meat and skin, raw Faisán, carne y piel, crudo	100 grams / gramos	181	9.29	22.7	177	5.3	12	1.15
Squab (pigeon), light meat only, raw Palomino (pichón), carne clara solamente, crudo	100 grams / gramos	134	4.52	21.76	57	5.1	10	2.31
Squab (pigeon), meat only, raw Palomino (pichón), carne solamente, crudo	100 grams / gramos	142	7.5	17.5	94	7.2	13	4.51
Squab (pigeon), meat and skin, raw Palomino (pichón), carne y piel, crudo	100 grams / gramos	294	23.8	18.47	243	5.2	12	3.54
Guinea Hen, meat only, raw Gallina de Guinea, carne solamente, cruda	100 grams / gramos	110	2.47	20.64	41	1.7	11	.77
Guinea Hen, meat and skin, raw Gallina de Guinea, carne y piel, cruda	100 grams / gramos	158	6.45	23.4	92	1.3	11	.84
Quail, meat and skin, raw Codorniz, carne y piel, cruda	100 grams / gramos	192	12.05	19.63	243	6.1	13	3.97

To access the USDA National Nutrient Database for Standard Reference, go to www.nal.usda.gov/fnic/foodcomp/search

Para ingresar a la base de datos nacional de nutrientes de referencia estándar del Departamento de Agricultura de E.U.A., visite: www.nal.usda.gov/fnic/foodcomp/search

NAMP
North American Meat Processors Association
Association Amérique du Nord des Transformateurs de Viande
Asociación Norteamericana de Procesadores de Carne

Beef Portion Cuts
Cortes Porcionados de Carne de Res

NAMP
NORTH AMERICAN MEAT PROCESSORS ASSOCIATION
ASSOCIATION AMÉRIQUE DU NORD DES TRANSFORMATEURS DE VIANDE
ASOCIACIÓN NORTEAMERICANA DE PROCESADORES DE CARNE

NAMP
NORTH AMERICAN MEAT PROCESSORS ASSOCIATION
ASSOCIATION AMÉRIQUE DU NORD DES TRANSFORMATEURS DE VIANDE
ASOCIACIÓN NORTEAMERICANA DE PROCESADORES DE CARNE

Veal Portion Cuts
Cortes Porcionados de Ternera

Item Pieza	Product Name Nombre del producto	Page Página

Pork Portion Cuts
Cortes Porcionados de Cerdo

NAMP
North American Meat Processors Association
Association Amérique du Nord des Transformateurs de Viande
Asociación Norteamericana de Procesadores de Carne

ndex / índice

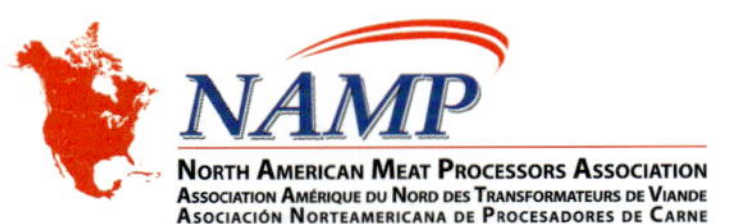

Center of the Plate Training®

from the producers of
The Meat Buyer's Guide®

Capacitación en ingredientes principales del plato

de los realizadores de la Guía
para Compradores de Carne®

Course Specifics

Center of the Plate Training® offered by the North American Meat Processors Association (NAMP) is a first-hand look at how carcasses are converted into portioned items commonly traded in the foodservice and retail meat business. The course covers all the major center of the plate protein items: beef, veal, lamb, pork, and poultry (in some locations).

This course is held two to three times annually across North America. It spans two to three days of classroom learning, with presentations by industry experts. You also will receive a copy of the NAMP *Meat Buyer's Guide®*, which is used extensively in the course.

What You Will Learn From This Course

- The IMPS/NAMP numbering system, purchase specified options, and standards common to the industry.

- A knowledge of meat items as described by IMPS and by NAMP's *Meat Buyer's Guide®*.

- Where meat products originate and how this affects their final use.

- The importance of standards and how they keep products consistent, wholesome, and fair throughout the market.

- Common defects or inconsistencies in meat products that you should look for to prevent dissatisfied customers or unpleasant dining experiences.

- Current trends in the foodservice industry, new menu ideas and options.

- How value is determined for different meat products and how this is affected by quality parameters.

If you're involved in the buying and selling of meat products - from restaurants and supermarkets to foodservice distributors and meat companies - gain a competitive edge by applying the valuable information you'll learn from this course.

Visit www.namp.com for more information on specific courses, locations, and dates.

Visite www.namp.com para obtener información adicional sobre cursos específicos, sitios y fechas.

Detalles del curso

La Capacitación en ingredientes principales del plato que ofrece la Asociación Norteamericana de Procesadores de Carne (NAMP) es una mirada de primera mano a la forma en que las canales se convierten en piezas porcionadas comúnmente comercializadas en la industria de servicios de alimentación y los negocios minoristas de carne. El curso comprende las principales piezas proteicas que constituyen los ingredientes principales del plato: carne de res, ternera, cordero, cerdo y aves (en algunos lugares).

Este curso se dicta dos o tres veces al año en toda Norteamérica. Abarca de dos a tres días de aprendizaje en un salón de clase, con presentaciones a cargo de expertos de la industria. También recibirá una copia de *La Guía para Compradores de Carne®* de NAMP (Asociación Norteamericana de Procesadores de Carne, por sus siglas en inglés) que se utilizará exhaustivamente en el curso.

Qué aprenderá en este curso

- El sistema de numeración IMPS/NAMP, las opciones especificadas de compra y las normas comunes de la industria.

- Un conocimiento de las piezas de carne como se describen en las IMPS (Especificaciones Institucionales de Compra de Carne, por sus siglas en inglés) y en *La Guía para Compradores de Carne®* de NAMP.

- Dónde se originan los productos de carne y cómo afecta esto su uso final.

- La importancia de las normas y cómo logran que los productos sean uniformes, saludables y buenos en todo el mercado.

- Defectos o anomalías en los productos de carne que debería buscar para evitar clientes insatisfechos o que tengan experiencias desagradables en la mesa.

- Las tendencias actuales de la industria de servicios de alimentación, nuevas ideas y opciones para su menú.

- Cómo se determina el valor de diferentes productos de carne y cómo éste se ve afectado por los parámetros de calidad.

Si participa en la compra y venta de productos de carne, ya sea en restaurantes y supermercados o distribuidores de la industria de servicios de alimentación y empresas de carne, obtenga una ventaja competitiva aplicando la valiosa información que aprenderá en este curso.

NORTH AMERICAN MEAT PROCESSORS ASSOCIATION
ASSOCIATION AMÉRIQUE DU NORD DES TRANSFORMATEURS DE VIANDE
ASOCIACIÓN NORTEAMERICANA DE PROCESADORES DE CARNE